HANGŬL-IN-A-HURRY CHART II
Vowels

Simple Vowels	"I" Diphthongs (vowel "i" added to	Other Diphthongs (combinations of various
아 a (fath...)		
야 ya (yar...)		
어 ŏ (hut)	에 e (met)	
여 yŏ (yearn)	예 ye (yes)	
오 o (home)	외 oe (Köln)	와 wa (wan) 왜 wae (wag)
요 yo (yoke)		
우 u (do)	위 wi (wield)	워 wŏ (won) 웨 we (wet)
유 yu (you)		
으 ŭ (taken)	의 ŭi (taken + we)	
이 i (ink)		

The "o" written with each vowel is an unvoiced consonant which functions to indicate where an initial consonant may be affixed to the vowel when writing a syllable. See the inside back cover for information on forming syllables.

ENGLISH-KOREAN PRACTICAL CONVERSATION DICTIONARY

(All-Romanized)

실용영한회화사전

Edited by
B.J. Jones & Gene S. Rhie

HOLLYM

First published in 1984
Seventh printing 1990
by Hollym International Corp.
18 Donald Place
Elizabeth, New Jersey 07208 U.S.A.

Published simultaneously in Korea
by Hollym Corporation; Publishers
14-5 Kwanchol-dong, Chongno-gu
Seoul 110-111 Korea
Phone:(02)735-7554   Fax:(02)730-5149

ISBN: 0-930878-22-1
Library of Congress Catalog Card Number: 83-81486
Printed in Korea

Preface

This dictionary is specially designed for an essential guidebook of Korean conversation. The book includes all the essential information as to basic Korean vocabularies used in everyday Korean conversation. The editors give special attention to a reviewed version of marking system by the Ministry of Education which accommodates McCune Reischauer system. Thus, the dictionary provides the newest and correct way of pronouncing Korean.

A special arrangement is also made in placing the order of vocabulary parts in such a way that the reader can learn Korean language more efficiently. For each entry, its synonyms and idiomatic usage are introduced first, followed by the romanized Korean translation and finally by its translation in Korean letters.

The dictionary provides many examples in complete Korean sentences in order to help the reader have a correct and useful knowledge of Korean language structure. The reader, through the examples shown in the dictionary, will find a correct usage of the verbs and adjectives of Korean.

Korean grammar is introduced and explained in a rather simple and clear way, yet providing a short cut way to learn Korean language more scientifically and efficiently. The proper usage of verbs in various forms is specially important part of Korean grammar. A linguistic and phonetical approach of Korean language is other unique feature of this dictionary.

B. J. Jones
Gene S. Rhie

The Korean Alphabet, *Han-gŭl*

The *han-gŭl* phonetic alphabet was invented by scholars commissioned by King Sejong of Yi dynasty and was promulgated in 1446 as an easy method for the common people to be able to read. Before that Korean used Chinese characters and study of the characters was limited to the upper class people. Korean, *han-gŭl* is one of the most phonetic alphabets and the system is orderly and easy to learn that one can imagine.

The Korean alphabet is so simple that its twenty-four letters can be learned in minutes with the aid of the *han-gŭl*-in-a-hurry charts at the inside front cover of this dictionary. The charts at the inside back cover illustrate how to write each *han-gŭl* letter and how to combine the letters into syllables. In Korean, *han-gŭl*, there are not as many tenses, not as many particles. Korean grammar is difficult for English-speaking people because the verb occurs at the end of sentence.

Korean consonants are pronounced much as they are in English, though they assume different shades of sound when they appear as initials, medials, or finals. The five stressed consonants are pronounced with greatest possible stress but with no expulsion of air. For example "tt"(ㄸ) is pronounced akin to the t of "stay." The aspirated consonants have an apostrophe after the romanized letter according the McCune-Reischauer System of Romanization. They are pronounced with a heavy expulsion of air. The "k"(ㅋ) is similar, for example, to the k of "kill." Vowels are pronounced essentially as noted on the inside front cover.

The Korean Letters and Their Sounds

(1) Vowels

1. Simple Vowels

Korean letter	Romanization	English sound
ㅏ	a	as *a* of f*a*ther
ㅑ	ya	as *ya* of *ya*rd
ㅓ	ŏ	as *u* of h*u*t
ㅕ	yŏ	as *you* of *you*ng
ㅗ	o	as *o* of h*o*me
ㅛ	yo	as *yo* of *yo*ke
ㅜ	u	as *o* of d*o*
ㅠ	yu	as *you* of *you*
ㅡ	ŭ	as *e* of tak*e*n
ㅣ	i	as *i* of *i*nk

2. Diphthongs

Korean letter	Romanization	English sound
ㅐ	ae	as *a* of h*a*t
ㅒ	yae	as *ya* of *ya*m
ㅔ	e	as *e* of m*e*t
ㅖ	ye	as *ye* of *ye*s
ㅚ	oe	as *ö* of K*ö*ln
ㅟ	wi	as *wie* of *wie*ld
ㅢ	ŭi	approximately the sound of *e* of tak*e*n followed by *e* of w*e*
ㅘ	wa	as *wa* of *wa*n
ㅝ	wŏ	as *wo* of *wo*n
ㅙ	wae	as *wa* of *wa*g
ㅞ	we	as *we* of *we*t

(2) Consonants

1. Simple Consonants

Korean letter	Romanization (position)			examples	English sound
	initial	medial	final		
ㄱ	k	k or g	k	*kolgyok* (골격) *kukka*(국가)	as *k*ing or *g*rocer (lightly aspirated)
ㄴ	n	n	n	always n	as *n*ame
ㄷ	t	t or d	n,t	*tatta*(닫다) *salda*(살다)	as *t*oy or *d*epend (lightly aspirated)
ㄹ	r	r or l	l	*radio*(라디오) *mulli*(물리)	as *r*ain or *l*i*l*y
ㅁ	m	m	m	always m	as *m*other
ㅂ	p	p or b	p	*pŏppok* (법복)	as *p*in or *b*ook (lightly aspirated)
ㅅ	s or sh	s	d,t n,s	*suttol*(숫돌)	as *s*ame(lightly pronounced)
ㅇ	not romanized		ng	*angyang* (앙양)	as ki*ng*
ㅈ	ch	ch or j	t	*chujŏnja* (주전자) *pit*(빗)	as *J*ohn
ㅊ	ch'	ch'	t	*ch'ach'ŭm* (차츰) *salkat*(살갗)	as *ch*urch
ㅋ	k'	k'	k	*k'ungk'ung* (쿵쿵) *puŏk*(부엌)	as *k*ill
ㅌ	t'	t'	t	*t'ant'anhan* (탄탄한) *pat*(밭)	as *t*ank
ㅍ	p'	p'	p	*p'ŏlp'ŭ*(펄프) *ap*(앞)	as *p*ump
ㅎ	h	h	-	*hwahae*(화해) *hwahak*(화학)	as *h*igh

2. Double Consonants

Korean letter	Romanization (position)				English sound
	initial	medial	final	examples	
ㄲ	kk	kk	k	*kk*a*k*ta(깎다) pa*kk*at(바깥)	as Ja*ck*
ㄸ	tt	tt	–	*tt*ok*tt*ok'an (똑똑한)	as s*t*ay
ㅃ	pp	pp	–	*pp*ŏt*pp*ŏt'an (뻣뻣한)	as s*p*y
ㅆ	ss	ss	t	*ss*ŭl*ss*ŭrhan (쓸쓸한) i*tt*a(있다)	as e*ss*ence
ㅉ	tch	tch	–	*tch*ap*tch*arhan (짭짤한)	as Li*tz*
ㄳ	not used be- tween vowels		ks(h) k	no*k*(넋) no*ksh*i(넋이)	
ㄵ	″		nj n	a*n*ta(앉다) a*nj*ŭn(앉은)	
ㄶ	″		n n	ma*n*t'a(많다) ma*n*ŭn(많은)	
ㄺ	″		k or lg k	i*k*ta(읽다) i*lg*ŭn(읽은) ta*k*(닭)	
ㄻ	″		m or lm m	sa*m*ta(삶다) sa*lm*ŭn(삶은) sa*m*(삶)	
ㄼ	″		p or lb p	ya*p*ta(얇다) ya*lb*ŭn(얇은)	
ㄽ	″		ls(h) l	to*l*(돐), to*lsh*i(돐이)	
ㄾ	″		lt' l	hu*l*ta(훑다) hu*lt'*ŭn(훑은)	
ㄿ	″		lp' p	ŭ*p*ta(읊다) ŭ*lp'*ŭn(읊은)	
ㅀ	″		l l	shi*l*t'a(싫다) shi*lk*'o(싫고)	
ㅄ	″		ps(h) p	ka*p*(값), ka*psh*i(값이)	

Korean Alphabet I

	ㄱ k(g)	ㄴ n	ㄷ t(d)	ㄹ r(l)	ㅁ m	ㅂ p(b)	ㅅ s
ㅏ a	가 k(g)a	나 na	다 t(d)a	라 r(l)a	마 ma	바 p(b)a	사 sa
ㅑ ya	갸 k(g)ya	냐 nya	댜 t(d)ya	랴 r(l)ya	먀 mya	뱌 p(b)ya	샤 sya
ㅓ ŏ	거 k(g)ŏ	너 nŏ	더 t(d)ŏ	러 r(l)ŏ	머 mŏ	버 p(b)ŏ	서 sŏ
ㅕ yŏ	겨 k(g)yŏ	녀 nyŏ	뎌 t(d)yŏ	려 r(l)yŏ	며 myŏ	벼 p(b)yŏ	셔 syŏ
ㅗ o	고 k(g)o	노 no	도 t(d)o	로 r(l)o	모 mo	보 p(b)o	소 so
ㅛ yo	교 k(g)yo	뇨 nyo	됴 t(d)yo	료 r(l)yo	묘 myo	뵤 p(b)yo	쇼 syo
ㅜ u	구 k(g)u	누 nu	두 t(d)u	루 r(l)u	무 mu	부 p(b)u	수 su
ㅠ yu	규 k(g)yu	뉴 nyu	듀 t(d)yu	류 r(l)yu	뮤 myu	뷰 p(b)yu	슈 syu
ㅡ ŭ	그 k(g)ŭ	느 nŭ	드 t(d)ŭ	르 r(l)ŭ	므 mŭ	브 p(b)ŭ	스 sŭ
ㅣ i	기 k(g)i	니 ni	디 t(d)i	리 r(l)i	미 mi	비 p(b)i	시 shi

Korean Alphabet II

ㅇ ng	ㅈ ch(j)	ㅊ ch'	ㅋ k'	ㅌ t'	ㅍ p'	ㅎ h
아 a	자 ch(j)a	차 ch'a	카 k'a	타 t'a	파 p'a	하 ha
야 ya	쟈 ch(j)ya	챠 ch'ya	캬 k'ya	탸 t'ya	퍄 p'ya	햐 hya
어 ŏ	저 ch(j)ŏ	처 ch'ŏ	커 k'ŏ	터 t'ŏ	퍼 p'ŏ	허 hŏ
여 yŏ	져 ch(j)yŏ	쳐 ch'yŏ	켜 k'yŏ	텨 t'yŏ	펴 p'yŏ	혀 hyŏ
오 o	조 ch(j)o	초 ch'o	코 k'o	토 t'o	포 p'o	호 ho
요 yo	죠 ch(j)yo	쵸 ch'yo	쿄 k'yo	툐 t'yo	표 p'yo	효 hyo
우 u	주 ch(j)u	추 ch'u	쿠 k'u	투 t'u	푸 p'u	후 hu
유 yu	쥬 ch(j)yu	츄 ch'yu	큐 k'yu	튜 t'yu	퓨 p'yu	휴 hyu
으 ŭ	즈 ch(j)ŭ	츠 ch'ŭ	크 k'ŭ	트 t'ŭ	프 p'ŭ	흐 hŭ
이 i	지 ch(j)i	치 ch'i	키 k'i	티 t'i	피 p'i	히 hi

Simplified Chart for the Romanization

Initial \ Final		ㄱ K	ㄴ N	ㄹ L R	ㅁ M	ㅂ P	ㅇ NG
ㅇ		g	n	r	m	b	ng
ㄱ	K	kk	n-g(k)	lg(k)	mg(k)	pk	ngg(k)
ㄴ	N	ngn	nn	ll	mn	mn	ngn
ㄷ	T	kt	nd(t)	lt(d)	md(t)	pt	ngd(t)
ㄹ	(R)	ngn	ll	ll	mn	mn	ngn
ㅁ	M	ngm	nm	lm	mm	mm	ngm
ㅂ	P	kp	nb(p)	lb(p)	mb(p)	pp	ngb(p)
ㅅ	S	ks	ns	ls	ms	ps	ngs
ㅈ	CH	kch	nj(ch)	lj(ch)	mj(ch)	pch	ngj(ch)
ㅊ	CH'	kch'	nch'	lch'	mch'	pch'	ngch'
ㅋ	K'	kk'	nk'	lk'	mk'	pk'	ngk'
ㅌ	T'	kt'	nt'	lt'	mt'	pt'	ngt'
ㅍ	P'	kp'	np'	lp'	mp'	pp'	ngp'
ㅎ	H	k'	nh	rh	mh	p'	ngh

Sound Changes

Changes of certain sound are necessary for linking words without a pause.

(1) When consonants *p*, *t*, or *k* are in the end of the word followed by a vowel of the next word, they are pronounced as *b*, *d*, or *g*:

pa*p*i→pa*b*i	rice(as subject)	밥이
ŏtŏmŏkta→ŏdŏmŏkta	beg food	얻어먹다
pyŏ*k*i→pyŏ*g*i	wall(as subject)	벽이

(2) If the word ends with the consonant *l* and is followed by a vowel, the sound of *l* is changed to *r*:

ki*l*i→ki*r*i	length	길이
pyŏ*l*ul→pyŏ*r*ŭl	star(as objective)	별을

(3) If the combinations are -*ln*-, -*mr*-, -*ngr*-, or -*nr*-, the sound changes as follows:

hi*l*nan→hi*ll*an	blame	힐난
yŏm*r*yŏ→yŏm*n*yŏ	concern	염려
sŭng*r*i→sŭng*n*i	victory	승리
pan*r*an→pa*ll*an	rebellion	반란

(4) When consonants *k*, *p*, or *t* are followed by *h*, *m*, *n*, *r*, or *s* of the next word, the sound changes as follows:

ku*kh*wa→ku*k'*wa	chrysanthemum	국화
ku*km*in→ku*ngm*in	nation	국민
pae*kn*yŏn→pae*ngn*yŏn	a hundred years	백년
mo*kr*yŏn→mo*ngn*yŏn	magnolia	목련

kŭphan→kŭp'an	urgent	급한
chipmada→chimmada	every house	집마다
apmun→ammun	front gate	앞문
sŏpri→sŏmni	providence	섭리
mathida→mach'ida	hit	맞히다
kŏjitmal→kŏjinmal	lie	거짓말
motnan→monnan	plain	못난
kkaekŭthan→kkaekŭt'an	clean	깨끗한
matsŭmnida→massŭmnida	be right	맞습니다

(5) There are some exceptions of above pattern. Examples are shown below:

A (Sound changes)

mulbyŏng→mulpyŏng	water bottle	물병
chŏldaejŏk→chŏltaejŏk	absolute	절대적
palgarak→palkarak	toe	발가락
kyŏljŏng→kyŏlchŏng	decision	결정
pŏmbŏp→pŏmpŏp	breaking the law	범법
shimda→shimta	plant	심다
momgap→momkap	ransom	몸값
momjit→momchit	gesture	몸짓
sanbul→sanpul	woodfire	산불
shinda→shinta	put on	신다
son-garak→sonkarak	finger	손가락
manjŏm→manchŏm	full marks	만점
hyŏngbŏp→hyŏngpŏp	criminal law	형법
yongdon→yongton	pocket money	용돈
chŭnggwŏn→chŭngkwŏn	stock	증권
changjŏm→changchŏm	merit	장점

B (Sound does not change)

kyŏlbak	binding	결박
cholda	doze	졸다
mulgŏn	thing	물건
maljoshim	care in speaking	말조심
nambu	southern part	남부

kam*d*ong	impression	감동
sŏ*mg*wang	flash	섬광
kam*j*a	potato	감자
chŏ*nb*o	telegram	전보
chan*d*i	lawn	잔디
sŏ*n-g*ŏ	election	선거
na*ngb*i	waste	낭비
no*ngd*am	joke	농담
ko*ngj*ang	factory	공장

For the words shown above no phonetical rules of pronunciation can easily be found, though there is some complicated pattern within the irregularities. A practical suggestion is to go by with individual word.

Phonetic Pattern

The formation of the Korean letters and words will help to follow the foregoing compact charts of the elements of the basic Korean characters and their phonemic rules. The reader will find the spelling rules.

1. The Korean alphabet consists of twenty-four letters, ten vowels and fourteen consonants. The individual letter has a phonetic value and independent form; two or more letters are written together as syllables as in Latin. These represent the phonemes of the Korean language.

The vowels are used only as medial sounds. These are: ㅏ a, ㅑ ya, ㅓ ŏ, ㅕ yŏ, ㅗ o, ㅛ yo, ㅜ u, ㅠ yu, ㅡ ŭ, ㅣ i(Among these ㅏ, ㅓ and ㅣ are used for modifying or compounding medial sound.); ㅐ ae, ㅒ yae, ㅔ e, ㅖ ye, ㅚ oe, ㅟ wi, ㅢ ŭi(modified by the ㅣ i); ㅘ wa, ㅝ wŏ (compounded with the ㅏ a, ㅓ ŏ); and ㅙ wae, ㅞ we (modified by the ㅏ a, ㅓ ŏ, ㅣ i in compound.)

The fourteen consonants are ㄱ kiyŏk, ㄴ niŭn, ㄷ tigŭt, ㄹ riŭl, ㅁ miŭm, ㅂ piŭp, ㅅ shiot, ㅇ iŭng, ㅈ chiŭt, ㅊ ch'iŭt, ㅋ k'iŭk, ㅌ t'iŭt, ㅍ p'iŭp, ㅎ hiŭt.

The name of each consonant contains two syllables; starting with the letter itself of the first syllable and ending with the same letter of the second syllable. Thus, when decoding the name of the consonant into sound, one can start sounding with that letter and also end with that letter.

The fourteen consonants also have both beginning and ending position. These consonants except for ㅇ ng, ㅊ ch', and ㅋ k' are combined to make double consonants. Usually double consonants are in the ending position, except for ㄲ kk, ㄸ tt, ㅃ pp, ㅆ ss, ㅉ tch. But ㄲ and ㅆ come in either position, beginning and ending.

To form a syllable or a word, a combination of consonants and vowels should be made either in left-to-right or top-to-bottom direction, Examples : 1) 가 ka, 개 kae, 꽤 kwae(simple consonants with various vowels); 2) 까 kka, 따 tta, 빠 ppa, 싸 ssa, 깨 kkae, 꾀 kkoe (double consonants with various vowels); 3) 박 pak (consonant +vowel+consonant), 백 paek (consonant+double vowel +consonant).

2. The meaning of simple and double consonants is different. Examples: 깨다 kkaeda(to break) and 개다 kaeda(to fold) or 찌다 tchida(to steam) and 지다 chida(to sink); or 빵 ppang(bread) and 방 pang(room).

3. In Korean language the accent is not articulate in syllable as in English, thus the intonations in Korean speech are rather even and smooth.

Korean Grammar

A few notes on grammatical details are provided for those who wish to grasp and understand the structure of Korean language and to have a further skill of Korean composition.

Article

Korean language does not have article like a or the in English. Also single and plural form is not as clear as English. Thus, 개 kae (dog) may mean *the dog*, *a dog*, *dogs* or *the dogs* depending on the context.

Table of Pronoun

English	Korean	English	Korean
I	nanŭn, naega	he	kŭnŭn, kŭga
we	urinŭn, uriga	his	kŭŭi
my	naŭi	him	kŭrŭl, kŭege
our	uriŭi	she	kŭ yŏjaga, kŭ yŏjanŭn
me	na-ege, narŭl	her	kŭ yŏjaŭi
us	uriege, urirŭl	her	kŭ yŏjarŭl, kŭ yŏja-ege
you	tangshinŭn, tangshini	they	kŭdŭrŭn, kŭdŭri
your	tangshinŭi	their	kŭdŭrŭi
you	tangshinege, tangshinŭl	them	kŭdŭrege, kŭdŭrŭl

Adjectives

The position of adjective in Korean language is before the noun. Korean adjective, like English adjective, modifies the noun by placing it in front of the noun: hŭin changmi 흰장미 *white rose*, yeppŭn sonyŏ 예쁜 소녀 *pretty girl*, chaemiinnŭn ch'aek 재미있는 책 *interesting book* etc.

I have a white rose.
Nanŭn <u>hŭin</u> changmirŭl kajigo issŭmnida.

Other function of adjective like in English is descriptive of the subject: hŭimnida 흽니다 *is white*, yeppŭmnida 예쁩니다 *is pretty*. Notice that these Korean words do not mean *white, pretty* but *is white, is pretty*.

This rose is white.   I changminŭn <u>hŭimnida.</u>
This book is interesting. I ch'aegŭn <u>chaemiissŭmnida.</u>

Numerals

Arabic numeral		Cardinal numeral	Ordinal numeral
0	yŏng		
1	il	hana	ch'ŏt(pŏn)tchae
2	i	tul	tultchae, tubŏntchae
3	sam	set	se(bŏn)tchae
4	sa	net	ne(bŏn)tchae
5	o	tasŏt	tasŏt(pŏn)tchae
6	yuk	yŏsŏt	yŏsŏt(pŏn)tchae
7	ch'il	ilgop	ilgop(pŏn)tchae
8	p'al	yŏdŏl	yŏdŏl(pŏn)tchae
9	ku	ahop	ahop(pŏn)tchae
10	ship	yŏl	yŏl(pŏn)tchae
11	shibil	yŏl hana	yŏl han(bŏn)tchae
12	shibi	yŏl tul	yŏl tu(bŏn)tchae
13	shipsam	yŏl set	yŏl se(bŏn)tchae

20	iship	sŭmul	sŭmu(bŏn)tchae
21	ishibil	sŭmul hana	sŭmul han(bŏn)tchae
22	ishibi	sŭmul tul	sŭmul tu(bŏn)tchae
30	samship	sŏrŭn	sŏrŭn(bŏn)tchae
40	saship	mahŭn	mahŭn(bŏn)tchae
50	oship	shwin	shwin(bŏn)tchae
60	yukship	yesun	yesun(bŏn)tchae
70	ch'ilship	irŭn	irŭn(bŏn)tchae
80	p'alship	yŏdŭn	yŏdŭn(bŏn)tchae
90	kuship	ahŭn	ahŭn(bŏn)tchae
100	paek	paek	paek(pŏn)tchae

For the numbers over hundred there is only way of counting.

200	ibaek	2,000	ich'ŏn
300	sambaek	3,000	samch'ŏn
400	sabaek	4,000	sach'ŏn
500	obaek	5,000	och'ŏn
600	yukpaek	6,000	yukch'ŏn
700	ch'ilbaek	7,000	ch'ilch'ŏn
800	p'albaek	8,000	p'alch'ŏn
900	kubaek	9,000	kuch'ŏn
1,000	ch'ŏn	10,000	man
20,000	iman	50,000	oman
100,000	shimman	1,000,000	paengman

Verbs

A characteristic of the Korean sentence is the verb expression at the end of the sentence. The verb in Korean functions as either *something happens, someone does something or something in a certain manner*.

Position of Verb

Note that the Korean verb is placed at the end of

the sentence in following example:

English structure : I read a book.

Korean structure : I <u>nŭn</u> a book <u>ŭl</u> read.

           (Na)   (ch'aek)   (iksŭmnida)

Verb Stem and Suffix

The verb in Korean consists of one verb stem plus one or more suffixes. For instance, the verb oda 오다 (*to come*) takes the suffixes in the following manner:

Korean	Stem-Suffix	Stem-Suffix	Meaning
오다	오-	o-	to come
옵니다	오-ㅂ니다	o-mnida	come
옵시다	오-ㅂ시다	o-pshida	let's come
옵니까	오-ㅂ니까	o-mnikka	do (you) come

Conjugation

In Korean dictionary, verbs are shown in present tense ending with -da -다.

kada 가다   I, you, we, they *go (or to go)*

oda 오다   I, you, we, they *come (or to come)*

However, in ordinary conversation the above forms of present tense are rarely heard. Instead, the suffixes such as -mnida -ㅂ니다(after vowel) or -ŭmnida -읍니다 (after consonant) are very common.

The following charts show changes of verb according to its tense. Please note that there are certain patterns (or rules) one can make from the examples which can be applied in making other various verb forms.

(1) Present tense

After	Suffix	Example	Meaning
Vowel	-mnida	sada 사다→samnida	to buy
Consonant	-ŭmnida	ch'amta참다→ch'amŭmnida	to endure

(2) Past tense

After		Suffix	Example	Meaning
Vowel	a	-ssŭmnida	sada사다→sassŭmnida	bought
	o	-assŭmnida	ssoda쏘다→ssoassŭmnida	shot
	e		peda베다→peŏssŭmnida	cut
	i	-ŏssŭmnida	kida기다→kiŏssŭmnida	crept
	u		chuda주다→chuŏssŭmnida	gave
	ha	-yŏssŭmnida	hada하다→hayŏssŭmnida	did
	oda	-wassŭmnida	oda오다→wassŭmnida	came
Consonant	a+c	-assŭmnida	ch'amta참다→ch'amassŭmnida	endured
	o+c		nokta녹다→nogassŭmnida	melted
	other vowel +consonant	-ŏssŭmnida	chŏpta접다·chŏbŏssŭmnida	folded
			ipta입다→ibŏssŭmnida	wore
			mutta묻다→murŏssŭmnida	asked

(3) Future tense

After	Suffix	Example	Meaning
Vowel	-gessŭmnida	sada사다→sagessŭmnida	I will buy
		hada하다→hagessŭmnida	I will do
Consonant	-k[g]essŭmnida	ipta입다→ipkessŭmnida	I will wear
		mutta묻다→mutkessŭmnida	I will ask

Omission of Subject

Like other language, it is not unusual in Korean language to drop the subject of sentence particularly when meaning is obvious without mentioning the details. Kamnida(*go*) may mean I, you, he, she, they, we am/is/are going. Kamnikka? (*go?*) may mean Is/Are you, he, she, they going?

Kamnida. Go.	(*I'm*) *going.*

Taegue kamnida. Taegu to go.	(*I'm*) *going to Taegu.*

Naeil Taegue kamnida.
Tomorrow Taegu to go.
             (*I'm*) *going to Taegu tomorrow.*

Nanŭn naeil Taegue kamnida.
I tomorrow Taegu to go.
             I'm going to Taegu tomorrow.

Declarative and Interrogative

Unlike English, Korean language has different suffixes for declarative and interrogative sentence respectively.

Sonyŏni kamnida.	*The boy is going.*
Sonyŏni kamnikka?	*Is the boy going?*

In above example, the suffix -da 다 is used for a declarative and -kka 까 for a interrogative sentence.

Negative Sentence

Negatives of Korean verbs may be formed in several ways but the easiest is simply to add the negative word an (*not*) before the verb.

Kamnida.	*He's going.*
An kamnida.	*He's not going.*
Kamnikka?	*Are you going?*
An kamnikka?	*Aren't you going?*

Another negative word that comes in handy is mot (*can't, unable to*).

Kamnida.	*I'm going.*
Mot kamnida.	*I can't go.*
Kamnikka?	*Is she going?*
Mot kamnikka?	*Can't she go?*

Yes and No

When Korean speakers answer "yes" or "no" questions, they agree or disagree with the question as in, "Yes, we have no apples." This differs from English usage when the question is in the negative. For examples:

Naeil kamnikka?	*Are you going tomorrow?*
Ne.	*Yes. (That's right, I'm going.)*
Anio.	*No. (That's not right, I'm not going.)*
An kamnikka?	*Aren't you going?*
Ne.	*Yes. (That's right, I'm not going.)*
Anio	*No. (That's not right, I'm going.)*

A

a *art. As an indefinite article,* **a** *is not translated in Korean.* ~ *hotel* hot'el 호텔/ ~ *ticket* ipchangkwŏn 입장권, ch'ap'yo 차표. *Can I get* ~ *ticket here?* Yŏgisŏ ch'ap'yorŭl sal su issŭmnikka? 여기서 차표를 살 수 있읍니까? (*When* ~ *means each, it may be translated by* il 일 *or* han 한.) *I'd like to stay for* ~ *week.* Han[il] chuil tongan sukpak'ago shipsŭmnida. 한[일] 주일 동안 숙박하고 싶습니다/ ~ *dollar* il tallŏ 일 달러/ *an hour ago* han shigan chŏn 한 시간 전/ *in* ~ *word* hanmadiro marhamyŏn 한마디로 말하면.

abandon *vt.* pŏrida 버리다, tannyŏmhada 단념하다, kŭmanduda 그만두다.

abbreviation *n.* saengnyak 생략, (*of symbolic characters*) yakcha 약자.

abdomen *n.* pae 배, pokpu 복부(腹部). *sleep upon the* ~ ŏptŭryŏ chada 엎드려 자다/ *I have a pain in my* ~. Paega ap'ŭmnida 배가 아픕니다.

abdominal *adj.* ~ *breathing* pokshik hohŭp 복식(腹式) 호흡/*an* ~ *operation* kaebok susul 개복(開腹) 수술/ ~ *pregnancy* pokkang imshin 복강 임신.

abduct *vt.* yugoehada 유괴하다, napch'ihada 납치하다. ~ *a person from his home* saramŭl yugoehada 사람을 유괴하다.

abductor *n.* yugoeja 유괴자.

abhor *vt.* mopshi shirŏhada 몹시 싫어하다. *I* ~ *snakes.* Nanŭn paemŭl mopshi shirŏhamnida. 나는 뱀을 몹시 싫어합니다.

abide *vi.,vt.* salda 살다, (*be faithful to*) …e ch'ungshirhada …에 충실하다, (*endure*) kyŏndida 견디다. ~ *for a time* chamshi salda 잠시 살다/ ~ *by a judgement* p'an-gyŏre pokchonghada 판결에 복종하다/ *law-abiding people* pŏbŭl chik'inŭn kungmin 법을 지키는 국민/ *Who can* ~ *that?* Kŭrŏn irŭl nuga ch'amŭl su itkessŭmnikka? 그런 일을 누가 참을 수 있겠읍니까?

ability *n.* nŭngnyŏk 능력, suwan 수완. *a man of* ~ suwan-ga 수완가/ *display one's* ~ chagiŭi suwanŭl parhwihada 자기의 수완을 발휘하다/ *He shows rare* ~ *in this direction.* Kŭnŭn i pangmyŏne pisanghan suwanŭl issŭmnida. 그는 이 방면에 비상한 수완을 가지고 있읍니다.

able *adj.* hal su innŭn 할 수 있는, himi innŭn 힘이 있는. *an* ~ *man* suwan-ga 수완가/ *I'm pleased that you will be* ~ *to come.* Sŏnsaengkkesŏ oshil su ittani much'ŏk pan-gapsŭmnida. 선생께서 오실 수 있다니 무척 반갑습니다 / *an* ~ *writer* yunŭnghan chakka 유능한 작

ablution *n.* mogyok 목욕, chaegye 재계.　　　　　　[가.

abnormal *adj.* isanghan 이상한, (*unnatural*) pujayŏnhan 부자연한. *an* ~ *condition* isanghan sangt'ae 이상한 상태.

aboard *adv.*, *prep.* pae[yŏlch'a, pihaenggi]e 배[열차, 비행기]에. *All* ~ *please.* Yŏrŏbun t'apsŭnghae chushipshio. 여러분 탑승해 주십시오.

abolish *vt.* p'yejihada 폐지하다. *We must* ~ *unnecessary punishments.* Pulp'iryohan hyŏngbŏrŭn p'yejihaeya hamnida. 불필요한 형벌은 폐지해야 합니다.

A-bomb *n.* wŏnja p'okt'an 원자 폭탄 (=*Atomic bomb*).

abound *vi.* p'ungbuhada 풍부하다, mant'a 많다. *Fish* ~*s in the river.* Kŭ kangenŭn mulkogiga manssŭmnida. 그 강에는 물고기가 많습니다/ *Korea* ~*s with rain.* Han-gugenŭn piga mani omnida. 한국에는 비가 많이 옵니다/ ~ *in natural resources* ch'ŏnyŏn chawŏni p'ungbuhada. 천연 자원이 풍부하다.

about *prep.* (*concerning*) ...e kwanhayŏ ...에 관하여. —*adv.* (*almost*) kŏŭi 거의, taeryak 대략, (*not far away in place or time*) tullee 둘레에, yŏgijŏgi 여기저기. *a book* ~ *gardening* wŏnyee kwanhan ch'aek 원예에 관한 책/ *What are you* ~? Muŏsŭl hago kyeshimnikka? 무엇을 하고 계십니까/ *What is it all* ~? Todaech'e musŭn malssŭmijiyo? 도대체 무슨 말씀이지요/ *Don't leave waste paper and empty bottles* ~ *in the park.* Kongwŏnesŏnŭn amudena hyujiwa pin pyŏngŭl pŏriji mashio. 공원에서는 아무데나 휴지와 빈 병을 버리지 마

시오/ *Don't drop cigarette butt* ~. Tambae kkong-ch'orŭl amudena pŏriji mashio. 담배 꽁초를 아무데나 버리지 마시오.

above *prep.* (*higher than*) ...poda wie …보다 위에, (*more than*) isangŭro 이상으로, (*beyond*) ...ŭl ch'owŏrhayŏ …을 초월하여. *The sun rose* ~ *the horizon.* Haega chip'yŏngsŏn wie ttŏollassŭmnida. 해가 지평선 위에 떠올랐읍니다/ *We were flying* ~ *the clouds.* Urinŭn kurŭm wirŭl nalgo issŏssŭmnida. 우리는 구름 위를 날고 있었읍니다/ *It weighs* ~ *ten tons.* Mugega ship t'on isangimnida. 무게가 10 톤 이상입니다/ ~ *all* (*more than anything else*) kŭ chungesŏdo 그 중에서도, t'ŭk'i 특히.

abroad *adv.* haeoee 해외에, oegugŭro 외국으로. —*n.* haeoe 해외. *Do you like to live* ~? Oegugesŏ salgirŭl choahashimnikka? 외국에서 살기를 좋아하십니까/ *He went* ~ *last year.* Kŭnŭn chinanhae haeoero ttŏnassŭmnida. 그는 지난해 해외로 떠났읍니다/ *from* ~ haeoerobut'ŏ 해외로부터.

absence *n.* pujae 부재. *during your* ~ tangshini ŏmnŭn tongane 당신이 없는 동안에/ ~ *from school* kyŏlsŏk 결석/ ~ *of mind* pangshim 방심(放心)/ *He called on me in my* ~. Naega ŏmnŭn tongane kŭga ch'ajawassŭmnida. 내가 없는 동안에 그가 찾아왔읍니다.

absent *adj.* pulch'amhan 불참한, kyŏlsŏk〔kyŏlgŭn〕han 결석〔결근〕한. —*vt.* kyŏlsŏk〔kyŏlgŭn〕hada 결석〔결근〕하다. *He was* ~ *from his work.* Kŭnŭn kyŏlgŭnhaessŭmnida. 그는 결근했읍니다/ *Why did you* ~ *yourself yesterday?* Ŏjenŭn wae kyŏlsŏk'aetchiyo? 어제는 왜 결석했지요?

absentee *n.* kyŏlgŭnja 결근자, kyŏlsŏkcha 결석자, pujaeja 부재자(不在者). *a long-term* ~ changgi kyŏlgŭnja 장기 결근자/ ~ *vote* pujaeja t'up'yo 부재자 투표. 「있는.

absent-minded *adj* ŏlppajin 얼빠진, mŏnghae innŭn 멍해

absolute *adj.* chŏltaeŭi 절대의, chŏltaejŏk 절대적. *an* ~ *majority* chŏltae tasu 절대 다수/ ~ *obedience* chŏltae pokchong 절대 복종/ ~ *right* chŏltae kwŏllyŏk 절대 권력.

absolutely *adv.* chŏltaero 절대로, mujokŏn 무조건. ~

right chŏltaero orŭn 절대로 옳은, (*in answer to a question*) kŭrŏk'omalgo 그렇고말고.

absorb *vt.* pparadŭrida 빨아들이다, hŭpsuhada 흡수하다. (*be*) ~*ed in* moltuhada 몰두하다, yŏlchunghada 열중하다/ *He was completely ~ed in reading.* Kŭnŭn toksŏe yŏlchunghago issŏssŭmnida. 그는 독서에 열중하고 있었읍니다.

abstain *vi.* kŭmanduda 그만두다, samgada 삼가다.

abstention *n.* kikwŏn 기권. ~ *from voting* t'up'yo kikwŏn 투표 기권.

absurd *adj.* t'ŏmuniŏmnŭn 터무니없는, ŏiŏmnŭn 어이없는. *Don't be ~!* Ŏiŏmnŭn chisŭn haji mashio. 어이없는 짓은 하지 마시오/ *What an ~ suggestion!* Maldo an toenŭn sori! 말도 안 되는 소리!

abundant *adj.* manŭn 많은, p'ungbuhan 풍부한. *an ~ harvest* p'ungjak 풍작/ *Is your country ~ in natural resources?* Tangshin naranŭn ch'ŏnyŏn chawŏni p'ungbuhamnikka? 당신 나라는 천연 자원이 풍부합니까?

academic *adj.* haksulchŏgin 학술적인, hagwŏnŭi 학원의. *the ~ year* hangnyŏndo 학년도/ *an ~ degree* hagwi 학위/ *Where can I see my ~ records?* Ŏdisŏ nae sŏngjŏkp'yorŭl pol su issŭmnikka? 어디서 내 성적표를 볼 수 있읍니까?

accept *vt.* padadŭrida 받아들이다, patta 받다. ~ *a gift* sŏnmurŭl patta 선물을 받다/ *Please ~ me as a friend.* Narŭl ch'in-guro sama chushio 나를 친구로 삼아 주시오/ *I can't ~ your apology.* Tangshinŭi sagwanŭn padadŭril su ŏpsŭmnida. 당신의 사과는 받아들일 수 없읍니다.

accident *n.* sago 사고, ubal sakŏn 우발 사건. *by ~* uyŏnhi 우연히/ *without ~* musahi 무사히/ *He was killed in a traffic ~.* Kŭnŭn kyot'ong sagoro chugŏssŭmnida. 그는 교통 사고로 죽었읍니다/ *There was an ~ on the Kyongbu line.* Kyŏngbusŏne sagoga palsaenghaessŭmnida. 경부선에 사고가 발생했읍니다/ ~ *insurance* sanghae pohŏm 상해(傷害) 보험.

accidentally *adv.* uyŏnhi 우연히.

accommodation *n.* sukpak shisŏl 숙박 시설. *Is there an ~*

facility on Mt. Sorak? Sŏraksanenŭn sukpak shisŏri toeŏ issŭmnikka? 설악산에는 숙박 시설이 되어 있읍니까?

accompany *vt.* …wa hamkke kada …와 함께 가다, tongbanhada 동반하다. *May I ~ you?* Hamkke kadŭrilkkayo? 함께 가드릴까요?

accomplish *vt.* iruda 이루다, sŏngch'wihada 성취하다. *~ a task* irŭl wansuhada 일을 완수하다/ *an ~ed fact* kijŏng sashil 기정 사실/ *I will ~ it by tomorrow.* Naeilkkaji wansuhagessŭmnida. 내일까지 완수하겠읍니다.

accord *vi.,vt.* ilch'ihada 일치하다, chohwahada 조화하다. *His deeds ~ with his words.* Kŭŭi ŏndongŭn ilch'ihago itta. 그의 언동은 일치하고 있다/ *~ with friends* ch'in-guwa hwahap'ada 친구와 화합(和合)하다. *—n.* (*agreement*) hyŏpchŏng 협정, (*will*) ŭiji 의지(意志). *of one's own ~* chajinhayŏ 자진하여/ *I did it of my own ~.* Nanŭn kŭgŏsŭl chajinhaesŏ hayŏssŭmnida. 나는 그것을 자진해서 하였읍니다.

accordance *n.* *in ~ with* …e ttara …에 따라, …kwa ilch'ihayŏ …과 일치하여. *In ~ with custom, they bowed to their teacher.* Kwallyee ttara kŭdŭrŭn sŏnsaengnimkke k'ŭnjŏrŭl haessŭmnida. 관례에 따라 그들은 선생님께 큰절을 했읍니다.

accordingly *adv.* ttarasŏ 따라서, kŭrŏmŭro 그러므로.

account *vi.,vt.* sŏlmyŏnghada 설명하다. …rago saenggak'ada …라고 생각하다. *—n.* kyesansŏ 계산서, (*explanation*) sŏlmyŏng 설명. *Can you ~ for the delay of the steamer?* Paenŭn wae nŭjŏtchiyo? 배는 왜 늦었지요/ *How do you ~ for it?* Kŭgŏsŭl ŏttŏk'e sŏlmyŏnghajiyo? 그것을 어떻게 설명하지요/ *I have an ~ with the Commercial Bank.* Nanŭn sangŏp ŭnhaengkwa kŏraega issŭmnida. 나는 상업 은행과 거래가 있읍니다/ *give a brief ~* kandanhi sŏlmyŏnghada 간단히 설명하다.

accountant *n.* hoegyesa 회계사, hoegyewŏn 회계원. *~ general* hoegye kwajang 회계 과장/ *the ~'s section* kyŏngnikwa 경리과.

accumulate *vt.* moŭda 모으다, ch'ukchŏk'ada 축적하다. *patiently ~ data* kosaenghayŏ charyorŭl moŭda 고생

하여 자료를 모으다.

accurate *adj*. chŏnghwak'an 정확한.

accuse *vt*. (*blame*) pinanhada 비난하다, (*indict*) kobar-[koso]hada 고발[고소]하다. *He was ~d of being a spy*. Kŭnŭn kanch'ŏpchoero kobaldanghaessŭmnida. 그는 간첩죄로 고발당했읍니다.

accuser *n*. kosoin 고소인.

accustom *vt*. iksukk'e hada 익숙케 하다. *We became ~ed to it*. Urinŭn kŏgie iksuk'aejyŏssŭmnida. 우리는 거기에 익숙해졌읍니다.

ache *vi*. ap'ŭda 아프다. —*n*. ap'ŭm 아픔. *My body ~s all over*. Nanŭn onmomi ap'ŭmnida. 나는 온몸이 아픕니다/ *My head ~s badly*. Nanŭn mŏriga mopshi ap'ŭmnida 나는 머리가 몹시 아픕니다/ *head~* tut'ong 두통/ *stomach~* pokt'ong 복통/ *tooth~* ch'it'ong 치통.

acid *adj*. shin 신. *~ taste* shinmat 신맛/ *A lemon is an ~ fruit*. Remonŭn shin kwairimnida. 레몬은 신 과일입니다.

acknowledge *vt*. injŏnghada 인정하다, (*express thanks for*) saryehada 사례하다. *I ~ it as true*. Nanŭn kŭgŏshi chinshirimŭl injŏnghamnida. 나는 그것이 진실임을 인정합니다/ *I ~d myself beaten*. Nanŭn chyŏttago marhaessŭmnida. 나는 졌다고 말했읍니다/ *gratefully ~ a favor* ŭnhyerŭl kamsahada 은혜를 감사하다.

acknowledgement *n*. sŭngin 승인, injŏng 인정, kamsa 감사, (*a receipt*) yŏngsujŭng 영수증.

acorn *n*. tot'ori 도토리.

acquaintance *n*. anŭn saram 아는 사람, ch'inji 친지. *an old ~* kumyŏn 구면(舊面).

acrobat *n*. kogyesa 곡예사.

across *adv*., *prep*. kŏnnŏsŏ 건너서, pandaetchoge 반대쪽에, shipcharo kyoch'ahayŏ 십자로 교차하여. *Can you swim ~?* Hŏmch'yŏ kŏnnŏl su issŭmnikka? 헤엄쳐 건널 수 있읍니까/ *I live ~ the river*. Nanŭn kang kŏnnŏe salgo issŭmnida. 나는 강 건너에 살고 있읍니다/ *I came ~ him on the street*. Kirŭl kadaga uyŏnhi kŭrŭl mannassŭmnida. 길을 가다가 우연히 그를 만났읍니다.

act *vi.* haenghada 행하다. —*n.* (*deed*) haengwi 행위, (*law*) pŏmnyŏng 법령, (*play*) mak 막. *He ~ed as guide to me.* Kŭga nae annaeyŏgŭl hae chuŏssŭmnida. 그가 내 안내역을 해 주었읍니다/ *You ~ed bravely.* Tangshinŭn yonggamhi haengdonghayŏssŭmnida. 당신은 용감히 행동하였 읍니다/ *I advise you to ~ sensibly.* Sŭlgiropke haengdonghashio. 슬기롭게 행동하시오/ *~ cautiously* choshimsŏng itke haengdonghada 조심성 있게 행동하다/ *~ decisively* tanhohi haengdonghada 단호히 행동하다/ *~ fair and square* kongmyŏng chŏngdaehage haengdonghada 공명 정대하게 행동하다/ *~ hastily* sŏdullŏ haengdonghada 서 둘러 행동하다/ *~ prudently* shinjunghi hada 신중히 하다/ *~ wisely* hyŏnmyŏnghage kulda 현명하게 굴다/ *an ~ of kindness* ch'injŏrhan haengdong 친절한 행동/ *The A~ was passed by Congress.* Kŭ pŏmnyŏngŭn kuk'oerŭl t'onggwahaessŭmnida. 그 법령은 국회를 통과했읍니다/ *A~ 1, Scene 3* ilmak samjang 1막 3장/ *first ~* sŏmak 서막/ *~ing manager* chibaein taeri 지배인 대리.

action *n.* haengwi 행위. *a bad ~* ak'aeng 악행 /*a good ~* sŏnhaeng 선행/ *mental ~* chŏngshin hwaltong 정신 활동 /*a man of ~* hwaltongga 활동가/ *~ film* hwalgŭk 활극.

active *adj.* hwaltongjŏgin 활동적인, hwalbarhan 활발한. *He is ~ in work.* Kŭnŭn hwalbarhi irhago issŭmnida. 그는 활발히 일하고 있읍니다/ *She has an ~ imagination.* Kŭnyŏnŭn sangsangnyŏgi wangsŏnghamnida. 그녀는 상 상력이 왕성합니다/ *an ~ volcano* hwarhwasan 활화산.

activity *n.* hwalbal 활발, hwaltongnyŏk 활동력. *one's time of full ~* hanch'angttae 한창때/ *be in ~* hwaltong chungida 활동 중이다.

actor *n.* paeu 배우. *a film ~* yŏnghwa paeu 영화 배우/ *a star ~* inki paeu 인기 배우.

actually *adv.* (*in fact*) shilchiro 실지로, shilchero 실제로, (*really*) ch'amŭro 참으로.

acute *adj.* kŭpsŏngŭi[in] 급성의[인]. *~ attack of appendicitis* kŭpsŏng maengjangyŏm 급성 맹장염/ *~ pneumonia* kŭpsŏng p'eryŏm 급성 폐렴.

add *vt*. tŏhada 더하다, kasanhada 가산하다. *an ~ed value tax* puga kach'ise 부가 가치세. *If you ~ 5 to 5, you get 10.* O-e orŭl tŏhamyŏn shibi toemnida. 5에 5를 더하면 10이 됩니다.

adding machine kyesan-gi 계산기.

addition *n*. tŏhagi 더하기, puga 부가. *in ~* kŭ wie 그 위에.

address *n*. chuso 주소. *Can you give me the ~ of Miss Lee?* I yangŭi chuso chom karŭch'yŏ chushigessŭmnikka? 이(李) 양의 주소 좀 가르쳐 주시겠읍니까/ *Here's my ~. Write to me when you have a time.* Igŏshi nae chusoimnida. Shigan issŭshimyŏn p'yŏnji chushipshio. 이것이 내 주소입니다. 시간 있으시면 편지 주십시오/ *Please give me your ~.* Chusorŭl karŭch'yŏ chushipshio. 주소를 가르쳐 주십시오/ *permanent ~* ponjŏk 본적.

addressee *n*. sushinin 수신인.

addresser *n*. palshinin 발신인.

adjourn *vt*. yŏn-gihada 연기하다. *The meeting was ~ed for a week.* Hoeŭinŭn ilchuilgan yŏn-gidoeŏssŭmnida. 회의는 1주일간 연기되었읍니다.

adjutant *n*. (*mil.*) pugwan 부관(副官).

administration *n*. haengjŏng 행정, (*control*) kwalli 관리, (*management*) kyŏngyŏng 경영. *business ~* saŏp kyŏngyŏng 사업 경영/ *military ~* kunjŏng 군정/ *personnel ~* insa kwalli 인사 관리.

admiral *n*. haegun taejang 해군 대장. *Fleet A~* haegun wŏnsu 해군 원수(元帥)/ *rear ~* haegun sojang 해군 소장/ *vice ~* haegun chungjang 해군 중장.

admire *vt*. kamt'anhada 감탄하다. *I ~ your dress.* Kŭ tŭresŭ mŏtchigunyo. 그 드레스 멋지군요/ *I ~ you for your effort in studying Korean.* Han-gungmarŭl paeunŭn noryŏgi nollapkunyo. 한국말을 배우는 노력이 놀랍군요.

admission *n*. ipchang 입장(入場). *~ fee* ipchangnyo 입장료/ *~ tax* ipchangse 입장세/ *~ ticket* ipchangkwŏn 입장권/ *A~ is free, sir.* Ipchangŭn muryoimnida. 입장은 무료입니다/ *How much is the ~ charge?* Ipchangnyonŭn ŏlmaimnikka? 입장료는 얼마입니까?

admit *vt.,vi*. nŏt'a 넣다, injŏnghada 인정하다. *I ~ that*

the statement is true. Kŭ mari sashirimŭl injŏnghamnida. 그 말이 사실임을 인정합니다.

admittance-fee *n.* ipchangnyo 입장료.

adopt *vt.* yangjaro samta 양자로 삼다, ch'aet'aek'ada 채택하다. *~ed daughter* yangnyŏ 양녀/ *~ed son* yangja 양자/ *They ~ed an orphan.* Kŭdŭrŭn koarŭl yangjaro samassŭmnida. 그들은 고아를 양자로 삼았읍니다. 「예배.

adoration *n.* (*veneration*) sungbae 숭배, (*worship*) yebae

adorn *vt.* changshik'ada 장식하다. *She ~ed herself with jewels.* Kŭnyŏnŭn posŏgŭro changshik'ago issŭmnida. 그녀는 보석으로 장식하고 있읍니다.

adult *n.* ŏrŭn 어른. *young ~s* ch'ŏngjangnyŏn 청장년(青壯年)/ *~ education* sŏngin kyoyuk 성인 교육.

advance *n.* chŏnjin 전진, chinbo 진보. *—vi.,vt.* chŏnjinhada 전진하다. *in ~* miri 미리/ *Send your luggage in ~.* Chimŭl miri palsonghashio. 짐을 미리 발송하시오/ *pay in ~* sŏnburhada 선불하다/ *~ payment* sŏnbul 선불.

advantage *n.* iik 이익. *the ~s of city life* toshi saenghwarŭi p'yŏnŭi 도시 생활의 편의/ *You have the ~ of me.* Chŏngmal molla poeŏssŭmnida. 정말 몰라 뵈었읍니다/ *What is the ~ of that?* Kŭgŏsŭi choŭn chŏmŭn muŏshimnikka? 그것의 좋은 점은 무엇입니까/ *I took ~ of that occasion.* Nanŭn kŭ kihoerŭl iyonghaessŭmnida. 나는 그 기회를 이용했읍니다.

advantageous *adj.* yurihan 유리한, yuyonghan 유용한.

adventure *n.* mohŏm 모험. *a tale of ~* mohŏmdam 모험담.

adventurer *n.* mohŏmga 모험가, (*impostor*) hyŏpchapkkun 협잡꾼.

adversary *n.* (*enemy*) chŏk 적, (*opponent*) sangdae 상대.

adverse *adj.* pandaeŭi 반대의. *~ winds* yŏkp'ung 역풍(逆風).

advertise *vi.,vt.* kwanggohada 광고하다. *~ in all newspapers* modŭn shinmune kwanggohada 모든 신문에 광고하다.

advertisement *n.* kwanggo 광고. *a help-wanted ~* kuin kwanggo 구인 광고/ *position-wanted ~* kujik kwanggo 구직 광고/ *an ~ column* kwanggonan 광고난.

advice *n.* ch'unggo 충고. *give* ~ ch'unggohada 충고하다/ *ask* ~ *of a person* namŭi choŏnŭl kuhada 남의 조언을 구하다/ *I want your* ~ *on the matter.* I ire kwanhaesŏ tangshinŭi ch'unggorŭl tŭtko shipsŭmnida. 이 일에 관해서 당신의 충고를 듣고 싶습니다/ *I came to you for* ~. Tangshinŭi ch'unggorŭl tŭrŭrŏ wassŭmnida. 당신의 충고를 들으러 왔습니다.

advisable *adj.* kwŏnhal manhan 권할 만한, hyŏnmyŏnghan 현명한. *It is* ~ *to go.* Kashinŭn p'yŏni chok'essŭmnida. 가시는 편이 좋겠습니다.

advise *vt.* ch'unggohada 충고하다. *I* ~*d him to be cautious.* Choshimhadorok kŭege ch'unggohaessŭmnida. 조심하도록 그에게 충고했습니다/ *I want a person who can* ~ *me.* Ch'unggorŭl chul su innŭn sarami p'iryohamnida. 충고를 줄 수 있는 사람이 필요합니다/ *What would you* ~ *me to see?* Muŏsŭl kugyŏnghalkkayo? 무엇을 구경할까요?

adviser, advisor *n.* choŏnja 조언자, komun 고문. *a legal* ~ pŏmnyul komun 법률 고문/ *a military* ~ kunsa komun 군사 고문/ *a technical* ~ kisul komun 기술 고문.

aerogram *n.* hanggong pongham yŏpsŏ 항공 봉함 엽서. *I'd like to have two* ~*s, please.* Hanggong pongham yŏpsŏrŭl tu chang chushio. 항공 봉함 엽서를 두 장 주시오.

affair *n.* sakŏn 사건, il 일. *business* ~*s* sangyong 상용 (商用)/ *a love* ~ yŏnae sakŏn 연애 사건 / *one's private* ~*s* sasaroun il 사사로운 일/ *Don't meddle with other people's* ~*s.* Namŭi ire kansŏp'aji mashio. 남의 일에 간섭하지 마시오.

affection *n.* aejŏng 애정. *the* ~ *of parent and child* pumowa ŏrini saiŭi aejŏng 부모와 어린이 사이의 애정.

affirm *vi.,vt.* tanŏnhada 단언하다. *I cannot* ~ *that he was there.* Kŭga kŏgie issŏttagonŭn tanŏnhal su ŏpsŭmnida. 그가 거기에 있었다고는 단언할 수 없습니다.

affliction *n.* kot'ong 고통, sunan 수난. *help people in* ~ kot'ongbannŭn saramdŭrŭl topta 고통받는 사람들을 돕다.

afford *vt.* ...hal yŏyuga itta...할 여유가 있다. *I cannot* ~ *a car.* Nanŭn ch'arŭl sal yŏyuga ŏpsŭmnida. 나는 차를 살 여유가 없습니다/ *I cannot* ~ *to be idle.* Nanŭn nolgo issŭl yŏyuga ŏpsŭmnida. 나는 놀고 있을 여유가 없읍니다.

afraid *adj.* turyŏwŏhayŏ 두려워하여, musŏun 무서운. *He is much ~ of the dog.* Kŭnŭn kaerŭl mopshi musŏwŏhamnida. 그는 개를 몹시 무서워합니다/ *I am ~ to go.* Nanŭn musŏwŏsŏ mot kagessŭmnida. 나는 무서워서 못 가겠읍니다.

after *adv.* twie 뒤에, najunge 나중에. —*prep.* …ŭi twie … 의 뒤에, …ŭi taŭme …의 다음에. —*conj.* …han taŭme …한 다음에, najunge 나중에. *You speak first, I will speak ~.* Mŏnjŏ malssŭmhashijiyo. Nanŭn najunge hagessŭmnida. 먼저 말씀하시지요. 나는 나중에 하겠읍니다/ *Come into the room ~ me.* Narŭl ttara pange tŭrŏoshio. 나를 따라 방에 들어오시오/ *Shut the door ~ you.* Tŭrŏomyŏn munŭl tadŭshio. 들어오면 문을 닫으시오. / *Let's begin the discussion ~ he comes.* Kŭga on taŭme t'ouirŭl shijak'apshida. 그가 온 다음에 토의를 시작합시다/ *day ~ day* nalmada 날마다/ *one another ~* ittarasŏ 잇따라서/ *one ~ the other* pŏn-gara 번갈아/ *year ~ year* haemada 해마다/ *~ all* kyŏlguk 결국.

afternoon *n.* ohu 오후. *this ~* onŭl ohu 오늘 오후/ *on Monday ~* wŏryoil ohue 월요일 오후에/ *Good ~.* Annyŏnghashimnikka? 안녕하십니까?

afterwards *adv.* kŭ hu 그 후, najunge 나중에. *They lived happily ever ~.* Kŭ hu kŭdŭrŭn haengbok'age chal sarassŭmnida. 그 후 그들은 행복하게 잘 살았읍니다.

again *adv.* tashi 다시, tto 또. *I hope to see you ~.* Tashi manna poepkessŭmnida. 다시 만나 뵙겠읍니다/ *Read it over ~.* Tashi han pŏn ilgŭshipshio. 다시 한 번 읽으십시오/ *Don't do that ~.* Tashinŭn kŭrŏji mashio. 다시는 그러지 마시오/ *I will never cry ~.* Tashinŭn ulji ank'essŭmnida. 다시는 울지 않겠읍니다 / *I hope you will soon be well ~.* Kot hoebok'ashigirŭl pimnida. 곧 회복하시기를 빕니다/ *If you fail the first time, try ~.* Ch'ŏtpŏntchae shilp'aehashimyŏn, tashi haeboshio. 첫번째 실패하시면 다시 해보시오/ *~ and ~* myŏt pŏnigo 몇 번이고.

against *prep. Don't stand leaning ~ the door.* Mune

kidae sŏji mashipshio. 문에 기대 서지 마십시오/ *Are you for or ~ the plan?* Tangshinŭn kŭ kyehoege ch'ansŏngimnikka, pandaeimnikka? 당신은 그 계획에 찬성입니까, 반대입니까?

age *n.* (*coll.*) nai 나이, (*pol.*) yŏnse 연세. *What is your ~?* Yŏnsega myŏch'ishimnikka? 연세가 몇이십니까/ *I am thirty years of ~.* Sŏrŭn sarimnida. 서른 살입니다/ *I am your ~.* Tangshin-gwa kat'ŭn naiyo. 당신과 같은 나이요/ *I have a son of your ~.* Na-egenŭn nŏmanhan adŭri itta. 나에게는 너만한 아들이 있다/ *You don't look your ~.* Yŏnseboda chŏlmŏ poishimnida. 연세보다 젊어 보이십니다/ *the air ~* hanggong shidae 항공 시대/ *the machine ~* kigye shidae 기계 시대.

agency *n.* taerijŏm 대리점. *an advertising ~* kwanggo taeriŏp 광고 대리업.

agent *n.* taeriin 대리인. *We have an ~ in Pusan.* Pusane taeriini issŭmnida. 부산에 대리인이 있읍니다/*a commission ~* wit'ak p'anmaein 위탁 판매인/ *a real estate ~* poktŏkpang 복덕방.

aggression *n.* konggyŏk 공격, ch'imnyak 침략.

aggressive *adj.* ch'imnyakchŏgin 침략적인, (*active*) hwaltongjŏgin 활동적인. *an ~ war* ch'imnyakchŏn 침략전/ *~ weapons* konggyŏk mugi 공격 무기.

ago *adv.* chŏne 전에. *ten years ~* ship nyŏn chŏn 십 년 전/ *three months ~* sŏk tal[sam kaewŏl] chŏne 석 달[삼 개월] 전에/ *seven days ~* ilchuil chŏne 일주일 전에/ *an hour ~* han shigan chŏne 한 시간 전에/ *a long time ~* orae chŏne 오래 전에/ *two nights ~* kŭjŏkke pame 그저께 밤에/ *My father died 5 years ~.* Abŏjikkesŏnŭn onyŏn chŏne toragasyŏssŭmnida. 아버지께서는 5년 전에 돌아가셨읍니다.

agony *n.* komin 고민, kot'ong 고통. *mental ~* pŏnmin 번민.

agree *vi.* tongŭihada 동의하다. *I cannot ~ with you.* Nanŭn tongŭihal su ŏpsŭmnida. 나는 동의할 수 없읍니다/ *We all ~ed on that terms.* Kŭ chokŏne modu ŭigyŏni ilch'ihayŏssŭmnida. 그 조건에 모두 의견이 일치하였읍니다/ *I ~ with you in your views.* Tangshinŭi kyŏnhaee tongŭihamnida. 당신의 견해에 동의합니다.

agreeable *adj.* kibun choŭn 기분 좋은. *She has an ~ voice.* Kŭnyŏŭi ŭmsŏngŭn tŭtkiga chossŭmnida. 그녀의 음성은 듣기가 좋습니다/ *~ manners* kibun choŭn t'aedo 기분 좋은 태도/ *Are you ~ to the proposal?* Kŭ cheŭie tongŭihae chushigessŭmnikka? 그 제의에 동의해 주시겠 읍니까?

agreement *n.* hyŏpchŏng 협정, kyeyak 계약. *sign an ~* hyŏpchŏnge sŏmyŏnghada 협정에 서명하다/ *make an ~* kyeyak'ada 계약하다/ *an ~ to rent a house* kaok imdae kyeyak 가옥 임대 계약/ *carry out an ~* kyeyagŭl ihaenghada 계약을 이행하다/ *violate an ~* kyeyagŭl p'agihada 계약을 파기하다/ *a ceasefire ~* chŏngjŏn hyŏpchŏng 정전

agriculture *n.* nongŏp 농업.   └(停戰) 협정.

ague *n.* hakchil 학질, ohan 오한.

ahead *adv. Go ~!* Mŏnjŏ hashipshio. 먼저 하십시오/ *Go ~!* (*continue speaking*) Kyesok'ashipshio. 계속하십시 오/ *Please go right ~.* Ŏsŏ mŏnjŏ tŭshijiyo. 어서 먼저 드시지요.

aid *vt.* topta 돕다, wŏnjohada 원조하다. *—n.* wŏnjo 원조. *~ goods* wŏnjo mulcha 원조 물자/ *first ~* ŭnggŭp ch'iryo 응급 치료/ *financial ~* kyŏngje wŏnjo 경제 원조.

aide-de-camp *n.* pugwan 부관(副官).

aim *vi.,vt.* kyŏnyanghada 겨냥하다. *—n.* kyŏnyang 겨냥, mokchŏk 목적. *What are you ~ing at?* Musŭn ttŭsŭl p'umko itchiyo? 무슨 뜻을 품고 있지요/ *My remarks did not ~ at you.* Tangshinŭl tugo han mari animnida. 당신을 두고 한 말이 아닙니다.

air *n.* konggi 공기. *fresh ~* shinsŏnhan konggi 신선한 공기/ *hot ~* ttŭgŏun konggi 뜨거운 공기/ *in the ~* kongjunge 공중에/ *Let's go out and have some fresh ~.* Pakkŭro naga shinsŏnhan konggirŭl mashipshida. 밖으로 나가 신 선한 공기를 마십시다/ *~ base* konggun kiji 공군 기지/ *~ force* konggun 공군/ *~ line* hanggong hoesa 항공 회사/ *~ raid* kongsŭp 공습.

air-condition *vt.* naengnanbang changch'irŭl hada 냉난방 장치를 하다. *This place is ~ed.* I kosenŭn naengnanbang changch'iga toeŏ issŭmnida. 이 곳에는 냉난방 장치가 되어 있읍니다. 「방 장치를 한.

air-conditioned *adj.* naengnanbang changch'irŭl han 냉난

air-conditioning *n.* naengnanbang changch'i 냉난방 장치. *Does the hotel have ∼?* Kŭ hot'erenŭn naengnanbang changch'iga wanbidoeŏ issŭmnikka? 그 호텔에는 냉난방 장치가 완비되어 있읍니까?

aircraft *n.* hanggonggi 항공기.

airfield *n.* pihaengjang 비행장.

airmail *n.* hanggong up'yŏn 항공 우편. *I would like to send this letter by ∼, please.* I p'yŏnjirŭl hanggong up'yŏnŭro puch'igo shipsŭmnida. 이 편지를 항공 우편으로 부치고 싶습니다/ *I'd like to have five 40 won ∼ stamps, please.* Sashibwŏntchari hanggong up'yorŭl tasŏt chang chushio. 40원짜리 항공 우표를 다섯 장 주시오.

airplane *n.* pihaenggi 비행기.

airport *n.* konghang 공항. *Please come to the ∼ an hour before the plane leaves.* Pihaenggi ttŭgi han shigan chŏne konghangŭro oshipshio. 비행기 뜨기 한 시간 전에 공항으로 오십시오.

airship *n.* pihaengsŏn 비행선.

airsick *adj.* pihaenggi mŏlmiga nan 비행기 멀미가 난. *Didn't you get ∼?* Pihaenggi mŏlminŭn anŭsyŏssŭmnikka? 비행기 멀미는 않으셨읍니까?

airstrip *n.* kasŏl[imshi] hwalchuro 가설[임시] 활주로.

alarm *n.* nollaum 놀라움, kyŏngbo 경보. *∼ bell* kyŏngjong 경종/ *∼ clock* chamyŏngjong 자명종/ *fire ∼* hwajae kyŏngbogi 화재 경보기/ *thief ∼* tonan kyŏngbogi 도난 경보기.

album *n.* sajinch'ŏp 사진첩, aelbŏm 앨범.

alibi *n.* hyŏnjang pujae chŭngmyŏng 현장 부재 증명, allibai 알리바이.

alien *adj.* oegugŭi 외국의. *—n.* oegugin 외국인. *an ∼ friend* ubangin 우방인/ *∼ property* oeguk chaesan 외국 재산/ *enemy ∼* chŏksŏng oegugin 적성(敵性) 외국인.

alike *adj.* talmŭn 닮은, pisŭt'an 비슷한. *young and old ∼* nosorŭl mangnonhago 노소(老少)를 막론하고/ *The two sisters are very much ∼.* Tu chamaenŭn mach'i ssangdongi kassŭmnida. 두 자매는 마치 쌍동이 같습니다/

They are all ~ to me. Na-egenŭn modu pisŭt'age po-imnida. 나에게는 모두 비슷하게 보입니다.

alive *adj.* sara innŭn 살아 있는. *Who is the greatest man ~?* Hyŏnjon inmul chunge nuga kajang widaehamni-kka? 현존 인물 중에 누가 가장 위대합니까/ *He is still ~.* Kŭnŭn ajik sara issŭmnida. 그는 아직 살아 있읍니다.

all *adj.* modŭn 모든, chŏnbuŭi 전부의, chŏn (*as a prefix*) 전(全). —*adv.* chŏnhyŏ 전혀, wanjŏnhi 완전히. —*n., pron.* modu 모두, chŏnbu 전부. ~ *the books* modŭn ch'aek 모든 책/ ~ *my friends* modŭn nae ch'in-gu 모든 내 친구/ ~ *Korea* chŏn Han-guk 전 한국/~ *the world* chŏnsegye 전 세계/ ~ *out* chŏnmyŏnjŏgin 전면적인/ ~ *of us* uri modu 우리 모두/ *They ~ went away.* Modu ttŏna pŏryŏssŭm-nida 모두 떠나 버렸읍니다/ *I'll take ~ of it.* Naega ta katko shipsŭmnida 내가 다 갖고 싶습니다/ *The steward-ess knows ~ about Korean history.* Kŭ sŭt'yuŏdisŭnŭn Han-guk yŏksa-e chŏngt'onghago issŭmnida. 그 스튜어 디스는 한국 역사에 정통하고 있읍니다/ ~ *alone* hollo 홀 로/ ~ *at once* kapchagi 갑자기/ ~ *of a sudden* pyŏran-gan 별안간/ *above* ~ kŭ chungesŏdo 그 중에서도/ *Not at* ~. *or Nothing at* ~. Ch'ŏnmaneyo 천만에요/ *Are you feeling* ~ *right?* Manjok'aseyo? 만족하세요?

alley *n.* twitkolmok 뒷골목, saetkil 샛길, osolkil 오솔길. *blind* ~ maktarŭn kolmok 막다른 골목/ ~ *cat* toduk ko-yangi 도둑 고양이.

alliance *n.* tongmaeng 동맹, hyŏmnyŏk 협력. *a defense* ~ pangwi tongmaeng 방위 동맹/ *A* ~ *for Progress* pal-chŏnŭl wihan tongmaeng 발전을 위한 동맹.

alligator *n.* agŏ 악어. ~ *handbag* agŏ haendŭbaek 악어 핸드백/ ~ *leather* agŏ kajuk 악어 가죽.

allotment *n.* haltang 할당, mok 몫.

allow *vt.,vi.* hŏrak'ada 허락하다, chuda 주다. *Please* ~ *me to carry your bag.* Kabangŭl unbanhae tŭrilkkayo? 가방을 운반해 드릴까요/ *It is* ~*ed by the law.* Pŏm-nyullossŏ hŏyonghago issŭmnida. 법률로써 허용하고 있 읍니다/ *A* ~ *me to introduce to you Mr. Lee.* I kunŭl sogaehamnida. 이 군을 소개합니다.

allowance *n.* sudang 수당, (*discount*) harin 할인, enuri 에누리. *I will give you an* ~ *of 20,000 won a month.* Han tare imanwŏnŭi sudangŭl tŭrijiyo. 한 달에 20,000원의 수당을 드리지요.

ally *vt.,vi.* tongmaenghada 동맹하다. —*n.* tongmaengguk 동맹국, yŏnhapkuk 연합국. *the Allied Powers* yŏnhapkuk 연합국/ *Atlantic Pact Allies* taesŏyang choyak kamaengguk 대서양 조약 가맹국.

almanac *n.* tallyŏk 달력, (*yearbook*) yŏn-gam 연감.

almighty *adj.* chŏnnŭnghan 전능한, mannŭngŭi 만능의. —*adv.* koengjanghi 굉장히. *the A~ God* chŏnnŭnghashin hanŭnim 전능하신 하느님/ ~ *dollar* mannŭngŭi ton 만능의 돈.

almost *adv.* kŏŭi 거의, taech'ero 대체로. *Dinner's* ~ *ready.* Shiksanŭn kŏŭi chunbiga toeŏssŭmnida. 식사는 거의 준비가 되었읍니다/ *I have* ~ *finished.* Nanŭn kŏŭi kkŭnnassŭmnida. 나는 거의 끝났읍니다.

alone *adj.* hollo 홀로, honjasŏ 혼자서. *Are you* ~? Honja kyeshimnikka? 혼자 계십니까/ *Leave me* ~, *please.* Chebal honja itke haejuseyo. 제발 혼자 있게 해주세요/ *Do you live* ~? Honja sashimnikka? 혼자 사십니까?

aloud *adv.* k'ŭn soriro 큰 소리로. *Please read the story* ~. Kŭ iyagirŭl k'ŭn soriro ilgŏ chushio. 그 이야기를 큰 소리로 읽어 주시오/ *Speak* ~, *please.* K'ŭn soriro malssŭmhae chushipshio. 큰 소리로 말씀해 주십시오.

alphabet *n.* alp'abet 알파벳, chamo 자모. *We have an* ~ *called han-gŭl.* Uriegenŭn han-gŭriran chamoga issŭmnida. 우리에게는 한글이란 자모가 있읍니다.

already *adv.* imi 이미, pŏlssŏ 벌써. *Have you had breakfast* ~? Pŏlssŏ ach'im shiksarŭl haessŭmnikka? 벌써 아침 식사를 했읍니까/ *When I arrived at the station, the train had* ~ *left.* Naega yŏge toch'ak'aessŭl ttae kich'anŭn imi ttŏnago ŏpsŏssŭmnida. 내가 역에 도착했을 때 기차는 이미 떠나고 없었읍니다.

also *adv.* yŏkshi 역시, ttohan 또한. *I* ~ *went.* Nado kassŭmnida. 나도 갔읍니다/ *Mr. Lee has* ~ *been to Saudi Arabia.* I kundo yŏkshi Saudi Arabiarŭl tanyŏwassŭmnida. 이 군도 역시 사우디아라비아를 다녀왔읍니다.

alter *vt.,vi.* pyŏn-gyŏnghada 변경하다, koch'ida 고치다. ~ *clothes* osŭl koch'ida 옷을 고치다.

although *conj.* pirok …ilchirado 비록 …일지라도, …iginŭn hana …이기는 하나. *A~ he is rich, he is not happy.* Kŭnŭn pujaiginŭn hana haengbok'ajinŭn mot'amnida. 그는 부자이기는 하나 행복하지는 못합니다/ *A~ he is very old yet he is quite strong.* Kŭnŭn mopshi nŭlgŏtchiman ajikto chŏngjŏnghamnida. 그는 몹시 늙었지만 아직도 정정합니다. 「고도 비행.

altitude *n.* nop'i 높이, haebal 해발. ~ *flight* kodo pihaeng

altogether *adv.* aju 아주, (*in all*) modu 모두, t'ongt'ŭrŏ 통틀어. *I don't ~ agree with you.* Tangshin-gwa aju ŭigyŏni ilch'ihanŭn kŏsŭn animnida. 당신과 아주 의견이 일치하는 것은 아닙니다/ *How much ~ ?* Modu ŏlmaimnikka? 모두 얼마입니까?

always *adv.* hangsang 항상, ŏnjena 언제나. *I am nearly ~ at home on Sunday.* Iryoirŭn kŏŭi ŏnjena chibe issŭmnida. 일요일은 거의 언제나 집에 있읍니다.

amaze *vt.* kkamtchak nollage hada 깜짝 놀라게 하다. *I was ~d at the news.* Kŭ soshigŭl tŭtko kkamtchak nollassŭmnida. 그 소식을 듣고 깜짝 놀랐읍니다.

ambassador *n.* taesa 대사(大使). *the U.S.~ to Korea* chuhan Miguk taesa 주한 미국 대사/ *the Korean ~ to the United States* chumi Han-guk taesa 주미 한국 대사.

ambition *n.* yamang 야망. *I have a great ~s.* Nanŭn k'ŭn yamangŭl p'umko issŭmnida. 나는 큰 야망을 품고 있읍니다/ *his life-long ~* kŭŭi p'ilsaengŭi yŏmwŏn 그의 필생의 염원/ *without ~* yongmangdo ŏpshi 욕망도 없이.

ambitious *adj.* yamange ch'an 야망에 찬. ~ *plan* yashimjŏgin kyehoek 야심적인 계획/ ~ *person* yashimga 야심가.

ambivalent *adj.* sorŏ yongnap'aji annŭn 서로 용납하지 않는, sanggŭk'anŭn 상극하는.

ambulance *n.* kugŭpch'a 구급차, aembyullŏnsŭ 앰뷸런스.

amend *vi.,vt.* koch'ida 고치다, sujŏnghada 수정하다. ~ *a constitution* kaehŏnhada 개헌하다.

America *n.* Amerik'a 아메리카 (*the United States of Amer-*

ica). *North* ~ Pungmi 북미/ *South* ~ Nammi 남미.

American *adj.* Amerik'aŭi 아메리카의, Migugŭi 미국의. —*n.* Migugin 미국인, (*language*) Migugŏ 미국어. *the* ~ *Embassy* Miguk taesagwan 미국 대사관/ *the* ~ *Consulate* Miguk yŏngsagwan 미국 영사관/ ~ *football* mishik ch'ŭkku 미식 축구.

amiable *adj.* kwiyŏmsŏng innŭn 귀염성 있는, sangnyanghan 상냥한. *an* ~ *woman* sangnyanghan puin 상냥한 부인.

ammunition *n.* t'anyak 탄약. *sporting* ~ suryŏbyong t'anyak 수렵용 탄약.

among *prep.* kaundee 가운데에, ...chunge ...중에. *I saw him* ~ *the crowd*. Kunjung soge innŭn kŭrŭl poassŭmnida. 군중 속에 있는 그를 보았읍니다/ *Divide the money* ~ *them*. Kŭdŭrege tonŭl nanuŏ chushipshio. 그들에게 돈을 나누어 주십시오/ ~ *others* kŭ chungesŏdo 그 중에서도, t'ŭk'i 특히.

amount *n.* yang 양(量), (*total*) ch'onggye 총계. —*vi.* ch'onggye ...i toeda 총계 ...이 되다, ...e haedanghada ...에 해당하다. *I have only a small* ~ *of money*. Nanŭn toni chogŭmbakke ŏpsŭmnida. 나는 돈이 조금밖에 없읍니다/ *My hotel bill* ~*ed to 40,000 won*. Sukpangnyonŭn samanwŏniŏssŭmnida. 숙박료는 4 만원이었읍니다/ *How much the whole* ~? Ch'ongaegi ŏlmana toemnikka? 총액이 얼마나 됩니까/ *a huge* ~ kŏaek 거액/ *a total* ~ ch'ongaek 총액.

ample *adj.* ch'ungbunhan 충분한, (*extensive*) nŏlbŭn 넓은. *an* ~ *supply of water* ch'ungbunhan mul konggŭp 충분한 물 공급/ *Will 5,000 won be* ~ *for your needs?* Och'ŏnwŏnimyŏn ch'ungbunhamnikka? 5 천원이면 충분합니까/ *an* ~ *bosom* p'ungmanhan kasŭm 풍만한 가슴.

amuse *vt.* chŭlgŏpke hada 즐겁게 하다. *I was quite* ~*d*. Chŏngmal chŭlgŏwŏssŭmnida. 정말 즐거웠읍니다/ *I* ~ *myself by reading*. Nanŭn toksŏrŭl chŭlgigo issŭmnida. 나는 독서를 즐기고 있읍니다/ *How do you* ~ *yourself in rainy weather?* Pionŭn narenŭn muŏsŭl hago chŭlgishimnikka? 비오는 날에는 무엇을 하고 즐기십니까?

amusement *n.* orak 오락, chŭlgŏum 즐거움. *popular* ~*s*

taejung orak 대중 오락.

analyze, analyse *vt.* punsŏk'ada 분석하다, (*examine critically*) kŏmt'ohada 검토하다.

ancestor *n.* chosang 조상, sŏnjo 선조. ~ *worship* chosang sungbae 조상 숭배/ *descend from* ~s chosangŭrobut'ŏ chŏnhayŏjida 조상으로부터 전하여지다.

anchor *n.* tat 닻. *cast* ~ tach'ŭl naerida 닻을 내리다/ *weigh* ~ tach'ŭl ollida 닻을 올리다.

anchor man (*radio or TV*) chinhaengja 진행자.

ancient *adj.* yennarŭi 옛날의, oraedoen 오래된. *in* ~ *days* mŏn yennare 먼 옛날에/ *an* ~ *looking hat* kushik moja 구식 모자/ *Koreans like to wear white clothes from* ~ *times.* Han-guk saramdŭrŭn mŏn yennalbut'ŏ hŭinosŭl chŭlgyŏ ipsŭmnida. 한국 사람들은 먼 옛날부터 흰옷을 즐겨 입습니다.

and *conj.* ...kwa[wa] ...과[와], ...mit ...및, kŭrigo 그리고. *you* ~ *I* tangshin-gwa na 당신과 나/ *a knife* ~ *fork* naip'ŭwa p'ok'ŭ 나이프와 포크/ *I bought two pencils, two notebooks,* ~ *an eraser.* Nanŭn yŏnp'il tu charu, kongch'aek tu kwŏn, kŭrigo chiugae han kaerŭl sassŭmnida. 나는 연필 두 자루, 공책 두 권, 그리고 지우개 한 개를 샀습니다.

anecdote *n.* irhwa 일화. *an amusing* ~ chaemiinnŭn irhwa 재미있는 일화/ *historical* ~s yŏksasangŭi irhwa 역사상의 일화/ ~s *about Admiral Yi Sun-shin* I Sunshin changgunŭi irhwa 이 순신 장군의 일화.

angel *n.* ch'ŏnsa 천사(天使).

anger *n.* noyŏum 노여움. *control one's* ~ noyŏumŭl ŏkchehada 노여움을 억제하다/ *show* ~ noyŏumŭl nat'anaeda 노여움을 나타내다/ *We parted in* ~. Urinŭn korŭl naego sŏro heŏjyŏssŭmnida. 우리는 골을 내고 서로 헤어졌습니다.

angle *n.* mot'ungi 모퉁이, kakto 각도. —*vi.* nakshijirhada 낚시질하다.

angler *n.* nakshikkun 낚시꾼.

angry *adj.* nohan 노한, sŏngnan 성난, hwanan 화난. *Are you* ~? Nohasyŏssŭmnikka? 노하셨습니까/ *Why are*

you ~ ? Wae nohashimnikka ? 왜 노하십니까/*I am not* ~.
Nohaji anassŭmnida. 노하지 않았읍니다/ *Don't be* ~ *with me*. Nahant'e hwanaeji mashipshio. 나한테 화내지 마십시오/ *an* ~ *look* hwanan ŏlgul 화난 얼굴/ *get* ~ nohada 노하다.

animal *n.* tongmul 동물, chimsŭng 짐승. *domestic* ~ kach'uk 가축/ *pet* ~*s* aewan'tongmul 애완 동물/ *wild* ~ yasu 야수/ ~ *fats* tongmulsŏng chibang 동물성 지방.

ankle *n.* palmok 발목. *I sprained my* ~ *by a fall*. Nŏmŏjyŏsŏ palmogŭl ppiŏssŭmnida. 넘어져서 발목을 삐었읍니다.

anniversary *n.* kinyŏmil 기념일. *wedding* ~ kyŏrhon kinyŏmil 결혼 기념일/ *the 60th* ~ *of one's birth* hoegap 회갑, hwan-gap 환갑.

announce *vt.* palp'yohada 발표하다, (*make known*) allida 알리다.

announcement *n.* kongp'yo 공표(公表), (*statement*) sŏngmyŏng 성명.

announcer *n.* ŏnaunsŏ 어나운서.

annoy *vt.* koerop'ida 괴롭히다, (*molest*) kollida 끓리다. *How* ~*ing* ! Chŏngmal kwich'ank'un ! 정말 귀찮군 !

annual *adj.* illyŏnŭi 일년의, haemadaŭi 해마다의. ~ *income* yŏnsuip 연수입(年收入)/ ~ *expenditure* sech'ul 세출/ *an* ~ *pension* yŏn-gŭm 연금(年金)/ *the* ~ *production* yŏn-gan saengsan-go 연간 생산고.

anonymous *adj.* ingmyŏngŭi 익명(匿名)의. ~ *contributions* ingmyŏng kibu 익명 기부/ *an* ~ *author* ingmyŏng chakka 익명 작가/ *an* ~ *letter* ingmyŏng t'usŏ 익명 투서.

another *adj.* tto hanaŭi 또 하나의, tarŭn 다른. *Will you have* ~ *cup of tea* ? Ch'a han chan tŏ hashigessŏyo ? 차(茶) 한 잔 더 하시겠어요/ *That is* ~ *matter*. Kŭgŏsŭn munjega tarŭmnida. 그것은 문제가 다릅니다/ ~ *day* tarŭn nal 다른 날/ ~ *place* tarŭn kot 다른 곳/ *one after* ~ ch'aryech'arye 차례차례/ *one* ~ sŏro 서로.

answer *vi.,vt.* taedap'ada 대답하다, (*respond to*) ŭnghada 응하다. —*n.* taedap 대답, hoedap 회답. *Bring an* ~. Hoedabŭl pada oshio. 회답을 받아 오시오/ *What shall I* ~ ? Mwŏrago taedap'alkkayo ? 뭐라고 대답할까요/ *Have you*

~*ed his letter?* Kŭŭi p'yŏnjie hoedap'aessŭmnikka? 그
의 편지에 회답했읍니까/~ *back* maldaekkuhada 말대꾸하다/
~ *for* ch'aegimŭl chida 책임을 지다, pojŭnghada 보증하다.

ant *n.* kaemi 개미.

anthology *n.* myŏngshisŏnjip 명시선집, myŏngmunjip 명문
집, chakp'umjip 작품집.

anthropology *n.* illyuhak 인류학.

anti- *pref.* pan 반, pi 비(非). ~ *-aircraft guns* kosap'o
고사포/~*-Communism* pan-gong 반공(反共)/ ~*-Semitism*
panyut'aejuŭi 반유태주의.

antibiotic *n.* hangsaeng mulchil 항생 물질.

antipathy *n.* pan-gam 반감(反感).

antique *n.* kcmul 고물(古物), (*curio*) koltongp'um 골동품.
~ *dealer* koltongp'umsang 골동품상/ *fake* ~ katcha koltongp'um 가짜 골동품.

anus *n.* hangmun 항문(肛門). *emit wind from the* ~. (=
break wind) panggwi kkwida 방귀 뀌다.

anxiety *n.* kŭnshim 근심, kŏkchŏng 걱정. *be in* ~ kŏk-
chŏnghago itta 걱정하고 있다/ *domestic* ~ chiban kŏkchŏng 집안 걱정/ *without* ~ kŏkchŏng ŏpshi 걱정 없이.

anxious *adj.* kŏkchŏnghanŭn 걱정하는, (*earnestly desirous*)
kalmanghanŭn 갈망하는. *Don't be* ~. Kŏkchŏnghaji mashio. 걱정하지 마시오/ *I'm very* ~ *about my son's health.*
Adŭrŭi kŏn-gangi mopshi kŏkchŏngdoemnida. 아들의 건
강이 몹시 걱정됩니다/ *We are really* ~ *for peace.* Urinŭn chŏngmal p'yŏnghwarŭl kalmanghago issŭmnida.
우리는 정말 평화를 갈망하고 있읍니다.

any *adj.* muŏn-ga 무언가, ŏlmaganŭi 얼마간의, muŏshidŭn
무엇이든, ...irado ...이라도. —*adv.* chogŭmŭn 조금은.
—*pron.* ŏnŭ kŏshin-ga 어느 것인가, nugun-ga 누군가. *Have
you* ~ *money with you?* Ton chom kajigo issŭmnikka?
돈 좀 가지고 있읍니까/ *Come* ~ *day you like.* Ŏnjego
choŭn nare oshipshio. 언제고 좋은 날에 오십시오/ *Is your
father* ~ *better?* Abŏjikkesŏn chom naajisyŏssŭmnikka?
아버지께선 좀 나아지셨읍니까/ *He is not* ~ *better.* Chogŭmdo naajiji anassŭmnida. 조금도 나아지지 않았읍니다/
Take ~ *you like.* Ŏnŭ kŏshina maŭme tŭnŭn kŏsŭl ka-

jishio. 어느 것이나 마음에 드는 것을 가지시오/ *If ~ of you know, tell me.* Tangshindŭl chung nugun-ga algo issŭmyŏn, marhae chushio. 당신들 중 누군가 알고 있으면 말해 주시오/ ~ *longer* i isangŭn 이 이상은/ ~ *one* nuguna 누구나/ *at* ~ *moment* ŏnjerado 언제라도/ *at* ~ *price* ŏttŏn hŭisaengŭl ch'irŭdŏrado 어떤 희생을 치르더라도/ *at* ~ *rate* amut'ŭn 아뭏든/ *in* ~ *case* ŏttŏn kyŏngurado 어떤 경우라도.

anybody *pron.* nugu 누구, nugun-ga 누군가. *Is there* ~ *here?* Nugu kyeshimnikka? 누구 계십니까/ *A*~ *can do that.* Nuguna hal su issŭmnida. 누구나 할 수 있읍니다/ *He doesn't lend his books to* ~. Kŭnŭn nuguegedo ch'aegŭl pillyŏ chuji anssŭmnida. 그는 누구에게도 책을 빌려 주지 않습니다.

anyhow *adv.* amut'ŭn 아뭏든, chwaugan 좌우간. *A*~ *I shall go and see you.* Amut'ŭn ch'ajaga poepkessŭmnida. 아뭏든 찾아가 뵙겠읍니다/ *It is too late now,* ~. Chwaugan chigŭmŭn nŏmu nŭssŭmnida. 좌우간 지금은 너무 늦습니다.

anyone *pron.*=*anybody.*

anything *pron.* (*positive*) muŏshidŭn 무엇이든, (*negative*) amugŏtto 아무것도, (*interrogative*) muŏshin-ga 무엇인가. *He can do* ~. Kŭnŭn muŏshidŭn hal su issŭmnida. 그는 무엇이든 할 수 있읍니다/ *A*~ *will do.* Muŏshidŭn chossŭmnida. 무엇이든 좋습니다/ *I couldn't see* ~. Amugŏtto pol su ŏpsŏssŭmnida. 아무것도 볼 수 없었읍니다/ *Have you* ~ *to say to me?* Na-ege muŏn-ga hal mari issŭmnikka? 나에게 무언가 할 말이 있읍니까?

anyway *adv.* =*anyhow. Thank you very much* ~. Chwaugan komapsŭmnida. 좌우간 고맙습니다.

apartment *n.* ap'at'ŭ 아파트. *I have a three room* ~. Nanŭn pangi set innŭn ap'at'ŭe salgo issŭmnida. 나는 방이 셋 있는 아파트에 살고 있읍니다.

ape *n.* wŏnsungi 원숭이, (*imitator*) hyungnaejangi 흉내장이. *play the* ~ hyungnaenaeda 흉내내다.

apologize *vi.* sagwahada 사과하다. *I must* ~ *for breaking a promise.* Yaksogŭl ŏgyŏ sagwadŭryŏya hagessŭmnida. 약속을 어겨 사과드려야 하겠읍니다/ *I* ~ *for what I said.*

Naega han mare taehae sagwadŭrimnida. 내가 한 말에 대해 사과드립니다.

apology *n.* sagwa 사과, sajoe 사죄. *I made an ～ for lateness.* Chigak'an te taehae sagwarŭl tŭryŏssŭmnida 지각한 데 대해 사과를 드렸읍니다/ *make a humble ～* kogae sugyŏ sagwahada 고개 숙여 사과하다.

apparent *adj.* myŏngbaek'an 명백한, (*seeming*) oegyŏnsangŭi 외견상의.

appeal *vi.,vt.* hosohada 호소하다, (*law*) hangsohada 항소하다, (*attract*) hŭngmirŭl kkŭlda 흥미를 끌다. *～ to the nation* kungminege hosohada 국민에게 호소하다 / *～ to a higher court* sanggŭp chaep'anso-e hangsohada 상급 재판소에 항소하다/ *Do these pictures ～ to you?* I kŭrimdŭri maŭme tŭshimnikka? 이 그림들이 마음에 드십니까?

appear *vi.* (*seem*) poida 보이다, (*come out*) nat'anada 나타나다. *Why does she ～ so sad?* Wae kŭnyŏnŭn kŭrŏk'e sŭlp'ŏ poijiyo? 왜 그녀는 그렇게 슬퍼 보이지요/ *The moon is ～ing.* Tari poimnida. 달이 보입니다.

appearance *n.* oegwan 외관(外觀), kŏnmoyang 겉모양. *an attractive ～* maeryŏkchŏgin oemo 매력적인 외모/ *judge by ～* oegwanŭro p'andanhada 외관으로 판단하다.

appendicitis *n.* maengjangyŏm 맹장염. *I was operated on for ～.* Nanŭn maengjangyŏm susurŭl padassŭmnida. 나는 맹장염 수술을 받았읍니다.

appendix *n.* purok 부록. *add an ～ to a book* ch'aege purogŭl puch'ida 책에 부록을 붙이다.

appetite *n.* shigyok 식욕. *How is your ～?* Shigyogŭn ŏttŏssŭmnikka? 식욕은 어떻습니까/ *I have no ～ at all.* Chogŭmdo shigyogi ŏpsŭmnida. 조금도 식욕이 없읍니다/ *loose one's ～* shigyogŭl ilt'a 식욕을 잃다/ *～ for knowledge* chishigyok 지식욕.

applaude *vi.* paksu kalch'aehada 박수 갈채하다.

applause *n.* paksu kalch'ae 박수 갈채. *There was a storm of ～.* Uroewa kat'ŭn paksu kalch'aega irŏnassŭmnida. 우뢰와 같은 박수 갈채가 일어났읍니다/ *win the ～ of audience* ch'ŏngjungŭi kalch'aerŭl patta 청중의 갈채를 받다.

apple *n.* sagwa 사과. *Would you like some ～ pie?* Aep'ŭl

p'airŭl chom tŭshigessŭmnikka? 애플 파이를 좀 드시겠읍
니까/ *green* ~ p'ussagwa 풋사과.

appliance *n.* kigu 기구, (*apparatus*) sŏlbi 설비.

applicant *n.* chiwŏnja 지원자, (*petitioner*) shinch'ŏngin 신
청인. *a job* ~ kujikcha 구직자.

application *n.* chimang 지망, (*request*) shinch'ŏng 신청.
~ *form* shinch'ŏng yongji[sŏshik] 신청 용지[서식]/
membership ~s ip'oe shinch'ŏngsŏ 입회(入會) 신청서/
a written ~ wŏnsŏ 원서.

apply *vi.,vt.* shinch'ŏnghada 신청하다. *A*~ *by letter*. Sŏmyŏnŭro shinch'ŏnghaseyo. 서면으로 신청하세요/ *A*~ *in
your own handwriting*. Chap'illossŏ shinch'ŏnghashipshio. 자필로써 신청하십시오/ *A*~ *personally*. Ponini sonsu shinch'ŏnghashipshio. 본인이 손수 신청하십시오.

appoint *vt.* immyŏnghada 임명하다, (*fix*) chŏnghada 정하
다. *He was* ~*ed Ambassador to the United States*.
Kŭnŭn chumi taesa-e immyŏngdoeŏssŭmnida. 그는 주미
대사에 임명되었읍니다/ *by the* ~*ed time* chijŏngdoen shi-

appointment *n.* yaksok 약속. ⌊gankkaji 지정된 시간까지.

appraise *vt.* kapsŭl maegida 값을 매기다, p'yŏngkahada
평가하다. ~ *property for taxation* kwaserŭl wihae cha-
sanŭl p'yŏngkahada 과세(課稅)를 위해 자산을 평가하다.

appreciate *vt.* kamsahada 감사하다. *We greatly* ~ *all
your help*. Yŏrŏbunŭi modŭn toume kip'i kamsahamnida. 여러분의 모든 도움에 깊이 감사합니다/ *I* ~ *it very
much*. Tangshinege kip'i kamsadŭrimnida. 당신에게 깊
이 감사드립니다.

appreciation *n.* kamsa 감사. *with* ~ kŭkchinhi saengga-
k'ayŏ 극진히 생각하여/ *That is a small token of my* ~.
Kŭgŏsŭn pyŏnbyŏnch'anŭn kŏshimnidaman chŏŭi kamsaŭi p'yoshiimnida. 그것은 변변찮은 것입니다마는 저의 감사
의 표시입니다.

apprentice *n.* kyŏnsŭpkong 견습공, (*pupil*) cheja 제자.
~s *to a printer* inswaeso kyŏnsŭpkong 인쇄소 견습공.

approach *vi.,vt.* tagagada 다가가다, chŏpkŭnhada 접근하다.
I ~*ed her*. Nanŭn kŭnyŏege tagagassŭmnida. 나는 그
녀에게 다가갔읍니다.

approval *n.* sŭngin 승인, tongŭi 동의. *We had his hearty ~.* Urinŭn kŭŭi yŏllyŏrhan tongŭirŭl ŏdŏssŭmnida. 우리는 그의 열렬한 동의를 얻었읍니다/ *I gave my ~.* Nanŭn sŭnginhayŏssŭmnida. 나는 승인하였읍니다.

approve *vt.* ch'ansŏnghada 찬성하다. sŭnginhada 승인하다. *I highly ~ of it.* Nanŭn kŭgŏsŭl yŏllyŏrhi ch'ansŏnghamnida. 나는 그것을 열렬히 찬성합니다/ *I can't ~ of your idea.* Tangshinŭi ŭigyŏne ch'ansŏnghal su ŏpsŭmnida. 당신의 의견에 찬성할 수 없읍니다.

apricot *n.* salgu 살구.

April *n.* sawŏl 사월(四月). *~ Fool(s') Day* manujŏl 만우절.

apron *n.* apch'ima 앞치마, eip'ŭrŏn 에이프런.

Arab *n.* Arabia saram 아라비아 사람. *the ~ League* Arap yŏnmaeng 아랍 연맹.

arbitrate *vt.* chungjaehada 중재하다. *~ a quarrel* ssaumŭl chungjaehada 싸움을 중재하다.

arbitration *n.* chungjae 중재.

arcade *n.* sangjŏmga 상점가. *a penny ~* ssaguryŏ sangjŏmga 싸구려 상점가.

arch *n.* ach'i 아치. *a triumphal ~* kaesŏnmun 개선문/ *a railway ~* (ch'ŏltoŭi) yukkyo (철도의) 육교.

archeology *n.* kogohak 고고학(考古學).

archery *n.* kungsul 궁술(弓術), yanggung 양궁.

architect *n.* kŏnch'ukka 건축가.

architecture *n.* kŏnch'uk 건축, kŏnch'uk'ak 건축학.

arctic *adj.* pukkŭgŭi 북극의. *—n. the A~* pukkŭk 북극/ *the A~ Ocean* pukkŭk'ae 북극해/ *the A~ zone* pukkŭktae 북극대(帶).

ardent *adj.* yŏllyŏrhan 열렬한. *~ love* yŏllyŏrhan sarang 열렬한 사랑.

area *n.* chiyŏk 지역, chigu 지구, chidae 지대. *an industrial ~* kongŏp chidae 공업 지대/ *residential ~* chut'aek chigu 주택 지구/ *the Seoul-Inchon ~* kyŏngin chigu 경인 지구.

argue *vi.,vt.* ŏnjaenghada 언쟁하다, tat'uda 다투다. *Why are you always arguing?* Wae tangshinŭn nŭl tat'ugiman hamnikka? 왜 당신은 늘 다투기만 합니까 / *I don't like to* ~ *about the price.* Mulgŏn kapsŭl kajigo tat'ugi shilssŭmnida. 물건 값을 가지고 다투기 싫습니다.

argument *n.* nonjaeng 논쟁, ŏnjaeng 언쟁.

arise *vi.* irŏnada 일어나다, (*appear*) nat'anada 나타나다.

aristocrat *n.* kwijok 귀족.

arithmetic *n.* sansu 산수. *mental* ~ amsan 암산(暗算).

arm *n.* p'al 팔, (*pl.*) (*weapon*) pyŏnggi 병기(兵器). —*vt.* mujangshik'ida 무장시키다. ~ *in* ~ p'are p'arŭl kkigo 팔에 팔을 끼고 / *heavily* ~*ed soldiers* chungmujanghan pyŏngsadŭl 중무장한 병사들.

armada *n.* hamdae 함대.

armament *n.* kunbi 군비. *the* ~ *industry* kunsa sanŏp 군사 산업 / *expansion of* ~ kunbi hwakchang 군비 확장 / ~ *expenditure* kunsabi 군사비.

armchair *n.* allak ŭija 안락 의자.

armistice *n.* hyujŏn 휴전. ~ *talk* hyujŏn hoedam 휴전 회담.

arms *n.* mugi 무기.

army *n.* yukkun 육군. *join the* ~ kune iptaehada 군에 입대하다 / *the Salvation A*~ kusegun 구세군.

aroma *n.* hyanggi 향기.

around *adv.*(*on every side*) sabange 사방에, (*not far away*) mŏlji anŭn kose 멀지 않은 곳에. *I heard noises all* ~. On sabange soŭmi tŭllyŏssŭmnida. 온 사방에 소음이 들렸습니다 / *Is there a hospital* ~? I kŭnch'ŏe pyŏngwŏni issŭmnikka? 이 근처에 병원이 있습니까?

arrange *vi.,vt.* chŏngdonhada 정돈하다, chojŏnghada 조정하다. *Would you please* ~ *this document?* Sŏryu chom chŏngnihae chushio. 서류 좀 정리해 주시오 / *Will you please* ~ *for my train ticket?* Ch'ap'yo chom chusŏnhae chushigessŭmnikka? 차표 좀 주선해 주시겠습니까?

arrangement *n.* chŏngdon 정돈, chunbi 준비. *flower* ~ kkotkkoji 꽃꽂이. *Have you made* ~*s for your journey to Cheju?* Chejuhaeng yŏhaeng chunbinŭn toeŏssŭmnikka? 제주행(行) 여행 준비는 되었습니까?

arrest *vt.* ch'ep'ohada 체포하다. —*n.* ch'ep'o 체포. *He was* ~*ed by the police.* Kŭnŭn kyŏngch'are ch'ep'odoeŏssŭmnida. 그는 경찰에 체포되었습니다/ *They made about fifty* ~s. Yak oshimmyŏngŭl ch'ep'ohaessŭmnida. 약 50 명을 체포했습니다.

arrival *n.* toch'ak 도착. *I shall let you know the time of my* ~. Naŭi toch'ak shiganŭl allyŏ tŭrigessŭmnida. 나의 도착 시간을 알려 드리겠습니다.

arrive *vi.* toch'ak'ada 도착하다. *What time is this train to* ~*in Seoul?* I yŏlch'anŭn myŏt shie Sŏure toch'ak'amnikka? 이 열차는 몇 시에 서울에 도착합니까/ *I just* ~*d from Pusan.* Panggŭm Pusanesŏ toch'ak'ayŏssŭmnida. 방금 부산에서 도착하였습니다/ *When will you be arriving, sir?* Ŏnje toch'ak'ashimnikka? 언제 도착하십니까?

arrogant *adj.* omanhan 오만한, kŏmanhan 거만한.

arrow *n.* hwasal 화살. *shoot an* ~ *into the air* kongjungŭl hyanghae hwarŭl ssoda 공중을 향해 화살을 쏘다/ ~*head* hwasalch'ok 화살촉.

arsenal *n.* chobyŏngch'ang 조병창. *a naval* ~ haegun kongch'ang 해군 공창.

art *n.* yesul 예술, (*fine arts*) misul 미술, (*skill*) kisul 기술. *graphic* ~ inswae yesul 인쇄 예술/ *plastic* ~s chohyŏng misul 조형 미술/ *an* ~ *exhibition* misul chŏllamhoe 미술 전람회/ *an* ~ *gallery* hwarang 화랑/ *He knows the* ~ *of making money.* Kŭnŭn tonpŏrihanŭn kisurŭl algo issŭmnida. 그는 돈벌이하는 기술을 알고 있읍니다.

artful *adj.* kyohwarhan 교활한, sudan choŭn 수단 좋은. *an* ~ *woman* sudan choŭn yŏin 수단 좋은 여인/ *an* ~ *trick* kyohwarhan sudan 교활한 수단.

article *n.* mulp'um 물품, (*provision*) chohang 조항, (*piece of writing*) kisa 기사(記事).

artificial *adj.* in-gongjŏgin 인공적인, (*opp. real*) mojoŭi 모조의. ~ *arm* ŭisu 의수(義手)/ ~ *flower* chohwa 조화 (造花)/ ~ *leg* ŭijok 의족(義足)/ ~ *teeth* ŭich'i 의치(義齒)/ *That trunk is made of* ~ *leather.* Kŭ kabangŭn injo kajugŭro mandŭrŏssŭmnida. 그 가방은 인조 가죽으로 만들었읍니다.

artillery *n.* taep'o 대포. ~ *fire* p'ohwa 포화/ ~ *man* p'obyŏng 포병/ *anti-aircraft* ～ kosap'odae 고사포대.

artisan *n.* chikkong 직공, kigyegong 기계공.

artist *n.* yesulga 예술가, (*of fine arts*) misulga 미술가.

as *adv.* I'm ～ *tall* ～ *you.* Nanŭn tangshinmank'ŭm k'ŭm-nida. 나는 당신만큼 큽니다/ *Today is not* ～ *warm* ～ *yesterday.* Onŭrŭn ŏj'emank'ŭm ttattŭt'aji anssŭmnida. 오늘은 어제만큼 따뜻하지 않습니다. —*conj. Do* ～ *I tell you.* Nae maldaero hashio. 내 말대로 하시오/ *She came* ～ *I was leaving.* Ttŏnaryŏdŏn ch'ame kŭnyŏga wassŭm-nida. 떠나려던 참에 그녀가 왔읍니다/ *I am not so young* ～ *you.* Nanŭn chanemank'ŭm chŏmchi anne. 나는 자네만큼 젊지 않네. —*prep. I regard him* ～ *a fool.* Nanŭn kŭrŭl paborago saenggak'amnida. 나는 그를 바보라고 생각합니다. *I will act* ～ *go-between.* Naega chungmaein yŏk'arŭl hagessŭmnida. 내가 중매인 역할을 하겠읍니다.

ascend *vi.,vt.* orŭda 오르다, ollagada 올라가다. ～ *a moun-tain* sane orŭda 산에 오르다/ ～ *the throne* wangwie orŭda 왕위에 오르다.

ascent *n.* orŭgi 오르기, orŭmakkil 오르막길. *I have never made the* ～ *of Mt. Halla.* Hallasan tŭngsanŭl haebon chŏgi ŏpsŭmnida. 한라산 등산을 해본 적이 없읍니다.

ash *n.* chae 재. ～ *tray* chaettŏri 재떨이.

ashamed *adj.* pukkŭrŏun 부끄러운. *I am* ～ *of doing so.* Kŭrŏn chisŭl haesŏ pukkŭrŏpsŭmnida. 그런 짓을 해서 부끄럽습니다/ *Aren't you* ～ *of your conduct?* Tangshinŭn chagi sohaengi pukkŭrŏpchi anssŭmnikka? 당신은 자기 소행이 부끄럽지 않습니까/ *I feel* ～. Pukkŭrŏpsŭmnida. 부끄럽습니다.

ashore *adv.* haebyŏne 해변에, mulkaro 물가로. *go* ～ sang-nyuk'ada 상륙하다/ *Please carry my things* ～. Nae chimŭl yangnyuk'ae chushio. 내 짐을 양륙(揚陸)해 주시오/ *Take me* ～ *please.* Haebyŏne teryŏda chushipshio. 해변에 데려다 주십시오.

Asia *n.* Asia 아시아.

Asiatic *adj.* Asiaŭi 아시아의. *the* ～ *continent* Asia tae-ryuk 아시아 대륙/ ～ *flu* Asia yuhaengsŏng kamgi 아시아 유행성 감기.

aside *adv.* kyŏt'ŭro 곁으로. *He took me* ~. Narŭl kyŏt'ŭro terigo kassŭmnida. 나를 곁으로 데리고 갔습니다/ *joking* ~ nongdamŭn chech'yŏnok'o 농담은 제쳐놓고.

ask *vt.* mutta 묻다, murŏ poda 물어 보다. *May I* ~ *your name and address?* Sŏnghamgwa chusorŭl allyŏ chushipshio. 성함과 주소를 알려 주십시오/ *Will you* ~ *her where she lives?* Kŭnyŏŭi chusorŭl murŏ poshiryŏmnikka? 그녀의 주소를 물어 보시렵니까/ *May I* ~ *you to repeat it again?* Tashi han pŏn toep'urihae chushiji ank'essŭmnikka? 다시 한 번 되풀이해 주시지 않겠습니까?

asleep *adj.,adv.* chamdŭrŏ 잠들어. *My train passed Taegu while I was fast* ~. Kip'i chamdŭn saie kich'anŭn Taegurŭl t'onggwahaessŭmnida. 깊이 잠든 사이에 기차는 대구 (大邱)를 통과했습니다/ *As soon as I lay down, I fell* ~. Tŭrŏnupchamaja nanŭn chami tŭrŏssŭmnida. 드러눕자마 자 나는 잠이 들었습니다.

asphalt *n.* asŭp'alt'ŭ 아스팔트.

aspiration *n.* yŏlmang 열망, p'obu 포부. *his* ~ *to be an actor* paeuga toeryŏnŭn kŭ ŭi p'obu 배우가 되려는 그의 포부/ *I have no* ~ *for fame.* Myŏngyenŭn paraji anssŭmnida. 명예는 바라지 않습니다.

aspire *vt.* yŏlmanghada 열망하다. ~ *to become a singer* kasurŭl chimanghada 가수를 지망하다.

aspirin *n.* asŭp'irin 아스피린.

ass *n.* tangnagwi 당나귀, (*stupid*) pabo 바보. *Don't make an* ~ *of me.* Narŭl pabo ch'wigŭp haji mashio. 나를 바보 취급 하지 마시오.

assassin *n.* amsalcha 암살자.

assault *n.* sŭpkyŏk 습격. *a violent* ~ maengsŭp 맹습.

assemble *vt.,vi.* moŭda 모으다, sojip'ada 소집하다, moida 모이다.

assembly *n.* chip'oe 집회. ~ *hall* hoeŭijang 회의장/ ~ *man* ŭiwŏn 의원(議員)/ *We call it the National A*~. Kuk'oerago purŭmnida. 국회(國會)라고 부릅니다.

assent *vi.* tongŭihada 동의하다. —*n.* tongŭi 동의. *I* ~ *to your views.* Tangshinŭi ŭigyŏne tongŭihamnida. 당신의 의견에 동의합니다/ *give a ready* ~ K'waehi sŭngnak'ada 쾌히 승낙하다.

assert vt. chujanghada 주장하다, (*declare*) tanŏnhada 단언
하다. *He ~ed that his son was innocent.* Kŭnŭn chagi
adŭri mujoerago tanŏnhaessŭmnida. 그는 자기 아들이 무
죄라고 단언했읍니다.

asset n. chasan 자산, chaesan 재산. *Good health is a*
great ~. Kŏn-gangŭn k'ŭn chasanimnida. 건강은 큰 자산
입니다/ *enemy ~* chŏksan 적산(敵産)/ *external ~s* haeoe chaesan 해외 재산.

assign vt. haltanghada 할당하다. *I ~ed the tasks to the*
committee. Nanŭn ŭiwŏndŭrege kakkak irŭl haltang-
haessŭmnida. 나는 의원들에게 각각 일을 할당했읍니다/ *I*
was ~ed to the position of manager. Chibaein charie
immyŏngdoeŏssŭmnida. 지배인 자리에 임명되었읍니다.

assignment n. haltang 할당, chijŏng 지정. *What is to-*
day's ~? Onŭl hal irŭn muŏshijiyo? 오늘 할 일은 무엇
이지요?

assist vt. topta 돕다, (*be present*) ch'amsŏk'ada 참석하다.

assistance n. toum 도움, wŏnjo 원조. *Thank you for*
your ~. Sugohae chusyŏsŏ kamsahamnida. 수고해 주셔서
감사합니다/ *Can I be of any ~ to you?* (*manager*)
Muŏsŭl sashiryŏmnikka? 무엇을 사시렵니까/ *financial ~*
chaejŏng wŏnjo 재정 원조.

assistant n. chosu 조수, pojoja 보조자. *a business ~* samuwŏn 사무원/ *a shop ~* chŏmwŏn 점원/ *an unpaid ~*
mugŭp chosu 무급 조수/ *~ professor* chogyosu 조교수.

association n. hyŏp'oe 협회, chohap 조합. *an alumni ~*
tongch'anghoe 동창회/ *a cooperative ~* hyŏptong chohap
협동 조합/*a credit ~* shinyong chohap 신용 조합/*a member*
of an ~ chohabwŏn 조합원/ *a trade ~* muyŏk hyŏp'oe
무역 협회.

assume vt. kajŏnghada 가정하다, ch'ujŏnghada 추정하다.

assurance n. hwakshin 확신, pojŭng 보증.

assure vt. changdamhada 장담하다, pojanghada 보장하다.
I ~ you there's no danger. Wihŏmhaji ant'anŭn kŏsŭl
pojŭnghamnida. 위험하지 않다는 것을 보증합니다/ *I can*
~ you there are very fresh. Igŏsŭn aju shingshing-

hamnida. 이것은 아주 싱싱합니다.

astonish vt. nollage hada 놀라게 하다. *I was much* ~*ed.* Nanŭn kkamtchak nollassŭmnida. 나는 깜짝 놀랐읍니다/ *I am* ~*ed to hear it.* Kŭ sorirŭl tŭtko kkamtchak nollassŭmnida. 그 소리를 듣고 깜짝 놀랐읍니다/ *Why, you* ~ *me!* Ya, nollassŏ! 야, 놀랐어!

astronomer n. ch'ŏnmunhakcha 천문학자.

astronomy n. ch'ŏnmunhak 천문학.

asylum n. *lunatic* ~ chŏngshin pyŏngwŏn 정신 병원.

at prep. ~ *home* chibesŏ 집에서/ ~ *the office* samushiresŏ 사무실에서/ ~ *the station* chŏnggŏjangesŏ 정거장에서/ *I was* ~ *home.* Nanŭn chibe issŏssŭmnida. 나는 집에 있었읍니다/ ~ *noon* chŏngo-e 정오에/ ~ *5 o'clock* tasŏssie 다섯시에/ *Please call on me* ~ *6 o'clock.* Yŏsŏssie ch'ajawa chushio. 여섯시에 찾아와 주시오/ *Look* ~ *the moon!* Tarŭl ch'yŏda poshio! 달을 쳐다 보시오/ *What are you aiming* ~*?* Muŏsŭl norigo issŭmnikka? 무엇을 노리고 있읍니까/ ~ *a low price* ssan kapsŭro 싼 값으로/ ~ *a good price* choŭn kapsŭro 좋은 값으로.

athlete n. undongga 운동가, kyŏnggija 경기자.

athletic adj. undongŭi 운동의, ch'eyugŭi 체육의. *an* ~ *meeting* undonghoe 운동회/ *an* ~ *field* undongjang 운동장.

athletics n. undong 운동, kyŏnggi 경기.

Atlantic adj. taesŏyangŭi 대서양의. —n. taesŏyang 대서양 (=*the* ~ *Ocean*).

atmosphere n. punwigi 분위기. *the conference* ~ kŭ hoeŭiŭi punwigi 그 회의의 분위기/ *a family* ~ kajŏng punwigi 가정 분위기.

atom n. wŏnja 원자.

atomic adj. wŏnjaŭi 원자의. ~ *age* wŏnja shidae 원자 시대/ ~ *bomb* wŏnja p'okt'an 원자 폭탄/ ~ *energy* wŏnjaryŏk 원자력/ ~ *nucleus* wŏnjahaek 원자핵/ ~ *pile* wŏnjaro 원자로/ ~ *theory* wŏnjaron 원자론/ ~ *warfare* wŏnp'okchŏn 원폭전/ ~ *weapons* wŏnja mugi 원자 무기.

atomizer n. punmugi 분무기.

atone vi. posanghada 보상하다. *How can I* ~*?* Ŏttŏk'e posanghalkkayo? 어떻게 보상할까요? 「…을 보상하다.

atonement n. posang 보상. *make* ~ *for* …ŭl posanghada

atrocious *adj.* chanak'an 잔악한, hyungak'an 흉악한. *an ~ crime* chanak'an pŏmjoe 잔악한 범죄/ *an ~ weather* koyak'an nalssi 고약한 날씨.

attach *vt.* puch'ida 붙이다. *~ labels to the luggage* chime kkorip'yorŭl puch'ida 짐에 꼬리표를 붙이다/ *a hospital ~ed to a university* taehak pusok pyŏngwŏn 대학 부속 병원/ *Is there a dining car ~ed to the train?* Yŏlch'a-e shiktangi tallyŏ issŭmnikka? 열차에 식당이 달려 있읍니까/ *a civilian ~ed to the Army* kunsok 군속(軍屬).

attache *n. military ~* taesagwanbu yukkun mugwan 대사관부 육군 무관.

attack *n.* konggyŏk 공격, (*seizure by disease*) palbyŏng 발병. *—vt.* konggyŏk'ada 공격하다. *make an ~ upon …ŭl* konggyŏk'ada …을 공격하다/ *an all-out ~* ch'onggonggyŏk 총공격/ *night ~* yasŭp 야습/ *a heart ~* shimjang mabi 심장 마비/ *an ~ of fever* paryŏl 발열(發熱)/ *Our soldiers ~ed the enemy.* Uri pyŏngsadŭri chŏgŭl konggyŏk'aessŭmnida. 우리 병사들이 적을 공격했읍니다/ *I was ~ed by a robber.* Todugege sŭpkyŏgŭl tanghaessŭmnida. 도둑에게 습격을 당했읍니다. / *I have been ~ed with influenza.* Yuhaengsŏng kamgie kŏllyŏssŭmnida. 유행성 감기에 걸렸읍니다.

attain *vt.* talsŏnghada 달성하다. *—vi.* irŭda 이르다. *~ one's end* mokchŏgŭl talsŏnghada 목적을 달성하다/ *~ one's hopes* hŭimangŭl iruda 희망을 이루다/ *~ to perfection* wansŏnghada 완성하다/ *~ to power* kwŏllyŏgŭl ŏtta 권력을 얻다.

attainment *n.* talsŏng 달성, (*ability*) chaenŭng 재능. *educational ~s* hagŏp 학업.

attempt *vt.* shidohada 시도하다. *—n.* shido 시도, kido 기도. *~ to conceal* sumgiryŏ hada 숨기려 하다/ *~ an excuse* pyŏnmyŏngharyŏ hada 변명하려 하다/ *give up an ~* kyehoegŭl p'ogihada 계획을 포기하다/ *make an ~ at suicide* chasarŭl kidohada 자살을 기도하다/ *a bold ~* taedamhan shido 대담한 시도/ *a silly ~* ŏrisŏgŭn shido 어리석은 시도/ *My first ~ has failed.* Naŭi ch'ŏt kyehoegŭn shilp'aehaessŭmnida. 나의 첫 계획은 실패했읍니다/ *I'll make my*

last ～. Majimak shidorŭl haebogessŭmnida. 마지막 시
도를 해보겠읍니다.

attend *vi.* ch'ulsŏk'ada 출석하다, ch'amsŏk'ada 참석하다,
(*wait upon*) shijungdŭlda 시중들다. *I* ～ *regularly at
church.* Nanŭn ŏnjena ppajiji ank'o kyohoee ch'ulsŏk'amnida. 나는 언제나 빠지지 않고 교회에 출석합니다/
Which doctor is ～*ing you?* Tamdang ŭisanŭn nugushimnikka? 담당 의사는 누구십니까?

attendance *n.* ch'ulsŏk 출석, ch'amsŏk 참석. *The meeting
had a large* ～. Kŭ moimenŭn chulsŏkchaga manassŭmnida. 그 모임에는 출석자가 많았읍니다/ *The* ～ *was poor.*
Ch'amsŏkchanŭn chŏgŏssŭmnida. 참석자는 적었읍니다.

attention *n.* chuŭi 주의(注意), (*an act of kindness*) chin-
jŏl 친절. *May I have your* ～, *please?* Chamkkan shillyehamnida. 잠깐 실례합니다/ *I thank you for your
kind* ～. Ch'injŏrhi hae chusyŏsŏ kamsahamnida. 친절히
해 주셔서 감사합니다.

attentive *adj.* seshimhan 세심한, shinjunghan 신중한. *She
was always* ～ *to her young brother.* Kŭnyŏnŭn ŏnjena namdongsaengege chasanghaessŭmnida. 그녀는 언제
나 남동생에게 자상했읍니다.

attest *vt.,vi.* chŭngmyŏnghada 증명하다, chŭngŏnhada 증
언하다. *I* ～*ed for him.* Kŭrŭl wihae chŭngŏnŭl haessŭmnida. 그를 위해 증언을 했읍니다.

attitude *n.* t'aedo 태도. *What* ～ *do you want me to take?*
Ŏttŏn t'aedorŭl ch'wiharan malssŭmimnikka? 어떤 태도
를 취하란 말씀입니까?

attorney *n.* pyŏnhosa 변호사. *A* ～ *General* kŏmch'al
ch'ongjang 검찰 총장/ *a letter of* ～ wiimchang 위임장.

attract *vt.* kkŭlda 끌다, yuinhada 유인하다. *I shouted to*
～ *attention.* Nanŭn chuŭirŭl kkŭlgi wihae sorich'yŏssŭmnida. 나는 주의를 끌기 위해 소리쳤읍니다.

attractive *adj.* maeryŏkchŏgin 매력적인. *Don't you think
it's very* ～? Kŭgŏshi maeu maeryŏkchŏgirago saenggakchi anssŭmnikka? 그것이 매우 매력적이라고 생각지 않
습니까?

auction *n.* kyŏngmae 경매.

auctioner *n.* kyŏngmaein 경매인.

audacious *adj.* taedamhan 대담한. ppŏnppŏnsŭrŏn 뻔뻔스런.

audience *n.* ch'ŏngjung 청중. *There was a large ~ in the hall.* Horenŭn ch'ŏngjungi manassŭmnida. 홀에는 청중이 많았습니다/ *a radio ~* radio ch'ŏngch'wija 라디오 청취자/ *a TV ~* t'ellebijŏn shich'ŏngja 텔레비젼 시청자.

auditorium *n.* kangdang 강당. *a main ~* taegangdang 대강당. *The graduation ceremony was held in the main ~.* Chorŏpshigŭn taegangdangesŏ kŏhaengdoeŏssŭmnida. 졸업식은 대강당에서 거행되었읍니다.

August *n.* p'arwŏl 팔월(八月).

aunt *n.* ajumŏni 아주머니.

austerity *n.* ŏmkyŏk 엄격, *(simple)* kanso 간소. *~ life* naep'ip saenghwal 내핍 생활.

Australia *n.* Osŭt'ŭreillia 오스트레일리아, Hoju 호주(濠洲).

author *n.* chŏja 저자, chakka 작가.

authoress *n.* yŏryu chakka 여류 작가.

authority *n.* kwŏnwi 권위, taega 대가(大家), *(pl.)* tangguk 당국, *(ground)* kŭn-gŏ 근거. *He is the highest ~ in modern architecture.* Kŭnŭn hyŏndae kŏnch'ugŭi ch'oego kwŏnwijaimnida. 그는 현대 건축의 최고 권위자입니다/ *the school authorities* hakkyo tangguk 학교 당국/ *On what ~ do you say so?* Ŏttŏn kŭn-gŏesŏ kŭrŏn marŭl hashimnikka? 어떤 근거에서 그런 말을 하십니까?

authorize *vt.* kwŏnhanŭl chuda 권한을 주다.

authorized *adj.* kongindoen 공인된. *an ~ textbook* kŏmjŏngp'il kyogwasŏ 검정필 교과서/ *an ~ translation* wŏnjŏjaŭi hŏgarŭl ŏdŭn pŏnyŏk 원저자의 허가를 얻은 번역.

autograph *n.* chap'il 자필(自筆).

automatic *adj.* chadongjŏk 자동적. *an ~ door* chadongshik mun 자동식 문/ *an ~ machine* chadong kigye 자동 기계/ *an ~ rifle* chadong soch'ong 자동 소총/ *I don't like ~ elevators.* Chadong ellibeit'ŏnŭn ŏtchŏnji shilt'anikkayo. 자동 엘리베이터는 어쩐지 싫다니까요.

automation *n.* chadong chojak 자동 조작, ot'omeisyŏn 오토메이션.

automobile *n.* chadongch'a 자동차.

autophone *n.* chadong chŏnhwa 자동 전화.

autumn *n.* kaŭl 가을.

autumnal *adj.* kaŭrŭi 가을의. ~ *equinox* ch'ubun 추분
(秋分). ~ *tints* tanp'ung 단풍.

available *adj.* yuhyohan 유효한. *How long is this ticket*
~? I p'yonŭn ŏlma tongan yuhyohamnikka? 이 표는 얼
마 동안 유효합니까/ *The ticket is* ~ *for one month.* I
p'yonŭn han tal tongan yuhyohamnida. 이 표는 한 달 동
안 유효합니다.

avalanche *n.* nunsat'ae 눈사태, (*rush*) swaedo 쇄도.

avaricious *adj.* yokshimmanŭn 욕심많은. *He is* ~ *of*
power. Kŭnŭn kwŏllyŏge kŭpkŭp'ago issŭmnida. 그는
권력에 급급하고 있읍니다.

avenue *n.* karosu kil 가로수 길, taero 대로.

average *n.* p'yŏnggyun 평균. *What is the* ~ *temperature*
of this town in August? I toshiŭi p'arwŏl p'yŏnggyun
kionŭn ŏlmaimnikka? 이 도시의 8월 평균 기온은 얼마입니
까/ *an article of* ~ *quality* pot'ongp'um 보통품, chungch'i 중치.

aviation *n.* pihaeng 비행, hanggong 항공. ~ *cap* pihaeng-
mo 비행모/ ~ *corps* hanggongdae 항공대/ ~ *ground* pihaengjang 비행장/ ~ *officer* konggun changgyo 공군 장교.

aviator *n.* pihaengsa 비행사.

aviatress, aviatrix *n.* yŏryu pihaengsa 여류 비행사 (=*a*
lady aviator)

avid *adj.* kegŏlsŭrŏun 게걸스러운. *be* ~ *of food* ŭmshigŭl
kegŏlsŭrŏpke t'amnaeda 음식을 게걸스럽게 탐내다.

avocation *n.* puŏp 부업, (*hobby*) ch'wimi 취미.

avoid *vt.* p'ihada 피하다. *Try to* ~ *danger.* Wihŏmŭn
p'ihadorok hashio. 위험은 피하도록 하시오/ *He* ~*ed giving*
me direct answers. Kŭnŭn chikchŏp taedap'agirŭl p'i-
haessŭmnida. 그는 직접 대답하기를 피했읍니다.

avouch *vt.,vi.* hwagŏnhada 확언하다, pojŭnghada 보증하
다. *I can* ~ *for the quality.* P'umjirŭl pojanghamnida.
품질을 보장합니다.

avow *vt.* kongŏnhada 공언하다, injŏnghada 인정하다. ~
oneself to be a patriot chashinŭl aegukcharago kongŏnhada 자신을 애국자라고 공언하다/ ~ *a fault* chalmosŭl

injŏnghada. 잘못을 인정하다.

awake *vi.,vt.* irŏnada 일어나다, irŭk'ida 일으키다. —*adj.* kkaeŏsŏ 깨어서, chaji ank'o 자지 않고. *I awoke from sleep.* Nanŭn chamesŏ kkaeŏssŭmnida. 나는 잠에서 깨었읍니다/ *I usually ~ at six.* Nanŭn yŏsŏssie irŏnamnida. 나는 여섯시에 일어납니다/ *I was wide ~ all night.* Pamsae han nundo puch'iji anassŭmnida. 밤새 한 눈도 붙이지 않았읍니다/ *~ old memories* yet kiŏgŭl pullŏirŭk'ida 옛 기억을 불러일으키다/ *~ to the danger* wihŏmŭl kkaedatta 위험을 깨닫다.

award *n.* sangp'um 상품(賞品). —*vt.* sangŭl chuda 상을 주다. *the Academy Award* ak'ademisang 아카데미상(賞)/ *a cash ~* sanggŭm 상금/ *a trophy ~* sangp'ae 상패/ *He was ~ed the first prize.* Kŭnŭn iltŭngsangŭl padassŭmnida. 그는 일등상을 받았읍니다.

aware *adj.* arach'arigo 알아차리고, kkaedatko 깨닫고. *be ~ of a danger* wihŏmŭl arach'arigo itta 위험을 알아차리고 있다/ *become ~ of* ...ŭl alda …을 알다.

away *adv.* ttŏrŏjyŏsŏ 떨어져서, mŏlli 멀리, chŏtchoguro 저쪽으로. *Keep the boy ~ from the fire.* Airŭl puresŏ mŏlli hashio. 아이를 불에서 멀리 하시오/ *My house is not far ~.* Uri chibŭn mŏlji anssŭmnida. 우리 집은 멀지 않습니다/ *Go ~!* Kashio! 가시오/ *Take them ~!* Tchoch'a pŏrishio. 쫓아 버리시오/ *He is ~ from home now.* Kŭnŭn chigŭm chibe ŏpsŭmnida. 그는 지금 집에 없읍니다/ *How long will you be ~?* Ŏnjekkaji naga issŭl yejŏngimnikka? 언제까지 나가 있을 예정입니까?

awe *n.* turyŏum 두려움. —*vt.* turyŏpke hada 두렵게 하다. *a feeling of ~* turyŏun kamjŏng 두려운 감정/ *be struck with ~* wiŏme nullida 위엄에 눌리다.

awful *adj.* turyŏun 두려운, mushimushihan 무시무시한. *The heat is ~ today.* Onŭrŭi tŏwinŭn mushimushihamnida. 오늘의 더위는 무시무시합니다.

awfully *adv.* musŏpke 무섭게, aju 아주. *I am ~ sorry.* Mianhagi tchagi ŏpsŭmnida. 미안하기 짝이 없읍니다.

awhile *adv.* chamkkan 잠깐, chamshi 잠시.

awkward *adj.* pulp'yŏnhan 불편한, ŏsaek'an 어색한. *This*

is an ~ *staircase*. I kyedanŭn pulp'yŏnhamnida. 이 계
단은 불편합니다/ *an* ~ *silence* ŏsaek'an ch'immuk 어색
한 침묵/ ~ *workman* sŏt'urŭn chikkong 서투른 직공.

awl *n.* songgot 송곳.

awning *n.* ch'ail 차일, ch'ayang 차양, ch'ŏnmak 천막.

ax, axe *n.* tokki 도끼. *grind an* ~ tokkirŭl kalda 도끼를

ax(e)man *n.* namukkun 나무꾼. 〔갈다.

azalea *n.* chindallae 진달래. *Do you have any potted* ~*s*?
Chindallae hwabunŭl kajigo issŭmnikka? 진달래 화분을
가지고 있읍니까?

azure *adj.* hanŭlsaegŭi 하늘색의. ~ *eyes* p'urŭn nun 푸른
눈/ *an* ~ *sky* p'urŭn hanŭl 푸른 하늘. —*n.* (*skyblue*)
hanŭlsaek 하늘색, (*blue*) namsaek 남색.

◂ B ▸

babe *n.* kannan ai 갓난 아이.

baby *n.* kannanagi 갓난아기. *a* ~ *boy* namja agi 남자 아
기/ *a* ~ *carriage* yumoch'a 유모차.

bachelor *n.* tokshin namja 독신 남자, ch'onggak 총각.

back *adv.* twiro 뒤로. —*vi.*,*vt.* hut'oehada 후퇴하다, huwŏnhada 후원하다. —*n.* tŭng 등, twi 뒤. *When will he
be* ~? Kŭnŭn ŏnje toraoshimnikka? 그이는 언제 돌아오
십니까/ *I hope you will* ~ *my plan*. Nae kyehoegŭl hu-
wŏnhae chushigi paramnida. 내 계획을 후원해 주시기 바
랍니다/ ~ *door* twinmun 뒷문/ ~ *mirror* paek mirŏ 백
미러/ ~ *seat* twitchari 뒷자리.

backbone *n.* tŭngppyŏ 등뼈, chungch'u 중추.

background *n.* paegyŏng 배경, kyŏngnyŏk 경력.

backyard *n.* twinmadang 뒷마당.

bad *adj.* nappŭn 나쁜. *That is too* ~. Kŭgŏ andwaetkunyo. 그거 안됐군요/ *Drinking is a* ~ *habit*. Ŭmju-
nŭn nappŭn pŏrŭshimnida. 음주는 나쁜 버릇입니다/ *She
feels* ~ *today*. Kŭnyŏnŭn onŭl momi p'yŏnch'anssŭmnida. 그녀는 오늘 몸이 편찮습니다/ *Don't let that fish
go* ~. *Put it in the fridge*. Saengsŏni sanghaji ant'orok

naengjanggo-e nŏushio. 생선이 상하지 않도록 냉장고에 넣
badge *n.* hwijang 휘장, paeji 배지. ㄴ으시오.
bag *n.* kabang 가방, paek 백. *Would you open your ~,*
please ? Kabangŭl yŏrŏ chushilkkayo ? 가방을 열어 주실까
요/ *I've left my ~ on the bus.* Kabangŭl pŏsŭe nok'o
naeryŏssŭmnida. 가방을 버스에 놓고 내렸읍니다.
baggage *n.* suhamul 수하물. *~ car* suhamulch'a 수하물차/
~ office suhamul ch'wigŭpso 수하물 취급소/ *~ room*
suhamul pogwanso 수하물 보관소/ *the ~ declaration*
form hyudaep'um shin-gosŏ 휴대품 신고서/ *Where can*
I get my ~ ? Suhamurŭn ŏdisŏ ch'assŭmnikka ? 수하물은
어디서 찾습니까/ *Is this all your ~ ?* Chimŭn igŏtppu-
nimnikka ? 짐은 이것뿐입니까/ *One of my ~ is missing.*
Hamuri hana ŏpsŭmnida. 하물이 하나 없읍니다.
bait *n.* mikki 미끼, mŏgi 먹이.
bake *vt.* kupta 굽다. *well ~d* chal kuwŏjin 잘 구워진/
a hard ~d cracker ttakttak'age kuun k'ŭraek'ŏ 딱
딱하게 구운 크래커/ *I think his plan is rather half*
~d. Kŭŭi kyehoegŭn mihŭp'an tega innŭn kŏt kassŭmnida. 그의 계획은 미흡한 데가 있는 것 같습니다.
baker *n.* ppang kumnŭn saram 빵 굽는 사람.
bakery *n.* ppangchip 빵집.
balance *n.* chŏul 저울, *(remainder)* chan-go 잔고. *—vt.*
ch'ŏngsanhada 청산(淸算)하다. *I have still a ~ at my*
bank. Ŭnhaengenŭn ajik chan-goga issŭmnida. 은행에는
아직 잔고가 있읍니다 /*Please ~ this account.* I kyesansŏrŭl ch'ŏngsanhae chushio. 이 계산서를 청산해 주시오.
balcony *n.* palk'oni 발코니, nodae 노대, *(in a theatre)*
t'ŭkpyŏlsŏk 특별석. *Two balconies, please.* T'ŭkpyŏl-
sŏgŭl tu chang chushio. 특별석을 두 장 주시오.
bald *adj.* pŏsŏjin 벗어진. *~ head* taemŏri 대머리 /*a ~*
mountain pŏlgŏsungi san 벌거숭이 산.
bale *n.* chimtchak 짐짝, kkurŏmi 꾸러미. *~s of cloth*
otkkurŏmi 옷꾸러미/ *~s of hay* kŏnch'o mungch'i 건초
뭉치.
ball *n.* kong 공, *(social dancing)* mudohoe 무도회. *base-*
~ yagu 야구/ *foot~* ch'ukku 축구/ *a tennis ~* chŏnggu

kong 정구 공/ ~*room* mudojang 무도장/ *You carry the* ~ *for me for the time being*. Tangbun-gan twinnirŭl put'aktŭrimnida. 당분간 뒷일을 부탁드립니다.

ballet *n.* palle 발레.

balloon *n.* kigu 기구, p'ungsŏn 풍선. *advertising* ~ aedŭbŏllun 애드벌룬/ ~ *satellite* p'ungsŏn wisŏng 풍선 위성/ ~ *fish* pogŏ 복어.

ballot *n.* t'up'yoji 투표지, t'up'yo 투표. *cast a* ~ t'up'yohada 투표하다/ *by secret* ~ pimil t'upyoro 비밀 투표로.

balsam *n.* pongsŏnhwa 봉선화.

bamboo *n.* tae 대. ~ *sprout* chuksun 죽순/ ~ *tree* taenamu 대나무/ *I will show you some excellent sofas made of* ~. Taero mandŭn hullyunghan sop'arŭl poyŏ tŭrigessŭmnida. 대로 만든 훌륭한 소파를 보여 드리겠읍니다.

bamboozle *vt.* sogida 속이다.

ban *n.* kŭmji 금지. —*vt.* kŭmjihada 금지하다. *The authorities* ~*ned the belly dance*. Tanggugŭn pelli taensŭrŭl kŭmjishik'yŏssŭmnida. 당국은 벨리 댄스를 금지시켰읍니다.

band *n.* aktan 악단, (*party*) tte 떼. *a brass* ~ ch'wiju aktan 취주 악단/ *a military* ~ yukkun kunaktae 육군 군악대/ *a* ~ *of robbers* toduktte 도둑떼.

bandage *n.* pungdae 붕대. —*vt.* pungdaerŭl kamta 붕대를 감다. *Why have you got a* ~ *on it*? Wae pungdaerŭl kamko issŭmnikka? 왜 붕대를 감고 있읍니까?

bandit *n.* sanjŏk 산적. *a mounted* ~ majŏk 마적(馬賊).

bank *n.* ŭnhaeng 은행, (*of a river*) tuk 둑. *commercial* ~ sangŏp ŭnhaeng 상업 은행/ *blood* ~ hyŏraek ŭnhaeng 혈액 은행/ ~ *account* ŭnhaeng kyechŏng 은행 계정/ *sand* ~ moraet'op 모래톱/ *After supper, let's walk along the river* ~. Chŏnyŏgŭl mŏkko nasŏ kangtugŭl ttara sanch'aek'apshida 저녁을 먹고 나서 강둑을 따라 산책합시다.

banker *n.* ŭnhaengga 은행가, chagŏptae 작업대.

bankrupt *n.* p'asanja 파산자. —*adj.* p'asanhan 파산한.

bankruptcy *n.* p'asan 파산, tosan 도산.

banner *n.* ki 기, kich'i 기치, (*streamer*) kitpal 깃발.

banquet *n.* yŏnhoe 연회. *wedding* ~ kyŏrhon p'iroyŏn 결혼 피로연/ *I will show you to the* ~ *room.* Yŏnhoejang-ŭro annaehae tŭrigessŭmnida. 연회장으로 안내해 드리겠읍니다.

baptism *n.* serye 세례, ch'imnye 침례.

baptize *vt.* serye [ch'imnye]rŭl chuda 세례 [침례]를 주다. *be* ~*d* serye[ch'imnye]rŭl patta 세례 [침례]를 받다.

bar *n.* maktaegi 막대기, (*for drinks*) pa 바. *parallel* ~*s* p'yŏnghaengbong 평행봉/*Gentleman, how are you? Something from the* ~? Annyŏnghaseyo. Surŭl han-jan tŭshilkkayo? 안녕하세요. 술을 한잔 드실까요?

barbarian *n.* yamanin 야만인. —*adj.* yamanjŏgin 야만적인.

barber *n.* ibalsa 이발사.

barbershop *n.* ibalso 이발소. *Where is a* ~? Ibalsonŭn ŏdi issŭmnikka? 이발소는 어디 있읍니까?

bare *adj.* pŏlgŏbŏsŭn 벌거벗은. ~ *head* maenmŏri 맨머리/ *with* ~ *hands* maensonŭro 맨손으로/ ~ *feet* maenbal 맨발.

bargain *n.* hŭngjŏng 흥정, ssaguryŏ mulgŏn 싸구려 물건. —*vi.* enurihada 에누리하다. *I will make a* ~ *with you.* Tangshin-gwa hŭngjŏngŭl hapshida. 당신과 흥정을 합시다/ *Is there any* ~ *sale going on now?* Chigŭm pa-genseil hanŭn koshi·issŭmnikka? 지금·바겐세일 하는 곳이 있읍니까/ *This is really a* ~. Igŏsŭn chŏngmal chal sashinŭn kŏshimnida. 이것은 정말 잘 사시는 것입니다.

bark *n.* namukkŏpchil 나무껍질. —*vi.* (*dogs*) kaega chitta 개가 짖다.

barley *n.* pori 보리. *boiled* ~ (*and rice*) poribap 보리밥.

barn *n.* kwang 광. *a cow* ~ somagu 소마구/ *an engine* ~ kigwan ch'ago 기관 차고.

barnyard *n.* twittŭl 뒤뜰.

barometer *n.* ch'ŏngugye 청우계, paromit'ŏ 바로미터.

barracks *n.* maksa 막사, pyŏngyŏng 병영(兵營). *army* ~ pyŏngsa 병사(兵舍).

barrel *n.* t'ong 통, (*gun*) p'oshin 포신, ch'ongyŏl 총열. *a* ~ *of beer* maekchu han t'ong 맥주 한 통.

barren *adj.* memarŭn 메마른, purimŭi 불임(不姙)의. *a* ~

soil memarŭn t'oji 메마른 토지/ *a ~ woman* airŭl nach'i mot'anŭn yŏin 아이를 낳지 못하는 여인.

barricade *n.* pangch'aek 방책, parik'eidŭ 바리케이드.

barrier *n.* ult'ari 울타리, kwanmun 관문. *Show your ticket at the ~.* Kaech'alguesŏ p'yorŭl poishipshio. 개찰구에서 표를 보이십시오.

barter *n.* mulmul kyohwan 물물 교환. *—vi.,vt.* mulmul kyohwanhada 물물 교환하다. *~ furs for powder* mop'iwa hwayagŭl kyohwanhada 모피와 화약을 교환하다.

base *n.* kich'o 기초, kiji 기지(基地). *—adj.* ch'ŏnhan 천한. *air ~* konggun kiji 공군 기지/ *naval ~* haegun kiji 해군 기지/ *He is guilty of ~ conduct.* Kŭnŭn haengshiri ch'ŏnhamnida. 그는 행실이 천합니다.

baseball *n.* yagu 야구. *play ~* yagurŭl hada 야구를 하다/ *How about going to a ~ game with me next Saturday?* Onŭn t'oyoil yagu kugyŏng an kashiryŏmnikka? 오는 토요일 야구 구경 안 가시렵니까/ *Let's go to Chamshil Stadium to see the Korea-Japan goodwill ~ game.* Chamshil undongjange hanil ch'insŏn yagu kyŏnggirŭl porŏ kapshida. 잠실 운동장에 한일 친선 야구 경기를 보러 갑시다.

basic *adj.* kich'ojŏgin 기초적인, kibonjŏgin 기본적인. *Well, you must remember a few ~ things.* Kŭlsseyo, kibonjŏgin kŏsŭl myŏt kaji ara tuŏya hal kŏshimnida. 글쎄요, 기본적인 것을 몇 가지 알아 두어야 할 것입니다.

basin *n.* taeya 대야, multongi 물동이. *a wash ~* sesu taeya 세수 대야/ *a ~ of water* mul han tongi 물 한 동이.

basket *n.* paguni 바구니, kwangjuri 광주리. *a shopping ~* shijang paguni 시장 바구니/ *a waste-paper ~* hyujit'ong 휴지통.

basketball *n.* nonggu 농구. *A Korean women's ~ team crushed the Indonesian team by 80 : 62.* Han-guk yŏja nonggut'imi Indoneshia t'imŭl p'alshiptae yukshibiro kyŏkp'ahaessŭmnida. 한국 여자 농구팀이 인도네시아 팀을 80대 62로 격파했읍니다.

baste *vt.* shich'ida 시치다, kabonghada 가봉하다.

bat *n.* paet'ŭ 배트, t'abong 타봉, *(animal)* pakchwi 박쥐.

bath *n.* mogyok 목욕. *sun ~* ilgwangyok 일광욕/*I want*

a single room with a ~ for tonight. Onŭlpam suk-pak'ago ship'ŭnde, yokshiri ttallin irinyong pangi issŭmnikka? 오늘밤 숙박하고 싶은데, 욕실이 딸린 일인용 방이 있읍니까/ *On what floor is a sauna ~?* Saunat'angŭn myŏt ch'ŭnge issŭmnikka? 사우나탕은 몇 층에 있읍니까?

bathe *vi.* myŏkkamta 멱감다, mogyok'ada 목욕하다.

bathing *n.* suyŏng 수영. *~ beach* haesuyokchang 해수욕장/ *(suit) ~ dress* suyŏngbok 수영복.

bathrobe *n.* hwajangbok 화장복.

bathroom *n.* mogyokt'ang 목욕탕, yokshil 욕실, hwajang-shil 화장실. *May I go to the ~?* Hwajangshil chom ssŏdo chok'essŭmnikka? 화장실 좀 써도 좋겠읍니까?

battery *n.* chŏnji 전지. *a dry ~* kŏnjŏnji 건전지/ *a storage ~* ch'ukchonji 축전지.

battle *n.* chŏnjaeng 전쟁. *an air ~* kongjungjŏn 공중전/ *~-field* chŏnjaengt'ŏ 전쟁터/ *a ~ for living* saenghwal chŏnsŏn 생활 전선.

bay *n.* man 만(灣). *the B~ of Kyonggi* kyŏnggiman 경기만(京畿灣).

be *v.(the original form of am, are, is, etc.)* ① *Before adjective* **be** *is translated by* …**mnida** …ㅂ니다(*for the present*), …**ŏssŭmnida** …었읍니다(*for the past*). *The world is round.* Chigunŭn tunggŭmnida. 지구는 둥급니다/ *He is ten years old.* Kŭnŭn yŏl sarimnida. 그는 열살입니다/ *She was happy.* Kŭnyŏnŭn haengbok'a-yŏssŭmnida. 그녀는 행복하였읍니다. ② *In other cases,* **be** *or* **there be** *is translated by* **issŭmnida** 있읍니다, *neg.* **ŏpsŭmnida** 없읍니다(*for the present*), *and by* **issŏssŭm-nida** 있었읍니다, *neg.* **ŏpsŏssŭmnida** 없었읍니다(*for the past*). ③ *In polite speech you may use* **kyeshimnida** 계십니다, *neg.* **an kyeshimnida** 안 계십니다(*for the present*), *and* **kyesyŏssŭmnida** 계셨읍니다, *neg.* **an kyesyŏssŭmnida** 안 계셨읍니다(*for the past*). *Is your father at home?* Abŏjinŭn chibe kyeshimnikka? 아버지는 집에 계십니까/ *How long have you been in Seoul?* Sŏurenŭn ŏlmana kyesyŏssŭmnikka? 서울에는 얼마나 계셨읍니까/ *How are you?* Ŏttŏssŭmnikka? 어떻습니까/ *I am fine, thank you.* Tŏkpune pyŏlt'al ŏpsŭmnida. 덕

분에 별탈 없읍니다/ *When is your birthday?* Tang-shinŭi saengirŭn ŏnjeimnikka? 당신의 생일은 언제입니까/ *What time should I be at the airport?* Myŏt shie konghangŭro kamyŏn toemnikka? 몇 시에 공항으로 가면 됩니까?

beach *n.* haebyŏn 해변, kaetpŏl 갯벌. *walk along the ~* haebyŏnŭl sanch'aek'ada 해변을 산책하다/ *Is there a good ~ around Pusan?* Pusan kŭnch'ŏe choŭn hae-suyokchangi issŭmnikka? 부산 근처에 좋은 해수욕장이 있읍니까/ *Yes, there are several good ~es.* Ne, myŏt kaeŭi choŭn haesuyokchangi issŭmnida. 네, 몇 개의 좋은 해수욕장이 있읍니다.

bead *n.* yŏmjual 염주알, kusŭl 구슬, (*pl.*) yŏmju 염주.

beak *n.* puri 부리.

beam *n.* kwangsŏn 광선, (*of building*) taedŭlpo 대들보.

bean *n.* k'ong 콩. *kidney ~s* kangnam-k'ong 강남콩/ *a red ~* p'at 팥/ *soya ~s* taedu 대두.

bear *n.* kom 곰. —*vi.,vt.* ch'amta 참다, ⟨yŏmju⟩ (*bring forth*) nat'a 낳다, (*carry*) narŭda 나르다, (*move*) naagada 나아가다. *I can't ~ this pain.* I kot'ongŭl ch'a-mŭl suga ŏpsŭmnida. 이 고통을 참을 수가 없읍니다/ *What year was he born in?* Kŭnŭn myŏnnyŏn saengimnikka? 그는 몇년 생입니까/ *He was born in Korea.* Kŭnŭn Han-gugesŏ t'aeŏnassŭmnida. 그는 한국에서 태어났읍니다/ *~ a heavy load* mugŏun chimŭl narŭda 무거운 짐을 나르다/ *B~ to the right at the next intersection.* Ta-ŭm kyoch'aro-esŏ orŭntchoguro naagashio. 다음 교차로에서 오른쪽으로 나아가시오.

beard *n.* suyŏm 수염. *grow a ~* suyŏmŭl kirŭda 수염을 기르다/ *shave the ~* suyŏmŭl kkakta 수염을 깎다.

bearing *n.* t'aedo 태도.

beast *n.* chimsŭng 짐승. *a wild ~* yasu 야수.

beat *vt.* ch'ida 치다, ttaerida 때리다. *He ~ the boy black and blue.* Kŭnŭn airŭl mŏngi tŭldorok ttaeryŏssŭmni-

da. 그는 아이를 멍이 들도록 때렸읍니다/ ～ *a drum*
pugŭl tudŭrida 북을 두드리다.

beautiful *adj.* arŭmdaun 아름다운. *You look ～ tonight.*
Onŭl pam arŭmdaushigunyo. 오늘 밤 아름다우시군요/
a ～ face yeppŭn ŏlgul 예쁜 얼굴/ *a ～ flower* arŭmdaun
kkot 아름다운 꽃.

beautifully *adv.* arŭmdapke 아름답게. *She plays the
piano ～.* Kŭnyŏnŭn p'ianorŭl arŭmdapke ch'imnida.
그녀는 피아노를 아름답게 칩니다.

beauty *n.* mi 미(美), arŭmdaum 아름다움, miin 미인. ～
artist miyongsa 미용사/ ～ *contest* miin taehoe 미인 대
회/ ～ *parlor*〔*shop*〕 mijangwŏn 미장원.

because *conj.* waenyahamyŏn 왜냐하면, ttaemune 때문에.
We stayed at home ～ it rained. Piga watki ttaemune
chibe issŏssŭmnida. 비가 왔기 때문에 집에 있었읍니다.

become *vi.,vt.* (…i) toeda (…이) 되다, *(suit)* ŏullida 어울리
다. *He became a doctor.* Kŭnŭn ŭisaga toeŏssŭmnida.
그는 의사가 되었읍니다/ *The weather has ～ cold.* Nalssiga ch'uwŏjyŏssŭmnida. 날씨가 추워졌읍니다/ *Does this
new dress ～ me?* I sae tŭresŭnŭn na-ege ŏullimnikka?
이 새 드레스는 나에게 어울립니까?

bed *n.* ch'imdae 침대. *go to ～* chamcharie tŭlda 잠자리에
들다/*How many ～s in a room?* Han pange ch'imdaega
myŏt kaeimnikka? 한 방에 침대가 몇 개입니까/ *We never
go to ～ till after midnight.* Yŏltushiga toel ttaekkaji
urinŭn chaji anssŭmnida. 12시가 될 때까지 우리는 자지 않
습니다/ *How long do you have to stay in ～?* Olmana
ibwŏnhaeya hamnikka? 얼마나 입원해야 합니까?

bedding *n.* ch'imgu 침구.

bedroom *n.* ch'imshil 침실. *My mother is in the ～ at the
end of the hall.* Ŏmŏninŭn pokto kkŭt'e innŭn ch'im-
shire kyeshimnida. 어머니는 복도 끝에 있는 침실에 계십니
bee *n.* pŏl 벌. 〔다.

beech *n.* nŏdobamnamu 너도밤나무.

beef *n.* soegogi 쇠고기. *Is this ～ too rare for you?* I koginŭn chŏm tŏl kuwŏjyŏssŭmnikka? 이 고기는 좀 덜 구
워졌읍니까?

beehive *n.* pŏlchip 벌집. ~ *culture* yangbong 양봉.

beer *n.* maekchu 맥주, piŏ 비어. *I want a ~, please.* Maekchurŭl han chan chuseyo. 맥주를 한 잔 주세요/ *Give me ~ and a hamburger, please.* Maekchuwa haembŏgŏrŭl chushio. 맥주와 햄버거를 주시오.

before *adv.,conj.* ap'e 앞에, chŏne 전에. *Please come ~ ten o'clock.* Yŏlshi chŏne wa chushio. 10시 전에 와 주시오/ *I've seen that film ~.* Ijŏne kŭ yŏnghwarŭl pon iri issŭmnida. 이전에 그 영화를 본 일이 있읍니다/ *I shall wait for you ~ that house.* Kŭ chip ap'esŏ kidarigessŭmnida. 그 집 앞에서 기다리겠읍니다/ *Do it now ~ you forget.* Itki chŏne chigŭm hashio. 잊기 전에 지금 하시오.

beg *vt.,vi.* ch'ŏnghada 청하다. *I ~ you to sit down.* Anjūshigi paramnida. 앉으시기 바랍니다/ *He ~ged (me) for some money.* Kŭnŭn ton chom tallago sajŏnghaessŭmnida. 그는 돈 좀 달라고 사정했읍니다.

beggar *n.* kŏji 거지.

begin *vt.,vi.* shijak'ada 시작하다, shijaktoeda 시작되다. *When did you ~ English?* Yŏngŏ kongburŭl ŏnje shijak'aessŭmnikka? 영어 공부를 언제 시작했읍니까/ *We shall ~ the meeting at seven o'clock.* Hoehabŭn ilgopshie shijak'al kŏshimnida. 회합은 일곱시에 시작할 것입니다.

beginner *n.* ch'oboja 초보자. *the ~ in English* Yŏngŏ ch'oboja 영어 초보자/ *a promising ~* chŏndo yumanghan ch'oboja 전도 유망한 초보자. 「ŭmbut'ŏ 처음부터.

beginning *n.* shich'o 시초, ch'o 초(初). *from the ~* ch'ŏ-

behalf *n.* *on ~ of* =*on one's ~* ...ŭl wihayŏ ···을 위하여, ...ŭl taeshinhayŏ ···을 대신하여. *I speak this on your ~.* Tangshinŭl wihae marhanŭn kŏshimnida. 당신을 위해 말하는 것입니다.

behave *vi.* haengdonghada 행동하다. *How did he ~?* Kŭŭi t'aedonŭn ŏttŏhaessŭmnikka? 그의 태도는 어떠했읍니까?

behind *adv.* twie 뒤에, paehue 배후에. *He was hiding ~ the door.* Kŭnŭn mun twie sumŏ issŏssŭmnida. 그는 문 뒤에 숨어 있었읍니다/ *They have a rich friend ~ them.* Kŭdŭrŭi paehuenŭn puhoga issŭmnida. 그들의 배후에는 부호가 있읍니다/ *Are you ~ with your work?* Iri milliji anassŭmnikka? 일이 밀리지 않았읍니까?

belief *n.* shinnyŏm 신념, shinang 신앙, soshin 소신(所信).

believe *vt.* mitta 믿다. *Don't you ~ in God?* Shinŭl mitchi anssŭmnikka? 신을 믿지 않습니까/ *I don't ~ it.* Midōjiji anssŭmnida. 믿어지지 않습니다.

bell *n.* chong 종, pangul 방울.

bellboy *n.* (*of hotel*) poi 보이, sahwan 사환. *The ~ will show you to your room.* Poiga pangkkaji annaehae tŭril kŏmnida. 보이가 방까지 안내해 드릴 겁니다.

bellows *n.* p'ulmu 풀무, (*of camera*) churŭm sangja 주름 상자.

belly *n.* pae 배, pokpu 복부. *an empty ~* kongbok 공복/ *the lower ~* araetpae 아랫배, habokpu 하복부.

belong *vi.* sok'ada 속하다, ...ŭi kŏshida …의 것이다. *These books ~ to me.* I ch'aektŭrŭn naegŏshimnida. 이 책들은 내것입니다/ *She doesn't ~ here.* Kŭnyŏnŭn irŏn kose issŭl yŏjaga animnida. 그녀는 이런 곳에 있을 여자가 아닙니다/ *Whom does this fountain pen ~ to?* I mannyŏnp'irŭn nuguŭi kŏshimnikka? 이 만년필은 누구의 것입니까?

belongings *n.* soyumul 소유물, hyudaep'um 휴대품, chaesan 재산.

below *prep.* ...poda mit'e …보다 밑에. *Shall I write my name above or ~ the line?* Irŭmŭn sŏn wie ssŭlkkayo, mit'e ssŭlkkayo? 이름은 선 위에 쓸까요, 밑에 쓸까요/ *Your work is ~ the average.* Tangshinŭi chakp'umŭn sujun ihaimnida. 당신의 작품은 수준 이하입니다/ *~ zero* yŏngha 영하(零下)/ *persons ~ fifty* oshipse ihaŭi saramdŭl 50세 이하의 사람들.

belt *n.* tti 띠, pelt'ŭ 벨트, (*zone*) chidae 지대. *leather ~* hyŏktae 혁대. 「hubo sŏnsu 후보 선수.

bench *n.* pench'i 벤치, kin ŭija 긴 의자. *~ warmer*

bend *vt.* kuburida 구부리다. —*vi.* kuburŏjida 구부러지다. *B~ the end of the wire up.* Ch'olsa kkŭt'ŭl wiro kuburishio. 철사 끝을 위로 구부리시오/ *The road ~s to the left here.* Kirŭn yŏgisŏ oentchogŭro kupsŭmnida. 길은 여기서 왼쪽으로 굽습니다.

beneath *prep.* paro mit'e 바로 밑에. *Let us rest ~ the*

tree. Namu mit'esŏ shwipshida. 나무 밑에서 쉽시다.

benefactor *n*. ŭnin 은인, (*patron*) huwŏnja 후원자.

benefit *n*. iik 이익, (*favor*) ŭnhye 은혜. *The money is to be used for the ~ of the poor*. Kŭ tonŭn kananhan saramŭl wihae ssŏyaman hamnida. 그 돈은 가난한 사람을 위해 써야만 합니다.

bequest *n*. yusan 유산, yujŭng 유증. *He left ~s of money to all his servants*. Haindŭl moduege tonŭl namgyŏ chuŏssŭmnida. 하인들 모두에게 돈을 남겨 주었읍니다.

beriberi *n*. (*med*.) kakki 각기 (脚氣).

berry *n*. changgwa 장과 (漿果). *straw~* yangttalgi 양딸기 / *rasp~* namuttalgi 나무딸기.

berth *n*. ch'imdae 침대. *Conductor, where is the ~?* Ch'ajang, ch'imdaenŭn ŏdi itchiyo? 차장, 침대는 어디 있지요/ *~ ticket* ch'imdaekwŏn 침대권.

beseech *vt*. kanch'ŏnghada 간청하다. *Spare him, I ~ you*. Put'agini chebal kŭrŭl yongsŏhae chushio. 부탁이니 제발 그를 용서해 주시오.

beside *prep*. ...ŭi kyŏt'e ...의 곁에. *Come and sit ~ me*. Nae kyŏt'e wa anjŭshio. 내 곁에 와 앉으시오.

besides *prep., adv*. ...oee 외에, kedaga 게다가. *I have three other hats ~ this*. Mojanŭn igŏ oeedo se kaega issŭmnida. 모자는 이거 외에도 세 개가 있읍니다/ *It's too late to go for a walk now, ~, it's beginning to rain*. Chigŭm sanch'aek'agienŭn nŏmu nŭssŭmnida, kedaga piga ogoyo. 지금 산책하기에는 너무 늦습니다, 게다가 비가 오고요.

best *adj*. kajang chohŭn 가장 좋은. —*adv*. kajang chal 가장 잘. —*n*. ch'oesang 최상. *Who is the ~ pupil in the class?* Hakkŭbesŏ nuga kajang usuhan haksaengimnikka? 학급에서 누가 가장 우수한 학생입니까/ *Show me the ~ you have*. Kajang chohŭn kŏsŭl poyŏ chushipshio. 가장 좋은 것을 보여 주십시오/ *I like this ~*. Nanŭn igŏsŭl kajang choahamnida. 나는 이것을 가장 좋아합니다/ *I will do my poor ~ to do so*. Mihŭp'ajiman ch'oesŏnŭl tahagessŭmnida. 미흡하지만 최선을 다하겠읍니다.

bet *n*. naegi 내기. —*vt., vi*. (*money*) kŏlda 걸다. *lose a ~* naegie chida 내기에 지다/ *win a ~* naegie igida 내기에 이

기다/ *Let us have a ~ on the result of the ball game.*
Kŭ yagu shihap, ŏnŭ tchogi iginŭn-ga naegihapshida.
그 야구 시합, 어느 쪽이 이기는가 내기합시다.

betray *vt.* paebanhada 배반하다, *(deceive)* sogida 속이다.
He ~ed my trust in him. Kŭnŭn nae shilloerŭl paeban-
haessŭmnida. 그는 내 신뢰를 배반했읍니다.

better *adj.* tŏ choŭn 더 좋은, poda naŭn 보다 나은. *Which*
is ~? Ŏnŭ kŏshi tŏ chŏssŭmnikka? 어느 것이 더 좋습니
까/ *This idea is ~ than mine.* I aidiŏnŭn naegŏtpoda
chossŭmnida. 이 아이디어는 내것보다 좋습니다/ *Does she*
seem to be any ~? Kŭnyŏnŭn chom choajin kŏt kassŭmnikka? 그녀는 좀 좋아진 것 같습니까/ *You had ~ bring*
your jacket when you go to the mountain. Sane kal
ttaenŭn chak'esŭl kajigo kanŭn kŏshi chossŭmnida. 산에
갈 때는 자켓을 가지고 가는 것이 좋습니다/ *She is ~ off*
now. Kŭnyŏnŭn chigŭm haengbok'age salgo issŭmnida.
그녀는 지금 행복하게 살고 있읍니다.

between *prep.* sai 사이, chunggan 중간. *the railway ~*
Seoul and Pusan Sŏul Pusan kanŭi ch'ŏlto 서울·부산
간의 철도/ *The event took place ~ 12 and 1 o'clock.*
Sakŏnŭn yŏltushiwa hanshi saie irŏnassŭmnida. 사건
은 12시와 1시 사이에 일어났읍니다/ *Let us keep this*
strictly ~ ourselves. I irŭn uridŭl saimanŭi illo hae
tupshida. 이 일은 우리들 사이만의 일로 해 둡시다/ *This is*
~ you and me ... Uridŭlkkiriŭi iyagijiman... 우리들끼
리의 이야기지만….

beware *vi.,vt.* choshimhada 조심하다, chuŭihada 주의하다.
B~ of pickpocket. Somaech'igirŭl choshimhashio. 소매
치기를 조심하시오.

beyond *prep.* chŏtchoge 저쪽에. *My house is ~ the bridge.*
Nae chibŭn tari chŏtchoge issŭmnida. 내 집은 다리 저쪽에
있읍니다/ *Don't stay out ~ 10 o'clock.* Yŏlshi nŏmtorok
pakke itchi marara. 10시 넘도록 밖에 있지 말아라/ *He*
lives ~ his income. Kŭnŭn suip isangŭi saenghwarŭl
hago issŭmnida. 그는 수입 이상의 생활을 하고 있읍니다.

Bible *n.* sŏnggyŏng 성경, sŏngsŏ 성서. *a B~ class* sŏnggyŏng yŏn-guhoe 성경 연구회/ *B~ society* sŏngsŏ hyŏ-

p'oe-성서 협회.

bicycle n. chajŏn-gŏ 자전거. _ride a_ ~ chajŏn-gŏrŭl t'ada 자전거를 타다/ _a_ ~ _race_ chajŏn-gŏ kyŏngju 자전거 경주/ _a_ ~ _trip_ chajŏn-gŏ yŏhaeng 자전거 여행.

bid vt. kapsŭl maegida 값을 매기다, marhada 말하다. _What shall I_ ~? Ŏlmarŭl purŭlkkayo? 얼마를 부를까요/ _B~ him come in._ Kŭege tŭrŏorago hashio. 그에게 들어오라 고 하시오.

big adj. k'ŭn 큰. _a_ ~ _boy_ k'ŭn sonyŏn 큰 소년/ _Is Seoul a_ ~ _city?_ Sŏurŭn k'ŭn toshiimnikka? 서울은 큰 도시입니 까/ _How_ ~ _is it?_ Ŏlmana k'ŭmnikka? 얼마나 큽니까?

bill n. kyesansŏ 계산서, (_beak_) puri 부리. _Please bring me my_ ~. Kyesansŏrŭl kajyŏoshio. 계산서를 가져오시오/ _Let me pay the_ ~. Kyesanŭn naega hagessŭmnida. 계 산은 내가 하겠읍니다/ ~ _of debt_ yaksok ŏŭm 약속 어음/ ~ _of exchange_ hwanŏŭm 환어음/ ~ _of sale_ maedo chŭngsŏ 매도 증서/ _I refuse to honor your_ ~. Tangshinŭi ŏŭmŭn chiburhal su ŏpsŭmnida. 당신의 어음은 지불할 수 없읍니다/ _The_ ~ _will soon fall due._ Kot ŏŭm chibul naltchaga tagaomnida. 곧 어음 지불 날짜가 다가옵니다.

billiard n. tanggu 당구. ~ _ball_ tanggugong 당구공/ ~ _hall_ tanggujang 당구장/ ~ _table_ tanggudae 당구대/ _Can you play_ ~_s?_ Tanggurŭl ch'il chul ashimnikka? 당구를 칠 줄 아십니까?

billion n. (_in U.S.A_) shibŏk 십억(10億), (_in England_) ilcho 일조(1兆).

bind vt.,vi. maeda 매다, mukta 묶다. ~ _a book_ chebon-hada 제본하다/ _They bound him hand and foot._ Kŭŭi sonbarŭl ta mukkŏssŭmnida. 그의 손발을 다 묶었읍니다.

binder n. chebonsa 제본사(製本師).

binding n. mukkŭm 묶음, chebon 제본(製本). _leather_ ~ kachuk chebon 가죽 제본/ ~ _medicine_ sŏlsayak 설사약.

binocular n. ssangan-gyŏng 쌍안경.

biography n. chŏn-gi 전기(傳記). _auto_~ chasŏjŏn 자서전.

birch n. chajangnamu 자작나무.

bird n. sae 새. ~ _cage_ saejang 새장/ ~ _fancier_ saejang-su 새장수.

birth *n.* ch'ulsaeng 출생. *give* ~ nat'a 낳다/ *His wife gave* ~ *to a son.* Kŭŭi anaega adŭrŭl naassŭmnida. 그의 아내가 아들을 낳았읍니다/ *a difficult* ~ nansan 난산/ *an untimely* ~ chosan 조산(早産)/ ~ *control* sana chehan 산아 제한.

birthday *n.* saengil 생일. ~ *present* saengil sŏnmul 생일 선물/ ~ *party* saengil chanch'i 생일 잔치/ *When is your* ~? Saengirŭn ŏnjeimnikka? 생일은 언제입니까/ *Happy* ~ *to you.* Saengirŭl ch'uk'ahamnida. 생일을 축하합니다.

birthplace *n.* ch'ulsaengji 출생지.

bishop *n.* chugyo 주교, sagyo 사교.

bit *n.* chagŭn chogak 작은 조각, chogŭm 조금. *a ~ of chalk* punp'il han kae 분필 한 개/ *I hope it rains a* ~. Piga chogŭm wassŭmyŏn hamnida. 비가 조금 왔으면 합니다/ *a little* ~ chogŭm 조금.

bite *vi.,vt.* mulda 물다, murŏttŭtta 물어뜯다/ *I was badly bitten by the mosquitoes.* Nanŭn mogiege mopshi mullyŏssŭmnida. 나는 모기에게 몹시 물렸읍니다.

bitter *adj.* ssŭn 쓴, (*painful*) ssŭrarin 쓰라린. —*n.* ssŭn maekchu 쓴 맥주. *a ~ taste* ssŭnmat 쓴맛/ ~ *experiences* ssŭrarin kyŏnghŏm 쓰라린 경험.

black *adj.* kŏmŭn 검은, ŏduun 어두운.

blackboard *n.* hŭkp'an 흑판, ch'ilp'an 칠판.

blacken *vt.* kŏmke hada 검게 하다, ŏdupke hada 어둡게 하다, (*slander*) hŏlttŭtta 헐뜯다.

blackmail *n.* konggal 공갈, kalch'wi 갈취.

blackmarket *n.* amshijang 암시장. 「kan 대장간.

blacksmith *n.* taejangjangi 대장장이. *a ~'s shop* taejang-black tea hongch'a 홍차.

bladder *n.* panggwang 방광, (*sack*) charu 자루. *a ~ of lard* pigye chumŏni 비계 주머니.

blade *n.* k'allal 칼날, (*leaf*) ip 잎, ipsagwi 잎사귀.

blame *vt.* namurada 나무라다. —*n.* pinan 비난, (*responsibility*) ch'aegim 책임. *I don't ~ you for doing that.* Tangshini kŭrŏk'e haettago haesŏ nappŭdagonŭn an hamnida. 당신이 그렇게 했다고 해서 나쁘다고는 안 합니다/

He laid all the ~ on me. Kŭnŭn modŭn ch'aegimŭl na-ege chiwŏssŭmnida. 그는 모든 책임을 나에게 지웠읍니다.

blank *adj.* kongbaegŭi 공백의. —*n.* kiip yongji 기입 용지. *a ~ cheque* paekchi sup'yo 백지 수표/ *Fill out this ~, please.* I yongjie kiip'ae chushio. 이 용지에 기입해 주시오.

blanket *n.* tamnyo 담요. *Please send another ~ to my room.* Nae pange tamnyo han chang tŏ katta chuseyo. 내 방에 담요 한 장 더 갖다 주세요.

blast *n.* tolp'ung 돌풍, (*explosion*) p'okpal 폭발.

blaze *n.* pulkil 불길. —*vi.* t'aorŭda 타오르다.

bleach *vt.* p'yobaek'ada 표백하다.

bleed *vi.* ch'urhyŏrhada 출혈하다. *You have nose ~ing.* K'o-e p'iga hŭrŭgo issŭmnida. 코에 피가 흐르고 있읍니다.

blend *vt.,vi.* honhap'ada 혼합하다. *~ed fabric* honbang chingmul 혼방 직물.

bless *vt.* ch'ukpok'ada 축복하다, ch'anmihada 찬미하다. *May you always be ~ed with good health.* Ŏnjena kŏn-ganghagirŭl pimnida. 언제나 건강하기를 빕니다.

blessing *n.* chukpok 축복, shinŭi ŭnch'ong 신의 은총. *ask God's ~* shinŭi ŭnch'ongŭl pilda 신의 은총을 빌다.

blind *adj.* nunmŏn 눈먼, maengmokchŏgin 맹목적인. *a ~ man* changnim 장님, sogyŏng 소경/ *a ~ obedience* maengjong 맹종/ *The soldier had been ~ed in the war.* Kŭ pyŏngsanŭn chŏnjaengesŏ shiryŏgŭl irŏssŭmnida. 그 병사는 전쟁에서 시력을 잃었읍니다.

blink *vi.* kkambakkŏrida 깜박거리다.

blister *n.* mulchip 물집. *I've ~s on my toes.* Palkarak saiga purŭt'ŏssŭmnida. 발가락 사이가 부르텄읍니다.

block *n.* k'ŭn tŏngŏri 큰 덩어리, (*of wood*) namu t'omak 나무 토막, (*a row of houses*) kuhoek 구획, pŭllok 블록, (*hindrance*)changae 장애. —*vt.* makta 막다, panghaehada 방해하다. *a wooden ~ marked with the letters of the Hangul alphabet* Han-gŭl alp'abeshi ssŭiŏjin namu t'omak 한글 알파벳이 씌어진 나무 토막/ *It is two ~s west, and two ~s north.* Sŏtchogŭro tu pŭllok, puktchogŭro tu pŭllok kan kose issŭmnida. 서쪽으로 두 블록, 북쪽으로 두 블록 간 곳에 있읍니다/ *Walk one ~ east.* Tongtcho-

gŭro han pŭllongman kŏrŏkashio. 동쪽으로 한 블록만 걸어
가시오/ *The road was ∼ed by the heavy snowfall.*
Toronŭn nune mak'yŏssŭmnida. 도로는 눈에 막혔읍니다.

blockade *n.* pongswae 봉쇄. *run the ∼* pongswaesŏnŭl
ttult'a 봉쇄선을 뚫다.

blockade runner mirhangja 밀항자, mirhangsŏn 밀항선.

blonde *adj.* kŭmbarŭi 금발의. *∼ hair* kŭmbal 금발. *—n.*
kŭmbarŭi yŏsŏng 금발의 여성.

blood *n.* p'i 피. *∼ bank* hyŏraek ŭnhaeng 혈액 은행/ *∼
doner* hŏnhyŏlja 헌혈자/ *∼ pressure* hyŏrap 혈압/ *∼
type* hyŏraek'yŏng 혈액형/ *∼ stain* p'itchaguk 핏자국/ *∼
vessel* hyŏlgwan 혈관.

bloodshot *adj.* p'itpari sŏn 핏발이 선, ch'unghyŏldoen 충혈
된. *Your eyes are ∼.* Nuni ch'unghyŏldoesyŏtkunyo. 눈
이 충혈되셨군요.

bloody *adj.* p'inanŭn 피나는. *∼ battle* p'ibirinnae nanŭn
ssaum 피비린내 나는 싸움.

bloom *n.* kkot 꽃. *in full ∼* manbarhayŏ 만발하여. *—vi.*
kkoch'i p'ida 꽃이 피다. *The rose ∼ed beautifully.* Kŭ
changmikkoch'ŭn arŭmdapke p'iŏssŭmnida. 그 장미꽃은
아름답게 피었읍니다/ *∼ into a prima donna* inki kasuro
ch'ulsehada 인기 가수로 출세하다.

blossom *n.* kkot 꽃. *come into ∼* kkoch'i p'igi shijak'ada
꽃이 피기 시작하다/ *decorate with ∼s* kkoch'ŭro kku-
mida 꽃으로 꾸미다.

blot *n.* ŏlluk 얼룩, ochŏm 오점. *—vt.* tŏrŏp'ida 더럽히다.
an ink ∼ ingk'ŭ ŏlluk 잉크 얼룩/ *I can't get out these
∼s.* I ŏllugŭn chiul suga ŏpsŭmnida. 이 얼룩은 지울 수
가 없읍니다/ *a ∼ upon Korean history* Han-guk yŏksasang hanaŭi ochŏm 한국 역사상 하나의 오점.

blotting paper apchi 압지.

blouse *n.* pŭllausŭ 블라우스, chagŏppok 작업복.

blow *vi.,vt.* pulda 불다, p'okparhada 폭발하다. *—n.* kang-
t'a 강타(強打). *The wind was ∼ing hard.* Parami kanghage pulgo issŏssŭmnida. 바람이 강하게 불고 있었읍니다/
My hat blew off. Parame mojaga pŏtkyŏjyŏssŭmnida.
바람에 모자가 벗겨졌읍니다/ *∼ out the gas* kasŭrŭl p'ok-

palshik'ida 가스를 폭발시키다/ *a death* ~ ch'imyŏngjŏk
t'agyŏk 치명적 타격/ *land a person a K.O.* ~ *on the
upper jaw* wit'ŏge K.O. p'ŏnch'irŭl mŏgida 위턱에 케
이오 펀치를 먹이다.

blue *adj.* p'urŭn 푸른. ~ *sky* p'urŭn hanŭl 푸른 하늘/ ~
jeans ch'ŏngbaji 청바지.

bluff *n.* hŏse 허세, ŭrŭmchang 으름장. —*vi.* hŏserŭl purida
허세를 부리다, ŭrŭmchangŭl not'a 으름장을 놓다. *He made
a* ~ *at hitting me.* Narŭl ttaeryŏ chugettago ŭrŭmchangŭl noassŭmnida. 나를 때려 주겠다고 으름장을 놓았읍니다.

blunder *n.* k'ŭn shilsu 큰 실수. —*vi.* k'ŭn shilsurŭl hada
큰 실수를 하다. *technical* ~s kisulsangŭi shilsu 기술상
의 실수. *My boss is hitting the ceiling because I made
a* ~. Naega shilsurŭl haetki ttaemune posŭga mopshi
hwarŭl naego issŭmnida. 내가 실수를 했기 때문에 보스가
몹시 화를 내고 있읍니다.

blunt *adj.* nari mudin 날이 무딘, (*brusk*) muttukttuk'an
무뚝뚝한, (*dull*) tunhan 둔한.

blush *vi.,vt.* ŏlgurŭl pulk'ida 얼굴을 붉히다. —*n.* hongjo 홍
조. *He* ~*ed at her.* Kŭnyŏrŭl pogo ŏlgurŭl pulk'yŏssŭmnida. 그녀를 보고 얼굴을 붉혔읍니다/ *I* ~*ed to hear
it.* Kŭ sorirŭl tŭtko nanŭn nach'ŭl pulk'yŏssŭmnida.
그 소리를 듣고 나는 낯을 붉혔읍니다.

boar *n.* sut'waeji 수퇘지. *wild* ~ mettwaeji 멧돼지.

board *n.* nŏlppanji 널빤지, (*table for meals*) shikt'ak 식탁,
(*council*) p'yŏngŭihoe 평의회. —*vi.* t'ada 타다. *a bulletin*
~ keship'an 게시판/ *a hospitable* ~ kŭkchinhi ch'arin
shikt'ak 극진히 차린 식탁/*a* ~ *of director* isahoe 이사회/
Please get on ~. Cha, t'ashipshio. 자, 타십시오/ *Here
is your* ~*ing pass.* T'apsŭngkwŏn yŏgi issŭmnida. 탑
승권 여기 있읍니다.

boardinghouse *n.* hasukchip 하숙집.

boast *vi.* charanghada 자랑하다. *That's nothing to* ~ *of.*
Kŭgŏsŭn kyŏlk'o charangkŏriga mot toemnida. 그것은
결코 자랑거리가 못 됩니다.

boat *n.* pot'ŭ 보트. ~ *race* pot'ŭ reisŭ 보트 레이스/ *ferry*
~ narutpae 나룻배/ *I'm going to travel by* ~. Paero

yŏhaengharyŏgo hamnida. 배로 여행하려고 합니다.

bob *vt.* tanballo hada 단발로 하다.

body *n.* mom 몸, shinch'e 신체, (*main part*) ponmun 본문 (本文), (*a group of persons*) chiptan 집단. *a human* ~ inch'e 인체/ *a dead* ~ shich'e 시체/ *the* ~ *of a motorcar* ch'ach'e 차체/ *the* ~ *of a letter* p'yŏnjiŭi ponmun 편지의 본문/ *an advisory* ~ komundan 고문단/ *a charitable* ~ chasŏn tanch'e 자선 단체. 「위병.

bodyguard *n.* kyŏnghowŏn 경호원, (*mil.*) howibyŏng 호

boil *n.* chonggi 종기, pusŭrŏm 부스럼. —*vt.* kkŭrida 끓이다. *I got a* ~ *on my neck.* Moge chonggiga nassŭmnida. 목에 종기가 났읍니다/ ~*ed egg* salmŭn talgyal 삶은 달걀.

boiler *n.* poillŏ 보일러. ~ *room* poillŏshil 보일러실.

boiling point pidŭngchŏm 비등점.

bold *adj.* taedamhan 대담한, (*impudent*) ppŏnppŏnsŭrŏn 뻔뻔스런. *a* ~ *bad man* taedamhan agin 대담한 악인/ *a* ~ *plan* taedamhan kyehoek 대담한 계획/ *as* ~ *as brass* ch'ŏlmyŏnp'ihan 철면피한/ ~ *faced* ppŏnppŏnsŭrŏn 뻔 뻔스런.

bolt *n.* (*of a door*) pitchang 빗장, (*thunder*~) pŏn-gae 번개, (*dart*) hwasal 화살.

bomb *n.* p'okt'an 폭탄. —*vt.* p'okkyŏk'ada 폭격하다. *an atomic* ~ wŏnja p'okt'an 원자 폭탄/ *a hydrogen* ~ suso p'okt'an 수소 폭탄.

bombardment *n.* p'okkyŏk 폭격. *air* ~ kongsŭp 공습.

bomber *n.* p'okkyŏkki 폭격기, p'okt'anbyŏng 폭탄병.

bonanza *n.* nodaji 노다지. *strike a* ~ k'ŭge hanmok boda 크게 한몫 보다/ *a* ~ *year* unsu choŭn hae 운수 좋은 해.

bond *n.* chŭngkwŏn 증권. *public* ~ kongch'ae 공채/*government* ~ kukch'ae 국채/ *a* ~*ed warehouse* pose ch'anggo 보세 창고/ ~*ed goods* posep'um 보세품/ ~ *of union* tan-gyŏl 단결.

bone *n.* ppyŏ 뼈. *old* ~*s* nogu 노구(老軀).

bonus *n.* sangyŏgŭm 상여금, ponŏsŭ 보너스. *The* ~ *is given twice a year.* Illyŏne tu pŏn sangyŏgŭmi chigŭptoemnida. 1년에 두 번 상여금이 지급됩니다.

book *n.* ch'aek 책. *a guest* ~ sukpakpu 숙박부/ *text*~

kyogwasŏ 교과서/ *reference* ~ ch'amgosŏ 참고서/ ~-*case* ch'aekchang 책장/ ~*store* sŏjŏm 서점/ ~*stand* sŏga 서가/ *B~s are sold on the fifth floor at the ~ department.* Ch'aegŭn och'ŭng sŏjŏkpuesŏ p'algo issŭmnida. 책은 5층 서적부에서 팔고 있읍니다.

booking-office (*railway stations*) ch'ulch'algu 출찰구, (*theater*) maep'yoso 매표소.

boom *n.* pyŏrak kyŏnggi 벼락 경기(景氣), pum 붐. *a ~ in real estate* pudongsan kyŏnggi 부동산 경기/ *Korean war* ~ Han-guk chŏnjaeng pum 한국 전쟁 붐.

boot *n.* changhwa 장화(長靴), kudu 구두. *leather* ~ kajuk kudu 가죽 구두/ *rubber* ~ komushin 고무신/~ *brush* kudutsol 구둣솔/ *Clean my* ~, *please.* Kudurŭl chom takka chushio. 구두를 좀 닦아 주시오.

booth *n.* nojŏm 노점, p'anjachip 판자집. *a phone* ~ chŏnhwashil 전화실/ *a polling* ~ t'up'yoso 투표소/ *Where's the ticket* ~ ? Maep'yosonŭn ŏdi issŭmnikka? 매표소는 어디 있읍니까?

booty *n.* yakt'alp'um 약탈품, nohoengmul 노획물. *a war* ~ chŏllip'um 전리품.

border *n.* kyŏnggye 경계, kukkyŏng 국경, (*edge*) kajangjari 가장자리. ~*line* kyŏnggyesŏn 경계선/ *the Korean-Manchurian* ~ hanman kukkyŏng 한만 국경.

bore *vt.* kumŏngŭl ttult'a 구멍을 뚫다, (*make weary*) chiruhage hada 지루하게 하다. ~ *a hole through the board* p'anja-e kumŏngŭl ttult'a 판자에 구멍을 뚫다/ *This music ~s me.* I ŭmagŭn shiltch'ŭngi namnida. 이 음악은 싫증이 납니다.

born *adj.* t'aeŏnan 태어난. *Where were you* ~ ? Ŏdisŏ t'aeŏnassŭmnikka? 어디서 태어났읍니까/ *I was* ~ *in Korea in 1950.* Nanŭn ch'ŏn kubaek oshimnyŏn Han-gugesŏ t'aeŏnassŭmnida. 나는 1950년 한국에서 태어났읍니다/ *a Seoul-born painter* Sŏul t'aesaengŭi hwaga 서울 태생의 화가/ *a* ~ *poet* t'agonan shiin 타고난 시인.

borrow *vt.* pilda 빌다, ch'ayonghada 차용하다. *Could I* ~ *some money from you?* Ton chom pillyŏ chushigessŭmnikka? 돈 좀 빌려 주시겠읍니까/ *Here's that book I ~ed* *from you.* Pillin ch'aek yŏgi issŭmnida. 빌린 책 여기 있읍니다.

bosom *n.* kasŭm 가슴. *a ~ friend* (tajŏnghan) ch'in-gu (다정한) 친구/ *have a full ~* kasŭmi p'ungmanhada 가슴이 풍만하다.

boss *n.* tumok 두목, posŭ 보스. *a party ~* chŏngdang posŭ 정당 보스/ *Who's the ~ in this house?* I chibŭi posŭnŭn nugushimnikka? 이 집의 보스는 누구십니까?

botanical garden(s) shingmurwŏn 식물원.

botany *n.* shingmurhak 식물학.

both *adj.,adv. & pron. I want ~ books.* Tu ch'aegi ta p'iryohamnida. 두 책이 다 필요합니다/ *B~ are absent.* Tul ta kyŏlsŏgimnida. 둘 다 결석입니다/ *I have made ~. Which would you really like?* Yangtchok ta chunbi-doeŏssŭmnida. Ŏnŭ tchogŭl choahashimnikka? 양쪽 다 준비되었읍니다. 어느 쪽을 좋아하십니까?

bother *vt.* koerop'ida 괴롭히다. *I am sorry to ~ you.* Panghaerŭl haesŏ mianhamnida. 방해를 해서 미안합니다/ *Don't ~ to see me to the door.* Hyŏn-gwankkaji chŏn-songhae chushil p'iryonŭn ŏpsŭmnida. 현관까지 전송해 주실 필요는 없읍니다/ *This tooth is ~ing me something awful, Doctor.* Sŏnsaengnim, i ippari chidok'i ap'ŭmnida. 선생님, 이 이빨이 지독히 아픕니다/ *Oh, ~!* Ai kwi-ch'ana! 아이, 귀찮아!

bottle *n.* pyŏng 병. *~ opener* pyŏngmagae ppobi 병마개 뽑이/ *~ stopper* pyŏngmagae 병마개/ *empty ~* pin pyŏng 빈 병.

bottom *n.* mitpadak 밑바닥. *the ~ of the cup* k'ŏbŭi mit-padak 컵의 밑바닥/ *from the ~ of my heart* ch'ungshi-mŭro 충심으로/ *What's your ~ price?* Ch'oejŏ kagyŏgŭn ŏlmaimnikka? 최저 가격은 얼마입니까?

bounce *vi.* ttwiŏorŭda 뛰어오르다. *~ about* kkangch'ong-kkangch'ong ttwiŏdanida 깡총깡총 뛰어다니다.

bound *adj.* ...haengŭi …행(行)의, *(destined)* haeya hal 해야 할. *This train is ~ for Suwon, not Inchon.* I yŏl-ch'anŭn Suwŏnhaengiji Inch'ŏnhaengi animnida. 이 열차는 수원행이지, 인천행이 아닙니다/ *You are ~ to do it.*

Tangshinŭn kŭ irŭl kkok haeya hamnida. 당신은 그 일을 꼭 해야 합니다.

boundary *n.* kyŏnggye 경계. ~ *line* kyŏnggyesŏn 경계선.

bouquet *n.* kkottabal 꽃다발.

bourgeois *n.* yusan kyegŭp 유산 계급, purŭjŭwa 부르즈「와.

bow *n.* hwal 활. —*vi.* mŏrirŭl sugida 머리를 숙이다. ~ *and arrow* hwalgwa hwasal 활과 화살/ *a* ~ *tie* nabi nekt'ai 나비 벡타이/ *I* ~*ed politely.* Nanŭn kongsonhi chŏrŭl haessŭmnida. 나는 공손히 절을 했읍니다.

bowels *n.* ch'angja 창자, naejang 내장.

bowl *n.* sabal 사발, konggi 공기. *a rice* ~ papkonggi 밥공기/ *a sugar* ~ sŏlt'ang tanji 설탕 단지/ *I ate three* ~*s of rice.* Nanŭn pabŭl se konggi mŏgŏssŭmnida. 나는 밥을 세 공기 먹었읍니다.

box *n.* sangja 상자. *document* ~ sŏryu sangja 서류 상자/ *the firstaid* ~ kugŭp sangja 구급 상자/ *mail* ~ uch'et'ong 우체통/ ~ *office* maep'yoso 매표소.

boxer *n.* kwŏnt'u sŏnsu 권투 선수.

boxing *n.* kwŏnt'u 권투. ~ *glove* kwŏnt'u changgap 권투 장갑/ ~ *match* kwŏnt'u shihap 권투 시합.

boy *n.* sonyŏn 소년, (*son*) adŭl 아들, (*young servant*) sahwan 사환. *a teen-age* ~ shiptae sonyŏn 10대 소년/*a bell* ~ sahwan 사환/ *I've a* ~ *and a girl.* Adŭl hana, ttal hana issŭmnida. 아들 하나, 딸 하나 있읍니다.

boycott *n.* pulmae tongmaeng 불매 동맹, poik'ot'ŭ 보이코트. —*vt.* poik'ot'ŭhada 보이코트하다. *a* ~ *of Japanese goods* Ilbon sangp'umŭi pulmae tongmaeng 일본 상품의 불매 동맹/ *examination* ~ suhŏm kŏbu 수험(受驗) 거부.

boyhood *n.* sonyŏn shidae 소년 시대, sonyŏn-gi 소년기.

boyish *adj.* ai kat'ŭn 아이 같은, misuk'an 미숙한.

bracelet *n.* p'altchi 팔찌. *How about a* ~? P'altchinŭn ŏttŏssŭmnikka? 팔찌는 어떻습니까?

brag *vt.* charanghada 자랑하다. —*n.* charang 자랑.

brain *n.* noe 뇌(腦), mŏri 머리. *have good* ~*s* mŏriga chot'a 머리가 좋다/ *He has no* ~*s.* Kŭnŭn mŏriga nappŭmnida. 그는 머리가 나쁩니다.

brake *n.* pŭreik'ŭ 브레이크. —*vt.* pŭreik'ŭrŭl kŏlda 브레

이크를 걸다. *an air* ~ konggi chedonggi 공기 제동기/ *The driver* ~*d suddenly*. Unjŏnsanŭn kŭp'i pŭreik'ŭrŭl palbassŭmnida. 운전사는 급히 브레이크를 밟았습니다.

bran *n*. milgiul 밀기울, kyŏ 겨.

branch *n*. kaji 가지, chijŏm 지점(支店). *break off a* ~ kajirŭl kkŏkta 가지를 꺾다/ *Where is the Tongdaemun* ~ *office of the Commercial Bank?* Sangŏp ŭnhaeng Tongdaemun chijŏmŭn ŏdiimnikka? 상업 은행 동대문 지점은 어디입니까?

brand *n*. sangp'yo 상표. *a standard* ~ p'yojunp'um 표준품/ *What* ~ *of whisky do you have?* Wisŭk'inŭn muŏshi issŭmnikka? 위스키는 무엇이 있읍니까/ *a well-known* ~ yumyŏng meik'ŏŭi sangp'um 유명 메이커의 상품.

brass *n*. notsoe 놋쇠. ~ *band* ch'wiju aktae 취주 악대, pŭrasŭ paendŭ 브라스 밴드.

brave *adj*. yonggamhan 용감한. *You are* ~ *for a woman*. Puinŭn yŏjarosŏ ch'am yonggamhamnida. 부인은 여자로서 참 용감합니다/ *Be* ~! Yonggirŭl naeshio. 용기를 내시오.

bravo *int*. pŭrabo 브라보, charhanda 잘한다.

brazen *adj*. ppŏnppŏnsŭrŏun 뻔뻔스러운. *a* ~ *voice* shikkŭrŏun malsori 시끄러운 말소리/ ~ *faced* ch'ŏlmyŏnp'iŭi 철면피의.

brazier, brasier *n*. hwaro 화로.

Brazil *n*. Pŭrajil 브라질.

breach *n*. wiban 위반, purihaeng 불이행. *a* ~ *of promise* yaksok wiban 약속 위반, wiyak 위약/ *a* ~ *of contract* kyeyak wiban 계약 위반.

bread *n*. ppang 빵. ~ *and butter* pŏt'ŏrŭl parŭn ppang 버터를 바른 빵.

breadth *n*. nŏbi 너비, p'ok 폭. *ten feet in* ~ p'ok ship p'it'ŭ 폭 10 피트.

break *vt*. kkaettŭrida 깨뜨리다, pusuda 부수다. ~ *a glass* yurirŭl kkaettŭrida 유리를 깨뜨리다/ *If you pull too hard, you will* ~ *the rope*. Churŭl nŏmu sege tanggimyŏn kkŭnŏjimnida. 줄을 너무 세게 당기면 끊어집니다/ *You have broken your promise*. Tangshinŭn yaksogŭl ŏgyŏssŭmnida. 당신은 약속을 어겼읍니다/ *Can you* ~ *this*

10, 000 won bill for me? I manwŏntchari chip'yerŭl chandonŭro pakkwŏ chushilkkayo? 이 10, 000 원짜리 지폐를 잔돈으로 바꿔 주실까요?

breakdown *n.* kojang 고장, punggoe 붕괴. *nervous* ~ shingyŏng soeyak 신경 쇠약/ *a ~ of machine* kigyeŭi p'ason 기계의 파손.

breakfast *n.* choban 조반. *Does the rate include* ~? I yogŭme chobani p'ohamdwae issŭmnikka? 이 요금에 조반이 포함돼 있읍니까/ *Would you be wanting* ~ *in your room?* Ach'im shiksanŭn pangesŏ hashiryŏmnikka? 아침 식사는 방에서 하시렵니까?

breakwater *n.* pangp'aje 방파제.

breast *n.* kasŭm 가슴, yubang 유방.

breath *n.* sum 숨, hohŭp 호흡. *Take a deep* ~. Sumŭl kilge shwiseyo. 숨을 길게 쉬세요.

breathe *vi., vt.* sumŭl shwida 숨을 쉬다, hohŭp'ada 호흡하다. *We* ~ *air.* Urinŭn konggirŭl hohŭp'amnida. 우리는 공기를 호흡합니다/ *He is still breathing.* Ajik sumi kkŭnŏjiji anassŭmnida. 아직 숨이 끊어지지 않았읍니다.

breathing *n.* hohŭp 호흡. *a deep* ~ shimhohŭp 심호흡/ *abdominal* ~ pokshik hohŭp 복식 호흡.

breed *vt.* (*produce*) nat'a 낳다, (*raise*) kirŭda 기르다, (*increase*) pŏnshik'ada 번식하다. ~ *cattle* kach'ugŭl kirŭda 가축을 기르다.

breeze *n.* sandŭlbaram 산들바람, mip'ung 미풍.

brew *vt.* yangjohada 양조하다, pitta 빚다.

brewery *n.* yangjojang 양조장.

bribe *n.* noemul 뇌물. —*vi., vt.* maesuhada 매수하다. *offer a* ~ noemurŭl mŏgida 뇌물을 먹이다/ *accept a* ~ noemurŭl patta 뇌물을 받다.

bribery *n.* chŭng[su]hoe 증[수]회. ~ *case* suroe sakŏn 수뢰 사건.

brick *n.* pyŏktol 벽돌. ~ *field* pyŏktol kongjang 벽돌 공장/ ~ *building* pyŏktol kŏnmul 벽돌 건물.

bride *n.* shinbu 신부.

bridegroom *n.* shillang 신랑.

bridge *n.* tari 다리, (*card game*) p'ŭriji 브리지. *a floating*

~pugyo 부교(浮橋)/*a suspension* ~ chŏkkyo 적교(吊橋)/
I like ~. *How about you?* Nanŭn pŭrijirŭl choahamnida. Tangshinŭn? 나는 브리지를 좋아합니다. 당신은?

bridle *n.* koppi 고삐.

brief *adj.* tchalbŭn 짧은, kan-gyŏrhan 간결한. *to be* ~
kandanhi marhamyŏn 간단히 말하면.

brier, briar *n.* tchille 찔레.

brigadier (**general**) (*Am.*) yukkun chunjang 육군 준장.

bright *adj.* pinnanŭn 빛나는, palgŭn 밝은, (*clever*) ch'ongmyŏnghan 총명한. ~ *faces* palgŭn p'yojŏng 밝은 표정/
Business is ~. Saŏbŭn pŏnch'anghamnida. 사업은 번창합
니다.

brighten *vt.,vi.* pakke hada 밝게 하다, myŏngnanghage
hada 명랑하게 하다. *What can we do to* ~ *the lives of
the poor?* Ŏttŏk'e hamyŏn kananhan saramdŭrŭi saenghwarŭl pakke hal su itchiyo? 어떻게 하면 가난한 사람들
의 생활을 밝게 할 수 있지요?

brilliant *adj.* pantchaginŭn 반짝이는, nunbushinŭn 눈부시
는. *a* ~ *record* hullyunghan kirok 훌륭한 기록/ *a* ~
mind ch'ŏnjaejŏgin mŏri 천재적인 머리.

brim *n.* kajangjari 가장자리, t'eduri 테두리. *a vase with a
broad* ~ t'eduriga nŏpchŏk'an hwabyŏng 테두리가 넓적
한 화병/ *the* ~ *of a hat* mojaŭi t'e 모자의 테.

bring *vt.* kajyŏoda 가져오다, teryŏoda 데려오다. *B*~ *me a
glass of water.* Murŭl han chan katta chushipshio. 물
을 한 잔 갖다 주십시오/ *Shall I* ~ *you a fork?* P'ok'ŭ-
rŭl katta tŭrilkkayo? 포크를 갖다 드릴까요? 「돼지털.

bristle *n.* ppŏtppŏt'an t'ŏl 뻣뻣한 털. *swine* ~ twaejit'ŏl

Britain *n.* Yŏngguk 영국(英國).

British *adj.* Yŏnggugŭi 영국의. *the B*~ *Commonwealth*
Yŏngyŏnbang 영연방(英聯邦)/ *the B*~ *Embassy* Yŏngguk taesagwan 영국 대사관/ *the B*~ *Empire* Taeyŏng
cheguk 대영 제국.

broad *adj.* nŏlbŭn 넓은, nŏlttaran 널따란.

broadcast *n.* pangsong 방송. *a filmed TV* ~ nok'wa
pangsong 녹화 방송/ *alive* ~ saengbangsong 생방송.

broadcasting *n.* pangsong 방송. *a* ~ *station* pangsongguk

방송국.

broad-minded *adj.* nŏgŭrŏun 너그러운, kwandaehan 관대한.

brochure *n.* soch'aekcha 소책자(小冊子), p'amp'ŭllet 팜플렛. *Do you sell an information* ~? Sŏlmyŏngsŏrŭl p'ashimnikka? 설명서를 파십니까/ *Here is a little* ~ *you might find interesting*. Chogŭman ch'aekchaga issŭmnida. Chaemiissŭshil kŏmnida. 조그만 책자가 있읍니다. 재미있으실 겁니다.

broil *vt.* pure kupta 불에 굽다, tchoeda 쬐다. ~*ed meat* pulgogi 불고기.

broker *n.* chunggaein 중개인, pŭrok'ŏ 브로커.

bronze *n.* ch'ŏngdong 청동. *B*~ *Age* ch'ŏngdonggi 청동기/ *a* ~ *statue* tongsang 동상(銅像).

brooch *n.* pŭroch'i 브로치, changshik p'in 장식 핀. *wear a* ~ pŭroch'irŭl talda 브로치를 달다.

brook *n.* shinae 시내, kaeul 개울, shilgaech'ŏn 실개천.

broom *n.* pi 비. *sweep with a* ~ piro ssŭlda 비로 쓸다.

brothel *n.* yugwak 유곽, maeŭmgul 매음굴.

brother *n.* hyŏngje 형제, *elder* ~ hyŏng 형/ *younger* ~ au 아우/ ~*s and sisters* hyŏngje chamae 형제 자매.

brother-in-law *n.* (*sister's husband*) maebu 매부, (*wife's brothers*) ch'ŏnam 처남, (*husband's brothers*) shisuk 시숙.

brow *n.* ima 이마, nunssŏp 눈썹 (=*eyebrow*).

brown *adj.* kalsaegŭi 갈색의. *a* ~ *eye* kalsaek nun 갈색 눈.

bruise *n.* t'abaksang 타박상. *I got a* ~. T'abaksangŭl ibŏssŭmnida. 타박상을 입었읍니다.

brush *n.* sol 솔, put 붓. *a writing* ~ mop'il 모필. *These Korean* ~*es are used by professional artists*. I Hangukche pusŭn misul chŏnmun-gadŭri sayonghamnida. 이 한국제 붓은 미술 전문가들이 사용합니다.

bubble *n.* kŏp'um 거품. *soap* ~*s* pinu kŏp'um 비누 거품/ *a water* ~ mulgŏp'um 물거품/ *blow soap* ~*s* pinu pangurŭl pulda 비누 방울을 불다.

bucket *n.* yangdongi 양동이, pakkessŭ 바께쓰.

bud *n.* ssak 싹, pongori 봉오리. —*vi.* ssakt'ŭda 싹트다. *How long will it take before the* ~*s blossom out into flowers?* Kkoch'i p'ijamyŏn ŏlmana issŏya hamnikka?

꽃이 피자면 얼마나 있어야 합니까?

Buddha *n.* Puch'ŏ 부처, Pult'a 불타.

Buddhism *n.* pulgyo 불교. *I believe in* ~. Nanŭn pulgyorŭl missŭmnida. 나는 불교를 믿습니다.

Buddhist *n.* pulgyo shinja 불교 신자.

budget *n.* yesan 예산.

buffalo *n.* mulso 물소.

buffet *n.* ch'anchang 찬장, kanishiktang 간이식당.

buffoon *n.* kwangdae 광대.

〈Puch'ŏ〉

bug *n.* konch'ung 곤충, pŏlle 벌레. *bed* ~ pindae 빈대.

bugbear *n.* tokkaebi 도깨비.

build *vt.* seuda 세우다, chitta 짓다. ~ *a house* chibŭl chitta 집을 짓다/ ~ *a fire* purŭl chip'ida 불을 지피다.

building *n.* kŏnmul 건물, pilding 빌딩. *a wooden* ~ mokcho kŏnmul 목조 건물/ *an attached* ~ pusok kŏnmul 부속 건물/ *a stone* ~ sŏkcho kŏnmul 석조 건물/ *a concrete steel* ~ ch'ŏlgŭn k'onk'ŭrit'ŭ kŏnmul 철근 콘크리트 건물.

bulb *n.* kugŭn 구근(球根). *electric* ~ chŏn-gu 전구(電球).

bulky *adj.* pup'iga k'ŭn 부피가 큰. *a* ~ *book* pup'iga k'ŭn ch'aek 부피가 큰 책.

bull *n.* hwangso 황소, suso 수소, suk'ŏt 수컷.

bullet *n.* t'anal 탄알, ch'ongal 총알.

bulletin *n.* keshi 게시(揭示). ~ *board* keship'an 게시판.

bullfight *n.* t'uu 투우. ~*er* t'uusa 투우사.

bump *n.* hok 혹. —*vi.* puditch'ida 부딪치다. *I got a bad* ~ *on my head.* Mŏrie k'ŭn hogi saenggyŏssŭmnida. 머리에 큰 혹이 생겼습니다/ *I* ~*ed my head against a wall.* Pyŏge mŏrirŭl puditch'yŏssŭmnida. 벽에 머리를 부딪쳤읍니다.

bumpkin *n.* shigolttŭgi 시골뜨기.

bumpy *adj.* ult'ungbult'unghan 울퉁불퉁한. *a* ~ *road* ult'ungbult'unghan kil 울퉁불퉁한 길.

bunch *n.* tabal 다발, songi 송이, muri 무리. *a* ~ *of keys* han tabarŭi yŏlsoe 한 다발의 열쇠/ *a* ~ *of grapes* p'odo han songi 포도 한 송이.

bundle *n*. kkurŏmi 꾸러미, tan 단, mukkŭm 묶음. —*vt*. taballo mukta 다발로 묶다. *I have a ~ of letters to answer.* Hoedabŭl haeya hal p'yŏnjiga santŏmigach'i ssayŏssŭmnida. 회답을 해야 할 편지가 산더미같이 쌓였읍니다/ *We ~d everything up.* Urinŭn modŭn kŏsŭl ta kkuryŏssŭmnida. 우리는 모든 것을 다 꾸렸읍니다.

bungalow *n*. panggallo 방갈로.

bunion *n*. t'inun 티눈.

buoy *n*. tchi 찌, pup'yo 부표. *life ~* kumyŏngdae 구명대.

burden *n*. mugŏun chim 무거운 짐, (*obligation*) pudam 부담, (*burdensome lot*) koeroum 괴로움.

bureau *n*. kuk 국(局), pu 부(部), samuso 사무소. *the B~ of the Mint* chop'yeguk 조폐국/ *an information ~* chŏngbobu 정보부/ *the Korea Tourist B~* Taehan yŏhaengsa 대한 여행사/ *Let me take you to a travel information ~*. Kwan-gwang annaeso-e mosyŏda tŭrijiyo. 관광 안내소에 모셔다 드리지요.

burglar *n*. totuk 도둑, kangdo 강도. *~ alarm* tonan kyŏngbogi 도난 경보기.

burial *n*. maejang 매장. *~ service* changnyeshik 장례식. *~ ground* changji 장지/ *~ mound* mudŏm 무덤.

burn *vt*. pult'aeuda 불태우다, kupta 굽다. —*vi*. t'ada 타다, teda 데다. *The house was ~ed down.* Chibi t'abŏryŏssŭmnida. 집이 타버렸읍니다.

burner *n*. pŏnŏ 버너. *an oil ~* sŏgyu nallo 석유 난로.

burst *vi*. t'ŏjida 터지다, (*bud*) p'iŏnada 피어나다. *My heart will ~.* Kasŭmi tchijŏjil kŏt katta. 가슴이 찢어질 것 같다/ *The buds are all ~ing.* Ssagi hanch'ang t'ŭgi shijak'aessŭmnida. 싹이 한창 트기 시작했읍니다.

bury *vt*. mutta 묻다, maejanghada 매장하다. *Did they ~ the hatchet?* Kŭdŭrŭn hwahaerŭl haessŭmnikka? 그들은 화해를 했읍니까?

bus *n*. pŏsŭ 버스. *sightseeing ~* kwan-gwang pŏsŭ 관광 버스/ *school ~* t'onghak pŏsŭ 통학 버스/ *~ fare* pŏsŭ yogŭm 버스 요금/ *~ stop* pŏsŭ chŏngnyujang 버스 정류장/ *Does this ~ go to Seoul Station?* I pŏsŭnŭn Sŏullyŏkkaji kamnikka? 이 버스는 서울역까지 갑니까/

Where can I take a number 60 ~? Yukshippŏn pŏsŭ-nŭn ŏdisŏ t'ajiyo? 60번 버스는 어디서 타지요/ *Is there a ~ stop near here?* I kŭnch'ŏe pŏsŭ chŏngnyujangi issŭmnikka? 이 근처에 버스 정류장이 있읍니까/ *Is there any ~ service to the center of the city?* Toshimjiro kanŭn pŏsŭp'yŏni issŭmnikka? 도심지로 가는 버스편이 있읍니까? 딸기나무.

bush *n.* kwanmok 관목, sup'ul 수풀. *a berry ~* ttalginamu

business *n.* yongmu 용무, pollil 볼일, (*matter*) il 일, (*occupation*) chigŏp 직업, (*buy and selling*) changsa 장사. *Have you any ~ with me?* Na-ege yongmuga issŭmnikka? 나에게 용무가 있읍니까/ *How is ~ these days?* Yojŭm iri chal toeshimnikka? 요즘 일이 잘 되십니까/ *It's none of your ~.* Tangshini al pa animnida. 당신이 알 바 아닙니다/ *What is your ~?* Chigŏbi muŏshimnikka? 직업이 무엇입니까/ *~ hours* yŏngŏp shigan 영업 시간.

business drink kyojesul 교제술.

businessman *n.* shirŏpka 실업가, sangin 상인.

busy *adj.* pappŭn 바쁜. *Are you ~ now?* Chigŭm pappŭ-shimnikka? 지금 바쁘십니까/ *This is our ~time.* Chigŭmi hanch'ang pappŭn ttaeimnida. 지금이 한창 바쁜 때입니다/ *If you're not ~ tomorrow afternoon, I'd like to come then.* Naeil ohu pappŭji anŭshimyŏn ch'aja poepko ship-sŭmnida. 내일 오후 바쁘지 않으시면 찾아 뵙고 싶습니다.

but *conj.,prep.* kŭrŏna 그러나, ...ŭl cheoehago …을 제외하고. *He worked hard ~ failed.* Kŭnŭn yŏlshimhi irhae-ssŭmnidaman shilp'aehaessŭmnida. 그는 열심히 일했읍니다만 실패했읍니다/ *I was not there ~ my brother was.* Nanŭn kŏgie ŏpsŏssŭna hyŏngi issŏssŭmnida. 나는 거기에 없었으나 형이 있었읍니다/ *He eats nothing ~ fruit.* Kŭnŭn kwailbakkenŭn amukŏtto mŏkchi anssŭmnida. 그는 과일밖에는 아무것도 먹지 않습니다.

butcher *n.* p'ujutkan 푸줏간, chŏngyukchŏm 정육점.

butter *n.* pŏt'ŏ 버터. *spread ~ on bread* ppange pŏt'ŏrŭl ch'irhada 빵에 버터를 칠하다.

butterfly *n.* nabi 나비, paramdungi 바람둥이.

buttocks *n.* kungdungi 궁둥이, ŏngdŏngi 엉덩이.

button *n.* tanch'u 단추. —*vt.* tanch'urŭl talda 단추를 달다. ~*hole* tanch'u kumŏng 단추 구멍.

buy *vt.* sada 사다. —*n.* san kŏt 산 것. *B~ me a drink, will you?* Sul hanjan an sa chugesso? 술 한잔 안 사 주겠소/ *I would ~ this, if I were you.* Naega sonnim kat'ŭmyŏn igŏsŭl sagessŭmnida. 내가 손님 같으면 이것을 사겠읍니다/ *I bought it at Midopa.* Midop'a-esŏ sassŭmnida. 미도파에서 샀읍니다.

buyer *n.* sanŭn saram 사는 사람, paiŏ 바이어. *You have a ~, you say?* Sal sarami ittanŭn malssŭmijiyo? 살 사람이 있다는 말씀이지요?

buzz *vi.* wingwinggŏrida 윙윙거리다, wingwing sorirŭl naeda 윙윙 소리를 내다. —*n.* soŭm 소음, (*phone call*) shinho sori 신호 소리. *My ears began ~ing.* Kwiga wingwinggŏrigi shijak'aessŭmnida. 귀가 윙윙거리기 시작 했읍니다/ *Give me a ~.* Chŏnhwa kŏrŏ chuseyo. 전화 걸어 주세요.

buzzer *n.* pŏjŏ 버저, kijŏk 기적, (*Eng.*) sairen 사이렌.

by *adv.* (*near, close at hand*) kyŏt'e 곁에, kakkai 가까이. *He hid the money when no body was ~.* Kŭnŭn kyŏt'e amudo ŏpsŭl ttae, kŭ tonŭl sumgyŏssŭmnida. 그는 곁에 아무도 없을 때, 그 돈을 숨겼읍니다. —*prep.* (*near*) kyŏt'e 곁에, kakkai 가까이. *Come and sit ~ me, please.* Iri wasŏ nae kyŏt'e anjŭshio. 이리 와서 내 곁에 앉으 시오/ *My house is ~ the park.* Uri chibŭn kongwŏn kŭnch'ŏe issŭmnida. 우리 집은 공원 근처에 있읍니다/(*past*) chinasŏ 지나서, kŏch'yŏsŏ 거쳐서. *Did you come ~ the nearest road?* Kajang kakkaun killo wassŭmnikka? 가 장 가까운 길로 왔읍니까/ (*during, in the course of*) kkajinŭn 까지는, saie 사이에. *Can you finish the work ~ tomorrow?* Naeilkkajinŭn kŭ irŭl kkŭnnael su issŭmnikka? 내일까지는 그 일을 끝낼 수 있읍니까/(*through the action*) ...e ŭihayŏ …에 의하여, ŭro 으로. *This stadium was designed ~ Mr. Kim.* I sŭt'adiumŭn Kimssie ŭihae sŏlgyedoeŏssŭmnida. 이 스타디움은 김씨에 의해 설계 되었읍니다/ *What do you mean ~ that?* Kŭgŏsŭn musŭn ttŭshijiyo? 그것은 무슨 뜻이지요/ *Don't judge any-*

one ~ appearance. Saramŭl oemoro p'andanhaji mashio. 사람을 외모로 판단하지 마시오/(*each separately*) *one ~ one* hanassik 하나씩/ *little ~ little* chogŭmssik 조금씩/(*to the amount of*) mank'ŭm 만큼/ *You are taller than I ~ a head.* Tangshinŭn naboda mŏri hanaga tŏ k'ŭmnida. 당신은 나보다 머리 하나가 더 큽니다/ *Can you get home ~ yourself?* Honja chibe kal su issŭmnikka? 혼자 집에 갈 수 있읍니까? *By the way, have you heard about Mr. Han?* Kŭrŏnde, Han kunŭi soshik tŭrŏssŭmnikka? 그런데 한 군(韓君)의 소식 들었읍니까?

bygone *adj.* kwagŏŭi 과거의, chinagan 지나간. —*n.* chinagan il 지나간 일. *Let ~s be ~s.* Kwagŏnŭn kkaekkŭshi ijŏbŏrija 과거는 깨끗이 잊어버리자.

bylaw *n.* naegyu 내규(內規), chŏnggwan 정관. *the ~ of a club* k'ŭllŏbŭi naegyu 클럽의 내규.

byname *n.* (*surname*) sŏng 성, pyŏlmyŏng 별명.

bypath *n.* yŏpkil 옆길, (*byway*) saetkil 샛길.

byproduct *n.* pusanmul 부산물.

bystander *n.* (*looker-on*) panggwanja 방관자, kugyŏngkkun 구경꾼. *send away the ~s* kugyŏngkkundŭrŭl tchotta 구경꾼들을 쫓다.

byway *n.* yŏpkil 옆길, yŏpkolmok 옆골목, saetkil 샛길.

byword *n.* hwaje kŏri 화제 거리. *She became the ~ of the village.* Kŭnyŏnŭn maŭrŭi hwaje kŏriga toeŏssŭmnida. 그녀는 마을의 화제 거리가 되었읍니다.

❧ C ❧

cab *n.* t'aekshi 택시. *If you need a ~, call the Mugunghwa C~ Company at 777-1234.* T'aekshiga p'iryohashimyŏn, ch'ilch'ilch'irŭi illisamsa mugunghwa t'aekshi hoesa-e chŏnhwarŭl kŏshipshio. 택시가 필요하시면 777-1234 무궁화 택시 회사에 전화를 거십시오.

cabbage *n.* yangbaech'u 양배추, k'aebiji 캐비지.

cabin *n.* odumakchip 오두막집, (*of ship*) sŏnshil 선실.

cabinet *n.* naegak 내각, (*furniture*) chang 장(欌).

cable *n.* kulgŭn patchul 굵은 밧줄, (*submarine*) haejŏ chŏnsŏn 해저 전선, (*cablegram*) haeoe chŏnbo 해외 전보. ~ *car* k'eibŭlk'a 케이블카/ *I'd like to send a ~ to Korea.* Han-guge chŏnborŭl ch'igo shipsŭmnida. 한국에 전보를 치고 싶습니다/ *Where can I take a ~ car ?* K'eibŭlk'anŭn ŏdisŏ t'ajiyo? 케이블카는 어디서 타지요?

cactus *n.* sŏninjang 선인장.

cadet *n.* sagwan hubosaeng 사관 후보생.

cage *n.* saejang 새장, uri 우리.. *bird*~ saejang 새장.

cake *n.* kwaja 과자. *This ~ is very delicious.* I kwajanŭn ch'am madissŭmnida. 이 과자는 참 맛있읍니다.

calamity *n.* chaenan 재난, purhaeng 불행. *suffer a ~* chaenanŭl tanghada 재난을 당하다/ *national ~* kungnan 국난.

calculate *vt.* kyesanhada 계산하다. *They usually ~ with the abacus.* Kŭdŭrŭn pot'ong chup'anŭro kyesanhamnida. 그들은 보통 주판으로 계산합니다.

calculation *n.* kyesan 계산, (*forecast*) yech'ŭk 예측. *I have made a mistake in my ~.* Nanŭn kyesanŭl chalmot'aessŭmnida. 나는 계산을 잘못했읍니다/ *upset the ~* yesangŭl twiŏpta 예상을 뒤엎다.

calendar *n.* tallyŏk 달력. *lunar ~* ŭmnyŏk 음력/ *solar ~* yangnyŏk 양력 / *Mark your ~ now.* (itchi ant'orok) tallyŏge p'yorŭl hashio. (잊지 않도록) 달력에 표를 하시오.

calf *n.* songaji 송아지.

calico *n.* ogyangmok 옥양목.

call *vt.* purŭda 부르다. —*vi.* (*telephone*) chŏnhwarŭl kŏlda 전화를 걸다, (*visit*) pangmunhada 방문하다. —*n.* t'onghwa 통화. *Shall I ~ a redcap ?* Chimkkunŭl purŭlkkayo? 짐꾼을 부를까요/ *Can you ~ a taxi for me ?* T'aekshirŭl pullŏ chuji ank'essŭmnikka? 택시를 불러 주지 않겠읍니까/ *How do you ~ this in Korean ?* Igŏsŭl Han-gungmallo mwŏrago hamnikka? 이것을 한국말로 뭐라고 합니까/ *Who is ~ ing, please ?* Chŏnhwa kŏshinŭn punŭn nugushimnikka? 전화 거시는 분은 누구십니까/ *I'm sorry to ~ you in this busy time.* Pappŭn shigane chŏnhwa kŏrŏ mianhamnida. 바쁜 시간에 전화 걸어 미안합니다/ *Would* *you please tell her to ~ me back?* Kŭnyŏege chŏnhwa kŏldorok chŏnhae chushigessŭmnikka? 그녀에게 전화 걸 도록 전해 주시겠읍니까/ *Were there any ~s, Miss Chong?* Misŭ Chŏng, na-ege chŏnhwa on te ŏmnayo? 미스 정, 나에게 전화 온 데 없나요/ *Please ~ me at this number.* I pŏnhoro chŏnhwa kŏro chushipshio. 이 번호로 전화 걸어 주시시오/ *I'll ~ again later.* Tashi chŏnhwa kŏlgessŭmnida. 다시 전화 걸겠읍니다/ *Miss Lee, you have a phone ~.* Misŭ Ri, chŏnhwa wassŭmnida. 미스 리, 전화 왔읍니다.

calligraphy *n.* sŏye 서예(書藝). *Are you interested in modern ~?* Hyŏndae sŏyee hŭngmirŭl kajishimnikka? 현대 서예에 흥미를 가지십니까/ *I have only read a few books on ~.* Sŏyee kwanhan ch'aegŭl myŏt kwŏn ilgŏ-ssŭl ppunimnida. 서예에 관한 책을 몇 권 읽었을 뿐입니다.

calling *n.* chŏmho 점호, (*profession*) chigŏp 직업.

calm *adj.* choyonghan 조용한, (*of sea*) chanjanhan 잔잔한. *Korea has been called a "land of morning ~".* Han-gugŭn 「choyonghan ach'imŭi nara」rago pullyŏ ogo issŭmnida. 한국은 「조용한 아침의 나라」라고 불려 오고 있읍니다.

camel *n.* nakt'a 낙타.

camellia *n.* tongbaengnamu 동백나무.

camera *n.* sajinki 사진기, k'amera 카메라.

cameraman *n.* sajinsa 사진사.

camouflage *n.* wijang 위장, k'amup'ŭllaji 카무플라지.

camp *n.* yayŏng 야영, k'aemp'ŭ 캠프.

campaign *n.* undong 운동, yuse 유세(遊說). *a political ~* chŏngch'i undong 정치 운동/*an election ~* sŏn-gŏ undong 선거 운동/ *~ speech* sŏn-gŏ yŏnsŏl 선거 연설.

campfire *n.* modakpul 모닥불, k'aemp'ŭp'aiŏ 캠프파이어. *Around the ~, we sang all together.* Modakpul chu-wiesŏ urinŭn modu noraerŭl pullŏssŭmnida. 모닥불 주위 에서 우리는 모두 노래를 불렀읍니다. 「핑.

camping *n.* yayŏng saenghwal 야영 생활, k'aemp'ing 캠

can *aux.v.* hal su itta 할 수 있다. *C~ you speak Korean?* Han-gungmarŭl hal su issŭmnikka? 한국말을 할 수 있읍니까/ *C~ you dance?* Ch'umŭl ch'ul su issŭmnikka? 춤을 출 수 있읍니까/ *C~ you tell me where the Choson Hotel is?* Chosŏn hot'eri ŏdi innŭnji karik'yŏ chushigessŭmnikka? 조선 호텔이 어디 있는지 가리켜 주시겠읍니까/ *You ~ go with us.* Uriwa hamkke kado chossŭmnida. 우리와 함께 가도 좋습니다/ *C~ it be true?* Kŭge chŏngmarimnikka? 그게 정말입니까/ *What ~ I do for you?* Muŏsŭl towa tŭrilkkayo? 무엇을 도와 드릴까요/ *I can't do without it.* Kŭgŏt ŏpshinŭn hal su ŏpsŭmnida. 그것 없이는 할 수 없읍니다.

can *n.* yangch'ŏlt'ong 양철통, kkangt'ong 깡통, (*water closet*) pyŏnso 변소. *Where is the ~?* Hwajangshirŭn ŏdiimnikka? 화장실은 어디입니까?

canal *n.* unha 운하. *the Suez ~* Suejŭ unha 수에즈 운하.

cancel *vt.* malsarhada 말살하다, ch'wisohada 취소하다. *I want to ~ my tour.* Yŏhaengŭl ch'wisohago shipsŭmnida. 여행을 취소하고 싶습니다/ *Please ~ this reservation and make it for the next flight.* I yeyagŭl ch'wisohago taŭm hanggongp'yŏnŭro chaba chushipshio. 이 예약을 취소하고 다음 항공편으로 잡아 주시시오/ *C~ all my appointments today.* Onŭl yaksogŭn modu ch'wisohashio. 오늘 약속은 모두 취소하시오.

cancer *n.* am 암(癌). *lung ~* p'yeam 폐암/ *breast ~* yubangam 유방암/ *~ of the stomach* wiam 위암/ *~ of the womb* chagungam 자궁암.

candidate *n.* huboja 후보자, chimangja 지망자.

candle *n.* yangch'o 양초.

candy *n.* sat'ang 사탕, k'aendi 캔디.

cane *n.* chip'angi 지팡이.

canned *adj.* t'ongjorimhan 통조림한. *~ goods* t'ongjorim chep'um 통조림 제품.

cannon *n.* taep'o 대포. *~ ball* p'ot'an 포탄.

cap *n.* moja 모자.

capacity *n.* suyongnyang 수용량, yongjŏk 용적, (*ability*) nŭngnyŏk 능력, (*function*) chagyŏk 자격.

capital *n.* sudo 수도(首都), (*money*) chabon 자본, (*capital letter*) taemuncha 대문자. *Seoul is the ~ city of the Republic of Korea.* Sŏurŭn Taehanmin-gugŭi sudoimnida. 서울은 대한민국의 수도입니다/ *private* ~ kaein chabon 개인 자본 / *with a small* ~ sojabonŭro 소자본으로.

capitalist *n.* chabon-ga 자본가.

captain *n.* yukkun taewi 육군 대위, (*navy*) taeryŏng 대령, (*merchant ship*) sŏnjang 선장.

capture *vt.* chapta 잡다, ŏtta 얻다.

car *n.* ch'a 차. *motor* ~ chadongch'a 자동차/ *street-* ~ chŏnch'a 전차/ *a sleeping* ~ ch'imdaech'a 침대차.

caravan *n.* taesang 대상(隊商).

carbon paper mukchi 묵지, poksaji 복사지.

card *n.* k'adŭ 카드. *post*~ yŏpsŏ 엽서/ *a visiting* ~ myŏngham 명함 / *a playing* ~ (*Western*) t'ŭrŏmp'ŭ 트럼프, (*Korean*) hwat'u 화투/ *May I have your* ~, *please?* Myŏngham kajigo issŭshimnikka? 명함 가지고 있으십니까/ *Excuse me, I don't have a calling* ~. Mianhajiman myŏnghami ŏpsŭmnida. 미안하지만 명함이 없습니다/ *Do you like to play* ~*s?* Hwat'unori choahashimnikka? 화투놀이 좋아하십니까?

cardinal *adj.* kibonjŏgin 기본적인. (*math.*) ~ *number* kisu 기수(基數). —*n.* ch'ugigyŏng 추기경.

care *n.* kŏkchŏng 걱정, (*heed*) chuŭi 주의, (*charge*) poho 보호. —*vi.* (*feel regard*) kwanshimŭl katta 관심을 갖다, (*like*) choahada 좋아하다, hago ship'ŏhada 하고 싶어하다. *family* ~*s* chiban kŏkchŏng 집안 걱정/ *Take* ~ *of yourself.* Mom choshimhashipshio. 몸 조심하십시오/ *Who will* ~ *for the children?* Aidŭrŭn nuga tolbolkkayo? 아이들은 누가 돌볼까요/ *Please write to me in* ~ *of Mr. Lee.* Issi pangŭro p'yŏnjirŭl hae chushipshio. 이(李)씨 방으로 편지를 해 주십시오/ *I don't* ~ *who you are.* Tangshini nugudŭn sanggwan ŏpsŭmnida. 당신이 누구든 상관 없습니다/ *Who* ~*s?* Al ke mwŏmnikka? 알 게 뭡니까/ *Would you* ~ *for some coffee?* K'op'i chom tŭshigessŭmnikka? 코피 좀 드시겠읍니까/ *Do you* ~ *for fried fish?* Saengsŏn p'ŭrairŭl choahashimnikka? 생선 프라이를 좋아하십니까?

careful *adj.* chuŭi kip'ŭn 주의 깊은, choshimsŏng innŭn 조심성 있는. *Be* ~ *not to break it.* Kkaeji ant'orok choshimhashio. 깨지 않도록 조심하시오.

carefully *adv.* chuŭi kipke 주의 깊게. *Carry the eggs* ~, *please*. Talgyarŭl chebal choshimhayŏ narŭshio. 달걀을 제발 조심하여 나르시오.

careless *adj.* choshimsŏng ŏmnŭn 조심성 없는. *He is* ~ *about his dress*. Kŭnŭn otch'arime mugwanshimhamnida. 그는 옷차림에 무관심합니다.

carelessly *adv.* sohorhage 소홀하게. *Don't do your work* ~. Irŭl sohorhi haji mashio. 일을 소홀히 하지 마시오.

cargo *n.* hwamul 화물. ~ *plane* hwamul susonggi 화물 수송기.

caricature *n.* manhwa 만화, p'ungja manhwa 풍자 만화.

carnival *n.* sayukche 사육제(謝肉祭).

carp *n.* ingŏ 잉어. *silver* ~ pungŏ 붕어.

carpenter *n.* moksu 목수, mokkong 목공.

carpet *n.* yungdan 융단.

carriage *n.* (*vehicle*) mach'a 마차, (*manner*) t'aedo 태도, (*transporting*) susong 수송. *sleeping* ~ ch'imdaech'a 침대차.

carrot *n.* tanggŭn 당근.

carry *vt.* unbanhada 운반하다, (*keep on hand*) hyudaehada 휴대하다. *May I* ~ *your suitcase?* Syut'ŭ k'eisŭrŭl unbanhae tŭrijiyo. 슈트 케이스를 운반해 드리지요/ *She was* ~*ing the baby in her arms*. Kŭnyŏnŭn agirŭl anko issŏssŭmnida. 그녀는 아기를 안고 있었읍니다/ *We don't* ~ *men's underwear*. Chŏhŭi kageesŏnŭn shinsayong naeŭinŭn ch'wigŭp'aji anssŭmnida. 저희 가게에서는 신사용 내의는 취급하지 않습니다.

cart *n.* chimmach'a 짐마차, talguji 달구지.

cartoon *n.* manhwa 만화. *animated* ~ manhwa yŏnghwa 만화 영화.

cartoonist *n.* manhwaga 만화가.

cartridge *n.* t'anyakt'ong 탄약통.

carve *vt.* saegida 새기다. ~ *a design on wood* namue toanŭl saegida 나무에 도안을 새기다.

carving *n.* chogak 조각. 「폭포.

cascade *n.* chagŭn p'okp'o 작은 폭포, in-gong p'okp'o 인공

case *n.* sangja 상자, (*occurrence*) sakŏn 사건. *I would like to report a* ~ *of lost money*. Ton punshire kwanhae shin-gohago shipsŭmnida. 돈 분실에 관해 신고하고 싶습니다/ *Would you tell me where to call in ～ of trouble, please?* Sago ttaenŭn ŏdiro yŏllak'amyŏn toenŭnjiyo? 사고 때는 어디로 연락하면 되는지요?

cash *n.* hyŏn-gŭm 현금. —*vt.* hyŏn-gŭmŭro pakkuda 현금으로 바꾸다. *We accept only ～.* Hyŏn-gŭmman passŭmnida. 현금만 받습니다/ *I want to ～ this check.* I sup'yorŭl hyŏn-gŭmŭro pakkugo shipsŭmnida. 이 수표를 현금으로 바꾸고 싶습니다.

cashier *n.* ch'ullapkye 출납계, hoegyegye 회계계. *Go to the ～'s desk.* Ch'ullapkyero kashipshio. 출납계로 가십시오/ *Please pay the ～.* Hoegyee chiburhashipshio. 회계에 지불하십시오.

casket *n.* chagŭn sangja 작은 상자, (*coffin*) kwan 관(棺).

cast *vt.* tŏnjida 던지다. —*n.* (*actors*) paeyŏk 배역.

castle *n.* sŏng 성(城).

casual *adj.* ttŭtpakkŭi 뜻밖의, uyŏnhan 우연한. *a ～ visitor* ttŭtpakke ch'ajaon sonnim 뜻밖에 찾아온 손님/ *a ～ fire* purŭiŭi hwajae 불의의 화재.

casualty *n.* (*mishap*) chaenan 재난, (*pl.*) sasangja 사상자. *a list of casualties* sasangja myŏngdan 사상자 명단.

cat *n.* koyangi 고양이.

catalog(ue) *n.* mongnok 목록, k'at'allogŭ 카탈로그.

cataract *n.* p'okp'o 폭포, hongsu 홍수.

catch *vt.* chapta 잡다, puttŭlda 붙들다, (*be in time for*) shigane taeda 시간에 대다, (*hit*) matta 맞다, (*incur*) kŏllida 걸리다, (*arrest*) kkŭlda 끌다. *How many fish did you ～?* Mulkogirŭl myŏt marina chabassŭmnikka? 물고기를 몇 마리나 잡았습니까/ *The thief was caught.* Todugŭn puttŭllyŏssŭmnida. 도둑은 붙들렸습니다/ *Did you ～ the train?* Kich'anŭn t'assŭmnikka? 기차는 탔습니까/ *～ a cold* kamgie kŏllida 감기에 걸리다/ *The house caught fire.* Chibe puri put'ŏssŭmnida. 집에 불이 붙었습니다/ *I don't quite ～ your meaning.* Tangshin marŭn chal ihaehaji mot'agessŭmnida. 당신 말은 잘 이해하지 못하겠습니다/ *I'm sure you'll ～ on soon.* Kot alge toel kŏshimnida. 곧 알게 될 것입니다.

catcher *n.* (*baseball*) p'osu 포수, k'aech'ŏ 캐처.

category *n.* chongnyu 종류, puryu 부류.

cathedral *n.* taesŏngdang 대성당. 「kyohoe 천주교회.

Catholic *n.* ch'ŏnjugyodo 천주교도. ~ *Church* ch'ŏnju-

Catholicism *n.* ch'ŏnjugyo 천주교.

cattle *n.* kach'uk 가축. ~ *pen* oeyangkan 외양간.

cause *n.* wŏnin 원인. —*vt.* irŭk'ida 일으키다. *What was the* ~? Wŏninŭn muŏshiŏssŭmnikka? 원인은 무엇이었읍니까/*What* ~*d his death?* Kŭnŭn wae chugŏssŭmnikka? 그는 왜 죽었읍니까?

caution *n.* choshim 조심, kyŏnggo 경고. —*vt.* kyŏnggohada 경고하다. *Take every* ~ *against error.* Shilsu ant'orok choshimhashio 실수 않도록 조심하시오/ *We were* ~*ed not to drive fast.* Kwasok unjŏnŭl ant'orok kyŏnggorŭl padassŭmnida. 과속 운전을 않도록 경고를 받았읍니다.

cautious *adj.* choshimsŏng innŭn 조심성 있는. *You must be* ~ *with the razor.* Myŏndohal ttaenŭn choshimhaeya hamnida. 면도할 때는 조심해야 합니다.

cave *n.* tonggul 동굴.

ceasefire *n.* hyujŏn 휴전(休戰). ~ *agreement* hyujŏn hyŏpchŏng 휴전 협정/ ~ *talks* hyujŏn hoedam 휴전 회담.

ceiling *n.* ch'ŏnjang 천장. *hit the* ~ mopshi sŏngnaeda 몹시 성내다/ *My boss is hitting the* ~ *because I made a blunder.* Naega shilsurŭl haetki ttaemune chuinŭn mopshi hwarŭl naego issŭmnida. 내가 실수를 했기 때문에 주인은 몹시 화를 내고 있읍니다.

celadon *n.* ch'ŏngja 청자(靑瓷). *It is a famous Koryo* ~. Kŭgŏsŭn yumyŏnghan Koryŏ ch'ŏngjaimnida. 그것은 유명한 고려 청자입니다.

celebrate *vt.* ch'uk'ahada 축하하다. ~ *one's birthday* saengirŭl ch'uk'ahada 생일을 축하하다/ *What are they celebrating?* Chŏ pundŭrŭn muŏsŭl ch'uk'ahago issŭmnikka? 저 분들은 무엇을 축하하고 있읍니까/ *They are celebrating the birth of Admiral Yi Sun-shin.* I Sun-shin changgunŭi t'ansaengŭl ch'uk'ahago issŭmnida. 이 순신 장군의 탄생을 축하하고 있읍니다.

celebrated *adj.* chŏmyŏnghan 저명한, yumyŏnghan 유명

한. *a picture by a ~ painter* yumyŏnghan hwagaŭi kŭrim 유명한 화가의 그림.

celebration *n.* ch'uk'a 축하, (*festival*) ch'ukche 축제, ch'uk'ahoe 축하회(祝賀會). *hold a ~* ch'uk'ahoerŭl yŏlda 축하회를 열다/ *in ~ of* ...ŭl ch'uk'ahayŏ …을 축하하여.

cemetery *n.* myoji 묘지, kongdong myoji 공동 묘지.

censor *n.* kŏmyŏlgwan 검열관.

censorship *n.* kŏmyŏl 검열.

census *n.* in-gu chosa 인구 조사. *carry out a ~* in-gu chosarŭl hada 인구 조사를 하다.

cent *n.* sent'ŭ 센트. *per ~* p'ŏsent'ŭ 퍼센트(%) / *five per ~* op'un 5푼(分)/ *ten per ~* irhal 1할(割)/ *not a single ~* tandon han p'undo ŏpshi 단돈 한 푼도 없이.

center, centre *n.* chungang 중앙, pokp'an 복판. *the ~ of Seoul* Sŏurŭi chungshimji 서울의 중심지/(*place of activity*) *Medical ~* chungang ŭiryowŏn 중앙 의료원/ *shopping ~* sangjŏmga 상점가/ *recreation ~* orakchang 오락장.

central *adj.* chungangŭi 중앙의, chungshimŭi 중심의. *the ~ figures* chungshim inmul 중심 인물.

century *n.* ilsegi 일세기.

cereal *n.* kongmul 곡물, kongnyu 곡류(穀類). *Do you keep ~s too?* Kongmuldo ch'wigŭp'ago issŭmnikka? 곡물도 취급하고 있읍니까?

ceremony *n.* ŭishik 의식(儀式), kyŏkshik 격식. *wedding* [*marriage*] *~* kyŏrhonshik 결혼식/ *graduation ~* choŏpshik 졸업식.

certain *adj.* hwakshirhan 확실한, t'ŭllimŏmnŭn 틀림없는. *~ evidence* hwakshirhan chŭnggŏ 확실한 증거/ *a ~ fact* t'ŭllimŏmnŭn sashil 틀림없는 사실/ *Are you ~ of that?* Kŭgŏsŭn hwakshirhamnikka? 그것은 확실합니까/ *He is ~ to come.* Kŭnŭn t'ullimŏpshi omnida. 그는 틀림없이 옵니다/ *for ~* t'ŭllimŏpshi 틀림없이.

certainly *adv.* hwakshirhi 확실히, (*in answer to questions*) mullonijiyo 물론이지요, kŭrŏk'omalgoyo 그렇고말고요. *Yes ~.* Mullonijiyo. 물론이지요/ *C~ not.* Ŏrimdo ŏpsŭmnida. 어림도 없읍니다/ *C~, won't you come in?* Algessŭmnida. Ŏsŏ tŭrŏooshijiyo. 알겠읍니다. 어서 들어오시지요.

certificate *n.* chŭngmyŏngsŏ 증명서, myŏnhŏchŭng 면허증. *medical* ~s chindansŏ 진단서/ *a health*~ kŏng-ang chŭngmyŏngsŏ 건강 증명서/ *a marriage* ~ honin chŭngmyŏngsŏ 혼인 증명서.

certification *n.* chŭngmyŏng 증명, myŏnhŏ 면허.

certify *vt.* chŭngmyŏnghada 증명하다.

chain *n.* sasŭl 사슬, (*fetters*) sokpak 속박. —*vt.* soesasŭllo maeda 쇠사슬로 매다. ~ *store* yŏnswaejŏm 연쇄점.

chair *n.* ŭija 의자. *rocking* ~ hŭndŭl ŭija 흔들 의자/ *Bath* ~ hwanja ŭija 환자(患者) 의자/ *swivel* ~ hoejŏn ŭija 회전 의자.

chairman *n.* ŭijang 의장(議長), wiwŏnjang 위원장.

chalk *n.* punp'il 분필, paengmuk 백묵.

chamber *n.* pang 방, tokpang 독방, (*bedroom*) ch'imshil 침실. ~*maid* hanyŏ 하녀.

champion *n.* usŭngja 우승자, ch'aemp'iŏn 챔피언, t'usa 투사, (*advocate*) onghoja 옹호자. *a boxing* ~ kwŏnt'u ch'aemp'iŏn 권투 챔피언/ *the* ~ *team* usŭngt'im 우승팀.

chance *n.* uyŏn 우연, (*opportunity*) kihoe 기회, (*luck*) un 운, (*probability*) kamang 가망. *Excuse me, but are you Mr. Kim by any* ~ ? Shillyejiman, hokshi Kim sŏnsaengi anishimnikka ? 실례지만, 혹시 김(金) 선생이 아니십니까/ *I met him by* ~. Uyŏnhi kŭ punŭl mannassŭmnida. 우연히 그 분을 만났읍니다/ *I seldom have a* ~ *to speak to foreigners.* Oeguk saramege marŭl hal kihoega chomch'ŏrŏm ŏpsŭmnida. 외국 사람에게 말을 할 기회가 좀처럼 없읍니다/ *Do you think we have a* ~ *for the pennant this year ?* Kŭmnyŏne usŭnghal kamangi ittago poshimnikka ? 금년에 우승할 가망이 있다고 보십니까?

change *n.* pyŏnhwa 변화, (*small coins*) chandon 잔돈, (*money returned as a balance*) kŏsŭrŭmton 거스름돈. —*vi.* pyŏnhada 변하다. —*vt.* pakkuda 바꾸다. *Have you got any* ~ ? Chandon ŏpsŭshimnikka ? 잔돈 없으십니까/ *You have given me the wrong* ~. Kŏsŭrŭmtoni t'ŭllimnida. 거스름돈이 틀립니다/ *Here is four bucks. Keep the* ~. Yŏgi sa tallŏ issŭmnida. Kŏsŭrŭmtonŭn kajishio. 여기 4달러 있읍니다. 거스름돈은 가지시오/ *Where do I* ~

the bus for the Medical Center? Chungang ŭiryowŏnŭro kajamyŏn ŏdisŏ pŏsŭrŭl kara t'aya hamnikka? 중앙 의료원으로 가자면 어디서 버스를 갈아 타야 합니까/ *Can you ~this five hundred won bill?* I obaegwŏnkwŏnŭl chandonŭro pakkuŏ chushigessŭmnikka? 이 500원을 잔 돈으로 바꾸어 주시겠읍니까?

channel *n.* suro 수로(水路), haehyop 해협, *(radio, TV)* ch'aenŏl 채널. *What's the KBS ~ giving us now?* KBS-esŏnŭn chigŭm muŏsŭl hago issŭmnikka? KBS에서는 지금 무엇을 하고 있읍니까?

chaos *n.* hondon 혼돈, taehollan 대혼란, mujilsŏ 무질서.

chap *vi.* salkach'i t'ŭda 살갗이 트다. *I have ~ped hands.* Soni t'ŏssŭmnida. 손이 텄읍니다 / *Her skin ~s easily.* Kŭnyŏŭi p'ibunŭn chal t'ŭmnida. 그녀의 피부는 잘 틉니다.

chapel *n.* yebaedang 예배당. *the Methodist ~* kamni kyo-hoe 감리 교회.

chapter *n.* chang 장(章), *(branch)* chibu 지부(支部). *the Inchon ~ of the Red Cross Society* chŏkshipchasa In-ch'ŏn chibu 적십자사 인천(仁川) 지부.

character *n.* *(letter)* kŭlcha 글자, sŏngkyŏk 성격, *(person)* inmul 인물, *(reputation)* p'yŏngp'an 평판. *Can you read a book in Chinese ~s?* Hancharo ssŭiŏjin ch'aegŭl ilgŭl su issŭmnikka? 한자(漢字)로 씌어진 책을 읽을 수 있 읍니까/ *a woman of noble ~* kogyŏrhan sŏngkyŏgŭi yŏin 고결한 성격의 여인/ *~ actor* sŏngkyŏk paeu 성격 배 우/ *He is a bad ~.* Kŭnŭn choch'i mot'an in-ganimnida. 그는 좋지 못한 인간입니다 / *He has a ~ for honesty.* Kŭnŭn chŏngjik'adanŭn p'yŏngimnida. 그는 정직하다는 평입니다.

characteristic *adj.* tokt'ŭk'an 독특한. —*n.* t'ŭkching 특 징. *facial ~s* ŏlgurŭi t'ŭkching 얼굴의 특징.

charcoal *n.* sut 숯, mokt'an 목탄.

charge *n.* *(burden)* chim 짐, pudam 부담, *(expense)* pi-yong 비용, *(responsibility)* ch'aegim 책임, *(indictment)* kobal 고발. —*vt.*(impose) pugwahada 부과하다, *(entrust)* matkida 맡기다, *(accuse)* kobarhada 고발하다, *(command)* myŏngnyŏnghada 명령하다. *Can you reverse the ~s?*

Yogŭmŭn sangdaebang pudamŭro hae chushipshio. 요금
은 상대방 부담으로 해 주십시오/ *How much do you ~ for
the room?* Pangkapsŭn ŏlmaimnikka? 방값은 얼마입니까/
Does the ~ include breakfast? Kŭ yogŭmenŭn ach'im
shiksaga p'ohamdoeŏ issŭmnikka? 그 요금에는 아침 식사가
포함되어 있읍니까/ *There is no ~ for delivery in the
city.* Shinae paedarŭn muryoimnida. 시내 배달은 무료입니
다/ *Give me someone in ~ of export.* Such'ul kwan-
gye ch'aegimja-ege taejushipshio. 수출 관계 책임자에게
대주십시오/ *I was in ~ of the office.* Naega kŭ yŏng-
ŏpsoŭi ch'aegimjayŏssŭmnida. 내가 그 영업소의 책임자였
읍니다/ *The fighting bull ~ed at the bullfighter.*
T'uuga t'uusarŭl hyanghae tolchinhaessŭmnida. 투우가
투우사를 향해 돌진했읍니다/ *Do you mean to ~ the guilt
on me?* Choerŭl na-ege ssŭiul chakchŏngio? 죄를 나에게
씌울 작정이오/ *He was arrested on ~ of murdering.*
Sarin hyŏmŭiro kŭnŭn ch'ep'odoeŏssŭmnida. 살인 혐의로
그는 체포되었읍니다/ *free of ~* muryo 무료/ *transportation ~* unim 운임.

charity *n.* chabishim 자비심, chasŏn 자선, (*subscription*)
kibugŭm 기부금. *~ concert* chasŏn ŭmak'oe 자선 음악회.

charm *n.* maeryŏk 매력.

charming *adj.* maeryŏkchŏgin 매력적인, (*delightful*) chŭlgŏun 즐거운. *a ~ young lady* maeryŏkchŏgin chŏlmŭn
yŏin 매력적인 젊은 여인.

chase *vt.* ch'ugyŏk'ada 추격하다, moranaeda 몰아내다. —*n.*
ch'ugyŏk 추격, (*hunting*) sanyang 사냥. *C~ that dog
out of the garden.* Chŏ kaerŭl chŏngwŏnesŏ tchoch'a
pŏrishio. 저 개를 정원에서 쫓아 버리시오.

chat *n.* chaptam 잡담. *Let's have a nice little ~.* Chom
chaeminanŭn chaptamirado haji ank'esso? 좀 재미나는
잡담이라도 하지 않겠소?

chatter *vi.* chikkŏrida 지껄이다. *~ noisily* shikkŭrŏpke
chaejalgŏrida 시끄럽게 재잘거리다/ *~ box* sudajangi 수다장
이.

chauffeur *n.* chagayong unjŏnsa 자가용 운전사.

cheap *adj.* ssan 싼, kapssan 값싼. *Have you anything
~er than this?* Igŏtpoda tŏ ssan kŏsŭn ŏpsŭmnikka? 이

것보다 더 싼 것은 없읍니까/ *Their goods are ~ and dependable.* Kŭdŭrŭi sangp'umŭn ssago shinyonghal su issŭmnida. 그들의 상품은 싸고 신용할 수 있읍니다.

cheat *vi.* sogida 속이다. *~ in the examination* shihŏmesŏ k'ŏningŭl hada 시험에서 커닝을 하다/ *I've been ~ed.* Nanŭn sogassŭmnida. 나는 속았읍니다/ *She ~ed me.* Kŭnyŏnŭn narŭl sogyŏssŭmnida. 그녀는 나를 속였읍니다.

check *n.* (*receipt*) yŏngsujŭng 영수증, sup'yo 수표. *—vt.* taejohada 대조하다, hwaginhada 확인하다, (*deposit*) matkida 맡기다. *—vi.* ~ *in* (*in hotel*) sukpagŭl shinch'ŏnghada 숙박을 신청하다/ ~ *out* kyesanhago naoda 계산하고 나오다/ *May I pay by ~?* Sup'yorŭl padŭshigessŭmnikka? 수표를 받으시겠읍니까/ *I want to cash this ~.* I sup'yo hyŏn-gŭmŭro pakkuŏ chushigessŭmnikka? 이 수표 현금으로 바꿔 주시겠읍니까/ *Do you accept traveller's ~s?* Yŏhaengja sup'yorŭl pada chushigessŭmnikka? 여행자 수표를 받아 주시겠읍니까/ *rubber*〔*bad*〕 ~ pudo sup'yo 부도 수표/ *May I have my ~, please?* Kyesanhae chushipshio. 계산해 주십시오/ *Separate ~s, please.* Ttarottaro kyesansŏrŭl chushipshio. 따로따로 계산서를 주십시오/ *Would you ~ the oil, please.* Kirŭmŭl poa chushigessŭmnikka? 기름을 보아 주시겠읍니까/ *Would you like to ~ your valuables?* Kwijungp'umŭn matkigessŭmnikka? 귀중품은 맡기겠읍니까/ *What time is the ~ing out time here?* Yŏgisŏnŭn hot'erŭl naganŭn shigani myŏt shijiyo? 여기서는 호텔을 나가는 시간이 몇 시지요/ *Have you ~ed up recently?* Ch'oegune chinch'arhae pon iri issŭmnikka? 최근에 진찰해 본 일이 있읍니까/ *Maybe you should go to see a doctor and get a ~up.* Ŭisakke chindanŭl pannŭn ke chok'essŭmnida. 의사께 진단을 받는 게 좋겠읍니다/ *Why don't you leave your baggage at the ~room?* Chimŭl hyudaep'um pogwanso-e matkimyŏn ŏttŏssŭmnikka? 짐을 휴대품 보관소에 맡기면 어떻습니까?

checkbook *n.* sup'yochang 수표장(帳).

cheek *n.* ppyam 뺨, pol 볼.

cheekbone *n.* kwangdaeppyŏ 광대뼈.

cheer *n.* (*applause*) kalch'ae 갈채, hwanho 환호, (*spirits*) kiun 기운, (*mood*) kibun 기분. —*vt.* kalch'aerŭl ponaeda 갈채를 보내다, (*comfort*) kippŭge hada 기쁘게 하다. —*vi.* kiunnada 기운나다. *a ~ leader* ŭngwŏndanjang 응원단장.

cheerful *adj.* kibunjoŭn 기분좋은, chŭlgŏun 즐거운. *a ~ day* chŭlgŏun haru 즐거운 하루/ *~ conversation* yuk'waehan taehwa 유쾌한 대화.

cheese *n.* ch'iju 치즈. *bread and ~* ch'ijŭrŭl parŭn ppang 치즈를 바른 빵. *Say, "~"!* Cha, usŭseyo! 자, 웃으세요!

chemical *adj.* hwahagŭi 화학의. —*n.* hwagongyakp'um 「화공약품.

chemist *n.* (*pharmacist*) yakchesa 약제사, (*expert in chemistry*) hwahakcha 화학자. *manufacturing ~* cheyaksa 제약사.

chemistry *n.* hwahak 화학.

cherry *n.* pŏtchi 버찌. *~ blossom* pŏtkkot 벚꽃/ *~ tree* pŏnnamu 벚나무/ *~ blossom viewing* pŏtkkonnori 벚꽃놀이/ *The ~ blossoms are at their best now.* Pŏtkkoch'i chigŭm hanch'angimnida. 벚꽃이 지금 한창입니다.

chess *n.* sŏyang changgi 서양 장기, ch'esŭ 체스. *Korean ~ changgi* 장기(將棋)/ *~ board* changgip'an 장기판/ *have a game of ~* changgirŭl tuda 장기를 두다/ *Let me challenge you to a game of ~.* Changgi han p'an tupshida. 장기 한 판 둡시다.

chest *n.* (*of body*) kasŭm 가슴, (*large box*) kwe 궤, (*of drawers*) otchang 옷장. *I have a pain in my ~.* Kasŭmi ap'ŭmnida. 가슴이 아픕니다/ *I want to buy some Korean ~s.* Han-gugŭi changŭl sago shipsŭmnida. 한국의 장(欌)을 사고 싶습니다.

chestnut *n.* pam 밤, (*tree*) pamnamu 밤나무.

chew *vt.,vi.* kkaemulda 깨물다, ssipta 씹다.

chewing gum kkŏm 껌.

chick *n.* pyŏngari 병아리, (*child*) ŏrin ai 어린 아이.

chicken *n.* tak 닭, (*young girl*) kyejibae 계집애.

chief *n.* chang 장(長). —*adj.* udumŏriŭi 우두머리의. *a section ~* kwajang 과장/ *the ~ of police* kyŏngch'alsŏjang 경찰서장.

chilblain *n.* tongsang 동상(凍傷).

child *n.* ai 아이, ŏrin ai 어린 아이. *a lost* ~ mia 미아(迷兒)/ *orphan* ~ koa 고아/ *a posthumous* ~ yubokcha 유복자.

chill *n.* han-gi 한기, ohan 오한.

chilly *adj.* ch'agaun 차가운, ŭsŭsŭhan 으스스한. *I feel* ~. Ohani tŭn kŏt kassŭmnida. 오한이 든 것 같습니다.

chimney *n.* kulttuk 굴뚝. ~ *sweeper* kulttuk ch'ŏngsobu 굴뚝 청소부.

chin *n.* t'ŏk 턱.

China *n.* Chungguk 중국(中國). *Red*[*Communist*] ~

china *n.* tojagi 도자기. [Chunggong 중공.

Chinese *n.* Chunggugin 중국인, Chunggugŏ 중국어. ~ *bellflower* toraji 도라지. ~ *ink* mŏk 먹.

chip *n.* t'omak 토막. —*vt.* kkakta 깎다. ~ *in* hanmok tŭlda 한몫 들다. *Let's* ~ *in to get her a present.* Chogŭmssik tonŭl naeŏ kŭnyŏege sŏnmurŭl hapshida. 조금씩 돈을 내어 그녀에게 선물을 합시다.

chirp *n.* tchaektchaek unŭn sori 쩍쩍 우는 소리. —*vi.* tchaektchaek ulda 쩍쩍 울다.

chisel *n.* kkŭl 끌, chŏng 정.

choice *n.* sŏnt'aek 선택, (*liking*) choahanŭn kŏt 좋아하는 것, (*things chosen*) korŭn mulgŏn 고른 물건. *Which is your* ~ ? Ŏnŭ kŏsŭl t'aek'ashigessŭmnikka ? 어느 것을 택하시겠읍니까/ *We have a lot* ~ *of bathing suits.* Uri kageenŭn kajigaji suyŏngbogi maryŏndoeŏ issŭmnida. 우리 가게에는 가지가지 수영복이 마련되어 있읍니다/ *What are the* ~s ? Muŏshi issŭmnikka ? 무엇이 있읍니까 ?

choke *vt.* chilshikshik'ida 질식시키다, (*fill up*) meuda 메우다. *The smoke almost* ~*d me.* Yŏn-giro sumi mak'il ppŏnhaessŭmnida. 연기로 숨이 막힐 뻔했읍니다/ *The garden is* ~*d with weeds.* Chapch'oga chŏngwŏnŭl mewŏssŭmnida. 잡초가 정원을 메웠읍니다.

choose *vt.*, *vi.* korŭda 고르다, sŏnt'aek'ada 선택하다. *Which would you* ~ *to buy ?* Ŏnŭ kŏsŭl sago shipsŭmnikka ? 어느 것을 사고 싶습니까/ *Which one will you* ~ ? Ŏnŭ kŏsŭl korŭshimnikka ? 어느 것을 고르십니까/ *I'll* ~ *this one.* Igŏsŭl korŭgessŭmnida. 이것을 고르겠읍니다.

chop *vt.* tchigŏsŏ charŭda 찍어서 자르다. ~ *a firewood* changjagŭl p'aeda 장작을 패다.

chopstick *n.* chŏtkarak 젓가락.

chorus *n.* hapch'ang 합창, hapch'angdae 합창대.

Christ *n.* Kŭrisŭdo 그리스도.

christen *vt.,vi.* seryerŭl chuda 세례를 주다, (*give a name*) myŏngmyŏnghada 명명(命名)하다. *The child was ~ed Mary*. Kŭ ainŭn Meriranŭn seryemyŏngŭl padassŭmnida. 그 아이는 메리라는 세례명을 받았읍니다.

Christian *n.* kidokkyo shinja 기독교 신자.

Christmas *n.* sŏngt'anjŏl 성탄절, k'ŭrisŭmasŭ 크리스마스. *~ Eve* k'ŭrisŭmasŭ chŏnya 크리스마스 전야(前夜).

chrysanthemum *n.* kuk'wa 국화. *grow ~* kuk'warŭl shimta 국화를 심다.

church *n.* kyohoe 교회, (*service*) yebae 예배. *What time does the ~ begin?* Yebaenŭn myŏt shie shijaktoemnikka? 예배는 몇 시에 시작됩니까/ *Don't you go to ~, then?* Kŭrŏm kyohoeenŭn an kashimnikka? 그럼 교회에는 안 가십니까?

cicada *n.* maemi 매미.

cigar *n.* yŏsongyŏn 여송연, shiga 시가.

cigaret(te) *n.* kwŏllyŏn 궐련, tambae 담배. *a pack of ~s* tambae han kap 담배 한 갑/ *~ butt* tambae kkongch'o 담배 꽁초/*May I have a ~?* Tambae han tae chushipshio. 담배 한 대 주십시오/ *How about smoking a ~?* Tambae han tae an p'iushigessŭmnikka? 담배 한 대 안 피우시겠읍니까?

cinema *n.* yŏnghwagwan 영화관. *There are many ~s in Seoul*. Sŏurenŭn manŭn yŏnghwagwani issŭmnida. 서울에는 많은 영화관이 있읍니다.

circle *n.* wŏn 원(圓), (*group of people*) tanch'e 단체, … kye …계(界). *educational ~s* kyoyukkye 교육계/ *economic ~s* kyŏngjegye 경제계/ *army ~s* kunin sahoe 군인 사회.

circular *adj.* tunggŭn 둥근. —*n.* hoeramchang 회람장.

circumference *n.* wŏndulle 원둘레, wŏnju 원주.

circumstance *n.* (*situation*) sajŏng 사정, hyŏngp'yŏn 형편, hwan-gyŏng 환경, (*case*) kyŏngu 경우. *in[under] these ~s* irŏn sajŏngŭro 이런 사정으로/ *They were under*

difficult ~s. Ŏryŏun sajŏnge noyŏ issŏssŭmnida. 어려운
사정에 놓여 있었읍니다.

circus *n.* kongmadan 곡마단, sŏk'ŏsŭ 서커스.

citizen *n.* shimin 시민. *the* ~s *of Seoul* Sŏul shimin
서울 시민.

citizenship *n.* shimin〔kongmin〕kwŏn 시민〔공민〕권.

city *n.* shi 시(市), toshi 도시. *a business* ~ sangŏp toshi
상업 도시/*a garden* ~ chŏnwŏn toshi 전원(田園) 도시/ *the*
~ *of Pusan* Pusanshi 부산시/ ~ *hall* shich'ŏng 시청/
Seoul is a very beautiful ~, *isn't it?* Sŏurŭn p'ŏk
arŭmdaun toshigunyo. 서울은 퍽 아름다운 도시군요.

civilian *n.* min-ganin 민간인, mun-gwan 문관(文官).

civilization *n.* munmyŏng 문명. *primitive* ~ wŏnshi munmyŏng 원시 문명/ *the white man's* ~ paegin munmyŏng
백인 문명/ *a machine* ~ kigye munmyŏng 기계 문명.

civil rights kongminkwŏn 공민권, inkwŏn 인권.

claim *n.* yogu 요구, ch'ŏnggu 청구, (*insistence*) chujang
주장. —*vt.* ch'ŏngguhada 청구하다, (*assert*) chujanghada
주장하다. *Does anyone* ~ *this umbrella?* I usanŭi imjanŭn an kyeshimnikka? 이 우산의 임자는 안 계십니까?

clam *n.* taehapchogae 대합조개.

clap *vt.,vi.* paksuch'ida 박수치다. *The audience* ~*ped for
five minutes.* Ch'ŏngjungdŭrŭn obun-ganina paksurŭl
ch'yŏssŭmnida. 청중들은 5분간이나 박수를 쳤읍니다.

clash *n.* ch'ungdol 충돌. —*vi.* ch'ungdorhada 충돌하다.

clasp *n.* kŏlsoe 걸쇠.

class *n.* (*sort*) chongnyu 종류, (*rank*) tŭnggŭp 등급,
(*social status*) kyegŭp 계급, (*student session*) hakkŭp
학급, suŏp 수업. *Two first* ~ *tickets to Pusan, please.*
Pusanhaeng iltŭng ch'ap'yo tu chang chushipshio. 부산행
1등 차표 두 장 주십시오/ *How much is a first* ~ *ticket
for Taegu?* Taeguhaeng iltŭngp'yonŭn ŏlmajiyo? 대구
(大邱)행 1등표는 얼마지요/ *I have* ~*es in the morning.*
Ojŏn chungenŭn suŏbi issŭmnida. 오전 중에는 수업이 있
읍니다.

classic *n.* kojŏn 고전. —*adj.* kojŏnjŏgin 고전적인. *What's
the most famous Korean* ~ *novel?* Kajang yumyŏnghan

Han-gugŭi kojŏn sosŏrŭn muŏshimnikka? 가장 유명한
한국의 고전 소설은 무엇입니까? 「고전 음악.

classical *adj.* kojŏnjŏgin 고전적인. ～*music* kojŏn ŭmak

claw *n.* (*of cat, hawk, etc.*) palt'op 발톱.

clay *n.* ch'arhŭk 찰흙, chinhŭk 진흙.

clean *adj.* kkaekkŭt'an 깨끗한. —*vt.* ch'ŏngsohada 청소하
다. ～*hands* kkaekkŭt'an son 깨끗한 손/ ～*air* malgŭn
konggi 맑은 공기/ *Wash it* ～. Kkaekkŭshi ssisŭshio. 깨
끗이 씻으시오/ *Give me a* ～*sheet of paper*. Kkaekkŭ-
t'an chongi han chang chushipshio. 깨끗한 종이 한 장 주
십시오/ *May I* ～*the room now?* Chigŭm pangch'ŏng-
sorŭl haedo chossŭmnikka? 지금 방청소를 해도 좋습니까/
Have this suit ～*ed.* I yangbogŭl set'ak'ae chushipshio.
이 양복을 세탁해 주십시오. 「리닝.

cleaning *n.* set'ak 세탁. *dry* ～ tŭrai k'ŭllining 드라이 클

clear *adj.* malgŭn 맑은, kkaekkŭt'an 깨끗한, (*bright*)
palgŭn 밝은, (*distinct*) ttoryŏt'an 또렷한.—*vt.* kkaekkŭshi ch'iuda 깨끗이 치우다. *a* ～*sky* malgŭn hanŭl 맑은
하늘/ *a* ～*voice* ttoryŏt'an moksori 또렷한 목소리/ ～*a
desk* ch'aeksangŭl malkkŭmhi hada 책상을 말끔히 하다.

clearly *adv.* ttokttok'i 똑똑히. *Please speak more* ～.
Chomdŏ ttokttok'i marhae chushipshio. 좀더 똑똑히 말해
주십시오.

clergyman *n.* moksa 목사, sŏngjikcha 성직자.

clerk *n.* samuwŏn 사무원, sŏgi 서기(書記). *a bank* ～ ŭn-
haengwŏn 은행원.

clever *adj.* yŏngnihan 영리한, (*adroit*) somssi choŭn 솜씨
좋은. *a* ～*boy* yŏngnihan sonyŏn 영리한 소년/ *a* ～
workman sungnyŏn-gong 숙련공.

client *n.* tan-gol sonnim 단골 손님, kogaek 고객.

climate *n.* kihu 기후. *a mild* ～ onhwahan kihu 온화한 기
후/ *a vile* ～ nappŭn kihu 나쁜 기후/ *a dry* ～ kŏnjohan
kihu 전조한 기후/ *How do you find the* ～*of Korea?*
Han-gŭgŭi kihurŭl ŏttŏk'e saenggak'ashimnikka? 한국의
기후를 어떻게 생각하십니까?

climax *n.* chŏlchŏng 절정, ch'oegojo 최고조. *reach the* ～
ch'oegojo-e tarhada 최고조에 달하다.

climb *vt.,vi.* orŭda 오르다, ollagada 올라가다. ~ *a tree* namue orŭda 나무에 오르다.

climber *n.* tŭngsan-ga 등산가.

climbing *n.* tŭngban 등반, tŭngsan 등산. *Will you go to the mountain* ~ *next Sunday?* Taŭm iryoire tŭngsan kashigessŭmnikka? 다음 일요일에 등산 가시겠읍니까?

clinch *vt.,vi.* choeda 죄다, matputtŭlda 맞붙들다.

cling *vi.* tallabutta 달라붙다, milch'ak'ada 밀착하다.

clinic *n.* (*hospital*) pyŏngwŏn 병원, (*medical office*) chillyoso 진료소. *I'm working at my father's* ~. Abŏji chillyoso-esŏ irŭl pogo issŭmnida. 아버지 진료소에서 일을 보고 있읍니다.

clip *n.* chongi chipke 종이 집게, k'ŭllip 클립. —*vt.,vi.* (*grip*) kkwak chwida 꽉 쥐다, (*trim*) kkakta 깎다. *I want some paper* ~*s.* Chongi chipkega myŏt kae p'iryohamnida. 종이 집게가 몇 개 필요합니다.

clock *n.* shigye 시계. *My* ~ *is out of order.* Nae t'aksang shigyenŭn kojangimnida. 내 탁상 시계는 고장입니다 / *The* ~ *goes fast.* I shigyenŭn pparŭmnida. 이 시계는 빠릅니다 / *an alarm* ~ chamyŏngjong 자명종.

clog *n.* (*pl.*) (*Korean wooden shoe*) namakshin 나막신.

close *adj.* (*intimate*) ch'inmirhan 친밀한, kakkaun 가까운. —*adv.* paro kyŏt'e 바로 곁에. —*vt.* (*shut*) tatta 닫다. —*vi.* tach'ida 닫히다. *Last night, I went from tavern to tavern with a few of my* ~ *friends.* Chinanbam nanŭn ch'inhan ch'in-gu myŏt myŏnggwa manŭn sulchibŭl toradanyŏssŭmnida. 지난밤 나는 친한 친구 몇 명과 많은 술집을 돌아다녔읍니다 / *I understand you live rather* ~ *to Mr. Park.* Paksshi chip kŭnch'ŏe sashindanŭn kŏl algo issŭmnida. 박씨(朴氏) 집 근처에 사신다는 걸 알고 있읍니다 / ~ *by* paro kyŏt'e 바로 곁에 / *I'll* ~ *the window right now.* Chigŭm kot ch'angmunŭl tatkessŭmnida. 지금 곧 창문을 닫겠읍니다. 「pyŏnso 변소.

closet *n.* pyŏkchang 벽장, (*privy*) pyŏnso 변소. *water* ~

cloth *n.* ch'ŏn 천, (*woven fabric*) otkam 옷감. *Please show me some samples of* ~. Otkam kyŏnbon chom poyŏ chushipshio. 옷감 견본 좀 보여 주십시오.

clothes *n.*(*dress*) ot 옷, ŭibok 의복. *Why are the Korean people called as "people of white ~ ?"* Han-guk saramŭn wae paegŭi minjogirago pulliŏjimnikka? 한국 사람은 왜 백의(白衣) 민족이라고 불리어집니까/*Please wear new ~.* Chebal sae osŭl ibŭshipshio. 제발 새 옷을 입으십 시오/ *~ line* ppallaetchul 빨랫줄.

cloud *n.* kurŭm 구름.

cloudy *adj.* hŭrin 흐린. *a ~ sky* hŭrin hanŭl 흐린 하늘/ *a ~ day* hŭrin nalssi 흐린 날씨/ *The radio says, it'll be ~ tomorrow.* Naeirŭn hŭrindago radioga pangsonghago issŭmnida. 내일은 흐린다고 라디오가 방송하고 있읍니다.

clown *n.* kwangdae 광대, iksalkkun 익살꾼.

club *n.* konbong 곤봉, (*society of persons*) k'ŭllŏp 클럽. *If you want to drink late, go to a night ~.* Nŭtkekkaji mashigo ship'ŭmyŏn nait'ŭ k'ŭllŏbŭro kashio. 늦게까지 마시고 싶으면 나이트 클럽으로 가시오.

clumsy *adj.* sŏt'urŭn 서투른, (*ill-adapted*) ŏsaek'an 어색한. *I'm ~ in speaking.* Nanŭn mari sŏt'umnida. 나는 말이 서툽니다/*a ~ apology* ŏsaek'an sagwa 어색한 사과.

coach *n.* mach'a 마차, (*railway*) kaekch'a 객차, (*trainer*) k'och'i 코치. —*vt.* k'och'ihada 코치하다, chidohada 지도하다. *a football ~* ch'ukku k'och'i 축구 코치/ *a swimming ~* suyŏng k'och'i 수영 코치.

coal *n.* sŏkt'an 석탄. *blind ~* muyŏnt'an 무연탄/ *~ mine* t'an-gaeng 탄갱/ *~ miner* ch'aet'anbu 채탄부/ *What is the name of the chief ~ mining district in Korea?* Han-gugŭi chuyo t'an-gwang chidaenŭn mwŏrago hamnikka? 한국의 주요 탄광 지대는 뭐라고 합니까?

coarse *adj.* kŏch'in 거친, (*crude*) chojap'an 조잡한, (*vulgar*) yabihan 야비한. *He is ~ in speech.* Kŭnŭn malt'uga kŏch'imnida. 그는 말투가 거칩니다.

coast *n.* haebyŏn 해변, haean 해안. *~line* haeansŏn 해안선. *~ guard* haean kyŏngbidae 해안 경비대.

coat *n.* chŏgori 저고리, sangŭi 상의(上衣), (*overcoat*) k'ot'ŭ 코트. *Can I take your ~?* K'ot'ŭrŭl pŏsŭshilkkayo? 코트를 벗으실까요?

cobbler *n.* kudu susŏn·gong 구두 수선공.

cobweb *n*. kŏmijul 거미줄, kŏmijip 거미집.

cock *n*. sut'ak 수탉.

cockroach *n*. pak'wi 바퀴, chindinmul 진딧물.

cocktail *n*. k'akt'eil 칵테일. *Would you care for a before-dinner* ∼? Shikchŏn k'akt'eirŭl hanjan hashigessŭmnikka? 식전(食前) 칵테일을 한잔 하시겠읍니까?

cocoon *n*. (nue)koch'i 누에(고치).

cod *n*. (*codfish*) taegu 대구. ∼-*liver oil* kanyu 간유.

code *n*. yak'o 약호(略號). *a secret* ∼ amho 암호/ *a telegraphic* ∼ chŏnshin puho 전신 부호.

coffee *n*. k'op'i 코피. *Give me a cup of* ∼, *please*. K'op'irŭl han chan chushipshio. 코피를 한 잔 주십시오/ *Here is your* ∼. K'op'irŭl kajigo wassŭmnida. 코피를 가지고 왔읍니다/ *Would you like some more* ∼? K'op'i chom tŏ tŭshigessŭmnikka? 코피 좀 더 드시겠읍니까/ *Bring us some good hot* ∼. Maditko ttakkŭnhan k'op'irŭl katta chushio. 맛있고 따끈한 코피를 갖다 주시오.

coffer *n*. kwe 궤, (*money box*) kŭmgo 금고.

coffin *n*. kwan 관(棺).

coin *n*. hwap'ye 화폐. *copper* ∼ tonghwa 동화/ *gold* ∼ kŭmhwa 금화/ *silver* ∼ ŭnhwa 은화/ *Can I buy old* ∼*s in the curio shop*? Koltongp'umjŏmesŏ yennal tongjŏnŭl sal su issŭmnikka? 골동품점에서 옛날 동전을 살 수 있읍니까/ *Here are ten five hundred won bills and eight coins*. Yŏgi obaegwŏnkwŏn yŏl changgwa tongjŏn yŏdŏl kaega issŭmnida. 여기 500 원권 열 장과 동전 여덟 개가 있읍니다.

coke *n*. (*Coca-Cola*) k'ok'ak'olla 코카콜라. *May I have a* ∼, *please*. K'ok'ak'ollarŭl chuseyo. 코카콜라를 주세요.

cold *adj*. ch'uun 추운, ssanŭrhan 싸늘한. —*n*. kamgi 감기. ∼ *cure* kamgiyak 감기약/ ∼ *reception* p'udaejŏp 푸대접/ ∼ *water* naengsu 냉수/ ∼ *wave* hanp'a 한파/ ∼ *war* naengjŏn 냉전/ *Eat it before it gets* ∼. Shikki chŏne tŭshipshio. 식기 전에 드십시오/ *I have a terrible* ∼. Nanŭn shimhan kamgie kŏllyŏssŭmnida. 나는 심한 감기에 걸렸읍니다.

collapse *vi*. munŏjida 무너지다, (*decline*) soet'oehada 쇠

퇴하다. —*n.* chwajŏl 좌절, wahae 와해.

collar *n.* k'alla 칼라, kit 깃.

colleague *n.* tongnyo 동료, tongŏpcha 동업자.

collect *vt.* moŭda 모으다, chingsuhada 징수하다. *I like to ～ stamps.* Nanŭn up'yo moŭnŭn kŏsŭl choahamnida. 나는 우표 모으는 것을 좋아합니다/ *～ waste articles* p'ye-p'umŭl sujip'ada 폐품을 수집하다.

collection *n.* sujip 수집, chingsu 징수. *My hobby is stamp ～.* Nae ch'wiminŭn up'yo sujibimnida. 내 취미는 우표 수집입니다/ *the ～ of taxes* segŭm chingsu 세금 징수.

college *n.* taehak 대학. *the C～ of Medicine* ŭikwa taehak 의과 대학/ *a junior ～* ch'ogŭp taehak 초급 대학/ *There are many ～s only for women in Seoul.* Sŏurenŭn yŏjadŭlmanŭi taehagi yŏrŏ kae issŭmnida. 서울에는 여자들만의 대학이 여러 개 있읍니다.

collide *vi.* pudich'ida 부딪히다, ch'ungdorhada 충돌하다.

collision *n.* ch'ungdol 충돌. *a railway bus ～* yŏlch'awa pŏsŭŭi ch'ungdol 열차와 버스의 충돌/ *The two trains came into ～.* Yŏlch'awa yŏlch'aga ch'ungdorhaessŭmnida. 열차와 열차가 충돌했읍니다.

colloquial *adj.* kuŏŭi 구어(口語)의, (*conversational*) hoehwaŭi 회화의.

colonel *n.* yukkun taeryŏng 육군 대령.

colony *n.* shingminji 식민지, (*group of people*) chiptan 집단, kŏryumin 거류민. *the American ～ in Seoul* Sŏurŭi Migugin kŏryumin 서울의 미국인 거류민/ *the ～ of artists* yesurin ch'on 예술인 촌.

colo(u)r *n.* saek 색. *bright ～* palgŭn saek 밝은 색/*dark ～* chinhan saek 진한 색/ *light ～* yŏlbŭn saek 엷은 색/ *natural ～* ch'ŏnyŏnsaek 천연색/ *water ～ painting* such'aehwa 수채화/ *Is this the only ～ you have?* Tarŭn saegŭn ŏpsŭmnikka? 다른 색은 없읍니까/ *The ～ becomes you.* Kŭ saegi tangshinege ŏullimnida. 그 색이 당신에게 어울립니다/ *Is this ～ fade-proof?* I saegŭn paraeji anssŭmnikka? 이 색은 바래지 않습니까?

column *n.* kidung 기둥, (*of newspaper*) nan 난(欄). *the sports ～* sŭp'och'ŭnan 스포츠난(欄).

comb *n.* pit 빗, (*of fowls*) pyŏt 볏.

combination *n.* kyŏrhap 결합, yŏnhap 연합.

come *vi.* oda 오다. *C~ here.* Iri oshio 이리 오시오/ *What time shall I ~?* Myŏt shie kalkkayo? 몇 시에 갈까요/ *When will she ~ home?* Kŭnyŏnŭn ŏnje chibe toraomnikka? 그녀는 언제 집에 돌아옵니까/ *Can you ~ over for dinner next Sunday?* Taŭm iryoil chŏnyŏk shiksae wa chushigessŭmnikka? 다음 일요일 저녁 식사에 와 주시겠읍니까/ *May I ~ to your office this afternoon?* Onŭl ohu samushillo kado kwaench'anssŭmnikka? 오늘 오후 사무실로 가도 괜찮습니까/ *Please ~ in and make yourself at home.* Ŏsŏ tŭrŏosyŏsŏ p'yŏnhi hashipshio. 어서 들어오셔서 편히 하십시오/ *Where do you ~ from?* Kohyangŭn ŏdishimnikka? 고향은 어디십니까/ *Oh, ~ on!* *I'm busy.* Aa ppalli hashio, nanŭn pappŭnikkayo. 아아, 빨리 하시오, 나는 바쁘니까요/ *Can you ~ down on this price?* Kapsŭl kkakkŭl su ŏpsŭmnikka? 값을 깎을 수 없읍니까/ *I can't ~ down that much.* Kŭrŏk'ekkajinŭn kkakkŭl su ŏpsŭmnida. 그렇게까지는 깎을 수 없읍니다.

comedian *n.* hŭigŭk paeu 희극 배우.

comedy *n.* hŭigŭk 희극.

comfortable *adj.* kibun choŭn 기분 좋은. *Are you ~ enough?* P'yŏnanhashimnikka? 편안하십니까/ *Please make yourself ~.* Pudi maŭm p'uk noŭshipshio. 부디 마음 푹 놓으십시오/ *That is a ~ chair.* Kŭgŏn p'yŏnanhan ŭijaimnida. 그건 편안한 의자입니다.

comic *adj.* usŭun 우스운, iksalmajŭn 익살맞은. —*n.* manhwa 만화. *Children like reading ~s.* Aidŭrŭn manhwaikkirŭl choahamnida. 아이들은 만화읽기를 좋아합니다.

command *vt.* myŏngnyŏnghada 명령하다. —*n.* myŏngnyŏng 명령, chihwi 지휘. *Do as I ~.* Myŏngnyŏngdaero hashio. 명령대로 하시오/ *Who ~s the army?* Nuga yukkunŭl chihwihamnikka? 누가 육군을 지휘합니까/ *The hill ~s a good view.* I ŏndŏgŭn chomangi ch'am chossŭmnida. 이 언덕은 조망이 참 좋습니다.

commemorate *vt.* kinyŏmhada 기념하다.

commence *vt.* shijak'ada 시작하다, kaeshihada 개시하다.

comment *n.* nonp'yŏng 논평. *No* ~*s.* Hal mal ŏpsŭmnida. 할 말 없읍니다.

commerce *n.* sangŏp 상업, (*trade*) muyŏk 무역. *domestic* ~ kungnae t'ongsang 국내 통상/ *overseas* ~ haeoe muyŏk 해외 무역/ *the Chamber of C*~ sanggong hoeŭiso 상공 회의소.

commercial *adj.* sangŏbŭi 상업의, muyŏgŭi 무역의. ~ *broadcasting* sangŏp pangsong 상업 방송/ ~ *salesman* oemu sawŏn 외무 사원.

commission *n.* immu 임무, (*authority*) chikkwŏn 직권, (*fee*) kujŏn 구전(口錢), susuryo 수수료. *Our salesman receives a ten percent* ~. Uri p'anmaewŏnŭn ship p'ŏsent'ŭŭi susuryorŭl passŭmnida. 우리 판매원은 10 퍼센트의 수수료를 받습니다.

committee *n.* wiwŏn 위원, wiwŏnhoe 위원회. *an advisory* ~ chamun wiwonhoe 자문 위원회/ *a financial* ~ chaejŏng wiwŏnhoe 재정 위원회.

common *adj.* pot'ongŭi 보통의, (*joint*) kongdongŭi 공동의, (*vulgar*) ch'ŏnhan 천한. ~ *manners* chŏsok'an t'aedo 저속한 태도.

common sense sangshik 상식. ~ *in law* pŏmnyul sangshik 법률 상식. *That is a matter of* ~. Kŭrŏn kŏsŭn sangshik munjeimnida. 그런 것은 상식 문제입니다.

commonwealth *n.* kukka 국가, (*democracy*) minjuguk 민주국, (*republic*) konghwaguk 공화국.

commotion *n.* tongyo 동요, sodong 소동.

communication *n.* chŏndal 전달,(*correspondence*) t'ongshin 통신, (*traffic*) kyot'ong 교통, (*connection*) yŏllak 연락. ~ *satellite* t'ongshin wisŏng 통신 위성/ *the Ministry of C*~ ch'eshinbu 체신부.

communism *n.* kongsanjuŭi 공산주의.

communist *n.* kongsanjuŭija 공산주의자, (*C*~) kongsandangwŏn 공산당원. ~ *party* kongsandang 공산당.

community *n.* tanch'e 단체, kongdong sahoe 공동 사회.

companion *n.* ch'in-gu 친구, tongbanja 동반자.

company *n.* (*companions*) pŏt 벗, tchak 짝, (*association*) kyoje 교제, (*guests*) sonnim 손님, (*party*) irhaeng 일행

(一行), (*mil.*) pobyŏng chungdae 보병 중대, (*firm*) hoesa 회사(會社). *Thank you very much for your* ~. Sŏnsaenggwa ŏullige toeŏ kamsahamnida. 선생과 어울리게 되어 감사합니다/ *He sees no* ~. Kŭnŭn myŏnhoerŭl sajŏrhago issŭmnida. 그는 면회를 사절하고 있읍니다/ *a concert* ~ aktan 악단(樂團)/ *a* ~ *of foot* pobyŏng chungdae 보병 중대/ *a* ~ *employee* hoesawŏn 회사원/ *an export*〔*import*〕 ~ such'ul〔suip〕 hoesa 수출〔수입〕회사/ *a jointstock* ~ chushik hoesa 주식 회사/ *a steamship* ~ kisŏn hoesa 기선 회사/ *a transportation* ~ unsong hoesa 운송 회사.

comparatively *adv.* pigyojŏg(ŭro) 비교적(으로).

compare *vt.* pigyohada 비교하다. *C*~ *two translations.* Tu kaji pŏnyŏgŭl pigyohae poshipshio. 두 가지 번역을 비교해 보십시오/ *Mine cannot be* ~*d to yours.* Naegŏsŭn tangshin kŏse pigil paga mot toemnida. 내것은 당신 것에 비길 바가 못 됩니다.

comparison *n.* pigyo 비교. *Make a careful* ~ *of them.* Kŭdŭrŭl chal pigyohae poshio. 그들을 잘 비교해 보시오.

compass *n.* nach'imban 나침반, k'omp'ŏsŭ 콤퍼스.

compassion *n.* tongjŏng 동정.

compel *vt.* ŏkchiro shik'ida 억지로 시키다, kangyohada 강요하다. *Can they* ~ *obedience from us?* Uriege pokchongŭl kangyohal su issŭmnikka? 우리에게 복종을 강요할 수 있읍니까/ *I was* ~*led to do so.* Kŭrihaji anŭl su ŏpsŏssŭmnida. 그리하지 않을 수 없었음니다.

compensation *n.* posanggŭm 보상금, (*salary*) ponggŭp 봉급, posu 보수. *accident* ~ chaehae posang 재해(災害) 보상/ *a satisfactory* ~ manjoksŭrŏn posu 만족스런 보수.

compete *vi.* kyŏngjaenghada 경쟁하다, tat'uda 다투다.

competition *n.* kyŏngjaeng 경쟁, (*contest*) shihap 시합. ~ *in armament* kunbi hwakchang kyŏngjaeng 군비 확장 경쟁/ *a boxing* ~ kwŏnt'u shihap 권투 시합.

competitor *n.* kyŏngjaengja 경쟁자, (*rival*) kyŏngjaeng sangdae 경쟁 상대.

complain *vi.* pulp'yŏnghada 불평하다, hosohada 호소하다. *We have nothing to* ~ *of.* Urinŭn amugŏtto pulp'yonghal kŏshi ŏpsŭmnida. 우리는 아무것도 불평할 것이 없읍니다.

complaint *n.* pulp'yŏng 불평, (*accusation*) koso 고소(告訴). *Have you any ~s to make?* Musŭn pulmani issŭmnikka? 무슨 불만이 있읍니까/ *Why don't you lodge a ~ against your noisy neighbors?* Wae shikkŭrŏun iuttŭrŭl kobarhaji anssŭmnikka? 왜 시끄러운 이웃들을 고발하지 않습니까?

complete *adj.* (*perfect*) wanjŏnhan 완전한, (*finished*) wansŏngdoen 완성된. —*vt.* wansŏnghada 완성하다, kkŭnnaeda 끝내다. *a ~ stranger* chŏnhyŏ morŭnŭn saram 전혀 모르는 사람/ *When will the work be ~?* Irŭn ŏnje kkŭnnagessŭmnikka? 일은 언제 끝나겠읍니까/ *I've ~d my task.* Nanŭn irŭl kkŭnnaessŭmnida. 나는 일을 끝냈읍니다.

complexion *n.* ŏlgulpit 얼굴빛.

complicated *adj.* pokchap'an 복잡한. *a ~ machine* pokchap'an kigye 복잡한 기계/ *Life is so ~ you know.* Insaengiran nŏmudo pokchap'agŏdŭnyo. 인생이란 너무도 복잡하거든요.

compliment *n.*(*greetings*) insamal 인사말, (*praise*) ch'ansa 찬사. *Give my ~s to your father.* Abŏnimkke anbu malssŭm chŏnhae chushipshio. 아버님께 안부 말씀 전해 주십시오/ *Thank you for your ~.* Ch'ingch'anhae chusyŏsŏ kamsahamnida. 칭찬해 주셔서 감사합니다.

compose *vt.* chakkok'ada 작곡하다, (*make up*) chorip'ada 조립하다.

composer *n.* chakkokka 작곡가. *Mr. Hong Nan-pa was a famous ~.* Hong Nanp'assinŭn yumyŏnghan chakkokkayŏssŭmnida. 홍 난파씨는 유명한 작곡가였읍니다.

composition *n.* kusŏng 구성, changmun 작문, kudo 구도.

compound *adj.* uran 울안, kunae 구내.

comprehension *n.* ihae 이해(理解). *The problem is beyond my ~.* Narosŏnŭn kŭ munjerŭl ihaehal suga ŏpsŭmnida. 나로서는 그 문제를 이해할 수가 없읍니다.

compromise *n.* t'ahyŏp 타협, (*middle course*) chŏlch'ung 절충, (*concession*) yangbo 양보. —*vt.* t'ahyŏp'ada 타협하다.

comrade *n.* tongji 동지, tongmu 동무.

conceal *vt.* kamch'uda 감추다, sumgida 숨기다.

conceive *vi.* imshinhada 임신하다, (*form in mind*) (maŭme) p'umta (마음에) 품다. *Why have you ∼d such a dislike for me?* Wae narŭl kŭt'orok shirŏhae watchiyo? 왜 나를 그토록 싫어해 왔지요?

concentration *n.* chipchung 집중, (*absorption*) chimnyŏm 집념.

concern *n.* kwanshim 관심, (*firm*) hoesa 회사, (*relation*) kwan-gye 관계, (*importance*) chungyosŏng 중요성. *I have no ∼ in this business.* I ire nanŭn kwan-gye ŏpsŭmnida. 이 일에 나는 관계 없읍니다.

concerning *prep.* ...e kwanhayŏ ⋯에 관하여. *I don't know anything ∼ this matter.* I kŏne taehaesŏ nanŭn amugŏtto morŭmnida. 이 건(件)에 대해서 나는 아무것도 모릅니다.

concert *n.* ŭmak'oe 음악회, hapchu 합주, k'onsŏt'ŭ 콘서트. *I'm looking for the ∼ hall.* Nanŭn ŭmak'oejangŭl ch'atko issŭmnida. 나는 음악회장을 찾고 있읍니다.

concession *n.* yangbo 양보, (*grant*) myŏnhŏ 면허, (*privilege*) t'ŭkkwŏn 특권.

conclusion *n.* chonggyŏl 종결, (*decision*) kyŏlchŏng 결정, (*concluding remark*) kyŏllon 결론.

condemn *vt.* (*blame*) ch'aengmanghada 책망하다, (*sentence*) sŏn-gohada 선고하다. *The prisoner was ∼ed to death.* Choeinŭn sahyŏng sŏn-gorŭl padassŭmnida. 죄인은 사형 선고를 받았읍니다.

condition *n.* sangt'ae 상태, (*terms*) chokŏn 조건. *on ∼ that* chokŏnŭro 조건으로/ *without ∼* mujokŏnŭro 무조건으로/ *I'm in the best of my physical ∼.* Nanŭn aju choŭn kŏn-gang sangt'aee issŭmnida. 나는 아주 좋은 건강 상태에 있읍니다/ *critical ∼* wihŏm sangt'ae 위험 상태/ *On what ∼ will you agree?* Ŏttŏn chokŏnimyŏn ŭnghashigessŭmnikka? 어떤 조건이면 응하시겠읍니까?

condolence *n.* choŭi 조의(弔意), chosa 조사(弔詞). *Please accept my ∼s.* Samga choŭirŭl p'yohamnida. 삼가 조의를 표합니다/ *express one's ∼* choŭirŭl p'yohada 조의를 표하다/ *telegram of ∼* chojŏn 조전(弔電).

conduct *n.* haengwi 행위, p'umhaeng 품행. —*vt.,vi.* haeng-donghada 행동하다, (*direct*) chihwihada 지휘하다. *good* ~ sŏnhaeng 선행/*scandalous* ~ mangch'ŭk'an haengshil 망측한 행실/ ~ *an orchestra* kwanhyŏnaktanŭl chihwi-hada 관현악단을 지휘하다.

conductor *n.* chihwija 지휘자, (*of trains*) ch'ajang 차장. *C*~, *where is the berth?* Ch'ajang, ch'imdaenŭn ŏdi itchiyo? 차장, 침대는 어디 있지요?

conductress *n.* yŏch'ajang 여차장. *Show this to the* ~. Igŏsŭl pŏsŭ annaeyangege poyŏ chuseyo. 이것을 버스 안 내양에게 보여 주세요.

confectionery *n.* kwajajŏm 과자점, chegwajŏm 제과점.

conference *n.* hoeŭi 회의, (*consultation*) ŭinon 의논. *a peace* ~ p'yŏnghwa hoeŭi 평화 회의/ *hold a* ~ hoeŭirŭl yŏlda 회의를 열다/ *Mr. Kim is in* ~ *now.* Misŭt'ŏ Ki-mŭn chigŭm hoeŭi chungimnida. 미스터 김(金)은 지금 회의 중입니다.

confess *vt.,vi.* chabaek'ada 자백하다, shiinhada 시인하다. (*Cath.*) kohaehada 고해(告解)하다. *He* ~*ed that he had stolen the money.* Kŭnŭn tonŭl humch'yŏttago cha-baek'aessŭmnida. 그는 돈을 훔쳤다고 자백했읍니다/ ~ *to a crime[fault]* choe[shilsu]rŭl shiinhada 죄[실수]를 시인하다.

confidence *n.* shinyong 신용, (*assurance*) hwakshin 확신, (*private secret*) pimil 비밀. *self* ~ chashin 자신(自信). *I've no* ~ *in you.* Nanŭn tangshinŭl shinyonghaji an-ssŭmnida. 나는 당신을 신용하지 않습니다.

confidential *adj.* kŭkpiŭi 극비의, (*private*) sachŏgin 사적(私的)인.

confirm *vt.* hwaginhada 확인하다, (*verify*) hwakchŭng-hada 확증하다. *Please* ~ *your telephone message by letter.* Chŏnhwa naeyongŭl sŏmyŏnŭro ch'uinhae chu-shipshio. 전화 내용을 서면으로 추인해 주십시오.

confiscate *vt.* molsuhada 몰수하다, apsuhada 압수하다. *Police* ~*d the liquor.* Kyŏngch'arŭn churyurŭl apsu-haessŭmnida. 경찰은 주류(酒類)를 압수했읍니다.

conflict *n.* ssaum 싸움, (*disagreement*) ch'ungdol 충돌.

—*vi.* ch'ungdorhada 충돌하다, (*fight*) ssauda 싸우다. *a ~ between father and son* pujaganŭi allyŏk 부자간의 알력/ *a domestic ~* kajŏng purhwa 가정 불화. 「자 왈.

Confucius *n.* Kongja 공자. *C~ said…* Kongja wal …공

confusion *n.* hollan 혼란, hondon 혼돈.

congratulate *vt.* ch'uk'ahada 축하하다. *I ~ you on passing the examination.* Hapkyŏgŭl ch'uk'ahamnida. 합격을 축하합니다.

congress *n.* hoeŭi 회의, (*C~*) ŭihoe 의회. *hold a ~* hoeŭirŭl yŏlda 회의를 열다/ *a party ~* tang taehoe 당(黨) 대회.

congressman *n.* kuk'oe ŭiwŏn 국회 의원.

connect *vt.,vi.* itta 잇다, yŏn-gyŏrhada 연결하다, (*associate with*) yŏllak'ada 연락하다. *Please ~ me with the advertising department.* Kwanggoburo taeŏ chushipshio. 광고 부로 대어 주십시오/ *Are you ~ed with one of the companies?* Ŏnŭ hoesawa kwan-gyehago kyeshimnikka? 어 느 회사와 관계하고 계십니까?

connection *n.* kwan-gye 관계, (*junction*) yŏllak 연락, (*relative*) ch'inch'ŏk 친척.

connoisseur *n.* kamjŏngga 감정가, kamshikka 감식가. *a ~ of antique* koltongp'um kamshikka 골동품 감식가.

conquer *vt.* chŏngbok'ada 정복하다.

conscience *n.* yangshim 양심(良心). *in (all) ~* yangshime pich'uŏ 양심에 비추어/ *I can't in ~ do such a thing.* Yangshimsang kŭrŏn chisŭn mot hagessŭmnida. 양심상 그런 짓은 못 하겠읍니다.

conscription *n.* chingbyŏng 징병. *He escaped ~ because he was too short.* Kŭnŭn k'iga chaga chingbyŏngi myŏnjedoeŏssŭmnida. 그는 키가 작아 징병이 면제되었읍니다.

consent *vi.* tongŭihada 동의하다, sŭngnak'ada 승낙하다. *I can't ~ to what you ask.* Put'agŭl padadŭril suga ŏpsŭmnida. 부탁을 받아들일 수가 없읍니다/ *I ~ to it.* Kŭgōse tongŭihamnida. 그것에 동의합니다.

consequence *n.* kyŏlgwa 결과, (*importance*) chungdae 중대(重大). *terrible ~* musŏun kyŏlgwa 무서운 결과/ *bring grave ~s* chungdaehan kyŏlgwarŭl kajyŏoda 중 대한 결과를 가져오다/ *a matter of ~* chungdae sakŏn 중

대 사전/ *people of* ~ chungyo inmul 중요 인물.

consequently *adv.* ttarasŏ 따라서.

consider *vt.* saenggak'ada 생각하다, (*contemplate*) koch'arhada 고찰하다, (*regard as*) kanjuhada 간주하다. *Please* ~ *my suggestion.* Naŭi cheanŭl koryŏhae chushipshio. 나의 제안을 고려해 주십시오/ ~ *coolly* naengjŏnghi saenggak'ada 냉정히 생각하다/ *I* ~*ed him to be a gentleman.* Nanŭn kŭrŭl shinsarago saenggak'aessŭmnida. 나는 그를 신사라고 생각했읍니다.

consideration *n.* koryŏ 고려, (*thoughtfulness*) tongjŏng 동정, (*importance*) chungyosŏng 중요성, (*reward*) posu 보수. *in* ~ *of* ch'amjak'ayŏ 참작하여/ *under* ~ koryŏ chung 고려 중/ *We have given a careful* ~ *to the point.* Kŭ chŏme taehaesŏnŭn ch'ungbunhi koryŏhaessŭmnida. 그 점에 대해서는 충분히 고려했읍니다.

consignment *n.* wit'ak hwamul 위탁 화물. ~ *goods* wit'ak p'anmaep'um 위탁 판매품/ ~ *sale* wit'ak p'anmae 위탁 판매.

conspicuous *adj.* nune chal ttŭinŭn 눈에 잘 띄는, (*remarkable*) chŏmyŏnghan 저명한. *Traffic signs should be* ~. Kyot'ong p'yojinŭn nune chal ttŭiŏya hamnida. 교통 표지는 눈에 잘 띄어야 합니다.

conspiracy *n.* ŭmmo 음모, kongmo 공모. *form a* ~ *against* ŭmmorŭl kkumida 음모를 꾸미다.

conspirator *n.* kongmoja 공모자, ŭmmoja 음모자.

conspire *vi.* kongmohada 공모하다, kyŏlt'ak'ada 결탁하다.

constant *adj.* pyŏnch'i annŭn 변치 않는, pudanhan 부단한.

constitution *n.* hŏnpŏp 헌법, (*physical structure*) ch'egyŏk 체격. *the* ~ *of the Republic of Korea* Taehanmin-guk hŏnpŏp 대한민국 헌법 / *a poor* ~ pinyak'an ch'egyŏk 빈약한 체격/ *It doesn't suit my* ~. Kŭgŏsŭn nae ch'ejire matchi anssŭmnida. 그것은 내 체질에 맞지 않습니다.

construct *vt.* (*erect*) seuda 세우다, (*build*) kŏnsŏrhada 건설하다, (*devise*) kusŏnghada 구성하다.

construction *n.* kŏnch'uk 건축, (*building*) kŏnmul 건물. *be under* ~ kŏnsŏl chungida 건설 중이다. *The temple is* *the most well-known* ~ *in orient.* Kŭ chŏrŭn tongyang-esŏ kajang irŭmnan kŏnch'ungmurimnida. 그 절은 동양에서 가장 이름난 건축물입니다.

consul *n.* yŏngsa 영사(領事). ~ *general* ch'ongyŏngsa 총영사. *She is Mrs. Kim, wife of the Korean* ~ *at Manila.* Kŭnyŏnŭn misesŭ Kimiranŭn saraminde, Manilla chujae Kim yŏngsaŭi puinimnida. 그녀는 미세스 김이라는 사람인데, 마닐라 주재 김 영사의 부인입니다.

consulate *n.* yŏngsagwan 영사관. ~ *general* ch'ongyŏngsagwan 총영사관.

consult *vt.* ŭigyŏnŭl mutta 의견을 묻다, (*refer to*) ch'amgohada 참고하다. —*vi.* ŭinonhada 의논하다. ~ *a doctor* ŭisaŭi chindanŭl patta 의사의 진단을 받다/ ~ *a dictionary* sajŏnŭl ch'atta 사전을 찾다 / *You can* ~ *about a job at the department of student affairs.* Haksaengkwa-esŏ chigŏbe kwanhan sangŭirŭl hal su issŭmnida. 학생과에서 직업에 관한 상의를 할 수 있읍니다.

consultant *n.* komun 고문, (*medical*) komun ŭisa 고문의사. *an engineering* ~ kisul komun 기술 고문.

consultation *n.* ŭinon 의논, sangdam 상담, (*medical*) chinch'al 진찰. *a family* ~ kajŏng sangdam 가정 상담/ *How much do you charge for a* ~? Chinch'allyonŭn irhoee ŏlmaimnikka? 진찰료는 1회에 얼마입니까/ ~ *fee* chinch'allyo 진찰료.

consumption *n.* sobi 소비, (*disease*) p'yepyŏng 폐병.

contact *vt.* yŏllagŭl ch'wihada 연락을 취하다. *Would you please* ~ *me?* Yŏllak'ae chushigessŭmnikka? 연락해 주시겠읍니까/ *Is there any way we can* ~ *to later?* Najunge yŏllaktŭril kiri itkessŭmnikka? 나중에 연락드릴 길이 있겠읍니까?

contagious *adj.* chŏnyŏmsŏngŭi 전염성의, (*catching*) omki shwiun 옮기 쉬운. *a* ~ *disease* chŏnyŏmpyŏng 전염병/ *Scarlet fever is* ~. Sŏnghongyŏrŭn chŏnyŏmhamnida. 성홍열은 전염합니다.

contain *vt.* p'ohamhada 포함하다, (*restrain*) nurŭda 누르다. *What does this box* ~? I sangja-enŭn muŏshi tŭrŏ issŭmnikka? 이 상자에는 무엇이 들어 있읍니까/ *How* *much does this bottle* ~ *?* I pyŏngŭn ŏlma tŭriimnikka? 이 병은 얼마 들이입니까/ *Can't you* ~ *your enthusiasm?* Yŏlchŏngŭl ŏngnurŭl su ŏptan marimnikka? 열정을 억누를 수 없단 말입니까?

contempt *n.* myŏlshi 멸시, kyŏngmyŏl 경멸, (*disgrace*) ch'iyok 치욕, moyok 모욕. *have[feel] a* ~ *for* ...ŭl kyŏngmyŏrhada ···을 경멸하다/ *in* ~ *of* ...ŭl mushihago ···을 무시하고.

content *n.* manjok 만족. —*adj.* manjok'an 만족한. *Are you* ~ *with your present salary?* Hyŏnjaeŭi ponggŭbe manjok'ashimnikka? 현재의 봉급에 만족하십니까?

contents *n.* naeyong 내용, (*of book*) mokch'a 목차.

contest *n.* kyŏngjaeng 경쟁. *a beauty* ~ miin taehoe 미인대회/ *a career* ~ ch'wijik shihŏm 취직 시험.

continent *n.* taeryuk 대륙.

continue *vt.* kyesok'ada 계속하다. —*vi.* kyesoktoeda 계속되다. *How far does this road* ~ *?* I kirŭn ŏlmana tŏ kyesoktoemnikka? 이 길은 얼마나 더 계속됩니까?

contract *n.* kyeyak 계약. —*vt.* kyeyak'ada 계약하다, (*enter into*) maetta 맺다, (*catch*) kŏllida 걸리다, (*shorten*) churida 줄이다. *cancel a* ~ kyeyagŭl haejehada 계약을 해제하다. *"I will" is* ~*ed to "I'll."* Ai wirŭn aillo tanch'uktoemnida. 아이 윌은 아일로 단축됩니다.

contradict *vt.* panbak'aha 반박하다, sangbanhada 상반하다. *Don't* ~ *me.* Nae marŭl panbak'aji mashio. 내 말을 반박하지 마시오.

contradiction *n.* panbak 반박, (*inconsistency*) mosun 모순. *There is much* ~ *in what you say.* Tangshinŭi marenŭn mosuni manssŭmnida. 당신의 말에는 모순이 많습니다.

contrary *adj.* pandaeŭi 반대의. —*n.* pandae 반대. *on the* ~ iwa pandaero 이와 반대로/ ~ *to one's expectation* yesanggwanŭn pandaero 예상과는 반대로.

contribute *vt.* (*subscribe*) kibuhada 기부하다, (*for newspapers*) kigohada 기고하다. —*vi.* (*assist*) topta 돕다, (*conduce*) konghŏnhada 공헌하다.

contribution *n.* kigo 기고, (*donation*) kibu 기부, (*service*) konghŏn 공헌.

control *n.* chibae 지배, (*restraint*) ŏkche 억제, (*management*) kwalli 관리. —*vt.*(*command*) ŏkchehada 억제하다, (*manage*) kwallihada 관리하다. *I got ~ of the factory.* Nanŭn kŭ kongjangŭl kwallihage toeŏssŭmnida. 나는 그 공장을 관리하게 되었읍니다.

convenient *adj.* p'yŏllihan 편리한, (*at hand*) sonshwiun 손쉬운. *What time should it be ~ for you?* Myŏt shiga p'yŏllihashimnikka? 몇 시가 편리하십니까/ *If it is ~ for you, would you please teach me English every Monday afternoon?* Hyŏngp'yŏni choŭshidamyŏn, mae wŏryoil ohue yŏngŏrŭl karŭch'yŏ chushigessŭmnikka? 형편이 좋으시다면, 매 월요일 오후에 영어를 가르쳐 주시겠읍니까?

convent *n.* sudowŏn 수도원.

conversation *n.* hoehwa 회화, taehwa 대화. *I'd like to study Korean ~.* Han-gugŏ hoehwarŭl paeugo shipsŭmnida. 한국어 회화를 배우고 싶습니다/ *I studied English at a ~ school.* Hoehwa hagwŏnesŏ yŏngŏrŭl paewŏssŭmnida. 회화 학원에서 영어를 배웠읍니다/ *I've enjoyed our ~.* Uri taehwanŭn chŭlgŏwŏssŭmnida. 우리 대화는 즐거웠읍니다.

convert *vt.* pakkuda 바꾸다, (*religion*) kaejonghada 개종하다. *~ a bedroom into sitting room* ch'imshirŭl kŏshillo pakkuda 침실을 거실로 바꾸다/ *~ people to Christianity* kidokkyoro kaejongshik'ida 기독교로 개종시키다.

convey *vt.* narŭda 나르다, unbanhada 운반하다.

convince *vt.* naptŭkshik'ida 납득시키다, ...ŭl mitke hada …을 믿게 하다.

cook *n.* yorisa 요리사, k'uk 쿡. —*vt.* yorihada 요리하다. *Do you know how to ~ Korean food?* Han-guk yorirŭl mandŭl chul ashimnikka? 한국 요리를 만들 줄 아십니까?

cool *adj.* sŏnŭrhan 서늘한, shiwŏnhan 시원한, (*unexcited*) ch'imch'ak'an 침착한, (*indifferent*) naengdamhan 냉담한. *This soup is not ~ enough to eat.* I sup'ŭnŭn mashigienŭn ajik tŏl shigŏssŭmnida. 이 수프는 마시기에는 아직 덜 식었읍니다/ *C~ off. Don't get mad, please.* Ch'imch'ak'ashipshio. Nŏmu hŭngbunhaji mashigo. 침착하십시오. 너무 흥분하지 마시고/ *They gave him a ~*

reception. Kŭdŭrŭn kŭrŭl naengdaehaessŭmnida. 그들
은 그를 냉대했읍니다.

cooperate *vi.* hyŏmnyŏk'ada 협력하다, (*contribute*) sŏro-
topta 서로 돕다.

cooperation *n.* hyŏmnyŏk 협력.

cooperative society sobi chohap 소비 조합.

copper *n.* kuri 구리, tong 동(銅). *a ~ coin* tongjŏn 동전/
a ~ medal tongmedal 동메달.

copy *n.* sabon 사본, (*photo*) poksa 복사, (*of picture*) mosa
모사, (*of book*) kwon 권(卷), pu 부(部). *—vt.* pekkida
베끼다, poksahada 복사하다. *We need a ~ of your family
register*. Tangshinŭi hojŏk tŭngboni p'iryohamnida. 당
신의 호적 등본이 필요합니다/ *Would you please ~ this
sentence in your notebook?* I munjangŭl not'ŭe pekki-
shipshio. 이 문장을 노트에 베끼십시오.

copyright *n.* p'ankwŏn 판권. *hold the ~ of* ...ŭi p'an-
kwŏnŭl soyuhada ···의 판권을 소유하다.

coral *n.* sanho 산호.

cord *n.* kkŭn 끈, (*small rope*) patchul 밧줄, k'odŭ 코드,
(*electr.*) chŏndŭngchul 전등줄. *vocal ~* sŏngdae 성대.

core *n.* sok 속, (*pith*) haekshim 핵심. *the ~ of a pear*
pae sok 배[梨] 속. 「크 마개」

cork *n.* k'orŭk'ŭ 코르크, (*stopper*) k'orŭk'ŭ magae 코르

corkscrew *n.* magaeppobi 마개뽑이.

corn *n.* oksusu 옥수수, (*callous*) mot 못, t'inun 티눈. *Could
I have some ~ plasters, please*. T'inunyagŭl chushipshio. 티눈약을 주십시오.

corner *n.* mot'ungi 모퉁이, (*nook*) kusŏk 구석. *Meet me
at the ~ of the street*. Kilmot'ungiesŏ mannapshida. 길
모퉁이에서 만납시다.

corporal *n.* (*mil.*) hasa 하사. *—adj.* shinch'eŭi 신체의.

corpse *n.* shich'e 시체, (*dead body*) songjang 송장.

correct *adj.* olbarŭn 올바른, (*exact*) chŏnghwak'an 정확
한, (*proper*) chŏktanghan 적당한. *—vt.* koch'ida 고치다,
sujŏnghada 수정하다. *Would you mind ~ing this
English letter?* I yŏngmun p'yŏnji chom koch'yŏ chushigessŭmnikka? 이 영문 편지 좀 고쳐 주시겠읍니까?

correspond *vi.* sŏshin wangnaerŭl hada 서신 왕래를 하다, (*agree*) ilch'ihada 일치하다.

correspondence *n.* t'ongshin 통신. ~ *course* t'ongshin kyoyuk 통신 교육/ ~ *department* munsŏkwa 문서과.

correspondent *n.* t'ongshinwŏn 통신원. *a special* ~ t'ŭkp'awŏn 특파원/ *a war* ~ chonggun kija 종군 기자.

corruption *n.* t'arak 타락, pup'ae 부패.

cosmetic *n.* hwajangp'um 화장품. *Where is the* ~ *section?* Hwajangp'umbunŭn ŏdiimnikka? 화장품부는 어디입니까?

cosmopolitan *n.* segyein 세계인, segyejuŭija 세계주의자.

cost *n.* (*price*) kap 값, kagyŏk 가격, (*expense*) piyong 비용. —*vt.* tŭlda 들다, ch'iida 치이다. *the* ~ *of living* saenghwalbi 생활비/ *production* ~s saengsanbi 생산비/ *How much does it* ~ *for cleaning?* Tangnŭnde ŏlmajiyo? 닦는데 얼마지요/ *Does it* ~ *much?* Pissage ch'iimnikka? 비싸게 치입니까/ *It* ~s *me too much.* Nŏmu pissamnida. 너무 비쌉니다/ *I don't know how much it'll* ~. Ŏlma tŭlchi morŭgessŭmnida. 얼마 들지 모르겠읍니다.

costume *n.* otch'arim 옷차림, pokchang 복장. *Korean* ~ *is very elegant.* Hanbogŭn chŏngmal uahagunyo. 한복은 정말 우아하군요.

cottage *n.* odumakchip 오두막집, (*vacation resort*) hyuyangji 휴양지.

cotton *n.* som 솜, mumyŏng 무명. ~ *cloth* myŏnp'o 면포/ ~ *thread* mumyŏngshil 무명실/ *sanitary* ~ t'alchimyŏn 탈지면/ ~ *plant* mok'wa 목화.

cough *n.* kich'im 기침. —*vi.* kich'imhada 기침하다. *a dry* ~ marŭn kich'im 마른 기침/ *a* ~ *medicine* kich'imnyak 기침약/ *I've had a slight* ~ *lately.* Yojŭm kich'imi chogŭm naomnida. 요즘 기침이 조금 나옵니다/ *Who is* ~*ing?* Nuga kich'imŭl hajiyo? 누가 기침을 하지요?

council *n.* hyŏbŭihoe 협의회, hoe 회(會). *family* ~ kajokhoeŭi 가족 회의/ ~ *room* hoeŭishil 회의실.

counselor *n.* komun 고문, choŏnja 조언자, (*embassy*) pŏmmugwan 법무관.

count *vt.* kyesanhada 계산하다, (*rely on*) ŭijihada 의지하다. —*n.* paekchak 백작. *Did you* ~ *the broken one?* Kkaejin kŏtto kyesane nŏŏssŭmnikka? 깨진 것도 계산에 넣었읍니까/ *Can you ~ to fifteen in Chinese?* Chunggung-mallo yŏl tasŏtkkaji sel su issŭmnikka? 중국말로 열 다섯까지 셀 수 있읍니까/ *You must not ~ upon me.* Narŭl kidaehaji mashipshio. 나를 기대하지 마십시오.

counter *n.* kyesandae 계산대, (*in a shop*) p'anmaedae 판매대. *You will find the camera ~ to the right as you get off.* Naerishimyŏn paro orŭntchoge k'amerabuga issŭmnida. 내리시면 바로 오른쪽에 카메라부(部)가 있읍니다.

counterfeit *adj.* wijoŭi 위조의, katchaŭi 가짜의. —*n.* katcha 가짜. —*vt.* wijohada 위조하다. *a ~ note* wijo chip'ye 위조 지폐 / *~ illness* kkoebyŏng 꾀병 / *This one thousand bill is a ~.* I ch'ŏnwŏntchari chip'yenŭn katchaimnida. 이 1,000원짜리 지폐는 가짜입니다.

country *n.* shigol 시골, (*nation*) nara 나라. *~ life* chŏnwŏn saenghwal 전원 생활/ *~ road* shigolgil 시골길/ *Do you like ~ life?* Chŏnwŏn saenghwarŭl choahashimnikka? 전원 생활을 좋아하십니까/ *My native ~ is Korea.* Naŭi chogugŭn Han-gugimnida. 나의 조국은 한국입니다.

countryman *n.* shigol saram 시골 사람, ch'onttŭgi 촌뜨기, (*compatriot*) hangohyang saram 한고향 사람.

couple *n.* tul 둘, (*pair*) han ssang 한 쌍, (*of people*) tu saram 두 사람, (*of animals*) tu mari 두 마리, (*of days*) it'ŭl 이틀, (*husband and wife*) pubu 부부. *They are a happy ~.* Kŭdŭrŭn haengbok'an pubuimnida. 그들은 행복한 부부입니다. ⌜hoesukwŏn 회수권.

coupon *n.* k'up'on 쿠폰, harinkwŏn 할인권. *~ ticket*

courage *n.* yonggi 용기. *develop ~* yonggirŭl kirŭda 용기를 기르다/ *reckless ~* mumohan yonggi 무모한 용기/ *Don't lose ~.* Yonggirŭl ilch'i mashio. 용기를 잃지 마시오.

course *n.* (*progress*) chinhaeng 진행, (*duration*) kwajŏng 과정, (*track*) nojŏng 노정(路程), (*line of action*) pangch'im 방침. *Bring us the next course, please.* Taŭm yorirŭl kajyŏda chushio. 다음 요리(料理)를 가져다 주시오/ *Take whatever ~ you think best.* Kajang chot'ago saenggaktoenŭn pangbŏbŭl ch'wihashio. 가장 좋다고 생각

되는 방법을 취하시오/ *of* ~ mullon 물론.

court *n.* (*yard*) madang 마당, ttŭl 뜰, (*law* ~) chaep'anso 재판소. *Which do you prefer for tennis, grass* ~*s or hard* ~*s?* Chŏnggu ch'inŭndenŭn chandi kujanggwa tandanhan kujangŭi ŏnŭ tchogi chŏssŭmnikka? 정구 치는데는 잔디 구장과 단단한 구장의 어느 쪽이 좋습니까?

courtesy *n.* (*politeness*) kongson 공손, (*favor*) hoŭi 호의.

cousin *n.* sach'on 사촌, chonghyŏngje 종형제. *second* ~*s* chaejong 재종, yukch'on 육촌.

cover *vt.* tŏpta 덮다, karida 가리다, (*extend over*) mich'ida 미치다. —*n.* ttukkŏng 뚜껑, tŏpkae 덮개. *C*~ *the table with a cloth.* T'eibŭre porŭl ssŭiushio. 테이블에 보를 씌우시오/ *When the water boils, take the* ~ *from the pan.* Muri kkŭlk'ŏdŭn nambittukkŏngŭl yŏshio. 물이 끓거든 남비뚜껑을 여시오.

cow *n.* amso 암소. *a milking* ~ chŏsso 젖소.

coward *n.* kŏpchangi 겁쟁이. —*adj.* kŏmmanŭn 겁많은, pigŏp'an 비겁한.

cowboy *n.* moktong 목동, k'auboi 카우보이.

cowpox *n.* (*med.*) udu 우두, chongdu 종두.

cozy *adj.* p'ogŭnhan 포근한, anŭk'an 아늑한, (*comfortable*) kibun joŭn 기분 좋은.

crab *n.* ke 게. *canned* ~ ke t'ongjorim 게 통조림.

crack *n.* kallajin kŭm 갈라진 금, (*chink*) t'ŭm 틈, (*shot*) palsa 발사, ch'alssak 찰싹. —*vi.* kkaejida 깨지다. —*vt.* pusuda 부수다. *There are dangerous* ~*s in the ice.* Pingp'ani kallajyŏ wihŏmhada. 빙판이 갈라져 위험하다/ *The dish* ~*ed.* Chŏpshiga kkaejyŏssŭmnida. 접시가 깨졌읍니다.

cradle *n.* yoram 요람, (*place of origin*) palsangji 발상지.

craftman *n.* kinŭnggong 기능공, changin 장인(匠人).

crane *n.* (*bird*) turumi 두루미, hak 학, (*a hoist*) kijunggi 기중기.

crash *n.* (*sound*) yoranhan sori 요란한 소리, (*collision*) ch'ungdol 충돌, (*ruin*) p'amyŏl 파멸, p'asan 파산(破産). —*vi.* pusŏjida 부서지다, munŏjida 무너지다, ch'ungdorhada 충돌하다.

crawl *vi.* kida 기다, kiŏgada 기어가다. ~ *on the belly*

paerŭl kkalgo kida 배를 깔고 기다.

crayon *n.* saengyŏnp'il 색연필, kŭreyong 크레용.

crazy *adj.* mich'in 미친. ~ *about* yŏlchunghanŭn 열중하는.
I'm ~ about cool jazz. K'ul chaejŭrŭl mopshi choahamnida. 쿨 재즈를 몹시 좋아합니다/ *You're ~ about
your wife.* Tangshinŭn anaeege holttak panhae itkunyo. 당신은 아내에게 홀딱 반해 있군요.

cream *n.* k'ŭrim 크림, yuji 유지(油脂). *With ~ and sugar?* K'ŭrimgwa sŏlt'angŭl nŏulkkayo? 크림과 설탕을 넣
을까요/ *How long will these ~ puffs keep?* I syu-
k'ŭrimŭn ŏlma tonganina tuŏdul su issŭmnikka? 이 슈
크림은 얼마 동안이나 두어둘 수 있읍니까?

create *vt.* ch'angjohada 창조하다, (*establish*) sŏllip'ada 설
립하다, (*cause*) irŭk'ida 일으키다.

creation *n.* ch'angjomul 창조물, ch'angsŏl 창설. *the ~ of
artists* yesulgadŭrŭi ch'angjangmul 예술가들의 창작물/
the latest Paris ~ P'ariŭi ch'oeshinhyŏng 파리의 최신형.

credential *n.* (*pl.*) shinimchang 신임장.

credit *n.* shinyong 신용, shinyong taebu 신용 대부, (*on ~*)
oesangŭro 외상으로. *You will lose your ~.* Tangshinŭn
shinyongŭl ilk'o mal kŏshimnida. 당신은 신용을 잃고 말 것
입니다/ *Please open a ~ in my favor.* Na-ege k'ŭre-
dit'ŭrŭl sŏlchŏnghae chuseyo. 나에게 크레디트를 설정해 주
세요/ *Can I buy this watch on ~?* I shigyerŭl oesangŭro
sal su issŭmnikka? 이 시계를 외상으로 살 수 있읍니까?

creditor *n.* ch'aetkwŏnja 채권자.

creep *vi.* kida 기다, salgŭmsalgŭm naagada 살금살금 나
아가다. —*n.* p'opok 포복, sŏhaeng 서행(徐行).

crescent *n.* (*a new moon*) ch'osŭngtal 초승달.

crest *n.* (*on animals' head*) pyŏt 벗, togamŏri 도가머리.

cricket *n.* kwitturami 귀뚜라미.

crime *n.* choe 죄, pŏmjoe 범죄. *commit a ~* choerŭl
pŏmhada 죄를 범하다.

criminal *n.* pŏmin 범인, choein 죄인. *a habitual ~* sangsŭppŏm 상습범/ ~ *court* hyŏngsa chaep'anso 형사 재판소.

crimson *n.* chinhongsaek 진홍색, tahong 다홍.

cripple *n.* chŏllŭmbari 절름발이, (*deformed*) pulguja 불구

자. *a* ~*d soldier* sangigunin 상이군인.

crisis *n.* wigi 위기, (*turning point*) kobi 고비. *financial* ~ kyŏngjejŏk wigi 경제적 위기 / *political* ~ chŏngch'ijŏk wigi 정치적 위기.

crisp *adj.* pasakpasak'an 바삭바삭한, (*of hair*) kopsŭlgopsŭrhan 곱슬곱슬한. *a* ~ *biscuit* pasakpasak'an pisŭk'it 바삭바삭한 비스킷.

critic *n.* pip'yŏngga 비평가, p'yŏngnon-ga 평론가. *an art* ~ misul pip'yŏngga 미술 비평가.

criticism *n.* pip'yŏng 비평, p'yŏngnon 평론.

criticize *vi.,vt.* pip'yonghada 비평하다.

crochet *n.* ttŭgaejil 뜨개질. *a* ~ *hook* k'obanŭl 코바늘.

crocodile *n.* agŏ 악어.

crooked *adj.* kuburŏjin 구부러진, (*not straight*) pitturŏjin 비뚤어진, (*dishonest*) pujŏngjik'an 부정직한. *You have got your hat on* ~. Mojaga pitturŏjyŏssŭmnida. 모자가 비뚤어졌읍니다.

crop *n.* suhwak 수확, (*harvest*) ch'usu 추수. *an abundant* ~ p'ungjak 풍작 / *a poor* ~ hyungjak 흉작 / *a rice* ~ ssallongsa 쌀농사.

cross *n.* shipchaga 십자가. —*vi.,vt.* kŏnnŏgada 건너가다, hoengdanhada 횡단하다. —*adj.* karoŭi 가로의. *Red C* ~ *Society* chŏkshipchasa 적십자사 / *Keep walking straight till you pass three* ~ *streets.* Negŏrirŭl set chinal ttaekkaji kotchang kŏrŏgashio. 네거리를 셋 지날 때까지 곧장 걸어가시오 / ~ *out* [*off*] chiuda 지우다 / ~ *one's name off* irŭmŭl chiuda 이름을 지우다.

crossroad *n.* shipcharo 십자로, negŏri 네거리. *We came to the* ~*s.* Urinŭn negŏriro nawassŭmnida. 우리는 네거리로 나왔읍니다.

crow *n.* kkamagwi 까마귀.

crowd *n.* kunjung 군중. —*vi.,vt.* moida 모이다, pumbida 붐비다. *It's lucky that the streets are not so* ~*ed.* Tahaenghi kŏrinŭn kŭdaji pumbiji ank'unyo. 다행히 거리는 그다지 붐비지 않군요 / *We* ~*ed round her with congratulations.* Urinŭn ch'uk'ahagi wihae kŭnyŏŭi chuwie moyŏdŭrŏssŭmnida. 우리는 축하하기 위해 그녀의 주위

에 모여들었읍니다.

crown *n.* wanggwan 왕관, *(top)* kkoktaegi 꼭대기. *the ～ of the head* mŏri kkoktaegi 머리 꼭대기.

cruel *adj.* chaninhan 잔인한. *a ～ master* chaninhan chuin 잔인한 주인.

crusade *n.* shipchagun 십자군, *(campaign)* hyŏkshin un-dong 혁신 운동. *a ～ against bribery* noemul paegyŏk undong 뇌물 배격 운동.

crush *vi.,vt.* tchigŭrŏttŭrida 찌그러뜨리다, *(squeeze)* ap-ch'ak'ada 압착하다, *(overwhelm)* aptohada 압도하다. *A Korean women's basketball team ～ed the Indonesian team by 80 : 62.* Han-guk yŏja nonggu t'imŭn Indone-shia t'imŭl p'alshiptae yukshibiro kyŏkp'ahaessŭmnida. 한국 여자 농구 팀은 인도네시아 팀을 80 대 62로 격파했읍니다.

crutch *n.* mokpal 목발, moktari 목다리. *I can probably get around on ～es.* Mokparŭl chipko kŏnil su issŭmnida. 목발을 짚고 거닐 수 있읍니다.

cry *n.* *(shout)* koham 고함, *(wailing)* ulbujijŭm 울부짖음. —*vi.* sorich'ida 소리치다, *(weep)* ulda 울다. *"Help ! Help !" he cried.* 「Saram sallyŏ ! Saram sallyŏ !」 hago kŭnŭn oech'yŏssŭmnida. 「사람 살려 ! 사람 살려 !」하고 그는 외쳤읍니다/ *"There, there ! Don't ～ !"* 「Cha, cha ulji marara !」「가, 자, 울지 말아라 !」

crystal *n.* sujŏng 수정.

cuckoo *n.* ppŏkkugi 뻐꾸기. *In the deep woods we listened to the ～s and larks.* Kip'ŭn supsogesŏ urinŭn ppŏkku-giwa chongdalsae urum sorirŭl tŭrŏssŭmnida. 깊은 숲속에서 우리는 뻐꾸기와 종달새 울음 소리를 들었읍니다.

cucumber *n.* oi 오이.

cue *n.* tangguch'ae 당구채, k'yu 큐.

cuff *n.* somaetpuri 소맷부리, *(of shirt)* k'ŏp'ŭsŭ 커프스. *I've lost one of my ～ links.* Hantchok k'ŏp'ŭsŭ tanch'urŭl irŏbŏryŏssŭmnida. 한쪽 커프스 단추를 잃어버렸읍니다.

cult *n.* *(rite)* ŭishik 의식, *(worship)* sungbae 숭배, *(devo-tion)* hŏnshin 헌신.

cultivate *vt.* kyŏngjak'ada 경작하다, *(grow)* kirŭda 기르

다, (*enlighten*) kyohwahada 교화하다.

culture *n.* (*civilization*) munhwa 문화, (*refinement*) kyo-yang 교양, (*cultivation*) chaebae 재배. —*vt.* chaebaehada 재배하다, yangshik'ada 양식하다. *Do you want to see natural pearls or ~d pearls?* Ch'ŏnyŏn chinjurŭl po-shigessŭmnikka, yangshik chinjurŭl poshigessŭmnikka? 천연 진주를 보시겠읍니까, 양식(養殖) 진주를 보시겠읍니까?

cunning *adj.* kyohwarhan 교활한, kansahan 간사한. *a ~ trick* kangye 간계(奸計).

cup *n.* chan 잔, k'ŏp 컵. *challenge ~* usŭngk'ŏp 우승컵. *I wish a ~ of tea.* Ch'a han chan chuseyo. 차 한 잔 주세요.

cupboard *n.* ch'anchang 찬장.

cure *n.* ch'iyu 치유, (*healing*) hoebok 회복. —*vi.,vt.*(*heal*) ch'iryohada 치료하다, natta 낫다. *What is the best ~ for a cough?* Kamgiŭi myoyagŭn muŏshijiyo? 감기의 묘약은 무엇이지요?

curio *n.* koltongp'um 골동품. *Where can I see Korean ~s?* Ŏdisŏ Han-guk koltongp'umŭl pol su issŭmnikka? 어디서 한국 골동품을 볼 수 있읍니까/ *In Insadong street, you can find many ~ shops.* Insadong kŏriesŏ manŭn koltongp'um sangjŏmŭl palgyŏnhal suga issŭmnida. 인사동(仁寺洞) 거리에서 많은 골동품 상점을 발견할 수가 있읍니다.

curiosity *n.* hogishim 호기심. *~ shop* koltongp'umjŏm 골동품점.

curious *adj.* (*strange*) isanghan 이상한, (*inquisitive*) ho-gishimi kanghan 호기심이 강한. *I'm ~ to know.* Nanŭn algo shipsŭmnida. 나는 알고 싶습니다/*Don't ask so many ~ questions.* Hogishime ch'an chilmunŭl kŭrŏk'e mani haji mashio. 호기심에 찬 질문을 그렇게 많이 하지 마시오.

curl *n.* (*of hair*) kosumŏri 고수머리, k'ŏl 컬. *How do you keep your hair in ~?* K'ŏrhan mŏriga ŏttŏk'e ha-myŏn an p'urŏjinŭnjiyo? 컬한 머리가 어떻게 하면 안 풀어지는지요?

currency *n.* t'onghwa 통화, (*vogue*) yuhaeng 유행. *gold ~* kŭmhwa 금화/ *paper ~* chip'ye 지폐/ *occupation ~*

kunp'yo 군표(軍票).

current adj. yut'ongdoenŭn 유통되는, t'onghwaŭi 통화의, (present) hyŏnjaeŭi 현재의. —n. (flow) hŭrŭm 흐름, (tendency) p'ungjo 풍조. the ~ month idal 이달/ ~ English shisa Yŏngŏ 시사 영어/ the ~ price shika 시가 (時價), shise 시세.

current account tangjwa kyejŏng 당좌 계정, pot'ong ye-gŭm 보통 예금. Is yours a ~ or a fixed account? po-t'ong yegŭmimnikka, animyŏn chŏnggi yegŭmimnikka? 보통 예금입니까, 아니면 정기 예금입니까?

curtain n. k'ŏt'ŭn 커튼, (in theatre) mak 막. Those are new ~s, aren't they? Igŏn sae k'ŏt'ŭni aniyeyo? 이건 새 커튼이 아니예요/ At what time does the ~ rise? Myŏt shie yŏn-gŭgi shijaktoemnikka? 몇 시에 연극이 시 작됩니까?

curve n. koksŏn 곡선. —vi.,vt. kuburŏjida 구부러지다.

cushion n. pangsŏk 방석, k'usyŏn 쿠션, (pillow) pegae 베개. Here's a ~ for you. I pangsŏge anjŭshipshio. 이 방석에 앉으십시오.

custody n. pogwan 보관, poho 보호, (imprisonment) kamgŭm 감금, kuryu 구류.

custom n. sŭpkwan 습관, p'ungsŭp 풍습. I thought this was an Korean ~. Yerobut'ŏŭi Han-guk p'ungsogin chul arassŭmnida. 예로부터의 한국 풍속인 줄 알았읍니다/ ~ house segwan 세관.

customer n. sonnim 손님, kogaek 고객, (patron) kŏraech'ŏ 거래처. I'm just a ~. Nado sonnimŭi han saramieyo. 나도 손님의 한 사람이에요.

cut vi.,vt. charŭda 자르다, kkŭnt'a 끊다, (curtail) sak-kamhada 삭감하다, (absent) kyŏlsŏk'ada 결석하다. C~ it short, please. Kandanhi marhae chuseyo. 간단히 말해 주세요/ I have ~ my finger. Sonkaragŭl peŏssŭmnida. 손가락을 베었읍니다/ Can you ~ it down to nine hun-dred won? Kubaegwŏnŭro kkakka chuji ank'essŏyo? 900 원으로 깎아 주지 않겠어요?

cute adj. kwiyŏun 귀여운. a ~ little girl kwiyŏun sonyŏ 귀여운 소녀/ She's awfully ~. Chŏngmal kwiyŏpke saenggyŏtkunyo. 정말 귀엽게 생겼군요.

cutting n. (*of clothes*) chaedan 재단, peŏnaegi 베어내기. *Your hair wants* ~. Tangshinŭn mŏrirŭl kkakkaya-gessŭmnida. 당신은 머리를 깎아야겠읍니다.

cuttlefish n. ppyŏojingŏ 뼈오징어, ojingŏ 오징어.

cycle n. (*round*) han bak'wi 한 바퀴, sunhwan 순환, (*bicycle*) chajŏn-gŏ 자전거. *the* ~ *of the seasons* kyejŏrŭi sunhwan 계절의 순환/ *boom and depression* ~s kyŏng-giwa pulgyŏnggiŭi sunhwan 경기와 불경기의 순환.

cyclopedia n. (*ency.*) paekkwa sajŏn 백과 사전.

cylinder n. wŏnt'ong 원통, kit'ong 기통, shillindŏ 실린더.

cynical adj. pikkonŭn 비꼬는, naengsojŏgin 냉소적인. *a* ~ *smile* pinjŏnggŏrinŭn usŭm 빈정거리는 웃음.

cynically adv. pikkoa 비꼬아, pikkodŭshi 비꼬듯이.

⟿ D ⟾

dad, daddy n. (*father*) appa 아빠, abŏji 아버지.

daffodil n. nap'alsusŏnhwa 나팔수선화.

dagger n. tando 단도(短刀), pisu 비수.

daily adj. maeirŭi 매일의, ilsangŭi 일상의. —n. ilgan shinmun 일간 신문. *a* ~ *bread* saenggye 생계/ *a* ~ *newspaper* ilgan shinmun 일간 신문/ *What's the* ~ *rate?* Haru yogŭmŭn ŏlmaimnikka? 하루 요금은 얼마입니까?

damage n. sonhae 손해, (*casualty*) p'ihae 피해. —vt. sonhaerŭl chuda 손해를 주다. *Let me pay for the* ~. Sonhaenŭn naega mulgessŭmnida. 손해는 내가 물겠읍니다.

dame n. (*Am.*) yŏja 여자. *Oh, she is a* ~! Kŭnyŏnŭn hyŏngp'yŏn ŏpsŭmnida. 그녀는 형편없읍니다.

damp adj. ch'ukch'uk'an 축축한, sŭp'an 습한. —n. sŭpki 습기. ~ *clothes* ch'ukch'uk'an ot 축축한 옷/ *Don't stay outside in the* ~. Sŭpki innŭn pakkat'e itchi mashio. 습기 있는 바깥에 있지 마시오.

dance n. ch'um 춤, muyong 무용, taensŭ 댄스. —v. ch'umch'uda 춤추다. *folk* ~ minsok muyong 민속 무용/ *a sword* ~ kŏmmu 검무(劍舞)/ *Will you* ~ *with me?* Chŏwa ch'umch'ushigessǔmnikka ? 저와 춤추시겠읍니까?

dancer *n.* muyongga 무용가, taensǒ 댄서.

dandelion *n.* mindǔlle 민들레.

dandruff *n.* (*on scalp*) pidǔm 비듬.

dandy *n.* mǒtchangi 멋장이, maepshikkun 맵시꾼.

danger *n.* wihǒm 위험. *be in* ~ *of* wihǒmi itta 위험이 있다/ ~ *signal* wihǒm shinho 위험 신호/ ~ *zone* wihǒm chidae 위험 지대/ *Well, scientists say that there's no* ~. Kǔrǒnde kwahakchadǔrǔn wihǒmi ǒptago hamnida. 그런데 과학자들은 위험이 없다고 합니다.

dangerous *adj.* wihǒmhan 위험한, wihǒmsǔrǒn 위험스런. *a* ~ *bridge* wihǒmhan tari 위험한 다리/ *The dog looks* ~. Chǒ kaenǔn sanawa poimnida. 저 개는 사나와 보입니다.

dare *vt.* kamhi ...hada 감히…하다, ...hal yonggiga itta ...할 용기가 있다. *How* ~ *you say such a thing?* Ǒtchi kamhi kǔrǒn marǔl hashimnikka? 어찌 감히 그런 말을 하십니까/ *I've never* ~*d* (*to*) *ask him.* Kamhi kǔege murǒboji mot'aessǔmnida. 감히 그에게 물어보지 못했읍니다/ *I* ~ *say* (*perhaps*) ama...il kǒshida 아마…일 것이다.

daring *adj.* yonggamhan 용감한, taedamhan 대담한. —*n.* (*audacity*) taedamsǒng 대담성. *a* ~ *robbery* taedamhan kangdo 대담한 강도.

dark *adj.* ǒduun 어두운, k'amk'amhan 캄캄한, (*color*) kǒmǔn 검은, (*sombre*) kǒmut'an 거뭇한. —*n.* ǒduum 어두움, amhǔk 암흑. *a* ~ *night* k'amk'amhan pam 캄캄한 밤/ ~ *room* amshil 암실/ *a* ~ *complexion* kǒmut'an p'ibusaek 거뭇한 피부색/ *It is already getting* ~. Nari pǒlssǒ ǒduwǒjyǒssǔmnida. 날이 벌써 어두워졌읍니다 / *Don't leave the child alone in the dark.* Kǔ airǔl honja ǒdum soge tuji mashio. 그 아이를 혼자 어둠 속에 두지 마시오/ *I don't like the* ~ *colors.* Nanǔn kǒmǔn saegǔl choahaji anssǔmnida. 나는 검은 색을 좋아하지 않습니다.

darling *adj.* kwiyǒun 귀여운. —*n.* kwiyǒun saram 귀여운 사람. *What a* ~ *little dog!* Ǒlmana kwiyǒun kaeimnikka ! 얼마나 귀여운 개입니까/ *She is a little* ~. Kunyǒnǔn kwiyŏun aiimnida. 그녀는 귀여운 아이입니다/ *Come here, my ~ !* Yaeya, iri on 애야 이리 온.

dash *n.* tolchin 돌진, (*short race*) tan-gŏri kyŏngju 단거리 경주. —*vt.* naedŏnjida 내던지다, (*shatter*) ttaeryŏ pusuda 때려 부수다. —*vi.* tolchinhada 돌진하다. *~ a mirror to pieces* kŏurŭl sansani pusuda 거울을 산산이 부수다/ *~ against* ch'ungdorhada 충돌하다/ *He made a ~ for the goal.* Kŭnŭn kyŏlsŭngchŏmŭl hyanghae tolchinhae kassŭmnida. 그는 결승점을 향해 돌진해 갔습니다.

date *n.* (*appointment*) yaksok 약속, teit'ŭ 데이트, (*on letters*) naltcha 날짜. *I've a ~ with him tomorrow.* Nanŭn naeil kŭwa mannal yaksogi twae issŭmnida. 나는 내일 그와 만날 약속이 돼 있습니다/ *What is the ~ today?* Onŭri myŏch'irijiyo? 오늘이 며칠이지요/ *out of ~* kushigŭi 구식(舊式)의/ *up to ~* ch'oeshinŭi 최신의, hyŏndaejŏgin 현대적인.

daughter *n.* ttal 딸, yŏshik 여식(女息). *I have two sons and one ~.* Na-egenŭn adŭl tul, ttal hanaga issŭmnida. 나에게는 아들 둘, 딸 하나가 있습니다/ *~-in-law* myŏnŭri 며느리, chabu 자부.

dawn *n.* saebyŏk 새벽. —*vi.* nari saeda 날이 새다.

day *n.* (*day time*) nat 낮, chugan 주간(晝間), (*period of 24 hours*) haru 하루, nal 날. (*epoch*) shidae 시대, tangdae 당대(當代). *all ~ long* chongil 종일/ *by ~* najenŭn 낮에는/ *~ after ~* nalmada 날마다/ *~ and night* pamnat 밤낮, chuya 주야/ *the ~ after tomorrow* more 모레/ *the ~ before yesterday* kŭjŏkke 그저께/ *from ~ to ~* nanari 나날이/ *in those ~s* kŭ muryŏp 그 무렵/ *one ~* (*past*) ŏnŭnal 어느날/ *the other ~* yojŏnnal 요전날, ilchŏne 일전에/ *some ~* ŏnjen-ganŭn 언젠가는/ *What ~ of the week is it today?* Onŭrŭn musŭn yoirimnikka? 오늘은 무슨 요일입니까/ *What ~ of the month is it today?* Onŭrŭn myŏch'irimnikka? 오늘은 며칠입니까/ *Today is the 25th of December.* Onŭrŭn shibiwŏl ishiboirimnida. 오늘은 12월 25일입니다.

daybreak *n.* saebyŏk 새벽, tongt'ŭllyŏk 동틀녘.

daydream *n.* paegilmong 백일몽, kongsang 공상.

daylight *n.* haetpyŏt 햇볕, ilgwang 일광.

daytime *n.* nat 낮, chugan 주간(晝間).

dead *adj.* chugŭn 죽은, (*inanimate*) saengmyŏng ŏmnŭn 생명 없는, (*faded*) malla chugŭn 말라 죽은, (*complete*) wanjŏnhan 완전한. *the ~ and the wounded* sasangja 사상자/ *~ sleep* kip'ŭn cham 깊은 잠. *—n.* saja 사자(死者). *I was ~ tired.* Nanŭn nokch'oga toeŏssŭmnida. 나는 녹초가 되었읍니다/ *We mourned for the ~.* Urinŭn koinŭl aedohayŏssŭmnida. 우리는 고인(故人)을 애도하였읍니다.

deadline *n.* magam shigan 마감 시간, ch'oejong kihan 최종 기한.

deaf *adj.* kwimŏgŏriŭi 귀머거리의, kwimŏgŭn 귀먹은. *a ~ person* kwimŏgŏri 귀머거리/ *He turned a ~ ear to my advice.* Kŭnŭn nae ch'unggorŭl tŭtchi anassŭmnida. 그는 내 충고를 듣지 않았읍니다.

deal *n.* (*business*) kŏrae 거래, (*amount*) pullyang 분량 (分量). *—vi.* (*act*) haengdonghada 행동하다, (*treat*) taruda 다루다, (*trade*) kŏraehada 거래하다. *—vt.* (*give*) chuda 주다. *a fair ~* kongjŏng kŏrae 공정 거래/ *a good ~ of* manŭn 많은, taryangŭi 다량의/ *Do you ~ with Smith, the grocer?* Shingnyop'umsang Sŭmidŭwa kŏraerŭl hamnikka? 식료품상 스미드와 거래를 합니까/ *How shall we ~ with this problem?* I munjerŭl ŏttŏk'e ch'ŏrihajiyo? 이 문제를 어떻게 처리하지요/ *You should ~ with him more politely.* Tangshinŭn kŭrŭl chomdŏ chŏngjunghi taehaeya hamnida. 당신은 그를 좀더 정중히 대해야 합니다.

dealer *n.* sangin 상인, changsu 장수. *a curio ~* koltongp'umsang 골동품상/ *a fish ~* saengsŏn changsu 생선 장수/ *a retail ~* somaesang 소매상/ *a real estate ~* pudongsan maemaeŏpcha 부동산 매매업자/ *a street ~* nojŏm sangin 노점 상인.

dean *n.* (*cathedral*) sajejang 사제장(司祭長), (*college*) hakchang 학장.

dear *adj.* (*costly*) kappissan 값비싼, (*important*) sojunghan 소중한, (*beloved*) kwiyŏun 귀여운. *That is too ~.* Kŭgŏsŭn nŏmu pissamnida. 그것은 너무 비쌉니다/ *Isn't* *she a ~?* Kŭnyŏnŭn kwiyŏpchi anssŭmnikka? 그녀는 귀엽지 않습니까/ *Honor is ~er to me than life.* Na-e-genŭn myŏngyega saengmyŏngboda kwijunghamnida. 나에게는 명예가 생명보다 귀중합니다.

death *n.* chugŭm 죽음, samang 사망. *~ agony* chugŭmŭi koeroum 죽음의 괴로움/ *~ day* kiil 기일(忌日)/ *~ rate* samangnyul 사망율/ *~ roll* samangja myŏngbu 사망자 명부/ *a notice of ~* samanggye 사망계/ *sudden ~* kŭpsa 급사(急死)/ *face ~* chugŭme chingmyŏnhada 죽음에 직면하다.

debenture *n.* sach'ae 사채. *~ stock[bond]* sach'aekwŏn 사채권.

debt *n.* pit 빚, puch'ae 부채, ch'aemu 채무. *a large ~* kŏaegŭi puch'ae 거액의 부채/ *a national ~* kukch'ae 국채/ *pay one's ~* pijŭl kapta 빚을 갚다/ *I have ~s.* Nanŭn piji issŭmnida. 나는 빚이 있읍니다/ *I'm out of ~.* Nanŭn piji ŏpsŭmnida. 나는 빚이 없읍니다/ *Don't run into ~.* Pijŭl chiji mashio. 빚을 지지 마시오.

debtor *n.* ch'aemuja 채무자, ch'aju 차주(借主).

debut *n.* ch'ŏnmudae ch'uryŏn 첫무대 출연, tebwi 데뷔.

decease *n.* samang 사망. —*vi.* chukta 죽다, samanghada 사망하다.

deceive *vt.,vi.* sogida 속이다, kimanhada 기만하다. *He entirely ~d us.* Kŭnŭn urirŭl wanjŏnhi sogyŏssŭmnida. 그는 우리를 완전히 속였읍니다.

deceiver *n.* sagikkun 사기꾼.

December *n.* shibiwŏl 12월, sŏttal 섣달.

decent *adj.* (*modest*) chŏmjanŭn 점잖은, kosanghan 고상한, (*proper*) ondanghan 온당한, (*respectable*) sangdanghan shinbunŭi 상당한 신분의, (*fair*) kŭrŏlssahan 그럴싸한.

decide *vt.,vi.* kyŏlchŏnghada 결정하다, (*settle*) haegyŏrhada 해결하다, (*law*) p'an-gyŏrhada 판결하다. *I ~d to be an engineer.* Nanŭn enjiniŏga toegiro kyŏlshimhaessŭmnida. 나는 엔지니어가 되기로 결심했읍니다.

decision *n.* kyŏlchŏng 결정, (*resolution*) kyŏlshim 결심.

deck *n.* (*of ship*) kapp'an 갑판, (*pack*) han pŏl 한 벌.

the upper ~ sanggapp'an 상갑판/ *a lower* ~ arae kapp'an 아래 갑판.

declaration *n.* (*announcement*) p'ogo 포고, (*proclamation*) sŏnŏn 선언, (*statement*) shin-go 신고.

declare *vt.,vi.* (*proclaim*) sŏnŏnhada 선언하다, (*report*) shin-gohada 신고하다. *I ~ this meeting closed.* P'yehoerŭl sŏnŏnhamnida 폐회를 선언합니다/ *Do you have anything to ~?* Shin-gohal kŏshi issŭmnikka? 신고할 것이 있읍니까?

decorate *vt.* changshik'ada 장식하다, (*reward*) hunjangŭl suyŏhada 훈장을 수여하다. *Several soldiers were ~d for bravery.* Myŏnmyŏt pyŏngsadŭri yonggamhaettŏn konguro hunjangŭi padassŭmnida. 몇몇 병사들이 용감했던 공으로 훈장을 받았읍니다.

decrease *vi.,vt.* chulda 줄다, kamsohada 감소하다. —*n.* kamso 감소.

dedicate *vt.* hŏnna[pongna]p'ada 헌납[봉납]하다, pach'ida 바치다, (*give up*) naedŏnjida 내던지다, (*inscribe*) hŏnjehada 헌제(獻題)하다. *To my uncle I ~ this volume.* Sukpunimkke i ch'aegŭl pach'imnida. 숙부님께 이 책을 바칩니다/ *The shrine is ~d to the memory of Admiral Yi Sun-shin.* I sadangŭn I Sunshin changgunŭl mosyŏ nok'o issŭmnida. 이 사당은 이 순신 장군을 모셔 놓고 있읍니다.

deduct *vt.* ppaeda 빼다, kongjehada 공제하다.

deed *n.* (*action*) haengwi 행위, (*exploit*) kongjŏk 공적, (*reality*) sashil 사실, (*law*) chŭngsŏ 증서. *a good ~* hullyunghan haengwi 훌륭한 행위/*a ~ of arms* muhun 무훈/*a ~ of contract* kyeyaksŏ 계약서.

deep *adj.* kip'ŭn 깊은, (*color*) chit'ŭn 짙은. *a ~ well* kip'ŭn umul 깊은 우물/ *a~ sigh* kip'ŭn hansum 깊은 한숨/*a ~ red* chit'ŭn ppalgang 짙은 빨강/*How ~ is this river?* I kangŭn ŏlmana kipsŭmnikka? 이 강은 얼마나 깊습니까?

deer *n.* sasŭm 사슴.

defeat *n.* p'aebae 패배, (*failure*) shilp'ae 실패. —*vt.* (*overcome*) chiuda 지우다, (*cause to fail*) muhyoro hada 무효로 하다.

defence, defense *n.* pangwi 방위, subi 수비. *air* ~ panggong 방공(防空)/ *air* ~ *manoeuvre* panggong yŏnsŭp 방공 연습/ *legal* ~ chŏngdang pangwi 정당 방위/ *national* ~ kukpang 국방.

defendant *n.* p'igo 피고, —*adj.* pigoŭi 피고의.

defer *vt.,vi.* yŏn-gihada 연기하다, chiyŏnhada 지연하다.

definitely *adv.* chŏltaero 절대로, chŏngmal 정말. *No. D*~ *not.* Anio, chŏltaero kŭrŏch'i anssŭmnida. 아니오, 절대로 그렇지 않습니다.

deformed *adj.* kihyŏngŭi 기형의, (*crippled*) pulguŭi 불구의. *a* ~ *child* kihyŏnga 기형아.

degree *n.* (*therm.*) to 도, (*extent*) chŏngdo 정도, (*univ.*) hagwi 학위. *The thermometer stood at 20* ~*s.* Ondogyenŭn ishiptorŭl karik'igo issŏssŭmnida. 온도계는 20도를 가리키고 있었읍니다/ *to a certain* ~ ŏnŭ chŏngdokkaji 어느 정도까지/ *to a high* ~ kodoro 고도로/ *I have attained the* ~ *of Master of Arts.* Nanŭn munhak sŏksa hagwirŭl hoektŭk'aessŭmnida. 나는 문학 석사 학위를 획득했읍니다.

delay *vt.,vi.* chiyŏnshik'ida 지연시키다, yŏn-gihada 연기하다, chich'ehada 지체하다. —*n.* yŏn-gi 연기. *We must start without* ~. Chich'e ŏpshi ttŏnaya hamnida. 지체 없이 떠나야 합니다/ *Don't* ~. Chich'ehaji mashio. 지체하지 마시오.

delicate *adj.* (*tender*) hŏyak'an 허약한, (*subtle*) mimyohan 미묘한, (*beautiful*) uahan 우아한. *a* ~ *child* hŏyak'an ai 허약한 아이/ *a* ~ *flower* uahan kkot 우아한 꽃.

delicious *adj.* madinnŭn 맛있는, chinmiŭi 진미의. *a* ~ *cake* madinnŭn kwaja 맛있는 과자/ *Oh, it is* ~! Ch'am madinneyo. 참 맛있네요.

delight *vt.* chŭlgŏpke hada 즐겁게 하다, kippŭge hada 기쁘게 하다. —*n.* kippŭm 기쁨. *We'd be* ~*ed to meet you.* Manna poeŏssŭmyŏn pan-gapkessŭmnida. 만나 뵈었으면 반갑겠읍니다/ *We are* ~*ed you could come.* Wa chusyŏsŏ much'ŏk pan-gapsŭmnida. 와 주서서 무척 반갑습니다.

delightful *adj.* kippŭn 기쁜, chŭlgŏun 즐거운. *Thank you for a* ~ *party.* Chŭlgŏun p'at'i kamsahamnida. 즐거운 파티 감사합니다.

deliver vt. (save) kuhada 구하다, (convey) chŏnhada 전하다, paedarhada 배달하다, (hand over) chuda 주다, (utter) yŏnsŏrhada 연설하다. Can I have it ~ed? Igŏl paedarhae chushigessŭmnikka? 이걸 배달해 주시겠읍니까/ I have to ~ in English. Yŏngŏro yŏnsŏrŭl haeya hamnida 영어로 연설을 해야 합니다/ Did you ~ my message to your father? Nae mal abŏnimkke chŏnhaessŭmnikka? 내 말 아버님께 전했읍니까?

delivery n. paedal 배달, indo 인도(引渡). Make it special ~, please. Soktallo haejushio. 속달로 해주시오/ We don't have ~ service. Paedarŭn haedŭriji anssŭmnida. 배달은 해드리지 않습니다.

delude vt. sogida 속이다, hyŏnhok'ada 현혹하다.

demand vt. (ask for) yoguhada 요구하다, (need) p'iryohada 필요하다. —n. yogu 요구, suyo 수요. ~ and supply suyo konggŭp 수요 공급.

demobilize vt. (army) chedaeshik'ida 제대시키다, (disband) haesanshik'ida 해산시키다.

democracy n. minjujuŭi 민주주의.

demon n. angma 악마. (devil) magwi 마귀. 「운동.

demonstration n. shiryŏn 실연(實演), shiwi undong 시위

denial n. pujŏng 부정(否定), (refusal) kŏbu 거부.

dense adj. (thick) chit'ŭn 짙은, ppaekppaek'an 빽빽한.

dental adj. ch'ikwaŭi 치과의. a ~ office ch'ikwa ŭiwŏn 치과 의원/ a ~ surgeon ch'ikwa ŭisa 치과 의사.

dentist n. ch'ikwa ŭisa 치과 의사.

deny vt. pujŏnghada 부정하다, (refuse) kŏjŏrhada 거절하다. It's true. You can't ~ it. Kŭgŏsŭn sashirio. Pujŏnghal suga ŏpsŭmnida. 그것은 사실이오. 부정할 수가 없읍니다.

depart vi. (start) ch'ulbarhada 출발하다, ttŏnada 떠나다. ~ from one's promise yaksogŭl ŏgida 약속을 어기다.

department n. (branch) pu 부(部), kuk 국(局), (Am.) sŏng 성(省). I'm looking for the toy ~. Wan-guburŭl ch'atko issŭmnida. 완구부를 찾고 있읍니다 / What do you think of our Korean ~ stores? Han-gugŭi paek'wajŏmŭl ŏttŏk'e saenggak'ashimnikka? 한국의 백화점을 어떻게 생각하십니까?

departure *n.* ch'ulbal 출발. *I had to postpone my* ~. Ch'ulbarŭl yŏn-gihaeya haessŭmnida. 출발을 연기해야 했읍니다/ *Which is the* ~ *platform?* Ŏnŭ tchogi ch'ulbal p'ŭllaetp'omimnikka? 어느 쪽이 출발 플랫폼입니까?

depend *vi.* ...e ŭijonhada ···에 의존하다, ...ŭl shilloehada ··· 을 신뢰하다. *Can I* ~ *upon this railway guide?* I ch'ŏlto annaesŏ midŏdo chossŭmnikka? 이 철도 안내서 믿어도 좋습니까/ *D*~ *upon it.* T'ŭllimŏpta 틀림없다.

dependent *n.* (*dependant*) puyang kajok 부양 가족, shik-kaek 식객. *How many* ~*s have you?* Kajogŭn myŏch'i-shimnikka? 가족은 몇이십니까?

deposit *n.* (*in a bank*) yegŭm 예금, (*earnest money*) pojŭnggŭm 보증금, (*sediment*) anggŭm 앙금. —*vt.* (*place*) not'a 놓다. (*put in a bank*) yegŭmhada 예금하다, (*settle*) karaanch'ida 가라앉히다. *I want to make a* ~. Yegŭmŭl hago shipsŭmnida. 예금을 하고 싶습니다/ *I cannot give a cash* ~. Hyŏn-gŭmŭronŭn pojŭnggŭmŭl nael suga ŏpsŭmnida. 현금으로는 보증금을 낼 수가 없읍니다/ *Please state the amount you wish to* ~. Yegŭmhashi-ryŏnŭn aeksurŭl chŏgŏ chushipshio. 예금하시려는 액수를 적어 주십시오/ *a current* ~ tangjwa yegŭm 당좌 예금/ *a fixed* ~ chŏnggi yegŭm 정기 예금.

depositor *n.* yegŭmja[ju] 예금자[주]. *Are you regular* ~? Chŏnggyu yegŭmjaishimnikka? 정규 예금자이십니까?

depression *n.* (*dullness*) pulgyŏnggi 불경기, purhwang 불황(不況), (*gloom*) ch'imul 침울. *agriculture* ~ nongŏbŭi pujin 농업의 부진/ *economical* ~ kyŏngjegyeŭi purhwang 경제계의 불황/ *mental* ~ ŭigi soch'im 의기 소침.

deprive *vt.* ppaeatta 빼앗다, pakt'arhada 박탈하다.

depth *n.* kip'i 깊이, (*pl.*) kip'ŭn kot 깊은 곳.

deputy *n.* taeriin 대리인, taerija 대리자. —*adj.* taeriŭi 대리의, pu 부(副). ~ *premier* pususang 부수상/ ~ *mayor* pushijang 부시장/ ~ *governer* pujisa 부지사.

derive *vt.,vi.* ikkŭrŏ naeda 이끌어 내다.

descend *vi.* (*come down*) naeryŏoda 내려오다, (*slope downward*) kyŏngsajida 경사지다.

descendant *n.* (*offspring*) chason 자손, huye 후예.

describe *vt.* marhada 말하다, sŏsurhada. 서술하다. *Can you ~ it to me?* Marhae chul su issŭmnikka? 말해 줄 수 있읍니까/*Please ~ what you saw.* Pon taero marhae chushio. 본 대로 말해 주시오.

desert *n.* samak 사막. —*vt.(abandon)* pŏrida 버리다, *(leave)* tomanghada 도망하다. *He ~ed his wife.* Kŭnŭn anaerŭl pŏryŏssŭmnida. 그는 아내를 버렸읍니다.

deserve *vt. (be worthy of)* kach'iga itta 가치가 있다, *(be entitled to)* chagyŏgi itta 자격이 있다. *You ~ a reward.* Sangŭl t'ashinŭn kŏsŭn tangyŏnhamnida. 상을 타시는 것은 당연합니다.

design *n. (outline)* toan 도안, *(idea)* koan 고안, *(plan)* kyehoek'ada 계획하다, *(intend)* kidohada 기도(企圖)하다. *I was unable to carry out my ~.* Kyehoegŭl shilch'ŏnhal suga ŏpsŏssŭmnida. 계획을 실천할 수가 없었읍니다/*What ~ was that?* Ŏttŏn tijainiŏnnayo? 어떤 디자인이었나요?

designer *n. (of sketches)* toan-ga 도안가, *(projector)* sŏlgyeja 설계자, *(of dresses)* tijainŏ 디자이너.

desire *vt.* parada 바라다. —*n.* yongmang 욕망. *We all ~ happiness and health.* Urinŭn ta haengbokkwa kŏn-gangŭl paramnida. 우리는 다 행복과 건강을 바랍니다/*What do you ~ me to do?* Naega muŏsŭl hagirŭl wŏnhashimnikka? 내가 무엇을 하기를 원하십니까?

desk *n.* ch'aeksang 책상.

despair *vi.* chŏlmanghada 절망하다, nakshimhada 낙심하다, *(give up)* p'ogihada 포기하다. —*n.* chŏlmang 절망, chap'ojagi 자포자기, tannyŏm 단념.

desperate *adj. (beyond hope)* chŏlmangjŏgin 절망적인, *(frantic)* p'ilsaŭi 필사의, *(reckless)* mumohan 무모한.

despise *vt.* kyŏngmyŏrhada 경멸하다, yatpoda 얕보다.

despite *prep. (=in spite of)* ...edo pulguhago ···에도 불구하고. *~ what she says* Kŭnyŏŭi maredo pulguhago 그녀의 말에도 불구하고.

dessert *n.* tijŏt'ŭ 디저트. *What kinds of ~s do you have?* Tijŏt'ŭenŭn ŏttŏn kŏshi issŭmnikka? 디저트에는 어떤 것이 있읍니까/*What will you have for ~s?* Tijŏt'ŭro muŏsŭl tŭshigessŭmnikka? 디저트로 무엇을 드시

겠읍니까?

destination *n.* mokchŏkchi 목적지, haengsŏnji 행선지.

destiny *n.* unmyŏng 운명, sungmyŏng 숙명.

destroy *vt.* p'agoehada 파괴하다, (*ruin*) mangch'ida 망치다, (*kill*) chugida 죽이다. *Don't ~ that box.* Kŭ sangjarŭl pusuji mashio. 그 상자를 부수지 마시오/ *The house was almost completely ~ed.* Chibi kŏŭi wanjŏnhi p'agoedoeŏssŭmnida. 집이 거의 완전히 파괴되었읍니다.

destroyer *n.* (*warship*) kuch'uk'am 구축함.

destruction *n.* p'agoe 파괴, (*ruin*) p'amyŏl 파멸.

destructionist *n.* p'agoejuŭija 파괴주의자.

destructive *adj.* p'agoejŏgin 파괴적인. *Are all small children ~?* Aidŭrŭn ta pusugirŭl choahamnikka? 아이들은 다 부수기를 좋아합니까?

detail *n.* (*item*) semok 세목, (*minute account*) sangsŏl 상설(詳說). *Please give me all the ~s.* Modŭn sebu sashirŭl marhae chushio. 모든 세부 사실을 말해 주시오/ *Don't omit a single ~.* Tan hanaŭi semokto saengnyak'aji mashio. 단 하나의 세목도 생략하지 마시오/ *in ~* sangsehi 상세히, semirhi 세밀히.

detective *n.* t'amjŏng 탐정, hyŏngsa 형사. *a ~story* t'amjŏng〔ch'uri〕 sosŏl 탐정〔추리〕 소설. 「kyŏlchŏng 결정.

determination *n.* (*resolution*) kyŏlshim 결심, (*decision*)

determine *vt.,vi.* (*decide*) kyŏlchŏnghada 결정하다, (*resolve*) kyŏlshimhada 결심하다. *We ~d to start early.* Iltchik ch'ulbarhagiro kyŏlshimhaessŭmnida. 일찍 출발하기로 결심했읍니다.

develop *vt.* palchŏnshik'ida 발전시키다. —*vi.* paltarhada 발달하다, (*photo*) hyŏnsanghada 현상(現像)하다. *We must ~ the natural resources of our country.* Uri nara ch'ŏnyŏn chawŏnŭl kaebarhaeya hamnida. 우리 나라 천연 자원을 개발해야 합니다/ *Please ~ these films.* I p'illŭmŭl hyŏnsanghayŏ chushio. 이 필름을 현상하여 주시오.

development *n.* paltal 발달, palchŏn 발전, (*growth*) sŏngjang 성장, (*exploitation*) kaebal 개발, (*photo*) hyŏnsang 현상.

device *n.* (*plan*) koan 고안, (*apparatus*) changch'i 장치,

(*stratagem*) ch'aengnyak 책략.

devil *n.* (*demon*) angma 악마, akkwi 악귀.

devilfish *n.* ojingŏ 오징어, nakchi 낙지, munŏ 문어.

devote *vt.* (*consecrate*) pach'ida 바치다, (*consign over*) matkida 맡기다. *I ~d my best to research.* Nanŭn on chŏngnyŏgŭl yŏn-gue pach'yŏssŭmnida. 나는 온 정력을 연구에 바쳤읍니다/ *Don't ~ too much time to games.* Norie nŏmu shiganŭl pach'iji marara. 놀이에 너무 시간을 바치지 말아라/ *be ~d to …e chŏnnyŏm〔moltu, yŏlchung〕hada …에 전념〔몰두, 열중〕하다.

devotion *n.* (*dedication*) hŏnshin 헌신, (*close attention*) chŏnnyŏm 전념, (*piety*) shinshim 신심(信心).

dew *n.* isŭl 이슬, *the ~ of tears* nunmul pangul 눈물 방울.

diabetes *n.* tangnyopyŏng 당뇨병. *It looks like she's got ~s.* Kŭnyŏnŭn tangnyopyŏnge kŏllin kŏt kassŭmnida. 그녀는 당뇨병에 걸린 것 같습니다.

diagram *n.* (*chart*) top'yo 도표, (*figure*) tohyŏng 도형.

dial *n.* taiŏl 다이얼, (*~ plate*) munchap'an 문자판, taiŏrŭl tollida 다이얼을 돌리다. *Would you clean the ~ of my wristwatch?* Nae shigye munchap'an chom takka chushigessŭmnikka? 내 시계 문자판 좀 닦아 주시겠읍니까/ *What number have you ~ed?* Myŏt pŏne kŏsyŏssŭmnikka? 몇 번에 거셨읍니까? 「taesa 대사.

dialog(ue) *n.* (*conversation*) taehwa 대화, (*of a play*)

diameter *n.* chikkyŏng 직경, chirŭm 지름. *the ~ of a tree trunk* namu tungch'iŭi chirŭm 나무 둥치의 지름.

diamond *n.* kŭmgangsŏk 금강석, taiamondŭ 다이아몬드.

diarrhoea *n.* sŏlsa 설사. *have ~* sŏlsahada 설사하다.

diary *n.* ilgi 일기, ilchi 일지(日誌).

dice *n.* chusawi 주사위. *play at ~* chusawinorirŭl hada 주사위놀이를 하다.

dictate *vt.* padassŭge hada 받아쓰게 하다, (*command*) myŏngnyŏnghada 명령하다.

dictation *n.* padassŭgi 받아쓰기, kusul 구술. *take ~ of …ŭl padassŭda …을 받아쓰다.

dictator *n.* tokchaeja 독재자, chibaeja 지배자. *the ~ of fashion* yuhaengŭi chibaeja 유행의 지배자.

dictionary *n.* sajŏn 사전. *English-Korean* ~ yŏnghan sajŏn 영한 사전, *Korean-English* ~ hanyŏng sajŏn 한영 사전/ *Biographical* ~ inmyŏng sajŏn 인명 사전.

die *vi.* chukta 죽다, (*wish very much*) kanjŏrhi parada 간절히 바라다. —*n.* (*dice*) chusawi 주사위. *We shall* ~ *someday.* Urinŭn ŏnjen-ganŭn chuksŭmnida. 우리는 언젠 가는 죽습니다/ *I'm dying from fatigue.* P'irohaesŏ chugŭl kŏnman kassŭmnida. 피로해서 죽을 것만 같습니다/ *We're all dying for a drink.* Hanjan hago ship'ŏ mot kyŏndigessŭmnida. 한잔 하고 싶어 못 견디겠습니다/ ~ *away* sarajida 사라지다/ ~ *from〔of〕* ...ŭro chukta …으 로 죽다/ ~ *out* somyŏrhada 소멸하다.

diet *n.* (*food*) ŭmshingmul 음식물, (*regimen*) kyujŏng-shik 규정식, shigi yopŏp 식이 요법, (*congress*) ŭihoe 의회, kuk'oe 국회. *I like a simple* ~ *best.* Nanŭn tambae-k'an ŭmshigŭl kajang choahamnida. 나는 담백한 음식을 가장 좋아합니다/ *the Korean home* ~ Han-gugŭi kajŏng ŭmshik 한국의 가정 음식/ *I'm on a* ~. Nanŭn kyujŏng-shigŭl mŏkko issŭmnida. 나는 규정식을 먹고 있습니다.

differ *vi.* tarŭda 다르다, t'ŭllida 틀리다. *I'm sorry to* ~ *from you about that question.* Yugamsŭrŏpchiman kŭ munjee kwanhaesŏnŭn tangshin-gwa ŭigyŏni tarŭmni-da. 유감스럽지만 그 문제에 관해서는 당신과 의견이 다릅니다.

difference *n.* ch'ai 차이, (*disagreement*) ŭigyŏn ch'ai 의 견 차이. *I can see a big* ~. K'ŭn ch'aiga ittago saeng-gak'amnida. 큰 차이가 있다고 생각합니다.

different *adj.* tarŭn 다른, ttan 딴. *That is quite* ~ *from this.* Kŭgŏsŭn igŏtkwanŭn chŏnhyŏ tarŭmnida. 그것은 이것과는 전혀 다릅니다/ *Show me a* ~ *one.* Tarŭn kŏsŭl poyŏ chushio. 다른 것을 보여 주시오.

difficult *adj.* ŏryŏun 어려운, kollanhan 곤란한, (*obstinate*) kkadaroun 까다로운. *English is not so* ~ *to learn.* Yŏngŏnŭn kŭdaji ŏryŏpchi anssŭmnida. 영어는 그다지 어렵지 않습니다/ *a* ~ *situation* kollanhan sat'ae 곤란한 사태/ *Please don't be so* ~. Chebal chom kŭrŏk'e kka-darŏpke kulji mashio. 제발 좀 그렇게 까다롭게 굴지 마 시오.

dig *vt.,vi.* p'ada 파다, p'anaeda 파내다, (*unearth*) k'aenaeda 캐내다. ~ *the ground* ttangŭl p'ada 땅을 파다/ ~ *potatoes* kamjarŭl k'aeda 감자를 캐다.

digest *vt.,vi.* sohwahada 소화하다, (*summarize*) yoyak'ada 요약하다. —*n.* taijesŭt'ŭ 다이제스트.

digestion *n.* sohwa 소화. 「갱부.

digger *n.* p'anŭn saram 파는 사람, (*miner*) kaengbu

dignity *n.* (*majesty*) wiŏm 위엄, (*grace*) p'umwi 품위. (*a high office*) kogwan 고관(高官). 「진퇴 유곡.

dilemma *n.* tillema 딜레마, kungji 궁지, chint'oe yugok

diligent *adj.* kŭnmyŏnhan 근면한, pujirŏnhan 부지런한. *a* ~ *person* pujirŏnhan saram 부지런한 사람/ *He is* ~ *at his lessons.* Kŭnŭn pujirŏnhi kongbuhago issŭmnida. 그는 부지런히 공부하고 있읍니다.

dim *adj.* hŭimihan 희미한, ŏdumch'imch'imhan 어둠침침한. *the* ~ *light of a candle* hŭimihan ch'otpul 희미한 촛불/ *a* ~ *room* ŏdumch'imch'imhan pang 어둠침침한 방.

dimension *n.* (*size*) ch'isu 치수, (*area*) myŏnjŏk 면적, (*capacity*) yongjŏk 용적. *What are the* ~*s of the room?* Pangŭn ŏlmana k'ŭmnikka? 방은 얼마나 큽니까?

diminish *vt.,vi.* churida 줄이다, chulda 줄다, kamsohada 감소하다. ~ *in population* in-guga chulda 인구가 줄다.

dimple *n.* pojogae 보조개.

dine *vi.* shiksarŭl hada 식사를 하다, chŏngch'anŭl mŏkta 정찬을 먹다. *dining car* shiktangch'a 식당차/*dining room* shiktang 식당/ *Would you guide me to the dining car?* Shiktangch'a-e annaehae chushigessŭmnikka? 식당차에 안내해 주시겠읍니까?

dinner *n.* chŏnyŏk shiksa 저녁 식사. *early* ~ och'an 오찬/ *late* ~ manch'an 만찬/ *When is* ~ *served?* Chŏnyŏk shiksanŭn myŏt shiimnikka? 저녁 식사는 몇 시입니까/ *Could you come to our house for* ~ *tomorrow evening?* Naeil chŏnyŏk uri chip manch'ane oshigessŭmnikka? 내일 저녁 우리 집 만찬에 오시겠읍니까/ *We are having a* ~ *party on Tuesday, the 2nd of July.* Ch'irwŏl iil, hwayoil, manch'anhoerŭl kajil yejŏngimnida. 7월 2일, 화요일, 만찬회를 가질 예정입니다/ *Thank you for the*

wonderful ～ *the other night.* Yojŏnnal pam yungsunghan shiksarŭl taejŏp'ae chusyŏsŏ kamsahamnida. 요전날
밤 융숭한 식사를 대접해 주셔서 감사합니다.

diploma *n.* (*charter*) myŏnhŏchang 면허장, (*of college*)
chorŏp chŭngsŏ 졸업 증서.

diplomacy *n.* oegyo 외교. *armed* ～ muryŏk oegyo 무력 외교.

diplomat *n.* oegyogwan 외교관, oegyoga 외교가.

direct *adj.* (*immediate*) chikchŏbŭi 직접의, (*straight*) ttokparŭn 똑바른. —*vt.* (*point or aim*) karik'ida 가리키다,
(*control*) kamdok'ada 감독하다. ～ *train* chik'aeng yŏlch'a 직행 열차/ *Would you* ～ *me to the little boy's room?*
Hwajangshirŭn ŏdijiyo? 화장실은 어디지요/ *I'll* ～ *you as
we go.* Kamyŏnsŏ karik'yŏ tŭrigessŭmnida. 가면서 가
리켜 드리겠읍니다/ *Who* ～*ed the film?* Kŭ yŏnghwa
kamdogŭn nuguimnikka? 그 영화 감독은 누구입니까?

direction *n.* (*course*) panghyang 방향, (*guidance*) chido
지도, (*control*) kwalli 관리, (*instr.*) chishi 지시. *in every*
～ sabangŭro 사방으로/ *in the reverse* ～ pandae panghyangŭro 반대 방향으로/ *In which* ～ *did he go?* Kŭnŭn
ŏnŭ panghyangŭro kassŭmnikka? 그는 어느 방향으로 갔읍
니까/ *You have been riding in the opposite* ～. Tangshinŭn pandae panghyangŭro kashigo itkunyo. 당신은 반
대 방향으로 가시고 있군요/ *Go in this* ～. Itchoguro kashipshio. 이쪽으로 가십시오/ ～*s for use* sayongpŏp 사
용법/ *detailed* ～*s inside* chasehan sayongpŏbi ane tŭrŏ
issŭmnida 자세한 사용법이 안에 들어 있읍니다.

director *n.* (*manager*) chibaein 지배인, (*of a company*)
chungyŏk 중역, isa 이사(理事). *a board of* ～*s* isahoe
이사회/ (*film*) kamdok 감독/ *a personnel* ～ insa pujang 인사 부장/ *a stage* ～ mudae kamdok 무대 감독.

directory *n.* (*book of names and addresses*) inmyŏngnok 인명록. *a telephone* ～ chŏnhwa pŏnhobu 전화 번호
부.

dirt *n.* (*dust*) ssŭregi 쓰레기, (*filth*) omul 오물.

dirty *adj.* (*soiled*) tŏrŏun 더러운, pulgyŏrhan 불결한,
(*stormy*) hŏmak'an 험악한, (*obscene*) sangsŭrŏun 상스
러운. *a* ～ *room* pulgyŏrhan pang 불결한 방/ *a* ～ *weather*
hŏmak'an nalssi 험악한 날씨/ *a* ～ *joke* sangsŭrŏun nong

dam 상스러운 농담.

disabled *adj.* pulguga toen 불구가 된, mot ssŭge toen 못 쓰게 된. *a ~ soldier* sangi kunin 상이 군인/ *a ~ car* p'yech'a 폐차.

disadvantage *n.* pulli 불리(不利), (*damage*) sonhae 손해.

disagree *vi.* ilch'ihaji ant'a 일치하지 않다. *I am sorry to ~ with you.* Tangshinŭi ŭigyŏn-gwanŭn tarŭndeyo. 당신의 의견과는 다른데요.

disagreeable *adj.* pul(yu)k'waehan 불(유)쾌한, shirŭn 싫은. *~ weather* pulk'waehan nalssi 불쾌한 날씨/ *a ~ fellow* shimsulgujŭn nyŏsŏk 심술궂은 녀석.

disappear *vi.* sarajida 사라지다, ŏpsŏjida 없어지다. *He ~ed into the night.* Kŭnŭn ŏdum sogŭro sarajyŏssŭmnida. 그는 어둠 속으로 사라졌습니다.

disappoint *vt.* shilmanghada 실망하다. *Please don't ~ me.* Narŭl shilmangshik'iji mashio. 나를 실망시키지 마시오/ *I was ~ed at your absence.* Chibe an kyesyŏsŏ shilmanghaessŭmnida. 집에 안 계셔서 실망했습니다.

disappointment *n.* shilmang 실망, nakshim 낙심. *I had a great ~.* Nanŭn k'ŭge shilmanghaessŭmnida. 나는 크게 실망했습니다/ *To my great ~, she refused.* Nakshim ch'ŏnmanhagedo kŭnyŏnŭn kŏjŏrhaessŭmnida. 낙심 천만하게도 그녀는 거절했습니다.

disapprove *vt.* ch'ansŏnghaji ant'a 찬성하지 않다, pulch'ansŏnghada 불찬성하다, (*condemn*) pinanhada 비난하다. *I wholly ~ of what you say.* Nanŭn tangshin marŭl chŏnchŏgŭro ch'ansŏnghal su ŏpsŭmnida. 나는 당신 말을 전적으로 찬성할 수 없습니다.

disarmament *n.* mujang haeje 무장 해제, (*reduction of armaments*) kunbi ch'ukso 군비 축소. *~ talks* kunch'uk hoeŭi 군축 회의.

disaster *n.* chaenan 재난, (*misfortune*) purhaeng 불행.

disc, disk *n.*(*phonograph*) rek'odŭ 레코드, ch'ugŭmgip'an 축음기판. *I can't find the ~ I want.* Naega ch'atko innŭn rek'odŭnŭn ŏpkunyo. 내가 찾고 있는 레코드는 없군요.

discharge *vt.* (*shoot*) palsahada 발사하다, (*unload*) chimŭl purida 짐을 부리다, (*dismiss*) haegohada 해고하다, p'urŏnot'a 풀어 놓다. *The servant was* ～d. Kŭ koyonginŭn haegodoeŏssŭmnida. 그 고용인은 해고되었읍니다.

disciple *n.* cheja 제자, munhasaeng 문하생.

discipline *n.* hullyŏn 훈련, (*order*) kyuyul 규율. —*vt.*(*train*) hullyŏnhada 훈련하다, (*punish*) chinggyehada 징계하다. *military* ～ kun-gi 군기(軍紀)/ *official* ～ kwan-gi 관기 (官紀)/ *Your child is well* ～*d.* Aiege kirŭl chal tŭryŏtkunyo. 아이에게 길을 잘 들였군요.

disclose *vt.* tŭrŏnaeda 드러내다, (*reveal*) p'ongnohada 폭로하다, (*make known*) palp'yohada 발표하다. *He* ～*d the secret to me.* Kŭnŭn na-ege pimirŭl t'ŏrŏnoassŭmnida. 그는 나에게 비밀을 털어놓았읍니다.

discount *n.* harin 할인, enuri 에누리. —*vt.* harinhada 할인 하다. *Can you give me a* ～? Harinhae chushigessŭmnikka? 할인해 주시겠읍니까/ *Perhaps we could give you a* ～. Chom ssage haedŭril su issŭmnida. 좀 싸게 해드릴 수 있읍니다/ *I'll give you a special* ～ *of five per cent.* T'ŭkpyŏrhi o p'osent'ŭ harinhae tŭrigessŭmnida. 특별히 5 퍼센트 할인해 드리겠읍니다.

discourage *vt.* shilmangshik'ida 실망시키다, nakshimk'e hada 낙심케 하다. *We were* ～*d at the news.* Kŭ nyusŭrŭl tŭtko shilmanghaessŭmnida. 그 뉴스를 듣고 실망했읍니다./ *Why are you* ～*d?* Wae nakshimhasyŏssŭmnikka? 왜 낙심하셨읍니까?

discover *vt.* palgyŏnhada 발견하다, (*realize*) alge toeda 알 게되다. *I never* ～*ed how to start the engine.* Paltongŭl ŏttŏk'e kŏnŭnji al su ŏpsŏssŭmnida. 발동을 어떻게 거는지 알 수 없었읍니다/ *Who* ～*ed America in 1492?* Ch'ŏn sabaek kuship inyŏn Amerik'arŭl palgyŏnhan saramŭn nuguimnikka? 1492년 아메리카를 발견한 사람은 누구입니까?

discreet *adj.* shinjunghan 신중한, punbyŏl innŭn 분별 있는.

discuss *vt.* t'oronhada 토론하다, ŭinonhada 의논하다. *I wish to* ～ *something personal.* Sachŏgin iyagirŭl chom hago shipsŭmnida. 사적(私的)인 이야기를 좀 하고 싶습니다.

discussion *n.* t'oron 토론, t'oŭi 토의, (*critical exam.*) shimŭi 심의. *We had a long* ～ *about the question.* Kŭ munjee taehae oraettongan t'oronhaessŭmnida. 그 문제

에 대해 오랫동안 토론했읍니다.

disdain *vt.* kyŏngmyŏrhada 경멸하다. —*n.* myŏlshi 멸시.

disease *n.* pyŏng 병, chilbyŏng 질병.

disembark *vt.,vi.* yangnyuk'ada 양륙하다, sangnyuk'ada 상륙하다〔shik'ida〕상륙하다〔시키다〕. 「망신.

disgrace *n.* pulmyŏngye 불명예, (*loss of honor*) mangshin

disguise *vt.* pyŏnjanghada 변장하다, kajanghada 가장하다, (*hide*) kamch'uda 감추다. —*n.* pyŏnjang 변장. ～ *one's nationality* kukchŏgŭl sumgida 국적을 숨기다/ *in* ～ pyŏnjanghayŏ 변장하여/ ～ *oneself as a beggar* kŏjiro pyŏnjanghada 거지로 변장하다.

disgust *vt.* chigŭtchigŭt'age hada 지긋지긋하게 하다, pulk'waehage hada 불쾌하게 하다. —*n.* shiltchŭng 싫증. *I'm* ～*ed with the man.* Kŭ sanaiege nŏndŏriga namnida. 그 사나이에게 넌더리가 납니다.

dish *n.* chŏpshi 접시, (*food as served*) yori 요리. ～ *cloth* haengju 행주/ *vegetable* ～*es* yach'ae yori 야채 요리/ *a side* ～ anju 안주/ *What* ～*es would you recommend to us today ?* Onŭl yorinŭn muŏshimnikka ? 오늘 요리는 무엇입니까 ?

dishonest *adj.* chŏngjik'aji mot'an 정직하지 못한, pulsŏngshirhan 불성실한. *a* ～ *act* pujŏng haengwi 부정 행위.

dishono(u)r *n.* pulmyŏngye 불명예, (*disgrace*) mangshin 망신. —*vt.* mangshinshik'ida 망신시키다. ～*ed bill* pudo sup'yo 부도 수표.

disinfect *vt.* sodok〔salgyun〕hada 소독〔살균〕하다.

disinfectant *n.* sodok〔salgyun〕je 소독〔살균〕제.

dislike *vt.* shirŏhada 싫어하다. —*n.* hyŏmo 혐오, pan-gam 반감. *I took a great* ～ *for him.* Nanŭn kŭrŭl much'ŏk shirŏhaessŭmnida. 나는 그를 무척 싫어했읍니다/ *I* ～ *this kind of work.* Nanŭn irŏn yuŭi chagŏbŭl shirŏhamnida. 나는 이런 유의 작업을 싫어합니다.

dismal *adj.* ŭmch'imhan 음침한, uurhan 우울한. ～ *weather* ŭmch'imhan nalssi 음침한 날씨/ *a* ～ *voice* uurhan moksori 우울한 목소리.

dismiss *vt.* (*discharge*) haegohada 해고하다, (*disband*)

haesanhada 해산하다, (*expel*) ch'ubanghada 추방하다.

disobedient *adj*. sunjongch'i annŭn 순종치 않는, kobun-gobunhaji annŭn 고분고분하지 않는.

disobey *vt.,vi*. sunjonghaji ant'a 순종하지 않다, (*order*) ŏgida 어기다. *Do you ever ~ your parents?* Tangshinŭn hangsang pumo-ege sunjonghaji anssŭmnikka? 당신은 항상 부모에게 순종하지 않습니까?

disorder *n*. (*confusion*) nanjap 난잡, mujilsŏ 무질서, (*tumult*) sodong 소동.

dispatch *n*. kŭpp'a 급파, (*a letter*) soktal up'yŏn 속달 우편 —*vt*. (*send off*) p'agyŏnhada 파견하다, (*a letter*) palsonghada 발송하다. *Please hurry up the ~ of these telegrams.* I chŏnborŭl ppalli ponaeshio. 이 전보를 빨리 보내시오/ *I'll ~ our delivery boy right away.* Paedarhanŭn airŭl kot ponaegessŭmnida. 배달하는 아이를 곧 보내겠습니다.

dispensary *n*. yakkuk 약국, (*factory*) chillyoso 진료소.

display *vt*. (*show*) poida 보이다, (*exhibit*) chinyŏrhada 진열하다. —*n*. chinyŏl 진열, (*show*) p'yoshi 표시. *Department stores ~ their goods in the windows.* Paek'wajŏmŭn chinyŏlchange sangp'umŭl chinyŏrhamnida. 백화점은 진열장에 상품을 진열합니다/ *How much is this string of pearls you have on ~ over here?* Yŏgi chinyŏldoen i chinju mokkŏrinŭn ŏlmana hamnikka? 여기 진열된 이 진주 목걸이는 얼마나 합니까/ *be on ~* chinyŏldoeŏ itta 진열되어 있다/ *~ case* chinyŏlchang 진열장.

dispose *vt.,vi*. (*arrange*) paeyŏrhada 배열하다, (*deal with*) ch'ŏrihada 처리하다. (*incline*) *be ~d to* ...hago shipta ...하고 싶다. *How can we ~ of all this rubbish?* I ssŭregirŭl ta ŏttŏk'e ch'ŏrihajiyo? 이 쓰레기를 다 어떻게 처리하지요/ *I'm not ~d to help that lazy fellow.* Kú keŭrŭn nyŏsŏgŭl topko shipchi anssŭmnida. 그 게으른 녀석을 돕고 싶지 않습니다.

dispute *vt.,vi*. (*debate*) maldat'umhada 말다툼하다, (*discuss*) nonŭihada 논의하다. —*n*. nonjaeng 논쟁, chaengŭi 쟁의(爭議). *a public ~* konggae t'oron 공개 토론/ *an employer-employee ~* nosaganŭi chaengŭi 노사간의 쟁의/ *a* *party* ∼ tangp'a ssaum 당파 싸움.

disregard *vt.* (*ignore*) mushihada 무시하다, kyŏngshihada 경시하다. —*n.* mushi 무시, mugwanshim 무관심.

dissolve *vi.,vt.* (*cause to melt*) nogida 녹이다, (*parl.*) haesanhada 해산하다. *D*∼ *the salt in water.* Sogŭmŭl mure nogishio. 소금을 물에 녹이시오/ *Parliament* ∼*d.* Kuk'oenŭn haesanhaessŭmnida. 국회는 해산했읍니다.

distance *n.* kŏri 거리, (*remote point*) mŏn kot 먼 곳, (*interval*) kan-gyŏk 간격. *What is the* ∼ *from here to Seoul?* Yŏgisŏ Sŏulkkaji ŏlmana mŏmnikka? 여기서 서울까지 얼마나 멉니까/ *I'd like to make a long* ∼ *call.* Changgŏri chŏnhwarŭl kŏlgo shipsŭmnida. 장거리 전화를 걸고 싶습니다/ *I saw some one in the* ∼. Mŏlli nugun-gaga poyŏssŭmnida. 멀리 누군가가 보였읍니다.

distant *adj.* (*far off*) mŏn 먼, (*time*) oraen 오랜, (*not friendly*) sŏrŭmhan 서름한. *We have always been rather* ∼. Urinŭn hangsang sŏrŭmsŏrŭmhan saiyŏssŭmnida. 우리는 항상 서름서름한 사이였읍니다.

distinctly *adv.* myŏnghwak'age 명확하게, ttoryŏshi 또렷이. *Please speak more* ∼. Chom tŏ myŏnghwak'age malssŭmhae chushipshio. 좀 더 명확하게 말씀해 주십시오/ *I* ∼ *told him what to do.* Nanŭn kŭege hal irŭl punmyŏnghi marhae chuŏssŭmnida. 나는 그에게 할 일을 분명히 말해 주었읍니다.

distinguish *v.* kubyŏrhada 구별하다, shikpyŏrhada 식별하다. ∼ *from* ...wa ...ŭl kubyŏrhada …와 …을 구별하다/ *I can* ∼ *right from wrong.* Nanŭn sŏnagŭl kubyŏrhal suga issŭmnida. 나는 선악(善惡)을 구별할 수가 있읍니다/ *What* ∼*es the hare from the rabbit?* Sant'okkiwa chipt'okkiŭi ch'ainŭn muŏshimnikka? 산토끼와 집토끼의 차이는 무엇입니까/ ∼ *oneself* yumyŏnghaejida 유명해지다.

distract *vt.* (*divert*) hŭttŭrida 흩뜨리다, (*confuse*) ŏjirŏp'ida 어지럽히다. *My ears are* ∼*ed by noises.* Shikkŭrŏwŏ kwiga wangwang ullimnida. 시끄러워 귀가 왕왕 울립니다.

distraction *n.* (*madness*) chŏngshin ch'angnan 정신 착란, (*amusement*) kibun chŏnhwan 기분 전환.

distress *n.* (*worry*) komin 고민, (*grief*) pit'an 비탄, (*poverty*) pin-gon 빈곤. —*vt.* (*afflict*) koerop'ida 괴롭히다, (*make miserable*) sŭlp'ŭge hada 슬프게 하다. *Don't ~ yourself.* Kŏkchŏnghaji mashio. 걱정하지 마시오.

distribute *vt.* (*allot*) nanuŏ chuda 나누어 주다, (*spread*) p'ŏttŭrida 퍼뜨리다, (*classify*) kubunhada 구분한다. *I ~d the sweets among the children.* Sat'angŭl aidŭrege nanuŏ chuŏssŭmnida. 사탕을 아이들에게 나누어 주었읍니다/ *D~ this money among you three.* I tonŭl tangshindŭl se puni nanuŏ kajishio. 이 돈을 당신들 세 분이 나누어 가지시오.

district *n.* chigu 지구(地區), (*region*) chibang 지방. *an agricultural ~* nongŏp chidae 농업 지대/*an electoral ~* sŏn-gŏgu 선거구/ *the theatrical ~* kŭkchangga 극장가/ *a ~ court* chibang pŏbwŏn 지방 법원.

disturb *vt.* panghaehada 방해하다, (*disarrange*) kyoranhada 교란하다. *Don't ~ yourself.* Kŭdaero kyeshipshio. 그대로 계십시오/ *I'm afraid I'm ~ing you.* Hokshi panghaega toeji anssŭmnikka? 혹시 방해가 되지 않습니까?

ditch *n.* torang 도랑, kaech'ŏn 개천.

dive *vi.* (*plunge into water*) ttwiŏdŭlda 뛰어들다, chamsuhada 잠수하다, taibinghada 다이빙하다. —*n.* chamsu 잠수.

divide *vt.,vi.* nanuda 나누다, (*set apart*) pullihada 분리하다, (*split up*) iganhada 이간한다. *D~ 8 by 2, and you get 4.* P'arŭl iro nanushio. Kŭrŏmyŏn saga toemnida. 8을 2로 나누시오. 그러면 4가 됩니다/ *D~ this for both of you.* Igŏsŭl tangshinne turisŏ nanushio. 이것을 당신네 둘이서 나누시오/ *We ~d the money equally.* Urinŭn kŭ tonŭl koru nanuŏ kajyŏssŭmnida. 우리는 그 돈을 고루 나누어 가졌읍니다.

dividend *n.* paedanggŭm 배당금. *The company paid a 10% ~ last year.* Kŭ hoesanŭn chinanhae ship p'ŏsent'ŭŭi paedanggŭmŭl chiburhaessŭmnida. 그 회사는 지난해 10퍼센트의 배당금을 지불했읍니다.

division *n.* nanugi 나누기, punhal 분할, (*mil.*) sadan 사단. *~ of labor* punŏp 분업.

divorce *n.* ihon 이혼. —*vt.* ihonhada 이혼하다. *a ~ suit* ihon sosong 이혼 소송/ ~ *procedure* ihon susok 이혼 수속/ *a* ~ *notice* ihon shin-go 이혼 신고/ *a* ~ *by agreement* habŭi ihon 합의 이혼.

dizziness *n.* hyŏn-gichŭng 현기증, atchirham 아찔함.

dizzy *adj.* hyŏn-gichŭngi nanŭn 현기증이 나는, ŏjirŏjirhan 어질어질한. *a* ~ *height* atchirhal mank'ŭm nop'ŭn kot 아찔할 만큼 높은 곳/ *I often get* ~ *spells.* Nanŭn ittagŭm ŏjirŏpsŭmnida. 나는 이따금 어지럽습니다.

do *vt.,vi.* (*act*) hada 하다, (*confer*) pep'ulda 베풀다, (*deal with*) ch'ŏrihada 처리하다, (*visit*) kugyŏnghada 구경하다, (*suit*) ssŭl manhada 쓸 만하다. —*aux.v.*(*ques., emph.*) *What are you ~ing now?* Chigŭm muŏsŭl hago kyeshimnikka? 지금 무엇을 하고 계십니까/ *I'll* ~ *what I can.* Ch'oesŏnŭl tahagessŭmnida. 최선을 다하겠습니다/ *Would you* ~ *me a favor?* Put'ak'aedo chossŭmnikka? 부탁해도 좋습니까/ *Will this racket* ~ *you?* I rak'esŭro ch'ungbunhalkkayo? 이 라켓으로 충분할까요/ *That will* ~ *me very well.* Kŭmanhamyŏn toemnida. 그만하면 됩니다/ *D~ come again.* Kkok tto oshipshio. 꼭 또 오십시오.

dock *n.* (*slip*) tok 독, sŏn-gŏ 선거(船渠).

dockyard *n.* (*shipyard*) chosŏnso 조선소(造船所).

doctor *n.* ŭisa 의사(醫師), (*degree*) paksa 박사. *a herb* ~ hanbangŭi 한방의(漢方醫)/ *a lady* ~ yŏŭisa 여의사/ *a quack* ~ tolp'ari ŭisa 돌팔이 의사/*D~ of Medicine* ŭihak paksa 의학 박사/ *Would you send for a* ~, *please?* Ŭisarŭl pullŏ chuseyo. 의사를 불러 주세요/ *I advise you to see the* ~. Ŭisahant'e ka poseyo. 의사한테 가 보세요.

document *n.* sŏryu 서류, munsŏ 문서. *official* ~ kongmunsŏ 공문서/ *legal* ~ pŏmnyul sŏryu 법률 서류.

dog *n.* kae 개. ~ *days* sambok 삼복/*a fierce* ~ maenggyŏn 맹견/ *a mad* ~ mich'in kae 미친 개/ *a hunting* ~ sanyangkae 사냥개/ *You* ~! I kaejashik! 이 개자식!

doll *n.* inhyŏng 인형. *a* ~ *play* inhyŏnggŭk 인형극 / *Do you have any Arirang dancing* ~ *s?* Arirang ch'umŭl ch'unŭn inhyŏng issŭmnikka? 아리랑 춤을 추는 인형 있습니까?

dollar *n.* tallŏ 달러, pul 불(弗). ~ *diplomacy* tallŏ oegyo 달러 외교/ *I sold it for a* ~. Kŭgŏsŭl il tallŏe p'arassŭmnida. 그것을 1달러에 팔았읍니다/ *I can't go beyond a* ~. Il tallŏ isangŭn kŏl su ŏpsŭmnida. 1달러 이상은 걸 수 없읍니다/ ~ *crisis* tallŏ wigi 달러 위기.

dolphin *n.* (*sea animal*) tolgorae 돌고래.

domestic *adj.* (*of the home*) kajŏngŭi 가정의, (*native*) kungnaeŭi 국내의. ~ *affairs* kasa 가사/ ~ *animals* kach'uk 가축/ ~ *industry* kanae kongŏp 가내 공업/ ~ *airline* kungnae hanggong 국내 항공/ ~ *mail* kungnae up'yŏn 국내 우편/ ~ *production* kuksanp'um 국산품.

domicile *n.* (*place of residence*) chuso 주소, (*abode*) chugŏ 주거, (*home*) chip 집. —*vi.* (*dwell*) salda 살다. *I'm* ~*d in Seoul.* Nae ponjŏkchinŭn Sŏurimnida. 내 본 적지는 서울입니다.

done *adj.* (*cooked*) igŭn 익은, kuwŏjin 구워진. *half-*~ pantchŭm igŭn 반쯤 익은/ *over-*~ nŏmu igŭn 너무 익은/ *under-*~ sŏrigŭn 설익은/ *I'd like mine well* ~, *please.* Naegŏsŭn passak kuwŏ chuseyo. 내것은 바싹 구워 주세요.

donkey *n.* tangnagwi 당나귀, (*silly person*) pabo 바보.

doom *n.* (*fate*) unmyŏng 운명, agun 악운, (*death*) chugŭm 죽음.

door *n.* mun 문, toŏ 도어, (*entrance*) ch'uripku 출입구. *back* ~ twinmun 뒷문/ *front* ~ ammun 앞문/*next* ~ iut 이웃/ *Wait a moment at the front* ~. Hyŏn-gwan ipkuesŏ chamkkan kidaryŏ chushipshio. 현관 입구에서 잠깐 기다려 주십시오/*Close the* ~ *after you, please.* Nagashin twi munŭl tada chuseyo. 나가신 뒤 문을 닫아 주세요/ ~ *mat* shin hŭkttŏlgae 신 흙떨개.

doorbell *n.* hyŏn-gwanŭi pel 현관의 벨, ch'oinjong 초인종.

doorman *n.* (*doorkeeper*) munjigi 문지기, suwi 수위.

doorway *n.* taemunkan 대문간, ch'uripku 출입구.

dope *n.* (*narcotic*) mach'wiyak 마취약.

dormitory *n.* kisuksa 기숙사, hapsukso 합숙소.

dot *n.* chŏm 점(點). —*vt.* chŏmŭl tchikta 점을 찍다. *a* ~*ted line* chŏmsŏn 점선.

double *adj.* tu paeŭi 두 배의, kapchŏrŭi 갑절의. —*n.* tu pae

두배, ibae 2배. —*vt.* tu paero hada 두 배로 하다. ~ *doors* ijungmun 이중문/ *a* ~ *bed* iinyong ch'imdae 2인용 침대/ *a* ~ *lock* ijung chamulsoe 2중 자물쇠/ *I want a* ~ *with a bath, please.* Yokt'angi ttallin iinyong pangi chok'essŭmnida. 욕탕이 딸린 2인용 방이 좋겠읍니다.

doubt *n.* ŭishim 의심, ŭihok 의혹. —*vt.* ŭishimhada 의심하다. *There is no* ~ *about it.* Kŭgŏse t'ŭllimi ŏpsŭmnida. 그것에 틀림이 없읍니다/ *He'll come back without* ~. Kŭnŭn t'ŭllimŏpshi toraol kŏshimnida. 그는 틀림없이 돌아올 것입니다/ *Do you* ~ *my word?* Nae marŭl mot mitkessŭmnikka? 내 말을 못 믿겠읍니까/ *I* ~ *he is a thief.* Kŭga todugirani midŏjiji anssŭmnida. 그가 도둑이라니 믿어지지 않습니다.

doubtful *adj.* (*uncertain*) hwakshilch'i anŭn 확실치 않은, (*ambiguous*) ŭishimsŭrŏun 의심스러운.

dough *n.* (*paste for bread*) milkaru panjuk 밀가루 반죽, (*money*) ton 돈, hyŏnch'al 현찰.

dove *n.* pidulgi 비둘기. *a* ~ *of peace* p'yŏnghwaŭi pidulgi 평화의 비둘기. ~ *cage* pidulgijang 비둘기장.

down *adv.* arae 아래, araero 아래로. *Put that gun* ~. Kŭ ch'ong naeryŏnoŭshio. 그 총 내려놓으시오/ *I'll come* ~ *soon.* Kot naeryŏgagessŭmnida. 곧 내려가겠읍니다.

downtown *n.* toshimji 도심지, sangga chidae 상가 지대. —*adj.* toshimjiŭi 도심지의. —*adv.* toshimjie[ro] 도심지에[로]. *I have to go* ~ *this afternoon.* Onŭl ohu sangga-e kaya hamnida. 오늘 오후 상가(商街)에 가야 합니다/ *You can buy it in a special shop in* ~ *Seoul.* Kŭgŏsŭn Sŏul shinae t'ŭkpyŏrhan sangjŏmesŏman sal su issŭmnida. 그것은 서울 시내 특별한 상점에서만 살 수 있읍니다.

doze *vi.* (*nap*) cholda 졸다, sŏnjam chada 선잠 자다. —*n.* (*light sleep*) chorŭm 졸음, sŏnjam 선잠.

dozen *n.* tasŭ 다스, t'a 타(打). *two* ~(*s*) *of pencil* yŏnp'il tu tasŭ 연필 두 다스. *I want three* ~ *of these.* 1-gŏt se tasŭga p'iryohamnida. 이것 세 다스가 필요합니다/ *Pack them in* ~*s.* Han tasŭssik ssashio. 한 다스씩 싸시오.

draft, draught *n.* (*bank bill*) hwanŏŭm 환어음, (*a plan*) ch'oan 초안, (*Am.*) (*conscription*) chingbyŏng 징병. *a* *bank* ~ ŭnhaeng ŏŭm 은행 어음/*Where can I cash this* ~? Ŏdisŏ i ŏŭmŭl pakkul su issŭmnikka? 어디서 이 어음을 바꿀 수 있읍니까/ ~ *beer* saengmaekchu 생맥주/ ~ *card* sojip yŏngchang 소집 영장.

drag *vt.* (*haul*) kkŭlda 끌다, (*trail*) chiljil kkŭlda 질질 끌다, (*dredge*) twijida 뒤지다, (*harrow*) korŭda 고르다.

dragon *n.* yong 용.

dragonfly *n.* (*large insect*) chamjari 잠자리.

drain *n.* such'ae 수채, hasudo 하수도. —*vt.* (*water*) ppajige hada 빠지게 하다. *Please don't* ~ *the bathtub.* T'angmurŭl hŭllyŏ pŏriji mashio. 탕물을 흘려 버리지 마시오.

drama *n.* (*play*) kŭk 극, yŏn·gŭk 연극. *the musical* ~ akkŭk 악극/ *the historical* ~ sagŭk 사극.

dramatic *adj.* kŭkchŏgin 극적인. *a* ~ *performance* yŏn·gi 연기/ ~ *changes* kŭkchŏk pyŏnhwa 극적 변화.

draper *n.* p'omoksang 포목상, chingmulsang 직물상.

draw *vt.* (*pull*) tanggida 당기다. (*inhale*) tŭrimashida 들이마시다, (*sketch*) kŭrida 그리다, (*take out*) kkŏnaeda 꺼내다. —*n.* (*tie*) musŭngbu 무승부. *Will you* ~ *me brief map to reach the Haeinsa temple?* Haeinsaro kanŭn yaktorŭl kŭryŏ chushigessŭmnikka? 해인사(海印寺)로 가는 약도를 그려 주시겠읍니까/ *The match ended in a* ~. Shihabŭn musŭngburo kkŭnnassŭmnida. 시합은 무승부로 끝났읍니다.

drawer *n.* (*of table*) sŏrap 서랍. *chest of* ~*s* changnong 장롱/*Open the second* ~ *from the top.* Wiesŏ tultchaepŏn sŏrabŭl yŏshio. 위에서 둘째번 서랍을 여시오/ *You will find it in the bottom* ~. Kŭgŏsŭn kajang arae sŏrabe issŭmnida. 그것은 가장 아래 서랍에 있읍니다/ *a desk* ~ ch'aeksang sŏrap 책상 서랍.

drawers *n.* p'aench'ŭ 팬츠, sokpaji 속바지, tŭrojŭ 드로즈. *bathing* ~ haesuyok p'aench'ŭ 해수욕 팬츠/ *Have my* ~ *pressed.* Nae p'aench'ŭrŭl taryŏ chushio. 내 팬츠를 다려 주시오.

dread *n.* kongp'o 공포. —*vt.* musŏwŏhada 무서워하다. *Do you* ~ *a visit to the dentist?* Ch'ikwa ŭisa-ege ch'ajaganŭn kŏshi musŏpsŭmnikka. 치과 의사에게 찾아가는 것이

무섭습니까?

dreadful *adj.* musŏun 무서운, mushimushihan 무시무시한. *What a ∼ story!* Ch'amŭro musŏun iyagigun! 참으로 무서운 이야기군/ *What a ∼ weather!* Ch'amŭro pulk'waehan nalssigun! 참으로 불쾌한 날씨군!

dream *n.* kkum 꿈. —*vt.,vi.* kkumŭl kkuda 꿈을 꾸다. *I had a ∼ about you last night.* Ŏjetpam tangshin kkumŭl kkuŏssŭmnida. 어젯밤 당신 꿈을 꾸었읍니다/ *I had awful ∼s.* Nanŭn musŏun kkumŭl kkuŏssŭmnida. 나는 무서운 꿈을 꾸었읍니다/ *My ∼ has been fulfilled.* Kkumi shirhyŏndoeŏssŭmnida. 꿈이 실현되었읍니다.

drench *vt.* hŭmppŏk chŏkshida 흠뻑 적시다. *I was ∼ed to the skin with rain.* Nanŭn pie hŭmppŏk chŏjŏssŭmnida. 나는 비에 흠뻑 젖었읍니다.

dress *n.* ot 옷, ŭibok 의복, dŭresŭ 드레스. —*vt.,vi.* osŭl ip'ida 옷을 입히다, osŭl ipta 옷을 입다. ∼*maker* yangjaesa 양재사/ *full ∼* chŏngjang 정장(正裝)/ *What do you think of the Korean ∼?* Hanbogŭl ŏttŏk'e saenggak'ashimnikka? 한복을 어떻게 생각하십니까/ *This is not an authentic Korean ∼.* Igŏn chintcha hanbogi animnida. 이건 진짜 한복이 아닙니다/ *What is the material of this ∼?* I tŭresŭŭi ch'ŏnŭn muŏshimnikka? 이 드레스의 천은 무엇입니까/ *Do I need to ∼ up?* Chŏngjangŭl haeya hamnikka? 정장을 해야 합니까?

dressing *n.* (*dress*) onmaemusae 옷매무새, (*sauce*) sosŭ 소스, mayonejŭ 마요네즈. ∼ *gown* hwajangot 화장옷/ ∼ *table* hwajangdae 화장대/ *What kind of salad ∼ do you have?* Saellŏdŭ tŭreshingi muŏjiyo? 샐러드 드레싱이 무어지요/ *What kind of ∼ do you want on your salad?* Saellŏdŭe ŏttŏn tŭreshingŭl wŏnhashimnikka? 샐러드에 어떤 드레싱을 원하십니까?

drift *n.* p'yoryu 표류, (*trend*) tonghyang 동향. —*vi.* p'yoryuhada 표류하다, ttŏdolda 떠돌다, (*go aimlessly*) mujakchŏng naagada 무작정 나아가다.

drill *n.* (*mil.*) kyoryŏn 교련(敎練), hullyŏn 훈련, (*tool*) songgot 송곳, tŭril 드릴. *fire ∼* panghwa hullyŏn 방화훈련.

drink *n.* ŭmnyo 음료. —*vt.*,*vi.* mashida 마시다. *soft* ～ ch'ŏng-nyang ŭmnyo 청량 음료/ *strong* ～ churyu 주류(酒類)/ *Let me buy you a* ～. Naega hanjan sagessŭmnida. 내가 한잔 사겠읍니다/ *Let's go out for a* ～, *shall we?* Nagasŏ hanjan halkkayo? 나가서 한잔 할까요/ *What would you like to* ～? Muŏsŭl mashigessŭmnikka? 무엇을 마시겠읍니까/ *Would you like something to* ～? Muŏn-ga mashil kŏsŭl tŭrilkkayo? 무언가 마실 것을 드릴 까요.

drinker *n.* sulkkun 술꾼, (*hard* ～) taejuga 대주가.

drip *vi.*,*vt.* (*in drops*) tŭtta 듣다, ttokttok ttŏrŏjida 똑똑 떨어지다.

drive *n.* unjŏn 운전, tŭraibŭ 드라이브. —*vt.*, *vi.* unjŏnhada 운전하다, tŭraibŭhada 드라이브하다. ～ *a nail home* mosŭl kip'i pakta 못을 깊이 박다/ *Can you* ～ *an automobile?* Chadongch'arŭl unjŏnhal chul ashimnikka? 자동차를 운전할 줄 아십니까/ *Have you had much experience in driving?* Unjŏn kyŏnghŏmŭn manŭshin-gayo? 운전 경험은 많으신가요/*How about a* ～ *to Kyongju?* Kyŏngjukkaji tŭraibŭhaji ank'essŭmnikka? 경주까지 드라이브하지 않겠 읍니까/ *Shall we* ～ *home or walk?* Chibe ch'aro kalkkayo, kŏrŏsŏ kalkkayo? 집에 차로 갈까요, 걸어서 갈까요?

driver *n.* unjŏnsa 운전사, (*of horses*) mabu 마부. *a taxi* ～ t'aekshi unjŏnsa 택시 운전사.

drop *n.* pangul 방울. —*vi.*,*vt.* ttŏrŏjida 떨어지다, ttŏrŏttŭrida 떨어뜨리다, (*send a message*) ssŏbonaeda 써보내다. *a* ～ *of rain* pitpangul 빗방울/*tear* ～*s* nunmul pangul 눈물 방울/ ～ *in* chamkkan tŭllŭda 잠깐 들르다/ *She* ～*ped the teapot.* Kŭnyŏnŭn ch'atchujŏnjarŭl ttŏrŏttŭryŏssŭmnida. 그녀는 찻주전자를 떨어뜨렸읍니다/ *Can you* ～ *the price a little?* Kapsŭl chom kkakkŭl su issŭmnikka? 값을 좀 깎을 수 있읍니까/ *Where shall I* ～ *you?* Ŏdisŏ naeryŏ tŭrilkkayo? 어디서 내려 드릴까요/ *May I* ～ *in sometime next week?* Taŭmchutchŭm tŭllŭlkkayo? 다음주쯤 들를까요/ *Would you like to* ～ *in to have a cup of tea?* Ch'a han chan hage tŭllŭshigessŏyo? 차 한 잔 하게 들르시겠어요/ *I'll* ～ *you a line.* P'yŏnji yŏllak tŭrigessŭmnida. 편지 연락 드리겠읍니다.

drown *vi.,vt.* ppajida 빠지다, iksahada 익사하다, ppattŭrida 빠뜨리다. ~ *oneself* t'ushin chasarhada 투신 자살하다. *He was* ~*ed at sea.* Kŭnŭn pada-esŏ iksahaessŭmnida. 그는 바다에서 익사했읍니다/ *They* ~*ed while swimming in a river.* Kangesŏ heŏm(ŭl) ch'idaga iksahaessŭmnida. 강에서 헤엄(을) 치다가 익사했읍니다.

drug *n.* yak 약, (*narcotics*) mach'wiyak 마취약. *an effective* ~ myoyak 묘약/ *a poisonous* ~ togyak 독약.

drugstore *n.* yakpang 약방.

drum *n.* puk 북. *beat a* ~ pugŭl ch'ida 북을 치다.

drummer *n.* kosu 고수(鼓手).

drunk *vi.,vt.* ch'wihan 취한, sulch'wihan 술취한. *I'm* ~ *on green tea.* Nanŭn nokch'a-e ch'wihaessŭmnida. 나는 녹차에 취했읍니다/ *He is dead* ~. Kondŭremandŭre ch'wihaessŭmnida. 곤드레만드레 취했읍니다.

drunkard *n.* sulkkun 술꾼, sulgorae 술고래, chujŏngbaengi 주정뱅이.

dry *adj.* marŭn 마른, (*of climate*) kŏnjohan 건조한. —*vt.,vi.* mallida 말리다, (*wipe away*) ssitta 씻다, marŭda 마르다. *a* ~ *battery* kŏnjŏnji 건전지/ ~ *milk* punyu 분유/ *We were* ~*ing our clothes in front of the fire.* Pul ap'esŏ osŭl malligo issŏssŭmnida. 불 앞에서 옷을 말리고 있었읍니다/ *D*~ *your hands on this towel.* I sugŏnŭro sonŭl takkŭshio. 이 수건으로 손을 닦으시오.

dry-clean *vt.* tŭrai k'ŭllininghada 드라이 클리닝하다. *Will you have this* ~*ed, please.* Igŏl tŭrai k'ŭllininghae chuseyo. 이걸 드라이 클리닝해 주세요.

dryer (*drier*) kŏnjogi 건조기, tŭraiŏ 드라이어.

duck *n.* ori 오리. *the domestic* ~ chibori 집오리/ *the wild* ~ murori 물오리.

due *adj.* (*payable*) chiburhaeya hal 지불해야 할, (*proper*) tangyŏnhan 당연한, (~ *to*) ...ttaemune ...때문에, (*appointed*) yejŏngin 예정인. *When is the rent* ~? Chipsenŭn ŏnje ch'irŭmnikka? 집세는 언제 치릅니까/ *My salary is* ~ *tomorrow.* Nae ponggŭbŭn naeirimnida. 내 봉급은 내일입니다/ *Our train is* ~ *at Seoul at 6.30 p.m.* Uri yŏlch'anŭn ohu yŏsŏssi pane Sŏure toch'ak'al yejŏngimnida. 우리 열차는 오후 6시 반에 서울에 도착할 예정입니다/ *D~ to his intemperance he lost his health.* Mujŏlche ttaemune kŭnŭn kŏn-gangŭl haech'yŏssŭmnida. 무절제 때문에 그는 건강을 해쳤읍니다.

duet *n.* ijungch'ang 이중창, ijungju 이중주. 「지위.

duke *n.* kongjak 공작. *rank of* ~ kongjagŭi chiwi 공작의

dull *adj.* (*blunt*) mudin 무딘, (*dim*) hŭrit'an 흐릿한, (*stupid*) udunhan 우둔한. *a* ~ *knife* mudin k'al 무딘 칼/ ~ *weather* hŭrit'an nalssi 흐릿한 날씨/ ~ *pupils* mŏriga tunhan haksaengdŭl 머리가 둔한 학생들.

dumb *adj.* mal mot hanŭn 말 못 하는, pŏngŏriŭi 벙어리의, (*Am.*) (*foolish*) udunhan 우둔한. *We must be kind to* ~ *animals.* Mal mot hanŭn chimsŭngegenŭn ch'injŏrhi taehaeya hamnida. 말 못 하는 짐승에게는 친절히 대해야 합니다/ *a blind and* ~ *school* nonga hakkyo 농아 학교.

dumbbell *n.* aryŏng 아령, (*dolt*) mŏngch'ŏngi 멍청이.

dummy *n.* (*straw man*) kkoktukkakshi 꼭둑각시, hŏsuabi 허수아비, (*model*) manek'in 마네킨, (*blockhead*) pabo 바보.

dumping *n.* t'umae 투매(投賣), tŏmp'ing 덤핑. *a* ~ *field* t'umae shijang 투매 시장/ ~ *ground* ssŭregi pŏrinŭn kot 쓰레기 버리는 곳.

duplicate *n.* sabon 사본(寫本), (*copy*) poksa 복사.

during *prep.* ...tongane ...동안에, ...hanŭn chung ...하는 중. ~ *life time* ilsaeng tongan 일생 동안/ ~ *one's illness* wabyŏngjung 와병중/ ~ *my absence* naega ŏmnŭn tongane 내가 없는 동안에/ ~ *the night* pamchunge 밤중에.

dusk *n.* ttangkŏmi 땅거미, hwanghon 황혼. *at* ~ haejil muryŏp 해질 무렵/ *from dawn till* ~ ach'imbut'ŏ chŏnyŏkkkaji 아침부터 저녁까지.

dust *n.* mŏnji 먼지, t'ikkŭl 티끌. —*vt., vi.* ch'ŏngsohada 청소하다. *With this, wipe the* ~ *from your face.* Igŏllo ŏlgurŭi mŏnjirŭl ssisŭshio. 이걸로 얼굴의 먼지를 씻으시오/ *Please* ~ *more carefully.* Chomdŏ choshimhayŏ ch'ŏngsohashio. 좀더 조심하여 청소하시오.

dustbin *n.* (*Am.*) (*ash can*) ssŭregit'ŏng 쓰레기통.

duster *n.* mŏnjittŏri 먼지떨이, ch'ongch'ae 총채.

dusty *adj.* mŏnjit'usŏngiŭi 먼지투성이의, mŏnjiga manŭn 먼지가 많은. *a ~ road* mŏnjit'usŏngiŭi kil 먼지투성이의 길/ *a ~ room* mŏnjit'usŏngiŭi pang 먼지투성이의 방.

Dutch *n.* Nedŏllandŭ saram 네덜란드 사람, Nedŏllandŭ mal 네덜란드 말. *go ~ kakcha pudamŭro hada* 각자 부담으로 하다/ *Let's go ~. Kakcha pudamŭro hapshida.* 각자 부담으로 합시다.

duty *n.* ŭimu 의무, ponbun 본분, (*tax*) chose 조세(租稅). *Don't forget your ~ to your parents. Pumo-e taehan ponbunŭl itchi mashio.* 부모에 대한 본분을 잊지 마시오/ *day*[*night*] *~ chugan*[*yagan*] kŭnmu 주간[야간] 근무/ *military duties kunmu* 군무/ *entertainment ~ yuhŭngse* 유흥세/ *death duties sangsokse* 상속세/ *transit ~ t'onghaengse* 통행세/ *off ~ pidangbŏn* 비당번/ *on ~ tangbŏn* 당번.

dwarf *n.* nanjangi 난장이. *—adj.* chagŭn 작은, kkomaŭi 꼬마의.

dwell *vi.* salda 살다, kŏjuhada 거주하다, (*brood over*) komgomi saenggak'ada 곰곰이 생각하다.

dweller *n.* (*resident*) kŏjuja 거주자, chumin 주민.

dwelling *n.* (*house*) chip 집, kŏch'ŏ 거처. *~ house chut'aek* 주택/sallimchip 살림집/ *~ place chuso* 주소/*a modern ~ munhwa chut'aek* 문화 주택/ *a rental ~ setchip* 셋집/ *You have changed your ~, haven't you? Isahashin ke animnikka?* 이사하신 게 아닙니까?

dye *n.* mulkam 물감, yŏmnyo 염료, (*tinge*) pitkkal 빛깔. *—vt.,vi.* yŏmsaek'ada 염색하다, muldŭlda 물들다. *~ a white dress blue hŭin osŭl ch'ŏngsaegŭro yŏmsaek'ada* 흰 옷을 청색으로 염색하다.

dye house yŏmsaekchip 염색집.

dye works yŏmsaek kongjang 염색 공장.

dynamic *adj.* himch'an 힘찬, tongch'ŏgin 동적인. *—n.* wŏndongnyŏk 원동력. *~ engineering kigye konghak* 기계 공학.

dynamite *n.* tainŏmait'ŭ 다이너마이트.

dynamo *n.* palchŏn-gi 발전기, tainŏmo 다이너모.

dynasty *n.* wangjo 왕조. *White ceramic of the Yi ~ is well*

known throughout the world. Ijo paekchanŭn chon se-
gyee chal allyŏjyŏ issŭmnida. 이조 백자는 전 세계에 잘
알려져 있읍니다/ *King Sejong of the Yi ~* Issi wang-
joŭi Sejong taewang 이씨(李氏) 왕조의 세종 대왕.

dysentery *n.* ijil 이질(痢疾), sŏlsapyŏng 설사병.

E

each *adj.* kakkagŭi 각각의, kakchaŭi 각자의. —*pron.* chŏmada 저마다, kakkak 각각. —*adv.* kakki 각기. *E~ country has its own customs.* Kak naranŭn kŭ t'ŭgyuŭi
p'ungsŭbi issŭmnida. 각 나라는 그 특유의 풍습이 있읍니다/
~ one of us uridŭl kakcha 우리들 각자/ *E~ of us
has his own desk.* Urinŭn chŏmada chagi ch'aeksangŭl
kajigo issŭmnida. 우리는 저마다 자기 책상을 가지고 있읍니
다/ *Give them two ~.* Kakki tu kaessik chushio. 각기
두 개씩 주시오/*love ~ other* sŏro saranghada 서로 사랑하
다/ *bow to ~ other* sŏro chŏrŭl hada 서로 절을 하다.

eager *adj.* yŏlmanghanŭn 열망하는, kanjŏrhi paranŭn 간
절히 바라는. *We are ~ for peace.* Urinŭn p'yŏnghwarŭl
kalmanghamnida. 우리는 평화를 갈망합니다/ *I'm not ~
to defend them.* Nanŭn kuji kŭdŭrŭl pyŏnhoharyŏnŭn
kosŭn animnida. 나는 굳이 그들을 변호하려는 것은 아닙니다.

eagerly *adv.* yŏlshimhi 열심히, kanjŏrhi 간절히.

eagle *n.* toksuri 독수리.

ear *n.* kwi 귀, (*corn*) isak 이삭. *~drop* (*earring*)
kwigŏri 귀걸이/ *~phone* iŏp'on 이어폰/ *~pick* kwii-
gae 귀이개/ *have a ~ for* ihaehada 이해하다/ *I've no ~
for music.* Nanŭn ŭmagŭl morŭmnida. 나는 음악을 모릅
니다/ *I could hardly believe my ~s.* Tojŏhi midŏjiji
anssŭmnida. 도저히 믿어지지 않습니다.

early *adj.* irŭn 이른. —*adv.* iltchigi 일찌기, ch'ogie 초기에.
an ~ spring irŭnbom 이른봄. *Mr. Kim, am I too ~?*
Misŭt'ŏ Kim, naega nŏmu iltchik on kŏt anyŏyo? 미스
터 김, 내가 너무 일찍 온 것 아녀요/ *~ in the morning*
ach'im iltchigi 아침 일찌기.

earn *vt.* pŏlda 벌다, (*by merit*) ŏtta 얻다. *How much do you ~ a month?* Han tare ŏlmana pŏshimnikka? 한 달에 얼마나 버십니까/ *~ one's living* saenghwalbirŭl pŏlda 생활비를 벌다.

earnest *adj.* chinjihan 진지한, yŏlsŏngjŏgin 열성적인. *—n.* chinshim 진심. *an ~ pupil* ch'akshirhan haksaeng 착실한 학생/ *I'm perfectly in ~, am not joking.* Chinjŏngimnida. Nongdami animnida. 진정입니다. 농담이 아닙니다.

earnestly *adv.* chinjŏng[chinshim]ŭro 진정[진심]으로.

earring *n.* kwigŏri 귀걸이, iŏring 이어링.

earth *n.* chigu 지구, (*ground*) ttang 땅, (*soil*) hŭk 흙. *The moon goes round the ~.* Tarŭn chigu tullerŭl tomnida. 달은 지구 둘레를 돕니다/ *the fertile ~* kirŭmjin ttang 기름진 땅/ *on ~* todaech'e 도대체, sesange 세상에/ *How on ~ did you know it?* Todaech'e ŏttŏk'e kŭgŏl aratchiyo? 도대체 어떻게 그걸 알았지요?

earthenware *n.* t'ogi 토기(土器), chilgŭrŭt 질그릇.

earthquake *n.* chijin 지진. *Did you feel the ~ this morning?* Onŭl ach'im chijinŭl asyŏssŭmnikka? 오늘 아침 지진을 아셨읍니까/ *We have seldom ~ in Korea.* Han-gugenŭn chijini tŭmumnida. 한국에는 지진이 드뭅니다.

earthworm *n.* chirŏngi 지렁이.

easel *n.* hwaga 화가(畵架), ijŭl 이즐.

easily *adv.* shwipke 쉽게, sonshwipke 손쉽게, (*readily*) sŏnttŭt 선뜻.

east *n.* tongtchŏk 동쪽. *the ~ wind* tongp'ung 동풍/ *the ~ coast* tonghaean 동해안/ *the Far E~* kŭktong 극동/ *the Middle E~* chungdong 중동.

Easter *n.* puhwalchŏl 부활절, puhwalche 부활제.

easy *adj.* shwiun 쉬운, yongihan 용이한, (*comfortable*) p'yŏnhan 편한, (*smooth*) pudŭroun 부드러운. *After the first one, it becomes ~.* Ch'ŏtpŏntchaeman kkŭnnaemyŏn taŭmŭn shwipke hal su issŭmnida. 첫번째만 끝내면 다음은 쉽게 할 수 있습니다/ *Take it ~.* Chebal sŏnggŭp'age kulji maseyo. 제발 성급하게 굴지 마세요. (*or*) Chebal milji maseyo. 제발 밀지 마세요.

eat *vt.* mŏkta 먹다, (*pol.*) chapsuda 잡수다. *Do you have*

anything to ~? Muŏn-ga mŏgŭl kŏshi ŏpsŭmnikka? 무언
가 먹을 것이 없읍니까/ *Is there anything you don't* ~?
Hokshi mot chapsushinŭn kŏshi issŭmnikka? 혹시 못 잡
수시는 것이 있읍니까/ *Shall we* ~ *at this restaurant?* I
resŭt'orangesŏ mŏgŭlkkayo? 이 레스토랑에서 먹을까요?

eaves *n.* ch'ŏma 처마, ch'aeng 챙.

ebb *n.* ~ *tide* ssŏlmul 썰물, (*decline*) soet'oe 쇠퇴.

echo *n.* meari 메아리, sanullim 산울림.

eclipse *n.* *solar* ~ ilshik 일식(日蝕)/ *lunar* ~ wŏlshik
월식(月蝕)/ *total* ~ kaegishik 개기식(皆旣蝕).

economic *adj.* kyŏngjesangŭi 경제상의, kyŏngjejŏk 경제적.
~ *circles* kyŏngjegye 경제계/ ~ *policy* kyŏngje chŏngch'aek 경제 정책/ ~ *blockade* kyŏngje pongswae 경제
economics *n.* kyŏngjehak 경제학.   [봉쇄.

economize *vt.* chŏryak'ada 절약하다. *We must* ~ *on light
and fuel.* Urinŭn chŏndŭnggwa yŏllyorŭl chŏryak'aeya
hamnida. 우리는 전등과 연료를 절약해야 합니다.

economy *n.* kyŏngje 경제, (*frugality*) chŏryak 절약, *national* ~ kukka kyŏngje 국가 경제/ *rural* ~ nongch'on
kyŏngje 농촌 경제/ *a man of* ~ chŏryakka 절약가/ *Do
you have any book on* ~? Kyŏngjee kwanhan sŏjŏgi
issŭmnikka? 경제에 관한 서적이 있읍니까?

edge *n.* (*of a blade*) nal 날, (*brink*) kajangjari 가장자리,
(*crest*) tŭngsŏngi 등성이.

edit *vt.* p'yŏnjip'ada 편집하다, (*publish*) kanhaenghada 간
행하다.

edition *n.* p'an 판(版), kanhaeng 간행. *a new* ~ shinp'an
신판/ *the first* ~ ch'op'an 초판/*a revised* ~ kaejŏngp'an
개정판/ *a cheap* ~ yŏmkap'an 염가판.

editor *n.* p'yŏnjipcha 편집자. *chief* ~ chup'il 주필.

editorial *n.* (*leader*) sasŏl 사설(社說). —*adj.* p'yŏnjibŭi
편집의. *an* ~ *office* p'yŏnjipshil 편집실/ *an* ~ *writer*
nonsŏl kija 논설 기자.

educate *vt.* kyoyuk'ada 교육하다, (*instruct*) hunyuk'ada
훈육하다. ~ *oneself* tok'ak'ada 독학하다/*Who will* ~ *the
children if their father dies?* Manil kŭdŭrŭi abŏjiga
chungnŭndamyŏn aidŭrŭi kyoyugŭn nuga shik'ijiyo? 만일

그들의 아버지가 죽는다면 아이들의 교육은 누가 시키지요?

education *n.* kyoyuk 교육, (*bring up*) yuksŏng 육성. *audiovisual* ~ shich'ŏnggak kyoyuk 시청각 교육/ *home* ~ kajŏng kyoyuk 가정 교육/ *industrial* ~ shirŏp kyoyuk 실업 교육/ *Ministry of E* ~ mun-gyobu 문교부.

eel *n.* paemjangŏ 뱀장어.

effect *n.* (*result*) kyŏlgwa 결과, (*efficacy*) hyohŏm 효험. *cause and* ~ wŏnin-gwa kyŏlgwa 원인과 결과/ *personal* ~s sojip'um 소지품/ *household* ~s kajae 가재(家財)/ *These are my personal* ~s. Igŏsŭn naŭi sojip'umimnida. 이것은 나의 소지품입니다.

effective *adj.* hyokwajŏgin 효과적인, yuhyohan 유효한. *This medicine is* ~ *against cancer*. I yagŭn ame chal tŭssŭmnida. 이 약은 암에 잘 듣습니다/ ~ *measures* hyokwajŏgin pangbŏp 효과적인 방법.

efficient *adj.* nŭngnyulchŏgin 능률적인, (*capable*) yunŭnghan 유능한. ~ *machines* nŭngnyulchŏgin kigye 능률적인 기계/ ~ *workmen* yunŭnghan chikkong 유능한 직공.

effort *n.* noryŏk 노력, (*strain*) nogo 노고. *with an* ~ aessŏsŏ 애써서/ *without* ~ himdŭlji ank'o 힘들지 않고/ *I'll make every* ~ *to help you*. Innŭn himŭl tahae towa tŭrigessŭmnida. 있는 힘을 다해 도와 드리겠읍니다.

egg *n.* al 알, (*a hen's* ~) talgyal 달걀. *the yellow of an* ~ talgyal norŭnjawi 달걀 노른자위/*a raw* ~ naldalgyal 날달걀/ *Will you have your* ~s *boiled or fried*? Talgyarŭn salma tŭrilkkayo, p'ŭrairo halkkayo? 달걀은 삶아 드릴까요, 프라이로 할까요?

ego *n.* (*self*) chagi 자기, chaa 자아(自我).

egoism *n.* igijuŭi 이기주의.

egoist *n.* igijuŭija 이기주의자.

eight *n.* yŏdŏl 여덟, p'al 팔(8). ~ *o'clock* yŏdŏlshi 여덟 시/ *a child of* ~ yŏdŏl saltchari ai 여덟 살짜리 아이.

eighteen *n.* yŏl yŏdŏl 열 여덟, shipp'al 십팔(18).

eighth *adj.* yŏdŏl pŏntchaeŭi 여덟 번째의, chep'arŭi 제 8의.

eighty *n.* yŏdŭn 여든, p'alship 팔십(80).

either *adj. & pron.* ŏnŭ hanaŭi 어느 하나의. —*conj.* (~ *or*) ...idŭn ttonŭn ...idŭn ...이든 또는 ...이든. *Do you*

- *know* ∼ *of the boys*? Tu sonyŏn chung ŏnŭ han sara-mŭl ashimnikka? 두 소년 중 어느 한 사람을 아십니까/ *Please* ∼ *come in or go out*. Tŭrŏoshidŭn-ga nagashidŭn-ga hashio. 들어오시든가 나가시든가 하시오.

elastic *adj.* (*flexible*) shinch'uksŏng innŭn 신축성 있는, (*springy*) t'allyŏksŏng innŭn 탄력성 있는. ∼ *regulation* yungt'ongsŏng innŭn kyuch'ik 융통성 있는 규칙/ *an* ∼ *cord* komujul 고무줄. 「통성.

elasticity *n.* t'allyŏk 탄력, (*flexibility*) yungt'ongsŏng 융-

elated *adj.* (*proud*) ŭigi yangyanghan 의기 양양한, (*in high spirits*) wŏn-gi wangsŏnghan 원기 왕성한.

elbow *n.* p'alkkumch'i 팔꿈치. *Take your* ∼*s off the desk*. Ch'aeksange p'alkkumch'irŭl chipchi mashio 책상에 팔꿈치를 짚지 마시오.

elder *adj.* sonwiŭi 손위의. —*n.* yŏnjangja 연장자. (*pl.*) sŏnbae 선배. ∼[*older*] *brother* hyŏng 형, (*polite*) hyŏngnim 형님/ ∼ *sister* nuna 누나, (*polite*) nunim 누님/ *Respect your* ∼ *s*. Sŏnbaerŭl chon-gyŏnghashio 선배를 존경하시오.

eldest *adj.* (=*oldest*) kajang naiga manŭn 가장 나이가 많은. *the* ∼ *brother*[*sister*] mat'yŏng[nuna] 맏형[누나].

elect *vt.* ppopta 뽑다, sŏnch'urhada 선출하다. *I was* ∼*ed to the chair*. Nanŭn ŭijange ppop-yŏssŭmnida. 나는 의장(議長)에 뽑혔습니다.

election *n.* sŏn-gŏ 선거. *a general* ∼ ch'ongsŏn-gŏ 총선거/ *an* ∼ *campaign* sŏn-gŏ undong 선거 운동/ *The* ∼ *is void*. Kŭ sŏn-gŏnŭn muhyoimnida. 그 선거는 무효입니다.

electric *adj.* chŏn-giŭi 전기의. *an* ∼ *car* chŏnch'a 전차/ *an* ∼ *fan* sŏnp'unggi 선풍기/ *an* ∼ *heater* chŏnyŏlgi 전열기/ *an* ∼ *lamp* chŏndŭng 전등/ *an* ∼ *phonograph* chŏn-ch'uk 전축/ *an* ∼ *washing machine* chŏn-gi set'akki 전기 세탁기/ *an* ∼ *railway* chŏn-gi ch'ŏlto 전기 철도.

electricity *n.* chŏn-gi 전기. *When did* ∼ *come to the village*? Kŭ maŭrenŭn ŏnje chŏn-giga tŭrŏwassŭmnikka? 그 마을에는 언제 전기가 들어왔읍니까?

electronic *adj.* chŏnjaŭi 전자(電子)의. *an* ∼ *calculator* chŏnja kyesan-gi 전자 계산기/ *an* ∼ *organ* chŏnja orŭgan

전자 오르간/ *an ~ microscope* chŏnja hyŏnmigyŏng 전자 현미경/ *~s* chŏnja konghak 전자 공학.

elegant *adj.* uahan 우아한, p'umwi innŭn 품위 있는, *(Am.)* *(fine)* mŏtchin 멋진. *an ~ young man* p'umwi innŭn chŏlmŭni 품위 있는 젊은이.

element *n.* yoso 요소, *(component)* sŏngbun 성분.

elementary *adj.* ch'oboŭi 초보의, ch'odŭngŭi 초등의. *~ education* ch'odŭng kyoyuk 초등 교육/ *~ (=primary) school* kungmin hakkyo 국민 학교/ *~ training* ch'obo hullyŏn 초보 훈련.

elephant *n.* k'okkiri 코끼리.

elevate *vt.* *(raise)* ollida 올리다, *(promote)* sŭngjinshik'ida 승진시키다, *(cheer)* kiunŭl puktoduda 기운을 북돋우다.

elevator *n.* *(lift)* sŭngganggi 승강기, ellibeit'ŏ 엘리베이터. *Do you see the ~ there?* Chŏgi ellibeit'ŏga poijiyo? 저기 엘리베이터가 보이지요/ *Take the ~ to the seventh floor.* Ellibeit'ŏro ch'ilch'ŭngkkaji ollagaseyo. 엘리베이터로 7층까지 올라가세요.

eleven *n.* yŏl hana 열 하나, shibil 십일(11). 「11의.

eleventh *n.* yŏl han pŏntchae 열 한 번째, cheshibirŭi 제

eliminate *vt.(exclude)* chegŏhada 제거하다, *(omit)* saengnyak'ada 생략하다, *(ignore)* mushihada 무시하다.

elm *n.* nŭrŭmnamu 느릅나무.

eloquence *n.* ungbyŏn 웅변. *fiery ~* yŏlbyŏn 열변.

eloquent *adj.* mal charhanŭn 말 잘하는, ungbyŏnŭi 웅변의. *~ speaker* ungbyŏn-ga 웅변가.

else *adv.* kŭ pakke 그 밖에, ttaro 따로. *someone ~* kŭ pakke nuga 그 밖에 누가 / *something ~* kŭ pakke muŏshi 그 밖에 무엇이/ *somewhere ~* kŭ pakke ŏdie 그 밖에 어디에/ *Did you see anybody ~?* Kŭ pakke nugurŭl mannassŭmnikka? 그 밖에 누구를 만났읍니까?

embark *vt.(board a ship)* paerŭl t'ada 배를 타다, *(depart)* ch'ulbŏmhada 출범하다.

embarrass *vt.* nanch'ŏhage hada 난처하게 하다, *(disturb)* panghaehada 방해하다. *~ing adj.* kwich'anŭn 귀찮은. *Don't ask ~ questions.* Kwich'anŭn chilmunŭl haji mashio. 귀찮은 질문을 하지 마시오. *~ment n.* tanghwang

당황, panghae 방해. *without* ~ tanghwanghaji ank'o 당황하지 않고.

embassy *n.* taesagwan 대사관. *Please call the Korean E*~. Han-guk taesagwane yŏllak'ae chushipshio. 한국 대사관에 연락해 주십시오.

embezzle *vt.* hoengnyŏnghada 횡령하다, ch'akpok'ada 착복하다. ~ *a large sum of public fund* kŏaegŭi kong-gumŭl hoengnyŏnghada 거액의 공금을 횡령하다.

emblem *n.* (*symbol*) sangjing 상징, p'yoji 표지.

embrace *vt.* p'oonghada 포옹하다, (*surround*) tullŏssada 둘러싸다, (*include*) p'ohamhada 포함하다.

embroider *vt.* sunot'a 수놓다. ~ *flowers on silk* pidane surŭl not'a 비단에 수를 놓다.

embroidery *n.* chasu 자수, sunok'i 수놓기. 「태아.

embryo *n.*(*germ*) ssinun 씨눈, pae 배(胚), (*human*) t'aea

emergency *n.* pisang sangt'ae 비상 상태, kin-gŭp sangt'ae 긴급 상태. ~ *call* pisang sojip 비상 소집/ ~ *exit* pisanggu 비상구/ ~ *measure* kin-gŭp choch'i 긴급 조치.

emigrant *n.* imin 이민. *Korean* ~*s for Brazil* Pŭrajillo kanŭn Han-guk imindŭl 브라질로 가는 한국 이민들.

emigrate *vi.* imin-gada 이민가다, ijuhada 이주하다. *A large number of people* ~*d to Paraguay from our country.* Uri nara-esŏ manŭn saramdŭri P'araguairo imin-gassŭmnida. 우리 나라에서 많은 사람들이 파라구아이로 이민갔습니다.

emigration *n.* imin 이민. ~ *law* iminpŏp 이민법.

emotion *n.* kamdong 감동, kamgyŏk 감격, (*feeling*) kam-jŏng 감정. *It's a matter of* ~. Kŭgŏsŭn kibun munjeji-yo. 그것은 기분 문제지요.

emperor *n.* hwangje 황제, chewang 제왕.

emphasize *vt.* kangjohada 강조하다, yŏksŏrhada 역설하다.

empire *n.* cheguk 제국(帝國).

employ *vt.* koyonghada 고용하다, (*use*) ssŭda 쓰다. *How many workmen do you* ~ *at your factory?* Tangshin kongjangesŏ chikkongŭl ŏlmana ssŭgo issŭmnikka? 당신 공장에서 직공을 얼마나 쓰고 있습니까/ *How do you* ~ *your spare time?* Yŏgarŭl ŏttŏk'e iyonghashimnikka? 여

가를 어떻게 이용하십니까?

employee *n.* koyongin 고용인, chongŏbwŏn 종업원.

employer *n.* koyongju 고용주, chuin 주인.

empress *n.* hwanghu 황후, wangbi 왕비.

empty *adj.* pin 빈, (*vacant*) konghŏhan 공허한. *a ~ box* pin sangja 빈 상자/ *an ~ stomach* kongbok 공복(空腹). —*vt.* piuda 비우다. *E~ your glass, please.* Chanŭl piushipshio. 잔을 비우십시오.

enamel *n.* enamel 에나멜, pŏmnang 법랑.

encircle *vt.* (*surround*) tullŏssada 둘러싸다.

enclose *vt.* (*a letter*) ponghae nŏt'a 봉해 넣다, (*surround*) tullŏssada 둘러싸다. *I'll ~ your letter with mine.* Tangshin p'yŏnjie naegŏtto hamkke nŏk'essŭmnida. 당신 편지에 내것도 함께 넣겠읍니다/ *The house is ~ d with walls,* Kŭ chibŭn tamŭro tullŏssayŏ issŭmnida. 그 집은 담으로 둘러싸여 있읍니다.

encore *n.* angk'orŭ 앙코르, chaech'ŏng 재청.

encourage *vt.* yonggirŭl puktoduda 용기를 북돋우다, (*incite*) kyŏngnyŏhada 격려하다. *I ~d him to study harder.* Kŭege tŏuk yŏlshimhi kongbuhadorok kyŏngnyŏhaessŭmnida. 그에게 더욱 열심히 공부하도록 격려했읍니다.

encyclop(a)edia *n.* paekkwa sajŏn 백과 사전.

end *n.* kkŭt 끝. (*tip*) maltan 말단, (*close*) chongmal 종말, (*conclusion*) kyŏlmal 결말, (*destruction*) myŏlmang 멸망, (*aim*) mokchŏk 목적, (*pl.*) tonggangi 동강이, (*part*) pangmyŏn 방면, tchok 쪽. —*vi., vt.* kkŭnnada 끝나다, kkŭnnaeda 끝내다. *from ~ to ~* kkŭt'esŏ kkŭtkkaji 끝에서 끝까지/ *to the ~ of the world* i sesangŭi chongmalkkaji 이 세상의 종말까지/ *gain one's ~s* mokchŏgŭl iruda 목적을 이루다/ *How does this story ~?* Ŏttŏk'e iyagiga kkŭnnamnikka? 어떻게 이야기가 끝납니까/ *Let's ~ our quarrel.* Ssaumŭn kŭmandupshida. 싸움은 그만둡시다/ *What will be the ~ of all this?* Todaech'e igŏsŭn ŏttŏk'e toelkkayo? 도대체 이것은 어떻게 될까요/ *Please investigate the matter at your ~.* I munjenŭn kŭtchogesŏ chosahae chushipshio. 이 문제는 그쪽에서 조사해 주십시오/ *in the ~* kyŏlguk 결국.

endeavo(u)r *n.* noryŏk 노력. *—vi.* noryŏk'ada 노력하다. *Please make every* ~ *to be here early*. Ppalli oshidorok ch'oesŏnŭl tahae chushipshio. 빨리 오시도록 최선을 다해 주십시오.

endless *adj.* kkŭdŏmnŭn 끝없는.

endorse *vt.* isŏhada 이서(裏書)하다, (*guarantee*) pojŭnghada 보증하다. *Will you* ~ *the check, please*? Sup'yo-e isŏhae chushigessŭmnikka? 수표에 이서해 주시겠읍니까?

endure *vt.* kyŏndida 견디다, (*bear*) ch'amta 참다, (*last*) chisok'ada 지속하다. *I can't* ~ *that woman*. Nanŭn kŭ yŏja-e taehaesŏ ch'amŭl suga ŏpsŭmnida. 나는 그 여자에 대해서 참을 수가 없읍니다/ *I can't* ~ *cold mutton*. Ch'an yanggoginŭn chilsaegimnida. 찬 양고기는 질색입니다/ *His work will* ~ *forever*. Kŭŭi chakp'umŭn yŏngwŏnhi namŭl kŏshimnida. 그의 작품은 영원히 남을 것입니다.

enema *n.* kwanjang 관장(灌腸).

enemy *n.* (*foe*) chŏk 적, chŏkkun 적군, (*of individuals*) wŏnsu 원수. *the* ~ *of health* kŏn-gangŭi chŏk 건강의 적.

energy *n.* (*vigor*) chŏngnyŏk 정력, wŏn-gi 원기, (*force*) him 힘, (*phys.*) enŏji 에너지. *I've lost all my* ~ Nanŭn ont'ong himi ppajigo marassŭmnida. 나는 온통 힘이 빠지고 말았읍니다/ *The world is faced with an* ~ *problem*. Segyenŭn enŏji munjee chingmyŏnhago issŭmnida. 세계는 에너지 문제에 직면하고 있읍니다.

engage *vt., vi.* (*promise*) yaksok'ada 약속하다, (*reserve*) yeyak'ada 예약하다, (*keep busy*) pappŭda 바쁘다, (*employ*) koyonghada 고용하다, (*betroth*) yak'onhada 약혼하다. *I'm* ~*d today at five o'clock* Onŭl tasŏssie yaksogi issŭmnida. 오늘 5시에 약속이 있읍니다/ *I've* ~*d rooms at the hotel*. Kŭ hot'ere pangŭl yeyak'ae tuŏssŭmnida. 그 호텔에 방을 예약해 두었읍니다/ *He* ~*d Mr. Han as his lawyer*. Hanssirŭl kŭŭi komun pyŏnhosaro koyonghaessŭmnida. 한(韓)씨를 그의 고문 변호사로 고용했읍니다/ *Are they* ~*d yet*? Kŭdŭrŭn pŏlssŏ yak'onŭl haessŭmnikka? 그들은 벌써 약혼을 했읍니까?

engagement *n.* (*promise*) yaksok 약속, (*contract*) kyeyak 계약, (*betrothal*) yak'on 약혼, (*business*) yongmu

용무, (*employment*) koyong 고용. *I'm sorry, I have a previous* ~. Chŏngmal mianhamnidaman sŏnyagi issŭmnida. 정말 미안합니다만 선약이 있습니다/ ~ *ring* yak'on panji 약혼 반지.

engine *n.* kigwan 기관, enjin 엔진, (*locomotive*) kigwanch'a 기관차. *a steam* ~ chŭnggi kigwan 증기 기관/ *an oil* ~ oil enjin 오일 엔진/ *a diesel* ~ tijel enjin 디젤 엔진/ *a three-cylinder* ~ samgit'ong enjin 삼기통 엔진.

engineer *n.* kisa 기사, konghakcha 공학자, (*mil.*) kongbyŏng 공병. *an air* ~ hanggong kisa 항공 기사/ *a civil* ~ t'omok kisa 토목 기사/ *a marine* ~ chosŏn kisa 조선 기사/ *a chief* ~ kisajang 기사장.

England *n.* Yŏngguk 영국.

English *adj.* (*of England*) Yŏnggugŭi 영국의, (*lang.*) Yŏngŏŭi 영어의,(*people*) Yŏngguginŭi 영국인의.—*n.* Yŏngŏ 영어. ~ *people* Yŏngguk kungmin 영국 국민/ *the* ~ *dictionary* Yŏngŏ sajŏn 영어 사전/ *What do you call this in* ~ ? Igŏsŭl Yŏngŏro muŏrago hamnikka ? 이것을 영어로 무어라고 합니까/ *Your* ~ *is so good.* Yŏngŏrŭl nŏmu chal hashinŭn-gunyo. 영어를 너무 잘 하시는군요.

Englishman *n.* Yŏngguk saram 영국 사람, Yŏngguguin 영국인.

engrave *vt.* chogak'ada 조각하다, saegida 새기다. *Could you* ~ *my name on it ?* Kŭ wie nae irŭmŭl saegil su issŭmnikka ? 그 위에 내 이름을 새길 수 있습니까?

engraving *n.* chogak 조각, (*picture*) p'anhwa 판화.

enigma *n.* (*riddle*) susukkekki 수수께끼.

enjoy *vt.* chŭlgida 즐기다, (*possess*) nurida 누리다, hyangyuhada 향유하다. *I* ~*ed it very much.* Maeu maditke mogŏssŭmnida. 매우 맛있게 먹었습니다/ *Did you* ~ *your trip ?* Yŏhaengŭn chŭlgŏwŏssŭmnikka ? 여행은 즐거웠습니까 ?/ *Frankly, I just don't* ~ *baseball.* Solchik'i marhaesŏ yagunŭn kŭdaji choahaji anssŭmnida. 솔직히 말해서 야구는 그다지 좋아하지 않습니다/ ~ *good health* kŏngangŭl nurida 건강을 누리다.

enjoyment *n.* hyangnak 향락, chŭlgŏum 즐거움. *I can read a novel in French with* ~. Nanŭn sosŏrŭl P'ŭrang-

sŭoro chaemiitke ilgŭl su issŭmnida. 나는 소설을 프랑스
어로 재미있게 읽을 수 있읍니다.

enlarge *vt.* (*make large*) k'ŭge hada 크게 하다, (*photo*)
hwaktaehada 확대하다, (*widen*) nŏlp'ida 넓히다. *Will
you please ~ this picture?* I sajinŭl hwaktaehae chushipshio. 이 사진을 확대해 주십시오/ *an ~d edition*
chŭngbop'an 증보판(增補版).

enlist *vi.* iptaehada 입대하다. —*vt.* (*enrole*) mobyŏnghada
모병하다. *~ in the army* yukkune iptaehada 육군에 입대
하다/ *~ a recruit* shinbyŏngŭl chingmohada 신병을 징
모하다.

enormous *adj.* kŏdaehan 거대한, (*huge*) maktaehan 막대
한. *an ~ sum of money* kŏaegŭi ton 거액의 돈.

enough *adj.* ch'ungbunhan 충분한. —*adv.* ch'ungbunhi 충
분히. *I've had ~, thank you.* Komapsŭmnida. Shilk'ŏt
mŏgŏssŭmnida. 고맙습니다. 실컷 먹었읍니다/ *Will 50,000
won be ~ for you?* Omanwŏnimyŏn nege chok'a-
nŭnya. (*to junior*) 5만원이면 네게 족하느냐/ *Are you
warm ~?* Ch'upchinŭn anŭshimnikka? 춥지는 않으십니
까/ *Is this good ~?* Igŏsŭro chossŭmnikka? 이것으로 좋
습니까/ *We have stayed long ~.* Much'ŏk orae mŏmullŏssŭmnida. 무척 오래 머물렀읍니다.

enrol(l) *vt.* (*enter*) myŏngbue ollida 명부에 올리다, (*enlist*)
pyŏngjŏge ollida 병적에 올리다, (*Am.*) (*enter a school*)
ip'akshik'ida 입학시키다.

entangle *vt.* ŏlk'ige hada 얽히게 하다, (*complicate*) pokchap'age hada 복잡하게 하다, (*entrap*) kon·gyŏnge ppattŭrida 곤경에 빠뜨리다.

enter *vt.*, *vi.* (*go into*) tŭrŏgada 들어가다, (*start*) shija-
k'ada 시작하다, (*join*) kaip'ada 가입하다, (*record*) kii-
p'ada 기입하다. *Where did the bullet ~ the body?* T'an-
hwanŭn mom ŏnŭ pubune pakhyŏssŭmnikka? 탄환은 몸
어느 부분에 박혔읍니까/ *She ~ed the beauty contest.*
Kŭnyŏnŭn miin sŏnbal taehoee ch'amgahaessŭmnida.
그녀는 미인 선발 대회에 참가했읍니다.

enterprise *n.* (*undertaking*) kiŏp 기업, saŏp 사업. *commercial ~* yŏngni saŏp 영리 사업/ *medium and small-*

sized ~ chungso kiŏp 중소 기업/ *philanthropic* ~ chasŏn saŏp 자선 사업/ *build an* ~ saŏbŭl irŭk'ida 사업을 일으키다.

entertain *vt.* (*guest*) hwandae[chŏptae]hada 환대[접대] 하다, (*amuse*) chŭlgŏpke hada 즐겁게 하다, (*harbor*) maŭme p'umta 마음에 품다/ ~ *friends to dinner* ch'ingudŭrege shiksarŭl taejŏp'ada 친구들에게 식사를 대접하다/ *I was* ~*ed by him.* Nanŭn kŭŭi hwandaerŭl padassŭmnida. 나는 그의 환대를 받았읍니다/ *He* ~*s his guests very poorly.* Kŭnŭn sonnim chŏptaega sŏt'umnida. 그는 손님 접대가 서툽니다/ *The magician* ~*ed the children.* Masulsanŭn aidŭrŭl chŭlgŏpke haessŭmnida. 마술사는 아이들을 즐겁게 했읍니다.

entertainer *n.* yŏnyein 연예인(演藝人). *a radio* ~ radio ch'uryŏnja 라디오 출연자/ *a video* ~ t'ellebijŏn ch'uryŏnja 텔레비전 출연자.

entertainment *n.* (*hospitality*) taejŏp 대접, (*reception*) yŏnhoe 연회, (*amusement*) orak 오락, (*public show*) yŏhŭng 여흥. *mass* ~ taejung orak 대중 오락/ *the* ~ *tax* yuhŭngse 유흥세.

enthusiasm *n.* (*zeal*) yŏlchung 열중, yŏlshim 열심.

enthusiastic *adj.* yŏllyŏrhan 열렬한, yŏlgwangjŏgin 열광적인. ~ *cheers* yŏllyŏrhan paksu kalch'ae 열렬한 박수 갈채.

entire *adj.* (*general*) ch'ŏnch'eŭi 전체의, (*whole*) on 온. —*n.* chŏnch'e 전체.

entirely *adv.* chŏnchŏgŭro 전적으로, (*solely*) oroji 오로지. *I owe my success* ~ *to you.* Nae sŏnggongŭn oroji tangshin tŏkpunimnida. 내 성공은 오로지 당신 덕분입니다.

entrance *n.* (*way in*) ipku 입구, (*portal*) hyŏn-gwan 현관. (*entering*) ipchang 입장(入場), (*admission*) ipchangkwŏn 입장권. ~ *examination* ip'ak shihŏm 입학 시험/ ~ *fee* ipchangnyo 입장료/ *I'll show you to the front* ~. Hyŏn-gwanŭro annaehagessŭmnida. 현관으로 안내하 겠읍니다/ *I just heard the results of the* ~ *examination.* Panggŭm ip'ak shihŏm kyŏlgwarŭl tŭrŏssŭmnida. 방금 입학 시험 결과를 들었읍니다.

entreat *vt.* kanch'ŏnghada 간청하다, kanjŏrhi parada 간절

히 바라다. *May I ~ a little favor of you?* Chogŭm
put'agi issŭmnidaman. 조금 부탁이 있읍니다만.

entree *n.* (*right, of entering*) ipchangkwŏn 입장권(權),
(*dish*) angt'ŭre 앙트레. *Does this lunch menu include
soup and ~?* I rŏnch'i menyuenŭn sup'ŭwa angt'ŭrega
p'ohamdoeŏ issŭmnikka? 이 런치 메뉴에는 수프와 앙트레
가 포함 되어 있읍니까?

entrenchment *n.* (*mil.*) ch'amho 참호, poru 보루.

entrust *vt.* matkida 맡기다, wiimhada 위임하다. *Can I ~
you the work to you?* or *Can I ~ you with the task?*
Tangshinege kŭ irŭl matkil su issŭlkkayo? 당신에게 그
일을 맡길 수 있을까요?

entry *n.* (*item*) chomok 조목, (*dictionary*) p'yojeŏ 표제
어, (*list*) ch'amgaja myŏngbu 참가자 명부, (*entrance*)
ipchang 입장(入場). *dictionary entries* sajŏnŭi p'yojeŏ
사전의 표제어 / *a large ~ for the marathon race* mara-
t'on kyŏngjuŭi manŭn ch'amgajadŭl 마라톤 경기의 많은
참가자들.

envelope *n.* pongt'u 봉투. *How much are these air mail
~s?* I hanggong up'yŏn pongt'unŭn ŏlmaimnikka? 이
항공 우편 봉투는 얼마입니까?

envious *adj.* (*be jealous*) shigishimi kanghan 시기심이
강한, (*feel envy*) purŏwŏhanŭn 부러워하는.

environment *n.* hwan-gyŏng 환경, (*surroundings*) chuwi
주위. *home ~* kajŏng hwan-gyŏng 가정 환경 / *social ~*
sahoejŏk hwan-gyŏng 사회적 환경.

envoy *n.* sajŏl 사절, (*special ~*) t'ŭksa 특사, kongsa 공사
(公使). *cultural ~* munhwa sajŏl 문화 사절 / *Korea's
goodwill ~s* Han-gugŭi ch'insŏn sajŏl 한국의 친선 사절.

envy *n.* sŏnmang 선망, shigi 시기. —*vt.* purŏwŏhada 부러워
하다, shigihada 시기하다. *I certainly ~ you.* Chŏngmal
purŏpsŭmnida. 정말 부럽습니다 / *I ~ your good fortune.*
Tangshinŭi haenguni purŏpsŭmnida. 당신의 행운이 부럽
습니다.

epidemic *n.* yuhaengpyŏng 유행병. *an influenza ~* yuhaengsŏng kamgi 유행성 감기. —*adj.* yuhaengsŏngŭi 유
행성의. *an ~ disease* chŏnyŏmpyŏng 전염병.

epilepsy *n.* kanjil 간질, chiralpyŏng 지랄병.

epoch *n.* (*period*) shidae 시대, shin-giwŏn 신기원.

epoch-making *adj.* hoekkijŏgin 획기적인

equal *adj.* (*the same*) kat'ŭn 같은, (*identical*) tongdŭng-han 동등한, (*capable*) kamdanghal su innŭn 감당할 수 있는. —*n.* tongdŭngja 동등자. ~ *in ability* nŭngnyŏgi kat'ŭn 능력이 같은.

equality *n.* p'yŏngdŭng 평등. ~ *between the sexes* namnyŏ tongkwŏn 남녀 동권.

equally *adv.* katke 같게, korŭge 고르게.

equator *n.* chŏkto 적도(赤道).

equinox *n.* *the autumnal* ~ ch'ubun 추분(秋分)/ *the vernal* [*spring*] ~ ch'unbun 춘분(春分).

equip *vt.* (*provide*) katch'uda 갖추다, (*fit out*) changbi-hada 장비하다, (*supply*) chunbihada 준비하다. *The soldiers were* ~*ped for combat.* Pyŏngsadŭrŭn chŏnt'u chunbirŭl katch'uŏssŭmnida. 병사들은 전투 준비를 갖추었 읍니다. 「장비.

equipment *n.* (*providing*) chunbi 준비, (*outfit*) changbi

erase *vt.*(*rub out*) chiuda 지우다, (*cross out*) sakchehada 삭제하다. ~ *pencil marks* yŏnp'il chagugŭl chiuda 연필 자국을 지우다.

eraser *n.* chiugae 지우개.

erotic *adj.* aeyogŭi 애욕의, (*amorous*) saekchŏngŭi 색정의. —*n.* (*erotic person*) hosaekka 호색가.

err *vi.* t'ŭllida 틀리다, kŭrŭch'ida 그르치다.

errand *n.* shimburŭm 심부름. *run*[*go on*] *an* ~ shimburŭm kada 심부름 가다/ *Can you do a little* ~ *for me?* Shimburŭm chom hae chushio. 심부름 좀 해 주시오/ *an* ~ *boy* shimburŭmkkun 심부름꾼, sahwan 사환.

error *n.* chalmot 잘못, kwashil 과실. *Correct* ~*s, if any.* Chalmoshi issŭmyŏn koch'ishio. 잘못이 있으면 고치시오.

eruption *n.* (*volcano*) p'okpal 폭발, punhwa 분화.

escalator *n.* esŭk'ŏlleit'ŏ 에스컬레이터, chadong kyedan 자동 계단. *Take the* ~. Esŭk'ŏlleit'ŏrŭl t'ashipshio. 에스 컬레이터를 타십시오.

escape *n.* tomang 도망, t'alch'ul 탈출. —*vi.* tomanghada

도망하다, taranada 달아나다, (*avoid*) momyŏnhada 모면
하다. *Is the gas escaping somewhere?* Ŏdisŏ kasŭga
saemnikka? 어디서 가스가 샙니까/ *How can we ~ being
seen?* Ŏttŏk'e hamyŏn namŭi nune ttŭiji anŭlkkayo?
어떻게 하면 남의 눈에 띄지 않을까요?

escort *vt.* howihada 호위하다. —*n.* howi 호위. *Who will
~ this young lady home?* Nuga i chŏlmŭn puinŭl
taegekkaji howihae tŭril kŏmnikka? 누가 이 젊은 부인을
댁에까지 호위해 드릴 겁니까?

espionage *n.* sŭp'ai 스파이, kanch'ŏp 간첩. *~ activities*
kanch'ŏp hwaltong 간첩 활동/ *an armed ~ agent* mujang
kanch'ŏp 무장 간첩.

essence *n.* ponjil 본질, chinsu 진수.

establish *vt.* (*set up*) sŏllip'ada 설립하다, (*fix*) hwang-
nip'ada 확립하다, (*prove*) hwakchŭnghada 확증하다,
(*constitute*) chejŏnghada 제정하다. *The church was
~ed in 1880.* Kŭ kyohoenŭn ch'ŏn p'albaek p'alshim-
nyŏne sŏlliptoeŏssŭmnida. 그 교회는 1880 년에 설립되었읍
establishment *n.* sŏllip 설립.   └니다.

estate *n.* chaesan 재산. *personal ~* tongsan 동산(動産)/
real ~ pudongsan 부동산.

esteem *n.* chon-gyŏng 존경. —*vt.* chonjunghada 존중하다.
I have a great ~ for his ability. Nanŭn kŭŭi suwane
kambok'ago issŭmnida. 나는 그의 수완에 감복하고 있읍니
다/ *I ~ your advise highly.* Tangshinŭi ch'unggorŭl
nop'i p'yŏngkahamnida. 당신의 충고를 높이 평가합니다.

estimate *vt., vi.* (*appraise*) p'yŏngkahada 평가하다,
(*judge*) p'andanhada 판단하다, (*calculate*) ch'usanhada
추산하다. —*n.* kyŏnjŏk 견적, (*rough calculation*) kaesan 개산(概算). *I ~d the loss at 7,000,000 won.* Son-
shirŭl ch'ilbaengmanwŏnŭro chabatta. 손실을 7 백만원으
로 잡았다/ *a written ~* kyŏnjŏksŏ 견적서.

eternal *adj.* (*everlasting*) yŏngwŏnhan 영원한, (*incessant*)
kkŭnimŏmnŭn 끊임없는/ *~ life* yŏngsaeng 영생/ *~
truth* yŏngwŏnhan chilli 영원한 진리.

etiquette *n.* yeŭi pŏmjŏl 예의 범절, yepŏp 예법, et'ik'et
에티켓.

Europe *n.* Yurŏp 유럽, Kuju 구주(歐洲).
European *n.* Yurŏp saram 유럽 사람. —*adj.* Yurŏbŭi 유럽의.
evacuate *vt.* (*mil.*) ch'ŏlsuhada 철수하다, (*remove*) sogae
〔p'inan, taep'i〕shik'ida 소개(疎開)〔피난, 대피〕시키다, (*va-
cate*) piuda 비우다.
evacuation *n.* (*mil.*) ch'ŏlsu 철수, (*physical*) paesŏl 배설.
evaporate *vt.,vi.* (*turn into vapor*) chŭngbalshik'ida 증
발시키다, chŭngbarhada 증발하다.
even *adj.* (*level*) p'yŏngp'yŏnghan 평평한. —*adv.* ...cho-
ch'ado …조차도, …majŏdo …마저도. *an ～ surface* p'yŏng-
p'yŏnghan p'yomyŏn 평평한 표면 / *～ teeth* korŭn ch'iyŏl
고른 치열(齒列) / *I never ～ opened the letter.* Nanŭn
p'yŏnji pongt'urŭl ttŭtchido anassŭmnida. 나는 편지 봉
투를 뜯지도 않았습니다 / *Please wait for me ～ if I'm
a little late.* Chogŭm nŭttŏrado kidaryŏ chushipshio.
조금 늦더라도 기다려 주십시오 / *～ if* pirok …ra halchi-
rado 비록 …라 할지라도 / *～ so* kŭrŏt'ason ch'idŏrado 그
렇다손 치더라도.
evening *n.* chŏnyŏk 저녁, pam 밤. *this ～* onŭl chŏnyŏk
오늘 저녁 / *yesterday ～* ŏje chŏnyŏk 어제 저녁 / *tomorrow
～* naeil chŏnyŏk 내일 저녁 / *Good ～!* Annyŏnghashimnikka! 안녕하십니까 / *On what ～ shall I attend you?*
Ŏnŭnal pame ch'aja poeolkkayo? 어느날 밤에 찾아 뵈올까
요 / *Will tomorrow ～ suit you?* Naeil chŏnyŏgi cho-
k'essŭmnikka? 내일 저녁이 좋겠습니까?
event *n.* (*happening*) sakŏn 사건, (*sports*) chongmok 종
목, (*result*) sŏngkwa 성과. *the chief ～s of 1983.* ch'ŏn
kubaek p'alship samnyŏnŭi chuyo sakŏndŭl 1983년의
주요 사건들 / *Which ～s have you entered for?* Ŏnŭ
kyŏnggi chongmoge ch'amgahaessŭmnikka? 어느 경기 종
목에 참가했습니까 / *at all ～s* hayŏt'ŭn 하여튼, chwaugan
좌우간 / *in the ～ of* …ŭi kyŏnguenŭn …의 경우에는.
eventually *adv.* kyŏlguk 결국, mach'imnae 마침내.
ever *adv.* (*formerly*) iltchigi 일찍이, (*always*) ŏnjena 언
제나, (*incessantly*) chulgot 줄곧, (*on any occasion*)
ŏnjen·ga 언젠가. *Have you ～ met him?* Kŭrŭl mannan
chŏgi issŭmnikka? 그를 만난 적이 있습니까 / *I've known*

him ~ since he was a boy. Kŭŭi ŏril ttaebut'ŏ chulgot algo issŭmnida. 그의 어릴 때부터 줄곧 알고 있습니다/ *Work hard as ~ as you can.* Hal su innŭn han yŏlshimhi irhashio. 할 수 있는 한 열심히 일하시오/ *Where~ did you lose it ?* Todaech'e ŏdisŏ kŭgŏsŭl punshirhaessŭmnikka ? 도대체 어디서 그것을 분실했읍니까/ *I wonder if I shall ~ see her again.* Tashi han pŏn kŭnyŏrŭl manna pol su issŭllŭnji morŭgessŭmnida. 다시 한 번 그녀를 만나 볼 수 있을는지 모르겠읍니다/ *for~* yŏngwŏnhi 영원히.

every *adj.* (*all*) modŭn 모든, (*each*) mae 매(每), mada 마다, (*all possible*) ongat 온갖. *~ man among you* nŏhŭidŭl modu 너희들 모두/ *~ boy* modŭn sonyŏn 모든 소년/ *~ day* maeil 매일/ *~ month* maedal 매달/ *~ year* maenyŏn 매년/ *~ fourth day* nahŭltchaemada 나흘째마다/ *~ third man* se saram chung han saram 세 사람 중 한 사람/ *I go there ~ other day.* Nanŭn haru kŏllŏ kamnida. 나는 하루 걸러 거기 갑니다/ *E~ third man has a car.* Se saram chung han saramŭn ch'arŭl kajigo issŭmnida. 세 사람 중 한 사람은 차를 가지고 있읍니다.

everybody *pron.* nugudŭnji 누구든지, nuguna (ta) 누구나 (다). *E~ knows that.* Nuguna ta algo issŭmnida. 누구나 다 알고 있읍니다/ *Not ~ can hear.* Nuguna ta tŭrŭl sunŭn ŏpsŭmnida. 누구나 다 들을 수는 없읍니다.

everyday *adj.* (*daily*) nalmadaŭi 날마다의, maeirŭi 매일의, (*usual*) ilsangŭi 일상의. *~ life* ilsang saenghwal

everyone *pron.* = *everybody*. ⌊일상 생활.

everything *pron.* muŏshina ta 무엇이나 다, mansa 만사, (*most important thing*) kajang sojunghan kŏt 가장 소중한 것. *Tell me ~ about it.* Kŭgŏse taehan modŭn kŏsŭl marhae chushio. 그것에 대한 모든 것을 말해 주시오/ *Thank you very much for ~.* Yŏrŏ kajiro kamsahamnida. 여러 가지로 감사합니다/ *Money is ~ to him.* Kŭegenŭn toni kajang sojunghamnida. 그에게는 돈이 가장 소중합니다.

everywhere *adv.* ŏdina 어디나, toch'ŏe 도처에. *~ about here* i kŭnch'ŏ ŏdisŏna 이 근처 어디서나/ *~ in the city* shinae toch'ŏe 시내 도처에.

evidence *n.* (*ground for belief*) chŭnggŏ 증거, (*clear-*

ness) myŏngbaek 명백, (*mark*) p'yoshi 표시. *certain* ~ hwakshirhan chŭnggŏ 확실한 증거/ *destroy the* ~ chŭnggŏrŭl inmyŏrhada 증거를 인멸하다.

evident *adj.* myŏngbaek'an 명백한, tturyŏt'an 뚜렷한.

evidently *adv.* myŏngbaek'i 명백히.

evil *adj.* (*bad*) nappŭn 나쁜, (*harmful*) haeroun 해로운, (*unlucky*) pulgirhan 불길한. —*n.* (*vice*) ak 악, (*wickedness*) hyungak 흉악, (*disaster*) chaehae 재해. ~ *tongue* toksŏl 독설/ *social* ~ sahoeak 사회악.

exact *adj.* (*accurate*) chŏnghwak'an 정확한, (*precise*) ŏmmirhan 엄밀한, (*strict*) ŏmjunghan 엄중한. *What is the* ~ *meaning of this word*? I marŭi chŏnghwak'an ttŭsŭn muŏshimnikka? 이 말의 정확한 뜻은 무엇입니까/ *an* ~ *memory* chŏnghwak'an kiŏk 정확한 기억/ *an* ~ *teacher* ŏmkyŏk'an sŏnsaengnim 엄격한 선생님.

exactly *adv.* chŏnghwak'age 정확하게, kkok 꼭, t'ŭllimŏpshi. *Your answer is* ~ *right.* Tangshinŭi taedabŭn kkok massŭmnida. 당신의 대답은 꼭 맞습니다/ *I'll be there* ~ *at five.* Chŏnggak tasŏssie kagessŭmnida. 정각 5시에 가겠읍니다/ *E* ~ *!* T'ŭllimŏpshi kŭrŏssŭmnida. 틀림없이 그렇습니다.

exaggerate *vt.* kwajanghada 과장하다, (*overstate*) hŏp'ungch'ida 허풍치다. *Don't* ~ *!* Hŏp'ung ttŏlji mashio. 허풍 떨지 마시오/ *You* ~ *the difficulties.* Tangshinŭn kon-gyŏngŭl kwajanghashinŭn-gunyo. 당신은 곤경을 과장하시는군요.

exaggeration *n.* kwajang 과장, hŏp'ung 허풍.

examination *n.* (*exam*) shihŏm 시험, (*inspection*) kŏmsa 검사, (*investigation*) chosa 조사. *an entrance* ~ ip'ak shihŏm 입학 시험/ *an oral* ~ kudushihŏm 구두 시험/ *pass an* ~ hapkyŏk'ada 합격하다/ *a physical* ~ shinch'e kŏmsa 신체 검사/ *medical* ~ chinch'al 진찰/ *undergo an* ~ kŏmsarŭl patta 검사를 받다/*under* ~ chosa chung 조사 중/ *We had a qualification* ~ *today.* Onŭl kŏmjŏng shihŏmŭl poassŭmnida. 오늘 검정 시험을 보았읍니다/ *fail in the* ~ nakchehada 낙제하다.

examine *vt.* (*test*) shihŏmhada 시험하다, (*inspect*) kŏmsaha-

example 156 **exchange**

da 검사하다, (*diagnose*) chinch'arhada 진찰하다. *Where shall we have our luggage ~d* ? Chimŭn ŏdisŏ kŏmsarŭl padaya hamnikka? 짐은 어디서 검사를 받아야 합니까/ *Have yourself carefully ~d.* Chasehi chinch'arŭl pada poshipshio. 자세히 진찰을 받아 보십시오.

example *n.* (*typical instance*) ye 예(例), (*sample*) kyŏnbon 견본, (*model*) mobŏm 모범. *I'll follow his ~.* Nanŭn kŭŭi yee ttarŭl kŏshimnida. 나는 그의 예에 따를 것입니다/ *Give me an ~, please.* Yerŭl tŭrŏ chushipshio. 예를 들어 주십시오/ *for ~* yerŭl tŭlmyŏn 예를 들면/ *a good ~* choŭn mobŏm[ponbogi] 좋은 모범[본보기].

exceedingly *adv.* koengjanghi 굉장히, mopshi 몹시. *an ~ difficult problem* mopshi ŏryŏun munje 몹시 어려운 문제.

excellency *n.* (*E~*) kak'a 각하. *Your E~* kak'a 각하.

excellent *adj.* usuhan 우수한, ttwiŏnan 뛰어난. *an ~ translation* hullyunghan pŏnyŏk 훌륭한 번역. *I'll show you some ~ sofas.* Hullyunghan sop'arŭl poyŏ tŭrigessŭmnida. 훌륭한 소파를 보여 드리겠습니다/ *I think you have done an ~ job.* Aju chal mandŭrŏssŭmnida. 아주 잘 만들었습니다.

except *prep.* cheoehago 제외하고, oeenŭn 외에는. *every day ~ Sunday* iryoirŭl ppaego maeil 일요일을 빼고 매일/ *~ for ...*oeenŭn ···외에는/ *We come to school every day ~ Sunday.* Iryoirŭl cheoehago maeil hakkyo-e kamnida. 일요일을 제외하고 매일 학교에 갑니다.

exception *n.* yeoe 예외. *without ~* yeoe ŏpshi 예외 없이/ *We'll make an ~ in your case.* Tangshinŭi kyŏngunŭn yeoero hagessŭmnida. 당신의 경우는 예외로 하겠습니다.

excessive *adj.* kwadohan 과도한, kŭktanjŏgin 극단적인. *an ~ demand* ŏmch'ŏngnan yogu 엄청난 요구/ *take ~ exercise* kwadohan undongŭl hada 과도한 운동을 하다.

exchange *vt.* kyohwanhada 교환하다, pakkuda 바꾸다. *—n.* kyohwan 교환, (*give and take*) chugobatki 주고받기, (*of coins*) hwanjŏn 환전(換錢), (*a place of~*) kŏraeso 거래소. *I'd like to ~ this sweater. It's too big.* I sŭwet'ŏrŭl kyohwanhaessŭmyŏn hamnida. Nŏmu k'ŭmnida. 이 스웨터를 교환했으면 합니다. 너무 큽니다/ *Can you*

~ *this 10,000 won bill into small coins*? I manwŏntchari chip'yerŭl chandonŭro pakkuŏ chushigessŭmni-
kka/ 이 만원짜리 지폐를 잔돈으로 바꾸어 주시겠읍니까/ *I'm
hereas an ~ student*. Nanŭn kyohwan haksaengŭro
yŏgi wa issŭmnida. 나는 교환 학생으로 여기 와 있읍니다.

excite *vt.* (*stimulate*) hŭngbunshik'ida 흥분시키다, (*arouse*)
irŭk'ida 일으키다. *Don't get* ~d. Hŭngbunhaji mashio.
흥분하지 마시오/ ~ *a riot* p'oktongŭl irŭk'ida 폭동을 일으
키다/ *You must be* ~d. Pan-gaushijiyo. 반가우시지요.

excursion *n.* sop'ung 소풍, yuram 유람. *a summer* ~
yŏrŭm sop'ung 여름 소풍/ *We took a nice* ~. Chaemiinnŭn sop'ungŭl haessŭmnida. 재미있는 소풍을 했읍니다.

excuse *vt.* (*apologize*) pyŏnmyŏnghada 변명하다, (*forgive*) yongsŏhada 용서하다. —*n.* (*apology*) pyŏnmyŏng
변명, (*pretext*) kushil 구실, (*pardon*) yongsŏ 용서. *E*~
me. Shillyehamnida. 실례합니다, Mianhamnida. 미안합니
다/ *E*~ *me but is the Kyongbok Palace near here*?
Shillyejiman Kyŏngbokkungŭn i kŭnch'ŏe issŭmnikka?
실례지만 경복궁은 이 근처에 있읍니까/ *I suppose you have
a good* ~. Musŭn iyuga innŭn tŭt'agunyo. 무슨 이유
가 있는 듯하군요.

exempt *vt.* myŏnjehada 면제하다. *I was* ~*ed from the
school fee*. Nanŭn suŏmnyorŭl myŏnjebadassŭmnida.
나는 수업료를 면제받았읍니다/ *These articles are* ~*ed
from customs duty*. I mulp'umdŭrŭn myŏnsep'umimnida. 이 물품들은 면세품입니다.

exercise *n.* (*of the body*) undong 운동, (*practice*) yŏnsŭp
연습, (*Am.*) (*ceremony*) ŭishik 의식(儀式). *lack of* ~
undong pujok 운동 부족/ *physical* ~ ch'ejo 체조/ *vocal*
~ palsŏng yŏnsŭp 발성 연습/ *drill* ~ kyoryŏn 교련/
opening[*closing*] ~ kae[p'ye]hoeshik 개[폐]회식/ *com-
mencement* ~ chorŏpshik 졸업식.

exhaust *vt.* (*use up*) ta ssŏbŏrida 다 써버리다, (*tire up*)
chich'ige hada 지치게 하다, (*draw off*) paech'urhada
배출하다. —*n.* paegi changch'i 배기 장치. *You must be* ~
ed. P'irohashijiyo. 피로하시지요/ *I'm completely* ~*ed*.
Wanjŏnhi nokch'oga toeŏssŭmnida. 완전히 녹초가 되었읍

니다.

exhibition *n.* pangnamhoe 박람회, chŏnshihoe 전시회. *an industrial* ~ sanŏp pangnamhoe 산업 박람회/ *an international* ~ man-guk pangnamhoe 만국 박람회/ *art* ~*s* misul chŏnshihoe 미술 전시회/ *a photo* ~ sajin chŏnshihoe 사진 전시회/ *Can I buy a ticket for the* ~ *here*? Yŏgisŏ chŏnshihoe kwallamkwŏnŭl sal su issŭmnikka? 여기서 전시회 관람권을 살 수 있읍니까/ *Is the* ~ *still on*? Chŏllamhoenŭn ajikto hago issŭmnikka? 전람회는 아직도 하고 있읍니까?

exile *n.* ch'ubang 추방, (*banishment*) yubae 유배(流配).

exit *n.* ch'ulgu 출구. *an emergency* ~ pisanggu 비상구.

exotic *adj.* oeraeŭi 외래의, igukchŏk 이국적. ~ *words* oeraeŏ 외래어/ ~ *fashion* oegukp'ung 외국풍.

expand *vi.,vt.* (*swell*) p'aengch'anghada 팽창하다, (*open out*) p'ŏjida 퍼지다, (*extend*) hwakchanghada 확장하다, (*dilate*) p'aengch'angshik'ida 팽창시키다. *Our foreign trade has* ~*ed during recent years.* Uri taeoe muyŏgŭn kŭnnyŏne hwakchanghayŏssŭmnida. 우리 대외 무역은 근년에 확장하였읍니다.

expect *vt.* (*look forward to*) kidaehada 기대하다, (*suppose*) ···irago saenggak'ada ···이라고 생각하다. *You are* ~*ing too much of her.* Kŭnyŏege nŏmu manŭn kŏsŭl kidaehashinŭngunyo. 그에게 너무 많은 것을 기대하시는군요/ *What time can we* ~ *you*? Myŏt shitch'ŭm oshinŭnjiyo? 몇 시쯤 오시는지요/ *We've been* ~*ing your call.* Tangshinŭi chŏnhwarŭl kidaryŏssŭmnida. 당신의 전화를 기다렸읍니다/ *Will he be late*? *I* ~ *so.* Kŭnŭn nŭjŭlkkayo? Nŭjŭrira saenggak'amnida. 그는 늦을까요? 늦으리라 생각합니다. 「da 원정하다.

expedition *n.* wŏnjŏng 원정(遠征). *go on an* ~ wŏnjŏngha-

expel *vt.* (*drive out*) naetchotta 내쫓다, ch'ubanghada 추방하다, (*dismiss*) haegohada 해고하다. ~ *a person from a country* kugoero ch'ubanghada 국외로 추방하다/ ~ *a bad boy from school* pullyang sonyŏnŭl t'oehakshik'ida 불량 소년을 퇴학시키다.

expenditure *n.* (*outlay*) chich'ul 지출, (*expense*) piyong

비용, kyŏngbi 경비, (*consumption*) somo 소모.

expense *n.* (*cost*) piyong 비용, (*expenditure*) chich'ul 지
출, (*loss*) sonshil 손실. *food* ~ shikpi 식비/ *living* ~*s*
saenghwalbi 생활비. *educational* ~*s* kyoyukpi 교육비/
social ~ kyojebi 교제비/ *traveling* ~*s* yŏbi 여비/ *Keep*
~*s as low as possible.* Toedorok piyongŭl churishio.
되도록 비용을 줄이시오/ *You must not spare* ~. Piyongŭl akkyŏsŏnŭn an toemnida. 비용을 아껴서는 안 됩니다/
I'll share the ~*s with you.* Piyongŭn tangshin-gwa
pundamk'iro hagessŭmnida. 비용은 당신과 분담키로 하겠
읍니다.

expensive *adj.* pissan 비싼, kappissan 값비싼. ~ *clothes*
pissan ot 비싼 옷/ *I'm afraid it's too* ~ *for me.* Nŏmu
pissan kŏt katkunyo. 너무 비싼 것 같군요/ *Do you have
a less* ~ *room?* Chom tŏl pissan pangŭn ŏpsŭmnikka?
좀 덜 비싼 방은 없읍니까?

experience *n.* kyŏnghŏm 경험. *Have you had any* ~?
Kyŏnghŏmi issŭshinjiyo? 경험이 있으신지요/ *I had an
interesting* ~ *the other day.* Ilchŏne nanŭn chaemiinnŭn
kyŏnghŏmŭl haessŭmnida. 일전에 나는 재미있는 경험을 했
읍니다/ *a man of* ~ kyŏnghŏmi manŭn saram 경험이
많은 사람.

expert *n.* chŏnmun-ga 전문가, myŏngsu 명수(名手). *an
agricultural* ~ nongŏp chŏnmun-ga 농업 전문가/ *a beauty*
~ miyongsa 미용사/ *an* ~ *in economics* kyŏngje chŏnmunga 경제 전문가/ *an chess* ~ chŏnmun kisa 전문 기
사(棋士).

expire *vi.,vt.* (*exhale*) sumŭl naeshwida 숨을 내쉬다, (*terminate*) man-giga toeda 만기가 되다. *When does your
driving licence* ~? Unjŏn myŏnhŏ man-ginŭn ŏnjeimnikka? 운전 면허 만기는 언제입니까?

explain *vt.* sŏlmyŏnghada 설명하다, (*interpret*) haesŏk'ada
해석하다. *Please* ~ *this problem to me.* I munjerŭl
sŏlmyŏnghae chushipshio. 이 문제를 설명해 주십시오/ *I
can't* ~ *it exactly.* Kŭgŏsŭl chŏnghwak'inŭn sŏlmyŏng-
hal su ŏpsŭmnida. 그것을 정확히는 설명할 수 없읍니다/
Please ~ *yourself in English.* Yŏngŏro sŏlmyŏnghae

chushio. 영어로 설명해 주시오.

explanation *n.* sŏlmyŏng 설명, haesŏl 해설. *Is the ~ given in English?* Yŏngŏ sŏlmyŏngi issŭmnikka? 영어 설명이 있읍니까/ *I should like to have ~.* Sŏlmyŏngŭl tŭrŏya hagessŭmnida. 설명을 들어야 하겠읍니다.

explode *vi.,vt.* p'okparhada[shik'ida] 폭발하다[시키다]. *The boiler ~d.* Poillŏga p'okparhayŏssŭmnida. 보일러가 폭발하였읍니다.

exploration *n.* t'amhŏm 탐험, tapsa 답사.

explore *vt.* t'amhŏmhada 탐험하다, (*pry into*) t'amsahada 탐사하다, (*search into*) yŏn-guhada 연구하다.

explorer *n.* t'amhŏmga 탐험가, t'amsaja 탐사자.

explosion *n.* p'okpal 폭발, p'okp'a 폭파. *the population ~* in-gu p'okpal 인구 폭발.

export *vt.* such'urhada 수출하다. —*n.* such'ul 수출. *an ~ ban* such'ul kŭmji 수출 금지/ *an ~ duty* such'ulse 수출세/ *the ~s of Korea to America* taemi Han-guk such'ulp'um 대미(對美) 한국 수출품/ *an ~ trader* such'ulsang 수출상/ *What are the chief ~s of Korea?* Han-gugŭi chuyo such'ulp'umŭn muŏshimnikka? 한국의 주요 수출품

exportation *n.* such'ul 수출. ⌊은 무엇입니까?

exporter *n.* such'urŏpcha 수출업자.

expose *vt.* (*uncover*) tŭrŏnaeda 드러내다, (*reveal*) p'ongnohada 폭로하다, (*exhibit*) chinyŏrhada 진열하다, (*photo*) noch'urhada 노출하다. *Don't ~ it to the sun.* Haetpyŏt'e kŭgŏsŭl tchoeji mashio. 햇볕에 그것을 쬐지 마시오.

express *vt.* (*in word*) p'yohyŏnhada 표현하다, (*say*) marhada 말하다. —*n.* (*train*) kŭp'aeng yŏlch'a 급행 열차, (*special delivery*) soktal 속달. *I'm afraid I can't ~ myself.* Chedaero marŭl mot hagetkunyo. 제대로 말을 못 하겠군요/ *The ~ for Pusan leaves on track No. 2.* Pusanhaeng kŭp'aeng yŏlch'anŭn ibŏnsŏnesŏ ch'ulbarhamnida. 부산행 급행 열차는 2번선에서 출발합니다/ *You'd better ~ the letter, it's urgent.* Kŭ p'yŏnjinŭn soktallo puch'ishipshio. Kŭp'anikkayo. 그 편지는 속달로 부치십시오. 급하니까요.

expression *n.* (*a look*) p'yojŏng 표정, (*verbal*) p'yohyŏn

표현. *a smiling* ~ unnŭn p'yojŏng 웃는 표정/ *change of* ~ ansaegŭi pyŏnhwa 안색의 변화/ *courteous* ~ chŏngjunghan p'yohyŏn 정중한 표현/ *vulgar* ~s yabihan p'yohyŏn 야비한 표현/ *Let me teach you some daily* ~s *in Korean.* Han-gugŏŭi ilsang p'yohyŏnŭl myŏt kae karŭch'yŏ tŭrigessŭmnida. 한국어의 일상 표현을 몇 개 가르쳐 드리겠읍니다.

extend *vt.,vi.* (*expand*) nŏlp'ida 넓히다, (*stretch out*) ppŏtta 뻗다, (*reach*) ...e irŭda …에 이르다. *Can't you* ~ *your visit for a few days?* Myŏch'il tŏ mŏmurŭl su ŏpsŭmnikka? 며칠 더 머무를 수 없읍니까/ *My garden* ~s *as far as the river.* Naŭi chŏngwŏnŭn kangkkaji ppŏdŏnaga issŭmnida. 나의 정원은 강(江)까지 뻗어나가 있읍니다.

extension *n.* (*expansion*) hwakchang 확장, (*stretching out*) yŏnjang 연장, (*annex*) chŭngch'uk 증축. *build an* ~ *to a hospital* pyŏngwŏnŭl chŭngch'uk'ada 병원을 증축하다. *His* ~ *number is 215, the Fuel Department.* Kuŭi kyohwan pŏnhonŭn ibaekshibobŏn yŏllyobuimnida. 그의 교환 번호는 215번, 연료부입니다.

extensive *adj.* (*wide*) nŏlbŭn 넓은, (*far reaching*) kwangbŏmwihan 광범위한. ~ *knowledge* kwangbŏmwihan chishik 광범위한 지식/ ~ *business* taegyumoŭi yŏngŏp 대규모의 영업.

exterior *n.* (*outside*) oebu 외부, (*outward aspect*) oegwan 외관. *a man of fine* ~ yongmoga arŭmdaun saram 용모가 아름다운 사람.

external *adj.* oebuŭi 외부의, oemyŏnŭi 외면의.

extinguish *vt.* (*put out*) kkŭda 끄다, (*destroy*) pangmyŏrhada 박멸하다. ~ *a fire* purŭl kkŭda 불을 끄다.

extinguisher *n.* sohwagi 소화기(消火器).

extra *adj.* (*additional*) yŏbunŭi 여분의, (*superior*) t'ŭkkŭbŭi 특급의. —*n.* hooe 호외(號外), (~ *charge*) halchŭnggŭm 할증금, (*cinema*) eksŭt'ŭrŏ 엑스트러. *pay a little* ~ *to a chauffeur.* Unjŏn kisa-ege t'ibŭl chogŭm chuda. 운전 기사에게 팁을 조금 주다.

extract *vt.* (*pull out*) ppoba naeda 뽑아 내다, (*excerpt*) palch'wehada 발췌하다. —*n.* ch'uch'ulmul 추출물, palch'we 발췌. ~ *a tooth* irŭl ppopta 이를 뽑다/ ~ *a bullet from a wound* sangch'ŏesŏ t'anhwanŭl ppoba naeda 상처에서 탄환을 뽑아 내다.

extraction *n.* (*extract*) ch'uch'ulmul 추출물, (*lineage*) hyŏlt'ong 혈통. *a man of humble* ~ t'aesaengi ch'ŏnhan saram 태생이 천한 사람/ *Americans of Korean* ~ Han-gukkye Migugin 한국계 미국인.

extraordinary *adj.* (*exceptional*) pisanghan 비상한, (*peculiar*) tokt'ŭk'an 독특한, (*additional*) imshiŭi 임시의. *a woman of* ~ *beauty* tŭmulge ponŭn miin 드물게 보는 미인/ *an* ~ *event* ibyŏn 이변(異變)/ *an* ~ *ambassador* t'ŭngmyŏng taesa 특명 대사/ *an* ~ *general meeting* imshi ch'onghoe 임시 총회.

extravagance *n.* sach'i 사치, (*wastefulness*) nangbi 낭비, (*unrestrained excess*) pangjong 방종.

extravagant *adj.* (*wasteful*) sach'isŭrŏun 사치스러운, (*unreasonable*) t'ŏmuniŏmnŭn 터무니없는, mumohan 무모한. *an* ~ *expenditure* mumohan chich'ul 무모한 지출/ *an* ~ *man* nangbibyŏgi shimhan saram 낭비벽이 심한 사람.

extreme *adj.* kŭktanjŏgin 극단적인, (*radical*) kwagyŏk'an 과격한, (*last*) maenkkŭt'ŭi 맨끝의. ~ *poverty* kŭkpin 극빈/ ~ *view* kwagyŏk'an kyŏnhae 과격한 견해/ *the* ~ *right[left]* kŭgu[kŭkchwa]p'a 극우〔극좌〕파.

extremely *adv.* kŭktanjŏguro 극단적으로, (*very*) mopshi 몹시.

eye *n.* nun 눈. *dull* ~*s* mŏnghan nŭn 멍한 눈/ *fine* ~*s* koun nun 고운 눈/ *hollow* ~*s* p'uk tŭrŏgan nun 푹 들어간 눈/ *large* ~*s* k'ŭn nun 큰 눈/ ~*glass* an-gyŏng 안경/ *Keep your* ~*s upon him.* Kŭrŭl chushihashio. 그를 주시하시오/ *Where are your* ~*s?* Tangshinŭi nunŭn ŏdi put'ŏ isso? 당신의 눈은 어디 붙어 있소?

eyeball *n.* nunal 눈알, an-gu 안구(眼球).

eyebrow *n.* nunssŏp 눈썹. *knit the* ~ nunsarŭl tchip'urida 눈살을 찌푸리다.

eyelash *n.* songnunssŏp 속눈썹.

eyelid *n.* nunkkap'ul 눈까풀.

eyesight *n.* shiryŏk 시력. *lose one's* ~ shilmyŏnghada 실

명하다, nuni mŏlda 눈이 멀다.

eyewitness *n.* mokkyŏkcha 목격자, shilchi chŭngin 실지
증인.

◆◆ **F** ◆◆

fable *n.* uhwa 우화(寓話).

fabric *n.* chingmul 직물, p'iryuk 피륙. *silk* ~ kyŏnjing-
mul 견직물/ *woolen* ~ mojingmul 모직물.

face *n.* ŏlgul 얼굴. —*vi.,vt.* ...e myŏnhada …에 면하다,
chingmyŏnhada 직면하다. *a smiling* ~ misohanŭn ŏlgul
미소하는 얼굴/ *Which way does your house* ~? Tangshinŭi chibŭn ŏnŭ tchogŭl hyanghae issŭmnikka? 당신의
집은 어느 쪽을 향해 있읍니까/ ~ *to* ~ ulgurŭl mattaego
얼굴을 맞대고.

facial *adj.* ŏlgurŭi 얼굴의. *a* ~ *massage* ŏlgul masaji 얼굴
마사지/ ~ *lifting* kaejang 개장(改裝)/ *I hear a lot of*
~ *lifting has been done.* Mani kaejangŭl hasyŏttajiyo.
많이 개장을 하셨다지요/ *I always make it a rule to get*
a ~ *as often as I can.* T'ŭmman issŭmyŏn ŏlgul masa-
jinŭn kkok hago issŭmnida. 틈만 있으면 얼굴 마사지는 꼭
하고 있읍니다.

facility *n.* (*special skill*) somssi 솜씨, (*pl.*) (*convenience*)
sŏlbi 설비, p'yŏnŭi 편의. *public facilities* konggong shisŏl
공공 시설/ *Is there an accommodation* ~ *on Mt. Sorak?*
Sŏraksanenŭn sukpak shisŏri issŭmnikka? 설악산에는 숙
박 시설이 있읍니까/ *Chamshil Stadium has facilities*
for night games. Chamshil undongjangŭn yagan
kyŏnggirŭl wihan shisŏrŭl katch'ugo issŭmnida. 잠실 운
동장은 야간 경기를 위한 시설을 갖추고 있읍니다.

fact *n.* sashil 사실. *in* ~ shilchero 실제로/*as a matter of* ~
sashirŭn 사실은/ *Tell me the* ~*s of the case.* Kŭ sakŏnŭi chinsangŭl marhae chushio. 그 사건의 진상을 말해
주시오.

factory *n.* kongjang 공장. ~ *workers* kongjang nodongja
공장 노동자/ *munition* ~ kunsu kongjang 군수 공장.

fade *vi.,vt.* (*lose color*) paraeda 바래다, (*wither*) shidŭlda 시들다, soet'oehada 쇠퇴하다. *Will the color in this material* ~ ? I otkamŭn saegi paraemnikka? 이 옷감은 색이 바랩니까?

fail *vi.,vt.* shilp'aehada 실패하다, (*bankrupt*) p'asanhada 파산하다, (*neglect, miss*) haji ant'a 하지 않다. *without* ~ pandŭshi 반드시, kkok 꼭. *I* ~*ed in my examination.* Shihŏme shilp'aehaessŭmnida. 시험에 실패했습니다/*Don't* ~ *to see Mt. Halla.* Hallasanŭl kkok poshipshio. 한라산을 꼭 보십시오/ *I shall write to you without* ~. Kkok p'yŏnjihagessŭmnida. 꼭 편지하겠습니다.

failure *n.* shilp'ae 실패, (*neglect*) t'aeman 태만, (*weakening*) soeyak 쇠약. *a dismal* ~ ch'amp'ae 참패/ *a heavy* ~ taeshilp'ae 대실패/*power* ~ chŏngjŏn 정전(停電).

faint *vi.* kijŏrhada 기절하다, (*dim*) hŭimihaejida 희미해지다. —*adj.* hŭimihan 희미한, (*weak*) yak'an 약한. —*n.* (*swoon*) kijŏl 기절. *I feel* ~. Mŏriga ŏtchirŏtchirhamnida. 머리가 어찔어찔합니다/ *We heard* ~ *sounds.* Hŭimihan sorirŭl tŭrŏssŭmnida. 희미한 소리를 들었습니다.

faintly *adv.* himŏpshi 힘없이, kanyalp'ŭge 가냘프게, hŭimihage 희미하게.

fair *adj.* (*beautiful*) arŭmdaun 아름다운, (*just*) kongp'yŏnghan 공평한, (*light-colored*) salkach'i hŭin 살갗이 흰. —*n.* pangnamhoe 박람회. *a* ~ *woman* arŭmdaun yŏja 아름다운 여자/ *Give your sister a* ~ *share of the cake.* Tangshin nuidongsaengege kwajarŭl kongp'yŏnghage nanuŏ chushio. 당신 누이동생에게 과자를 공평하게 나누어 주시오/ *You have a* ~ *complexion.* Tangshin ŏlgurŭn hŭigunyo. 당신. 얼굴은 희군요/ *a world's* ~ man-guk pangnamhoe 만국 박람회.

fairly *adv.* kongp'yŏnghage 공평하게, (*pretty*) kkwae 꽤.

fairy *n.* yojŏng 요정(妖精). ~ *tale* tonghwa 동화.

faith *n.* (*trust*) shinyong 신용, (*belief*) shinang 신앙, (*fidelity*) shinŭi 신의. *Have you any* ~ *in what he says?* Kŭŭi marŭl missŭmnikka? 그의 말을 믿습니까/ *I haven't much* ~ *in this medicine.* Nanŭn i yagŭl kŭdaji mitchi anssŭmnida. 나는 이 약을 그다지 믿지 않습니다.

faithful *adj.* (*loyal*) sŏngshirhan 성실한.

faithless *adj.* (*disloyal*) pulsŏngshirhan 불성실한.

fall *vi.* ttŏrŏjida 떨어지다, (*tumble*) nŏmŏjida 넘어지다, (*decline*) naerida 내리다. —*n.* nak'a 낙하, (*pl.*) (*waterfall*) p'okp'o 폭포, (*Am.*) (*season*) kaŭl 가을. *A child fell from a stair.* Kyedanesŏ aiga ttŏrŏjyŏssŭmnida. 계단에서 아이가 떨어졌읍니다/ *Prices are ~ing.* Mulkaga ttŏrŏjigo issŭmnida. 물가가 떨어지고 있읍니다/ *The rain was ~ing steadily.* Piga kkŭnimŏpshi naerigo issŏssŭmnida. 비가 끊임없이 내리고 있었읍니다/ *I had a hard ~.* Nanŭn hodoege nŏmŏjyŏssŭmnida. 나는 호되게 넘어졌읍니다/ *~ back* mullŏsŏda 물러서다/ *~ behind* ...e twijida ...에 뒤지다/ *~ in* pyŏngdŭlda 병들다/ *~ short of* ...e mich'iji mot'ada ...에 미치지 못하다.

false *adj.* (*untrue*) kŏjisŭi 거짓의, (*wrong*) chalmottoen 잘못된, (*unfaithful*) pulsŏngshirhan 불성실한, (*not real*) katchaŭi 가짜의. *a ~ alarm* hŏwi kyŏngbo 허위 경보/ *give a ~ impression* kŭrŭttoen insangŭl chuda 그릇된 인상을 주다/ *a ~ hair* kabal 가발/ *a ~ coin* katcha ton 가짜 돈, wip'ye 위폐/ *Your report is utterly ~.* Tangshinŭi pogonŭn chŏnhyŏ ŏngt'oriyo. 당신의 보고는 전혀 엉터리요.

falter *vi.,vt.* (*stagger*) pit'ŭlgŏrida 비틀거리다, (*stammer*) marŭl tŏdŭmta 말을 더듬다, (*waver*) mŏmutkŏrida 머뭇거리다.

fame *n.* myŏngsŏng 명성, sep'yŏng 세평.

familiar *adj.* (*intimate*) ch'inhan 친한, (*well-known*) chal allyŏjyŏ innŭn 잘 알려져 있는, (*common*) hŭnhan 흔한. *Don't be too ~ with him.* Kŭwa nŏmu ch'inhage chinaeji mashio. 그와 너무 친하게 지내지 마시오/ *I have been ~ with him.* Nanŭn kŭwa ch'inhage chinaewassŭmnida. 나는 그와 친하게 지내왔읍니다.

family *n.* kajŏng 가정, kajok 가족, (*descent*) kamun 가문. *a ~ name* sŏng 성(姓)/ *Have they any ~?* Chŏbundŭregenŭn chanyŏga issŭmnikka? 저분들에게는 자녀가 있읍니까/ *I have a large ~.* Nanŭn kajogi manssŭmnida. 나는 가족이 많습니다/ *We are a ~ of six in all.* Kajogŭn

modu yŏsŏt saramimnida. 가족은 모두 여섯 사람입니다/
What is your ~ *name?* Tangshinŭi sŏngŭn muŏshimnikka? 당신의 성은 무엇입니까?

famine *n.* (*starvation*) kigŭn 기근, kumjurim 굶주림.

famous *adj.* yumyŏnghan 유명한, irŭm nop'ŭn 이름 높은.
Where is the ~ *Pulguksa temple?* Yumyŏnghan Pulguksanŭn ŏdi issŭmnikka? 유명한 불국사(佛國寺)는 어디
있읍니까/ *What is Kyongju* ~ *for?* Kyŏngjunŭn muŏsŭro yumyŏnghamnikka? 경주(慶州)는 무엇으로 유명합니
까?

fan *n.* puch'ae 부채, (*enthusiast*) p'aen 팬. *an electric* ~
sŏnp'unggi 선풍기/ *a baseball* ~ yagu p'aen 야구 팬/
Here is a ~. Yŏgi puch'aega issŭmnida. 여기 부채가 있
읍니다/ *I'm not much of a music* ~. Nanŭn pyŏllo
ŭmagŭl choahaji anssŭmnida. 나는 별로 음악을 좋아하지
않습니다.

fanatic *n.* (*zealot*) kwangshinja 광신자.

fancy *n.* (*imagination*) kongsang 공상, (*whim*) pyŏndŏk
변덕, (*liking*) kiho 기호. —*vt.* (*imagine*) kongsanghada
공상하다, (*suppose*) saenggak'ada 생각하다, (*like*) choahada 좋아하다. —*adj.* kongdŭryŏ kkumin 공들여 꾸민.
I have a ~ *that he will not come.* Kŭga oji anŭl kŏt kat'ŭn
saenggagi tŭmnida. 그가 오지 않을 것 같은 생각이 듭니다/
I have a great ~ *for travelling.* Nanŭn much'ŏk yŏhaengŭl choahamnida. 나는 무척 여행을 좋아합니다/ *Here's
a* ~ *one made of alligator skin.* Yŏgi agŏ kajugŭro
mandŭn aju hullyunghan kŏshi issŭmnida. 여기 악어 가
죽으로 만든 아주 훌륭한 것이 있읍니다/ *Just* ~ *!* Chom
saenggak'ae poshio! 좀 생각해 보시오!

fang *n.* songgonni 송곳니, (*poisonous tooth*) toga 독아.

fantastic *adj.* (*fanciful*) kongsangjŏgin 공상적인, (*odd*)
koehan 괴이한, (*unreal*) kŭn·gŏ ŏmnŭn 근거 없는. ~
dreams koesanghan kkum 괴상한 꿈. *I think it looks
too* ~. Che saenggagenŭn nŏmu pyŏlla poinŭn kŏt kassŭmnida. 제 생각에는 너무 별나 보이는 것 같습니다.

far *adj.* mŏn 먼, mŏnamŏn 머나먼. —*adv.* mŏlli 멀리. *a*
~ *country* mŏn nara 먼 나라/ *the F*~ *East* kŭktong

극동/ *How* ~ *is it from here?* Yŏgisŏ ŏlmana mŏmni-kka? 여기서 얼마나 멉니까/ *How* ~ *are you going?* Ŏdi-kkaji kashimnikka? 어디까지 가십니까/ *I will go with you as* ~ *as Pusan.* Pusankkaji tonghaenghagessŭmnida. 부산까지 동행하겠읍니다/ *This is* ~ *better.* I kŏshi hwŏl-ssin chŏssŭmnida. 이것이 훨씬 좋습니다/ *by* ~ hwŏlssin 훨씬, aju 아주/ *so* ~ chigŭmkkaji 지금까지.

fare *n.* (*charge*) yogŭm 요금, (*passengers*) sŭnggaek 승객, (*food*) ŭmshingmul 음식물. —*vi.* (*proceed*) toeŏgada 되어가다, (*get on*) chinaeda 지내다, (*food*) ŭmshigŭl mŏkta 음식을 먹다. *a taxi* ~ t'aekshi yogŭm 택시 요금/*at half* ~ panaegŭro 반액으로/ *How much is the* ~*?* Yo-gŭmŭn ŏlmaimnikka? 요금은 얼마입니까/ *Do I pay the* ~ *in advance?* Yogŭmŭn sŏnburimnikka? 요금은 선불입니까/ *All* ~*s, please!* Sonnimdŭl modu t'ajushipshio. 손님들 모두 타주십시오/ *a coarse* ~ nappŭn ŭmshik 나쁜 음식/ *How did the enterprise* ~*?* Saŏbŭn chal toeŏssŭm-nikka? 사업은 잘 되었읍니까/ *How* ~*s it with you?* Chal toeŏ kamnikka? 잘 되어 갑니까?

farewell *n.* chakpyŏl 작별, chakpyŏl insa 작별 인사. —*adj.* songbyŏrŭi 송별의. —*int.* (*good-bye*) annyŏng 안녕. *a* ~ *party* songbyŏryŏn 송별연/ *a* ~ *speech* kobyŏlsa 고별사/ *I must bid you* ~. Chakpyŏl insa tŭryŏyagessŭmnida. 작별 인사 드려야겠읍니다/ *say* ~ chakpyŏl insa hada 작별 인사 하다.

farm *n.* nongjang 농장, nongji 농지, (~*house*) nongga 농가. —*vt.* (*cultivate*) kyŏngjak'ada 경작하다.

farmer *n.* nongbu 농부, nongjangju 농장주.

farming *n.* (*agriculture*) nongŏp 농업, nonggyŏng 농경. *dairy* ~ nangnong 낙농/ *egg* ~ yanggyeŏp 양계업/ *oyster* ~ kul yangshik 굴 양식.

farther *adj., adv.* tŏ mŏn[mŏlli] 더 먼[멀리]. *I can't go any* ~. I isang tŏ kal su ŏpsŭmnida. 이 이상 더 갈 수 없읍니다.

farthest *adj., adv.* kajang mŏn[mŏlli] 가장 먼[멀리].

fascinate *vt.* maŭmŭl hollida 마음을 홀리다, (*charm*) maehok'ada 매혹하다.

fascinating *adj.* maehokchŏgin 매혹적인, hwangholk'e hanŭn 황홀케 하는. *a ~ voice* maehokchŏgin moksori 매혹적인 목소리/ *To us Korean, of course, it doesn't seem ~ at all.* Mullon uridŭl Han-guginegenŭn chogŭmdo maehokchŏgŭronŭn poiji anssŭmnida. 물론 우리들 한국인에게는 조금도 매혹적으로는 보이지 않습니다.

fashion *n.* (*vogue*) yuhaeng 유행, (*manner*) pangshik 방식, (*style*) hyŏng 형(型). —*vt.* (*make*) mandŭlda 만들다. *follow the ~* yuhaengŭl chotta 유행을 좇다/ *the fall ~* kaŭlch'ŏl yuhaeng 가을철 유행/ *When did this style of dress come into ~?* I ot sŭt'airŭn ŏnje yuhaenghage toeŏssŭmnikka? 이 옷 스타일은 언제 유행하게 되었읍니까/ *I always do a thing in my own ~.* Nanŭn ŏnjena nae pangshiktaero hamnida. 나는 언제나 내 방식대로 합니다.

fashionable *adj.* yuhaenghanŭn 유행하는, shisogŭi 시속(時俗)의. *I don't like ~ songs.* Nanŭn yuhaenggarŭl choahaji anssŭmnida. 나는 유행가를 좋아하지 않습니다.

fast *adj.* (*prompt*) chaepparŭn 재빠른, (*firmly fixed*) kojŏngdoen 고정된. —*adv.* (*tightly*) tandanhi 단단히, (*soundly*) kip'i 깊이. —*n.* tanshik 단식(斷食). *a ~ train* pparŭn yŏlch'a 빠른 열차/ *My watch is five minutes ~.* Nae shigyenŭn obun pparŭmnida. 내 시계는 5분 빠릅니다/ *Make the door ~.* Mundansogŭl hashio. 문단속을 하시오/ *a ~ sleep* kip'ŭn cham 깊은 잠/ *sleep ~* p'uk chada 푹 자다/ *a ~ of three days* samilganŭi tanshik 3일간의 단식.

fasten *vt.,vi.* tongyŏmaeda 동여매다, tandanhi kojŏngshik'ida 단단히 고정시키다. *Have you ~ed all the doors?* Munŭl tandanhi kŏrŏssŭmnikka? 문을 단단히 걸었읍니까/ *Please show me how to ~ this seat belt.* I chwasŏk pelt'ŭrŭl choenŭn pangbŏbŭl karŭch'yŏ chushipshio. 이 좌석 벨트를 죄는 방법을 가르쳐 주십시오.

fat *adj.* (*well-fed*) saltchin 살찐, (*fertile*) piok'an 비옥한. —*n.* pigye 비계, chibang 지방. *a ~ woman* ttungttunghan yŏin 뚱뚱한 여인/ *~ lands* okt'o 옥토(沃土)/ *I don't like ~.* Nanŭn pigyerŭl choahaji anssŭmnida. 나는 비계를 좋아하지 않습니다.

fatal adj. ch'imyŏngjŏgin 치명적인, (*fateful*) sungmyŏng-jŏgin 숙명적인. a ~ disease pulch'iŭi pyŏng 불치의 병/ a ~ wound ch'imyŏngsang 치명상/ a ~ day unmyŏng-ŭi nal 운명의 날.

fatality n. (*disaster*) chaenan 재난, (*death*) chugŭm 죽음, (*destiny*) unmyŏng 운명, sungmyŏng 숙명.

fate n. (*destiny*) unmyŏng 운명, (*destruction*) p'amyŏl 파멸, (*death*) chugŭm 죽음. decide one's ~ unmyŏngŭl kyŏlchŏnghada 운명을 결정하다/meet one's ~ chukta 죽다.

father n. abŏji 아버지, (*honorific*) abŏnim 아버님, puch'in 부친. ~-in-law changin 장인, shiabŏji 시아버지/ step~ kyebu 계부/ foster ~ yangbu 양부.

fatherland n. choguk 조국(=*mother country*).

fathom n. kil 길[尋]. —vt. chaeda 재다, (*understand*) aranaeda 알아내다. twelve ~(s) yŏl tu kil 열 두 길/ I cannot ~ his meaning. Kŭŭi ŭidorŭl ihaehal suga ŏp-sŭmnida. 그의 의도를 이해할 수가 없읍니다.

fatigue n. p'iro 피로, p'igon 피곤, (*toil*) nogo 노고. —vt., vi. chich'ida 지치다. mental ~ chŏngshinjŏk p'iro 정신적 피로/ physical ~ yukch'ejŏk p'iro 육체적 피로.

fault n. (*defect*) kyŏlchŏm 결점, (*mistake*) chalmot 잘못, (*weak point*) tanchŏm 단점. It is not your ~. Tangshin chalmoshi animnida. 당신 잘못이 아닙니다/Who is in ~? Nuga nappŭmnikka? 누가 나쁩니까?

favo(u)r n. (*good grace*) ŭnhye 은혜, hoŭi 호의, (*aid*) chiji 지지, put'ak 부탁, (*letter*) p'yŏnji 편지. —vt. ŭnhye-rŭl pep'ulda 은혜를 베풀다, (*approve of*) ch'ansŏnghada 찬성하다. Can you do me a ~? Put'ak hana tŭrŏ chushi-gessŭmnikka? 부탁 하나 들어 주시겠읍니까/ Do me a little ~, will you? Che put'ak chom tŭrŏ chushigessŭmni-kka? 제 부탁 좀 들어 주시겠읍니까/ I have received your ~. P'yŏnji pada poassŭmnida. 편지 받아 보았읍니다/ Will you ~ us with a song? Norae han kok tŭllyŏ chushipshio. 노래 한 곡 들려 주십시오/ Will you ~ me with your company? Pudi ch'amsŏk'ae chushipshio. 부디 참석해 주십시오.

favo(u)rable adj. hoŭijŏgin 호의적인, (*advantageous*)

yurihan 유리한, (*hopeful*) yumanghan 유망한.

favo(u)rite *adj.* (*preferred*) maŭme tŭnŭn 마음에 드는, aju choahanŭn 아주 좋아하는. *What is your* ~ *meal?* Ŏttŏn shiksarŭl choahashimnikka? 어떤 식사를 좋아하십니까/ *Who is your* ~ *singer?* Choahashinŭn kasunŭn nuguimnikka? 좋아하시는 가수는 누구입니까/ *Lilies are my* ~ *flower.* Paek'abŭn naega choahanŭn kkoch'imnida. 백합은 내가 좋아하는 꽃입니다.

fear *n.* (*awe*) kongp'o 공포, turyŏum 두려움, (*anxiety*) kŏkchŏng 걱정. —*vt., vi.* musŏwŏhada 무서워하다, kŏkchŏnghada 걱정하다. *Have you any* ~ *?* Musŭn kŏkchŏngirado issŭmnikka? 무슨 걱정이라도 있읍니까?

fearful *adj.* (*awful*) musŏun 무서운.

feast *n.* (*festival*) ch'ukche 축제, (*banquet*) chanch'i 잔치. *a wedding* ~ kyŏrhon chanch'i 결혼 잔치.

feat *n.* (*exploit*) kongjŏk 공적, (*merits*) hun-gong 훈공.

feather *n.* kit 깃. *tail* ~s kkorigit 꼬리깃.

feature *n.* (*appearance*) yongmo 용모, (*characteristic*) t'ŭkching 특징, (*highlight*) inki p'ŭro 인기 프로. *Your eyes are your best* ~. Tangshinŭi nuni kajang arŭmdapsŭmnida. 당신의 눈이 가장 아름답습니다/ *facial* ~s imokkubi 이목구비(耳目口鼻)/ *radio* ~s radio inki p'ŭro 라디오 인기 프로.

February *n.* iwŏl 2월. 「연합.

federation *n.* (*union*) tongmaeng 동맹, (*league*) yŏnhap

fee *n.* (*charge*) yogŭm 요금, susuryo 수수료, (*tip*) t'ip 팁. *an admission* ~ ipchangnyo 입장료/ *a school* ~ suŏmnyo 수업료/ *How much is the entrance* ~ *?* Ipchangnyonŭn ŏlmaimnikka? 입장료는 얼마입니까?

feeble *adj.* (*weak*) yak'an 약한, (*faint*) kiryŏgi ŏmnŭn 기력이 없는. *a* ~ *body* yakch'e 약체/ *a* ~ *mind* pagyak'an chŏngshin 박약한 정신.

feed *vt., vi.* (*give food to*) mŏgŭl kŏsŭl chuda 먹을 것을 주다, (*nourish*) kirŭda 기르다, (*supply*) konggŭp'ada 공급하다.

feeder *n.* yŏmult'ong 여물통, kuyu 구유.

feel *vt., vi.* nŭkkida 느끼다, (*touch*) manjyŏ poda 만져 보다,

tŏdŭmta 더듬다. *How do you ~ about this?* Yŏgie taehae ŏttŏk'e saenggak'ashimnikka? 여기에 대해 어떻게 생각하십니까/ *I don't ~ well.* Kibuni choch'i anssŭmnida. 기분이 좋지 않습니다/ *I ~ the same way.* Nado tonggamimnida. 나도 동감입니다/ *I do hope you will ~ better.* Pyŏnghwani naŭshigirŭl pimnida. 병환이 나으시기를 빕니다/ *F~ how cold my hands are.* Nae soni ŏlmana ch'agaunji manjyŏ poshipshio. 내 손이 얼마나 차가운지 만져 보십시오.

feeling *n.* (*sense*) kamgak 감각, (*sensation*) kibun 기분, (*emotion*) kamjŏng 감정. *a bad ~* akkamjŏng 악감정/ *~ of duty* ch'aegimgam 책임감/ *a ~ of security* anjŏngam 안전감/ *I have no personal ~ against him.* Kŭege kaeinjŏgin pan-gamŭn ŏpsŭmnida. 그에게 개인적인 반감은 없읍니다.

feign *vt.,vi.* (*pretend*) ...in ch'ehada ...인 체하다, (*forge*) wijohada 위조하다. *~ illness* kkoebyŏngŭl purida 꾀병을 부리다/ *~ another's voice* namŭi moksorirŭl hyŭngnaenaeda 남의 목소리를 흉내내다.

fellow *n.* (*companion*) ch'in-gu 친구, (*comrade*) tongnyo 동료, (*chap*) nyŏsŏk 녀석, sanai 사나이. *school ~s* hagu 학우, tongch'angsaeng 동창생/*a jobless ~* shirŏpcha 실업자/ *Poor ~!* Pulssanghan nyŏsŏk! 불쌍한 녀석/ *I never saw a more obstinate ~.* Chŏwa kach'i kojip sen nomŭn poji mot'aessŭmnida. 저와 같이 고집 센 놈은 보지 못했읍니다.

female *n.* (*woman*) yŏja 여자, (*animal*) amk'ŏt 암컷. —*adj.* yŏsŏngŭi 여성의, amk'ŏsŭi 암컷의. *a ~ child* yŏja ai 여자 아이/*a ~ dog* amk'ae 암캐/ *~ workers* yŏgong 여공(女工).

fence *n.* (*barrier*) ult'ari 울타리, (*fencing*) kŏmsul 검술, p'enshing 펜싱. —*vi.,vt.* ult'arirŭl ch'ida 울타리를 치다, p'enshingŭl hada 펜싱을 하다. *Can you ~?* P'enshingŭl hal chul ashimnikka? 펜싱을 할 줄 아십니까?

fern *n.* yangch'iryu 양치류. *a ~ brake* kosari 고사리.

ferry *n.* narutpae 나룻배. *~boat* narutpae 나룻배, yŏllaksŏn 연락선/ *Where do I take a ~?* Yŏllaksŏnŭn ŏdisŏ t'amnikka? 연락선은 어디서 탑니까?

fertile *adj.* piok'an 비옥한, (*productive*) tasanin 다산(多産)인. ~ *land* piok'an t'oji 비옥한 토지/ *a* ~ *egg* sujŏngnan 수정란.

fertilizer *n.* (*manure*) piryo 비료, kŏrŭm 거름, (*chemical* ~) hwahak piryo 화학 비료.

festival *n.* (*feast*) ch'ukche 축제, chanch'i 잔치, (*festal day*) ch'ukcheil 축제일. *the New Year's* ~ sŏllal ch'ukche 설날 축제.

fetch *vt.* (*go and get*) kasŏ kajigo oda 가서 가지고 오다, (*bring*) teryŏoda 데려오다. *Please* ~ *the child from school.* Hakkyo-e kasŏ ku ai chom teryŏoseyo. 학교에 가서 그 아이 좀 데려오세요/ *F*~ *a doctor at once.* Kot ŭisarŭl pullŏ oshio. 곧 의사를 불러 오시오.

feudal *adj.* ponggŏnjŏgin 봉건적인. *the* ~ *age* ponggŏn shidae 봉건 시대/ *the* ~ *system* ponggŏn chedo 봉건 제도/ *a* ~ *lord* yŏngju 영주(領主).

fever *n.* yŏl 열(熱), yŏlbyŏng 열병, (*craze*) yŏlgwang 열광. *a high* ~ koyŏl 고열/ *typhoid* ~ changjilbusa 장질부사/ *Do you have a* ~? Shinyŏri issŭmnikka? 신열(身熱)이 있읍니까/ *I have a little* ~. Yakkan yŏri issŭmnida. 약간 열이 있읍니다.

few *adj.* (*not many*) sosuŭi 소수의, yakkanŭi 약간의, kŏŭi ŏmnŭn 거의 없는. —*n.* sosu 소수, tuset 두셋. *Can I borrow your typewriter for a* ~ *days?* Tangshin t'aip'ŭrait'ŏrŭl myŏch'il pillyŏ chuseyo. 당신 타이프라이터를 며칠 빌려 주세요/ *I'll be there in a* ~ *minutes.* Myŏt pun twimyŏn kŏgi tangdohal kŏshimnida. 몇 분 뒤면 거기 당도할 것입니다.

fiancé *n.* (*male*) yak'onja 약혼자.

fiancée *n.* (*female*) yak'onnyŏ 약혼녀.

fiber, fibre *n.* sŏmyu 섬유, (*texture*) ch'ŏn 천, (*character*) sojil 소질. *chemical* ~ hwahak sŏmyu 화약 섬유/ *stable* ~ injo sŏmyu 인조 섬유/*a man of the political* ~ chŏngch'ijŏk sojiri innŭn saram 정치적 소질이 있는 사람.

field *n.* tŭl 들, pŏlp'an 벌판, (*patch*) pat 밭, (*scope*) punya 분야. *an oil* ~ yujŏn 유전/ *a rice* ~ non 논/ *a* *wheat* ~ milbat 밀밭/ *the* ~ *of medicine* ŭihak punya 의학(醫學) 분야.

fierce *adj.* (*wild*) sanaun 사나운, (*violent*) maengnyŏrhan 맹렬한, (*intense*) chidok'an 지독한. ~ *dogs* sanaun kae 사나운 개/ ~ *hatred* chidok'an chŭngoshim 지독한 증오심.

fifty *n.* shwin 쉰, oship 오십(50).

fig *n.* (*tree*) muhwagwa 무화과, (*dress*) pokchang 복장.

fight *n.* (*combat*) chŏnt'u 전투, (*struggle*) kyŏkt'u 격투. —*vt.,vi.* (*have a battle*) jŏnt'uhada 전투하다, (*contend*) tat'uda 다투다, (*strive*) punt'uhada 분투하다. *a dog* ~ kaessaum 개싸움/ *a sham* ~ moŭijŏn 모의전/ *loose a* ~ ssaume chida 싸움에 지다/ *win one's* ~ ssaume igida 싸움에 이기다/ *a* ~ *against disease* t'ubyŏng 투병/ ~*ing spirit* t'uji 투지.

figure *n.* (*shape*) moyang 모양, (*image*) ch'osang 초상, (*personage*) myŏngsa 명사, (*number*) sucha 수자. —*vt., vi.* (*portray*) kŭrida 그리다, (*indicate*) nat'anaeda 나타내다, (*calculate*) kyesanhada 계산하다. *We bought the house at a high* ~. Chibŭl pissage sassŭmnida. 집을 비싸게 샀읍니다/ *a world* ~ segyejŏk inmul 세계적 인물.

file *n.* (*row*) yŏl 열(列), (*folder*) sŏryuch'ŏl 서류철, (*tool*) chul 줄. —*vt.* (*documents*) ch'ŏrhada 철하다, (*rasp*) ssŭlda 쓸다. *Where is the* ~ *of Dong-a Daily News?* Tongailbo ch'ŏrŭn ŏdi issŭmnikka? 동아일보 철은 어디 있읍니까?

filial *adj.* ~ *devotion* hyosŏng 효성/ ~ *piety* hyodo 효도.

fill *vt.,vi.* (*make full*) ch'aeuda 채우다, (*stop up*) meuda 메우다, makta 막다. *F*~ *up your bathtub and pans with water.* Yokt'anggwa nambiedo murŭl ch'aewŏ chushio. 욕탕과 남비에도 물을 채워 주시오/ *Please* ~ *in this embarkation card.* Ch'ulguk k'adŭe kiip'ae chushio. 출국 카드에 기입해 주시오.

filling station chuyuso 주유소 (=*gas station*).

film *n.* p'illŭm 필름, (*movie*) yŏnghwa 영화. *a silent* ~ musŏng yŏnghwa 무성 영화/ *a sound* ~ yusŏng yŏnghwa 유성 영화/ *a* ~ *studio* yŏnghwa ch'waryŏngso 영화 촬영소/ *Let me have a roll of black and white* ~. Hŭkpaek p'illŭm han t'ong chushipshio. 흑백 필름 한 통 주십시오.

filter *n.* yŏgwagi 여과기, (*photo*) p'ilt'ŏ 필터.

filth *n.* (*trash*) ssŭregi 쓰레기, (*foul matter*) omul 오물.

filthy *adj.* (*unclean*) pulgyŏrhan 불결한, (*foul*) tŏrŏun 더러운, (*obscene*) ŭmt'anghan 음탕한.

fin *n.* (*of a fish*) chinŭrŏmi 지느러미. 「jŏgin 최종적인.

final *adj.* (*last*) ch'oehuŭi 최후의, (*decisive*) ch'oejong-

finally *adv.* mach'imnae 마침내, kyŏlguk 결국.

finance *n.* chaejŏng 재정, chaemu 재무. *the Ministry of F~* chaemubu 재무부.

financial *adj.* chaejŏngsangŭi 재정상의. *~ support* chaejŏng wŏnjo 재정 원조/ *~ difficulties* chaejŏngnan 재정난/ *~ standing* chaejŏng sangt'ae 재정 상태.

find *vt.,vi.* (*discover*) palgyŏnhada 발견하다, (*recover*) ch'ajanaeda 찾아내다. *Where can I ~ a taxi?* T'aekshinŭn ŏdisŏ chabŭl su issŭmnikka? 택시는 어디서 잡을 수 있읍니까/ *What do you ~ most interesting about our city?* Uri toshiesŏ muŏshi kajang hŭngmiga issŭmnikka? 우리 도시에서 무엇이 가장 흥미가 있읍니까/ *I couldn't ~ my way out.* Ch'ulgurŭl ch'ajŭl suga ŏpsŏssŭmnida. 출구를 찾을 수가 없었읍니다.

fine *adj.* (*nice*) hullyunghan 훌륭한, (*bright*) malgŭn 맑은, sangk'waehan 상쾌한, (*handsome*) mimoŭi 미모의, (*minute*) kanŭdaran 가느다란. *Thanks. I had a ~ time.* Kamsahamnida. Chal norassŭmnida. 감사합니다. 잘 놀았읍니다/ *I feel very ~.* Maeu kibuni chossŭmnida. 매우 기분이 좋습니다/ *I want some finer thread.* Chom tŏ kanŭn shirŭl chushipshio. 좀 더 가는 실을 주십시오/ *sand* mosae 모세, semorae 세모래.

finger *n.* sonkarak 손가락. *fore~* chipkesonkarak 집게손가락/ *middle ~* kaundetsonkarak 가운뎃손가락/ *ring ~* mumyŏngji 무명지/ *little ~* saekkisonkarak 새끼손가락.

fingernail *n.* sont'op 손톱.

fingerprint *n.* chimun 지문.

finish *vt.,vi.* (*terminate*) kkŭnnaeda 끝내다, (*complete*) wallyohada 완료하다, (*perfect*) wansŏnghada 완성하다. *Have you ~ed that book yet?* Kŭ ch'aek ta ilgŏssŭm-

nikka? 그 책 다 읽었읍니까/ *Yes, I have ~ed it.* Ne,
kkŭnnaessŭmnida. 네, 끝냈읍니다/ *I'm ~ed for the
day.* Onŭl irŭn kkŭnnassŭmnida. 오늘 일은 끝났읍니다/
I have now ~ed with her. Kŭnyŏwa chŏlgyohaessŭm-
nida. 그녀와 절교했읍니다.

fir *n.* chŏnnamu 전나무.

fire *n.* pul 불, *(conflagration)* hwajae 화재. *—vt.,vi.* purŭl
puch'ida 불을 붙이다, *(shoot)* palp'ohada 발포하다,
(dismiss) haegohada 해고하다. ~ *alarm* hwajae kyŏngbogi 화재 경보기/ ~ *insurance* hwajae pohŏm 화재 보험/
~ *man* sobangsu 소방수/ ~ *work* pulkkot 불꽃/ *Make
a ~ in the stove.* Nallo-e purŭl chip'ishio. 난로에 불을 지
피시오/ *We have frequent ~s in Pusan.* Pusanenŭn
chaju hwajaega palsaenghamnida. 부산에는 자주 화재가
발생합니다.

firefly *n.* kaettongbŏlle 개똥벌레.

firm *adj.* *(solid)* kyŏn-gohan 견고한, *(steady)* hwakkohan 확고한. *—n.* *(company)* sanghoe 상회, hoesa 회사.
~ *ground* kudŭn ttang 굳은 땅/a ~ *faith* hwakkohan
shinnyŏm 확고한 신념/an *exporting* ~ such'ul sangsa 수
출 상사/ *an engineering* ~ t'ogŏn hoesa 토건 회사.

first *adj.* ch'ŏtchaeŭi 첫째의, cheirŭi 제 1 의. *—adv.* ch'oech'oro 최초로. *—n.* cheil 제 1, ch'ŏtchae 첫째. *the ~ day
of the month* ch'oharu 초하루/*the ~ chapter* cheilchang
제 1 장/~ *class* iltŭng 1 등/*for the ~ time* ch'ŏŭmŭro 처음
으로/*This is my ~ time staying here.* Yŏgie mŏmunŭn
kŏsŭn ibŏni ch'ŏŭmimnida. 여기에 머무는 것은 이번이 처음
입니다/*Do this~.* Igŏsŭl mŏnjŏ hashio. 이것을 먼저 하시오/
~ *of all* chŏtchaero 첫째로/ *at ~* ch'ŏŭmenŭn 처음에는/
I found English difficult at ~. Nanŭn ch'ŏŭm Yŏngŏga ŏryŏptanŭn kŏsŭl arassŭmnida. 나는 처음 영어가 어
렵다는 것을 알았읍니다/ *the ~ on earth* ch'ŏnha ilp'um
천하 일품.

fish *n.* mulkogi 물고기, saengsŏn 생선. *a ~ market* saengsŏn shijang 생선 시장/ *roast ~* saengsŏn kui 생선 구이/
sliced raw ~ saengsŏnhoe 생선회.

fisherman *n.* ŏbu 어부, *(angler)* nakshikkun 낚시꾼.

fishery *n.* ŏŏp 어업, susanŏp 수산업.

fishing *n.* kogijabi 고기잡이, nakshijil 낚시질. ~ *boat* ŏsŏn 어선/ ~ *net* ŏmang 어망/ ~ *rod* nakshittae 낚싯대/*Do you like* ~ ? Nakshirŭl choahashimnikka? 낚시를 좋아하십니까/ *How about going* ~ *on coming Sunday?* Onŭn iryoil nakshiharŏ kaji ank'essŭmnikka? 오는 일요일 낚시하러 가지 않겠읍니까?   「비린내.

fishy *adj.* pirinnae nanŭn 비린내 나는. *a* ~ *smell* pirinnae

fist *n.* chumŏk 주먹. *I struck him with my* ~. Chumŏgŭro kŭrŭl ttaeryŏ chuŏssŭmnida. 주먹으로 그를 때려 주었읍니다.

fit *adj.* (*suitable*) chŏk'ap'an 적합한, (*proper*) mattanghan 마땅한, (*qualified*) chagyŏgi innŭn 자격이 있는. —*vi.,vt.* (*adapt*) almatta 알맞다, chŏk'ap'ada 적합하다. —*n.* (*spasm*) palchak 발작(發作), kyŏngnyŏn 경련. *The food was not* ~ *to eat.* Kŭ ŭmshigŭn mŏgŭl suga ŏpsŏssŭmnida. 그 음식은 먹을 수가 없었읍니다/*You are not* ~ *for the position.* Tangshinŭn kŭ chigwie chŏgimi animnida. 당신은 그 직위에 적임이 아닙니다/*Do you think it will* ~ *me?* Na-ege almajŭlkkayo? 나에게 알맞을까요/*a fainting* ~ *cholto* 졸도/*in a* ~ *of anger* hwatkime 홧김에.

fitting *n.* (*tailoring*) kabong 가봉. *You can have a* ~ *on Tuesday of next week.* Taŭmchu hwayoire kabongi toegessŭmnida. 다음주 화요일에 가봉이 되겠읍니다.

five *n.* tasŏt 다섯, o 오(5).

fix *vt.,vi.* (*make firm*) kojŏngshik'ida 고정시키다, (*set*) changch'ihada 장치하다, (*decide*) chŏnghada 정하다, (*repair*) koch'ida 고치다. *Is yours a current or a* ~ed *account?* Pot'ong yegŭmimnikka animyŏn chŏnggi yegŭmimnikka? 보통 예금입니까 아니면 정기 예금입니까/*Let us* ~ *a date for our excursion.* Sop'ung naltcharŭl kyŏlchŏnghapshida. 소풍 날짜를 결정합시다/*Do you think you could* ~ *it?* Surihal su innŭnjiyo? 수리할 수 있는지요?

flag *n.* ki 기(旗). *the national* ~ kukki 국기/*hoist the national* ~ kukkirŭl keyanghada 국기를 게양하다/*lower the* ~ kirŭl naerida 기를 내리다/*wave* ~s kirŭl hŭndŭlda 기를 흔들다.

flagman *n.* kisu 기수(旗手).

flagstaff *n.* kittae 깃대.

flame *n.* pulkkot 불꽃. —*vi.* (*blaze*) t'aorŭda 타오르다.

flank *n.* yŏpkuri 옆구리. 「ssak ch'ida 찰싹 치다.

flap *vt.,vi.* (*flutter*) p'ŏlrŏkkŏrida 펄럭거리다, (*beat*) ch'al-

flash *n.* sŏmgwang 섬광, pŏntchŏgim 번쩍임, (*photo*) p'ŭl-
laeshi 플래시. *a ~ of lightning* pŏn-gaepit 번개빛/ *in a
~ sunshikkane* 순식간에.

flat *adj.* (*level*) p'yŏngp'yŏnghan 평평한, (*dull*) mumi
kŏnjohan 무미 건조한, (*plain*) solchik'an 솔직한. *a ~ roof*
p'yŏngp'yŏnghan chibung 평평한 지붕/*The spare tire is
~.* Sŭp'eŏ t'aiŏga ppangkkuna issŭmnida 스페어 타이어가
빵꾸나 있읍니다/ *a ~ lecture* kimppajin kangŭi 김빠진 강
의/ *a ~ refusal* solchik'an kŏjŏl 솔직한 거절.

flatter *vt.* ach'ŏmhada 아첨하다, allanggŏrida 알랑거리다.
Oh, you ~ me. Nŏmu ch'uŏ ollishinŭn-gunyo. 너무 추어
올리시는군요/ *I am ~ed.* Ch'ingch'anhae chuŏ kippŭgunyo. 칭찬해 주어 기쁘군요. 「거리는 사람.

flatterer *n.* ach'ŏmkkun 아첨꾼, allanggŏrinŭn saram 알랑

flattery *n.* ach'ŏm 아첨, ch'irenmal 치렛말.

flavo(u)r *n.* (*taste*) mat 맛, p'ungmi 풍미, (*smell*) hyanggi 향기. *a kimchi ~* kimch'i mat 김치 맛/ *I like this ~.*
Nanŭn i hyanggiga chossŭmnida. 나는 이 향기가 좋습니다.

flaw *n.* (*crack*) hŭm 흠, kŭm 금, (*defect*) kyŏlchŏm 결점.

flea *n.* pyŏruk 벼룩.

flee *vi.,vt.* (*run away*) tomanghada 도망하다. *He fled by
night.* Kŭnŭn yagan tojurŭl haessŭmnida. 그는 야간 도주
를 했읍니다.

fleet *n.* hamdae 함대. *the Pacific F~* t'aep'yŏngyang
hamdae 태평양 함대.

flesh *n.* sal 살, salk'ogi 살코기, (*human body*) yukch'e 육체.

flexible *adj.* hwigi shwiun 휘기 쉬운.

flight *n.* (*flying*) pihaeng 비행, (*running away*) tomang
도망. *a night ~* yagan pihaeng 야간 비행/*a nonstop air ~*
much'angnyuk pihaeng 무착륙 비행/*Is there a morning
~ to Cheju-do?* Chejudohaeng ach'im pihaenggiga i-
ssŭmnikka? 제주도행(行) 아침 비행기가 있읍니까/ *I hope*

you have a comfortable ~! Chŭlgŏun pihaenggi yŏ-haengi toeshigirŭl! 즐거운 비행기 여행이 되시기를!

float *n.* (*raft*) ttenmok 뗏목, (*bob*) nakshitchi 낚시찌. —*vi.*, *vt.* ttŭda 뜨다, (*circulate*) p'ŏttŭrida 퍼뜨리다. *What is that ~ing on the water?* Mul wie ttŏ innŭn chŏgŏsŭn muŏshimnikka? 물 위에 떠 있는 저것은 무엇입니까?

flood *n.* hongsu 홍수. —*vi.*,*vt.* pŏmnamhada 범람하다, (*rush*) swaedohada 쇄도하다. *I have a ~ of callers.* Sonnimi hongsuch'ŏrŏm millyŏdŭmnida. 손님이 홍수처럼 밀려듭니다/ *I am ~ed with orders.* Chumuni swaedohago issŭmnida. 주문이 쇄도하고 있읍니다.

floor *n.* maru 마루, (*storey*) ch'ŭng 층, *first* ~ ilch'ŭng 1층/*Put them down on the* ~. Kŭgŏttŭrŭn marue tushipshio. 그것들은 마루에 두십시오/ *Take the escalator to the fourth* ~. Esŭk'ŏlleit'ŏrŭl t'ago sach'ŭnguro kashipshio. 에스컬레이터를 타고 4층으로 가십시오.

florist *n.* kkotchangsu 꽃장수.

flour *n.* karu 가루, punmal 분말, milkaru 밀가루. ~ *bag* milkaru pudae 밀가루 부대.

flow *vi.* hŭrŭda 흐르다.

flower *n.* kkot 꽃. *artificial* ~ chohwa 조화/ *the national* ~ kuk'wa 국화(國花)/ ~ *arrangement* kkotkkoji 꽃꽂이/ ~ *bed* hwadan 화단.

flu *n.* yuhaengsŏng kamgi 유행성 감기, tokkam 독감. *Have you had ~ shots?* Tokkam yebang chusarŭl majassŭmnikka? 독감 예방 주사를 맞았읍니까/ *I think I'm coming down with the* ~. Nanŭn tokkame kŏllin moyangie-yo. 나는 독감에 걸린 모양이에요.

fluently *adv.* yuch'anghage 유창하게. *He speaks four languages* ~. Kŭnŭn sagae kugŏrŭl yuch'anghage marhamnida. 그는 4개 국어를 유창하게 말합니다.

flush *vi.*,*vt.* (*turn red*) pulgŏjida 붉어지다, (*flow rapidly*) walk'ak ssodajida 왈칵 쏟아지다. ~ *toilet* suseshik pyŏnso 수세식 변소.

flute *n.* p'iri 피리, p'ŭllut'ŭ 플루트.

flutter *vi.*,*vt.* (*bird*) nalgaech'ida 날개치다, (*wave*) p'ŏllŏ-gida 펄럭이다.

fly *n.* p'ari 파리. —*vi.,vt.* (*birds or airplanes*) nalda 날다, nallida 날리다, (*run away*) tomangch'ida 도망치다. *We are going to* ~. Pihaenggiro kal chakchŏngimnida. 비행기로 갈 작정입니다/ *Why did you* ~ *off the handle*? Wae kŭch'ŏrŏm nohaessŭmnikka? 왜 그처럼 노(怒)했읍니까?

foam *n.* kŏp'um 거품. —*vi.* kŏp'umi ilda 거품이 일다.

focus *n.* ch'ochŏm 초점, (*center*) chungshim 중심. *bring into* ~ ch'ochŏme match'uda 초점에 맞추다/ *out of* ~ p'int'ŭga an matta 핀트가 안 맞다.

fodder *n.* saryo 사료(飼料), mŏgi 먹이. 「nongmu 농무.

fog *n.* an-gae 안개. *a dense* ~ chit'ŭn an-gae 짙은 안개,

fold *vt.,vi.* chŏpta 접다, (*wrap*) ssada 싸다. —*n.* churŭm 주름. *a* ~*ing screen* pyŏngp'ung 병풍. *When I finish my letter, I* ~ *it.* P'yŏnjirŭl ta ssŭmyŏn kŭgŏsŭl chŏpsŭmnida. 편지를 다 쓰면 그것을 접습니다.

folk *n.* (*people*) saramdŭl 사람들, (*one's family*) kajok 가족. *poor* ~*s* kananhan saramdŭl 가난한 사람들/~ *dance* minsok muyong 민속 무용/ *I want a record of Korean* ~ *songs.* Han-guk minyo rek'odŭrŭl han chang sago shipsŭmnida. 한국 민요 레코드를 한 장 사고 싶습니다.

follow *vt.,vi.* (*come after*) ttarŭda 따르다, (*understand*) ihaehada 이해하다, (*succeed*) twirŭl itta 뒤를 잇다. *Will you* ~ *me, please*? Iri oshijiyo. 이리 오시지요/ *I don't quite* ~ *you.* Musŭn malssŭminji chal morŭgessŭmnida. 무슨 말씀인지 잘 모르겠습니다.

follower *n.* (*attendant*) suhaengwŏn 수행원, (*adherent*) puha 부하, (*disciple*) cheja 제자.

following *adj.* taŭmŭi 다음의. *the* ~ *day* taŭmnal 다음날/ *the* ~ *month* taŭmtal 다음달/*the* ~ *person* taŭm saram 다음 사람/ *the* ~ *year* taŭmhae 다음해.

fond *adj.* choahanŭn 좋아하는. *be* ~ *of*...ŭl choahada …을 좋아하다/ *I am very* ~ *of sleeping late.* Nanŭn nŭtchamŭl choahamnida. 나는 늦잠을 좋아합니다/ *Are you* ~ *of wine*? Surŭl choahashimnikka? 술을 좋아하십니까?

food *n.* ŭmshik 음식, shingnyang 식량. *Korean* ~ Han-guk ŭmshik 한국 음식, hanshik 한식/ *vegetable* ~ ch'aeshik채식. *Do you like foreign* ~ ? Yangshigŭl choaha-shimnikka? 양식을 좋아하십니까?

fool *n.* pabo 바보, mŏngch'ŏngi 멍청이. *April Fools' Day* manujŏl 만우절.

foolish *adj.* (*silly*) ŏrisŏgŭn 어리석은, (*ridiculous*) ssuk-sŭrŏun 쑥스러운. *a* ~ *person* ŏrisŏgŭn saram 어리석은 사람/ *a* ~ *idea* ssuksŭrŏun saenggak 쑥스러운 생각.

foot *n.* pal 발, (*step*) kŏrŭm 걸음, (*measure of length*) p'it'ŭ 피트. *Can I go there on* ~ ? Kŏrŏsŏ kal su issŭm-nikka? 걸어서 갈 수 있읍니까/ ~ *rule* p'it'ŭ cha 피트 자 [尺]/ ~ *man* mabu 마부/ ~ *path* podo 보도/ ~ *race* tobo kyŏngju 도보 경주/ ~ *step* palchaguk 발자국.

football *n.* ch'ukku 축구. *F* ~ *games are played mostly in Hyochang Stadium.* Ch'ukku kyŏngginŭn taegae Hyo-ch'ang undongjangesŏ yŏllimnida. 축구 경기는 대개 효창 운동장에서 열립니다/ ~ *match* ch'ukku shihap 축구 시합/ ~ *player* ch'ukku sŏnsu 축구 선수.

for *prep.* (*in behalf of*) ...ŭl wihayŏ ...을 위하여, (*in place of*)...ŭl taeshinhayŏ ...을 대신하여, (*in return for*) ...ŭi posangŭro ...의 보상으로, (*corresponding to*) ...e taeŭng-hayŏ ...에 대응하여, (*adapted to*) ...e almajŭn ...에 알맞은, (*for the purpose of*) ...ŭl wihayŏ ...을 위하여, (*in the direction of*) ...ŭl hyanghayŏ ...을 향하여, (*during*) ...ŭi sai ...의 사이. *What can I do* ~ *you*? Muŏsŭl haedŭrilkka-yo? 무엇을 해드릴까요/ *What's this* ~ ? Igŏsŭn muŏse ssŭnŭn kŏshimnikka? 이것은 무엇에 쓰는 것입니까/ *I'll be here* ~ *just two days.* I kosenŭn it'ŭlman itkessŭmnida. 이 곳에는 이틀만 있겠읍니다.

forbid *vt.* (*prohibit*) kŭmhada 금하다, (*prevent*) panghae-hada 방해하다. *Wine is forbidden here.* Yŏgisŏnŭn ŭmjuga kŭmjidoeŏ issŭmnida. 여기서는 음주가 금지되어 있읍니다/ *I* ~ *you to use that word.* Kŭ marŭl sayong-haji mashio. 그 말을 사용하지 마시오.

force *n.* (*strength*) him 힘, (*power*) pyŏngnyŏk 병력, (*pl.*) kundae 군대. —*vt.*(*press*) kangyohada 강요하다. *the* ~ *of nature* chayŏnŭi him 자연의 힘/ *the Air F* ~ konggun 공군/ *the U.S. Armed F* ~ s Migun 미군/ *I am sorry to*

~ *business on you.* Kangjero irŭl shik'yŏ mianhamnida. 강제로 일을 시켜 미안합니다.

forecast *n.* yebo 예보. —*vt.* yebohada 예보하다. *a weather* ~ ilgi yebo 일기 예보.

forehead *n.* ima 이마.

foreign *adj.* oegugŭi 외국의, oeraeŭi 외래의. *a* ~ *country* oeguk 외국/ ~ *language* oegugŏ 외국어/ *the Ministry of F*~ *Affairs* oemubu 외무부/ *the F*~ *Minister* oemubu changgwan 외무부 장관.

foreigner *n.* oegugin 외국인, oeguk saram 외국 사람. *Are there many* ~*s in Seoul?* Sŏurenŭn oegugini man-ssŭmnikka? 서울에는 외국인이 많습니까?

foresee *vt.* yegyŏnhada 예견하다, miri alda 미리 알다. *We foresaw the war.* Urinŭn chŏnjaengul miri arassŭmnida. 우리는 전쟁을 미리 알았읍니다.

foresight *n.* (*prevision*) sŏn-gyŏn 선견, (*forecast*) yegyŏn 예견.

forest *n.* sup 숲. *a dense* ~ millim 밀림/ *primeval* ~ wŏnshirim 원시림.

forestry *n.* sallimhak 산림학, imŏp 임업.

foretell *vt.* (*tell beforehand*) yegohada 예고하다, (*predict*) yeŏnhada 예언하다.

forever *adv.* (*eternally*) yŏngguhi 영구히, (*continually*) kkŭnimŏpshi 끊임없이.

forge *vt.,vi.* (*metal*) pyŏrida 벼리다, (*money*) wijohada 위조하다. —*n.* (*smithy*) taejangkan 대장간.

forget *vt.,vi.* itta 잊다, (*leave behind*) nok'o oda 놓고 오다. *Don't* ~ *to post the letters.* Itchi malgo kkok p'yŏnjirŭl puch'ishio. 잊지 말고 꼭 편지를 부치시오/ *I forgot it in the train.* Kich'a soge kŭgŏsŭl nok'o wassŭmnida. 기차 속에 그것을 놓고 왔읍니다.

forget-me-not *n.* (*flower*) mulmangch'o 물망초.

forgive *vt.* yongsŏhada 용서하다. *F*~ *me for coming so late.* Nŭjŭn kŏsŭl yongsŏhashipshio. 늦은 것을 용서하십시오/ *Will you* ~ *me?* Yongsŏhae chushigessŭmnikka? 용서해 주시겠읍니까?

fork *n.* (*for food*) p'ok'ŭ 포크, (*prong*) soesurang 쇠스

랑, (*crossroad*) pun-gichŏm 분기점. *a dinner ~* shiksa-yong p'ok'ŭ 식사용 포크/ *a hay ~* kŏnch'oyong soesŭ-rang 전초용 쇠스랑.

form *n.* (*shape*) hyŏngt'ae 형태, (*appearance*) moyang 모양, (*style*) yangshik 양식, (*formula*) sŏshik 서식(書式). —*vi.,vt.*(*shape*) hyŏngt'aerŭl iruda 형태를 이루다, (*organize*) kusŏnghada 구성하다. *Would you fill out this ~?* I yongjie kiip'ae chushipshio. 이 용지에 기입해 주십시오.

formal *adj.* hyŏngshikchŏgin 형식적인, (*regular*) chŏng-shigŭi 정식의.

former *adj.* (*earlier*) ijŏnŭi 이전의, (*old*) yennarŭi 옛날의, (*the ~*) chŏnjaŭi 전자(前者)의.

formerly *adv.* ijŏne 이전에, yennare 옛날에.

fortify *vt.* (*strengthen*) kanghwahada 강화하다, (*build forts*) ch'uksŏnghada 축성하다. *a fortified zone* yosae chidae 요새 지대.

fortnight *n.* (*two weeks*) ijugan 2주간.

fortunately *adj.* un jok'e 운 좋게, tahaenghi 다행히. *F~ the weather was good.* Tahaenghido nalssiga choassŭm-nida. 다행히도 날씨가 좋았읍니다.

fortune *n.* (*good luck*) un 운, haengun 행운, (*wealth*) chaesan 재산. *~ teller* chŏmjangi 점장이/ *a man of ~* chaesan-ga 재산가.

forty *n.* saship 사십(40), mahŭn 마흔.

forward *adv.*(*onwards*) ap'ŭro 앞으로. —*vt.*(*send*) ponaeda 보내다, (*send ~*) chŏnsonghada 전송(轉送)하다. *look ~ to* kidaehada 기대하다/ *Please ~ my mail to this address.* Up'yŏnmurŭn i chusoro chŏnsonghae chushipshio. 우편물은 이 주소로 전송해 주십시오/ *I'm looking ~ to seeing you.* Tashi manna poepkirŭl kidaehamnida. 다시 만나 뵙기를 기대합니다.

foster *vt.* (*nurse*) kirŭda 기르다. —*adj.* yangyugŭi 양육의. *a ~ daughter* suyangttal 수양딸, yangnyŏ 양녀/ *a ~ father* suyang abŏji 수양 아버지, yangbu 양부/ *a ~ son* suyang adŭl 수양 아들, yangja 양자.

found *vt.,vi.* (*establish*) ch'angnip[ch'angsŏr]hada 창립[창설]하다, seuda 세우다. *They ~ed a hospital in Seoul.*

Kŭdŭrŭn Sŏure pyŏngwŏnŭl sewŏssŭmnida. 그들은 서울
에 병원을 세웠읍니다／ ~ *a city* toshirŭl kŏllip'ada 도시를
건립하다.

foundation *n.* (*base*) t'odae 토대, (*establishing*) ch'ang-
gŏn 창건, (*endowment*) chaedan 재단.

founder *n.* ch'angnipcha 창립자, shijo 시조(始祖). *Who's
the ~ of Korea?* Han-gugŭi shijonŭn nuguimnikka?
한국의 시조는 누구입니까？

foundry *n.* chumul kongjang 주물 공장. *an iron*[*glass*,
type] ~ ch'ŏlmul[yuri, hwalcha] kongjang 철물[유리, 활
자] 공장.

fountain *n.* (*natural*) saem 샘, (*artificial*) punsu 분수.
~ *pen* mannyŏnp'il 만년필.

four *n.* sa 사(4), net 넷.

fourteen *n.* shipsa 십사(14), yŏl net 열 넷.

fourteenth *adj.* cheshipsa 제 14, yŏl netchae 열 네째.

fourth *adj.* chesa 제 4, netchae 네째.

fowl *n.* tak 닭, (*poultry*) kagŭm 가금.

fox *n.* yŏu 여우.

fraction *n.* (*scrap*) p'ap'yŏn 파편, chogak 조각, (*arith.*)
punsu 분수. 「골절.

fracture *n.* (*breaking*) p'ayŏl 파열, (*of bone*) kolchŏl

fragile *adj.* (*easily broken*) pusŏjigi shwiun 부서지기 쉬운,
(*frail*) hŏyak'an 허약한.

frame *n.* (*photo*) t'ŭl 틀, aekcha 액자. *—vt.* ~ *a
photograph* sajinŭl aekcha-e kkiuda 사진을 액자에 끼우다.

France *n.* P'ŭrangsŭ 프랑스.

frank *adj.* (*candid*) solchik'an 솔직한. *to be ~ with you*
solchik'i marhajamyŏn 솔직히 말하자면.

frankly *adv.* solchik'i 솔직히, t'ŏnok'o 터놓고. *F~
(speaking), I don't like him.* Solchik'i marhaesŏ kŭga
shilssŭmnida. 솔직히 말해서 그가 싫습니다.

fraternal *adj.* (*brotherly*) hyŏngjeŭi 형제의, (*friendly*)
uaeŭi 우애의. ~ *love* uae 우애.

fraternity *n.* uae 우애, tongp'oae 동포애, (*Am.*) (*soc. of
students*) haksaenghoe 학생회.

fraud *n.* sagi 사기. *a marriage* ~ kyŏrhon sagi 결혼 사기.

free *adj.* (*without payment*) muryoŭi 무료의, (*liberated*) chayuroun 자유로운, (*at leisure*) han-gahan 한가한. *You can get this tax ~.* Igŏsŭn myŏnsero sashil su issŭmnida. 이것은 면세로 사실 수 있읍니다/ *Are you ~ tomorrow?* Naeil shigani issŭshimnikka? 내일 시간이 있으십니까?

freedom *n.* (*liberty*) chayu 자유, (*independence*) tongnip 독립. ~ *of religion* chonggyoŭi chayu 종교의 자유/ ~ *of speech* ŏllonŭi chayu 언론의 자유.

freely *adv.* chayuropke 자유롭게.

freeze *vi.,vt.* ŏlda 얼다. *What freezing weather!* Toege ch'uun nalssigun! 되게 추운 날씨군!

freight *n.* (*cargo*) hwamul 화물, (*carriage charges*) unim 운임. ~ *car* hwamulch'a 화물차.

freighter *n.* (*cargo vessel*) hwamulsŏn 화물선.

French *adj.* P'ŭrangsŭŭi 프랑스의. —*n.* (*language*) purŏ 불어(佛語), (*the F~*) P'ŭrangsŭ kungmin 프랑스 국민.

Frenchman *n.* P'ŭrangsŭ saram 프랑스 사람.

frequent *adj.* (*often happening*) pinbŏnhan 빈번한, (*habitual*) sangsŭpchŏgin 상습적인.

frequently *adv.* chaju 자주, pinbŏnhi 빈번히.

fresh *adj.* (*new*) saeroun 새로운, (*newly made*) kat naon 갓 나온, (*cool*) shiwŏnhan 시원한. *Is there any ~ news?* Musun saeroun nyusŭga issŭmnikka? 무슨 새로운 뉴스가 있읍니까/ ~ *milk* shinsŏnhan uyu 신선한 우유/ ~ *breeze* shiwŏnhan sandŭlbaram 시원한 산들바람.

freshman *n.* (*college*) shinipsaeng 신입생, irhangnyŏnsaeng 1학년생.

friar *n.* t'akpalsŭng 탁발승, sudosŭng 수도승. 「충돌.

friction *n.* (*rubbing*) mach'al 마찰, (*clash*) ch'ungdol

Friday *n.* kŭmyoil 금요일. *Black ~* pulgirhan kŭmyoil 불길한 금요일.

friend *n.* ch'in-gu 친구, tongmu 동무. *a girl ~* yŏja ch'in-gu 여자 친구/*a good ~* ch'inhan ch'in-gu 친한 친구/ *a true ~* chinshirhan ch'in-gu 진실한 친구/ *Bring your ~ with you.* Ch'in-gurŭl terigo oshio. 친구를 데리고 오시오./*We are great ~s.* Urinŭn ch'inhan ch'in-gu saiimnida. 우리는 친한 친구 사이입니다.

friendly *adj.* ch'inhan 친한, *(amicable)* uhojŏgin 우호적인. *Would you mind a ~ tip?* Naega hanmadi haedo chok'essŭmnikka? 내가 한마디 해도 좋겠읍니까?

friendship *n.* ujŏng 우정, uae 우애.

fright *n.* kongp'o 공포, nollam 놀람.

frighten *vt.* kkamtchak nollage hada 깜짝 놀라게 하다, kŏbŭl chuda 겁을 주다. *I was badly ~ed.* Nanŭn kkamtchak nollassŭmnida. 나는 깜짝 놀랐읍니다/ *Did the noise ~ you?* Kŭ sorie nollassŭmnikka? 그 소리에 놀랐읍니까?

frightful *adj.* *(dreadful)* mushimushihan 무시무시한, *(horrible)* kkŭmtchik'an 끔찍한.

fringe *n.* *(edge)* kaduri changshik 가두리 장식, *(tuft)* sul 술, *(border)* pyŏnduri 변두리.

frock *n.* sangŭi 상의(上衣), p'ŭrokk'ot'ŭ 프록코트.

frog *n.* kaeguri 개구리, *table[edible] ~s* shigyong kaeguri 식용 개구리.

from *prep.* ...ŭrobut'ŏ ...으로부터, ...esŏ ...에서, *(out of)* ...esŏ naon ...에서 나온. *~ beginning to end* ch'ŏŭmbut'ŏ kkŭtkkaji 처음부터 끝까지/ *~ Seoul to Pusan* Sŏuresŏ Pusankkaji 서울에서 부산까지/ *a letter ~ my friend* ch'in-gurobut'ŏ on p'yŏnji 친구로부터 온 편지/ *die ~ fatigue* p'iroro chukta 피로로 죽다/ *Where are you ~?* Kohyangi ŏdishimnikka? 고향이 어디십니까?

front *n.* *(forward part)* chŏnmyŏn 전면, ap 앞, *(fore side)* chŏngmyŏn 정면(正面), *(line of battle)* chŏnsŏn 전선. *a ~ seat* apchari 앞자리/ *the ~ page of a newspaper* shinmun cheilmyŏn 신문 제1면/ *Wait for me in ~ of the hotel.* Hot'el ap'esŏ kidarishio. 호텔 앞에서 기다리시오/ *I'll give you the ~ desk.* Chŏpsugyee taeŏ tŭrigessŭmnida. 접수계에 대어 드리겠읍니다/ *My brother is now at the ~.* Hyŏngŭn chigŭm ilsŏne naga issŭmnida. 형은 지금 일선에 나가 있읍니다.

frontier *n.* kukkyŏng chibang 국경 지방, pyŏn-gyŏng 변경.

frost *n.* sŏri 서리. *We have had the first ~ of the year.* Ch'ŏtsŏriga naeryŏssŭmnida. 첫서리가 내렸읍니다.

frostbite *n.* tongsang 동상(凍傷).

frown *vi.* ŏlgurŭl tchip'urida 얼굴을 찌푸리다.

frozen *adj.* (*congealed*) ŏn 언, naengdonghan 냉동한, ~ *fish* naengdongŏ 냉동어.

frugal *adj.* (*economical*) kŏmsohan 검소한.

fruit *n.* kwail 과일, kwashil 과실. *a* ~ *dealer* kwail chang-su 과일 장수/ *a* ~ *shop* kwailjŏm 과일점.

frustrate *vt.,vi.* (*baffle*) chwajŏlshik'ida 좌절시키다.

fry *vt.,vi.* kirŭme t'wigida 기름에 튀기다.

frying pan p'ŭrai nambi 프라이 남비, p'ŭrai p'aen 프라이 팬.

fuel *n.* yŏllyo 연료. ~ *gas* yŏllyo kasŭ 연료 가스.

fugitive *n.* (*deserter*) tomangja 도망자, (*refugee*) mang-myŏngja 망명자.

fulfil(l) *vt.* (*perform*) tahada 다하다, (*carry out*) ihaeng-hada 이행하다. ~ *one's promise* yaksogŭl ihaenghada 약속을 이행하다.

full *adj.* kadŭk ch'an 가득 찬, (*whole*) chŏnbuŭi 전부의. —*n.* chŏnbu 전부(全部). *The box is* ~. Sangjanŭn kkwak ch'a issŭmnida. 상자는 꽉 차 있읍니다/ *This bottle is only half* ~. I pyŏngŭn panbakke ch'a itchi anssŭm-nida. 이 병은 반밖에 차 있지 않습니다/ *at* ~ *speed* chŏn-songnyŏguro 전(全)속력으로/ ~ *dress* chŏngjang 정장 (正裝)/ ~ *moon* manwŏl 만월/ *Please write your name in* ~. Sŏngmyŏngŭl (churiji malgo) chŏnbu ssŭshipshio. 성명을 (줄이지 말고) 전부 쓰십시오/ *I'm really* ~. Chŏng-mal paega purŭmnida. 정말 배가 부릅니다.

full-time *adj.* chŏnshigan kŭnmuŭi 전시간 근무의, chŏnim-ŭi 전임(專任)의.

fun *n.* (*merriment*) changnan 장난, (*joke*) nongdam 농담, (*amusement*) chaemi 재미. *make* ~ *of* ...ŭl nollida …을 놀리다. *What* ~! Igŏ chaemiitkun! 이거 재미있군/ *We had great* ~ *at the party.* P'ati chŏngmal chaemiissŏ-ssŭmnida. 파티 정말 재미있었습니다/ *Please have* ~! Chaemi poshipshio! 재미 보십시오!

fund *n.* chagŭm 자금, (*pl.*) chaewŏn 재원. *operating* ~*s* unyŏng chagŭm 운영 자금/ *We have no* ~*s in our hands.* Urinŭn sujunge chagŭmi ŏpsŭmnida. 우리는 수중

에 자금이 없읍니다.

funeral *n.* changnyeshik 장례식. ~ *service* changnyeshik 장례식/ *a public* ~ sahoejang 사회장/ *a state* ~ kukchang 국장/ *The* ~ *will be held on Monday*. Changnyeshigŭn wŏryoire kŏhaengdoemnida. 장례식은 월요일에 거행됩니다.

funnel *n.* (*boat*) kulttuk 굴뚝, (*pouring*) kkalttaegi 깔때기.

funny *adj.* (*laughable*) usŭun 우스운, (*strange*) isanghan 이상한. *That is* ~. Igŏn isanghagunyo. 이건 이상하군요/ *a* ~ *column* manhwanan 만화난(欄).

fur *n.* mop'i 모피. *a* ~ *coat* mop'i k'ot'ŭ 모피 코트/ *a fox* ~ yŏu mop'i 여우 모피.

furious *adj.* (*raging*) kyŏkpunhan 격분한, (*violent*) maengnyŏrhan 맹렬한, (*fierce*) nanp'ok'an 난폭한.

furiously *adv.* maengnyŏrhi 맹렬히.

furnace *n.* (*blast* ~) yonggwangno 용광로, (*fireplace*) hwaro 화로.

furnish *vi.,vt.* (*provide*) konggŭp'ada 공급하다, (*fit up*) sŏlbihada 설비하다.

furniture *n.* kagu 가구. *I have ordered new* ~. Sae kagurŭl chumunhaessŭmnida. 새 가구를 주문했읍니다.

furrow *n.* patkorang 밭고랑, (*wrinkle*) churŭm 주름.

further *adv.* (*in addition*) tŏugi 더우기, kŭ wie 그 위에, (*farther*) tŏ mŏlli 더 멀리. *I have nothing* ~ *to say*. Tŏ isang hal mari ŏpsŭmnida. 더 이상 할 말이 없읍니다/ *We must get* ~ *information*. Tŏ manŭn chŏngborŭl ŏdŏyagessŭmnida. 더 많은 정보를 얻어야겠읍니다.

fury *n.* (*wild anger*) kyŏkpun 격분, (*violence*) kwangp'o 광포, (*raging*) maengwi 맹위.

fuse *n.* p'yujŭ 퓨즈, tohwasŏn 도화선. —*vt.,vi.* (*melt*) nogida 녹이다, (*join*) yunghapshik'ida 융합시키다, (*dissolve*) nokta 녹다.

fuss *n.* (*bustle*) yadanbŏpsŏk 야단법석.

futile *adj.* (*useless*) ssŭlteŏmnŭn 쓸데없는, (*frivolous*) hach'anŭn 하찮은.

future *n.* mirae 미래, changnae 장래. *in the near* ~ kakkaun changnaee 가까운 장래에.

✦ G ✦

gab *n.* suda 수다, (*idle talk*) chaptam 잡담. *Stop your* ∼.
Ip takch'ishio. 입 닥치시오.

gadget *n.* (*accessory*) pusokp'um 부속품.

gag *n.* immagae 입마개, chaegal 재갈. ∼ *man* hŭigŭk
paeu 희극 배우.

gaiety *n.* (*merriment*) k'waehwal 쾌활, (*brightness*)
hwaryŏ 화려.

gain *vt.,vi.* (*get*) ŏtta 얻다, (*win*) igida 이기다, (*reach*)
toch'ak'ada 도착하다, (*increase*) nŭlda 늘다, (*watch,
clock*) shigyega tŏ kada 시계가 더 가다. —*n.* (*profit*) iik
이익, (*increase*) chŭngga 증가. *I have* ∼*ed five pounds
this summer.* Kŭmnyŏn yŏrŭm ch'ejungi o p'aundŭ
nŭrŏssŭmnida. 금년 여름 체중이 5파운드 늘었읍니다/ *My
watch* ∼*s three minutes a day.* Nae shigyenŭn haru
sambun tŏ kamnida. 내 시계는 하루 3분 더 갑니다.

gait *n.* kŏrŭmgŏri 걸음걸이, (*Am.*) sokto 속도.

gaiter *n.* kakpan 각반.   「응답.

gall *n.* ssŭlgaejŭp 쓸개즙, ssŭlgae 쓸개. *bear* ∼ ungdam

gallery *n.* (*fine arts*) hwarang 화랑. *the National G*∼
kungnip misulgwan 국립 미술관.

gallon *n.* kaellon 갤론. *sell by the* ∼ kaellondang ŏlma-
ssigŭro p'alda 갤론당 얼마씩으로 팔다.

gallows *n.* (*scaffold*) kyosudae 교수대, (*punishment*)
kyosuhyŏng 교수형.

gamble *vi.* (*play for money*) tobak'ada 도박하다, naegi-
hada 내기하다. —*n.* tobak 도박. ∼ *at cards* naegi k'a-
dŭnorirŭl hada. 내기 카드놀이를 하다.

gambler *n.* norŭmkkun 노름꾼, tobakkun 도박꾼.

game *n.* (*play*) nori 놀이, (*sporting contest*) kyŏnggi
경기, shihap 시합, (*prey*) sanyangkam 사냥감. *the
Olympic G*∼*s* ollimp'ik taehoe 올림픽 대회/ *Will you
have a* ∼ ? Shihap han p'an hashiryŏmnikka ? 시합 한
판하시렵니까/ *What did you think of the* ∼ *last*

night? Ŏjetpam shihabŭl ŏttŏk'e saenggak'ashimnikka? 어젯밤 시합을 어떻게 생각하십니까/ *card* ∼ k'adŭnori 카드놀이.

gang *n.* (*group*) iltan 일단, (*Am.*) nori tongmu 놀이 동무. *a* ∼ *of children* han muriŭi ŏrinidŭl 한 무리의 어린이들.

gap *n.* (*opening*) kumŏng 구멍, (*break*) pint'ŭm 빈틈, (*interval*) kan-gyŏk 간격.

gape *vi.* (*yawn*) hap'umhada 하품하다. —*n.* hap'um 하품.

garage *n.* ch'ago 차고. *an auto* ∼ chadongch'a ch'ago 자동차 차고.

garden *n.* chŏngwŏn 정원, ttŭl 뜰. *a flower* ∼ hwawŏn 화원.

gardener *n.* chŏngwŏnsa 정원사.

gargle *vi.* mogŭl kashida 목을 가시다.

garland *n.* (*wreath*) hwahwan 화환.

garlic *n.* manŭl 마늘.

garrison *n.* (*troops*) subidae 수비대.

garter *n.* yangmal taenim 양말 대님.

〈manŭl〉

gas *n.* kasŭ 가스, (*Am.*) kasollin 가솔린, hwiballyu 휘발유. *poison* ∼ tokkasŭ 독가스/ ∼ *lamp* kasŭdŭng 가스등/ ∼ *mask* pangdongmyŏn 방독면/∼ *station* chuyuso 주유소/ *We are getting out of* ∼, *ma'am.* Puin, hwiballyuga ta toeŏ kamnida. 부인, 휘발유가 다 되어 갑니다.

gasoline *n.* kasollin 가솔린, hwiballyu 휘발유.

gasp *vi.,vt.* hŏlttŏkkŏrida 헐떡거리다, sumch'ada 숨차다.

gate *n.* mun 문. *back* ∼ twinmun 뒷문/ *front* ∼ ammun 앞문. *What* ∼ *does flight 42 leave from*? Sashibibŏn kinŭn myŏt pŏn keit'ŭesŏ ch'ulbarhamnikka? 42번 기(機)는 몇 번 게이트에서 출발합니까?

gather *vt.,vi.* (*assemble*) moŭda 모으다, (*collect*) sujip'ada 수집하다, (*pick*) ttada 따다, (*infer*) ch'uch'ŭk'ada 추측하다. *Please* ∼ *me some flowers.* Kkoch'ŭl myŏt songi ttada chushipshio. 꽃을 몇 송이 따다 주십시오/ *What did you* ∼ *from his statement*? Kŭŭi mare ţaehae ŏttŏk'e saenggak'aessŭmnikka? 그의 말에 대해 어떻게 생각했읍니까?

gathering *n.* chip'oe 집회, sujip 수집.

gauge n. kyegi 계기(計器). —vi. (measure) ch'ŭkchŏnghada 측정하다. a rain ~ uryanggye 우량계/ a wind ~ p'ungsokkye 풍속계.

gauze n. kaje 가제. bandage ~ pungdaeyong kaje 붕대용 가제.

gay adj. (merry) k'waewharhan 쾌활한, (showy) hwaryŏhan 화려한. I don't feel very ~. Momi chom choch'i anssŭmnida. 몸이 좀 좋지 않습니다/ the ~ quarters hwaryugye 화류계.

gaze vi (look fixedly) ŭngshihada 응시하다.

gee int. chŏrŏn! 저런! nollassŏ! 놀랐어! G~, I don't know. Kŭlsse, chal morŭgennŭndeyo. 글쎄, 잘 모르겠는데요/G~ whiz! (Am.) Ai kkamtchagiya! 아이 깜짝이야!

gelatin(e) n. agyo 아교, chellat'in 젤라틴.

gem n. (jewel) posŏk 보석, ok 옥(玉).

general adj. (usual) ilbanjŏgin 일반적인, (whole) ch'ongch'ejŏgin 총체적인, (vague) magyŏnhan 막연한. —n. yukkun taejang 육군 대장. in ~ ilbanjŏguro 일반적으로/ a four star ~ sasŏng changgun 사성 장군.

generally adv. (usually) ilbanjŏguro 일반적으로, (widely) nŏlli 널리, (as a rule) pot'ong 보통. What time do you ~ get up? Taegang myŏt shie irŏnamnikka? 대강 몇 시에 일어납니까?

generation n. (period) shidae 시대(時代), (descendants) chason 자손, (origination) palsaeng 발생. future ~ huse 후세(後世)/ the present ~ hyŏndae 현대/ from ~ to ~ taedaero 대대로/ the ~ of gas kasŭŭi palsaeng 가스의 발생.

genius n. (prodigy) ch'ŏnjae 천재. a mathematical ~ suhagŭi ch'ŏnjae 수학의 천재.

gentle adj. (mild) onhwahan 온화한, (kind) sangnyanghan 상냥한, (decent) chŏmjanŭn 점잖은. a ~ manner chŏmjanŭn t'aedo 점잖은 태도.

gentleman n. shinsa 신사. a middle-aged ~ chungnyŏn shinsa 중년 신사.

genuine adj. (true) chintchaŭi 진짜의, (sincere) sŏngsirhan 성실한. I hope these stones are ~. Chintcha posŏgimenŭn t'ŭllimi ŏpketchiyo? 진짜 보석임에는 틀림이 없겠지요?

geography *n.* chiri 지리. *human* ~ inmun chiri 인문 지

geology *n.* chijirhak 지질학. 리.

geometry *n.* kihahak 기하학.

germ *n.* (*microbe*) segyun 세균, misaengmul 미생물.

German *adj.* Togirŭi 독일의. —*n.* Togil saram 독일 사람.

Germany *n.* Togil 독일. *West G*~ Sŏdok 서독/ *made in* ~ Togilche 독일제.

gesture *n.* momchit 몸짓, sonchit 손짓, chesŭch'ŏ 제스처.

get *vt.,vi.* (*obtain*) ŏtta 얻다, (*earn*) pŏlda 벌다, (*catch*) chapta 잡다, (*reach*) irŭda 이르다, (*cause*) ...hage hada ...하게 하다. ~ *along* saragada 살아가다/ ~ *down* naeryŏgada 내려가다/ ~ *in* tŭrŏgada 들어가다/ ~ *off* naerida 내리다/ ~ *on* (*car,train,etc.*) t'ada 타다/ ~ *out* nagada 나가다/ ~ *over* (*recover*) hoebok'ada 회복하다, (*surmount*) kŭkpok'ada 극복하다/ ~ *to* toch'ak'ada 도착하다/ ~ *up* irŏnada 일어나다/ *I'll* ~ *you a ticket for Pusan.* Pusanhaeng p'yorŭl sadŭrigessŭmnida. 부산행 표를 사드리겠습니다/ *Will you* ~ *me at the station tomorrow?* Naeil yŏgŭro majungnawa chushigessŭmnikka? 내일 역으로 마중나와 주시겠읍니까/ *We* ~ *along fine.* Modu ŭijok'e chinaego issŭmnida. 모두 의좋게 지내고 있읍니다/ *Mr. Driver, I want to* ~ *off here.* Unjŏnsu yangban, yŏgisŏ naeryŏ chuseyo. 운전수 양반, 여기서 내려 주세요/ *You'll* ~ *over it soon.* Kot hoebogi toel kŏshimnida. 곧 회복이 될 것입니다/ *When can you* ~ *through with your work?* Ŏnjekkaji wansŏnghal su issŭmnikka? 언제까지 완성할 수 있읍니까/ *Do you know how to* ~ *to my house?* Chŏŭi chibŭl algo kyeshimnikka? 저의 집을 알고 계십니까/ *I hope you* ~ *well soon.* Sok'i hoebok'ashigirŭl pimnida. 속히 회복하시기를 빕니다.

ghost *n.* yuryŏng 유령, hŏkkaebi 허깨비.

giant *n.* kŏin 거인. *a* ~ *in the business world* shirŏpkyeŭi kŏmul 실업계의 거물.

gift *n.* (*present*) sŏnmul 선물, (*talent*) chaenŭng 재능. *a New Year's* ~ saehae sŏnmul 새해 선물/ *to offer a* ~ sŏnmullo chuda 선물로 주다/ *You sure get the* ~ *of* *gab*. Tangshinŭn chŏngmal malchaegani issŭmnida. 당신은 정말 말재간이 있읍니다.

gimlet *n*. songgot 송곳, nasa songgot 나사 송곳.

ginger *n*. saenggang 생강. ～ *tea* saenggangch'a 생강차.

ginseng *n*. insam 인삼. *Korean* ～ Koryŏ insam 고려 인삼/ *Korean* ～ *tea* insamch'a 인삼차.

giraffe *n*. kirin 기린, chirap'ŭ 지라프.

girdle *n*. (*belt*) tti 띠, hŏritti 허리띠.

girl *n*. sonyŏ 소녀, kyejibai 계집 아이. *a decent* ～ yanggachip ttanim 양가집 따님/ *a business* ～ yŏsamuwŏn 여사무원/ *a factory* ～ yŏgong 여공/ ～ *friend* yŏja ch'in-gu 여자 친구.

give *vt.,vi.* (*bestow*) chuda 주다, (*hold*) kaech'oehada 개최하다, (*entrust*) matkida 맡기다/ *Please* ～ *me a glass of water*. Mul han chanman chushipshio. 물 한 잔만 주십시오/ *G*～ *the porter your bags*. Kabangŭl chimkkunege matkishio. 가방을 짐꾼에게 맡기시오/ ～ *away* (*secret*) nusŏrhada 누설하다/ ～ *in* (*surrender*) hangbok'ada 항복하다/ ～ *up* p'ogihada 포기하다.

glacier *n*. pingha 빙하. ～ *epoch* pingha shidae 빙하시대.

glad *adj*. kippŭn 기쁜, chŭlgŏun 즐거운. *I am very* ～ *to see you*. Manna poeŏ maeu pan-gapsŭmnida. 만나 뵈어 매우 반갑습니다/ *We are so* ～ *you could come*. Irŏk'e osyŏsŏ chŏngmal pan-gapsŭmnida. 이렇게 오셔서 정말 반갑습니다/ *I'm* ～ *you like it*. Maŭme tŭshindani pan-gapsŭmnida. 마음에 드신다니 반갑습니다.

glance *vi.,vt.* hilkkŭt poda 힐끗 보다. —*n*. ilgyŏn 일견(一見). *at a* ～ ŏllŭn poasŏ 얼른 보아서.

glare *vi.,vt.* (*shine strongly*) nunbushige pinnada 눈부시게 빛나다, (*stare fiercely*) noryŏboda 노려보다. —*n*. (*strong light*) sŏmgwang 섬광.

glaring *adj*. (*dazzling*) nunbushin 눈부신.

glass *n*. (*substance*) yuri 유리, (*cup*) chan 잔, k'ŏp 컵. *looking* ～ kŏul 거울/ *eye* ～ an-gyŏng 안경/ ～ *works* (*factory*) yuri kongjang 유리 공장/ *safety* ～ anjŏn yuri 안전 유리/ *Fill your* ～. Chanŭl ch'aeuseyo. 잔을 채우세요/ *Can I have another* ～ *of water*? Mul han chan tŏ chushiryŏmnikka? 물 한 잔 더 주시렵니까/ *I can't see without my ~es.* An-gyŏng ŏpshinŭn pol suga ŏpsŭmnida. 안경 없이는 볼 수가 없읍니다/ *rimless ~es* t'e ŏmnŭn an-gyŏng 테 없는 안경.

glide *vi.* mikkŭrŏjida 미끄러지다.

glider *n.* hwalgonggi 활공기, kŭllaidŏ 글라이더.

globe *n.* (*ball*) kong 공, (*the earth*) chigu 지구. ~*fish* pogŏ 복어.

gloom *n.* (*darkness*) ŏdum 어둠, (*melancholy*) uul 우울.

gloomy *adj.* (*dismal*) ch'imurhan 침울한, (*dreary*) ŭmsanhan 음산한. *The weather is ~ today.* Onŭl nalssiga ŭmsanhamnida. 오늘 날씨가 음산합니다/ *Why are you so ~ today?* Onŭl wae kŭrŏk'e uurhashimnikka? 오늘 왜 그렇게 우울하십니까?

glorious *adj.* (*honorable*) yŏnggwangsŭrŏun 영광스러운, (*magnificent*) changŏmhan 장엄한, (*splendid*) hullyunghan 훌륭한.

glory *n.* (*honor*) yŏnggwang 영광, (*splendor*) hwaryŏ 화려, (*brilliant sight*) changgwan 장관.

glove *n.* changgap 장갑, kŭllŏbŭ 글러브. *leather ~* kajuk changgap 가죽 장갑. *Excuse my ~s.* Changgap kkin ch'aero shillyehamnida. 장갑 낀 채로 실례합니다/ *~ fight* kwŏnt'u 권투.

glow *n.* (*white heat*) paegyŏl 백열, (*brightness*) kwangch'ae 광채, (*flushing*) hongjo 홍조. —*vi.* ppalgak'e taraorŭda 빨갛게 달아오르다.

glue *n.* agyo 아교, (*starch*) p'ul 풀. —*vt.* agyoro puch'ida 아교로 붙이다.

gnaw *vt.,vi.* (*bite*) kalgamŏkta 갉아먹다, ssolda 쏠다, (*torment*) koerop'ida 괴롭히다.

go *vi.* (*move away*) kada 가다, (*depart*) ttŏnada 떠나다, (*reach*) todarhada 도달하다, (*operate*) chagyonghada 작용하다, (*progress*) chinhaenghada 진행하다, (*be spent on*) sayongdoeda 사용되다, (*die*) chukta 죽다. *Where do you want to ~?* Ŏdiro kashiryŏmnikka? 어디로 가시렵니까/ *Let's ~ for a walk.* Sanch'aek'arŏ kapshida. 산책하러 갑시다/ *How ~es it?* Ŏttŏk'e chinaeshimnikka?

어떻게 지내십니까/ *How much of your money ~es on food*? Shikpinŭn ŏlmana tŭshimnikka? 식비는 얼마나 드십니까/ *He is ~ing, poor fellow*! Kŭnŭn chugŏ kago issŭmnida, pulssanghan kŏt! 그는 죽어 가고 있읍니다, 불쌍한 것/ *~ away* kabŏrida 가버리다/ *~ back* toragada 돌아가다/ *~ down* naeryŏgada 내려가다/ *~ into* …ŭro tŭrŏgada …으로 들어가다/ *~ out* oech'urhada 외출하다/ *~ through* t'onggwahada 통과하다/ *~ up* orŭda 오르다/ *~ with* …wa tonghaenghada …와 동행하다.

goal *n.* (*sports*) kyŏlsŭngchŏm 결승점, kol 골, (*object*) mokchŏk 목적.

goat *n.* yŏmso 염소.

god *n.* (*deity*) shin 신, (*G~*) hanŭnim 하느님, (*idol*) usang 우상. *thank G~* komawara 고마와라/ *G~ bless me*! ik'ŭ 이크, ŏmŏna! 어머나/ *O, G~*! Yadannannŭnde! 야단났는데/ *pray to G~* hanŭnimkke pilda 하느님께 빌다/ *swear by G~* hanŭnimkke maengsehada 하느님께 맹세하다/ *~father* taebu 대부(代父)/ *~mother* taemo 대모.

goddess *n.* yŏshin 여신. *the G~ of Liberty* chayuŭi yŏshin 자유의 여신.

gold *n.* kŭm 금. *~ coin* kŭmhwa 금화/ *~ foil* kŭmbak 금박/ *~fish* kŭmbungŏ 금붕어/ *~ mine* kŭmgwang 금광/ *~ ring* kŭmbanji 금반지/ *~ watch* kŭmshigye 금시계.

golden *adj.* kŭmpich'ŭi 금빛의. *~ earing* kŭmgwigŏri 금귀걸이/ *~ hair* kŭmbal 금발.

golf *n.* kolp'ŭ 골프. *play at ~* kolp'ŭrŭl ch'ida 골프를 치다/ *~ course[links]* kolp'ŭjang 골프장/ *~ club* kolp'ŭch'ae 골프채.

gong *n.* ching 징. *Has the ~ sounded for dinner yet?* Chŏnyŏk shiksa chongi pŏlssŏ ullyŏssŭmnikka? 저녁 식사 종이 벌써 울렸읍니까?

good *adj.* (*nice*) choŭn 좋은, (*virtuous*) ch'ak'an 착한, (*excellent*) hullyunghan 훌륭한. —*n.* sŏn 선(善), (*benefit*) iik 이익, (*pl.*) sangp'um 상품. *Show me some ~ cloth, please.* Kogŭp ch'ŏnŭl poyŏ chushio. 고급 천을 보여 주시오/

My sight is still ~. Nae shiryŏgŭn ajik chossŭmnida. 내 시력은 아직 좋습니다/ *G~ morning !* Annyŏnghashim-nikka ? 안녕하십니까/ *How ~ of you !* Ch'amŭro ch'injŏrhagido hasyŏra ! 참으로 친절하기도 하셔라/ *This medicine will do you* ~. I yagŭn chal tŭrŭl kŏshimnida. 이 약은 잘 들을 것입니다/ *domestic* ~s kuksanp'um 국산품/ *imported* ~s suipp'um 수입품.

good-by(e) *int.* annyŏng! 안녕 ! —*n.* (*farewell*) chakpyŏl insa 작별 인사. *say ~ to* chakpyŏl insarŭl hada 작별 인사를 하다/ *I must say ~ now.* Ije sŭlsŭl shillyehaeyage-ssŭmnida. 이제 슬슬 실례해야겠읍니다/ *G~ for today !* Onŭrŭn igŏllo shillyehamnida. 오늘은 이걸로 실례합니다.

goose *n.* kŏwi 거위.

gospel *n.* pogŭm 복음.

gossip *n.* (*idle talk*) handam 한담, chaptam 잡담, koship 고십. *the ~ column* koshimnan 고십난(欄).

gourd *n.* horibyŏngbak 호리병박, chorong-bak 조롱박.

govern *vt.,vi.* (*rule*) tasŭrida 다스리다, (*control*) ŏkchehada 억제하다.   ⟨chorongbak⟩

government *n.* (*politics*) chŏngch'i 정치, (*ruling*) chibae 지배, (*the ministry*) chŏngbu 정부. *the G~ of Korea* Han-guk chŏngbu 한국 정부/ ~ *office* kwanch'ŏng 관청/ ~ *official* kwalli 관리.

governor *n.* (*of a province*) chisa 지사, (*of bank*) ch'ongjae 총재. *a deputy ~* pujisa 부지사.

gown *n.* (*a loose robe*) kin udot 긴 웃옷, kaun 가운.

graceful *adj.* uahan 우아한, chŏmjanŭn 점잖은.

grade *n.* (*degree*) tŭnggŭp 등급, (*mark*) p'yŏngchŏm 평점, (*form*) hakkŭp 학급. *the first ~* iltŭng 1등/ *pay ~* ponggŭmnyul 봉급률.

gradually *adv.* sōsōhi 서서히, chŏmch'a 점차.

graduate *n.* (*from a univ.*) chorŏpsaeng 졸업생. —*vt.,vi.* chorŏp'ada 졸업하다. *a ~ of Seoul National University* Sŏul taehakkyo chorŏpsaeng 서울 대학교 졸업생/ ~-*to-be* chŏrŏp yejŏngja 졸업 예정자/ *At what university were* *you ~ed?* Ŏnŭ taehagŭl chorŏp'aessŭmnikka? 어느 대학을 졸업했읍니까?

graft *n.* (*corruption*) tokchik 독직, (*bribe*) suhoe 수회 (收賄). ~ *scandal* suhoe sakŏn 수회 사건.

grain *n.* (*cereals*) kongmul 곡물, (*single seed*) nadal 낟알.

grammar *n.* (*as a science*) munpŏp 문법. *Your ~ is shocking.* Tangshin marŭn munpŏbi ŏngmangimnida. 당신 말은 문법이 영망입니다.

gramophone *n.* (*phonograph*) ch'ugŭmgi 축음기.

grand *adj.* (*imposing*) ungdaehan 웅대한, (*splendid*) changnyŏhan 장려한, (*luxurious*) hohwaroun 호화로운. *We had a ~ time.* Aju yuk'waehan shiganŭl ponaessŭmnida. 아주 유쾌한 시간을 보냈읍니다.

grandchild *n.* (*male*) sonja 손자, (*female*) sonnyŏ 손녀.

granddaughter *n.* sonnyŏ 손녀.

grandfather *n.* harabŏji 할아버지, chobu 조부.

grandmother *n.* halmŏni 할머니, chomo 조모.

grandnephew *n.* chongson 종손(從孫).

grandniece *n.* chongsonnyŏ 종손녀.

grandparent *n.* chobumo 조부모.

grandson *n.* sonja 손자(孫子).

granite *n.* hwagangam 화강암, ssuktol 쑥돌.

grant *vt.* (*allow*) hŏrak'ada 허락하다, (*give*) suyŏhada 수여하다, (*admit*) ...irago injŏnghada …이라고 인정하다. *—n.* (*subsidy*) pojogŭm 보조금. *He was ~ed a pension.* Kŭnŭn yŏn-gŭmŭl t'age toeŏssŭmnida. 그는 연금을 타게 되었읍니다/ *I will make you a ~ of one million won a year.* Illyŏne paengmanwŏn pojohae tŭrigessŭmnida. 1년에 100만원 보조해 드리겠읍니다.

grape *n.* p'odo 포도. ~ *sugar* p'ododang 포도당.

grasp *n.* (*grip*) kkwak chwida 꽉 쥐다, (*seize upon*) puttŭlda 붙들다, (*understand*) ihaehada 이해하다. *I ~ed his right hand firmly.* Nanŭn kŭŭi orŭnsonŭl kkwak chwiŏssŭmnida. 나는 그의 오른손을 꽉 쥐었읍니다.

grass *n.* p'ul 풀, (*turf*) chandi 잔디. *Keep off the ~.* Chandirŭl papchi mashio. 잔디를 밟지 마시오/ *We sat on the ~es and had our lunch.* Urinŭn chandie anjasŏ chŏmshimŭl mŏgŏssŭmnida. 우리는 잔디에 앉아서 점심을 먹었읍니다.

grateful *adj.* kamsahanŭn 감사하는. *I am ~ for your kindness.* Ch'injŏrhi haejusyŏsŏ kamsahamnida. 친절히 해주셔서 감사합니다.

gratitude *n.* kamsa 감사.

grave *n.* (*tomb*) mudŏm 무덤, myo 묘. *~stone* pisŏk 비석/ *~yard* myoji 묘지.

gravel *n.* chagal 자갈. *a ~ path* chagalkil 자갈길.

gravitation *n.* illyŏk 인력(引力), chungnyŏk 중력.

gray, grey *adj.* hoesaegŭi 회색의. *—n.* hoesaek 회색.

grease *n.* (*fat*) kirŭm 기름, chibang 지방.

great *adj.* (*big*) k'ŭn 큰, (*prominent*) widaehan 위대한. *a ~ mistake* k'ŭn chalmot 큰 잘못/ *a ~ man* wiin 위인 (偉人)/ *a ~ number of* koengjanghi manŭn 굉장히 많은/ *~-grandfather* chŭngjobu 증조부/ *G~ Britain* Tae Pŭrit'ŭn sŏm 대 브리튼 섬, Yŏngguk 영국.

Greece *n.* Kŭrisŭ 그리스.

greedy *adj.* (*ravenous*) mopshi kumjurin 몹시 굶주린, (*desirous*) kalmanghanŭn 갈망하는, (*covetous*) yokshim manŭn 욕심 많은.

Greek *adj.* Kŭrisŭŭi 그리스의. *—n.* Kŭrisŭin 그리스인.

green *adj.* noksaegŭi 녹색의, ch'orokpich'ŭi 초록빛의. *—n.* noksaek 녹색. *~belt* nokchidae 녹지대, kŭrinbelt'ŭ 그린벨트/ *~grocer* ch'aeso changsu 채소 장수/ *~house* onshil 온실.

greet *vt.* (*salute*) insahada 인사하다.

greeting *n.* insa 인사, hwanyŏngŭi mal 환영의 말, (*pl.*) insamal 인사말. *~ card* insachang 인사장, ch'uk'achang 축하장/ *wedding ~s* kyŏrhon ch'uksa 결혼 축사.

grief *n.* (*sorrow*) sŭlp'ŭm 슬픔, pit'an 비탄, pit'ong 비통, (*distress*) konoe 고뇌.

grieve *vt.,vi.* sŭlp'ŭge hada 슬프게 하다, (*distress*) koerop'ida 괴롭히다, (*lament*) pit'anhada 비탄하다.

grill *n.* (*gridiron*) sŏksoe 석쇠, (*~ food*) pulgogi 불고기, (*~room*) kŭril 그릴.

grind *vt.,vi.* ppat'a 빻다, (*grate*) kalda 갈다. *~ coffee* *beans* k'op'ik'ongŭl ppat'a 코피콩을 빻다/ ~ *one's teeth* irŭl kalda 이를 갈다.

grocer *n.* shingnyop'um sangin 식료품 상인, shingnyo chap'wasang 식료 잡화상.

grocery *n.* shingnyo chap'waryu 식료 잡화류.

groom *n.* (*horse driver*) mabu 마부, (*bride~*) shillang 신랑.

gross *n.* (*12 dozen*) kŭrosŭ 그로스, shibi tasŭ 12 다스. —*adj.* ~ *amount* ch'ongaek 총액/ ~ *income* ch'ongsuip 총수입/ ~ *error* ŏmch'ŏngnan shilsu 엄청난 실수.

ground *n.* (*land*) t'oji 토지, (*play~*) undongjang 운동장, (*base*) kŭn-gŏ 근거.

group *n.* chiptan 집단, muri 무리. *What ~ of language does Korean belong to?* Han-gugŏnŭn ŏnŭ ŏgune sok'amnikka? 한국어는 어느 어군에 속합니까/ *a ~ of girls* han muriŭi sonyŏ 한 무리의 소녀.

grow *vi.,vt.* (*become larger*) sŏngjanghada 성장하다, (*become*) ...ŭro toeda …으로 되다, (*cultivate*) chaebaehada 재배하다, (*develop*) paltalshik'ida 발달시키다. *You seem to ~ younger, every time I see you.* Mannal ttaemada tangshinŭn chŏlmojinŭn kŏt kassŭmnida. 만날 때마다 당신은 젊어지는 것 같습니다/ *Will you ~ some medical herbs for me?* Yakch'orŭl chom chaebaehae chushigessŭmnikka? 약초를 좀 재배해 주시겠읍니까/ *a grown-up person* ŏrŭn 어른.

growth *n.* sŏngjang 성장.

grudge *n.* wŏnhan 원한. *harbor a ~* wŏnhanŭl p'umta 원한을 품다/ *I bear him no ~.* Kŭege amurŏn wŏnhando ŏpsŭmnida. 그에게 아무런 원한도 없읍니다/ *Why do you hold a ~ against her?* Wae kŭnyŏrŭl chŏktaeshihashimnikka? 왜 그녀를 적대시하십니까?

grumble *vt.,vi.* (*complain*) pulp'yŏnghada 불평하다, (*murmur*) t'udŏlgŏrida 투덜거리다. —*n.* pulp'yŏng 불평. *He is always grumbling.* Kŭnŭn ŏnjena pulp'yŏngŭl hago issŭmnida. 그는 언제나 불평을 하고 있읍니다/ *What are you grumbling?* Muŏsŭl t'udŏldaego issŭmnikka? 무엇을 투덜대고 있읍니까?

guarantee *n.* (*person*) pojŭngin 보증인, (*money*) pojŭnggŭm 보증금, (*security*) tambo 담보, (*actor, etc.*) ch'uryŏnnyo 출연료. —*vt.* (*insure*) pojŭnghada 보증하다. *What ~ can you offer?* Ŏttŏn tamborŭl chegonghal su issŭmnikka? 어떤 담보를 제공할 수 있습니까/ *I can offer my house as a ~.* Tamborosŏ nae chibŭl chegonghal su issŭmnida. 담보로서 내 집을 제공할 수 있습니다/ *This camera is ~d for one year.* I k'ameranŭn illyŏn-gan pojŭnghamnida. 이 카메라는 1년간 보증합니다.

guarantor *n.* pojŭngin 보증인.

guard *n.* (*warden*) suwi 수위, (*sentry*) poch'o 보초, (*escort*) kyŏnghowŏn 경호원, (*Am.*) (*conductor*) ch'ajang 차장. —*vt.* kyŏnggyehada 경계하다.

guardian *n.* (*protector*) pohoja 보호자, (*legal*) hugyŏnin 후견인. *~ angel* suhoŭi ch'ŏnsa 수호의 천사, suhoshin 수호신.

guess *vt., vi.* (*surmise*) ch'uch'ŭk'ada 추측하다, aramach'ida 알아맞히다, (*think*) saenggak'ada 생각하다. —*n.* (*conjecture*) ch'uch'ŭk 추측. *Can you ~ my age?* Nae nairŭl aramach'il su issŭmnikka? 내 나이를 알아맞힐 수 있습니까/ *G~ what I'm thinking.* Naega muŏsŭl saenggak'ago innŭn-ga aramach'yŏ poshio. 내가 무엇을 생각하고 있는가 알아맞혀 보시오/ *by ~* ŏrimjaba 어림잡아.

guest *n.* (*visitor*) sonnim 손님. *~ of honor* chubin 주빈/ *state ~* kukpin 국빈/ *~room* kaekshil 객실/ *I would like you to be my ~.* Nae sonnimi toeŏ chusyŏssŭmyŏn hamnida. 내 손님이 되어 주셨으면 합니다/ *Please be my ~.* Naega naegessŭmnida. 내가 내겠읍니다.

guidance *n.* (*leadership*) chido 지도, (*guide*) annae 안내. *personal ~* kaein chido 개인 지도/ *vocational ~* chigŏp chido 직업 지도.

guide *n.* (*usher*) annaeja 안내자, (*leader*) chidoja 지도자, (*guidebook*) annaesŏ 안내서. —*vt.* (*lead*) annaehada 안내하다, (*direct*) chidohada 지도하다. *I want a ~ who speaks English.* Yŏngŏrŭl hal su innŭn annaejaga p'iryohamnida. 영어를 할 수 있는 안내자가 필요합니다/ *Do you have a ~book of Korea?* Han-guk annaesŏga issŭmnikka? 한국 안내서가 있읍니까?

guided missile yudot'an 유도탄.

g(u)ild n. (*association*) chohap 조합, kildŭ 길드.

guilt n. (*guilty conduct*) pŏmjoe haengwi 범죄 행위, (*wrongdoing*) pihaeng 비행, (*sin*) choe 죄. *confess one's* ～ pŏmhaengŭl chabaek'ada 범행을 자백하다/ *a partner in* ～ kongbŏmja 공범자. 「는.

guiltless adj. kyŏlbaek'an 결백한, choega ŏmnŭn 죄가 없

guilty adj. (*criminal*) yujoeŭi 유죄의, (*feeling guilt*) maŭme k'engginŭn 마음에 켕기는. *What crime was he* ～ *of?* Kŭga musŭn choerŭl chiŏttŏn-gayo? 그가 무슨 죄를 지었던가요?

guinea pig morŭmot'ŭ 모르모트, kini p'igŭ 기니 피그.

guise n. (*disguise*) kajang 가장, pyŏnjang 변장, (*appearance*) oegwan 외관(外觀). 「를 치다.

guitar n. kit'a 기타. *play* (*on*) *the* ～ kit'arŭl ch'ida 기타

gulf n. man 만(灣).

gull n. (*sea* ～) kalmaegi 갈매기.

gulp vt. kkulkkŏkkulkkŏk mashida 꿀꺽꿀꺽 마시다, ch'amta 참다, samk'ida 삼키다. ―n. han mogŭm 한 모금. *Don't swallow your meals at a* ～. Shiksarŭl tansume samk'iji mashio. 식사를 단숨에 삼키지 마시오.

gum n. (*rubber*) komu 고무, (*Am.*) (*chewing* ～) ch'uinggŏm 추잉껌, (*pl.*) (*of the mouth*) inmom 잇몸.

gun n. (*rifle*) ch'ong 총, (*cannon*) taep'o 대포. *an air* ～ konggich'ong 공기총/ *shot* ～ yŏpch'ong 엽총/ ～*fire* p'ohwa 포화/ ～*lock* pangasoe 방아쇠/ ～*man* p'osu 포수/ ～*powder* hwayak 화약.

gunnery n. (*operation of guns*) p'osul 포술(砲術).

gush vi.,vt. (*issue with force*) naeppumta 내뿜다, (*spout*) punch'urhada 분출하다. ―n. yuch'ul 유출, punch'ul 분출. *a* ～ *of oil* sŏgyuŭi punch'ul 석유의 분출.

gut n. (*bowels*) naejang 내장, (*entrails*) ch'angja 창자, *blind* ～ maengjang 맹장.

gutter n. (*groove*) hom 홈, (*ditch*) torang 도랑, (*slums*) pinmin-gul 빈민굴.

guy n. (*fellow*) nom 놈, nyŏsŏk 녀석. *a queer* ～ koe-

sanghan nyŏsŏk 괴상한 녀석/ *a silly* ～ ŏrisŏgŭn nom 어
리석은 놈.

gymnasium *n.* (*gym*) ch'eyukkwan 체육관. *What number
bus goes to Changchung G～?* Myŏt pŏn pŏsŭga
Changch'ung ch'eyukkwanŭro kamnikka? 몇 번 버스가
장충 체육관으로 갑니까?　　　　　　　　　　　　　「사.

gymnast *n.* ch'ejo sŏnsu 체조 선수, ch'ejo kyosa 체조 교

gymnastics *n.* ch'ejo 체조.

gynecologist *n.* puinkwa ŭisa 부인과 의사.　　　　　「소녀.

gypsy, gipsy *n.* chipshi 집시. *a ～ girl* chipshi sonyŏ 집시

H

haberdasher *n.* chap'wa sangin 잡화 상인.

habit *n.* (*custom*) sŭpkwan 습관, (*usual behaviour*)
sŭpsŏng 습성, pŏrŭt 버릇. *good ～* choŭn pŏrŭt 좋은 버릇/
domestic ～s kap'ung 가풍/ *the reading ～* toksŏbyŏk
독서벽/ *Beware of the bad ～.* Nappŭn pŏrŭsŭl choshimhashio. 나쁜 버릇을 조심하시오.

habitation *n.* chuso 주소.

habitual *adj.* (*customary*) sŭpkwanjŏgin 습관적인, (*usual*)
p'yŏngsoŭi 평소의. *a ～ liar* sangsŭpchŏgin kŏjinmalchangi
상습적인 거짓 말장이.

haggard *adj.* (*gaunt*) yŏwin 여윈, mallappajin 말라빠진.

haggle *vi.* kapsŭl kkakta 값을 깎다, enurihada 에누리하다.

hail *n.* (*winter ～*) ssarangnun 싸락눈, (*summer ～*) ubak
우박, (*cheer*) hwanho 환호. *—vt.* (*welcome*) hwanyŏnghada 환영하다, (*call*) purŭda 부르다. *Let's ～ a taxi,
shall we?* T'aekshirŭl purŭlkkayo? 택시를 부를까요?

hair *n.* t'ŏl 털, (*～ of the head*) mŏrik'arak 머리카락.
comb one's ～ mŏrirŭl pitta 머리를 빗다/ *curl one's ～*
mŏrirŭl chijida 머리를 지지다/ *I would like to have my
～ set.* Mŏrirŭl set'ŭhae chushipshio. 머리를 세트해 주십시
오/ *～brush* mŏritsol 머릿솔/ *～cut* ibal 이발/ *～-
dresser* ibalsa 이발사/ *～pin* mŏrip'in 머리핀/ *～ -tweezers*
chokchipke 족집게/ *Just a ～cut, please.* Ibalman hae-

juseyo. 이발만 해주세요.

hale *adj.* (*robust*) t'ŭnt'ŭnhan 튼튼한, (*healthy*) kŏnganghan 건강한.

half *n.* pan 반, chŏlban 절반. —*adj.* panŭi 반의. —*adv.* pantchŭm 반쯤. *more than* ～ pan isang 반 이상/ *two and a* ～ tu kae pan 두 개 반/ ～ *an hour* = *a* ～ *hour* pan shigan 반 시간/ ～ *price* panaek 반액/ ～ *year* pan nyŏn 반 년/ *Just* ～ *a cup, please.* Pan k'ŏmman chuseyo. 반 컵만 주세요/ *Let's share the expenses* ～ *and* ～. Piyongŭn panbanŭro nanupshida. 비용은 반반으로 나눕시다/ *Cut this bread in* ～. I ppangŭl panŭro charŭshipshio. 이 빵을 반으로 자르십시오/ *I have read* ～ *the book.* Ku ch'aegŭi panŭl ilgŏssŭmnida. 그 책의 반을 읽었읍니다/ ～ *brother* ŭibut hyŏngje 의붓 형제, paedarŭn hyŏngje 배다른 형제/ ～-*breed* honhyŏra 혼혈아/ ～-*moon* pandal 반달.

hall *n.* (*for meetings*) hoegwan 회관, hol 홀, (*of univ.*) kangdang 강당, (*for meals*) shiktang 식당, (*passage*) pokto 복도. *city* ～ shich'ŏng 시청/ *dining* ～ shiktang 식당/ *lecture* ～ kangdang 강당/ *music* ～ ŭmaktang 음악당/ *Walk to the end of the* ～. Pokto kkŭtkkaji kŏrŏgashio. 복도 끝까지 걸어가시오.

hallo *int.* (*hullo*) yŏboseyo 여보세요, yaa 야아.

halt *vi.,vt.* (*stop*) mŏmch'wŏ sŏda 멈춰 서다.

hamburger *n.* haembŏgŏ 햄버거. *Give me beer and a* ～, *please.* Maekchuwa haembŏgŏrŭl chushio. 맥주와 햄버거를 주시오.

hamlet *n.* (*small village*) chagŭn maŭl 작은 마을, ch'ollak 촌락.

hammer *n.* mangch'i 망치, haemŏ 해머.

hand *n.* son 손, (*of a timepiece*) panŭl 바늘. —*vt.* (*transfer*) nŏmgyŏjuda 넘겨주다. *left* ～ oenson 왼손/ *right* ～ orŭnson 오른손/ *both* ～*s* yangson 양손/ *the minute* ～ punch'im 분침/ *at* ～ kakkaie 가까이에/ *clap one's* ～*s* paksuch'ida 박수치다/ *shake one's* ～ aksuhada 악수하다/ ～ *over* nŏmgyŏjuda 넘겨주다/ *Would you like to wash your* ～*s?* Sonŭl ssisŭshigessŭmnikka? 손을 씻

으시겠읍니까/ *Would you be kind enough to* ~ *me a cup?* Mianhajiman k'ŏbŭl chom chibŏ chushigessŭmnikka? 미안하지만 컵을 좀 집어 주시겠읍니까?

handbag *n.* haendŭbaek 핸드백, sonkabang 손가방.

handbook *n.* p'yŏllam 편람, annaesŏ 안내서.

handcart *n.* chimsure 짐수레, sonsure 손수레.

handful *n.* hanjum 한줌, (*small number*) sosu 소수. *a* ~ *of children* sosuŭi aidŭl 소수의 아이들.

hand glass sonkŏul 손거울.

handicap *n.* (*disadvantage*) pullihan chokŏn 불리한 조건, haendik'aep 핸디캡. —*vt.* pullihan chokŏnŭl puch'ida 불리한 조건을 붙이다/ *industrial* ~*s* sanŏpsang pullihan chokŏn 산업상 불리한 조건.

handkerchief *n.* sonsugŏn 손수건.

handle *n.* (*of tool, cup, door, etc.*) sonjabi 손잡이, charu 자루, haendŭl 핸들. —*vt.* (*manipulate*) taruda 다루다. *The* ~ *is broken.* Haendŭri kojangna issŭmnida. 핸들이 고장나 있읍니다/ *H*~ *this parcel with care.* I chimŭl chuŭihayŏ tarushipshio. 이 짐을 주의하여 다루십시오/ *Do you also* ~ *chicken meat?* Takkogido p'ashimnikka? 닭고기도 파십니까?

hand-made *adj.* sonŭro mandŭn 손으로 만든.

handsome *adj.* (*comely*) chal saenggin 잘 생긴, (*fine*) hullyunghan 훌륭한, (*ample*) kkwae manŭn 꽤 많은. *a* ~ *man* minamja 미남자/ *a* ~ *present* p'ujimhan sŏnmul 푸짐한 선물.

handwriting *n.* p'ilchŏk 필적.

handy *adj.* (*convenient*) almajŭn 알맞은, p'yŏllihan 편리한, (*skillful*) somssi innŭn 솜씨 있는. *a* ~ *tool* p'yŏllihan togu 편리한 도구/ *come in* ~ ssŭlmoga itta 쓸모가 있다/ *She is* ~ *with the needle.* Kŭnyŏnŭn panŭjil somssiga chossŭmnida. 그녀는 바느질 솜씨가 좋습니다.

hang *vt.,vi.* (*suspend*) maedalda 매달다, kŏlda 걸다, (*strangle*) kyosarhada 교살(絞殺)하다, (*depend*) ...e tallyŏ itta ...에 달려 있다. *H*~ *your coat on that hook.* Chŏ otkŏrie k'ot'ŭrŭl kŏshipshio. 저 옷걸이에 코트를 거십시오/ *H*~ *on, please.* Suhwagirŭl tŭn ch'ae kidaryŏ

chushipshio. 수화기를 든 채 기다려 주십시오/ *Please ~
up.* Chŏnhwarŭl kkŭnŏ chuseyo. 전화를 끊어 주세요.

hanger *n.* otkŏri 옷걸이.

hanger-on *n.* shikkaek 식객, (*dependent*) puha 부하.

hangover *n.* (*illness*) sukch'wi 숙취(宿醉), (*survival*)
yumul 유물. *Oh, that is too bad. H~?* Kŭgŏt ch'am
andwaetkunyo. Sukch'wi aniseyo? 그것 참 안됐군요. 숙
취 아니세요?

happen *n.* (*occur*) irŏnada 일어나다, (*chance*) uyŏnhi
...hada 우연히 ...하다, (*befall to*) takch'yŏoda 닥쳐오다.
What~ed to your leg? Tarika ŏttŏk'e twaessŭmnikka?
다리가 어떻게 됐읍니까/ *How did it ~?* Ŏttŏk'e hada
kŭrŏk'e toeŏtchiyo? 어떻게 하다 그렇게 되었지요/ *I ~ed
to be there.* Nanŭn uyŏnhi kŏgi issŏssŭmnida. 나는 우
연히 거기 있었읍니다.

happening *n.* (*event*) sakŏn 사건. *a strange ~* isanghan
sakŏn 이상한 사건/ *world ~s* segyeŭi tonghyang 세계의
동향.

happiness *n.* haengbok 행복, haengun 행운.

happy *adj.* (*fortunate*) haengbok'an 행복한, (*glad*)
kippŭn 기쁜. *a ~ life* haengbok'an saenghwal 행복한
생활/ *a ~ union* haengbok'an kyŏrhon 행복한 결혼/ *I
shall be very ~ to see you.* Kkok mannabogo shipsŭmnida. 꼭 만나보고 싶습니다/ *You look ~ today.* Onŭrŭn
haengbok'age poinŭn-gunyo. 오늘은 행복하게 보이는군요/
She was not ~. Kŭnyŏnŭn haengbok'aji mot'aessŭmnida. 그녀는 행복하지 못했읍니다.

harbo(u)r *n.* (*port*) hanggu 항구, (*in compound*) ...hang
...항(港). *enter a ~* ip'anghada 입항하다/ *a commercial ~*
muyŏk'ang 무역항/ *Inchon ~* Inch'ŏnhang 인천항/ *a
military ~* kunhang 군항.

hard *adj.* (*solid*) ttakttak'an 딱딱한, (*difficult*) ŏryŏun
어려운. —*adv.* (*earnestly*) yŏlshimhi 열심히. *This pencil
is too ~ to write with.* I yŏnp'irŭn ssŭgie nŏmu ttakttak'amnida. 이 연필은 쓰기에 너무 딱딱합니다/ *This
problem is too ~.* I munjenŭn nŏmu ŏryŏpsŭmnida.
이 문제는 너무 어렵습니다/ *This has been a ~ day for
you.* Onŭrŭn kosaengi manassŭmnida. 오늘은 고생이 많

았읍니다/ *I'm* ~ *up*. Nanŭn yojŭm kungsaek'amnida. 나는 요즘 궁색합니다/ *You must work* ~. Yŏlshimhi irhaeyaman hamnida. 열심히 일해야만 합니다/ *It is raining* ~. Piga mopshi omnida. 비가 몹시 옵니다.

harden *vt.,vi.* (*solidify*) tandanhage hada 단단하게 하다, (*make hardy*) kanghage hada 강하게 하다. ~ *the body* shinch'erŭl tallyŏnshik'ida 신체를 단련시키다.

hardly *adv.* (*scarcely*) kŏŭi …anida 거의 …아니다. *I* ~ *know her*. Nanŭn kŭnyŏrŭl kŏŭi morŭmnida. 나는 그녀를 거의 모릅니다/ *I can* ~ *believe it*. Kŏŭi midŭl su ŏpsŭmnida. 거의 믿을 수 없읍니다.

hardship *n.* konan 고난, kosaeng 고생. *experience* ~*s* konanŭl kyŏkta 고난을 겪다.

hardware *n.* ch'ŏlmul 철물, (*computer*) hadŭweŏ 하드웨어.

hare *n.* sant'okki 산토끼. —*vi.* chilchuhada 질주하다.

harm *n.* (*damage*) hae 해, sonhae 손해, (*injury*) sonsang 손상. —*vt.* (*hurt*) haech'ida 해치다. *I mean no* ~. Chogŭmdo agŭinŭn ŏpsŭmnida. 조금도 악의는 없읍니다/ *A few drinks will do you no* ~. Sul myŏt chantchŭmŭn haeropchi anŭl kŏshimnida 술 몇 잔쯤은 해롭지 않을 것입

harmful *adj.* haeroun 해로운. ㄴ니다.

harmless *adj.* haega ŏmnŭn 해가 없는, muhaeŭi 무해의.

harmony *n.* (*music*) hwasŏng 화성, (*concord*) chohwa 조화, hwahap 화합. *color* ~ saegŭi chohwa 색의 조화/ *live in* ~ hwamok'age chinaeda 화목하게 지내다.

harness *n.* magu 마구(馬具). —*vt.* magurŭl ch'aeuda 마구를 채우다.

harp *n.* hap'ŭ 하프. —*vi.* hap'ŭrŭl t'ada 하프를 타다.

harrow *n.* ssŏre 써레.

harsh *adj.* (*coarse*) kŏch'in 거친, (*bitter*) ssŭn 쓴, (*stern*) ŏmkyŏk'an 엄격한, (*discordant*) kwie kŏsŭllinŭn 귀에 거슬리는. *a* ~ *texture* kkŏch'ilkkŏch'irhan ch'ŏn 꺼칠꺼칠한 천/ *a* ~ *voice* kŏsen moksori 거센 목소리.

harvest *n.* (*crop*) suhwak 수확, ch'usu 추수. *abundant* ~ p'ungjak 풍작/ *bad* ~ hyungjak 흉작/ *the time of* ~ suhwakki 수확기.

hash vt. (chop up) tajida 다지다, chōmida 저미다, (make a mess of) ŏngmanguro mandŭlda 엉망으로 만들다.

haste n. (hurry) sŏdurŭm 서두름, sŏnggŭp 성급. Make ~. Sŏdurŭshio. 서두르시오/ We have made all possible ~. Urinŭn toedorok sŏdullŏssŭmnida. 우리는 되도록 서둘렀읍니다/ Don't do things in ~. Irŭl sŏdullŏsŏnŭn an toemnida. 일을 서둘러서는 안 됩니다.

hasten vt.,vi. (speed up) chaech'ok'ada 재촉하다, (hurry) sŏdurŭda 서두르다. I ~ed to the spot. Nanŭn hyŏnjie tallyŏgassŭmnida. 나는 현지에 달려갔읍니다/ Why do you ~ so? Wae kŭrŏk'e sŏdurŭshimnikka? 왜 그렇게 서두르십니까?

hat n. moja 모자. pot ~ chungsanmo 중산모/ silk ~ shilk'ŭ haet'ŭ 실크 해트/ soft ~ chungjŏlmo 중절모/ straw ~ milchip moja 밀짚 모자/ ~ hanger[rack] mojagŏri 모자걸이/ Put on your ~. Mojarŭl ssŭshipshio. 모자를 쓰십시오/ Take off your ~ in the room. Shillaeesŏnŭn mojarŭl pŏsŭshipshio. 실내에서는 모자를 벗으십시오.

hatch vi.,vt. puhwahada 부화하다, arŭl kkada 알을 까다.

hatchet n. (small ax) sondokki 손도끼, tokki 도끼. bury the ~ hwahaehada 화해하다/ Did they bury the ~? Kŭdŭrŭn hwahaehaessŭmnikka? 그들은 화해했읍니까?

hate vt. (detest) miwŏhada 미워하다, (dislike) shirŏhada 싫어하다. We ~ injustice. Pujŏngŭl miwŏhamnida. 부정(不正)을 미워합니다/ I ~ to study. Nanŭn kongbuga shilssŭmnida. 나는 공부가 싫습니다.

hatred n. (loathing) mium 미움, (ill will) angshim 앙심.

hatter n. mojajŏm 모자점.

haughty adj. (arrogant) kŏmanhan 거만한. ~ air kŏnbangjin t'aedo 건방진 태도.

haul vt.,vi. chabadanggida 잡아당기다.

haunt vt.,vi. (frequent) chaju tŭnadŭlda 자주 드나들다, (obsess) tallabutta 달라붙다. —n. (resort) chaju taninŭn kot 자주 다니는 곳, (den) sogul 소굴. be ~ed by fears kŏkchŏngi put'ŏdanida 걱정이 붙어다니다/ a holiday ~ hyuirŭi hwallak changso 휴일의 환락 장소/ the ~s of thieves todugŭi sogul 도둑의 소굴.

have *vt.* (*possess*) kajida 가지다, (*obtain, receive*) ŏtta 얻다, patta 받다, (*eat*) mŏkta 먹다, (*drink*) mashida 마시다, (*wear*) ipta 입다, (*experience*) kyŏnghŏmhada 경험하다, (~ *to do*) haji anŭmyŏn an toeda 하지 않으면 안되다. *How many children do you* ~ ? Ainŭn myŏch'ina toeshimnikka? 아이는 몇이나 되십니까/ *H*~ *you any money with you?* Ton kajin kŏt issŭmnikka? 돈 가진 것 있읍니까/ *I had on two flannel shirts.* Nanŭn p'ŭllannel syassŭrŭl tu changina ipko issŏssŭmnida. 나는 플란넬 샤쓰를 두 장이나 입고 있었읍니다/ *Did you* ~ *a good holiday?* Hyuga chaemiissŏssŭmnikka? 휴가 재미있었읍니까/ *You* ~ *to go at once.* Tangshinŭn kot kaya hamnida. 당신은 곧 가야 합니다/ *I must* ~ *these shoes repaired.* I kudurŭl susŏnhaeyagessŭmnida. 이 구두를 수선해야겠읍니다/ *When did you* ~ *your haircut?* Ŏnje ibarŭl haessŭmnikka? 언제 이발을 했읍니까?

hawk *n.* mae 매, (*sharper*) sagikkun 사기꾼.

hawker *n.* (*peddler*) haengsangin 행상인.

hay *n.* kŏnch'o 건초.

hazard *n.* (*danger*) wihŏm 위험, (*risk*) mohŏm 모험, (*chance*) un 운.

haze *n.* ajiraengi 아지랭이, an-gae 안개.

hazy *adj.* (*misty*) an-gae kkin 안개 낀, ajiraengi kkin 아지랭이 낀, hŭrin 흐린. ~ *weather* hŭrin nalssi 흐린 날씨.

he *pron.* kŭnŭn[ga] 그는[가], (*that man*) chŏ saramŭn[i] 저 사람은[이].

head *n.* (*of the body*) mŏri 머리, (*intellect*) chinŭng 지능, (*boss*) udumŏri 우두머리, (*top*) kkoktaegi 꼭대기, (*front*) ammyŏn 앞면. *Hit him on the* ~. Kŭŭi mŏrirŭl ttaerishio. 그의 머리를 때리시오/ *Hold up your* ~. Mŏrirŭl tŭshio. 머리를 드시오/ *a household* ~ hoju 호주(戶主)/ *the* ~ *of the family* kajang 가장/ *a section* ~ pu[kwa]-jang 부[과]장/ *the* ~ *teacher* kyogam 교감(校監)/ *You have a good* ~ *for business.* Tangshinŭn saŏbe t'agonan chaenŭngi issŭmnida. 당신은 사업에 타고난 재능이 있읍니다/ *H*~*s or tails?* Ammyŏnio, twinmyŏnio? 앞면이오, 뒷면이오/ *keep one's* ~ ch'imch'ak'ada 침착하다/

lose one's ~ tanghwanghada 당황하다/ ~*ing* p'yoje 표제/ ~*line* chemok 제목/ ~*light* hedŭrait'ŭ 헤드라이트/ ~*master* kyojang 교장.

headache *n.* tut'ong 두통. *I have a bad* ~. Nanŭn tut'ongi maeu shimhamnida. 나는 두통이 매우 심합니다.

headquarter *n.* (*pl.*) ponbu 본부, saryŏngbu 사령부. *the general* ~*s*[GHQ] ch'ongsaryŏngbu 총사령부.

heal *vt.,vi.* koch'ida 고치다. *The ointment* ~*ed his wound*. I koyagŭro kŭŭi sangch'ŏga naassŭmnida. 이 고약으로 그의 상처가 나았읍니다.

health *n.* kŏn-gang 건강. *How is your* ~ *of late?* Yojŭm kŏn-gangŭn ŏttŏssŭmnikka? 요즘 건강은 어떻습니까? *Thank you, I am enjoying excellent* ~. Komapso, aju kŏn-ganghamnida. 고맙소, 아주 건강합니다/ *My* ~ *isn't any too good*. Kŏn-gangi shint'ongch'i anssŭmnida. 건강이 신통치 않습니다/ *You will ruin your* ~. Tangshinŭn kŏn-gangŭl ilk'o mal kŏshimnida. 당신은 건강을 잃고 말 것입니다/ *To your* ~! (*toast*) Kŏn-gangŭl wihayo! 건강을 위하여/ *public* ~ kongjung wisaeng 공중 위생/ ~ *examination* kŏn-gang chindan 건강 진단/ *the Ministry of H*~ *and Social Affairs* pogŏn sahoebu 보건 사회부.

healthy *adj.* kŏn-ganghan 건강한, kŏnjanghan 건장한. *The children look very* ~. Kŭ aidŭrŭn maeu kŏn-ganghae poimnida. 그 아이들은 매우 건강해 보입니다/ *I hope you're quite* ~. Kŏn-ganghashigirŭl pimnida. 건강하시기를 빕니다.

heap *n.* (*mound*) mudŏgi 무더기, tŏmi 더미. ―*vt.* (*pile up*) ssaa ollida 쌓아 올리다. *a dump* ~ ssŭregi tŏmi 쓰레기 더미/ *a* ~ *of money* manŭn ton 많은 돈/ *I've a* ~ *of work to do*. Hal iri santŏmi kassŭmnida. 할 일이 산더미 같습니다.

hear *vt.,vi.* tŭtta 듣다, …*i* tŭllida …이 들리다, (*learn*) tŭrŏ alda 들어 알다. *Please* ~ *me out*. Kkŭtkkaji tŭrŏ chushio. 끝까지 들어 주시오/ *Did you* ~ *him go out?* Kŭga naganŭn sorirŭl tŭrŏssŭmnikka? 그가 나가는 소리를 들었읍니까/ *Have you heard the news?* Soshigŭl tŭrŏssŭmnikka? 소식을 들었읍니까?

heart *n.* (*organ of the body*) shimjang 심장, (*bosom*) kasŭm 가슴, (*mind*) maŭm 마음, (*affection*) aejŏng 애정, (*courage*) yonggi 용기. *My ～ beat fast at the news.* Kŭ soshigŭl tŭtko nae shimjangŭn magu ttwiŏssŭmnida. 그 소식을 듣고 내 심장은 마구 뛰었읍니다/ *I love you with all my ～.* Chinshimŭro saranghamnida. 진심으로 사랑합니다/ *～ disease* shimjangpyŏng 심장병/ *～ failure* shimjang mabi 심장 마비.

heartbeat *n.* shimjangŭi kodong 심장의 고동.

heartless *adj.* mujŏnghan 무정한, pakchŏnghan 박정한. *a ～ woman* pakchŏnghan yŏin 박정한 여인.

hearty *adj.* (*sincere*) chinjŏnghan 진정한, (*robust*) kŏnganghan 건강한. *a ～ welcome* ttattŭt'an hwanyŏng 따뜻한 환영/ *a ～ fellow* kŏn-ganghan sanai 건강한 사나이.

heat *n.* (*hotness*) tŏwi 더위, (*of fever*) yŏl 열. *—vt.* (*make hot*) teuda 데우다, (*excite*) hŭngbunshik'ida 흥분시키다. *I can't stand ～.* Tŏwinŭn chilsaegimnida. 더위는 질색입니다/ *What do you think of this ～?* I tŏwinŭn ŏttŏssŭmnikka? 이 더위는 어떻습니까/ *I couldn't sleep for the ～.* Tŏwi ttaemune chal suga ŏpsŏssŭmnida. 더위 때문에 잘 수가 없었읍니다/ *He was ～ed with passion.* Kŭnŭn mopshi hŭngbunhago issŏssŭmnida. 그는 몹시 흥분하고 있었읍니다.

heater *n.* chŏnyŏlgi 전열기, hit'ŏ 히터.

heathen *n.*(*pl.*) (*pagan*) igyodo 이교도, ibangin 이방인. *—adj.* igyodoŭi 이교도의.

heave *vt.,vi.* (*raise*) tŭrŏ ollida 들어 올리다, (*give a sigh*) hansumŭl shwida 한숨을 쉬다.

heaven *n.* (*sky*) hanŭl 하늘, kongjung 공중, (*home of God*) ch'ŏndang 천당, (*Buddhism*) kŭngnak 극락, (*God*) hanŭnim 하느님. *By H～(s)!* Maengsek'o! 맹세코/ *Good H～s!* Yadannanne! 야단났네/ *Thank H～!* Komawara! 고마와라/ *～ and earth* ch'ŏnji 천지.

heavenly *adj.* (*celestial*) hanŭrŭi 하늘의, (*holy*) sŏngsŭrŏun 성스러운. *～body* ch'ŏnch'e 천체.

heavy *adj.* (*weighty*) mugŏun 무거운, (*severe*) shimhan 심한, (*oppressive*) taptap'an 답답한. *This box is terribly*

~. I sangjanŭn mopshi mugŏpsŭmnida. 이 상자는 몹시 무
겹습니다/ a ~ wound chungsang 중상(重傷)/ a ~ rain
p'ogu 폭우/ a ~ heart taptap'an shimjŏng 답답한 심정.

heavyweight n. (boxing) hebikŭp sŏnsu 헤비급 선수.

Hebrew n. (Jew) Hebŭrai saram 헤브라이 사람, yut'aein
유태인, (language) Hebŭraiŏ 헤브라이어(語).

hedge n. sanult'ari 산울타리.

heed n. (mind) chuŭi 주의, choshim 조심, yuŭi 유의.
—vt. chuŭihada 주의하다. Take ~ of such men! Kŭrŏn
saramdŭrŭl chuŭihashio. 그런 사람들을 주의하시오.

heel n. twikkumch'i 뒤꿈치. high ~ shoes haihil 하이힐.

height n. (altitude) nop'i 높이, (stature) k'i 키. What
is your ~? Tangshin k'inŭn olmana toeshimnikka? 당
신 키는 얼마나 되십니까/ I am six feet in ~. Nae k'inŭn
yuk p'it'ŭimnida. 내 키는 6피트입니다/ the ~ of a building kŏnmurŭi nop'i 건물의 높이.

heir n. (successor) sangsogin 상속인, hugyeja 후계자. Who
is the ~ to this large fortune? I manŭn chaesanŭi
sangsoginŭn nuguimnikka? 이 많은 재산의 상속인은 누구
입니까?

heiress n. yŏja sangsogin 여자 상속인.

heirloom n. (ancestral treasure) kabo 가보(家寶).

hell n. (inferno) chiok 지옥, (Hades) chŏsŭng 저승.
What's the ~! Pirŏmŏgŭl! 빌어먹을/ What the ~ are
you doing? Todaech'e tangshinŭn muŏsŭl hago issŏyo?
도대체 당신은 무엇을 하고 있어요/ Oh, ~! Chegiral 제기
랄!

hello int. yŏboseyo! 여보세요! —n. (greeting) insa 인사.
Say ~ to your wife for me. Puinkke anbu chŏnhashio.
부인께 안부 전하시오.

helmet n. ch'ŏlmo 철모, helmet moja 헬멧 모자.

help vt.,vi. (aid) topta 돕다, (rescue) kuhada 구하다.
—n. (assistance) wŏnjo 원조, (relief) kujo 구조. Would
you ~ me, please? Chom towa chushilkkayo? 좀 도와 주
실까요/ Can I ~ you with anything? Mwŏ towa tŭril
kŏshi ŏpsŭlkkayo? 뭐 도와 드릴 것이 없을까요/ Sorry, I
can't ~ you. Mianhajiman towa tŭril suga ŏpsŭmnida.

미안하지만 도와 드릴 수가 없읍니다/ *I can't ~ laughing.*
Utchi anŭl suga ŏpsŭmnida. 웃지 않을 수가 없읍니다/
H~ yourself to a candy. K'aendi hana tŭshipshio. 캔디
하나 드십시오.

helper *n.* choryŏkcha 조력자, chosu 조수(助手).

helpful *adj.* yuyonghan 유용한.

helpless *adj.* (*needy*) ŭijihal kot ŏmnŭn 의지할 곳 없는,
(*powerless*) muryŏk'an 무력한.

hem *n.* (*cloth*) kajangjari 가장자리, (*margin*) ka 가.

hemisphere *n.* (*half sphere*) pan-guch'e 반구체. *the
Northern H~* pukpan-gu 북반구.

hemorrhage *n.* ch'urhyŏl 출혈. *cerebral ~* noech'urhyŏl
뇌출혈, noeirhyŏl 뇌일혈.

hemp *n.* sam 삼, taema 대마.

hen *n.* amt'ak 암닭.

hence *adv.* (*from now*) chigŭmbut'ŏ 지금부터, (*from
here*) yŏgisŏbut'ŏ 여기서부터, (*therefore*) kŭrŏmŭro 그
러므로. *a week ~* chigŭmbut'ŏ ilchuil hue 지금부터 1주
일 후에.

hencoop *n.* takchang 닭장, tunguri 둥우리.

her *pron.* kŭ yŏjarŭl〔ege〕 그 여자를〔에게〕, kŭ yŏjaŭi 그
여자의. *Give ~ the book.* Kŭnyŏege kŭ ch'aegŭl chushio.
그녀에게 그 책을 주시오/ *We like ~.* Urinŭn kŭnyŏrŭl
choahamnida. 우리는 그녀를 좋아합니다/ *H~ father is
dead.* Kŭnyŏŭi abŏjinŭn chugŏssŭmnida. 그녀의 아버지
는 죽었읍니다.

herb *n.* p'ul 풀, ch'obon 초본. *medical ~* yakch'o 약초/
poisonous ~ tokch'o 독초.

herd *n.* tte 떼. *a ~ of elephants* k'okkiri tte 코끼리 떼.

here *adv.* (*in this place*) yŏgi 여기, (*to this place*)
yŏgiro 여기로, iri 이리. *I live ~.* Yŏgi salgo issŭmnida.
여기 살고 있읍니다/ *Put the box ~.* Sangjarŭl yŏgi
noŭshio. 상자를 여기 놓으시오/ *Get out of ~!* Nagashio. 나가시오/ *H~ you are.* Cha, yŏgi issŭmnida. 자,
여기 있읍니다/ *H~ comes the bus!* Pŏsŭga watkunyo.
버스가 왔군요/ *H~'s to you!* Ch'ukpae! 축배/ *~ and
there* yŏgijŏgie 여기저기에.

hereafter *adv.* kŭmhu 금후, changch'a 장차. ap'ŭro 앞으로. *I shall be careful* ~. Ap'ŭro chuŭihagessŭmnida. 앞으로 주의하겠읍니다.

heredity *n.* yujŏn 유전.

heritage *n.* (*patrimony*) sangsok chaesan 상속 재산, (*inherited lot*) yusan 유산. *cultural* ~ munhwa yusan 문화 유산.

hero *n.* (*man of great deeds*) yŏngung 영웅, (*protagonist*) chuin-gong 주인공.

heroine *n.* (*female*) yŏgŏl 여걸, yŏjangbu 여장부, (*of a novel, etc.*) yŏjuin-gong 여주인공.

herring *n.* ch'ŏngŏ 청어.

hesitate *vi.* (*falter*) mangsŏrida 망설이다, chujŏhada 주저하다. *Don't* ~ *to tell me your opinion.* Chujŏ malgo ŭigyŏnŭl marhashipshio. 주저 말고 의견을 말하십시오/ *Why do you* ~? Wae mangsŏrishimnikka? 왜 망설이십니까/ *We have no time to* ~. Mangsŏrigo issŭl shigani ŏpsŭmnida. 망설이고 있을 시간이 없읍니다.

hesitation *n.* chujŏ 주저, mangsŏrim 망설임. *Please call on me without* ~. Chujŏhaji mashigo ch'ajaoshipshio. 주저하지 마시고 찾아오십시오.

hiccup, hiccough *n.* ttalkkukchil 딸꾹질.

hide *vt.,vi.* (*conceal*) kamch'uda 감추다, sumta 숨다. —*n.* (*animal's skin*) kajuk 가죽, p'ihyŏk 피혁. *He hid money under the pillow.* Kŭnŭn pegae mit'e tonŭl kamch'uŏssŭmnida. 그는 베개 밑에 돈을 감추었읍니다/ *Where was the criminal hiding?* Pŏminŭn ŏdi sumŏ issŏssŭmnikka? 범인은 어디 숨어 있었읍니까/ *You had better* ~. Sumnŭn ke chossŭmnida. 숨는 게 좋습니다/ *a raw* ~ saenggajuk 생가죽.

high *adj.* nop'ŭn 높은, (*superior*) kogŭbŭi 고급의. ~ *school* kodŭng hakkyo 고등 학교. —*adv.* nopke 높게. *a* ~ *mountain* nop'ŭn san 높은 산/ *a* ~ *building* nop'ŭn kŏnmul 높은 건물/ *How* ~ *is Mt. Nam?* Namsanŭn ŏlmana nopsŭmnikka? 남산은 얼마나 높습니까/ *a* ~ *official* kogŭp kwalli 고급 관리/ *The price is too* ~. Kapshi nŏmu pissamnida. 값이 너무 비쌉니다/ *climb* ~ *on the* *ladder* sadarie nop'i orŭda 사다리에 높이 오르다.

high-class *adj.* kogŭbŭi 고급의.

highway *n.* kongno 공로, kansŏn toro 간선 도로.

hike *vt.* (*tramp*) t'ŏbŏkt'ŏbŏk kŏtta 터벅터벅 걷다, haik'ing-hada 하이킹하다. —*n.* tobo yŏhaeng 도보 여행.

hiker *n.* tobo yŏhaengja 도보 여행자.

hiking *n.* haik'ing 하이킹, tŭngsan 등산. *I'm planning on going* ~. Nanŭn haik'ingŭl kal ch'amimnida. 나는 하이킹을 갈 참입니다.

hill *n.* (*a small mountain*) chagŭn san 작은 산, ŏndŏk 언덕. *down* ~ naerimakkil 내리막길/ *up* ~ orŭmakkil 오르막길. *The sun was rising over the* ~s. T'aeyangi san wie ttŏorŭgo issŏssŭmnida. 태양이 산 위에 떠오르고 있었읍니다.

him *pron.* (*dative*) kŭege 그에게, (*accusative*) kŭrŭl 그를. *Give* ~ *the money*. Kŭege tonŭl chushio. 그에게 돈을 주시오/ *I saw* ~ *yesterday*. Ŏje kŭrŭl poassŭmnida. 어제 그를 보았읍니다.

himself *pron.* ku chashin 그 자신. *Did you see the manager* ~? Paro kŭ chibaeinŭl poassŭmnikka? 바로 그 지배인을 보았읍니까/ *by* ~ chagi honjasŏ 자기 혼자서/ *The widower lives by* ~. Kŭ horabinŭn honja salgo issŭmnida. 그 홀아비는 혼자 살고 있읍니다.

hinder *vt.* (*prevent*) panghaehada 방해하다. *Don't* ~ *me in my work*. Nae irŭl panghaehaji mashio. 내 일을 방해하지 마시오.

hint *n.* (*suggestion*) amshi 암시, hint'ŭ 힌트. —*vi.,vt.* amshi[shisa]hada 암시[시사]하다. *Will you give me a* ~? Hint'ŭrŭl chushiji ank'essŭmnikka? 힌트를 주시지 않겠읍니까/ *Why not give him a* ~? Kŭege hint'ŭrŭl chudorok hapshida. 그에게 힌트를 주도록 합시다.

hip *n.* ŏngdŏngi 엉덩이, hip'ŭ 히프.

hippopotamus *n.* hama 하마.

hire *n.* koyong 고용, se 세. —*vt.* (*engage*) koyonghada 고용하다, (*automobile, etc.*) sak naego pillida 삯 내고 빌리다. *automobiles for* ~ chŏnse chadongch'a 전세 자동차/ *Do you keep boats on* ~? Chŏnse pot'ŭga issŭmnikka?

전세 보트가 있읍니까?

historian *n.* yŏksaga 역사가, sahakcha 사학자.

historic *adj.* (*notable in history*) yŏksasang yumyŏnghan 역사상 유명한. *a ~ spot* sajŏk 사적(史蹟)/ *a ~ event* yŏksajŏk sakŏn 역사적 사건.

historical *adj.* (*pertaining to history*) yŏksaŭi 역사의, yŏksasangŭi 역사상의. *a ~ novel* yŏksa sosŏl 역사 소설/ *a ~ science* yŏksahak 역사학, sahak 사학(史學).

history *n.* yŏksa 역사. *the ~ of Korea* Han-guk yŏksa 한국 역사/ *Oriental ~* tongyangsa 동양사/ *How long is the Korean ~?* Han-guk yŏksanŭn ŏlmana orae toeŏssŭmnikka? 한국 역사는 얼마나 오래 되었읍니까/ *Is this your personal ~?* Igŏshi tangshin iryŏksŏimnikka? 이것이 당신 이력서입니까?

hit *vt.,vi.* (*strike*) ch'ida 치다. *~ against* puditch'ida 부딪치다, (*guess right*) aramach'ida 알아맞히다. *—n.* (*blow*) t'agyŏk 타격, (*success*) sŏnggong 성공, hit'ŭ 히트. *H~ hard!* Sege ch'ishio. 세게 치시오/ *Don't ~ my cat.* Nae koyangirŭl ttaeriji mashio. 내 고양이를 때리지 마시오/ *I ~ my forehead against a pole.* Imarŭl chŏnjue puditch'yŏssŭmnida. 이마를 전주에 부딪쳤읍니다/ *I ~ him a blow.* Kŭrŭl han tae ch'yŏssŭmnida. 그를 한 대 쳤읍니다/ *Have you a list of the latest ~ song?* Ch'oegŭnŭi hit'ŭsong risŭt'ŭga issŭmnikka? 최근의 히트송 리스트가 있읍니까/ *The new play is quite a ~.* Kŭ shin-gŭgŭn taedanhan hit'ŭimnida. 그 신극(新劇)은 대단한 히트입니다.

hive *n.* (*beehive*) pŏlchip 벌집.

hoard *n.* (*store*) chŏjang 저장. *—vt.,vi.* (*save*) chŏjanghada 저장하다, kanjik'ada 간직하다.

hoarse *adj.* (*husky*) mogi shwin 목이 쉰. *~ voice* mokshwin sori 목쉰 소리.

hobby *n.* ch'wimi 취미, (*recreation*) torak 도락. *Do you have any hobbies?* Musŭn ch'wimirŭl kajigo issŭmnikka? 무슨 취미를 가지고 있읍니까/ *My ~ is stamp collection.* Nae ch'wiminŭn up'yo sujibimnida. 내 취미는 우표 수집입니다.

hockey *n.* hak'i 하키. *ice ~* aisŭ hak'i 아이스 하키.

hoe *n.* kwaengi 꽹이. —*vt.,vi.* kwaengijirhada 꽹이질하다.

hog *n.* (*pig*) twaeji 돼지.

hoist *vt.* (*lift up*) ollida 올리다. —*n.*(*lift*) sŭngganggi 승강기, (*crane*) kijunggi 기중기. ~ *a flag* kirŭl talda 기를 달다.

hold *vt.,vi.* (*grasp*) chwida 쥐다, (*contain*) tamta 담다, (*possess*) katko itta 갖고 있다, (*conduct*) kaech'oehada 개최하다. *H~ the line, please.* Chŏnhwa kk'ŭnch'i malgo kidaryŏ chushipshio. 전화 끊지 말고 기다려 주십시오/ *Would you mind ~ing my dog for a minute?* Chamkkan nae kaerŭl anko kyeshipshio. 잠깐 내 개를 안고 계십시오/ *Do you think this bag will ~ very much?* I kabangŭn mani tŭrŏgalkkayo? 이 가방은 많이 들어갈까요/ *The National Athletic Meet will be held on the third of October.* Chŏn-guk ch'eyuk taehoenŭn shiwŏl samire kaech'oedoemnida. 전국 체육 대회는 10월 3일에 개최됩니다.

holder *n.* sojija 소지자. *a license ~* myŏnhŏchang sojija 면허장 소지자/ *a share ~* chuju 주주(株主).

holdup *n.* (*highway robber*) nosang kangdo 노상 강도, kwŏnch'ong kangdo 권총 강도.

hole *n.* kumŏng 구멍. *a mouse's ~* chwigumŏng 쥐구멍/ *make a ~* kumŏngŭl p'ada 구멍을 파다.

holiday *n.* (*vacation*) hyuil 휴일, (*feast day*) myŏngjŏl 명절. *a national ~* kukkyŏngil 국경일/ *Have a good ~.* Hyuil chŭlgŏpke shwiseyo. 휴일 즐겁게 쉬세요/ *Where are you going for your ~s this winter?* Kŭmnyŏn kyŏul hyuga-enŭn ŏdiro kashil chakchŏngimnikka? 금년 겨울 휴가에는 어디로 가실 작정입니까/ ~ *clothes* naduri ot 나들이 옷.

holiday-maker *n.* yuramja 유람자. *tempt ~s from abroad* haeoe yuramjarŭl yuch'ihada 해외 유람자를 유치하다.

Holland *n.* Nedŏllandŭ 네덜란드.

hollow *n.* (*depression*) umuk'an kot 우묵한 곳, (*basin*) punji 분지(盆地). —*vt.* (*make hollow*) kumŏngŭl ttult'a 구멍을 뚫다.

holy *adj.* (*sacred*) shinsŏnghan 신성한, (*divine*) kŏruk'an 거룩한. ~ *ground* sŏngji 성지(聖地)/ ~ *love* kŏruk'an sarang 거룩한 사랑.

home n. (*house*) chip 집, taek 댁, (*household*) kajŏng 가정, (*native land*) kohyang 고향, (*native country*) pon-guk 본국. —adv. chibe 집에, chiburo 집으로. *Is this the ~ of Mr. Lee?* I sŏnsaengnim taegishijyo? 이(李) 선생님 댁이시죠/ *How can I get to your ~?* Taegenŭn ŏttŏk'e kamyŏn toemnikka? 댁에는 어떻게 가면 됩니까/ *a middle class ~* chungnyu kajŏng 중류 가정/ *a ~ life* kajŏng saenghwal 가정 생활/ *Please make yourself at ~.* Chebal p'yŏnhi anjúshipshio. 제발 편히 앉으십시오./ *products* kuksanp'um 국산품/ *Is he ~ yet?* Pŏlssŏ kwigahaessŭmnikka? 벌써 귀가했읍니까?

homeland n. kohyang 고향, (*native land*) koguk 고국.

homesick adj. hoehyangpyŏngŭi 회향병의, kohyangi kŭriun 고향이 그리운. *be ~ for Korea* Han-gugi kŭripta 한국이 그립다.

homesickness n. (*nostalgia*) hyangsu 향수.

homework n. sukche 숙제.

honest adj. (*upright*) chŏngjik'an 정직한, (*sincere*) sŏngshirhan 성실한, (*candid*) solchik'an 솔직한. *I shall be quite ~ with you.* Tangshinegenŭn chŏngjik'i marhae tŭrijyo. 당신에게는 정직히 말해 드리죠/ *be ~ with you* solchik'i marhaesŏ 솔직히 말해서.

honey n. pŏlkkul 벌꿀.

honeymoon n. mirwŏl 밀월. *~ trip* shinhon yŏhaeng 신혼 여행.

honorary adj. myŏngyeŭi 명예의. *an ~ doctor's degree* myŏngye paksa hagwi 명예 박사 학위/ *an ~ post* myŏngyejik 명예직/ *an ~ president* myŏngye hoejang 명예 회장.

hono(u)r n. (*glory*) myŏngye 명예, (*self-respect*) chajonshim 자존심, (*esteem*) chon-gyŏng 존경, (*pl.*) (*decoration*) hunjang 훈장. —vt. (*show honor to*) myŏngyerŭl chuda 명예를 주다, (*respect*) chon-gyŏnghada 존경하다. *I deem it an ~ to accept your invitation.* Ch'odaehae chusyŏsŏ yŏnggwangŭro saenggak'amnida. 초대해 주셔서 영광으로 생각합니다/ *You are an ~ to your family.* Tangshinŭn chibanŭi charangimnida. 당신은 집안의 자랑입니다/

We gave dinner in his ~. Kŭrŭl wihae manch'anŭl pep'urŏssŭmnida. 그를 위해 만찬을 베풀었읍니다/ *I have the* ~ *to inform you that....* Samga ... allyŏ tŭrimnida. 삼가 …알려 드립니다/ *graduate with* ~s udŭnguro chorŏp'ada 우등으로 졸업하다/ *Will you* ~ *me with a visit?* Pangmunhae chushimyŏn yŏnggwangigessŭmnida. 방문해 주시면 영광이겠읍니다.

hono(u)rable *adj.* chon-gyŏnghal manhan 존경할 만한, myŏngyeroun 명예로운. *an* ~ *position* myŏngyeroun chiwi 명예로운 지위, myŏngyejik 명예직.

hood *n.* tugŏn 두건, hudŭ 후드.

hoof *n.* palgup 발굽, mal palgup 말 발굽.

hook *n.* (*bent piece of metal*) kalgori 갈고리, (*fish*~) nakshi panŭl 낚시 바늘, (*for dresses*) huk tanch'u 훅 단추.

hoop *n.* t'e 테, kullŏngsoe 굴렁쇠.

hop *vi.,vt.* (*leap*) ttwida 뛰다, (*dance*) ch'umch'uda 춤추다.

hope *n.* hŭimang 희망, (*expectation*) kidae 기대, (*possibility*) kamang 가망. —*vt.,vi.* (*wish*) parada 바라다, (*expect*) kidaehada 기대하다. *I don't really have much* ~. Sashil kŭdaji kidaehaji anssŭmnida. 사실 그다지 기대하지 않습니다/ *You are my last* ~. Tangshinŭn naŭi majimak hŭimangimnida. 당신은 나의 마지막 희망입니다/ *I* ~ *to see you again.* Tashi mannagirŭl paramnida. 다시 만나기를 바랍니다/ *I* ~ *so.* Kŭraessŭmyŏn chok'essŭmnida. 그랬으면 좋겠읍니다/ *I* ~ *not.* Kŭrŏch'i ank'irŭl paramnida. 그렇지 않기를 바랍니다/ *I* ~ *you'll like it.* Maŭme tŭshimyŏn chok'essŭmnida. 마음에 드시면 좋겠읍니다/ *I* ~ *it will be fine tomorrow.* Naeirŭn malgŭrira saenggak'amnida. 내일은 맑으리라 생각합니다/ *I* ~ *to come back next year.* Naenyŏne toraorirago saenggak'amnida. 내년에 돌아오리라고 생각합니다.

hopeful *adj.* (*having hope*) hŭimange ch'an 희망에 찬, (*promising*) yumanghan 유망한. *I'm* ~ *of success.* Sŏnggonghariranŭn hŭimangŭl p'umko issŭmnida. 성공하리라는 희망을 품고 있읍니다.

hopeless *adj.* hŭimang ŏmnŭn 희망 없는, (*desperate*) chŏlmangjŏgin 절망적인. *I'm ~ of success.* Nanŭn sŏnggong-ŭl tannyŏmhago issŭmnida. 나는 성공을 단념하고 있읍니다/ *a ~ illness* kamang ŏmnŭn pyŏng 가망 없는 병.

horizon *n.* chip'yŏngsŏn 지평선.

horizontal *adj.* (*level*) sup'yŏngŭi 수평의. *~ bars* ch'ŏl-bong 철봉.

horn *n.* (*of animals*) ppul 뿔, (*wind instrument*) ppul-lap'al 뿔나팔, (*music*) horŭn 호른. *a motor ~* chadong-ch'a kyŏngjŏk 자동차 경적.

horrible *adj.* (*dreadful*) musŏun 무서운, (*frightful*) momsŏrich'inŭn 몸서리치는, (*unpleasant*) pulk'waehan 불쾌한. *~ crimes* kkŭmtchik'an pŏmjoe 끔찍한 범죄/ *~ weather* chidok'an nalssi 지독한 날씨.

horrify *vt.* sorŭmkkich'ige hada 소름끼치게 하다, musŏpke hada 무섭게 하다. *We were horrified by what we saw.* Kŭ kwanggyŏnge tŭngkori ossak'aessŭmnida. 그 광경에 등골이 오싹했읍니다.

horror *n.* kongp'o 공포, chŏnyul 전율. *the ~s of modern warfare* kŭndaejŏnŭi kongp'o 근대전의 공포/ *I saw a wonderful ~ movie the other day.* Myŏch'il chŏn nanŭn nollaun koegi yŏnghwarŭl poassŭmnida. 며칠 전 나는 놀라운 괴기 영화를 보았읍니다.

horse *n.* mal 말. *mount〔ride〕a ~* marŭl t'ada 말을 타다/ *I have never been on a ~ in my life.* Nanŭn yŏt'ae marŭl t'abon chŏgi ŏpsŭmnida. 나는 여태 말을 타본 적이 없읍니다.

horsefly *n.* malp'ari 말파리, tŭnge 등에.

horsepower *n.* maryŏk 마력(馬力).

horse race *n.* kyŏngma 경마.

hose *n.* (*tube*) hosŭ 호스, komugwan 고무관, (*stockings*) kin yangmal 긴 양말.

hospital *n.* pyŏngwŏn 병원. *a general ~* chonghap pyŏng-wŏn 종합 병원/ *enter a ~* ibwŏnhada 입원하다/ *leave a ~* t'oewŏnhada 퇴원하다/ *I hear you've been in ~.* Ibwŏnhago kyesyŏttagoyo. 입원하고 계셨다고요/ *Which ~ were you in?* Ŏnŭ pyŏngwŏne ibwŏnhaessŭmnikka? 어느 병원에 입원했읍니까?

hospitality *n.* (*friendly reception*) hwandae 환대, hudae 후대(厚待).

host *n.* (*landlord*) chuin 주인. *play ~ to...* ...ŭl ch'odaehada ...을 초대하다/ *I understand your country is playing ~ to the Olympics.* Kwigugesŏ ollimp'igi kaech'oedoendajiyo. 귀국에서 올림픽이 개최된다지요.

hostess *n.* (*a female host*) anchuin 안주인, (*in hotel, etc.*) yŏjuin 여주인, hosŭt'esŭ 호스테스.

hostility *n.* (*enmity*) chŏkkaeshim 적개심, (*attack*) chŏktae haengwi 적대 행위.

hot *adj.* ttŭgŏun 뜨거운, tŏun 더운, (*ardent*) yŏllyŏrhan 열렬한. *a ~ day* tŏun nal 더운 날/ *~ water* tŏun mul 더운 물/ *Awfully ~ , isn't it ?* Mopshi tŏpkunyo. 몹시 덥군요.

hotel *n.* hot'el 호텔, (*inn*) yŏgwan 여관. *What ~ are you staying at ?* Ŏnŭ yŏgwane t'usuk'ago kyeshimnikka ? 어느 여관에 투숙하고 계십니까/ *Is there a pub in this ~ ?* I hot'ere sulchibi issŭmnikka ? 이 호텔에 술집이 있읍니까/ *Take me to the Plaza H~ , please.* (*to cabman*) P'ŭllaja hot'elkkaji kapshida. 플라자 호텔까지 갑시다.

hothouse *n.* (*greenhouse*) onshil 온실. *a ~ plant* onshil shingmul 온실 식물.

hound *n.* sanyangkae 사냥개, (*blood~*) kyŏngch'algyŏn 경찰견.

hour *n.* (han) shigan (한) 시간. *half an ~* pan shigan 반 시간, samshippun 30분/ *a quarter of an ~* shibobun 15분/ *business ~s* yŏngŏp shigan 영업 시간/ *office ~s* chimmu shigan 집무 시간/ *How many ~s does it take to Inchon ?* Inch'ŏnkkaji myŏt shigan kŏllimnikka ? 인천까지 몇 시간 걸립니까/ *It will take about two ~s.* Yak tu shigan kŏllimnida. 약 두 시간 걸립니다.

house *n.* chip 집. *my ~* naŭi chip 나의 집/ *your ~* tangshin taek 당신 댁/ *movie ~* yŏnghwagwan 영화관/ *rental ~* setchip 셋집/ *store ~* ch'anggo 창고/ *tile-roofed ~* kiwajip 기와집/ *thatch-roofed ~* ch'ogajip 초가집/ *one storied ~* tanch'ŭngchip 단층집/ *two storied ~* ich'ŭngchip 2층집/ *Where is your ~ ?* Taegi ŏdishimnikka ?

댁이 어디십니까/ *I've heard much about your beautiful
~*. Chibi arŭmdaptanŭn marŭn mani tŭtko issŭmnida. 집이 아름답다는 말은 많이 듣고 있읍니다/ *~keeper*
chubu 주부/ *~maid* kajŏngbu 가정부.

housewife *n.* kajŏng chubu 가정 주부.

housework *n.* chibannil 집안일, sallimsari 살림살이.

how *adv.* (*in what way*) ŏttŏk'e 어떻게, (*to what extent*)
ŏlmamank'ŭm 얼마만큼, (*why*) wae 왜. *H~ are you
getting on?* Ŏttŏk'e chinaeshimnikka? 어떻게 지내십니까/
H~ do you call this in Korea? Igŏsŭl Han-gungmallo
muŏrago hamnikka? 이것을 한국말로 무어라고 합니까/ *H~
about Hotel Shilla?* Shilla hot'erŭn ŏttŏssŭmnikka? 신
라 호텔은 어떻습니까/ *H~ about going to a ball game?*
Yagu shihabe an kagessŭmnikka? 야구 시합에 안 가겠읍니
까/ *H~ old are you?* Myŏt sarimnikka? 몇 살입니까/
H~ do you sell these apples? I sagwanŭn ŏlmajyo? 이
사과는 얼마죠/ *H~ is it (that) you are late?* Wae
chigagŭl haessŭmnikka? 왜 지각을 했읍니까/ *H~ kind
of you!* Ch'am ch'injŏldo hasyŏra! 참 친절도 하셔라/
H~ many are there? Ŏlmana mani issŭmnikka? 얼마나
많이 있읍니까/ *H~ much do you want?* Ŏlmana p'iryohamnikka? 얼마나 필요합니까/ *H~ are you?* (*salute*)
Annyŏnghashimnikka? 안녕하십니까/ *H~ do you do?*
Ch'ŏŭm poepkessŭmnida. 처음 뵙겠읍니다.

however *adv.* (*despite which*) amuri ...haedo 아무리 …해
도. —*conj.* (*nevertheless*) kŭrŏch'iman 그렇지만. *H~
tired you may be, you must do it.* Amuri kodanhadŏra-
do kŭgŏsŭl haeyaman hamnida. 아무리 고단하더라도 그것
을 해야만 합니다/ *H~ can I do the work in a day?* Todaech'e ŏttŏk'e naega kú irŭl harue hal su itkessŭmnikka? 도대체 어떻게 내가 그 일을 하루에 할 수 있겠읍니까/
I hate concerts, ~ I shall go to this one. Ŭmak'oenŭn
shilssŭmnida. Kŭrŏch'iman ibŏnenŭn kagessŭmnida. 음
악회는 싫습니다. 그렇지만 이번에는 가겠읍니다.

howl *vi.,vt.* (*wail*) ulbujitta 울부짖다, (*wind*) wingwing
sorinaeda 윙윙 소리내다.

hub *n.* (*nave*) pak'wit'ong 바퀴통, (*center*) chungshim 중

심. *a* ~ *of commerce* sangŏbŭi chungshim 상업의 중심.

huddle *vi.,vt.* (*crowd*) mollyŏdŭlda 몰려들다, (*press*) milda 밀다. —*n.* (*confusion*) honjap 혼잡.

hue *n.* (*color*) saek 색, (*tint*) pitkkal 빛깔.

hug *vt.* (*embrace*) kkyŏanta 껴안다, kkŭrŏanta 끌어안다. —*n.* (*tight embrace*) p'oong 포옹. *Give me a* ~, *darling.* Kkyŏana chuseyo, ne! 껴안아 주세요, 네!

huge *adj.* (*gigantic*) kŏdaehan 거대한, (*enormous*) maktaehan 막대한. *a* ~ *sum of money* maktaehan kŭmaek 막대한 금액.

hull *n.* (*husk*) kkŏpchil 껍질, (*pod*) kkot'uri 꼬투리. *remove the* ~*s of* kkŏpchirŭl pŏtkida 껍질을 벗기다.

hullo(a) *int.* ŏi 어이! yŏboseyo 여보세요!

hum *vi.,vt.* (*drone*) waengwaenggŏrida 왱왱거리다. ~ *a song* k'onnorae purŭda 콧노래 부르다. —*n.* (~*ming noise*) wingwing sori 윙윙 소리.

human *adj.* (*of man*) in-ganŭi 인간의, saramŭi 사람의, (*opp. animal*) in-ganjŏgin 인간적인. ~ *being* in-gan 인간/ ~ *body* inch'e 인체/ ~ *life* saramŭi saengmyŏng 사람의 생명/ ~ *nature* in-gansŏng 인간성/ ~ *rights* inkwŏn 인권.

humane *adj.* (*compassionate*) injŏng innŭn 인정 있는 (*merciful*) chabiroun 자비로운. ~ *feelings* chabishim 자비심/ ~ *treatment* indojŏk ch'ŏu 인도적 처우.

humanity *n.* (*human nature*) in-gansŏng 인간성, (*benevolence*) inae 인애(仁愛), (*mankind*) illyu 인류. *an act of* ~ chasŏn haengwi 자선 행위/ *a friend of* ~ illyuŭi pŏt 인류의 벗.

humankind *n.* illyu 인류, in-gan 인간.

humble *adj.* (*lowly*) pich'ŏnhan 비천한, (*modest*) kyŏmsonhan 겸손한, (*mean*) ch'orahan 초라한. —*vt.* (*abase*) p'umwirŭl ttŏrŏttŭrida 품위를 떨어뜨리다. *a* ~ *occupation* ch'ŏnhan chigŏp 천한 직업/ *a* ~ *request* kyŏmsonhan yogu 겸손한 요구/ *a* ~ *home* ch'orahan chip 초라한 집.

humbly *adv.* kyŏmson[kyŏmhŏ]hage 겸손[겸허]하게. *That young man spoke* ~. Kŭ ch'ŏngnyŏnŭn kyŏmsonhage marhaessŭmnida. 그 청년은 겸손하게 말했읍니다.

humidity *n.* (*dampness*) sŭpki 습기, sŭpto 습도. *determine the* ~ sŭptorŭl chaeda 습도를 재다.

humiliate *vt.* (*disgrace*) ch'angp'irŭl chuda 창피를 주다.

humiliation *n.* ch'angp'i 창피, kuryok 굴욕. *We can't sit down quietly under that* ~. Kŭrŏn kuryogŭl patko mungmuk'i issŭl sunŭn ŏpsŭmnida. 그런 굴욕을 받고 묵묵히 있을 수는 없읍니다.

humo(u)r *n.* (*comicality*) yumŏ 유머, iksal 익살, (*disposition*) kijil 기질, (*mood*) kibun 기분. *a sense of* ~ yumŏ kamgak 유머 감각/ *in good* ~ kibuni choasŏ 기분이 좋아서/ *I am in no* ~. Nanŭn kibuni choch'i anssŭmnida. 나는 기분이 좋지 않습니다.

humo(u)rist *n.* iksalkkun 익살꾼.

humo(u)rous *adj.* iksalmajŭn 익살맞은. *a* ~ *writer* yumŏ chakka 유머 작가/ *a* ~ *look* iksalmajŭn nunchit 익살맞은

hump *n.* (*round lump*) yukpong 육봉, hok 혹. 눈짓.

hunchback *n.* kopsadŭngi 꼽사등이.

hundred *n.* paek 백(100). ~ *times* paek pae 백 배(倍). *a few* ~ *people* subaek myŏngŭi saramdŭl 수백 명의 사람들/ ~*s of people* manŭn saramdŭl 많은 사람들.

hundredth *n.,adj.* paek pŏntchae(ŭi) 백 번째(의).

hundredthly *adv.* paek pŏntchaero 백 번째로.

hunger *n.* (*famine*) kumjurim 굶주림, (*craving for food*) kongbok 공복, (*strong desire*) kalmang 갈망. *die of* ~ kulmŏ chukta 굶어 죽다/ ~ *for fame* myŏngsŏnge taehan kalmang 명성에 대한 갈망.

hungry *adj.* *be* ~ paegop'ŭda 배고프다, shijanghada 시장하다. *I'm very* ~ *now.* Chigŭm mopshi shijanghamnida. 지금 몹시 시장합니다.

hunt *vt.,vi.* sanyanghada 사냥하다, (*search*) ch'atta 찾다. —*n.* (*hunting*) sanyang 사냥. ~ *the hare* t'okki sanyangŭl hada 토끼 사냥을 하다/ ~ *for a job* ilcharirŭl ch'atta 일자리를 찾다/ *I've been* ~*ing for your house for twenty minutes.* Ishippun tonganina taegŭl ch'ajassŭmnida. 20분 동안이나 댁을 찾았습니다.

hunter *n.* sanyangkkun 사냥꾼. 「사냥 갑시다.

hunting *n.* sanyang 사냥. *Let us go* ~ Sanyang kapshida.

hurdle *n.* (*barrier*) changaemul 장애물, hŏdŭl 허들. ~ *race* changaemul kyŏngju 장애물 경주.

hurl *vt.* (*throw*) tŏnjida 던지다. ~ *a spear at a tiger* horangiege ch'angŭl tŏnjida 호랑이에게 창을 던지다.

hurrah *int.* manse! 만세! *H*~ *for the Queen!* Yŏwang manse! 여왕 만세!

hurricane *n.* t'aep'ung 태풍, p'okp'ung 폭풍.

hurry *vi.,vt.* sŏdurŭda 서두르다, (*urge*) chaech'ok'ada 재촉하다. —*n.* (*haste*) sŏdurŭm 서두름. *Don't* ~ . Sŏdurŭji mashio. 서두르지 마시오/ *H*~ *up!* Ppalli (hashio)! 빨리 (하시오)/ *I am in a* ~ . Nanŭn sŏdurŭgo issŭmnida. 나는 서두르고 있습니다/ *Why are you in such a* ~ ? Wae kŭrŏk'e sŏdurŭshimnikka? 왜 그렇게 서두르십니까?

hurt *vt.,vi.* (*do harm*) sangch'ŏrŭl ip'ida 상처를 입히다, (*suffer pain*) ap'ŭda 아프다. *Did you* ~ *yourself?* Tach'yŏssŭmnikka? 다쳤읍니까/ *Did I* ~ *you?* Kibun sanghaessŏyo? 기분 상했어요/ *It* ~*s me to cough.* Kich'imŭl hani ap'ŭmnida. 기침을 하니 아픕니다/ *My eyes* ~ . Nuni ap'ŭmnida. 눈이 아픕니다.

husband *n.* namp'yŏn 남편. *my* ~ chuin 주인/ *a devoted* ~ aech'ŏga 애처가/ *Is your* ~ *interested in baseball?* Pakkat yangbanŭn yagurŭl choahashimnikka? 바깥 양반은 야구를 좋아하십니까?

hush *vt.,vi.* (*make silent*) choyonghage hada 조용하게 하다. *H*~ ! *Be silent!* Shwit! Choyonghi hashio. 쉿! 조용히 하시오/ ~ *money* immagŭm ton 입막음 돈.

husk *n.* (*of seeds*) kkŏpchil 껍질.

hustle *vi.,vt.* (*jostle*) kŏch'ilge milda 거칠게 밀다, (*impel*) kangyohada 강요하다. ~ *a person aside* yŏp'ŭro mirŏjŏch'ida. 옆으로 밀어젖히다/ *I won't be* ~*d.* Kangyonŭn patchi ank'essŭmnida. 강요는 받지 않겠읍니다. 「퀀셋.

hut *n.* (*cabin*) odumakchip 오두막집. *Quonset* ~ k'wŏnset

hutch *n.* (*box*) sangja 상자, (*chest*) k'ŭn kwe 큰 궤.

hybrid *n.* chapchong 잡종, honhyŏra 혼혈아. *A mule is a* ~ *animal.* Nosaenŭn chapchong tongmurimnida. 노새는 잡종 동물입니다.

hydroelectric *adj.* suryŏk palchŏnŭi 수력 발전의. ~ *power plant* suryŏk palchŏnso 수력 발전소. 「소 폭탄.

hydrogen *n.* suso 수소(水素). *a* ~ *bomb* suso p'okt'an 수

hydrophobia *n.* kongsupyŏng 공수병, (*rabies*) kwanggyŏn-pyŏng 광견병.

hygiene *n.* wisaenghak 위생학, wisaeng 위생. *mental* ~ chŏngshin wisaeng 정신 위생/ *public* ~ kongjung wisaeng 공중 위생.

hymen *n.* ch'ŏnyŏmak 처녀막.

hymn *n.* (*psalm*) ch'ansongga 찬송가, (*song of praise*) ch'an-ga 찬가.

hypnotism *n.* ch'oemyŏnsul 최면술.

hypocrisy *n.* wisŏn 위선.

hypocrite *n.* wisŏnja 위선자. *play the* ~ shich'imirŭl tteda 시치미를 떼다.

hypodermic *adj.* (*under the skin*) p'ihaŭi 피하의. ~ *injection* p'iha chusa 피하 주사.

hysteria *n.* hisŭt'eri 히스테리.

I *pron.* na 나, (*to superior*) chŏ 저. *I'm Mr. Han.* Na-nŭn Hanimnida. 나는 한(韓)입니다/ *It is* ~ *who am to blame.* Chega nappŭmnida. 제가 나쁩니다/ ~ *am sure.* T'ŭllimŏpsŏyo. 틀림없어요.

ice *n.* ŏrŭm 얼음, (~ *cream*) aisŭk'ŭrim 아이스크림. *We shall have* ~ *tomorrow.* Naeirŭn ŏrŭmi ŏl kŏshimnida. 내일은 얼음이 얼 것입니다/ *a strawberry* ~ ttalgi aisŭk'ŭ-rim 딸기 아이스크림/ ~ *bag* orŭm pegae 얼음 베개.

icebox *n.* naengjanggo 냉장고.

icebreaker *n.* swaebingsŏn〔gi〕 쇄빙선〔기〕.

icicle *n.* kodŭrŭm 고드름.

idea *n.* (*opinion*) ŭigyŏn 의견, (*notion*) ch'aksang 착상, (*impression*) insang 인상, (*knowledge*) chishik 지식. *What is the* ~? Ŏtchŏl chakchŏngimnikka? 어쩔 작정입니까/ *Do you have any good* ~ *for me?* Choŭn aidiŏnŭn ŏpsŭmnikka? 좋은 아이디어는 없읍니까/ *I have no* ~ *what you mean.* Musŭn ttŭshinji morŭgessŭmnida. 무슨 뜻인지 모르겠읍니다.

ideal *n.* (*perfection*) isang 이상, (*model*) chŏnhyŏng 전형. —*adj.* isangjŏgin 이상적인. *a lofty* ~ nop'ŭn isang 높은 이상/ *realize one's* ~ isangŭl shirhyŏnhada 이상을 실현하다/ *Yi Sunshin is my* ~ *of a hero.* I Sunshinŭn naŭi isangjŏgin yŏngungimnida. 이 순신은 나의 이상적인 영웅입니다/ *an* ~ *husband〔wife〕* isangjŏgin namp'yŏn 〔anae〕 이상적인 남편〔아내〕.

idealist *n.* isangga 이상가, isangjuŭija 이상주의자.

identification *n.* ~ *card* shinbun chŭngmyŏngsŏ 신분 증명서/ *May I see your* ~ *card?* Shinbun chŭngmyŏngsŏrŭl poyŏ chushigessŭmnikka? 신분 증명서를 보여 주시겠읍니까?

idiom *n.* kwanyonggu 관용구, sugŏ 숙어.

idiot *n.* paekch'i 백치, (*fool*) pabo 바보. *What an* ~ *I am!* Nayamallo pabogunyo! 나야말로 바보군요!

idle *adj.* (*lazy*) keŭrŭn 게으른, (*unemployed*) hal il ŏmnŭn 할 일 없는, (*worthless*) muik'an 무익한. *I can't afford to be* ~. Keŭrŭmŭl p'iul suga ŏpsŭmnida. 게으름을 피울 수가 없읍니다/ *Don't listen to* ~ *gossip.* Ssŭlteŏmnŭn yaeginŭn tŭtchi mashio. 쓸데없는 얘기는 듣지 마시오/ ~ *hours* han-gahan shigan 한가한 시간.

idleness *n.* nat'ae 나태, keŭrŭm 게으름, muwi 무위.

idol *n.* usang 우상. *a popular screen* ~ inki yŏnghwa paeu 인기 영화 배우/ *Don't make an* ~ *of wealth.* Purŭl sungbaehaji mashio. 부(富)를 숭배하지 마시오.

if *conj.* (*in case that*) manil …iramyŏn 만일 …이라면, (*even if*) …ilchirado …일지라도, (*whether*) …inji aninji …인지 아닌지. *If you ask him, he will help you.* Kŭ punege put'ak'amyŏn towa chul kŏshimnida. 그 분에게 부탁하면 도와 줄 것입니다/ *I asked* ~ *he was married.* Kyŏrhonŭl haennŭnji murŏ poatchiyo. 결혼을 했는지 물어 보았지요/ *Can you tell me* ~ *the bus for Youido stops here?* Yŏŭidohaeng pŏsŭga yŏgi sŏmnikka? 여의도행(行) 버스가 여기 섭니까/ ~ *only* …ŭl hal suman ittamyŏn …을 할 수만 있다면/ ~ *you please* pudi 부디, choesonghajiman 죄송하지만.

ignorance n. (lack of knowledge) mushik 무식, muji 무지, (want of educ.) muhak 무학.

ignorant adj. mushik'an 무식한, (not aware) morŭnŭn 모르는. My grandfather was quite ~ . Uri harabŏjinŭn tot'ong mushikchayŏssŭmnida. 우리 할아버지는 도통 무식 자였읍니다/ I was ~ of the fact. Nanŭn kŭ sashirŭl morŭgo issŏssŭmnida. 나는 그 사실을 모르고 있었읍니다.

ignore vt. (disregard) mushihada 무시하다. be ~d by superiors sangsarobut'ŏ mushidanghada 상사로부터 무시 당하다.

ill adj. (sick) pyŏngdŭn 병든, (bad) nappŭn 나쁜, (unwell) kibuni nappŭn 기분이 나쁜, (hostile) shimsulgujŭn 심술궂은. How long has your mother been ~ ? Chadangkkesŏnŭn ŏnjebut'ŏ alk'o kyeshimnikka ? 자당께서는 언제부터 앓고 계십니까/ ~ manners pŏrŭdŏmnŭn t'aedo 버릇없는 태도/ ~ fame akp'yŏng 악평.

illegal adj. (unlawful) pulpŏbŭi 불법의. an ~ action pulpŏp haengwi 불법 행위/an ~ operation nakt'ae 낙태.

illegitimate adj. (unlawful) wibŏbŭi 위법의, pulpŏbŭi 불법의, (bastard) sŏch'urŭi 서출의. an ~ child sasaenga 사생아.

illiterate adj. mushik'an 무식한, munmaengŭi 문맹의.

illness n. pyŏng 병. a severe ~ chungbyŏng 중병.

illogical adj. (not logical) chorie matchi annŭn 조리에 맞지 않는.

ill-treat vt. p'udaejŏp'ada 푸대접하다, haktaehada 학대하다.

illuminate vt. pich'uda 비추다, chomyŏnghada 조명하다.

illumination n. chomyŏng 조명. stage ~ mudae chomyŏng 무대 조명.

illusion n. (unreal image) hwan-gak 환각, (delusion) hwansang 환상, ch'akkak 착각. a sweet ~ chŭlgŏun hwansang 즐거운 환상.

illustrate vt. (exemplify) sŏlmyŏnghada 설명하다, (provide with pictures) kŭrimŭl nŏt'a 그림을 넣다.

image n. (likeness) sang 상, (portrait) ch'osang 초상,

(*form*) moyang 모양, (*psych.*) shimsang 심상, (*idea*)
kaenyŏm 개념. *an ～ of Buddha* pulsang 불상/ *an ～ of
Virgin Mary* sŏngmo Mariasang 성모 마리아상/ *Did God
create man in his own ～?* Shinŭn saramŭl kkok chagi
moyangdaero mandŭrŏssŭlkkayo? 신은 사람을 꼭 자기
모양대로 만들었을까요/ *How can we improve our ～?*
Ŏtchihamyŏn uri imijirŭl chok'e hal su issŭlkkayo? 어
찌하면 우리 이미지를 좋게 할 수 있을까요?

imaginary *adj.* (*visionary*) sangsangŭi 상상의, (*supposed*)
kasangŭi 가상의. *an ～ enemy* kasang chŏk 가상 적.

imagination *n.* sangsang 상상, sangsangnyŏk 상상력. *He
hasn't much ～.* Kŭ saramŭn sangsangnyŏgi pinyak'amnida. 그 사람은 상상력이 빈약합니다/ *Novelists use their
～.* Sosŏlganŭn sangsangnyŏgŭl kusahamnida. 소설가는
상상력을 구사합니다.

imagine *vt.* sangsanghada 상상하다, (*suppose*) chimjak'a-
da 짐작하다. *Can you ～ life without electricity?*
Chŏn-gi ŏmnŭn saenghwarŭl sangsanghal su issŭmnikka? 전기 없는 생활을 상상할 수 있읍니까/ *I can't ～
who the man is.* Kŭ namjaga nuguinji chimjagi an
kamnida. 그 남자가 누구인지 짐작이 안 갑니다.

imbecile *n.* (*foolish person*) pabo 바보, chŏnŭngja 저능
자. —*adj.* (*feeble*) hŏyak'an 허약한, (*stupid*) chŏnŭnghan 저능한.

imitate *vt.* (*copy*) mobanghada 모방하다, (*mimic*) hyungnaenaeda 흉내내다. *You should ～ great men.* Hullyunghan saramŭl ponbadaya hamnida 훌륭한 사람을 본받아야
합니다.

imitation *n.* (*sham*) katcha 가짜, mojo 모조, (*copy*) mo-
bang 모방. *～ gem* mojo posŏk 모조 보석/ *～ leather* injo
kaʼjuk 인조 가죽/ *Beware of ～s.* Mojop'ume chuŭihashio.
모조품에 주의하시오.

immaterial *adj.* (*spiritual*) chŏngshinjŏgin 정신적인,
(*not important*) hach'anŭn 하찮은.

immediate *adj.* (*direct*) chikchŏbŭi 직접의, (*instant*)
chŭksŏgŭi 즉석의, (*present*) tangmyŏnhan 당면한. *the ～
cause* chikchŏp wŏnin 직접 원인/ *an ～ answer* chŭktap

즉답.

immediately *adv.* (*at once*) chŭkshi 즉시, kot 곧. *You may leave ~ he comes.* Kŭ sarami omyŏn kot kado chossŭmnida. 그 사람이 오면 곧 가도 좋습니다.

immemorial *adj.* (*exceedingly remote*) mŏn yennarŭi 먼 옛날의, (*ancient*) t'aegoŭi 태고의.

immense *adj.* (*very large*) kwangdaehan 광대한, (*immeasurable*) hanŏmnŭn 한없는.

immensely *adv.* muhanhi 무한히, (*greatly*) aju 아주, taedanhi 대단히.

immigrant *n.* imin 이민(移民).

immigrate *vi.* iminoda 이민(移民)오다.

immigration *n.* imin 이민. *an ~ law* iminpŏp 이민법/ *I'll take you to the ~ office.* Ipkuk kwalli samuso-e annaehagessŭmnida 입국 관리 사무소에 안내하겠읍니다.

imminent *adj.* (*very near*) paktuhan 박두한, (*impending*) imbak'an 임박한.

immoral *adj.* (*wicked*) pudodŏk'an 부도덕한, (*lewd*) ŭmt'anghan 음탕한. *You ~ swindler!* I mottoen sagikkun kat'ŭni! 이 못된 사기꾼 같으니!

immovable *adj.* (*firm*) umjigiji annŭn 움직이지 않는, hwakkohan 확고한.

impact *n.* (*collision*) ch'ungdol 충돌, (*shock*) ch'unggyŏk 충격.

impair *vt.,vi.* (*make worse*) haech'ida 해치다, (*injure*) sonsanghada 손상하다. *~ one's health by overwork* kwaroro kŏn-gangŭl haech'ida 과로로 건강을 해치다.

impartial *adj.* (*fair*) kongp'yŏnghan 공평한, (*just*) chŏngdanghan 정당한.

impassable *adj.* t'onggwahal su ŏmnŭn 통과할 수 없는.

impasse *n.* (*blind alley*) maktarŭn kolmok 막다른 골목.

impatient *adj.* (*not patient*) ch'amŭlsŏng ŏmnŭn 참을성 없는, (*irritable*) sŏnggŭp'an 성급한. *I am ~ for his arrival.* Kŭŭi toch'agŭl ch'ojohage kidarigo issŭmnida. 그의 도착을 초조하게 기다리고 있읍니다.

impel *vt.* (*push*) milgo nagada 밀고 나가다, (*force*) ŏkchiro shik'ida 억지로 시키다. *I was ~led to go.* Nanŭn kaji anŭl su ŏpsŏssŭmnida. 나는 가지 않을 수 없었읍니다.

imperfect *adj.* purwanjŏnhan 불완전한. *an ~ vision* purwanjŏnhan shiryŏk 불완전한 시력.

imperial *adj.* (*of an empire*) chegugŭi 제국의, (*of an emperor*) chewangŭi 제왕의. *the ~ family* hwangjok 황

imperialism *n.* chegukchuŭi 제국주의. 「족.

impertinent *adj.* (*insolent*) kŏnbangjin 건방진, (*not to the point*) chŏkchŏlch'i anŭn 적절치 않은. *an ~ boy* pŏrŭdŏmnŭn ai 버릇없는 아이.

implement *n.* (*tool*) togu 도구, (*utensil*) kigu 기구. *—vt.* (*complete*) wansŏnghada 완성하다, (*fill out*) poch'unghada 보충하다. *a farm(ing) ~* nonggigu 농기구.

implicate *vt.* (*entangle*) kwallyŏnshik'ida 관련시키다, (*include*) naep'ohada 내포하다.

implore *vt.* (*entreat*) t'anwŏnhada 탄원하다.

imply *vt.* (*mean*) ŭimihada 의미하다, (*hint*) amshihada 암시하다. *What do you mean to ~?* Ŏttŏn ttŭsŭro malssŭmhashinŭnjiyo? 어떤 뜻으로 말씀하시는지요/ *Do you ~ that he is dishonest?* Kŭ sarami chŏngjik'aji ant'anŭn ttŭshimnikka? 그 사람이 정직하지 않다는 뜻입니까?

impolite *adj.* (*rude*) pŏrŭdŏmnŭn 버릇없는, muryehan 무례한.

import *vt.* suip'ada 수입하다. *—n.* (*importation*) suip 수입. *~ed goods* suipp'um 수입품/ *direct ~* chiksuip 직수입/ *an excess of ~s* suip ch'ogwa 수입 초과/ *~ permit* suip hŏga 수입 허가/ *~ prohibition* suip kŭmji 수입 금지/ *taxes on ~s* suipp'um se 수입품 세/ *Korea ~s wool from Australia.* Han-gugŭn Hojuesŏ yangmorŭl suip'amnida. 한국은 호주에서 양모를 수입합니다.

important *adj.* (*significant*) chungyohan 중요한, (*eminent*) hullyunghan 훌륭한, (*precious*) kwijunghan 귀중한. *an ~ position* chungyohan chiwi 중요한 지위/ *an ~ part* chungyohan yŏk'al 중요한 역할/ *I have something ~ to tell you.* Tangshinege tŭril chungyohan malssŭmi issŭmnida. 당신에게 드릴 중요한 말씀이 있읍니다.

importation *n.* suip 수입, suipp'um 수입품.

importer *n.* suipsang 수입상.

impose *vt.,vi.* (*lay*) pugwahada 부과하다, (*palm off*) sogyŏ ttŏmatkida 속여 떠맡기다.

impossible *adj.* pulganŭnghan 불가능한. *an ~ scheme* pulganŭnghan kyehoek 불가능한 계획/ *Don't ask me to do the ~*. Na-ege pulganŭnghan irŭn put'ak'aji mashio. 나에게 불가능한 일은 부탁하지 마시오.

impostor *n.* (*deceiver*) sagikkun 사기꾼, (*swindler*) hyŏpchapkkun 협잡꾼.

impotent *adj.* (*powerless*) muryŏk'an 무력한, (*weak*) hŏyak'an 허약한.

impractical *adj.* pishiryongjŏgin 비실용적인.

impresario *n.* (*promoter*) hŭnghaengju 흥행주, (*organizer*) chuch'oeja 주최자.

impress *vt.* (*imprint*) tchikta 찍다, (*fix deeply*) insangŭl chuda 인상을 주다. *How did Seoul ~ you?* Sŏurŭi insangi ŏttŏssŭmnikka? 서울의 인상이 어떻습니까/ *I'm ~. ed !* Kamgyŏk'aessŭmnida. 감격했읍니다.

impression *n.* (*effect on the feeling*) insang 인상, (*effect on the senses*) nŭkkim 느낌, (*influence on the intellect*) kammyŏng 감명. *What is your first ~ of Korea?* Han-gugŭi ch'ŏdinsangŭn ŏttŏssŭmnikka? 한국의 첫인상은 어떻습니까/ *a deep ~* kip'ŭn insang 깊은 인상/ *a good ~* choŭn insang 좋은 인상/ *She gave me a good ~.* Kŭ yŏjabunŭn na-ege choŭn insangŭl chuŏssŭmnida. 그 여자분은 나에게 좋은 인상을 주었읍니다.

impressive *adj.* (*moving*) insangjŏgin 인상적인. *He made an ~ speech.* Kŭnŭn insangjŏgin yŏnsŏrŭl haessŭmnida. 그는 인상적인 연설을 했읍니다.

imprison *vt.* (*put in prison*) t'uok'ada 투옥하다, (*confine*) kamgŭmhada 감금하다.

improbable *adj.* issŭl pŏp'aji anŭn 있을 법하지 않은. *Such a story is ~.* Kŭwa kat'ŭn iyaginŭn midŏjiji anssŭmnida. 그와 같은 이야기는 믿어지지 않습니다.

improper *adj.* (*unsuitable*) pujŏktanghan 부적당한, (*erroneous*) kŭrŭttoen 그릇된.

improve *vt.,vi.* (*make better*) kaesŏnhada 개선하다, (*reform*) kaeryanghada 개량하다, (*make good use of*) iyonghada 이용하다. *I'm sure things will ~* . Sat'aenŭn pandŭshi choajigetchiyo. 사태는 반드시 좋아지겠지요.

improvement *n.* (*betterment*) kaesŏn 개선, hyangsang 향상. *There is need for ~ in your handwriting.* (*to inferior*) Nŏnŭn kŭlssirŭl chomdŏ chal ssŏyagetta. 너는 글씨를 좀더 잘 써야겠다.

impudent *adj.* (*rudely bold*) ppŏnppŏnsŭrŏn 뻔뻔스런, (*insolent*) kŏnbangjin 건방진. *an ~ request* ppŏnppŏnsŭrŏn yogu 뻔뻔스런 요구.

impulse *n.* (*propulsion*) ch'ungdong 충동, (*impetus*) ch'ŭjinnyŏk 추진력, (*stimulus*) chagŭk 자극. *a sudden ~* sun-ganjŏgin ch'ungdong 순간적인 충동/ *the sexual ~* sŏngyok 성욕(性慾)/ *receive a great ~* k'ŭn chagŭgŭl patta 큰 자극을 받다.

impure *adj.* (*not pure*) pulsunhan 불순한, (*dirty*) pulgyŏrhan 불결한.

impute *vt.* (*attribute*) …ŭi t'asŭro tollida …의 탓으로 돌리다. *We shouldn't ~ the accident to the driver's carelessness.* Kŭ sagorŭl unjŏnsaŭi pujuŭiro tollyŏsŏnŭn an toemnida. 그 사고를 운전사의 부주의로 돌려서는 안 됩니다.

in *prep.* (*place*) …ŭi ane …의 안에, (*time*) …e …에, naee 내에, (*inside*) soge 속에, (*of dress*) …ŭl ipko …을 입고, (*condition*) …hayŏ …하여. *I'll see if Mr. Lee is ~* . Isshiga kyeshinŭnji pogo ogessŭmnida. 이(李)씨가 계시는지 보고 오겠읍니다/ *Is there anyone ~* ? Chibe nuga issŭmnikka? 집에 누가 있읍니까/ *I shall be back ~ a few days.* Myŏch'il naee toraogessŭmnida. 며칠 내에 돌아오겠읍니다/ *Can you finish the work ~ an hour?* Han shigan inaee kŭ irŭl kkŭnnael su issŭmnikka? 한 시간 이내에 그 일을 끝낼 수 있읍니까/ *~ the morning* ach'ime 아침에/ *~ the evening* chŏnyŏge 저녁에/ *What is there ~ the box?* Sangja soge innŭn kŏsŭn muŏshimnikka? 상자 속에 있는 것은 무엇입니까/ *What shall I go ~* ? Muŏsŭl ipko kalkkayo? 무엇을 입고 갈까요/ *I can't go out ~ these clothes.* Irŏn osŭl ipkonŭn nagal su ŏpsŭmnida. 이런 옷을 입고는 나갈 수 없읍니다/ *~ poor health* kŏn-gangi nappasŏ 건강이 나빠서/ *~ debt* pijŭl chigo 빚을 지고/ *~*

poverty kananhayŏ 가난하여.

inability *n.* munŭng 무능, muryŏk 무력.

inaccurate *adj.* (*incorrect*) pujŏnghwak'an 부정확한, (*wrong*) t'ŭllin 틀린. 「불충분한.

inadequate *adj.* pujŏktanghan 부적당한, pulch'ungbunhan

inadvisable *adj.* kwŏnhal su ŏmnŭn 권할 수 없는, (*not wise*) hyŏnmyŏnghaji mot'an 현명하지 못한.

inanimate *adj.* (*not alive*) saengmyŏngi ŏmnŭn 생명이 없는, (*dull*) hwalgi ŏmnŭn 활기 없는.

inaugurate *vt.* (*install in office*) ch'wiimshigŭl hada 취임식을 하다, (*initiate*) shijak'ada 시작하다.

inauguration *n.* (*inaugural ceremony*) ch'wiimshik 취임식, (*dedication ceremony*) naksŏngshik 낙성식.

inborn *adj.* (*natural*) t'agonan 타고난, (*innate*) sŏnch'ŏnjŏgin 선천적인.

inbound *adj.* pon-gugŭro toraganŭn 본국으로 돌아가는.

incapable *adj.* hal nŭngnyŏgi ŏmnŭn 할 능력이 없는, (*incompetent*) munŭnghan 무능한. 「탄.

incendiary *adj.* panghwaŭi 방화의. ~ *bomb* soit'an 소이

incense *n.* hyang 향(香). ~ *burner* hyangno 향로.
—*vt.* (mopshi) kollage hada (몹시) 골나게 하다.

incessant *adj.* (*ceaseless*) kkŭnimŏmnŭn 끊임없는, yŏnsokchŏgin 연속적인. *We have had a week of ~ rain.* Chinan ilchuil tongan kyesok piga naeryŏssŭmnida. 지난 1주일 동안 계속 비가 내렸읍니다.

inch *n.* (*measure of length*) inch'i 인치. *I'm an ~ or two shorter than you.* Nanŭn tangshinboda k'iga handu inch'i chaksŭmnida. 나는 당신보다 키가 한두 인치 작습니다/ ~ *by* ~ chogŭmssik 조금씩.

incident *n.* (*happening*) irŏnan il 일어난 일, (*event*) sakŏn 사건. —*adj.* (*apt to occur*) irŏnagi shwiun 일어나기 쉬운.

incidentally *adv.* (*by chance*) uyŏnhi 우연히, (*unexpectedly*) ttŭtpakke 뜻밖에.

incisor *n.* amni 앞니.

incite *vt.* (*stir up*) chagŭk[sŏndong]hada 자극[선동]하다.

inclination *n.* (*slope*) kyŏngsa 경사, (*tendency*) kyŏng-

hyang 경향, (liking) kiho 기호. He showed no ~ to leave.
Kŭnŭn ttŏnaryŏnŭn kisaegi ŏpsŏssŭmnida. 그는 떠나려는
기색이 없었읍니다/ That task is my ~. Kŭ irŭn naega
choahanŭn irimnida. 그 일은 내가 좋아하는 일입니다.

incline vt.,vi. (lean) kiulda 기울다, (dispose) maŭm
naek'ige hada 마음 내키게 하다, (tend) kyŏnghyangi itta
경향이 있다. —n. (slope) kyŏngsamyŏn 경사면. I am ~ed
to agree. Kwayŏn kŭrŏt'ago nanŭn saenggak'amnida.
과연 그렇다고 나는 생각합니다/ run down an ~ pit'arŭl
tallyŏ naeryŏgada 비탈을 달려 내려가다.

include vt. (contain) p'ohamhada 포함하다. The price ~s
carriage. Paedallyorŭl p'ohamhan kagyŏgimnida. 배달
료를 포함한 가격입니다/ Does this bill ~ all expenses?
I kyesansŏe modŭn piyongi p'ohamdoeŏ issŭmnikka? 이
계산서에 모든 비용이 포함되어 있읍니까?

income n. (earnings) suip 수입, sodŭk 소득. cash ~ hyŏn-
gŭm suip 현금 수입/ national ~ kungmin sodŭk 국민
소득/ net ~ sunsuip 순수입/ yearly ~ yŏnsu 연수/ Did
you file the ~ tax return? Sodŭkserŭl wannap'asyŏssŭmnikka? 소득세를 완납하셨읍니까?

incompetent adj. (incapable) munŭnghan 무능한, (unfit)
pujŏktanghan 부적당한.

incomplete adj. (not complete) purwanjŏnhan 불완전한,
pulch'ungbunhan 불충분한.

inconvenient adj. (unhandy) pulp'yŏnhan 불편한, (caus-
ing trouble) kwich'anŭn 귀찮은. You have come at a
very ~ time. Aju choch'i anŭl ttae osyŏssŭmnida. 아주
좋지 않을 때 오셨읍니다/ Would the afternoon be ~?
Ohumyŏn hyŏngp'yŏni nappŭshimnikka? 오후면 형편이
나쁘십니까/ Well, today is rather ~. Onŭrŭn chom
an toegessŭmnida. 오늘은 좀 안 되겠읍니다.

incorrect adj. (inaccurate) olch'i anŭn 옳지 않은, (wrong)
t'ŭllin 틀린, (improper) t'adangch'i anŭn 타당치 않은.
Your pronunciation is ~. Tangshinŭi parŭmŭn chŏnghwak'aji anssŭmnida. 당신의 발음은 정확하지 않습니다.

increase vt.,vi. (size) k'ŭge hada 크게 하다, (number)
nŭllida 늘리다, nŭrŏnada 늘어나다, (degree) ollida 올리다.

—n. chŭngga 증가. *The driver ~d speed.* Unjŏnsanŭn soktorŭl ollyŏssŭmnida. 운전사는 속도를 올렸읍니다/ *Is the consumption of beer still on the ~?* Maekchu sobiryangi ajikto nŭlgo issŭmnikka? 맥주소비량이 아직도 늘고 있읍니까?

incubator *n.* (*hatching eggs*) puran-gi 부란기, (*rearing weak babies*) poyukki 보육기, ink'yubeit'ŏ 인큐베이터.

incurable *adj.* pulch'iŭi 불치의. *~ disease* pulch'ipyŏng 불치병. *That's ~, isn't it?* Chal an nannŭn pyŏng animnikka? 잘 안 낫는 병 아닙니까?

indecent *adj.* (*unseemly*) kkolsanaun 꼴사나운, (*obscene*) ch'ujap'an 추잡한.

indeed *adj.* (*to be sure*) ch'amŭro 참으로, kwayŏn 과연. *Thank you very much ~.* Chŏngmal komapsŭmnida. 정말 고맙습니다/ *Very cold ~.* Ch'amŭro ch'upkunyo. 참으로 춥군요/ *Yes, ~!* Chŏngmal kŭrŏk'omalgoyo. 정말 그렇고말고요.

indefinite *adj.* (*vague*) aemaehan 애매한, (*unlimited*) hanŏmnŭn 한없는. *an ~ answer* aemaehan taedap 애매한 대답/*for an ~ time* ŏnjekkajina 언제까지나.

independence *n.* (*freedom from control*) tongnip 독립, *~ day* tongnip kinyŏmil 독립 기념일/ *live a life of ~* chahwarhada 자활하다.

independent *adj.* (*autonomous*) tongnibŭi 독립의, chajujŏgin 자주적인. *an ~ life* tongnip saenghwal 독립 생활/ *an ~ state* tongnip kukka 독립 국가.

index *n.* (*of books*) saegin 색인, indeksŭ 인덱스. *~ number* chisu 지수(指數)/ *a price ~* mulka chisu 물가 지수.

India *n.* Indo 인도.

Indian *adj.* Indoŭi 인도의. —n. Indoin 인도인. *~ ink* mŏk 먹〔墨〕/ *the ~ Ocean* indoyang 인도양.

indicate *vt.* (*point out*) chijŏk'ada 지적하다, (*show*) nat'anaeda 나타내다, (*hint*) amshihada 암시하다.

indifferent *adj.* (*uninterested*) mugwanshimhan 무관심한, (*unfeeling*) ssalssarhan 쌀쌀한, (*commonplace*) p'yŏngbŏmhan 평범한. *I am ~ about my appearance.* Nanŭn momch'arime kwanshimi ŏpsŭmnida. 나는 몸차림에 관심

이 없읍니다.

indigestion *n.* sohwa pullyang 소화 불량. *I have* ~. Sohwaga an toemnida. 소화가 안 됩니다.

indignant *adj.* pun-gaehan 분개한. *I was* ~ *at their mean actions.* Kŭdŭrŭi piyŏrhan t'aedo-e nanŭn pun-gaehaessŭmnida. 그들의 비열한 태도에 나는 분개했읍니다.

indirect *adj.* (*roundabout*) mŏlli tonŭn 멀리 도는, (*not straightforward*) kanjŏpchŏgin 간접적인. *an* ~ *road* toraganŭn kil 돌아가는 길/ ~ *lighting* kanjŏp chomyŏng 간접 조명/ ~ *taxes* kanjŏpse 간접세.

indirectly *adv.* kanjŏpchŏgŭro 간접적으로.

indispensable *adj.* (*absolutely essential*) ŏpsŏsŏnŭn an toenŭn 없어서는 안 되는, p'ilsujŏgin 필수적인.

indisposition *n.* (*slight illness*) kabyŏun pyŏng 가벼운 병.

individual *adj.* (*single*) tandogŭi 단독의, (*private*) kaeinjŏgin 개인적인, (*separate*) kaegaeŭi 개개의. ~ *instruction* kaein kyosu 개인 교수/ *an* ~ *enterprise* kaein kiŏp 개인 기업/ *an* ~ *home* kaein chut'aek 개인 주택.

individualism *n.* kaeinjuŭi 개인주의.

individuality *n.* (*peculiar character*) kaesŏng 개성.

indoor *adj.* (*in the house*) ongnaeŭi 옥내의, shillaeŭi 실내의. ~ *games* shillae orak 실내 오락/ *an* ~ *swimming-bath* shillae suyŏngjang 실내 수영장.

indoors *adv.* ongnaeesŏ 옥내에서, shillaeesŏ 실내에서. *stay* ~ chibane t'ŭrŏbak'ida 집안에 틀어박히다/ *live* ~ chibanesŏman salda 집안에서만 살다.

inducement *n.* (*attraction*) yuin 유인, (*incentive*) chagŭk 자극, (*motive*) tonggi 동기.

indulge *vt.,vi.* (*gratify*) manjokshik'ida 만족시키다, (*pamper*) chemŏttaero hage hada 제멋대로 하게 하다, (~ *in*) ...e ppajida...에 빠지다. *I have* ~*d in cake and ice cream.* Nanŭn kwajawa aisŭk'ŭrimŭl shilk'ŏt mŏgŏssŭmnida. 나는 과자와 아이스크림을 실컷 먹었읍니다/ *I never* ~*d in such sexual pleasures.* Kŭ kat'ŭn chusaege ppajin chŏgi ŏpsŭmnida. 그 같은 주색에 빠진 적이 없읍니다.

industrial *adj.* kongŏbŭi 공업의, sanŏbŭi 산업의. ~ *alcohol* kongŏmyong alk'ol 공업용 알콜/*an* ~ *nation* kongŏp kukka 공업 국가/ *an ~ town* kongŏp toshi 공업 도시.

industry *n.* kongŏp 공업, sanŏp 산업, (*diligence*) kŭnmyŏn 근면. *a domestic ~* kajŏng kongŏp 가정 공업/ *heavy ~* chunggongŏp 중공업/ *machine-driven ~* kigye kongŏp 기계 공업/ *commerce and ~* sanggongŏp 상공업.

inequality *n.* pulp'yŏngdŭng 불평등. *~ of treatment* ch'abyŏl taeu 차별 대우.

inevitable *adj.* (*unavoidable*) p'ihal su ŏmnŭn 피할 수 없는. *Such accidents are ~.* Kŭrŏn sagonŭn p'ihal suga ŏpsŭmnida. 그런 사고는 피할 수가 없읍니다.

inevitably *adv.* p'ihal su ŏpshi 피할 수 없이.

inexpensive *adj.* (*cheap*) kapssan 값싼, (*not ~*) piyongi an tŭnŭn 비용이 안 드는.

inexperienced *adj.* kyŏnghŏmi ŏmnŭn 경험이 없는. *He was ~ in women.* Kŭnŭn yŏja kyŏnghŏmi ŏpsŏssŭmnida. 그는 여자 경험이 없었습니다. 「t'urŭn 서투른.

inexpert *adj.* (*unskilful*) misuk'an 미숙한, (*clumsy*) sŏ-

infallible *adj.* (*free from error*) chalmoshi chŏnhyŏ ŏmnŭn 잘못이 전혀 없는, (*unfailing*) hwakshirhan 확실한. *~ remedies* t'ŭk'yoyak 특효약.

infamous *adj.* (*disgraceful*) pulmyŏngyesŭrŏun 불명예스러운, (*notorious*) angmyŏngnop'ŭn 악명높은.

infant *n.* yua 유아, yŏnga 영아.

infantry *n.* pobyŏng 보병.

infect *vt.* chŏnyŏmshik'ida 전염시키다. *She is ~ed with tuberculosis.* Kŭnyŏnŭn kyŏrhaege kŏllyŏ issŭmnida. 그녀는 결핵에 걸려 있습니다. 「병.

infection *n.* chŏnyŏm 전염, (*disease*) chŏnyŏmpyŏng 전염

infectious *adj.* chŏnyŏmŭi 전염의. *~ disease* chŏnyŏmpyŏng 전염병/ *a case of ~ disease* chŏnyŏmpyŏng hwanja 전염병 환자.

infer *vt.* (*conclude*) ch'uronhada 추론하다.

inference *n.* (*conclusion*) ch'uron 추론, ch'uch'ŭk 추측. *by ~* ch'uch'ŭkk'ŏndae 추측컨대/ *draw an ~* kyŏllonŭl naerida 결론을 내리다.

inferior *adj.* (*beneath*) araeŭi 아래의, (*lower in grade*) hagŭbŭi 하급의, (*of poor quality*) hadŭngŭi 하등의.

—*n.* sonaraet saram 손아랫 사람. *an ~ officer* hagŭp
kwalli 하급 관리 / *This article is ~ to the sample.* I mul-
p'umŭn kyŏnbonboda mot'amnida. 이 물품은 견본보다
못합니다.

inferiority *n.* (*inferior condition*) yŏlse 열세, (*bad quality*) hadŭng 하등. *a feeling of ~* yŏltŭnggam 열등감 /
~ complex yŏltŭngŭishik 열등의식, yŏltŭnggam 열등감.

infirm *adj.* (*weak*) yak'an 약한, (*unstable*) hwakkohaji
mot'an 확고하지 못한. *an ~ constitution* hŏyak'an ch'e-
jil 허약한 체질.

inflame *vt.,vi.* (*set on fire*) purŭl puch'ida 불을 붙이다,
(*stimulate*) chagŭk'ada 자극하다. *an ~d eye* ch'unghyŏldoen nun 충혈된 눈.

inflation *n.* (*currency*) t'onghwa p'aengch'ang 통화 팽창,
inp'ŭlle 인플레.

influence *n.* (*effect*) yŏnghyang 영향, (*power*) seryŏk
세력. *I have no ~ over that man.* Nanŭn chŏ saramege
amu wiryŏkto ŏpsŭmnida. 나는 저 사람에게 아무 위력도
없읍니다.

influential *adj.* (*potent*) yuryŏk'an 유력한. *an ~ politician* yuryŏk'an chŏngch'iga 유력한 정치가.

influenza *n.* yuhaengsŏng kamgi 유행성 감기.

inform *vt.,vi.* (*tell*) allida 알리다, (*notify*) t'ongjihada
통지하다. *Have you ~ed them of your departure?*
Ch'ulbarhashindanŭn kŏl kŭdŭrege allyŏssŭmnikka?
출발하신다는 걸 그들에게 알렸읍니까?

information *n.* (*knowledge*) chishik 지식, (*news*) chŏngbo
정보, soshik 소식, (*informing*) t'ongji 통지. *Where can I
get the tourism ~?* Odisŏ yŏhaeng chishigŭl ŏdŭl su
issŭmnikka? 어디서 여행 지식을 얻을 수 있읍니까 / *Here
is some ~ on the Cheju Island.* Yŏgi Chejudo-e kwanhan
charyoga issŭmnida. 여기 제주도에 관한 자료가 있읍니다 /
I'd like to get some ~ about Korean colleges. Han-gugŭi
taehage kwanhan chŏngborŭl ŏtko shipsŭmnida. 한국의
대학에 관한 정보를 얻고 싶습니다 / *Where is the information bureau?* Annaesonŭn ŏdimnikka? 안내소는 어딥니까?

ingenious *adj.* (*clever*) yŏngnihan 영리한, (*inventive*) palmyŏngŭi chaegani innŭn 발명의 재간이 있는, (*exquisite*) chŏnggyohan 정교한.

ingratitude *n.* paeŭn mangdŏk 배은 망덕.

ingredient *n.* (*constituent*) sŏngbun 성분, wŏllyo 원료. *the ~s of a cake* kwajaŭi wŏllyo 과자의 원료.

inhabitant *n.* chumin 주민. *the ~s tax* chuminse 주민세. *How many ~s are there in this town?* I maŭrŭi chuminŭn ŏlmana toemnikka? 이 마을의 주민은 얼마나 됩니까?

inhale *vt.* sumŭl tŭrishwida 숨을 들이쉬다. *~ air* konggirŭl tŭrimashida 공기를 들이마시다/ *~ tobacco smoke* tambae yŏn-girŭl tŭrimashida 담배 연기를 들이마시다.

inherit *vt.,vi.* sangsok'ada 상속하다, iŏbatta 이어받다. *The eldest son ~ed a large fortune from his father.* Kŭ changjanŭn abŏjiŭi manŭn chaesanŭl sangsokpadassŭmnida. 그 장자는 아버지의 많은 재산을 상속받았습니다. *She ~ed her mother's good look.* Kŭnyŏnŭn ŏmŏniŭi mimorŭl iŏbadassŭmnida. 그녀는 어머니의 미모를 이어받았습니다.

inheritance *n.* sangsok 상속, (*property*) yusan 유산. *~ taxes* sangsokse 상속세.

inhuman *adj.* (*brutal*) chaninhan 잔인한, mujabihan 무자비한. *~ treatment* haktae 학대.

initial *adj.* ch'ŏnmŏriŭi 첫머리의. —*n.* (*letter*) mŏrigŭlcha 머리글자. *the ~ stage* ch'ŏttangye 첫단계/ *an ~ letter* ch'ŏtkŭlcha 첫글자/ *What is your ~s?* Irŭmŭi mŏrigŭlchanŭn muŏshimnikka? 이름의 머리글자는 무엇입니까?

initiative *n.* (*first step*) cheilbo 제일보, (*leading movement*) chudokwŏn 주도권. *have the ~* chudokwŏnŭl katta 주도권을 갖다.

injection *n.* chusa 주사. *get[have] an ~* chusarŭl matta 주사를 맞다/ *preventive ~* yebang chusa 예방 주사.

injure *vt.* (*damage*) sangch'ŏrŭl ip'ida 상처를 입히다. *My brother was badly ~d on both legs.* Tongsaengŭn tu tarie chungsangŭl ibŏssŭmnida. 동생은 두 다리에 중상을 입었습니다.

injury *n.* (*hurt*) sangch'ŏ 상처, (*damage*) sonhae 손해. *receive a slight ~ to one's head* mŏrie kyŏngsangŭl ipta 머리에 경상을 입다.

injustice *n.* (*injust action*) pujŏng haengwi 부정 행위.

ink *n.* ingk'ŭ 잉크. *Indian* ~ mŏk 먹.

inkstone *n.* pyŏru 벼루.

inland *adj.* (*interior*) naeryugŭi 내륙의, (*domestic*) kungnaeŭi 국내의. ~ *area* naeryuk chibang 내륙 지방/ ~ *trade* kungnae muyŏk 국내 무역.

inmate *n.* (*lodger*) tonggŏin 동거인.

〈pyŏru〉

inn *n.* (*small hotel*) yŏinsuk 여인숙. *During my trip I want to try a Korean* ~. Yŏhaeng chung Han-gukshik yŏgwanedo mukko shipsŭmnida. 여행 중 한국식 여관에도 묵고 싶습니다.

inner *adj.* (*internal*) anŭi 안의, naebuŭi 내부의, (*mental*) chŏngshinŭi 정신의. *an* ~ *room* naeshil 내실/ *the* ~ *life* chŏngshin saenghwal 정신 생활.

inning *n.* (*baseball, etc.*) hoe 회(回), ining 이닝. *the first* ~ cheirhoe 제 1 회.

innocent *adj.* (*pure*) sun-gyŏrhan 순결한, (*guiltless*) kyŏlbaek'an 결백한, (*entirely lacking*) chŏnhyŏ ŏmnŭn 전혀 없는. *an* ~ *child* sunjinhan ai 순진한 아이/ *a Chinese servant,* ~ *of Korean* Han-gungmarŭl morŭnŭn Chunggugin hain 한국말을 모르는 중국인 하인.

inoculate *vt.* (*vaccinate*) chŏpchonghada 접종하다.

inquire, enquire *vt.,vi.* (*ask*) mutta 묻다, (*examine*) chosahada 조사하다. *I will* ~ *again as to that matter.* Kŭ ire kwanhae tashi mutko shipsŭmnida. 그 일에 관해 다시 묻고 싶습니다/ *We must* ~ *into the incident.* Kŭ sakŏnŭl kyumyŏnghaeya hamnida. 그 사건을 규명해야 합니다.

inquiry,enquiry *n.* (*asking*) munŭi 문의, (*investigation*) chosa 조사. *I made a personal* ~ *on the spot.* Nanŭn hyŏnjangesŏ kaeinjŏguro chosahae poassŭmnida. 나는 현장에서 개인적으로 조사해 보았읍니다/ ~ *office* annaeso 안내소/ ~ *agency* hŭngshinso 흥신소.

insane *adj.* (*mad*) mich'in 미친. *an* ~ *person* mich'i-gwangi 미치광이/ *an* ~ *asylum* chŏngshin pyŏngwŏn

정신 병원.

inscription n. (*on tombstone*) pimun 비문, (*on books*) sŏmyŏng 서명.

insect n. (*small creature*) konch'ung 곤충, pŏlle 벌레.

insert vt. (*put into*) kkiwŏnŏt'a 끼워넣다, (*publish*) kejaehada 게재하다. *I wish to ~ in the contract the following.* Kyeyaksŏe taŭm sahangŭl kkiwŏnŏk'o shipsŭmnida. 계약서에 다음 사항을 끼워넣고 싶습니다.

inside n. antchok 안쪽, naebu 내부. —adv. antchogŭro 안쪽으로, (*Am.*) (*within*) naee 내에. —adj. antchogŭi 안쪽의, naebuŭi 내부의. *the ~ of a box* sangja sok 상자 속/ *Look ~.* Anŭro poshio. 안으로 보시오.

insignificant adj. (*unimportant*) hach'anŭn 하찮은, (*trifling*) sasohan 사소한, (*meaningless*) muŭimihan 무의미한.

insist vt.,vi. (*assert*) chujanghada 주장하다, kangyohada 강요하다. *I ~ed that he should come with us.* Nanŭn kŭga uriwa hamkke kaya handago chujanghaessŭmnida. 나는 그가 우리와 함께 가야 한다고 주장했읍니다/ *I'll have another glass if you ~.* Kŭt'orok kwŏnhashimyŏn han chan tŏ mashigessŭmnida. 그토록 권하시면 한 잔 더 마시겠읍니다.

insomnia n. pulmyŏnchŭng 불면증. *I'm suffering from ~.* Pulmyŏnchŭngŭro kosaenghago issŭmnida. 불면증으로 고생하고 있읍니다.

inspect vt. (*examine*) kŏmsahada 검사하다, (*troops*) sayŏrhada 사열하다. *You have to ~ everything carefully.* Kolgoru salp'yŏya hamnida. 골고루 살펴야 합니다.

inspection n. kŏmsa 검사, kŏmyŏl 검열. *a medical ~* shinch'e kŏmsa 신체 검사/ *sanitary ~* wisaeng kŏmsa 위생 검사/ *safety ~* anjŏn kŏmsa 안전 검사.

inspector n. (*of factory, mine*) kamdokkwan 감독관, (*of school*) changhakkwan 장학관.

inspiration n. yŏnggam 영감, insŭp'ireisyŏn 인스피레이션.

install vt. (*induct*) ch'wiimshik'ida 취임시키다, (*equip with*) changch'ihada 장치하다.

installation n. (*appointment*) immyŏng 임명, (*equip-*

ment) changbi 장비.

instal(l)ment *n.* (*part payment*) punnap 분납. *monthly* ~ wŏlbu 월부/ *We're paying for the television by monthly* ~. T'ellebijŏn taegŭmŭl wŏlburo naego issŭmnida. 텔레비전 대금을 월부로 내고 있읍니다.

instance *n.* (*example*) pogi 보기, shillye 실례, (*case*) kyŏngu 경우. *for* ~ yerŭl tŭlmyŏn 예를 들면/ *in this* ~ i kyŏngu 이 경우.

instant *adj.* (*immediate*) chŭkshiŭi 즉시의, (*the present month*) idarŭi 이달의, (*urgent*) kin-gŭp'an 긴급한. —*n.* (*moment*) chŭkshi 즉시, sun-gan 순간. ~ *death* chŭksa 즉사/ ~ *coffee* insŭt'ŏnt'ŭ k'op'i 인스턴트 코피/ *for an* ~ chamkkan sai 잠깐 사이:

instantly *adj.* tangjang 당장, kot 곧. *I telegraphed* ~ *I arrived there.* Toch'ak'aja kot chŏnborŭl ch'yŏssŭmnida. 도착하자 곧 전보를 쳤읍니다.

instead *adv.* taeshinŭro 대신으로. *Give me this* ~ *of that.* Kŭgŏt malgo igŏsŭl chushipshio 그것 말고 이것을 주십시오/ *If you can't go, let him go* ~. Tangshini kal su ŏpsŭmyŏn kŭ saramŭl taeshin ponaeshio. 당신이 갈 수 없으면 그 사람을 대신 보내시오.

instinct *n.* ponnŭng 본능. *the sexual* ~ sŏngŭi ponnŭng 성의 본능/ *by* ~ ponnŭngjŏgŭro 본능적으로.

instinctive *adj.* ponnŭngjŏgin 본능적인. *an* ~ *sense* ponnŭngjŏgin kamgak 본능적인 감각.

instinctively *adv.* ponnŭngjŏgŭro 본능적으로.

institute *vt.* (*set up*) sŏllip'ada 설립하다, (*begin*) shijak'ada 시작하다, (*appoint*) immyŏnghada 임명하다. —*n.*(*society*) hyŏp'oe 협회. *a research* ~ yŏn-guso 연구소.

institution *n.* (*society*) hak'oe 학회, (*established custom*) chedo 제도, (*establishment*) sŏllip 설립. *a charitable* ~ chasŏn tanch'e 자선 단체/ *a public* ~ konggong kigwan 공공 기관/ *the* ~ *of slavery* noye chedo 노예 제도/ *the* ~ *of laws* pŏmnyurŭi chejŏng 법률의 제정.

instruct *vt.* (*teach*) karŭch'ida 가르치다, (*inform*) allida 알리다, (*direct*) chishihada 지시하다.

instruction *n.* (*teaching*) kyosu 교수, (*information*)

chishik 지식, (*direction*) chishi 지시. *military* ~ kunsa kyoyuk 군사 교육/ *oral* ~ kudu chishi 구두 지시/ *violate* ~s chishirŭl ŏgida 지시를 어기다/ *Do you have a booklet of operating* ~s? Sayongpŏp sŏlmyŏngsŏga issŭmnikka? 사용법 설명서가 있읍니까?

instructor *n.* (*teacher*) kyosa 교사, (*Am.*) kangsa 강사. *a foreign* ~ oegugin kangsa 외국인 강사/ *a gymnastic* ~ ch'eyuk kyosa 체육 교사/ *an* ~ *in English* yŏngŏ kyosa 영어 교사.

instrument *n.* (*tool*) kigu 기구, (*means*) sudan 수단. *musical* ~ akki 악기/ *optical* ~ kwanghak kigu 광학 기구/ *string* ~ hyŏnakki 현악기.

insufficient *adj.* (*not enough*) pulch'ungbunhan 불충분한, (*inadequate*) pujŏktanghan 부적당한. *an* ~ *supply of coal* sŏkt'anŭi konggŭp pujok 석탄의 공급 부족.

insult *vt.* ch'angp'i chuda 창피 주다. —*n.* (*insolence*) moyok 모욕, (*abuse*) yok 욕.

insurance *n.* pohŏm 보험. *an* ~ *contract* pohŏm kyeyak 보험 계약/ *an* ~ *premium* pohŏmnyo 보험료/ *fire*[*health, life, marine, unemployment*] ~ hwajae[kŏn-gang, saengmyŏng, haesang, shirŏp] pohŏm 화재[건강, 생명, 해상, 실업] 보험.

insure *vt.* pohŏme tŭlda 보험에 들다, (*guarantee*) pojŭnghada 보증하다. *Would you like it* ~*d?* Pohŏme tŭlgessŭmnikka? 보험에 들겠읍니까/ *How much was the house* ~*d for?* Kŭ chibŭn pohŏme ŏlmana tŭrŏssŭmnikka? 그 집은 보험에 얼마나 들었읍니까?

intellect *n.* chisŏng 지성. *a man of* ~ chisŏngin 지성인.

intellectual *adj.* chishigŭi 지식의, chinŭngŭi 지능의. *an* ~ *life* chichŏk saenghwal 지적 생활/ *an* ~ *offence* chinŭngbŏm 지능범.

intelligence *n.* (*intellect*) chinŭng 지능, (*sagacity*) ch'ongmyŏng 총명, (*information*) chŏngbo 정보. *a man with average* ~ pot'ong chinŭngŭl kajin saram 보통 지능을 가진 사람/ *the Central I~ Agency* chungang chŏngboguk 중앙 정보국.

intelligent *adj.* (*rational*) ijijŏgin 이지적인, chichŏgin 지적

인, (*acute*) ch'ongmyŏnghan 총명한. *an* ~ *child* ch'ong-myŏnghan ai 총명한 아이/ *an* ~ *question* chaech'i innŭn tappyŏn 재치 있는 답변.

intend *vt.* (*plan*) …hal chakchŏngida …할 작정이다, (*mean*) ŭimihada 의미하다. *I* ~ *to do the work.* Nanŭn kŭ irŭl hal chakchŏngimnida. 나는 그 일을 할 작정입니다/ *What do you* ~ *to do today?* Onŭrŭn muŏsŭl haryŏmnikka? 오늘은 무엇을 하렵니까/ *What do you* ~ *by these words?* I marŭn musŭn ttŭshijiyo? 이 말은 무슨 뜻이지요?

intense *adj.* (*violent*) kyŏngnyŏrhan 격렬한, (*eager*) yŏllyŏrhan 열렬한, (*serious*) shimgak'an 심각한. ~ *cold* hok'an 혹한/ ~ *love* yŏllyŏrhan sarang 열렬한 사랑/ *an* ~ *face* shimgak'an ŏlgul 심각한 얼굴.

intention *n.* (*purpose*) ŭido 의도, (*conception*) kaenyŏm 개념. *Do you have any* ~ *of going there?* Tangshinŭn kŏgie kal saenggagi issŭmnikka? 당신은 거기에 갈 생각이 있읍니까/ *Many thanks for your kind* ~*s.* Yŏrŏ kaji ch'injŏl kamsahamnida. 여러 가지 친절 감사합니다.

intercourse *n.* *friendly* ~ uho kwan-gye 우호 관계/ *social* ~ sagyo 사교/ *diplomatic* ~ oegyo 외교/ *illicit* ~ kant'ong 간통/ *sexual* ~ sŏnggyo 성교.

interest *n.* (*pleasurable concern*) hŭngmi 흥미, (*intellectual curiosity*) kwanshim 관심, (*importance*) chungyosŏng 중요성, (*pl.*) (*profit*) iik 이익, (*rate*) ija 이자. —*vt.* (*attract attention*) hŭngmirŭl irŭk'ida 흥미를 일으키다. *Do you have any particular field of* ~? T'ŭk'i hŭngmirŭl kajishin punyaga issŭmnikka? 특히 흥미를 가지신 분야가 있읍니까/ *I'll do the best for your* ~*s.* Tangshinŭi iigŭl wihae ch'oesŏnŭl tahagessŭmnida. 당신의 이익을 위해 최선을 다하겠읍니다/ *I've lent him the money at 5 per cent* ~. Kŭege op'un ijaro tonŭl pillyŏ chuŏssŭmnida. 그에게 5푼 이자로 돈을 빌려 주었읍니다/ *Are you* ~*ed in skiing?* Sŭk'i choahashimnikka? 스키 좋아하십니까/ *I'm* ~*ed in Buddhist temple.* Sach'are kwanshimi issŭmnida. 사찰에 관심이 있읍니다.

interesting *adj.* hŭngmi〔chaemi〕 innŭn 흥미〔재미〕있는.

an ~ book chaemiinnŭn ch'aek 재미있는 책/ *an ~ topic* chaeminanŭn hwaje 재미나는 화제.

interfere *vi.* (*meddle*) kansŏp'ada 간섭하다, (*hinder*) hwebanghada 훼방하다. *Please don't ~ in my business.* Chebal nae ire ch'amgyŏnhaji mashio. 제발 내 일에 참견하지 마시오/ *You have no right to ~ between us.* Tangshinŭn uri tu saramege kansŏp'al kwŏllinŭn ŏpsŭmnida. 당신은 우리 두 사람에게 간섭할 권리는 없읍니다/ *Don't ~ with this machine.* I kigyee hamburo sondaeji mashio. 이 기계에 함부로 손대지 마시오.

interior *adj.* (*inside*) antchogŭi 안쪽의, (*inland*) naeryugŭi 내륙의. —*n.* naebu 내부, an 안. *~ decoration* shillae changshik 실내 장식/ *the house ~s* shillae 실내.

interlude *n.* (*interval*) makkan 막간, (*music*) kanjugok 간주곡.

intermarriage *n.* kukche kyŏrhon 국제 결혼.

intermission *n.* (*pause*) chungdan 중단, (*in theatres*) makkan 막간, (*at concert or cinema*) hyushik shigan 휴식 시간. *without ~* kkŭnimŏpshi 끊임없이.

intern *n.* int'ŏn 인턴, shilsŭp ŭisa 실습 의사.

internal *adj.* (*inner*) anŭi 안의, naebuŭi 내부의, (*domestic*) kungnaeŭi 국내의. *for ~ use* (*medicine*) naebogyongŭi 내복용의/ *~ wars* naeran 내란.

international *adj.* kukchejŏgin 국제적인. *an ~ conference* kukche hoeŭi 국제 회의/ *~ game* kukche kyŏnggi 국제 경기/ *an ~ language* kukcheŏ 국제어/ *~ relation* kukche kwan-gye 국제 관계/ *~ trade* kukche muyŏk 국제 무역/ *~ treaty* kukche choyak 국제 조약.

interpret *vt.*, *vi* (*construe*) haesŏk'ada 해석하다, (*translate orally*) t'ongyŏk'ada 통역하다. *Will you please ~ for me?* T'ongyŏk chom haejushio. 통역 좀 해주시오.

interpretation *n.* (*explanation*) haesŏk 해석, sŏlmyŏng 설명, (*oral translation*) t'ongyŏk 통역.

interpreter *n.* t'ongyŏkcha[kwan] 통역자[관].

interrogation *n.* (*question*) chilmun 질문, (*inquiry*) shimmun 심문. *~ mark* ŭimun puho 의문 부호.

interrupt *vt.* (*break in upon*) makta 막다, (*hinder*)

panghaehada 방해하다. *Please don't* ~. Chebal panghaehaji mashio. 제발 방해하지 마시오/ *Don't* ~ *me when*
I'm busy. Pappŭl ttae hwebang noch'i mashio. 바쁠 때
훼방 놓지 마시오.

interruption *n.* (*break*) chungdan 중단, (*interference*)
panghae 방해.

intersection *n.* kyoch'achŏm 교차점, hoengdanno 횡단로.
Now turn left at the next ~. Taŭm kyoch'achŏmesŏ
oentchoguro toshio. 다음 교차점에서 왼쪽으로 도시오.

interval *n.* (*space*) kan-gyŏk 간격, kŏri 거리, (*time*) sai
사이, kigan 기간, (*music*) hyuge shigan 휴게 시간. *I'm*
delighted to see you after so long an ~. Oraenmane
manna poeŏ pan-gapkunyo. 오랜만에 만나 뵈어 반갑군요/
at ~s kan-gyŏgŭl tugo 간격을 두고.

interview *n.* (*meeting*) myŏnhoe 면회, (*with pressmen*)
int'ŏbyu 인터뷰, (*conference*) hoedam 회담. —*vt.*
myŏnhoehada 면회하다, hoegyŏnhada 회견하다. *When*
will you grant me an ~? Ŏnje myŏnhoehal su itkessŭmnikka? 언제 면회할 수 있겠읍니까/ *I* ~*ed him at his*
home. Kŭ saram chibesŏ kŭrŭl myŏnhoehaessŭmnida.
그 사람 집에서 그를 면회했읍니다.

intimate *adj.*(*close*) ch'inmirhan 친밀한, (*private*) ilshin-
sangŭi 일신상의. *an* ~ *friend* ch'in-gu 친구/ *an* ~ *diary*
kaein ilgi 개인 일기.

into *prep.* an[sog]e 안[속]에, an[sog]ŭro 안[속]으로.
Come ~ *the house.* Chip anŭro tŭrŏoshio. 집 안으로 들어
오시오/ *Throw it* ~ *the fire.* Pul soge chibŏ nŏushio. 불
속에 집어 넣으시오.

intolerance *n.* p'yŏnhyŏp 편협.

intolerant *adj.* p'yŏnhyŏp'an 편협한, (*bigoted*) kojip pul-
t'ongŭi 고집 불통의.

intoxicate *vt.* (*make drunk*) ch'wihage hada 취하게 하다.
I was so ~*d that I could not walk.* Nanŭn nŏmu
ch'wihae kŏrŭl suga ŏpsŏssŭmnida. 나는 너무 취해 걸을
수가 없었읍니다.

introduce *vt.* (*make known*) sogaehada 소개하다, (*lead*)
kkŭrŏdŭrida 끌어들이다. *May I* ~ *Mr. Kim, our man-*

ager? Chŏhŭi chibaein Kimssirŭl sogaehalkkayo? 저희 지배인 김씨를 소개할까요/ *May I ~ myself?* Che sogaerŭl hagessŭmnida. 제 소개를 하겠읍니다/ *I should like to be ~d to her.* Kŭnyŏege sogaehae chushimyŏn hamnida. 그녀에게 소개해 주시면 합니다.

introduction *n.* (*of a person to another*) sogae 소개, (*of a book*) mŏrimal 머리말, sŏmun 서문. *a letter of ~* sogaechang 소개장.

intrude *vi.,vt.* (*push in*) ch'imip'ada 침입하다, panghaehada 방해하다. *I hope I'm not intruding.* Panghaedoejinŭn annŭnjiyo. 방해되지는 않는지요/ *May I ~ on your privacy?* Panghaehaedo chok'essŭmnikka? 방해해도 좋겠읍니까?

invade *vt.* (*attack*) ch'yŏdŭrŏoda 쳐들어오다, (*violate*) ch'imhaehada 침해하다.

invader *n.* ch'imnyakcha 침략자.

invalid *adj.* (*feeble*) hŏyak'an 허약한, (*of no force*) muhyoŭi 무효의. *—n.* (*disabled person*) pyŏngja 병자. *an ~ soldier* sangibyŏng 상이병/ *an ~ cheque* muhyo sup'yo 무효 수표.

invaluable *adj.* maeu kwijunghan 매우 귀중한. *Her services are ~ to me.* Kŭnyŏŭi sugonŭn naege issŏ nŏmuna kapchin kŏshimnida. 그녀의 수고는 내게 있어 너무나 값진 것입니다.

invasion *n.* ch'imnyak 침략.

invent *vt.* (*contrive*) palmyŏnghada 발명하다, (*false story*) kkumyŏnaeda 꾸며내다. *King Sejong of the Yi dynasty ~ed the Hangul about 500 years ago.* Ijo Sejongkkesŏ yak obaengnyŏn chŏn han-gŭrŭl palmyŏnghayŏssŭmnida. 이조 세종께서 약 500 년 전 한글을 발명하였읍니다.

invention *n.* (*thing invented*) palmyŏngp'um 발명품.

inventor *n.* palmyŏngga 발명가.

inventory *n.* (*detailed list*) chaesan mongnok 재산 목록, (*catalogue*) sangp'um mongnok 상품 목록, (*stock*) chaegop'um 재고품. 「주다.

invest *vt.* (*lay out*) t'ujahada 투자하다, (*endow*) chuda

investigate *vt.,vi.* chosahada 조사하다.

investigation *n.* (*inquiry*) chosa 조사, (*research*) yŏngu 연구. *make an* ~ chosahada 조사하다/ *be under* ~ chosa chungida 조사 중이다.

investigator *n.* chosagwan 조사관, yŏn-guga 연구가.

investment *n.* t'uja 투자.

invisible *adj.* nune poiji annŭn 눈에 보이지 않는.

invitation *n.* ch'odae 초대. *Many thanks for your kind* ~. Ch'odaehae chusyŏsŏ kamsahamnida. 초대해 주셔서 감사합니다.

invite *vt.* (*ask to come*) ch'odaehada 초대하다, (*ask for*) ch'ŏnghada 청하다. *May I* ~ *you to a dinner at Korean restaurant*? Han-guk ŭmshikchŏmesŏ chŏnyŏk ch'odaerŭl hago shipsŭmnida. 한국 음식점에서 저녁 초대를 하고 싶습니다/ *I hope you will* ~ *us again sometime.* Amutchorok tashi ch'odaehae chushipshio. 아무쪼록 다시 초대해 주십시오/ *Thanks for inviting me.* Ch'odaehae chusyŏsŏ komapsŭmnida. 초대해 주셔서 고맙습니다.

invoice *n.* songchang 송장(送狀). *an export[import]* ~ such'ul[suip] songchang 수출[수입] 송장.

IOC *International Olympic Committee* kukche ollimp'ik wiwŏnhoe 국제 올림픽 위원회.

IOU (=*I owe you*) ch'ayong chŭngsŏ 차용 증서.

Ireland *n.* Aillaendŭ 아일랜드, Eire 에이레.

iris *n.* putkkot 붓꽃.

Irishman *n.* Aillaendŭ saram 아일랜드 사람.

iron *n.* soe 쇠, ch'ŏl 철, (*flatiron*) tarimi 다리미. —*vt.* tarimijirhada 다리미질하다. *cast* ~ chuch'ŏl 주철/ *sheet* ~ ch'ŏlp'an 철판/ *an electric* ~ chŏn-gi tarimi 전기 다리미/ *Please* ~ *my shirt.* Syassŭrŭl chom taryŏ chushipshio. 샤쓰를 좀 다려 주십시오.

ironical *adj.* pikkonŭn 비꼬는, pinjŏngdaenŭn 빈정대는. *an* ~ *remark* pikkonŭn mal 비꼬는 말/ *an* ~ *smile* naengso 냉소.

irony *n.* pikkogi 비꼬기, pinjŏngdaem 빈정댐.

irregular *adj.* pulgyuch'ik'an 불규칙한. *an* ~ *life* pulgyuch'ik'an saenghwal 불규칙한 생활/ *an* ~ *marriage* chŏngshik anin honin 정식 아닌 혼인.

irresponsible *adj.* much'aegimhan 무책임한. *an ~ behavior* much'aegimhan haengdong 무책임한 행동.

irrigation *n.* kwan-gae 관개, multaegi 물대기.

irritate *vt.* (*provoke*) hwanage hada 화나게 하다, (*make sore*) arige hada 아리게 하다. *The thick smoke ~d my eyes.* Tok'an yŏn-gie nae nuni aryŏssŭmnida. 독한 연기에 내 눈이 아렸읍니다.

irritation *n.* andal 안달, sŏngnam 성남.

island *n.* sŏm 섬. *an uninhabited ~* muindo 무인도/ *a solitary ~* oettan sŏm 외딴 섬.

isolate *vt.* (*detach*) pullihada 분리하다, (*separate*) kyŏngnihada 격리하다.

isolation *n.* korip 고립, kyŏngni 격리.

issue *n.* (*flowing out*) yuch'ul 유출, (*publication*) parhaeng 발행, (*subject debated*) munje 문제. —*vt., vi.* (*send forth*) naeda 내다, (*make public*) palp'ohada 발포하다, (*publish*) parhaenghada 발행하다. *I never miss an ~.* Nanŭn mae ho ppajiji ank'o samnida. 나는 매 호(號) 빠지지 않고 삽니다/ *a recent ~ ch'oegŭnho* 최근 호/ *This book was ~d recently.* I ch'aegŭn ch'oegŭne palgandoeŏssŭmnida. 이 책은 최근에 발간되었읍니다.

it *pron.* kŭgŏsŭn 그것은, kŭgŏshi 그것이, kŭgŏsŭl 그것을. *It is in my desk.* Kŭgŏsŭn nae ch'aeksang ane issŭmnida. 그것은 내 책상 안에 있읍니다/ *I like ~.* Kŭgŏsŭl choahamnida. 그것을 좋아합니다. *It is very often omitted in the Korean translation. Who is ~?* Nugushimnikka? 누구십니까/ *It snows.* Nuni omnida 눈이 옵니다/ *Is ~ difficult to learn written Chinese?* Hanjchanŭn paeugiga ŏryŏpsŭmnikka? 한자는 배우기가 어렵습니까? *When used impersonally* **It** *is not translated. It was I.* Nayŏssŭmnida. 나였읍니다/ *It is Sunday.* Iryoirimnida. 일요일입니다/ *It looks like rain.* Piga ol kŏt kassŭmnida. 비가 올 것 같습니다.

Italian *n.* (*person*) It'allia saram 이탈리아 사람, (*language*) It'allia mal 이탈리아 말.

Italy *n.* It'allia 이탈리아.

itch *n.* (*itchy feeling*) karyŏum 가려움, (*scabies*) om 옴.

item *n.* chomok 조목, p'ummok 품목. *How many ~s are there on the list?* Kŭ risŭt'ŭenŭn myŏt p'ummogi tŭrŏ issŭmnikka? 그 리스트에는 몇 품목이 들어 있읍니까/ *a chief ~* chuyo hangmok 주요 항목.

itinerary *n.* (*plan of travel*) yŏjŏng 여정, (*record of travel*) yohaeng ilgi 여행 일기. *Include these places on your ~.* Idŭl changsodo yŏjŏnge nŏŭishipshio. 이들 장소도 여정에 넣으십시오.

itself *pron.* kŭ chach'e 그 자체. *by ~* honjasŏ 혼자서/ *in ~* pollae 본래/ *of ~* chŏjŏllo 저절로/ *Put it by ~.* Ttaro tushio. 따로 두시오.

ivory *n.* sanga 상아(象牙). *artificial ~* injo sanga 인조 상아/ *~ chopsticks* sanga chŏtkarak 상아 젓가락/ *~ tower* sangat'ap 상아탑.

ivy *n.* tamjaengi 담쟁이.

---★◀ **J** ▶★---

jab *n.* (*boxing*) chaep 잽, (*injection*) chusa 주사. *Have you had your cholera ~s yet?* K'ollera chusarŭl majassŭmnikka? 콜레라 주사를 맞았읍니까?

jack *n.* (*tool*) chaek 잭.

jacket *n.* chak'et 자켓. *a sports ~* undongbok 운동복.

jade *n.* pich'wi 비취.

jail *n.* (*prison*) kyodoso 교도소, kamok 감옥. *a detention ~* yuch'ijang 유치장/ *a ~ bird* sangsŭppŏm 상습범.

jam *n.* chaem 잼. *apple ~* sagwa chaem 사과 잼/ *strawberry ~* ttalgi chaem 딸기 잼/ *bread and ~* chaem parŭn ppang 잼 바른 빵.

janitor *n.* (*doorkeeper*) munjigi 문지기, suwi 수위.

January *n.* irwŏl 1월, chŏngwŏl 정월(正月).

Japan *n.* Ilbon 일본.

Japanese *n.* (*person*) Ilbon saram 일본 사람, (*language*) Ilbonŏ 일본어.

jar *n.* hangari 항아리, tanji 단지. *a ~ of pickles* kimch'i han tanji 김치 한 단지.

jaw *n.* t'ŏk 턱. *Oh, shut your* ~ *!* Takch'yŏ! 닥쳐!

jazz *n.* chaejŭ ŭmak 재즈 음악. ~ *band* chaejŭ aktan 재즈 악단.

jealous *adj.* saemi manŭn 샘이 많은. *a* ~ *wife* saemi manŭn anae 샘이 많은 아내.

jealousy *n.* shisaem 시샘, chilt'u 질투.

jeer *n.* (*taunt*) chorong 조롱. —*vi.* choronghada 조롱하다.

jelly *n.* umu 우무, hanch'ŏn 한천.

jellyfish *n.* haep'ari 해파리.

jerk *vt., vi.* hwaek chabadanggida 홱 잡아당기다. —*n.* hwaek chabadanggim 홱 잡아당김. *pull with a* ~ hwaek chabach'aeda 홱 잡아채다.

jest *n.*(*fun*) nongdam 농담, (*joke*) iksal 익살. —*vi.*(*joke*) nongdamŭl hada 농담을 하다. *Don't* ~ *about serious things.* Chinjihan ire shirŏpshi kulji mashio. 진지한 일에 실없이 굴지 마시오.

Jesus *n.* Yesu (Kŭrisŭdo) 예수 (그리스도).

jet plane chet'ŭgi 제트기.

Jew *n.* yut'aein 유태인.

jewel *n.* posŏk 보석. *a precious* ~ kappissan posŏk 값비싼 보석.

jewl(l)er *n.* posŏksang 보석상.

jingle *n.* ttallangttallang 딸랑딸랑, tchirŭrŭng 찌르릉. —*vi.* ttallangttallang〔tchirŭrŭng〕 sori nada 딸랑딸랑〔찌르릉〕소리 나다.

job *n.* (*work*) il 일, (*employment*) chigŏp 직업, (*post*) chiwi 지위. *a big* ~ k'ŭn il 큰 일/ *hunt a* ~ ilcharirŭl ch'atta 일자리를 찾다/ *lose one's* ~ shilchik'ada 실직하다/ *a side* ~ puŏp 부업/ *Do you want to take the* ~? Kŭ ilcharirŭl katko shipso? 그 일자리를 갖고 싶소/ *I want a* ~ *with your company.* Tangshin hoesa-e ch'wijik'ago shipsŭmnida. 당신 회사에 취직하고 싶습니다/ ~ *hunting* kujik undong 구직 운동/ *You got a* ~? Ch'wijik'aessŭmnikka? 취직했읍니까?

jobber *n.* p'ump'arikkun 품팔이꾼, inbu 인부.

jobbery *n.* ikwŏn undong 이권 운동, tokchik 독직.

jobless *adj.* (*unemployed*) mujigŭi 무직의. *mobilize the ~ for public works* konggong saŏbe shirŏpcharŭl tongwŏnhada 공공 사업에 실업자를 동원하다.

john *n.* (*water-closet*) pyŏnso 변소, hwajangshil 화장실. *Where is the ~?* Hwajangshirŭn ŏdijiyo? 화장실은 어디지요/ *May I go to the ~?* Hwajangshire kado chossŭmnikka? 화장실에 가도 좋습니까?

join *vt., vi.* (*unite*) kyŏrhap'ada 결합하다, (*connect*) yŏngyŏlshik'ida 연결시키다, (*become a member of*) kaip'ada 가입하다. *May I ~ you?* Hanmok kkiŏ chushigessŭmnikka? 한목 끼어 주시겠읍니까/ *Would you like to ~ us?* Hamkke ŏullyŏ chushiryŏmnikka? 함께 어울려 주시렵니까/ *Will you ~ us in a walk?* Hamkke sanch'aek'ashiji ank'essŭmnikka? 함께 산책하시지 않겠읍니까?

joiner *n.* kagujangi 가구장이, (*Am.*) (*carpenter*) somokchangi 소목장이.

joint *n.* (*seam*) iŭmsae 이음새, (*of the body*) kwanjŏl 관절, (*junction*) chŏp'ap 접합, (*disreputable places*) tobakchang 도박장. —*adj.* (*common*) kongdongŭi 공동의. *a bamboo ~* taemadi 대마디/ *finger ~s* sonkaragŭi kwanjŏl 손가락의 관절/ *a ~ debtor* yŏndae ch'aemuja 연대 채무자/ *a ~ author* kongjŏja 공저자.

joke *n.* (*jest*) nongdam 농담, iksal 익살. —*vi., vt.* (*banter*) nollida 놀리다. *for a ~* nongdam samasŏ 농담 삼아서/ *in ~* nongdamŭro 농담으로/ *It is no ~.* Nongdami anio. 농담이 아니오/ *None of your ~s.* Nongdam mashio. 농담 마시오/ *How can you be angry at such an innocent ~?* Kŭrŏn choeŏmnŭn nongdame ŏttŏk'e hwarŭl naeshimnikka? 그런 죄없는 농담에 어떻게 화를 내십니까?

joker *n.* (*jester*) iksalkkun 익살꾼, (*merry fellow*) changnankkun 장난꾼, (*fool*) ŏritkwangdae 어릿광대.

jolly *adj.* (*merry*) myŏngnanghan 명랑한, (*gay*) yuk'waehan 유쾌한. —*adv.* (*very*) maeu 매우, mopshi 몹시. *a ~ fellow* k'waenama 쾌남아/ *~ book* chaemiinnŭn ch'aek 재미있는 책/ *We had a ~ good time.* Maeu chaemiissŏssŭmnida. 매우 재미있었읍니다.

jostle *vt.* (*push roughly*) ttŏmilda 떠밀다, (*elbow*) milch'igo nagada 밀치고 나가다. *We were ~d by the crowd.* Urinŭn kunjungdŭrege ttŏmillyŏssŭmnida. 우리는 군중들 에게 떠밀렸읍니다.

journal *n.* (*daily newspaper*) shinmun 신문, (*magazine*) chapchi 잡지, (*diary*) ilgi 일기. *How many weekly ~s do you read?* Chuganjinŭn myŏt chongnyu poshimnikka? 주간지는 몇 종류 보십니까/ *the Economic J~* kyŏngjeji 경제지/ *keep a ~* ilgirŭl chŏkta 일기를 적다.

journalist *n.* shinmun chapchi kija 신문 잡지 기자.

journey *n.* (*travel*) yŏhaeng 여행. —*vi.* yŏhaenghada 여행 하다. *a ~ by rail* kich'a yŏhaeng 기차 여행/*Let us proceed with our ~.* Cha, yŏhaengŭl ttŏnapshida. 자 여행을 떠납 시다/ *a school ~* suhak yŏhaeng 수학 여행/ *I wish you a safe ~.* Tojung musahashigirŭl pimnida. 도중 무사하시 기를 빕니다.

joy *n.* (*delight*) kippŭm 기쁨, hwanhŭi 환희. *~s and sorrows* kippŭmgwa sŭlp'ŭm 기쁨과 슬픔/ *tears of ~* kippŭmŭi nunmul 기쁨의 눈물/ *I was mad with ~ at the news.* Kŭ soshigŭl tŭtko mich'il tŭshi kippŏhaessŭmni-da. 그 소식을 듣고 미칠 듯이 기뻐했읍니다.

joyful *adj.* kippŭn 기쁜, chŭlgŏun 즐거운.

joyous *adj.* chŭlgŏun 즐거운(=*joyful*).

jubilant *adj.* (*triumphant*) kippŭme ch'an 기쁨에 찬.

jubilee *n.* (*anniversary*) kinyŏm 기념. *the silver[golden] ~* ŭnhon[kŭmhon]shik 은혼[금혼]식.

judge *n.* (*public officer*) p'ansa 판사, (*umpire*) shimp'an 심판, (*connoisseur*) kamjŏngga 감정가. —*vt.* (*try*) shim-p'anhada 심판하다. *Don't ~ a man by his looks.* Oemo-ro saramŭl p'andanhaji mashio. 외모로 사람을 판단하지 마 시오/ *I can't ~ whether he was right or wrong.* Kŭga orannŭnji nappannŭnji p'andanhal suga ŏpsŭmnida. 그 가 옳았는지 나빴는지 판단할 수가 없읍니다/ *Judging from what you say, he ought to succeed.* Tangshin mallo p'andanhandamyŏn t'ŭllimŏpshi kŭnŭn sŏnggonghal kŏ-shimnida. 당신 말로 판단한다면 틀림없이 그는 성공할 것입 니다.

judg(e)ment *n.* (*judging*) shimp'an 심판, (*good sense*) p'andannyŏk 판단력, (*opinion*) ŭigyŏn 의견. *Beware of hasty* ~. Soktanŭl naeriji ant'orok choshimhashio. 속단을 내리지 않도록 조심하시오/ *a man of* ~ yangshigŭl kajin saram 양식을 가진 사람/ *in my* ~ nae ŭigyŏnŭronŭn 내 의견으로는.

judicious *adj.* (*discreet*) saryŏ kip'ŭn 사려 깊은, (*wise*) ch'ongmyŏnghan 총명한.

jug *n.* (*pot for liquids*) mulpyŏng 물병, (*for beer*) chokki 조끼. *a* ~ *of beer* maekchu han chokki 맥주 한 조끼.

juggle *n.* (*sleight of hands*) yosul 요술, (*imposture*) sagi 사기, hyŏpchap 협잡. ~ *with words* mallo ŏlbŏmurida 말로 얼버무리다.

juggler *n.* (*conjurer*) yosuljangi 요술장이, (*trickster*) sagikkun 사기꾼.

juice *n.* chŭp 즙, aek 액(液). *grape* ~ p'odojŭp 포도즙/ *lemon* ~ remonjŭp 레몬즙/ *I'd like to have tomato* ~ *and bacon.* T'omat'o chusŭwa peik'ŏnŭl chushio. 토마토 주스와 베이컨을 주시오.

July *n.* ch'irwŏl 7월.

jumble *n.* (*medley*) chaptongsani 잡동사니, (*disorder*) hollan 혼란. —*vt., vi.* (*mix*) twibŏmbŏgi toeda 뒤범벅이 되다.

jump *n.* (*leap*) ttwiŏorŭgi 뛰어오르기, toyak 도약. —*vi.* ttwida 뛰다. —*vt.* ttwiŏnŏmta 뛰어넘다. *He* ~*ed up with joy.* Kŭnŭn kippŏsŏ kkŏngch'ung ttwiŏssŭmnida. 그는 기뻐서 껑충 뛰었읍니다/*Don't* ~ *to conclusion.* Soktanhaji mashipshio. 속단하지 마십시오.

juncture *n.* (*critical moment*) wigi 위기, (*junction*) chŏp'apchŏm 접합점. *at this* ~ i chungdaehan shigie 이 중대한 시기에.

June *n.* yuwŏl 6월.

jungle *n.* millim (chidae) 밀림 (지대), chŏnggŭl 정글.

junior *n.* (*younger*) yŏnsoja 연소자, hubae 후배. —*adj.* (*younger*) yŏnhaŭi 연하의, (*of lower position*) hagŭbŭi 하급의. *I'm your* ~ *by two years.* Nanŭn tangshinboda inyŏn sonaraeimnida. 나는 당신보다 2년 손아래입니다.

junk *n.* (*Chinese ship*) chŏngk'ŭ 정크, (*trash*) p'yemul

폐물.

jurisdiction *n.* (*legal power*) sabŏpkwŏn 사법권, (*extent of authority*) kwanhalkwŏn 관할권. ~ *over foreigners* oegugine taehan sabŏpkwŏn 외국인에 대한 사법권.

jury *n.* paeshim 배심. *a* ~ *system* paeshim chedo 배심 제도.

just *adj.* (*right*) olbarŭn 올바른, (*fair*) kongjŏnghan 공정한, (*lawful*) chŏngdanghan 정당한. —*adv.* (*but a moment before*) ije 이제, mak 막, (*exactly*) paro 바로, kkok 꼭, (*approximately*) taech'ung 대충, (*hardly*) kakkasŭro 가까스로, (*only, merely*) chogŭm 조금, tanji 단지. *I've had dinner.* Ije mak chŏnyŏk shiksarŭl tŭrŏssŭmnida. 이제 막 저녁 식사를 들었읍니다/ *That's* ~ *what I was going to say.* Kŭgŏshi paro naega marharyŏdŏn kŏshimnida. 그것이 바로 내가 말하려던 것입니다/ *J*~ *taste this!* Igŏt mat chom poshio. 이것 맛 좀 보시오/ *J*~ *a moment, please.* Chamkkan kidaryŏ chushio. 잠깐 기다려 주시오/ *I have come here* ~ *to see you.* Taman tangshinŭl mannarŏ yŏgikkaji wassŭmnida. 다만 당신을 만나러 여기까지 왔읍니다/ ~ *now* panggŭm 방금.

justice *n.* (*righteousness*) chŏngŭi 정의, (*justness*) chŏngdang 정당, (*a judge*) pŏpkwan 법관. *I saw the* ~ *of your remarks.* Tangshin parŏni chŏngdanghadanŭn kŏl arassŭmnida. 당신 발언이 정당하다는 걸 알았읍니다/ *a court of international* ~ kukche chaep'anso 국제 재판소/ *a chief* ~ (*Am.*) chaep'anjang 재판장.

justify *vt., vi.* (*prove to be just*) chŏngdanghwahada 정당화하다. *You can hardly* ~ *such conduct.* Kŭrŏn haengdongŭl olt'ago hal sunŭn ŏpsŭmnida. 그런 행동을 옳다고 할 수는 없읍니다.

justly *adv.* (*rightly*) chŏngdanghage 정당하게, (*fairly*) kongjŏnghage 공정하게, (*exactly*) chŏnghwak'age 정확하게.

justness *n.* (*propriety*) olbarŭm 올바름, (*fairness*) kongjŏng 공정, (*exactness*) chŏnghwak 정확.

juvenile *adj.* (*young*) nai ŏrin 나이 어린, sonyŏn sonyŏŭi 소년 소녀의. ~ *court* sonyŏnwŏn 소년원/ ~ *delinquency* sonyŏn pŏmjoe 소년 범죄/ *Do you have a serious* ~ *de-*

linquency problem in Korea? Han-gugedo shimgak'an sonyŏn pŏmjoe munjega issŭmnikka? 한국에도 심각한 소년 범죄 문제가 있읍니까?

---❧ **K** ❧---

kaleidoscope *n.* manhwagyŏng 만화경.

keen *adj.* (*sharp*) nalk'aroun 날카로운, (*cutting*) ppyŏe sŭmyŏdŭnŭn 뼈에 스며드는, (*eager*) yŏlshimin 열심인, (*Am.*) (*charming*) yeppŭn 예쁜, (~ *on*) (*fond of*) mopshi choahanŭn 몹시 좋아하는. *a ~ knife* nalk'aroun k'al 날카로운 칼/ *a ~ wind* ppyŏe sŭmyŏdŭnŭn param 뼈에 스며드는 바람/ *be ~ on* (*making*) *money* tonbŏrie yŏlchunghada 돈벌이에 열중하다/ *I am ~ to go abroad.* Oeguge kago ship'ŏ chukkessŭmnida. 외국에 가고 싶어 죽겠읍니다/ *I'm not very ~ on jazz.* Chaejüenŭn kŭdaji hŭngmiga ŏpsŭmnida. 재즈에는 그다지 흥미가 없읍니다.

keep *vt.,vi.* (*hold*) chinida 지니다, (*observe*) chik'ida 지키다, (*care for*) tolboda 돌보다, (*detain*) puttŭrŏ tuda 붙들어 두다, (*run*) kyŏngyŏnghada 경영하다, (*continue*) kyesok'ada 계속하다, (*restrain*) chejihada 제지하다. *Will you ~ these things safe for me?* I mulgŏnŭl anjŏnhage pogwanhae chushigessŭmnikka? 이 물건을 안전하게 보관해 주시겠읍니까/ *Just ~ the change.* Kŏsŭrŭmtonŭn kŭman tuseyo. 거스름돈은 그만 두세요/ *K~ this well in mind.* Chal kiŏk'ae tushipshio. 잘 기억해 두십시오/ *How long may I ~ this book?* I ch'aek ŏnjekkaji pillil su issŭmnikka? 이 책 언제까지 빌릴 수 있읍니까/ *I'm sorry I've kept you waiting.* Kidarige haesŏ mianhamnida. 기다리게 해서 미안합니다/ *What kept you?* Muŏt ttaemune mot watchiyo? 무엇 때문에 못 왔지요/ *K~ off the grass.* Chandie tŭrŏgaji mashio. 잔디에 들어가지 마시오.

keeper *n.* (*guardian*) kwalliin 관리인, (*protector*) pohoja 보호자, (*proprietor*) kyŏngyŏngju 경영주. *door~* munjigi 문지기/ *goal~* munjigi 문지기, kolk'ip'ŏ 골키퍼/

shop~ kage chuin 가게 주인.

kennel *n.* kaejip 개집.

kernel *n.* (*of a fruit*) in 인(仁), (*grain*) nadal 낟알, (*core*) haekshim 핵심.

kerosene·kerosine *n.* tŭngyu 등유(燈油). *a ~ lamp* sŏgyu namp'o 석유 남포. *How do you light this ~ stove?* I sŏgyu nallonŭn ŏttŏk'e purŭl puch'imnikka? 이 석유 난로는 어떻게 불을 붙입니까?

kettle *n.* chujŏnja 주전자. *How much is a ~ of makkoli?* Makkŏlli han chujŏnjanŭn ŏlmaimnikka? 막걸리 한 주전자는 얼마입니까?

key *n.* yŏlsoe 열쇠. *~hole* yŏlsoe kumŏng 열쇠 구멍/ *a bunch of ~s* yŏlsoe mukkŭm 열쇠 묶음/ *Do you know where my car ~s are?* Nae ch'a yŏlsoega ŏdi innŭnji ashio? 내 차 열쇠가 어디 있는지 아시오?

kick *vt., vi.* ch'ada 차다. —*n.* ch'agi 차기. *I ~ed him on the head.* Kŭŭi mŏrirŭl ch'assŭmnida. 그의 머리를 찼읍니다.

kid *n.* (*young goat*) yŏmso saekki 염소 새끼, (*child*) ai 아이, (*leather*) k'idŭ kajuk 키드 가죽. —*vi.,vt.* (*jest*) nongdamhada 농담하다. *You must be ~ding.* Nongdamishigetchiyo. 농담이시겠지요.

kidnap *vt.* (*abduct*) yugoehada 유괴하다, napch'ihae kada 납치해 가다. *I understand you have very few ~ping cases in Korea.* Han-gugenŭn yugoe sakŏni aju chŏktajiyo. 한국에는 유괴 사건이 아주 적다지요.

kidney *n.* shinjang 신장, k'ongp'at 콩팥.

kill *vt.,vi.* chugida 죽이다. *He was ~ed in a railway accident.* Kŭnŭn ch'ŏlto sagoro chugŏssŭmnida. 그는 철도 사고로 죽었읍니다/ *~ oneself* chasarhada 자살하다.

kind *n.* (*sort*) chongnyu 종류. —*adj.* (*tender*) ch'injŏrhan 친절한. *What ~ of work are you in?* Musŭn irŭl hago kyeshimnikka? 무슨 일을 하고 계십니까/ *What ~ of a man would you like for a husband?* Namp'yŏnŭro ŏttŏn saramŭl choahamnikka? 남편으로 어떤 사람을 좋아합니까/ *May I have another glass of the same ~?* Kat'ŭn kŏsŭro han chan tŏ chuseyo. 같은 것으로 한 잔

더 주세요/ *Will you be ~ enough to close the door?* Mian-hajiman mun chom tada chushigessŭmnikka? 미안하지만 문 좀 닫아 주시겠읍니까/ *~ of (somewhat)* taso 다소/ *You look ~ of tired.* Tangshinŭn chom chich'in kŏt ka-sso. 당신은 좀 지친 것 같소.

kindergarten *n.* yuch'iwŏn 유치원.

kindly *adj.* ch'injŏrhan 친절한. *—adv.* ch'injŏrhage 친절하게, *(agreeably)* kikkŏi 기꺼이. *Will you ~ show me the way to the station?* Yŏguro kanŭn kil chom kari-k'yŏ chushigessŭmnikka? 역으로 가는 길 좀 가리켜 주시겠읍니까?

kindness *n.* *(goodness)* ch'injŏl 친절, *(love)* aejŏng 애정, *(favor)* hoŭi 호의, *(kind behavior)* ch'injŏrhan t'aedo 친절한 태도. *Thank you for your ~.* Ch'injŏrhi hae chu-syŏsŏ kamsahamnida. 친절히 해 주셔서 감사합니다/ *Do me the ~ to hold your tongues.* Chebal chom choyong-hi hae chushio. 제발 좀 조용히 해 주시오.

king *n.* wang 왕. *the great ~* widaehan wang 위대한 왕/ *the late ~* sŏnwang 선왕(先王).

kingdom *n.* *(monarchical state)* wangguk 왕국, *(realm)* yŏngyŏk 영역, *(domain)* ...kye ...계. *the animal ~* tongmulgye 동물계/ *the ~ of science* kwahakkye 과학계.

kiss *n.* k'isŭ 키스, immatch'um 입맞춤. *—vt.* immatch'u-da 입맞추다, k'isŭhada 키스하다. *Do me a~, won't you?* K'isŭhae chushigesso? 키스해 주시겠소?

kitchen *n.* puŏk 부엌, chubang 주방. *~ maid* kajŏngbu 가정부.

kite *n.* *(bird)* solgae 솔개, *(toy)* yŏn 연(鳶). *~ flying* yŏnnalligi 연날리기.

kitten *n.* *(young cat)* saekki koyangi 새끼 고양이, *(flapper girl)* malgwal-lyangi 말괄량이.

knapsack *n.* paenang 배낭.

knead *vt.* *(dough)* panjuk'ada 반죽하다, *(massage)* anmahada 안마하다.

⟨yŏn⟩

knee *n.* murŭp 무릎. *I begged her forgiveness on my ~s.* Murŭbŭl kkulk'o kŭnyŏŭi yongsŏrŭl pirŏssŭmnida.

무릎을 꿇고 그녀의 용서를 빌었읍니다.

kneel *vi.* murŭbŭl kkult'a 무릎을 꿇다. *Everyone knelt in prayer.* Modŭn sarami murŭbŭl kkulk'o kidohaessŭmnida. 모든 사람이 무릎을 꿇고 기도했읍니다.

knife *n.* k'al 칼, naip'ŭ 나이프. *a kitchen* ~ puŏkk'al 부엌칼/ *a pocket* ~ chumŏnik'al 주머니칼/ *sharpen a* ~ k'arŭl kalda 칼을 갈다/ *Would you please lend me your* ~? K'al chom pillyŏ chushigessŭmnikka? 칼 좀 빌려 주시겠읍니까?

knit *vt.,vi.* (*yarn*) ttŭda 뜨다, (*joint*) chŏp'ap'ada 접합하다, (*unite*) kyŏrhap'ada 결합하다. ~ *wool into stockings* t'ŏlshillo yangmarŭl ttŭda 털실로 양말을 뜨다.

knitting *n.* ttŭgaejil 뜨개질. *a* ~ *machine* p'yŏnmulgi 편물기.

knob *n.* sonjabi 손잡이. *a door* ~ mun sonjabi 문 손잡이/ *This* ~ *doesn't work.* I sonjabinŭn kojangimnida. 이 손잡이는 고장입니다.

knock *vt.,vi.* (*rap*) tudŭrida 두드리다, (*strike*) ch'ida 치다. —*n.* (*blow*) kut'a 구타, (*rap*) tudŭrim 두드림, (*boxing*) noktaun 녹다운. *Come in, don't* ~. Tŭrŏoshio, nok'ŭhal p'iryoga ŏpsŭmnida. 들어오시오, 노크할 필요가 없읍니다/ *Someone is* ~*ing at the door.* Nugun-gaga munŭl tudŭrigo issŭmnida. 누군가가 문을 두드리고 있읍니다/ *Please* ~ *at the door before entering.* Tŭrŏogi chŏne nok'ŭrŭl hashipshio. 들어오기 전에 노크를 하십시오/ *He was* ~*ed out in one round.* Kŭ saramŭn ch'ŏt raundŭesŏ noktaun tanghaessŭmnida. 그 사람은 첫 라운드에서 녹다운 당했읍니다.

knot *n.* (*tie*) maedŭp 매듭. —*vt.,vi.* maetta 맺다. *undo a* ~ maedŭbŭl p'ulda 매듭을 풀다.

know *vt.,vi.* (*understand*) alda 알다, (*recognize*) injŏnghada 인정하다, (*be acquainted with*) …wa anŭn saida …와 아는 사이다. *Do you* ~ *Korean?* Han-gungmarŭl ashimnikka? 한국말을 아십니까/ *I* ~ *him to be honest.* Kŭ sarami chŏngjik'adanŭn kŏsŭl algo issŭmnida. 그 사람이 정직하다는 것을 알고 있읍니다/ *I* ~ *him by his voice.* Ŭmsŏngŭro kŭ saramŭl al su issŭmnida. 음성으로 그 사

람을 알 수 있읍니다/ *Be sure to let me* ~, *okay?* Kkok allyŏ chuseyo, ashigetchiyo? 꼭 알려 주세요, 아시겠지요/ *Have you known him long?* Kŭbun-gwa ashin chi orae toeshimnikka? 그분과 아신 지 오래 되십니까?

know-how *n.* (*Am.*) (*knowledge*) chishik 지식, (*technique*) kisul 기술, (*method*) pigyŏl 비결. *scientific* ~ kwahak chŏk ch'ŏri pangbŏp 과학적 처리 방법.

knowledge *n.* (*information*) chishik 지식, (*perception*) inshik 인식, (*understanding*) ihae 이해, (*familiarity*) ch'insuk 친숙, (*learning*) hangmun 학문. *gain* ~ chishigŭl ŏtta 지식을 얻다/ *up-to-date* ~ ch'oeshinŭi chishik 최신의 지식/ *I have no* ~ *of his whereabout.* Kŭ sarami ŏdi innŭnji morŭgessŭmnida. 그 사람이 어디 있는지 모르겠읍니다/ *Has he any* ~ *of Korean?* Kŭ saramŭn Han-gungmarŭl algo issŭmnikka? 그 사람은 한국말을 알고 있읍니까/ *My* ~ *of Mr. Park is slight.* Nanŭn Pakssirŭl chal morŭmnida. 나는 박씨를 잘 모릅니다/ *to one's* ~ (*so far as one knows*) anŭn pa-enŭn 아는 바에는.

knuckle *n.* (*finger-joint*) sonkarak madi 손가락 마디, (*knee-joint*) murŭp kwanjŏl 무릎 관절. —*vi.,vt.* chumŏgŭro ch'ida 주먹으로 치다.

Korea *n.* Han-guk 한국. *The Republic of K* ~ Taehanmin-guk 대한민국/ *North K* ~ Puk'an 북한/ *Oh you are from Korea, are you?* Han-gugesŏ oshin punigunyo. 한국에서 오신 분이군요.

Korean *adj.* Han-gugŭi 한국의. —*n.* (*person*) Han-gugin 한국인, (*language*) Han-gugŏ 한국어. *Where can I buy the* ~ *History?* Ŏdisŏ Han-guksarŭl sal su issŭmnikka? 어디서 한국사를 살 수 있읍니까/ *What do you call it in* ~? Kŭgŏsŭl Han-gungmallo muŏrago hamnikka? 그것을 한국말로 무어라고 합니까/ *a* ~ *American* Han-gukkye Migugin 한국계 미국인.

—≪ **L** ≫—

label *n.* ttakchi 딱지, ret'erŭ 레테르. —*vt.* ttakchirŭl

puch'ida 딱지를 붙이다.

labo(u)r *n.* nodong 노동. ~ *dispute* nodong punjaeng 노동 분쟁/ *L~ Day* nodongjŏl 노동절/ *L~ Union* nodong chohap 노동 조합.   「부두 노동자.

labo(u)rer *n.* nodongja 노동자. *a dock* ~ pudu nodongja

lace *n.* (*fabric*) reisŭ 레이스, (*of boots*) kudukkŭn 구두 끈. *undo the* ~ *of boots* kudukkŭnŭl p'ulda 구두끈을 풀 다. —*vt.,vi.* kkŭnŭro mukta〔maeŏjida〕 끈으로 묶다〔매 어지다〕.

lack *n.* (*deficiency*) kyŏlp'ip 결핍, (*shortage*) pujok 부 족. —*vt.,vi.* (*be wanting*) …i ŏpta …이 없다. ~ *of sleep* sumyŏn pujok 수면 부족/ *the* ~ *of funds* chagŭm pujok 자금 부족/ *We don't* ~ *for food.* Shingnyangi pujok'a- jinŭn anssŭmnida. 식량이 부족하지는 않습니다.

lacquer *n.* ot 옻, raek'ŏ 래커. *What are these* ~*ed dishes used for?* I ch'ilgi chŏpshinŭn muŏse ssŭmnikka? 이 칠 기 접시는 무엇에 쑵니까/ ~*ed ware* ch'ilgi 칠기.

lad *n.* (*youth*) chŏlmŭni 젊은이, (*boy*) sonyŏn 소년. *a promising* ~ yumanghan ch'ŏngnyŏn 유망한 청년.

ladder *n.* sadaktari 사다리. *Steady the* ~ *while I get on.* Naega orŭnŭn tongane sadaktarirŭl kkok puttŭrŏ chuseyo. 내가 오르는 동안에 사다리를 꼭 붙들어 주세요.

ladle *n.* kukcha 국자.

lady *n.* kwibuin 귀부인, sungnyŏ 숙녀, puin 부인. *ladies and gentlemen* shinsa sungnyŏ 신사 숙녀/ *young* ~ agassi 아가씨/ *a* ~ *doctor* yŏŭisa 여의사/ *the first* ~ taet'ong- nyŏng puin 대통령 부인/ ~*-killer* saekkol 색골/ *Are you the* ~ *of the house?* I taek ajumŏnishimnikka? 이 댁 아주머니십니까/ *Where is the* ~*'s room?* Hwajangshirŭn ŏdijiyo? 화장실은 어디지요?

ladylike *adj.* (*genteel*) chŏmjanŭn 점잖은, (*fragile*) yu- yak'an 유약한.

lake *n.* hosu 호수, (*in compound words*) ho 호. *Sanjong L~* Sanjŏng hosu 산정(山井) 호수.

lame *adj.* chŏllŭmbari 절름발이. *walk* ~ chŏlttukkŏrida 절뚝거리다/ ~ *in the left leg* oentchok tarirŭl chŏlda 왼 쪽 다리를 절다.

lamp *n.* laemp'ŭ 램프, tŭng 등(燈). *an electric* ~ chŏndŭng 전등/ *a phosphorescent* ~ hyŏnggwangdŭng 형광등/ ~ *shade* raemp'ŭŭi kat 램프의 갓.

lance *n.* ch'ang 창(槍).

land *n.* (*soil*) ttang 땅, yukchi 육지, (*state*) nara 나라, (*district*) chibang 지방. —*vi.,vt.* (*disembark*) sangnyuk'ada 상륙하다, (*alight*) ch'angnyuk'ada 착륙하다. *Do you own much* ~ *here*? Yŏgi soyujiga manssŭmnikka? 여기 소유지가 많습니까/ *Are you going by* ~ *or by sea?* Yungnoro kashimnikka, animyŏn haeroro kashimnikka? 육로로 가십니까, 아니면 해로로 가십니까/ *We shall* ~ *at Kimpo Airport in five minutes.* Obun humyŏn Kimp'o konghange ch'angnyuk'amnida. 5분 후면 김포 공항에 착륙합니다.

landing *n.* sangnyuk 상륙, ch'angnyuk 착륙, (*a platform in a staircase*) ch'ŭnggyech'am 층계참. ~ *field* pihaengjang 비행장/ ~ *strip* hwalchuro 활주로/ *make a forced* ~ pulshich'ak'ada 불시착하다.

landlord *n.* chuin 주인, kajang 가장.

landscape *n.* p'unggyŏng 풍경, chŏnmang 전망.

lane *n.* (*narrow road*) chobŭn kil 좁은 길, (*alley*) kolmokkil 골목길.

language *n.* (*human speech*) ŏnŏ 언어, mal 말, (*in compound words*) ŏ 어(語). *Korean* ~ Han-gugŏ 한국어/ *English* ~ Yŏngŏ 영어/ *Chinese* ~ Chunggugŏ 중국어/ *foreign* ~ oegugŏ 외국어/ *What's the* ~ *of Korea?* Han-gugŭi ŏnŏnŭn muŏshimnikka? 한국의 언어는 무엇입니까/ *What is your first* ~ ? Mogugŏnŭn muŏshijiyo? 모국어는 무엇이지요?

lantern *n.* ch'orong 초롱. *a paper* ~ chedŭng 제등(提燈)/ *a* ~ *procession* chedŭng haengnyŏl 제등 행렬.

lap *n.* murŭp 무릎. —*vt.* (*lick*) halta 핥다, (*enfold*) ssada 싸다. *The mother had the baby on her* ~ . Ŏmŏninŭn chŏnmŏgirŭl murŭbe anko issŏssŭmnida. 어머니는 젖먹이를 무릎에 안고 있었읍니다.

lapse *n.* (*passing*) kyŏnggwa 경과, (*error*) kwashil 과실. *after a three-month* ~ samgaewŏri chinan twi 3개월

이 지난 뒤/ *a ~ of memory* kiŏgǔi ch'ago 기억의 착오.

lard *n.* twaeji kirǔm 돼지 기름, radǔ 라드.

large *adj.* (*big*) k'ǔn 큰, (*spacious*) nŏlbǔn 넓은, (*numerous*) manǔn 많은, (*liberal*) kwandaehan 관대한. *a ~ room* nŏrǔn pang 너른 방/ *a ~ income* k'ǔn suip 큰 수입/ *a ~ population* manǔn in-gu 많은 인구/ *a ~ heart* kwandaehan maǔm 관대한 마음.

lark *n.* (*skylark*) chongdari 종다리, chongdalsae 종달새.

lash *n.* (*of whip*) ch'aetchik kkǔn 채찍 끈, (*eyelash*) songnunssǒp 속눈썹. —*vt.,vi.* (*thrash*) ttaerida 때리다.

lass *n.* (*girl, maid*) sonyŏ 소녀.

last *adj.* (*final*) ch'oehuǔi 최후의, (*latest*) ch'oegǔnǔi 최근의. —*adv.* ch'oehuro 최후로, majimagǔro 마지막으로. —*n.* (*end*) ch'oehu 최후, chongmal 종말. —*vi.* (*continue*) kyesok'ada 계속하다, (*endure*) kyŏndida 견디다. *Where were you ~ night?* Ŏjetpame ŏdi kyesyŏtchiyo? 어젯 밤에 어디 계셨지요/ *When were you ~ in New York?* Ch'oegǔn Nyuyoge kyesyŏttŏn ke ŏnjeimnikka? 최근 뉴욕에 계셨던 게 언제입니까/ *I'm planning a little trip about the ~ of this month.* Idal malkke kandanhan yŏhaengǔl ttŏnal yejŏngimnida. 이달 말께 간단한 여행을 떠날 예정입니다/ *How long will the fine weather ~?* Choǔn nalssiga ŏlmana kyesoktoelkkayo? 좋은 날씨가 얼마나 계속될까요?

lasting *adj.* (*durable*) kyesoktoenǔn 계속되는, (*enduring*) orae kanǔn 오래 가는, (*permanent*) yŏnggujŏgin 영구적인.

latch *n.* kŏlsoe 걸쇠, pitchang 빗장. —*vt.,vi.* kŏlsoerǔl kŏlda 걸쇠를 걸다.

late *adj.* (*opp. early*) nǔjǔn 늦은, (*recent*) ch'oegǔnǔi 최근의, (*dead*) chakkohan 작고한, ko 고(故). —*adv.* nǔjŏsŏ 늦어서. *I'm sorry to be ~.* Nǔjŏ mianhamnida. 늦어 미안합니다/ *I am afraid we are ~.* Ammanhaedo nǔjǔl kŏt katkunyo. 암만해도 늦을 것 같군요/ *I'll be about 10 minutes ~.* Shippun chŏngdo nǔjǔl kŏt kassǔmnida. 10분 정도 늦을 것 같습니다/ *the ~st news* ch'oeshin nyusǔ 최신 뉴스/ *her ~ husband* koini toen namp'yŏn 고인이 된 남편, mangbu 망부(亡夫)/ *the ~ Dr. Chang* ko Chang paksa 고(故) 장 박사.

lately *adv.* (*of late*) ch'oegŭn 최근, yojŭŭm 요즈음.

later *adj.* tŏ nŭjŭn 더 늦은. —*adv.* hue 후에, najunge 나중에. *See you ~*. Najunge poepkessŭmnida. 나중에 뵙겠읍니다/ *I will call ~*. Najunge chŏnhwa kŏlgessŭmnida. 나중에 전화 걸겠읍니다.

lather *n.* pinu kŏp'um 비누 거품.

Latin *adj.* Rat'inŭi 라틴의. —*n.* (*language*) Rat'inŏ 라틴어, (*person*) Rat'in saram 라틴 사람. *L~ America* chungnammi chiyŏk 중남미 지역/ *the ~ language* Rat'inŏ 라틴어.

latitude *n.* wido 위도. *north ~* pugwi 북위/ *38 degrees north ~* samp'alsŏn 38선(線).

latter *adj.* twiŭi 뒤의, hujaŭi 후자의. —*n.* (*the ~*) huja 후자. *the ~ half of the year* haban-gi 하반기(下半期)/ *I have a brother and a sister; the former is in Pusan, but the ~ is in Kwangju.* Naegenŭn hyŏngnimgwa nunimi issŭmnida. Chŏnjanŭn Pusane itko, hujanŭn Kwangjue samnida. 내게는 형님과 누님이 있읍니다. 전자는 부산에 있고, 후자는 광주에 삽니다.

laugh *vi.,vt.* utta 웃다. —*n.* usŭm 웃음. *~ loudly* kkŏlkkŏl utta 껄껄 웃다. *What are you ~ing at?* Mwŏl pogo utko issŭmnikka? 뭘 보고 웃고 있읍니까/ *We had a good ~ over it.* Kŭraesŏ urinŭn hanbat'ang usŏssŭmnida. 그래서 우리는 한바탕 웃었읍니다/ *burst into a ~* usŭmŭl t'ŏttŭrida 웃음을 터뜨리다/ *an agreeable ~* k'waehwarhan usŭm 쾌활한 웃음/ *~ at ...*ŭl piutta ...을 비웃다.

laughingstock *n.* usŭmkŏri 웃음거리. *become a ~ for others* namŭi usŭmkŏriga toeda 남의 웃음거리가 되다.

laughter *n.* usŭm 웃음. *burst into ~* usŭmŭl t'ŏttŭrida 웃음을 터뜨리다/ *an outburst of ~* p'okso 폭소.

launch *vt.,vi.* (*set afloat*) chinsushik'ida 진수시키다, (*start*) shijak'ada 시작하다. —*n.* (*a steam boat*) ttokttaksŏn 똑딱선. *~ing ceremony* chinsushik 진수식.

laundry *n.* (*room, building*) set'akso 세탁소, (*clothes,* *etc.*) set'angmul 세탁물, ppallaetkam 빨랫감. *I'd like to send a couple of shirts to* ~ . Syassŭ tu pŏrŭl set'akso-e ponaeyagessŭmnida. 샤쓰 두 벌을 세탁소에 보내야겠읍니다/ *I haven't received my* ~ *yet.* Ajik set'angmuri an torawassŭmnida. 아직 세탁물이 안 돌아왔읍니다.

laurel *n.* (*tree*) wŏlgyesu 월계수.

lavatory *n.* (*for washing one's hands, etc.*) semyŏnso 세면소, hwajangshil 화장실, (*privy*) pyŏnso 변소. *Where is the* ~? Hwajangshirŭn ŏdijyo? 화장실은 어디죠/ *May I use your* ~? Hwajangshil chom ssŭgo shipsŭmnida. 화장실 좀 쓰고 싶습니다.

lavish *vt.* (*spend freely*) nangbihada 낭비하다. —*adj.* (*generous*) taebŏmhan 대범한. ~ *money on the poor* kananhan saramŭl wihae akkimŏpshi tonŭl ssŭda 가난한 사람을 위해 아낌없이 돈을 쓰다.

law *n.* pŏp 법, pŏmnyul 법률. *the constitutional* ~ hŏnpŏp 헌법/ *civil* ~ minpŏp 민법/ *martial* ~ kyeŏmnyŏng 계엄령/ *the anti-communist* ~ pan-gongpŏp 반공법/ *We are equal before the* ~. Pŏp ap'esŏ urinŭn ta p'yŏngdŭnghamnida. 법 앞에서 우리는 다 평등합니다.

lawn *n.* (*sod*) chandi 잔디. ~ *mower* chandi kkangnŭn kigye 잔디 깎는 기계.

lawyer *n.* (*jurist*) pŏmnyulga 법률가, (*attorney*) pyŏnhosa 변호사. *Who is to act as* ~ *for him?* Nuga kŭ saramŭi pyŏnhosaga toel kŏshimnikka? 누가 그 사람의 변호사가 될 것입니까?

laxative *n.* haje 하제, wanwhaje 완화제

lay *vt.,vi.* (*cause to lie*) nup'ida 눕히다, (*put*) not'a 놓다, (*eggs*) nat'a 낳다. *I laid myself upon the bed.* Nanŭn ch'imdaee nuwŏssŭmnida. 나는 침대에 누웠읍니다/ *L*~ *it on the table.* T'eibŭl wie kŭgŏsŭl tushio. 테이블 위에 그것을 두시오/ *How many eggs does this hen* ~ *each week?* I amt'agŭn maeju arŭl myŏt kae nassŭmnikka? 이 암탉은 매주 알을 몇 개 낳습니까/ *Are your hens* ~*ing yet?* Tangshinne amt'agŭn pŏlssŏ arŭl nassŭmnikka? 당신네 암탉은 벌써 알을 낳습니까?

lazy *adj.* (*idle*) keŭrŭn 게으른, (*sluggish*) nŭrin 느린.

a ~ fellow keŭrŭmjangi 게으름장이/ *You're the laziest man I have ever seen.* Tangshingach'i keŭrŭn saramŭn saengjŏn ch'ŏŭm poassŭmnida. 당신같이 게으른 사람은 생전 처음 보았읍니다.

lead *n.* (*metal*) nap 납, (*guidance*) chido 지도. —*vt.,vi.* (*guide*) annaehada 안내하다, (*direct*) chihwihada 지휘하다, (*run*) tadarŭda 다다르다. *May I ~ the way?* Naega annaehae tŭrilkkayo? 내가 안내해 드릴까요/ *Who's going to ~ off?* Nuga mŏnjŏ shijak'amnikka? 누가 먼저 시작합니까/ *Where does this road ~?* Igŏn ŏdi kanŭn kirijiyo? 이건 어디 가는 길이지요/ *I don't think it will ~ to a good result.* Choŭn kyŏlgwarŭl kajyŏooriragonŭn saenggakchi anssŭmnida. 좋은 결과를 가져오리라고는 생각지 않습니다.

leader *n.* (*chief*) t'ongsolcha 통솔자, (*guide*) chidoja 지도자, (*mus.*) chihwija 지휘자. *a band ~* aktae chihwija 악대 지휘자/ *a cheer ~* ŭngwŏndanjang 응원단장.

leadership *n.* chihwi 지휘, t'ongsol 통솔.

leading *adj.* (*chief*) chuyohan 주요한. —*n.* (*guidance*) chido 지도, (*direction*) chihwi 지휘. *a ~ part* chuyŏk 주역(主役)/ *a ~ singer* illyu kasu 일류 가수/ *Who is the ~ character of the play?* I yŏn-gŭgŭi chuyŏgŭn nuguimnikka? 이 연극의 주역은 누구입니까?

leaf *n.* (*of plant*) ip 잎, (*petal*) kkonnip 꽃잎, (*page*) ch'aekchang 책장. *fallen ~* nagyŏp 낙엽/ *tinted leaves* tanp'ung 단풍/ *This book wants two leaves.* I ch'aegŭn tu changi ppajyŏ issŭmnida. 이 책은 두 장이 빠져 있읍니다.

leaflet *n.* (*young leaf*) chagŭn ip 작은 잎, (*printed sheet*) rip'ŭllet 리플렛.

league *n.* (*alliance*) tongmaeng 동맹, (*confederation*) yŏnmaeng 연맹. *the L~ of Nations* kukche yŏnmaeng 국제 연맹/ *a ~ game* rigŭjŏn 리그전(戰).

leak *n.* (*crack*) saenŭn kumŏng 새는 구멍, (*liquid getting out*) saenŭn mul 새는 물. —*vi.,vt.* saeda 새다. *~ a secret* pimirŭl nusŏrhada 비밀을 누설하다/ *Who ~ed the news to the press?* Kŭ nyusŭrŭl nuga shinmune allyŏssŭmnikka? 그 뉴스를 누가 신문에 알렸읍니까?

leakage *n.* (*leak*) saeŏnaom 새어나옴, (*of electricity*) nujŏn 누전, (*transpiring*) t'allo 탄로. *electric* ~ nujŏn 누전.

lean *adj.* (*thin*) yŏwin 여윈, (*meager*) memarŭn 메마른, (*barren*) pulmoŭi 불모의. —*vi.,vt.* (*bend toward*) kiurŏjida 기울어지다, (*rely on*) kidaeda 기대다. *a* ~ *person* mallakkaengi 말라깽이/ ~ *against the wall* pyŏge kidaeda 벽에 기대다.

leap *vi.,vt.* (*jump*) ttwida 뛰다. —*n.* (*bound*) ttwigi 뛰기. ~ *into a taxi* t'aekshie ttwiŏorŭda 택시에 뛰어오르다.

learn *vt.,vi.* paeuda 배우다, (*memorize*) oeda 외다, (*become informed*) alda 알다, (*hear*) tŭtta 듣다. *Where did you* ~ *Japanese?* Ŏdisŏ Ilbonŏrŭl paewŏssŭmnikka? 어디서 일본어를 배웠읍니까/ *I* ~*ed English under a foreign teacher.* Oegugin kyosa mit'esŏ Yŏngŏrŭl paewŏssŭmnida. 외국인 교사 밑에서 영어를 배웠읍니다.

learned *adj.* (*well-informed*) hakshigi innŭn 학식이 있는. *a* ~ *man* hakcha 학자.

learning *n.* (*knowledge*) hangmun 학문, (*erudition*) hakshik 학식, (*studying*) haksŭp 학습.

lease *n.* (*contract*) imdaech'a kyeyak 임대차 계약. —*vt.* imdaehada 임대하다, sedŭlda 세들다. *I have a long* ~ *of this house.* Changgi kyeyagŭro i chibŭl pilligo issŭmnida. 장기 계약으로 이 집을 빌리고 있읍니다.

least *adj.* (*smallest*) ch'oesoŭi 최소의. —*adv.* kajang chŏkke 가장 적게. —*n.* ch'oeso(ryang) 최소(량). *at* ~ chŏgŏdo 적어도, ch'oesohan 최소한/ *You'll need ten thousand won at* ~. Chŏgŏdo manwŏnŭn p'iryohal kŏshimnida. 적어도 만원은 필요할 것입니다/ *I am not in the* ~ *afraid of it.* Kŭrŏn kŏsŭn chogŭmdo turyŏpchi anssŭmnida. 그런 것은 조금도 두렵지 않습니다.

leather *n.* kajuk 가죽, p'ihyŏk 피혁, kajuk kabang 가죽 가방. *a* ~ *belt* kajuk tti 가죽 띠/ ~ *gloves* kajuk changgap 가죽 장갑.

leave *vi.,vt.* (*depart*) ttŏnada 떠나다, (*not touch*) kŭdaero tuda 그대로 두다, (*depart without taking*) tugo kada

두고 가다, (*allow*) pangch'ihada 방치하다. —*n.* (*permission*) hŏrak 허락, (*holiday*) hyuga 휴가, (*farewell*) chakpyŏl 작별. *What time does this bus ~?* I pŏsŭnŭn myŏt shie ttŏnamnikka? 이 버스는 몇 시에 떠납니까/ *Tonight I'm leaving for Pusan.* Onŭlpam Pusanŭro ttŏnamnida. 오늘밤 부산으로 떠납니다/ *May I ~ my baggage here until Sunday?* Iryoilkkaji chimŭl yŏgi tuŏdo chossŭmnikka? 일요일까지 짐을 여기 두어도 좋습니까/ *I have left my bag on the bus.* Paegŭl pŏsŭe nok'o naeryŏssŭmnida. 백을 버스에 놓고 내렸읍니다/ *Please ~ it if you don't feel like eating it.* Chapsushigi kŏbuk'ashimyŏn namgishijiyo. 잡수시기 거북하시면 남기시지요/ *Grant me ~ of absence for a week.* Ilchuilgan kyŏlgŭnŭl hŏgahae chushipshio. 1주일간 결근을 허가해 주십시오/ *I took my ~.* Hyugarŭl ŏdŏssŭmnida. 휴가를 얻었읍니다.

lecture *n.* (*discourse*) kangŭi 강의, (*speech*) kangyŏn 강연, (*scolding*) hun-gye 훈계. *a ~ on Korean history* Han-guksa-e kwanhan kangŭi 한국사에 관한 강의.

lecturer *n.* yŏnsa 연사, (*of college*) kangsa 강사. *a full-time ~* chŏnim kangsa 전임 강사.

leech *n.* kŏmŏri 거머리.

leek *n.* puch'u 부추.

left *adj.* oentchogŭi 왼쪽의. —*n.* oentchok 왼쪽. *on the ~* oentchoge 왼쪽에/ *to the ~* oentchogŭro 왼쪽으로/ *the ~ side* chwach'ŭk 좌측/ *the ~-hand* oenson 왼손/ *~ wing* chwaik 좌익/ *~-handed* oensonjabiŭi 왼손잡이의/ *a ~-handed person* oensonjabi 왼손잡이/ *Make a turn to the ~ at the next corner.* Taŭm mot'ungiesŏ oentchogŭro toshio. 다음 모퉁이에서 왼쪽으로 도시오.

leftist *n.* chwap'a 좌파, kŭpchinp'a 급진파.

leftover *n.* namŏji 나머지, chanjonmul 잔존물.

leg *n.* tari 다리. *long ~s* kin tari 긴 다리/ *the ~s of a table* ch'aeksang tari 책상 다리/ *artificial ~* ŭijok 의족 (義足)/ *bandy ~* antchangdari 안짱다리/ *I hurt my ~.* Tarirŭl tach'yŏssŭmnida. 다리를 다쳤읍니다.

legacy *n.* yusan 유산.

legal *adj.* pŏmnyurŭi 법률의, happŏpchŏgin 합법적인. *a* ~ *adviser* pŏmnyul komun 법률 고문/ ~ *interest* pŏpchŏng ija 법정 이자/ ~ *wife* ponch'ŏ 본처.

legation *n.* kongsagwan 공사관. *the staff of the Korean L*~ Han-guk kongsagwan chigwŏn 한국 공사관 직원.

legend *n.* chŏnsŏl 전설.

legendary *adj.* chŏnsŏlchŏgin 전설적인. ~ *heroes* chŏnsŏl-sangŭi yŏngungdŭl 전설상의 영웅들.

leggings *n.* (*pl.*) kakpan 각반, chŏnggangibaji 정강이받이.

legible *adj.* (*easily read*) ikki shwiun 읽기 쉬운. ~ *writing* ikki shwiun p'ilchŏk 읽기 쉬운 필적.

legislation *n.* (*making of laws*) ippŏp 입법, (*laws*) pŏmnyul 법률.

legislature *n.* (*law-making body*) ippŏppu 입법부.

legitimate *adj.* (*lawful*) happŏbŭi 합법의, (*reasonable*) hamnijŏgin 합리적인, (*regular*) chŏngt'ongŭi 정통의. *a* ~ *child* chŏkcha 적자(嫡子)/ *a* ~ *drama* ponkyŏk kŭk 본격 극.

leisure *n.* (*spare time*) yŏga 여가, t'ŭm 틈. *I am seldom at* ~. Nanŭn chomch'ŏrŏm tchami ŏpsŭmnida. 나는 좀처럼 짬이 없습니다/ *I shall be at* ~ *the day after tomorrow.* Morenŭn t'ŭmi issŭl kŏmnida. 모레는 틈이 있을 겁니다.

lemonade *n.* remonsu 레몬수, remoneidŭ 레모네이드.

lend *vt.* (*loan*) pillyŏ chuda 빌려 주다. *Will you* ~ *me your dictionary?* Sajŏn chom pillyŏ chushigessŭmnikka? 사전 좀 빌려 주시겠읍니까/ *I will* ~ *you my ball pen.* Nae polp'enŭl pillyŏ tŭrijiyo. 내 볼펜을 빌려 드리지요.

lender *n.* pillyŏ chunŭn saram 빌려 주는 사람. *money* ~ taegŭmŏpcha 대금업자.

length *n.* kiri 길이. *What is its* ~? Kirinŭn ŏlmana toemnikka? 길이는 얼마나 됩니까/ *It measures 20 meters in* ~. Kirinŭn iship mit'ŏimnida. 길이는 20미터입니다/ *I feel the* ~ *of your skirt is too short.* Tangshin ch'ima-nŭn nŏmu tchalbŭn kŏt kassŭmnida. 당신 치마는 너무 짧은 것 같습니다/ *at* ~ (*at last*) tŭdiŏ 드디어.

lengthen *vt., vi.* (*make longer*) kilge hada 길게 하다,

(*prolong*) nŭrida 늘이다, (*grow longer*) kirŏjida 길어
지다. *The days ~ in March.* Samwŏrenŭn haega kirŏ-
jimnida. 3월에는 해가 길어집니다.

lens *n.* renjŭ 렌즈. *a ~ of eyeglasses* an-gyŏng renjŭ
안경 렌즈/ *train the ~es on* renjŭrŭl match'uda 렌즈를
맞추다.

leopard *n.* (*panther*) p'yobŏm 표범.

less *adj.* (*in size*) poda chagŭn 보다 작은, (*in quantity*)
poda chŏgŭn 보다 적은. *—adv.* poda chŏkke 보다 적게.
The height of the tree is ~ than that of the tower. Chŏ
namuŭi nop'inŭn chŏ t'ap nop'iboda nassŭmnida. 저 나무
의 높이는 저 탑 높이보다 낮습니다/ *I have ~ money than
you.* Tangshinboda kajin toni chŏksŭmnida. 당신보다 가
진 돈이 적습니다/ *Eat ~, drink ~.* Tŏl mŏkko, tŏl mashipshio. 덜 먹고 덜 마십시오.

lesson *n.* (*school subject*) hakkwa 학과, (*school work*)
suŏp 수업, (*chapter*) kwa 과(課), (*study*) kongbu 공부,
(*instruction*) kyohun 교훈. *Have you finished your
~s for tomorrow?* Naeil hakkwa yesŭbŭn mach'yŏssŭmnikka? 내일 학과 예습은 마쳤습니까/ *L~ three.*
chesamgwa 제 3 과/ *the first ~* cheilgwa 제 1 과/ *I am
taking ~s on the piano.* P'iano resŭnŭl patko issŭmnida.
피아노 레슨을 받고 있읍니다/ *I wish to take Korean ~s.*
Han-gugŏ kongburŭl hago shipsŭmnida. 한국어 공부를 하
고 싶습니다/ *What ~ do we have in the first hour?*
Ch'ŏtchae shiganŭn musŭn suŏbijiyo? 첫째 시간은 무슨
수업이지요/ *What ~ have you learned from this story?*
I iyagiesŏ ŏttŏn kyohunŭl padassŭmnikka? 이 이야기에
서 어떤 교훈을 받았읍니까?

let *vt.* ...shik'ida ...시키다, (*allow to*) ...hage hada ...하게
하다, (*lend*) pillida 빌리다. *L~ us go.* Kapshida. 갑시
다/ *L~ me take there.* Chega kŭ kosŭro moshigessŭmnida.
제가 그 곳으로 모시겠읍니다/ *Please ~ me know what
happens.* Musŭn iri issŭmyŏn pudi allyŏ chushipshio.
무슨 일이 있으면 부디 알려 주십시오/ *Let's start at once.*
Kot ttŏnapshida. 곧 떠납시다/ *Would you ~ me know
when the bus gets there?* Pŏsŭga kŭ kose taŭmyŏn allyŏ

chushigessŏyo? 버스가 그 곳에 닿으면 알려 주시겠어요/ *L~ me off at the 5th floor.* Och'ŭngesŏ naeryŏ chushio. 5 층에서 내려 주시오/ *L~ us pray.* Tagach'i kidohapshida. 다같이 기도합시다/ *L~ me alone.* Narŭl honja itke hae chushio. 나를 혼자 있게 해 주시오.

letter *n.* (*character*) kŭlcha 글자, muncha 문자, (*written message*) p'yŏnji 편지, sŏmyŏn 서면. *a capital* ~ taemuncha 대문자. *Please write in block* ~s. Hwalchach'ero ssŏ chushipshio. 활자체로 써 주십시오/ *To whom do you write* ~s? Nuguege p'yŏnjirŭl ssŭshimnikka? 누구에게 편지를 쓰십니까/ *I have some* ~s *to write.* Ssŏya hal p'yŏnjiga myŏt t'ong issŭmnida. 써야 할 편지가 몇 통 있읍니다/ *Thank you very much for your kind letter.* P'yŏnji komapke padassŭmnida. 편지 고맙게 받았읍니다/ *Please write me a* ~ *when you arrive there.* Toch'ak'ashimyŏn kot p'yŏnji chushipshio. 도착하시면 곧 편지 주십시오/ *Please forward my letters to this address.* Na-ege chushil p'yŏnjinŭn i chusoro ponae chushipshio. 나에게 주실 편지는 이 주소로 보내 주십시오/ *a love* ~ yŏnae p'yŏnji 연애 편지/ *a* ~ *of introduction* sogaechang 소개장/ *a* ~ *of recommendation* ch'uch'ŏnchang 추천장.

lettuce *n.* sangch'i 상치. ~-*wrapped rice* sangch'issam 상치쌈/ *I would like to have a cheeseburger with* ~ *and tomato.* Ch'ijŭbŏgŏrŭl sangch'iwa t'omat'orŭl kyŏttŭryŏ chushio. 치즈버거를 상치와 토마토를 결들여 주시오.

level *n.* (*plane surface*) sup'yŏng 수평, (*flat area*) p'yŏngji 평지. —*adj.* (*even*) p'yŏngp'yŏnghan 평평한, (*horizontal*) sup'yŏngŭi 수평의. *1,000 meters above sea* ~ haebal ch'ŏn mit'ŏ 해발 1,000 미터/ *water* ~ sujun 수준/ *cultural* ~ munhwa sujun 문화 수준/*the highest* ~ ch'oego sujun 최고 수준/*a* ~ *crossing* kŏnnŏlmok 건널목.

lever *n.* chirettae 지렛대.

levy *n.* (*assessment*) chingse 징세. —*vt.* (*assess*) pugwahada 부과하다, (*collect*) chingsuhada 징수하다, (*enrol*) sojip'ada 소집하다.

liable *adj.* (*apt*) ...hagi shwiun ...하기 쉬운, (*responsible*) ch'aegimi innŭn 책임이 있는, (*subject to*) pokchonghaeya hal 복종해야 할. *Is a man ~ for his wife's debts?* Nam-janŭn anaeŭi pijŭl kap'ŭl ch'aegimi issŭmnikka? 남자는 아내의 빚을 갚을 책임이 있읍니까/ *I am ~ to seasickness.* Nanŭn paenmŏlmirŭl chal hamnida. 나는 뱃멀미를 잘 합니다.

liaison *n.* (*mil.*) yŏllak 연락. *~ officer* yollak changgyo 연락 장교.

liar *n.* kŏjinmaljangi 거짓말장이. *You are a ~.* Kŏjinmal marara 거짓말 말아라.

liberal *adj.* (*generous*) huhan 후한, (*abundant*) p'ungbu-han 풍부한, (*free*) chayuroun 자유로운. *a ~ giver* akkimŏpshi chal chunŭn saram 아낌없이 잘 주는 사람/ *a ~ supply of food* p'ungbuhan shingnyang konggŭp 풍부한 식량 공급/ *~ education* kyoyang kyoyuk 교양 교육/ *the L~ Party* chayudang 자유당.

liberalism *n.* chayujuŭi 자유주의.

liberate *vi.* (*set free*) haebanghada 해방하다, (*release*) sŏkpanghada 석방하다. *~ a slave* noyerŭl haebanghada 노예를 해방하다.

liberty *n.* (*freedom*) chayu 자유, (*presumptuous act*) pangja 방자(放恣). *I shall be at ~ this afternoon.* Onŭl ohunŭn han-gahamnida. 오늘 오후는 한가합니다/ *You are at ~ to go or stay.* Kadŭn mŏmurŭdŭn tangshin chayuimnida. 가든 머무르든 당신 자유입니다.

library *n.* (*building*) tosŏgwan 도서관, (*study*) sŏjae 서재, (*collection of books*) changsŏ 장서. *Would you show me the way to the national ~?* Kungnip tosŏgwane kanŭn kirŭl karŭch'yŏ chushigessŭmnikka? 국립 도서관에 가는 길을 가르쳐 주시겠읍니까?

license *n.* (*authorization*) myŏnhŏ 면허, (*permission*) hŏrak 허락, (*certificate of permission*) myŏnhŏchang 면허장, kamch'al 감찰. *a driver's ~* chadongch'a unjŏn myŏnhŏ 자동차 운전 면허/ *a temporary ~* imshi myŏnhŏ 임시 면허/ *a ~ fee* myŏnhŏse 면허세/ *a business[trade] ~* yŏngŏp kamch'al 영업 감찰/ *Show me your ~.* Myŏn-hŏchangŭl poyŏ chushio. 면허장을 보여 주시오.

lick *vt.* halta 핥다. *The cat was ~ing its paws.* Koyang-iga che parŭl halko issŏssŭmnida. 고양이가 제 발을 핥고 있었읍니다.

lid *n.* (*cover*) ttukkŏng 뚜껑, (*eye~*) nunkkŏp'ul 눈꺼풀. *the ~ of a box* sangja ttukkŏng 상자 뚜껑/ *Take the ~ off.* Ttukkŏngŭl yŏshio. 뚜껑을 여시오/ *Put the ~ on.* Ttukkŏngŭl tadŭshio. 뚜껑을 닫으시오.

lie *vi.* (*~ down*) nupta 눕다, (*be situated*) wich'ihada 위치하다, (*speak falsely*) kŏjinmarhada 거짓말하다. —*n.* (*falsehood*) kŏjinmal 거짓말. *L~ down a moment.* Chamkkan nuushipshio. 잠깐 누우십시오/ *You are lying to me.* Na-ege kŏjinmarŭl hashinŭn-gunyo 나에게 거짓말을 하시는군요/ *Don't tell a ~!* Kŏjinmal mashio! 거짓말 마시오/ *Japan ~s to the east of Korea.* Ilbonŭn Han-gugŭi tongtchoge wich'ihago issŭmnida. 일본은 한국의 동쪽에 위치하고 있읍니다.

lieutenant *n.* (*army*) yukkun chungwi 육군 중위, (*navy*) haegun taewi 해군 대위. *a second ~* sowi 소위/ *~ general* yukkun chungnyŏng 육군 중령/ *~ commander* haegun soryŏng 해군 소령.

life *n.* (*power of living*) saengmyŏng 생명, (*duration of existence*) sumyŏng 수명, ilsaeng 일생, (*manner of existence*) saenghwal 생활, (*biography*) chŏn-gi 전기(傳記), (*liveliness*) hwalgi 활기. *Is there any ~ on the planet Mars?* Hwasŏngenŭn saengmuri issŭmnikka? 화성에는 생물이 있읍니까/ *a busy ~* pappŭn saenghwal 바쁜 생활/ *a frugal ~* kŏmsohan saenghwal 검소한 생활/ *happy ~* haengbok'an saenghwal 행복한 생활/ *modern ~* hyŏndae saenghwal 현대 생활/ *urban ~* toshi saenghwal 도시 생활/ *Do you enjoy reading the lives of great men?* Wiinjŏnŭl chŭlgyŏ ilgŭshimnikka? 위인전을 즐겨 읽으십니까/ *Put more ~ into your work.* Ire chomdŏ chŏngnyŏgŭl ssodŭshipshio. 일에 좀더 정력을 쏟으십시오/ *~boat* kumyŏngjŏng 구명정/ *~ member* chongshin hoewŏn 종신 회원/ *~ sentence* mugi chingyŏk 무기 징역.

lift *vt., vi.* (*raise up*) tŭrŏ ollida 들어 올리다, (*move upward*) ollagada 올라가다. —*n.* (*elevator*) sŭngganggi

승강기, (*a ride*) sŭngch'a 승차(乘車). *This box is too heavy for me to ~.* I sangjanŭn nŏmu mugŏwŏ tŭl suga ŏpsŭmnida. 이 상자는 너무 무거워 들 수가 없읍니다/ *This window won't ~.* I ch'angmunŭn ollagaji anssŭmnida. 이 창문은 올라가지 않습니다/ *take the ~ to the tenth floor* shipch'ŭngkkaji ellibeit'ŏrŭl t'ago kada 10층까지 엘리베이터를 타고 가다.

light *n.* (*beam*) pit 빛, (*ray*) kwangsŏn 광선, (*lamp~*) tŭngpul 등불, (*brightness*) kwangmyŏng 광명. —*vt., vi.* purŭl k'yŏda 불을 켜다. —*adj.* (*not heavy*) kabyŏun 가벼운. *sun~* haetpit 햇빛/ *moon ~* talpit 달빛/ *gas~* kasŭdŭng 가스등/ *electric ~* chŏndŭng 전등. *We need more ~.* Tŏ manŭn kwangsŏni p'iryohamnida. 더 많은 광선이 필요합니다/ *Turn the ~s on.* Purŭl k'yŏshio. 불을 켜시오/ *Please give me a ~.* Purŭl chom pillyŏ chushio. 불을 좀 빌려 주시오/ *Put out the ~s before leaving a room.* Pangesŏ nagal ttaenŭn purŭl kkŭshio. 방에서 나갈 때는 불을 끄시오/ *How do you ~ this kerosene stove?* I sŏgyu sŭt'obŭnŭn ŏttŏk'e purŭl puch'imnikka? 이 석유 스토브는 어떻게 불을 붙입니까/ *I have to get a ~ summer suit somewhere.* Ŏdisŏ kabyŏun habogŭl sayagessŭmnida. 어디서 가벼운 하복(夏服)을 사야겠읍니다/ *I want to read something ~.* Chom kabyŏun kŏsŭl ikko shipsŭmnida. 좀 가벼운 것을 읽고 싶습니다.

lighten *vt.* (*make light*) pakke hada 밝게 하다, (*illuminate*) pich'uda 비추다, (*make less heavy*) kabyŏpke hada 가볍게 하다.

lightning *n.* pŏn-gae 번개, pyŏrak 벼락. *L~ flashed.* Pŏngaetpuri pŏntchŏk'aessŭmnida. 번갯불이 번쩍했읍니다/ *The tree has been struck by ~.* Chŏ namue pyŏragi ttŏrŏjyŏssŭmnida. 저 나무에 벼락이 떨어졌읍니다.

like *adj.* (*similar*) pisŭt'an 비슷한, (*alike*) talmŭn 닮은. —*vt., vi.* (*be fond of*) choahada 좋아하다. —*n.* pisŭt'an kŏt 비슷한 것. *Do you have another just ~ this?* Igŏtkwa kkok kat'ŭn kŏsŭn ŏpsŭmnikka? 이것과 꼭 같은 것은 없읍니까/ *I'd like to see what Korea is really ~.* Han-gugŭi chintcha mosŭbŭl pogo shipkunyo. 한국의 진짜

모습을 보고 싶군요/ *What would you ~ to drink?* Mwŏl
mashigessŭmnikka? 뭘 마시겠읍니까/ *Do you ~ fish?*
Saengsŏnŭl choahashimnikka? 생선을 좋아하십니까/ *How
do you ~ your tea?* Hongch'aga ŏttŏssŭmnikka? 홍차가
어떻습니까/ *Would you ~ to have pulgogi?* Pulgogirŭl
tŭshigessŭmnikka? 불고기를 드시겠읍니까/ *I'm glad you
~ it.* Mame tŭshindani kippŭgunyo. 맘에 드신다니 기쁘
군요.

likely *adj. & adv.* (*probably*) ama 아마, (*reasonable*)
kŭrŏlssahan 그럴싸한, (*suitable*) chŏk'ap'an 적합한.
Which are the most ~ candidate? Ōnŭ huboga kajang
yumanghamnikka? 어느 후보가 가장 유망합니까/ *I shall
very ~ be here again next month.* Ama naedaltchŭm
tashi i kose oge toel kŏshimnida. 아마 내달쯤 다시 이 곳에
오게 될 것입니다.

likewise *adv.* (*similarly*) mach'an-gajiro 마찬가지로.
—*conj.* (*too*) tto 또.

liking *n.* (*fondness*) choaham 좋아함, kiho 기호. *Is it to
your ~?* Maŭme tŭshimnikka? 마음에 드십니까/ *It is
much to my ~.* Ssŏk maŭme tŭmnida. 썩 마음에 듭니다.

lily *n.* nari 나리, narikkot 나리꽃.

limb *n.* (*of man or animal*) sonbal 손발, (*wing*) nalgae
날개, (*branch*) kaji 가지. *He lost a ~ in battle.* Kŭ
saramŭn chŏnjaengesŏ p'arŭl[tarirŭl] hana irŏssŭmnida.
그 사람은 전쟁에서 팔을[다리를] 하나 잃었읍니다.

lime *n.* sŏk'oe 석회.

limelight *n.* kakkwang 각광(脚光).

limit *n.* (*bound*) chehan 제한, (*pl.*) (*extent*) pŏmwi 범위.
—*vt.*(*restrict*) chehanhada 제한하다. *within ~* chŏktanghage 적당하게/ *without ~* mujehanŭro 무제한으로/ *I'm
willing to help you within ~s.* Tangshinŭl chŏkchŏr-
hi topko shipsŭmnida. 당신을 적절히 돕고 싶습니다.

limitation *n.* (*limiting*) hanjŏng 한정, (*bound*) han-gye
한계, (*restriction*) chehan 제한.

limited *adj.* (*restricted*) yuhanŭi 유한(有限)의. *~ express*
t'ŭkkŭp yŏlch'a 특급 열차/ *~ company* yuhan ch'aegim
hoesa 유한 책임 회사(*Ltd.*).

limp *vi.* chŏllŭmgŏrida 절름거리다.

line *n.* (*cord*) kkŭn 끈, chul 줄, (*a long narrow mark*) sŏn 선(線), (*row*) yŏl 열(列), (*lineage*) kyet'ong 계통, (*course*) nosŏn 노선, (*trade*) changsa 장사, (*a short letter*) tanshin 단신(短信). —*vt.,vi.* (*mark with line*) sŏnŭl kŭtta 선을 긋다, (*form a line*) yŏrŭl chitta 열을 짓다. *hang the clothes on the* ~ osŭl ppallaetchure nŏlda 옷을 빨랫줄에 널다/ *I'm sorry the* ~ *is busy.* Choesonghajiman kyesok t'onghwa chungieyo. 죄송하지만 계속 통화 중이에요/ *Hold the* ~, *please.* Kkŭnch'i malgo chamshi kidaryŏ chushio. 끊지 말고 잠시 기다려 주시오/ *Let's stand in a* ~. Churŭl sŏpshida. 줄을 섭시다/ *What* ~ *are you in?* Musŭn irŭl hashimnikka? 무슨 일을 하십니까/ *I carry on the work as a side* ~. Puŏbŭro kŭ irŭl hago issŭmnida. 부업으로 그 일을 하고 있읍니다/ *Drop me a* ~ *to say how you're getting on.* Ŏttŏk'e chinaenŭnji myŏt chul ssŏ ponaeshipshio. 어떻게 지내는지 몇 줄 써 보내십시오/ *the Kyongbu L*~ kyŏngbusŏn 경부선(京釜線)/ *the North Atlantic Air L*~ puktaesŏyang hanggong hoesa 북대서양 항공 회사.

lineage *n.* (*pedigree*) kagye 가계(家系), hyŏlt'ong 혈통. *a woman of high* ~ myŏngmunŭi puin 명문의 부인.

linen *n* amap'o 아마포(亞麻布), rinnerŭ 린네르.

liner *n.* (*ship or aircraft*) chŏnggisŏn[hanggonggi] 정기선[항공기]. *a trans-Atlantic* ~ taesŏyang hoengdan chŏnggisŏn 대서양 횡단 정기선.

linguist *n.* ŏhakcha 어학자.

lining *n.* (*of dresses*) an 안. *an overcoat with a fur* ~ mop'iro anŭl taen oet'u 모피로 안을 댄 외투.

link *n.* (*of a chain*) kori 고리.

lion *n.* saja 사자, (*person*) yongmaengsŭrŏun saram 용맹스러운 사람.

lip *n.* ipsul 입술. *curl one's* ~ ibŭl ppijukkŏrida 입을 삐죽거리다/ *She pressed her* ~*s to mine.* Kŭ yŏjanŭn chagi ipsullo nae ipsurŭl nullŏssŭmnida. 그 여자는 자기 입술로 내 입술을 눌렀읍니다.

lipstick *n.* ipsul yŏnji 입술 연지.

liquid *n.* aekch'e 액체. ~ *air* aekch'e konggi 액체 공기/ ~ *fuel* aekch'e yŏllyo 액체 연료.

liquidate *vt.,vi.* (*settle*) ch'ŏngsanhada 청산하다. ~ *the past* kwagŏrŭl ch'ŏngsanhada 과거를 청산하다.

liquor *n.* sul 술, (*foreign* ~) yangju 양주. *Makkolli is the most traditional Korean* ~. Makkŏllinŭn kajang chŏnt'ongjŏgin Han-guk surimnida. 막걸리는 가장 전통적 인 한국 술입니다.

list *n.* (*table*) illamp'yo 일람표, (*roll*) myŏngbu 명부, (*catalogue*) mongnok 목록. *a membership* ~ hoewŏn myŏngbu 회원 명부/ *the casualty* ~s sasangja myŏngbu 사상자(死傷者) 명부/ *price* ~ chŏngkap'yo 정가표/ *We didn't find the name in the* ~. Myŏngbuenŭn kŭ irŭmi ŏpsŭmnida. 명부에는 그 이름이 없습니다.

listen *vt.,vi.* tŭtta 듣다. ~ *to music* ŭmagŭl tŭtta 음악 을 듣다/ *L*~ *to what I say.* Nae marŭl kwidama tŭrŭshio. 내 말을 귀담아 들으시오/ *Pardon, mademoiselle, I wish to* ~ *to your heart.* Agassi, ch'ŏngjinŭl haeyagen-nŭndeyo. 아가씨, 청진(聽診)을 해야겠는데요.

literal *adj.* (*word for word*) muncha kŭdaeroŭi 문자 그 대로의, (*accurate*) chŏnghwak'an 정확한. ~ *error* ocha 오자(誤字)/ *a* ~ *translation* chigyŏk 직역.

literary *adj.* munhagŭi 문학의. *a* ~ *columns* munyeran 문예란/ *a* ~ *man* munin 문인/ ~ *pursuits* munp'irŏp 문필업(文筆業).

literature *n.* munhak 문학. *classic* ~ kojŏn munhak 고 전 문학/ *modern* ~ hyŏndae munhak 현대 문학/ *popular* ~ taejung munhak 대중 문학/ *English* ~ yŏngmunhak 영문학.

little *adj.* (*not big*) chagŭn 작은, (*not much*) chŏgŭn 적은, (*young*) nai ŏrin 나이 어린, (*petty*) pyŏnbyŏnch'i anŭn 변변치 않은. —*n.* (*not much*) chogŭm 조금. *a* ~ *boy* kwiyŏun ai 귀여운 아이/ *a* ~ *thing* hach'anŭn kŏt 하찮은 것/ *I have a* ~ *money.* Toni chogŭm issŭmnida. 돈이 조금 있습니다/ *I have* ~ *money.* Toni kŏŭi ŏpsŭm-nida. 돈이 거의 없습니다/ *Won't you stay a* ~ *time with me?* Chamshi nawa kach'i issŏ chuji ank'essŭmnikka?

잠시 나와 같이 있어 주지 않겠읍니까/ I have very ~ time for reading. Toksŏhal shigani kŏŭi ŏpsŭmnida. 독서할 시간이 거의 없읍니다.

live vt.,vi. (dwell) salda 살다, kŏjuhada 거주하다, (make a life) saenghwarhada 생활하다, (exist) salda 살다, saengjonhada 생존하다. Where do you ~ ? Ŏdisŏ salgo issŭmnikka? 어디서 살고 있읍니까/ Are your parents still living in Seoul? Yangch'inŭn ajik Sŏuresŏ salgo kyeshimnikka? 양친은 아직 서울에서 살고 계십니까/ Her memory will always ~. Kŭ yŏjaŭi kiŏgŭn yŏngwŏnhi ich'yŏjiji anŭl kŏshimnida. 그 여자의 기억은 영원히 잊혀 지지 않을 것입니다.

livelihood n. saenggye 생계, sallim 살림. earn one's ~ by teaching kyojigŭro saenggyerŭl seuda 교직으로 생계 를 세우다/ have no means of ~ saenggyega magyŏnhada 생계가 막연하다.

lively adj. (vigorous) hwalgich'an 활기찬, p'alp'arhan 팔팔한, (vivid) sŏnmyŏnghan 선명한.

liver n. kanjang 간장(肝臟). ~ trouble kanjangpyŏng 간장 병/ ~ cancer kanam 간암.

livestock n. kach'uk 가축. ~ farming mokch'uk 목축.

living adj. (alive) sara innŭn 살아 있는, (contemporary) hyŏnjonhanŭn 현존하는, (active) hwalbarhan 활발한. —n. (livelihood) saenggye 생계. all ~ things modŭn saengmul 모든 생물/ ~ English hyŏndae Yŏngŏ 현대 영어/ ~ language hyŏndaeŏ 현대어/ ~ faith yŏllyŏrhan shinang 열렬한 신앙/thrifty ~ chŏryak saenghwal 절약 생 활/What does he do for his ~ ? Kŭ saramŭi saengŏbŭn muŏshimnikka? 그 사람의 생업은 무엇입니까/ ~ room (sitting room) kŏshil 거실, kŏch'ŏpang 거처방.

load n. (burden) chim 짐, (charge) pudam 부담. —vt., vi. chimŭl shitta 짐을 싣다. a heavy ~ mugŏun chim 무 거운 짐/ groan under a heavy ~ of taxation mugŏun segŭme hŏdŏgida 무거운 세금에 허덕이다.

loaf n. (~ of bread) ppang han tŏngi 빵 한 덩이. The ~ has risen in price. Ppang kapshi ollassŭmnida. 빵 값이 올랐읍니다.

loan n.(*lending*) taebu 대부, (*money lent*) ch'ayonggǔm 차용금, ch'agwan 차관. *government* ~s kukch'ae 국채/ *a foreign* ~ oech'ae 외채.

lobby n. (*entrance hall*) hyǒn-gwan hol 현관 홀, (*passageway*) pokto 복도, nangha 낭하. *the* ~ *of hotel* hot'el pokto 호텔 복도/ *We shall meet at the* ~ *of the Choson Hotel.* Chosǒn hot'el pokto-esǒ mannapshida. 조선 호텔 복도에서 만납시다.

lobster n. kajae 가재.

local adj. chibangǔi 지방의. ~ *color* chibangsaek 지방색/ *a* ~ *paper* chibang shinmun 지방 신문/ *Can I make a* ~ *call, please?* Shinae chǒnhwarǔl kǒlgo ship'ǔndeyo. 시내 전화를 걸고 싶은데요.

locate vt.,vi. (*place*) charijapta 자리잡다, (*settle*) chǒngjuhada 정주하다. *Where is the Kyongbok Palace* ~d? Kyǒngbokkungǔn ǒdi issǔmnikka? 경복궁은 어디 있읍니까/ *Where is the new factory to be* ~d? Sae kongjangǔn ǒdi sewǒjimnikka? 새 공장은 어디 세워집니까?

location n. (*position*) wich'i 위치, (*movie*) yaoe ch'waryǒng(jang) 야외 촬영(장).

lock n. chamulsoe 자물쇠. —vt.,vi. (*fasten*) chamulsoerǔl chamgǔda 자물쇠를 잠그다. *This* ~ *is broken.* I chamulsoega kojangnassǔmnida. 이 자물쇠가 고장났읍니다/ *The door* ~s *by itself.* Toǒnǔn chadongjǒgǔro tach'yǒssǔmnida. 도어는 자동적으로 닫혔읍니다.

locomotive n. (~ *engine*) kigwanch'a 기관차. *an electric* ~ chǒn-gi kigwanch'a 전기 기관차.

locust n. mettugi 메뚜기, (*Am.*) (*cicada*) maemi 매미.

lodge vt.,vi. (*stay*) mukta 묵다, t'usuk'ada 투숙하다. —n. (*hut*) odumak 오두막, (*guard office*) suwishil 수위실. *Where are you lodging now?* Ǒdisǒ mukko kyeshimnikka? 어디서 묵고 계십니까/ *I'm lodging at Mr. and Mrs. Pak.* Paksshi pubu taegesǒ mukko issǔmnida. 박(朴)씨 부부 댁에서 묵고 있읍니다.

lodging n. (*boarding*) hasuk 하숙, (*dwelling place*) sukso 숙소. ~ *house* hasukchip 하숙집/ *Send them over to my* ~s. Nae hasugǔro ponae chushio. 내 하숙으로 보내 주

시오/ *Where can we find ~s for the night?* Pame ŏdisŏ mugŭl su issŭlkkayo? 밤에 어디서 묵을 수 있을까요?
log *n.* t'ongnamu 통나무.
logic *n.* nolli 논리, nollihak 논리학. *formal ~* hyŏngshik
nollihak 형식 논리학.
logical *adj.* nollijŏgin 논리적인. *a ~ mind* nollijŏk sago
논리적 사고(思考).
loin *n.* hŏri 허리. *~ cloth* kandanhan sogot 간단한 속옷.
loiter *vt.,vi.* (*linger*) pindunggŏrida 빈둥거리다, (*dally*)
kkumulgŏrida 꾸물거리다.
lonely *adj.* (*solitary*) kodok'an 고독한, (*lonesome*) ssŭlssŭrhan 쓸쓸한, oeroun 외로운. *a ~ traveller* kodok'an
nagŭne 고독한 나그네/ *a ~ life* oeroun saenghwal 외로운
생활/ *I feel ~.* Nanŭn ssŭlssŭrhamnida. 나는 쓸쓸합니
다.
lonesome *adj.* (*lonely*) ssŭlssŭrhan 쓸쓸한. *a ~ journey*
ssŭlssŭrhan yŏhaeng 쓸쓸한 여행/ *feel ~* ssŭlssŭrhada
쓸쓸하다.
long *adj.* (*lengthy*) kin 긴, (*tall*) nop'ŭn 높은, (*duration*) oraen 오랜. *—vi.* (*yearn*) yŏlmanghada 열망하다.
—n. changshigan 장시간. *How ~ is the River Naktong?*
Naktonggangŭn kiriga ŏlmana toemnikka? 낙동강은 길이
가 얼마나 됩니까/ *This room is ten feet ~.* I pangŭn
kiriga ship p'it'ŭimnida. 이 방은 길이가 10피트입니다/ *How
~ have you been in Korea?* Han-guge oshin chi ŏlmana
toeshimnikka? 한국에 오신 지 얼마나 되십니까/ *How ~ will
it take to reach L.A.?* Rosŭaenjellesŭkkaji kanŭn te
myŏch'irina kŏllimnikka? 로스앤젤레스까지 가는 데 며칠이
나 걸립니까/ *Can't you stay ~er?* Chomdŏ ittaga kashiji ank'essŭmnikka? 좀더 있다가 가시지 않겠습니까/ *I
won't be ~.* Kot toraogessŭmnida. 곧 돌아오겠습니다/
How ~ are the holidays? Hyuganŭn ŏlma tonganimni-
kka? 휴가는 얼마 동안입니까/ *We are ~ing for peace.*
Urinŭn mopshi p'yŏnghwarŭl parago issŭmnida. 우리는
몹시 평화를 바라고 있습니다/ *I'm ~ing to see you.* Much'ŏk manna pogo shipsŭmnida. 무척 만나 보고 싶습니다/
Will you be away for ~? Oraettongan ttŏna kyeshil

kŏmnikka? 오랫동안 떠나 계실 겁니까/ *I shall see you before* ~. Kot mannage toel kŏshimnida. 곧 만나게 될 것입니다/ *So* ~ *!* Chal ka! 잘 가 !

longevity *n.* (*long life*) changsu 장수(長壽). *the secret of* ~ changsuŭi pigyŏl 장수의 비결.

longitude *n.* kyŏngdo 경도.

look *vt.,vi.* (*see*) poda 보다, (*stare*) nunyŏgyŏ poda 눈여겨 보다, (*face*) ...e myŏnhada …에 면하다, (*seem*)...ŭro poida …으로 보이다. —*n.* (*appearance*) oegwan 외관, (*countenance*) ansaek 안색, (*glance*) ilgyŏn 일견. *Doctor, will you* ~ *at my ankle?* Ŭisa sŏnsaengnim, nae palmogŭl pwa chushigessŭmnikka? 의사 선생님, 내 발목을 봐 주시겠읍니까/ *Are you still* ~*ing for a job?* Ajikto ilcharirŭl ch'atko issŭmnikka? 아직도 일자리를 찾고 있읍니까/ *L*~ *to your manners, my boy.* Yaeya, haengshirŭl choshimhaera. 애야, 행실을 조심해라/ *L*~ *in a mirror.* Kŏurŭl poshio. 거울을 보시오/ *I'm just* ~*ing.* Kŭjŏ kugyŏnghanŭn kŏmnida. 그저 구경하는 겁니다/ *What number are you* ~*ing for?* Ŏnŭ pŏnhorŭl ch'ajŭshimnikka? 어느 번호를 찾으십니까/ *That* ~*s good.* Chal ŏullisyŏ. 잘 어울리셔/ *You don't* ~ *your age.* Chagi naironŭn poiji anssŭmnida. 자기 나이로는 보이지 않습니다/ *Does this hat* ~ *well on me?* I moja na-ege chal ŏullimnikka? 이 모자 나에게 잘 어울립니까/ *I'm* ~*ing forward to your visiting here.* Tangshini i kosŭl ch'aja chushigirŭl kodaehago issŭmnida. 당신이 이 곳을 찾아 주시기를 고대하고 있읍니다/ *I don't like his* ~. Nanŭn kŭ saramŭi ŏlguldo pogi shilssŭmnida. 나는 그 사람의 얼굴도 보기 싫습니다/ *Do not judge of a man by his* ~*s.* Saramŭl oegwanŭro p'andanhaji mashio. 사람을 외관으로 판단하지 마시오/ *May I take a* ~ *at the T.V Guide?* T'ellebijŏn annaerŭl chom poyŏ chushigessŭmnikka? 텔레비전 안내를 좀 보여 주시겠읍니까/ ~ *after* (*take care of*) ...ŭl tolboda …을 돌보다.

looker-on *n.* kugyŏngkkun 구경꾼.

looking glass kŏul 거울.

loop *n.* (*link*) kori 고리, rup'ŭ 루프.

loose *adj.* (*slack*) hŏlgŏun 헐거운, (*free to move*) hŭndŭllinŭn 흔들리는, (*inexact*) haehan 해이한, (*wanton*) pangjonghan 방종한, (*flabby*) ch'uk nŭrŏjin 축 늘어진. *It's too ~ around the waist.* Hŏri pubuni nŏmu hŏllŏnghamnida. 허리 부분이 너무 헐렁합니다/ *Let ~ !* Noa chushipshio. 놓아 주십시오.

loosen *vt.,vi.* (*untie*) p'ulda 풀다, (*slacken*) nŭsŭnhage hada 느슨하게 하다, nŭsŭnhaejida 느슨해지다.

loot *n.* (*spoil*) chŏllip'um 전리품, (*plundering*) yakt'al 약탈. —*vt.* (*pillage*) yakt'arhada 약탈하다.

lord *n.* (*chief*) tumok 두목, (*master*) chuin 주인, (*ruler*) chibaeja 지배자, (*sovereign*) kunju 군주, (*Christ*) chu 주(主), (*Eng.*) kyŏng 경(卿). 「자동차.

lorry *n.* (*truck*) t'ŭrŏk 트럭, hwamul chadongch'a 화물

lose *vt.,vi.* (*fail to keep*) ilt'a 잃다, (*get rid of*) momyŏnhada 모면하다, (*miss*) mot tŭtta 못 듣다, (*fail to catch*) noch'ida 놓치다, (*fail*) shilp'aehada 실패하다, (*be defeated*) chida 지다, (*suffer loss*) sonhaeboda 손해보다. *I have lost my ticket.* Ch'ap'yorŭl punshirhaessŭmnida. 차표를 분실했읍니다/ *Don't ~ your heart.* Kiunŭl naeshipshio. 기운을 내십시오/ *I tried not to ~ a word of the speech.* Nanŭn kŭ yŏnsŏresŏ han madido noch'iji anŭryŏgo noryŏk'aessŭmnida. 나는 그 연설에서 한 마디도 놓치지 않으려고 노력했읍니다/ *I've just lost his name.* Kŭ saramŭi irŭmŭl kkamppak ijŏssŭmnida. 그 사람의 이름을 깜빡 잊었읍니다/ *Japan lost the game to Korea by 10 to 8.* Ilbonŭn Han-guk'ant'e shiptae p'allo chyŏssŭmnida. 일본은 한국한테 10대 8로 졌읍니다/ *You will ~ nothing by waiting.* Kidaryŏsŏ sonhaebol kŏsŭn ŏpsŭl kŏshimnida. 기다려서 손해볼 것은 없을 것입니다/ *How much did he ~ on the transaction?* Kŭ kŏraeesŏ kŭ saramŭn ŏlmana sonhaerŭl poassŭmnikka? 그 거래에서 그 사람은 얼마나 손해를 보았읍니까/ *My watch ~s two minutes a day.* Nae shigyenŭn harue ibun nŭssŭmnida. 내 시계는 하루에 2분 늦습니다.

loss *n.* (*losing*) punshil 분실, (*opp. gain*) sonhae 손해, (*death*) samang 사망. *a great ~* k'ŭn sonshil 큰 손실/

What is the estimated ~? Sonhaeaegŭn taeryak ŏlmana toemnikka? 손해액은 대략 얼마나 됩니까/ *I am at a* ~ *what to do.* Ŏtchihaeya choŭlchi nanch'ŏhamnida. 어찌해야 좋을지 난처합니다.

lost *adj.* (*that was lost*) irŭn 잃은, (*missing*) haengbang pulmyŏngŭi 행방 불명의. *a* ~ *child* mia 미아(迷兒)/ *Where is the* ~ *and found office?* Yushilmulgyenŭn ŏdiimnikka? 유실물계는 어디입니까/ *I'd like to report a case of* ~ *money.* Ton punshire kwanhae shin-gohago ship'ŭndeyo. 돈 분실에 관해 신고하고 싶은데요.

lot *n.* (*lottery*) chebi 제비, (*fate*) unmyŏng 운명, (*plot*) puji 부지(敷地), (*multitude*) taryang 다량. *draw* ~*s* chebirŭl ppopta 제비를 뽑다/ *The* ~ *fell to me.* Naega tangch'ŏmdoeŏssŭmnida. 내가 당첨되었읍니다/ *Let's cast* ~*s for the first move.* Chebiro sunbŏnŭl chŏnghapshida. 제비로 순번을 정합시다/ *Thanks a* ~. Taedanhi kamsahamnida. 대단히 감사합니다.

lottery *n.* pokkwŏn 복권, (*drawing*) ch'uch'ŏm 추첨. *draw* ~ chebirŭl ppopta 제비를 뽑다.

lotus *n.* yŏn 연(蓮).

loud *adj.* (*not quiet*) moksoriga k'ŭn 목소리가 큰, (*noisy*) shikkŭrŏun 시끄러운, (*showy*) yahan 야한. *Don't talk so* ~. Kŭrŏk'e k'ŭge marhaji mashio. 그렇게 크게 말하지 마시오/ *Please speak a little* ~*er.* Chomdŏ k'ŭge marhae chushio. 좀더 크게 말해 주시오/ *It is too* ~. Nŏmu hwaryŏhagunyo. 너무 화려하군요/ ~ *speaker* hwaksŏnggi 확성기.

loudly *adv.* k'ŭn soriro 큰 소리로.

lounge *n.* (*in hotel or club*) hyugeshil 휴게실, sagyoshil 사교실/~ *hall* orakshil 오락실.

lounge chair (*sofa*) sop'a 소파.

lousy *adj.* (*foul*) tŏrŏun 더러운, (*vile*) yabihan 야비한.

love *n.* (*affection*) sarang 사랑, (*fondness*) aeho 애호, (*sexual affection*) yŏnae 연애, (*sweetheart*) aein 애인. —*vt.* saranghada 사랑하다, (*worship*) sungbaehada 숭배하다, (*like*) choahada 좋아하다. *mother's* ~ ŏmŏniŭi sarang 어머니의 사랑/ ~ *for one's country* chogugae 조국애/ ~ *letter* yŏnae p'yŏnji 연애 편지/ ~ *story* yŏnae so-

sŏl 연애 소설/ *Give my best ~ to your parents*. Pumonimkke anbu chŏnhashio. 부모님께 안부 전하시오/ *My
wife would ~ to meet you*. Urijip saramdo kkok hanbŏn manna poassŭmyŏn hamnida. 우리집 사람도 꼭 한번
만나 보았으면 합니다/ *I ~ you*. Saranghamnida. 사랑합
니다.

lovely *adj*. (*beautiful*) arŭmdaun 아름다운, (*charming*)
kwiyŏun 귀여운, (*noble*) hullyunghan 훌륭한. *How ~ !*
Chŏngmal arŭmdawa ! 정말 아름다와/ *That is a ~
scarf*. Mŏtchin sŭk'ap'ŭrogunyo. 멋진 스카프로군요/
Sunmi, thank you once again for a ~ evening. Sunmi,
chŭlgŏun chŏnyŏk p'at'i tashi han pŏn kamsahaeyo.
순미, 즐거운 저녁 파티 다시 한 번 감사해요.

lover *n*. (*sweetheart*) aein 애인, yŏnin 연인, (*admirer*)
aehoga 애호가. *a pair of happy ~s* han ssangŭi
haengbok'an yŏnin 한 쌍의 행복한 연인/ *a music ~*
ŭmak aehoga 음악 애호가.

low *adj*. (*not high*) najŭn 낮은, (*cheap*) ssan 싼, (*vulgar*) yabihan 야비한, (*feeble*) yak'an 약한. *a ~ fence*
najŭn ult'ari 낮은 울타리/ *How can you sell your merchandise for such a ~price?* Ŏttŏk'e igach'i ssage p'al
su issŭmnikka ? 어떻게 이같이 싸게 팔 수 있읍니까/
wages pakpong 박봉/ *a man of ~ birth* t'aesaengi ch'ŏnhan saram 태생이 천한 사람.

lower *adj*. *~ animals* hadŭng tongmul 하등 동물. —*vt*.
(*bring down*) natch'uda 낮추다, naerida 내리다, (*de-
grade*) ttŏrŏttŭrida 떨어뜨리다, (*weaken*) yak'washik'i-
da 약화시키다. *~ the price* kapsŭl natch'uda 값을 낮추다.

loyal *adj*. (*faithful*) ch'ungsŏngsŭrŏn 충성스런, sŏngshirhan 성실한. *a ~ husband* sŏngshirhan namp'yŏn 성실한
남편.

lubricate *vt*. (*grease*) kirŭmŭl ch'ida 기름을 치다.

lubrication oil yunhwallyu 윤활유.

luck *n*. (*fortune*) un 운, haengun 행운. *good ~* haengun
행운/ *Good ~ !* Haengunŭl pimnida! 행운을 빕니다/
Good ~ to you both. Tu punŭi haengbogŭl pimnida.
두 분의 행복을 빕니다/ *I'm in ill ~ tonight*. Onŭl chŏ-

nyŏgŭn chaesuga ŏpsŭmnida. 오늘 저녁은 재수가 없읍
니다.

lucky *adj.* (*fortunate*) unsu choŭn 운수 좋은, haengunŭi
행운의. *How ~ you are!* Tangshinŭn ch'am uni chossŭmnida. 당신은 참 운이 좋습니다/ *I'm very ~ to learn
English from you.* Sŏnsaengnimege yŏngŏrŭl paeuge
toeŏ chŏngmal haengunimnida. 선생님에게 영어를 배우게
되어 정말 행운입니다/ *We are terribly ~ today.* Onŭrŭn aju chaesuga chossŭmnida. 오늘은 아주 재수가 좋습
니다.

luggage *n.* (*baggage*) suhamul 수하물. *hand ~* suhamul
수하물/ *a ~ ticket* suhamul inhwanp'yo 수하물 인환표/
a ~ office suhamul ch'wigŭpso 수하물 취급소/ *a ~ van*
hwach'a 화차/ *How many pieces of ~ do you have?*
Chimŭn myŏt kaena toemnikka? 짐은 몇 개나 됩니까/
Please take this ~ down. I chimŭl naeryŏ chushipshio.
이 짐을 내려 주십시오.

lukewarm *adj.* mijigŭnhan 미지근한. *~ water* mijigŭnhan mul 미지근한 물/ *~ attitude* mijigŭnhan t'aedo
미지근한 태도.

lull *vt.,vi.* (*soothe*) tallaeda 달래다, (*fall quiet*) karaanta 가라앉다. *~ a baby to sleep* ŏrinirŭl tallaesŏ chaeuda
어린이를 달래서 재우다/ *The wind ~ed.* Parami mŏjŏ-
ssŭmnida. 바람이 멎었읍니다.

lullaby *n.* (*cradlesong*) chajangga 자장가.

lumber *n.* (*timber*) chaemok 재목, mokchae 목재. *—vi.*
k'ungk'ung kŏtta 쿵쿵 걷다. *building ~* kŏnch'uk mokchae 건축 목재. *A heavy truck ~ed by.* Mugŏun t'ŭrŏ-
gi tŏlk'ŏdŏnggŏrimyŏ chinagassŭmnida. 무거운 트럭이 덜
커덩거리며 지나갔읍니다.

lump *n.* tŏngŏri 덩어리. *~ sugar* kaksŏlt'ang 각설탕/ *One
~ of sugar and cream, please.* Kaksŏlt'ang han kaewa
k'ŭrimŭl chuseyo. 각설탕 1개와 크림을 주세요.

lunar *adj.* *~ calendar* ŭmnyŏk 음력/ *~ eclipse* wŏlshik
월식/ *~ rainbow* talmuri 달무리.

lunatic *n.* (*crazy person*) mich'igwangi 미치광이. *~ asylum* chŏngshin pyŏngwŏn 정신 병원.

lunch *n.* chŏmshim 점심, (*Am.*) kyŏngshiksa 경식사. *Let us take* ~. Chŏmshim mŏgŭpshida. 점심 먹읍시다/ *What will you have for* ~? Chŏmshim shiksa-e muŏl chapsushimnikka? 점심 식사에 무얼 잡수십니까/ *a box* ~ toshirak 도시락/ *Does this* ~ *menu include soup and entree?* I chŏmshim menyuenŭn sup'ŭwa angt'ŭrega tŭrŏ issŭmnikka? 이 점심 메뉴에는 수프와 앙트레가 들어 있읍니까/ *How about having* ~ *with me tomorrow?* Naeil chŏhago chŏmshim kach'i haji ank'essŭmnikka? 내일 저하고 점심 같이 하지 않겠읍니까? / *Come on, let's have* ~ *at the Japanese restaurant.* Cha, chŏmshimŭn ilshikchibesŏ hapshida. 자, 점심은 일식집에서 합시다/ *Don't forget to bring your* ~ *box.* Toshirak kajyŏonŭn kot itchi mashio. 도시락 가져오는 것 잊지 마시오.

luncheon *n.* chŏmshim 점심, och'an 오찬. *a* ~ *party* och'anhoe 오찬회.

lunchtime *n.* chŏmshim shigan 점심 시간.

lung *n.* p'ye 폐(肺), hŏp'a 허파. ~ *cancer* p'yeam 폐암.

lure *n.* (*decoy*) mikki 미끼. —*vt.* (*entice*) yuhok'ada 유혹하다.

lurk *vi.* (*be hidden*) sumta 숨다, (*be latent*) chambok'ada 잠복하다, (*prowl*) mollae tanida 몰래 다니다.

lust *n.* (*strong desire*) yongmang 욕망, (*lewd desire*) sŏngyok 성욕(性慾).

luster, lustre *n.* (*gloss*) yun 윤, kwangt'aek 광택, (*glory*) yŏnggwang 영광. *Your hair always has wonderful* ~. Taegŭi mŏrinŭn ŏnjena arŭmdaun yuni nago itkunyo. 댁의 머리는 언제나 아름다운 윤이 나고 있군요.

luxurious *adj.* sach'isŭrŏun 사치스러운, hohwaroun 호화로운. *a* ~ *hotel* hohwaroun hot'el 호화로운 호텔/ *a* ~ *life* sach'isŭrŏn saenghwal 사치스런 생활.

luxury *n.* sach'i 사치, (*things*) sach'ip'um 사치품. *That's quite a sum. I couldn't afford to such* ~. Ŏmch'ŏngnan kapshigunyo. Kŭrŏk'e sach'ihan kŏsŭn sal suga ŏpsŭmnida. 엄청난 값이군요. 그렇게 사치한 것은 살 수가 없읍니다.

lynch *n.* sahyŏng 사형(私刑), rinch'i 린치.

⟨ M ⟩

ma'am *n.* (*madam*) puin 부인(夫人), manim 마님. *Thank you*, ～. Komapsŭmnida, puin. 고맙습니다, 부인.

machine *n.* kigye 기계. *a sewing* ～ chaebongt'ŭl 재봉틀/ *a vending* ～ chadong p'anmaegi 자동 판매기/ *a washing* ～ set'akki 세탁기/ *Keep off the* ～. Kigyee sondaeji mashio. 기계에 손대지 마시오.

machinery *n.* (*machines*) kigyeryu 기계류, (*mechanism*) kigu 기구.

mad *adj.* (*insane*) mich'in 미친, (*eager*) yŏlchunghan 열중한, (*angry*) hwaga nan 화가 난. *I am* ～ *about the stage.* Nanŭn yŏn-gŭge yŏlchunghago issŭmnida. 나는 연극에 열중하고 있읍니다/ *Don't get* ～, *please.* Chebal hwarŭl naeji mashio. 제발 화를 내지 마시오.

madam *n.* madam 마담, (*lady*) puin 부인, (*Am.*) (*mistress*) chubu 주부. *M*～ *Chang* Chang madam 장(張) 마담/ *May I speak to the* ～ *of the house?* Chubunim chom taejushiryŏmnikka? 주부님 좀 대주시렵니까?

made *adj.* (*artificially produced*) mandŭn 만든, ...che ...제(製). *M*～ *in Korea* Han-gukche 한국제/ *M*～ *in U.S.A.* Migukche 미국제/ *home*～*goods* kuksanp'um 국산품.

magazine *n.* (*periodical*) chapchi 잡지. *weekly* ～ chuganji 주간지/ *monthly* ～ wŏlganji 월간지.

magic *n.* (*sorcery*) mabŏp 마법, (*conjuring*) yosul 요술.

magician *n.* (*wizard*) mabŏpsa 마법사, (*conjurer*) yosulchangi 요술장이.

magistrate *n.* *a civil* ～ mun-gwan 문관/ *a judicial* ～ sabŏpkwan 사법관/ (*justice of the peace*) ch'ian p'ansa 치안 판사.

magnanimous *adj.* kwandaehan 관대한.

magnet *n.* (*lodestone*) chasŏk 자석. *a horseshoe* ～ malgup chasŏk 말굽 자석.

magnetism *n.* chagi 자기(磁氣).

magnificent *adj.* (*grand*) changŏmhan 장엄한, (*splen-*

did) kŭnsahan 군사한, mŏtchin 멋진.

magnify *vt*. (*make greater*) hwaktaehada 확대하다, (*exaggerate*) kwajanghada 과장하다.

ma(h)jong *n*. (*Chinese game*) majak 마작(麻雀).

maid *n*. (*girl*) sonyŏ 소녀, (*virgin*) ch'ŏnyŏ 처녀. ~- *servant* hanyŏ 하녀/ *house*~ kajŏngbu 가정부/ *kitchen* ~ shingmo 식모.

maiden *n*. (*young unmarried woman*) ch'ŏnyŏ 처녀. —*adj*. (*unmarried*) ch'ŏnyŏŭi 처녀의. *a* ~ *voyage* ch'ŏnyŏ hanghae 처녀 항해/ *a* ~ *speech* ch'ŏnyŏ yŏnsŏl 처녀 연설.

mail *n*. (*letters, etc.*) up'yŏnmul 우편물, p'yŏnji 편지. —*vt*. (*send by post*) usonghada 우송하다. *Is there any* ~ *for me* ? Na-ege on p'yŏnjiga issŭmnikka? 나에게 온 편지가 있읍니까/ *Air* ~ *or surface* ~ ? Hanggong p'yŏnŭro hashiryŏmnikka, paep'yŏnŭro hashiryŏmnikka? 항공편으로 하시렵니까, 배편으로 하시렵니까/ *I want to* ~ *these, please.* Igŏl puch'igo shipsŭmnida. 이걸 부치고 싶습니다/ ~ *box* uch'et'ong 우체통/ ~ *carrier* uch'ebu 우체부/ ~ *order* t'ongshin p'anmae 통신 판매.

main *adj*. (*chief*) chuyohan 주요한, (*leading*) yuryŏk'an 유력한. *one's* ~ *business* ponjik 본직/ *the* ~ *office* pon-guk[jŏm] 본국[점]/ *the* ~ *street* pŏnhwaga 번화가/ *the* ~ *land* pont'o 본토/ *Where is the* ~ *office of the Choheung Bank* ? Chohŭng ŭnhaeng ponjŏmŭn ŏdi issŭmnikka? 조흥 은행 본점은 어디 있읍니까?

maintain *vt*. (*keep*) yujihada 유지하다, (*support*) puyanghada 부양하다, (*assert*) chujanghada 주장하다.

maintenance *n*. (*upkeep*) pojon 보존, (*continuation*) chisok 지속, (*support*) puyang 부양, (*assertion*) chu- ⌐jang 주장.

maize *n*. (*Indian corn*) oksusu 옥수수. └

majestic, majestical *adj*. (*stately*) wiŏm innŭn 위엄 있는, tangdanghan 당당한.

majesty *n*. (*dignity*) chonŏm 존엄, (*title of king, etc.*) p'yeha 폐하. *the present M*~ kŭmsang p'yeha 금상 폐하/ *Her M*~ *the Empress* hwanghu p'yeha 황후 폐하.

major *adj*. (*greater*) k'ŭn tchogŭi 큰 쪽의, (*chief*) chuyohan 주요한. —n. (mil.) yukkun soryŏng 육군 소령. —vi. (specialize) chŏn-gonghada 전공하다. *What are you ~-ing in?* Musŭn kwamogŭl chŏn-gonghashimnikka? 무슨 과목을 전공하십니까?

majority n. (greater number) taedasu 대다수, (plurality) kwabansu 과반수, tasup'a 다수파, (full age) sŏngnyŏn 성년(成年). *gain a ~* kwabansurŭl hoektŭk'ada 과반수 를 획득하다/ *a ~ party* tasudang 다수당(多數黨)/ *decide by ~* tasuro chŏnghada 다수로 정하다.

make vt.,vi. (manufacture) mandŭlda 만들다, (construct) chitta 짓다, (compel) ...hage hada ⋯하게 하다, (prove) ...i toeda ⋯이 되다, (devise) koanhada 고안하다, (gain) ŏtta 얻다, (reach) toch'ak'ada 도착하다, (understand) ihaehada 이해하다. *What do you ~ with flour?* Milka-ruro muŏsŭl mandŭmnikka? 밀가루로 무엇을 만듭니까/ *We ~ our clothes from cloth.* Urinŭn ch'ŏnŭro osŭl mandŭmnida. 우리는 천으로 옷을 만듭니다/ *What ~s the grass grow?* Muŏshi p'urŭl charage hamnikka? 무엇이 풀을 자라게 합니까/ *Who made this ridiculous rule?* Nuga i usŭkkwangsŭrŏn kyuch'igŭl mandŭrŏnae-ssŭmnikka? 누가 이 우스꽝스런 규칙을 만들어냈읍니까/ *We made for home together.* Urinŭn hamkke chibŭro toragassŭmnida. 우리는 함께 집으로 돌아갔읍니다.

maker n. chejakcha 제작자. *dress~* yangjaesa 양재사/ *a holiday~* sop'unggaek 소풍객/ *a trouble~* malssŏng-kkurŏgi 말썽꾸러기.

makeup n. (composition) kusŏng 구성, hwajang 화장.

Malay n. Mallei mal 말레이 말. —adj. Mallei pandoŭi 말

Malayan n. Mallei saram 말레이 사람. ⌊레이 반도의.

male (man) namja 남자, (~ animal) suk'ŏt 수컷. —adj. namjaŭi 남자의, suk'ŏsŭi 수컷의. *a ~ person* namja 남자/ *a ~ cat* suk'oyangi 수코양이.

malicious adj. (spiteful) agŭi innŭn 악의 있는, shimsul-gujŭn 심술궂은.

malignant adj. (very evil) aksŏngŭi 악성의. *~ glances* chŏgŭirŭl p'umŭn shisŏn 적의를 품은 시선/ *~ cancer* ak-sŏng am 악성 암.

mammoth *n.* maemŏdŭ 매머드. —*adj.* (*huge*) kŏdaehan 거대한. *a ~ tanker* kŏdaehan〔maemŏdŭ〕yujosŏn 거대한 〔매머드〕유조선.

man *n.* (*human being*) in-gan 인간, (*male*) namja 남자, (*person*) saram 사람. *a ~ of action* hwaltongga 활동가/ *a ~ of wealth* puja 부자(富者)/ *Can I recognize the ~ ?* Kŭ saramŭl arabol su issŭlkkayo? 그 사람을 알아볼 수 있을까요?

manage *vt., vi.* (*control*) kwallihada 관리하다, (*handle*) taruda 다루다, (~ *to do*) irŏkchŏrŏk …hada 이럭저럭 …하다. *No, thank you. I can ~.* Kwaench'anssŭmnida. Honjasŏ hal su issŭmnida. 괜찮습니다. 혼자서 할 수 있읍니다/ *I'll ~ it somehow.* Ŏttŏk'edŭn haebogessŭmnida. 어떻게든 해보겠읍니다.

management *n.* (*control*) kwalli 관리, (*handling*) ch'wigŭp 취급, (*direction*) kyŏngyŏng 경영. *personnel ~* in-sa kwalli 인사 관리/ *factory ~* kongjang kyŏngyŏng 공장 경영.

manager *n.* chibaein 지배인. *a hotel ~* hot'el chibaein 호텔 지배인/ *a business ~* yŏngŏp pujang 영업 부장/ *Get me the ~.* Chibaeinŭl pullŏ chushio. 지배인을 불러 주시오.

managing *adj.* kwallihanŭn 관리하는. *a ~ director* chŏnmu isa 전무 이사.

mandate *n.* (*order*) chiryŏng 지령, (*a commission*) wiim 위임. —*vt.* wiim t'ongch'ihada 위임 통치하다. *a ~d territory* wiim t'ongch'iryŏng 위임 통치령.

maneuver, manoeuvre *n.* (*mil.*) kidong yŏnsŭp 기동 연습, (*intrigue*) ch'aengnyak 책략. —*vt., vi.* kidong yŏnsŭbŭl hada 기동 연습을 하다.

manhood *n.* sanaidaum 사나이다움. *reach ~* sŏngnyŏni toeda 성년(成年)이 되다.

mania *n.* (*craze*) yŏlgwang 열광, yŏlchung 열중, …kwang …광(狂). *the collecting ~* sujipkwang 수집광/ *a photo ~* sajin-gwang 사진광.

maniac *adj.* (*mad*) mich'in 미친. —*n.* (*madman*) mich'igwangi 미치광이.   「shihada 명시하다.

manifest *vt.* myŏngbaek'age hada 명백하게 하다, myŏng-

manifesto *n.* (*proclamation*) sŏnŏn 선언, sŏngmyŏng 성명. *a political* ~ chŏnggang 정강(政綱).

mankind *n.* (*human race*) illyu 인류, (*human beings*) in-gan 인간, (*male sex*) namsŏng 남성, namja 남자. *M*~ *is corrupted.* Illyunŭn pup'aehaessŭmnida. 인류는 부패했읍니다.

manner *n.* (*behavior*) t'aedo 태도, (*pl.*) (*etiquette*) yejŏl 예절, (*habits*) p'ungsŭp 풍습, (*way*) yangshik 양식. *I don't like his* ~. Kŭ saramŭi t'aedoga shilssŭmnida. 그 사람의 태도가 싫습니다/ *I must teach him* ~s. Kŭ saramŭi pŏrŭsŭl koch'yŏ chuŏya hagessŭmnida. 그 사람의 버릇을 고처 주어야 하겠읍니다/ *in this* ~ irŏn pangshigŭro 이런 방식으로.

mansion *n.* k'ŭn chŏt'aek 큰 저택. *private* ~ sajŏ 사저 (私邸).

manual *adj. a* ~ *labor* son il 손 일. —*n.* (*small book*) p'yŏllam 편람, (*handbook*) annaesŏ 안내서. *a desk* ~ t'aksang p'yŏllam 탁상 편람.

manufacture *n.* chejo 제조. —*vt.* chejohada 제조하다. *a Korean* ~ Han-guk chep'um 한국 제품.

manufacturer *n.* chejoŏpcha 제조업자.

manure *n.* piryo 비료, kŏrŭm 거름.

manuscript *n.* won-go 원고. *an unfinished* ~ miwansŏng wŏn-go 미완성 원고.

many *adj.* manŭn 많은, (*numerous*) tasuŭi 다수의. —*n.* tasu 다수, (*people*) manŭn saram 많은 사람, (*things*) manŭn kŏt 많은 것. *Did you see* ~ *people?* Manŭn saramŭl mannassŭmnikka? 많은 사람을 만났읍니까/ *Do you need so* ~? Kŭrŏk'e mani p'iryohashimnikka? 그렇게 많이 필요하십니까/ *There are* ~ *who think so.* Kŭrŏk'e saenggak'anŭn sarami manssŭmnida. 그렇게 생각하는 사람이 많습니다/ *How* ~ *pears are left in the box?* Sangja-e paega myŏt kae nama issŭmnikka? 상자에 배가 몇 개 남아 있읍니까/ *How* ~ *times did you go to Cheju?* Chejuenŭn myŏt pŏn kassŭmnikka? 제주에는 몇 번 갔읍니까/ *M*~ *times.* Yŏrŏ pŏn. 여러 번/ *a good* ~ kkwae manŭn 꽤 많은.

map 291 **market**

map *n.* chido 지도. *a ~ of Korea* Han-guk chido 한국 지도.

maple *n.* tanp'ung 단풍. *~ tree* tanp'ungnamu 단풍나무.

marble *n.* taerisŏk 대리석. *a ~ statue* taerisŏksang 대리 석상.

March *n.* samwŏl 3월.

march *n.* (*parade*) haengjin 행진, (*music*) haengjin-gok 행진곡. *—vi.* haengjinhada 행진하다. *The troops ~ed by.* Pudaega haengjinhae chinagassŭmnida. 부대가 행진 해 지나갔읍니다/ *a funeral ~* changsonggok 장송곡/ *a wedding ~* kyŏrhon haengjin-gok 결혼 행진곡.

margin *n.* (*border*) kajangjari 가장자리, (*profit*) p'an-mae suik 판매 수익. *The price leaves no ~ of profit.* Kŭ kapsŭronŭn iigi ŏpsŭmnida. 그 값으로는 이익이 없읍 니다.

marine *adj.* (*oceanic*) padaŭi 바다의, haeyangŭi 해양의, (*nautical*) sŏnbagŭi 선박의. *~ products* haesanmul 해 산물/ *~ insurance* haesang pohŏm 해상 보험/ *~ corps* haebyŏngdae 해병대.

mark *n.* (*sign*) kiho 기호, (*symbol*) puho 부호, (*trace*) chaguk 자국, (*trade ~*) sangp'yo 상표, (*target*) p'yo-jŏk 표적, (*standard*) p'yojun 표준, (*grade ~*) chŏmsu 점수. *—vt.* (*make a ~*) p'yorŭl hada 표를 하다. *a question ~* ŭimunp'yo 의문표/ *rub off pencil ~s* yŏnp'il cha-gugŭl chiuda 연필 자국을 지우다/ *Don't put chalk ~ on fences.* (*to inferiors*) Tamjange paengmuk chagugŭl tchikchi marara. 담장에 백묵 자국을 찍지 말아라/ *Have I a ~ on my face?* Nae ŏlgure ŏllugi issŭmnikka? 내 얼굴 에 얼룩이 있읍니까/ *a trade ~* sangp'yo 상표/ *hit the ~* myŏngjunghada 명중하다/ *a failure ~* nakchechŏm 낙제점/*How many ~s did I get in history?* Chŏŭi yŏksa chŏmsunŭn myŏt chŏmimnikka? 저의 역사 점수는 몇 점입 니까/ *get good ~s* choŭn chŏmsurŭl ttada 좋은 점수를 따다.

market *n.* shijang 시장. *~ place* changt'ŏ 장터/ *a fish ~* ŏshijang 어시장/*a vegetable ~* ch'ŏnggwa shijang 청과 시 장/*~ prices* shijang kagyŏk 시장 가격/*the stock ~* chŭngkwŏn shijang 증권 시장/ *a black* ~ amshijang 암시장.

marriage *n.* kyŏrhon 결혼. *a* ~ *ceremony* kyŏrhonshik 결혼식/ *an international* ~ kukche kyŏrhon 국제 결혼/ *a love* ~ yŏnae kyŏrhon 연애 결혼. 「척추.

marrow *n.* (*pith*) ppyŏgol 뼈골. *the spinal* ~ ch'ŏkch'u

marry *vt.,vi.* (*wed*) kyŏrhonhada 결혼하다. *When did you get married?* Ŏnje kyŏrhonhaessŭmnikka? 언제 결혼했읍니까/ *We have been married three years.* Kyŏrhonhan chi samnyŏni toemnida. 결혼한 지 3년이 됩니다/ *She is married to a foreigner.* Kŭ yŏjanŭn oegugin-gwa kyŏrhonhaessŭmnida. 그 여자는 외국인과 결혼했읍니다.

Mars *n.* hwasŏng 화성, kunshin 군신.

marsh *n.* (*swamp*) nŭp 늪. ~ *gas* met'an kasŭ 메탄 가스.

marshal *n.* (*mil.*) yukkun wŏnsu 육군 원수(元帥).

martial *adj.* (*warlike*) chŏnjaengŭi 전쟁의, (*militant*) hojŏnjŏgin 호전적인. ~ *music* kunak 군악/ ~ *law* kyeŏmnyŏng 계엄령/ *court* ~ kunpŏp hoeŭi 군법 회의.

martini *n.* mat'ini 마티니. *May I have a* ~, *please?* Mat'inirŭl han chan chushilkkayo? 마티니를 한 잔 주실까요/ *We don't have* ~*s, I'm sorry.* Mianhajiman mat'iniga ŏpkunyo. 미안하지만 마티니가 없군요.

martyr *n.* sun-gyoja 순교자, (*victim*) hŭisaengja 희생자. *a* ~ *to lover* sarangŭi sun-gyoja 사랑의 순교자.

marvel(l)ous *adj.* (*wonderful*) nollaun 놀라운, (*singular*) kiihan 기이한. *How* ~ ! Nollapkunyo ! 놀랍군요/ *She is a* ~ *pianist.* Kŭ yŏjanŭn mŏtchin p'ianisŭt'ŭimnida. 그 여자는 멋진 피아니스트입니다.

mash *vt.* (*crush*) chinnigida 짓이기다.

mask *n.* kamyŏn 가면, t'al 탈. *wear a* ~ kamyŏnŭl ssŭda 가면을 쓰다/ *put off* ~ kamyŏnŭl pŏtta 가면을 벗다/ *a* ~ *drama* kamyŏn-gŭk 가면극.

〈t'al〉

mason *n.* sŏkkong 석공, sŏksu 석수.

masquerade *n.* kajang mudohoe 가장 무도회.

mass *n.* (*lump*) tŏngŏri 덩어리, (*the* ~*es*) taejung 대중, (*group*) chiptan 집단, (*Chr.*) misa 미사. *a* ~ *of earth* hŭktŏngŏri 흙덩어리/ ～ *media* taejung maech'e 대중 매체/ ～ *production* taeryang saengsan 대량 생산/ *go to* ～ misa-e kada 미사에 가다.

massage *n.* masaji 마사지, anma 안마. *facial* ～ anmyŏn masaji 안면 마사지/ *Have you tried* ～? Masajihae poassŭmnikka? 마사지해 보았읍니까?

mast *n.* (*of a ship*) tottae 돛대.

master *n.* (*of the house*) chuin 주인, (*employer*) koyongju 고용주, (*owner*) soyuja 소유자, (*teacher*) kyosa 교사, (*leader*) chidoja 지도자, (*art, etc.*) taega 대가, (*M～*) sŏksa 석사. —*vt.* (*subdue*) chŏngbok'ada 정복하다. *My* ～ *is very strict.* Uri chuinŭn maeu ŏmhamnida. 우리 주인은 매우 엄합니다/ *a music* ～ ŭmak kyosa 음악 교사/ *M～ of Arts* munhak sŏksa 문학 석사.

masterpiece *n.* kŏlchak 걸작. *a world* ～ segyejŏk myŏngjak 세계적 명작.

mat *n.* totchari 돗자리, kŏjŏk 거적. *a door* ～ toŏ maet'ŭ 도어 매트.

match *n.* (*for ignition*) sŏngnyang 성냥, (*peer*) sangdae 상대, (*contest*) shihap 시합, (*marriage*) kyŏrhon 결혼. —*vi.* (*suit*) ŏullida 어울리다. *Have you got any* ～*es?* Sŏngnyang issŭmnikka? 성냥 있읍니까/ ～ *box* sŏngnyangkap 성냥갑/ *Did you see the boxing* ～ *last night?* Ŏjetpam kwŏnt'u shihap poassŭmnikka? 어젯밤 권투 시합 보았읍니까?

mate *n.* (*companion*) tongnyo 동료, (*spouse*) paeuja 배우자. *school* ～*s* hagu 학우. *Find me the* ～ *of this glove.* I changgabŭi han tchagŭl ch'aja chushio. 이 장갑의 한 짝을 찾아 주시오.

material *adj.* mulchirŭi 물질의, (*important*) chungyohan 중요한. —*n.* (*stuff*) chaeryo 재료. ～ *civilization* mulchil munmyŏng 물질 문명/ ～ *evidence* chungdaehan chŭnggŏ 중대한 증거/ *raw* ～ wŏllyo 원료/ *What kind of* ～ *is this?* Igŏsŭn musŭn chaeryoimnikka? 이것은 무슨 재료입니까?

maternal *adj.* (*motherly*) ŏmŏniŭi 어머니의, mosŏngŭi 모성의. ～ *love* mosŏngae 모성애/ ～ *association* ŏmŏnihoe 어머니회.

mathematics *n.* suhak 수학.

matter *n.* (*subject*) munje 문제, (*business*) il 일, (*substance*) mulchil 물질, (*material*) chaeryo 재료. —*vi.* (*signify*) chungyohada 중요하다. *a ~ of money* ton munje 돈 문제/ *I will ask some one about that ~.* Kŭ munjerŭl nuguege murŏ pogessŭmnida. 그 문제를 누구에게 물어 보겠읍니다/ *What is the ~ with you?* Ŏtchidoen irimnikka? 어찌된 일입니까/ *liquid ~* aekch'e 액체/ *mineral ~* kwangmulchil 광물질/ *What kind of ~ is this?* Igŏsŭn musŭn chaeryoimnikka? 이것은 무슨 재료입니까/ *What does it ~?* Kŭge ŏttŏt'an marimnikka? 그게 어떻단 말입니까/ *It doesn't ~ much.* Pyŏllil animnida. 별일 아닙니다/ *a ~ of course* tangyŏnhan il 당연한 일/ *a matter of fact* sashilsangŭi munje 사실상의 문제.

mattress *n.* ch'imdaeyong yo 침대용 요, maet'ŭrisŭ 매트리스.

mature *adj.* (*ripe*) sŏngsuk'an 성숙한, (*well thought-out*) sukkohan 숙고한, (*due*) man-giŭi 만기의. —*vt.,vi.* (*ripen*) ikta 익다. *persons of ~ years* sŏngsuk'an saramdŭl 성숙한 사람들/ *a ~ mind* wŏnsuk'an chŏngshin 원숙한 정신/ *~ plans* shinjunghan kyehoek 신중한 계획/ *a ~d bill* man-gidoen ŏŭm 만기된 어음.

maturity *n.* (*ripeness*) sŏngsuk 성숙, (*expiration*) man-gi 만기(滿期). *early ~* chosuk 조숙/ *pay at ~* man-gie chiburhada 만기에 지불하다.

May *n.* owŏl 5월. *a ~ queen* owŏrŭi yŏwang 5월의 여왕/ *the ~ Festival* owŏrŭi ch'ukche 5월의 축제.

may *aux. v.* (*possibility*) *You ~call him a hero.* Kŭ saramŭl yŏngungirago hal su issŭmnida. 그 사람을 영웅이라고 할 수 있읍니다/ (*permission*) *M~ I smoke?* Tambae p'iwŏdo chossŭmnikka? 담배 피워도 좋습니까/ *Yes, you ~.* Ne, p'iushipshio. 네 피우십시오/ (*guess*) *I ~ be late.* Nanŭn nŭjŭlchido morŭmnida. 나는 늦을지도 모릅니다/ (*wonder*) *How old ~ she be?* Kŭ yŏjanŭn myŏt sarilkkayo? 그 여자는 몇 살일까요/ (*purpose*) *Work hard that you ~ succeed.* Sŏnggonghadorok yŏlshimhi noryŏk'ashio. 성공하도록 열심히 노력하시오/ (*wish or prayer*) *M~ you both be happy*! Tu punŭi haengbogŭl pimnida. 두 분의 행복을 빕니다.

maybe *adv.* (*perhaps*) ama 아마, ŏtchŏmyŏn 어쩌면. *M~ he is an American.* Kŭ saramŭn ama Miguk saramil kŏmnida. 그 사람은 아마 미국 사람일 겁니다/ *M~ so.* Ama kŭrŏl kŏshimnida. 아마 그럴 것입니다/ *I thought ~ you were a Japanese.* Ilboninilchido morŭndago saenggak'aessŭmnida. 일본인일지도 모른다고 생각했습니다.

mayor *n.* shijang 시장(市長). *the ~ of Seoul* Sŏul shijang 서울 시장/ *a ~'s mansion* shijang kwansa 시장 관사.

me *pron.* (*accusative*) narŭl 나를, (*dative*) na-ege 나에게. *He saw ~.* Kŭ saramŭn narŭl poassŭmnida. 그 사람은 나를 보았읍니다/ *Please give ~ a glass of water.* (Na-ege) mul han k'ŏp chushipshio. (나에게) 물 한 컵 주십시오.

meadow *n.* mokchang 목장.

meal *n.* (*food*) shiksa 식사. *morning ~* choban 조반/ *noon ~* chŏmshim 점심/ *evening ~* chŏnyŏk shiksa 저녁 식사/ *M~s will be served in the plane.* Shiksanŭn kinaeesŏ chegonghamnida. 식사는 기내에서 제공합니다/ *I want my ~s brought to my room.* Shiksanŭn nae pangŭro kajyŏda chushio. 식사는 내 방으로 가져다 주시오/ *Thank you for the wonderful ~.* Hullyunghan shiksa kamsahamnida. 훌륭한 식사 감사합니다/ *eating between ~s* kanshik 간식.

mean *adj.* (*base*) piyŏrhan 비열한, (*shabby*) ch'orahan 초라한, (*stingy*) insaek'an 인색한. —*vt.* (*signify*) ŭimihada 의미하다, (*intend*) hal chakchŏngida 할 작정이다. —*n.* (*way*) pangbŏp 방법, sudan 수단. *Don't be so ~ to your little brother.* Tongsaengege chom chŏmjank'e kushio. 동생에게 좀 점잖게 구시오/ *He is very ~ about money.* Kŭ saramŭn tone mopshi insaek'amnida. 그 사람은 돈에 몹시 인색합니다/ *What do you ~ by this word?* I marŭn musŭn ttŭshimnikka? 이 말은 무슨 뜻입니까/ *I see what you ~.* Malssŭm aradŭtkessŭmnida. 말씀 알아듣겠습니다/ *use every ~s* modŭn sudanŭl tahada 모든 수단을 다하다/ *by foul ~s* pujŏng sudanŭro 부정(不正) 수

단으로.

meaning *n.* (*sense*) ttŭt 뜻, ŭimi 의미, (*intent*) ŭido 의도. *a wide* ~ nŏlbŭn ŭimi 넓은 의미/ *My* ~ *was innocent*. Che ŭidonŭn sunsuhan kŏshiŏssŭmnida. 제 의도는 순전한 것이었습니다.

meanwhile *adv.* kŭ tongane 그 동안에. *in the* ~ irŏkchŏrŏk'anŭn tongane 이럭저럭하는 동안에.

measles *n.* hongyŏk 홍역. *catch the* ~ hongyŏge kŏllida 홍역에 걸리다/ *All my children have had the* ~. Uri aidŭrŭn modu hongyŏgŭl kkŭnnaessŭmnida. 우리 아이들은 모두 홍역을 끝냈습니다.

measure *n.* (*dimensions*) ch'isu 치수. —*vt.* (*calculate*) ch'ŭkchŏnghada 측정하다. *Will you take my* ~? Nae ch'isurŭl chae chushiryŏmnikka? 내 치수를 제 주시렵니까/ *Can you* ~ *accurately*? Chŏnghwak'i chael su issŭmnikka? 정확히 잴 수 있습니까?

measurement *n.* ch'isu 치수. *Please take my* ~s. Ch'isurŭl chae chuseyo. 치수를 제 주세요.

meat *n.* (*animal flesh*) kogi 고기. *lecn* ~ salk'ogi 살코기/ *fresh* ~ shingshinghan kogi 싱싱한 고기.

mechanic *n.* (*artisan*) chikkong 직공, (*motor* ~) kigyegong 기계공.

mechanical *adj.* kigyeŭi 기계의, kigyejŏgin 기계적인. *a* ~ *doll* kigye changch'iŭi inhyŏng 기계 장치의 인형/ ~ *movements* kigyejŏk tongjak 기계적 동작.

mechanism *n.* (*machinery*) kigye changch'i 기계 장치, kigu 기구(機構), (*mechanical operation*) kigye chagyong 기계 작용. *the* ~ *of the body* shinch'eŭi kujo 신체의 구조/ *the* ~ *of government* chŏngbu kigu 정부 기구.

medal *n.* medal 메달, (*mil.*) hunjang 훈장. *a gold* ~ kŭmmedal 금메달/ *a silver* ~ ŭnmedal 은메달/ *a bronze* ~ tongmedal 동메달.

meddle *vi.* (*interfere*) kansŏp'ada 간섭하다, (*tamper*) chumurŭda 주무르다. *Don't* ~ *in my affairs*. Nae ire kansŏp'aji mashio. 내 일에 간섭하지 마시오/ *Who's been meddling with my papers*? Nuga nae sŏryurŭl kŏndŭryŏssŭmnikka? 누가 내 서류를 건드렸습니까?

meddler *n.* (*busybody*) kansŏpcha 간섭자.

mediate *vt.*,*vi.* (*reconcile*) chungjaehada 중재하다, (*intercede*) hwahaeshik'ida 화해시키다.

mediator *n.* chungjaein 중재인, chojŏngja 조정자.

medical *adj.* ŭihagŭi 의학의. *a ~ examination* kŏn-gang chindan 건강 진단/ *~ inspection* kŏmyŏk 검역/ *a ~ student* ŭihakto 의학도.

medicine *n.* yak 약. *Take this ~ three times a day.* I yagŭl harue se pŏnssik tŭshipshio. 이 약을 하루에 세 번씩 드십시오/ *Bring me some ~ for airsickness.* Pihaenggi mŏlmi yagŭl chuseyo. 비행기 멀미 약을 주세요.

meditate *vt.*,*vi.* (*ponder*) sukkohada 숙고하다, (*plan*) kyehoek'ada 계획하다. *~ on one's past life* chinagan saengaerŭl muksanghada 지나간 생애를 묵상하다/ *~ revenge* poksurŭl kyehoek'ada 복수를 계획하다.

meditation *n.* (*pondering*) sukko 숙고, (*quiet thought*) myŏngsang 명상.

Mediterranean Sea chijunghae 지중해.

medium *adj.* (*middle*) chungganŭi 중간의, (*moderate*) pot'ongŭi 보통의. *—n.* chunggan 중간. *How would you like your steak? M~, please.* Sŭt'eik'ŭnŭn ŏttŏk'e kuwŏ tŭrilkkayo? Pot'ongŭro kuwŏ chuseyo. 스테이크는 어떻게 구워 드릴까요? 보통으로 구워 주세요/ *a ~ size one* chungganch'i 중간치.

meet *vi.*,*vt.* (*encounter*) mannada 만나다, (*welcome*) majunghada 마중하다. *I'm very glad to ~ you.* Manna poepke toeŏ pan-gapsŭmnida. 만나 뵙게 되어 반갑습니다/ *Let's ~ at seven Sunday morning.* Iryoil ach'im ilgopshie mannapshida. 일요일 아침 7시에 만납시다.

meeting *n.* (*congregation*) hoehap 회합, (*encounter*)mannam 만남, (*gathering*) moim 모임, (*interview*) myŏnhoe 면회. *an alumni ~* tongch'anghoe 동창회/ *a general ~ of shareholders* chuju ch'onghoe 주주 총회/ *a mass ~ of citizens* shimin taehoe 시민 대회/ *the opening of a ~* kaehoe 개회.

melancholy *n.* (*gloom*) uul 우울. *—adj.* (*gloomy*) uur-han 우울한.

mellow *adj.* (*ripe*) igŭn 익은, (*sweet*) kammiroun 감미

로운.

melody *n.* (*harmony*) sŏnyul 선율, mellodi 멜로디, (*tune*) kokcho 곡조. *old Korean melodies* Han-gugŭi yet kagok 한국의 옛 가곡.

melon *n.* mellon 멜론, ch'amoe 참외, (*Am.*) ingyŏ iik 잉여 이익. *a water* ~ subak 수박.

melt *vi.,vt.* nokta 녹다, nogida 녹이다. *This cake* ~*s in the mouth.* I k'eik'ŭnŭn ip anesŏ sarŭrŭ noksŭmnida. 이 케이크는 입 안에서 사르르 녹습니다.

member *n.* (*limb*) sonbal 손발, (*of an assoc.*) hoewŏn 회원, (*of a company*) hoesawŏn 회사원, (*of a group*) tanwŏn 단원. *a regular* ~ chŏnghoewŏn 정(正)회원/ *a* ~ *of the National Assembly* kuk'oe ŭiwŏn 국회 의원/ *Is Korea a* ~ *to the United Nations?* Han-gugŭn yuen hoewŏn-gugimnikka? 한국은 유엔 회원국입니까?

memorandum *n.* kaksŏ 각서, pimangnok 비망록, (*memo*) memo 메모, (*company*) chŏnggwan 정관.

memorial *n.* kinyŏmmul 기념물, (*monument*) kinyŏmbi 기념비. *a* ~ *day* kinyŏmil 기념일/ *a* ~ *service* ch'udoshik 추도식.

memory *n.* kiŏk 기억, kiŏngnyŏk 기억력. *You have a splendid* ~. Tangshinŭi kiŏngnyŏgŭn nollapsŭmnida. 당신의 기억력은 놀랍습니다.

mend *vt.,vi.* (*repair*) surihada 수리하다, koch'ida 고치다, (*patch up*) kipta 깁다, (*darn*) kkwemaeda 꿰매다. *I had my shoes* ~*ed.* Nanŭn kudurŭl koch'yŏssŭmnida. 나는 구두를 고쳤읍니다.

menses *n.* wŏlgyŏng 월경. *have the* ~ wŏlgyŏnghada 월경하다/ *be in one's* ~ wŏlgyŏng chungida 월경 중이다.

mental *adj.* chŏngshinŭi 정신의. ~ *age* chŏngshin yŏllyŏng 정신 연령/ *a* ~ *disease* chŏngshinpyŏng 정신병/ ~ *disorder* chŏngshin isang 정신 이상/~ *test* chinŭng kŏmsa 지능 검사/~ *effort(s)* chŏngshinchŏk noryŏk 정신적 노력.

mention *vt.* (*speak about*) marhada 말하다, (*write about*) ssŭda 쓰다. *My father has often* ~*ed you to me.* Taegŭi malssŭmŭn appaga chaju hasyŏssŭmnida. 댁의 말씀은 아빠가 자주 하셨읍니다/ *Don't* ~ *it.* Ch'ŏnmanŭi malssŭm 천만의 말씀.

menu *n.* (*bill of fare*) menyu 메뉴, shiktanp'yo 식단표.
Let me look at the ~, *please.* Menyu chom poyŏ chushio.
메뉴 좀 보여 주시오/ *Here is the* ~ *and wine list.* Me-
nyuwa churyu risŭt'ŭga yŏgi issŭmnida. 메뉴와 주류 리
스트가 여기 있읍니다.

mercantile *adj.* (*commercial*) sangŏbŭi 상업의. *the* ~
field sangŏpkye 상업계/ *a* ~ *paper* sangŏp ŏŭm 상업 어
음/ ~ *law* sangpŏp 상법.

merchandise *n.* (*goods*) sangp'um 상품. *general* ~ cha-
p'wa 잡화/ *returned* ~ panp'um 반품(返品).

merchant *n.* sangin 상인. *a retail* ~ somaesangin 소매상
인/ *a wholesale* ~ tomaesangin 도매상인.

merciful *adj.* (*compassionate*) injŏng manŭn 인정 많은,
(*lenient*) kwandaehan 관대한. ~ *to others* namege in-
jŏngi mant'a 남에게 인정이 많다.

merciless *adj.* mujabihan 무자비한.

mercury *n.* suŭn 수은, (*thermometer*) ondogye 온도계.

mercy *n.* (*compassion*) chabi 자비, (*blessing*) ŭnhye 은
혜. *That is a* ~ ! Kŭgŏt ch'am komapkunyo. 그것 참
고맙군요/ *We must be thankful for small mercies.*
Chagŭn ŭnhyeedo kamsahaeya hamnida. 작은 은혜에도
감사해야 합니다/ *M* ~ ! Chŏrŏn! 저런!

mere *adj.* (*simple*) tansunhan 단순한. *She is a* ~ *child.*
Kŭ yŏja ainŭn ajik ŏrinie chinaji anssŭmnida. 그 여자
아이는 아직 어린이에 지나지 않습니다/ ~ *formality* tansunhan hyŏngshik 단순한 형식.

merely *adv.* (*only*) tanji 단지, ojik 오직. *I* ~ *asked his*
name. Kŭŭi irŭmŭl murŏssŭl ppunimnida. 그의 이름을
물었을 뿐입니다.

merit *n.* (*excellence*) changchŏm 장점, (*worth*) kach'i 가
치, (*pl.*) (*deserts*) konggwa 공과(功過). *have both* ~ *s*
and demerits changdanchŏmŭl kajigo itta 장단점을 가지
고 있다/ *a person of* ~ *s* kongnoja 공로자.

merry *adj.* (*gay*) k'waehwarhan 쾌활한, (*joyous*) chŭlgŏun 즐거운. *a* ~ *laugh* myŏngnanghan usŭm 명랑한 웃
음/ *I wish you a* ~ *Christmas.* K'ŭrisŭmasŭrŭl ch'uk'a-

hamnida. 크리스마스를 축하합니다/ *the ~ month of May* chŭlgŏun owŏl 즐거운 5월.

merry-go-round *n*. hoejŏn mongma 회전 목마.

merry-making *n*. (*fun*) hwallak 환락, (*festivity*) chanch'i 잔치.

mesh *n*. (*of net*) kŭmulk'o 그물코, (*snare*) olgami 올가미.

mess *n*.(*disorder*) hollan 혼란. *You have made a ~ of the job.* Tangshini irŭl mangch'yŏ noassŭmnida. 당신이 일을 망쳐 놓았읍니다/ *~ hall* shiktang 식당/ *~ up* mujilsŏ 무질서.

message *n*. (*information*) soshik 소식, (*verbal*) chŏn-gal 전갈, (*appeal*) kyosŏ 교서(敎書). *Is there any ~?* Chŏnhashil malssŭmirado issŭmnikka? 전하실 말씀이라도 있읍니까/ *May I leave a ~?* Malssŭm chom chŏnhae chushilkkayo? 말씀 좀 전해 주실까요/ *May I take a ~?* Chŏnhashil malssŭmi issŭshinjiyo? 전하실 말씀이 있으신지요?

messenger *n*. (*envoy*) shimburŭmkkun 심부름꾼, (*carrier*) paedarin 배달인.

metal *n*. kŭmsok 금속. *alloyed ~* hapkŭm 합금/ *~ work* kŭmsok segongp'um 금속 세공품/ *Is it made of wood or ~?* Kŭgŏsŭn mokcheimnikka, kŭmsokcheimnikka? 그것은 목제입니까, 금속제입니까?

metallic *adj*. kŭmsogŭi 금속의.

meteor *n*. (*shooting star*) yusŏng 유성, (*~ite*) unsŏk 운석(隕石).

meteorological *adj*. kisangŭi 기상의. *~ observatory* kisangdae 기상대/ *~ station* ch'ŭk'uso 측후소.

meter, metre *n*. (*measure*) mit'ŏ 미터, (*gauge*) kyeryanggi 계량기. *an electric ~* chŏn-gi kyeryanggi 전기 계량기/ *a water ~* sudo kyeryanggi 수도 계량기.

method *n*. pangbŏp 방법. *a practical ~* shilchejŏgin pangbŏp 실제적인 방법/ *a scientific ~* kwahakchŏk pangbŏp 과학적 방법.

methodical *adj*. (*systematic*) chojikchŏgin 조직적인.

Methodist *n*. kamnigyo shinja 감리교 신자.

metric system mit'ŏpŏp 미터법.

metropolis *n*. (*capital*) sudo 수도, (*centre*) chungshimj

중심지.

Mexico *n.* Mekshik'o 멕시코.

microbe *n.* (*germ*) segyun 세균.

microphone *n.* hwaksŏnggi 확성기, maik'ŭrop'on 마이크로폰.

microscope *n.* hyŏnmigyŏng 현미경. *an electron* ~ chŏnja hyŏnmigyŏng 전자 현미경.

middle *adj.* han-gaundeŭi 한가운데의, chungganŭi 중간의. —*n.* chungang 중앙, han-gaunde 한가운데. *the* ~ *finger* kaundetsonkarak 가운뎃손가락/ *a* ~ *school* chunghakkyo 중학교/*the M*~ *East* chungdong 중동/ ~ *age* chungnyŏn 중년/ *the* ~ *class* chungnyu kyegŭp 중류 계급.

middleman *n.* (*intermediary*) chunggaein 중개인, (*broker*) pŭrok'ŏ 브로커.

midnight *n.* hanbamchung 한밤중, chajŏng 자정.

midst *n.* hanbokp'an 한복판. —*adv.* hanbokp'ane 한복판에.

midway *adj.* (*halfway*) chungdoŭi 중도의. —*n.* chungdo 중도.

midwife *n.* sanp'a 산파, chosanwŏn 조산원.

mien *n.* (*manner*) momgajim 몸가짐, (*appearance*) p'ungch'ae 풍채. *her sorrowful* ~ kŭ yŏjaŭi sŭlp'ŭn mosŭp 그 여자의 슬픈 모습/ *his warlike* ~ kŭŭi hojŏnjŏgin t'aedo 그의 호전적인 태도.

might[1] *n.* (*power*) him 힘, (*ability*) nŭngnyŏk 능력, (*physical force*) wallyŏk 완력. *armed* ~ muryŏk 무력 (武力)/ *with all one's* ~ himkkŏt 힘껏.

might[2] *aux.v.* (*past form of may*) *How old* ~ *she be?* Myŏt sarina toeŏssŭlkkayo? 몇 살이나 되었을까요?

mild *adj.* (*gentle*) onhwahan 온화한, (*amiable*) sangnyanghan 상냥한, (*soft*) pudŭrŏun 부드러운. *a* ~ *climate* onhwahan kihu 온화한 기후/ ~ *cheese* pudŭrŏun ch'ijŭ 부드러운 치즈.

mile *n.* mail 마일. *How much is a* ~ *in kilometers?* Il mairŭn myŏt k'illoimnikka? 1마일은 몇 킬로입니까?

military *adj.* yukkunŭi 육군의. ~ *academy* yukkun sagwan hakkyo 육군 사관 학교/ ~ *policeman* hŏnbyŏng 헌병/ ~ *service* pyŏngyŏk 병역/ *a* ~ *hospital* yukkun pyŏngwŏn 육군 병원.

milk *n.* uyu 우유. *Give me a bottle of* ~. Uyu han pyŏng chushio. 우유 한 병 주시오.

milkman *n.* uyu paedalbu 우유 배달부.

milkpowder *n.* punyu 분유.

Milky Way ŭnhasu 은하수.

mill *n. a saw~* chejaeso 제재소/ *a spinning* ~ pangjik kongjang 방직 공장/ *a water* ~ mullebanga 물레방아/ *a wind~* p'ungch'a 풍차.

millet *n.* kijang 기장.

million *n.* paengman 백만. ~*s of* subaengmanŭi 수백만의.

million(n)aire *n.* paengman changja 백만 장자.

millstone *n.* maettol 맷돌.

<maettol>

mimic *vt.* (*imitate*) hyungnaenaeda 흉내내다. —*adj.* mobangŭi 모방의. —*n.* hyungnaejangi 흉내장이.

mince *vt.* (*hash*) chalge ssŏlda 잘게 썰다. ~*d meat* (~*meat*) tajin kogi 다진 고기.

mind *n.* (*soul*) maŭm 마음, (*thought*) saenggak 생각, (*intent*) ŭihyang 의향. —*vt.,vi* (*heed*) chuŭihada 주의하다, (*care about*) yŏmnyŏhada 염려하다, (*take care of*) tolboda 돌보다. *What is on your* ~? Hago ship'ŭn malssŭmŭn muŏshinjiyo? 하고 싶은 말씀은 무엇인지요/ *I'm of your* ~. Kat'ŭn ŭigyŏnimnida. 같은 의견입니다/ *Do you* ~ *if I smoke?* Tambae p'iwŏdo chossŭmnikka? 담배 피워도 좋습니까/ *Would you* ~ *passing me that plate?* Kŭ chŏpshi chom iriro chushigessŭmnikka? 그 접시 좀 이리로 주시겠읍니까/ *Never* ~! Yŏmnyŏ mashio. 염려 마시오/ *M*~ *your own business!* Tangshin irina chal hashio. 당신 일이나 잘 하시오!

mine[1] *pron.* naegŏt 내것. *Is this book yours or* ~? I ch'aegŭn tangshin kŏshimnikka, animyŏn naŭi kŏshimnikka? 이 책은 당신 것입니까, 아니면 나의 것입니까/ *That umbrella is* ~. Kŭ usanŭn naegŏshimnida. 그 우산은 내것입니다.

mine² *n.* (*pit*) kwangsan 광산. *a coal* ~ t'an-gwang 탄광/ *a gold* ~ kŭmgwang 금광/ *a* ~ *worker* kwangsan no-dongja 광산 노동자.

miner *n.* kwangbu 광부.

mineral *n.* kwangmul 광물, (*chem.*) mugimul 무기물. ~ *resources* kwangmul chawŏn 광물 자원/ ~ *waters* t'an-sansu 탄산수/ *We need various vitamins and* ~s. Yŏrŏ kaji pit'amin-gwa mugimuri p'iryohamnida. 여러 가지 비타민과 무기물이 필요합니다.

miniature *n.* (*epitome*) ch'ukto 축도.

minimum *n.* ch'oesohando 최소한도. —*adj.* (*smallest possible*) ch'oesohan 최소한.

minister *n.* (*pastor*) moksa 목사, (*secretary*) changgwan 장관, (*envoy*) kongsa 공사(公使). *Prime M*~ kungmu ch'ongni 국무 총리/ *the M*~ *of Foreign Affairs* oemubu changgwan 외무부 장관/ *the M*~ *of Defense* kukpangbu changgwan 국방부 장관/ *the M*~ *of Education* mun-gyobu changgwan 문교부 장관/ *the M*~ *of Home Affairs* naemubu changgwan 내무부 장관/ *the M*~ *of Culture and Information* mun-gongbu changgwan 문공부 장관/ *the M*~ *of Justice* pŏmmubu changgwan 법무부 장관/ *Vice M*~ ch'agwan 차관.

ministry *n.* (*cabinet*) naegak 내각, (*of the church*) sŏngjik 성직(聖職). *the M*~ *of Transportation* kyot'ongbu 교통부.

minor *n.* (*infant*) misŏngnyŏn 미성년. —*adj.* (*smaller*) chagŭn p'yŏnŭi 작은 편의, (*lesser*) sosuŭi 소수의. *We can't sell cigarettes to* ~s. Misŏngnyŏnegenŭn tambaerŭl p'al su ŏpsŭmnida. 미성년에게는 담배를 팔 수 없읍니다.

minority *n.* (*smaller number*) sosu 소수, (*opp. to majority*) sosup'a 소수파, (*legal infancy*) misŏngnyŏn 미성년(未成年).

mint *n.* (*for coinage*) chop'yeguk 조폐국, (*herb*) pak'a 박하. *the Korea M*~ *Corporation* Han-guk chop'ye kong sa 한국 조폐 공사.

minute *n.* pun 분(分). *in a* ~ kot 곧/ *We arrived here a*

few ~s ahead of the time. Isambun chŏne toch'a-
k'aessŭmnida. 2, 3분 전에 도착했읍니다.

miracle *n.* (*supernatural event*) kijŏk 기적, (*marvel*)
shin-gihan il 신기한 일. *the ~ of Asia* Asiaŭi kijŏk 아시
아의 기적.

mirror *n.* kŏul 거울. *Look at yourself in the ~.* Kŏure
chashinŭl pich'uŏ poshipshio. 거울에 자신을 비추어 보십시
오/ *Would you like to use a ~?* Kŏurŭl ssŭshige-
ssŭmnikka? 거울을 쓰시겠읍니까?

miscarriage *n.* (*failure*) shilsu 실수, (*abortion*) yusan 유
산. *have a ~* yusanhada 유산하다.

mischief *n.* (*prank*) changnan 장난. *do ~* changnanhada 장난하다/ *Tell the children to keep out of ~.* Chang-
nanhaji maldorok aidŭrege irŭshipshio. 장난하지 말도록
아이들에게 이르십시오.

mischievous *adj.* (*harmful*) haeroun 해로운, (*naughty*)
changnankkurŏgiŭi 장난꾸러기의. *a ~ child* changnan-
kkurŏgi 장난꾸러기.

miser *n.* kudusoe 구두쇠, norangi 노랑이.

miserable *adj.* (*pitiable*) pulssanghan 불쌍한, (*wretched*)
pich'amhan 비참한, (*poor*) pyŏnbyŏnch'anŭn 변변찮은.
a ~ life pich'amhan saenghwal 비참한 생활.

misery *n.* (*suffering*) kot'ong 고통, (*poverty*) pin-gon
빈곤, (*discontent*) pulp'yŏng punja 불평 분자. *live in ~
and want* kot'onggwa pin-gon soge salda 고통과 빈곤 속
에 살다.

misfortune *n.* (*ill luck*) purun 불운, (*adversity*) yŏk-
kyŏng 역경, (*calamity*) chaenan 재난.

mishap *n.* (*mischance*) chaenan 재난, (*unhappiness*) purun 불운. *industrial ~s* sanŏpchae 산업재(產業災)/*a traffic ~* kyot'ong sago 교통 사고.

misinform *vt.* chalmot allida 잘못 알리다. *I find I was
~ed about it.* Nanŭn kŭgŏsŭl chalmot tŭrŭn kŏsŭl arassŭmnida. 나는 그것을 잘못 들은 것을 알았읍니다.

misinformation *n.* obo 오보(誤報).

misjudge *vt.* (*judge wrongly*) op'anhada 오판하다, (*un-
derrate*) yatpoda 얕보다.

mislay *vt.* (*lose*) tugo ijŏbŏrida 두고 잊어버리다, (*misplace*) chalmot tuda 잘못 두다. *I have mislaid my passport.* Yŏkwŏnŭl ŏdi tuŏnnŭnji ijŏtkunyo. 여권을 어디 두었는지 잊었군요.

mislead *vt.* (*lead astray*) chalmot indohada 잘못 인도하다, (*delude*) sogida 속이다.

misplace *vt.* chalmot tuda 잘못 두다. *You may have ～d it.* Ŏdi kŭgŏl chalmot tuŏtketchiyo. 어디 그걸 잘못 두었겠지요.

misprint *n.* oshik 오식.

miss *vt.,vi.* (*fail to hit*) noch'ida 놓치다, (*notice absence of*) ŏpsŭmŭl alda 없음을 알다, ŏpsŏsŏ sŏpsŏp'ada 없어서 섭섭하다. —*n.* (*failure*) shilch'aek 실책, (*omission*) t'allak 탈락. *I have ～ed the train.* Kich'arŭl noch'yŏssŭmnida. 기차를 놓쳤읍니다/ *Have you ～ed anything?* Muŏsŭl irŏssŭmnikka? 무엇을 잃었읍니까/ *We shall ～ you badly.* Tangshini an kyeshimyŏn maeu ssŭlssŭrhagetkunyo. 당신이 안 계시면 매우 쓸쓸하겠군요/ *Missing home, aren't you?* Kohyang saenggak nashijiyo? 고향 생각 나시지요?

Miss *n.* yang 양(孃), misŭ 미스. ～ *Lee* I yang 이 양. *Good morning, ～!* Sŏnsaengnim, annyŏng! 선생님, 안녕!

mission *n.* (*delegation*) sajŏltan 사절단, (*religious institution*) chŏndohoe 전도회. *a trade ～ to South America* Nammi p'agyŏn muyŏk sajŏltan 남미 파견 무역 사절단/ ～ *school* chŏndo hakkyo 전도 학교.

missionary *n.* sŏn-gyosa 선교사. *a foreign ～* oegugin sŏn-gyosa 외국인 선교사/ ～ *work* chŏndo saŏp 전도 사업.

misspell *vt.* ch'ŏlcharŭl chalmot ssŭda 철자를 잘못 쓰다. *a misspelt word* ch'ŏlchaga t'ŭllin tanŏ 철자가 틀린 단어/ *These words are often ～ed even among American people.* I tanŏnŭn kakkŭm Migugindŭl saiesŏdo ch'ŏlchaga t'ŭllinŭn suga issŭmnida. 이 단어는 가끔 미국인들 사이에서도 철자가 틀리는 수가 있읍니다.

mist *n.* (*fog*) an-gae 안개. *an evening ～* chŏnyŏk an-gae 저녁 안개.

mistake *n.* chalmot 잘못, t'ŭllim 틀림. —*vt.,vi.* t'ŭllida

틀리다. *There is a ~ in the bill.* Kyesansŏe t'ŭllin tega itkunyo. 계산서에 틀린 데가 있군요/ *I made no ~ in selection.* Nae sŏnt'aegenŭn t'ŭllimi ŏpsŭmnida. 내 선택에는 틀림이 없읍니다/ *I took your umbrella by ~.* Chalmot'ayŏ tangshin usanŭl kajyŏwassŭmnida. 잘못하여 당신 우산을 가져왔읍니다/ *I mistook you for your brother.* Tangshinŭl tangshin hyŏngnimŭro chalmot poassŭmnida. 당신을 당신 형님으로 잘못 보았읍니다/ *I was mistaken for a spy.* Nanŭn kanch'ŏbŭro oinŭl padassŭmnida. 나는 간첩으로 오인을 받았읍니다.

mister *n.* ssi 씨(氏), sŏnsaengnim 선생님. *Mr. Kang* Kangssi 강씨, Kang sŏnsaengnim 강 선생님.

mistress *n.* (*Mrs.*) chubu 주부, anchuin 안주인, (*title of courtesy*) yŏsa 여사, (*female teacher*) yŏgyosa 여교사, (*paramour*) chŏngbu 정부. *Is your ~ at home?* Puinŭn taege kyeshimnikka? 부인은 댁에 계십니까/ *keep a ~* ch'ŏbŭl tuda 첩을 두다.

mistrust *vt.* shinyonghaji ant'a 신용하지 않다. *We ~ such a guy.* Kŭrŏn nomŭn mitchi anssŭmnida. 그런 놈은 믿지 않습니다.

misunderstand *vt.* ohaehada 오해하다. *I am misunderstood.* Nanŭn ohaerŭl patko issŭmnida. 나는 오해를 받고 있읍니다/ *You have misunderstood my advice.* Tangshinŭn nae ch'unggorŭl ohaehasyŏssŭmnida. 당신은 내 충고를 오해하셨읍니다.

misunderstanding *n.* (*mistake*) ohae 오해, (*disagreement*) purhwa 불화.

mix *vt.,vi.* (*mingle together*) sŏkta 섞다, honhap'ada 혼합하다, (*combine*) sŏkkida 섞이다. *M~ them well.* Chal sŏkkŭshipshio. 잘 섞으십시오/ *Never ~ them up.* Sŏkchi mashipshio. 섞지 마십시오.

mixture *n.* (*mixing*) honhap 혼합, (*blend*) honhammul 혼합물. *a ~ of sand and cement* moraewa shiment'ŭŭi honhammul 모래와 시멘트의 혼합물.

moan *n.* (*groan*) shinŭm 신음, (*lament*) hant'an 한탄. —*vi.,vt.* shinŭmhada 신음하다.

mob *n.* (*rabble*) p'okto 폭도, (*masses*) taejung 대중,

(*crowd*) kunjung 군중. ~ *psychology* kunjung shimni
군중 심리.

mobilize *vt.* (*troops, ships*) tongwŏnhada 동원하다.

mock *vt.,vi.* (*ridicule*) piutta 비웃다, (*imitate*) hyungnaenaeda 흉내내다. —*n.* (*jeer*) chorong 조롱. *Why do
you ~ at me?* Wae narŭl choronghashio? 왜 나를 조롱하
시오?

mode *n.* (*manner*) yangshik 양식, (*fashion*) yuhaeng 유
행. *a ~ of life* saenghwal yangshik 생활 양식/ *the latest
~s* ch'oeshin yuhaeng 최신 유행.

model *n.* (*pattern*) mohyŏng 모형, (*example*) ponbogi 본
보기, (*exemplar*) mobŏm 모범, (*for artist's pose*) model
모델. *a fashion ~* p'aesyŏn model 패션 모델/ *act as a ~*
moderi toeda 모델이 되다/ *This ~ is very popular.*
I hyŏngi maeu inkiga issŭmnida. 이 형이 매우 인기가
있읍니다.

moderate *adj.* (*reasonable*) on-gŏnhan 온건한, (*medium*)
chŏktanghan 적당한, (*fair*) susuhan 수수한. —*n.*
(*political party*) on-gŏnp'a 온건파. *The hotel is ~ in
its charges.* Kŭ hot'erŭi yogŭmŭn chŏktanghamnida.
그 호텔의 요금은 적당합니다/ *a ~ income* almajŭn suip 알
맞은 수입/ *a ~ request* muri ŏmnŭn yogu 무리 없는 요구.

modern *adj.* (*recent*) hyŏndaeŭi 현대의, kŭndaeŭi 근대의,
(*up-to-date*) shinshigŭi 신식의. ~ *history* kŭndaesa 근대
사/ ~ *style* hyŏndaeshik 현대식.

modernize *vt.* hyŏndaehwahada 현대화하다.

modest *adj.* (*humble*) kyŏmsonhan 겸손한, (*decent*) yam-
jŏnhan 얌전한, (*moderate*) susuhan 수수한, (*shy*) su-
jubŭn 수줍은. *He is very ~.* Kŭ punŭn maeu kyŏmson-
hamnida. 그 분은 매우 겸손합니다/ ~ *speech* kyŏmsonhan
malssi 겸손한 말씨.

modify *vt.* (*change*) pyŏn-gyŏnghada 변경하다, (*lessen*)
kyŏnggamhada 경감하다, (*gram.*) (*qualify*) sushik'ada
수식하다. *You had better ~ your tone.* Ŏjorŭl natch'unŭn
p'yŏni chok'essŭmnida. 어조를 낮추는 편이 좋겠읍니다.

Mohammedan *n.* hoegyodo 회교도. —*adj.* hoegyoŭi 회교
의. *a ~ country* hoegyoguk 회교국.

moist *adj.* (*damp*) ch'ukch'uk'an 축축한, sŭpkich'an 습기찬. ~ *ground* ch'ukch'uk'an ttang 축축한 땅.

moisture *n.* (*dampness*) sŭpki 습기.

mold *n.* (*matrix*) chuhyŏng 주형, kŏp'ujip 거푸집, (*form*) moyang 모양, (*pattern*) mohyŏng 모형, (*mildew*) komp'angi 곰팡이.

moldy *adj.* (*musty*) komp'angnae nanŭn 곰팡내 나는. *become* ~ komp'angi sŭlda 곰팡이 슬다/ ~ *food* komp'angnae nanŭn ŭmshik 곰팡내 나는 음식.

mole *n.* (*animal*) tudŏji 두더지, (*on skin*) samagwi 사마귀, (*breakwater*) pangp'aje 방파제.

molehill *n.* tudŏji kumŏng 두더지 구멍. *make a mountain out of a* ~ ch'imsobongdaehada 침소봉대하다.

moment *n.* (*instant*) sun-gan 순간, (*time*) ttae 때. *Please wait a* ~. Chamkkan kidaryŏ chushipshio. 잠깐 기다려 주십시오/ *I can't tell you at this* ~. Chigŭmŭn marhal su ŏpsŭmnida. 지금은 말할 수 없읍니다/ *Won't you come in for a* ~? Chamshi tŭrŏoshipshio. 잠시 들어오십 시오/ *I'll be with you in a* ~. Kot kagessŭmnida. 곧 가 겠읍니다.

monarch *n.* (*king*) kunju 군주.

monastery *n.* (*of male*) sudowŏn 수도원. *join a* ~ sudowŏne tŭrŏgada 수도원에 들어가다.

Monday *n.* wŏryoil 월요일.

money *n.* ton 돈, kŭmjŏn 금전. *How would you like your* ~? Tonŭl ottŏk'e tŭrilkkayo? 돈을 어떻게 드릴까 요/ *That is a lot of* ~. Kŭgŏsŭn sangdanghan kŭmaegimnida. 그것은 상당한 금액입니다/*make* ~ tonŭl pŏlda 돈을 벌다/ *borrow* ~ tonŭl pillida 돈을 빌리다/ *paper* ~ chip'ye 지폐/ *counterfeit* ~ wijo hwap'ye 위조 화폐/ ~ *box* chŏgŭmt'ong 저금통/ *I have no* ~ *with me.* Kajin toni ŏpsŭmnida. 가진 돈이 없읍니다/ ~ *order* hwan 환(換)/ ~ *changer* hwan-gŭmsang 환금상.

monkey *n.* wŏnsungi 원숭이. ~ *business* hyŏpchap 협잡/ *You little* ~! Yo changnankkurŏgiya! 요 장난꾸러기야!

monopoly *n.* chŏnmae 전매. ~ *goods* chŏnmaep'um 전매 품/ *the M*~ *Office* chŏnmaech'ŏng 전매청.

monsoon *n.* kyejŏlp'ung 계절풍.

monster *n.* (*griffin, etc.*) koemul 괴물, (*freak of nature*) kihyŏngmul 기형물. *an ugly* ~ ch'uhan koemul 추한 괴물.

month *n.* tal 달, wŏl 월. *this* ~ idal 이달/ *last* ~ chinandal 지난달/ *next* ~ taŭmtal 다음달/ *one* ~ han tal 한 달/ *In which* ~ *were you born?* Tangshinŭn ŏnŭ tare t'aeŏnassŭmnikka? 당신은 어느 달에 태어났읍니까/ *How many* ~*s have you been in Korea?* Han-guge wasŏ myŏt tari toeŏssŭmnikka? 한국에 와서 몇 달이 되었읍니까/ *Only three* ~*s.* Kyŏu sŏk tal toeŏssŭmnida. 겨우 석 달 되었읍니다.

monthly *adj.* maedarŭi 매달의. —*n.* (*periodicals*) wŏlgan chapchi 월간 잡지. ~ *instalment* wŏlbu 월부/ ~ *salary* wŏlgŭp 월급.

monument *n.* (*memorial*) kinyŏmbi 기념비. *ancient* ~ yŏksajŏk kinyŏmmul 역사적 기념물/ *natural* ~ ch'ŏnyŏn kinyŏmmul 천연 기념물.

mood *n.* (*feeling*) kibun 기분, shimjŏng 심정. *a gloomy* ~ uurhan kibun 우울한 기분/ *a festive* ~ ch'ukche kibun 축제 기분/ *I am not in the* ~ *for seeing anyone.* Nugurŭl manna pol kibuni naji anssŭmnida. 누구를 만나 볼 기분이 나지 않습니다.

moon *n.* tal 달. *a full* ~ manwŏl 만월/ *a new* ~ ch'osŭngtal 초승달/ *an old* ~ kŭmŭmtal 그믐달/ *At what time does the* ~ *rise?* Myŏt shie tari ttŭmnikka? 몇 시에 달이 뜹니까/ *Won't you come out somewhere to view the* ~? Ŏdi talgugyŏng kaji ank'essŭmnikka? 어디 달구경 가지 않겠읍니까/ *an eclipse of the* ~ wŏlshik 월식.

moonlight *n.* talpit 달빛, wŏlgwang 월광. *a* ~ *night* talpam 달밤/ ~ *sonata* wŏlgwanggok 월광곡.

moor *vt.* chŏngbakshik'ida 정박시키다.

mop *n.* mop 몹, kin charu tallin kŏlle 긴 자루 달린 걸레.

moral *adj.* (*virtuous*) todŏkchŏgin 도덕적인, (*ethical*) yullijŏgin 윤리적인. —*n.* (*maxim*) kyohun 교훈, (*morality*) tŏk'aeng 덕행, (*ethics*) yulli 윤리. *a* ~ *question* todŏkchŏk munje 도덕적 문제/ *public* ~*s* sahoeŭi p'unggi 사회의 풍기/ *social* ~ kongjung todŏk 공중 도덕.

morale *n.* sagi 사기(士氣). *have high* ~ sagiga wangsŏng-hada 사기가 왕성하다.

morality *n.* todŏk 도덕.

more *adj.* tŏ manŭn 더 많은. —*adv.* tŏuk 더욱. *Would you like some* ~ *soup?* Sup'ŭrŭl chomdŏ tŭrilkkayo? 수프를 좀더 드릴까요/ *May I have one* ~? Hana tŏ kajyŏdo chossŭmnikka? 하나 더 가져도 좋습니까/ *You need to sleep* ~. (*to inferior*) Chanenŭn chomdŏ chaya hane. 자네는 좀더 자야 하네/ *Once* ~, *please.* Tashi han pŏn put'ak'amnida. 다시 한 번 부탁합니다/ *I can't walk any* ~. Ijenŭn tŏ kŏrŭl suga ŏpsŭmnida. 이제는 더 걸을 수가 없습니다/ *I have got* ~ *and* ~ *interest in English.* Yŏngŏga chŏmjŏm chaemiissŏjimnida. 영어가 점점 재미 있어집니다/ *I have* ~ *materials than you.* Tangshinboda manŭn chaeryorŭl kajigo issŭmnida. 당신보다 많은 재료를 가지고 있습니다/ *She is* ~ *or less crazy.* Kŭ yŏjanŭn yakkan mŏriga isanghamnida. 그 여자는 약간 머리가 이상합니다/ *The* ~ *I know him, the* ~ *I like him.* Kŭ saramŭl almyŏn alsurok tŏuk choajimnida. 그 사람을 알면 알수록 더욱 좋아집니다.

morning *n.* ach'im 아침, (*before noon*) ojŏn 오전. *this* ~ onŭl ach'im 오늘 아침/ *tomorrow* ~ naeil ach'im 내일 아침/ *yesterday* ~ ŏje ach'im 어제 아침/ *early* ~ irŭn ach'im 이른 아침/ *from* ~ *till evening* ach'imbut'ŏ chŏnyŏkkaji 아침부터 저녁까지/ *Good* ~. (*greeting*) Annyŏnghashim-nikka 안녕하십니까.

mortar *n.* (*bowl*) chŏlgu 절구, (*lime, etc.*) morŭt'arŭ 모르타르.

mortgage *n.,vt.* chŏdang (chapta) 저당 (잡다). ~ *a house* chibŭl chŏdang chapta 집을 저당 잡다.

mosquito *n.* mogi 모기. *a* ~ *net* mogijang 모기장/ *I was bitten by* ~*es.* Mogihant'e mullyŏssŭmnida. 모기한테 물렸읍니다.

moss *n.* ikki 이끼.

most *adj.* kajang manŭn 가장 많은, taegaeŭi 대개의. —*adv.* kajang 가장, much'ŏk 무척. —*n.* (*majority*) ch'oedasu 최다수. ~ *people* taebubunŭi saramdŭl 대부분의 사람들/

a ~ *beautiful woman* much'ŏk arŭmdaun yŏja 무척 아
름다운 여자/ *M*~ *of the Korean think so.* Taedasuŭi
Han-guginŭn kŭwa kach'i saenggak'amnida. 대다수의 한
국인은 그와 같이 생각합니다/ *I think she is seventeen at
the* ~. Kikkŏt'aeya yŏrilgop sal[shipch'ilse] tchŭmiget-
chiyo. 기껏해야 열일곱 살[17세]쯤이겠지요/ *These goods,
for the* ~ *part, are made in factories.* I sangp'umŭn
taebubun kongjangesŏ mandŭrŏjimnida. 이 상품은 대부
분 공장에서 만들어집니다.

moth *n.* (*larva*) nabang 나방, (*clothes* ~) chombŏlle 좀
벌레. ~*-eaten* chommŏgŭn 좀먹은/ ~ *ball* chomnyak
좀약.

mother *n.* ŏmŏni 어머니, moch'in 모친. *grand*~ halmŏni
할머니/ ~ *in law* shiŏmŏni 시어머니, changmo 장모/ *step-*
~ kyemo 계모/ *M*~'*s Day* ŏmŏninal 어머니날.

motherly *adj.* ŏmŏnidaun 어머니다운. ~ *affection* ŏmŏniŭi
aejŏng 어머니의 애정.

motion *n.* (*movement*) undong 운동, (*carriage*) tongjak
동작, (*gesture*) momchit 몸짓, (*proposal*) tongŭi 동의(動
議), (*action of the bowels*) taesobyŏn 대소변. *a rapid* ~
pparŭn undong 빠른 운동/*a slow* ~ nŭrin undong 느린 운
동/ *make a* ~ tongŭihada 동의하다/ *second a* ~ tongŭie
ch'ansŏnghada 동의에 찬성하다/ *I have not had a* ~ *for
several days.* Nanŭn i myŏch'il tongan pyŏnŭl poji
anassŭmnida. 나는 이 며칠 동안 변 보지 않았읍니다.

motionless *adj.* umjigiji annŭn 움직이지 않는.

motion picture yŏnghwa 영화.

motor *n.* paltonggi 발동기, mot'ŏ 모터. ~*boat* mot'ŏbot'ŭ
모터보트/ ~*cycle* ot'obai 오토바이/ ~ *pool* chuch'ajang
주차장.

motorcar *n.* (*automobile*) chadongch'a 자동차.

motto *n.* p'yoŏ 표어, mot'o 모토.

mount *vt.,vi.* (*go up*) orŭda 오르다. —*n.* (*mountain*) san
산. ~ *a hill* ŏndŏge orŭda 언덕에 오르다/ *M*~ *Kum-
gang* Kŭmgangsan 금강산/ *M*~ *Sorak* Sŏraksan 설악산.

mountain *n.* san 산, (*pl.*) sanmaek 산맥. *What's the
highest* ~ *in Korea?* Han-gugesŏ kajang nop'ŭn sanŭn

muŏshimnikka? 한국에서 가장 높은 산은 무엇입니까/ *Mt. Paektu is the highest* ~. Paektusani kajang nop'ŭn sanimnida. 백두산이 가장 높은 산입니다.

mountaineer *n.* tŭngsan-ga 등산가. ~*ing* tŭngsan 등산.

mountainous *adj.* sani manŭn 산이 많은. *Korea is a* ~ *country*. Han-gugŭn sani manssŭmnida. 한국은 산이 많습니다.

mourn *vt.,vi.* sŭlp'ŏhada 슬퍼하다. ~ *for a dead child* chugŭn airŭl sŭlp'ŏhada 죽은 아이를 슬퍼하다.

mourning *n.* (*for the dead*) sang 상(喪). *We are in* ~. Chŏhŭinŭn sangchungimnida. 저희는 상중(喪中)입니다/ ~ *badge* sangjang 상장/ ~ *card* pugo 부고(訃告).

mourner *n.* aedoja 애도자. *the chief* ~ sangju 상주.

mouse *n.* saengjwi 생쥐. *a field* ~ tŭlchwi 들쥐/ ~ *trap* chwidŏt 쥐덫.

m(o)ustache *n.* k'otsuyŏm 콧수염. *wear a* ~ k'otsuyŏmŭl kirŭgo itta 콧수염을 기르고 있다.

mouth *n.* ip 입. *open one's* ~ ibŭl pŏllida 입을 벌리다/ *shut one's* ~ ibŭl tamulda 입을 다물다/ *wipe one's* ~ ibŭl ssitta 입을 씻다/ *the* ~ *of a river* kanggu 강구(江口)/ *from* ~ *to* ~ ibesŏ ibŭro 입에서 입으로.

move *vt.,vi.* umjigida 움직이다. *Don't* ~ *the table.* T'eibŭrŭl umjigiji mashio. 테이블을 움직이지 마시오/ *M*~ *your chair nearer to the fire.* Nallo-e kakkai taga anjŭseyo. 난로에 가까이 다가 앉으세요/ *Will you just* ~ *off?* Chogŭm pik'yŏ chushipshio. 조금 비켜 주십시오/ *When are you moving?* Ŏnje isahashimnikka? 언제 이사하십니까/ *We have* ~*d to No.1 Samchong-dong.* Samch'ŏng-dong ilbŏnjiro isahayŏssŭmnida. 삼청동 1번지로 이사하였읍니다/ *I was deeply* ~*d.* Nanŭn kip'i kamdonghaessŭmnida. 나는 깊이 감동했읍니다/ ~ *about* toradanida 돌아다니다/ ~ *away* ttŏnada 떠나다/ ~ *back* mullŏsŏda 물러서다/ ~ *out* omgyŏ kada 옮겨 가다.

movement *n.* (*moving*) undong 운동, hwaltong 활동, (*gesture*) tongjak 동작, momchit 몸짓, (*activities*) haengdong 행동, tongjŏng 동정. *the new community* ~ saemaŭl undong 새마을 운동/ *a temperance* ~ kŭmju undong 금주 운동/ *a boycott* ~ pulmae undong 불매 운동/ *Let me know all your ~s while you are there.* Kŭ kose kyeshinŭn tongan tongjŏngŭl natnach'i allyŏ chushipshio. 그 곳에 계시는 동안 동정을 낱낱이 알려 주십시오.

movie *n.* (*motion picture*) yŏnghwa 영화. *Have you seen any good ~ lately?* Ch'oegŭne chaeminanŭn yŏnghwarŭl poassŭmnikka? 최근에 재미나는 영화를 보았읍니까/ *I'd like to see a first-run ~.* Kaebong yŏnghwarŭl pogo shipsŭmnida. 개봉(開封) 영화를 보고 싶습니다.

mow *vt.* (*cut grass*) peda 베다. ~ *the lawn* chandirŭl kkakta 잔디를 깎다.

mower *n.* p'ul penŭn saram 풀 베는 사람, (~*ing machine*) chandi kkangnŭn kigye 잔디 깎는 기계.

much *adj.* manŭn 많은. —*adv.* mani 많이. *How ~ flour do you want?* Milkaruga ŏlmana p'iryohashimnikka? 밀가루가 얼마나 필요하십니까/ *You have given me too ~.* Nŏmu mani chusyŏssŭmnida. 너무 많이 주셨읍니다/ *How ~ of this paper have you?* I chonginŭn ŏlmana issŭmnikka? 이 종이는 얼마나 있읍니까/ *I enjoyed it very ~.* P'ŏk chŭlgŏwŏssŭmnida. 퍽 즐거웠읍니다/ *You must work ~ harder.* Tŏ yŏlshimhi irhaeya hamnida. 더 열심히 일해야 합니다/ *I can't make ~ of it.* Taedanhan kŏshiragonŭn saenggaktoeji anssŭmnida. 대단한 것이라고는 생각되지 않습니다/ *Can you let me have this ~?* Na-ege imank'ŭm chul su issŭmnikka? 나에게 이만큼 줄 수 있읍니까/ *as ~ as ...mank'ŭm ···만큼/ *Bring me as ~ as you can.* Toel su innŭn taero mani katta chushipshio. 될 수 있는 대로 많이 갖다 주십시오.

mud *n.* chinhŭk 진흙.

muddy *adj.* chinhŭkt'usŏngiŭi 진흙투성이의, chinch'angŭi 진창의. *a ~ road* chinch'angkil 진창길.

muffler *n.* (*scarf*) moktori 목도리.

mulberry *n.* ppongnamu 뽕나무. *the fruit of the ~* odi 오디.

mule *n.* nosae 노새.

multiply *vi.*, *vt.* (*math.*) kop'ada 곱하다. ~ *2 by 2* ie irŭl kop'ada 2에 2를 곱하다/ ~ *two numbers together*

tu surŭl kop'ada 두 수를 곱하다/ 5 *multiplied by 3 is*
15. O kop'agi samŭn shibo. 5 곱하기 3은 15.

mumble *vt., vi. (mutter)* chungŏlgŏrida 중얼거리다. *Don't*
~ *your words. (to inferior)* Chungŏlgŏriji marara. 중
얼거리지 말아라.

municipal *adj.* shiŭi 시(市)의. *a* ~ *office* shich'ŏng 시청.

munition *n.* kunsup'um 군수품. *a* ~s *factory* kunsu
kongjang 군수 공장.

murder *n.* sarin 살인. —*vt. (kill)* chugida 죽이다. *an*
attempted ~ sarin misu 살인 미수/ *commit* ~ sarinŭl
pŏmhada 살인을 범하다/ *sex* ~ ch'ijŏng sarin 치정 살인/
a case of ~ sarin sakŏn 살인 사건/ *Did you read about*
the ~ *in the newspapers?* Shinmune pododoen sarin sakŏnŭl ilgŏssŭmnikka? 신문에 보도된 살인 사건을 읽었읍
니까?

murderer *n.* sarinja 살인자.

muscle *n.* kŭnyuk 근육.

museum *n.* pangmulgwan 박물관. *the National M*~
kungnip pangmulgwan 국립 박물관/ *the science* ~ kwahak pangmulgwan 과학 박물관/ *Is the* ~ *open now?*
Pangmulgwane tŭrŏgal su issŭmnikka? 박물관에 들어갈
수 있읍니까?

mushroom *n.* pŏsŏt 버섯.

music *n.* ŭmak 음악. *What kind of* ~ *do you like?* Ŏttŏn
ŭmagŭl choahashimnikka? 어떤 음악을 좋아하십니까/ *I*
like Korean ~s. Han-guk ŭmagŭl choahamnida. 한국
음악을 좋아합니다/ *a* ~ *hall* ŭmak kamsangshil 음악 감상
실/ *a* ~ *school* ŭmak hakkyo 음악 학교/ *a* ~ *teacher*
ŭmak sŏnsaeng 음악 선생/ *play* ~ ŭmagŭl yŏnjuhada
음악을 연주하다.

musician *n.* ŭmakka 음악가.

must *aux. v. (be obliged to)* haeyaman handa 해야만
한다, *(be certain to)* ...ime t'ŭllimŏpta …임에 틀림없다.
M~ *you go so soon?* Kŭrŏk'e ppalli kaya hamnikka?
그렇게 빨리 가야 합니까/ *Yes, I* ~. Ne, ppalli kaya
hamnida. 네, 빨리 가야 합니다/ *We* ~ *not be late.* Nŭ-
jŏsŏnŭn an toemnida. 늦어서는 안 됩니다/ *You* ~ *know.*

Ara tuŏya hamnida. 알아 두어야 합니다/ *You ~ have been aware of it.* Algo issŏssŭme t'ŭllimŏpsŭmnida. 알고 있었음에 틀림없읍니다/*You ~ be joking !* Nongdam-igetchiyo ! 농담이겠지요 !

mustard *n.* kyŏja 겨자.

muster *vt.,vi.* (*gather*) sojip'ada 소집하다, (*assemble*) chip'ap'da 집합하다. *Go and ~ all the men you can find.* Kasŏ ch'ajŭl su innŭn chŏnwŏnŭl sojip'ashio. 가서 찾을 수 있는 전원을 소집하시오.

musty *adj.* (*moldy*) komp'angnae nanŭn 곰팡내 나는. ~ *room* komp'angnae nanŭn pang 곰팡내 나는 방/ *This bread smells ~.* I ppangŭn komp'angnaega namnida. 이 빵은 곰팡내가 납니다.

mute *adj.* (*dumb*) pŏngŏriŭi 벙어리의, (*silent*) marŏmnŭn 말없는. —*n.* pŏngŏri 벙어리. *a ~ appeal* muŏnŭi hoso 무언의 호소/ *a ~ deaf* nongaja 농아자.

mutilate *vt.* (*limbs, etc.*) chŏltanhada 절단하다, (*disfigure*) pulguro mandŭlda 불구로 만들다.

mutiny *n.* (*rebellion*) pallan 반란. —*vi.* (*revolt*) p'oktongŭl irŭk'ida 폭동을 일으키다.

mutter *vt.,vi.* (*murmur*) soksagida 속삭이다, (*grumble*) chungŏlgŏrida 중얼거리다. *Are you ~ing threats at me?* Na-ege hyŏppak'anŭn kŏmnikka ? 나에게 협박하는 겁니까/ *What is he ~ing?* Kŭ saramŭn muŏsŭl chungŏl-gŏrigo issŭmnikka ? 그 사람은 무엇을 중얼거리고 있읍니까?

mutton *n.* yanggogi 양고기.

mutual *adj.* (*interchanged*) sŏroŭi 서로의, sanghoŭi 상호의, (*common*) kongt'ongŭi 공통의. *a ~ contract* sangho kyeyak 상호 계약/ *a ~ defense treaty* sangho pangwi choyak 상호 방위 조약/ *~ aid* sangho pujo 상호 부조/ *by ~ consent* habŭie ttara 합의에 따라/ *The pleasure is ~, I assure you.* Na yŏkshi pan-gapki tchagi ŏpsŭmnida. 나 역시 반갑기 짝이 없읍니다.

muzzle *n.* (*of animals*) chudungi 주둥이, (*of guns*) ch'onggu 총구, (*bit*) chaegal 재갈. —*vt.* (*impose silence on*) ibŭl tamulge hada 입을 다물게 하다. *The dog has a ~ over his mouth.* Kŭ kaenŭn ibe chaegarŭl mulgo issŭmnida. 그 개는 입에 재갈을 물고 있읍니다.

my *pron.* naŭi 나의, nae 내. ~ *father* naŭi abŏji 나의 아
버지/ ~ *room* nae pang 내 방/ *Where's ~ hat?* Nae
mojanŭn ŏdi itchiyo? 내 모자는 어디 있지요/ *M~! you
look nice.* Ya! nŭlssinhagunyo. 야! 늘씬하군요.

myriad *adj.* (*numberless*) musuhan 무수한, (*various*) kaji
kaksaegŭi 가지 각색의.

myriad-minded *adj.* chaegani mugung mujinhan 재간이
무궁 무진한.

myself *pron.* na chashin 나 자신. *I did it* ~. Na chashini hayŏssŭmnida. 나 자신이 하였읍니다/ *I am not* ~.
Momi naegŏt katchi anssŭmnida. 몸이 내것 같지 않습니
다/ *by* ~ honjasŏ 혼자서, tandoguro 단독으로/ *for* ~
sonsu 손수.

mysterious *adj.* (*full of mystery*) shinbihan 신비한, (*obscure*) mohohan 모호한, (*puzzling*) pulgasaŭihan 불가
사의한. *a* ~ *crime* pulgasaŭihan pŏmjoe 불가사의한 범죄.

mystery *n.* shinbi 신비, pulgasaŭi 불가사의, (~ *story*)
ch'uri sosŏl 추리 소설/ *solve a* ~ shinbirŭl p'ulda 신비를
풀다/ *Is it true that Korea is full of* ~? Han-gugŭn
shinbie ch'a ittanŭn ke sashirimnikka? 한국은 신비에 차
있다는 게 사실입니까?

mystic *adj.* (*occult*) pipŏbŭi 비법의, (*esoteric*) milgyoŭi
밀교(密教)의. —*n.* shinbiga 신비가. ~ *rites* milgyo ŭishik 밀교 의식. 「하다.

mystify *vt.* (*perplex*) ŏridungjŏrhage hada 어리둥절하게

myth *n.* shinhwa 신화(神話), (*legend*) chŏnsŏl 전설.
ancient Greek ~*s* kodae Kŭrisŭ shinhwa 고대 그리스
신화.

mythical *adj.* (*of myths*) shinhwaŭi 신화의, (*not real*)
kagongŭi 가공의.

mythologist *n.* shinhwahakcha 신화학자.

mythology *n.* (*myths*) shinhwa 신화, (*science*) shinhwahak
신화학. *According to the Korean* ~, *Tan-gun is the
founder of this country.* Han-gugŭi shinhwa-e ttarŭmyŏn
Tan-guni i naraŭi shijoimnida. 한국의 신화에 따르면 단군
(檀君)이 이 나라의 시조(始祖)입니다.

---※ N ※---

nab *vt.* (*catch*) putchapta 붙잡다, (*arrest*) ch'ep'ohada 체포하다. *The patrol ship ~bed illegal fishing boat.* Kyŏngbijŏngi pulpŏp ŏsŏnŭl nap'ohaessŭmnida. 경비정 이 불법 어선을 나포했읍니다.

nag *vt.,vi.* sŏnggashige chansorihada 성가시게 잔소리하다. *I wish you would stop ~ging me.* Chebal chansori chom haji maseyo. 제발 잔소리 좀 하지 마세요.

nail *n.* (*fingers*) sont'op 손톱, (*toes*) palt'op 발톱, (*instrument*) mot 못. —*vt.* mosŭl pakta 못을 박다. *~ cutter* sont'opkkakki 손톱깎이/ *trim one's~s* sont'obŭl kkakta 손톱을 깎다/ *Don't have your finger~s long.* Sont'obŭl kilge kirŭji mashio. 손톱을 길게 기르지 마시오/ *Isn't the box ~ed up yet?* I sangjanŭn ajik motchirŭl an haessŭmnikka? 이 상자는 아직 못질을 안 했읍니까?

naive *adj.* (*simple*) tansunhan 단순한, (*artless*) sobak'an 소박한, (*unsophisticated*) sunjinhan 순진한. *She is ~.* Kŭ yŏjanŭn sunjinhamnida. 그 여자는 순진합니다.

naked *adj.* (*bare*) pŏlgŏbŏsŭn 벌거벗은, nach'eŭi 나체의, (*exposed*) tŭrŏnan 드러난. *stark ~* shiroragi hana kŏlch'iji anŭn 실오라기 하나 걸치지 않은/ *~ feet* maenbal 맨발/ *fight with ~ fists* maenjumŏgŭro ssauda 맨주먹으로 싸우다.

name *n.* irŭm 이름, myŏngch'ing 명칭. *a family ~* (*surname*) sŏng 성(姓). *the christian ~* seryemyŏng 세례명/ *an assumed ~* kamyŏng 가명/ *a pen ~* p'ilmyŏng 필명/ *May I have your ~, please?* Shillyejiman nugushinjiyo? 실례지만 누구신지요/ *May I have your ~ and address?* Sŏnghamgwa chusorŭl karŭch'yŏ chushigessŭmnikka? 성함과 주소를 가르쳐 주시겠읍니까/ *His ~ is Lee Min-kyu.* Kŭŭi irŭmŭn I Min-kyuimnida. 그의 이름은 이 민규입니다/ *Did he leave his ~?* Kŭbunŭn irŭmŭl allyŏ nok'o kassŭmnikka? 그분은 이름을 알려 놓고 갔읍니까/ *I can't recall his ~ right now.* Kŭbunŭi irŭmi ŏllŭn saeng-

gangnaji annŭn-gunyo. 그분의 이름이 얼른 생각나지 않는
군요/ *There is no one here by that* ∼. Kŭrŏn irŭm kajin
punŭn yŏgi ŏpsŭmnida. 그런 이름 가진 분은 여기 없습니다/
Will you please give me your ∼ *card?* Myŏnghamŭl
han chang chushipshio. 명함을 한 장 주십시오.

nap *n.* (*of fabrics*) pop'ul 보풀, (*doze*) natcham 낮잠.
take a ∼ natcham chada 낮잠 자다/ *I take a* ∼ *after
lunch.* Chŏmshimŭl mŏkko namyŏn natchamŭl chamnida.
점심을 먹고 나면 낮잠을 잡니다.

nape *n.* moktŏlmi 목덜미.

napkin *n.* (*table* ∼) naepk'in 냅킨, (*Am.*) (*diaper*) ki-
jŏgwi 기저귀. *a paper* ∼ chongi naepk'in 종이 냅킨/ ∼
ring naepk'in ring 냅킨 링.

narcissus *n.* susŏnhwa 수선화.

narcotic *n.* mach'wije 마취제. ∼*s ring* mayak milmae-
dan 마약 밀매단.

narrow *adj.* chobŭn 좁은. *a* ∼ *alley* chobŭn kolmokkil
좁은 골목길/ *a* ∼*-minded person* p'yŏnhyŏp'an saram 편
협한 사람/*have a* ∼ *escape* kusa ilsaengŭro ppajyŏnaoda
구사 일생으로 빠져나오다.

nasal *adj.* k'oŭi 코의. ∼ *sound* k'otsori 콧소리.

nasty *adj.* (*dirty*) tŏrŏun 더러운, nappŭn 나쁜, (*ill-natured*) shimsulgujŭn 심술궂은. *a* ∼ *book* ch'ujap'an
ch'aek 추잡한 책/ *Don't be so* ∼ *to me.* Kŭrŏk'e shim-
sulburiji mashio. 그렇게 심술부리지 마시오.

nation *n.* kungmin 국민, kukka 국가. *the Korean* ∼ Han-
guk kungmin 한국 국민/ *civilized* ∼*s* munmyŏng kungmin 문명 국민/ *an industrial* ∼ kongŏp kukka 공업 국
가/ *neutral* ∼*s* chungnipkuk 중립국.

national *adj.* kungminŭi 국민의, kukkaŭi 국가의. *a* ∼
anthem kukka 국가/ *a* ∼ *flag* kukki 국기/ *a* ∼ *cemetery*
kungnip myoji 국립 묘지/*a* ∼ *park* kungnip kongwŏn 국
립 공원/ *a* ∼ *holiday* kukkyŏngil 국경일/ *the* ∼ *railways*
kugyu ch'ŏlto 국유 철도.

nationalism *n.* kukkajuŭi 국가주의, minjokchuŭi 민족주
의, aegukshim 애국심.

nationalist *n.* minjokchuŭija 민족주의자.

nationality *n.* (*character*) kungminsŏng 국민성, (*membership*) kukchŏk 국적. *May I ask your* ~? Ŏnŭ nara punishimnikka? 어느 나라 분이십니까?

native *adj.* (*opp. to foreign*) chagugŭi 자국의, (*indigenous*) t'osanŭi 토산(土産)의. —*n.* t'och'angmin 토착민. *one's* ~ *place* kohyang 고향/ ~ *country* moguk 모국/ ~ *language* mogugŏ 모국어/ ~ *pottery* t'osan tojagi 토산 도자기.

natural *adj.* (*not artificial*) chayŏnŭi 자연의, ch'ŏnyŏnŭi 천연의, (*innate*) t'agonan 타고난. ~ *resources* ch'ŏnyŏn chawŏn 천연 자원/ ~ *gifts* ch'ŏnbuŭi chaenŭng 천부의 재능.

naturalize *vt.,vi.* kwihwahada 귀화하다. *She was* ~*d in Korea.* Kŭ yŏjanŭn Han-guge kwihwahaessŭmnida. 그 여자는 한국에 귀화했읍니다.

nature *n.* chayŏn 자연, (*character*) sŏngjil 성질. *the laws of* ~ chayŏnŭi pŏpch'ik 자연의 법칙/ ~ *cure* chayŏn yopŏp 자연 요법/ *good* ~ ch'ak'an sŏngjil 착한 성질/ *ill* ~ nappŭn sŏngjil 나쁜 성질/ *by* ~ namyŏnsŏbut'ŏ 나면서부터, pollae 본래.

naught, nought *n.* (*zero*) yŏng 영, chero 제로, (*nothing*) mu 무(無). *come to* ~ shilp'aero kkŭnnada 실패로 끝나다/ *His efforts came to* ~. Kŭ saramŭi noryŏgŭn sup'oro toragassŭmnida. 그 사람의 노력은 수포로 돌아갔읍니다.

naughty *adj.* (*wrong*) nappŭn 나쁜, (*disobedient*) haengshil nappŭn 행실 나쁜/ ~ *stories* ŭmt'anghan iyagi 음탕한 이야기/ *a* ~ *child* haengshil nappŭn ai 행실 나쁜 아이.

nausea *n.* yokchigi 욕지기, (*sea sickness*) paenmŏlmi 뱃멀미. *feel* ~ mesŭkkŏpta 메스껍다/ *I have a bit of* ~. Kut'oga irŏnamnida 구토가 일어납니다.

naval *adj.* haegunŭi 해군의. *a* ~ *office* haegun changgyo 해군 장교/ *the* ~ *academy* haegun sagwan hakkyo 해군 사관 학교.

navel *n.* paekkop 배꼽. *the* ~ *cord* t'aetchul 탯줄.

navigation *n.* hanghae 항해. *ocean* ~ wŏnyang hanghae 원양 항해/ *aerial* ~ hanggong 항공/ ~ *light* (*of airplane*) p'yojidŭng 표지등.

navy *n.* haegun 해군. *a ~ plane* haegun-gi 해군기(機)/ *a ~ flag* haegun-gi 해군기(旗)/ *the N~ Department* (*Am.*) haegunsŏng 해군성/ *N~ Day* haegunŭi nal 해군의 날.

near *adv.* kakkai 가까이. —*prep.* (*close to*) kŭnch'ŏe 근처에. —*adj.* kakkaun 가까운. —*vt.*, *vi.* kakkai kada 가까이 가다. *There is a church ~ my house.* Nae chip kakkai kyohoega issŭmnida. 내 집 가까이 교회가 있읍니다/ *Come and sit ~ me.* Wasŏ nae kyŏt'e anjŭshio. 와서 내 곁에 앉으시오/ *We passed Taejon several hours ago, and we must be ~ing Taegu.* Myŏt shigan chŏne Taejŏnŭl t'onggwahaessŭmŭro chigŭm Taegue kakkai ogo issŭl kŏmnida. 몇 시간 전에 대전을 통과했으므로 지금 대구에 가까이 오고 있을 겁니다.

nearly *adv.* (*almost*) kŏŭi 거의, taeryak 대략. *I'm ~ ready.* Kŏŭi chunbiga toeŏssŭmnida. 거의 준비가 되었읍니다/ *She ~ fell into the river.* Kŭ yŏjanŭn hamat'ŏmyŏn kange ppajil ppŏnhaessŭmnida. 그 여자는 하마터면 강에 빠질 뻔했읍니다/ *not ~* tojŏhi ... anida 도저히… 아니다/ *~ all* kŏŭi chŏnbu 거의 전부.

neat *adj.* (*trim*) malssuk'an 말쑥한, (*elegant*) p'umwi innŭn 품위 있는, (*tidy*) choch'orhan 조촐한, (*skillful*) somssi innŭn 솜씨 있는. *a ~ desk* chŏngdondoen ch'aeksang 정돈된 책상/ *a ~ dress* pumwi innŭn ot 품위 있는 옷/ *She is always ~ and tidy.* Kŭ yŏjanŭn hangsang malssuk'an ch'arimŭl hago issŭmnida. 그 여자는 항상 말쑥한 차림을 하고 있읍니다.

necessarily *adv.* pandŭshi 반드시. *You don't ~ have to attend.* Kkok ch'ulsŏk'aeyaman hal p'iryonŭn ŏpsŭmnida. 꼭 출석해야만 할 필요는 없읍니다.

necessary *adj.* (*required*) p'iryohan 필요한, (*inevitable*) p'ihal su ŏmnŭn 피할 수 없는. *Your help is ~.* Tangshinŭi toumi p'iryohamnida. 당신의 도움이 필요합니다/ *Was it ~ for you to go yesterday?* Ŏje kayaman haessŭmnikka? 어제 가야만 했읍니까/ *Sleep is ~ to health.* Chamŭn kŏn-gange p'iryohamnida. 잠은 건강에 필요합니다.

necessity *n.* (*need*) p'iryo 필요, (*something necessary*)

p'ilsup'um 필수품. *I'm under the ~ of leaving home.*
Nanŭn pudŭgi chibŭl ttŏnayaman hamnida. 나는 부득이
집을 떠나야만 합니다/ *the necessities of life* saenghwal
p'ilsup'um 생활 필수품.

neck *n.* mok 목. *the ~ of a bottle* pyŏngŭi mok 병의 목/
a long, slender ~ kilgo, kanŭdaran mok 길고 가느다란
목/ *She embraced his ~.* Kŭ yŏjanŭn kŭŭi mogŭl
kkŭrŏanassŭmnida. 그 여자는 그의 목을 끌어안았습니다.

neckerchief *n.* moktori 목도리, moksugŏn 목수건.

necklace *n.* mokkŏri 목걸이. *wear a ~* mokkŏrirŭl hada
목걸이를 하다/ *a pearl ~* chinju mokkŏri 진주 목걸이.

necktie *n.* nekt'ai 넥타이. *bow ~* nabi nekt'ai 나비 넥타이/
Would you show me the ~, please? Chŏ nekt'ai chom
poyŏ chushilkkayo? 저 넥타이 좀 보여 주실까요/ *Where
did you buy this ~?* Ŏdisŏ i nekt'airŭl sassŭmnikka?
어디서 이 넥타이를 샀습니까?

need *n.* (*requirement*) soyong 소용, (*necessity*) p'iryo
필요, (*poverty*) pin-gon 빈곤. —*vt.* (*require*) p'iryoro
hada 필요로 하다, …hal p'iryoga itta …할 필요가 있다.
—*aux. v.* haji anŭmyŏn an toenda 하지 않으면 안 된다/
I have ~ of money. Nanŭn toni p'iryohamnida. 나는
돈이 필요합니다/ *Is there any ~ to hurry?* Sŏdurŭl
p'iryoga issŭmnikka? 서두를 필요가 있습니까/ *What do
you ~?* Muŏshi p'iryohamnikka? 무엇이 필요합니까/ *I
~ some salt.* Sogŭmi p'iryohamnida. 소금이 필요합니다.

needle *n.* panŭl 바늘. *~ case* panŭlssam 바늘쌈/ *the eyes
of a ~* panŭlkwi 바늘귀/ *pine ~s* sollip 솔잎.

needlework *n.* panŭjil 바느질, chasu 자수.

negative *adj.* (*saying no*) pujŏngjŏgin 부정적인, (*not
positive*) sogŭkchŏgin 소극적인, (*contrary*) pandaeŭi
반대의. —*n.* (*phot.*) wŏnp'an 원판. *a ~ sentence* pujŏng-
mun 부정문/ *My request received a ~.* Nae yogunŭn
kŏjŏldanghaessŭmnida. 내 요구는 거절당했습니다/ *develop
a ~* hyŏnsanghada 현상(現像)하다.

neglect *vt.* (*disregard*) keŭllihada 게을리하다. —*n.* (*lack
of care*) t'aeman 태만, mushi 무시. *You've ~ed to
clean your shoes.* Kudu tangnŭn kŏsŭl ijŏssŏtkunyo.

구두 닦는 것을 잊었었군요/ *Don't ~ your work.* Irŭl keŭllihaji mashio. 일을 게을리하지 마시오.

negligence *n.* (*neglect*) t'aeman 태만, (*indifference*) mugwanshim 무관심.

negligent *adj.* (*neglectful*) t'aemanhan 태만한, (*indifferent*) mugwanshimhan 무관심한. ᆨ관 교섭.

negotiation *n.* kyosŏp 교섭. *loan ~* ch'agwan kyosŏp 차

Negro, negro *n.* hŭgin 흑인, kkamdungi 깜둥이.

neighbo(u)r *n.* iutsaram 이웃사람, iut 이웃. *my next-door ~* iutchip saram 이웃집 사람/ *We are next-door ~s.* Urinŭn iutkanimnida. 우리는 이웃간입니다.

neighbo(u)rhood *n.* (*vicinity*) kŭnch'ŏ 근처, (*neighbors*) iutsaramdŭl 이웃사람들. *Is this a quiet ~?* I kŭnch'ŏnŭn choyonghamnikka? 이 근처는 조용합니까/ *Do you live in this ~?* I kŭnch'ŏe sashimnikka? 이 근처에 사십니까/ *Is there a house to let in your ~?* Taegŭi iuse setchibi issŭmnikka? 댁의 이웃에 셋집이 있읍니까?

neither *pron., adv. I like ~ of them.* Ŏnŭ kŏtto maŭme an tŭmnida. 어느 것도 마음에 안 듭니다/ *If you don't go, ~ shall I.* Tangshini an kashimyŏn nado an kagessŭmnida. 당신이 안 가시면 나도 안 가겠읍니다/ *N~ you nor I.* Tangshindo anigo nado animnida. 당신도 아니고 나도 아닙니다.

neon *n.* neon 네온. *a ~ sign* neon sain 네온 사인.

nephew *n.* (*one's brother's son*) chok'a 조카, (*one's sister's son*) saengjil 생질.

nerve *n.* (*nervous fiber*) shin-gyŏng 신경, (*courage*) yonggi 용기, (*audacity*) tamnyŏk 담력. *~ war* shin-gyŏngjŏn 신경전.

nervous *adj.* (*of the nerve*) shin-gyŏngŭi 신경의, shin-gyŏngjirin 신경질인, (*irritable*) hŭngbunhagi shwiun 흥분하기 쉬운. *What are you so ~ about?* Muŏt ttaemune kŭrŏk'e hŭngbunhago issŭmnikka? 무엇 때문에 그렇게 흥분하고 있읍니까/ *Don't be so ~.* Nŏmu shin-gyŏngjirŭl naeji mashio. 너무 신경질을 내지 마시오.

nest *n.* saedunguri 새둥우리, saejip 새집. *a sparrow's ~* ch'amsaejip 참새집.

net *n.* kŭmul 그물. —*adj.* chŏng 정(正), sun 순(純). *fishing* ~s ŏmang 어망/ *a mosquito* ~ mogijang 모기장/ ~ *price* chŏngka 정가/ ~ *profit* suniik 순이익.

network *n.* pangsongmang 방송망.

neuralgia *n.* shin-gyŏngt'ong 신경통. *suffer from* ~ shin-gyŏngt'ongŭl alt'a 신경통을 앓다.

neutral *adj.* chungnibŭi 중립의. *a* ~ *nation* chungnipkuk 중립국/ *a* ~ *zone* chungnip chidae 중립 지대.

never *adv.* kyŏlk'o[chŏltaero, tashinŭn] ...anida[ant'a] 결코[절대로, 다시는] ...아니다[않다]. *I* ~ *slept a wink all night*. Pamsaedorok hanjamdo chaji mot'aessŭmnida. 밤새도록 한잠도 자지 못했습니다/ *N*~ *mind!* Yŏmnyŏ mashio! 염려 마시오/ *I* ~ *said so*. Kŭrŏk'e marhan chŏgŭn ŏpsŭmnida. 그렇게 말한 적은 없습니다.

nevertheless *conj., adv.* (*yet*) kŭrŏch'iman 그렇지만, (*all the same*) yŏkshi 역시.

new *adj.* (*opp. old*) saeroun 새로운, (*renewed*) saerowajin 새로와진, (*recently appointed*) shinimŭi 신임의. ~ *clothes* sae ot 새 옷/ ~ *furniture* sae kagu 새 가구/ *the* ~ *minister* saero on moksanim 새로 온 목사님/ *You see, I'm* ~ *in Seoul*. Sŏul on chi ŏlma an toemnida. 서울 온 지 얼마 안 됩니다.

news *n.* (*tidings*) soshik 소식, (*reports*) podo 보도, (*of newspaper*) kisa 기사, (*something new*) saeroun il 새로운 일. *Have you heard the* ~ ? Kŭ soshik tŭrŏssŭmnikka? 그 소식 들었습니까/ *Happy* ~ ? Choŭn soshigimnikka? 좋은 소식입니까/ *Is there any* ~ ? Musŭn saektarŭn iri issŭmnikka? 무슨 색다른 일이 있습니까/ *I was shocked at the* ~. Kŭ soshik tŭtko kkamtchak nollassŭmnida. 그 소식 듣고 깜짝 놀랐습니다/ *reliable* ~ midŭl manhan podo 믿을 만한 보도/ *front-page* ~ ilmyŏn kisa 일면 기사/ *radio* ~ pangsong nyusŭ 방송 뉴스/ ~ *boy* shinmun paedalbu 신문 배달부/ ~ *agency* t'ongshinsa 통신사.

newspaper *n.* shinmun(ji) 신문(지). *daily* ~ ilgan shinmun 일간 신문/ *morning* ~ chogan shinmun 조간 신문/ *evening* ~ sŏkkan shinmun 석간 신문/ *What* ~ *do you* *read?* Musŭn shinmunŭl poshimnikka? 무슨 신문을 보십니까/ *I read it in a* ~. Shinmunesŏ kŭgŏsŭl poassŭmnida. 신문에서 그것을 보았읍니다.

newspaperman *n.* shinmun kija 신문 기자.

New Year saehae 새해, shinnyŏn 신년. *New Year's Day* sŏllal 설날/ *New Year's Eve* sŏttal kŭmŭmnal 설달 그믐날/ *New Year's greetings* sebae 세배/ *A Happy New Year.* Saehaee pok mani padŭshipshio. 새해에 복 많이 받으십시오.

next *adj.* (*nearest*) taŭmŭi 다음의, (*neighboring*) yŏp'ŭi 옆의. —*adv.* (*after this*) taŭme 다음에. —*prep.* ...taŭmŭi [e] ...다음의[에]. *What is the* ~ *article?* Taŭmŭn muŏsŭl tŭrilkkayo? 다음은 무엇을 드릴까요/ ~ *week* taŭm chu 다음 주/ ~ *month* taŭmtal 다음달/ *Is he coming this weekend or* ~ *weekend?* Kŭ punŭn ibŏn chumare oshimnikka, taŭm chumare oshimnikka? 그 분은 이번 주말에 오십니까, 다음 주말에 오십니까?/ *the* ~ *door* iut chip 이웃집/ *My house is* ~ *to the temple.* Uri chibŭn chŏl yŏp'e issŭmnida. 우리 집은 절 옆에 있읍니다/ *What shall I do* ~? Taŭmŭn muŏsŭl halkkayo? 다음은 무엇을 할까요/ *What will you take* ~? Taŭmŭn muŏsŭl tŭshigesso? 다음은 무엇을 드시겠소/ *What is the* ~ *station?* Taŭmŭn musŭn yŏgijiyo? 다음은 무슨 역이지요/ *We live* ~ *door to each other.* Urinŭn iuse salgo issŭmnida. 우리는 이웃에 살고 있읍니다.

nice *adj.* (*good*) choŭn 좋은, (*agreeable*) chŭlgŏun 즐거운, (*pleasant*) mŏtchin 멋진, (*tasty*) madinnŭn 맛있는. ~ *weather* choŭn nalssi 좋은 날씨/ *I hope you have a* ~ *trip to Pusan.* Pusan chal tanyŏoshipshio. 부산 잘 다녀오십시오/ *Have a* ~ *weekend!* Chŭlgŏun chumarŭl ponaeshipshio! 즐거운 주말을 보내십시오/ *It was* ~ *talking with you.* Malssŭm nanuge toen kŏsŭl kippŭge saenggak'amnida. 말씀 나누게 된 것을 기쁘게 생각합니다 / ~ *dishes* madinnŭn yori 맛있는 요리/ *It is* ~ *of you to* ...hae chusyŏsŏ komapsŭmnida ...해 주셔서 고맙습니다.

nickname *n.* pyŏlmyŏng 별명.

niece *n.* chok'attal 조카딸, chillyŏ 질녀.

night *n.* pam 밤, yagan 야간. *at ~* pame 밤에/ *all ~ (long)* pamsaedorok 밤새도록/ *every ~* pammada 밤마다/ *last ~* kanbam 간밤/ *~ and day* chuya(ro) 주야(로)/ *over ~* pamsaedorok 밤새도록/ *mid~* hanbamchung 한밤중/ *~clothes* chamot 잠옷/ *~ school* yagan hakkyo 야간 학교/ *How many ~s will you stay?* Myŏch'il pam mugŭshiryŏmnikka? 며칠 밤 묵으시렵니까/ *Let us stay here for the ~.* Onŭlpamŭn yŏgisŏ mugŭpshida. 오늘밤은 여기서 묵읍시다/ *He works day and ~.* Kŭ saramŭn pamnajŭro irhamnida. 그 사람은 밤낮으로 일합니다/ *My husband is working ~s this week.* Uri kŭinŭn ibŏn chuil yagŭnhashimnida. 우리 그이는 이번 주일 야근하십니다.

nightingale *n.* *a Korean ~* kkoekkori 꾀꼬리.

nightmare *n.* angmong 악몽, suma 수마. *Night after night I was oppressed by a ~.* Pammada nanŭn angmonge shidallyŏssŭmnida. 밤마다 나는 악몽에 시달렸읍니다.

nighty *n.* *(nightgown)* chamot 잠옷.

nimble *adj.* *(quick)* chaepparŭn 재빠른, minch'ŏp'an 민첩한. *~ fingers* chaepparŭn sonkarak 재빠른 손가락.

nine *n.* ahop 아홉, ku 구(9).

nineteen *n.* yŏrahop 열아홉, shipku 십구(19).

nineteenth *n.* yŏrahop pŏntchae 열아홉 번째, cheshipku 제 19, *(of the month)* shipkuil 19일.

ninetieth *n.* ahŭn pŏntchae 아흔 번째, cheguship 제 90.

ninety *n.* ahŭn 아흔, kuship 90.

ninth *n.* ahop pŏntchae 아홉 번째, chegu 제 9, *(of the month)* kuil 9 일.

nip *vt., vi.* *(pinch)* kkojipta 꼬집다, *(bite)* kkaemulda 깨물다, *(clip)* challanaeda 잘라내다, *(run)* ttwida 뛰다.

nipple *n.* chŏtkkokchi 젖꼭지. *rosy ~s* pulgŭrehan chŏtkkokchi 불그레한 젖꼭지.

no *adv.* anio 아니오. *Will you come? No.* Oshigessŭmnikka? 오시겠읍니까? Anio. 아니오/ *Is it Monday today? No, it isn't.* Onŭri wŏryoirin-gayo? Anio. 오늘이 월요일인가요? 아니오. *(To a question in the negative the Korean generally uses no*[anio] *for yes, and yes*[ye] *for no.) Isn't it Monday today? No, it isn't.* Onŭri wŏryoil

animnikka? Ye, animnida. 오늘이 월요일 아닙니까? 예,
아닙니다/ *Aren't you busy? No, I'm not.* Pappŭji
anssŭmnikka? Ye, pappŭji anssŭmnida. 바쁘지 않습니까?
예, 바쁘지 않습니다.

noble *adj.* (*high-minded*) kosanghan 고상한, (*stately*)
tangdanghan 당당한, (*aristocratic*) kwijogŭi 귀족의.

nobleman *n.* kwijok 귀족.

nobody *pron.* amudo …anida 아무도 …아니다. *N~ came
to me.* Amudo narŭl mannarŏ oji anassŭmnida. 아무도
나를 만나러 오지 않았읍니다/ *N~ was at home when
I arrived.* Naega toch'ak'aessŭl ttae amudo chibe
ŏpsŏssŭmnida. 내가 도착했을 때 아무도 집에 없었읍니다.

noise *n.* (*unpleasant sound*) soŭm 소음, (*outcry*) koham
고함. *Don't make so much ~!* Ttŏdŭlji mashio. 떠들지
마시오/ *What's that ~?* Chŏ shikkŭrŏun sorinŭn muŏshimnikka? 저 시끄러운 소리는 무엇입니까/ *I can not sleep
for the ~.* Soŭm ttaemune chamŭl chal suga ŏpsŭmnida. 소음 때문에 잠을 잘 수가 없읍니다.

noisy *adj.* shikkŭrŏun 시끄러운. *a ~ city* shikkŭrŏun toshi
시끄러운 도시/ *Good gracious, children, why are you
so ~ today?* Ya, yaedŭra, onŭrŭn wae iri shikkŭrŏpchi?
야, 애들아, 오늘은 왜 이리 시끄럽지?

none *pron.* (*no persons*) amudo …ant'a 아무도 …않다,
(*not any*) chogŭmdo …ant'a 조금도 …않다. *N~ of them
came.* Kŭ saramdŭrŭn amudo oji anassŭmnida. 그 사
람들은 아무도 오지 않았읍니다/ *Have you any money
left? I have ~ left.* Toni ŏlmana namassŭmnikka?
Chogŭmdo namchi anassŭmnida. 돈이 얼마나 남았읍니까?
조금도 남지 않았읍니다/ *N~ for me, thanks.* Komawayo.
Ijen ch'ungbunhaeyo [Tŏ mot mŏkkessŏyo]. 고마와요.
이젠 충분해요[더 못 먹겠어요].

nonsense *n.* (*absurd word, conduct, etc.*) pabogat'ŭn sori
바보같은 소리, ŏngt'ŏri ŏmnŭn chit 엉터리 없는 짓. *Stop
your ~.* Pabogat'ŭn chit kŭman hashio. 바보같은 짓 그만
하시오/ *You are talking ~!* Ŏrisŏgŭn sorirŭl hashinŭn-gunyo. 어리석은 소리를 하시는군요/ *What (a) ~!*
T'ŏmuniŏmnŭn sori! 터무니없는 소리!

nook *n.* (*corner*) kusŏk 구석, (*remote spot*) oettan kot 외딴 곳, pyŏkchi 벽지. *search every* ~ kusŏkkusŏk twijida 구석구석 뒤지다.

noon *n.* chŏngo 정오, (*midday*) hannat 한낮. *at* ~ chŏngo-e 정오에/ *before* ~ ojŏne 오전에/ ~ *of night* hanbamchung 한밤중.

nor *conj. I have neither time* ~ *money.* Nanŭn shigando tondo ŏpsŭmnida. 나는 시간도 돈도 없읍니다/ *You don't like it,* ~ *do I.* Tangshindo kŭgŏsŭl an choahajiman nado kŭrŏssŭmnida. 당신도 그것을 안 좋아하지만 나도 그렇습니다/ *I have not yet visited Chejudo* ~ *Hongdo.* Nanŭn ajik Chejudodo Hongdodo kaboji mot'aessŭmnida. 나는 아직 제주도도 홍도(紅島)도 가보지 못했읍니다.

normal *adj.* (*standard*) p'yojunŭi 표준의, (*regular*) chŏnggyuŭi 정규의, chŏngsangŭi 정상의, (*average*) p'yŏnggyunŭi 평균의. *a* ~ *state* p'yojun sangt'ae 표준 상태/ *the* ~ *procedure* chŏnggyu chŏlch'a 정규 절차/ *the* ~ *temperature* p'yŏngon 평온(平溫)/ *My pulse is* ~. Nae maekpagŭn chŏngsangimnida. 내 맥박은 정상입니다.

north *n.* puk 북(北), puktchok 북쪽. —*adj.* pugŭi 북의. *N*~ *Korea* Puk'an 북한/ *the* ~ *pole* pukkŭk 북극/ *the N*~ *Sea* puk'ae 북해/ *Which way is* ~? Ŏnŭ tchogi puktchogimnikka? 어느 쪽이 북쪽입니까/ *It lies thirty miles* ~ *of Pusan.* Kŭ kosŭn Pusanesŏ puktchogŭro samship mail toenŭn kose issŭmnida. 그 곳은 부산에서 북쪽으로 30마일 되는 곳에 있읍니다.

nose *n.* k'o 코. *a flat* ~ napchakk'o 납작코/ *blow one's* ~ k'orŭl p'ulda 코를 풀다/ *wipe one's* ~ k'orŭl takta 코를 닦다/ ~ *bleed* k'op'i 코피/ *My* ~ *is stuffed up with a cold.* Kamgiro k'oga meŏssŭmnida. 감기로 코가 메었습니다.

nosegay *n.* (*bouquet*) kkottabal 꽃다발. [니다.

nostalgia *n.* hyangsu 향수(鄉愁).

nostril *n.* k'otkumŏng 콧구멍.

not *adv.* animnida 아닙니다, anssŭmnida 않습니다. *I don't know.* Nanŭn morŭmnida. 나는 모릅니다/ *Can not you come?* Ol su ŏpsŭmnikka? 올 수 없읍니까/ *Won't you go with us?* Uriwa hamkke kaji ank'essŭmnikka? 우

리와 함께 가지 않겠읍니까/ *Can you come next week?*
I'm afraid ~. Taŭm chue ol su issŭmnikka? Ama ol su
ŏpsŭl kŏmnida. 다음 주에 올 수 있읍니까? 아마 올 수 없을
겁니다/ *Are you tired? N*~ *at all.* P'irohashimnikka?
Chogŭmdo p'irohaji anssŭmnida. 피로하십니까? 조금도
피로하지 않습니다/ *Thank you very much. N*~ *at all.*
Komapsŭmnida. Ch'ŏnmaneyo. 고맙습니다. 천만에요/
Why ~? Nuga aniraeyo? 누가 아니래요?

notable *adj.* (*remarkable*) chŏmyŏnghan 저명한, (*note-*
worthy) chumok'al manhan 주목할 만한. *a* ~ *person*
chŏmyŏng insa 저명 인사.

notary *n.* (~ *public*) kongjŭngin 공증인. *a* ~ *office*
kongjŭngin samuso 공증인 사무소.

note *n.* (*memorandum*) memo 메모, (*annotation*) chuhae
주해, (*record*) kirok 기록, (*bill*) chip'ye 지폐. —*vt.*
(*take* ~ *of*) chŏkta 적다. ~ *book* kongch'aek 공책/
I will take a ~ *of your address.* Tangshinŭi chusorul
chŏgŏ tugo shipsŭmnida. 당신의 주소를 적어 두고 싶습니
다/ *foot* ~s kakchu 각주(脚註)/ *a bank* ~ ŭnhaengkwŏn
은행권/ *a promissory* ~ yaksok ŏŭm 약속 어음/ *Give*
me the change in ~s. Kŏsŭrŭmtonŭn chip'yero chushipshio. 거스름돈은 지폐로 주십시오.

nothing *pron.* amugŏtto ...ŏpta 아무것도 ...없다. *I know*
~ *about it.* Kŭgŏse taehae amugŏtto morŭmnida. 그것에
대해 아무것도 모릅니다/ *I have* ~ *particular to do.*
T'ŭkpyŏrhi hal irŭn ŏpsŭmnida. 특별히 할 일은 없읍니다/
What's wrong with you? N~ *serious.* Musŭn iri
issŏssŭmnikka? Amugŏtto animnida. 무슨 일이 있었읍니
까? 아무것도 아닙니다/ *N*~ *was the matter.* Amu il
ŏpsŏssŭmnida. 아무 일 없었읍니다/ *Did I mean to insult*
him? N~ *of that kind.* Naega kŭrŭl moyok'aryŏ
haettagoyo? Ch'ŏnmanŭi malssŭm. 내가 그를 모욕하려
했다고요? 천만의 말씀/ *I got the ticket for* ~. Kong-
tcharo kŭ p'yorŭl ŏdŏssŭmnida. 공짜로 그 표를 얻었읍
니다.

notice *n.* (*notification*) konggo 공고, (*information*) t'ongji 통지, (*observation*) chumok 주목, (*warning*) yego

예고. —*vt.* (*perceive*) arach'arida 알아차리다, (*observe*) chumok'ada 주목하다. *send a ~* t'ongjirŭl naeda 통지를 내다/ *without ~* yego ŏpshi 예고 없이/ *post a ~ on a board* keship'ane keshihada 게시판에 게시하다/ *I didn't take particular ~*. Nanŭn pyŏllo chuŭihaji anassŭmnida. 나는 별로 주의하지 않았습니다/ *a written ~* t'ongjisŏ 통지서/ *absence without ~* mudan kyŏlgŭn 무단 결근/ *We expect a week's ~*. Ilchuil chŏne yegohae chushipshio. 1주일 전에 예고해 주십시오/ *I didn't ~ you.* Tangshinŭl araboji mot'aetkunyo. 당신을 알아보지 못했군요/ *I ~d that he left early.* Kŭ sarami iltchik ttŏnan kŏsŭl arach'aryŏssŭmnida. 그 사람이 일찍 떠난 것을 알아차렸습니다.

notify *vt.* (*inform*) t'ongjihada 통지하다, (*announce*) palp'yohada 발표하다. *We'll ~ you by mail about the results of this interview.* Myŏnjŏp kyŏlgwanŭn u-p'yŏnŭro t'ongjihae tŭrigessŭmnida. 면접 결과는 우편으로 통지해 드리겠습니다.

notion *n.* (*opinion*) kyŏnhae 견해, (*idea*) ŭihyang 의향. *I have no ~ to go abroad.* Oeguge kal saenggagŭn ŏpsŭmnida. 외국에 갈 생각은 없습니다.

notorious *adj.* (*infamous*) angmyŏng nop'ŭn 악명 높은, p'yŏngi nappŭn 평이 나쁜. *He is ~ as a "dead beat."* Kŭ saramŭn "ton ttemŏkki"ro yumyŏnghamnida. 그 사람은 "돈 떼먹기"로 유명합니다.

notwithstanding *prep.* ...edo pulguhago …에도 불구하고. *N~ his protest, I shall go.* Kŭ saramŭi pandaeedo pulguhago nanŭn kaya hamnida. 그 사람의 반대에도 불구하고 나는 가야 합니다.

noun *n.* (*gram.*) myŏngsa 명사(名詞).

nourish *vt.* (*feed*) kirŭda 기르다, (*cherish*) maŭme p'umta 마음에 품다. *~ an infant with milk* ŏrinaerŭl uyuro kirŭda 어린애를 우유로 기르다.

nourishment *n.* (*nutriment*) chayangmul 자양물.

novel *n.* sosŏl 소설.

novelist *n.* sosŏlga 소설가.

November *n.* shibirwŏl 11월.

now *adv.* chigŭm 지금. *just* ~ chigŭm mak 지금 막/
right ~ chigŭm tangjang 지금 당장/ *from* ~ chigŭmbut'ŏ
지금부터/ *till* ~ chigŭmkkaji 지금까지/ *I saw him just* ~.
Panggŭm kŭ saramŭl mannassŭmnida. 방금 그 사람을
만났읍니다/ *Do your homework right* ~. (*to inferior*)
Chigŭm tangjang sukcherŭl hayŏra. 지금 당장 숙제를 하
여라/ *What is on* ~? Chigŭm mwŏl hago issŭmnikka?
지금 뭘 하고 있읍니까/ ~ *and then* ttaettaero 때때로.

nowadays *adv.* yojŭŭm 요즈음. *N*~ *children prefer TV*
to reading. Yojŭŭm aidŭrŭn toksŏboda t'ellebijŏnŭl tŏ
choahamnida. 요즈음 아이들은 독서보다 텔레비전을 더 좋아
합니다.

nowhere *adv.* amudedo ...ant'a[ŏpta] 아무데도 …않다[없
다]. *Where did you go? N*~. Ŏdi katta wassŭmnikka?
Amudedo kaji anassŭmnida. 어디 갔다 왔읍니까? 아무데
도 가지 않았읍니다.

nuclear *adj.* wŏnjaŭi 원자의, haegŭi 핵의. ~ *bomb* wŏnja
p'okt'an 원자 폭탄/ ~ *energy* wŏnjaryŏk 원자력/ ~ *reac-*
tor wŏnjaro 원자로/ ~ *war* haekchŏnjaeng 핵전쟁/ ~
weapon haengmugi 핵무기.

nude *adj.* almomŭi 알몸의, nach'eŭi 나체의. —*n.* nach'e
나체. *the beauty of the* ~ nach'emi 나체미/ *a* ~ *statue*
nach'esang 나체상.

nuisance *n.* (*annoying action*) tut'ongkŏri 두통거리,
(*troubles*) sŏnggashin il[saram] 성가신 일[사람]. *What*
a ~ *that child is!* Chŏ aenŭn ch'am kwich'anssŭmnida.
저 애는 참 귀찮습니다.

nullify *vt.* (*make ineffective*) muhyoro hada 무효로 하다,
(*cancel*) ch'wiso[p'agi]hada 취소[파기]하다. ~ *a con-*
tract kyeyagŭl p'agihada 계약을 파기하다.

numb *adj.* mabidoen 마비된. *My fingers are* ~ *with cold.*
Ch'uwi ttaemune nae sonkaragi mabidoŏssŭmnida. 추
위 때문에 내 손가락이 마비되었읍니다.

number *n.* (*sum*) su 수(數), (*numeral*) sucha 숫자, pŏnho
번호, ho 호(號). *What is your room* ~? Taegŭi pangŭn
myŏt hoshirimnikka? 댁의 방은 몇 호실입니까/*Please call*
me at this ~. I pŏnhoro chŏnhwa kŏrŏ chushipshio. 이

번호로 전화 걸어 주십시오/ *Wrong* ∼, *I'm sorry*. Chŏn-hwa pŏnhoga t'ŭllimnida. 전화 번호가 틀립니다/ *odd* ∼ holsu 홀수/ *even* ∼ tchaksu 짝수/ *a large* ∼ *of people* manŭn saramdŭl 많은 사람들.

numerous *adj.* sumanŭn 수많은.

nun *n.* sunyŏ 수녀.

nurse *n.* (*wet* ∼) yumo 유모, (*a hospital* ∼) kanhowŏn 간호원. —*vt.,vi.* (*the sick*) kanhohada 간호하다, (*suckle*) chŏjŭl mŏgida 젖을 먹이다. *a dry* ∼ pomo 보모/ *a staff* ∼ suganhowŏn 수간호원.

nursery *n.* (*room for children*) ŏrini pang 어린이 방, (*for plants*) myop'an 묘판, onsang 온상.

nut *n.* hodu 호두.

nutrition *n.* yŏngyang 영양. *Take care of the* ∼ *of children*. Aidŭl yŏngyange choshimhashipshio. 아이들 영양에 조심하십시오.

nylon *n.* naillon 나일론. ∼ *stockings* naillon yangmal 나일론 양말.

※ **O** ﹖

O *int.* *O dear me!* Ŏmŏna! 어머나! Irŏn! 이런! *O no.* Wŏn ch'ŏnmane. 원 천만에.

oak *n.* ch'amnamu 참나무.

oar *n.* no 노(櫓). *pull an* ∼ norŭl chŏtta 노를 젓다.

oat *n.* kwiri 귀리.

oath *n.* maengse 맹세. *on my* ∼ maengsek'o 맹세코/ *make* ∼ maengsehada 맹세하다/ *I didn't say anything to him about you, on my* ∼. Chŏngmariji kŭ saramhant'e tang-shin marŭn an haessŭmnida. 정말이지 그 사람한테 당신 말은 안 했읍니다.

obedience *n.* pokchong 복종. *absolute* ∼ chŏltae pokchong 절대 복종/ *blind* ∼ maengjong 맹종.

obedient *adj.* (*dutiful*) sunjonghanŭn 순종하는, yusun-han 유순한. ∼ *children* yusunhan aidŭl 유순한 아이들/ *The child is* ∼ *to his parents*. Kŭ ainŭn pumo-ege chal sunjonghamnida. 그 아이는 부모에게 잘 순종합니다.

obey *vt.,vi.* pokchonghada 복종하다, ttarŭda 따르다. *Soldiers must ~ orders.* Kuninŭn myŏngnyŏnge pokchonghaeya hamnida. 군인은 명령에 복종해야 합니다.

obituary *n.* samangŭi 사망의. *an ~ notice* pugo 부고(訃告).

object *n.* (*thing*) mulgŏn 물건, (*goal*) mokchŏk 목적, (*gram.*) mokchŏgŏ 목적어. —*vi.* pandaehada 반대하다. *What is your ~ for coming here?* Yŏgi oshin mokchŏgi muŏshimnikka? 여기 오신 목적이 무엇입니까/ *I don't ~ to a good glass of wine.* Kogŭp sul han chantchŭmŭn shilch'i anssŭmnida. 고급 술 한 잔쯤은 싫지 않습니다/ *Do you ~ to my opening the door?* Munŭl yŏrŏdo kwaench'anssŭmnikka? 문을 열어도 괜찮습니까?

objection *n.* (*opposition*) pandae 반대, (*reluctance*) shilchŭng 싫증, (*drawback*) nanchŏm 난점. *I have no ~ to it.* Kŏgie taehae iŭinŭn ŏpsŭmnida. 거기에 대해 이의는 없습니다/ *We have no ~ to your marriage.* Tangshinŭi kyŏrhone pandaehaji anssŭmnida. 당신의 결혼에 반대하지 않습니다.

obligation *n.* (*duty*) ŭimu 의무, (*debt*) ch'aemu 채무, (*debt of gratitude*) ŭnhye 은혜. *I have an ~ to help him.* Kŭ saramŭl toul ŭimuga issŭmnida. 그 사람을 도울 의무가 있읍니다.

oblige *vt.* (*compel*) kangyohada 강요하다, (*favor*) ŭnhyerŭl pep'ulda 은혜를 베풀다. *I was ~d to go yesterday.* Ŏje kayaman haessŭmnida. 어제 가야만 했읍니다/ *Could you ~ me with a thousand won?* Ch'ŏnwŏnman pillyŏ chushigessŭmnikka? 1,000원만 빌려 주시겠읍니까/ *Please do so to ~ me.* Narŭl poa kŭrŏk'e hae chushipshio. 나를 보아 그렇게 해 주십시오/ *I'm much ~d (to you).* Taedanhi kamsahamnida. 대단히 감사합니다.

obscene *adj.* ŭmnanhan 음란한. *~ pictures* ch'unhwa 춘화.

obscure *adj.* (*vague*) aemaehan 애매한, (*dim*) ŏsŭmp'urehan 어슴푸레한.

observation *n.* (*notice*) kwanch'al 관찰, (*watching*) kamshi 감시. *escape ~* kamshirŭl p'ihada 감시를 피하다.

observatory *n.* *an astronomical* ~ ch'ŏnmundae 천문대/ *a meteorological* ~ kisangdae 기상대, ch'ŭk'uso 측후소.

observe *vi.,vt.* (*watch*) kwanch'arhada 관찰하다, (*keep*) chik'ida 지키다, (*remark*) marhada 말하다. *We must* ~ *the laws.* Pŏmnyurŭl chik'yŏya hamnida 법률을 지켜야 합니다/*O*~ *traffic signals.* Kyot'ong shinhorŭl chik'ishio. 교통 신호를 지키시오.

observer *n.* kwanch'alja 관찰자, kwanch'ŭkcha 관측자.

obstacle *n.* (*hindrance*) panghae(mul) 방해(물). *an* ~ *race* changaemul kyŏngju 장애물 경주.

obstetrician *n.* sanbuinkwa ŭisa 산부인과 의사.

obstinate *adj.* (*stubborn*) wan-gohan 완고한. *an* ~ *person* kojipchangi 고집장이.

obstruct *vi.,vt.* (*hinder*) panghaehada 방해하다, (*block up*) karomakta 가로막다.

obtain *vt.,vi.* (*gain*) ŏtta 얻다, sone nŏt'a 손에 넣다, (*prevail*) yuhaenghada 유행하다. *Where can I* ~ *the book?* Kŭ ch'aegŭl ŏdisŏ sal su issŭmnikka? 그 책을 어디서 살 수 있읍니까/*The custom still* ~*s in districts.* Kŭ p'ungsŭbi ajik chibangesŏnŭn yuhaenghago issŭmnida. 그 풍습이 아직 지방에서는 유행하고 있읍니다.

obvious *adj.* (*evident*) ppanhan 빤한, chal poinŭn 잘 보이는, myŏngbaek'an 명백한.

occasion *n.* (*opportunity*) kihoe 기회, (*case*) kyŏngu 경우. *I never have had* ~ *to use it.* Kŭgŏsŭl sayonghal kihoega ŏpsŏssŭmnida. 그것을 사용할 기회가 없었읍니다/ *I will reserve it for another* ~. Kŭ kŏnŭn tarŭn kihoero mirugessŭmnida. 그 것은 다른 기회로 미루겠읍니다/ *on this* ~ *i kihoe* 이 기회에.

occasionally *adv.* ittagŭm 이따금, kakkŭm 가끔.

occidental *adj.* sŏyangŭi 서양의. ~ *manner* sŏyangshik 서양식/ ~ *civilization* sŏyang munmyŏng 서양 문명.

occupation *n.* (*business*) il 일, (*seizure*) chomnyŏng 점령, (*job*) chigŏp 직업. *a manufacturing* ~ chejoŏp 제조업/ *What is your* ~? Chigŏbi muŏshijiyo? 직업이 무엇이지요/ *an army of* ~ chŏmnyŏnggun 점령군.

occupy *vt.* (*take up*) ch'ajihada 차지하다, (*engage*) chong-

sahada 종사하다, (*seize upon*) chŏmyuhada 점유하다,
(*live in*) salda 살다. *I'm now occupied in writing*. Chigŭm chōsure chongsahago issŭmnida. 지금 저술에 종사하
고 있읍니다/ *My sister occupies an important position
in that company*. Nae nuidongsaengŭn kŭ hoesa-esŏ
chungyohan chiwie issŭmnida. 내 누이동생은 그 회사에서
중요한 지위에 있읍니다.

occur *vi*. (*happen*) irŏnada 일어나다, (*come to mind*)
saenggagi ttŏorŭda 생각이 떠오르다, (*appear*) nat'anada
나타나다. *When did the accident* ∼? Kŭ sagonŭn ŏnje
irŏnatchiyo? 그 사고는 언제 일어났지요/ *His name doesn't* ∼ *to me now*. Chigŭm kŭūi irŭmi saenggangnaji
anssŭmnida. 지금 그의 이름이 생각나지 않습니다/ *Black
sheep* ∼ *in all families*. Malssŏngkkunŭn nwijibena
innŭn pŏbimnida. 말썽꾼은 뉘집에나 있는 법입니다.

occurrence *n*. (*accident*) sakŏn 사건, il 일. *an everyday
∼* ilsang innŭn il 일상 있는 일/ *an unfortunate ∼* purhaenghan sakŏn 불행한 사건/ *This is a common ∼*. Igŏsŭn
pot'ong innŭn irimnida. 이것은 보통 있는 일입니다.

ocean *n*. taeyang 대양(大洋). *the Atlantic ∼* taesŏyang
대서양/ *the Pacific ∼* t'aep'yŏngyang 태평양.

o'clock *n*. shi 시(時). *sharp at two ∼* chŏnggak tushie 정
각 2시에/ *I'll be back by nine ∼*. Ahopshikkajinŭn toraogessŭmnida. 9시까지는 돌아오겠읍니다.

October *n*. shiwŏl 10월.

octopus *n*. munŏ 문어, (*small ∼*) nakchi 낙지.

oculist *n*. ankwa ŭisa 안과 의사.

odd *adj*. (*strange*) isanghan 이상한, (*not paired*) holsuŭi
홀수의, (*extra*) namŏjiŭi 나머지의. *It's ∼ you don't
know*. Tangshini morŭdani isanghagunyo. 당신이 모르다니
이상하군요/ *He is an ∼-looking old man*. Kŭnŭn isanghage saenggin noinimnida. 그는 이상하게 생긴 노인입니
다/ *an ∼ number* holsu 홀수/ *You may keep the ∼
change*. Usurinŭn nŏŏ tushio. 우수리는 넣어 두시오/ *∼s
and ends* chaptongsani 잡동사니.

odo(u)r *n*. (*fragrance*) hyanggi 향기, (*smell*) naemsae
냄새. *sweet ∼* hyanggi 향기/ *foul ∼* akch'wi 악취/ *body*

~ ch'ech'wi 체취.

of prep. (belonging to) the children ~ a family kajŏngŭi aidŭl 가정의 아이들/ (made from) a house ~ bricks pyŏktollo mandŭn chip 벽돌로 만든 집/ (quality) a look ~ pity tongjŏnghanŭn ŏlgul 동정하는 얼굴/ (away from) north ~ Seoul City Sŏurŭi puktchok 서울의 북쪽/ (concerning) think well ~ someone nugurŭl chok'e saenggak'ada 누구를 좋게 생각하다/ (through) die ~ illness pyŏngŭro chukta 병으로 죽다/ (out of) She came ~ a noble family. Kŭ yŏjanŭn kwijok ch'ulshinida. 그 여자는 귀족 출신이다/ (among) some ~ us uridŭl chung myŏt saram 우리들 중 몇 사람.

off adv. (away) mŏlli 멀리, ttŏrŏjyŏsŏ 떨어져서, (not on) ttŏnasŏ 떠나서, (wholly) wanjŏnhi 완전히. —prep. (away from)...ŭrobut'ŏ ···으로부터, (deviating) pŏsŏnasŏ 벗어나서, (to seaward) appadaro 앞바다로. How far ~ is the town? Five miles ~. Kŭ maŭrŭn ŏlmana mŏmnikka? O mail ttŏrŏjyŏ issŭmnida. 그 마을은 얼마나 멉니까? 5마일 떨어져 있읍니다/ I was ~ on a skiing trip. Nanŭn sŭk'i yŏhaengŭl ttŏnassŭmnida. 나는 스키 여행을 떠났읍니다/ Please let me ~ here. Yŏgisŏ naeryŏ chushio. 여기서 내려 주시오/ Thank you for coming out to see me ~. Chŏnsongnawa chusyŏsŏ komapsŭmnida. 전송나와 주셔서 고맙습니다/ Kanghwa is an island ~ Inchon harbor. Kanghwanŭn Inch'ŏn appada-e innŭn sŏmimnida. 강화는 인천 앞바다에 있는 섬입니다/ Can you take something ~ the price? Kapsŭl chom kkakkŭl su ŏpsŭmnikka? 값을 좀 깎을 수 없읍니까/ Well,it's hard to say ~ hand. Kŭraeyo, tangjang taedap'agin kollanhamnida. 그래요, 당장 대답하긴 곤란합니다/ Keep ~ the grass. Chandie tŭrŏgaji mashio. 잔디에 들어가지 마시오/ I am ~ duty today. Nanŭn onŭl pibŏnimnida. 나는 오늘 비번입니다/ Please turn ~ the light before you go to bed. Ch'wich'im chŏne purŭl kkŏ chushipshio. 취침 전에 불을 꺼 주십시오.

offend vt.,vi. (make angry) nohage hada 노하게 하다, (displease) piwirŭl kŏsŭrŭda 비위를 거스르다. I am sorry you are ~ed. Piwirŭl sanghage haedŭryŏ mianhamnida. 비위를 상하게 해드려 미안합니다/ *Why are you ∼ed at me?* Wae na·ege hwarŭl naeshimnikka? 왜 나에게 화를 내십니까?

offense, offence *n.* (*transgression*) panch'ik 반칙, (*insult*) moyok 모욕, (*anger*) noyŏum 노여움, (*attack*) konggyŏk 공격. *a first ∼* ch'obŏm 초범/ *a previous ∼* chŏnkwa 전과(前科)/ *take ∼ at* ...ege hwarŭl naeda ...에게 화를 내다/ *weapons of ∼* konggyŏngyong mugi 공격용 무기/ *No ∼!* Agŭiro han marŭn anio. 악의로 한 말은 아니오.

offensive *adj.* (*disagreeable*) pulk'waehan 불쾌한, (*insolent*) pŏrŭdŏmnŭn 버릇없는, (*aggressive*) konggyŏk-chŏgin 공격적인. *an ∼ odor* koyak'an naemsae 고약한 냄새/ *∼ manners* pŏrŭdŏmnŭn t'aedo 버릇없는 태도/ *∼ weapons* konggyŏk mugi 공격 무기.

offer *vt.,vi.* (*present*) chegonghada 제공하다, (*propose*) cheŭihada 제의하다, (*dedicate*) pach'ida 바치다. —*n.* (*proposal*) shinch'ŏng 신청, cheŭi 제의. *I have been ∼ed a job in Korea.* Han-gugesŏ ilcharirŭl hana chugettago hamnida. 한국에서 일자리를 하나 주겠다고 합니다/ *It's the best price I can ∼.* Igŏsŭn hankkŏt naerin kapshimnida. 이것은 한껏 내린 값입니다/ *He ∼ed to help me.* Kŭ sarami narŭl topkettago nasŏssŭmnida. 그 사람이 나를 돕겠다고 나섰읍니다/ *Don't accept his ∼.* Kŭ saramŭi shinch'ŏngŭn patchi mashio. 그 사람의 신청은 받지 마시오/ *I declined her ∼.* Kŭ yŏjaŭi cheŭirŭl kŏjŏrhaessŭmnida. 그 여자의 제의를 거절했읍니다.

offering *n.* (*sacrifice*) chemul 제물, (*collection*) hŏn·gŭm 헌금, (*gift*) sŏnmul 선물.

office *n.* (*rooms of business*) samuso 사무소, (*buildings of government*) kwanch'ŏng 관청, (*position*) kwanjik 관직, (*duty*) chingmu 직무. *Where is your ∼?* Samusonŭn ŏdi issŭmnikka? 사무소는 어디 있읍니까/ *Our ∼ closes at six.* Uri samushirŭn yosŏssie tassŭmnida. 우리 사무실은 6시에 닫습니다/ *a lawyer's ∼* pŏmnyul samuso 법률 사무소/ *∼ boy* sahwan 사환/ *∼ girl* yŏsamuwŏn 여사무원.

officer *n.* changgyo 장교. ~s *and men* changbyŏng 장병/ *a military* ~ yukkun changgyo 육군 장교/ *a naval* ~ haegun changgyo 해군 장교/ *a public* ~ kongmuwŏn 공무원/ *the medical* ~ *of health* kŏmyŏkkwan 검역관.

official *adj.* (*public*) kongchŏgin 공적인, (*formal*) kongshigŭi 공식의. —*n.* kwalli 관리, kongmuwŏn 공무원. *an* ~ *residence* konggwan 공관/ *an* ~ *visit* kongshik pangmun 공식 방문/ *public* ~s kongmuwŏn 공무원/ *high* ~s kogwan 고관/ *emigration and immigration* ~s ch'uripkuk kwalli 출입국 관리/ *an embassy* ~ taesagwan chigwŏn 대사관 직원. 「son 자손.

offspring *n.* (*children*) chashik 자식, (*descendants*) cha-

often *adv.* chongjong 종종, chaju 자주. *How* ~ *do the buses run?* Pŏsŭnŭn ŏlmana chaju tanimnikka? 버스는 얼마나 자주 다닙니까/ *We* ~ *go there.* Kŏgie chaju kamnida. 거기에 자주 갑니다/ *Please come* ~. Chaju oshipshio. 자주 오십시오.

oil *n.* kirŭm 기름, oil 오일. —*vt.* kirŭmŭl ch'ida 기름을 치다. ~ *burner* oil pŏnŏ 오일 버너/ ~ *field* yujŏn 유전(油田)/ ~ *lamp* sŏgyu raemp'ŭ 석유 램프/ ~ *station* chuyuso 주유소/ ~ *stove* sŏgyu nallo 석유 난로/ *volatile* ~ hwiballyu 휘발유.

ointment *n.* yŏn-go 연고, koyak 고약.

OK, O.K. *adj.,adv. & v.* (*all right*) chot'a 좋다, (*correct*) t'ŭllimŏpta 틀림없다.

old *adj.* (*aged*) nŭlgŭn 늙은, (*worn*) nalgŭn 낡은, (*of age*) myŏt sarŭi 몇 살의. *an* ~ *man* noin 노인/ *an* ~ *house* nalgŭn chip 낡은 집, kuok 구옥/ *How* ~ *is he?* Kŭ saramŭn myŏt sarimnikka? 그 사람은 몇 살입니까/ *How much* ~*er is he than you?* Kŭ saramŭn tangshinboda myŏt sal wiimnikka? 그 사람은 당신보다 몇 살 위입니까/ *He is two years* ~*er than I.* Naboda tu sal wiimnida. 나보다 두 살 위입니다/ *I am thirty years* ~. Nanŭn sŏrŭn sarimnida. 나는 서른 살입니다/ ~ *boy* tongch'angsaeng 동창생/ ~ *fashioned* kushigŭi 구식의/ ~ *maid* oldŭmisŭ 올드미스, noch'ŏnyŏ 노처녀. 「올리브유.

olive *n.* ~ *tree* kamnamnamu 감람나무/ ~ *oil* ollibŭyu

Olympic *adj*. ollimp'igŭi 올림픽의. —*n*. (*pl*.) ollimp'ik kyŏnggi 올림픽 경기. *the* ~ *games* kukche ollimp'ik kyŏnggi taehoe 국제 올림픽 경기 대회/ *the Korea* ~ *Committee* taehan ollimp'ik wiwŏnhoe 대한 올림픽 위원회/ *an* ~ *village* ollimp'ik ch'on 올림픽 촌(村)/ *the* ~ *flame* ollimp'ik sŏnghwa 올림픽 성화/ *Next* ~ *will be held in Seoul*. Taŭm ollimp'igŭn Sŏuresŏ yŏllimnida. 다음 올림픽은 서울에서 열립니다.

omen *n*. (*foreboding*) chŏnjo 전조. *evil* ~ hyungjo 흉조/ *good* ~ kilcho 길조.

ominous *adj*. (*inauspicious*) pulgirhan 불길한, (*threatening*) hŏmak'an 험악한. *an* ~ *dream* pulgirhan kkum 불길한 꿈.

omission *n*. (*leaving out*) saengnyak 생략, nurak 누락, (*neglect*) t'aeman 태만, (*slip*) shilsu 실수. *There is an* ~ *in this account*. I kyesane ppattŭrin tega itkunyo. 이 계산에 빠드린 데가 있군요/ *without* ~ ppajimōpshi 빠짐 없이.

omit *vt*. (*leave out*) saengnyak'ada 생략하다, ppaeda 빼다, (*neglect*) keŭllihada 게을리하다. *This chapter may be* ~*ted*. I changŭn ppaedo chossŭmnida. 이 장(章)은 빼도 좋습니다/ *Don't* ~ *clearing your teeth*. Yangch'ijirŭl keŭllihaji mashio. 양치질을 게을리하지 마시오.

on *prep*. (*touching*) chŏp'ayŏ 접하여, (*toward*) myŏnhayŏ 면하여, hyanghayŏ 향하여, (*ground*) ...ranŭn iyuro ...라는 이유로, (*above*) 위에, (*concerning*) kwanhae 관해, (*at the time*) ttae 때. *a picture* ~ *the wall* pyŏge kŏllyŏ innŭn kŭrim 벽에 걸려 있는 그림/ *face* ~ *the sea* pada-e myŏnhada 바다에 면하다/ *have a hat* ~ *one's head* mojarŭl ssŭgo itta 모자를 쓰고 있다/ *a book* ~ *war* chŏnjaenge kwanhan ch'aek 전쟁에 관한 책/ ~ *Monday* wŏryoire 월요일에/ ~ *the morning* ach'ime 아침에/ ~ *fire* pult'ago 불타고/ *Have you a match* ~ *you?* Sŏngnyang issŭmnikka? 성냥 있읍니까/ *Don't try it* ~ *him*. Kŭ saramege kŭrŏn chisŭl haji mashio. 그 사람에게 그런 짓을 하지 마시오/ *O*~ *what ground do you think it is a lie?* Musŭn kŭn-gŏro kŏjinmarira saenggak'ashimnikka? 무슨 근거로 거짓말이라 생각하십 니까/ *I congratulate you ~ your success.* Sŏnggongŭl ch'uk'ahamnida. 성공을 축하합니다/ *The drinks are ~ me.* Sulgapsŭn naega naegesso. 술값은 내가 내겠소.

once *adv.* (*one time*) han pŏn 한 번, (*formerly*) iltchigi 일찌기, (*before*) chŏne 전에. *I wind up my watch ~ a day.* Shigyerŭl haru han pŏn kamsŭmnida. 시계를 하루 한 번 감습니다/ *I should like to see her ~ before I go.* Kagi chŏne kŭnyŏrŭl han pŏn manna pogo shipsŭmnida. 가기 전에 그녀를 한 번 만나 보고 싶습니다/ *O~ I lived in Pusan.* Chŏne Pusane san chŏgi issŭmnida. 전에 부산에 산 적이 있읍니다/ ~ *more* han pŏn tŏ 한 번 더/ *at ~* kot 곧/ *all at ~* kapchagi 갑자기.

one *adj.* (*single*) hanaŭi 하나의, (*a certain*) ŏttŏn 어떤, ŏnŭ 어느. —*n.* hana 하나, il 일. —*pron.* (*person*) saram 사람. ~ *man* han saram 한 사람/ ~ *hand* han son 한 손/ ~ *more* tto hana 또 하나/ ~ *man* ~ *vote* irin ilp'yo 1인 1표/ *I saw him again ~ day.* Ŏnŭ nal nanŭn kŭ saramŭl tashi mannassŭmnida. 어느 날 나는 그 사람을 다시 만났읍니다/ *I met her ~ evening last week.* Chinan chu ŏnŭ nal chŏnyŏk kŭ yŏjarŭl mannassŭmnida. 지난 주 어느 날 저녁 그 여자를 만났읍니다/ *O~ must do one's duty.* Saramŭn chagi ŭimurŭl tahaeya hamnida. 사람은 자기 의무를 다해야 합니다/ ~ *another* sŏro 서로/ ~ *by* ~ hanassik 하나씩/ ~ *after another* ch'aryero 차례로/ *the* ~ ... *the other* chŏnja ... huja 전자 …후자.

onion *n.* yangp'a 양파. *I'll start with the ~ soup, please.* Usŏn yangp'a sup'ŭrŭl kajyŏoshio. 우선 양파 수프를 가져오시오/ *Hot dog with ~ and pickles, please.* Hat togŭe yangp'awa p'ik'ŭrŭl nŏŏ chushio. 핫 도그에 양파와 피클을 넣어 주시오.

onlooker *n.* kugyŏngkkun 구경꾼.

only *adj.* (*sole*) yuirhan 유일한, tanji...manŭi 단지…만의. —*adv.* (*merely*) taman 다만, ppun 뿐. *He is the ~ son.* Kunŭn tan hanaŭi〔oe〕 adŭrimnida. 그는 단 하나의 〔외〕 아들입니다/ *one's ~ friend* yuirhan ch'in-gu 유일

한 친구/ *the ~ survival* yuirhan saengjonja 유일한 생
존자/ *I have ~ two dictionaries.* Sajŏnŭn tu kwŏn-
ppunimnida. 사전은 두 권뿐입니다/ *I posted the letter
~ yesterday.* Kŭ p'yŏnjinŭn taman ŏje puch'yŏssŭl
ppunimnida. 그 편지는 다만 어제 부쳤을 뿐입니다/ *You
have ~ to wait.* Kidarigo itkiman hamyŏn toemnida.
기다리고 있기만 하면 됩니다.

open *vt.,vi.* yŏlda 열다, yŏllida 열리다. *O~ the door softly.* Munŭl salmyŏshi yŏshipshio. 문을 살며시 여십시오/
O~ your book at page 5. O p'eijirŭl p'yŏshio. 5페이
지를 펴시오/ *Shall I ~ another bottle?* Tto han pyŏng
ttal[yŏl]kkayo? 또 한 병 딸[열]까요/ *What time does
the bank ~?* Ŭnhaengŭn myŏt shie yŏmnikka? 은행은
몇 시에 엽니까/ *When does the school ~ again?* Hakkyonŭn tto ŏnje shijak'amnikka? 학교는 또 언제 시작합니
까/ *Leave the door ~.* Munŭl yŏrŏ tushipshio. 문을 열
어 두십시오/ *~ air* ogoe 옥외/ *~ game* op'ŭn keim 오픈
게임/ *~ letter* konggaechang 공개장.

opener *n.* magaeppobi 마개뽑이, kkangt'ongttagae 깡통따
개. *a can ~* kkangt'ongttagae 깡통따개.

opening *n.* (*beginning*) shijak 시작, (*gap*) t'ŭm 틈,
(*vacancy*) pinjari 빈자리. *the ~ time* kaejŏm shigan 개점
시간/ *the ~ of a speech* yŏnsŏrŭi shijak 연설의 시작/ *an
~ in a fence* ŭlt'ari t'ŭm[kaegumŏng] 울타리 틈[개구
멍]/ *look out for an ~* ilcharirŭl ch'atta 일자리를 찾다.

open-minded *adj.* solchik'an 솔직한.

opera *n.* kagŭk 가극, op'era 오페라. *~ house* op'era
kŭkchang 오페라 극장/ *~ singer* op'era kasu 오페라 가
수/ *Are you fond of ~?* Op'erarŭl choahashimnikka?
오페라를 좋아하십니까?

operate *vt.,vi.* (*work*) umjigida 움직이다, (*run*) kyŏngyŏnghada 경영하다, (*be effective*) hyokwarŭl naeda
효과를 내다, (*surgery*) susurhada 수술하다. *The sight-
seeing train is ~d everyday between Seoul and Pusan.* Sŏulgwa Pusan saienŭn maeil kwan-gwang yŏlch'aga tanigo issŭmnida. 서울과 부산 사이에는 매일 관광
열차가 다니고 있습니다/ *This medicine ~s well.* I ya-

gŭn chal tŭssŭmnida. 이 약은 잘 듣습니다/ *I had my nose ~d on*. Nanŭn k'orŭl susurhaessŭmnida. 나는 코를 수술했읍니다/ *operating room* susulshil 수술실.

operation *n*. (*working*) chagyong 작용, (*mil*.) chakchŏn 작전, (*surgery*) susul 수술. *come into ~* shilshihada 실시하다. *When does the plan come into ~?* Kŭ kyehoegŭn ŏnje shilch'ŏnhamnikka? 그 계획은 언제 실천합니까/ *a plan of ~s* chakchŏn kyehoek 작전 계획/ *a feint ~* yangdong chakchŏn 양동 작전/ *undergo an ~* susurŭl patta 수술을 받다/ *He died after an ~ from cancer*. Kŭ saramŭn am susul twie chugŏssŭmnida. 그 사람은 암 수술 뒤에 죽었읍니다.

operative *n*. (*factory hand*) chikkong 직공.

operator *n. a telephone ~* chŏnhwa kyohwansu 전화 교환수/ *a wireless ~* musŏn kisa 무선 기사.

opinion *n*. (*view*) ŭigyŏn 의견, kyŏnhae 견해, (*belief*) soshin 소신(所信), (*estimate*) p'yŏngka 평가. *public ~* yŏron 여론/ *according to my ~* nae ŭigyŏnŭronŭn 내 의견으로는/ *Tell me your ~ about it*. Kŭ ire taehae ŭigyŏnŭl malssŭmhae chushio. 그 일에 대해 의견을 말씀해 주시오/ *Are you of the same ~?* Kat'ŭn ŭigyŏnishimnikka? 같은 의견이십니까/ *I have a favorable ~*. Nanŭn houirŭl kajigo issŭmnida. 나는 호의를 가지고 있읍니다/ *pro-Korean ~s* ch'inhanjŏgin yŏron 친한(親韓) 적인 여론/ *What's your ~ of that man?* Chŏ saramŭl ŏttŏk'e saenggak'ashimnikka? 저 사람을 어떻게 생각하십니까?

opium *n*. ap'yŏn 아편. *an ~ eater〔smoker〕* ap'yŏnjangi 아편장이/ *an ~ den* ap'yŏn-gul 아편굴.

opponent *n*. (*in fight*) chŏksu 적수, (*in game*) sangdae 상대, (*in business*) kyŏngjaengja 경쟁자.

opportunity *n*. (*good chance*) kihoe 기회, (*favorable time*) chŏkki 적기(適期). *seize an ~* kihoerŭl chapta 기회를 잡다/ *I had not the ~ to speak with him*. Kŭ saramgwa iyagihal kihoega ŏpsŏssŭmnida. 그 사람과 이야기할 기회가 없었읍니다/ *Don't pass up this ~*. I kihoerŭl noch'iji mashio. 이 기회를 놓치지 마시오/ *I think* *the* ~ *has gone*. Kihoenŭn sarajyŏttago saenggak'amnida. 기회는 사라졌다고 생각합니다.

oppose *vt.* pandaehada 반대하다. *I am very much* ~*d to your opinion*. Tangshin ŭigyŏnenŭn aju pandaeimnida. 당신 의견에는 아주 반대입니다/ *I have nothing to* ~ *to your marriage*. Tangshinŭi kyŏrhone pandaehal iyuga ŏpsŭmnida. 당신의 결혼에 반대할 이유가 없습니다.

opposite *adj.* (*facing*) majŭnp'yŏnŭi 맞은편의, (*contrary*) pandaeŭi 반대의. *I took a seat* ~ *to him*. Kŭ saram majŭnp'yŏne charirŭl chabassŭmnida. 그 사람 맞은편에 자리를 잡았습니다/ *We live on the* ~ *side of the street*. Urinŭn i kil kŏnnŏp'yŏne salgo issŭmnida. 우리는 이 길 건너편에 살고 있습니다/ *the* ~ *direction* pandae panghyang 반대 방향.

opposition *n.* pandae 반대, (*party*) yadang 야당. *My wife has an* ~ *to my project*. Anaenŭn nae kyehoege pandaehamnida. 아내는 내 계획에 반대합니다/ *We need a stronger* ~. Tŏ kangnyŏk'an yadangi p'iryohamnida. 더 강력한 야당이 필요합니다.

oppress *vt.* (*weigh down*) appak'ada 압박하다, (*treat harshly*) haktaehada 학대하다.

oppression *n.* (*burdening*) appak 압박, (*hardship*) kollan 곤란, (*depression*) uul 우울. *a sense of* ~ appakkam 압박감.

oppressive *adj.*(*tyrannical*) ŏgapchŏgin 억압적인, (*gloomy*) taptap'an 답답한. ~ *heat* tchinŭn tŭt'an tŏwi 찌는 듯한 더위/ ~ *weather* summak'inŭn nalssi 숨막히는 날씨.

optical *adj.* (*visual*) shiryŏgŭi 시력의, kwanghagŭi 광학의. *Where can I find* ~ *instrument?* Kwanghak kigye nŭn ŏdi issŭmnikka? 광학 기계는 어디 있습니까?

optimism *n.* nakch'ŏnjuŭi 낙천주의.

optimist *n.* nakch'ŏn-ga 낙천가, nakch'ŏnjuŭija 낙천주의자. *a born* ~ t'agonan nakch'ŏn-ga 타고난 낙천가.

or *conj.* ttonŭn 또는. *Which do you like better, coffee* ~ *tea?* K'op'iwa ch'a chungesŏ onŭ kŏsŭl tŏ choahamnikka? 코피와 차 중에서 어느 것을 더 좋아합니까/ *Which* *is older, Mr. Kim ～ I?* Kimssiwa nanŭn ŏnŭ tchogi naiga manssŭmnikka? 김씨와 나는 어느 쪽이 나이가 많습니까/ *I don't want any tea ～ coffee.* Nanŭn ch'ado k'op'ido p'iryoŏpsŭmnida. 나는 차도 코피도 필요없읍니다/ *We must work ～ (else) starve.* Irŭl an hamyŏn kulmŭl subakke ŏpsŭmnida. 일을 안 하면 굶을 수밖에 없읍니다/ *Hurry up, ～ else you'll be late.* Sŏdurŭship-shio, kŭrŏch'i anŭmyŏn nŭssŭmnida. 서두르십시오, 그렇지 않으면 늦습니다/ *I want a hundred ～ so.* Paekkae-tchŭm p'iryohamnida. 100개쯤 필요합니다.

orator *n.* ungbyŏn-ga 웅변가, pyŏnsa 변사.

oratory *n.* ungbyŏn(sul) 웅변(술).

orchard *n.* kwasuwŏn 과수원, *(apples)* sagwanamu pat 사과나무 밭.

orchestra *n.* kwanhyŏnaktan 관현악단, ok'esŭt'ŭra 오케스트라. *a symphony ～* kyohyangaktan 교향악단.

orchid *n.* nanch'o 난초.

order *n.* *(sequence)* sunsŏ 순서, *(arrangement)* chilsŏ 질서. —*vt.* *(command)* myŏngnyŏnghada 명령하다, *(request to supply)* chumunhada 주문하다. *Is your passport in ～?* Yŏkwŏnŭn chedaero toeŏ issŭmnikka? 여권은 제대로 되어 있읍니까/ *Bell is out of ～. Please knock.* Perŭn kojangimnida. Nok'ŭhashipshio. 벨은 고장입니다. 노크하십시오/ *This machine is out of ～.* I ki-gyenŭn kojangimnida. 이 기계는 고장입니다/ *by ～ of receipt* sŏnch'aksunŭro 선착순으로/ *What ～ did you give him?* Kŭ saramege muŏrago myŏngnyŏnghayŏssŭmnikka? 그 사람에게 무어라고 명령하였읍니까/ *I ～ed him to go.* Karago myŏngnyŏnghaessŭmnida. 가라고 명령했읍니다/ *May I take your ～?* Chumunŭl padŭl-kkayo? 주문을 받을까요/ *I have ～ed flowers for your wife.* puinkke ponae tŭril kkoch'ŭl chumunhaessŭmni-da. 부인께 보내 드릴 꽃을 주문했읍니다/ *in ～ to, in ～ that ...* hagi wihaesŏ …하기 위해서.

ordinary *adj.* *(usual)* pot'ongŭi 보통의, *(mediocre)* p'yŏngbŏmhan 평범한. *an ～ express* pot'ong kŭp'aeng yŏlch'a 보통 급행 열차/ *～ mail* pot'ong up'yŏn 보통 우편/

This is an ~ ticket. Igŏsŭn pot'ong sŭngch'akwŏnim-nida. 이것은 보통 승차권입니다/ *the ~ rate* pot'ong yo-gŭm 보통 요금/ *an ~ standard of living* pot'ong saeng-hwal sujun 보통 생활 수준/ *~ dress* p'yŏngbok 평복.

ore *n.* kwangsŏk 광석. *~ of gold* kŭmgwang 금광.

organ *n.* (*instrument*) orŭgan 오르간, p'unggŭm 풍금, (*of body*) kigwan 기관. *pipe ~* p'aip'ŭ orŭgan 파이프 오르간/ *mouth ~* hamonik'a 하모니카/ *~s of digestion* sohwagi 소화기/ *the sex ~* saengshikki 생식기.

organization *n.* (*system*) chojik 조직, kigwan 기관, (*formation*) kusŏng 구성.

organize *vt.* (*form*) chojik'ada 조직하다, (*institute*) ch'angnip'ada 창립하다. *~ a party* chŏngdangŭl cho-jik'ada 정당을 조직하다/ *~ a factory* kongjangŭl sŏl-lip'ada 공장을 설립하다.

orient *n.* (*the O~*) tongyang 동양. —*adj.* tongyangŭi 동양의. *the extreme ~* kŭktong 극동.

Oriental *n.* (*person*) tongyangin 동양인. —*adj.* tongyang-ŭi 동양의. *~ civilization* tongyang munmyŏng 동양 문명/ *~ music* tongyang ŭmak 동양 음악/ *~ painting* tongyanghwa 동양화.

origin *n.* (*source*) kŭnwŏn 근원, (*beginning*) paltan 발단, (*birth*) t'aesaeng 태생. *~ of a quarrel* ssaumŭi paltan 싸움의 발단/ *the ~s of civilization* munnyŏngŭi kiwŏn 문명의 기원/ *a man of humble ~* ch'ulshini ch'ŏnhan saram 출신이 천한 사람.

original *adj.* (*first*) ch'oech'oŭi 최초의, (*not copied*) wŏnbonŭi 원본의, (*inventive*) tokch'angjŏgin 독창적인. —*n.* (*model*) wŏnbon 원본, (*cause*) wŏnin 원인, (*parentage*) t'aesaeng 태생. *the ~ edition* wŏnp'an 원판/ *the ~ plan* wŏnan 원안/ *Who wrote the ~ story?* Wŏn-jakchanŭn nuguimnikka? 원작자는 누구입니까/ *This is a copy; the ~ is in the Haeinsa Temple.* Igŏsŭn sa-bonimnida. Wŏnbonŭn Haeinsa-e issŭmnida. 이것은 사본입니다. 원본은 해인사에 있읍니다/ *Where is the ~ of this translation?* I pŏnyŏgŭi wŏnsŏnŭn ŏdi issŭmni-kka? 이 번역의 원서는 어디 있읍니까?

ornament *n.* (*decoration*) changshik 장식, (*grace*) myŏngye 명예. —*vt.* changshik'ada 장식하다. *a personal* ~ changshin-gu 장신구/ *It is used as an* ~. Kŭgŏsŭn changshigŭro ssŭyŏjimnida. 그것은 장식으로 쓰여집니다.

orphan *n.* koa 고아. *a war* ~ chŏnjaeng koa 전쟁 고아.

orphanage *n.* koawŏn 고아원.

orthodox *adj.* (*conventional*) chŏngt'ongjŏgin 정통적인, (*religion*) chŏnggyoŭi 정교(正敎)의. *O*~ *Church* chŏnggyohoe 정교회/ *the* ~ *party* chŏngt'ongp'a 정통파.

ostrich *n.* t'ajo 타조.

other *adj.* tarŭn 다른, ttan 딴. —*pron.* (*person*) tarŭn saram 다른 사람, (*thing*) tarŭn kŏt 다른 것. *Have you any* ~ *question?* Tarŭn chilmunŭn ŏpsŭmnikka? 다른 질문은 없읍니까/ *Give me some* ~ *ones.* Tarŭn kŏsŭl chushio. 다른 것을 주시오/*Where are the* ~ *boys?* Tarŭn aidŭrŭn ŏdi issŭmnikka? 다른 아이들은 어디 있읍니까/ *I'm busy now; ask me about it some* ~ *time.* Chigŭmŭn pappŭmnida. Onjen-ga tarŭn ttaee wasŏ munŭihashio. 지금은 바쁩니다. 언젠가 다른 때에 와서 문의하시오/ *How many* ~ *brothers have you?* Tto hyŏngjega myŏch'ina issŭmnikka? 또 형제가 몇이나 있읍니까/ *Do good to* ~s Namege ch'ak'age hashio 남에게 착하게 하시오/ *among* ~s t'ŭk'i 특히/ *every* ~ hana kŏllŏ 하나 걸러/ *Please write on every* ~ *line.* Han chul kŏllŏ ssŭshipshio. 한 줄 걸러 쓰십시오/ *in* ~ *words* pakkwŏ marhamyŏn 바꿔 말하면/ *the* ~ *day* yojŏnnal 요전날.

otherwise *adv.* (*or else*) kŭrŏch'i anŭmyŏn 그렇지 않으면, (*differently*) talli 달리. *Go at once,* ~ *you will be too late.* Kot kashio, kŭrŏch'i anŭmyŏn nŭjŭl kŏmnida. 곧 가시오, 그렇지 않으면 늦을 겁니다/ *I think* ~. Nanŭn kŭrŏk'e saenggak'aji anssŭmnida. 나는 그렇게 생각하지 않습니다.

ought *aux.v.* (*should*) hayŏya handa 하여야 한다. *O*~ *I to go?* Naega kaya hamnikka? 내가 가야 합니까/*You* ~ *to start at once.* Chŭkshi ttŏnaya hamnida. 즉시 떠나야 합니다/ *I* ~ *to go to the bank this morning.* Onŭl ojŏne ŭnhaenge kaya hamnida. 오늘 오전에 은행에 가야

합니다/ *You ~ to have consulted him.* Kŭ saramgwa
ŭinonŭl haessŏya hanŭnde. 그 사람과 의논을 했어야 하는데.

our *pron.* uriŭi 우리의. *~ house* uri chip 우리 집/ *~ country*
ŭri nara 우리 나라/ *~s* uriŭi kŏt 우리의 것.

ourselves *pron.* uri chashin 우리 자신. *Let us go ~.* Uri
chashini kapshida. 우리 자신이 갑시다/ *We must not
spoil ~.* Uri chashinŭl mangch'yŏsŏnŭn an toemnida.
우리 자신을 망쳐서는 안 됩니다.

out *adv.* pakkŭro 밖으로. *—n.* pakkat 바깥, oebu 외부.
My father is ~ on business. Abŏjinŭn polnillo oech'ul
chungishimnida. 아버지는 볼일로 외출 중이십니다/ *I found
him ~.* Kaboni oech'urhago ŏpsŏssŭmnida. 가보니 외출
하고 없었읍니다/ *I happened to be ~ when he called.*
Kŭ sarami wassŭl ttae nanŭn mach'im oech'ul chungi-
ŏssŭmnida. 그 사람이 왔을 때 나는 마침 외출 중이었읍니다/
Put the cigarette ~. Tambaetpurŭl kkŭshio. 담뱃불을
끄시오/ *My watch is five minutes ~.* Nae shigyenŭn
obun t'ŭllimnida. 내 시계는 5분 틀립니다/ *Choose one
~ of these ten.* I yŏl kae chungesŏ hanarŭl korŭshio.
이 열 개 중에서 하나를 고르시오/ *~ of question* ŭishimhal
yŏji ŏpshi 의심할 여지 없이/ *in and ~* anp'ak 안팎.

outbreak *n.* palbal 발발, palsaeng 발생.

outcast *n.* *(vagabond)* pangnangja 방랑자, *(homeless
wanderer)* yurangja 유랑자, *(refuse)* ssŭregi 쓰레기.

outdoor *adj.* *(outside the house)* ogoeŭi 옥외의, *(in the
open air)* yaoeŭi 야외의. *—n.* *(pl.)* yaoe 야외, ogoe 옥
외. *an ~ dress* oech'ulbok 외출복/ *an ~ game* ogoe
kyŏnggi 옥외 경기.

outfit *n.* ch'aebi 채비, changbi 장비. *a bath ~* mogyok kigu 목욕 기구/ *a travel ~* yŏhaeng changbi 여행 장비/ *a
ski ~* sŭk'i yonggu 스키 용구.

outing *n.* *(excursion)* sop'ung 소풍, sanch'aek 산책. *go
for an ~* sop'unggada 소풍가다/ *an auto ~* chadongch'a
yŏhaeng 자동차 여행.

outlaw *n.* *(outcast)* purangja 부랑자, *(habitual criminal)*
sangsŭppŏm 상습범, mubŏpcha 무법자.

outlay *n.* *(outgoings)* chich'ul 지출, *(expenses)* kyŏngbi

경비. *with a small* ~ chŏgŭn piyongŭro 적은 비용으로/ *I cannot afford such an* ~. Kŭgat'ŭn chich'urŭn kamdanghal su ŏpsŭmnida. 그같은 지출은 감당할 수 없읍니다.

outline *n.* (*contour*) yun-gwak 윤곽, (*rough draft*) mitkŭrim 밑그림, (*summary*) kaeyo 개요. *an* ~ *of English grammar* yŏngmunpŏp kaeyo 영문법 개요/ *Please make an* ~ *map showing the way to your house.* Tangshin taegŭro kanŭn yaktorŭl kŭryŏ chushio. 당신 댁으로 가는 약도를 그려 주시오. 「식의.

out-of-date *adj.* shidaee twijin 시대에 뒤진, kushigŭi 구

output *n.* (*production*) saengsannyang 생산량, (*power*) ch'ullyŏk 출력. *increase the* ~ saengsan-gorŭl nop'ida 생산고를 높이다/ *the total* ~ ch'ongsaengsan-go 총생산고.

outrage *n.* p'ok'aeng 폭행. *commit an* ~ *on* ...e p'ok'aengŭl kahada …에 폭행을 가하다/ *a serious* ~ shimhan p'ok'aeng 심한 폭행.

outside *n.* (*exterior*) oebu 외부, pakkatchok 바깥쪽, (*personal appearance*) oegwan 외관. *the* ~ *of a house* chip pak 집 밖/ *open the door from* ~ pakkesŏ munŭl yŏlda 밖에서 문을 열다/ *Don't judge a person from the* ~. Saramŭl oemoro p'andanhaji mashio. 사람을 외모로 판단하지 마시오.

outsider *n.* munoehan 문외한, kugoeja 국외자. *He is a rank* ~. Kŭ saramŭn chŏnhyŏ munoehanimnida. 그 사람은 전혀 문외한입니다.

outskirt *n.* (*border*) pyŏnduri 변두리, (*suburb*) kyooe 교외. *I live on the* ~*s of the city.* Nanŭn kyooee salgo issŭmnida. 나는 교외에 살고 있읍니다/ *the* ~*s of Seoul* Sŏul kŭn-gyo 서울 근교.

outspoken *adj.* solchik'an 솔직한. ~ *comments* kit'anŏmnŭn nonp'yŏng 기탄없는 논평.

outstanding *adj.* (*striking*) tturyŏt'an 뚜렷한, nune ttŭinŭn 눈에 띄는, (*not paid*) mot kap'ŭn 못 갚은. *an* ~ *person* ttwiŏnan inmul 뛰어난 인물/ ~ *debts* mot kap'ŭn pit 못 갚은 빚. 「shikchŏgin 형식적인.

outward *adj.* (*outer*) oebuŭi 외부의, (*formal*) hyŏng-

oval *adj.* t'awŏnhyŏngŭi 타원형의.

oven *n.* sot 솥, kama 가마, hwadŏk 화덕. *a baker's ~* ppang kumnŭn kama 빵 굽는 가마.

over *adj.* (*above*) wie 위에, (*on high*) nop'ŭn kose 높은 곳에, (*across*) nŏmŏro 너머로, (*finished*) kkŭnnago 끝나고, (*once more*) toep'urihayŏ 되풀이하여. *Spread a cloth ~ that table.* Shikt'age t'eibŭlporŭl kkashio. 식탁에 테이블보를 까시오/ *She put her hands ~ her face.* Kŭ yŏjanŭn tu sonŭro ŏlgurŭl karyŏssŭmnida. 그 여자는 두 손으로 얼굴을 가렸읍니다./ *Come ~ and see me some time.* Onjego tto nollŏ oshipshio. 언제고 또 놀러 오십시오/ *Thanks for asking me ~ tonight.* Onŭlpam pullŏ chusyŏsŏ kamsahamnida. 오늘밤 불러 주셔서 감사합니다/ *School is ~ at 2.* Hakkyonŭn tushie kkŭnnamnida. 학교는 2시에 끝납니다./ *Go back and do it ~.* Ch'ŏŭmbut'ŏ tashi haeboshio. 처음부터 다시 해보시오/ *~ again* toep'urihayŏ 되풀이하여/ *~ and ~* yŏrŏ pŏn 여러 번/ *~ there* chŏtchoge 저쪽에.

overalls *n.* chagŏppok 작업복.

overcast *adj.* (*clouded over*) chanttŭk hŭrin 잔뜩 흐린, (*gloomy*) ŭmch'imhan 음침한.

overcharge *n.* enuri 에누리, pudanghan kap 부당한 값. —*vi.*,*vt.* enurihada 에누리하다. *We were ~d for the eggs.* Talgyarŭl pissage sassŭmnida. 달걀을 비싸게 샀읍니다/ *That grocer never ~s.* Chŏ shikp'um kagenŭn chŏltaero pagajirŭl ssŭiuji anssŭmnida. 저 식품 가게는 절대로 바가지를 씌우지 않습니다.

overcoat *n.* oet'u 외투, obŏ(k'ot'ŭ) 오버(코트).

overcome *vt.* igyŏ naeda 이겨 내다. *~ temptation* yuhogŭl igyŏ naeda 유혹을 이겨 내다.

overcrowded *adj.* honjap'an 혼잡한. *The bus is ~.* Pŏsŭ ga mopshi pumbimnida. 버스가 몹시 붐빕니다.

overflow *n.* (*flood*) hongsu 홍수, (*excess*) kwaing 과잉. —*vi.*,*vt.* (*flow over*) nŏmch'ida 넘치다, pŏmnamhada 범람하다. *the ~ of population* in-gu kwaing 인구 과잉/ *The Han River has ~ed (its banks).* Han-gangi pŏmnamhaessŭmnida. 한강(漢江)이 범람했읍니다.

overgrow *vt.* (*grow over*) musŏnghada 무성하다, (*outgrow*) nŏmu k'ŏjida 너무 커지다. *Weeds ~ the garden.* Ttŭre chapch'oga musŏnghamnida. 뜰에 잡초가 무성합니다/ *an ~ing town* palchŏnhanŭn ŭp 발전하는 읍.

overhaul *vt.* punhaehayŏ surihada 분해하여 수리하다. *~ an engine* enjinŭl punhaehayŏ surihada 엔진을 분해하여 수리하다.

overhear *vi.,vt.* yŏttŭtta 엿듣다. *I ~d him saying so.* Kŭ sarami kŭrŏn marŭl hanŭn kŏsŭl yŏttŭrŏssŭmnida. 그 사람이 그런 말을 하는 것을 엿들었읍니다.

overheat *n.* kwayŏl 과열. —*vt.* kwayŏrhada 과열하다.

overjoy *vt.* mopshi kippŏhada 몹시 기뻐하다. *The children were ~ed to see me.* Ŏrinidŭrŭn narŭl pogo kippŏ nalttwiŏssŭmnida. 어린이들은 나를 보고 기뻐 날뛰었읍니다.

overland *adj.* yungnoŭi 육로의. —*adv.* yungnoro 육로로. *an ~ journey* yungno yŏhaeng 육로 여행/ *travel ~* yungnoro kada 육로로 가다.

overlook *vt.* (*look down*) naeryŏdaboda 내려다보다, (*fail to notice*) ppattŭrida 빠뜨리다, (*excuse*) nun-gama chuda 눈감아 주다. *I'll ~ your behavior this time.* (*to inferior*) Ibŏnmanŭn ne haengwirŭl nun-gama chugetta. 이번만은 네 행위를 눈감아 주겠다/ *~ a line in reading* han chul ppattŭrigo ikta 한 줄 빠뜨리고 읽다/ *~ a printer's error* oshigŭl mot pogo nŏmŏgada 오식(誤植)을 못 보고 넘어가다.

oversea(s) *adv.* haeoero〔esŏ〕 해외로〔에서〕. —*adj.* haeoeŭi 해외의. *an ~ trade* haeoe muyŏk 해외 무역/ *an ~ travel* haeoe yŏhaeng 해외 여행/ *live ~* haeoee kŏjuhada 해외에 거주하다/ *the Korea O~ Development Corporation.* Han-guk haeoe kaebal kongsa 한국 해외 개발 공사.

overseer *n.* kamdok 감독, chikkongjang 직공장.

oversleep *vt.* (*sleep beyond*) nŏmu chada 너무 자다. *I overslept and was late for work.* Nŭtcham chadaga chikchange nŭjŏssŭmnida. 늦잠 자다가 직장에 늦었읍니다.

overthrow *vt.* (*upset*) twijibŏŏpta 뒤집어엎다, (*vanquish*) kyŏkp'ahada 격파하다. *~ the government* chŏngburŭl twijibŏŏpta 정부를 뒤집어엎다.

overturn *vt.,vi.* (*overthrow*) nŏmŏttŭrida 넘어뜨리다, (*up-set*) twijibŏŏpta 뒤집어엎다. *The boat ~ed.* Pot'ŭga twijip'yŏssŭmnida. 보트가 뒤집혔습니다.

overweight *n.* (*extra weight*) ch'ogwa chungnyang 초과 중량. —*adj.* chungnyang ch'ogwaŭi 중량 초과의. *an ~ bag* chungnyangi ch'ogwadoen p'odae 중량이 초과된 포대/ *If your luggage is ~ you'll have to pay extra.* Chim mugega ch'ogwahamyŏn yogŭmŭl tŏ naeya hamnida. 짐 무게가 초과하면 요금을 더 내야 합니다/ *Are they ~?* Chungnyang ch'ogwaimnikka? 중량 초과입니까?

overwhelm *vt.* (*overpower*) aptohada 압도하다. *Your kindness quite ~s me.* Ch'injŏre taehae muŏra kamsahal mari ŏpsŭmnida. 친절에 대해 무어라 감사할 말이 없습니다.

overwork *vt.,vi.* hoksahada 혹사하다, nŏmu irhada 너무 일하다. —*n.* kwaro 과로. *~ an employee* koyonginŭl hoksahada 고용인을 혹사하다/ *He fell ill from ~.* Kŭ saramŭn kwaro ttaemune pyŏnge kŏllyŏssŭmnida. 그 사람은 과로 때문에 병에 걸렸습니다.

owe *vt.,vi.* (*be indebted*) pitchigo itta 빚지고 있다, (*be obliged*) ŭnhyerŭl ipko itta 은혜를 입고 있다. *I ~ Mr. Kim 10,000 won.* Nanŭn Kimssiege piji manwŏn issŭmnida. 나는 김씨에게 빚이 만(萬) 원 있습니다/ *I ~ my success to you.* Nae sŏnggongŭn tangshin tŏkt'aegimnida. 내 성공은 당신 덕택입니다/ *How much do I ~ you?* Ŏlma tŭrimyŏn toejiyo? 얼마 드리면 되지요/ *I ~ him a grudge.* Kŭege yugami issŭmnida. 그에게 유감이 있습니다/ *I ~ no thanks to her.* Kŭ yŏja-ege amu ŭnhyedo ipchi anassŭmnida. 그 여자에게 아무 은혜도 입지 않았습니다/ *I ~ for your services.* Himssŏ chusyŏsŏ kamsahamnida. 힘써 주셔서 감사합니다/ *owing to ...*ttaemune ...때문에/ *O~ to the rain, we could not come.* Pi ttaemune ol su ŏpsŏssŭmnida. 비 때문에 올 수 없었습니다.

owl *n.* olppaemi 올빼미, puŏngi 부엉이.

own *adj.* (*of oneself*) chagiŭi 자기의. —*vt.,vi.* (*possess*) soyuhada 소유하다. *This is my ~ house.* Igŏshi nae chibimnida. 이것이 내 집입니다/ *I saw it with my ~*

eyes. Nae nunŭro chikchŏp poassŭmnida. 내 눈으로 직접
보았읍니다/ *Who ~s this car?* I ch'anŭn nuguŭi soyuimnikka? 이 차는 누구의 소유입니까/ *Mr. Kim ~s it.*
Kimssiŭi soyuimnida. 김씨의 소유입니다.

owner *n.* (*proprietor*) imja 임자, soyuja 소유자. *Who is
the ~ of this car?* I ch'a imjanŭn nuguimnikka? 이 차
임자는 누구입니까/ *Mr. Park is the ~.* Pakssiimnida.

ownership *n.* soyu(kwŏn) 소유(권). ⌐박씨입니다.

ox *n.* (*male of cattle*) suso 수소, hwangso 황소.

oxtail *n.* soekkori 쇠꼬리. ⌐호흡기.

oxygen *n.* sanso 산소. *an ~ inhaler* sanso hohŭpki 산소

oyster *n.* kul 굴. *fried ~s* kult'wigim 굴튀김/ *raw ~*
saenggul 생굴/ *May I eat ~s in this season?* Yojŭm
kurŭl mŏgŏdo chossŭmnikka? 요즘 굴을 먹어도 좋습니까/
O~s are specially good in cold season. Kulmasŭn
kyŏure pyŏlmiimnida. 굴맛은 겨울에 별미입니다.

P

pace *n.* (*step*) hanbaltchak 한발짝, (*stride*) han-gŏrŭm
한걸음, (*speed*) sokto 속도. —*vt.* (*measure by ~s*) kŏrŭ-
mŭro chaeda 걸음으로 재다. *walk at a quick ~* ch'ongch'ongkŏrŭmŭro kŏtta 총총걸음으로 걷다/ *I cannot keep
~ with you.* Tangshinŭl ttaragal suga ŏpsŭmnida. 당신
을 따라갈 수가 없읍니다.

pacific *adj.* (*peaceable*) p'yŏnghwajŏgin 평화적인, (*tranquil*) chanjanhan 잔잔한. *the P~ Ocean* t'aep'yŏngyang 태평양.

pacifism *n.* p'yŏnghwajuŭi 평화주의, panjŏnnon 반전론.

pacifist *n.* p'yŏnghwajuŭija 평화주의자.

pacify *vt.* (*calm*) tallaeda 달래다, (*quiet*) karaanch'ida
가라앉히다.

pack *n.* (*bundle*) kkurŏmi 꾸러미, (*gang*) hanp'ae 한패.
—*vt.,vi.* kkurida 꾸리다, p'ojanghada 포장하다. *Give
me a ~ of cigarette, please.* Tambae han kap chushio.
담배 한 갑 주시오/ *Can you ~ doll and send it to the*

United States for me? Kŭ inhyŏngŭl p'ojanghayŏ Migugŭro ponae chul su issŭmnikka? 그 인형을 포장하여 미국으로 보내 줄 수 있읍니까?

package *n.* (*parcel*) sop'o 소포, (*bundle*) tabal 다발. *I would like to send this ∼ to New York.* I sop'orŭl Nyuyoge puch'igo shipsŭmnida. 이 소포를 뉴욕에 부치고 싶습니다/ ∼ *paper* p'ojangji 포장지.

packer *n.* chim kkurinŭn saram 짐 꾸리는 사람, p'ojangŏpcha 포장업자.

pact *n.* (*contract*) kyeyak 계약, (*agreement*) hyŏpchŏng 협정, (*treaty*) choyak 조약. *a trade* ∼ t'ongsang hyŏpchŏng 통상 협정.

pad *n. a blotting* ∼ apchi 압지/ *a drawing* ∼ tohwaji ch'ŏp 도화지 첩/ *a shoulder* ∼ ŏkkaebaji 어깨받이/ *a stamp* ∼ sŭt'aemp'ŭ inju 스탬프 인주.

paddy *n.* (*rice*) pyŏ 벼, ssal 쌀.

paddyfield *n.* (*rice field*) non 논.

padlock *n.* maengkkongi chamulsoe 맹꽁이 자물쇠. *I would like to see some* ∼*s that are burglarproof.* Tonan pangjiyong maengkkongi chamulsoerŭl poyŏ chushio. 도난 방지용 맹꽁이 자물쇠를 보여 주시오.

page *n.* p'eiji 페이지, myŏn 면(面). *Open* (*your book*) *at* ∼ 5. O p'eijirŭl p'yŏshio. 5 페이지를 펴시오/ *You will find it on* ∼ 12. Kŭgŏsŭn shibi p'eijie issŭmnida 그것은 12 페이지에 있읍니다.

pageant *n.* (*splendid display*) changgwan 장관, (*parade*) haengnyŏl 행렬, (*outdoor play*) yaoegŭk 야외극.

pagoda *n.* t'ap 탑. *a five-storied* ∼ och'ŭngt'ap 5 층탑.

pail *n.* mult'ong 물통, yangdongi 양동이.

pain *n.* (*ache*) ap'ŭm 아픔, (*suffering*) kot'ong 고통, (*anxiety*) kŭnshim 근심, (*pl.*)(*effort*) sugo 수고, (*trouble*) kosaeng 고생. —*vi.* (*ache*) ap'ŭda 아프다. —*vt.* (*cause* ∼ *to*) kot'ongŭl chuda 고통을 주다. *Where do you feel* ∼? Ŏdiga ap'ŭshimnikka? 어디가 아프십니까/ *I have got a* ∼ *in my left shoulder.* Oentchok ŏkkaega a'pŭmnida. 왼쪽 어깨가 아픕니다/ *I've got a terrible* ∼. Mopshi ap'ŭmnida. 몹시 아픕니다/ *spare no* ∼*s to* ...*e* sugorŭl akkiji annŭnda…에 수고를 아끼지 않는다/ *cry with* ~ koerowa sorirŭl chirŭda 피로와 소리를 지르다/ *It ~s me deeply.* Kŭgŏshi mopshi kŏkchŏngimnida. 그것이 몹시 걱정입니다.

painful *adj.* ap'ŭn 아픈, (*toilsome*) kodoen 고된. *The task was ~ to me.* Kŭ irŭn kodoeŏssŭmnida. 그 일은 고되었읍니다/ *a ~ duty* kodoen immu 고된 임무.

paint *n.* p'eint'ŭ 페인트, kŭrimmulkam 그림물감. —*vt.,vi.* (*portray*) kŭrida 그리다, (*coat*) p'eint'ŭrŭl ch'irhada 페인트를 칠하다. *Wet[Fresh]* ~. P'eint'ŭ chuŭi 페인트 주의/ *water* ~ susŏng p'eint'ŭ 수성 페인트/ *The ~ is off in places.* Kundegunde ch'iri pŏtkyŏjyŏ issŭmnida. 군 데군데 칠이 벗겨져 있읍니다.   「화가.

painter *n.* (*workman*) ch'iljangi 칠장이, (*artist*) hwaga

painting *n.* kŭrim 그림. *oil* ~ yuhwa 유화/ *water color* ~ such'aehwa 수채화/ *a nude* ~ nach'ehwa 나체화.

pair *n.* (*set of two*) han ssang 한 쌍, (*mated couple*) pubu 부부, (*fellow*)han tchak 한 짝. *a ~ of shoes* kudu han k'yŏlle 구두 한 켤레/ *a ~ of trousers* paji han pŏl 바지 한 벌/*I'll get you another ~ of gloves.* (*to inferior*) Changgabŭl tto han k'yŏlle sa chuma. 장갑을 또 한 켤레 사 주마/ *How many ~s of socks do you have?* Yangmarŭn myŏt k'yŏlle kajigo issŭmnikka? 양말은 몇 켤레 가지고 있읍니까/ *the happy* ~ haengbok'an pubu 행복한 부부/ *I have lost the ~ to this glove.* I changgap han tchagŭl irŏssŭmnida. 이 장갑 한 짝을 잃었읍니다/ *Where is the ~ to this sock?* I yangmal han tchak ŏdi itchiyo? 이 양말 한 짝 어디 있지요?

pajamas *n.* p'ajama 파자마, chamot 잠옷.

pal *n.* (*friend*) ch'in-gu 친구. *a pen* ~ p'yŏnji ch'in-gu 편지 친구.

palace *n.* kungjŏn 궁전. *picture[cinema]* ~ yŏnghwagwan 영화관.

palate *n.* (*roof of the mouth*) ipch'ŏnjang 입천장.

pale *adj.* (*wan*) ch'angbaek'an 창백한, (*dim*) yŏlbŭn 엷은. *You look* ~. Ŏlguri ch'angbaek'ashimnida. 얼굴이 창백하십니다/ ~ *blue* yŏlbŭn nampit 엷은 남빛.

palm *n.* (*of hand*) sonpadak 손바닥, (*tree*) chongnyŏ 종려. *read one's* ~ sonkŭmŭl poda 손금을 보다.

palmistry *n.* sonkŭmbogi 손금보기, susangsul 수상술.

palsy *n.* (*paralysis*) chungp'ung 중풍, mabi 마비.

pamphlet *n.* p'amp'ŭllet 팜플렛, soch'aekcha 소책자.

pan *n.* nambi 남비. *a frying* ~ p'ŭraip'aen 프라이팬/ *a stew* ~ sŭt'yu nambi 스튜 남비.

pander *n.* (*pimp*) ttujangi 뚜장이, p'oju 포주.

pane *n.* p'anyuri 판유리. *window* ~ ch'angyuri 창유리.

pang *n.* (*sharp pain*) ssushigo ap'ŭm 쑤시고 아픔, (*mental torture*) sangshim 상심. *the* ~*s of hunger* churimŭi kot'ong 주림의 고통.

panic *n.* (*sudden fright*) kongp'o 공포, (*econ.*) konghwang 공황. *a* ~ *age* konghwang shidae 공황 시대/*financial* ~ kyŏngje konghwang 경제 공황.

pant *n.* (*gasp*) hŏlttŏkkŏrim 헐떡거림, (*throb*) kodong 고동. —*vi.,vt.* hŏlttŏkkŏrida 헐떡거리다. *The runner* ~*ed after the race.* Chujanŭn talligiga kkŭnnan twi hŏlttŏkkŏryŏssŭmnida. 주자는 달리기가 끝난 뒤 헐떡거렸읍니다.

pantry *n.* (*larder*) shingnyŏp'umshil 식료품실, (*housemaid's* ~) shikkishil 식기실.

pants *n.* (*pl.*)(*trousers*) paji 바지, (*drawers*) p'aench'ŭ 팬츠. *corduroy* ~ k'orŭden paji 코르덴 바지/ *knee* ~ panbaji 반바지.

papa *n.* (*daddy*) appa 아빠.

paper *n.* chongi 종이, (*newspaper*) shinmunji 신문지, (*essay*) nonmun 논문. (*pl.*) sŏryu 서류. *art* ~ at'ŭji 아트지/ *blank* ~ paekchi 백지/ *brown* ~ p'ojangji 포장지/ *plotting* ~ panganji 방안지(方眼紙)/ *toilet* ~ hyuji 휴지/ *wrapping* ~ p'ojangji 포장지/ ~ *clip* chongi kkiugae 종이 끼우개/ ~ *money* chip'ye 지폐/ *a sheet of* ~ chongi han chang 종이 한 장/ *Is there any interesting news in the* ~? Shinmune musŭn chaeminanŭn nyusŭga issŭmnikka? 신문에 무슨 재미나는 뉴스가 있읍니까?

par *n.* (*comm.*) aengmyŏn kagyŏk 액면 가격. *at* ~ aengmyŏn kagyŏgŭro 액면 가격으로/ *above* ~ aengmyŏn isangŭro 액면 이상으로/ *Shares have fallen below* ~

Chushigi aengmyŏn iharo ttŏrŏjyŏssŭmnida. 주식이 액면 이하로 떨어졌읍니다.

parachute *n.* nak'asan 낙하산, p'arasyut'ŭ 파라슈트.

parade *n.* (*marching*) haengnyŏl 행렬, (*troops*) yŏlbyŏng 열병, (*display*) kwashi 과시. *a funeral* ∼ changŭi haeng-nyŏl 장의 행렬/ *a street* ∼ kadu haengnyŏl 가두 행렬.

paradise *n.* (*heaven*) ch'ŏn-guk 천국, nagwŏn 낙원, (*Budd.*) kŭngnak 극락. *a* ∼ *on earth* chisangŭi nagwŏn 지상의 낙원.

parallel *adj.* p'yŏnghaengŭi 평행의. —*n.* p'yŏnghaengsŏn 평행선, (*geog.*) wisŏn 위선(緯線). *Korea has been divided at the 38th* ∼ *of the north latitude.* Han-gugŭn samp'alsŏnesŏ punhaldoeŏ issŭmnida. 한국은 38 선에서 분할되어 있읍니다.

paralysis *n.* mabi 마비, (*palsy*) chungp'ung 중풍. *infan-tile* ∼ soa mabi 소아 마비/ ∼ *of the heart* shimjang mabi 심장 마비.

parasite *n.* (*insect*) kisaengch'ung 기생충, (*person*) shik-kaek 식객.

parasol *n.* p'arasol 파라솔, (*sunshade*) yangsan 양산. *This is a* ∼. *You can't use it in the rain.* Igŏsŭn p'ara-sorimnida. Piol ttaenŭn sayonghal su ŏpsŭmnida. 이것은 파라솔입니다. 비올 때는 사용할 수 없읍니다.

paratroops *n.* nak'asan pudae 낙하산 부대.

parcel *n.* (*package*) chimbottari 짐보따리, (*post*) sop'o 소포. *Will you carry this* ∼ *for me?* I chimbottari chom tŭrŏda chushigessŭmnikka? 이 짐보따리 좀 들어다 주시겠읍니까/ *Please send this* ∼ *by registered post.* I sop'orŭl tŭnggi up'yŏnŭro ponae chushio. 이 소포를 등기 우편으로 보내 주시오/ *Handle this* ∼ *with care.* I chimŭl choshim-hayŏ ch'wigŭp'ashio. 이 짐을 조심하여 취급하시오/ *undo a* ∼ sop'orŭl kkŭrŭda 소포를 끄르다.

parch *vt.,vi.* (*roast*) pokta 볶다, (*scorch*) passak malli-da 바싹 말리다. ∼*ed peas* pokkŭn k'ong 볶은 콩. *I am* ∼*ed with thirst.* Mogi passak marŭmnida. 목이 바싹 마릅니다.

pardon *vt.* (*forgive*) yongsŏhada 용서하다. —*n.* yongsŏ

용서. *P~ me for interrupting you.* Panghaega toeŏ
mianhamnida. 방해가 되어 미안합니다/ *P~ me for being
late.* Nŭtke wasŏ choesonghamnida. 늦게 와서 죄송합니다/
P~ my saying so. Kŭrŏn marŭl haesŏ mianhamnida.
그런 말을 해서 미안합니다/ *I beg your ~ for disturbing
you.* P'yerŭl kkich'yŏ choesonghamnida. 폐를 끼쳐 죄송
합니다/ *I beg your ~, but which way is to the Myong-
dong?* Shillyeimnidaman Myŏngdongŭn ŏnŭ tchoguro
kamyŏn toemnikka? 실례입니다만 명동은 어느 쪽으로 가면
됩니까/ *Beg your ~?* Tashi han pŏn malssŭmhae chushigessŏyo? 다시 한 번 말씀해 주시겠어요?

parent *n.* yangch'in 양친, pumo 부모. *May I introduce
you to my ~s?* Pumonimkke sogaehae tŭrilkkayo? 부모
님께 소개해 드릴까요/ *Are your ~s living?* Yangch'in-
kkesŏnŭn saengjonhae kyeshimnikka? 양친께서는 생존해
계십니까/ *~ company* mohoesa 모(母)회사.

parish *n.* kyogu 교구(敎區).

park *n.* kongwŏn 공원, (*Am.*) (*car ~*) chuch'ajang 주
차장. —*vt.* chuch'ahada 주차하다, (*put*) tuda 두다. *a
national ~* kungnip kongwŏn 국립 공원/ *Sajik P~* Sajik-
kongwŏn 사직 공원/ *Where can we ~ (the car)?* Ŏdie
chuch'ahal su issŭmnikka? 어디에 주차할 수 있읍니까?

parking *n.* chuch'a 주차. *a ~ lot* chuch'ajang 주차장/ *No
P~* chuch'a kŭmji 주차 금지/ *a ~ violation* chuch'a wiban 주차 위반.

parley *n.* tamp'an 담판. —*vt.,vi.* tamp'anhada 담판하다.

parliament *n.* ŭihoe 의회, kuk'oe 국회. *Member of P~*
kuk'oe ŭiwŏn 국회 의원/ *P~ meets tomorrow.* Ku-
k'oega naeil yŏllimnida. 국회가 내일 열립니다.

parlo(u)r *n.* (*private*) kŏshil 거실, (*official*) ŭngjŏpshil
응접실. *a beauty ~* mijangwŏn 미장원/ *a hairdresser's
~ ibalgwan* 이발관/ *billiard ~* tanggujang 당구장.

parrot *n.* aengmusae 앵무새.

part *n.* (*section*) pubun 부분, (*share*) mok 몫, (*role*)
yŏk'al 역할, (*concern*) kwan-gye 관계, (*side*) tchok
쪽, (*district*) chibang 지방, (*ability*) chaenŭng 재능.
—*vt.,vi.* (*separate*) nanuda 나누다, (*go apart*) heŏjida 헤

어지다. *I like the last ~ of the play most.* Kŭ yŏn-gŭgŭi majimak pubuni kajang chossŭmnida. 그 연극의 마지막 부분이 가장 좋습니다/ *I lost ~ of my money.* Tonŭl ŏlmagan irŏbŏryŏssŭmnida. 돈을 얼마간 잃어버렸습니다/ *I'll do my ~.* Nae ponbunŭl tahagessŭmnida. 내 본분을 다하겠읍니다/ *I have a personal ~ in it.* Kŏgie tae-hae chikchŏp kwan-gyega issŭmnida. 거기에 대해 직접 관계가 있읍니다/ *What ~ of Korea do you come from?* Han-gugŭi ŏnŭ chibang ch'ulshinimnikka? 한국의 어느 지방 출신입니까/ *a woman without ~s* munŭnghan yŏin 무능한 여인/ *I ~ed from her at Pusan Station.* Kŭ yŏjawa Pusanyŏgesŏ heŏjyŏssŭmnida. 그 여자와 부산역에서 헤어졌읍니다/ *We must ~ now.* Ije heŏjyŏyagessŭm-nida. 이제 헤어져야겠읍니다/ *for my ~* narosŏnŭn 나로서는/ *for the most ~* taegae 대개/ *in ~* ŏnŭ chŏngdo 어느 정도/ *take ~ in* ch'amgahada 참가하다.

particular *adj.* (*especial*) kakpyŏrhan 각별한, (*distinct*) kaegaeŭi 개개의, (*striking*) tturyŏt'an 뚜렷한, (*de-tailed*) sangsehan 상세한. —*n.* (*details*) myŏngse 명세. *I have nothing ~ to do.* Kakpyŏrhi hal irŭn ŏpsŭmni-da. 각별히 할 일은 없읍니다/ *Why did you choose this ~ chair?* Wae tŭkpyŏrhi i ŭijarŭl t'aek'aessŭmnikka? 왜 특별히 이 의자를 택했읍니까/ *Give me a ~ account of the expenses?* Sangsehan kyesansŏrŭl chushipshio. 상세한 계산서를 주십시오/ *a bill of ~s* myŏngsesŏ 명세서/ *I re-member one of them in ~.* T'ŭk'i kŭdŭl chung han saramŭl kiŏk'amnida. 특히 그들 중 한 사람을 기억합니다/ *in ~* t'ŭk'i 특히.

particularly *adv.* t'ŭkpyŏrhi 특별히. *I ~ asked him to be careful.* Choshimharago kakpyŏrhi put'ak'aessŭmnida. 조심하라고 각별히 부탁했읍니다/ *Do you want to go? No, not ~.* Kago shipsŭmnikka? Anyo, pyŏllo. 가고 싶습니까? 아뇨, 별로.

parting *n.* (*separation*) chakpyŏl 작별. —*adj.* chakpyŏ-rŭi 작별의. *a ~ greeting* chakpyŏl insa 작별 인사/ *a ~ gift* chakpyŏl sŏnmul 작별 선물.

partition *n.* kanmagi 간막이. *a ~ wall* kanmagi pyŏk 간

막이 벽.

partner *n.* (*associate*) tchakp'ae 짝패, (*companion*) sang-daeja 상대자, p'at'ŭnŏ 파트너. *one's life* ~ paeuja 배우자/ *a dancing* ~ taensŭ p'at'ŭnŏ 댄스 파트너/ *Miss Lee, I'm quite proud of having you for a* ~. Misŭ Ri, tang-shinŭi p'at'ŭnŏga doen kŏsŭl yŏnggwangŭro saenggak'amnida. 미스 리, 당신의 파트너가 된 것을 영광으로 생각합니다.   「hammyŏng hoesa 합명 회사.

partnership *n.* (*association*) yŏnhap 연합, (*business*)

party *n.* (*social gathering*) p'at'i 파티, moim 모임, (*political*) chŏngdang 정당. *a dinner* ~ manch'anhoe 만찬회/ *a send off* ~ songbyŏrhoe 송별회/ *When does the* ~ *take place?* P'at'inŭn ŏnje yŏllimnikka? 파티는 언제 열립니까/ *Would you like to come to our* ~? Uri p'at'ie oshiji ank'essŭmnikka? 우리 파티에 오시지 않겠읍니까/ *Thank you very much for inviting me to the* ~. P'at'ie ch'odaehae chusyŏsŏ taedanhi kamsahamnida. 파티에 초대해 주셔서 대단히 감사합니다/ *the Communist P* ~ kongsandang 공산당/ *Do you have many parties in your country?* Kwigugenŭn chŏngdangi man-ssŭmnikka? 귀국에는 정당이 많습니까?

pass *n.* (*passage*) t'onghaeng 통행, (*free ticket*) p'aesŭ 패스, (*exam.*) hapkyŏk 합격. —*vi.,vt.* (*go by*) chinaga-da 지나가다, (*exam.*) hapkyŏk'ada 합격하다, (*hand over*) kŏnneda 건네다. *an admission* ~ muryo ipchangkwŏn 무료 입장권/ *a* ~ *on a railway* ch'ŏlto muryo sŭngch'a-kwŏn 철도 무료 승차권/ *Please let me* ~. Chom china-gagessŭmnida. 좀 지나가겠읍니다/ *Will you kindly allow me to* ~? Mianhajiman chinagado chossŭmnikka? 미안하지만 지나가도 좋습니까/ *The candidates* ~*ed* (*the exam*). Chimangjadŭrŭn (shihŏme) hapkyŏk'aessŭmni-da. 지망자들은 (시험에) 합격했읍니다/ *We have to* ~ *the Customs before we leave.* Ttŏnagi chŏne segwanŭl t'onggwahaeya hamnida. 떠나기 전에 세관을 통과해야 합니다/ *Would you* ~ *the salt please.* Sogŭm chom kŏnne chushipshio. 소금 좀 건네 주십시오.

passage *n.* (*passing*) t'onghaeng 통행, (*way*) t'ongno

통로, (*journey*) yŏhaeng 여행, (*voyage*) hanghae 항해, (*corridor*) pokto 복도.

passenger *n.* (*train, bus*) sŭnggaek 승객, (*boat*) sŏn-gaek 선객. ~ *boat* yŏgaeksŏn 여객선/ ~ *car* kaekch'a 객차/ ~ *list* sŏn-gaek myŏngbu 선객 명부.

passer-by, passerby *n.* t'onghaengin 통행인.

passing *n.* (*passage*) t'onghaeng 통행, (*death*) chugŭm 죽음, (*enactment*) t'onggwa 통과, (*exam.*) hapkyŏk 합격.

passion *n.* (*intense emotion*) yŏlchŏng 열정, (*rage*) kyŏkpun 격분, (*ardent love*) yŏllyŏrhan sarang 열렬한 사랑, (*enthusiasm*) yŏlshim 열심. *the tender* ~ aejŏng 애정/ *a foolish* ~ ch'ijŏng 치정(痴情)/ *a* ~ *for fame* myŏngyeyok 명예욕/ *get into a* ~ pŏlk'ŏk sŏngŭl naeda 벌컥 성을 내다.

passionate *adj.* (*ardent*) yŏllyŏrhan 열렬한, (*quick-tempered*) sŏngmiga kŭp'an 성미가 급한. *a* ~ *love* yŏllyŏrhan sarang 열렬한 사랑/ *a* ~ *speech* yŏlbyŏn 열변/ *a man of* ~ *nature* sŏngmi kŭp'an saram 성미 급한 사람.

passport *n.* yŏkwŏn 여권, p'aesŭp'ot'ŭ 패스포트. *apply to the authorities for* ~ tangguge yŏkwŏnŭl shinch'ŏnghada 당국에 여권을 신청하다/ *a* ~ *for America* Miguk'aeng yŏkwŏn 미국행(行) 여권/ *Let me have your* ~. P'aesŭp'ot'ŭ chom poyŏ chushipshio. 패스포트 좀 보여 주십시오/ *Where is the* ~ *control?* Yŏkwŏn shimsakwanŭn ŏdijiyo? 여권 심사과는 어디지요?

password *n.* amho 암호.

past *n.* kwagŏ 과거. —*adj.* (*gone by*) chinagan 지나간, kwagŏŭi 과거의, (*just passed*) panggŭm chinan 방금 지난. *in the* ~ kwagŏ-e 과거에/ *We know nothing of her* ~. Kŭ yŏjaŭi kwagŏnŭn morŭmnida. 그 여자의 과거는 모릅니다/ *the* ~ *month* chinan tal 지난 달/ *during the* ~ *week* chinan chuil tongane 지난 주일 동안에/ *the* ~ *president* chŏn hoejang 전 회장/ *It is twenty minutes* ~ *two.* Tushi ishippunimnida. 2시 20분입니다.

paste *n.* p'ul 풀. —*vt.* p'ullo parŭda 풀로 바르다. *thin* ~ mulgŭn p'ul 묽은 풀/ ~ *up posters* p'osŭt'ŏrŭl puch'ida

포스터를 붙이다.

pasteboard *n.* p'anji 판지, mabunji 마분지.

pastime *n.* (*amusement*) orak 오락, (*recreation*) soilkŏri 소일거리. *a national* ~ kungmin orak 국민 오락.

pastor *n.* (*minister*) moksa 목사, (*priest*) sŭngnyŏ 승려.

pastry *n.* saenggwaja 생과자.

pasture *n.* (*grassland*) mokchang 목장, mokch'o 목초.

pat *vt.,vi.* (*tap*) kabyŏpke tudŭrida 가볍게 두드리다. ―*n.* (*light blow*) t'okt'ok ch'im 톡톡 침. *He~ted me on the back.* Ŏkkaerŭl tudŭrimyŏ ch'ingch'anhaessŭmnida. 어깨를 두드리며 칭찬했읍니다.

patch *n.* hŏnggŏp 헝겊. ―*vt.* hŏnggŏbŭl tŏttaeda 헝겊을 덧대다/ *P~ up this coat.* I chŏgorie hŏnggŏbŭl taeŏsŏ kiwŏ chushio. 이 저고리에 헝겊을 대어서 기워 주시오.

patent *n.* chŏnmae t'ŭk'ŏ 전매특허. *the P~ Bureau* t'ŭk'ŏguk 특허국/ *hold a* ~ *right* t'uk'ŏkwŏnŭl kajida 특허권을 가지다.

path *n.* (*footway*) osolkil 오솔길, (*track*) t'ongno 통로. *Keep to the* ~ *or you may lose your way.* Kŭ kirŭl ttaragaji anŭmyŏn kirŭl ilk'o mal kŏmnida. 그 길을 따라가지 않으면 길을 잃고 말 겁니다/ ~*way* chobŭn kil 좁은 길.

pathway *n.* (*path*) osolkil 오솔길, (*track*) podo 보도.

patience *n.* (*forbearance*) ch'amŭlsŏng 참을성, (*endurance*) innae 인내. *I have lost* ~ *with you.* Tangshinegenŭn ch'amŭl suga ŏpsŭmnida. 당신에게는 참을 수가 없읍니다/ *Have* ~ *for another day or two.* Haru it'ŭlman tŏ ch'ama chushipshio. 하루 이틀만 더 참아 주십시오.

patient *adj.* ch'amŭlsŏng innŭn 참을성 있는. ―*n.* hwanja 환자. *Be* ~ *with children.* Aidŭregenŭn ch'amŭlsŏng itke taehashio. 아이들에게는 참을성 있게 대하시오/ *a hospital* ~ pyŏngwŏn hwanja 병원 환자/ *a surgical* ~ susul hwanja 수술 환자/ *The* ~ *is progressing favorable.* Hwanjanŭn kyŏnggwaga chossŭmnida. 환자는 경과가 좋습니다.

patriot *n.* aegukcha 애국자.

patriotic *adj.* aegugŭi 애국의. *a* ~ *song* aegukka 애국가/

a ~ movement aeguk undong 애국 운동/ *the Ladies P~ Society* aeguk puinhoe 애국 부인회.

patriotism *n.* aegukshim 애국심.

patrol *n.* sunch'al 순찰. *~ boat* ch'ogyejŏng 초계정/ *a police ~ car* kyŏngch'al sunch'alch'a 경찰 순찰차.

patrolman *n.* (*Am.*) sunch'al kyŏngch'al 순찰 경찰.

patron *n.* (*sponsor*) huwŏnja 후원자, (*client*) tan-gol sonnim 단골 손님. *a cinema ~* yŏnghwa p'aen 영화 팬/ *I hope that you will also become one of my ~.* Kwihakkesŏdo nae huwŏnjaŭi han puni toeŏ chushipshio. 귀하께서도 내 후원자의 한 분이 되어 주십시오.

patronage *n.* (*support*) huwŏn 후원, (*encouragement*) ch'anjo 찬조, (*customers*) tan-gol kŏrae 단골 거래. *May we expect your continued ~ of our hotel ?* Ap'ŭro kyesok chŏhŭi hot'erŭl ch'aja chushipshio. 앞으로 계속 저희 호텔을 찾아 주십시오.

pattern *n.* (*model*) mohyŏng 모형, (*sample*) kyŏnbon 견본, (*example*) mobŏm 모범, (*design*) munŭi 무늬. *a ~ wife* mobŏmjŏgin anae 모범적인 아내/ *a ~ book* kyŏnbonch'aek 견본책/ *Please show me some ~s of cloth.* Ch'ŏnŭi kyŏnbonŭl chom poyŏ chushio. 천의 견본을 좀 보여 주시오.

pause *n.* (*suspense*) mŏmch'um 멈춤, (*hesitation*) chujŏ 주저. *—vi.* (*stop*) mŏmch'uda 멈추다, (*intermit*) chungdanhada 중단하다, (*linger*) mangsŏrida 망설이다.

pave *vt.* (*road*) kkalda 깔다, p'ojanghada 포장하다. *~ a road with asphalt* asŭp'alt'ŭro tororŭl p'ojanghada 아스팔트로 도로를 포장하다.

pavement *n.* p'ojang toro 포장 도로.

pavilion *n.* (*large tent*) k'ŭn ch'ŏnmak 큰 천막.

paw *n.* appal 앞발. *a dog's ~* kaeŭi pal 개의 발.

pawn *n.* (*pledge*) tambomul 담보물, (*chessman*) chol 졸 (卒). *My watch is in ~.* Nae shigyenŭn chŏdangchap'yŏssŭmnida. 내 시계는 저당잡혔읍니다.

pay *n.* (*payment*) chibul 지불, (*salary*) ponggŭp 봉급, (*wage*) imgŭm 임금. *—vt.* ch'irŭda 치르다, chiburhada 지불하다. *daily ~* ilgŭp 일급(日給)/ *overtime ~* shiganoe

sudang 시간외 수당/ ~ *day* ponggŭmnal 봉급날/ *What* ~ *does he get?* Kŭ saramŭi ponggŭbŭn ŏlmaimnikka? 그 사람의 봉급은 얼마입니까/ *What is the* ~? Ponggŭbŭn ŏlmaimnikka? 봉급은 얼마입니까/ *How much are you willing to* ~? Olma yesanhago issŭmnikka? 얼마 예산하고 있읍니까/ *I'll* ~ *for tonight.* Onŭl chŏnyŏgŭn naega sagessŭmnida. 오늘 저녁은 내가 사겠읍니다/ *Have you paid all your debts yet?* Pijŭn pŏlssŏ ta kap'assŭmnikka? 빚은 벌써 다 갚았읍니까/ *Come on, I'm* ~*ing.* Cha, naega sagessŭmnida. 자, 내가 사겠읍니다/ *Please* ~ *more attention to your work.* Tangshin ire chomdŏ chuŭirŭl kiurishio. 당신 일에 좀더 주의를 기울이시오.

payment *n.* (*paying*) chibul 지불, (*sum paid*) chiburaek 지불액, (*reward*) posu 보수. *the date of* ~ chibul naltcha 지불 날짜/ *advance* ~ sŏnbul 선불/ *cash* ~ hyŏn-gŭm chibul 현금 지불/ *The* ~ *is due on the 30th of this month.* Idal samshibire chiburhagiro toeŏ issŭmnida. 이달 30 일에 지불하기로 되어 있읍니다.

pea *n.* wanduk'ong 완두콩. *green* ~*s* kŭrinp'isŭ 그린 피스, ch'ŏngwandu 청완두.

peace *n.* (*opp. war*) p'yŏnghwa 평화, (*quiet*) p'yŏngon 평온, (*mutual concord*) hwahap 화합(和合). *domestic* ~ kajŏngŭi p'yŏnghwa 가정의 평화/ *world* ~ segye p'yŏnghwa 세계 평화/ *the P* ~ *Corps* p'yŏnghwa pongsadan 평화 봉사단/ ~ *treaty* p'yŏnghwa choyak 평화 조약/ *We are at* ~ *with all the nations.* Urinŭn modŭn narawa hwach'inhago issŭmnida. 우리는 모든 나라와 화친하고 있읍니다/ *Leave me in* ~. Choyonghi itke hae chushio. 조용히 있게 해 주시오.

peaceful *adj.* (*peaceable*) p'yŏnghwaroun 평화로운, (*quiet*) choyonghan 조용한. *a* ~ *country* p'yŏnghwaroun nara 평화로운 나라/ *a* ~ *evening* koyohan pam 고요한 밤/ ~ *industry* p'yŏnghwa sanŏp 평화 산업.

peach *n.* poksunga 복숭아. ~ *blossom* poksungakkot 복숭아꽃/ *canned* ~*es* poksunga t'ongjorim 복숭아 통조림.

peacock *n.* kongjak 공작.

peak *n.* (*summit*) sankkoktaegi 산꼭대기, (*highest point*) chŏlchŏng 절정, (*pointed end*) kkŭt 끝.

pearl *n.* chinju 진주. *an artificial* ～ injo chinju 인조 진주/ *a cultured* ～ yangshik chinju 양식 진주/ *a sham* ～ katcha chinju 가짜 진주/ *I want to see some* ～ *necklaces*. Chinju mokkŏrirŭl poyŏ chushio. 진주 목걸이를 보여 주시오.

peasant *n.* (*farmer*) nongbu 농부, (*rustic*) shigolttŭgi 시골뜨기. *a* ～ *girl* shigol ch'ŏnyŏ 시골 처녀.

pebble *n.* choyaktol 조약돌, chagal 자갈.

peck *vt.,vi.* tchoda 쪼다.

peculiar *adj.* (*unique*) tokt'ŭk'an 독특한, (*special*) t'ŭksuhan 특수한, (*strange*) isanghan 이상한. *The custom is quite* ～ *to this country*. Kŭ sŭpkwanŭn i nara t'ŭgyuhan kŏshimnida. 그 습관은 이 나라 특유한 것입니다/ *These expressions are* ～ *to Korean language*. Irŏn p'yohyŏnpŏbŭn Han-gugŏ-e t'ŭgyuhan kŏshimnida. 이런 표현법은 한국어에 특유한 것입니다.

pedantic *adj.* hakchain ch'ehanŭn 학자인 체하는, anŭn ch'ehanŭn 아는 체하는. *Don't be so* ～. Nŏmu anŭn ch'ehaji mashio. 너무 아는 체하지 마시오.

peddle *vi.,vt.* haengsangŭl hada 행상(行商)을 하다. ～ *out English* igotchŏgot tanimyŏ Yŏngŏrŭl karŭch'ida. 이곳저곳 다니며 영어를 가르치다/ *She* ～*s vegetables*. Kŭ yŏjanŭn yach'ae haengsangŭl hamnida. 그 여자는 야채 행상을 합니다.

peddler *n.* haengsangin 행상인.

pedestrian *n.* (*walker*) pohaengja 보행자. ～*s' crossing* hoengdan podo 횡단 보도.

pedigree *n.* (*list of ancestors*) chokpo 족보, (*lineage*) hyŏlt'ong 혈통.

peel *vt.,vi.* kkŏpchirŭl pŏtkida 껍질을 벗기다. ～ *a banana* panana kkŏpchirŭl pŏtkida 바나나 껍질을 벗기다/ *The wallpaper is* ～*ing off*. Pyŏkchiga pŏtkyŏjigo issŭmnida. 벽지가 벗겨지고 있읍니다.

peep *vi.* (*peer slyly*) yŏtpoda 엿보다, (*emerge*) nat'anada 나타나다. —*n.* (*glimpse*) yŏtpŏm 엿봄. *Don't* ～ *into* *the room.* Pangŭl tŭryŏdaboji mashio. 방을 들여다보지 마시오/ *Get a ~ inside.* Sogŭl tŭryŏdaboshio. 속을 들여다보시오.

peer *n.* (*equal*) tongnyo 동료, (*nobleman*) kwijok 귀족. —*vt.,vi.* (*look sharply*) chasehi poda 자세히 보다.

peg *n.* namumot 나무못, (*stake*) malttuk 말뚝. *a hat ~* mojagŏri 모자걸이/ *Just fetch me the hat on the ~, there is a good boy.* (*to inferior*) Ch'ak'an aiya, kŭ moja chom katta chwŏ! 착한 아이야, 그 모자 좀 갖다 줘!

pelt *n.* (*raw hide*) saenggajuk 생가죽, (*fur*) t'ŏlgajuk 털가죽.

pen *n.* (*for writing*) p'en 펜, (*pen nib*) p'ench'ok 펜촉, (*fold*) uri 우리. *~ holder* p'entae 펜대/ *~ name* p'il-myŏng 필명/ *~ pal* p'enp'al 펜팔/ *Is this ball-point ~ 100 won each?* I polp'enŭn han charue paegwŏnimnikka? 이 볼펜은 한 자루에 100 원입니까?

penalty *n.* (*punishment*) hyŏngbŏl 형벌, (*fine*) pŏlgŭm 벌금, (*in sport*) panch'ik 반칙. *the death ~* sahyŏng 사형/ *The referee awarded a ~.* Shimp'anŭn p'enŏlt'irŭl chuŏssŭmnida. 심판은 페널티를 주었읍니다/ *~ kick* p'enŏlt'i k'ik 페널티 킥.

pencil *n.* yŏnp'il 연필. *a color ~* saengnyŏnp'il 색연필/ *an eyebrow ~* nunssŏp kŭrigae 눈썹 그리개/ *Sharpen this ~, please.* I yŏnp'il chom kkakka chushipshio. 이 연필 좀 깎아 주십시오/ *~ case* p'ilt'ong 필통/ *~ sharpener* yŏnp'ilkkakki 연필깎이. 「한반도.

peninsula *n.* pando 반도. *the Korean P~* hanbando

penknife *n.* chumŏnik'al 주머니칼.

penmanship *n.* sŭpcha 습자, p'ilpŏp 필법, (*style of handwriting*) p'ilchŏk 필적.

pennant *n.* samgakki 삼각기, p'enŏnt'ŭ 페넌트.

pension *n.* (*annuity*) yŏn-gŭm 연금, (*bounty*) changnyŏ-gŭm 장려금. *an old-age ~* yangno yŏn-gŭm 양로 연금/ *He lives on a ~.* Kŭ saramŭn yŏn-gŭmŭro saenghwar-hamnida. 그 사람은 연금으로 생활합니다.

peony *n.* chagyak 작약. *a tree ~* moran 모란/ *a ~ blossom* morankkot 모란꽃.

people *n.* (*individual*) saram 사람, (*nation*) kungmin 국민, (*race*) minjok 민족, (*family*) kajok 가족. *the Korean* ~ Han-guk saram 한국 사람/ *white* ~ paegin 백인/ *young* ~ chŏlmŭn saram 젊은 사람/ *How many* ~, *sir?* Myŏt punishijyo? 몇 분이시죠/ *My* ~ *live in the country.* Uri kajogŭn shigoresŏ salgo issŭmnida. 우리 가족은 시골에서 살고 있읍니다.

pepper *n.* huch'u 후추, (*red* ~) koch'u 고추. *ground* ~ huch'utkaru 후춧가루/ *sprinkle* ~ huch'urŭl ch'ida 후추를 치다/ ~*box* huch'ut'ong 후추통.

peppermint *n.* pak'a 박하.

per *prep.* (*for each*) ...mada ...마다, ...tang ...당, (*for*) ...ap'e ... 앞에, ...e taehayŏ ...에 대하여, (*by means of*) ...ŭro ...으로. *The admission fee is 1,000 won* ~ *person.* Ipchangnyonŭn irindang ch'ŏnwŏnimnida. 입장료는 1인당 1,000원입니다/ ~ *post* up'yŏnŭro 우편으로/ *What is the price of a room* ~ *day?* Haru pangsenŭn ŏlmaimnikka? 하루 방세는 얼마입니까/ *Eighty won* ~ *hundred grams.* Paek kŭraemdang p'alshibwŏnimnida. 100그램당 80원입니다.

perceive *vt.* (*through senses*) kamjihada 감지하다, (*grasp*) p'och'ak'ada 포착하다, (*understand*) ihaehada 이해하다.

percentage *n.* (*proportion*) paekpunnyul 백분율, (*commission*) kujŏn 구전, (*rake-off*) paedang 배당. *a* ~ *of* 2 paekpunŭi i 100분의 2/ *mortality* ~ samangnyul 사망률/ *unemployment* ~ shirŏmnyul 실업률/ *He received a large* ~.. Kŭ saramŭn manŭn kujŏnŭl padassŭmnida. 그 사람은 많은 구전을 받았읍니다.

perch *n.* (*roost*) hwaettae 홰대, (*high position*) nop'ŭn chiwi 높은 지위. —*vi.* (*alight*) naeryŏanta 내려앉다.

perfect *adj.* wanjŏnhan 완전한. —*vt.* (*complete*) wansŏnghada 완성하다. *He is a quite* ~ *gentleman.* Kŭ saramŭn chŏngmal hullyunghan shinsaimnida. 그 사람은 정말 훌륭한 신사입니다.

perfectly *adv.* wanjŏnhi 완전히, kkok 꼭. *Your trousers fit* ~. Tangshin pajinŭn kkok massŭmnida. 당신 바지는 꼭 맞습니다/ *You are* ~ *right.* Chŏnchŏgŭro tangshin mari olssŭmnida. 전적으로 당신 말이 옳습니다.

perfection *n.* (*completion*) wansŏng 완성, (*faultlessness*) wanjŏn 완전, (*excellence*) usu 우수. *You will find ~ of service at the hotel.* Chŏ hot'erŭi sŏbisŭnŭn wanjŏnhamnida. 저 호텔의 서비스는 완전합니다.

perform *vt.* (*do*) haenghada 행하다, (*accomplish*) sŏngch'wihada 성취하다, (*carry out*) ihaenghada 이행하다, (*act, play*) kongyŏnhada 공연하다. *~ a task* irŭl hada 일을 하다/ *~ your promise* yaksogŭl ihaenghada 약속을 이행하다/ *Are they ~ing now?* Yojŭm yŏnjuhago issŭmnikka? 요즘 연주하고 있읍니까?

performance *n.* (*execution*) shirhaeng 실행, (*work*) chagŏp 작업, (*operation*) unjŏn 운전, (*play, sing*) kongyŏn 공연. *I want to hear a ~ of the Seoul Symphony.* Sŏul shimp'oniŭi kongyŏnŭl tŭtko shipsŭmnida. 서울 심포니의 공연을 듣고 싶습니다/ *At what time will the ~ begin?* Kongyŏnŭn myŏt shie shijaktoemnikka? 공연은 몇 시에 시작됩니까?

perfume *n.* hyangsu 향수. *spray ~* hyangsurŭl ppurida 향수를 뿌리다.

perhaps *adv.* (*probably*) ama 아마, (*maybe*) ŏtchŏmyŏn 어쩌면. *P~ he is English.* Ama kŭ saramŭn Yŏngguginin-ga pomnida. 아마 그 사람은 영국인인가 봅니다/ *It will ~ rain tomorrow.* Naeirŭn ama piga olchido morŭmnida. 내일은 아마 비가 올지도 모릅니다.

peril *n.* (*danger*) wihŏm 위험. *Keep off at your ~.* Wihŏmhani kakkai kaji mashio. 위험하니 가까이 가지 마시오/ *Touch that at your ~.* Kŏgi sondaemyŏn wihŏmhamnida. 거기 손대면 위험합니다.

period *n.* (*era*) shigi 시기, (*term*) kigan 기간, (*present time*) hyŏndae 현대, (*sign*) chongjibu 종지부, (*pl.*) (*menses*) wŏlgyŏng 월경. *I lived in Seoul for a ~.* Chamshi Sŏure san chŏgi issŭmnida. 잠시 서울에 산 적이 있읍니다/ *a girl of the ~* hyŏndae yŏsong 현대 여성/ *Has she already had her first ~?* Pŏlssŏ ch'ogyŏngŭl shijak'aessŭmnikka? 벌써 초경(初經)을 시작했읍니까?

permanent *adj.* (*perpetual*) yŏnggujŏgin 영구적인, (*fixed*)

sangsŏrŭi 상설(常設)의. —*n.* (~ *wave*) p'ŏmŏ 퍼머.
~ *address* ponjŏk 본적/ *I'd like to have a* ~, *please.*
P'ŏmŏrŭl hae chuseyo. 퍼머를 해 주세요.

permission *n.* (*permitting*) hŏga 허가, (*consent*) sŭng-nak 승낙, (*licence*) myŏnhŏ 면허. *You need a special*
~ *for Panmunjom tourism.* P'anmunjŏmŭl yŏhaengha-jamyŏn t'ŭkpyŏrhan hŏgaga p'iryohamnida. 판문점을
여행하자면 특별한 허가가 필요합니다/ *Where do I get* ~?
Ŏdisŏ hŏgarŭl passŭmnikka? 어디서 허가를 받습니까?

permit *vt.* (*allow*) hŏgahada 허가하다, (*admit of*) in-jŏnghada 인정하다. —*n.* (*licence*) hŏgachŭng 허가증,
(*permission*) hŏga 허가. *P*~ *me to introduce myself.*
Che sogaerŭl hagessŭmnida. 제 소개를 하겠읍니다/ *Is it*
~*ted to take photographs?* Sajinŭl tchigŏdo chossŭm-nikka? 사진을 찍어도 좋습니까/ *You won't get into*
the Atomic Research Station without a ~. Hŏgachŭng
ŏpshi wŏnja yŏn-guso-e tŭrŏgal su ŏpsŭmnida. 허가증 없
이 원자.연구소에 들어갈 수 없읍니다.

perpendicular *adj.* sujigŭi 수직의.

perpetual *adj.* (*eternal*) yŏnggujŏgin 영구적인, (*con-stant*) kkŭnimŏmnŭn 끊임없는, (*permanent*) chong-shinŭi 종신(終身)의. ~ *punishment* chongshinhyŏng 종신
형/ *a* ~ *annuity* chongshin yŏn-gŭm 종신 연금.

perpetuate *vt.* (*make perpetual*) yŏngsokshik'ida 영속시키
다. ~ *one's name* kiri irŭmŭl namgida 길이 이름을 남
기다.

perplex *vt.* (*embarrass*) nanch'ŏhage mandŭlda 난처하게
만들다, (*tangle*) hollank'e hada 혼란케 하다. *I was* ~*ed*
for an answer. Muŏra taedap'aeya halchi mollassŭm-nida. 무어라 대답해야 할지 몰랐읍니다/ *be* ~*ed about*
[*at*] ...e kominhada …에 고민하다.

persecution *n.* pak'ae 박해. *religious* ~ chonggyosangŭi
pak'ae 종교상의 박해.

persevere *vi.* (*endure*) kyŏndida 견디다, (*continue*
steadily) kkujunhi kyesok'ada 꾸준히 계속하다.

Persian *n.* P'erŭshia saram 페르시아 사람. —*adj.* P'erŭshi-aŭi 페르시아의.

persimmon *n.* kam 감, *dried* ~s kotkam 곶감.

person *n.* (*human being*) saram 사람, (*in compounds*) in 인(人), (*fellow*) nom 놈, nyŏsŏk 녀석. *You are just the ~ I'd like to see.* Tangshinŭl mach'im mannaryŏ hadŏn ch'amiŏsso 당신을 마침 만나려 하던 참이었소/ *ten ~s* yŏl saram 열 사람, shibin 10인/ *Who is this ~?* Inomŭn nugujiyo? 이놈은 누구지요/ *in ~ (personally)* momso 몸소, chikchŏp 직접/ *Can't I see him in ~?* Chikchŏp mannaboel su ŏpsŭmnikka? 직접 만나 뵐 수 없읍니까?

personal *adj.* (*individual*) kaeinŭi 개인의, (*one's own*) chagiŭi 자기의, (*private*) sayongŭi 사용(私用)의. *a ~ history* iryŏksŏ 이력서/ *a ~ letter* sashin 사신(私信)/ *~ opinion* kaeinŭi ŭigyŏn 개인의 의견/ *a ~ interview* chikchŏp myŏnhoe 직접 면회/ *Excuse me for asking a ~ question.* Sachŏgin kŏsŭl murŏ choesonghamnida. 사적인 것을 물어 죄송합니다/ *Is this your ~ history?* Igŏshi tangshinŭi iryŏksŏimnikka? 이것이 당신의 이력 서입니까?

personality *n.* (*personal character*) inkyŏk 인격, (*personal quality*) kaesŏng 개성, (*pl.*) inshin konggyŏk 인신 공격.

personnel *n.* (*staff*) chigwŏn 직원, inwŏn 인원. *P~ Section, please.* Insakwa-e put'ak'amnida. 인사과에 부탁 합니다/ *May I have your P~ Department, please?* Insakwaro taeŏ chushimyŏn kamsahagessŭmnida. 인사과 로 대어 주시면 감사하겠읍니다.

perspiration *n.* (*sweat*) ttam 땀, (*sweating*) parhan 발한.

perspire *vi,vt.* ttamŭl hŭllida 땀을 흘리다.

persuade *vt.* (*induce*) sŏltŭk'ada 설득하다, (*convince*) mitke hada 믿게 하다. *I'm half ~d to buy them.* Sago ship'ŭn saenggagi tŭnŭn-gunyo. 사고 싶은 생각이 드는군 요.

pest *n.* (*pestilence*) p'esŭt'ŭ 페스트, hŭksapyŏng 흑사병, (*nuisance*) kwich'anŭn saram 귀찮은 사람.

pet *n.* (*favorite*) kwiyŏmdungi 귀염둥이. —*adj.* kwiyŏ-wŏhanŭn 귀여워하는. —*vt.* (*fondle*) kwiyŏwŏhada 귀여

워하다. *a ~ child* kwiyŏmdungi 귀염둥이/ *a ~ name*
aech'ing 애칭/ *~ a dog* kaerŭl kwiyŏwŏhada 개를 귀여
워하다.

petition *n.* (*appeal*) t'anwŏn 탄원, (*formal request*)
chinjŏng 진정. *a written ~* chinjŏngsŏ 진정서/ *present
a ~* chinjŏngsŏrŭl naeda 진정서를 내다.

petrol *n.* (*gasoline*) kasollin 가솔린, hwiballyu 휘발유.
I've run out of ~. Hwiballyuga ttŏrŏjyŏssŭmnida. 휘발
유가 떨어졌읍니다.

petroleum *n.* sŏgyu 석유. *crude ~* chungyu 중유(重油)/
a ~ plant sŏgyu kongjang 석유 공장.

petticoat *n.* sokch'ima 속치마, sŭk'ŏt'ŭ 스커트.

petty *adj.* (*minor*) chagŭn 작은, (*trifling*) shishihan 시시
한. *~ cash* chandon 잔돈/ *~ shopkeepers* kumŏng kage
chuin 구멍 가게 주인/ *~ troubles* shishihan kŏkchŏngkŏri 시시한 걱정거리.

pew *n.* (*chair*) ŭija 의자, (*seat*) chwasŏk 좌석. *Take
a ~.* Anjŭshipshio. 앉으십시오/ *Can't you find a ~
somewhere?* Ŏdi anjŭl chari ŏpsŭmnikka? 어디 앉을
자리 없읍니까?

phantom *n.* (*ghost*) yuryŏng 유령, (*apparition*) hŏkkaebi
허깨비. *~ ship* yuryŏngsŏn 유령선.

pharmacist *n.* yakchesa 약제사.

pharmacy *n.* (*dispensary*) yakkuk 약국. *Go to the ~
section.* Maeyakpuro kashipshio. 매약부로 가십시오.

pheasant *n.* kkwŏng 꿩.

phenomenon *n.* hyŏnsang 현상.

philanthropist *n.* pagaejuŭija 박애주의자, (*charitable
person*) chasŏn-ga 자선가.

philatelist *n.* up'yo sujipka 우표 수집가.

philology *n.* ŏnŏhak 언어학.

philosopher *n.* chŏrhakcha[ka] 철학자[가].

philosophy *n.* chŏrhak 철학. *the ~ of life* insaeng ch'ŏrhak 인생 철학/ *a ~ of living* chŏse ch'ŏrhak 처세 철
학.

phoenix *n.* pulsajo 불사조, (*Chinese ~*) ponghwangsae
봉황새.

phone *n.* (*telephone*) chŏnhwa 전화. —*vi.,vt.* chŏnhwahada 전화하다. *Mr. Kim, you have a ~ call.* Kim sŏnsaeng-nim, chŏnhwa wassŭmnida. 김 선생님, 전화 왔읍니다/ *She is on the ~ now.* Puinŭn chigŭm chŏnhwarŭl patko issŭm-nida. 부인은 지금 전화를 받고 있읍니다/ *I am calling from a public ~.* Kongjung chŏnhwarŭl kŏlgo issŭm-nida. 공중 전화를 걸고 있읍니다.

photograph *n.* sajin 사진. —*vt.,vi.* sajinŭl tchikta 사진을 찍다, sajine tchik'ida 사진에 찍히다. *Will you take my ~ with my camera, please?* Nae k'ameraro sajin chom tchigŏ chushigessŭmnikka? 내 카메라로 사진 좀 찍어 주시겠읍니까/ *a ~ in natural colors* k'ŏllŏ sajin 컬러 사진.

photographer *n.* sajinsa 사진사.

phrase *n.* ku 구(句), sugŏ 숙어. *a catch- ~* p'yoŏ 표어, k'aech'ip'ŭreijŭ 캐치프레이즈/ *a sporting ~* sŭp'och'ŭ yongŏ 스포츠 용어.

physic *n.* (*drug*) yak 약, (*cathartic*) haje 하제(下劑).

physician *n.* ŭisa 의사, naekwaŭi 내과의(內科醫). *a quack ~* tolp'ari ŭisa 돌팔이 의사/ *a visiting ~* wangjinŭi 왕진의(往診醫)/ *the ~ in charge* chuch'iŭi 주치의/ *Call a ~, please.* Ŭisarŭl chom pullŏ chushipshio. 의사를 좀 불러 주십시오.

physics *n.* (*science*) mullihak 물리학.

piano *n.* p'iano 피아노. *play (on) the ~* p'ianorŭl ch'ida 피아노를 치다/ *take ~ lessons* p'ianorŭl paeuda 피아노를 배우다.

pick *vt.,vi.* (*pierce*) tchirŭda 찌르다, (*peck*) tchoda 쪼다, (*select*) korŭda 고르다, (*gather*) chupta 줍다. *P~ out the best.* Kajang choŭn kŏsŭl korŭshipshio. 가장 좋은 것을 고르십시오/ *What time should I ~ you up?* Myŏt shie t'aeurŏ kalkkayo? 몇 시에 태우러 갈까요/ *Come and ~ me up.* Wasŏ teryŏga chushipshio. 와서 데려가 주십시오/ *We'll send a car to ~ you up at five.* Tasŏssie ch'arŭl ponaegessŭmnida. 다섯시에 차를 보내겠읍니다.

pickles *n.* kimch'i 김치. *cabbage ~* paech'u kimch'i 배추 김치/ *cucumber ~* oi kimch'i 오이 김치/ *radish ~* muu-

gimch'i 무우김치 / *These are ~ which I made myself.*
Naega mandŭn kimch'iyeyo. 내가 만든 김치예요.

pickpocket *n.* somaech'igi 소매치기. *Beware of ~s.*
Somaech'igi choshim! 소매치기 조심!

picnic *n.* sop'ung 소풍, p'ik'ŭnik 피크닉. *We are going
to a ~ tomorrow.* Urinŭn naeil sop'unggamnida. 우리는
내일 소풍갑니다 / *a ~ party* yayuhoe 야유회.

picture *n.* (*painting*) kŭrim 그림, (*photo*) sajin 사진,
(*pl.*) (*motion picture*) yŏnghwa 영화. *I'd like to take
your ~. Is it all right?* Tangshinŭi sajin tchigŏdo
kwaench'anssŭmnikka? 당신의 사진 찍어도 괜찮습니까?
You look good in this ~. Tangshin i sajine chal tchik-
k'yŏssŏyo. 당신 이 사진에 잘 찍혔어요 / *Can you frame
this ~ for me?* I kŭrim aekcha-e nŏŏ chushigessŭmnikka? 이 그림 액자에 넣어 주시겠습니까 / *We don't go often
to the ~s.* Urinŭn yŏnghwa porŏ chaju kaji anssŭmnida.
우리는 영화 보러 자주 가지 않습니다 / *a ~ book* kŭrim-
ch'aek 그림책 / *a ~ gallery* hwarang 화랑 / *a ~ house*
yŏnghwagwan 영화관 / *a nude ~* nach'ehwa 나체화.

picturesque *adj.* kŭrimgat'ŭn 그림같은. *a ~ village* kŭrimgat'ŭn maŭl 그림같은 마을.

pie *n.* p'ai 파이. *fruit ~s* kwail p'ai 과일 파이 / *a meat ~*
kogi p'ai 고기 파이.

piece *n.* (*bit*) han chogak 한 조각, (*portion*) ilbu 일부,
(*coin*) chuhwa 주화. *a ~ of bread* ppang han chogak
빵 한 조각 / *in ~s* chogakchogak 조각조각 / *May I have
two ~s of this cake?* I k'eikŭ tu chogak mŏgŏdo chossŭmnikka? 이 케이크 두 조각 먹어도 좋습니까? / *Will you
have another ~ of cake?* K'eik'ŭ han chogak tŏ tŭshigessŭmnikka? 케이크 한 조각 더 드시겠습니까? / *Does this
machine take to ~s?* I kigyenŭn punhaehal su issŭmnikka? 이 기계는 분해할 수 있습니까? / *a gold ~* kŭmhwa
금화 / *a nickel ~ of 100 won* paegwŏn tchari paektong-
hwa 100원 짜리 백동화.

pier *n.* (*wharf*) pudu 부두, sŏnch'ang 선창, (*breakwater*)
pangp'aje 방파제, (*of a bridge*) kyogak 교각. *From
what ~ does the ship for Hongkong sail?* Hongk'ong

kanŭn paenŭn ŏnŭ puduesŏ ch'urhanghamnikka ? 홍콩
가는 배는 어느 부두에서 출항합니까?

pierce *vt., vi.* (*stab*) kkwettult'a 꿰뚫다, (*make a hole*)
kumŏngŭl ttult'a 구멍을 뚫다, (*bore into*) torip'ada 돌
입하다.

pierrot *n.* p'iero 피에로, ŏritkwangdae 어릿광대.

piety *n.* (*godliness*) kyŏnggŏn 경건, (*devotedness*) kong-
gyŏng 공경. *filial* ∼ hyodo 효도.

pig *n.* (*hog*) twaeji 돼지. *a young* ∼ twaeji saekki 돼지
새끼/ ∼ *iron* sŏnch'ŏl 선철.

pigeon *n.* (*dove*) pidulgi 비둘기. *a carrier* ∼ chŏnsŏgu
전서구.

pile *n.* (*heap*) mudŏgi 무더기, (*large amount*) tasu 다수,
taeryang 대량. —*vt., vi.* (*load*) ssaa ollida 쌓아 올리다.
People died in ∼s. Saramdŭri mudŏgiro chugŏssŭmnida.
사람들이 무더기로 죽었읍니다/ *a* ∼ *of books* subuk'age
ssain ch'aek 수북하게 쌓인 책/ *a* ∼ *money* kŏaegŭi ton
거액의 돈/ *an atomic* ∼ wŏnjaro 원자로/ ∼ *up wealth*
chaemurŭl ssaa ollida 재물을 쌓아 올리다.

piles *n.* ch'ijil 치질(痔疾). *a victim of* ∼ ch'ijil hwanja
치질 환자.

pilfer *vt.* chomdodukchirhada 좀도둑질하다.

pilferer *n.* chomdoduk 좀도둑.

pilgrim *n.* (*palmer*) sullyeja 순례자, (*wanderer*) pangnangja 방랑자, (*traveller*) nagŭne 나그네.

pill *n.* hwanyak 환약, allyak 알약. *I'm on vitamin* ∼s.
Pit'aminjerŭl changbok'ago issŭmnida. 비타민제(劑)를
장복하고 있읍니다/ ∼ *box* hwanyak sangja 환약 상자.

pillage *n.* (*plunder*) yakt'al 약탈, (*sack*) yakt'alp'um
약탈품. —*vt., vi.* (*despoil*) yakt'arhada 약탈하다.

pillar *n.* (*column*) kidung 기둥, (*important support*)
chusŏk 주석(柱石). *Right there behind that* ∼. Paro
kŭ kidung twie issŭmnida. 바로 그 기둥 뒤에 있읍니다/
a ∼ *of the Liberal Party* chayudangŭi chungjin 자유당
의 중진.

pillow *n.* pegae 베개.

pilot *n.* (*of ships*) suro annaein 수로 안내인, (*of*

aircrafts) chojongsa 조종사. *a sky* ～ pihaenggi chojongsa 비행기 조종사.

pimp *n.* (*pander*) ttujangi 뚜장이, (*procurer*) p'oju 포주.

pimple *n.* yŏdŭrŭm 여드름. *P～s began to break out on my chin.* Nae t'ŏge yŏdŭrŭmi nagi shijak'aessŭmnida. 내 턱에 여드름이 나기 시작했습니다.

pin *n.* p'in 핀. —*vt.* p'inŭro kkotta 핀으로 꽂다. *a hair* ～ mŏrip'in 머리핀/ *a safety* ～ anjŏnp'in 안전핀.

pinch *vt.,vi.* kkojipta 꼬집다, (*nip*) saie kkiuda 사이에 끼우다, (*constrict*) choeda 죄다, (*steal*) humch'yŏ naeda 훔쳐 내다. *He ～ed the boy's cheek.* Kŭnŭn sonyŏnŭi ppyamŭl kkojibŏssŭmnida. 그는 소년의 뺨을 꼬집었읍니다/ *I ～ed my finger in the doorway.* Munt'ŭme sonkaragi kkiyŏssŭmnida. 문틈에 손가락이 끼였읍니다/ *Who's ～ed my dictionary?* (*to inferior*) Nuga nae sajŏnŭl humch'yŏnna? 누가 내 사전을 훔쳤나?

pine *n.* sol 솔. ～*tree* sonamu 소나무/ ～*needles* sollip 솔잎.

pineapple *n.* p'ainaep'ŭl 파인애플.

ping-pong *n.* t'akku 탁구, p'ingp'ong 핑퐁.

pink *n.* punhongpit 분홍빛. *a ～ skirt* punhong ch'ima 분홍 치마/ *I think I'll buy some of these ～ roses for my wife.* Anaeege punhongpit changmirŭl sada chunŭn ke chok'essŭmnida. 아내에게 분홍빛 장미를 사다 주는 게 좋겠읍니다.

pint *n.* (*measure*) p'aint'ŭ 파인트. *Give me a ～ of bitter, please.* Pit'ŏrŭl han p'aint'ŭ chushio. 비터를 한 파인트 주시오.

pious *adj.* (*devout*) kyŏnggŏnhan 경건한, tokshirhan 독실한, (*worthy*) kyarŭk'an 갸륵한. *a ～ believer in Buddhism* tokshirhan pulgyo shinja 독실한 불교 신자.

pipe *n.* (*for fluid*) kwan 관, p'aip'ŭ 파이프, (*for smoking*) tambaettae 담뱃대(*Korean style*). *a drain ～* paesugwan 배수관/ *a hydraulic[water] ～* sudogwan 수도관/ *a tobacco ～* tambaettae 담뱃대/ ～*line* songyugwan 송유관.

pirate *n.* (*sea robber*) haejŏk 해적, (*plagiarist*) p'yojŏlcha

표절자. *a ~ ship* haejŏksŏn 해적선/ *a ~ edition* haejŏk-p'an 해적판.

piss *vi.* (*make water*) sobyŏnŭl poda 소변을 보다. **—***n.* (*urine*) ojum 오줌, sobyŏn 소변.

pistol *n.* kwŏnch'ong 권총, p'isŭt'ol 피스톨. *a toy ~* changnankam kwŏnch'ong 장난감 권총/ *a burglar with a ~* kwŏnch'ong kangdo 권총 강도.

pit *n.* (*cavity*) kudŏngi 구덩이, (*pitfall*) hamjŏng 함정, (*coal mine*) t'an-gaeng 탄갱.

pitch *vt., vi.* (*throw*) tŏnjida 던지다, (*roll,rock*) aptwiro hŭndŭllida 앞뒤로 흔들리다. *Our boat ~ed heavily.* Uri paenŭn shimhage araewiro hŭndŭllyŏssŭmnida. 우리 배는 심하게 아래위로 흔들렸읍니다.

pitcher *n.* (*baseball*) t'usu 투수, (*jug*) mulchujŏnja 물주전자.

pitchfork *n.* (*rake*) kalk'wi 갈퀴.

⟨kalk'wi⟩

pith *n.* (*spinal cord*) ch'ŏksu 척수.

pitiful *adj.* (*compassionate*) injŏng manŭn 인정 많은, (*touching*) kayŏpsŭn 가엾은. *It was too ~ to watch.* Kayŏpsŏ ch'ama pol suga ŏpsŏssŭmnida. 가엾어 차마 볼 수가 없었읍니다.

pity *n.* (*compassion*) pulssanghi yŏgim 불쌍히 여김, (*sympathy*) tongjŏng 동정, (*regret*) aesŏk'am 애석함. **—***vt., vi.* pulssanghi yŏgida 불쌍히 여기다. *That's a ~.* Kŭgŏt ch'am ttak'agunyo. 그것 참 딱하군요/ *Have ~ on that poor old man.* Kŭ pulssanghan noinŭl kayŏpshi yŏgishio. 그 불쌍한 노인을 가엾이 여기시오/ *What a ~!* A, kayŏpsŏra! 아, 가엾어라/ *My heart swelled with ~.* Pulssanghaesŏ kasŭmi miŏjinŭn tŭt'aessŭmnida. 불쌍해서 가슴이 미어지는 듯했읍니다/ *I ~ you if you think so.* Tangshini kŭrŏk'e saenggak'ashindamyŏn chŏngmal ttak'amnida. 당신이 그렇게 생각하신다면 정말 딱합니다.

place *n.* (*spot*) changso 장소, kot 곳. **—***vt.* (*put*) tuda 두다. *Can you tell me the best ~ to stay in Seoul?* Sŏuresŏ t'usuk'agi kajang choŭn kosŭl karŭchy'ŏ chushio. 서울에서 투숙하기 가장 좋은 곳을 가르쳐 주시오/ *Is this the right ~ to take a down train?* Namhaeng yŏlch'anŭn yŏgisŏ t'ajiyo? 남행(南行) 열차는 여기서 타지요/ *Go back to your ~, please.* Tangshin chariro toragaship-shio. 당신 자리로 돌아가십시오/ *Where shall I ~ the flower vase?* Kkotpyŏngŭl ŏdida tulkkayo? 꽃병을 어디다 둘까요/ *I'll teach in ~ of your teacher.* Tangshin sŏnsaengnim taeshine naega karŭch'igesso. 당신 선생님 대신에 내가 가르치겠소/ *Your question is out of ~.* T'ŏmuniŏmnŭn chilmunigunyo. 터무니없는 질문이군요.

plague *n.* (*epidemic*) chŏnyŏmpyŏng 전염병. *the black ~* hŭksapyŏng 흑사병.

plain *n.* (*moor*) pŏlp'an 벌판, (*level ground*) p'yŏngji 평지, (*~ cloth*) muji 무지(無地). —*adj.* (*simple*) sobak'an 소박한, (*evident*) myŏngbaek'an 명백한, (*homely*) kŏmsohan 검소한, (*not handsome*) motsaenggin 못생긴. *What kind of tie are you looking for? P~ or stripe?* Ŏttŏn t'airŭl ch'ajŭshimnikka, muji, ttonŭn chulmunŭi? 어떤 타이를 찾으십니까, 무지(無地) 또는 줄무늬/ *I am a tall woman, ~ and skinny.* Nanŭn k'iman kŭgo, ppyŏman angsanghan monnan yŏjayeyo. 나는 키만 크고 뼈만 앙상한 못난 여자예요.

plan *n.* (*scheme*) kyehoek 계획, (*diagram*) tomyŏn 도면. —*vt.* (*arrange beforehand*) kyehoek'ada 계획하다, (*make a design*) sŏlgyehada 설계하다. *a city ~* toshi kyehoek 도시 계획/ *I have a ~ to go on a tour to Kyongju next summer.* Onŭn yŏrŭmenŭn Kyŏngju kwan-gwangŭl hal yejŏngimnida. 오는 여름에는 경주 관광을 할 예정입니다/ *I'm ~ning another enterprise.* Saeroun saŏbŭl kyehoek'ago issŭmnida. 새로운 사업을 계획하고 있읍니다.

plane *n.* (*level surface*) p'yŏngmyŏn 평면, (*Am.*) (*airplane*) pihaenggi 비행기. —*adj.* (*flat*) p'yŏngp'yŏnghan 평평한.

planet *n.* haengsŏng 행성(行星), yusŏng 유성.

plank *n.* nŏlppanji 널빤지.

plant *n.* (*vegetable*) shingmul 식물, (*factory*) kongjang 공장. —*vt.* (*sow*) shimta 심다. *a tropical ~* yŏltae shingmul 열대 식물/ *a pot ~* punjae 분재/ *a printing ~* inswae kongjang 인쇄 공장/ *a soap-making* ~ pinu kongjang 비누 공장/ *Let's* ~ *trees in the streets.* Kŏrie namurŭl shimcha. 거리에 나무를 심자.

plantation *n.* (*large farm*) nongwŏn 농원.

plaster *n.* (*gyps*) sŏkko 석고, (*patch*) koyak 고약. *a* ~ *figure* sŏkkosang 석고상/ *put on a* ~ koyagŭl parŭda 고약을 바르다.

plastic *n.* (*pl.*) p'ŭllast'ik 플라스틱, hapsŏng suji 합성 수지. —*adj. a* ~*operation* sŏnghyŏng susul 성형 수술.

plate *n.* (*dish*) chŏpshi 접시, (*sheet metal*) p'an-gŭm 판금 (板金). —*vt.* (*gild*) togŭmhada 도금하다. *a bread* ~ ppang chŏpshi 빵 접시/ *an iron* ~ ch'ŏlp'an 철판/ (*photo.*) *a negative* ~ wŏnp'an 원판/ *a door* [*name*] ~ munp'ae 문패/ ~*d spoon* togŭmhan sutkarak 도금한 숟가락/ *They are 300 won per* ~. Han chŏpshie sambaegwŏnimnida. 한 접시에 300원입니다/ *I'll take two* ~*s full.* Tu chŏpshi kadŭk sagessŭmnida. 두 접시 가득 사겠읍니다.

platform *n.* (*dais*) tan 단, (*in railway station*) p'ŭllaetp'om 플랫폼. *a lecture* ~ kangdan 강단(講壇)/ *Which* ~ *does the Seoul-Pusan line leave from?* Kyŏngbusŏn yŏlch'anŭn ŏnŭ p'ŭllaetp'omesŏ ch'ulbarhamnikka? 경부(京釜)선 열차는 어느 플랫폼에서 출발합니까/ *P* ~ *number four.* Sabŏn p'ŭllaetp'omimnida. 4번 플랫폼입니다.

platinum *n.* paekkŭm 백금. ~*ring* paekkŭm panji 백금 반지.

play *vt.,vi* (*sport*) nolda 놀다, (*perform music*) yŏnjuhada 연주하다, (*act*) yŏgŭl hada 역(役)을 하다. —*n.* (*fun*) nori 놀이, (*game*) kyŏnggi 경기, (*drama*) yŏn-gŭk 연극, (*gambling*) naegi 내기. *Let's go out and* ~. (*to inferior*) Nagasŏ nolcha. 나가서 놀자/ *Will you* ~ *chess with me?* Nawa changgi han p'an tushigessŭmnikka? 나와 장기 한 판 두시겠읍니까/ *You* ~ *the piano, don't you?* P'iano ch'il chul ashijiyo? 피아노 칠 줄 아시지요/ *I would like to see a Korean* ~. Han-guk yŏn-gŭgŭl pogo shipsŭmnida. 한국 연극을 보고 싶습니다.

player *n.* (*of games*) sŏnsu 선수, (*actor*) paeu 배우, (*performer*) yŏnjuja 연주자.

playground *n.* undongjang 운동장, norit'o 놀이터.
playmate *n.* (*playfellow*) nori ch'in-gu 놀이 친구.
playwright *n.* kŭkchakka 극작가.
plea *n.* (*excuse*) kushil 구실, (*entreaty*) kanch'ŏng 간청, (*in law*) sosong 소송. *on the ~ of illness* ap'ŭdanŭn kushillo 아프다는 구실로/ *He resigned under the ~ of ill health.* Kŏn-gangŭl iyuro kŭ saramŭn sajik'aessŭmnida. 건강을 이유로 그 사람은 사직했읍니다/ *make a ~ for mercy* chabirŭl kanch'ŏnghada 자비를 간청하다.
plead *vt.,vi.* (*appeal*) t'anwŏnhada 탄원하다, (*defend*) pyŏnhohada 변호하다, hangbyŏnhada 항변하다. *How do you ~ ?* Ŏttŏk'e tappyŏnhajiyo? 어떻게 답변하지요/ *I ~ed for him in vain.* Kŭrŭl wihae pyŏnhohaessŭna soyongi ŏpsŏssŭmnida. 그를 위해 변호했으나 소용이 없었읍니다.
pleasant *adj.* (*comfortable*) kibun joŭn 기분 좋은, (*cheerful*) k'waehwarhan 쾌활한, (*fair*) nalssi choŭn 날씨 좋은.
please *vt.,vi.* (*delight*) kippŭge hada 기쁘게 하다, (*be agreeable*) maŭme tŭlda 마음에 들다. *What ~ you best ?* Muŏshi kajang maŭme tŭshimnikka 무엇이 가장 마음에 드십니까/ *I'm very ~d to hear it.* Kŭ marŭl tŭrŭni pan-gapkunyo. 그 말을 들으니 반갑군요/ (*The English "please" is translated into Korean as* "chebal", "chom" *or* "chushipshio" *etc.*) *P~ fill out the guarantee card.* Pojŭng k'adŭe kiip'ae chushipshio. 보증 카드에 기입해 주십시오/ *One moment, ~.* Chamshi kidaryŏ chushipshio. 잠시 기다려 주십시오/ *Hold the line, ~.* Kŭdaero chamshi kidaryŏ chushipshio. 그대로 잠시 기다려 주십시오/ *Close the door, ~.* Munŭl chom tada chushio. 문을 좀 닫아 주시오.
pleasure *n.* (*delight*) kippŭm 기쁨, (*sensual gratification*) k'waerak 쾌락, (*amusement*) wian 위안, (*desire*) yokku 욕구. *May I have the ~ of taking a glass of wine with you ?* Hanjan kach'i haji ank'essŭmnikka ? 한잔 같이 하지 않겠읍니까/ *With ~, I'll go with you.* Kikkŏi hamkke kagessŭmnida. 기꺼이 함께 가겠읍니다/~

boat yuramsŏn 유람선/ ~ *trip* yuram yŏhaeng 유람 여행.

pleat *n.* churŭm 주름. —*vt.* churŭmjapta 주름잡다. *a* ~*ed* *skirt* churŭm ch'ima 주름 치마.

plebiscite *n.* (*referendum*) kungmin t'up'yo 국민 투표, ilban t'up'yo 일반 투표.

pledge *n.* (*mortgage*) chŏdang 저당, (*pawn*) chŏdang-mul 저당물, (*solemn promise*) sŏyak 서약, (*security*) pojŭng 보증. —*vt.* (*pawn*) chŏdanghada 저당하다, (*plight*) sŏyak'ada 서약하다, (*toast*) ch'ukpaerŭl tŭlda 축배를 들다. *I gave her a ring as a* ~. Sŏyagŭi p'yojŏgŭro kŭnyŏege panjirŭl chuŏssŭmnida. 서약의 표적으로 그녀에게 반지를 주었습니다/ *Let us* ~ *our master's health.* Chuinnimŭi kŏn-gangŭl wihae ch'ukpaerŭl tŭpshida. 주인님의 건강을 위해 축배를 듭시다.

plenty *n.* (*abundance*) manŭm 많음, taryang 다량, (*enough*) ch'ungbun 충분. *Six will be* ~. Yŏsŏt kae-myŏn ch'ungbunhamnida. 여섯 개면 충분합니다.

plight *n.* (*condition*) hyŏngp'yŏn 형편, (*predicament*) kon-gyŏng 곤경. —*vt.* (*pledge*) maengsehada 맹세하다.

plot *n.* (*intrigue*) ŭmmo 음모, (*ground*) chagŭn t'ŏ 작은 터. —*vt.* (*conspire*) kongmohada 공모하다, (*plan*) kye-hoek'ada 계획하다. *What* ~ *are you brewing?* Musŭn ŭmmorŭl kkumigo issŭmnikka? 무슨 음모를 꾸미고 있읍니까/ *a political* ~ chŏngch'ijŏk ŭmmo 정치적 음모/ *We are* ~*ting how we shall spend our holidays.* Hyu-irŭl ŏttŏk'e chinaelkka kyehoek chungimnida. 휴일을 어떻게 지낼까 계획 중입니다/ *a building* ~ kŏnch'uk puji 건축 부지.

plow, plough *n.* chaenggi 쟁기. —*vi.,vt.*(*till*) chaenggiro kalda 쟁기로 갈다.

pluck *vi.,vt.* (*pull off*) chabattŭtta 잡아뜯다, (*pick*) tta-da 따다. *Has this goose been* ~*ed?* I kŏwinŭn t'ŏri ttŭtkyŏssŭmnikka? 이 거위는 털이 뜯겼읍니까/ *P~ up!* *you aren't hurt badly.* Himŭl naeshio. Sangch'ŏnŭn ka-byŏpsŭmnida. 힘을 내시오. 상처는 가볍습니다.

plug *n.* (*stopper*) magae 마개, (*elect.*) p'ŭllŏgŭ 플러그. —*vt.* (*stop up*) t'ŭrŏmakta 틀어막다. *a fire* ~ sohwajŏn

소화전/ ～ *in the TV set* t'el-
lebijŏne p'ŭllŏgŭrŭl kkotta 텔
레비전에 플러그를 꽂다.

plum *n*. oyat 오얏. ～ *blossom*
maehwa 매화.

plumb *n*. ch'u 추(錘).

plumber *n*. yŏn-gong 연공(鉛工).

plume *n*. (*feather*) kit 깃.

plump *adj*. (*fat*) ttungttunghan 뚱뚱한, ⟨maehwa⟩
(*fleshy*) t'oshilt'oshirhan 토실토실한. *a baby with a* ～
cheeks pori p'odongp'odonghan agi 볼이 포동포동한 아기.

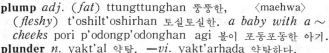

plunder *n*. yakt'al 약탈. —*vi*. yakt'arhada 약탈하다.

plunge *vi*.,*vt*. (*leap in*) ttwiŏdŭlda 뛰어들다, (*rush in*)
torip'ada 돌입하다. —*n*. (*plunging*) ttwiŏdŭlgi 뛰어들
기, (*rapid dash*) torip 돌입.

plural *adj*. poksuŭi 복수의. —*n*. (*compound number*)
poksu 복수. *What is the* ～ (*form*) *of sheep?* "Sheep"ŭi
poksunŭn muŏshimnikka? Sheep의 복수는 무엇입니까?

plus *prep*. ...ŭl tŏhayŏ... 을 더하여. *Two* ～ *five is seven*.
Tul tŏhagi tasŏsŭn ilgop. 둘(2) 더하기 다섯(5)은 일곱(7).
5 ～ *5 equals 10*. O tŏhagi onŭn ship. 5 더하기 5는 10.

pneumonia *n*. p'yeryŏm 폐렴. *acute* ～ kŭpsŏng p'yeryŏm
급성 폐렴.

pocket *n*. hojumŏni 호주머니, p'ok'et 포켓. *a trousers* ～
paji chumŏni 바지 주머니. *Put this into your* ～. Hoju-
mŏnie nŏŏ tushio. 호주머니에 넣어 두시오/ ～ *book* tonchi-
gap 돈지갑, (*notebook*) such'ŏp 수첩/ ～ *money* yongton
용돈.

pockmark *n*. mama chaguk 마마 자국.

poem *n*. shi 시(詩). *How do you like this* ～? I shinŭn
ŏttŏssŭmnikka? 이 시는 어떻습니까/ *a Chinese* ～ hanshi
한시. *an epic*[*lyric*] ～ sŏsa[sŏjŏng]shi 서사[서정]시.

poet *n*. shiin 시인.

poetess *n*. (*woman poet*) yŏryu shiin 여류 시인.

poetry *n*. (*poems*) shi 시, (*verse*) shiga 시가(詩歌),
(*poetical works*) shijakp'um 시작품.

point *n*. (*dot*) chŏm 점, (*tip*) kkŭt 끝, (*pith*) yochŏm 요

점. —*vt.,vi.* (*indicate*) chishihada 지시하다. *a decimal* ~
sosuchŏm 소수점/ *freezing* ~ pingchŏm 빙점/ *the* ~ *of
a needle* panŭlkkŭt 바늘끝/ *I don't see your* ~. Malssŭ-
mŭi yojirŭl morŭgessŭmnida. 말씀의 요지를 모르겠읍니다/
I can't understand that ~ *of view.* Nanŭn kŭ kyŏnhae-
rŭl ihaehal suga ŏpsŭmnida. 나는 그 견해를 이해할 수가
없읍니다/ *Can you* ~ *out the man you suspect ?* Ŭisim
kanŭn saramŭl chijŏk'ae chul su issŭmnikka? 의심 가는
사람을 지적해 줄 수 있읍니까/ *two* ~ *one* ichŏm il 2.1/ *a
weak* ~ yakchŏm 약점.

poison *n.* tok 독. —*vt.* (*kill by*~) toksarhada 독살하다,
(*harm by*~) togŭl nŏt'a 독을 넣다. *neutralize* ~
togŭl ŏpsaeda 독을 없애다/ *put* ~ *into* ...e togul sŏkta
...에 독을 섞다.

poisonous *adj.* togi innŭn 독이 있는. ~ *gas* yudok kasŭ
유독 가스/ ~ *plants* yudok shingmul 유독 식물.

poke *vt.* (*thrust*) tchirŭda 찌르다, (*prod*) ssushida 쑤시
다. ~ (*up*) *the dying fire* kkŏjinŭn purŭl ssusyŏ irŭ-
k'ida 꺼지는 불을 쑤셔 일으키다.

pole *n.* (*piece of wood*) maktaegi 막대기, (*astron.*) kŭk
극(極). *a flag* ~ kittae 깃대/ *a telephone* ~ chŏnju 전
주(電柱)/ *the North P*~ pukkŭk 북극/ *the South P*~
namgŭk 남극.

police *n.* kyŏngch'al 경찰, (~*man*) kyŏnggwan 경관. ~
box p'ach'ulso 파출소/ ~ *station* kyŏngch'alsŏ 경찰서/
Oh, there comes a ~*man.* A, chŏgi sun-gyŏngi onŭn-
gunyo. 아, 저기 순경이 오는군요/ *Where is the nearest
* ~ *station ?* Kajang kakkaun kyŏngch'alsŏnŭn ŏdi issŭmnikka ? 가장 가까운 경찰서는 어디 있읍니까/ *Call the* ~.
Kyŏnggwanŭl pullŏ chushio. 경관을 불러 주시오/ ~*man*
kyŏngch'algwan 경찰관.

policy *n.* (*political measures*) chŏngch'aek 정책, (*method*) pangch'im 방침, (*contr. of insurance*) pohŏm
chŭngkwŏn 보험 증권. *an anti-Communist* ~ pan-gong
chŏngch'aek 반공 정책/ *foreign policies* oegyo chŏngch'aek 외교 정책/ *a business* ~ yŏngŏp pangch'im 영업 방
침/ *alter one's* ~ pangch'imŭl pakkuda 방침을 바꾸다/ *a

fire-insurance ~ hwajae pohŏm chŭngkwŏn 화재 보험
증권/ ~ *maker* chŏngch'aek suripcha 정책 수립자/ ~
holder pohŏm kyeyakcha 보험 계약자.

polio *n.* soa mabi 소아 마비. *A few years ago,* ~ *was in-*
curable. Myŏt nyŏn chŏnman haedo, soa mabinŭn pulch'ipyŏngiŏssŭmnida. 몇 년 전만 해도 소아 마비는 불치병
이었읍니다.

polish *vt.* (*make smooth*) takta 닦다, (*make elegant*)
tadŭmta 다듬다. *P~ my shoes, please.* Kudu chom takka chushio. 구두 좀 닦아 주시오.

polite *adj.* (*courteous*) kongsonhan 공손한, (*refined*)
p'umwi innŭn 품위 있는.

politely *adv.* kongsonhi 공손히. *bow* ~ kongsonhi chŏr-
hada 공손히 절하다/ *speak* ~ kongsonhi marhada 공손
히 말하다.

political *adj.* chŏngch'ijŏgin 정치적인. ~ *circles* chŏnggye
정계/ *a* ~ *movement* chŏngch'i undong 정치 운동/ ~ *par-*
ty chŏngdang 정당.

politician *n.* chŏngch'iga 정치가, chŏnggaek 정객.

politics *n.* chŏngch'i 정치, (*science*) chŏngch'ihak 정치학.
Do you have any book on ~ ? Chŏngch'ie kwanhan
ch'aegi issŭmnikka? 정치에 관한 책이 있읍니까?

poll *vt.* (*vote*) t'up'yohada 투표하다. —*n.* (*voting*) t'u-
p'yo 투표, (*number of votes*) tŭkp'yosu 득표수, (*pl.*)
t'up'yoso 투표소. *go to the* ~ t'up'yoharŏ kada 투표하러
가다/ *How stands the* ~ ? T'up'yo kyŏlgwanŭn ŏttŏssŭmnikka? 투표 결과는 어떻습니까/ *Mr. Lee* ~ed *over*
30,000 votes. Issinŭn samman p'yo isangŭl ŏdŏssŭmnida. 이(李)씨는 3만 표 이상을 얻었읍니다.

pollution *n.* oyŏm 오염. *air* ~ taegi oyŏm 대기 오염/ *en-*
vironmental ~ hwan-gyŏng oyŏm 환경 오염.

polygamy *n.* ilbu dach'ŏ 일부 다처.

polyglot *n.* sugae kugŏ-e nŭngt'onghan saram 수개 국어에
능통한 사람. *You are quite a* ~. Tangshinŭn yŏrŏ nara
marŭl chal hashinŭn-gunyo. 당신은 여러 나라 말을 잘 하시
는군요.

pomade *n.* p'omadŭ 포마드.

pomegranate *n.* sŏngnyu 석류(石榴). *a* ~ *tree* sŏngnyunamu 석류나무.

pond *n.* mot 못, nŭp 늪. *a lotus* ~ yŏnmot 연못/ *a culture* ~ yangŏjang 양어장.

ponder *vt.,vi.* (*consider deeply*) sukkohada 숙고하다, (*meditate*) komgomi saenggak'ada 곰곰이 생각하다.

pool *n.* (*puddle*) murungdŏngi 물웅덩이, (*swimming* ~) p'ul 풀. *a bathing* ~ suyŏngjang 수영장.

poor *adj.* (*needy*) kananhan 가난한, (*pitiable*) pulssanghan 불쌍한, (*unfortunate*) purhaenghan 불행한, (*clumsy*) sŏt'urŭn 서투른. *a* ~ *family* kananhan kajŏng 가난한 가정/ *P*~ *fellow!* Pulssanghaera! 불쌍해라/ *a* ~ *picture* sŏt'urŭn kŭrim 서투른 그림/ *I am* ~ *in mathematics.* Nanŭn suhagŭl chal mot'amnida. 나는 수학을 잘 못합니다.

pop *vi.* ~ *the question* (*woo*) kuhonhada 구혼하다/ *Why don't you* ~ *the question?* Wae kuhonŭl haji anssŭmnikka? 왜 구혼을 하지 않습니까?

pope *n.* Roma kyohwang 로마 교황, pŏbwang 법왕(法王).

poplar *n.* p'op'ŭlla 포플라. *the white* ~ paegyang 백양.

poppy *n.* yanggwibi 양귀비.

popular *adj.* (*of the people*) taejungŭi 대중의, (*generally liked*) inki innŭn 인기 있는, (*famous*) p'yŏngi choŭn 평이 좋은. ~ *song* taejung kayo 대중 가요/ *a* ~ *magazine* taejung chapchi 대중 잡지/ *What is the most* ~ *sports in Korea?* Han-gugesŏ kajang inki innŭn sŭp'och'ŭnŭn muŏshimnikka? 한국에서 가장 인기 있는 스포츠는 무엇입니까?

popularity *n.* inki 인기(人氣). *win* ~ inkirŭl ŏtta 인기를 얻다/ ~ *poll* inki t'up'yo 인기 투표.

population *n.* in-gu 인구. *What's the* ~ *of Korea?* Han-gugŭi in-gunŭn ŏlmaimnikka? 한국의 인구는 얼마입니까/ *The* ~ *of Korea is now calculated at forty millions.* Han-gugŭi in-gunŭn chigŭm sach'ŏnmanŭro ch'usandoemnida. 한국의 인구는 지금 4천만으로 추산됩니다/ *the total* ~ ch'ongin-gu 총인구/ *urban* ~ toshi in-gu 도시 인구.

porcelain *n.* chagi 자기(瓷器), sagi kŭrŭt 사기 그릇. ~ *dishes* sagi chŏpshi 사기 접시.

porch *n.* hyŏn-gwan 현관. *the front ~* ammun hyŏn-gwan 앞문 현관.

pork *n.* twaejigogi 돼지고기.

porridge *n.* (*gruel*) chuk 죽. *a bowl of ~* chuk han kŭrŭt 죽 한 그릇.

port *n.* (*harbor*) hanggu 항구. *a ~ city* hanggu toshi 항구 도시/ *We shall be in ~ before long.* Mŏlji ana hanggue taŭl kŏshimnida. 멀지 않아 항구에 닿을 것입니다/ *enter ~* ip'anghada 입항하다/ *~ dues* ip'angse 입항세/ *leave ~* ch'urhanghada 출항하다.

porter *n.* (*gatekeeper*) munjigi 문지기, (*carrier*) chimkkun 짐꾼, (*redcap*) p'ot'ŏ 포터. *The hotel ~ will call a taxi for you.* Hot'el suwiga t'aekshirŭl pullŏ chul kŏshimnida. 호텔 수위가 택시를 불러 줄 것입니다/ *P~, come here.* Chimkkun, iri oshio. 짐꾼, 이리 오시오.

portion *n.* (*part*) ilbu 일부, pubun 부분, (*share*) mok 몫.

portrait *n.* (*likeness*) ch'osanghwa 초상화, (*image*) yusamul 유사물. *a self~* chahwasang 자화상/ *You are the very ~ of your mother.* Tangshinŭn ŏmŏni kŭdaeromnida. 당신은 어머니 그대롭니다.

Portugal *n.* P'orŭt'ugal 포르투갈.

pose *n.* (*attitude*) chase 자세, p'ojŭ 포즈. *—vt.* chaserŭl ch'wihada 자세를 취하다. *Will you ~ with me for a picture?* Sajinŭl tchikko ship'ŭnde hamkke sŏ chushijiyo. 사진을 찍고 싶은데 함께 서 주시지요.

position *n.* (*rank*) chiwi 지위, (*site*) wich'i 위치, (*attitude*) t'aedo 태도, (*point of view*) kyŏnhae 견해, (*job*) kŭnmuch'ŏ 근무처. *What ~ are you on the team?* Kŭ t'imesŏ muŏl hago kyeshijiyo? 그 팀에서 무얼 하고 계시지요/ *On the pitcher's ~s.* T'usuolshida. 투수올시다/ *What's your ~ on this problem?* I munjee taehae ŏttŏk'e saenggak'ashimnikka? 이 문제에 대해 어떻게 생각하십니까/ *I'm not in a ~ to answer that questions.* Kŭ murŭme taehae taedap'al ch'ŏjiga mot toemnida. 그 물음에 대해 대답할 처지가 못 됩니다.

positive *adj.* (*definite*) hwakshirhan 확실한, (*convinced*) chashin innŭn 자신 있는, (*active*) chŏkkŭkchŏgin 적극

적인. *I'm ~ that it is so*. Kŭrŏt'ago hwakshinhamnida. 그렇다고 확신합니다/ *Don't be too ~*. Nŏmu chashin itke marhaji mashio. 너무 자신 있게 말하지 마시오.

possess *vt*. (*own*) kajida 가지다, (*dominate*) chibaehada 지배하다, (*control by an evil spirit*) angma-ege hollida 악마에게 홀리다. *~ a house and a car* chipkwa ch'arŭl kajigo itta. 집과 차를 가지고 있다.

possession *n*. (*holding*) soyu 소유, (*occupation*) chŏmyu 점유, (*pl.*) (*property*) chaesan 재산. *in ~ of ...ŭl soyuhago itta* ···을 소유하고 있다/ *I was not in ~ of the key*. Nanŭn yŏlsoerŭl kajigo itchi anassŭmnida. 나는 열쇠를 가지고 있지 않았읍니다.

possible *adj*. (*that can be*) kanŭnghan 가능한, hal su innŭn 할 수 있는. *Come as quickly as ~*. Toel su innŭndaero ppalli oshio. 될 수 있는 대로 빨리 오시오/ *Call on me, if (it is) ~*. Toel su issŭmyŏn ch'ajawa chushio. 될 수 있으면 찾아와 주시오.

possibly *adv*. (*perhaps*) ama 아마, ŏtchŏmyŏn 어쩌면, (*by any possibility*) ŏttŏk'edŭnji haesŏ 어떻게든지 해서. *Will they increase your salary? P~*. Tangshin ponggŭbŭl ollyŏ chulkkayo? Ama, ollyŏ chugetchiyo. 당신 봉급을 올려 줄까요? 아마, 올려 주겠지요/ *Can you ~ lend me 10,000 won?* Ŏttŏk'e haesŏrado manwŏnman tollyŏ chushil su ŏpsŭlkkayo? 어떻게 해서라도 10,000 원만 돌려 주실 수 없을까요?

post *n*. (*mail*) up'yŏn(mul)우편(물), (*station*) pusŏ 부서 (部署), (*pillar*) kidung 기둥. —*vt*. (*mail*) usonghada 우송하다. *Take these letters to (the) ~*. I p'yŏnjirŭl uch'et'onge nŏushio. 이 편지를 우체통에 넣으시오/ *Where is the nearest ~ office?* Kajang kakkaun uch'egugŭn ŏdijiyo? 가장 가까운 우체국은 어디지요?

postage *n*. up'yŏn yogŭm 우편 요금, (*~ stamp*) up'yo 우표. *How much is ~ for this registered letter?* I tŭnggi p'yŏnjiŭi yogŭmŭn ŏlmaimnikka? 이 등기 편지의 요금은 얼마입니까/ *Is this ~ correct?* I up'yonŭn paro put'ŏssŭmnikka? 이 우표는 바로 붙었읍니까/ *a ~ stamp* up'yo 우표.

postcard *n.* up'yŏn yŏpsŏ 우편 엽서. *a picture* ~ kŭrim yŏpsŏ 그림 엽서/ *a return* ~ wangbok yŏpsŏ 왕복 엽서.

posterity *n.* (*descendants*) chason 자손.

postman *n.* uch'ebu 우체부, up'yŏn paedalbu 우편 배달부.

postmaster *n.* uch'egukchang 우체국장.

postpone *vt.* (*put off*) yŏn-gihada 연기하다. *How long is the party* ~*d?* P'at'inŭn ŏnjekkaji yŏn-gidoeŏssŭmnikka? 파티는 언제까지 연기되었읍니까.

postponement *n.* yŏn-gi 연기, twiro mirugi 뒤로 미루기.

pot *n.* (*jar*) tanji 단지, (*pan*) nambi 남비, (*bowl*) sabal 사발. *a jam* ~ chaem tanji 잼 단지/ *a coffee* ~ k'op'i chujŏnja 코피 주전자/ *a flower* ~ hwabun 화분/ *We also handle various* ~*ted plants.* Yŏrŏ kaji punjaedo ch'wigŭp'amnida. 여러 가지 분재도 취급합니다.

potato *n.* kamja 감자. *boiled* ~*es* salmŭn kamja 삶은 감자/ *fried* ~*es* t'wigin kamja 튀긴 감자/ *mashed* ~ chinnigin kamja 짓이긴 감자.

pottery *n.* (*ceramics*) tojagi 도자기. 「ssamji 담배 쌈지.

pouch *n.* (*sack*) chumŏni 주머니. *a tobacco* ~ tambae

pound *n.* (*weight*) p'aundŭ 파운드. *How much is this per* ~? Han p'aundŭdang ŏlmajiyo? 한 파운드당 얼마지요/ *half a* ~ pan p'aundŭ 반 파운드.

pour *vt.* (*into a glass*) putta 붓다, (*fill*) ttarŭda 따르다, (*flow*) ssotta 쏟다, (*of rain*) p'ŏputta 퍼붓다. *P~ yourself another cup of coffee.* K'op'i han chan tŏ ttara mashipshio. 코피 한 잔 더 따라 마십시오.

poverty *n.* (*being poor*) kanan 가난, (*lack*) kyŏlp'ip 결핍. *extreme* ~ kŭkpin 극빈/ *live in* ~ kananhage salda 가난하게 살다.

powder *n.* (*dust*) karu 가루, (*cosmetic* ~) hwajangbun 화장분, (*medicine*) karuyak 가루약. —*vt.* (*face* ~) punch'irhada 분칠하다. ~ *box* punkap 분갑/ *Excuse me. Where is the* ~ *room?* Hwajangshirŭn ŏdimnikka? 화장실은 어딘니까?

power *n.* (*force*) him 힘, (*ability*) nŭngnyŏk 능력, (*authority*) kwŏllyŏk 권력, (*energy*) tongnyŏk 동력, (*state*) kangguk 강국. *horse* ~ maryŏk 마력/ *I'll do* *everything in my* ~ *to help*. Him charanŭn tekkaji muŏdŭn towa tŭrigessŭmnida. 힘 자라는 데까지 무어든 도와 드리겠읍니다/ *electric* ~ chŏllyŏk 전력/ *water* ~ suryŏk 수력/ ~ *failure* chŏngjŏn 정전(停電)/ ~ *plant* palchŏnso 발전소/ *the Allied* ~s tongmaengguk 동맹국/ *the great* ~s yŏlgang 열강(列強).

powerful *adj.* kangnyŏk'an 강력한, kanghan 강한.

power house palchŏnso 발전소.

powerless *adj.* muryŏk'an 무력한, munŭnghan 무능한.

practical *adj.* (*opp. theoretical*) shilchejŏgin 실제적인, (*useful*) shiryongjŏgin 실용적인, (*actual*) shilchiŭi 실지의. ~ *English* shiryong Yŏngŏ 실용 영어/ ~ *experience* shilchi kyŏnghŏm 실지 경험.

practically *adv.* shilchero 실제로, (*almost*) kŏŭi 거의. *We have had* ~ *no fine weather this month*. I tarenŭn shilchero choŭn nalssinŭn ŏpsŏssŭmnida. 이 달에는 실제로 좋은 날씨는 없었읍니다.

practice *n.* (*exercise*) yŏnsŭp 연습, (*performance*) shilch'ŏn 실천, (*custom*) kwansŭp 관습. —*vt.,vi.* (*exercise*) yŏnsŭp'ada 연습하다, (*carry out*) shirhaenghada 실행하다, (*establish*) kaeŏp'ada 개업하다. *You will improve by* ~. Yŏnsŭbŭl hamyŏn hyangsanghamnida 연습을 하면 향상합니다/ *Let's have a* ~ *game*. Yŏnsŭp kyŏnggirŭl hapshida. 연습 경기를 합시다/ *corrupt* ~s p'yesŭp 폐습/ *an evil* ~ aksŭp 악습/ *a habitual* ~ sangsŭp 상습/ *the* ~ *of a lawyer* pyŏnhosaŏp 변호사업/ *a physician in* ~ kaeŏbŭi 개업의(開業醫)/ *I'm practicing up on the art of self-defence*. Nanŭn hoshinsurŭl yŏnsŭp'ago issŭmnida. 나는 호신술을 연습하고 있읍니다.

prairie *n.* taech'owŏn 대초원, (*meadow*) mokchang 목장.

praise *n.* (*commendation*) ch'ingch'an 칭찬, (*veneration*) ch'anyang 찬양, (*glorification*) ch'anmi 찬미. —*vt.* (*applaud*) ch'ingch'anhada 칭찬하다, (*glorify*) ch'anmihada 찬미하다. *I* ~*d her for her filial piety*. Nanŭn kŭ yŏjaŭi hyosŏngŭl ch'ingch'anhaessŭmnida. 나는 그 여자의 효성을 칭찬했읍니다.

praiseworthy *adj.* ch'ingch'anhal manhan 칭찬할 만한.

pray *vi.,vt.* (*beg earnestly*) pilda 빌다, (*entreat*) kanch'ŏnghada 간청하다, (*please*) amutchorok 아무쪼록, pudi 부디. ~ *for the success of...* ...ŭi sŏnggongŭl pilda ...의 성공을 빌다/ *P*~ *come with me.* Chebal chŏwa hamkke kajushipshida. 제발 저와 함께 가주십시다.

prayer *n.* kido 기도. *a morning*[*evening*] ~ ach'im [chŏnyŏk] kido 아침[저녁] 기도/ *a* ~ *for rain* kiu 기우 (祈雨)/ *a* ~ *to Buddha* yŏmbul 염불.

preacher *n.* (*clergyman*) chŏndosa 전도사.

precaution *n.* (*careful foresight*) kyŏnggye 경계, choshim 조심, (*measures*) yebich'aek 예비책. *You should take an umbrella as a* ~. Yebich'aegŭro usanŭl hyudaehashio. 예비책으로 우산을 휴대하시오/ *air raid* ~s kongsŭp kyŏnggye kyŏngbo 공습 경계 경보/ *take* ~s *against* ...ŭl kyŏnggyehada ...을 경계하다.

precede *vt.,vi.* (*go before*) ...e apsŏda ...에 앞서다.

precious *adj.* (*valuable*) kwijunghan 귀중한, (*costly*) pissan 비싼, (*very dear*) kwiyŏun 귀여운, (*perfect*) sunjŏnhan 순전한. —*adv.* (*very*) maeu 매우. ~ *metals* kwigŭmsok 귀금속/ ~ *stones* posŏk 보석/ *a* ~ *fool* sunjŏnhan pabo 순전한 바보/ *I have* ~ *little money left.* Namŭn toniragonŭn kŏŭi ŏpsŭmnida. 남은 돈이라고는 거의 없읍니다.

precipice *n.* (*steep cliff*) nangttŏrŏji 낭떠러지, pyorang 벼랑, chŏlbyŏk 절벽. *Keep off from the* ~. Chŏlbyŏge chŏpkŭnhaji mashio. 절벽에 접근하지 마시오.

precise *adj.* (*exact*) chŏnghwak'an 정확한, (*just*) kkok tŭrŏmannŭn 꼭 들어맞는, (*meticulous*) kkomkkomhan 꼼꼼한. *the* ~ *amount* chŏnghwak'an pullyang 정확한 분량/ *a* ~ *man* kkomkkomhan saram 꼼꼼한 사람.

precisely *adv.* chŏnghwak'i 정확히. *Tell me* ~ *what you want.* Muŏsŭl wŏnhashinŭnji chŏnghwak'i malssŭmhashipshio. 무엇을 원하시는지 정확히 말씀하십시오.

precision *n.* (*accuracy*) chŏnghwak 정확, (*exactness*) chŏngmil 정밀. *a* ~ *instrument* chŏngmil kigye 정밀 기계/ ~ *gauge* chŏngmil kyegi 정밀 계기.

precocious *adj.* (*premature*) chosuk'an 조숙한, (*plant*) oldoen 올된. *a* ~ *child* chosuk'an ai 조숙한 아이.

predicament *n.* kon-gyŏng 곤경. *I was in a dreadful* ~. Nanŭn shimhan kon-gyŏnge ppajyŏ issŏssŭmnida. 나는 심한 곤경에 빠져 있었읍니다.

predict *vt.,vi.* (*prophesy*) yeŏnhada 예언하다, (*foretell*) yegohada 예고하다, (*forecast*) yebohada 예보하다. *The weather forecast* ~*s rain.* Ilgi yebonŭn piga ondago hamnida. 일기 예보는 비가 온다고 합니다.

preface *n.* (*foreword*) mŏrimal 머리말, sŏmun 서문.

prefer *vt.* (*like better*) ohiryŏ ...ŭl tŏ choahada 오히려 ...을 더 좋아하다. ~ *to* ...ŭl tŏ choahada ...을 더 좋아하다. *What color would you* ~? Ŏnŭ saegŭl tŏ choahashimnikka? 어느 색을 더 좋아하십니까/ *I'll* ~ *this way of eating to formal dinners.* Yangshigŭl katch'un shiksaboda ige tŏ chŏssŭmnida. 양식을 갖춘 식사보다 이게 더 좋습니다.

pregnant *adj.* imshinhan 임신한. *a* ~ *woman* imbu 임부/ *be six months* ~ imshin yukkaewŏrida 임신 6개월이다.

prejudice *n.* (*bias*) p'yŏn-gyŏn 편견, (*preoccupation*) sŏnipkyŏn 선입견. *Throw aside your* ~*s.* P'yŏn-gyŏnŭl pŏrishio. 편견을 버리시오/ *Let us cast away all* ~*s.* Modŭn p'yŏn-gyŏnŭl pŏripshida. 모든 편견을 버립시다.

prelude *n.* (*music*) sŏgok 서곡, chŏnjugok 전주곡.

premier *n.* (*prime minister*) susang 수상, kungmu ch'ongni 국무 총리. *an ex-*~ chŏn susang 전(前) 수상/ *a deputy* ~ pususang 부수상.

premium *n.* (*reward*) p'osanggŭm 포상금, p'ŭrimiŏm 프리미엄, (*insurance due*) pohŏmnyo 보험료.

preparation *n.* chunbi 준비. ~*s for exam* shihŏm chunbi 시험 준비/ *Don't try to do it without* ~. Chunbi ŏpshi kŭgŏsŭl shidohaji mashio. 준비 없이 그것을 시도하지 마시오.

prepare *vt.* (*make ready*) maryŏnhada 마련하다, chunbihada 준비하다, (*compound*) chojehada 조제하다. ~ *a meal* shiksa chunbirŭl hada 식사 준비를 하다/ *How do the Koreans usually* ~ *tuna?* Han-guk saramdŭrŭn pot'ong tarangŏrŭl ŏttŏk'e hae moksŭmnikka? 한국 사람들은 보통 다랑어를 어떻게 해 먹습니까?

prescribe *vt.,vi.* (*ordain*) kyujŏnghada 규정하다, (*order*) chishihada 지시하다, (*med.*) ch'ŏbanghada 처방하다.

prescription *n.* (~ *slip*) ch'ŏbangjŏn 처방전. *Please prepare some medicine according to this* ~. I ch'ŏbangdaero yagŭl chojehae chushio. 이 처방대로 약을 조제해 주시오.

present *adj.* (*not absent*) ch'ulsŏk'an 출석한, (*existing*) innŭn 있는, (*current*) hyŏnjaeŭi 현재의. —*n.* (~ *time*) hyŏnjae 현재, (*gift*) sŏnmul 선물. —*vt.* (*offer*) sŏnsahada 선사하다, (*show*) poida 보이다, (*submit*) chech'urhada 제출하다. *Were you* ~ *at the ceremony?* Ŭishige ch'amsŏk'asyŏssŭmnikka? 의식(儀式)에 참석하셨읍니까/ *I have no money to spare at* ~. Chigŭm yŏbunŭi toni ŏpsŭmnida. 지금 여분의 돈이 없읍니다/ *That'll be enough for the* ~. Tangbun-gan kŭgŏsŭro ch'ungbunhamnida. 당분간 그것으로 충분합니다/ *I'll make you a* ~ *of my old car*. Nae chunggoch'arŭl tangshinhant'e sŏnmurhagessŭmnida. 내 중고차를 당신한테 선물하겠읍니다/ *Thank you for the* ~. Sŏnmul kamsahamnida. 선물 감사합니다/ *Allow me to* ~ *Mr. Lee to you*. Issirŭl sogaehamnida. 이(李)씨를 소개합니다/ *at* ~ hyŏnjae 현재, chigŭm 지금/ *for the* ~ tangbun-gan 당분간.

presently *adv.* (*soon*) kot 곧, inae 이내, (*at present*) hyŏnjae 현재. *I'll be with you* ~. Kot tangshinhant'e kagessŭmnida. 곧 당신한테 가겠읍니다.

preservative *n.* (*antiseptic*) pangbuje 방부제.

preserve *vt.* (*keep safe*) pojonhada 보존하다, (*retain*) yujihada 유지하다, (*conserve*) chŏjanghada 저장하다, chŏrida 절이다. ~ *health* kŏn-gangŭl yujihada 건강을 유지하다/ ~ *peaches* poksungarŭl chŏjanghada 복숭아를 저장하다/ ~ *in salt*[*sugar*] sogŭm[sŏlt'ang]e chŏrida 소금[설탕]에 절이다.

president *n.* (*of republic*) taet'ongnyŏng 대통령, (*of company*) sajang 사장, (*of university*) ch'ongjang 총장, (*of party*) ch'ongjae 총재.

press *vt.,vi.* (*weigh upon*) nurŭda 누르다, appak'ada 압박하다, (*urge on*) kangyohada 강요하다, (*iron*) tari-

da 다리다. —n. (newspapers) shinmun 신문, (printing)
inswae 인쇄, (machine) apch'akki 압착기, (bookshelves)
ch'aekchang 책장. I am ~ed for money. Tone tcho-
dŭlligo issŭmnida. 돈에 쪼들리고 있읍니다/ I want to
have my trousers ~ed. Paji chom taryŏ chushio. 바지
좀 다려 주시오/ the Associated P~ yŏnhap t'ongshin 연
합 통신/ the daily ~ ilgan shinmun 일간 신문/ My novel
is in the ~. Nae sosŏrŭn inswae chungimnida. 내 소설
은 인쇄 중입니다/ I keep some of my books in the ~.
Yakkanŭi sŏjŏgŭn ch'aekchange nŏŏ tugo issŭmnida.
약간의 서적은 책장에 넣어 두고 있읍니다.

pressure n. (oppression) appak 압박, (stress) amnyŏk
압력, (compulsion) kangje 강제. air ~ kiap 기압/ blood
~ hyŏrap 혈압/ high blood ~ kohyŏrap 고혈압/ ~
gauge amnyŏkkye 압력계.

prestige n. (credit) wishin 위신, (fame) myŏngsŏng 명성.

presume vt.,vi. (suppose) ch'uch'ŭk'ada 추측하다, kajŏnghada 가정하다, (venture) kamhi ...hada 감히 ...하다. I ~
this to be a final decision. Igŏshi ch'oejong kyŏlchŏng-
irago saenggak'amnida. 이것이 최종 결정이라고 생각합니
다/Dr. Chong, I ~. Chŏngbaksashijiyo. 정박사시지요/ I
won't ~ to disturb you. P'yega an toellŭnjiyo. 폐가
안 될는지요/ May I ~ to advise you? Choŏnŭl tŭryŏ-
do toegessŭmnikka? 조언을 드려도 되겠읍니까?

pretend vt.,vi. (simulate) ...in ch'ehada ...인 체하다,
(feign) kajanghada 가장하다, (venture) kamhi...hada
감히 ...하다. They ~ed not to see us. Kŭ saramdurŭn
urirŭl mot pon ch'ehaessŭmnida. 그 사람들은 우리를 못
본 체했읍니다/ ~ illness kkoebyŏngŭl alt'a 꾀병을 앓다.

pretense, pretence n. (plea) kushil 구실, p'inggye 핑계,
(sham) sogimsu 속임수, (make believe) kamyŏn 가면.
His grief is all a ~. Kŭ saramŭi sŭlp'ŭmŭn kamyŏne
chinaji anssŭmnida. 그 사람의 슬픔은 가면에 지나지 않습
니다.

pretext n. (pretence) kushil 구실, (excuse) pyŏnmyŏng
변명. make[find] a ~ of ...ŭi kushirŭl mandulda
[ch'atta] ...의 구실을 만들다[찾다]/ He cheated me under

~ *of friendship.* Kŭnŭn ujŏngŭl kushil sama narŭl sogyŏssŭmnida. 그는 우정을 구실 삼아 나를 속였읍니다.

pretty *adj.* (*attractive*) yeppŭn 예쁜. —*adv.* (*fairly*) kkwae 꽤, (*considerably*) sangdanghi 상당히. *a ~ girl* yeppŭn sonyŏ 예쁜 소녀/ *a ~ child* kwiyŏun ai 귀여운 아이/ *P~ good!* Kkwae chok'unyo. 꽤 좋군요/ *a ~ sum of money* kkwae manŭn kŭmaek 꽤 많은 금액/ *I feel ~ well today.* Onŭrŭn kkwae kibuni chossŭmnida. 오늘은 꽤 기분이 좋습니다.

prevail *vi.* (*be victorious*) igida 이기다, (*be predominant*) usehada 우세하다, (*be prevalent*) yuhaenghada 유행하다, (*persuade*) sŏlbok'ada 설복하다. *We have ~ed over our enemies.* Urinŭn chŏgege igyŏssŭmnida. 우리는 적에게 이겼읍니다/ *This custom ~s in the south.* I p'ungsŭbŭn nambuesŏ yuhaenghago issŭmnida. 이 풍습은 남부에서 유행하고 있읍니다.

prevent *vt.* (*hinder*) panghaehada 방해하다, (*keep from*) mot'age hada 못하게 하다, (*guard against*) pohohada 보호하다. *What ~ed you from coming?* Muŏt ttaemune oji mot'aetchiyo? 무엇 때문에 오지 못했지요?

previous *adj.* (*prior*) ijŏnŭi 이전의, (*foregoing*) ap'ŭi 앞의, (*premature*) nŏmu irŭn 너무 이른. *a ~ engagement* sŏnyak 선약(先約)/*without ~ notice* yego ŏpshi 예고 없이/ *What is your ~ employer's?* Chŏnjigi ŏdijiyo? 전직(前職)이 어디지요?

prey *n.* mŏgi 먹이, (*victim*) hŭisaeng 희생. —*vi.* chabamŏkta 잡아먹다. *beast of ~* maengsu 맹수

price *n.* (*charge*) kap 값, kagyŏk 가격, (*cost*) taeka 대가 (代價), (*reward*) sanggŭm 상금. *What ~ are you asking?* Kapsŭn ŏlmajiyo? 값은 얼마지요/ *The ~ is all right for me.* Kapsŭn chŏktanghamnida. 값은 적당합니다/ *Will you cut down the ~ a little?* Chom kkakka chushigessŭmnikka? 좀 깎아 주시겠읍니까/ *I'll do it at any ~.* Ŏttŏn taekarŭl ch'irŭdŏrado hagessŭmnida. 어떤 대가를 치르더라도 하겠읍니다/ *a fixed ~* chŏngka 정가(定價)/ *the ceiling ~* ch'oego kagyŏk 최고 가격/ *the floor ~* ch'oejŏ kagyŏk 최저 가격/ *the retail ~* somae kagyŏk

소매 가격/ *the wholesale* ~ tomae kagyŏk 도매 가격/ ~ *tag* chŏngch'al 정찰, chŏngkap'yo 정가표.

prick *vt.,vi.* (*pierce slightly*) tchirŭda 찌르다, ssushida 쑤시다, (*pain*) koerop'ida 괴롭히다, (*raise*) seuda 세우다. *My fingers are ~ing.* Sonkaragi mopshi ssushimnida. 손가락이 몹시 쑤십니다/ *The dog ~ed up its ears.* Kaega kwirŭl tchunggŭt sewŏssŭmnida. 개가 귀를 쫑긋 세웠읍니다.

pride *n.* (*boast*) charang 자랑, (*arrogance*) kyoman 교만, (*self-respect*) chajonshim 자존심. *Pulguk Temple is the ~ of Korea.* Pulguksanŭn han-gugŭi charangimnida. 불국사는 한국의 자랑입니다/ *hurt one's ~* chajonshimŭl sanghada 자존심을 상하다.

priest *n.* (*monk*) sŭngnyŏ 승려, (*minister*) moksa 목사. *Buddhist ~* chung 중, sŭngnyŏ 승려/ *Catholic ~* shinbu 신부/ *Protestant ~* moksa 목사.

primary *adj.* (*original*) pollaeŭi 본래의, (*first*) ch'oech'oŭi 최초의, (*principal*) chudoen 주된, (*elementary*) ch'oboŭi 초보의. *the ~ colors* wŏnsaek 원색/ *a ~ school* kungmin hakkyo 국민 학교.

prime *adj.* (*first*) cheirŭi 제1의, (*chief*) chuyohan 주요한, (*original*) pollaeŭi 본래의. —*n.* (*beginning*) ch'oech'o 최초, (*youth*) ch'ŏngch'un 청춘, (*best time*) chŏnsŏnggi 전성기. *the P~ Minister* kungmu ch'ŏngni 국무 총리/ *~ of life* hanch'angttae 한창때/ *When is a man in his ~?* Saramŭi chŏnsŏnginŭn ŏnjejiyo? 사람의 전성기는 언제지요/ *~ cost* wŏnka 원가.

primitive *adj.* (*primeval*) wŏnshiŭi 원시의, (*uncivilized*) migaehan 미개한. —*n.* (*prehistoric man*) wŏnshiin 원시인. *~ customs* wŏnshijŏk kwansŭp 원시적 관습.

prince *n.* (*son of king*) wangja 왕자, hwangt'aeja 황태자, (*title of nobility*) kongjak 공작. *the Crown P~* hwangt'aeja 황태자.

princess *n.* (*daughter of king*) kongju 공주, wangnyŏ 왕녀.

principal *adj.* (*chief*) chuyohan 주요한, (*first*) cheirŭi 제1의. —*n.* (*head*) tumok 두목, (*head of school*) kyojang 교장. *the ~ actress* chuyŏn yŏbaeu 주연 여배우/ *a* *lady* ~ yŏgyojang 여교장.

principle *n.* (*fundamental doctrine*) wŏlli 원리, (*rule*) pŏpch'ik 법칙. *the guiding* ~ chido wŏlli 지도 원리/ *the root* ~*s* kibon wŏnch'ik 기본 원칙.

print *n.* (*printing*) inswae 인쇄, (*printed matter*) inswaemul 인쇄물, (*mark*) chaguk 자국. —*vt.* inswaehada 인쇄하다. *in* ~ inswaedoen 인쇄된/ *His novel is in* ~. Kŭ saramŭi sosŏrŭn chigŭm p'algo issŭmnida. 그 사람의 소설은 지금 팔고 있읍니다/ *foot*~ palchaguk 발자국/ *finger*~*s* chimun 지문/ *How many copies shall I* ~? Myŏt chang inswaehalkkayo? 몇 장 인쇄할까요?

printer *n.* (*person*) inswaeŏpcha 인쇄업자, (*instrument*) inswaegi 인쇄기.

printing *n.* (*act of* ~) inswae 인쇄, (*art of* ~) inswaesul 인쇄술, (*printed matter*) inswaemul 인쇄물, (*photo*) inhwa 인화. *three-colored* ~ samsaekp'an 삼색판/ ~ *office* inswaeso 인쇄소.

prison *n.* kyodoso 교도소, (*gaol*) kamok 감옥. *a* ~ *officer* kyodogwan 교도관/ *a* ~ *guard* kansu 간수/ *a* ~ *life* kamoksari 감옥살이.

prisoner *n.* choesu 죄수. ~ *of war* p'oro 포로/ *a political* ~ chŏngch'ibŏm 정치범.

privacy *n.* (*private life*) sasaenghwal 사생활, (*secrecy*) pimil 비밀. *I don't want my* ~ *disturbed*. Sasaenghwarŭl panghaedanghago shipchi anssŭmnida. 사생활을 방해당하고 싶지 않습니다.

private *adj.* (*not public*) sachŏgin 사적인, (*personal*) kaeinjŏgin 개인적인, (*secret*) pimirŭi 비밀의. ~ *life* sasaenghwal 사생활/ *a* ~ *teacher* kajŏng kyosa 가정 교사/ *a* ~ *school* sarip hakkyo 사립 학교/ *I can only tell you in* ~. Tan turi issŭl ttaeman marhal su issŭmnida. 단 둘이 있을 때만 말할 수 있읍니다.

privilege *n.* (*special right*) t'ŭkkwŏn 특권, (*special favor*) t'ukchŏn 특전.

prize *n.* sang(p'um) 상(품). —*vt.* (*esteem*) chonjunghada 존중하다. *the Nobel Peace P*~ Nobel p'yŏnghwasang 노벨 평화상/ *the first* ~ iltŭngsang 1등상/ *a* ~ *winner* susangja 수상자/ ~ *money* sanggǔm 상금/ *We ~ liberty more than life*. Saengmyǒngbodado chayurǔl chonjunghamnida. 생명보다도 자유를 존중합니다.

pro *pref*. (*favoring*) ch'in 친(親). ~ *Korea* ch'inhan 친한(親韓)/ ~ *America* ch'inmi 친미(親美).

probability *n*. (*likelihood*) kongsan 공산(公算), (*math*.) hwangnyul 확률. *There is no ~ of his coming*. Kǔ saramǔn ol kǒt katchi anssǔmnida. 그 사람은 올 것 같지 않습니다/ *in all ~* shipchung p'algunǔn 십중 팔구는.

probable *adj*. (*likely to be*) issǔmjik'an 있음직한, (*promising*) yumanghan 유망한. *a ~ winner* usǔng hubo 우승 후보.

probably *adv*. (*perhaps*) ama 아마, (*most likely*) taegae 대개. *P~ you are right*. Ama tangshin malssǔmi olk'etchiyo. 아마 당신 말씀이 옳겠지요/ *Will he come? P~ not*. Kǔ saramǔn olkkayo? Ama an ol kǒmnida. 그 사람은 올까요? 아마 안 올 겁니다.

problem *n*. (*question*) munje 문제, (*difficult question*) nanmun 난문, (*doubt*) ǔimun 의문. *a social ~* sahoe munje 사회 문제/ *a ~ child* munjea 문제아/ *I have many problems to solve*. Na-egenǔn haegyǒrhal munjega mani issǔmnida. 나에게는 해결할 문제가 많이 있읍니다.

procedure *n*. (*process*) chǒlch'a 절차, susok 수속. *according to the ~* chǒlch'a-e ttara 절차에 따라/ *Have you finished your checkin ~?* Ch'ek'ǔin chǒlch'anǔn kkǔnnaessǔmnikka? 체크인 절차는 끝냈읍니까/ *How long will the whole ~ take?* Susogǔl kkǔnnaeryǒmyǒn ǒlmana kǒllimnikka? 수속을 끝내려면 얼마나 걸립니까?

proceed *vi*. (*go forward*) naagada 나아가다, (*continue*) kyesok'ada 계속하다, (*issue*) palsaenghada 발생하다. *Let us ~ to business*. Ire ch'aksuhapshida. 일에 착수합시다/ *You may ~ to the custom office*. Segwan tchogǔro kǒrǒgashio. 세관 쪽으로 걸어가시오.

proceeding *n*. (*the minutes*) hoeǔirok 회의록, (*legal action*) sosong chǒlch'a 소송 절차, (*measure*) pangch'aek 방책. *take legal ~s against* ...ǔl kisohada…을 기소하다/ *What is our best way of ~?* Ch'oesǒnǔi pangch'aegǔn muŏshimnikka? 최선의 방책은 무엇입니까?

process *n.* (*course*) kwajŏng 과정, (*method*) pangbŏp 방법, (*operation*) chagyong 작용. *the ~ of growth* sŏngjang kwajŏng 성장 과정/ *By what ~ is the cloth made?* Ch'ŏnŭn ŏttŏn pangbŏbŭro mandŭrŏjimnikka? 천은 어떤 방법으로 만들어집니까/ *the digestive ~* sohwa chagyong 소화 작용.

procession *n.* (*parade*) haengnyŏl 행렬(行列). *a funeral ~* changnyeshik haengnyŏl 장례식 행렬/ *We had a lantern ~.* Urinŭn chedŭng haengnyŏrŭl haessŭmnida. 우리는 제등 행렬을 했읍니다/ *in ~* haengnyŏrŭl chiŏ 행렬을 지어.

proclaim *vt.* (*make public*) kongp'ohada 공포하다, (*declare*) sŏnŏnhada 선언하다.

proclamation *n.* (*declaration*) sŏnŏn 선언, (*statement*) sŏngmyŏng 성명(聲明), (*public ~*) kongp'o 공포(公布).

procure *vt.* (*obtain*) sone nŏt'a 손에 넣다, (*cause*) irŭk'ida 일으키다. *Can you ~ me some specimens?* P'yobonŭl chom ŏdŏ chul su issŭmnikka? 표본을 좀 얻어 줄 수 있읍니까/ *His pride ~d his downfall.* Kŭ saramŭn challan ch'ehada shinserŭl mangch'yŏssŭmnida. 그 사람은 잘난 체하다 신세를 망쳤읍니다.

produce *vt.,vi.* (*yield*) saengsanhada 생산하다, (*make*) mandŭlda 만들다, (*show*) poida 보이다, (*stage*) sangyŏnhada 상연하다. *We must ~ more food.* Shingnyangŭl tŏ saengsanhaeya hamnida. 식량을 더 생산해야 합니다/ *~ one's ticket* p'yorŭl naeboida 표를 내보이다.

producer *n.* (*manufacturer*) saengsanja 생산자, (*of film*) chejakcha 제작자, (*of play*) yŏnch'ulga 연출가, (*radio, etc.*) p'ŭrodyusŏ 프로듀서.

product *n.* (*produce*) saengsanp'um 생산품, (*amount produced*) saengsan-go 생산고, (*manufacture*) chejakp'um 제작품, (*result*) kyŏlgwa 결과. *farm ~s* nongsanmul 농산물/ *marine ~* haesanmul 해산물/ *factory ~s* kongjang chep'um 공장 제품.

production *n.* (*producing*) saengsan 생산, (*manufacture*) chejak 제작, (*work*) chakp'um 작품. *mass ~* taeryang saengsan 대량 생산/ *a native ~* kuksanp'um 국산품/ *the*

~ *of films* yŏnghwa chejak 영화 제작/ *an artistic* ~ yesul chakp'um 예술 작품.

profession *n.* (*vocation*) chigŏp 직업, (*professed faith*) shinang kobaek 신앙 고백, (*declaration*) sŏnŏn 선언(宣言). *What is his* ~ ? *He is a lawyer by* ~. Kŭ saramŭi chigŏbŭn muŏshimnikka? Kŭ saramŭi chigŏbŭn pyŏnhosaimnida. 그 사람의 직업은 무엇입니까? 그 사람의 직업은 변호사입니다.

professional *adj.* (*of profession*) chigŏbŭi 직업의, (*opp. amateur*) chŏnmunŭi 전문의. —*n.* (*expert*) chŏnmunga 전문가, p'ŭro 프로. *You are like a* ~ *cook.* Tangshinŭn yori chŏnmun-ga kassŭmnida. 당신은 요리 전문가 같습니다/ *a* ~ *boxer* p'ŭro kwŏnt'uga 프로 권투가.

professor *n.* (*of univ.*) kyosu 교수. *an associate* ~ pukyosu 부교수/ *an assistant* ~ chogyosu 조교수/ *an exchange* ~ kyohwan kyosu 교환 교수.

proficient *adj.* (*skilled*) nŭngnanhan 능란한, suktaldoen 숙달된, (*competent*) yunŭnghan 유능한.

profile *n.* (*of face*) yŏmmosŭp 옆모습, (*outline*) yungwak 윤곽, p'ŭrop'il 프로필.

profit *n.* (*gain*) iik 이익, (*interest*) ija 이자(利子), (*benefit*) tŭk 득(得). —*vi.,vt.* (*make gains*) iigŭl poda 이익을 보다. *I have read it with* ~. Kŭgŏsŭl ikko tŭgŭl poassŭmnida. 그것을 읽고 득을 보았습니다/ *Have you* ~ed *by the experience?* Kŭ kyŏnghŏmi toumi toesyŏnnŭnjiyo? 그 경험이 도움이 되셨는지요?

program(me) *n.* p'ŭrogŭraem 프로그램, (*plan*) kyehoek 계획, (*schedule*) yejŏngp'yo 예정표. *What is the* ~ *for tomorrow?* Naeirŭi yejŏngŭn ŏttŏk'e toeŏ issŭmnikka? 내일의 예정은 어떻게 되어 있읍니까/ *a business* ~ saŏp kyehoek 사업 계획/ *radio* ~s pangsong p'ŭrogŭraem 방송 프로그램.

progress *n.* (*moving forward*) chŏnjin 전진, (*advancement*) chinbo 진보, (*course*) kyŏnggwa 경과. —*vi.* (*advance*) chinhaenghada 진행하다, (*improve*) chinbohada 진보하다. *But I'm afraid I'm not making much* ~. Hajiman, nanŭn pyŏllo chinbohanŭn kŏt katchiga anssŭmnida. 하지만 나는 별로 진보하는 것 같지가 않습니다/ *I ~ed favorably and recovered very quickly.* Kyŏnggwaga choasŏ kot hoebok'ayŏssŭmnida. 경과가 좋아서 곧 회복하였읍니다.

prohibit *vt.* (*forbid*) kŭmhada 금하다, (*prevent*) pangjihada 방지하다. *It is ~ed by the law.* Kŭgŏsŭn pŏburo kŭmhago issŭmnida. 그것은 법으로 금하고 있읍니다.

prohibition *n.* (*forbidding*) kŭmji 금지.

project *n.* (*plan*) kyehoek 계획, (*design*) sŏlgye 설계. —*vt.,vi.* (*plan*) kyehoek'ada 계획하다, (*protrude*) t'wiŏnaoda 튀어나오다. *a business ~* saŏp kyehoek 사업 계획/ *a home ~* kajŏng shilsŭp 가정 실습.

prolong *vt.* (*make longer*) yŏnjanghada 연장하다.

prominent *adj.* (*well-known*) chŏmyŏnghan 저명한, (*conspicuous*) nune ttŭinŭn 눈에 띄는, (*projecting*) tolch'urhan 돌출한. *a ~ businessman* chŏmyŏnghan shirŏpka 저명한 실업가/ *~ eyes* t'ungbangulnun 퉁방울눈.

promise *n.* (*engagement*) yaksok 약속, (*contract*) kyeyak 계약, (*hope*) kidae 기대, hŭimang 희망. —*vi., vt.* yaksok'ada 약속하다. *He ~d to help me.* Kŭbunŭn wŏnjorŭl yaksok'aessŭmnida. 그분은 원조를 약속했읍니다/ *Forgive me for breaking a ~.* Yaksok mot chik'in kŏt yongsŏhashipshio. 약속 못 지킨 것 용서하십시오/ *Is there any ~ for my English?* Nae Yŏngŏe taso kamangsŏngi poimnikka? 내 영어에 다소 가망성이 보입니까?

promising *adj.* (*hopeful*) chŏndo yumanghan 전도 유망한. *a ~ youth* yumanghan ch'ŏngnyŏn 유망한 청년.

promissory *adj.* yaksogŭi 약속의, yakchŏnghan 약정한. *~ note* yaksok ŏŭm 약속 어음.

promote *vt.* (*advance*) chin-gŭpshik'ida 진급시키다, (*further*) chojanghada 조장하다, (*help forward*) ch'okchinhada 촉진하다. *He was ~d sergeant.* Kŭ saramŭn chungsaro chin-gŭptoeŏssŭmnida. 그 사람은 중사로 진급 되었읍니다.

promotion *n.* (*advancement*) sŭngjin 승진, chin-gŭp 진급, (*encouragement*) changnyŏ 장려. *I gave him a dictionary to celebrate his ~.* Chin-gŭp sŏnmullo kŭege

sajŏnŭl chuŏssŭmnida. 진급 선물로 그에게 사전을 주었읍
니다. *win[gain]* ~ chin-gŭp'ada 진급하다.

prompt *adj.* *(quick)* chaepparŭn 재빠른, *(immediate)* chŭkshiŭi 즉시의. —*vt.* *(incite)* chagŭk'ada 자극하다. *a* ~
reply chŭktap 즉답/ *What ~ed you to do this rash
act?* Muŏt ttaemune kŭrŏn kyŏngsorhan chisŭl hasyŏssŭmnikka? 무엇 때문에 그런 경솔한 짓을 하셨읍니까?

promptly *adv.* kot 곧, chaeppalli 재빨리.

pronounce *vi., vt.* *(articulate)* parŭmhada 발음하다, *(declare)* tanŏnhada 단언하다. *How do you ~ the word?*
Kŭ tanŏnŭn ŏttŏk'e parŭmhamnikka? 그 단어는 어떻게
발음합니까/ *I ~ the pears unripe.* Tanŏnhajiman i
paenŭn ikchi anassŭmnida. 단언하지만 이 배는 익지 않았
읍니다.

pronunciation *n.* parŭm 발음. *Which of these three ~s
do you recommend?* I se parŭm chungesŏ ŏnŭ kŏsŭl
kwŏnhashimnikka? 이 세 발음 중에서 어느 것을 권하십니까?

proof *n.* *(evidence)* chŭnggŏ 증거, *(demonstration)*
chŭngmyŏng 증명, *(printing)* kyojŏngswae 교정쇄.
Can you give ~ of your nationality? Tangshinŭi kukchŏgŭl chŭngmyŏnghal su issŭmnikka? 당신의 국적을 증
명할 수 있읍니까/ *water~* pangsuŭi 방수의/ *fire~*
panghwaŭi 방화의/ *~reader* kyojŏngja 교정자/ *~ sheet*
kyojŏngswae 교정쇄.

prop *n.* *(support)* pŏt'immok 버팀목, *(supporter)* chijija
지지자. —*vt.* pŏt'ida 버티다, chijihada 지지하다.

propaganda *n.* sŏnjŏn 선전. *a ~ bill* sŏnjŏn ppira 선전
삐라/ *~ effects* sŏnjŏn hyokwa 선전 효과.

propagate *vt., vi.* *(spread)* pogŭp'ada 보급하다, *(increase)*
pŏnshikshik'ida 번식시키다.

proper *adj.* *(fit)* chŏktanghan 적당한, *(peculiar)* koyuŭi
고유의, *(accurate)* orŭn 옳은, *(polite)* yeŭibarŭn 예의바
른. *Is this the ~ tool for the job?* Kŭ ire igŏshi
chŏktanghan yŏnjangimnikka? 그 일에 이것이 적당한 연
장입니까/ *customs ~ to Korean* Han-guk saram koyuŭi
p'ungsok 한국 사람 고유의 풍속.

properly *adv.* *(fitly)* chŏktanghage 적당하게.

property *n.* (*asset*) chaesan 재산, (*estate*) soyuji 소유지, (*possession*) soyumul 소유물. *Whom does this ~ belong to?* I chaesanŭn nuguŭi soyuimnikka? 이 재산은 누구의 소유입니까/ *I have a small ~ in Shihŭng.* Shihŭnge chogŭmahan t'ojiga issŭmnida. 시흥에 조그마한 토지가 있읍니다/ *a man of ~* chaesan-ga 재산가.

prophecy *n.* yeŏn 예언. *a startling ~* nollaun yeŏn 놀라운 예언.

prophesy *vt., vi.* yeŏn〔yech'ŭk〕hada 예언〔예측〕하다.

prophet *n.* yeŏnja 예언자, yeboja 예보자. *a weather ~* (*Am.*) ilgi yeboja 일기 예보자.

proportion *n.* (*ratio*) piyul 비율, (*part*) pubun 부분, (*balance*) kyunhyŏng 균형, (*share*) mok 몫. *the ~ of three to one* samdae irŭi piyul 3대 1의 비율/ *The building is out of ~.* Kŭ kŏnmurŭn kyunhyŏngi chap'yŏ itchi anssŭmnida. 그 건물은 균형이 잡혀 있지 않습니다/ *My house is very small in ~ to yours.* Taege pihamyŏn nae chibŭn maeu chaksŭmnida. 댁에 비하면 내 집은 매우 작습니다.

proposal *n.* (*offer*) shinch'ŏng 신청, (*proposition*) cheŭi 제의, (*wooing*) kuhon 구혼. *Hear his ~.* Kŭŭi cheŭirŭl tŭrŭshio. 그의 제의를 들으시오/ *I have had a ~.* Nanŭn kuhonŭl padassŭmnida. 나는 구혼을 받았읍니다.

propose *vi., vt.* (*offer*) shinch'ŏnghada 신청하다, (*suggest*) cheanhada 제안하다, (*intend*) kyehoek'ada 계획하다, (*woo*) kuhonhada 구혼하다. *I ~ starting early.* Iltchik ttŏnal kŏsŭl cheŭihamnida. 일찍 떠날 것을 제의합니다/ *I ~ Mr. Park for chairman.* Pakssirŭl ŭijange ch'uch'ŏnhamnida. 박씨를 의장에 추천합니다/ *I ~ to take my holiday in June.* Yuwŏre hyugarŭl ŏdŭl kyehoegimnida. 6월에 휴가를 얻을 계획입니다.

proposition *n.* (*proposal*) cheŭi 제의, (*assertion*) chujang 주장(主張), (*Am.*) (*undertaking*) kiŏp 기업(企業).

proprietor *n.* (*owner*) soyuja 소유자, (*manager*) kyŏngyŏngja 경영자, (*of land*) chiju 지주(地主). *the ~s of the hotel* hot'erŭi soyuja 호텔의 소유자/ *a land ~* chiju 지주.

prose *n.* sanmun 산문.

prospect *n.* (*expectation*) kidae 기대, (*view*) chŏnmang 전망(展望), (*mental view*) kamang 가망, (*landscape*) kyŏngch'i 경치. *I see no ～ of his recovery.* Kŭ sarami hoebok'al kamangŭn ŏpsŭmnida. 그 사람이 회복할 가망은 없읍니다/ *Is there no ～ of your visiting us soon?* Kot pangmunhae chushil kamangŭn ŏpsŭshimnikka? 곧 방문해 주실 가망은 없으십니까/ *Is there any ～ of success?* Sŏnggonghal kamangsŏngi poimnikka? 성공할 가망성이 보입니까/ *The hotel has a good ～.* Kŭ hot'erŭn chŏnmangi chossŭmnida. 그 호텔은 전망이 좋습니다.

prosperity *n.* (*flourish*) pŏnyŏng 번영, (*success*) sŏnggong 성공. *national ～* kukkaŭi pŏnyŏng 국가의 번영/ *I wish you all ～.* Sŏnggongŭl pimnida. 성공을 빕니다.

prosperous *adj.* (*flourishing*) pŏnch'anghanŭn 번창하는, (*favorable*) sunjoroun 순조로운. *a ～ business* pŏnch'anghanŭn changsa 번창하는 장사/ *～ years* pŏnyŏnghanŭn yŏndae 번영하는 연대.

prostitute *n.* (*harlot*) maech'unbu 매춘부, ch'angnyŏ 창녀. *～ quarters* yugwak 유곽.

prostitution *n.* maech'un 매춘, maeŭm 매음.

protect *vt.* (*guard*) pohohada 보호하다, (*defend*) makta 막다. *～ one's country* nararŭl chik'ida 나라를 지키다/ *P～ your eyes from the sun.* Haetpit'esŏ nunŭl pohohashio. 햇빛에서 눈을 보호하시오.

protection *n.* (*protecting*) poho 보호, (*patronage*) huwŏn 후원.

protector *n.* (*guardian*) pohoja 보호자.

protein *n.* tanbaekchil 단백질.

protest *vi., vt.* (*object*) hangŭihada 항의하다, (*assert*) chujanghada 주장하다. ―*n.* (*dissent*) hangŭi 항의, (*disapproval*) pandae 반대. *He ～ed the boy's innocence.* Kŭ saramŭn sonyŏnŭi mujoerŭl chujanghaessŭmnida. 그 사람은 소년의 무죄를 주장했읍니다/ *a ～ demonstration* hangŭi temo 항의 데모.

protestant *n.* shin-gyodo 신교도.

proud *adj.* (*self-respectful*) charangsŭrŏun 자랑스러운,

(*haughty*) kyomanhan 교만한, (*grand*) tangdanghan 당당한. *You must be very ～ of your daughter*. Ttanimi p'ŏk charangsŭrŏpketkunyo. 따님이 퍽 자랑스럽겠군요/ *Korea is ～ of her long history*. Han-gugŭn kin yŏksarŭl charanghago issŭmnida. 한국은 긴 역사를 자랑하고 있읍니다.

prove *vt.*, *vi.* (*demonstrate*) chŭngmyŏnghada 증명하다, (*turn out*) p'anmyŏngdoeda 판명되다. *Can you ～ it?* Chŭngmyŏnghal su issŭmnikka? 증명할 수 있읍니까/ *The document was ～d to be false*. Kŭ sŏryunŭn wijoimi p'anmyŏngdoeŏssŭmnida. 그 서류는 위조임이 판명되었읍니다.

proverb *n.* soktam 속담.

provide *vt.*, *vi.* (*get ready*) chunbihada 준비하다, (*supply*) konggŭp'ada 공급하다. *We must ～ for our visitors*. Sonnimŭl majŭl chunbirŭl haeya hamnida. 손님을 맞을 준비를 해야 합니다/ *Can you ～ me with these goods by tomorrow?* Naeilkkaji i mulgŏndŭrŭl konggŭp'ae chul su issŭmnikka? 내일까지 이 물건들을 공급해 줄 수 있읍니까?

province *n.* (*state*) chu 주, (*prefecture*) do 도(道), (*rural regions*) shigol 시골. *How many ～s are there in Korea?* Han-gugenŭn myŏt kaeŭi doga issŭmnikka? 한국에는 몇 개의 도(道)가 있읍니까?

provision *n.* (*supplies of food*) shingnyang 식량, (*preparation*) chunbi 준비, (*stipulation*) kyujŏng 규정. *I require ～s for the journey*. Yŏhaengnyong shingnyangi p'iryohamnida. 여행용 식량이 필요합니다/ *We ran short of ～s*. Shingnyangi pujok'aessŭmnida. 식량이 부족했읍니다/ *general ～s* ilban kyujŏng 일반 규정/ *punitive ～s* pŏlch'ik 벌칙.

provisional *adj.* (*temporal*) imshiŭi 임시의. *a ～ government* imshi chŏngbu 임시 정부/ *a ～ agreement* imshi hyŏpchŏng 임시 협정.

provocation *n.* (*irritation*) yagorŭge ham 약오르게 함, (*incitement*) tobal 도발. *feel ～* sŏngnaeda 성내다/ *give ～* sŏngnage hada 성나게 하다.

provoke *vt.* (*make angry*) hwanage hada 화나게 하다,

(*instigate*) puch'ugida 부추기다, (*stir up*) tobarhada 도발하다. *If you ~ the dog, it will attack you.* Kaerŭl chipchŏkŏrimyŏn mullimnida. 개를 집적거리면 물립니다/ *I'm ~ed at his impudence.* Kŭjaŭi muryehamŭl poni hwaga namnida. 그자의 무례함을 보니 화가 납니다/ *~ laughter* usŭmŭl chaanaeda 웃음을 자아내다/ *~ a quarrel* ssaumŭl kŏrŏ oda 싸움을 걸어 오다.

prudence *n.* (*discretion*) punbyŏl 분별, shinjungham 신중함, (*economy*) alttŭrham 알뜰함. *Use your ~ a bit more.* Chomdŏ shinjunghi hashio. 좀더 신중히 하시오.

prudent *adj.* (*cautious*) shinjunghan 신중한, (*discreet*) punbyŏl innŭn 분별 있는. *a ~ housekeeper* alttŭrhan chubu 알뜰한 주부/ *be ~ with utterance* marŭl samgada 말을 삼가다.

prune *n.* (*plum*) oyat 오얏, (*silly guy*) pabo 바보. —*vt.* (*cut off*) kajirŭl ch'ida 가지를 치다. *You poor ~!* Pabo! 바보/ *~ off dead branches* marŭn kajirŭl charŭda 마른 가지를 자르다.

psalm *n.* (*hymn*) ch'ansongga 찬송가, sŏngga 성가.

psychologist *n.* shimnihakcha 심리학자.

psychology *n.* shimnihak 심리학, shimni 심리.

pub *n.* (*public house*) sŏnsulchip 선술집. *Is there a ~ in this hotel?* I hot'erenŭn sŏnsulchibi issŭmnikka? 이 호텔에는 선술집이 있읍니까?

puberty *n.* sach'un-gi 사춘기, myoryŏng 묘령(妙齡).

public *adj.* (*opp. private*) konggongŭi 공공의, (*of the people*) kongjungŭi 공중의, (*open to all*) konggaeŭi 공개의. —*n.* (*people in general*) kongjung 공중, (*community*) sahoe 사회. *Where can I find a ~ telephone?* Kongjungchŏnhwanŭn ŏdi issŭmnikka? 공중 전화는 어디 있읍니까/ *~ officer* kongmuwŏn 공무원/ *a ~ school* kongnip hakkyo 공립 학교/ *the buying ~* sobijach'ŭng 소비자층.

publicity *n.* (*advertisement*) kwanggo 광고, (*notoriety*) chuji 주지(周知), (*good reputation*) hop'yŏng 호평. *press ~* shinmun kwanggo 신문 광고/ *seek ~* chagi sŏnjŏn hada 자기 선전 하다/ *~ department* kwanggobu 광고부.

publish *vt.* (*make public*) palp'yohada 발표하다. (*promulgate*) kongp'ohada 공포(公布)하다, (*book, paper, etc.*) ch'ulp'anhada 출판하다. *When will the book be ~ed?* Ku ch'aegun ŏnje ch'ulp'andoemnikka? 그 책은 언제 출판됩니까?

puff *n.* (*whiff*) huk pulgi 혹 불기, (*sound of whiff*) huk punun sori 혹 부는 소리, —*vt.,vi.* (*blow in ~s*) hukhuk naeppumta 혹혹 내뿜다, (*smoke with ~s*) ppŏkkŭmppŏkkŭm p'iuda 뻐끔뻐끔 피우다, (*pant*) hŏlttŏkkŏrida 헐떡거리다/ *I gave two or three ~s to put out the candle.* Ch'otpurul kkuryŏgo tusŏnŏ pŏn hukhuk purŏssŭmnida. 촛불을 끄려고 두서너 번 혹혹 불었읍니다/ *He ~ed smoke into my face.* Kŭnŭn nae ŏlgure yŏngirul naeppumŏssŭmnida. 그는 내 얼굴에 연기를 내뿜었읍니다.

pull *vt., vi.* (*draw*) chabadanggida 잡아당기다, (*tug*) kkŭlda 끌다, (*extract*) ppopta 뽑다, (*row*) chŏtta 젓다, (*cheat*) sogida 속이다. *P~ your chair up to the table.* Uijarul t'eibŭl kakkai kkŭrŏdanggishio. 의자를 테이블 가까이 끌어 당기시오/ *Help! P~ me out!* Sallyŏ chushio. Kkŭrŏnae chushio. 살려 주시오. 끌어내 주시오/ *Now, all ~ together.* Cha, tagach'i chŏupshida. 자, 다같이 저웁시다/ *Don't ~ any tricks.* Chaeju puriji mashio. 재주 부리지 마시오/ *~ down* kkŭrŏnaerida 끌어내리다/ *~ on* (*shoes*) shinta 신다, (*gloves*) kkida 끼다/ *P~ your gloves on quickly.* Ppalli changgabŭl kkishio. 빨리 장갑을 끼시오/ *~ out* (*grass*) ppopta 뽑다, (*revolver*) ppaeda 빼다.

pullover *n.* p'ulobŏ 풀오버. *What is this ~ made of?* I p'ulobŏŭi chaeryonŭn muŏjiyo? 이 풀오버의 재료는 무어지요?

pulp *n.* (*of wood*) p'ŏlp'ŭ 펄프, (*of fruit*) kwayuk 과육.

pulpit *n.* sŏlgyodan 설교단, yŏndan 연단.

pulsate *vi.* (*beat*) maegi ttwida 맥이 뛰다, (*throb*) kodonghada 고동하다.

pulse *n.* maekpak 맥박. *feel the ~* maegŭl chipta 맥을 집다/ *The ~ is still beating.* Maekpagŭn ajik ttwigo issŭmnida. 맥박은 아직 뛰고 있읍니다.

pump *n.* p'ŏmp'ŭ 펌프. —*vt.* (*liquid*) p'ŏmp'ŭro p'uda 펌프로 푸다, (*air*) konggirŭl nŏt'a 공기를 넣다. *an air* ~ konggi p'ŏmp'ŭ 공기 펌프/ *a fire* ~ sobang p'ŏmp'ŭ 소방 펌프/ *a spray* ~ punmugi 분무기/ ~ *water up* p'ŏmp'ŭro murŭl p'ŏollida 펌프로 물을 퍼올리다/ ~ *up a tire* t'aiŏe konggirŭl nŏt'a 타이어에 공기를 넣다.

pumpkin *n.* hobak 호박.

punch *n.* (*blow*) p'ŏnch'i 펀치. *get a* ~ *on the head* mŏrie p'ŏnch'irŭl matta 머리에 펀치를 맞다/ *a boxer with a strong* ~ p'ŏnch'iga sen kwŏnt'u sŏnsu 펀치가 센 권투 선수.

punctual *adj.* (*on time*) shiganŭl ŏmsuhanŭn 시간을 엄수하는, (*not late*) chich'e ŏmnŭn 지체 없는.

punctually *adv.* shigandaero 시간대로, chich'e ŏpshi 지체 없이. *The train arrived* ~. Yŏlch'anŭn chŏnggage toch'ak'aessŭmnida. 열차는 정각에 도착했습니다.

puncture *n.* ppangkku 빵꾸. —*vi.* ppangkkunada 빵꾸나다. *We had one of the car tires* ~d *on the way.* Tojungesŏ t'aiŏ hanaga ppangkkunassŭmnida. 도중에서 타이어 하나가 빵꾸났습니다.

punish *vt.* (*chastise*) pŏljuda 벌주다, ch'ŏbŏrhada 처벌하다, (*treat severely*) ttaeryŏ nup'ida 때려 눕히다. *Don't* ~ *the boy.* Kŭ sonyŏnŭl ch'ŏbŏrhaji mashipshio. 그 소년을 처벌하지 마십시오/ *The boxer* ~ed *his opponent severely.* Kŭ kwŏnt'u sŏnsunŭn tojŏnjarŭl ttaeryŏ nup'yŏssŭmnida. 그 권투 선수는 도전자를 때려 눕혔습니다.

punishment *n.* ch'ŏbŏl 처벌, hyŏngbŏl 형벌. *a lenient* ~ kwandaehan ch'ŏbŏl 관대한 처벌/ *a pecuniary* ~ pŏlgŭmhyŏng 벌금형/ (*a*) *capital* ~ sahyŏng 사형.

pupil *n.* (*scholar*) haksaeng 학생, (*disciple*) cheja 제자, (*of the eye*) nuntongja 눈동자. *primary* ~s kungmin hakkyo haksaeng 국민 학교 학생/ *become a* ~ *of* cheja-ga toeda 제자가 되다.

puppet *n.* (*marionette*) kkoktukkakshi 꼭둑각시, (*dummy*) koeroe 괴뢰. *a* ~ *government* koeroe chŏngbu 괴뢰 정부.

purchase *vt.* (*buy*) sada 사다, kuip'ada 구입하다. —*n.* kumae 구매. *a* ~ *contract* kumae kyeyak 구매 계약/

a purchasing department kumaebu 구매부/ *a purchasing price* kumae kagyŏk 구매 가격.

pure *adj.* (*unmixed*) sunsuhan 순수한, (*clear*) kkaekkŭt'an 깨끗한, (*chaste*) sun-gyŏrhan 순결한. ~ *gold* sun-gŭm 순금/ ~ *air* kkaekkŭt'an konggi 깨끗한 공기/ ~ *love* sun-gyŏrhan sarang 순결한 사랑/ *It's* ~ *silk.* Kŭgŏsŭn sun-gyŏnimnida. 그것은 순견입니다.

purge *n.* (*cleanup*) sukch'ŏng 숙청, (*aperient*) haje 하제 (下劑). —*vt.* (*cleanse*) kkaekkŭshi hada 깨끗이 하다, (*from party, etc.*) sukch'ŏnghada 숙청하다.

purify *vt.* (*make pure*) ch'ŏnggyŏrhi hada 청결히 하다, (*refine*) chŏngjehada 정제하다.

purple *adj.* chajusaek 자주색, poratpit 보랏빛. *She is attired in* ~. Kŭ yŏjanŭn chajusaek osŭl ipko issŭmnida. 그 여자는 자주색 옷을 입고 있읍니다.

purpose *n.* (*aim*) mokchŏk 목적, (*intent*) ŭido 의도, (*effect*) hyokwa 효과. *For what* ~ *did you do it?* Ŏttŏn mokchŏgŭro haessŭmnikka? 어떤 목적으로 했읍니까/ *on* ~ koŭiro 고의로, ilburŏ 일부러/ *You did it on* ~. Tangshinŭn koŭiro haessŭmnida. 당신은 고의로 했읍니다.

purse *n.* chigap 지갑. *leather* ~ kajuk chigap 가죽 지갑/ *My* ~ *is gone!* Chigabi ŏpsŏjyŏssŭmnida. 지갑이 없어졌읍니다/ *I have one thousand won in my* ~. Nae chigabenŭn ch'ŏnwŏni tŭrŏ issŭmnida. 내 지갑에는 1,000원이 들어 있읍니다/ *the public* ~ kukko 국고(國庫).

purser *n.* (*of ship, airplane, etc.*) samujang 사무장.

pursue *vt., vi.* (*chase*) twitchotta 뒤쫓다, (*carry on*) sok'aenghada 속행하다.

pus *n.* korŭm 고름.

push *vt., vi.* (*press forward*) milda 밀다, (*impel*) milgo naagada 밀고 나아가다, (*urge*) kangyohada 강요하다. —*n.* (*shove*) milgi 밀기. *P*~ *it a little to the right.* Orŭntchogŭro yakkan mirŏ chushipshio. 오른쪽으로 약간 밀어 주십시오/ *Stop* ~*ing at the back!* Twiesŏ milji mashio. 뒤에서 밀지 마시오.

put *vt., vi.* (*place*) tuda 두다, not'a 놓다. *Where shall I* ~ *this suitcase?* I kabangŭl ŏdida tulkkayo? 이 가방

을 어디다 둘까요/ ～ *aside* chech'yŏ not'a 제쳐 놓다/ *If you want the article, I will ～ it aside for you.* I mulgŏni p'iryohashimyŏn ttaro ch'iwŏ tugessŭmnida. 이 물건이 필요하시면 따로 치워 두겠읍니다/ *P～ them back just as they were.* Ponshi ittŏn taero toedollyŏ noŭshio. 본시 있던 대로 되돌려 놓으시오/ *P～ down that gun!* Kŭ ch'ongŭl naeryŏnoŭshio. 그 총을 내려놓으시오/ *P～ down here your name and address, please.* Yŏgie sŏnghamgwa chusorŭl chŏgŏ chushipshio. 여기에 성함과 주소를 적어 주십시오/ *I'll not ～ off any longer.* Tŏ isang kidariji ank'essŭmnida. 더 이상 기다리지 않겠읍니다/ *The meeting was ～ off.* Hoeŭinŭn yŏn-gidoeŏssŭmnida. 회의는 연기되었읍니다/ *～ on* ipta 입다/ *I ～ on my clothes in a hurry.* Nanŭn sŏdullŏ osŭl ibŏssŭmnida. 나는 서둘러 옷을 입었읍니다/*P～ on the light.* Purŭl k'yŏshipshio. 불을 켜십시오/ *～ out(extinguish)* purŭl kkŭda 불을 끄다/ *P～ it out, please.* Kŭgŏsŭl chom kkŏjushio. 그것을 좀 꺼주시오/ *P～ your hand up.* Sonŭl tŭshio. 손을 드시오/ *Will you ～ us up for the night?* Harutpam t'usukshik'yŏ chushiryŏmnikka? 하룻밤 투숙시켜 주시렵니까? / *Did you ～ milk in my coffee?* Nae k'ŏp'ie uyurŭl t'assŭmnikka? 내 커피에 우유를 탔읍니까/ *How shall I ～ it?* Ŏttŏk'e p'yohyŏnhalkkayo? 어떻게 표현할까요?

puzzle *n.* (*riddle*) susukkekki 수수께끼, (*quiz*) k'wijŭ 퀴즈, (*hard question*) nanmunje 난문제. —*vt.,vi.* (*perplex*) ŏtchŏlchul morŭge hada 어쩔줄 모르게 하다. *I'm ～d what to do.* Ŏtchŏmyŏn choŭlchi morŭgessŭmnida. 어쩌면 좋을지 모르겠읍니다.

pyramid *n.* kŭmjat'ap 금자탑, p'iramit 피라밋.

pyjamas *n.* (*pajamas*) chamot 잠옷, p'ajama 파자마.

---

quack *n.* (*charlatan*) tolp'ari ŭisa 돌팔이 의사, (*imposter*) sagikkun 사기꾼. —*vi.* (*play the ～*) ŏngt'ŏri ch'iryorŭl hada 엉터리 치료를 하다.

quail *n.* (*bird*) mech'uragi 메추라기, mech'uri 메추리.

quaint *adj.* (*queer*) myohan 묘한, kibarhan 기발한, (*odd*) koesanghan 괴상한. *a ~ old house* koesanghan nalgŭn chip 괴상한 낡은 집.

quake *vi.* (*sway*) hŭndŭllida 흔들리다, (*shake*) ttŏlda 떨다. —*n.* (*tremor*) chindong 진동. *~ with fear* kongp'oe ttŏlda 공포에 떨다.

qualification *n.* (*requirement*) chagyŏk 자격, (*limits*) chehan 제한, (*reservation*) chokŏn 조건. *obtain a ~* chagyŏgŭl ŏtta 자격을 얻다/ *~s of the applicant* shinch'ŏngja chagyŏk 신청자 자격/ *without ~* mujokŏn 무조건.

qualified *adj.* (*competent*) chagyŏgi innŭn 자격이 있는, (*limited*) chokŏnbuŭi 조건부의.

qualify *vt., vi.* (*make competent*) chagyŏgŭl chuda 자격을 주다, (*modify*) sushik'ada 수식하다. *Do you ~ to vote?* T'up'yo chagyŏgi issŭmnikka? 투표 자격이 있읍니까/ *You are well qualified for this post.* Tangshinŭn i charie aju chŏkkyŏkchaimnida. 당신은 이 자리에 아주 적격자입니다.

quality *n.* (*degree of excellence*) p'umjil 품질, (*excellence*) yangjil 양질, (*characteristic*) t'ŭksŏng 특성. *first-class ~* iltŭngp'um 1등품/ *Haven't you any better ~?* Tŏ choŭn kŏsŭn ŏpsŭmnikka? 더 좋은 것은 없읍니까/ *We manufacture goods of various qualities.* Yŏrŏ kaji chirŭi sangp'umŭl mandŭlgo issŭmnida. 여러 가지 질의 상품을 만들고 있읍니다/ *We aim at ~ rather than quantity.* Yangboda chirŭl mokp'yoro hago issŭmnida. 양보다 질을 목표로 하고 있읍니다/ *You have many good qualities.* Tangshinŭn changchŏmi manssŭmnida. 당신은 장점이 많습니다.

quantity *n.* (*amount*) pullyang 분량, (*numbers*) suryang 수량, (*pl.*) (*large amount*) taeryang 대량, tasu 다수. *a large ~ of sugar* manŭn yangŭi sŏlt'ang 많은 양의 설탕/ *What ~ do you want?* Ŏlmana p'iryohashimnikka? 얼마나 필요하십니까/ *We've quantities of rain this month.* Idarenŭn piga mani wassŭmnida. 이달에는 비가 많이 왔

읍니다/ *There is only a small ～ left.* Chogŭmbakke nama itchi anssŭmnida. 조금밖에 남아 있지 않습니다/ *a certain ～* yakkannyang 약간량/ *a fixed ～* ilchŏngnyang 일정량/ *a small ～* soryang 소량, chogŭm 조금.

quarantine *n.* (*medical inspection*) kŏmyŏk 검역(檢疫), (*of ship*) kŏmyŏk chŏngsŏn 검역 정선(停船). *pass a ～* kŏmyŏgŭl t'onggwahada 검역을 통과하다/ *a ～ against cholera* k'olleraŭi kŏmyŏk 콜레라의 검역/ *This ship is detained in ～.* I paenŭn kŏmyŏk ttaemune chŏngsŏnhago issŭmnida. 이 배는 검역 때문에 정선하고 있읍니다.

quarrel *n.* ssaum 싸움, maldat'um 말다툼. —*vi.* ssauda 싸우다, maldat'umhada 말다툼하다. *a family ～* chiban ssaum 집안 싸움/*a matrimonial ～* pubu ssaum 부부 싸움/ *Don't ～ over such a trifling matter.* Kŭrŏn shishihan illo ssauji mashio. 그런 시시한 일로 싸우지 마시오.

quarrelsome *adj.* shibi choahanŭn 시비 좋아하는.

quarry *n.* (*stone ～*) ch'aesŏkchang 채석장, (*prey*) sanyangkam 사냥감.

quarter *n.* sabunŭi il 1/4, (*Am.*) ishibo sent'ŭ 25센트, (*place*) chidae 지대, (*lodgings*) sukso 숙소, (*direction*) panghyang 방향. *a ～ of a mile* sabunŭi il mail 1/4 마일/*a ～ of an hour* shibobun 15분/ *I pay my rent every ～.* Sam kaewŏlmada chipserŭl ch'irŭmnida. 3개월마다 집세를 치릅니다/ *It is a ～ after three.* Seshi shibobunimnida. 3시 15분입니다/ *It is a ～ to three.* Seshi shibobun chŏnimnida. 3시 15분 전입니다/ *I'd like to change a dollar to ～s, please.* Tallŏrŭl sent'ŭhwaro pakkwŏ chushipshio. 달러를 센트화(貨)로 바꿔 주십시오/ *modern living ～s* munhwa chut'aekka 문화 주택가/ *From what ～ does the wind blow?* Paramŭn ŏnŭ panghyangesŏ purŏ ogo issŭmnikka? 바람은 어느 방향에서 불어 오고 있읍니까?

quarterly *n.* kyeganji 계간지(季刊誌).

quartermaster *n.* (*mil.*) pogŭpkye 보급계. *Q～ Corps* pyŏngch'am pudae 병참 부대.

quay *n.* pudu 부두, sŏnch'ang 선창. *I met him on the ～ at Pusan.* Pusan puduesŏ kŭ saramŭl mannassŭmnida.

부산 부두에서 그 사람을 만났읍니다/ *moor a steamer alongside the* ~ pudue paerŭl taeda 부두에 배를 대다.

queen *n.* yŏwang 여왕. *a* ~ *of society* sagyogyeŭi yŏwang 사교계의 여왕/ *a* ~ *bee* yŏwangbŏl 여왕벌.

queer *adj.* (*odd*) koesanghan 괴상한, (*doubtful*) susanghan 수상한. *a* ~ *character* koesanghan saram 괴상한 사람/ *That's* ~. Kŏ susanghande! 거 수상한데/ *There is something* ~ *about him.* Chŏ saramŭn ŏdinji susanghagunyo. 저 사람은 어딘지 수상하군요.

quest *n.* (*search*) t'amsaek 탐색, susaek 수색. *in* ~ *of* ...ŭl ch'aja …을 찾아/ *He went off in* ~ *of food.* Yangshigŭl kuharŏ kassŭmnida. 양식을 구하러 갔읍니다.

question *n.* (*inquiry*) chilmun 질문, (*problem*) munje 문제. —*vt., vi.* (*inquire*) chilmunhada 질문하다, (*interrogate*) shimmunhada 심문하다, (*study*) yŏn-guhada 연구하다. *May I ask you a* ~? Han kaji chilmunhaedo chossŭmnikka? 한 가지 질문해도 좋습니까/ *Why do you ask me such a* ~? Wae kŭrŏn chilmunŭl hashimnikka? 왜 그런 질문을 하십니까/ *What you say is out of* ~. Tangshinŭi malssŭmŭn munjega an toemnida. 당신의 말씀은 문제가 안 됩니다/ *Where's the man in* ~? Munjeŭi kŭ saramŭn ŏdi issŭmnikka? 문제의 그 사람은 어디 있읍니까/ *I was* ~*ed by the police.* Nanŭn kyŏngch'arŭi shimmunŭl padassŭmnida. 나는 경찰의 심문을 받았읍니다.

questionable *adj.* (*doubtful*) mishimtchŏgŭn 미심쩍은, (*uncertain*) hwakshilch'i anŭn 확실치 않은. *a* ~ *statement* ŭishimsŭrŏun chinsul 의심스러운 진술/ ~ *conduct* punmyŏngch'i anŭn haengwi 분명치 않는 행위.

question(n)aire *n.* chirŭisŏ 질의서, angk'et'ŭ 앙케트. *fill out a* ~ chirŭisŏe kiip'ada 질의서에 기입하다.

question-answer *n.* chirŭi ŭngdapsŏ 질의 응답서. *a great* "~" hullyunghan ch'amgosŏ 훌륭한 참고서.

quick *adj.* (*rapid*) pparŭn 빠른, (*prompt*) nallaen 날랜, (*acute*) yeminhan 예민한. —*adv.* ppalli 빨리. *Be* ~ *about it.* Ppalli hashio. 빨리 하시오/ *Try to be a little* ~*er.* Chomdŏ ppalli hadorok hashio. 좀더 빨리 하도록 하시오/ *Can't you run* ~*er?* Tŏ ppalli tallil su ŏpsŭmnikka? 더 빨리 달릴 수 없읍니까?

quickly *adv.* ppalli 빨리. *You speak too* ~. Malssŭmi nŏmu pparŭshimnida. 말씀이 너무 빠르십니다/ *Bring it here*, ~. Ppalli kajyŏoshio. 빨리 가져오시오/ *(to driver) Get along as* ~ *as you can*. Toel su innŭn taero ppalli tallishio. 될 수 있는 대로 빨리 달리시오/ *I* ~ *changed my clothes*. Nanŭn ppalli osŭl kara ibŏssŭmnida. 나는 빨리 옷을 갈아 입었읍니다/ *Call a doctor* ~. Ppalli ŭisarŭl pullŏ chushipshio. 빨리 의사를 불러 주십시오.

quiet *adj.* *(still)* choyonghan 조용한, *(gentle)* onhwahan 온화한, *(not showy)* susuhan 수수한. —*n.* *(stillness)* choyongham 조용함, *(rest)* hyushik 휴식, *(peace)* p'yŏngon 평온. *Be* ~! Choyonghi hashio. 조용히 하시오/ *I'm spending a* ~ *life here*. Yŏgisŏ p'yŏngonhan saeng-hwarŭl ponaego issŭmnida. 여기서 평온한 생활을 보내고 있읍니다/ *How long do I have to keep* ~? Myŏch'irina anjŏngŭl ch'wihaeya hamnikka? 며칠이나 안정을 취해야 합니까/ *Show me something more* ~. Chomdŏ susuhan kŏsŭl poyŏ chushio. 좀더 수수한 것을 보여 주시오/ *Here are some with* ~*er designs*. Yŏgi han-gyŏl tŏ susuhan munŭiga issŭmnida. 여기 한결 더 수수한 무늬가 있읍니다.

quill *n.* *(feather)* kit 깃.

quilt *n.* ibul 이불. *spread one's* ~*s* iburŭl p'yŏda 이불을 펴다.

quit *vt.* *(leave)* ttŏnada 떠나다, *(give up)* p'ogihada 포기하다, *(stop)* kŭmanduda 그만두다. *You had better* ~ *smoking and drinking*. Tambaewa surŭn kkŭnnŭn ke chossŭmnida. 담배와 술은 끊는 게 좋습니다/ *Did you* ~ *smoking?* Tambaenŭn kkŭnŏssŭmnikka? 담배는 끊었읍니까?

quite *adv.* *(completely)* aju 아주, wanjŏnhi 완전히, *(practically)* shilchero 실제로, *(somewhat)* kkwae 꽤. *Are you* ~ *sure?* Chŏngmal chashin issŭmnikka? 정말 자신 있읍니까/ *I am* ~ *tired*. Nanŭn aju chich'yŏssŭm-nida. 나는 아주 지쳤읍니다/ *I* ~ *like her*. Nanŭn kŭnyŏ-rŭl kkwae choahamnida. 나는 그녀를 꽤 좋아합니다.

quiver *vi.*, *vt.* *(tremble)* ttŏlda 떨다, *(shake)* hŭndŭlda

혼들다. —*n.* (*tremor*) chindong 진동, ttŏllim 떨림. *Her lips were ~ing with fear.* Kŭnyŏŭi ipsurŭn kongp'o-e ttŏlgo issŏssŭmnida. 그녀의 입술은 공포에 떨고 있었읍니다/ *a ~ing leaf* nabukkinŭn ipsagwi 나부끼는 잎사귀.

quiz *n.* (*questioning*) mutki 묻기, (*interrogation*) chilmun 질문, (*joke*) changnan 장난, (*radio, etc.*) k'wijŭ 퀴즈. *~ show* k'wijŭ p'ŭro 퀴즈 프로/ *~master* k'wijŭ p'ŭroŭi sahoeja 퀴즈 프로의 사회자.

quota *n.* (*share*) mok 몫, (*proportion*) haltangnyang 할당량. *reach the full ~* chŏngwŏne tarhada 정원(定員)에 달하다/ *the export ~ system* such'ul haltangje 수출 할당제.

quotation *n.* (*citation*) inyong 인용, (*price*) shise 시세, shika 시가. *exchange ~s* hwanyul shise 환율 시세/ *black-market ~s* amshise 암시세(暗時勢).

quote *vt., vi.* (*cite*) inyonghada 인용하다, (*refer to*) yero tŭlda 예(例)로 들다. *Let me ~ you the words of Confucius.* Kongja malssŭmŭl inyonghagessŭmnida. 공자(孔子) 말씀을 인용하겠읍니다/ *Can you ~ (me) a recent instance?* Ch'oegŭnŭi saryerŭl poyŏ chul su issŭmnikka? 최근의 사례를 보여 줄 수 있읍니까?

-- R --

rabbit *n.* t'okki 토끼. *~ hutch* t'okkijang 토끼장/ *~ hunting* t'okki sanyang 토끼 사냥.

rabies *n.* kwanggyŏnpyŏng 광견병, (*hydrophobia*) kongsupyŏng 공수병.

race *n.* (*competition*) kyŏngju 경주, (*tribe*) injong 인종. —*vi., vt.* (*compete*) kyŏngju[kyŏngjaeng]hada 경주[경쟁]하다. *a boat ~* pot'ŭ kyŏngju 보트 경주/ *a horse ~* kyŏngma 경마/ *a Marathon ~* marat'on kyŏngju 마라톤 경주/ *the yellow ~* hwangsaek injong 황색 인종/ *the Korean ~* Han-guk minjok 한국 민족/ *~ prejudice* injongjŏk p'yŏn-gyŏn 인종적 편견/ *Don't ~ your engine.* Enjinŭl hŏttolge haji mashio. 엔진을 헛돌게 하지 마시오.

racing *n.* kyŏngju 경주, (*horse* ~) kyŏngma 경마. *automobile* ~ chadongch'a kyŏngju 자동차 경주/ *horse* ~ kyŏngma 경마.

rack *n.* (*shelves*) shirŏng 시렁, sŏnban 선반, (*hanger*) kŏri 걸이. *Don't put it on the* ~. Kŭgŏsŭl sŏnbane tuji mashio. 그것을 선반에 두지 마시오/ *a hat*~ mojagŏri 모자걸이.

radar *n.* chŏnp'a t'amjigi 전파 탐지기, reida 레이다, ~ *installation* reida changch'i 레이다 장치.

radiant *adj.* (*shining*) pinnanŭn 빛나는, (*luminous*) palgŭn 밝은. *the* ~ *sun* ch'allanhan t'aeyang 찬란한 태양/ *a* ~ *face* palgŭn p'yojŏng 밝은 표정.

radiation *n.* (*radiated rays*) pangsasŏn 방사선. ~ *chemistry* pangsasŏn hwahak 방사선 화학/ ~ *therapy* pangsasŏn yopŏp 방사선 요법.

radiator *n.* (*for heat*) naenggakki 냉각기, radieit'ŏ 라디에이터. *This car has a fan-cooled* ~. I ch'a-enŭn songp'ungshik naenggakkiga tallyŏ issŭmnida. 이 차에는 송풍식 냉각기가 달려 있읍니다.

radical *adj.* (*basic*) kich'ojŏgin 기초적인, (*extreme*) kŭpchinjŏgin 급진적인. *a* ~ *principle* kich'o wŏlli 기초 원리/ ~ *ideas* kŭpchin sasang 급진 사상/*a* ~ *element* kŭpchin punja 급진 분자.

radio *n.* radio 라디오. *a portable* ~ hyudaeyong radio 휴대용 라디오/ *listen to* ~ radiorŭl tŭtta 라디오를 듣다/ *put on*[*off*] *the* ~ radiorŭl k'yŏda[kkŭda] 라디오를 켜다[끄다]/ *I heard it over the* ~. Radio-esŏ tŭrŏssŭmnida. 라디오에서 들었읍니다/ *Shall I turn on the* ~? Radiorŭl t'ŭlkkayo? 라디오를 틀까요/ *I studied English by* ~. Radioro yŏngŏ kongburŭl haessŭmnida. 라디오로 영어 공부를 했읍니다/ ~ *announcer* radio ŏnaunsŏ 라디오 어나운서/ ~ *station* musŏn chŏnshin-guk 무선 전신국.

radioactivity *n.* pangsanŭng 방사능.

radiogram *n.* musŏn chŏnbo 무선 전보.

radish *n.* muu 무우. *pickled* ~ muugimch'i 무우김치/ *dried* ~ *slice* muumallaengi 무우말랭이/ ~ *shreds* muuch'ae 무우채.

raft *n.* tt'enmok 뗏목.

rag *n.* (*tatter*) nŏngma 넝마, nudŏgi 누더기, (*newspapers*) shinmunji 신문지. *My coat was worn to* ~s. K'ot'ŭga nalgasŏ nudŏgiga toeŏssŭmnida. 코트가 낡아서 누더기 가 되었읍니다/ *Why do you read that worthless* ~? Muŏt ttaemune kŭrŏn ssŭlmo ŏmnŭn shinmunŭl po-shimnikka? 무엇 때문에 그런 쓸모 없는 신문을 보십니까?

rage *n.* (*fury*) kyŏngno 격노, (*vehement desire*) yŏlmang 열망, (*great fashion*) taeyuhaeng 대유행. —*vi.,vt.* (*rave*) sanapke nalttwida 사납게 날뛰다, (*scold*) yadanch'ida 야단치다, (*prevail*) yuhaenghada 유행하다. *in a* ~ hwat-kime 홧김에/ *It is now all the* ~ *in Korea.* Kŭgŏsŭn chigŭm Han-gugesŏ taeyuhaengimnida. 그것은 지금 한국 에서 대유행입니다/ *The storm* ~d *all day.* P'okp'ung-uga haru chongil sanapke purŏssŭmnida. 폭풍우가 하루 종일 사납게 불었읍니다.

raid *n.* (*sudden attack*) sŭpkyŏk 습격, kisŭp 기습, (*police*) kŏmgŏ 검거. —*vi., vt.* (*attack*) sŭpkyŏk'ada 습격하다, (*police*) tŏpch'ida 덮치다. *an air* ~ kongsŭp 공습.

rail *n.* (*railway*) reil 레일, ch'ŏlto 철도, (*hand*~) nan-gan 난간, (*fence*) ult'ari 울타리. *The train went off the* ~s. Kich'aga t'alsŏnhayŏssŭmnida. 기차가 탈선하였 읍니다/ *wooden* ~s namu ult'ari 나무 울타리/ *metal* ~s soebuch'i nan-gan 쇠붙이 난간.

railing *n.* nan-gan 난간.

railroad *n.* (*Am.*) ch'ŏlto 철도. *a* ~ *company* ch'ŏlto hoesa 철도 회사/ *a* ~ *accident* ch'ŏlto sago 철도 사고/*the Office of R*~s ch'ŏltoch'ŏng 철도청.

railway *n.* (*Brit.*) ch'ŏlto 철도.. *a* ~ *employee* ch'ŏlto chongŏbwŏn 철도 종업원/ *an electric* ~ chŏnch'ŏl 전철 (電鐵)/ ~ *fares* ch'ŏlto yogŭm 철도 요금/ *a scenic* ~ kwan-gwang ch'ŏlto 관광 철도/ *a* ~ *station* kich'ayŏk 기 차역/ *underground* ~ (*Am.*) chihach'ŏl 지하철/ *Where is the* ~ *station?* Kich'ayŏgŭn ŏdi issŭmnikka? 기차역 은 어디 있읍니까/ *Take me to the* ~ *station.* Kich'ayŏ-gŭro narŭl teryŏda chushipshio. 기차역으로 나를 데려다 주

십시오.

rain n. pi 비. —vi.,vt. piga oda 비가 오다, pirŭl naerida
비를 내리다. *a fine* ～ isŭlbi 이슬비/ *a heavy* ～ p'ogu
폭우/ *the* ～s changmach'ŏl 장마철/ *We shall have* ～.
Piga ol kŏshimnida. 비가 올 것입니다/ *Looks like* ～,
doesn't it? Piga ol kŏt katchiyo? 비가 올 것 같지요/
We have been having a lot of ～ *lately, haven't we?*
Yojŭm yŏn-gŏp'u manŭn piga ogo itkunyo. 요즘 연거푸
많은 비가 오고 있군요/ *Do you think it will* ～ *tomorrow?* Naeil piga ogessŭmnikka? 내일 비가 오겠읍니까/
I wonder if it's going to ～ *tomorrow.* Naeirŭn piga
ol kŏt katchi anssŭmnida. 내일은 비가 올 것 같지 않습
니다.

rainbow n. mujigae 무지개.

raincoat n. reink'ot'ŭ 레인코트, piot 비옷.

raindrop n. pitpangul 빗방울, naksutmul 낙수물.

rainstorm n. p'okp'ungu 폭풍우.

rainy adj. piga onŭn 비가 오는. *a* ～ *day* pionŭn nal 비오는
날/ *the* ～ *season* changmach'ŏl 장마철/ *for the* ～ *day*
manirŭl wihayŏ 만일을 위하여/ *You must save money
for a* ～ *day.* Manirŭi kyŏngue taebihayŏ tonŭl chŏch'uk'aeya hamnida. 만일의 경우에 대비하여 돈을 저축해
야 합니다.

raise vt. (*move upward*) ollida 올리다, (*hoist*) tŭlda 들
다, (*breed*) kirŭda 기르다, (*grow*) chaebaehada 재배하
다, (*collect*) moŭda 모으다. *We* ～d *the boy in our
arms.* Kŭ airŭl tu p'allo ana ollyŏssŭmnida. 그 아이를
두 팔로 안아 올렸읍니다/ *My uncle* ～s *chickens, hogs
and cattle.* Uri ajŏssinŭn takkwa twaejiwa sorŭl
kirŭmnida. 우리 아저씨는 닭과 돼지와 소를 기릅니다.

raisin n. kŏnp'odo 건포도.

rake n. (*tool*) kalk'wi 갈퀴.

ramble vi. (*roam*) ŏsŭllŏngŏsŭllŏng kŏnilda 어슬렁어슬렁
거닐다. *I'm fond of rambling among the trees.* Sup'ul
sairŭl kŏnilgi choahamnida. 수풀 사이를 거닐기 좋아합
니다.   「esŏ salda 농장에서 살다.

ranch n. (*farm*) nongjang 농장. *live on the* ～ nongjang-

random *adj.* *at* ~ takch'inŭn taero 닥치는 대로/ *He fired a shot at* ~. Kŭ saramŭn takch'inŭn taero magu ssoassŭmnida. 그 사람은 닥치는 대로 마구 쏘았읍니다.

rank *n.* (*row*) chul 줄, (*station*) chiwi 지위, kyegŭp 계급. *front* ~ apchul 앞줄/ *rear* ~ twitchul 뒷줄/ *first* ~ ilgŭp 1급/ *man of high* ~ kowich'ŭngŭi saram 고위층의 사람.

ransom *vt.* (*redeem by paying*) momkapsŭl patko sŏkpanghada 몸값을 받고 석방하다. ~ *a kidnapped diplomat* napch'idoen oegyogwanŭl sŏkpanghada 납치된 외교관을 석방하다.

rap *vt., vi.* ttokttok tudŭrida 똑똑 두드리다. —*n.*(*knocking sound*) tudŭlginŭn sori 두들기는 소리. *I heard a* ~ *on the door*. Mun tudŭrinŭn sorirŭl tŭrŏssŭmnida. 문 두드리는 소리를 들었읍니다. 「kangganhada 강간하다.

rape *vt.* (*take by force*) kangt'arhada 강탈하다, (*violate*)

rapid *adj.* (*quick*) pparŭn 빠른, (*steep*) kap'arŭn 가파른. —*n.*(*pl.*) (*swift current*) kŭmnyu 급류. *a* ~ *train* pparŭn yŏlch'a 빠른 열차/ *a* ~ *journey* kŭp'an yŏhaeng

rapidly *adv.* ppalli 빨리. 「급한 여행.

rare *adj.* (*scarce*) tŭmun 드문, chin-gwihan 진귀한, (*thin*) hŭibak'an 희박한, (*underdone*) sŏrigŭn 설익은. *a* ~ *book* chin-gwihan ch'aek 진귀한 책/ *I would like it* ~, *please*. Naegŏsŭn saltchak ik'yŏ chuseyo. 내것은 살짝 익혀 주세요/ *I ordered mine* ~. Saltchak ik'in kŏsŭl chumunhaessŏyo. 살짝 익힌 것을 주문했어요.

rarely *adv.* (*seldom*) chomch'ŏrŏm ...ant'a 좀처럼 ...않다. *I* ~ *meet him*. Nanŭn chomch'ŏrŏm kŭ saramŭl mannaji mot'amnida. 나는 좀처럼 그 사람을 만나지 못합니다.

rascal *n.* (*rogue*) ak'an 악한, purhandang 불한당, (*to inferior*) *You little* ~! Yo kkoma nyŏsŏk! 요 꼬마 녀석/ *What an impudent* ~! I purhandang kat'ŭn nom! 이 불한당 같은 놈!

raspberry *n.* (*fruit*) namuttalgi 나무딸기.

rat *n.* chwi 쥐. ~*trap* chwidŏt 쥐덫/ *catch a* ~ *by the trap* tŏch'ŭro chwirŭl chapta 덫으로 쥐를 잡다.

rate *n.* (*ratio*) piyul 비율, (*price*) shise 시세, (*charge*) yogŭm 요금. *competitive* ∼ kyŏngjaengnyul 경쟁율/ *fertility* ∼ ch'ulsannyul 출산율/ *mortality* ∼ samangnyul 사망율/ *What is the present* ∼ *of exchange?* Hyŏnjae hwanyurŭn ŏlmaimnikka? 현재 환율은 얼마입니까/ *What are the* ∼*s?* Yogŭmi ŏlmajiyo? 요금이 얼마지요/ *Would you show me a list of your* ∼*s?* Yogŭmp'yorŭl poyŏ chushio. 요금표를 보여 주시오/*at any* ∼ ŏtchaettŭn 어쨌든, amut'ŭn 아뭏든/ *Well, at any* ∼, *I will wait for you till noon.* Amut'ŭn chŏngokkaji kidarigessŭmnida. 아뭏든 정오까지 기다리겠읍니다.

rather *adv.* (*preferably*) ohiryŏ 오히려, ch'arari 차라리, (*somewhat*) taso 다소, kkwae 꽤, (*sure*) kŭrŏk'omalgo 그렇고말고. *I would* ∼ *you come tomorrow than today.* Onŭlboda ohiryŏ naeil wa chuŏssŭmyŏn chok'esso. 오늘보다 오히려 내일 와 주었으면 좋겠소/ *I* ∼ *think you may be mistaken.* Tangshini chalmot saenggak'ago innŭn kŏt kassŭmnida. 당신이 잘못 생각하고 있는 것 같습니다/ *Do you like this? R*∼. Igŏsŭl choahashimnikka? Choahadamadayo. 이것을 좋아하십니까? 좋아하다마다요.

ration *n.* (*mil.*) harubunŭi shingnyang 하루분의 식량. ∼ *bread* kunyong ppang 군용 빵/ ∼ *food* kunyong shikp'um 군용 식품.

rational *adj.* isŏngi innŭn 이성(理性)이 있는, (*reasonable*) hamnijŏgin 합리적인. *a* ∼ *man* torirŭl anŭn saram 도리를 아는 사람/ ∼ *conduct* hamnijŏgin haengwi 합리적인 행위.

rattle *vi.,vt.* tŏlgŏktŏlgŏk sorinada 덜걱덜걱 소리나다. —*n.* tŏlgŏktŏlgŏk'anŭn sori 덜걱덜걱하는 소리. *The windows were rattling in the wind.* Ch'angmuni parame tŏlgŏkkŏrigo issŏssŭmnida. 창문이 바람에 덜걱거리고 있었읍니다/ *The old bus* ∼*d along over the stony road.* Nalgŭn pŏsŭnŭn tolkirŭl tŏlgŏdŏkkŏrimyŏ tallyŏssŭmnida. 낡은 버스는 돌길을 덜거덕거리며 달렸읍니다.

rattrap *n.* chwidŏt 쥐덫, nan-guk 난국.

ravage *n.* (*destruction*) p'agoe 파괴, (*devastation*) hwangp'ye 황폐, (*damage*) sonhae 손해. *blood* ∼ suhae 수해.

rave *vi.,vt.* (*talk wildly*) hŏtsorihada 헛소리하다, (*talk* *enthusiastically*) chŏngshinŏpshi chikkŏrida 정신없이 지껄이다. *You're raving mad !* Chŏngshin nagatkunyo ! 정신 나갔군요 !

raven *n.* (*bird*) kalgamagwi 갈가마귀. *R~s croak.* Kalgamagwiga umnida. 갈가마귀가 웁니다.

raw *adj.* (*uncooked*) nalgŏsŭi 날것의, (*rare*) sŏrigŭn 설익은, (*unexperienced*) misuk'an 미숙한. ~ *materials* wŏllyo 원료/ ~ *meat* nalkogi 날고기/ *Would you like to eat ~ fish ?* Hoerŭl chapsushigessŭmnikka ? 회를 잡수 시겠읍니까/ *I've heard that you eat ~ fish in Korea.* Han-gugesŏnŭn saengsŏnŭl nallo mŏngnŭndago hadŏgunyo. 한국에서는 생선을 날로 먹는다고 하더군요.

rawhide *n.* saenggajuk 생가죽. ~ *boots* saenggajuk kudu 생가죽 구두/*a ~ whip* saenggajuk hoech'ori 생가죽 회초리.

ray *n.* kwangsŏn 광선, (*light*) pit 빛. *the ~s of the sun* t'aeyang kwangsŏn 태양 광선/*the ~ of the moon* talpit 달빛/ *an X-~ photograph* eksŭrei sajin 엑스레이 사진.

razor *n.* myŏndok'al 면도칼. *a safety ~* anjŏn myŏndok'al 안전 면도칼/ *Don't use the ~ against the grain.* Myŏndojirŭl kŏkkuro haji mashipshio. 면도질을 거꾸로 하지 마 십시오.

reach *vt., vi.* (*get to*) toch'ak'ada 도착하다, (*extend*) irŭda 이르다, (*stretch out*) ppŏtta 뻗다, (*hand over*) kŏnne chuda 건네 주다, (*communicate with*) yŏllak'ada 연락하다. *Your letter ~ed me today.* Tangshin p'yŏnjiga onŭl toch'ak'aessŭmnida. 당신 편지가 오늘 도착했읍니다/ *My land ~es as far as the river.* Nae ttangŭn kangkkaji ppŏch'yŏ issŭmnida. 내 땅은 강(江)까지 뻗쳐 있읍 니다/ *Reach me the pen.* Kŭ p'enŭl chibŏ chushio. 그 펜을 집어 주시오/ *Where can I ~ you?* Ŏdida yŏllagŭl halkkayo ? 어디다 연락을 할까요/ *You can ~ me at 435-5510.* Sasamo ooilgongŭro kŏshimyŏn toemnida. 435-5510으로 거시면 됩니다.

react *vi.* (*act in response*) panŭnghada 반응하다, (*act in return*) panjagyŏnghada 반작용하다, (*act in opposition*) pandaehada 반대하다. *How did he ~ when he heard the news ?* Kŭ soshigŭl tŭtko kŭ saramŭn ŏttŏk'e naoptikka? 그 소식을 듣고 그 사람은 어떻게 나옵디까?

reaction *n.* (*against*) pandong 반동, (*response*) panŭng 반응, (*influence*) yŏnghyang 영향. *What was his ~ to your proposal?* Tangshinŭi cheŭie taehae kŭ saramŭi panŭngŭn ŏttŏhaessŭmnikka? 당신의 제의에 대해 그 사람의 반응은 어떠했읍니까?

reactionary *adj.* pandongjŏgin 반동적인. —*n.* (~ *statesman*) pandong chŏngch'iga 반동 정치가.

reactor *n.* (*nuclear* ~) wŏnjaro 원자로.

read *vt.* ikta 읽다, (*indicate*) p'yoshihada 표시하다, (~ *like*) ...wa kach'i ssŭiŏ itta …와 같이 쓰어 있다. *Can you ~ Chinese characters?* Hancharŭl ilgŭl chul ashimnikka? 한자를 읽을 줄 아십니까/*Can the child ~ the clock yet?* Aiga pŏlssŏ shigyerŭl pol chul amnikka? 아이가 벌써 시계를 볼 줄 압니까/ *What does the thermometer ~?* Ondogyenŭn myŏt toimnikka? 온도계는 몇 도입니까/ *It ~s as follows.* Taŭmgwa kach'i ssŭiŏ issŭmnida. 다음과 같이 쓰어 있읍니다.

reader *n.* (*person*) tokcha 독자, (*book*) tokpon 독본. *the general* ~ ilban tokcha 일반 독자/ *an English* ~ yŏngŏ tokpon 영어 독본/ *a side* ~ pudokpon 부독본/ *proof*~ kyojŏngwŏn 교정원.

reading *n.* toksŏ 독서. ~ *room* tosŏshil 도서실, yŏllamshil 열람실/ *Do you do much* ~? Toksŏ mani hashimnikka? 독서 많이 하십니까?

ready *adj.* (*prepared*) chunbidoen 준비된, (*willing*) kikkŏi ...hanŭn 기꺼이 …하는, (*prompt*) shinsok'an 신속한, (*handy*) kot ssul su innŭn 곧 쓸 수 있는. *Are you* ~? Chunbinŭn toeŏssŭmnikka? 준비는 되었읍니까/ *Let's get* ~ *to get off.* Naeril chunbirŭl hapshida. 내릴 준비를 합시다/ *a* ~ *reply* chŭktap 즉답(即答)/ *Please get your passport and disembarkation card* ~. Yŏkwŏn-gwa ipkuk k'adŭrŭl chunbihae chushipshio. 여권과 입국 카드를 준비해 주십시오.

readymade *adj.* kisŏngp'umŭi 기성품의. *I'd like a* ~ *clothes.* Kisŏngbogŭl sagessŭmnida. 기성복을 사겠읍니다/ ~ *shoes* kisŏnghwa 기성화/ *a* ~ *shop* kisŏngbok

kage 기성복 가게.
real *adj.* (*actual*) shilcheŭi 실제의, (*true*) chŏngmarŭi 정말의, (*genuine*) chintchaŭi 진짜의. *Who is the ~ manager of the business?* Nuga i sangsaŭi chintcha chibaeinimnikka? 누가 이 상사의 진짜 지배인입니까/ *Is this ~ gold?* Igŏsŭn sun-gŭmimnikka? 이것은 순금입니까/ *We had a ~ good time.* Chŏngmal chŭlgŏwŏssŭmnida. 정말 즐거웠읍니다/ ~ *estate* pudongsan 부동산.
realist *n.* hyŏnshilchuŭija 현실주의자.
reality *n.* (*actuality*) hyŏnshil 현실, (*fact*) sashil 사실, (*truth*) chinshil 진실.
realization *n.* shirhyŏn 실현.
realize *vt.* (*make real*) shirhyŏnhada 실현하다, (*understand*) kkaedatta 깨닫다, (*gain*) pŏlda 벌다, (*exchange for cash*) hyŏn-gŭmŭro pakkuda 현금으로 바꾸다. *I never ~d that.* Kŭrŏhan kŏsŭn chŏnhyŏ kkaedatchi mot'aessŭmnida. 그러한 것은 전혀 깨닫지 못했읍니다/ *Does he ~ his error yet?* Kŭ saramŭn chagi chalmosŭl kkaedatko issŭmnikka? 그 사람은 자기 잘못을 깨닫고 있읍니까/ *You had better ~ at once.* Kot tonŭro pakkunŭn kŏshi chok'essŭmnida. 곧 돈으로 바꾸는 것이 좋겠읍니다/ ~ *one's dream* kkumŭl shirhyŏnhada 꿈을 실현하다.
really *adv.* shilchero 실제로, chŏngmallo 정말로. *R~?* Chŏngmarimnikka? 정말입니까/ *Not ~!* Sŏlma! 설마/ *Tell me what you ~ think.* Tangshinŭi chinshimŭl marhae chushio. 당신의 진심을 말해 주시오/ *We ~ wanted you to come.* Chŏngmal oshigirŭl paraessŭmnida. 정말 오시기를 바랬읍니다.
reap *vi., vt.* (*cut*) peŏdŭrida 베어들이다, (*harvest*) suhwak'ada 수확하다. ~ *grain* kokshigŭl kŏduda 곡식을 거두다/ ~ *a field* patkokshigŭl suhwak'ada 밭곡식을 수확하다.
rear *vt.* (*bring up*) kirŭda 기르다, (*breed*) sayuk'ada 사육하다. —*adj.* (*back*) paehuŭi 배후의. —*n.* (*back*) twittchok 뒤쪽, (*army*) hubang pudae 후방 부대. (*Where's toy department?*) *It's on five, ~.* Och'ŭng antchoge issŭmnida. 5층 안쪽에 있읍니다.
reason *n.* (*cause*) iyu 이유, (*rationality*) isŏng 이성(理

性), (*motive*) tonggi 동기. —*vt.*, *vi.* (*draw conclusions*) ch'urihada 추리하다, (*form judgments*) p'andanŭl naerida 판단을 내리다, (*examine critically*) kŏmt'ohada 검토하다. *I don't know the* ~. Nanŭn kŭ iyurŭl morŭmnida. 나는 그 이유를 모릅니다/ *I cannot understand the* ~. Kŭ iyurŭl ihaehal suga ŏpsŭmnida. 그 이유를 이해할 수가 없습니다.

reasonable *adj.* (*sensible*) punbyŏl innŭn 분별 있는, (*fair*) ondanghan 온당한, (*moderate*) kapshi chŏktanghan 값이 적당한. *You must be* ~. Punbyŏri issŏya hamnida. 분별이 있어야 합니다/ ~ *terms* ondanghan chokŏn 온당한 조건/ *The price is quite* ~. Kapsŭn chŏktanghamnida. 값은 적당합니다.

rebel *n.* panyŏkcha 반역자. —*vi.* (*revolt*) pallanŭl irŭk'ida 반란을 일으키다, (*disobey*) kŏyŏk'ada 거역하다.

rebellion *n.* (*revolt*) pallan 반란, (*riot*) p'oktong 폭동. *raise a* ~ pallanŭl irŭk'ida 반란을 일으키다/ *put down a* ~ pallanŭl chinap'ada 반란을 진압하다.

rebuild *vt.* chaegŏnhada 재건하다, (*reconstruct*) kaech'uk'ada 개축하다. *a rebuilt typewriter* chaesaeng t'ajagi 재생 타자기/ ~ *a house* chibŭl kaech'uk'ada 집을 개축하다.

recall *vt.* (*remember*) saenggak'ae naeda 생각해 내다, sanggihada 상기하다. ~ *old faces* yet ŏlguldŭrŭl sanggihada 옛 얼굴들을 상기하다/ *I can't* ~ *the name now.* Tangjang kŭ irŭmi saenggangnaji annŭn-gunyo. 당장 그 이름이 생각나지 않는군요.

receipt *n.* yŏngsujŭng 영수증. *I want a* ~, *please.* Yŏngsujŭngŭl chuseyo. 영수증을 주세요/ *Here's your* ~. Yŏngsujŭng yŏgi issŭmnida. 영수증 여기 있습니다/ *Do you have the* ~? Yŏngsujŭng kajigo kyeshimnikka? 영수증 가지고 계십니까?

receive *vi.*, *vt.* (*accept*) patta 받다, (*admit*) majadŭrida 맞아들이다. *When did you* ~ *the letter?* Ŏnje p'yŏnjirŭl padassŭmnikka? 언제 편지를 받았습니까/ *You'll* ~ *a warm welcome when you come to Korea.* Han-guge oshimyŏn ttattŭt'an hwanyŏngŭl padŭl kŏshimnida. 한국

에 오시면 따뜻한 환영을 받을 것입니다.

receiver *n.* (*person*) such'wiin 수취인, (*instrument*)
(*telephone*) suhwagi 수화기, (*radio, etc.*) sushin-gi 수신
기. *I picked up the ~ and answered instantly.* Nanŭn
suhwagirŭl tŭrŏ ollija chŭksŏgesŏ taedap'aessŭmnida.
나는 수화기를 들어 올리자 즉석에서 대답했읍니다/ *a radio ~*
radio sushin-gi 라디오 수신기.

recent *adj.* (*late*) ch'oegŭnŭi 최근의, (*new*) saeroun 새
로운. *a ~ event* ch'oegŭnŭi sakŏn 최근의 사건/ *~ news*
ch'oegŭn soshik 최근 소식.

recently *adv.* (*lately*) ch'oegŭne 최근에. *This book was
issued ~.* I ch'aegŭn ch'oegŭne ch'ulp'andoeŏssŭmni-
da. 이 책은 최근에 출판되었읍니다.

reception *n.* (*welcoming*) hwanyŏng 환영, (*entertainment*)
hwanyŏnghoe 환영회, p'at'i 파티. *a farewell ~* songbyŏryŏn 송별연/ *a wedding ~* kyŏrhon p'iroyŏn 결혼 피
로연/ *a welcome ~* hwanyŏnghoe 환영회/ *hold a ~*
hwanyŏnghoerŭl yŏlda 환영회를 열다/ *~ day* myŏnhoeil
면회일/ *~ room* ŭngjŏpshil 응접실.

recess *n.* (*repose*) hyushik 휴식, (*vacation*) hyuga 휴가,
(*pl.*) (*quiet nook*) kipsuk'an kot 깊숙한 곳. *a ten
minutes' ~* shippun-gan hyushik 10분간 휴식/ *the Christmas holiday ~* K'ŭrisŭmasŭ hyuga 크리스마스 휴가.

recipe *n.* (*prescription*) ch'ŏbang 처방, (*receipt*) yoripŏp
요리법. *May I borrow your ~ book?* Yorich'aek chom
pillyŏ chushigessŭmnikka? 요리책 좀 빌려 주시겠읍니까?

recipient *n.* pannŭn saram 받는 사람, suryŏngja 수령자.

reciprocal *adj.* (*mutual*) sŏroŭi 서로의, (*done in return*)
podabŭi 보답의. *~ visits* sangho pangmun 상호 방문/ *a
~ gift* tamnye sŏnmul 답례 선물.

reciprocate *vt.* (*interchange*) chugobatta 주고받다, (*return*) podap'ada 보답하다. *~ favors* sŏro houirŭl pe-
p'ulda 서로 호의를 베풀다/ *I ~ your good wishes.* Ho-
ŭie taehae kamsahamnida. 호의에 대해 감사합니다.

recital *n.* (*musical performance*) tokch'anghoe 독창회.
a piano ~ p'iano tokchuhoe 피아노 독주회/ *a ~ of songs*
kagok tokch'anghoe 가곡 독창회.

recite *vt.* (*read aloud*) nangsonghada 낭송하다, (*narrate*) iyagihada 이야기하다. ~ *a poem* shirŭl nangsonghada 시를 낭송하다/ ~ *one's adventures* mohŏmdamŭl hada 모험담을 하다.

reckless *adj.* punbyŏrŏmnŭn 분별없는, mumohan 무모한. ~ *driving* mumohan unjŏn 무모한 운전/ ~ *expenditure* mumohan chich'ul 무모한 지출.

reckon *vi.*, *vt.* (*count*) kyesanhada 계산하다, (*suppose*) ...irago saenggak'ada ···이라고 생각하다, (*depend on*) kidaehada 기대하다. *I* ~ *50 of them.* Kyesanhae poni oshibi toemnida. 계산해 보니 50이 됩니다/ *I* ~ *that he will come.* Kŭ saramŭn ol kŏshimnida. 그 사람은 올 것 입니다/ *I* ~ *on your help.* Tangshinŭi toumŭl kidaehamnida. 당신의 도움을 기대합니다.

reclaim *vt.* (*make cultivable*) kaeganhada 개간하다, (*reform*) kyohwahada 교화(敎化)하다. ~*ed land* maech'ukchi 매축지/ ~ *a criminal* choesurŭl kyodohada 죄수를 교도하다.

recline *vi.*, *vt.* (*lean against*) kidaege hada 기대게 하다, (*lie down*) tŭrŏnupta 드러눕다, (*rely*) ŭijihada 의지하다. ~ *on a couch* sop'a-e kidaeda 소파에 기대다/ ~ *against the wall* pyŏge kidaeda 벽에 기대다/ *He* ~*d on a rug.* Kŭ saramŭn yungdan wie tŭrŏnuwŏssŭmnida. 그 사람은 융단 위에 드러누웠읍니다.

recognition *n.* (*recognizing*) injŏng 인정, (*acceptance*) sŭngin 승인, (*notice*) arabogi 알아보기. *win public* ~ ilbanege injŏngŭl patta 일반에게 인정을 받다/*the* ~ *of a new government* sae chŏngbuŭi sŭngin 새 정부의 승인/ *official* ~ kongin 공인(公認).

recognize *vt.* (*know again*) araboda 알아보다, (*acknowledge*) injŏnghada 인정하다, (*appreciate*) ch'ihahada 치하하다. *Pardon me, but I couldn't* ~ *you.* Araboji mot'ae choesonghamnida. 알아보지 못해 죄송합니다.

recollect *vi.*, *vt.* (*remember*) hoesanghada 회상하다, saenggak'ae naeda 생각해 내다. *I cannot* ~ *who he is.* Chŏ puni nuguinji saenggagi an namnida. 저분이 누구인지 생각이 안 납니다.

recollection *n.* (*remembrance*) hoesang 회상, (*reminiscence*) ch'uŏk 추억. *I may have said so, but I have no ~ of it.* Kŭwa kach'i marhaennŭnjinŭn morŭna kiŏgi ŏpsŭmnida. 그와 같이 말했는지는 모르나 기억이 없습니다.

recommend *vt.* (*speak favorably of*) ch'uch'ŏnhada 추천하다, (*advise*) kwŏn-gohada 권고하다. *Will you please ~ me a good hotel?* Choŭn hot'erŭl sogaehae chushiji ank'essŭmnikka? 좋은 호텔을 소개해 주시지 않겠습니까/ *Whom do you ~?* Ŏnŭ punŭl ch'uch'ŏnhashiryŏmnikka? 어느 분을 추천하시렵니까/ *Can you ~ a doctor?* Ŭisa sŏnsaengnimŭl sogaehae chushigessŭmnikka? 의사 선생님을 소개해 주시겠습니까/ *What do you ~?* Muŏshi choŭlkkayo? 무엇이 좋을까요?

recommendation *n.* ch'uch'ŏn 추천. *a letter of*~ ch'uch'ŏnchang 추천장/ *Have you any further ~?* Kŭ pakke kwŏn-gohae chushil chŏmŭn ŏpsŭmnikka? 그 밖에 권고해 주실 점은 없습니까?

recompense *n.* (*requital*) podap 보답, (*reward*) posu 보수, (*amends*) posang 보상. *work without ~* posu ŏpshi irhada 보수 없이 일하다/ *I cannot cancel the contract without some ~.* Ŏlmaganŭi posang ŏpshinŭn kŭ kyeyagŭl ch'wisohal su ŏpsŭmnida. 얼마간의 보상 없이는 그 계약을 취소할 수 없습니다.

reconcile *vt.* (*make friends again*) hwahaehada 화해하다. (*adjust*) chojŏnghada 조정하다. *We became ~d.* Urinŭn hwahaehaessŭmnida. 우리는 화해했습니다/ *He refused to become ~d with his brother.* Kŭ saramŭn chagi auwa hwahaehagirŭl kŏbuhaessŭmnida. 그 사람은 자기 아우와 화해하기를 거부했습니다.

reconciliation *n.* (*reconciling*) hwahae 화해.

reconsider *vt.* chaegohada 재고하다. *I would advise you to ~ your intended resignation.* Sajigŭi ttŭsŭn chaegohae poshipshio. 사직의 뜻은 재고해 보십시오.

record *n.* (*written note*) kirok 기록, (*career*) kyŏngnyŏk 경력, (*in competition*) kirok 기록, (*disk*) ŭmban 음반. *family ~* chokpo 족보/*school ~s* hakkyo sŏngjŏk 학교 성적/ *hold the world's ~* segye kirogŭl poyuhada 세계

기록을 보유하다/ *set up a new ~* shin-girogŭl seuda 신기록을 세우다/ *Where can I see my academic ~s?* Ŏdisŏ nae sŏngjŏgŭl pol su issŭmnikka? 어디서 내 성적을 볼 수 있읍니까/ *I want a ~ of Korean folk songs.* Hanguk minyo rek'odŭrŭl sago shipsŭmnida. 한국 민요 레코드를 사고 싶습니다/ *Where's the ~ section?* Rek'odŭ p'anŭn kosŭn ŏdijiyo? 레코드 파는 곳은 어디지요?

recorder *n.* nogŭmgi 녹음기, tŭngnokcha 등록자.

recover *vt., vi. (regain)* hoebok'ada 회복하다, *(make up for)* poch'unghada 보충하다. *Has your wife quite ~ed?* Puinŭn wanjŏnhi hoebok'asyŏssŭmnikka? 부인은 완전히 회복하셨읍니까/ *How long will I take to ~?* Hoebok'ajamyŏn ŏlmana kŏllilkkayo? 회복하자면 얼마나 걸릴까요/ *I hope you will soon ~.* Kot hoeboktoeshirira missŭmnida. 곧 회복되시리라 믿습니다/ *We soon ~ed lost time.* Hŏbidoen shiganŭl inae poch'unghaessŭmnida. 허비된 시간을 이내 보충했읍니다.

recreation *n. (amusement)* orak 오락, rek'ŭrieisyŏn 레크리에이션, *(refreshment)* wŏn-gi hoebok 원기 회복, hyuyang 휴양. *What kind of ~ do you like?* Ŏttŏn oragŭl choahashimnikka? 어떤 오락을 좋아하십니까/ *We often go to the department store for ~.* Chongjong nollŏ paek'wajŏme kamnida. 종종 놀러 백화점에 갑니다.

recruit *n.* shinbyŏng 신병. *—vt., vi (enlist)* chingjip'ada 징집하다, *(recover)* poch'unghada 보충하다.

rectify *vt. (correct)* sujŏnghada 수정하다, *(adjust)* chojŏnghada 조정하다, *(refine)* chŏngnyuhada 정류하다. *~ mistake* chalmosŭl koch'ida 잘못을 고치다/ *rectified alcohol* chŭngnyudoen alk'ol 증류된 알콜.

rector *n. (clergyman)* moksa 목사, *(of school)* kyojang 교장, *(of college)* hakchang 학장.

red *adj. (color)* ppalgan 빨간, *(communistic)* kongsanjuŭiŭi 공산주의의. *—n. (color)* ppalgang 빨강, *(communist)* kongsanjuŭija 공산주의자, ppalgaengi 빨갱이. *~ wine* ppalgan p'odoju 빨간 포도주/R~ *China* Chunggong 중공/ *the R~ Army* pulgŭn kundae 붉은 군대, kongsan-gun 공산군/ R~ *Cross* chŏkshipcha 적십자/ *the R~ Sea*

honghae 홍해/ *Tell me how you like me in* ∼? Ppalgan
osŭl ibŭn naega ŏttŏssŭmnikka? 빨간 옷을 입은 내가 어
떻습니까?

reduce *vt.* (*bring down*) churida 줄이다, (*cut down*)
ch'uksohada 축소하다, (*subdue*) chŏngbok'ada 정복하다.
If you ∼ *the price, I'll buy it.* Kapsŭl chom kkakka
chumyŏn sagessŭmnida. 값을 좀 깎아 주면 사겠읍니다/
∼ *one's expenses* kyŏngbirŭl churida 경비를 줄이다/
∼ *speed* songnyŏgŭl churida 속력을 줄이다.

reduction *n.* (*discount*) harin 할인, (*reducing*) ch'ukso
축소. *Do you give a* ∼ *for a month's stay?* Han tal
tusuk'amyŏn harinhae chumnikka? 한 달 투숙하면 할
인해 줍니까/ *You will have a* ∼ *for cash.* Hyŏn-gŭm
naeshimyŏn harinhae tŭrimnida. 현금 내시면 할인해 드립
니다/ *What* ∼ *can you make?* Ŏlmana harinhamnikka?
얼마나 할인합니까/ *We will· give you a special* ∼ *of
five percent.* O p'ŏsent'ŭ t'ŭkpyŏl harinhae tŭrigessŭmnida. 5% 특별 할인해 드리겠읍니다/ *arms* ∼ kunbi
ch'ukso 군비 축소/ *a personnel* ∼ kamwŏn 감원.

reed *n.* kaltae 갈대.

reel *n.* (*spool*) ŏlle 얼레, shilgamkae 실감개. *news* ∼
nyusŭ yŏnghwa 뉴스 영화.

refer *vi., vt.* (*make reference*) ŏn-gŭp'ada 언급하다,
ch'amgohada 참고하다, (*quote*) inyonghada 인용하다.
R∼ *to your dictionary as often as you can.* Toedorok
sajŏnul ch'ajabodorok hashio. 되도록 사전을 찾아보도록 하
시오/ *Don't* ∼ *to this matter again, please.* Chebal i
munjenŭn chaeronhaji mashio. 제발 이 문제는 재론하지 마
시오/*Does that remark* ∼ *to me?* Narŭl tugo hashinŭn
malssŭmimnikka? 나를 두고 하시는 말씀입니까?

reference *n.* (*consulting*) ch'amgo 참고, (*inquiry*) cho-
hoe 조회, (*mention*) ŏngŭp 언급, (*testimonial*) chŭngmyŏngsŏ 증명서, (*surety*) shinwŏn pojŭngin 신원 보증인.
∼ *book* ch'amgosŏ 참고서/ *You should make* ∼ *to a
dictionary.* Sajŏnŭl ch'aja boaya hamnida. 사전을 찾아보
아야 합니다/ *Who are your* ∼*s?* Pojŭnginŭn nuguimnikka? 보증인은 누구입니까?

refine *vt., vi.* (*make pure*) chŏngjehada 정제하다. ~ *oil* chŏngyuhada 정유(精油)하다.

refined *adj.* (*purified*) chŏngjehan 정제한, (*elegant*) p'umwi innŭn 품위 있는. ~ *oil* chŏngyu 정유/ *a* ~ *gentleman* p'umwi innŭn shinsa 품위 있는 신사.

refinery *n. oil* ~ chŏngyu kongjang 정유 공장.

reflect *vt.* (*throw back*) pansahada 반사하다, (*mirror*) pich'uda 비추다, (*express*) nat'anaeda 나타내다, (*think*) kip'i saenggak'ada 깊이 생각하다. *Look at trees ~ed in the lake.* Hosue pich'in namudŭrŭl poshio. 호수에 비친 나무들을 보시오/ *I want time to* ~. Saenggak'al shiganŭl chushipshio. 생각할 시간을 주십시오/ *R~ upon all I have said to you.* Chigŭm naega han marŭl saenggak'ae poshio. 지금 내가 한 말을 생각해 보시오.

reform *vt., vi.* (*amend*) kaeryanghada 개량하다, (*renovate*) hyŏkshinhada 혁신하다. —*n.* (*improvement*) kaeryang 개량, (*amendment*) kaeshim 개심(改心). ~ *a system of education* kyoyuk chedorŭl kaehyŏk'ada 교육 제도를 개혁하다/ *a land* ~ t'oji kaehyŏk 토지 개혁.

refrain *vi.* (*abstain*) samgada 삼가다, (*forbear*) ch'amta 참다. *Please* ~ *from spitting in public places.* Konggong changso-esŏ ch'imbaennŭn irŭn samgashio. 공공 장소에서 침뱉는 일은 삼가시오/ *Please* ~ *from smoking.* Tambaerŭl chom samgashipshio. 담배를 좀 삼가십시오/ *I couldn't* ~ *from laughing.* Nanŭn usŭmŭl ch'amŭl suga ŏpsŏssŭmnida. 나는 웃음을 참을 수가 없었읍니다.

refreshment *n.* (*light meal*) kandanhan shiksa 간단한 식사, tagwa 다과(茶菓). *We were entertained with* ~*s.* Tagwa taejŏbŭl padassŭmnida. 다과 대접을 받았읍니다/ ~ *car* shikdangch'a 식당차.

refrigerator *n.* naengjanggo 냉장고. 「난처.

refuge *n.* (*shelter*) p'inan 피난, (*asylum*) p'inanch'ŏ 피

refugee *n.* p'inanmin 피난민. ~ *camps* nanmin suyongso 난민 수용소/ *a political* ~ mangmyŏngja 망명자.

refund *n.* panhwan 반환. —*vt.* panhwanhada 반환하다. *I want to cancel my tour. Can I get a* ~? Yŏhaengŭl ch'wisohago shipsŭmnida. Panhwanhae chushigessŭmnikka? 여행을 취소하고 싶습니다. 반환해 주시겠읍니까?

refusal *n.* (*denial*) kŏjŏl 거절, kŏbu 거부.

refuse *vi., vt.* kŏjŏrhada 거절하다, kŏbuhada 거부하다. *We were modestly ~d.* Urinŭn pogi chok'e kŏjŏldanghaessŭmnida. 우리는 보기 좋게 거절당했읍니다/ *~a request* put'agŭl kŏjŏrhada 부탁을 거절하다.

regard *vt.* (*consider*) ...rago saenggak'ada …라고 생각하다, (*respect*) chonjunghada 존중하다, (*gaze at*) ŭngshihada 응시하다, (*heed*) chuŭihada 주의하다. —*n.* (*pl.*) anbu 안부, munan 문안. *I ~ him as a friend.* Kŭ saramŭl ch'in-guro saenggak'amnida 그 사람을 친구로 생각합니다/ *My best ~s to your wife.* Puinkke anbu chŏnhashio. 부인께 안부 전하시오.

regarding *prep.* ...e kwanhayŏ …에 관하여. *I know nothing ~ the matter.* Kŭ ire kwanhaesŏnŭn amugŏtto morŭmnida. 그 일에 관해서는 아무것도 모릅니다.

regardless *adj.* (*heedless*) kwanshimi ŏmnŭn 관심이 없는, (*ignoring*) mushihanŭn 무시하는. *~ of* kwan-gye ŏpshi 관계 없이/ *I shall go ~ of the weather.* Nalssie kwan-gye ŏpshi kagessŭmnida. 날씨에 관계 없이 가겠읍니다.

regime *n.* (*political system*) chŏngch'e 정체(政體), (*institution*) chedo 제도. *puppet ~* koeroe chŏngkwŏn 괴뢰 정권.

regiment *n.* (*mil.*) yŏndae 연대. *a ~ of foot* pobyŏng yŏndae 보병 연대.

region *n.* (*area*) chiyŏk 지역, (*belt*) chidae 지대. *an oil ~* yujŏn chidae 유전(油田) 지대/ *a troubled ~* punjaeng chiyŏk 분쟁 지역.

register *vt.* (*record*) tŭngnok'ada 등록하다, (*letter*) tŭnggiro puch'ida 등기로 부치다. —*n.* (*~ book*) tŭngnokpu 등록부, (*automatic recorder*) tŭngnokki 등록기. *a hotel ~* sukpakpu 숙박부/ *a cash ~* kŭmjŏn tŭngnokki 금전 등록기/ *Where can I ~ for the English course?* Yŏng-ŏban tŭngnogŭn ŏdisŏ hamnikka? 영어반 등록은 어디서 합니까/ *I want to ~ this letter.* I p'yŏnjirŭl tŭnggiro puch'igo shipsŭmnida. 이 편지를 등기로 부치고 싶습니다/ *How much postage for this ~ed letter?* I tŭnggi p'yŏnjienŭn ŏlmatchari up'yorŭl puch'yŏya hamnikka? 이 등기 편지에는 얼마짜리 우표를 부쳐야 합니까?

registration *n.* tŭngnok 등록, tŭnggi 등기.

registry office tŭnggiso 등기소.

regret *n.* (*repentance*) huhoe 후회, (*grief*) sŭlp'ŭm 슬픔, (*disappointment*) shilmang 실망, (*pl.*) (*refusal*) kŏjŏl 거절. —*vt.* (*repent*) huhoehada 후회하다, (*mourn*) sŭlp'ŏhada 슬퍼하다. *I have no ~s.* Huhoehaji anssŭmnida 후회하지 않습니다/ *Please accept my ~s.* Yugamijiman sajŏrhamnida. 유감이지만 사절합니다/ *I ~ being unable to help.* Towa tŭriji mot'ae yugamimnida. 도와 드리지 못해 유감입니다/ *I ~ to say that I am unable to help you.* Yugamsŭrŏpchiman towa tŭril suga ŏpsŭmnida. 유감스럽지만 도와 드릴 수가 없습니다.

regular *adj.* (*formal*) chŏngshigŭi 정식의, (*well-ordered*) kyuch'ikchŏgin 규칙적인, (*periodic*) chŏnggijŏgin 정기적인, (*Am.*) (*authorized*) kongindoen 공인(公認)된. *I have no ~ introduction.* Chŏngshik sogaechangŭn ŏpsŭmnida. 정식 소개장은 없습니다/the *~ course* chŏnggyu kwajŏng 정규 과정/ *a ~ army* chŏnggyugun 정규군/ *keep ~ hours* kyuch'ikchŏk saenghwarŭl hada 규칙적 생활을 하다/ *a ~ meeting* chŏnggijŏk hoehap 정기적 회합/ *customers* tan-gol sonnim 단골 손님.

regulation *n.* (*rule*) kyuch'ik 규칙. *school ~s* kyoch'ik 교칙/ *traffic ~s* kyot'ong kyuch'ik 교통 규칙.

rehearsal *n.* (*play, music, etc.*) yŏnsŭp 연습, (*trial performance*) yehaeng yŏnsŭp 예행 연습. *a dress ~* mudae yŏnsŭp 무대 연습.

rehearse *vt., vi.* yehaeng yŏnsŭbŭl hada 예행 연습을 하다.

reign *n.* (*rule*) chibae 지배, (*sway*) t'ongch'i 통치. —*vi.* t'ongch'ihada 통치하다.

rein *n.* (*bridle*) koppi 고삐, (*restraint*) kyŏnje 견제.

reinforce *vt.* (*strengthen*) poganghada 보강하다. ~*ed concrete* ch'ŏlgŭn k'onk'ŭrit'ŭ 철근 콘크리트.

reissue *n.* (*second issue*) chaep'an 재판. —*vt.* chaebarhaenghada 재발행하다. *May I have them ~d?* Chaebarhaenghae chusyŏssŭmyŏn hamnida. 재발행해 주셨으면

합니다.

reject vt. (*refuse to receive*) mullich'ida 물리치다, (*throw away*) pŏrida 버리다. ~ *a plea* ch'ŏngŭl mullich'ida 청(請)을 물리치다/ *He was ~ed for physical defects.* Shinch'ejŏk kyŏrham ttaemune t'allaktoeŏssŭmnida. 신체적 결함 때문에 탈락되었읍니다.

rejoice vi., vt. (*delight*) kippŏhada 기뻐하다, (*gladden*) kippŭge hada 기쁘게 하다. *I'm ~d at your success.* Sŏnggonghasyŏsŏ kippŭmnida. 성공하셔서 기쁩니다.

relate vt., vi. (*tell*) marhada 말하다, (*ally by kinship*) ...kwa ch'inch'ŏgida …과 친척이다. *Are you ~d to Mr. Pak?* Pakssihago ch'inch'ŏgishimnikka? 박씨하고 친척이십니까/ *I am not ~d to him in any way.* Amut'ŭn nanŭn kŭűi ch'inch'ŏgi animnida. 아뭏든 나는 그의 친척이 아닙니다.

relation n. (*connection*) kwan-gye 관계, (*relative*) ch'inch'ŏk 친척. *diplomatic* ~s oegyo kwan-gye 외교 관계/ *Korean-American* ~s hanmi kwan-gye 한미 관계/ *blood* ~s hyŏryŏn 혈연.

relative n. ch'inch'ŏk 친척. *Do you have ~s in this country?* Uri nara-e ch'inch'ŏgirado kyeshimnikka? 우리 나라에 친척이라도 계십니까/ *I have no ~s in this town.* I maŭrenŭn ch'inch'ŏgi ŏpsŭmnida. 이 마을에는 친척이 없읍니다/ *a distant* ~ mŏn ch'inch'ŏk 먼 친척.

relax vt., vi. (*loosen*) nŭtch'uda 늦추다, (*ease*) shwida 쉬다. *Come in and* ~ *for a few minutes.* Chamshi tŭrŏwasŏ shwiŏ kashio. 잠시 들어와서 쉬어 가시오/ *Let us stop working and* ~ *for an hour.* Irŭl chungdanhago han shiganman shwipshida. 일을 중단하고 1시간만 쉽시다.

release vt. (*let go*) p'urŏ chuda 풀어 주다, (*set free*) sŏkpanghada 석방하다. ~ *a bomb* p'okt'anŭl t'uhahada 폭탄을 투하하다/ ~ (*a person*) *from office* haeimhada 해임하다/ *You just stand there and* ~ *the shutter.* Kŏgi sŏsŏ syŏt'ŏman nullŏ chushipshio. 거기 서서 셔터만 눌러 주십시오.

reliable adj. midŭl su innŭn 믿을 수 있는, midŭmjik'an 믿음직한. *a* ~ *man* midŭmjik'an saram 믿음직한 사람/

Can I have a ~ watch for fifty thousand won? Oman-wŏn naemyŏn midŭl manhan shigyerŭl sal su issŭmni-kka? 5만원 내면 믿을 만한 시계를 살 수 있읍니까?

reliance *n.* (*trust*) midŭm 믿음, (*confidence*) shinyong 신용. *Do you place much ~ on your doctor?* Tangshinŭn ŭisarŭl mani missŭmnikka? 당신은 의사를 많이 믿습니까?

relic *n.* (*pl.*) (*remnant*) yumul 유물, (*remains*) yujŏk 유적, (*souvenir*) kinyŏmp'um 기념품. *a ~ of the past* kwagŏŭi yumul 과거의 유물/ *a historic ~* yŏksasangŭi yujŏk 역사상의 유적/ *Are many precious cultural ~s preserved in the National Museum?* Kungnip pangmul-gwanenŭn kwijunghan munhwajŏk yumuri pogwandoeŏ issŭmnikka? 국립 박물관에는 귀중한 문화적 유물이 보관되어 있읍니까?

relief *n.* (*aid*) kujo 구조, (*removal*) chegŏ 제거, (*comfort*) wian 위안, (*in sculpture*) yanggak 양각. *a ~ fund* kuje kigŭm 구제 기금/ *Speak English. I know it well. Thank you, that's a great ~.* Yŏngŏro malssŭmhaseyo. Chal aradŭssŭmnida. Komawayo, kŭgŏt ch'am tahaeng-igunyo. 영어로 말씀하세요. 잘 알아듣습니다. 고마와요, 그것 참 다행이군요.

relieve *vt.* (*rescue*) kujehada 구제하다, (*give ease*) anshim-shik'ida 안심시키다, (*mitigate*) tŏrŏ chuda 덜어 주다, (*release from duty*) kyodaeshik'ida 교대시키다. *~ the poor* pinminŭl kujehada 빈민을 구제하다/ *I was ~d at the news.* Kŭ soshigŭl tŭtko anshimhaessŭmnida. 그 소식을 듣고 안심했읍니다/ *Let me ~ you of your suitcase.* Yŏhaeng kabangŭl tŭrŏ tŭrijiyo. 여행 가방을 들어 드리지요/ *You shall be ~d at 10:30.* Yŏlshi pane kyodaehae tŭrigesso. 10시 반에 교대해 드리겠소.

religion *n.* chonggyo 종교. *believe in ~* chonggyorŭl mitta 종교를 믿다/ *Buddhist ~* pulgyo 불교/ *the Christian ~* kidokkyo 기독교.

religious *adj.* chonggyoŭi 종교의, (*devout*) shinangi ki-p'ŭn 신앙이 깊은, (*pious*) kyŏnggŏnhan 경건한. *a ~ book* chonggyo sŏjŏk 종교 서적/ *a ~ life* shinang saeng-hwal 신앙 생활/ *~ services* yebae 예배.

relish *vt.* (*taste*) matpoda 맛보다, (*enjoy*) chŭlgida 즐기다. —*n.* (*taste*) mat 맛, (*flavor*) p'ungmi 풍미, (*liking*) kiho 기호. *I have no ~ for that sort of novels.* Kŭwa kat'ŭn sosŏrŭn choahaji anssŭmnida. 그와 같은 소설은 좋아하지 않습니다.

reluctant *adj.* majimot'ae hanŭn 마지못해 하는, (*unwilling*) shirŏhanŭn 싫어하는. *He gave me ~ assistance.* Kŭ saramŭn majimot'ae narŭl towa chuŏssŭmnida. 그 사람은 마지못해 나를 도와 주었습니다. 「어하면서.

reluctantly *adv.* majimot'ae 마지못해, shirŏhamyŏnsŏ 싫

rely *vi.* (*depend on*) ŭijihada 의지하다, (*trust*) mitta 믿다. *You may ~ upon my remittance.* Kkok songgŭmhae tŭrigessŭmnida. 꼭 송금해 드리겠읍니다/ *R~ on my promise.* Yaksogŭn kkok chik'igesso. 약속은 꼭 지키겠소.

remain *vi.* (*be left*) namta 남다, (*stay*) mŏmurŭda 머무르다. *Please ~ in your seat.* Chwasŏgŭl ttŏnaji mashipshio. 좌석을 떠나지 마십시오.

remainder *n.* (*surplus*) namŏji 나머지, (*the rest*) namŭn saram 남은 사람. *Keep the ~ for yourself.* Namŏjinŭn tangshini kajishipshio. 나머지는 당신이 가지십시오.

remark *vt., vi.* (*say*) marhada 말하다, (*make comment*) p'yŏnghada 평하다, (*notice*) chumok'ada 주목하다. —*n.* (*short statement*) mal 말, (*comment*) nonp'yŏng 논평.

remarkable *adj.* (*noteworthy*) chumok'al manhan 주목할 만한, (*striking*) tturyŏt'an 뚜렷한. *He is ~ for his diligence.* Kŭnŭn imanjŏmanhan kŭnmyŏn-gaga animnida. 그는 이만저만한 근면가가 아닙니다/ *a ~ event* chumok'al sakŏn 주목할 사건.

remedy *n.* (*cure*) yopŏp 요법, (*medicine*) yak 약, (*redress*) kujech'aek 구제책. *Is there any ~ for fever?* Muŏn-ga haeyŏlchega ŏpsŭmnikka? 무언가 해열제가 없읍니까?

remember *vt., vi.* (*recall*) saenggak'ae naeda 생각해 내다, (*have in mind*) kiŏk'ago itta 기억하고 있다. *I can't ~ his name.* Kŭ saramŭi irŭmi saenggangnaji anssŭmnida. 그 사람의 이름이 생각나지 않습니다/ *Do you ~ where you put the key?* Yŏlsoe tun kosŭl kiŏk'ago issŭmnikka? 열쇠 둔 곳을 기억하고 있읍니까?

remembrance *n.* (*memory*) kiŏk 기억, (*souvenir*) kinyŏm-mul 기념물. *I have no ~ of it.* Kŭgŏshi chogŭmdo kiŏng-naji anssŭmnida. 그것이 조금도 기억나지 않습니다/ *I send a small ~.* Pyŏnbyŏnch'i mot'an sŏnmurŭl ponae tŭ-rimnida. 변변치 못한 선물을 보내 드립니다.

remind *vt.* (*make think*) saenggangnage hada 생각나게 하다, (*make remember*) ilkkaeuda 일깨우다. *You ~ me of my brother.* Tangshinŭl poni nae au saenggagi namni-da. 당신을 보니 내 아우 생각이 납니다. / *I ~ed her to go home before dark.* Kŭnyŏege ŏdupki chŏne chibe kadorok illŏ chuŏssŭmnida. 그녀에게 어둡기 전에 집에 가도록 일러 주었읍니다.

remit *vt.*, *vi.* (*send money*) songgŭmhada 송금하다, *Kindly ~ by cheque.* Sup'yoro songgŭmhae chuship-shio. 수표로 송금해 주십시오/ *~ money to a person* nu-guege tonŭl puch'ida 누구에게 돈을 부치다.

remittance *n.* (*money sent*) songgŭm 송금. *~ charge* songgŭm susuryo 송금 수수료/ *telegraphic ~* chŏnshin-hwan 전신환.

remorse *n.* (*repentance*) huhoe 후회, (*pangs of con-science*) yangshimŭi kach'aek 양심의 가책. *I felt ~ for what I had done.* Naega han chisŭl huhoehayŏssŭmni-da. 내가 한 짓을 후회하였읍니다.

remove *vt.*, *vi.* (*move*) omgida 옮기다, (*take away*) ch'iuda 치우다, (*take off*) pŏtta 벗다. *We are removing to the city next week.* Naeju shinaero isahamnida. 내주 시내로 이사합니다/ *R~ the dishes from the table.* Shikt'agesŏ shikkirŭl ch'iwŏ chushio. 식탁에서 식기를 치워 주시오.

rend *vi.*, *vt.* (*tear*) tchitta 찢다, (*split*) tchogaeda 쪼개다. *She rent up all her clothes.* Kŭ yŏjanŭn chagi osŭl kalgigalgi tchijŏssŭmnida. 그 여자는 자기 옷을 갈기갈기 찢었읍니다.

render *vt.* (*give*) chuda 주다, (*give in return*) tamnye-hada 답례하다, (*pay*) pach'ida 바치다. *Can I ~ any aid?* Muŏsŭl towa tŭrilkkayo? 무엇을 도와 드릴까요/ *~ thanks* tamnyehada 답례하다/ *~ him a service* kŭ saramege pongsahada 그 사람에게 봉사하다.

renew *vt., vi.* (*make again*) chaesaenghada 재생하다, (*replace*) saero kalda 새로 갈다, (*recover*) hoebok'ada 회복하다, (*repeat*) toep'urihada 되풀이하다. ~ *the carpets* yungdanŭl saero kalda 융단을 새로 갈다/ *This contract has to be ~ed.* I kyeyagŭn kaengshinhaeya hamnida. 이 계약은 갱신해야 합니다.

renounce *vt., vi.* (*give up*) pŏrida 버리다, (*disclaim*) puinhada 부인하다. ~ *a right* kwŏllirŭl p'ogihada 권리를 포기하다/ ~ *smoking and drinking* kŭmyŏn kŭmjuhada 금연 금주하다/ ~ *one's friend* chŏlgyohada 절교하다.

rent *n.* (*of a house*) chipse 집세, (*of land*) ttangse 땅세, (*of rooms*) pangse 방세. —*vt.* (*let for* ~) pillyŏ chuda 빌려 주다. *What is the charge for* ~? Imdaeryonŭn ŏlmaimnikka? 임대료는 얼마입니까/ *a room for* ~ sepang 세방/ *a house for* ~ setchip 셋집/ *I have ~ed a new house.* Sae chibe sedŭrŏssŭmnida. 새 집에 세들었읍니다/ *I'd like to* ~ *a car, please.* Ch'arŭl pilligo shipsŭmnida. 차를 빌리고 싶습니다.

repair *vt.* (*mend*) koch'ida 고치다, surihada 수리하다, (*restore*) torik'ida 돌이키다, (*make amends for*) posanghada 보상하다. —*n.* (*repairing*) suri 수리, (*good condition*) suri sangt'ae 수리 상태. ~ *a puncture* ppangkkurŭl ttaeuda 빵꾸를 때우다/ *Where can I* ~ *my watch?* Ŏdisŏ shigyerŭl surihal su issŭmnikka? 어디서 시계를 수리할 수 있읍니까/ *Please* ~ *this radio.* I radiorŭl surihae chushio. 이 라디오를 수리해 주시오/ *automobile* ~s chadongch'a suri 자동차 수리/ *a* ~ *shop* suri kongjang 수리 공장/ *This* ~s *will cost about 5,000 won.* Suribinŭn och'ŏnwŏn karyangimnida. 수리비는 5천원 가량입니다.

repay *vt., vi.* (*pay back*) kapta 갚다, (*make return for*) podap'ada 보답하다. *If you lend me ten thousand won, I'll* ~ *you next week.* Manwŏnman pillyŏ chushimyŏn naejue kap'a tŭrigessŭmnida. 만원만 빌려 주시면 내주에 갚아 드리겠읍니다.

repeat *vt., vi.* (*do again*) toep'urihada 되풀이하다, (*say again*) toep'uri marhada 되풀이 말하다, (*recite*) amsong-

hada 암송하다. *I'm sorry, but would you ~ it again?*
Mianhajiman han pŏn tŏ malssŭmhae chushigessŭmnikka? 미안하지만 한 번 더 말씀해 주시겠읍니까/ *Please ~
what you said.* Tashi han pŏn malssŭmhae chushipshio.
다시 한 번 말씀해 주십시오/ *Would you mind reciting
your name?* Sŏnghamŭl han pŏn tŏ illŏ chushigessŭmnikka? 성함을 한 번 더 일러 주시겠읍니까?

repel *vt.*, *vi.* (*drive back*) mullich'ida 물리치다, (*disgust*)
pulk'waegamŭl chuda 불쾌감을 주다.

repent *vt.*, *vi.* (*regret*) huhoehada 후회하다, nwiuch'ida
뉘우치다. *You shall ~ this.* Kkok huhoehage toel t'eni
tugo poshio. 꼭 후회하게 될 테니 두고 보시오/ *I ~ed my
kindness.* Naega pep'un ch'injŏri huhoedoedŏgŭnyo.
내가 베푼 친절이 후회되더군요.

replace *vt.* (*put back*) tollyŏ chuda 돌려 주다, (*take the
place of*) taeshin tŭrŏanta 대신 들어앉다, (*repay*) kapta
갚다. *R~ the book on the shelf.* Ch'aegŭl ch'aekchange
toro kkojŭshio. 책을 책장에 도로 꽂으시오/*Please ~ this
clock's hands with new ones.* I shigye panŭrŭl sae
kŏtkwa pakkuŏ chushipshio. 이 시계 바늘을 새 것과 바
꾸어 주십시오/ *We'll ~ it.* Pakkwŏ tŭrigessŭmnida. 바
꿔 드리겠읍니다.

reply *vi.*, *vt.* (*respond*) taedap'ada 대답하다. —*n.* (*answer*) taedap 대답, (*response*) hoedap 회답. *Please ~ as
soon as you can.* Toedorok ppalli hoedabŭl chushipshio.
되도록 빨리 회답을 주십시오/ *I cannot ~ for a few days.*
Suillaero hoedabŭl tŭril suga ŏpsŭmnida. 수일내로 회답
을 드릴 수가 없읍니다/*I expect your prompt ~.* Chosok'i
hoedap chushigirŭl paramnida. 조속히 회답 주시기를 바람
니다. *~ (postal) card* wangbok yŏpsŏ 왕복 엽서.

report *n.* (*account*) pogo 보고, podo 보도, (*rumor*) somun
소문, (*bang*) p'osŏng 포성(砲聲). —*vt.* (*inform*) pogo-
hada 보고하다, (*tell about*) chŏnhada 전하다. *an
interim ~* chunggan pogo 중간 보고/ *a ~ card* sŏngjŏkp'yo 성적표/ *I shall ~ you to the superiors.* (*to
inferior*) Chanerŭl sangsa-ege pogohagenne. 자네를 상
사에게 보고하겠네.

reporter *n.* (*newspaper writer*) shinmun kija 신문 기자.

represent *vt.* (*stand for*) taep'yohada 대표하다, (*explain*) sŏlmyŏnghada 설명하다, (*describe*) myosahada 묘사하다, (*perform*) yŏnch'urhada 연출하다. *He ~ed Korea at the conference.* Kŭ punŭn Han-gugŭl taep'yohayŏ hoeŭie ch'amsŏk'aessŭmnida. 그 분은 한국을 대표하여 회의에 참석했읍니다.

representative *n.* (*delegate*) taep'yoja 대표자, (*congressman*) kuk'oe ŭiwŏn 국회 의원, (*example*) kyŏnbon 견본, *a legal ~* pŏpchŏng taeriin 법정 대리인.

repress *vt.* (*restrain*) ŏngnurŭda 억누르다, (*supress*) chinap'ada 진압하다. *~ a sneeze* chaech'aegirŭl ch'amta 재채기를 참다.

reprint *n.* (*new impression*) chaep'an 재판, (*off print*) palch'we inswae 발췌 인쇄. —*vt.* tashi tchikta 다시 찍다.

repro *n.* (*document, film, etc.*) poksa 복사.

reproach *vt.* (*blame*) namurada 나무라다, (*scold*) kkujitta 꾸짖다. —*n.* (*censure*) ch'aengmang 책망, (*blame*) pinan 비난. *Why do you ~ him?* Wae kŭ saramŭl namuramnikka? 왜 그 사람을 나무랍니까?

republic *n.* konghwaguk 공화국. *the R~ of Korea* Taehanmin-guk 대한민국/ *the ~ of letters* mundan 문단.

repulse *vt.* (*drive back*) kyŏkt'oehada 격퇴하다, (*repel*) panbak'ada 반박하다, kŏjŏrhada 거절하다. —*n.* (*repelling*) kyŏkt'oe 격퇴, (*refusal*) kŏjŏl 거절.

reputation *n.* (*fame*) p'yŏngp'an 평판, myŏngsŏng 명성. *I know him well by ~.* Kŭ saramŭn p'yŏngi choa nado chal algo issŭmnida. 그 사람은 평이 좋아 나도 잘 알고 있읍니다.

request *n.* (*asking*) yogu 요구, (*entreaty*) kanch'ŏng 간청. —*vt.* (*beg for*) yoch'ŏnghada 요청하다, (*solicit*) put'ak'ada 부탁하다. *I would like to make a ~.* Hangaji put'agi issŭmnida. 한가지 부탁이 있읍니다/ *I consent to your ~.* Tangshinŭi put'agŭl tŭrŏ tŭrigessŭmnida. 당신의 부탁을 들어 드리겠읍니다/ *I ~ you to send money at once.* Kot songgŭmhae chushipshio. 곧 송금해 주십시오.

require *vt., vi.* (*need*) p'iryohada 필요하다, (*demand*)

yoguhada 요구하다. *We ~ extra help*. T'ŭkpyŏrhan wŏnjoga p'iryohamnida. 특별한 원조가 필요합니다.

requisite *n.* (*things needed*) p'ilsup'um 필수품. *toilet ~s* hwajang yongp'um 화장 용품. *We supply every ~ for travel*. Modŭn yŏhaeng yongp'umŭl konggŭp'amnida. 모든 여행 용품을 공급합니다.

rescue *vt.* (*save from danger*) kuhae naeda 구해 내다, (*deliver*) kujohada 구조하다. *—n.* (*deliverance*) kuch'ul 구출. *a ~ boat* kujosŏn 구조선/ *a ~ party* kujodae 구조대/ *~ work* kujo chagŏp 구조 작업/ *~ a child from drowning* mure ppajin airŭl kuch'urhada 물에 빠진 아이를 구출하다.

research *n.* (*investigation*) chosa yŏn-gu 조사 연구. *—vi.* yŏn-gu chosahada 연구 조사하다. *a ~ institute* yŏn-guso 연구소/ *~ expenses* yŏn-gubi 연구비.

resemble *vt.* (*be like*) …ŭl tamta …을 닮다, (*similar to*) pisŭt'ada 비슷하다. *Your younger brother ~s you very much*. Tangshinŭi tongsaengŭn tangshinŭl mani talmassŭmnida. 당신의 동생은 당신을 많이 닮았읍니다.

resent *vt.* (*feel angry at*) pun-gaehada 분개하다, hwanaeda 화내다. *Does he ~ my being here*. Kŭ saramŭn naega yŏgi innŭn kŏsŭl motmattanghae hamnikka? 그 사람은 내가 여기 있는 것을 못마땅해 합니까? 「성 잘 내는.

resentful *adj.* pun-gaehanŭn 분개하는, sŏng chal naenŭn

resentment *n.* pun-gae 분개, wŏnhan 원한.

reservation *n.* (*keeping back*) poryu 보류, (*arranging in advance*) yeyak 예약. *secure sleeping car ~* ch'imdaech'arŭl yeyak'ada 침대차를 예약하다/ *Have you made a hotel ~?* Hot'el yeyagŭl hasyŏssŭmnikka? 호텔 예약을 하셨읍니까/ *I have ~s for four*. Ne saram yeyagŭl hae tuŏssŭmnida. 네 사람 예약을 해 두었읍니다.

reserve *vt.* (*keep*) pojonhada 보존하다, (*retain*) poryuhada 보류하다, (*arrange for in advance*) yeyak'ada 예약하다. *R~ your strength for the climb*. Tŭngsanŭl wihae himŭl akkyŏ tushio. 등산을 위해 힘을 아껴 두시오/ *I have ~d a room through my travel agent*. Yŏhaengsarŭl t'onghae pangŭl yeyak'ae tuŏssŭmnida. 여행사를 통해 방

을 예약해 두었읍니다/ *Are the seats* ~*d*? Chwasŏgŭn chijŏngimnikka. 좌석은 지정입니까? 「외에서 살다.

reside *vi.* (*live*) salda 살다. ~ *abroad* haeoeesŏ salda 해

residence *n.* (*house*) chut'aek 주택, chŏt'aek 저택, (*residing*) kŏju 거주. *an official* ~ konggwan 공관. *I met her at the* ~ *of Mr. Chong.* Chŏngssiŭi chŏt'aegesŏ kŭ yŏjarŭl mannassŭmnida. 정씨의 저택에서 그 여자를 만났읍니다. 「han Migugin 주한 미국인.

resident *n.* kŏjuja 거주자. *American* ~*s in Korea.* chu-

resign *vi.*, *vt.* (*give up office*) saimhada 사임하다, (*retire*) t'oejik'ada 퇴직하다, (*abandon*) p'ogihada 포기하다. *Why did you* ~ *your post?* Wae sajik'asyŏssŭmnikka? 왜 사직하셨읍니까/ ~ *from public life* kongjik saenghwaresŏ ŭnt'oehada 공직 생활에서 은퇴하다.

resignation *n.* *a written* ~ sap'yo 사표/ *offer one's* ~ sap'yorŭl naeda 사표를 내다/ *accept one's* ~ sap'yorŭl surihada 사표를 수리하다/ *general* ~ ch'ongsajik 총사직.

resin *n.* suji 수지(樹脂), songjin 송진.

resist *vt.*, *vi.* (*oppose*) pandaehada 반대하다, (*withstand*) kyŏndida 견디다, (*abstain from*) samgada 삼가다. *I could* ~ *no longer.* Tŏ isang kyŏndil suga ŏpsŏssŭmnida. 더 이상 견딜 수가 없었읍니다/*I can't* ~ *a cigarette.* Tambaeramyŏn sajŏgŭl mot ssŭmnida. 담배라면 사족을 못 씁니다.

resistance *n.* (*resisting*) chŏhang 저항, panhang 반항. ~ *movement* chŏhang undong 저항 운동.

resolution *n.* kyŏrŭi 결의, kyŏlshim 결심. *a firm* ~ kudŭn kyŏlshim 굳은 결심/ *form a* ~ kyŏlshimhada 결심하다.

resolve *vt.*, *vi.* (*decide*) kyŏlshimhada 결심하다, (*solve*) p'ulda 풀다, (*separate*) punhaehada 분해하다. *I* ~*d to give up smoking.* Tambaerŭl kkŭnk'iro kyŏlshimhayŏssŭmnida. 담배를 끊기로 결심하였읍니다/ *All doubts were* ~*d.* Modŭn ŭishimŭn p'ullyŏssŭmnida. 모든 의심은 풀렸읍니다.

resort *n.* (*place frequented*) norit'ŏ 놀이터, yuwŏnji 유원지. *Walker Hill is one of the famous* ~*s in Seoul.* Wŏk'ŏhirŭn Sŏuresŏ yumyŏnghan yuwŏnjiŭi hanaimnida. 워커힐은 서울에서 유명한 유원지의 하나입니다/ *a health* ~ hyuyangji 휴양지/ *a summer* ~ p'isŏji 피서지.

resource *n.* (*pl.*) chawŏn 자원. *natural* ~s ch'ŏnyŏn chawŏn 천연 자원/ *national* ~s kukkaŭi chawŏn 국가의 자원/ *exploit oil* ~s sŏgyu chawŏnŭl kaebarhada 석유 자원을 개발하다/*Korea is rich in human* ~s. Han-gugŭn inchŏk chawŏni p'ungbuhamnida. 한국은 인적 자원이 풍부합니다.

respect *vt.* (*honor*) chon-gyŏnghada 존경하다, (*esteem*) chonjunghada 존중하다, (*heed*) koryŏhada 고려하다. —*n.* chon-gyŏng 존경, chonjung 존중. *I* ~ *your opinions.* Tangshinŭi ŭigyŏnŭl chonjunghamnida. 당신의 의견을 존중합니다/ *Do you* ~ *the laws of your country?* Naraŭi pŏbŭl chik'ishimnikka? 나라의 법을 지키십니까/ *I* ~ *him as my superior.* Kŭ punŭl sŏnbaerosŏ chon-gyŏnghamnida. 그 분을 선배로서 존경합니다.

respectable *adj.* (*estimable*) chon-gyŏnghal manhan 존경할 만한, (*decent*) chŏmjanŭn 점잖은, (*fair*) sangdanghan 상당한.

respectful *adj.* (*polite*) kongsonhan 공손한, chŏngjunghan 정중한.

respectively *adv.* chŏmada 저마다, kakki 각기.

respiration *n.* (*breathing*) hohŭp 호흡. *artificial* ~ in-gong hohŭp 인공 호흡.

respite *n.* (*delay*) yŏn-gi 연기, yuye 유예, (*lull*) ttŭmham 뜸함. ~ *for the murderer* sarinbŏme taehan chip'aeng yuye 살인범에 대한 집행 유예.

respond *vi.* (*reply*) taedap'ada 대답하다, (*react*) panŭnghada 반응하다.

respondent *n.* ŭngdapcha 응답자, p'igo 피고. 「반응.

response *n.* (*answer*) ŭngdap 응답, (*reaction*) panŭng

responsibility *n.* ch'aegim 책임. *Where shall we place the* ~ *for it?* I ch'aegimŭn nuguege issŭmnikka? 이 책임은 누구에게 있읍니까/ *I will assume the* ~. Kŭ ch'aegimŭl chigesŭmnida. 그 책임을 지겠읍니다.

responsible *adj.* ch'aegim innŭn 책임 있는. *I'm not* ~ *for it.* Nae ch'aegimi animnida. 내 책임이 아닙니다/ *Who* *is ~ for it?* Nuguŭi ch'aegimimnikka? 누구의 책임입니까/ *How far are we ~ for it?* Ŏnŭ sŏnkkaji ch'aegimjyŏya hamnikka? 어느 선까지 책임져야 합니까?

rest *n.* (*repose*) hyushik 휴식, (*mental peace*) anjŏng 안정, (*sleep*) cham 잠, (*remainder*) namŏji 나머지. —*vi.* (*stop work*) shwida 쉬다, (*take repose*) chada 자다, (*pause*) chŏngjihada 정지하다, (*lean*) kidaeda 기대다. *Let's take a ~.* Chom shwipshida. 좀 쉽시다/ *Keep the ~ for yourself.* Namŏjinŭn tŭrigessŭmnida. 나머지는 드리겠읍니다/ *Are you quite ~ed?* P'uk shwiŏssŭmnikka? 푹 쉬었읍니까/ *I think you are taking a ~.* Hyushigŭl ch'wihago kyeshinŭn-gŭnyo. 휴식을 취하고 계시는군요/ *R~ the ladder against the wall.* Sadaktarirŭl pyŏge kidae noŭshio. 사다다리를 벽에 기대 놓으시오.

restaurant *n.* shiktang 식당, ŭmshikchŏm 음식점. *Is there a good ~ around here?* I kŭnch'ŏ choŭn ŭmshikchŏmi issŭmnikka? 이 근처 좋은 음식점이 있읍니까/ *Maybe we can go to a Chinese ~.* Chungguk yorina mŏgŭrŏ kaji ank'essŭmnikka? 중국 요리나 먹으러 가지 않겠읍니까/ *a Chinese ~* Chungguk ŭmshikchŏm 중국 음식점.

resting place hyushikch'ŏ 휴식처, (*landing*) ch'ŭnggyech'am 층계참.

restless *adj.* puranhan 불안한, tŭlttŭn 들뜬.

restore *vt.* (*bring back*) toedollida 되돌리다, (*give back*) tollyŏ chuda 돌려 주다, (*reinstate*) pokchikshik'ida 복직시키다, (*reconstruct*) chaegŏnhada 재건하다.

restrain *vt.* (*hold back*) ŏkchehada 억제하다, (*check*) pangjihada 방지하다.

restraint *n.* (*checking*) ŏkche 억제, (*restraining*) sokpak 속박. *without ~* chayuroi 자유로이.

restriction *n.* (*limitation*) chehan 제한, (*reserve*) sayang 사양. *place ~s on foreign trade* haeoe muyŏgŭl chehanhada 해외 무역을 제한하다. 「shil 화장실.

rest room (*of station, theater*) pyŏnso 변소, hwajang-

result *n.* (*effect*) kyŏlgwa 결과. *Have you seen the football ~s?* Ch'ukku kyŏlgwarŭl posyŏssŭmnikka? 축구 결과를 보셨읍니까/ *test ~s* shihŏm sŏngjŏk 시험 성적/ *a* *table of* ～s sŏngjŏkp'yo 성적표.

resume *vt.*, *vi.* (*begin again*) tashi shijak'ada 다시 시작하다, (*take back*) hoebok'ada 회복하다. *Let's* ～ *where we left off.* Akka kkŭnnan tesŏbut'ŏ tashi shijak'apshida. 아까 끝난 데서부터 다시 시작합시다.

resurrect *vt.* (*reanimate*) tashi sallida 다시 살리다, (*being back into use*) puhwalshik'ida 부활시키다, (*dig out*) p'anaeda 파내다.

resurrection *n.* puhwal 부활. *the R*～ Kŭrisŭdoŭi puhwal 그리스도의 부활.

retail *n.* somae 소매. ―*vt.* somaehada 소매하다. ―*adv.* somaero 소매로. *a* ～ *price* somae kagyŏk 소매 가격/ *a* ～ *shop* somaejŏm 소매점/ *Do you sell wholesale or* ～? Tomaero p'amnikka, somaero p'amnikka? 도매로 팝니까, 소매로 팝니까?

retailer *n.* somae sangin 소매 상인.

retain *vt.* (*keep*) poryuhada 보류하다, (*preserve*) poyuhada 보유하다, (*hire*) koyonghada 고용하다, (*keep in mind*) kiŏk'ada 기억하다. 「앙갚음하다.

retaliate *vi.* (*revenge*) pobok'ada 보복하다, anggap'ŭmhada

retaliation *n.* angap'ŭm 앙갚음, pobok 보복, *a measure of* ～ pobok sudan 보복 수단. 「hada 더디게 하다.

retard *vt.* (*make slow*) nŭtch'uda 늦추다, (*delay*) tŏdige

retire *vi.* (*go back*) mullŏgada 물러가다, (*from office*) t'oejik'ada 퇴직하다, (*go to bed*) chamcharie tŭlda 잠자리에 들다. ～ *from ring* ringesŏ ŭnt'oehada 링에서 은퇴하다/ *My wife usually* ～*s at 11 o'clock.* Nae anaenŭn pot'ong yŏrhanshie chamnida. 내 아내는 보통 11시에 잡니다.

retired *adj.* (*from society*) ŭnt'oehan 은퇴한, (*from business*) t'oejik'an 퇴직한, (*from service*) t'oeyŏk'an 퇴역한. *a* ～ *life* ŭnt'oe saenghwal 은퇴 생활.

retort *vt.*,*vi.* (*reply sharply*) maldaekkuhada 말대꾸하다.

retreat *n.* (*withdrawing*) hut'oe 후퇴, t'oegak 퇴각. ―*vi.* (*go back*) mullŏgada 물러가다, (*withdraw*) ch'ŏlsuhada 철수하다. 「회고[회상]하다.

retrospect *n.* hoego 회고, ―*vt.*,*vi.* hoego[hoesang]hada

return *vi.*, *vt.* (*go back*) torao[ga]da 돌아오[가]다, (*repay*)

tollyŏ chuda 돌려주다. *When will you ～?* Ŏnje tora-
gashimnikka? 언제 돌아가십니까/ *I've just ～ed.* Panggŭm torawassŭmnida. 방금 돌아왔읍니다/ *When will
you ～ the book?* Kŭ ch'aek ŏnje tollyŏ chushiryŏmnikka? 그 책 언제 돌려 주시렵니까/ *R～ it back to me.* Na-
ege tollyŏ chushipshio. 나에게 돌려 주십시오/ *a ～ ticket*
wangbokp'yo 왕복표/ *What shall I give you in ～ for
this present?* I sŏnmurŭi tamnyero muŏsŭl tŭrilkkayo?
이 선물의 답례로 무엇을 드릴까요?

reveal *vt. (disclose)* nat'anaeda 나타내다, *(show)* poida
보이다, *(make known)* allyŏ chuda 알려 주다, *(divulge)*
p'ongnohada 폭로하다.

revel *vi. (feast)* sul mashimyŏ hŭngch'ŏnggŏrida 술 마시며
흥청거리다, *(make merry)* hŭngch'ŏnggŏrimyŏ nolda 흥
청거리며 놀다. *—n. (carousal)* suljanch'i 술잔치, chuyŏn
주연(酒宴), *(merrymaking)* yuhŭng 유흥. *Our ～s now
are ended.* Chuyŏnŭn ije kkŭnnassŭmnida. 주연은 이제
끝났읍니다.

revelation *n. (revealing)* p'ongno 폭로, *(disclosure)*
palgak 발각, *(religion)* kyeshi 계시, *(surprise)* ttŭtpakkŭi il 뜻밖의 일. *It was a ～ to me.* Naegenŭn ttŭtpakkŭi iriŏssŭmnida. 내게는 뜻밖의 일이었읍니다.

revel(l)er *n.* nanbongkkun 난봉꾼, pangt'angja 방탕자.

revelry *n. (merrymaking)* hwallak 환락, yuhŭng 유흥.

revenge *vt.,vi. (vengeance)* poksu 복수. *—vt.,vi. (avenge)*
anggap'ŭmhada 앙갚음하다. *You have won the game;
I must now have my ～.* Tangshini igyŏssŭnikka ije
naega pobok'al ch'aryeimnida. 당신이 이겼으니까 이제 내
가 보복할 차례입니다.

revenue *n. (of individual)* suip 수입, sodŭk 소득, *(of
State)* seip 세입. *national ～* kukka seip 국가 세입/ *a
～ stamp* suip inji 수입 인지.

reverence *n. (esteem)* chon-gyŏng 존경, *(pious feeling)*
kyŏnggŏnhan maŭm 경건한 마음, *(deep bow)* kyŏngnye
경례. *I retired with two profound ～s.* Tu pŏn kyŏng-
nyerŭl olligo mullŏnassŭmnida. 두 번 경례를 올리고 물
러났읍니다.

reverend *n.* (*clergyman*) moksa 목사, (*holy father*) shin-b 신부. *Rev. Chang* Chang shinbunim 장신부님.

reverse *vt.* (*turn upside down*) kŏkkuro hada 거꾸로 하다, (*transpose*) pakkwŏ not'a 바꿔 놓다. —*n.* (*contrary*) pandae 반대. —*adj.* (*opposite*) 반대의. *Can you ~ the charges?* Yogŭmŭn sangdaebangi muldorok hae chushipshio. 요금은 상대방이 물도록 해 주십시오/ *Is he rich? No, quite the ~.* Kŭ punŭn pujaimnikka? Anyo, chŏngbandaeimnida. 그 분은 부자입니까? 아뇨, 정반대입니다.

review *n.* (*troop ~*) yŏlbyŏng 열병(閱兵), (*criticism*) p'yŏngnon 평론, (*magazine*) chapchi 잡지. —*vt.* (*inspect*) kŏmnyŏrhada 검열하다, (*write ~s*) p'yŏngnonhada 평론하다, (*examine again*) poksŭp'ada 복습하다. *a military ~* yŏlbyŏngshik 열병식/ *a weekly ~* chugan p'yŏngnon 주간 평론/ *a book ~* sŏp'yŏng 서평.

revise *vt.* (*reexamine*) kyojŏnghada 교정하다, (*amend*) sujŏnghada 수정하다. *~d edition* kaejŏngp'an 개정판.

revoke *vt., vi.* (*repeal*) haeyak'ada 해약하다, (*cancel*) ch'wisohada 취소하다.

revolt *n.* (*rebellion*) pallan 반란. —*vi., vt.* (*rebel*) panyŏk'ada 반역하다, (*be disgusted*) piwie kŏsŭllida 비위에 거슬리다. *My stomach ~s at such food.* Kŭrŏn ŭmshigŭl mŏgŭmyŏn nanŭn t'ohamnida. 그런 음식을 먹으면 나는 토합니다.

revolution *n.* hyŏngmyŏng 혁명. *a military ~* kunsa hyŏngmyŏng 군사 혁명.

reward *n.* (*repayment*) posu 보수, (*prize*) sang 상, (*repay*) podap'ada 보답하다. *I ask no ~.* Nanŭn posurŭl paraji anssŭmnida. 나는 보수를 바라지 않습니다/ *I ~ed him for his services.* Kŭ saramŭi kongno-e podap'aessŭmnida. 그 사람의 공로에 보답했읍니다.

rewrite *vt.* tashi ssŭda 다시 쓰다, koch'yŏ ssŭda 고쳐 쓰다.

rheumatism *n.* ryumŏt'ijŭm 류머티즘. *acute[chronic] ~* kŭpsŏng[mansŏng] ryumŏt'ijŭm 급성[만성] 류머티즘/ *suffer from ~* ryumŏt'ijŭmŭl alt'a 류머티즘을 앓다.

rhythm *n.* ridŭm 리듬, yultong 율동. 「쇠갈비.

rib *n.* kalbittae 갈빗대, nŭkkol 늑골. *~s of beef* soegalbi

ribbon *n.* ribon 리본, tti 띠. *wear a* ~ ribonŭl talda 리본을 달다/ *a typewriter* ~ t'ajagi ribon 타자기 리본.

rice *n.* (*plant*) pyŏ 벼, (*raw grain*) ssal 쌀, (*cooked*) pap 밥, *cook* ~ pabŭl chitta 밥을 짓다/ *The Koreans live on* ~. Han-guk saramŭn ssarŭl chushigŭro hamnida. 한국 사람은 쌀을 주식으로 합니다/ *Would you like to have* ~? Pabŭl chashigessŭmnikka? 밥을 자시겠읍니까/ ~ *cake* ttŏk 떡/ ~ *field* non 논.

rich *adj.* (*wealthy*) ton manŭn 돈 많은, (*abundant*) p'ungbuhan 풍부한. —*n.* (*pl.*) pu 부(富). *a* ~ *person* puja 부자/ *become* ~ pujaga toeda 부자가 되다/ *Korea is* ~ *in historic remains.* Han-gugenŭn kojŏgi p'ungbuhamnida. 한국에는 고적이 풍부합니다.

rid *vt.* (*free*) ŏpsaeda 없애다, (*remove*) chegŏhada 제거하다. *get* ~ *of* (*get free from*) …ŭl pŏsŏnada …을 벗어나다, tchoch'a pŏrida 쫓아 버리다. *How can we get* ~ *of this unwelcome visitor?* I pulch'ŏnggaegŭl ŏttok'e tchoch'a pŏrindam! 이 불청객을 어떻게 쫓아 버린담/ *I cannot get* ~ *of my cold.* Kamgirŭl ttel suga ŏpsŭmnida. 감기를 뗄 수가 없읍니다.

riddle *n.* (*puzzle*) susukkekki 수수께끼. *R*~ *me a* ~, *what's this?* I susukkekki aramatch'wŏ pwayo. 이 수수께끼, 알아맞춰 봐요.

ride *n.* t'agi 타기. —*vi.*, *vt.* t'ada 타다. ~ *a horse* marŭl molda 말을 몰다/ ~ *in a bus* pŏsŭrŭl t'ada 버스를 타다/ *Let me have a* ~ *in your car.* Tangshin ch'a-e chom t'aewŏ chushio. 당신 차에 좀 태워 주시오/ *You can't* ~ *in this car with this ticket.* I p'yo kajigonŭn t'al su ŏpsŭmnida. 이 표 가지고는 탈 수 없읍니다.

ridge *n.* (*of mount*) sandŭngsŏngi 산등성이, (*of roof*) yongmaru 용마루.

ridiculous *adj.* usŭun 우스운, pabo kat'ŭn 바보 같은. *You look* ~ *in those blue jeans.* Ch'ŏngbajirŭl ipko innŭn tangshin kkori usŭpkunyo. 청바지를 입고 있는 당신 꼴이 우습군요.

riding *n.* sŭngma 승마. ~ *boots* sŭngmahwa 승마화/ *a* ~ *crop* malch'aetchik 말채찍/ *a* ~ *suit* sŭngmabok 승마복.

rifle *n*. (*just*) soch'ong 소총. *shoot a* ~ ch'ongŭl ssoda 총을 쏘다/ *a toy* ~ changnankam soch'ong 장난감 소총.

right *adj*. (*just*) parŭn 바른, (*correct*) chŏnghwak'an 정확한, (*true*) chintcha 진짜, (*opp. left*) orŭntchogŭi 오른쪽의. —*n*. (*privilege*) kwŏlli 권리, (*direction*) orŭntchok 오른쪽, uch'ŭk 우측/ *Is your watch* ~ ? Tangshin shigyenŭn massŭmnikka ? 당신 시계는 맞습니까/ *You are perfectly* ~. Chidanghan malssŭmimnida. 지당한 말씀입니다/ *human* ~s inkwŏn 인권/ *You have no* ~ *to come in*. Tangshinŭn tŭrŏol kwŏlliga ŏpsŭmnida. 당신은 들어올 권리가 없습니다/ *Take the first turning to the* ~. Ch'ŏttchae mot'ungiesŏ uch'ŭgŭro toshipshio. 첫째 모퉁이에서 우측으로 도십시오/*the* ~ *hand* orŭnson 오른손/ *the* ~ *wing* uik 우익, up'a 우파/ *I think it's all* ~, *too*. Kŭgŏtto chot'ago saenggak'amnida. 그것도 좋다고 생각합니다.

rim *n*. (*margin*) kajangjari 가장자리, (*edge*) t'e 테, t'eduri 테두리. *the* ~ *of an eyeglass* an-gyŏngt'e 안경테.

ring *n*. (*for fingers*) panji 반지, (*arena*) kwŏnt'u shihapchang 권투 시합장. —*vi.,vt.* (*sound*) ullida 울리다, (*telephone*) chŏnhwarŭl kŏlda 전화를 걸다. *That's a nice* ~. Kŭgŏsŭn choŭn panjiimnida/ 그것은 좋은 반지입니다/ *a diamond*[*gold, jeweled*] ~ taia[kŭm, posŏk] panji 다이아[금, 보석] 반지/ *Just* ~ *the bell near the exit*. Ch'ulgu kyŏte innŭn perŭl ullishipshio. 출구 곁에 있는 벨을 울리십시오/ *Please* ~ *me up at ten*. Yŏlshie chŏnhwa kŏrŏ chushipshio. 10시에 전화 걸어 주십시오. 「장.

rink *n*. (*for skating*) shillae sŭk'eit'ŭjang 실내 스케이트

rinse *vt*. (*wash lightly*) hengguda 헹구다. ~ *out clothes* osŭl hengguda 옷을 헹구다/ ~ *out one's mouth* ibŭl kashida 입을 가시다.

riot *n*. (*uprising*) p'oktong 폭동, (*disturbance*) sodong 소동. *raise a* ~ sodongŭl irŭk'ida 소동을 일으키다/ *a student* ~ hagwŏn soyo 학원 소요.

rip *vt., vi*. (*tear*) tchitta 찢다. —*n*. (*rent*) tchijŏjin t'ŭm 찢어진 틈. ~ *open an envelope* pongt'urŭl tchijŏ yŏlda 봉투를 찢어 열다.

ripe *adj.* (*mature*) igŭn 익은. *Are these grapes* ~? I p'odonŭn igŏssŭmnikka? 이 포도는 익었읍니까/ ~ *fruit* igŭn kwail 익은 과일.

ripen *vi.,vt.* (*become ripe*) ikta 익다, (*make ripe*) ik'ida 익히다.

ripple *n.* (*little waves*) chanmulkyŏl 잔물결. —*vi.* chanmulkyŏri ilda 잔물결이 일다.

rise *vi.* (*go up*) orŭda 오르다, (*sun, moon, etc.*) ttŭda 뜨다, (*stand up*) irŏsŏda 일어서다, (*get up*) irŏnada 일어나다, (*go higher*) orŭda 오르다. *Has the moon risen yet?* Pŏlssŏ tari ttŏssŭmnikka? 벌써 달이 떴읍니까/ ~ *from a chair* ŭija-esŏ irŏsŏda 의자에서 일어서다/ *Prices are rising.* Mulkaga orŭmnida. 물가가 오릅니다.

risk *n.* (*danger*) wihŏm 위험, (*hazard*) mohŏm 모험. —*vt.* (*expose to peril*) wit'aeropke hada 위태롭게 하다, (*venture*) naegŏlda 내걸다. *at the* ~ *of* ...ŭl murŭpssŭgo ...을 무릅쓰고/ *at all* ~s ŏttŏn wihŏmŭl murŭpssŭgorado 어떤 위험을 무릅쓰고라도.

rite *n.* (*ceremony*) ŭishik 의식, (*observance*) kwallye 관례. *burial* ~s changnyeshik 장례식/ *the* ~s *of hospitality* sonnim chŏptae 손님 접대.

rival *n.* (*competitor*) kyŏngjaengja 경쟁자, (*equal*) chŏksu 적수(敵手), raibŏl 라이벌. ~ *firms* kyŏngjaeng hoesa 경쟁 회사/ ~ *lovers* yŏnjŏk 연적(戀敵)/ *business* ~ sangjŏk 상적(商敵).

river *n.* nae 내, kang 강. *What's the name of this* ~? I kangŭi irŭmŭn muŏshimnikka? 이 강의 이름은 무엇입니까/ *What's the longest* ~ *in Korea?* Han-gugesŏ cheil kin kangŭn muŏshimnikka? 한국에서 제일 긴 강은 무엇입니까/ *The Yalu R~ is the longest one in Korea.* Amnokkangi Han-gugesŏ kajang kin kangimnida. 압록강이 한국에서 가장 긴 강입니다/ ~*side* kangbyŏn 강변.

road *n.* (*way*) kil 길, toro 도로. *a broad* ~ nŏlbŭn toro 넓은 도로/ *a motor* ~ chadongch'a kil 자동차 길/ *a steep* ~ pit'alkil 비탈길/ *an uphill* ~ orŭmakkil 오르막길/ *a downhill* ~ naerimakkil 내리막길/ *Where does this* ~ *lead to?* I kirŭn ŏdiro kanŭn kirimnikka? 이 길은 어디로

가는 길입니까/ *This ~ leads to Suwon.* I kirŭn Suwŏn kanŭn kirimnida. 이 길은 수원 가는 길입니다/ *~side* kilka 길가.

roar *vi., vt.* (*bellow*) ŭrŭrŏnggŏrida 으르렁거리다, (*shout*) kohamch'ida 고함치다. —*n.* (*of animal*) ŭrŭrŏnggŏrinŭn sori 으르렁거리는 소리, (*of human*) nosŏng 노성, (*of cannon*) p'osŏng 포성. *the ~s of tiger* horangi urŭm sori 호랑이 울음 소리/ *You need not ~.* Kŭrŏk'e kohamch'il p'iryoga ŏpsŭmnida. 그렇게 고함칠 필요가 없읍니다/ *I heard the waves ~ing.* Kōsen p'ado sorirŭl tŭrŏssŭmnida. 거센 파도 소리를 들었읍니다.

roast *n.* (*~ meat*) kuun kogi 구운 고기, pulgogi 불고기. —*vt.* kupta 굽다. *~ beef* soegogi pulgogi 쇠고기 불고기/ *~ pork* twaejigogi pulgogi 돼지고기 불고기.

rob *vt.* (*plunder*) ppaeatta 빼앗다, (*steal*) humch'ida 훔치다. *I was ~bed of my watch.* Nanŭn shigyerŭl ppaeatkyŏssŭmnida. 나는 시계를 빼앗겼읍니다/ *I heard your house was ~bed last night.* Ōjetpam todugi turŏttajiyo. 어젯밤 도둑이 들었다지요.

robber *n.* kangdo 강도. *a ~ in a bank* ŭnhaeng kangdo 은행 강도.

robbery *n.* todukchil 도둑질, kangdojil 강도질.

robe *n.* *a bath ~* hwajangbok 화장복/ *official ~s* kwanbok 관복/ *a lawyer's ~* pŏppok 법복.

rock *n.* (*stone*) pawi 바위, (*pl.*) amch'o 암초. *on the ~* (*wrecked*) chwach'ohan 좌초한/ *Their marriage is on the ~.* Kŭ saramdŭrŭi kyŏrhonŭn p'at'an sangt'aeimnida. 그 사람들의 결혼은 파탄 상태입니다/ *Give me a Scotch on the ~s, please.* Sŭk'och'i on tŏ rok'ŭrŭl chuseyo. 스코치 온 더 로크를 주세요.

rocking chair hundŭrŭija 흔들의자 (=*rocker*).

rod *n.* (*thin bar*) maktaegi 막대기, (*pole*) changtae 장대, (*whip*) hoech'ori 회초리. *a lightning ~* p'iroech'im 피뢰침/ *give the ~* maejirhada 매질하다.

rogue *n.* (*rascal*) ak'an 악한, (*vagabond*) purangja 부랑자, kaegujangi 개구장이. *You dear little ~!* I kaegujangi kat'ŭn nom! 이 개구장이 같은 놈!

role *n.* (*part*) yŏk'al 역할, (*function*) immu 임무. *play an important* ∼ chungyohan yŏk'arŭl hada 중요한 역할을 하다/ *title* ∼ chuyŏk 주역(主役).

roll *n.* (*small bread*) roulppang 로울빵, (*list of name*) myŏngbu 명부, (*of paper*) turumari 두루마리. *—vi.,vt.* (∼ *over*) kurŭda 구르다, (*wind*) kamta 감다, malda 말다. *an employment* ∼ chigwŏn myŏngbu 직원 명부/ *the* ∼ *of voters* t'up'yoja myŏngbu 투표자 명부/ *Let me have a* ∼ *of black and white film.* Hŭkpaek p'illŭm han t'ong chuseyo. 흑백 필름 한 통 주세요/ *R*∼ *up that map on the wall.* Pyŏge kŏllin chidorŭl mashipshio. 벽에 걸린 지도를 마십시오.

Roman *adj.* Romaŭi 로마의. ∼ *Catholic* Roma k'at'ollik kyodo 로마 카톨릭 교도/ ∼ *law* Roma pŏp 로마 법.

romance *n.* (*love story*) romaensŭ 로맨스, yŏnae iyagi 연애 이야기, chŏn-gi sosŏl 전기(傳奇) 소설.

romantic *adj.* nangmanjŏgin 낭만적인.

roof *n.* chibung 지붕. *a thatched* ∼ ch'oga chibung 초가 지붕/ *a* ∼ *tile* chibung kiwa 지붕 기와.

room *n.* (*chamber*) pang 방, shil 실(室), (*space*) chari 자리. *I want a* ∼, *please.* Pangi issŭmnikka? 방이 있읍니까/ *How many beds in a* ∼? Pangenŭn ch'imdaega myŏt kae issŭmnikka? 방에는 침대가 몇 개 있읍니까/ *The* ∼ *you are looking for is number 312.* Ch'ajŭshinŭn pangŭn sambaekshibi hoshirimnida. 찾으시는 방은 312호실입니다/ *Is there* ∼ *for me in the car?* Kŭ ch'a-e naega tŭrŏgal chariga issŭmnikka? 그 차에 내가 들어갈 자리가 있읍니까?

roost *n.* (*perch*) hwae 홰, takchang 닭장.

rooster *n.* (*cock*) sut'ak 수탉.

root *n.* ppuri 뿌리, (*cause*) kŭn-wŏn 근원.

rope *n.* saekki 새끼, patchul 밧줄, rop'ŭ 로프. *Can you reach the* ∼? Rop'ŭe soni tassŭmnikka? 로프에 손이 닿습니까/ ∼*skipping* chullŏmki 줄넘기/ ∼ *ladder* saekki sadaktari 새끼 사다리.

rosary *n.* (*Cath.*) mukchu 묵주, (*Budd.*) yŏmju 염주.

rose *n.* changmi 장미. *a wild* ∼ tŭlchangmi 들장미. *I*

would like to buy a few ~*s.* Changmikkoch'ŭl chom sago shipsŭmnida. 장미꽃을 좀 사고 싶습니다/ *the R*~ *of Sharon* mugunghwa 무궁화.

rosé *n.* roje 로제, changmipit p'odoju 장미빛 포도주. *Make it* ~, *please.* Rojero hae chushio. 로제로 해 주시오.

rot *vi.,vt.* (*decay*) ssŏkta 썩다. —*n.* (~*ting*) pup'ae 부패.

rotary *n.* (*traffic circle*) rot'ŏri 로터리, kyoch'aro 교차로. *the R*~ *Club* rot'ŏri k'ŭllŏp 로터리 클럽.

rotate *vi.* (*revolve*) hoejŏnhada 회전하다, (*alternate*) kyodaehada 교대하다.

rotten *adj.* (*decayed*) ssŏgŭn 썩은, (*corrupt*) pup'aehan 부패한, (*unpleasant*) pulk'waehan 불쾌한. *the* ~ *government officials* pup'aehan kwalli 부패한 관리/ ~ *eggs* ssŏgŭn talgyal 썩은 달걀/*I'm feeling* ~ *today.* Onŭrŭn kibuni nappŭmnida. 오늘은 기분이 나쁩니다.

rouge *n.* (*lipstick*) yŏnji 연지, rujŭ 루즈. *put on* ~ yŏnjirŭl tchikta 연지를 찍다.

rough *adj.* (*not smooth*) kŏch'in 거친, (*uneven*) ult'ung-bult'unghan 울퉁불퉁한, (*rude*) nanp'ok'an 난폭한, (*stormy*) hŏmhan 험한. *a* ~ *skin* kŏch'in p'ibu 거친 피부/ *a* ~ *road* ult'ungbult'unghan kil 울퉁불퉁한 길/ *a* ~ *boy* nanp'ok'an sonyŏn 난폭한 소년/ ~ *weather* hŏmhan nalssi 험한 날씨/ *a* ~ *estimate* kaesan 개산.

round *adj.* tunggŭn 둥근. *a* ~ *table* tunggŭn t'eibŭl 둥근 테이블. *a* ~ *trip* ilchu yŏhaeng 일주 여행/ *a* ~-*trip ticket* wangbok sŭngch'akwŏn 왕복 승차권/ *Please give me a* ~ *trip ticket for Pusan.* Pusanhaeng wangbok ch'ap'yorŭl han chang chushio. 부산행(行) 왕복 차표를 한 장 주시오/ *all the year* ~ illyŏn naenae 일년 내내.

route *n.* (*road*) kil 길, t'ongno 통로, (*line*) hangno 항로. *an air* ~ hanggongno 항공로.

routine *n.* p'ane pak'in il 판에 박힌 일. *daily* ~ ilgwa 일과.

row *n.* (*line*) chul 줄, (*rank*) yŏl 열(列). —*vt., vi.* (*use* ~*s*) norŭl chŏtta 노를 젓다. *in the front* ~ apchure 앞 줄에/*the first* ~ ch'ŏttchae chul 첫째 줄/ ~ *a boat* paerŭl chŏtta 배를 젓다/ *Shall we* ~ *back to the shore?* Paerŭl chŏŏ tashi haeanŭro toragalkkayo? 배를 저어 다시 해안으로 돌아갈까요?

royal *adj.* (*of a king*) wangŭi 왕의. *the* ~ *family* wangshil 왕실/ *a* ~ *palace* wanggung 왕궁.

royalty *n.* (*on a book*) inse 인세(印稅), (*on patent*) t'ŭk'ŏkwŏn sayongnyo 특허권 사용료.

rub *vt.* pibida 비비다, (*scrub*) munjirŭda 문지르다, (*clean*) takta 닦다. *He was* ~*bing his hands together.* Kŭ saramŭn tu sonŭl pibigo issŏssŭmnida. 그 사람은 두 손을 비비고 있었읍니다/ *R*~ *this oil on your skin.* P'ibue i kirŭmŭl parŭshio. 피부에 이 기름을 바르시오/ *R*~ *the surface dry.* P'yomyŏnŭl takka naeshio. 표면을 닦아 내시오.

rubber *n.* komu 고무, (*eraser*) chiugae 지우개, (*pl.*) (*overshoes*) tŏtshin 덧신. ~ *boots* komu changhwa 고무 장화/ ~ *shoes* komushin 고무신/ *a* ~ *stamp* komu tojang 고무 도장/ *crude* ~ saenggomu 생고무.

rubbing *n.* t'appon 탑본(搨本). *make a* ~ *of* tapponŭl ttŭda 탑본을 뜨다.

rubbish *n.* ssŭregi 쓰레기. *a pile of* ~ ssŭregi tŏmi 쓰레기 더미/ ~ *gatherer* ssŭregikkun 쓰레기꾼/*Dump no* ~ *here.* Yŏgie ssŭregirŭl pŏriji mashio. 여기에 쓰레기를 버리지 마시오/ *Where can I dump this* ~? I ssŭregirŭl ŏdida pŏrilkkayo? 이 쓰레기를 어디다 버릴까요?

ruby *n.* rubi 루비, hongok 홍옥.

rucksack *n.* paenang 배낭, ruksaek 룩색.

rudder *n.* (*of boats, etc.*) k'i 키, panghyangt'a 방향타.

rude *adj.* (*impolite*) muryehan 무례한, (*without culture*) kyoyang ŏmnŭn 교양 없는, (*crude*) kŏch'in 거친, (*primitive*) yamanjŏgin 야만적인. *a* ~ *fellow* pŏrŭdŏmnŭn nyŏsŏk 버릇없는 녀석/ *a* ~ *reply* muryehan taedap 무례한 대답/ ~ *waves* kŏch'in p'ado 거친 파도/*our* ~ *forefathers* uriŭi migaehan chosangdŭl 우리의 미개한 조상들/ *What a* ~ *reply!* I ŏlmana muryehan taedabimnikka! 이 얼마나 무례한 대답입니까/ *Was I being* ~? Shillyenŭn an toeŏnnŭnjiyo? 실례는 안 되었는지요?

ruffian *n.* (*cruel man*) ak'an 악한, kkangp'ae 깡패.

rug *n.* (*floor covering*) yungdan 융단, kkalgae 깔개, yangt'anja 양탄자, (*blanket*) tamyo 담요. *a hearth* ~ nallo kkalgae 난로 깔개.

ruin *n.* (*collapse*) punggoe 붕괴, (*destruction*) p'amyŏl 파멸, (*downfall*) mollak 몰락, (*corruption*) t'arak 타락, (*remains*) p'yehŏ 폐허. —*vt.*, *vi.* (*destroy*) p'amyŏl-shik'ida 파멸시키다, (*spoil*) mangch'ida 망치다.

rule *n.* (*regulation*) kyuch'ik 규칙, (*control*) chibae 지배, (*instruction*) myŏngnyŏng 명령, (*ruler*) cha 자. —*vt.* *vi.* (*control*) chibaehada 지배하다, (*decide*) p'an-gyŏr hada 판결하다. *My* ~ *is to get up at seven and have breakfast at eight.* Ilgopshie irŏna yŏdŏlshie ach'imŭ mŏngnŭn kŏshi nae kyuch'igimnida. 7시에 일어나 8시에 아침을 먹는 것이 내 규칙입니다.

ruler *n.* chibaeja 지배자, (*for measuring*) cha 자, (*for bookkeeping*) pugibong 부기봉.

rummage *vt.*, *vi.* (*hunt through*) satsach'i twijida 샅샅이 뒤지다. ~ *in the desk drawer for* ch'aeksang sŏ rabesŏ ...ŭl twijida 책상 서랍에서 …을 뒤지다.

rumo(u)r *n.* (*popular report*) somun 소문, p'ungmun 풍문. *start a* ~ somunnaeda 소문내다.

rumple *vt.* (*crumple*) kugida 구기다, (*ruffle*) hŏngk'ŭld 헝클다. *I have just done my hair, so please don't* ~ *i* Panggŭm mŏri sŏnjirŭl haessŭni chebal hŏngk'ŭl mashio. 방금 머리 손질을 했으니 제발 헝클지 마시오.

run *vi.*, *vt.* (*move swiftly on foot*) tallida 달리다, (*flee* tomangch'ida 도망치다, (*flow*) hŭrŭda 흐르다, (*man age*) kyŏngyŏnghada 경영하다, (*be a candidate*) ch'u mahada 출마하다, (*convey*) narŭda 나르다. —*n.* (*running* talligi 달리기, (*of performance*) sangyŏn kigan 상연 간. *We ran to help him.* Kŭ saramŭl tourŏ tallyŏg ssŭmnida. 그 사람을 도우러 달려갔습니다 / *Are you ning in the 100 meters?* Paek mit'ŏ kyŏngjue ch'u chŏnhashimnikka? 100미터 경주에 출전하십니까 / ~ *fo election to the National Assembly* kuk'oeŭiwŏne ch'u mahada 국회의원에 출마하다 / ~ *a hotel*[*restauran* *hospital*] hot'el[yojŏng, pyŏngwŏn]ŭl kyŏngyŏnghada 호텔[요정, 병원]을 경영하다/ *Would you ~ me up to town?* Shinaekkaji t'aewŏda chushigessŭmnikka? 시내까지 태워다 주시겠읍니까/*Can we have a trial ~ in the new car?* Sae ch'arŭl hanbŏn shisŭnghal su issŭlkkayo? 새 차를 한번 시승(試乘)할 수 있을까요/*Are the ~s frequent?* Ch'ap'yŏnŭn chaju issŭmnikka? 차편은 자주 있읍니까/*The play had a ~ of six months.* Kŭ yŏn-gŭgŭn yukkaewŏlgan yŏnsok kongyŏndoeŏssŭmnida. 그 연극은 6개월간 연속 공연되었읍니다/ *~ away* tomangch'ida 도망치다/ *We've ~ out of letter paper.* P'yŏnjijirŭl ta ssŏ pŏryŏssŭmnida. 편지지를 다 써 버렸읍니다/*My brother was ~ over by a taxi.* Nae tongsaengi t'aekshie ch'iŏssŭmnida. 내 동생이 택시에 치었읍니다/ *I'm ~ning short of money.* Toni ttŏrŏjyŏ kungsaek'amnida. 돈이 떨어져 궁색합니다.

runabout *n.* (*vagabond*) pangnangja 방랑자, (*carriage*) sohyŏng chadongch'a 소형 자동차.

runaway *n.* (*fugitive*) tomangja 도망자.

runner *n.* (*racer*) kyŏngjuja 경주자, (*of baseball*) chuja 주자(走者), (*fugitive*) tomangja 도망자.

rupture *n.* (*breaking*) p'ayŏl 파열, (*quarrel*) purhwa 불화. —*vt., vi.* tchitta 찢다, tchijŏjida 찢어지다. *the ~ of a blood vessel* hyŏlgwanŭi p'ayŏl 혈관의 파열/ *a ~ between friends* ch'in-gu saiŭi purhwa 친구 사이의 불화.

rural *adj.* shigorŭi 시골의. *~ people* shigol saram 시골 사람/ *~ manners* shigol p'ungsŭp 시골 풍습.

rush *n.* (*onset*) tolchin 돌진, (*urgent pressure*) punmang 분망, (*sudden demands*) kŭpsuyo 급수요. —*vi., vt.* (*dash*) ttwiŏdŭlda 뛰어들다, (*act rashly*) sŏnggŭp'i hada 성급히 하다. *I'm in ~, you may take your time.* Nanŭn pappŭji anŭnikka ch'ŏnch'ŏnhi hashipshio. 나는 바쁘지 않으니까 천천히 하십시오/*I don't like the ~ of city life.* Nanŭn punmanghan toshi saenghwarŭl choahaji anssŭmnida. 나는 분망한 도시 생활을 좋아하지 않습니다/ *the ~ hour* rŏshi awŏ 러시 아워/*We were caught in the ~ hour traffic.* Rŏshi awŏŭi kyot'ong ttaemune kkom-

tchak mot'aessŭmnida. 러시 아워의 교통 때문에 꼼짝 못했
읍니다/ *I have to ~ to Seoul Station by two.* Tushikka j
Sŏulyŏge kŭp'i kaya hamnida. 2시까지 서울역에 급히 가
야 합니다/ *We were in a hurry. Please ~ our orders*
Pappŭmnida. Chumunhan kŏt ppalli chuseyo. 바쁩니다.
주문한 것 빨리 주세요.

Russia *n.* Rŏshia 러시아, Soryŏn 소련. *Soviet ~* Sobiet'
Rŏshia 소비에트 러시아.

Russian *n.* (*person*) Rŏshiain 러시아인, (*language*) Rŏ
shiaŏ 러시아어. —*adj.* Rŏshiaŭi 러시아의. *~ revolutio*
Rŏshia hyŏngmyŏng 러시아 혁명.

rust *n.* nok 녹. —*vi.* noksŭlda 녹슬다. *gather ~* noksŭld
녹슬다/ *remove ~* nogŭl takta 녹을 닦다/ *This knif*
resists ~. I naip'ŭnŭn nogi sŭlji anssŭmnida. 이 나c
프는 녹이 슬지 않습니다.

rustic *n.* (*countryman*) shigolttŭgi 시골뜨기, (*farmer*
nongbu 농부.

rusty *adj.* nŏksŭn 녹슨. *a ~ blade* noksŭn k'al 녹슨 칼
Your head is getting ~, I fear. Tangshin mŏrinŭ
noksŭnŭn kŏt kat'ayo. 당신 머리는 녹스는 것 같아요.

rut *n.* (*wheel track*) pak'wi chaguk 바퀴 자국, (*fixe*
way) p'ane pak'in pangshik 판에 박힌 방식, sangt'u
투, sangnye 상례.

ruthless *adj.* (*merciless*) mujabihan 무자비한. *a ~ tyra*
mujabihan p'okkun 무자비한 폭군.

rye *n.* homil 호밀. *~ bread* hŭkppang 흑빵. *How muc*
is this loaf of ~ bread? I hŭkppangŭn ŏlmaimnikka
이 흑빵은 얼마입니까?

—❦ **S** ❦—

Sabbath *n.* anshigil 안식일. *keep the ~* anshigirŭl chik
da 안식일을 지키다.

sabotage *n.* t'aeŏp 태업, sabot'ajŭ 사보타즈. *acts of*
sabot'ajŭ haengwi 사보타즈 행위.

sack *n.* (*large cloth bag*) charu 자루, pudae 부대. *t*

~s *of potatoes* kamja tu pudae 감자 두 부대.

acred *adj.* (*holy*) shinsŏnghan 신성한, (*consecrated*) shinege pach'in 신에게 바친, (*inviolable*) shinsŏng pulgach'imhan 신성 불가침한. *a* ~ *building* shinjŏn 신전/ ~ *music* chonggyo ŭmak 종교 음악.

acrifice *n.* (*offering to god*) chemul 제물, (*voluntary loss*) hŭisaeng 희생. —*vt.* (*devote*) hŭisaenghada 희생하다. *By* ~ *do you mean loss of money?* Hŭisaengirani sonhaerŭl posyŏttanŭn malssŭmimnikka? 희생이라니 손해를 보셨다는 말씀입니까/ *We are prepared to make great* ~*s.* K'ŭn hŭisaengŭl ch'irŭl kagoga toeŏ issŭmnida. 큰 희생을 치를 각오가 되어 있읍니다.

ad *adj.* (*grieving*) sŭlp'ŭn 슬픈, (*deplorable*) t'ongt'anhal 통탄할. *Why is he looking so* ~? Wae chŏ punŭn chŏrŏk'e sŭlp'ŏ poimnikka? 왜 저 분은 저렇게 슬퍼 보입니까/ *Don't be so* ~. Nŏmu sŭlp'ŏhaji maseyo. 너무 슬퍼하지 마세요.

addle *n.* anjang 안장.

afe *n.* (*strongbox*) kŭmgo 금고. —*adj.* (*secure*) anjŏnhan 안전한, (*careful*) choshimsŏng innŭn 조심성 있는. *Is this beach* ~ *for bathing?* I haebyŏnesŏ heŏmch'yŏdo anjŏnhamnikka? 이 해변에서 헤엄쳐도 안전합니까/ *Is your dog* ~? Tangshinŭi kaenŭn mulji anssŭmnikka? 당신의 개는 물지 않습니까/ *Keep it in a* ~ *place.* Kŭgŏsŭl anjŏnhan kose pogwanhashio. 그것을 안전한 곳에 보관하시오.

afely *adv.* anjŏnhage 안전하게, musahi 무사히.

afety *n.* anjŏn 안전. *a* ~ *belt* kumyŏngdae 구명대/ *a* ~ *pin* anjŏnp'in 안전핀/*a* ~ *razor* anjŏn myŏndok'al 안전 면도칼/*a* ~ *zone* anjŏn chidae 안전 지대/~ *for life and property* saengmyŏnggwa chaesanŭi anjŏn 생명과 재산의 안전.

ail *n.* tot 돛, (*ships*) pae 배, (*voyage*) hanghae 항해. —*vi., vt.* (*put to sea*) ch'ulbŏmhada 출범하다, (*navigate*) hanghaehada 항해하다. *lift a* ~ toch'ŭl ollida 돛을 올리다/ *lower a* ~ toch'ŭl naerida 돛을 내리다/ *furl a* ~ toch'ŭl malda 돛을 말다/*We had an easy* ~. Urinŭn p'yŏnhan hanghaerŭl haessŭmnida. 우리는 편한 항해를 했읍니다/ *It will take about eight hours to* ~ *from*

Pusan to Cheju. Pusanesŏ Chejukkaji paero yŏdŏ
shigantchŭm kŏllimnida. 부산에서 제주도까지 배로 여덟 시
간쯤 걸립니다. 「수병.

sailor *n.* (*seaman*) sŏnwŏn 선원, (*bluejacket*) subyŏng

saint *n.* sŏngja 성자, (*S~*) sŏng 성(聖). *S~ Luke* sŏng
Nuga 성(聖) 누가.

sake *n.* (*purpose*) mokchŏk 목적, (*because of*) iyu 이유,
(*interest*) iik 이익. *I'll help you for your sister's ~*
Tangshin nuirŭl wihae tangshinŭl topkesso. 당신 누이를
위해 당신을 돕겠소/ *art for art's ~* yesurŭl wihan yesu
예술을 위한 예술/ *for God's ~*, *for Heaven's ~*, *for*
pity's ~ chebal 제발/ *Save me for God's ~*. Cheba
kuhae chushio. 제발 구(救)해 주시오/ *for one's name'*
~ myŏngyerŭl wihae 명예를 위해.

salad *n.* saellŏdŭ 샐러드. *fruit ~* kwail saellŏdŭ 과일 샐러
드/ *vegetable ~* yach'ae saellŏdŭ 야채 샐러드/ *I'd lik*
a ~, please. Saellŏdŭrŭl chuseyo. 샐러드를 주세요/ *Le*
me try chef's ~. Chubangjangŭi saellŏdŭrŭl mŏgŏ
polkkayo? 주방장의 샐러드를 먹어 볼까요?

salary *n.* (*pay*) ponggŭp 봉급, kŭmnyo 급료, (*monthly*
wŏlgŭp 월급/ *a commencing ~* ch'obong 초봉/ *lo*
salaries pakpong 박봉/*I expect a moderate ~.* Pot'on
wŏlgŭbŭn padaya hagessŭmnida. 보통 월급은 받아야 하겠
읍니다.

sale *n.* p'anmae 판매, (*amount sold*) maesanggo 매상고
auction ~ kyŏngmae 경매/ *bargain ~* ssaguryŏ p'anma
싸구려 판매/ *instalment ~* wŏlbu p'anmae 월부 판매/ *I*
this house for ~? I chibŭn p'al kŏshimnikka? 이 집은
팔 것입니까/ *Don't you have ~s tax in Korea?* Han
gugenŭn p'anmaesega ŏpsŭmnikka? 한국에는 판매세가
없읍니까/ *S~s are down a bit.* Maesanggoga chon
churŏssŭmnida. 매상고가 좀 줄었읍니다. 「원

salesman *n.* p'anmaewŏn 판매원, (*Am.*) oep'anwŏn 외판

sales promotion p'anmae hwaltong 판매 활동.

saliva *n.* ch'im 침, t'aaek 타액. *swallow one's ~* ch'imŭ
samk'ida 침을 삼키다/*run ~* ch'imŭl hŭllida 침을 흘리다

salmon *n.* yŏnŏ 연어.

salt *n.* sogŭm 소금. *May I trouble you for the* ~ ? Sogŭm chom chibŏ chushiji ank'essŭmnikka? 소금 좀 집어 주시지 않겠읍니까? 「kogi 절인 고기.

salted *adj.* sogŭme chŏrin 소금에 절인. ~ *meat* chŏrin

salty *adj.* tchan 짠. *a* ~ *taste* tchanmat 짠맛 / *This soup is somewhat* ~. I kugŭn yakkan tchamnida. 이 국은 약간 짭니다.

salutation *n.* insa 인사. *exchange* ~s sŏro insahada 서로 인사하다 / *bow in* ~ insaro mŏrirŭl sugida 인사로 머리를 숙이다.

salute *n.* (*bow*) chŏl 절, (*greeting*) insa 인사, (*military*) kyŏngnye 경례. —*vt.* (*greet*) insahada 인사하다. *They* ~*d each other with a bow.* Sŏro chŏrŭl hayŏssŭmnida. 서로 절을 하였읍니다.

salvation *n.* kuje 구제. *the S*~ *Army* kusegun 구세군.

same *adj.* (*identical*) kat'ŭn 같은, (*similar*) pisŭt'an 비슷한. *I have the* ~ *watch as you have.* Nado tangshingwa kat'ŭn shigyerŭl kajigo issŭmnida. 나도 당신과 같은 시계를 가지고 있읍니다 / *We are all going the* ~ *way.* Urinŭn modu kat'ŭn kirŭl kago issŭmnida. 우리는 모두 같은 길을 가고 있읍니다 / *Enjoy your stay here. I wish the* ~. Chŭlgŏpke mŏmurŭshipshio. Taekkesŏdoyo. 즐겁게 머무르십시오. 댁께서도요 / *Don't all speak at the* ~ *time.* Moduga tongshie marhaji mashio. 모두가 동시에 말하지 마시오 / *all the* ~ kkok kat'ŭn 꼭 같은, amuraedo choŭn 아무래도 좋은 / *It is all the* ~ *to me.* Na-egenŭn amuraedo chossŭmnida. 나에게는 아무래도 좋습니다.

sample *n.* (*specimen*) kyŏnbon 견본, p'yobon 표본. *a* ~ *copy* kyŏnbonch'aek 견본책 / *a trade* ~ sangp'um kyŏnbon 상품 견본 / *Show me a* ~, *please.* Kyŏnbonŭl poyŏ chushio. 견본을 보여 주시오 / *come[be] up to* ~ kyŏnbongwa katta 견본과 같다.

sanction *n.* (*approval*) sŭngin 승인, (*consent*) ch'ansŏng 찬성, (*penalty*) chejae 제재. —*vt.* (*approve*) hŏgahada 허가하다, (*authorize*) shiinhada 시인하다. *economic* ~s kyŏngjejŏk chejae 경제적 제재 / *apply* ~ *against* ...e chejaerŭl kahada ...에 제재를 가하다.

sand *n.* morae 모래. ~*bag* morae chumŏni 모래 주머니/ ~*paper* sap'o 사포(砂布)/ *fine* ~ mosae 모새/ *sprinkle* ~ moraerŭl ppurida 모래를 뿌리다.

sandy *adj.* (*of sand*) moraeŭi 모래의, (*gritty*) kkalkkarhan 깔깔한, (*yellowish*) moraepich'ŭi 모래빛의. ~ *hair* yŏnhan kalsaek mŏri 연한 갈색 머리.

sanitary *adj.* (*hygienic*) wisaengjŏgin 위생적인. *a* ~ *belt* wisaengdae 위생대/ ~ *facilities* wisaeng shisŏl 위생 시설/ ~ *room* wisaengshil 위생실/~ *thought* wisaeng kwannyŏm 위생 관념.

sap *n.* (*of plant*) chin 진, suaek 수액, (*vigor*) hwallyŏk 활력. *rubber* ~ komujin 고무진.

sarcastic *adj.* pikkonŭn 비꼬는, nollinŭn 놀리는.

sardine *n.* chŏngŏri 정어리. *canned* ~*s* chŏngŏri t'ongjorim 정어리 통조림.

sash *n.* (*band*) tti 띠, (*of window*) saeshi 새시. *She has a* ~ *around her waist.* Kŭ yŏjanŭn hŏrie ttirŭl turŭgo issŭmnida. 그 여자는 허리에 띠를 두르고 있습니다.

Satan *n.* (*Devil*) angma 악마, sat'an 사탄.

satchel *n.* (*small bag*) sonkabang 손가방.

satellite *n.* (*planet*) wisŏng 위성, (*attendant*) ch'ujongja 추종자, (*state*) wisŏngguk 위성국. ~ *cities* wisŏng toshi 위성 도시/ *artificial* ~ in-gong wisŏng 인공 위성.

satin *n.* (*fabric*) kongdan 공단.

satire *n.* p'ungja 풍자. *a* ~ *on modern civilization* hyŏndae munmyŏnge taehan p'ungja 현대 문명에 대한 풍자.

satisfaction *n.* manjok 만족. *a feeling of* ~ manjokkam 만족감/ *I heard the news with great* ~. Nanŭn kŭ soshigŭl tŭtko maeu manjok'ayŏssŭmnida. 나는 그 소식을 듣고 매우 만족하였습니다.

satisfactory *adj.* (*contented*) manjok'an 만족한, (*sufficient*) ch'ungbunhan 충분한, (*adequate*) almajŭn 알맞은, (*good*) choŭn 좋은. *Would that be* ~? Kŭgŏsŭro manjok'ashimnikka? 그것으로 만족하십니까/ *These goods are by no means* ~. I sangp'umdŭrŭn tomuji maŭme tŭlji anssŭmnida. 이 상품들은 도무지 마음에 들지 않습니다/ ~ *results* choŭn kyŏlgwa 좋은 결과.

satisfy *vt.,vi.* (*make content*) manjokshik'ida 만족시키다, (*convince*) naptŭkshik'ida 납득시키다, (*compensate*) paesanghada 배상하다. *I am satisfied with your explanation.* Tangshin sŏlmyŏnge manjok'amnida. 당신 설명에 만족합니다/ ~ *an obligation* pijŭl kapta 빚을 갚다.

Saturday *n.* t'oyoil 토요일.

sauce *n.* sosŭ 소스, (*Korean*) kanjang 간장. *put* ~ *on* sosŭrŭl ch'ida 소스를 치다.

saucer *n.* patch'im chŏpshi 받침 접시. *a flying* ~ pihaeng chŏpshi 비행 접시.

saucy *adj.* (*impudent*) ppŏnppŏnsŭrŏn 뻔뻔스런. *You are getting too* ~. (*to inferior*) Nŏnŭn chinach'ige kŏnbangjida. 너는 지나치게 건방지다.

savage *adj.* (*wild*) yamansŭrŏun 야만스러운. —*n.* yamanin 야만인. ~ *tribes* yamanjok 야만족.

save *vt., vi.* (*rescue*) kuhae naeda 구해 내다, (*reserve*) chŏch'uk'ada 저축하다, (*be frugal*) chŏryak'ada 절약하다. —*prep.* (*except*) ...ŭl cheoehago ...을 제외하고. *He* ~*d me from drowning.* Kŭ sarami naega mure ppajin kŏsŭl kuhae chuŏssŭmnida. 그 사람이 내가 물에 빠진 것을 구해 주었습니다/ *I* ~ *20 percent of my pay every month.* Maewŏl ponggŭbŭi iharŭl chŏch'uk'amnida. 매월 봉급의 2 할을 저축합니다/ *You can* ~ *two hours by taking the express.* Kŭp'aengŭl t'amyŏn tu shigan iltchik tassŭmnida. 급행을 타면 두 시간 일찍 닿습니다.

saw *n.* (*tool*) t'op 톱. —*vi., vt.* t'oburo k'yŏda 톱으로 켜다. *This wood* ~*s easily.* I namunŭn t'opchirhagi shwipsŭmnida. 이 나무는 톱질하기 쉽습니다/ ~ *dust* t'oppap 톱밥/ ~ *mill* chejaeso 제재소.

say *vt., vi.* (*speak*) marhada 말하다, (*honorific*) malssŭmhashida 말씀하시다, (*let us* ~) marhajamyŏn 말하자면. *How do you* ~ *this in English?* Igŏsŭl Yŏngŏro muŏrago marhamnikka? 이것을 영어로 무어라고 말합니까/ *Did you* ~ *anything?* Musŭn malssŭmŭl hasyŏssŭmnikka? 무슨 말씀을 하셨습니까/ *You may well* ~ *so.* Kŭrŏk'e malssŭmhashinŭn kŏtto tangyŏnhamnida. 그렇게 말씀하

시는 것도 당연합니다/ Do you ～ so? Chŏngmarimnikka?
정말입니까/ You don't ～ so. Sŏlma! 설마/ What do
you ～ to taking a walk? Sanch'aek'aji ank'essŭmnikka?
산책하지 않겠읍니까/ What ～ you to 500 won? Obaeg-
wŏnimyŏn ŏttŏssŭmnikka? 500원이면 어떻습니까?

saying n. soktam 속담. an old ～ yennal soktam 옛날
속담.

scab n. (of wound) ttakchi 딱지, (skin disease) p'ibu-
pyŏng 피부병.

scabbard n. (of sword) k'alchip 칼집.

scaffold n. (platform) palp'an 발판, (gallows) ch'ŏ-
hyŏngdae 처형대.

scald vt. tege hada 데게 하다. ～ one's hand with hot
water ttŭgŏun mure sonŭl teda 뜨거운 물에 손을 데다.

scale n. (of fish) pinŭl 비늘, (balance) chŏul 저울. Have
you removed the ～s? Pinŭrŭn pŏtkisyŏssŏyo? 비늘은
벗기셨어요/ a platform ～ anjŭnbaengi chŏul 앉은뱅이 저
울/ a folding ～ chŏpcha 접자.

scandal n. (disgrace) ch'umun 추문, (harmful gossip)
pibang 비방, (corruption) pujŏng sakŏn 부정 사건. Don't
listen to ～. Pibange kwirŭl kiuriji mashio. 비방에 귀를
기울이지 마시오.

scar n. sangch'ŏ chaguk 상처 자국.

scarce adj. (insufficient) mojaranŭn 모자라는, (rare)
tŭmun 드문. Eggs are ～ and expensive. Talgyari
mojara kapshi pissamnida. 달걀이 모자라 값이 비쌉니다.

scarcely adj. (hardly) kanshinhi 간신히, kyŏu 겨우,
(probably not) kŏŭi ...anida 거의 ...아니다. She is ～
thirteen years old. Kŭ yŏja ainŭn kyŏu yŏl se sari
toelkkamalkka hamnida. 그 여자 아이는 겨우 열 세 살이
될까말까 합니다/ I ～ know him. Nanŭn kŭ saramŭl
kŏŭi morŭmnida. 나는 그 사람을 거의 모릅니다.

scarcity n. (shortage) pujok 부족, (dearth) kigŭn 기근.
food ～ shingnyang pujok 식량 부족/labor ～ nodongnyŏk
pujok 노동력 부족/ job ～ ch'wijingnan 취직난/ a year
of great ～ kigŭnŭi hae 기근의 해.

scare vt. (frighten) kkamtchak nollage hada 깜짝 놀라게

하다. *Don't be* ~*d*. Nollaji mashio. 놀라지 마시오/ *I'm*
~*d*. Kkamtchak nollassŭmnida. 깜짝 놀랐읍니다.

scarecrow *n*. hŏsuabi 허수아비. *set up a* ~ hŏsuabirŭl
seuda 허수아비를 세우다.

scarf *n*. moktori 목도리, sŭk'ap'ŭ 스카프.

scarlet *n*. chinhongsaek 진홍색. ~*fever* sŏnghongyŏl 성
홍열.

scatter *vt., vi*. (*strew*) ppurida 뿌리다, hŭttŭrida 흩뜨리
다, (*disperse*) tchoch'a pŏrida 쫓아 버리다. *The police*
~*ed the mob*. Kyŏnggwani p'oktorŭl tchoch'a pŏryŏssŭmnida. 경관이 폭도를 쫓아 버렸읍니다/ *The park was*
~*ed with rubbish*. Kongwŏnenŭn ssŭregiga hŭt'ŏjyŏ
issŏssŭmnida. 공원에는 쓰레기가 흩어져 있었읍니다.

scavenger *n*. ch'ŏngsobu 청소부. *a municipal* ~ shich'ŏng
ch'ŏngsobu 시청 청소부.

scene *n*. (*place*) changmyŏn 장면, (*setting*) paegyŏng
배경, (*view*) kwanggyŏng 광경. *The sunrise was a*
beautiful ~. Haedojinŭn arŭmdaun kwanggyŏngiŏssŭm-
nida. 해돋이는 아름다운 광경이었읍니다.

scenery *n*. (*landscape*) p'unggyŏng 풍경, (*stage settings*)
mudae paegyŏng 무대 배경. *grand* ~ ungdaehan p'unggyŏng 웅대한 풍경/ *stage* ~ mudae paegyŏng 무대 배경.

scent *n*. (*smell*) naemsae 냄새, (*perfume*) hyanggi 향기,
(*liquid*) hyangsu 향수. *the* ~ *of roses* changmi hyanggi
장미 향기/ *a bottle of* ~ hyangsu han pyŏng 향수 한 병.

schedule *n*. (*list*) illamp'yo 일람표, (*timetable*) shiganp'yo
시간표, (*program*) yejŏng 예정. *a* ~ *of prices* mulka-
p'yo 물가표/ *a sailing* ~ ch'ulbŏm yejŏngp'yo 출범 예정
표/ *What is our* ~ *for tomorrow?* Naeil yejŏngŭn
muŏshimnikka? 내일 예정은 무엇입니까/ *You were* ~*d*
to come for yesterday. Tangshinŭn ŏje oshil yejŏngiŏ-
ssŭmnida. 당신은 어제 오실 예정이었읍니다/ *The ship is*
~*d to sail on April 10th*. Paenŭu sawŏl shibil ch'ŭl-
bŏmhal yejŏngimnida. 배는 4월 10일 출범할 예정입니다/
according to ~ yejŏngdaero 예정대로.

scheme *n*. (*plan*) kyehoek 계획, (*device*) an 안(案),
(*intrigue*) ŭmmo 음모. —*vt., vi*. (*plan*) kyehoek'ada

계획하다, (*plot*) ŭmmorŭl kkumida 음모를 꾸미다.

scholar *n.* (*learned man*) hakcha 학자, (*student*) haksaeng 학생. *a great* ~ taehakcha 대학자/ *an English* ~ Yŏngŏ hakcha 영어 학자/ *a backward* ~ chŏnŭnghan haksaeng 저능한 학생.

scholarship *n.* changhakkŭm 장학금. *I studied in America on a* ~. Nanŭn changhakkŭmŭl ŏdŏ Migugesŏ kongbuhaessŭmnida. 나는 장학금을 얻어 미국에서 공부했읍니다/ *win a* ~ changhakkŭmŭl ŏtta 장학금을 얻다.

school *n.* (*institution*) hakkyo 학교, (*lesson*) suŏp 수업. *a primary* ~ kungmin hakkyo 국민 학교/ *a high* ~ kodŭng hakkyo 고등 학교/ *a commercial high* ~ sangŏp kodŭng hakkyo 상업 고등 학교/*a public* ~ kongnip hakkyo 공립 학교/*a private* ~ sarip hakkyo 사립 학교/*a graduate* ~ taehagwŏn 대학원/ *I leave for* ~ *at* 8. Yŏdŏlshie hakkyoro ttŏnamnida. 8시에 학교로 떠납니다/ *We have no* ~ *today*. Onŭrŭn suŏbi ŏpsŭmnida. 오늘은 수업이 없읍니다/ *enter a* ~ ip'ak'ada 입학하다/ *a* ~ *boy* haksaeng 학생.

science *n.* (*branch of knowledge*) kwahak 과학, (*learning*) hangmun 학문. *natural* ~s chayŏn kwahak 자연 과학/ *social* ~s sahoe kwahak 사회 과학/ *the Ministry of S*~ *and Technology* kwahak kisulch'ŏ 과학 기술처/ *the S*~ *Museum* kwahak pangmulgwan 과학 박물관/ ~ *fiction* (*S.F.*) kwahak sosŏl 과학 소설.

scientist *n.* kwahakcha 과학자.

scissors *n.* (*pl.*) kawi 가위. *a pair of* ~ kawi han charu 가위 한 자루/ *I want some* ~. Kawiga p'iryohamnida. 가위가 필요합니다/ *Where are my* ~? Kawiga ŏdi issŭmnikka? 가위가 어디 있읍니까?

scold *vt., vi.* (*blame*) kkujitta 꾸짖다. *Why do you* ~ *him?* Wae kŭ saramŭl kkujissŭmnikka? 왜 그 사람을 꾸짖습니까/ *He was* ~*ed about it*. Kŭ il ttaemune kkujŭngŭl tŭrŏssŭmnida. 그 일 때문에 꾸중을 들었읍니다.

scoop *n.* (*ladle*) kukcha 국자. —*vt.* (*dip out*) p'uda 푸다, (*dig out*) p'anaeda 파내다.

scorch *vt.* (*singe*) kŭsŭllida 그슬리다, (*parch*) t'aeuda

태우다. *You ~ed my shirt when you ironed it.* Tari·
mijirhamyŏnsŏ nae syassŭrŭl t'aewŏtkunyo. 다리미질하
면서 내 샤쓰를 태웠군요.

score *n.* (*point*) tŭkchŏm(su) 득점(수). *What is the ~ ?*
Myŏt chŏm ttassŭmnikka ? 몇 점 땄읍니까/ *Korea won
the game with the ~ of 7 to 3.* Han·gugi ch'iltae sa·
mŭro igyŏssŭmnida. 한국이 7 대 3으로 이겼읍니다.

Scotch *n.* (*~ whisky*) Sŭk'ot'ŭllaendŭsan wisŭk'i 스코틀
랜드산(產) 위스키/ *May I have ~ and soda ?* Wisŭk'i
sodarŭl chushilkkayo ? 위스키 소다를 주실까요?

scoundrel *n.* (*rascal*) aktang 악당, ak'an 악한.

scour *vi., vt.* (*polish*) munjillŏ takta 문질러 닦다. *~ the
rust off* nogŭl pŏtkida 녹을 벗기다.

scout *n.* (*reconnaissance*) ch'ŏk'u 척후, (*patrolman*)
sunch'arwŏn 순찰원. —*vi.* (*reconnoiter*) chŏngch'arhada
정찰하다. *the Boy S~* sonyŏndan 소년단, poisŭk'aut'ŭ
보이 스카우트.

scram *int.,vi.* (*be off*) *S~ !* Taranashio ! 달아나시오/ *I told
him to ~.* Tomangch'irago marhaessŭmnida. 도망치라고
말했읍니다.

scramble *vi., vt.* (*climb*) kiŏorŭda 기어오르다, (*struggle
to secure*) sŏro ppaeatta 서로 빼앗다. *~ up a hill* sane
kiŏorŭda 산에 기어오르다/ *They ~d for pennies thrown
to them.* Ppurin tongjŏnŭl sŏro ppaeasassŭmnida. 뿌린
동전을 서로 빼앗았읍니다/ *~d eggs* p'urŏ pokkŭn talgyal
풀어 볶은 달걀.

scrap *n.* (*fragments*) chogak 조각, (*newspaper cuttings*)
oryŏnaen kŏt 오려낸 것. *~s of paper* chongi chogak 종
이 조각/ *~book* sŭk'ŭraeppuk 스크랩북.

scratch *n.* (*slight cuts*) kŭlk'in sangch'ŏ 긁힌 상처. —*vt.,
vi.* (*rub with fingernail*) halk'wida 할퀴다, (*grate
against*) munjirŭda 문지르다. *It's only a ~.* Kŭjŏ
kabyŏun sangch'ŏe chinaji anssŭmnida. 그저 가벼운 상
처에 지나지 않습니다/ *Who has ~ed the paint ?* Nuga
p'eint'ŭch'irŭl kŭlgŏ naessŭmnikka ? 누가 페인트칠을 긁
어 냈읍니까/ *Never ~ a mosquito bite.* Mogiga mun
charinŭn kŭkchi mashio. 모기가 문 자리는 긁지 마시오.

scream *n.* (*shrill cry*) oemadi sori 외마디 소리, pimyŏng 비명. —*vi.*, *vt.* (*make a sharp cry*) pimyŏngŭl chirŭda 비명을 지르다, (*laugh heartily*) kkalkkal utta 깔깔 웃다. *I heard a ～ for help.* Kuhae tallanŭn oemadi sorirŭl tŭrŏssŭmnida. 구해 달라는 외마디 소리를 들었읍니다.

screen *n.* (*partition*) kanmagi 간막이, (*curtain*) mak 막, (*movie pictures*) ŭnmak 은막, (*folding ～*) pyŏngp'ung 병풍. —*vt.* (*hide*) karomakta 가로막다, (*project*) sang-yŏnghada 상영하다. *a radar ～* reidamang 레이다망/ *a smoke ～* yŏnmak 연막/ *～ actors* yŏnghwa paeu 영화 배우/ *What's on the ～ now?* Chigŭm muŏsŭl sangyŏngha-go issŭmnikka? 지금 무엇을 상영하고 있읍니까/ *set up a ～* pyŏngp'ungŭl seuda 병풍을 세우다.

screw *n.* (*mech. device*) nasa 나사, (*propeller*) ch'ujin-gi 추진기. —*vt.*, *vi.* nasaro choeda 나사로 죄다. *The ～ is loose.* Nasaga p'urŏjyŏssŭmnida. 나사가 풀어졌읍니다/ *Give the ～ another turn.* Nasarŭl han pŏn tŏ tollishio. 나사를 한 번 더 돌리시오.

scribe *n.* (*copyist*) p'ilgija 필기자, (*clerk*) sŏgi 서기.

Scripture *n.* (*the Bible*) sŏnggyŏng 성경, sŏngsŏ 성서.

scroll *n.* turumari 두루마리.

scrub *vt.*, *vi.* pukpuk munjirŭda 북북 문지르다. *～ the floor* marutpadagŭl munjirŭda 마룻바닥을 문지르다.

sculptor *n.* chogakka 조각가.

sculpture *n.* chogak 조각. —*vt.*, *vi.* chogak'ada 조각하다.

scum *n.* (*froth*) kŏp'um 거품, (*dregs*) ssŭregi 쓰레기. *You filthy ～!* I pappŏlle kat'ŭn nom! 이 밥벌레 같은 놈!

sea *n.* pada 바다. *at ～* pada-esŏ 바다에서/ *by ～* (*by ship*) paero 배로/ *～ bathing* haesuyok 해수욕/ *～ beach* hae-byŏn 해변/ *～ coast* haebyŏn 해변/ *～ gull* kalmaegi 갈매기/ *～ port* hanggu 항구/ *～ shore* haean 해안/ *～ side* padatka 바닷가/ *～ sickness* paenmŏlmi 뱃멀미/ *I was at the ～ last summer.* Chinan yŏrŭmŭn padatka-esŏ chinaessŭmnida. 지난 여름은 바닷가에서 지냈읍니다/ *Let's walk as far as the ～.* Haeankkaji kŏrŏgapshida. 해안까지 걸어갑시다/ *I feel ～ sick. Please give me a remedy.* Paenmŏlmiga namnida. Yagŭl chushipshio. 뱃

멀미가 납니다. 약을 주십시오.

seal n. (*tight closure*) pongin 봉인, (*stamp*) tojang 도장, (*sea animal*) mulkae 물개. —vt. (*mark with a ~*) tojangŭl tchikta 도장을 찍다, (*close tightly*) ponghada 봉하다. *Please show it to me before you ~ it up.* Ponghagi chŏne hanbŏn poyŏ chushio. 봉하기 전에 한번 보여 주시오.

sea level haemyŏn 해면(海面). *above sea level* haebal 해발 (海拔)/ *1,000 meters above sea level.* haebal ch'ŏn mit'ŏ 해발 1,000 미터.

seam n. solgi 솔기, iŭn chari 이은 자리. *~stress* ch'immo 침모(針母), yŏja chaebongsa 여자 재봉사. —vt.(*join with a ~*) kkwemaeda 꿰매다.

seaman n. (*sailor*) sŏnwŏn 선원, (*bluejacket*) subyŏng 수병.

sear vt. (*wither*) shidŭlge hada 시들게 하다, (*scorch*) kŭsŭllida 그슬리다.

search n. (*quest*) susaek 수색, (*inquiry*) shimmun 심문, (*investigation*) chosa 조사. —vt., vi. (*explore*) ch'atta 찾다, twijida 뒤지다, (*examine closely*) chasehi salp'ida 자세히 살피다. *a ~ warrant* susaek yŏngchang 수색 영장/ *What are you ~ing for?* Muŏsŭl ch'atko issŭmnikka? 무엇을 찾고 있읍니까/ *I'm ~ing for my watch.* Shigyerŭl ch'atko issŭmnida. 시계를 찾고 있읍니다/ *~light* t'amjodŭng 탐조등, sŏch'irait'ŭ 서치라이트.

season n. kyejŏl 계절, ch'ŏl 철. —vt. (*flavor*) mattŭrida 맛들이다. *the rainy [tourist] ~* changma[kwan-gwang] ch'ŏl 장마[관광]철/ *the four ~s* sach'ŏl 사철/ *the baseball ~* yagu sijŭn 야구 시즌/ *out of ~* ch'ŏri chinan 철이 지난/ *Is this the ~ for strawberries?* Chigŭmi ttalgich'ŏrimnikka? 지금이 딸기철입니까/ *This meat should be ~ed with salt.* I koginŭn sogŭmŭro kanŭl match'uŏya hamnida. 이 고기는 소금으로 간을 맞추어야 합니다.

seasoning n. (*spices*) chomiryo 조미료, yangnyŏm 양념.

seat n. (*thing to sit on*) chwasŏk 좌석, (*chair*) ŭija 의자, (*bench*) pench'i 벤치. *Please take a ~.* Charie anjŭshipshio. 자리에 앉으십시오/ *Is this ~ taken?* I charie nu-

ga issŭmnikka? 이 자리에 누가 있읍니까/ *Is this ~ free?*
I charinŭn piŏ issŭmnikka? 이 자리는 비어 있읍니까/ *May
I have a two thousand won ~, please?* Ich'onwŏntchari
chwasŏgŭl han chang chuseyo. 2,000 원짜리 좌석을 한 장
주세요/ *Please be ~ed over there for a moment.* Chŏgi
chamkkan anja kyeshipshio. 저기 잠깐 앉아 계십시오/ *I
want to reserve a ~.* Chwasŏgŭl yeyak'ago shipsŭmnida. 좌석을 예약하고 싶습니다.

second *adj.* cheiŭi 제 2 의, tultchaeŭi 둘째의. —*n.* (*time*)
ch'o 초(秒). *Pusan is the ~ city in Korea.* Pusanŭn
Han-gugŭi cheiŭi toshiimnida. 부산은 한국의 제 2 의 도시
입니다/*Wait a ~.* Chamkkanman kidarishipshio. 잠깐만
기다리십시오/ *We must not lose a ~.* Ilch'odo ŏmul-
gŏril sunŭn ŏpsŭmnida. 1초도 어물거릴 수는 없읍니다/ *a ~
cabin* idŭng sŏnshil 2등 선실/ *~hand* chunggoŭi 중고
(中古)의/ *a ~ helping* ttŏ han kŭrŭt 또 한 그릇/ *~ lieutenant* yukkun sowi 육군 소위/ *~ cousin* chaejong 재종
(再從)/ *~ nature* cheiŭi ch'ŏnsŏng 제 2 의 천성.

secret *n.* pimil 비밀, (*key*) pigyŏl 비결. —*adj.* pimirŭi
비밀의. *Let's have no ~s between us.* Uridŭlkkirinŭn
pimiri ŏptorok hapshida. 우리들끼리는 비밀이 없도록 합시
다/ *Can you keep a ~?* Pimirŭl chik'il su issŭmnikka?
비밀을 지킬 수 있읍니까/ *Oh, I have the ~!* A (kŭ
pigyŏrŭl) arassŭmnida. 아, (그 비결을) 알았읍니다/ *break
a ~* pimirŭl nusŏrhada 비밀을 누설하다/ *a ~ ballot* mugimyŏng t'up'yo 무기명 투표.

secretary *n.* (*clerk*) sŏgi 서기, (*private ~*) pisŏ 비서,
(*cabinet minister*) changgwan 장관. *a first ~ of the
embassy* taesagwan iltŭng sŏgigwan 대사관 1 등 서기관/
May I see the ~ in charge of foreign trade? Oeguk
muyŏk tamdang pisŏrŭl poelkka hamnida. 외국 무역 담
당 비서를 뵐까 합니다/ *He is ~ to Mr. Chong.* Kŭbunŭn
Chŏngssiŭi pisŏimnida. 그분은 정(鄭)씨의 비서입니다/
The S~ of State (*Am.*) kungmu changgwan 국무 장관/
a ~general samu ch'ongjang 사무 총장.

sect *n.* (*denomination*) chongp'a 종파, (*school*) hakp'a
학파. *a religious ~* chongp'a 종파.

section *n.* (*part*) pubun 부분, (*district*) kuyŏk 구역, (*dept.*) kwa 과(課). *divide the cake into* ~s k'eik'ŭrŭl yŏrŏ t'omaguro charŭda 케이크를 여러 토막으로 자르다/ *the business* ~ *of a town* shinae sangŏp chigu 시내 상 업 지구/ *Export S*~, *please.* Such'ulkwa-e put'ak'amnida. 수출과에 부탁합니다.

secure *adj.* (*safe*) anjŏnhan 안전한, (*firm*) t'ŭnt'ŭnhan 튼튼한, (*certain*) hwakshirhan 확실한. —*vt.* (*obtain*) ŏtta 얻다, (*guard*) chik'ida 지키다. *Our victory is* ~. Uriŭi sŭngninŭn hwakshirhamnida. 우리의 승리는 확실합 니다/ *Is that ladder* ~? Chŏ sadarinŭn t'ŭnt'ŭnhamnikka? 저 사다리는 튼튼합니까/ *Please* ~ *a seat for me.* Charirŭl hana hwakpohae chushipshio. 자리를 하나 확보 해 주십시오.

security *n.* (*pledge*) tambo 담보, chŏdang 저당, (*guarantee*) pojŭng 보증, (*pl.*) yuka chŭngkwŏn 유가 증권. *What* ~ *can you offer for it?* Muŏsŭl chŏdanghashigessŭmnikka? 무엇을 저당하시겠읍니까/ *Is there any* ~ *against H-bombs?* Sup'oge taehan musŭn pangŏ sudani issŭmnikka? 수폭(水爆)에 대한 무슨 방어 수단이 있읍니까/ *securities market* chŭngkwŏn shijang 증권 시장/ ~ *guard* kyŏngbiwŏn 경비원.

seduce *vt.* (*lead astray*) nappŭn killo ikkŭlda 나쁜 길로 이끌다, (*tempt into sin*) aguro yuhok'ada 악으로 유혹하 다, (*corrupt*) t'arakshik'ida 타락시키다. ~ *a girl by fair speech* kamŏnŭro sonyŏrŭl yuhok'ada 감언(甘言)으 로 소녀를 유혹하다.

see *vt.*, *vi.* (*look at*) poda 보다, (*meet*) mannada 만나다, (*understand*) alda 알다, (*escort*) paeunghada 배웅하다, (*attend*) tolboda 돌보다. *Would you like to* ~ *the album?* Sajinch'ŏbŭl poshigessŏyo? 사진첩을 보시겠어요/ *What have you seen in Seoul?* Sŏuresŏ muŏsŭl posyŏssŭmnikka? 서울에서 무엇을 보셨읍니까/ *I saw him in the street.* Kŏriesŏ kŭbunŭl poassŭmnida. 거리에서 그분을 보았읍 니다/ *Can I* ~ *you tomorrow afternoon?* Naeil ohue manna poel su issŭlkkayo? 내일 오후에 만나뵐 수 있을까 요/ *My, it's good to* ~ *you.* (*to equal*) Ya, nŏrŭl mannasŏ pan-gapta. 야, 너를 만나서 반갑다/ *S~ you again.* Tashi poepkessŭmnida. 다시 뵙겠읍니다/ *May I ~ them?* Ponae chushilkkayo? 보내 주실까요/ *Don't you ~ what I mean?* Nae marŭl mot aradŭtkesso? 내 말을 못 알아듣겠소/ *You~?* Algetchyo? 알겠죠/ *I ~.* Arassŏyo. 알았어요/ *I don't ~ why he doesn't come.* Wae an onŭnji morŭgessŭmnida. 왜 안 오는지 모르겠읍니다/ *I'll ~ you off at the station.* Yŏgesŏ paeunghagessŭmnida. 역에서 배웅하겠읍니다/ *I was ~n off by many of my friends.* Manŭn ch'in-gudŭrŭi chŏnsongŭl padassŭmnida. 많은 친구들의 전송을 받았읍니다/ *I'll ~ to the patient.* Hwanjanŭn naega tolbogessŭmnida. 환자는 내가 돌보겠읍니다/ *Let me ~!* Kŭlsseolshida. 글쎄올시다/ *We will ~ about it.* Koryŏhae popshida. 고려해 봅시다.

seed *n.* ssi 씨, chongja 종자. *sow ~s* ssirŭl ppurida 씨를 뿌리다/ *~ a field with corn* pat'e oksusu ssirŭl ppurida 밭에 옥수수씨를 뿌리다.

seek *vt., vi.* (*search*) ch'atta 찾다, (*try to obtain*) ŏdŭryŏgo hada 얻으려고 하다, (*pursue*) norida 노리다, (*ask for*) yoguhada 요구하다, (*inquire into*) yŏn-guhada 연구하다. *I have been ~ing it all round.* Yŏgijŏgi ch'aja hemaeŏssŭmnida. 여기저기 찾아 헤매었읍니다/ *I will ~ my doctor's advise.* Ŭisa sŏnsaengnimŭi ch'unggorŭl ŏdŭryŏgo hamnida. 의사 선생님의 충고를 얻으려고 합니다.

seem *vi.* (*appear*) poida 보이다, (*look like*) …in kŏt katta …인 것 같다. *She ~s (to be) a kind woman.* Kŭ puinŭn ch'injŏrhan saram kassŭmnida. 그 부인은 친절한 사람 같습니다/ *You ~ tired.* P'irohashin kŏt katkunyo. 피로하신 것 같군요/ *I don't ~ to have you down.* Taegŭi sŏnghamŭl chŏgŏ noch'i anŭn kŏt kassŭmnida. 댁의 성함을 적어 놓지 않은 것 같습니다.

seismograph *n.* chijin-gye 지진계.

seize *vt., vi.* (*grasp*) putchapta 붙잡다, (*understand*) p'aak'ada 파악하다, (*take forcibly*) ppaeatta 빼앗다. *The policeman ~d the thief.* Kyŏnggwani todugŭl putchabassŭmnida. 경관이 도둑을 붙잡았읍니다/ *I was ~d with terror.* Nanŭn kongp'o-e sarojap'yŏssŭmnida.

나는 공포에 사로잡혔습니다.

seldom *adv.* (*rarely*) tŭmulge 드물게, chomch'ŏrŏm …haji ant'a 좀처럼 …하지 않다. *I ～ go out.* Nanŭn oech'ur-hanŭn iri tŭmumnida. 나는 외출하는 일이 드뭅니다/ *I ～ have a chance to speak to foreigners.* Oeguk saramgwa iyagihal kihoega chomch'ŏrŏm ŏpsŭmnida. 외국 사람과 이야기할 기회가 좀처럼 없습니다.

select *vt.* (*pick out*) korŭda 고르다, ppopta 뽑다. —*adj.* (*chosen*) ppobŭn 뽑은. *S～ the book you want.* Katko ship'ŭn ch'aegŭl korŭshipshio. 갖고 싶은 책을 고르십시오.

selection *n.* (*choice*) sŏnt'aek 선택, (*things chosen*) chŏngsŏnp'um 정선품. *a musical ～* palch'wegok 발췌곡/ *We have a very wide ～ of dolls.* Yŏrŏ kaji inhyŏngŭl mani katch'uŏ noassŭmnida. 여러 가지 인형을 많이 갖추어 놓았습니다.

self *n.* (*one's own person*) chagi 자기, chasin 자신. —*pref.* chashini 자신(自身)이, momso 몸소. *my poor～* pojalkŏdŏmnŭn na chashin 보잘것없는 나 자신/ *our two selves* uri tu saram 우리 두 사람/ *Please accept our thanks to Mr. Kim and ～.* Kimssiwa tangshin chashin-kke kamsadŭrimnida. 김씨와 당신 자신께 감사드립니다/～-*control* chaje 자제(自制)/ ～-*defence* chawi 자위(自衛)/ ～-*determination* chagyŏl 자결(自決)/ ～-*educated* to-k'agŭi 독학의/ ～-*respect* chajonshim 자존심/ ～-*satisfaction* chagi manjok 자기 만족.

self-acting *adj.* chadong(shig)ŭi 자동(식)의.

sell *vt.,vi.* p'alda 팔다. *Do you ～ wine?* P'odoju p'ashimnikka? 포도주 파십니까/ *Where do they ～ men's shoes?* Namja kudunŭn ŏdisŏ p'amnikka? 남자 구두는 어디서 팝니까/ *I am sorry, it's sold out.* Mianhajiman p'umjŏrimnida. 미안하지만 품절입니다/ *Is the book ～ing well?* I ch'aegŭn chal p'allimnikka? 이 책은 잘 팔립니까/ *I won't ～ it for thousand won less.* Ch'ŏnwŏn iharonŭn p'algo shipchi anssŭmnida. 1,000원 이하로는 팔고 싶지 않습니다/ *That merchant ～s dear.* Chŏ changsunŭn pissage p'amnida. 저 장수는 비싸게 팝니다.

semester *n.* irhakki 1 학기. *When does the spring ～ begin* *in Korea?* Han-gugesŏnŭn pom hakkiga ŏnje shijak-toemnikka? 한국에서는 봄 학기가 언제 시작됩니까?

senate *n.* (*Am.*) sangwŏn 상원(上院).

send *vt.* (*forward*) ponaeda 보내다, (*by post*) puch'ida 부치다. *Please ~ up a bellboy.* Poirŭl ponae chuseyo. 보이를 보내 주세요/ *Would you please ~ this to Korea?* Igŏsŭl Han-guge ponae chushigessŭmnikka? 이것을 한국에 보내 주시겠읍니까/ *S~ these flowers to Miss Lee.* I kkoch'ŭl I yangege ponae chushio. 이 꽃을 이 양에게 보내 주시오/ *How much will it cost to ~ it by air mail.* Hanggongp'yŏnŭro puch'ijamyŏn ŏlmajiyo? 항공편으로 부치자면 얼마지요/ *S~ for a doctor, please.* Ŭisarŭl pullŏ chushipshio. 의사를 불러 주십시오.

sender *n.* palsongin 발송인.

send-off *n.* chŏnsong 전송. *receive a hearty ~* yŏllyŏrhan chŏnsongŭl patta 열렬한 전송을 받다/ *We will give him a good ~.* Kŭ saramŭl yŏllyŏrhage chŏnsonghal chak-chŏngimnida. 그 사람을 열렬하게 전송할 작정입니다.

senior *adj.* (*older*) sonwiŭi 손위의, (*in rank*) sanggŭbŭi 상급의. —*n.* (*age*) yŏnjangja 연장자, (*rank*) sanggŭpcha 상급자. *He is two years ~ to me.* Kŭ saramŭn naboda tu sal wiimnida. 그 사람은 나보다 두 살 위입니다/ *He is my ~ by two years.* Kŭinŭn naboda inyŏn yŏnsangimnida. 그이는 나보다 2년 연상입니다/ *a ~ officer* sanggwan 상관/ *a ~ high school* kodŭng hakkyo 고등 학교.

sensation *n.* (*feeling*) nŭkkim 느낌, kamgak 감각, (*excited feeling*) kamdong 감동, (*excited reaction*) sŏnp'ung 선풍, senseisyŏn 센세이션. *a ~ of fear* kong-p'ogam 공포감/ *I have a ~ of giddiness.* Hyŏn-gichŭngi namnida. 현기증이 납니다/ *a profound ~* kip'ŭn kam-dong 깊은 감동/ *create a wonderful ~* iltae sŏnp'ŭngŭl irŭk'ida 일대 선풍을 일으키다/ *The news created a great ~.* Kŭ soshigŭn k'ŭn sŏnp'ungŭl irŭk'yŏssŭmni-da. 그 소식은 큰 선풍을 일으켰읍니다.

sensational *adj.* sesangŭl nollage hanŭn 세상을 놀라게 하는. *a ~ murder* sesangŭl nollage hanŭn sarin 세상을 놀라게 하는 살인.

sense *n.* (~ *organ*) kamgak 감각, (*perception*) chigak 지각, (*recognition*) inshik 인식, (*practical judgement*) p'andannyŏk 판단력, (*meaning*) ŭimi 의미. —*vt.* (*feel*) nŭkkida 느끼다, (*understand*) kkaedatta 깨닫다. *the five* ~*s* ogam 오감/ *the sixth* ~*s* yukkam 육감/ *keen* ~*s* yeminhan kamgak 예민한 감각/ *Has a plant* ~? Shingmuredo kamgagi issŭmnikka? 식물에도 감각이 있읍니까/ *common* ~ sangshik 상식/ *in a broad* ~ nŏlbŭn ttŭsesŏ 넓은 뜻에서/ *What is the* ~ *of this passage?* I kujŏrŭi ttŭsŭn muŏshimnikka? 이 구절의 뜻은 무엇입니까/ *Can you make* ~ *of what he says?* Kŭ saram marŭl aradŭtkessŭmnikka? 그 사람 말을 알아듣겠읍니까/ *I* ~*d the danger.* Nanŭn wihŏmŭl nŭkkyŏssŭmnida. 나는 위험을 느꼈읍니다.

sensible *adj.* (*sagacious*) ch'ongmyŏnghan 총명한, (*wise*) hyŏnmyŏnghan 현명한. *a* ~ *woman* hyŏnmyŏnghan yŏja 현명한 여자/ *a* ~ *idea* hyŏnmyŏnghan saenggak 현명한 생각/ *That was very* ~ *of you!* Kŭgŏt ch'am chal haetkunyo! 그것 참 잘 했군요!

sensitive *adj.* (*susceptible*) min-gamhan 민감한, (*easily hurt*) sanghagi shwiun 상하기 쉬운, (*touchy*) shin-gyŏngjilchŏgin 신경질적인. *She is very* ~. Kŭ yŏjanŭn maeu sin-gyongjilchŏgimnida. 그 여자는 매우 신경질적입니다.

sensual *adj.* (*carnal*) kwannŭngjŏgin 관능적인, (*lewd*) ŭmnanhan 음란한. ~ *enjoyment* yukch'ejŏk hyangnak 육체적 향락/ ~ *life* pangt'ang saenghwal 방탕 생활.

sentence *n.* munjang 문장, (*judgment*) p'an-gyŏl 판결. —*vt.* p'an-gyŏrhada 판결하다. *The accused was* ~*d to death.* P'igonŭn sahyŏngŭl sŏn-gobadassŭmnida. 피고는 사형을 선고받았읍니다.

sentimental *adj.* (*emotional*) kamsangjŏgin 감상적인, tajŏngdagamhan 다정다감한. ~ *music* kamsangjŏgin ŭmak 감상적인 음악/ *Put such* ~ *feelings out of your mind.* Kŭrŏn kamsangjŏgin saenggagŭn kŭmandushio. 그런 감상적인 생각은 그만두시오.

sentry *n.* poch'o 보초, ch'obyŏng 초병. ~ *box* ch'oso 초소 (哨所)/ ~ *go* poch'o kŭnmu 보초 근무/ *stand on* ~ poch'o sŏda 보초 서다.

separate adj. (*apart*) kallajin 갈라진, (*individual*) kaegaeŭi 개개의. —vt., vi. (*divide*) tteŏnot'a 떼어 놓다, pullihada 분리하다. *a ~ account* pyŏlto kyesan 별도 계산/ *~ trade* tandok yŏngŏp 단독 영업/ *Cut it into three ~ parts.* Se kaero charŭshio. 세 개로 자르시오/ *How long had they been ~d?* Kŭdŭrŭn ŏlma tongan pyŏlgŏhayŏssŭmnikka? 그들은 얼마 동안 별거하였읍니까?

separately adv. ttarottaro 따로따로. *Wrap them ~, will you?* Ttarottaro p'ojanghae chushigessŭmnikka? 따로따로 포장해 주시겠읍니까?

separation n. (*partition*) pulli 분리, (*sorting*) pullyu 분류, (*limited divorce*) pyŏlgŏ 별거.

September n. kuwŏl 9월.

sequence n. (*succession*) yŏnsok 연속, (*result*) kwigyŏl 귀결, (*order*) sunsŏ 순서, (*serial*) yŏnsongmul 연속물. *a ~ of bad harvest* ittarŭn hyungjak 잇따른 흉작/ *in ~* ch'aryech'aryero 차례차례로/ *a ~ to a story* huiltam 후일담.

serenade n. soyagok 소야곡, serenade 세레나데.

serene adj. (*clear*) malge kaen 맑게 갠, (*calm*) koyohan 고요한, (*tranquil*) ch'imch'ak'an 침착한. *a ~ sky* malgŭn hanŭl 맑은 하늘/ *a ~ life* p'yŏngonhan saenghwal 평온한 생활/ *a ~ smile* chanjanhan miso 잔잔한 미소.

sergeant n. sangsa 상사(上士). *~ major* t'ŭngmu sangsa 특무 상사/ *a police ~* kyŏngsa 경사.

sericulture n. yangjam 양잠.

serious adj. (*important*) chungdaehan 중대한, (*grave*) shimgak'an 심각한, (*critical*) widok'an 위독한, (*earnest*) ch'akshirhan 착실한. *a ~ mistake* chungdaehan chalmot 중대한 잘못/ *What has made you so ~?* Wae kŭrŏk'e shimgak'aejyŏssŭmnikka? 왜 그렇게 심각해졌읍니까/ *a ~ illness* chungbyŏng 중병/ *Please be ~ about your work.* Irŭl ch'akshirhage hashio. 일을 착실하게 하시오/ *a ~ worker* ch'akshirhan ilkkun 착실한 일꾼.

seriously adv. chinjihage 진지하게, chinjŏngŭro 진정으로. *Don't take what he says ~.* Kŭ saram marŭl chinjiha-

ge padadŭriji mashio. 그 사람 말을 진지하게 받아들이지 마
시오/ *S*~, *I really want you to come.* Nongdam mashigo, chŏngmal oseyo. 농담 마시고, 정말 오세요.

sermon *n.* sŏlgyo 설교. *listen to a* ~ sŏlgyorŭl tŭtta 설
교를 듣다.

serpent *n.* paem 뱀.

servant *n.* (*man*~) hain 하인, mŏsŭm 머슴, (*maid*~)
hanyŏ 하녀. *He has many* ~*s.* Kŭ saramŭn manŭn
hainŭl ssŭgo issŭmnida. 그 사람은 많은 하인을 쓰고 있읍
니다/ *a public* ~ kongbok 공복(公僕).

serve *vt., vi.* (*attend*) shijungdŭlda 시중들다, (*work for*)
kŭnmuhada 근무하다, (*supply*) konggŭp'ada 공급하다,
(*tennis*) sŏbŭrŭl nŏt'a 서브를 넣다. —*n.* (*tennis, etc.*)
sŏbŭ 서브. *I was* ~*d with tea and cake.* Ch'awa
k'eik'ŭŭi taejŏbŭl padassŭmnida. 차와 케이크의 대접을 받
았읍니다/ *May I* ~ *you some coffee?* K'ŏp'i tŭshigessŭmnikka? 커피 드시겠읍니까/ *My sister* ~*s in a
company as a typist.* Nae nui tongsaengŭn hoesa t'aja-
suro kŭnmuhago issŭmnida. 내 누이 동생은 회사 타자수로
근무하고 있읍니다/ *Whose* ~ *is it?* Nuga sŏbŭhal ch'a-
ryeimnikka? 누가 서브할 차례입니까?

service *n.* (*act of serving*) pongsa 봉사, (*devotions*)
yebae 예배, (*armed forces*) pyŏngyŏk 병역, (*expert
help*) sŏbisŭ 서비스, (*tennis*) sŏbŭ 서브. *Hey, can we
get some* ~ *over here?* Ibwayo, yŏgido chumunŭl pada-
gayo. 이봐요, 여기도 주문을 받아가요/ *We are at your*
~, *sir.* Punbudaero moshigessŭmnida. 분부대로 모시겠읍
니다/ *Does this sum include the* ~ *charge?* I aeksue-
nŭn sŏbisŭryoga tŭrŏ issŭmnikka? 이 액수에는 서비스료
가 들어 있읍니까/ *morning*[*evening*] ~ ach'im[chŏnyŏk]
yebae 아침[저녁] 예배/ *home* ~ pon-guk kŭnmu 본국 근
무/ *public* ~ kongmu 공무/ *Whose* ~ *is it?* Nuga sŏbŭhal ch'aryeimnikka? 누가 서브할 차례입니까/ ~ *station*
chuyuso 주유소.

session *n.* (*term*) hoegi 회기, (*semester*) hakki 학기,
(*assembly*) kaehoe 개회, (*court*) kaejŏng 개정(開廷),
(*comm.*) kaejang 개장. *the autumn* ~ kaŭl kaehoe 가

을 개회/ *a full* ∼ ch'onghoe 총회/ *morning* [*afternoon*] ∼ ojŏn[ohu] suŏp 오전[오후] 수업/ *hold a night* ∼ yagan hoeŭirŭl yŏlda 야간 회의를 열다.

set *n.* (*pair*) han pŏl 한 벌, han set'ŭ 한 세트, (*build*) mommae 몸매, (*of hair*) mŏri moyang 머리 모양. —*vt.*, *vi.* (*put*) tuda 두다, not'a 놓다, (*fix*) changch'ihada 장치하다, (*start*) shijak'ada 시작하다, (*go down*) chida 지다(沒), (*hair*) set'ŭhada 세트하다. —*adj.* (*fixed*) ilchŏnghan 일정한. *A shampoo and* ∼, *please.* Mŏrirŭl kamko set'ŭrŭl hae chuseyo. 머리를 감고 세트를 해 주세요/ *Please* ∼ *my hair in this style.* I sŭt'aillo hae chuseyo. 이 스타일로 해 주세요/ *I must* ∼ *about my packing.* Chimŭl kkuryŏyagessŭmnida. 짐을 꾸려야겠읍니다/ *I'll* ∼ *this aside for future use.* Pich'uk'ae tuŏttaga changnaee ssŭgessŭmnida. 비축해 두었다가 장래에 쓰겠읍니다/ *How should I* ∼ *myself down in the hotel register?* Hot'el sukpakkyerŭl ŏttŏk'e chŏkchiyo? 호텔 숙박계를 어떻게 적지요/ *Is this condition* ∼ *forth in the agreement?* Kyeyaksŏe i chokŏni tŭrŏ issŭmnikka? 계약서에 이 조건이 들어 있읍니까/ *They* ∼ *out at dawn.* Kŭ saramdŭrŭn saebyŏge ch'ulbarhaessŭmnida. 그 사람들은 새벽에 출발했읍니다/ *I shall* ∼ *up as a dentist.* Ch'ikwa pyŏngwŏnŭl ch'aril chakchŏngimnida. 치과 병원을 차릴 작정입니다.

settle *vt.*, *vi.* (*fix*) chŏnghada 정하다, (*solve*) haegyŏrhada 해결하다, (*establish*) chŏngjuhada 정주하다, (*quiet*) karaanch'ida 가라앉히다, (*pay*) ch'ŏngsanhada 청산하다. *What have you* ∼*d on?* Ŏttŏn chokŏnŭro kyŏlchŏnghaessŭmnikka? 어떤 조건으로 결정했읍니까/ *I should like to* ∼ *in Korea.* Han-guge chŏngjuhago shipsŭmnida. 한국에 정주하고 싶습니다/ *Have a brandy— it will* ∼ *your nerve.* Pŭraendirŭl han chan tŭshipshio. Shin-gyŏngi karaanjŭl kŏshimnida. 브랜디를 한 잔 드십시오. 신경이 가라앉을 것입니다/ *Will you* ∼ *for me?* Sem chom ch'irŏ chushigesso? 셈 좀 치러 주시겠소?

settlement *n.* chŏngch'ak 정착, chŏngju 정주, (*conclusion*) haegyŏl 해결, (*arrangement*) chojŏng 조정, (*payment*) chibul 지불, *(welfare establishment)* pokchi tanch'e 복지 단체.

seven *n.* ilgop 일곱, ch'il 칠(7). *Oh, I'm on cloud* ~. Ah, nanŭn kippŏsŏ chukkessŏyo. 아, 나는 기뻐서 죽겠어요.

seventeen *n.* yŏl ilgop 열 일곱, shipch'il 십칠(17).

seventeenth *n:*, *adj.* yŏl ilgoptchae(ŭi) 열 일곱째(의), cheshipch'il(ŭi) 제 17(의).

seventh *n.*, *adj.* ilgoptchae(ŭi) 일곱째(의), chech'il(ŭi) 「제 7(의).

seventy *n.*, *adj.* irhŭn(ŭi) 일흔(의), ch'ilship(ŭi) 70(의).

sever *vt.* *(cut off)* kkŭnt'a 끊다, *(divide)* karŭda 가르다, kyŏngnihada 격리하다, *(estrange)* purhwahage hada 불화하게 하다.

several *adj.* yŏrŏsŭi 여럿의, ...myŏt ...몇. —*n.* *(persons or things)* yŏrŏ saram 여러 사람, yŏrŏ kae 여러 개. *I've read the book* ~ *times.* Nanŭn kŭ ch'aegŭl myŏt ch'arye ilgŏssŭmnida. 나는 그 책을 몇 차례 읽었읍니다/ *We have* ~ *Kims. Do you know where he works?* Kimssiga yŏrŏ pun issŭmnida. Ŏnŭ pusŏesŏ irhago issŭmnikka? 김씨가 여러 분 있읍니다. 어느 부서에서 일하고 있읍니까?

severe *adj.* *(strict)* ŏmgyŏk'an 엄격한, *(violent)* kyŏngnyŏrhan 격렬한, *(grave)* chunghan 중한, *(plain)* susuhan 수수한. *a* ~ *punishment* ŏmbŏl 엄벌/ ~ *rain* p'ogu 폭우/ ~ *cold* shimhan ch'uwi 심한 추위/ *a* ~ *illness* chungbyŏng 중병(重病).

sew *vt.*, *vi.* kipta 깁다, kkwemaeda 꿰매다. ~ *a dress* osŭl kkwemaeda 옷을 꿰매다/ *She has been* ~*ing all evening.* Kŭ yŏjanŭn chŏnyŏk naenae panŭjirŭl hago issŏssŭmnida. 그 여자는 저녁 내내 바느질을 하고 있었읍니다/ ~*ing machine* chaebongt'ŭl 재봉틀.

sewage *n.* shigungch'ang 시궁창.

sewer *n.* *(main drain)* hasudogwan 하수도관, *(seamstress)* ch'immo 침모.

sex *n.* sŏng 성(性), *the male* ~ namsŏng 남성, *(of animals)* suk'ŏt 수컷. *the female*〔*fair*〕~ yŏsŏng 여성, *(of animals)* amk'ŏt 암컷/ ~ *appeal* sŏngchŏk maeryŏk 성적 매력/ ~ *education* sŏnggyoyuk 성교육.

sexual *adj.* sŏngchŏgin 성적인. ~ *appetite* sŏngyok 성욕/

$\sim$ *disease* sŏngpyŏng 성병/ $\sim$ *intercourse* sŏnggyo 성교.

shabby *adj.* (*poorly dressed*) ch'orahan 초라한, (*well-worn*) haejin 해진. *a* $\sim$ *overcoat* haejin oet'u 해진 외투/ *You look rather* $\sim$ *in those clothes.* Kŭrŏn osŭl ibŭni chom ch'orahage poimnida. 그런 옷을 입으니 좀 초라하게 보입니다.

shackle *n.* (*fetters*) soegorang 쇠고랑, (*manacle*) sugap 수갑, (*restraint*) sokpak 속박.

shade *n.* (*opp. light*) kŭnŭl 그늘, (*blind*) ch'ayang 차양, (*awning*) ch'ail 차일, (*lamp* $\sim$) kat 갓. *Keep in the* $\sim$; *it is cooler.* Kŭnŭre kyeshipshio, tŏ sŏnsŏnhanikkayo. 그늘에 계십시오, 더 선선하니까요/ *Pull up the* $\sim$. Ch'ayangŭl ollishio. 차양을 올리시오/ *a lamp* $\sim$ raemp'ŭ kat 램프 갓/ *a window* $\sim$ pŭllaindŭ 블라인드.

shadow *n.* kŭrimja 그림자.

shaft *n.* (*arrow*) hwasal 화살, (*handle*) charu 자루, (*axle*) kultae 굴대. *a ventilating* $\sim$ hwan-gigaeng 환기갱(換氣坑).

shake *vi.,vt.* (*tremble*) ttŏlda 떨다, (*wave*) hŭndŭlda 흔들다. —*n.* (*vibration*) chindong 진동, (*handshake*) aksu 악수. *Her voice shook with emotion.* Kŭ yŏjaŭi moksorinŭn kamdongŭro ttŏllyŏssŭmnida. 그 여자의 목소리는 감동으로 떨렸읍니다/ *S* $\sim$ *the bottle well.* Pyŏngŭl chal hŭndŭshio. 병을 잘 흔드시오/ *Do you* $\sim$ *hands every time you meet a friend?* Ch'in-gurŭl mannal ttaemada aksurŭl hamnikka? 친구를 만날 때마다 악수를 합니까/ *I shook him warmly by the hand.* Kŭiwa yŏllyŏrhan aksurŭl hayŏssŭmnida. 그이와 열렬한 악수를 하였읍니다.

shall *aux. v.* (*with the 1st person*) ...hal kŏshida 할 것이다, (*affirm*) ...shik'ida …시키다, hage hada 하게 하다/ *I* $\sim$ *be very happy to see you.* Kikkŏi mannagessŭmnida. 기꺼이 만나겠읍니다/ *I* $\sim$ *feel much obliged to you.* (Kŭrŏk'e hae chushimyŏn) maeu komapkessŭmnida. (그렇게 해 주시면) 매우 고맙겠읍니다/ *S* $\sim$ *I have him call you?* Kŭga tangshinkke chŏnhwahadorok halkkayo? 그가 당신께 전화하도록 할까요/ *You* $\sim$ *have the money tomorrow.* Naeil tonŭl tŭrigessŭmnida. 내일

돈을 드리겠읍니다.

shallow *adj.* (*not deep*) yat'ŭn 얕은, (*superficial*) ch'on-bak'an 천박한. ～ *water* yat'ŭn mul 얕은 물/ *a* ～ *dish* yat'un chŏpshi 얕은 접시/ ～ *talk* ch'ŏnbak'an iyagi 천박한 이야기.

shame *n.* (*disgrace*) ch'angp'i 창피, mangshin 망신, (*dishonor*) pulmyŏngye 불명예, (*hard luck*) nŏmuhan il 너무한 일. *I cannot do it for very* ～. Ch'angp'ihaesŏ mot hagessŭmnida. 창피해서 못 하겠읍니다/ *I was put to* ～. Mangshinŭl tanghaessŭmnida. 망신을 당했읍니다/ *What a* ～! Ige musŭn ch'angp'inya! 이게 무슨 창피냐/ *Why*, ～ *on you, man!* (*to equals*) Nŏ, ch'angp'ihaji anni? 너, 창피하지 않니/ *What a* ～ *to treat you like that!* Tangshinŭl kŭrŏk'e taehadani nŏmuhamnida. 당신을 그렇게 대하다니 너무합니다.

shameful *adj.* ch'isasŭrŏn 치사스런.

shameless *adj.* pukkŭrŏmŭl morŭnŭn 부끄럼을 모르는, p'aryŏmch'ihan 파렴치한.

shape *n.* (*form*) moyang 모양, (*appearance*) oegwan 외관. —*vt., vi.* (*form*) moyangŭl iruda 모양을 이루다. *a round* ～ wŏnhyŏng 원형/ *What* ～ *shall I make the meeting seats?* Hoehap chwasŏgŭn ŏttŏn moyanguro mandŭlkkayo? 회합 좌석은 어떤 모양으로 만들까요?

share *n.* (*portion*) mok 몫, (*part*) yŏk'al 역할, (*stock*) chu 주(株). —*vt., vi.* (*divide*) punbaehada 분배하다, (*use together*) kach'ihada 같이하다. *Please let me go* ～*s with you in the taxi fare.* T'aekshi yogŭmŭn hamkke naepshida. 택시 요금은 함께 냅시다/ *Your* ～ *of the expenses is 5,000 won.* Piyong chung tangshin pudamŭn och'ŏnwŏnimnida. 비용 중 당신 부담은 5,000 원입니다/ *I have no* ～ *in the matter.* Nanŭn kŭ ire kwan-gyega ŏpsŭmnida. 나는 그 일에 관계가 없읍니다/ *an ordinary* ～ t'ongsangju 통상주/ *If you have an umbrella, let me* ～ *it with you.* Usan kajigo kyeshimyŏn nado kach'i kapshida. 우산 가지고 계시면 나도 같이 갑시다/ ～ *holder* chuju 주주(株主)/ ～*holder meeting* chuju ch'onghoe 주주 총회.

shark *n.* (*sea-fish*) sangŏ 상어, (*swindler*) sagikkun 사

기꾼.

sharp *adj.* (*not blunt*) nalk'aroun 날카로운, yerihan 예리한, (*cutting well*) chal peŏjinŭn 잘 베어지는, (*pointed*) ppyojok'an 뾰족한, (*steep*) hŏmhan 험한, (*of sounds*) nalk'aroun 날카로운. *a ~ knife* chal tŭnŭn k'al 잘 드는 칼/ *a ~ needle* ppyojok'an panŭl 뾰족한 바늘.

sharper *n.* *a pencil ~* yŏnp'ilkkakki 연필깎이. *Please show me some pencil ~s.* Yŏnp'ilkkakki chom poyŏ chushipshio. 연필깎이 좀 보여 주십시오.

sharpen *vt.*, *vi.* (*whet*) kalda 갈다, (*pencil, etc.*) kkakta 깎다, (*point*) ppyojok'age hada 뾰족하게 하다.

shatter *vt.*, *vi.* (*break into pieces*) pusuda 부수다, (*damage*) sonsangshik'ida 손상시키다, (*disable*) mangch'ida 망치다.

shave *n.* (*shaving*) myŏndo 면도. —*vt.*, *vi.* (*with razors*) myŏndohada 면도하다, (*with planes*) kkakta 깎다. *Give me a ~ and a haircut, please.* Myŏndowa ibal chom hae chushio. 면도와 이발 좀 해 주시오.

shaver *n.* (*razor*) myŏndogi 면도기. *electric ~* chŏn-gi myŏndogi 전기 면도기. *Are you taking this ~ abroad?* I myŏndoginŭn oegugŭro kajigo kashil kŏmnikka? 이 면도기는 외국으로 가지고 가실 겁니까?

shavings *n.* (*of wood*) taep'aetpap 대팻밥.

shawl *n.* syol 숄, ŏkkaegŏri 어깨걸이.

she *pron.* kŭ yŏjanŭn[ga] 그 여자는[가], (*in honorific*) kŭbunŭn[i] 그분은[이].

shear *n.* (*pl*) (*large scissors*) k'ŭn kawi 큰 가위. —*vt.* (*clip*) charŭda 자르다, (*cut*) peda 베다.

sheath *n.* (*of swords*) k'alchip 칼집.

shed *n.* (*barn*) hŏtkan 헛간, kang 강, (*storage*) ch'anggo 창고. —*vt.* (*pour out*) hŭllida 흘리다. *an army ~* pyŏngsa 병사(兵舍)/ *a car ~* ch'ago 차고/ *~ tears* nunmurŭl hŭllida 눈물을 흘리다/ *~ blood* p'irŭl hŭllida 피를 흘리다.

sheep *n.* yang 양(羊).

sheer *adj.* (*utter*) sunjŏnhan 순전한, (*very thin*) maeu yalbŭn 매우 얇은, (*steep*) kap'arŭn 가파른. *a ~ waste of time* sunjŏnhan shigan nangbi 순전한 시간 낭비/

stockings of ～ *nylon* yalbŭn naillon sŭt'ak'ing 얇은 나
일론 스타킹

sheet *n.* (*cloth*) shit'ŭ 시트, (*paper*) han chang 한 장.
change the ～*s on one's bed* ch'imdaeŭi shit'ŭrŭl kalda
침대의 시트를 갈다/ *a* ～ *of paper* chongi han chang
종이 한 장/ *How many* ～*s are there in the box?* Sangja-enŭn myŏt chang tŭrŏ issŭmnikka? 상자에는 몇 장 들
어 있읍니까/ *I'll take both* ～ *music and the record.*
Akpowa rek'odŭrŭl sagessŭmnida. 악보와 레코드를 사겠
읍니다/ ～ *glass* p'anyuri 판유리.

sheik, sheikh *n.* (*Am.*) (*lady-killer*) minamja 미남자,
hosaekkun 호색꾼. *He is a* ～ *among young ladies.* Kŭ
namjanŭn chŏlmŭn yŏjadŭrege inkiga issŭmnida. 그 남
자는 젊은 여자들에게 인기가 있읍니다.

shelf *n.* sŏnban 선반, shirŏng 시렁. *a book* ～ ch'aekkoji
책꽂이/ *a continental* ～ taeryukpung 대륙붕/ *You will
find the goods on the shelves over there.* Kŭ sang-
p'umŭn chŏtchok sŏnban wie issŭmnida. 그 상품은 저쪽
선반 위에 있읍니다.

shell *n.* (*of turtles, nuts, etc.*) kkŏpchil 껍질, (*of clam*)
chogabi 조가비, (*bullet*) t'anp'i 탄피.

shelter *n.* (*refuge*) p'inanch'ŏ 피난처, taep'iso 대피소,
(*shed*) hŏtkan 헛간, (*air raid* ～) panggongho 방공호,
(*protection*) poho 보호. —*vt., vi.* (*house*) sumgida 숨
기다, (*protect*) pohohada 보호하다. *a bomb* ～ panggongho 방공호/ *We are* ～*ed from the enemy's fire.*
Urinŭn chŏgŭi p'ohwarobut'ŏ wŏnhorŭl patko issŭmnida. 우리는 적의 포화(砲火)로부터 원호를 받고 있읍니다.

shepherd *n.* (*sheepherder*) yangch'igi 양치기, moktong
목동, (*pastor*) moksa 목사.

shield *n.* (*defensive armor*) pangp'ae 방패.

shin *n.* chŏnggangi 정강이. *kick a person on the* ～
chŏnggangirŭl ch'ada 정강이를 차다.

shine *vi., vt.* (*gleam*) pinnada 빛나다, pantchagida 반짝이
다, (*polish*) kwangnaeda 광내다. —*n.* (*light*) haetpit
햇빛, (*luster*) yun 윤. *Have you* ～*d your shoes?* Kudurŭl takkassŭmnikka? 구두를 닦았읍니까?

ship *n.* pae 배, sŏnbak 선박. —*vi., vt.* (*embark*) paerŭl t'ada 배를 타다, (*send by* ~) paero susonghada 배로 수송하다, (*Am.*) (*by cars*) unbanhada 운반하다. *a freight* ~ hwamulsŏn 화물선/ *a merchant* ~ sangsŏn 상선/ *steam-* ~ kisŏn 기선/ *a war* ~ kunham 군함/ *a sailing* ~ tottan pae 돛단 배/ *Can you* ~ *these goods to Korea?* I hwamurŭl Han-gugŭro susonghal su issŭmnikka? 이 화물을 한국으로 수송할 수 있읍니까/ ~*board* kapp'an 갑판/ ~*building yard* chosŏnso 조선소/ ~*mate* sŏnwŏn 선원/ *I want to make a* ~ *to Hong Kong.* Hongk'ongkkaji hwamurŭl ponaego shipsŭmnida. 홍콩까지 화물을 보내고 싶습니다/ ~*wreck* nanp'asŏn 난파선.

shipment *n.* sŏnjŏk 선적, paee shitki 배에 싣기.

shipping *n.* sŏnbak 선박. ~ *agent* sŏnbak taerijŏm 선박 대리점/ ~ *business* haeunŏp 해운업/ ~ *charges* sŏnjŏk piyong 선적 비용/ ~ *bill* sŏnha chŭngkwŏn 선하 증권.

shirt *n.* syassŭ 샤쓰, wai syassŭ 와이 샤쓰. *in one's* ~ syassŭ paramŭro 샤쓰 바람으로/ *Send this* ~ *to the laundry.* I syassŭrŭl set'akso-e ponaeshipshio. 이 샤쓰를 세탁소에 보내십시오.

shiver *vi.* (*tremble*) ttŏlda 떨다. —*n.* (*shake*) ttŏlgi 떨기, chŏnyul 전율. *It gives me the cold* ~*s when I think of it.* Saenggangman haedo momi ossak'aejimnida. 생각만 해도 몸이 오싹해집니다.

shock *n.* (*percussion*) ch'unggyŏk 충격, syok'ŭ 쇼크, —*vt.* ch'unggyŏgŭl chuda 충격을 주다, (*surprise*) nollage hada 놀라게 하다. *I felt a* ~. Nanŭn ch'unggyŏgŭl padassŭmnida. 나는 충격을 받았읍니다/ *I got a great* ~. Kkamtchak nollassŭmnida. 깜짝 놀랐읍니다/ *I'm* ~*ed to hear of his death.* Kŭ sarami chugŏttanŭn soshigŭl tŭtko kkamtchak nollassŭmnida. 그 사람이 죽었다는 소식을 듣고 깜짝 놀랐읍니다.

shoe *n.* kudu 구두, shin 신. *high* ~*s* changhwa 장화/ *rubber* ~*s* komushin 고무신/ *sports* ~*s* undonghwa 운동화/ ~*brush* kudutsol 구둣솔/ ~*black or* (~*shine boy*) kudu takkki 구두 닦기/ ~*horn* kudut chugŏk 구둣 주걱/ ~ *polish* kuduyak 구두약/ ~ *lace* kudukkŭn

구두끈/ *put on* ~s kudurŭl shinta 구두를 신다/ *take off*
~s kudurŭl pŏtta 구두를 벗다/ *What size of* ~s *do you*
wear? Shinŭn myŏt saijŭrŭl shinŭshimnikka? 신은 몇
사이즈를 신으십니까/ *You may keep your* ~s *on.* Kudunŭn an pŏsŏdo chossŭmnida. 구두는 안 벗어도 좋습니다.

shoot *vt., vi.* (*fire*) ssoda 쏘다, sagyŏk'ada 사격하다,
(*sprout*) ssagi t'ŭda 싹이 트다. *I shot the wild boar dead*
in two bullets. Kŭ mettwaejirŭl tan tu pallo ssoa chu-
gyŏssŭmnida. 그 멧돼지를 단 두 발로 쏘아 죽였습니다/ ~
an arrow hwarŭl ssoda 활을 쏘다/ *He* ~s *well.* Kŭ saramŭn sagyŏk somssiga chossŭmnida. 그 사람은 사격 솜
씨가 좋습니다/ *A plant* ~s *out buds.* Shingmuri ssagŭl
t'ŭmnida. 식물이 싹을 틉니다.

shop *n.* (*store*) kage 가게, sangjŏm 상점, (*workroom*)
chagŏpchang 작업장. *a cake* ~ kwajajŏm 과자점/ *a*
coffee ~ tabang 다방/ *a fruit* ~ kwailchŏm 과일점/
What do they sell in the ~? Chŏ kageesŏ muŏsŭl p'algo
issŭmnikka? 저 가게에서 무엇을 팔고 있습니까/ *That* ~
sells dear. Chŏ kagenŭn pissage p'amnida. 저 가게는
비싸게 팝니다/ *I deal at his* ~. Nanŭn kŭ saram ka-
gewa tan-gorimnida. 나는 그 사람 가게와 단골입니다/ *a*
print ~ inswae kongjang 인쇄 공장/ *a repair* ~ suri
kongjang 수리 공장.

shopping *n.* mulgŏnsagi 물건사기, changbogi 장보기,
syop'ing 쇼핑. *a* ~ *bag* changpaguni 장바구니/ ~ *center*
syop'ing sent'ŏ 쇼핑 센터/ *I want to go* ~. Changborŏ
kago shipsŭmnida. 장보러 가고 싶습니다/ *I did a lot*
of ~ *in that store.* Chŏ kageesŏ manŭn syop'ingŭl
haessŭmnida. 저 가게에서 많은 쇼핑을 했습니다.

shore *n.* padatka 바닷가, haean 해안. *the* ~ *patrol* haean
kyŏngch'al 해안 경찰/ ~ *leave* sangnyuk hŏga 상륙 허가/
go on ~ sangnyuk'ada 상륙하다.

short *adj.* (*not long*) tchalbŭn 짧은, (*low*) k'iga chagŭn
키가 작은, (*brief*) kandanhan 간단한, (*scanty*) pujok'an
부족한, (*near*) kakkaun 가까운. *How* ~ *do you want*
your hair? Ŏlmana tchalke kkakkŭlkkayo? 얼마나 짧게
깎을까요?/ *I'm* ~ *of cash.* Hyŏnch'ari pujok'amnida.

현찰이 부족합니다/ *We are ~ of hands.* Ilsoni mojaramnida. 일손이 모자랍니다/ *a ~ distance* kakkaun kŏri 가까운 거리/ *~ cut* chirŭmkil 지름길.

shorthand *n.* sokki(sul) 속기(술). *How good is your ~?* Sokkinŭn ŏnŭ chŏngdo hashimnikka? 속기는 어느 정도 하십니까/ *in ~* (*in a word*) yok'ŏndae 요컨대.

shorten *vt., vi.* (*make shorter*) tchalke hada 짧게 하다, (*abbreviate*) saengnyak'ada 생략하다, (*curtail*) churida 줄이다, (*decrease*) churŏdulda 줄어들다, (*become shorter*) tchalbajida 짧아지다. *Please have this coat ~ed.* I udosŭi kijangŭl churyŏ chushipshio. 이 웃옷의 기장을 줄여 주십시오.

should *aux. v.* (*pt. of shall*) (*expressing duty*) *You ~n't speak so loud.* Kŭrŏk'e k'ŭn soriro marhaji mashio. 그렇게 큰 소리로 말하지 마시오/ *I ~ go to the post office.* Uch'eguge kaya hamnida. 우체국에 가야 합니다/ *I ~ help him.* Kŭ saramŭl towa chuŏya hamnida. 그 사람을 도와 주어야 합니다. (*expressing opinion*) *I ~ like to go.* Kabogo shipkunyo. 가보고 싶군요/ *S~ you like tea?* Ch'a tŭshigessŏyo? 차 드시겠어요/ *What time ~ I pick you up?* Myŏt shie moshirŏ kalkkayo? 몇 시에 모시러 갈까요/ (*advice, convenience*) *You ~ try.* Hae poshinŭn ke choŭl kŏshimnida. 해 보시는 게 좋을 것입니다/ *You ~ consult a doctor.* Ŭisaŭi chinch'arŭl pannŭn ke chok'essŭmnida. 의사의 진찰을 받는 게 좋겠읍니다/ *Which way ~ I take?* Ŏnŭ kirŭl kamyŏn toemnikka? 어느 길을 가면 됩니까?

shoulder *n.* ŏkkae 어깨. *—vt., vi.* (*carry on the ~*) ŏkkaec meda 어깨에 메다. *pat on the ~* ŏkkaerŭl tudŭrida 어깨를 두드리다/ *Give me a ~massage.* Nae ŏkkae chorchumullŏ chushio. 내 어깨 좀 주물러 주시오.

shout *n.* (*loud cry*) koham 고함, hamsŏng 함성. *—vi., vt.* (*cry out*) oech'ida 외치다, (*take or laugh loudly*) K'ŭn soriro chikkŏrida[utta] 큰 소리로 지껄이다[웃다]. *Don't ~ at me.* Na-ege kohamch'iji mashio. 나에게 고함치지 마시오/ *I'm not deaf, you needn't ~.* Kwimŏgŏriga aninikka kohamŭl chirŭl p'iryoga ŏpsŭmnida. 귀머거리가 아니니까 고함을 지를 필요가 없읍니다.

shovel *n.* sap 삽.

show *n.* (*attraction*) kugyŏngkŏri 구경거리, (*exhibition*) chŏllamhoe 전람회. *—vt., vi.*(*point out*) karik'ida 가리 키다, (*guide*) annaehada 안내하다, (*become visible*) poida 보이다. *Have you seen any good ~s lately?* Yojŭm choŭn syorŭl poassŭmnikka? 요즘 좋은 쇼를 보 았읍니까/ *Good ~s!* Chal haesso. 잘 했소/*S~ me the way to the Kyongbok Palace.* Kyŏngbokkung kanŭn kirŭl karik'yŏ chushipshio. 경복궁 가는 길을 가리켜 주 십시오/ *Would you ~ me around the city, if you have time?* Shigani issŭshimyŏn shinaerŭl annaehae chushio. 시간이 있으시면 시내를 안내해 주시오/ *S~ him in.* Kŭ punŭl annaehae oshio. 그 분을 안내해 오시오/ *S~ your ticket, please.* P'yorŭl poyŏ chushipshio. 표를 보여 주십 시오/ *S~ this to the conductress.* Annaeyangege igŏ-sŭl poishio. 안내양에게 이것을 보이시오.

showcase *n.* chinyŏlchang 진열장.

shower *n.* (*passing rain*) sonagi 소나기, (*~ bath*) syawŏ 샤워. *Do you have a vacancy with a ~?* Syawŏ ttallin pin pangi issŭmnikka? 샤워 딸린 빈 방이 있읍니까/ *A single with a ~ will do.* Syawŏ ttallin tokpangimyŏn toemnida. 샤워 딸린 독방이면 됩니다.

showy *adj.* (*striking*) nune ttŭinŭn 눈에 띄는, (*gaudy*) yahan 야한.

shrew *n.* (*scolding woman*) pagaji kŭngnŭn yŏja 바가지 긁는 여자.

shrewd *adj.* (*clever*) yŏngnihan 영리한, (*acute*) yemin-han 예민한, (*keen-witted*) pint'ŭmŏmnŭn 빈틈없는. *a ~ businessman* pint'ŭmŏmnŭn shirŏpka 빈틈없는 실업가/ *~ at a bargain* kŏraee pint'ŭmi ŏpta 거래에 빈틈이 없다.

shriek *n.* pimyŏng 비명, tchaenŭn tŭt'an sori 째는 듯한 소리. *give a ~* pimyŏngŭl chirŭda 비명을 지르다.

shrill *adj.* nalk'aroun 날카로운. *—vi., vt.* nalk'aroun sorirŭl naeda 날카로운 소리를 내다. *I ~ed with joy.* Nalk'aroun sorirŭl chirŭmyŏ kippŏhaessŭmnida. 날카로 운 소리를 지르며 기뻐했읍니다.

shrimp *n.* saeu 새우. *fried ~s* saeu t'wigim 새우 튀김/

salted ~s saeujŏt 새우젓.

shrink *vi.,vt.* (*contract*) ogŭradŭlda 오그라들다, (*lessen*) chulda 줄다. *Will this soap* ~ *woolen clothes?* I pinunŭn mojigŭl ogŭradŭlge hamnikka? 이 비누는 모직을 오그라들게 합니까/ *Our resources are gradually* ~*ing.* Uri chawŏnŭn chŏmjŏm churŏ kamnida. 우리 자원은 점점 줄어 갑니다/ *Flannel* ~s *in the wash.* P'ŭllannerŭn set'ak'amyŏn ogŭradŭmnida. 플란넬은 세탁하면 오그라듭니다.

shroud *n.* suŭi 수의(壽衣), (*veil*) changmak 장막.

shrub *n.* k'i chagŭn namu 키 작은 나무, kwanmok 관목. *a* ~ *zone* kwanmok chidae 관목 지대.

shrug *vi., vt.* (ŏkkaerŭl) ŭssŭk'ada (어깨를) 으쓱하다. *He just* ~*ged his shoulders.* Kŭ saramŭn taman ŏkkaerŭl ŭssŭk'aessŭmnida. 그 사람은 다만 어깨를 으쓱했읍니다.

shudder *vi.* (*shiver*) momŭl ttŏlda 몸을 떨다. —*n.* chŏnyul 전율. *I* ~ *at the sight of blood.* P'irŭl poja momi ttŏllimnida. 피를 보자 몸이 떨립니다/ *A* ~ *passed over me.* Chŏnshini ossak'aessŭmnida. 전신이 오싹했읍니다.

shuffle *vt., vi.* (*mix*) twisŏkta 뒤섞다, (*shift*) pakkuda 바꾸다.

shun *vt.* (*avoid*) p'ihada 피하다. ~ *temptation* yuhogŭl p'ihada 유혹을 피하다.

shut *vt., vi.* (*close*) tatta 닫다, tach'ida 닫히다. *S*~ *the door, please.* Munŭl tadŭshipshio. 문을 닫으십시오/ *This door won't* ~. I munŭn tach'yŏjiji anssŭmnida. 이 문은 닫혀지지 않습니다/ *Tell him to* ~ *up.* Kŭ saramege ip chom takch'irago hashio. 그 사람에게 입 좀 닥치라고 하시오.

shutter *n.* (*outer door*) tŏnmun 덧문, (*of camera*) syŏt't'ŏ 셔터. *You just stand there and release the* ~. Kŏgi sŏsŏ syŏt'ŏman nullŏ chushio. 거기 서서 셔터만 눌러 주시오.

shy *adj.* (*bashful*) pukkŭrŏwŏhanŭn 부끄러워하는, (*reluctant*) kkŏrinŭn 꺼리는, (*Am.*) (*lacking*) pujok'an 부족한. *Don't be* ~. Pukkŭrŏwŏhaji mashio. 부끄러워하지 마시오/ *Why are you* ~? Wae pukkŭrŏwŏhamnikka? 왜 부끄러워합니까/ *Don't be* ~ *of telling me what you*

want. Wŏnhanŭn kŏsŭl mangsŏriji malgo marhashio. 원
하는 것을 망설이지 말고 말하시오/ *We are* ~ *of funds*.
Chagŭmi pujok'amnida. 자금이 부족합니다.

sick *adj*. (*ill*) pyŏngnan 병난, allŭn 앓는, (*nauseated*)
mesŭkkŏun 메스꺼운, (*longing*) kŭriwŏhanŭn 그리워하
는. *Are you* ~ ? P'yŏnch'anŭshimnikka? 편찮으십니까/
You look very ~. Maeu p'yŏnch'anŭn kŏt kassŭmnida.
매우 편찮은 것 같습니다/ *I feel* ~. (*Am*.) Momi ap'ŭmnida. 몸이 아픕니다. (*Brit*.) Mesŭkkŏpsŭmnidạ. 메스껍
습니다/ *I'm going to be* ~. T'ohal kŏt kassŭmnida.
토할 것 같습니다/ *car* ~ ch'amŏlmihanŭn 차멀미하는/
sea ~ paenmŏlmihanŭn 뱃멀미하는/ *home* ~ kohyang kŭ-
⌐rinŭn 고향 그리는.

sickroom *n*. pyŏngshil 병실.

sickle *n*. nat 낫.

sickness *n*. pyŏng 병. *fake* ~ kkoebyŏng 꾀병/ *a severe*
~ chungbyŏng 중병/ *sea* ~ paenmŏlmi 뱃멀미.

side *n*. (*direction*) tchok 쪽, (*party*) p'yŏn 편, (*of body*)
yŏpkuri 옆구리. *the left* ~ oentchok 왼쪽/ *the right* ~
orŭntchok 오른쪽/ *the back* ~ twitchok 뒤쪽/ *the front* ~
aptchok 앞쪽/ *the right* [*wrong*] ~ (*of cloth*) kŏt[an]-
tchok 겉[안]쪽/ ~ *effect* pujagyong 부작용/ ~ *way* podo
보도, yŏpkil 옆길/ *Look on the reverse* ~ *of this wrap-*
per. I p'yojiŭi twinmyŏnŭl poshio. 이 표지의 뒷면을 보시
오/ *I said to a friend at my* ~. Nae yŏptchoge innŭn
ch'in-guege marhaessŭmnida. 내 옆쪽에 있는 친구에게 말
했읍니다/ *Which* ~ *are you on*? Ŏnŭ p'yŏnimnikka?
어느 편입니까/ *I feel a pain in my* ~. Yŏpkuriga ap'ŭmnida. 옆구리가 아픕니다/ *What is the price of that* ~
dish? Chŏ anjuŭi kapsŭn ŏlmaimnikka? 저 안주의 값은
얼마입니까?

siege *n*. p'owi 포위. ~ *warfare* p'owijŏn 포위전.

sieve *n*. ch'e 체. —*vt*. ch'ejirhada 체질하다.

sift *vt*. (*sieve*) ch'ero ch'ida 체로 치다. ~ *sand over the*
ground moraerŭl ch'ero ch'ida 모래를 체로 치다.

sigh *n*. hansum 한숨. —*vi*., *vt*. hansum shwida 한숨 쉬다.
draw a ~ hansum shwida 한숨 쉬다/ *Why do you* ~ ?
Wae hansumŭl shwishimnikka? 왜 한숨을 쉬십니까?

sight *n.* (*vision*) shiryŏk 시력, (*scene*) kwanggyŏng 광경, (*famous places*) myŏngsŭngji 명승지. *far* ~ wŏnshi 원시/ *short* ~ kŭnshi 근시/ *loss of* ~ shilmyŏng 실명(失明)/ *My* ~ *is dim.* Nuni ch'imch'imhamnida. 눈이 침침 합니다/ *I know him by* ~. Kŭ saramgwanŭn anmyŏni issŭmnida. 그 사람과는 안면이 있읍니다/ *Get out of my* ~. Nae ap'esŏ kkŏjishio. 내 앞에서 꺼지시오/ *What a* ~ *you are.* Tangshin kkori mwŏyo! 당신 꼴이 뭐요/ *I want to do the* ~s *of the city.* Shinae kugyŏngŭl hago shipsŭmnida. 시내 구경을 하고 싶습니다.

sightseeing *n.* kwan-gwang 관광, kugyŏng 구경. *go* ~ kugyŏngharŏ kada 구경하러 가다/ *a* ~ *bus* kwan-gwang pŏsŭ 관광 버스/ *Nice day for* ~, *isn't it?* Kwan-gwang hagienŭn choŭn nalssijiyo? 관광하기에는 좋은 날씨지요/ *Are there any* ~ *buses?* Kwan-gwang pŏsŭga issŭmnikka? 관광 버스가 있읍니까/ *What time does the* ~ *train leave?* Kwan-gwang yŏlch'anŭn myŏt shie ch'ulbarhamnikka? 관광 열차는 몇 시에 출발합니까?

sightseer *n.* kugyŏngkkun 구경꾼, kwan-gwanggaek 관광객. *attract many* ~s manŭn kwan-gwanggaegŭl yuch'ihada 많은 관광객을 유치하다.

sign *n.* (*signal*) shinho 신호, (*gesture*) sonchit 손짓, (*token*) p'yojŏk 표적, (*mark*) p'yoshi 표시, (*signboard*) kanp'an 간판. —*vi.*, *vt.* (*put one's name on*) sŏmyŏnghada 서명 하다, (*give a* ~ *to*) shinhohada 신호하다. *I see no* ~ *of rain.* Piga ol kŏt katchi anssŭmnida. 비가 올 것 같지 않 습니다/ *Are dark clouds a* ~ *of rain?* Kŏmŭn kurŭmŭn pi ol chojimimnikka? 검은 구름은 비 올 조짐입니까/ *Where shall I* ~? *Right here. On the dotted line.* Ŏdie sŏmyŏng halkkayo? Paro yŏgie. Chŏmsŏnŭl ttara sŏmyŏnghae chushio. 어디에 서명할까요? 바로 여기에. 점선을 따라 서명해 주시오/ *Will you* ~ *those papers?* I sŏryue sŏmyŏnghae chushio. 이 서류에 서명해 주시오/ *The policeman* ~ed *them to stop.* Kyŏnggwanŭn kŭdŭrege sŏrago shinhohaetta. 경관은 그들에게 서라고 신호했다/ ~ *board* kanp'an 간판/ ~ *painter* kanp'anjangi 간판장이/ ~ *a check* sup'yo-e sŏmyŏnghada 수표에 서명하다/ ~ *and seal* sŏmyŏng narinhada 서명 날인하다.

signal *n.* (*sign*) shinho 신호, (*alarm*) kyŏngbo 경보. *an automatic* ~ chadong shinho 자동 신호/ *a caution* ~ kyŏnggye kyŏngbo 경계 경보/ *a distress* ~ chonan shinho 조난 신호/ *a go* ~ ch'ŏngshinho 청신호/ *a red* ~ chŏkshinho 적신호, pulgŭn shinho 붉은 신호/ *a starting* ~ ch'ulbal shinho 출발 신호/ *traffic* ~s kyot'ong shinho 교통 신호/ *a* ~ *fire* ponghwa 봉화/ *a* ~ *lamp* shinhodŭng 신호등/ *make a* ~ shinhorŭl hada 신호를 하다.

signature *n.* sŏmyŏng 서명. *May I have your* ~ *here, please.* Yŏgie sŏmyŏnghae chushipshio. 여기에 서명해 주십시오/ *Full* ~? Sainŭn p'ul neimŭro hanŭn kŏmnikka? 사인은 풀 네임으로 하는 겁니까?

signet *n.* (*seal*) tojang 도장, injang 인장.

silence *n.* ch'immuk 침묵. *keep* ~ ch'immugŭl chik'ida 침묵을 지키다/ *break* (*the*) ~ ch'immugŭl kkaettŭrida 침묵을 깨뜨리다.

silent *adj.* choyonghan 조용한. *a* ~ *prayer* mukto 묵도/ *Be* ~! Choyonghashio 조용하시오/ *You had better be* ~. Tangshinŭn chamjak'o innŭn kŏshi chossŭmnida. 당신은 잠자코 있는 것이 좋습니다/ *We will be* ~ *about your conduct.* Tangshinŭi haengwie taehaesŏnŭn marhaji ank'essŭmnida. 당신의 행위에 대해서는 말하지 않겠읍니다.

silk *n.* pidan 비단, myŏngju 명주. ~ *clothes* pidanot 비단옷/ ~ *thread* pidanshil 비단실/ *artificial* ~ injogyŏn 인조견/ *raw* ~ saengsa 생사/ *She is dressed in* ~. Kŭ yŏinŭn pidanosŭl ipko issŭmnida. 그 여인은 비단옷을 입고 있읍니다/ *Is this made of* ~? Igŏsŭn pidanshillo mandŭn kŏshimnikka? 이것은 비단실로 만든 것입니까/ ~*worm* nue 누에/ ~*worm cocoon* koch'i 고치/ ~ *mill* chesa kongjang 제사 공장.

sill *n.* (*threshold*)munchibang 문지방. *door* ~ munchibang 문지방/ *window* ~ ch'angt'ŏk 창턱.

silly *adj.* (*stupid*) ŏrisŏgŭn 어리석은. —*n.* (*fool*) pabo 바보. *a* ~ *guy* pabo 바보/ *Don't be* ~! Mŏngch'ŏnghage kulji malge! 멍청하게 굴지 말게/ (*to equals*) *You were very* ~ *to trust him.* Kŭ saramŭl mittani tangshindo

kkwae paborogunyo. 그 사람을 믿다니 당신도 꽤 바보로군
요/ *I know it's* ~, *but I can't help it.* Ŏrisŏgŭn churŭn
aljiman hal su ŏpsŭmnida. 어리석은 줄은 알지만 할 수 없
읍니다.

silver *n.* ŭn 은. ~ *coins* ŭnhwa 은화/ ~ *hair* ŭnbal 은발/
~ *medal* ŭnmedal 은메달/ ~*ware* ŭngŭrŭt 은그릇.

similar *adj.* (*resembling*) pisŭt'an 비슷한, (*same kind*)
kat'ŭn chongnyuŭi 같은 종류의. *My wife and I have* ~
tastes in music. Anaewa nanŭn ŭmage pisŭt'an ch'wimirŭl katko issŭmnida. 아내와 나는 음악에 비슷한 취미를
갖고 있읍니다/ *They are quite* ~ *to those in Korea.*
Han-gugŭi kŭgŏtkwa pisŭt'agunyo. 한국의 그것과 비슷하
군요.

simple *adj.* (*easy*) kandanhan 간단한, (*not combined*)
tansunhan 단순한, (*plain*) kŏmsohan 검소한, (*foolish*)
pabogat'ŭn 바보같은. *a* ~ *matter* kandanhan il 간단한 일/
the ~ *life* kŏmsohan saenghwal 검소한 생활/ *a* ~ *soldier*
cholbyŏng 졸병/ ~-*minded* sunjinhan 순진한.

simplicity *n.* tansun 단순, (*plainness*) kanso 간소, komso
검소.

sin *n.* (*transgression*) choe 죄, (*error*) kwashil 과실,
(*offence*) wiban 위반. *commit a* ~ choerŭl pŏmhada 죄
를 범하다/ *forgive a* ~ choerŭl yongsŏhada 죄를 용서하
다/ *original* ~ wŏnjoe 원죄.

since *adv.* (*subsequently*) kŭ hu 그 후, irae 이래. —*prep.*
(*till, by*) ...put'ŏ tchuk ...부터 쪽. —*conj.* (*continuously
from...*) ...ttaebut'ŏ tchuk ...때부터 쪽. *Ever* ~ *I came
to Korea I have lived in this house.* Han-guge on irae
tchuk i chibe salgo issŭmnida. 한국에 온 이래 쪽 이 집에
살고 있읍니다/ *I haven't heard from him* ~ *last March.*
Chinan samwŏl ihubut'ŏ kŭbunŭi soshigi ŏpsŭmnida. 지
난 3월 이후부터 그분의 소식이 없읍니다/ *How long is it*
~ *you were in Seoul?* Sŏul kyeshin chi ŏlmana toeshimnikka? 서울 계신 지 얼마나 되십니까/ *ever* ~ kŭ hu chulgot
그 후 줄곧/ *I have ever* ~*given up smoking.* Orae
chŏne tambaerŭl kkŭnŏssŭmnida. 오래 전에 담배를 끊었
읍니다/ *not long* ~ paro ŏlma chŏne 바로 얼마 전에.

sincere *adj.* (*true*) chinshirhan 진실한, (*honest*) sŏngshir-han 성실한. *a ~ friend* chinshirhan ch'in-gu 진실한 친구.

sing *vi., vt.* noraehada 노래하다, (*of birds*) chijŏgwida 지저귀다. *Will you ~ me a song?* Norae han kok pullŏ chushio. 노래 한 곡 불러 주시오/ *I can't ~.* Purŭl chul morŭmnida. 부를 줄 모릅니다/ *Please ~ a Korean song.* Han-guk norae han kok pullŏ chushipshio. 한국 노래 한 곡 불러 주십시오/ *Birds were ~ing merrily.* Saedŭri chŭlgŏpke chijŏgwigo issŏssŭmnida. 새들이 즐겁게 지저귀고 있었읍니다.

singe *vt.* (*burn a little*) kŭullida 그을리다, (*hair*) chijida 지지다.

singer *n.* kasu 가수.

single *n.* (*room*) tokpang 독방, (*ticket*) p'yŏndo ch'ap'yo 편도 차표, (*tennis*) tanshik shihap 단식 시합. —*adj.* (*one only*) tanirŭi 단일의, (*not married*) tokshinŭi 독신의, (*for one person*) irinyongŭi 1인용의. *a ~ house* tandok kaok 단독 가옥/ *a ~ man* tokshin namja 독신 남자/ *a ~ life* tokshin saenghwal 독신 생활/ *What's the daily rate for a ~?* Tokpangŭn haru ŏlmaimnikka? 독방은 하루 얼마입니까/ *A ~ room with a bath is 25,000 won.* Yokshiri ttallin tokpangŭn imanoch'ŏnwŏnimnida. 욕실이 딸린 독방은 25,000원입니다/ *A ~ with a shower will do.* Syawŏga ttallin tokpangimyŏn toemnida. 샤워가 딸린 독방이면 됩니다.

singular *adj.* (*single*) tandogŭi 단독의, (*strange*) isang-han 이상한, (*eccentric*) koetchaŭi 괴짜의. *the ~ number* tansu 단수/ *~ clothes* isanghan pokchang 이상한 복장/ *~ habits* koesanghan pŏrŭt 괴상한 버릇.

sink *vi., vt.* (*go down*) karaanta 가라앉다, (*sun, etc.*) chida 지다. —*n.* (*of kitchen*) shingk'ŭdae 싱크대. *The ship sank.* Paenŭn karaanjassŭmnida. 배는 가라앉았읍니다/ *S~ or swim, I will try.* Chugi toedŭn pabi toedŭn haebogessŭmnida. 죽이 되든 밥이 되든 해보겠읍니다.

sinless *adj.* choeŏmnŭn 죄없는.

sinner *n.* (*transgressor*) choein 죄인, (*rogue*) ak'an 악한. *You, young ~!* Yo, akchira! 요, 악질아!

sip *vt., vi.* han mogŭmssik mashida 한 모금씩 마시다. —*n.*

han mogŭm 한 모금. ~ (*up*) *one's coffee* k'op'irŭl han mogŭmssik mashida. 코피를 한 모금씩 마시다/ *I'll just take a* ~. Han mogŭmman mashigessŭmnida. 한 모금만 마시겠읍니다.

sir *n.* (*Korean polite title*) nim 님, sŏnsaeng 선생, (*cap.*) kyŏng 경(卿). *Good morning,* ~? Annyŏnghi chumusyŏssŭmnikka? 안녕히 주무셨읍니까/ *Yes,* ~ Ne 네 (*respectful term*)/ *S*~ *Walter Scott* Wŏlt'ŏ Sŭk'ot'ŭ kyŏng 월터 스코트 경(卿).

siren *n.* (*whistle*) sairen 사이렌, kijŏk 기적(汽笛), (*nymph*) yojŏng 요정(妖精), (*witch*) manyŏ 마녀. *The* ~ *blows.* Saireni ullimnida. 사이렌이 울립니다.

sister *n.* chamae 자매, nui 누이. *my elder* ~ nui 누이, nunim 누님 (*honorific*)/ *my younger* ~ nuidongsaeng 누이동생/ *your elder* ~ tangshinŭi nunim 당신의 누님 (*honorific*)/ *your younger* ~ tangshinŭi nuidongsaeng 당신의 누이동생, tangshinŭi maessi 당신의 매씨(妹氏) (*honorific*)/ ~-*in-law* hyŏngsu 형수, kyesu 계수, ch'ŏhyŏng 처형, ch'ŏje 처제, ŭijamae 의자매.

sit *vi.,vt.* anta 앉다. *Please* ~ *down.* Anjŭshipshio. 앉으십시오/ *Won't you* ~ *down?* Anjŭseyo. 앉으세요/ *S*~ *on this chair.* I ŭija-e anjŭseyo. 이 의자에 앉으세요/ *Just* ~ *me up a little.* Chom irŭk'yŏ chushio. 좀 일으켜 주시오.

site *n.* (*lot*) puji 부지, (*place*) changso 장소. *a building* ~ kŏnmul puji 건물 부지/ *a ceremonial* ~ shikchang 식장.

situated *adj.* (*located*) …e innŭn …에 있는. *Where is your apartment* ~? Taegŭi ap'at'ŭnŭn ŏdi issŭmnikka? 댁의 아파트는 어디 있읍니까/ *My apartment is* ~ *at the riverside of the Han-gang.* Uri ap'at'ŭnŭn Han-gangbyŏne issŭmnida. 우리 아파트는 한강변에 있읍니다.

situation *n.* (*location*) wich'i 위치, (*circumstance*) ch'ŏji 처지, (*job*) ilchari 일자리. *a delicate* ~ mimyohan hyŏngse 미묘한 형세. *How's the world* ~ *lately?* Yojŭm segye chŏngsega ŏttŏssŭmnikka? 요즘 세계 정세가 어떻습니까/ *We have the same* ~ *in Korea, too.* Han-gukto yŏkshi kat'ŭn ch'ŏjiimnida. 한국도 역시 같은 처지입니다/ *He has a good* ~. Kŭ saramŭn choŭn ilcharirŭl kajigo issŭmnida. 그 사람은 좋은 일자리를 가지고 있읍니다/ *I'm unable to find a ~.* Ilcharirŭl ch'ajŭl suga ŏpsŭmnida. 일자리를 찾을 수가 없읍니다.

six *n.* (*bigness*) yŏsŏt 여섯, yuk 육(6). —*adj.* yŏsŏsŭi 여섯의, yugŭi 의. *~ men* yŏsŏt saram 여섯 사람/ *~ days* yŏtsae 엿새.

six-shooter *n.* yugyŏnbal kwŏnch'ong 6연발 권총. yuk'yŏlp'o 육혈포.

sixteen *n.* yŏl yŏsŏt 열 여섯, shimnyuk 십육(16). *a girl of sweet ~* kkottaun ip'al ch'ŏngch'un 꽃다운 이팔 청춘.

sixth *n.* yŏsŏt pŏntchae 여섯 번째, cheyuk 제 6. —*adj.* yŏsŏt pŏntchaeŭi 여섯 번째의. *the ~ day of month* ch'o-yŏtsaennal 초엿샛날.

sixty *n.* yesun 예순, yukship 육십(60).

size *n.* (*bigness*) k'ŭgi 크기, (*measurement*) ch'isu 치수, saijŭ 사이즈. *What ~ do you want?* Saijŭnŭn ŏlmajiyo? 사이즈는 얼마지요/ *Do you know your ~ in centimeters?* Ch'isurŭl sent'iro algo kyeshimnikka? 치수를 센티로 알고 계십니까/ *What ~ is your hat?* Taegŭi moja ch'isunŭn ŏlmajiyo? 댁의 모자 치수는 얼마지요/ *This ~ is too large [small].* I ch'isunŭn nŏmu k'ŭm[chaksŭm]nida. 이 치수는 너무 큼[작슴]니다.

skate *n.* (*pl.*) sŭk'eit'ŭ kudu 스케이트 구두. —*vi.* sŭk'eit'ŭrŭl t'ada 스케이트를 타다. *May I use these ~s?* I sŭk'eit'ŭrŭl ssŏdo chossŭmnikka? 이 스케이트를 써도 좋습니까/ *Do you ~?* Sŭk'eit'ŭrŭl t'al chul ashimnikka? 스케이트를 탈 줄 아십니까/ *I cannot ~.* Sŭk'eit'ŭrŭl t'al chul morŭmnida. 스케이트를 탈 줄 모릅니다.

skating *n.* sŭk'eit'ing 스케이팅, ŏrŭmjich'igi 얼음지치기. *a ~ rink* shillae sŭk'eit'ŭjang 실내 스케이트장/ *~ shoes* sŭk'eit'ŭ kudu 스케이트 구두.

skeleton *n.* haegol 해골, (*framework*) ppyŏdae 뼈대. *He looks like a living ~.* Kŭ saramŭn sara innŭn haegol kassŭmnida. 그 사람은 살아 있는 해골 같습니다.

sketch *n.* (*rough drawing*) sŭk'ech'i 스케치, (*outline*) yun-gwak 윤곽, (*from nature*) sasaeng 사생. —*vt., vi.* sasaenghada 사생하다. *I am doing a ~ of flowers.* Kkoch'ŭl sasaenghago issŭmnida. 꽃을 사생하고 있읍니

다/ *My sister often goes into the country to* ∼. Nae nuinŭn sŭk'ech'iharŏ chaju shigore kamnida. 내 누이는 스케치하러 자주 시골에 갑니다/ ∼ *book* sŭk'ech'ibuk 스케치북, sasaengch'ŏp 사생첩/ ∼ *map* yakto 약도.

ski *n.* sŭk'i 스키. *I bought a pair of* ∼s. Nanŭn sŭk'irŭl hana sassŭmnida. 나는 스키를 하나 샀습니다/ *I have never been on* ∼s. Sŭk'irŭl t'abon chŏgi ŏpsŭmnida. 스키를 타본 적이 없읍니다.

skiing *n.* (*ski running*) sŭk'it'agi 스키타기. *Then you must be able to do a lot of* ∼. Kŭrŏshidamyŏn sŭk'inŭn mani t'ashigetkunyo. 그러시다면 스키는 많이 타시겠군요.

skill *n.* (*knack*) somssi 솜씨, (*expertness*) chŏnmun kisul 전문 기술. *a man of* ∼ noryŏnhan saram 노련한 사람/ *reading* ∼s toksŏsul 독서술/ *I failed to show my usual* ∼. P'yŏngsoŭi somssirŭl parhwihaji mot'aessŭmnida. 평소의 솜씨를 발휘하지 못했읍니다.

skil(l)ful *adj.* somssi choŭn 솜씨 좋은, nŭngsuk'an 능숙한. *He is not very* ∼ *with his chopsticks*. Kŭ saramŭn chŏtkarak ssŭnŭn pŏbi mopshi sŏt'urŭmnida. 그 사람은 젓가락 쓰는 법이 몹시 서투릅니다/ *a* ∼ *surgeon* nŭngsuk'an oekwa ŭisa 능숙한 외과 의사.

skin *n.* (*of persons*) p'ibu 피부, salkat 살갗, (*hide*) kajuk 가죽, (*rind*) kkŏpchil 껍질. —*vt.* (*animals*) kajugŭl pŏtkida 가죽을 벗기다, (*fruits*) kkŏpchirŭl pŏtkida 껍질을 벗기다. *fair* [*yellow, black*] ∼ hŭin [noran, kŏmŭn] p'ibu 흰 [노란, 검은] 피부/ *Would you show me a watch band made of* ∼. Kajugŭro mandŭn shigyechul hana poyŏ chuseyo. 가죽으로 만든 시계줄 하나 보여 주세요/ *I was wet to the* ∼. Nanŭn hŭmppŏk chŏjŏssŭmnida. 나는 흠뻑 젖었읍니다.

skip *vi., vt.* (*jump rope*) chullŏmkihada 줄넘기하다, (*pass over*) kŏnnŏttwida 건너뛰다.

skipping *n.* chullŏmki 줄넘기.

skirt *n.* sŭk'ŏt'ŭ 스커트, ch'ima 치마, (*of garments*) charak 자락, (*slang*) (*woman*) yŏja 여자.

skull *n.* tugaegol 두개골.

sky *n.* hanŭl 하늘. *the blue* ∼ p'urŭn hanŭl 푸른 하늘/

the clear ~ malgŭn hanŭl 맑은 하늘/ *the cloudy* ~ hŭrin hanŭl 흐린 하늘/ *We didn't see the* ~ *for weeks.* Yŏrŏ chuil tongan p'urŭn hanŭrŭl mot poassŭmnida. 여러 주일 동안 푸른 하늘을 못 브았읍니다/ ~ *blue* hanŭlsaek 하늘색.

skylark *n.* chongdari 종다리, chongdalsae 종달새.

skyscraper *n.* mach'ŏllu 마천루.

slack *adj.* (*loose*) nŭsŭnhan 느슨한, (*slow*) nŭrin 느린, (*not active*) pulgyŏnggiŭi 불경기의. —*vt., vi.* (*slacken*) nŭtch'uda 늦추다. *Business is* ~ *this week.* I chuirŭn changsaga pulgyŏnggiimnida. 이 주일은 장사가 불경기입 니다/ *Can't you* ~ *up a little?* Chom ch'ŏnch'ŏnhi kal su ŏpsŭmnikka? 좀 천천히 갈 수 없읍니까?

slacks *n.* sŭllaeksŭ 슬랙스, paji 바지. *I would like to find a pair of* ~. Pajirŭl pogo ship'ŭndeyo. 바지를 보고 싶은데요.   「sanghada 중상하다.

slander *n.* chungsang 중상, pibang 비방. —*vt.* chung-

slang *n.* sogŏ 속어, (*jargon*) t'ŭksu yongŏ 특수 용어. *American* ~ Miguk sogŏ 미국 속어/ *college* ~ taehak-saeng yongŏ 대학생 용어/ *service* ~ kundae yongŏ 군대 용어/ *sports* ~ sŭp'och'ŭ yongŏ 스포츠 용어.

slap *vt.* ch'alssak ch'ida 찰싹 치다. *I* ~*ped him on the back.* Kŭ saramŭi tŭngŭl ch'alssak ttaeryŏ chuŏssŭm-nida. 그 사람의 등을 찰싹 때려 주었읍니다.

slate *n.* sŏkp'an 석판, sŭlleit'ŭ 슬레이트. *roofing* ~ chi-bung inŭn sŭlleit'ŭ 지붕 이는 슬레이트/ ~ *pencil* sŏkp'il 석필.

slaughter *n.* (*butchering*) tosal 도살, (*massacre*) haksal 학살, (*genocide*) taeryang haksal 대량 학살. —*vt.* tosal〔haksal〕hada 도살〔학살〕하다.

slave *n.* noye 노예. ~ *ship* noyesŏn 노예선.

slay *vt.* (*murder*) chugida 죽이다, sarhaehada 살해하다.

sledge *n.* ssŏlmae 썰매. *carry by* ~ ssŏlmaero narŭda 썰 매로 나르다.

sleep *n.* cham 잠, sumyŏn 수면. —*vi.* (*fall asleep*) chada 자다, chamjada 잠자다. *How many hours' ~ do you need?* Myŏt shigan chumusyŏya hamnikka? 몇 시간 주무

서야 합니까/ I had a good ∼ last night. Ōjetpam chal
chassŭmnida. 어젯밤 잘 잤읍니다/ Do you ever talk in
your ∼? Chamkkodaehanŭn iri issŭmnikka? 잠꼬대하는
일이 있읍니까/ I don't ∼ well at night. Pame chamŭl
chal iruji mot'amnida. 밤에 잠을 잘 이루지 못합니다/ I
slept very badly last night. Ōjetpam t'ong chaji mo-
t'aessŭmnida. 어젯밤 통 자지 못했읍니다/ ∼walking
mongyupyŏng 몽유병/ ∼ing car ch'imdaech'a 침대차/
∼ing pill sumyŏnje 수면제/ ∼ing room ch'imshil 침실/
Has this train a ∼ing car? I yŏlch'anŭn ch'imdaech'aga issŭmnikka? 이 열차는 침대차가 있읍니까?

sleepy adj. (drowsy) chollinŭn 졸리는.

sleeve n. somae 소매. roll up one's ∼ somaerŭl kŏdŏ ollida
소매를 걷어 올리다.

slender adj. (slim) nalssinhan 날씬한, (slight) kanyal-
p'ŭn 가냘픈, (scanty) pinyak'an 빈약한. a ∼ hope
kanyalp'ŭn hŭimang 가냘픈 희망/ a ∼ income pinyak'an
suip 빈약한 수입.

slice n. chogak 조각. —vt. yalke ssŏlda 얇게 썰다. a ∼ of
bread ppang han chogak 빵 한 조각/ How thick do you
want the ∼s? Ōnŭ chŏngdoŭi tukkero ssŏrŏ tŭrilkkayo?
어느 정도의 두께로 썰어 드릴까요/ S∼ the beef thin. Soe-
gogirŭl yalke ssŏrŏ chushio. 쇠고기를 얇게 썰어 주시오.

slide vi., vt. (slip) mikkŭrŏjida 미끄러지다. —n. (photo)
sŭllaidŭ 슬라이드. Let's ∼ down this grassy slope. P'uri
musŏnghan pit'arŭl mikkŭrŏjyŏ naeryŏgapshida. 풀이 무
성한 비탈을 미끄러져 내려갑시다/ S∼ the drawer into
its place. Sŏrabŭl chejarie mirŏ nŏushio. 서랍을 제자리
에 밀어 넣으시오.

sliding n. a ∼ door midaji 미닫이.

slight adj. (inconsiderable) yakkanŭi 약간의, (trivial)
kabyŏun 가벼운, (slender) kanŭn 가는, (frail) murŭn
무른. a ∼ increase yakkanŭi chŭngga 약간의 증가/ a ∼
wound kabyŏun sangch'ŏ 가벼운 상처/ a ∼ person hol-
tchuk'an saram 홀쭉한 사람/ I have not the ∼est doubt.
Nanŭn chogŭmdo ŭishimhaji anssŭmnida. 나는 조금도 의
심하지 않습니다/ I have a ∼ cold. Nanŭn yakkan kamg

kiuni issŭmnida. 나는 약간 감기 기운이 있읍니다.

slightly *adj.* chogŭm 조금, yakkan 약간.

slim *adj.* (*slender*) kanŭdaran 가느다란. *a ~ leg* kanŭdaran tari 가느다란 다리.

sling *n.* (*band*) ŏkkaee kŏnŭn pungdae 어깨에 거는 붕대. *I had to carry my arm in a ~.* P'arŭl pungdaero ŏkkae kŏlgo tanyŏyaman haessŭmnida. 팔을 붕대로 어깨에 걸고 다녀야만 했읍니다.

slip *n.* (*trip*) hŏttidim 헛디딤, (*stumble*) nŏmŏjim 넘어짐, (*mistake*) shilsu 실수, (*error in speech*) shirŏn 실언, (*string*) chongi chogak 종이 조각. *—vi., vt.* (*slide*) mikkŭrŏjida 미끄러지다, (*escape secretly*) mollae taranada 몰래 달아나다. *It's a ~ of the tongue.* Shirŏnŭl haessŭmnida. 실언을 했읍니다/ *Give me a ~ of paper.* Chongi chogak han changman chushio. 종이 조각 한 장만 주시오/ *I ~ped past without a sound.* Nanŭn soriŏpshi saltchak chinach'yŏssŭmnida. 나는 소리없이 살짝 지나쳤읍니다/ *I must ~ out to post a letter.* P'yŏnjirŭl puch'irŏ cḥamkkan nagaya hagessŭmnida. 편지를 부치러 잠깐 나가야 하겠읍니다.

slipper *n.* (*pl.*) shillaehwa 실내화, sŭllip'ŏ 슬리퍼. *Please put on these ~s.* I sŭllip'ŏrŭl shinŭshipshio. 이 슬리퍼를 신으십시오.

slippery *adj.* mikkŭrŏun 미끄러운. *~ roads* mikkŭrŏun kil 미끄러운 길.

slit *n.* kallajin t'ŭm 갈라진 틈. *—vi., vt.* (*cut apart*) tchaeŏ karŭda 쩨어 가르다/ *~ an envelope open* pongt'urŭl tchitta 봉투를 찢다.

slogan *n.* p'yoŏ 표어, sŭllogŏn 슬로건. *political ~s* chŏngch'i p'yoŏ 정치 표어.

slope *n.* (*incline*) pit'al 비탈, (*slant*) kyŏngsa 경사. *—vi., vt.* (*incline*) kiurŏjida 기울어지다, pit'aljida 비탈지다. *mountain ~s* sanbit'al 산비탈/ *ski ~s* sŭk'i hwalchuro 스키 활주로.

slot *n.* kumŏng 구멍. *a ~ machine* chadong p'anmaegi 자동 판매기.

slow *adj.* (*not fast*) nŭrin 느린, (*behind time*) nŭjŭn 늦

은, (*dull*) tunhan 둔한. —*vi.*, *vt.* (*retard*) songnyŏgŭl churida 속력을 줄이다. *a ～ train* wanhaeng yŏlch'a 완행 열차/ *My watch is three minutes ～.* Nae shigyenŭn sambun nŭssŭmnida. 내 시계는 3분 늦습니다/ *I'm very ～ in understanding.* Nanŭn mopshi ihaeryŏgi tunhamnida. 나는 몹시 이해력이 둔합니다/ *Go ～ here.* Yŏgisŏnŭn ch'ŏnch'ŏnhi kapshida. 여기서는 천천히 갑시다/ *The road is slippery, you had better ～ down.* Kiri mikkŭrŏuni ch'ŏnch'ŏnhi kŏnnŭn ke chok'essŭmnida. 길이 미끄러우니 천천히 걷는 게 좋겠읍니다.

slowly *adv.* ch'ŏnch'ŏnhi 천천히. *Speak more ～, please.* Chomdŏ ch'ŏnch'ŏnhi malssŭmhashipshio. 좀더 천천히 말씀하십시오/ *Let's go ～.* Ch'ŏnch'ŏnhi kapshida. 천천히 갑시다.

sluggard *n.* (*idler*) nomp'angi 놈팡이, (*lounger*) kŏndal 건달.

sluggish *adj.* (*lazy*) keŭrŭn 게으른, (*inactive*) kkumulgŏrinŭn 꾸물거리는.

sluice *n.* (*dock gate*) sumun 수문.

slumber *n.* (*light sleep*) sŏnjam 선잠. —*vi.*, *vt.* (*sleep lightly*) sŏnjamjada 선잠자다, (*doze*) cholda 졸다.

sly *adj.* (*cunning*) kyohwarhan 교활한, (*stealthy*) ŏngk'ŭmhan 엉큼한. *a ～ person* kyohwarhan in-gan 교활한 인간/ *on the ～* nammollae 남몰래.

smack *n.* (*with one's tongue*) hyŏrŭl ch'am 혀를 참, (*loud kiss*) tchok'anŭn k'isŭ 쪽하는 키스. —*vi.*, *vt.* (*click tongue*) hyŏrŭl ch'ada 혀를 차다, (*slap*) ch'alssak ttaerida 찰싹 때리다. *He gave her a hearty ～.* Kŭnŭn kŭ yŏja-ege shinnanŭn k'isŭrŭl haessŭmnida. 그는 그 여자에게 신나는 키스를 했읍니다.

small *adj.* (*size*) chagŭn 작은, (*quantity*) chŏgŭn 적은. *This pair of shoes are too ～ for me.* I kudunŭn na-ege nŏmu chaksŭmnida. 이 구두는 나에게 너무 작습니다/ *a ～ room* chagŭn pang 작은 방/ *a ～ income* chŏgŭn suip 적은 수입/ *in ～ numbers* chŏgŭn suro 적은 수로.

smallpox *n.* ch'ŏnyŏndu 천연두.

smart *adj.* (*clever*) chaech'i innŭn 재치 있는, (*brisk*) min-

ch'ŏp'an 민첩한, (*stylish*) santtŭt'an 산뜻한. —*vi.*
(*sting*) ssŭrida 쓰리다. *a ~ student* chaech'i innŭn haksaeng 재치 있는 학생/ *a ~ pace* minch'ŏp'an palkŏrŭm
민첩한 발걸음/ *You look very ~.* Maeu santtŭt'ae poimnida. 매우 산뜻해 보입니다/ *The wound ~s.* Sangch'ŏga
ssŭrimnida. 상처가 쓰립니다.

smash *vt., vi.* (*crush*) ttaeryo pusuda 때려 부수다, (*hit
hard*) tudŭlgyŏ p'aeda 두들겨 패다. *~ a window* ch'angmunŭl ttaeryŏ pusuda 창문을 때려 부수다/ *I ~ed the man
on the nose.* Kŭ sanaiŭi k'orŭl kalgyŏ chuŏssŭmnida.
그 사나이의 코를 갈겨 주었습니다.

smear *vt., vi.* (*stain*) tŏrŏp'ida 더럽히다, (*paint*) ch'irhada
칠하다. *It ~s easily.* Tŏrŏmŭl chal t'amnida. 더럼을 잘
탑니다/ *~ butter on a plate* chŏpshie pŏt'ŏrŭl parŭda 접
시에 버터를 바르다.

smell *n.* (*odor*) naemsae 냄새, (*scent*) hyanggi 향기,
(*stink*) akch'wi 악취. —*vt., vi.* (*sniff*) naemsaerŭl
matta 냄새를 맡다, (*emit odor*) naemsaega nada 냄새가
나다. *I can't bear the ~ of tobacco.* Tambae naemsaenŭn
ch'amŭl suga ŏpsŭmnida. 담배 냄새는 참을 수가 없읍니다/
What a ~! Naemsaega koyak'agunyo! 냄새가 고약하군
요/ *Do you ~ anying unusual?* Isanghan naemsaega
naji anssŭmnikka? 이상한 냄새가 나지 않습니까/ *I can ~
something burning.* Muŏn-ga t'anŭn naemsaega namnida. 무언가 타는 냄새가 납니다/ *~ good[bad]* choŭn
[nappŭn] naemsaega nada 좋은[나쁜] 냄새가 나다.

smile *n.* miso 미소. —*vi.* misohada 미소하다, panggŭt
utta 방긋 웃다. *with a ~ on one's lips* ipsure misorŭl
ttigo 입술에 미소를 띠고/ *Who are you smiling at?*
Nugurŭl pogo usŭshimnikka? 누구를 보고 웃으십니까/
She ~d to me from her window. Kŭ yŏjanŭn ch'ang-
ka-esŏ na-ege misorŭl chiŏssŭmnida. 그 여자는 창가에서
나에게 미소를 지었읍니다.

smith *n.* (*blacksmith*) taejangjangi 대장장이, (*blacksmith's
shop*) taejangkan 대장간.

smoke *n.* yŏn-gi 연기, (*tobacco*) tambae 담배. —*vi., vt.*
(*emit ~*) yŏn-girŭl naeda 연기를 내다, (*burn tobacco*)

tambaerŭl p'iuda 담배를 피우다/ *I'm choking with the* ~.
Yŏn-gie chilshik'al kŏt kassŭmnida. 연기에 질식할 것 같
습니다/ *cigarette* ~ tambae yŏn-gi 담배 연기/ *I do smell*
~; *where is it?* Yŏn-gi naemsaega nanŭn koshi ŏdijiyo?
연기 냄새가 나는 곳이 어디지요/ *How about a* ~? Han tae
p'iushigessŭmnikka? 한 대 피우시겠읍니까/ *Have a* ~. Han
tae t'aeushijiyo. 한 대 태우시지요/ *May I* ~? Tambae
p'iwŏdo chossŭmnikka? 담배 피워도 좋습니까/ *Do you
mind if I* ~? Tambae p'iwŏdo kwaench'anssŭmnikka?
담배 피워도 괜찮습니까/ *You have to cut out smoking for
your health*. Kŏn-gangŭl wihae tambaerŭl kkŭnŭsyŏya
hamnida. 건강을 위해 담배를 끊으셔야 합니다/ *smoking
room* kkigyŏnshil 끽연실/ ~ *screen* yŏnmak 연막.

smoky *adj*. yŏn-gi nanŭn 연기 나는, maeun 매운, yŏn-giga
manŭn 연기가 많은.

smooth *adj*. (*not rough*) maekkŭrŏun 매끄러운, (*even*)
korŭn 고른, (*mild*) pudŭrŏun 부드러운, (*favorable*)
sunjoroun 순조로운. *a* ~ *floor* maekkŭrŏun maru 매끄
러운 마루/ *The way is now* ~. Hyŏnjae kirŭn korŭm-
nida. 현재 길은 고릅니다/ *a* ~ *salad dressing* pudŭrŏun
saellŏdŭ tŭreshing 부드러운 샐러드 드레싱.

smoothly *adv*. sunjoropke 순조롭게. *Everything went* ~
with me. Modŭn iri na-egenŭn sunjorowassŭmnida. 모든
일이 나에게는 순조로왔읍니다.

smother *vt., vi*. (*suffocate*) chilshikshik'ida 질식시키다,
(*choke*) tŏp'ŏ kkŭda 덮어 끄다. *I was* ~*ed by the
crowd*. Kunjungdŭllo chilshik'al chigyŏngiŏssŭmnida
군중들로 질식할 지경이었읍니다/ *We* ~*ed the fire with
sand*. Moraerŭl kkiŏnjŏ purŭl kkŏssŭmnida. 모래를 끼
얹어 불을 껐읍니다.

smudge *n*. ochŏm 오점, ŏlluk 얼룩, tŏrŏum 더러움.

smug *adj*. toksŏnjŏgin 독선적인, chŏmjanppaenŭn 점잔빼는

smuggle *vt*. milsuip〔milsuch'ur〕hada 밀수입〔밀수출〕하다
He ~*d in a valuable camera*. Kŭ saramŭn pissan sa
jinkirŭl milsuip'ayŏssŭmnida. 그 사람은 비싼 사진기를 밀
수입하였읍니다/ ~*d goods* milsup'um 밀수품.

smuggler *n*. milsukkun 밀수꾼, milsuŏpcha 밀수업자.

snack *n.* (*light meal*) kabyŏun shiksa 가벼운 식사. ~ *bar* kani shiktang 간이 식당/ *Let's have a* ~ *at that* ~ (*bar*). Chŏ sŭnaegesŏ kabyŏun shiksarŭl hapshida. 저 스낵에서 가벼운 식사를 합시다.

snail *n.* talp'aengi 달팽이.

snake *n.* paem 뱀. *a poisonous* ~ toksa 독사.

snap *vi., vt.* (*break suddenly*) ttak purŏttŭrida 딱 부러뜨리다, (*photo*) ch'alkkak tchikta 찰깍 찍다, (*close with sound*) sorirŭl naemyŏ tach'ida 소리를 내며 닫히다. *The rope* ~*ped.* Patchuri t'uk kkŭnŏjyŏssŭmnida. 밧줄이 툭 끊어졌읍니다.

snapshot *n.* sŭnaep sajin 스냅 사진.

snare *n.* (*trap*) tŏt 덫, (*temptation*) yuhok 유혹.

snatch *vi., vt.* (*seize suddenly*) chabach'aeda 잡아채다. *He* ~*ed the letter out of my hand.* Kŭnŭn nae sonesŏ p'yŏnjirŭl ch'aegassŭmnida. 그는 내 손에서 편지를 채갔읍니다.

sneak *vi.* mollae tomangch'ida 몰래 도망치다. ~ *to a corner* mollae kusŏgŭro p'ihada 몰래 구석으로 피하다.

sneer *vi.* (*jeer*) piutta 비웃다, naengsohada 냉소하다, choronghada 조롱하다. —*vt.* piusŭmyŏ marhada 비웃으며 말하다, kyŏngmyŏrhada 경멸하다. —*n.* naengso 냉소, kyŏngmyŏl 경멸.

sneeze *n.* chaech'aegi 재채기. —*vi.* chaech'aegihada 재채기하다. *Use a handkerchief when you* ~. Chaech'aegihal ttaenŭn sonsugŏnŭl ssŭshio. 재채기할 때는 손수건을 쓰시오.

snore *n.* k'ogonŭn sori 코고는 소리. —*vi.* k'orŭl kolda 코를 골다.

snow *n.* nun 눈. *We had* ~ *last night.* Ŏjetpame nuni wassŭmnida. 어젯밤에 눈이 왔읍니다/ *It looks like* ~, *doesn't it ?* Nuni naeril kŏt kassŭmnida. 눈이 내릴 것 같습니다/ *a heavy* ~ p'oksŏl 폭설/ *powdery* ~ ssarangnun 싸락눈/ *S*~ *melts.* Nuni nongnŭnda. 눈이 녹는다/ ~*ball* nuntŏngi 눈덩이/ ~*man* nunsaram 눈사람/ ~*slide* nunsat'ae 눈사태/ ~*storm* nunbora 눈보라/ *We had a snowfall of ten centimeters.* Nuni ship sent'ina wassŭmnida. 눈이 10센티나 왔읍니다.

so *adv.* kŭrŏk'e 그렇게, kŭraesŏ 그래서. —*conj.* kŭrŏmŭro

그러므로. —*int.* twaessŏ 됐어. *Do it* ~. Kŭrŏk'e hashio. 그렇게 하시오/ *Don't walk* ~ *fast*. Kŭrŏk'e ppalli kŏtchi mashio. 그렇게 빨리 걷지 마시오/ *She asked me to go,* ~ *I went*. Kŭ yŏjaga kadallago haessŏyo, kŭraesŏ katchiyo. 그 여자가 가달라고 했어요, 그래서 갔지요/ ~ *long* (*good-bye*) annyŏng 안녕/ *How is your business? So-so.* Saŏbŭn chal toeshimnikka? Kŭjŏ kŭrŏssŭmnida. 사업은 잘 되십니까? 그저 그렇습니다/ *I was* ~ *hungry that I could not walk*. Nŏmu paega kop'a kŏrŭl suga ŏpsŏssŭmnida. 너무 배가 고파 걸을 수가 없었읍니다.

soak *vi., vt.* (*steep*) chŏtta 젖다, (*permeate*) paeŏdŭlda 배어들다, (*drench*) chŏkshida 적시다. *I was* ~*ed to the skin*. Nanŭn hŭmppŏk chŏjŏssŭmnida. 나는 흠뻑 젖었읍니다/ *S*~ *the cloth in the dye*. Ch'ŏnŭl mulkame tamgushio. 천을 물감에 담그시오.

soap *n.* pinu 비누. *toilet* ~ sesu pinu 세수 비누/ *laundry* ~ set'ak pinu 세탁 비누/ ~ *powder* karu pinu 가루 비누.

soar *vi.* (*fly upward*) nara orŭda 날아 오르다, (*prices*) p'oktŭnghada 폭등하다.

sob *vi.* hŭnŭkkyŏ ulda 흐느껴 울다. —*n.* hŭnŭkkim 흐느낌.

sober *adj.* (*not drunk*) sul ch'wihaji anŭn 술 취하지 않은. ~ *up* suri kkaeda 술이 깨다/ *Does he ever go to bed* ~ ? Ch'wihaji ank'o chamcharie tŭn iri issŭmnikka? 취하지 않고 잠자리에 든 일이 있읍니까?

so-called *adj.* irŭnba 이른바, sowi 소위. *We went to the* ~ *circus*. Sowi kongmadaniran terŭl kaboassŭmnida. 소위 곡마단이란 데를 가보았읍니다.

soccer *n.* ch'ukku 축구. *a* ~ *game* ch'ukku kyŏnggi 축구 경기/ *a* ~ *player* ch'ukku sŏnsu 축구 선수.

sociable *adj.* sagyojŏgin 사교적인. —*n.*(*gathering*) ch'inmok'oe 친목회/ *a* ~ *person* sagyoga 사교가/ *a church* ~ kyohoe ch'inmok'oe 교회 친목회.

social *adj.* sahoeŭi 사회의, sahoejŏk 사회적. ~ *life* sahoe saenghwal 사회 생활/ ~ *problems* sahoe munje 사회 문제/ ~ *work* sahoe saŏp 사회 사업.

socialism *n.* sahoejuŭi 사회주의.

socialist *n.* sahoejuŭija 사회주의자.

society *n.* (*community*) sahoe 사회, (*association*) hyŏp'oe 협회, hoe 회, (*institution*) hak'oe 학회, (*union*) chohap 조합. *high*[*polite*] ~ sangnyu sahoe 상류 사회/ *modern industrial societies* hyŏndae sanŏp sahoe 현대 산업 사회/ *the Asiatic S*~ Ashia hyŏp'oe 아시아 협회/ *the philosophical*~ ch'ŏrhak'oe 철학회/ *a cooperative* ~ sobi chohap 소비 조합.

sock *n.* yangmal 양말. *darn* ~s yangmarŭl kipta 양말을 집다/ *a pair of* ~s yangmal han k'yŏlle 양말 한 켤레.

socket *n.* (*eye* ~) nunkumŏng 눈구멍, (*for electric light*) sok'etŭ 소케트.

soda *n.* soda 소다. ~-*water* sodasu 소다수.

soft *adj.* (*not hard*) pudŭroun 부드러운, (*smooth*) podŭlbodŭrhan 보들보들한. *a* ~ *hand* podŭlbodŭrhan son 보들보들한 손/ *a* ~ *smile* pudŭroun miso 부드러운 미소/ ~ *drink* ch'ŏngnyang ŭmnyo 청량 음료/ ~*ware* (*computer*) sop'ŭt'ŭweŏ 소프트웨어.

soften *vt.* pudŭrŏpke hada 부드럽게 하다.

softly *adv.* pudŭrŏpke 부드럽게.

soil *n.* (*earth*) hŭk 흙, (*ground*) t'oji 토지, (*filth*) omul 오물. —*vt.* (*stain*) tŏrŏp'ida 더럽히다. ~ *one's clothes* osŭl tŏrŏp'ida 옷을 더럽히다.

sojourn *vi.* ch'eryuhada 체류하다, mukta 묵다. —*n.* (*brief stay*) ch'ejae 체재.

solder *n.* ttaemnap 땜납. —*vi.* napttaemhada 납땜하다.

soldier *n.* kunin 군인, pyŏngsa 병사. *a foot* ~ pobyŏng 보병.

sole *adj.* (*single*) tan hanaŭi 단 하나의, (*unique*) tokt'ŭk'an 독특한. —*n.* (*of foot*) palpadak 발바닥, (*of shoes*) kuduch'ang 구두창. *the* ~ *agent* ch'ong taeriin 총 대리인/ *walk on the* ~ *of the foot* maenballo kŏtta 맨발로 걷다.

solemn *adj.* (*magnificent*) ŏmsuk'an 엄숙한, (*ceremonious*) kyŏkshigŭl ch'arinŭn 격식을 차리는. *a* ~ *oath* ŏmsuk'an sŏyak 엄숙한 서약/ *You look very* ~. Mopshi chŏmjank'e poinŭn-gunyo. 몹시 점잖게 보이는군요.

solicit *vt., vi.* (*ask earnestly*) kanch'ŏnghada 간청하다,

(*beg for*) chorŭda 조르다, (*tempt*) yuhok'ada 유혹하다.
I ~ed him for his help. Kŭbunŭi choryŏgŭl kanch'ŏng-
haessŭmnida. 그분의 조력을 간청했읍니다.

solicitor *n.* kanch'ŏngin 간청인, (*suitor*) kuhonja 구혼자,
(*Brit.*) samu pyŏnhosa 사무 변호사.

solid *adj.* (*hard*) ttanttanhan 딴딴한, (*firm*) t'ŭnt'ŭnhan
튼튼한, (*firmly united*) ilch'i tan-gyŏrhan 일치 단결한.
a ~ ball ttanttanhan kong 딴딴한 공/ *a ~ house* t'ŭn-
t'ŭnhan chip 튼튼한 집/ *We are ~ for peace.* Urinŭn
hanagach'i p'yŏnghwarŭl chijihamnida. 우리는 하나같이
평화를 지지합니다.

solitary *adj.* (*lonely*) kodok'an 고독한, (*alone*) honja-
ppunin 혼자뿐인, (*secluded*) oettan 외딴. *a ~ life* tokshin saenghwal 독신 생활/ *a ~ house* oettan chip 외딴 집.

solo *n.* (*music*) tokch'ang 독창, tokchu 독주. —*adj.*
(*alone*) tandogŭi 단독의. *a violin ~* paiollin tokchugok
바이올린 독주곡/ *a vocal ~* tokch'ang 독창/ *a ~ flight*
tandok pihaeng 단독 비행.

soloist *n.* (*of songs*) tokch'angga 독창가, (*of instruments*)
tokchuga 독주가.

solution *n.* (*solving*) haegyŏl 해결, (*explanation*) sŏlmyŏng 설명, (*dissolving*) nogim 녹임, yonghae 용해,
(*chem.*) aekch'e 액체. *Is there no other ~?* Talli hae-
gyŏlch'aegŭn ŏpsŭmnikka? 달리 해결책은 없읍니까?

solve *vt.* (*clear up*) p'ulda 풀다, (*explain*) sŏlmyŏnghada
설명하다. *~ a problem* munjerŭl p'ulda 문제를 풀다.

some *adj.* (*certain*) ŏttŏn 어떤, (*a number of, a quantity*
of) ŏlmaganŭi 얼마간의, (*about*) yak 약, (*considerable*)
kwae manŭn 꽤 많은. *S~ children learn language*
easily. Ŏttŏn ainŭn marŭl shwipke paeumnida. 어떤 아이
는 말을 쉽게 배웁니다/ *Please have ~ cake.* Kwaja chom
tŭshipshio. 과자 좀 드십시오/ *Give me ~ more.* Chomdŏ
chushipshio. 좀더 주십시오/ *Aren't there ~ stamps in*
that drawer? Kŭ sŏrap soge up'yo myŏt chang ŏpsŭmnikka? 그 서랍 속에 우표 몇 장 없읍니까/ *I waited ~ 10*
minutes. Yak shippun tongan kidaryŏssŭmnida. 약 10
분 동안 기다렸읍니다/ *I stayed there for ~ days.* Kkwae

yŏrŏ nal kŏgisŏ mŏmullŏssŭmnida. 째 여러 날 거기서 머물
렀읍니다/ ~ of these days ilgan 일간/ ~other time
ŏnjen-ga tashi 언젠가 다시/ in ~ way or other irŏkchŏrŏk 이럭저럭.

somebody *pron.* nugun-ga 누군가, ŏttŏn saram 어떤 사람.
I'll get ~ who speaks English. Yŏngŏ hal chul anŭn
punŭl taedŭrigessŭmnida. 영어 할 줄 아는 분을 대드리겠읍
니다.

someday *adv.* ŏnjen-ga 언젠가, hunnal 훗날.

somehow *adv.* (*in one way or another*) ŏttŏk'e haesŏdŭnji
어떻게 해서든지, (*in some way or other*) amut'ŭn 아뭏
든, (*for some reason or other*) ŏtchŏnji 어쩐지. *We shall
get there ~.* Ŏttŏk'e haesŏrado kŏgie toch'ak'al kŏshimnida. 어떻게 해서라도 거기에 도착할 것입니다/ *S~ I
don't trust that man.* Ŏtchŏnji kŭ saramŭn midŏpchiga
anssŭmnida. 어쩐지 그 사람은 미덥지가 않습니다.

something *pron.* muŏshin-ga 무엇인가, (*little*) chogŭm 조
금. *I want ~ to eat.* Muŏn-ga mŏgŭl kŏsŭl chom chushipshio. 무언가 먹을 것을 좀 주십시오/ *This is ~ for you.*
Igŏ pada chuseyo. 이거 받아 주세요/ *at two ~* tushi
chogŭm chinasŏ. 2시 조금 지나서.

sometime *adv.* ŏnjen-ga 언젠가. *I saw him ~ in April.*
Sawŏl ŏnjen-ga kŭbunŭl poassŭmnida. 4월 언젠가 그
분을 보았읍니다/ *Come over ~.* Tto nollŏ oseyo. 또 놀러
오세요.

sometimes *adv.* ttaettaero 때때로, kakkŭm 가끔. *S~ we
go to the cinema.* Urinŭn ttaettaero yŏnghwagwane
kamnida. 우리는 때때로 영화관에 갑니다/ *I ~ have letters
from him.* Kakkŭm kŭegesŏ p'yŏnjiga omnida. 가끔 그
에게서 편지가 옵니다.

somewhat *adv.* (*to some extent*) ŏnŭ chŏngdo 어느 정도,
(*a little*) yakkan 약간, chom 좀. *I was ~ surprised.*
Nanŭn yakkan nollassŭmnida. 나는 약간 놀랐읍니다/ *We
have arrived ~ late.* Chom nŭtke toch'ak'aessŭmnida.
좀 늦게 도착했읍니다.

somewhere *adv.* ŏdinji 어딘지, ŏdin-ga-e 어딘가에. *I have
left my gloves ~.* Changgabŭl ŏdin-ga-e tugo wassŭm-

nida. 장갑을 어딘가에 두고 왔읍니다/ *I'm sure I've seen him* ~. Punmyŏnghi ŏdin-ga-esŏ pon ŏlgurimnida. 분명히 어딘가에서 본 얼굴입니다.

son *n.* (*male child*) adŭl 아들. *my* ~ adŭllom 아들놈/ *your* ~ adŭnim 아드님/ *the S*~ *of God* hanŭnimŭi adŭl 하느님의 아들/ ~*-in-law* sawi 사위, yangja 양자.

song *n.* norae 노래. *a children's* ~ tongyo 동요/ *a folk* ~ minyo 민요/ *a popular* ~ yuhaengga 유행가/ *a sacred* ~ sŏngga 성가/ *Let us have a* ~. Nuguna han kok purŭshio. 누구나 한 곡(曲) 부르시오.

soon *adv.* (*in a short time*) kot 곧, inae 이내, (*early*) iltchik 일찍, (*quickly*) ppalli 빨리. *We shall* ~ *start.* Kot ch'ulbarhamnida. 곧 출발합니다/ *Come back* ~. Kot toraoshio! 곧 돌아오시오/ *Must you leave so* ~ ? Kŭrŏk'e iltchik ch'ulbarhaeya hamnikka? 그렇게 일찍 출발해야 합니까/ *We've arrived too* ~. Nŏmu iltchik tochak'aessŭmnida. 너무 일찍 도착했읍니다/ *Do it* ~ ! Ppalli hashio. 빨리 하시오/ *Go out as* ~ *as you have finished it.* Mach'igŏdŭn kot nagashio. 마치거든 곧 나가시오/ *pretty* ~ ŏlma an kasŏ 얼마 안 가서, kot 곧/ *I'm going out pretty* ~. Kot oech'urhamnida. 곧 외출합니다.

soot *n.* kŏmdaeng 검댕, kŭŭrŭm 그을음.

soothe *vt.* (*calm down*) tallaeda 달래다, (*comfort*) wirohada 위로하다, (*allay*) karaanch'ida 가라앉히다. ~ *a crying baby* unŭn airŭl tallaeda 우는 아이를 달래다.

sore *n.* (*ulcer*) chonggi 종기, (*bruise*) sangch'ŏ 상처. —*adj.* (*painful*) ap'ŭn 아픈, ssŭrin 쓰린, (*severe*) shimhan 심한. *cure a* ~ sangch'ŏrŭl koch'ida 상처를 고치다/ *reopen old* ~*s* oraedoen sangch'ŏrŭl kŏndŭrida 오래된 상처를 건드리다/ *a running* ~ korŭmi hŭrŭnŭn chonggi 고름이 흐르는 종기/ *I've got a* ~ *throat.* Mokkumŏngi ap'ŭmnida. 목구멍이 아픕니다.

sorry *adj.* (*feeling regret*) kayŏpke yŏginŭn 가엾게 여기는, (*express apology*) mianhan 미안한, (*pitiable*) pulssanghan 불쌍한. *I am* ~ *for your father's death.* Abŏnimi toragasyŏttani andwaetkunyo. 아버님이 돌아가셨다니 안됐군요/ *I'm* ~ *to hear it.* Kŭgŏ ch'am an-

dwaessŭmnida. 그거 참 안됐읍니다/ *I am ~*. Yugamimnida. 유감입니다/ *I'm ~ to have kept you waiting*.
Kidarige haesŏ mianhamnida. 기다리게 해서 미안합니다/
I'm very ~. Taedanhi mianhamnida. 대단히 미안합니다/
I'm ~ I was not at home. Oech'urhago ŏpsŏsŏ mianhamnida. 외출하고 없어서 미안합니다/ *I'm ~ I have done
you wrong*. Tangshinege mianhan chisŭl haessŭmnida.
당신에게 미안한 짓을 했읍니다/ *a ~ excuse* kujilgujirhan
pyŏnmyŏng 구질구질한 변명.

sort *n*. (*kind*) chongnyu 종류, (*quality*) p'umjil 품질.
—*vt*. (*classify*) pullyuhada 분류하다. *What ~ of man
is he?* Chŏ saramŭn ŏttŏn saramimnikka? 저 사람은 어
떤 사람입니까/ *We talked of all ~s of subjects*. On-gat
munjee taehaesŏ iyagihaessŭmnida. 온갖 문제에 대해 이
야기했읍니다/ *Do you mean to insult me? Nothing of
the ~*. Narŭl moyŏk'al semio? Ch'ŏnmanŭi malssŭm.
나를 모욕할 셈이오? 천만의 말씀/ *a ~ of* ilchongŭi 일종의.

soul *n*. (*spirit*) yŏnghon 영혼, nŏk 넋, (*mind*) chŏngshin
정신, (*person*) saram 사람, (*courage*) kibaek 기백.
She sold her ~ for money. Kŭ yŏinŭn tonŭl wihae
nŏksŭl p'arassŭmnida. 그 여인은 돈을 위해 넋을 팔았읍니
다/ *I didn't see a ~ in the street*. Kŏrienŭn saramira-
gonŭn ŏpsŏssŭmnida. 거리에는 사람이라고는 없었읍니다/
a good ~ sŏllyanghan saram 선량한 사람/ *an honest ~*
chŏngjik'an saram 정직한 사람/ *He has no ~*. Kŭ
saramŭn kibaegi ŏpsŭmnida. 그 사람은 기백이 없읍니다.

sound *n*. sori 소리, ŭmhyang 음향. —*vi*., *vt*. (*make a ~*)
soriga nada 소리가 나다. —*adj*. (*healthy*) kŏnjŏnhan
전전한. *the ~ of a bugle* nap'al sori 나팔 소리/ *I can't
hear the ~*. Soriga tŭlliji anssŭmnida. 소리가 들리지 않
습니다/ *I heard an ominous ~ nearby*. Kakkaiesŏ
pulgirhan sorirŭl tŭrŏssŭmnida. 가까이에서 불길한 소리를
들었읍니다/ *The trumpet ~ed*. Nap'al soriga nassŭmnida.
나팔 소리가 났읍니다/ *Your English ~s pretty good*.
Taegŭi Yŏngŏnŭn maeu hullyunghan tŭt'amnida. 댁의
영어는 매우 훌륭한 듯합니다/ *It all ~s the same to me*.
Na-egenŭn moduga ttokkach'i tŭllimnida. 나에게는 모두

가 똑같이 들립니다/ *a ~ sleep* kip'ŭn cham 깊은 잠/ *a ~ body* kŏnjŏnhan yukch'e 건전한 육체.

soup *n.* sup'ŭ 수프, kuk 국. *chicken ~* takkogi sup'ŭ 닭고기 수프/ *What kind of ~ will you have?* Sup'ŭnŭn muŏshi issŭmnikka? 수프는 무엇이 있읍니까/ *I want the ~ of the day, please.* Onŭl t'ŭkche sup'ŭrŭl chushio. 오늘 특제 수프를 주시오.

sour *adj.* (*acid*) shin 신, shik'ŭmhan 시큼한, (*unpleasant*) pulk'waehan 불쾌한, (*bad-tempered*) shimsulgujŭn 심술궂은. *a ~ apple* shin sagwa 신 사과/ *Most green fruit is ~.* P'urŭn kwairŭn taegae shimnida. 푸른 과일은 대개 십니다/ *a ~ smell* shin naemsae 신 냄새/ *a ~ fellow* pulk'waehan sanai 불쾌한 사나이/ *~ looks* ppurut'unghan p'yojŏng 뿌루퉁한 표정.

source *n.* (*origin*) wŏnch'ŏn 원천, (*provenance*) ch'ulch'ŏ 출처, (*cause*) wŏnin 원인. *The news comes from a reliable ~.* Kŭ nyusŭnŭn midŭl manhan soshikt'ongesŏ nawassŭmnida. 그 뉴스는 믿을 만한 소식통에서 나왔읍니다/ *a news ~* nyusŭŭi ch'ulch'ŏ 뉴스의 출처.

south *n.* namtchok 남쪽, nambu 남부. *~east* namdong 남동/ *~west* namsŏ 남서/ *north and ~* nambuk 남북/ *S~ Korea* Namhan 남한/ *the S~ Pole* namgŭk 남극.

southern *adj.* namtchogŭi 남쪽의.

souvenir *n.* (*memento*) kinyŏmp'um 기념품, (*gift*) sŏnmul 선물. *Here's a ~ for you.* Sŏnmul padŭshipshio. 선물 받으십시오/ *I think this will make a good ~.* Choŭn sŏnmuri toel chul amnida. 좋은 선물이 될 줄 압니다.

sovereign *n.* (*ruler*) kunju 군주.

Soviet *n.* (= *the ~ Union*) Soryŏn 소련.

sow *n.* (*female pig*) amt'waeji 암퇘지. —*vt., vi.* (*scatter seeds*) ppurida 뿌리다. *~ seed* ssirŭl ppurida 씨를 뿌리다/ *~ field with barley* pat'e porissirŭl ppurida 밭에 보리씨를 뿌리다.

soy, soya *n.* kanjang 간장. *~ bean* k'ong 콩.

space *n.* konggan 공간, uju 우주, (*room*) pin kot 빈 곳, (*interval*) kan-gyŏk 간격, (*distance*) kŏri 거리, (*area*) changso 장소. *~ship* ujusŏn 우주선/ *~ travel* uju yŏhaeng 우주 여행/ *Have you enough ~ to work in?* Irhal chariga nŏngnŏk'amnikka? 일할 자리가 넉넉합니까/ *an open ~* pint'ŏ 빈터.

spacious *adj.* (*vast*) nŏltchik'an 널찍한. *a ~ room* nŏltchik'an pang 널찍한 방.

spade *n.* (*tool*) sap 삽, karae 가래, (*of playing cards*) sŭp'eidŭ 스페이드.

Spain *n.* Sŭp'ein 스페인.

Spanish *n.* (*person*) Sŭp'ein saram 스페인 사람, (*language*) Sŭp'einŏ 스페인어(語). —*adj.* Sŭp'einŭi 스페인의. *How do you say this in ~?* Sŭp'einŏro igŏsŭl mwŏrago hamnikka? 스페인어로 이것을 뭐라고 합니까?

spank *vt.* (*slap*) ch'alssak ttaerida 찰싹 때리다, polgirŭl ch'ida 볼기를 치다. *You are going to get a ~ing!* (*to inferior*) Nenomŭn polgirŭl majayagetta! 네놈은 볼기를 맞아야겠다!

spare *adj.* (*reserved*) yebiŭi 예비의, (*extra*) yŏbunŭi 여분의, (*scanty*) mojaranŭn 모자라는. —*vi.*, *vt.* (*refrain from using*) akkida 아끼다, (*use economically*) chŏryak'ada 절약하다, (*dispense with*) nanuŏ chuda 나누어 주다. *We have no ~ room in our house.* Uri chibenŭn yebiyong ch'imshiri ŏpsŭmnida. 우리 집에는 예비용 침실이 없읍니다/ *I have no ~ time.* Shiganŭi yŏyuga ŏpsŭmnida. 시간의 여유가 없읍니다/ *S~ no expense.* Piyongŭl akkiji mashio. 비용을 아끼지 마시오/ *Can you ~ me a few minutes?* Naege myŏt punman shiganŭl naejushigessŭmnikka? 내게 몇 분만 시간을 내주시겠읍니까/ *Have you any ticket to ~?* Yŏbunŭi p'yoga issŭmnikka? 여분의 표가 있읍니까?

spark *n.* (*of fire*) pulkkot 불꽃, (*flash*) sŏmgwang 섬광.

sparkle *n.* pult'i 불티. —*vi.* (*emit sparks*) pulkkoch'ŭl t'wigida 불꽃을 튀기다, (*glitter*) pantchagida 반짝이다. *Her eyes ~d with joy.* Kŭ yŏjaŭi nunŭn kippŭmŭro pantchagyŏssŭmnida. 그 여자의 눈은 기쁨으로 반짝였읍니다.

sparrow *n.* ch'amsae 참새.

spasm *n.* (*convulsion*) kyŏngnyŏn 경련. *a ~ of the stomach* wigyŏngnyŏn 위경련.

speak *vi.*, *vt.* (*say*) marhada 말하다, (*talk*) iyagihada 이
야기하다, (*make a speech*) yŏnsŏrhada 연설하다. *Can
you ~ Korean?* Han-gungmarŭl hal chul ashimnikka?
한국말을 할 줄 아십니까/ *I ~ Korean just a little.* Han-
gungmarŭl chogŭm hal chul amnida. 한국말을 조금 할
줄 압니다/ *Will you ~ up?* Chomdŏ k'ŭn soriro malssŭmhae chushilkkayo? 좀더 큰 소리로 말씀해 주실까요/
Would you please ~ a little more slowly? Chom ch'ŏnch'ŏnhi malssŭmhae chushigessŭmnikka? 좀 천천히 말씀
해 주시겠읍니까/ *I'll get someone who ~ English.* Yŏngŏrŭl hal chul anŭn saramŭl taedŭrigessŭmnida. 영어를
할 줄 아는 사람을 대드리겠읍니다/ *May I ~ with you?*
Iyagi kach'i nanuŏdo chok'essŭmnikka? 이야기 같이 나누
어도 좋겠읍니까/ *Hello, May I ~ to Mr. Choe?* Ch'oe-
ssiege chom taeŏ chuseyo. 최(崔)씨에게 좀 대어 주세요/
Who is ~ing please? (*on telephone*) Nugushimnikka?
누구십니까/ *This is Mr. Kim ~ing.* Kimimnida. 김
(金)입니다.

speaker *n.* (*orator*) yŏnsa 연사, (*lecturer*) kangsa 강사,
(*loudspeaker*) sŭp'ik'ŏ 스피커. *an after-dinner ~*
manch'an huŭi yŏnsa 만찬 후의 연사/ *foreign ~s of
Korean* Han-gungmarŭl hanŭn oegugin 한국말을 하는 외
국인.

speaking *n.* (*talk*) iyagi 이야기, (*oratory*) yŏnsŏl 연설.

spear *n.* (*lance*) ch'ang 창.

special *adj.* (*particular*) t'ŭkpyŏrhan 특별한, (*extraordinary*) imshiŭi 임시의, (*private*) chŏnyongŭi 전용의,
(*specialized*) chŏnmunŭi 전문의. —*n.* (*person or thing*)
t'ukpyŏrhan saram[kŏt] 특별한 사람[것], (~ *train*)
imshi yŏlch'a 임시 열차. *a ~ case* t'ŭngnye 특례/ *There
is a ~ train leaving at 7 : 30 in the morning.* Ach'im
ilgopshi pane ttŏnanŭn imshi yŏlch'aga issŭmnida. 아침
7시 반에 떠나는 임시 열차가 있읍니다/ *Is this a ~ product of Korea?* Igŏshi Han-guk t'ŭksanmurimnikka? 이
것이 한국 특산물입니까/ *Give me a 1,500 won ~.* Ch'ŏn-
obaegwŏntchari t'ŭkpyŏl chŏngshigŭl chushio. 1,500
원짜리 특별 정식을 주시오/ *What is today's ~?* Onŭrŭi

t'ŭkpyŏl yorinŭn muŏshimnikka? 오늘의 특별 요리는 무
엇입니까? 「의(專門醫).

specialist *n.* chŏnmun-ga 전문가, *(doc.)* chŏnmunŭi 전문

speciality *n.* *(special product)* t'ŭksanmul 특산물, *(special manufacture)* t'ŭkchep'um 특제품, *(noted product)* myŏngsanmul 명산물. *Ginseng is a ~ of Kanghwa.* Insamŭn Kanghwaŭi t'ŭksanmurimnida. 인삼은 강화(江華)의 특산물입니다.

specialize *vi., vt.* *(major)* chŏn-gonghada 전공하다, *(limit)* kuk'anhada 국한하다, *(specify)* t'ŭksuhwahada 특수화하다. *What do you ~ in?* Muŏl chŏn-gonghashimnikka? 무얼 전공하십니까?

specially *adv.* t'ŭkpyŏrhi 특별히, *(on purpose)* ilburŏ 일부러. *I came here ~ to see you.* Tangshinŭl mannarŏ ilburŏ wassŭmnida. 당신을 만나러 일부러 왔읍니다.

specialty *n.* *(=speciality)* *(special manufacture)* t'ŭkchep'um 특제품. *a local ~* myŏngmul 명물/ *I'd like today's ~, please.* Onŭrŭi t'ŭkche yorirŭl put'ak'amnida. 오늘의 특제 요리를 부탁합니다/ *This rice cake is a ~ of Pusan.* I ttŏgŭn Pusanŭi myŏngmurimnida. 이 떡은 부산의 명물입니다.

specific *n.* *(~ remedy)* t'ŭk'yoyak 특효약, myoyak 묘약. *a ~ against headache* tut'ongŭi t'ŭk'yoyak 두통의 특효약/ *Quinine is a ~ for malaria.* K'ininenŭn mallariaŭi t'ŭk'yoyagimnida. 키니네는 말라리아의 특효약입니다.

specification *n.* *(pl.)* myŏngsesŏ 명세서. *building ~s* kŏnch'uk myŏngsesŏ 건축 명세서.

specimen *n.* *(sample)* p'yobon 표본, kyŏnbon 견본. *Can you show me some ~s of your work?* Chakp'umŭi kyŏnbonŭl chom poyŏ chushigessŭmnikka? 작품의 견본을 좀 보여 주시겠읍니까/ *zoological ~s* tongmul p'yobon 동물 표본.

spectacle *n.* *(sight)* kwanggyŏng 광경, *(grand sight)* changgwan 장관, *(show)* kugyŏngkŏri 구경거리, *(pl.)* *(glasses)* an-gyŏng 안경. *put on[wear] ~s* an-gyŏngŭl kkida 안경을 끼다/ *take off ~s* an-gyŏngŭl pŏtta 안경을 벗다.

spectator *n.* (*onlooker*) kugyŏngkkun 구경군, kwan-gaek
관객, (*witness*) mokkyŏkcha 목격자.

specter, spectre *n.* (*ghost*) yuryŏng 유령, (*goblin*) tokkaebi 도깨비.

speculate *vi.* (*think*) saenggak'ada 생각하다, (*ponder*)
sasaek'ada 사색하다, (*gamble*) t'ugihada 투기하다. ∼
in oil shares sŏgyujue t'ugihada 석유주(石油株)에 투기
하다.

speculation *n.* (*meditation*) sasaek 사색, (*conjecture*)
ch'uch'ŭk 추측, (*stockjobbing*) t'ugi 투기. *I'm sorry to
disturb your* ∼. Sasaegŭl panghaehae mianhamnida.
사색을 방해해 미안합니다/ *I bought it on* (*a*) ∼. Yohaeng-
surŭl kŏlgo kŭgŏsŭl sassŭmnida. 요행수를 걸고 그것을 샀
읍니다.

speech *n.* (*address*) yŏnsŏl 연설, (*language*) mal 말. *a
farewell* ∼ kobyŏl yŏnsŏl 고별 연설/ *a congratulatory* ∼
ch'uksa 축사/ *His* ∼ *is not clear*. Kŭ saramŭi marŭn
punmyŏngch'i anssŭmnida. 그 사람의 말은 분명치 않습
니다.

speed *n.* (*swiftness*) shinsok 신속, (*velocity*) sokto 속도.
at full ∼ chŏnsongnyŏguro 전속력으로/ *a* ∼ *limit* sokto
chehan 속도 제한.

speedy *adj.* pparŭn 빠른, chaepparŭn 재빠른.

spell *n.* (*magic formula*) chumun 주문, (*enchantment*)
maryŏk 마력, (*short period*) chamshi 잠시. —*vt., vi.*
(*words*) ch'ŏlchahada 철자하다, (*decipher*) p'andok'ada
판독하다. *a magic* ∼ maryŏk 마력/ *be under the* ∼ *of
beauty* arŭmdaume hollida 아름다움에 홀리다/ *How do
you* ∼ *your name?* Taegŭi sŏnghamŭl ŏttŏk'e ssŭ-
nŭnjiyo? 댁의 성함을 어떻게 쓰는지요/ *Would you please*
∼ *the word?* Sŭp'ellingŭl karŭch'yŏ chushilkkayo?
스펠링을 가르쳐 주실까요?

spend *vt., vi.* (*pay out*) sobihada 소비하다, (*pass*) ponaeda
보내다, chinaeda 지내다. *How much have you spent?*
Ŏlmana ssŭsyŏssŭmnikka? 얼마나 쓰셨읍니까/ *How do
you* ∼ *your leisure?* Yŏgarŭl ŏttŏk'e chinaeshimnikka?
여가를 어떻게 지내십니까?

sphere *n.* (*globe*) ku 구(球), (*ball*) kong 공, (*scope*) pŏmwi 범위. *a heavenly* ~ ch'ŏnch'e 천체 / *a* ~ *of activity* hwaltong pŏmwi 활동 범위.

spice *n.* (*seasoning*) yangnyŏm 양념, chomiryo 조미료, (*flavor*) mat 맛, (*smack*) kimi 기미(氣味). *Could you show me where you have* ~*s?* Yangnyŏmŭn ŏdi itchiyo? 양념은 어디 있지요 / *a* ~ *of humor* haehangmi 해학미 / *a* ~ *of wildness* kŏch'in kimi 거친 기미.

spider *n.* kŏmi 거미. *a* ~*'s web* kŏmijul 거미줄.

spike *n.* (*of sports shoes*) sŭp'aik'ŭ 스파이크, (*big nail*) k'ŭn mot 큰 못.

spill *vt.*, *vi.* (*let run*) hŭllida 흘리다, ŏpchirŭda 엎지르다, hŭrŭda 흐르다. *I'm sorry, I've* ~*ed some coffee on your rug.* Mianhaeyo. Yangt'anja wie k'op'irŭl ŏpchillŏssŏyo. 미안해요. 양탄자 위에 코피를 엎질렀어요.

spin *vt.*, *vi.* (*yarn*) chatta 잣다, (*weave*) pangjŏk'ada 방적하다, (*twirl*) tollida 돌리다. ~ *a top* p'aengirŭl tollida 팽이를 돌리다.

spinach *n.* shigŭmch'i 시금치.

spindle *n.* (*for spinning*) puk 북, (*axle*) kultae 굴대.

spine *n.* (*backbone*) ch'ŏkch'u 척추, tŭngppyŏ 등뼈.

spinning *n.* pangjŏk 방적.

spiral *adj.* (*screwed*) nasŏnhyŏngŭi 나선형의, (*coiled*) pibikkoin 비비꼬인. —*n.* (*helix*) nasŏn 나선. *a* ~ *staircase* nasŏnhyŏng kyedan 나선형 계단 / *a* ~ *spring* nasŏn yongsuch'ŏl 나선 용수철.

spirit *n.* (*soul*) chŏngshin 정신, (*vigor*) kiun 기운, (*ghost*) yuryŏng 유령, (*pl.*) (*alcohol*) alk'ol 알콜, (*mood*) kibun 기분, (*courage*) yonggi 용기. *a military* ~ kunin chŏngshin 군인 정신 / *Put a little more* ~ *into your work.* Ire chomdŏ kiunŭl naeshio. 일에 좀더 기운을 내시오 / *You are quite out of* ~*s.* Chŏngmal kiuni ŏpkunyo. 정말 기운이 없군요 / *I drink no* ~*s.* Tokchunŭn an mashimnida. 독주(毒酒)는 안 마십니다.

spiritual *adj.* (*of the spirit*) chŏngshinjŏgin 정신적인, (*sacred*) sunggohan 숭고한, (*religious*) chonggyojŏgin 종교적인.

spit *n.* (*saliva*) ch'im 침. —*vi.*, *vt.* ch'imŭl paetta 침을

뱉다, (*spew out*) t'ohada 토하다. *Please don't ~ in the car.* Ch'a anesŏ ch'imŭl paetchi mashipshio. 차 안에서 침을 뱉지 마십시오.

spite *n.* (*malice*) agŭi 악의, (*grudge*) wŏnhan 원한. *in ~ of* ...edo pulguhago ...에도 불구하고/ *I went to school in ~ of my sickness.* Ap'ŭndedo pulguhago nanŭn hak-kyo-e kassŭmnida. 아픈데도 불구하고 나는 학교에 갔읍니다.

spittoon *n.* t'agu 타구.

splash *vt., vi.* (*spatter*) t'wigida 튀기다, t'wida 튀다. —*n.* (*~ing*) t'wigim 튀김, (*~ing sound*) t'ŏmbŏng 텀벙. *We had our car all ~ed with mud.* Uri ch'anŭn ont'ong hŭkt'angmurŭl twijibŏssŏssŭmnida. 우리 차는 온통 흙탕물을 뒤집어썼읍니다.

splendid *adj.* (*magnificent*) changŏmhan 장엄한, (*admirable*) hullyunghan 훌륭한, (*grand*) ungjanghan 웅장한, (*excellent*) ch'oegoŭi 최고의. *a ~ palace* ungjanghan kungjŏn 웅장한 궁전/ *We had a ~ time.* Ch'oegoro chaemiissŏssŭmnida. 최고로 재미있었읍니다.

splice *vt.* (*join*) itta 잇다, (*get married*) kyŏrhonhada 결혼하다. —*n.* (*grafting*) chŏmmok 접목, (*marriage*) kyŏrhon 결혼. *We decided to get ~d in October.* Shiwŏre kyŏrhonhagiro hayŏssŭmnida. 10월에 결혼하기로 하였읍니다.

splinter *n.* p'ap'yŏn 파편. *a ~ of a bomb* p'okt'anŭi p'ap'yŏn 폭탄의 파편.

split *vt., vi.* (*crack*) tchogaeda 쪼개다, (*cleave*) tchitta 찢다, (*share*) nanuda 나누다, (*disunite*) punyŏlshik'ida 분열시키다. —*n.* (*crack*) kallajin t'ŭm 갈라진 틈, (*fragment*) p'ap'yŏn 파편, (*rupture*) punyŏl 분열, (*faction*) tangp'a 당파. *My head is ~ting.* Mŏriga t'ŏjil tŭshi ap'ŭmnida. 머리가 터질 듯이 아픕니다/ *Let's ~ the cost of the meal.* Shiksabinŭn nanuŏ naepshida. 식사비는 나누어 냅시다.

spoil *vt., vi.* (*ruin*) mangch'ida 망치다, (*damage*) haech'ida 해치다, (*plunder*) kangt'arhada 강탈하다. *Don't ~ appetite by eating sweets.* Tan-gŏsŭl mŏkko immat p'oriji mashio. 단것을 먹고 입맛 버리지 마시오/ *a spoilt* *child* pŏrŭdŏmnŭn ai 버릇없는 아이.

spokesman *n.* taebyŏnja 대변자.

sponge *n.* haemyŏn 해면. *This ~ cake is very good.* I sŭp'onji k'eik'ŭnŭn maeu madissŭmnida. 이 스폰지 케이크는 매우 맛있읍니다.

sponsor *n.* (*surety*) pojŭngin 보증인, (*promoter*) palgiin 발기인, (*supporter*) huwŏnja 후원자, (*commercial radio, TV*) sŭp'onsŏ 스폰서. —*vt.* (*support*) huwŏnhada 후원하다, (*vouch for*) pojŭnghada 보증하다. *a TV ~* t'ellebijŏn sŭp'onsŏ 텔레비전 스폰서/ *be ~ed by ...*ŭi chuch'oero ...의 주최(主催)로.   「로.

sponsorship *n.* *under the ~ of ...*ŭi huwŏnŭro ...의 후원으

spontaneous *adj.* (*voluntary*) chabalchŏgin 자발적인, (*natural*) chayŏnjŏgin 자연적인, (*self-acting*) chadongjŏgin 자동적인. *~ movement* chadong undong 자동 운동/ *He made a ~ offer of help.* Chajinhayŏ topkettago nasŏssŭmnida. 자진하여 돕겠다고 나섰읍니다.

spool *n.* (*bobbin*) shilp'ae 실패, (*reel*) shilgamkae 실감개.

spoon *n.* sutkarak 숟가락. *a tea ~* ch'atsutkarak 찻숟가락/ *a table ~* papsutkarak 밥숟가락/ *Would you like to use a ~?* Sutkaragŭro tŭshiryŏmnikka? 숟가락으로 드시렵니까?

sport *n.* sŭp'och'ŭ 스포츠, undong kyŏnggi 운동 경기, (*fun*) chaemi 재미, (*jest*) nongdam 농담. —*vi., vt.* (*play*) nolda 놀다, (*frolic*) changnanhada 장난하다. *indoor ~s* ogoe undong 옥외 운동/ *indoor ~s* shillae undong 실내 운동/ *The ~s were postponed.* Undonghoenŭn yŏn-gidoeŏssŭmnida. 운동회는 연기되었읍니다/ *a ~s magazine* sŭp'och'ŭ chapchi 스포츠 잡지/ *~sman* undongga 운동가.

spot *n.* (*speck*) chŏm 점, panjŏm 반점, (*stain*) ŏlluk 얼룩, (*place*) changso 장소. *How did I get this ~?* I ŏllugŭn ŏtchihayŏ mudŏssŭlkkayo? 이 얼룩은 어찌하여 묻었을까요/ *I can't get out these ~s.* I ŏllugŭl chiul suga ŏpsŭmnida. 이 얼룩을 지울 수가 없읍니다/ *Is there any interesting ~ to visit?* Kabol manhan tega issŭmnikka? 가볼 만한 데가 있읍니까/ *This is a good ~.* I kosŭn choŭn changsoimnida. 이 곳은 좋은 장소입니다.

spotlight *n.* (*of stage*) kakkwang 각광, sŭp'ot'ŭrait'ŭ 스포트라이트, (*public notice*) chumok 주목.

sprain *vt.* ppida 삐다. *I've ~ed my ankle.* Palmogŭl ppiŏssŭmnida. 발목을 삐었읍니다.

spray *n.* (*from water*) mulbora 물보라, (*small branch*) chan-gaji 잔가지, (*intrument*) punmugi 분무기. —*vt.,vi.* mulborarŭl nallida 물보라를 날리다.

spread *vt., vi.* (*unfold*) p'yŏda 펴다, (*overlay*) parŭda 바르다, (*scatter*) ppurida 뿌리다, (*become expanded*) p'ŏjida 퍼지다. *S~ out your fingers.* Sonkaragŭl p'yŏshio. 손가락을 펴시오/ *~ butter on bread* Ppange pŏt'ŏrŭl parŭda 빵에 버터를 바르다/ *The powder doesn't ~ well.* Kŭ punŭn chal p'ŏjiji anayo. 그 분(粉)은 잘 펴지지 않아요.

spring *n.* (*springtime*) pom 봄, (*fountain*) saem 샘, (*elastic device*) yongsuch'ŏl 용수철. —*vt., vi.* (*jump*) ttwiŏorŭda 뛰어오르다, (*arise*) saenggida 생기다. *in the early ~* ch'obome 초봄에/ *hot ~s* onch'ŏn 온천/ *the ~ of a watch* t'aeyŏp 태엽/ *~board* ttwimp'an 뜀판/ *~tide* pomch'ŏl 봄철.

sprinkle *vt., vi.* (*spray*) ppurida 뿌리다, (*strew*) hŭtppurida 흩뿌리다. *~ water on the flower* kkoch'e murŭl ppurida 꽃에 물을 뿌리다.

sprout *n.* (*shoot*) saessak 새싹. —*vi.,vt.* ssagi t'ŭda 싹이 트다. *bamboo ~s* chuksun 죽순.

spur *n.* (*for horsemen*) pakch'a 박차. —*vt., vi.* (*urge*) pakch'arŭl kahada 박차를 가하다.

spy *n.* kanch'ŏp 간첩, sŭp'ai 스파이. —*vt., vi.* (*watch secretly*) yŏmt'amhada 염탐하다, (*descry*) t'amjihada 탐지하다. *a newtwork of spies* kanch'ŏmmang 간첩망/ *an industrial ~* sanŏp sŭp'ai 산업 스파이.

squander *vt.* (*waste*) nangbihada 낭비하다. *~ one's money in drink* ŭmjue tonŭl nangbihada 음주에 돈을 낭비하다.

squanderer *n.* nangbiga 낭비가.

square *n.* (*plane figure*) chŏngsagak'yŏng 정사각형, p'yŏngbang 평방(平方), (*open space*) kwangjang 광장.

—*adj.*(*four cornered*) nemoŭi 네모의. *a public* ~ kwang-jang 광장/ *two* ~ *miles* ip'yŏngbang mail 2평방 마일.

squash *vt.* (*crush*) tchigŭrŏttŭrida 찌그러뜨리다, ŭkkaeda 으깨다. —*n.* (*vegetable*) hobak 호박. *Don't sit on my hat; you'll* ~ *it flat.* Nae moja-e anchi mashio. Tchigŭ-rŏjinikkayo. 내 모자에 앉지 마시오. 찌그러지니까요.

squat *vi.* (*crouch*) ungk'ŭrigo anta 웅크리고 앉다. *Find somewhere to* ~. Ŏdi anjŭl terŭl ch'ajaboshio. 어디 앉을 데를 찾아보시오.

squeeze *vt.* (*press*) choeda 죄다, (*wring*) tchanaeda 짜내다, (*force into*) pijipko tŭrŏgada 비집고 들어가다, (*hug*) kkok kkyŏanta 꼭 껴안다. ~ *a lemon dry* remonŭl passak tchada 레몬을 바싹 짜다/ *Can I* ~ *in?* Pijipko tŭrŏgal su issŭmnikka? 비집고 들어갈 수 있읍니까/ *S*~ *yourselves a little.* Chomdŏ choeŏ anja chushipshio. 좀더 죄어 앉아 주십시오.

squint *n.* sap'allun 사팔눈. —*vi.* (*look askance*) kyŏn nunjirhada 곁눈질하다. *a man with a* ~ sap'alttŭgi 사팔뜨기.

squirrel *n.* taramjwi 다람쥐.

stab *vi.*, *vt.* (*pierce*) tchirŭda 찌르다. ~ *oneself with a dagger* tandoro chasarhada 단도로 자살하다.

stable *n.* (*for cattle*) magutkan 마굿간. —*adj.* (*firm*) anjŏnhan 안전한. *What we need is a* ~ *government.* Uriege p'iryohan kŏsŭn anjŏngdoen chŏngbuimnida. 우리에게 필요한 것은 안정된 정부입니다.

stadium *n.* kyŏnggijang 경기장. *Where is Hyochang S*~? Hyoch'ang undongjangŭn ŏdi issŭmnikka? 효창 운동장은 어디 있읍니까/ *the Olympic* ~ *at Seoul.* Sŏurŭi ollimp'ik kyŏnggijang 서울의 올림픽 경기장/ *a baseball*~ yagujang 야구장.

staff *n.* (*stick*) maktaegi 막대기, (*pole*) changtae 장대, (*personnel*) chigwŏn 직원, (*military*) ch'ammo 참모. *How large a* ~ *will you need?* Ŏlmana chigwŏni piryo-hashimnikka? 얼마나 직원이 필요하십니까/ *I'm a member of the* ~. Kŭ sŭt'aep'ŭŭi han saramimnida. 그 스태프의 한 사람입니다.

stag *n.* (*male deer*) susasŭm 수사슴. ~ *party* namjadŭl-manŭi hoehap 남자들만의 회합.

stage *n.* (*theatre*) mudae 무대, (*scene of action*) hwal-tong mudae 활동 무대/ ~ *career* mudae saenghwal 무대 생활/ ~ *drama* mudaegŭk 무대극/ *a* ~ *setting* mudae changch'i 무대 장치/ *a revolving* ~ hoejŏn mudae 회전 무대.

stagger *vi.,vt.* (*reel*) pit'ŭlgŏrida 비틀거리다, (*hesitate*) mangsŏrida 망설이다, (*become confused*) ŏridungjŏrhada 어리둥절하다. *I was* ~*ed by the news.* Nanŭn kŭ soshi-gŭl tŭtko ŏridungjŏrhaessŭmnida. 나는 그 소식을 듣고 어리둥절했읍니다.

stagnant *adj.* (*not flowing*) koeŏ innŭn 괴어 있는, (*foul*) ssŏgŭn 썩은, (*not active*) ch'imch'ehan 침체한. *The market is extremely* ~. Shijangŭn mopshi ch'imch'e-hago issŭmnida. 시장은 몹시 침체하고 있읍니다.

stain *n.* (*blot*) ŏlluk 얼룩, (*spot*) ochŏm 오점. —*vt., vi.* (*make foul*) tŏrŏp'ida 더럽히다, (*become stained*) tŏrŏ-wŏjida 더러워지다. *ink* ~ ingk'ŭ ŏlluk 잉크 얼룩/ *Your collar has a* ~ *on it.* K'alla-e ŏllugi chyŏtkunyo. 칼라에 얼룩이 졌군요/ ~*ed glass* ch'aksaek yuri 착색 유리.

stainless *adj.* noksŭlji annŭn 녹슬지 않는.

stair *n.* (*steps*) kyedan 계단, (*pl.*) sadaktari 사닥다리. *screw* ~*s* nasŏnshik kyedan 나선식 계단/ *Walk up the* ~*s to the third floor.* Kyedanŭro samch'ŭngkkaji ollagashio. 계단으로 3층까지 올라가시오/ *down*~*s* arae ch'ŭng 아래층/ *up*~*s* wich'ŭng 위층.

staircase *n.* kyedan 계단. *a wooden* ~ mokcho kyedan 목조 계단/ *a back* ~ twitchok kyedan 뒤쪽 계단.

stake *n.* malttuk 말뚝, maktaegi 막대기.

stale *adj.* (*not fresh*) shinsŏnhaji anŭn 신선하지 않은, (*rotten*) sanghan 상한, (*flat*) kimppajin 김빠진, (*trite*) k'yek'yemugŭn 케케묵은/ ~ *bread* sanghan ppang 상한 빵/ ~ *beer* kimppajin maekchu 김빠진 맥주/ *a* ~ *joke* k'yek'yemugŭn nongdam 케케묵은 농담.

stalk *n.* (*stem*) chulgi 줄기. *an asparagus* ~ asŭp'aragŏ-sŭŭi chulgi 아스파라거스의 줄기.

stall *n.* (*stand*) maejŏm 매점, (*stable*) magutkan 마굿간.
a news ~ shinmun maejŏm 신문 매점.

stammer *vi.,vt.* (*stutter*) marŭl tŏdŭmta 말을 더듬다. *He*
~*s badly.* Kŭ saramŭn mopshi marŭl tŏdŭmsŭmnida.
그 사람은 몹시 말을 더듬습니다.

stamp *n.* (*seal*) tojang 도장, (*postage* ~) up'yo 우표,
(*postmark*) soin 소인. *a rubber* ~ komuin 고무인(印)/
May I have your personal ~? Tojang chom chushigessŭmnikka? 도장 좀 주시겠읍니까/ *My hobby is* ~ *collection.* Nae ch'wiminŭn up'yo sujibimnida. 내 취미는
우표 수집입니다/ *How much is an airmail* ~ *for Korea?*
Han-gukkajiŭi hanggong up'yonŭn ŏlmaimnikka? 한국
까지의 항공 우표는 얼마입니까/ *Give me five 50 won* ~*s.*
Oshibwŏnchari up'yo tasŏt chang chuseyo. 50원짜리 우
표 다섯 장 주세요.

stand *n.* (*rest*) patch'imtae 받침대, (*rack*) kŏri 걸이,
(*booth*) maejŏm 매점, (*grandstand*) kwallamsŏk 관람
석, (*station*) changso 장소. —*vi., vt.* (*be on one's feet*)
sŏda 서다, (*set upright*) seuda 세우다, (*stand up*)
irŏsŏda 일어서다, (*endure*) kyŏndida 견디다. *a music*~
akpodae 악보대/ *a news*~ shinmun p'anmaedae 신문 판
매대/ *the grand*~ t'ŭkpyŏl kwallamsŏk 특별 관람석/ *a
bus* ~ pŏsŭ chŏngnyujang 버스 정류장/ *We do business
at the old* ~. Pondi changso-esŏ yŏngŏp'ago issŭmnida.
본디 장소에서 영업하고 있읍니다/ *S*~ *up, please.* Irŏsŏ-
shipshio. 일어서십시오/ *S*~ *the bottle on the table.* Kŭ
pyŏngŭl t'akcha wie seushio. 그 병을 탁자 위에 세우시오/
S~ *them in a row.* Han chullo seushio. 한 줄로 세우시오/
We had to ~ *all the way in the bus.* Pŏsŭesŏ chulgot
sŏ issŏyaman haessŭmnida. 버스에서 줄곧 서 있어야만 했
읍니다/ *I can't* ~ *him.* Kŭ saramegenŭn ch'amŭl suga
ŏpsŭmnida. 그 사람에게는 참을 수가 없읍니다/ *I can't* ~
this heat any longer. Ije i tŏwirŭl kyŏndil suga ŏpsŭmnida. 이제 이 더위를 견딜 수가 없읍니다/ *Will you* ~ *us
champagne?* Syamp'ein hanjan sashigesso? 샴페인 한잔
사시겠소/ *If you* ~ *me up, I'll flatten you.* Parammac-
ch'imyŏn nŭlssinhage ttaeryŏ chul t'enikkayo. 바람맞

히면 늘쩐하게 때려 줄 테니까요.

standard *n.* (*criterion*) p'yojun 표준, kijun 기준, (*flag*) ki 기, (*emblem*) kijang 기장. *the ~ language* p'yojunmal 표준말/ *living ~* saenghwal sujun 생활 수준/ *the ~ time* p'yojunshi 표준시/ *a ~ writer* illyu chakka 일류 작가/ *Upon what~ is she judged?* Kŭ yŏinŭn ŏttŏn kijunesŏ pip'anŭl patko issŭmnikka? 그 여인은 어떤 기준에서 비판을 받고 있읍니까/ *The work was a low ~.* Kŭ chakp'umŭn chungnyu ihayŏssŭmnida. 그 작품은 중류 이하였읍니다.

stanza *n.* (*poem*) chŏl 절, yŏn 연(聯).

staple *n.* (*production*) chusanmul 주산물, (*fiber*) sŏmyu 섬유. *~ food* chushik 주식(主食)/ *~ fiber* injo sŏmyu 인조 섬유.

star *n.* (*astr.*) pyŏl 별, (*fortune*) unsu 운수, (*leading actor*) sŭt'a 스타, (*prominent person*) kŏmul 거물/ *a fixed ~* hangsŏng 항성/ *a wondering ~* haengsŏng 행성(行星)/ *Oh, there goes a shooting ~!* A, chŏgi pyŏlttongbyŏri! 아, 저기 별똥별이/ *What do the ~s foretell?* Unsega ŏttŏssŭmnikka? 운세가 어떻습니까/ *She always wanted to be a movie ~.* Kŭ yŏjanŭn hangsang yŏnghwa paeuga toego ship'ŏhaessŭmnida. 그 여자는 항상 영화 배우가 되고 싶어했읍니다.

starch *n.* p'ul 풀. *—vt.* p'urŭl mŏgida 풀을 먹이다.

stare *vt., vi.* (*gaze*) ppanhi poda 빤히 보다, noryŏboda 노려보다. *Why do you ~ me in the face?* Wae nae ŏlgurŭl noryŏboshimnikka? 왜 내 얼굴을 노려보십니까?

start *vi., vt.* (*set out*) ch'ulbarhada 출발하다, (*begin*) shijak'ada 시작하다, (*rise*) irŏnada 일어나다, (*be startled*) kkamtchak nollada 깜짝 놀라다. *—n.* (*beginning*) shijak 시작, (*outset*) ch'aksu 착수, (*~ing point*) ch'ulbalchŏm 출발점, (*lead*) apchang 앞장, (*slight shock*) kkamtchak nollam 깜짝 놀람. *We ~ed at six.* Yŏsŏssie ch'ulbarhaessŭmnida. 6시에 출발했읍니다/ *Have you ~ed working yet?* Pŏlssŏ irŭl shijak'aessŭmnikka? 벌써 일을 시작했읍니까/ *Who ~ed the fire?* Purŭn nuga naessŭmnikka? 불은 누가 냈읍니까/ *I awoke with a ~.*

Kkamtchak nolla nunŭl ttŏtchiyo. 깜짝 놀라 눈을 떴지요/ *I'll give you 5 meters* ～. O mit'ŏ apsewŏ tŭrijiyo. 5 미터 앞세워 드리지요.

startle *vt., vi.* (*surprise*) kkamtchak nollage hada〔nollada〕 깜짝 놀라게 하다〔놀라다〕/ *I was ～d at the news.* Kŭ nyusŭrŭl tŭtko kkamtchak nolassŭmnida. 그 뉴스를 듣고 깜짝 놀랐습니다.

starve *vi., vt.* (*die from hunger*) kulmŏ chukta 굶어 죽다, (*be very hungry*) mopshi paegop'ŭda 몹시 배고프다. *I'm starving.* Paega kop'a chukkessŭmnida. 배가 고파 죽겠습니다/ *I'm almost ～d.* Aju shijanghamnida. 아주 시장합니다/ *What's for dinner? I'm simply starving.* Chŏnyŏk panch'ani muŏshijiyo? Mopshi shijanghaeyo. 저녁 반찬이 무엇이지요? 몹시 시장해요.

state *n.* (*condition*) sangt'ae 상태, (*nation*) kukka 국가. —*vt.* (*say*) marhada 말하다, iyagihada 이야기하다. *I'm in a bad ～ of health.* Nanŭn kŏn-gang sangt'aega nappŭmnida. 나는 건강 상태가 나쁩니다/ *What ～ are you from?* Ŏnŭ nara-esŏ osyŏssŭmnikka? 어느 나라에서 오셨읍니까/ *Please ～ the amount.* Kŭmaegŭl malssŭmha shipshio. 금액을 말씀하십시오.

statement *n.* (*stating*) chinsul 진술, (*spoken declaration*) sŏngmyŏng 성명, (*accounting*) kyesansŏ 계산서. *We can hardly credit his ～.* Kŭ saramŭi chinsurŭl kŏŭi midŭl suga ŏpsŭmnida. 그 사람의 진술을 거의 믿을 수가 없읍니다/ *a joint ～* kongdong sŏngmyŏng 공동 성명/ *an official ～* kongshik sŏngmyŏng 공식 성명.

statesman *n.* (*politician*) chŏngch'iga 정치가. *a constructive ～* kŏnsŏlchŏgin chŏngch'iga 건설적인 정치가/ *a warrior ～* kunin-chŏngch'iga 군인·정치가.

station *n.* (*of railway*) yŏk 역(驛), chŏnggŏjang 정거장. *Can you tell me how to get to Seoul S～?* Sŏulyŏk kanŭn kirŭl karŭch'yŏ chushio. 서울역 가는 길을 가르쳐 주시오/ *Is there a railway ～ around here?* I kŭnch'ŏe kich'ayŏgi issŭmnikka? 이 근처에 기차역이 있읍니까/ *May I go to the ～ to see my friend off?* Ch'in-gurŭl chŏnsongharŏ yŏkkaji katta wado chossŭmnikka?

친구를 전송하러 역까지 갔다 와도 좋습니까?

stationer *n.* munbanggujŏm 문방구점.

stationery *n.* munbanggu 문방구. 「계표.

statistics *n.* t'onggye 통계. *a table of* ~ t'onggyep'yo 통

statue *n.* chosang 조상(彫像). *a bronze* ~ tongsang 동상 (銅像)/ *a plaster* ~ sŏkkosang 석고상/ *Whose* ~ *is that?* Kŭ tongsangŭn nuguŭi kŏshimnikka? 그 동상은 누구의 것입니까?

stay *vi., vt.* (*remain*) mŏmurŭda 머무르다, (*sojourn*) mukta 묵다. *How long are you going to* ~ *in Seoul?* Sŏure ŏlma tongan mŏmurŭshimnikka? 서울에 얼마 동안 머무르십니까/ *I'm going to* ~ *three nights.* Samilgan mŏmurŭgessŭmnida. 3일간 머무르겠습니다/ *Enjoy your* ~ *here.* Chaemiitke mugŭshipshio. 재미있게 묵으십시오/ *Can't you* ~ *longer?* Chomdŏ ittaga kashiji ank'essŭmnikka? 좀더 있다가 가시지 않겠습니까/ *How about* ~*ing for dinner?* Kyeshidaga kach'i shiksana hapshida. 계시다가 같이 식사나 합시다.

stay-at-home *n.* anpang saennim 안방 샌님.

steady *adj.* (*firm*) hwakkohan 확고한, (*regular*) hangyŏlgat'ŭn 한결같은, (*steadfast*) ch'akshirhan 착실한. *Hold the ladder* ~. Sadarirŭl tandanhi chaba chushio. 사다리를 단단히 잡아 주시오.

steak *n.* pulgogi 불고기, sŭt'eik'ŭ 스테이크/ *beef*~ pip'ŭ sŭt'eik'ŭ 비프 스테이크/ *I'll have a* ~ *dinner, please.* Pulgogi chŏngshigŭl chushio. 불고기 정식을 주시오/ *How would you like your* ~? *Medium, please.* Sŭt'eik'ŭnŭn ŏttŏk'e kuwŏ tŭrilkkayo? Pot'ongŭro kuwŏ chushio. 스테이크는 어떻게 구워 드릴까요? 보통으로 구워 주시오.

steal *vt., vi.* humch'ida 훔치다. *I have had my watch stolen.* Shigyerŭl todungmajassŭmnida. 시계를 도둑맞았습니다/ *My umbrella was stolen.* Yangsanŭl todungmajassŭmnida. 양산을 도둑맞았습니다.

steam *n.* (*water* ~) chŭnggi 증기, kim 김. ~*boat* kisŏn 기선/ ~ *engine* chŭnggi kigwan 증기 기관.

steamer *n.* (*steamship*) kisŏn 기선. *a ferry* ~ yŏllaksŏn 연락선/ *a pleasure* ~ yuramsŏn 유람선.

steamship *n.* (*steamer*) kisŏn 기선.

steel *n.* kangch'ŏl 강철.

steep *adj.* (*precipitous*) kap'arŭn 가파른, hŏmhan 험한, (*excessive*) ŏmch'ŏngnan 엄청난. *a ~ slope* kap'arŭn pit'al 가파른 비탈/ *That's a very ~ price for a brooch.* Pŭroch'i kap ch'igonŭn nŏmu pissamnida. 브로치 값 치고는 너무 비쌉니다.

steer *vt.*, *vi.* (*guide*) k'irŭl chapta 키를 잡다, (*follow*) ttaragada 따라가다. *Where are you ~ing for?* Ŏdiro kashimnikka? 어디로 가십니까/ *We ~ed for the railway station.* Yŏgŭl hyanghae kassŭmnida. 역을 향해 갔읍니다.

steersman *n.* k'ijabi 키잡이.

stem *n.* (*of plants*) chulgi 줄기.

stencil *n.* sŭt'ensŭl 스텐슬. *~ paper* wŏnji 원지(原紙).

stenographer *n.* sokkisa 속기사.

stenography *n.* (*shorthand*) sokki(sul) 속기(술).

step *n.* (*pace*) kŏrŭm 걸음, (*gait*) kŏrŭmgŏri 걸음걸이, (*football*) palchaguk sori 발자국 소리, (*stairway*) ch'ŭngch'ŭngdae 층층대, (*measure*) choch'i 조치. *—vi.*, *vt.* (*walk*) kŏtta 걷다, (*feet*) naeditta 내딛다, (*tread*) papta 밟다. *Mind the ~.* Pal mit'ŭl choshimhashipshio. 발 밑을 조심하십시오/ *Please watch your ~.* Pal choshim hashipshio. 발 조심 하십시오/ *I heard a light ~ on the stairs.* Kyedanesŏ kabyŏun palchaguk soriga tŭllyŏssŭmnida. 계단에서 가벼운 발자국 소리가 들렸읍니다/ *What is the next ~?* Taŭm choch'inŭn muŏshimnikka? 다음 조치는 무엇입니까/ *S~ forward, please.* Ap'ŭro naoshipshio. 앞으로 나오십시오/ *Hey, Kim, ~ inside.* Ŏi Kimgun, anŭro tŭrŏwa. 어이, 김군, 안으로 들어와/ *Somebody ~ped on my foot.* Nuga nae parŭl palbassŭmnida. 누가 내 발을 밟았읍니다/ *~child* ŭibut chashik 의붓 자식/ *~daughter* ŭibuttal 의붓딸/ *~father* kyebu 계부/ *~mother* kyemo 계모/ *~brother* paedarŭn hyŏngje 배다른 형제/ *~sister* paedarŭn chamae 배다른 자매.

stereo *n.* ipch'e 입체. *a ~ camera* ipch'e sajinki 입체 사진기/ *a ~ picture* ipch'e sajin 입체 사진.

stereotype *n.* yŏnp'an 연판(鉛版).

sterile *adj.* (*not fertile*) memarŭn 메마른, (*barren*) airŭl mot nannŭn 아이를 못 낳는. *a ~ woman* airŭl mot nannŭn yŏin 아이를 못 낳는 여인/ *~ soil* memarŭn ttang 메마른 땅.

stern *adj.* (*severe*) ŏmhan 엄한, ŏmkyŏk'an 엄격한. —*n.* (*of ship*) komul 고물. *a ~ face* ŏmsuk'an ŏlgul 엄숙한 얼굴/ *a ~ taskmaster* ŏmkyŏk'an shipchang 엄격한 십장.

steward *n.* (*in ship*) ch'wisabanjang 취사반장, (*in hospital, etc.*) yongdogye 용도계, (*manager*) chipsa 집사, kansa 간사.

stewardess *n.* sŭt'yuŏdisŭ 스튜어디스. *a KAL ~* taehan hanggong sŭt'yuŏdisŭ 대한 항공 스튜어디스.

stick *n.* (*thin branch*) namu maktaegi 나무 막대기, (*cane*) chip'angi 지팡이. —*vt., vi.* (*thrust*) tchirŭda 찌르다, (*fix on to*) tallaputta 달라붙다, (*paste*) puch'ida 붙이다, (*adhere*) kosuhada 고수하다. *a golf ~* kolp'ŭch'ae 골프채/ *a yard ~* yadŭ cha 야드 자[尺]/ *S~ the fork into the potato.* Kamjarŭl p'ok'ŭro tchigŭshio. 감자를 포크로 찍으시오/ *Glue ~s to the finger.* Agyoga sonkarage tŭllōbussŭmnida. 아교가 손가락에 들러붙습니다/ *S~ right where you are.* Chigŭm innŭn charie kŭdaero kyeshipshio. 지금 있는 자리에 그대로 계십시오.

sticky *adj.* (*adhesive*) kkŭnjŏkkŭnjŏk'an 끈적끈적한, (*humid*) kkŭnkkŭnhan 끈끈한. *My shirt is ~ with sweat.* Syassŭga ttamŭro kkŭnkkŭnhada. 샤쓰가 땀으로 끈끈하다.

stiff *adj.* (*hard*) ttakttak'an 딱딱한, (*no moving freely*) ppakppak'an 빡빡한, (*dense*) kŏltchuk'an 걸쭉한. *I've a ~ shoulder.* Ŏkkaega ppŏgŭnhamnida. 어깨가 뻐근합니다.

still *adj.* (*quiet*) koyohan 고요한, (*motionless*) umjigiji annŭn 움직이지 않는. —*adv.* (*even now*) ajikto 아직도, (*yet*) tŏuk 더욱. *Keep your feet ~.* Parŭl umjigiji mashio. 발을 움직이지 마시오/ *Please keep ~ while I take your photograph.* Sajinŭl tchingnŭn tongan kamanhi kyeseyo. 사진을 찍는 동안 가만히 계세요/ *Will you ~ be here when I return?* Naega toraol ttaekkaji yŏgie

itkessŭmnikka? 내가 돌아올 때까지 여기에 있겠읍니까/ ～
less tŏuk ....anida 더욱 …아니다/ ～ *more* tŏgundana…
ida 더군다나 …이다.

sting *n.* (*prick*) panŭl 바늘, kashi 가시, (*of insect*) ch'im
침, (*pain*) ap'ŭm 아픔. —*vt., vi.* (*prick*) ssoda 쏘다,
tchirŭda 찌르다, (*cause sharp pain*) ssushida 쑤시다.
Have you any ointment to put on these ～s? Ssoin te
parŭnŭn yŏn-goga issŭmnikka? 쏘인 데 바르는 연고가 있
읍니까/ *I was stung by a bee.* Nanŭn pŏre ssoyŏssŭm-
nida. 나는 벌에 쏘였읍니다.

stingy *adj.* (*miserly*) insaek'an 인색한. *Don't be so ～
with the sugar!* Sŏlt'ang kajigo kŭrŏk'e insaek'age
kulji mashio. 설탕 가지고 그렇게 인색하게 굴지 마시오/ *a
～ fellow* kudusoe 구두쇠.

stink *n.* (*bad smell*) akch'wi 악취. —*vi., vt.* akch'wirŭl
p'unggida 악취를 풍기다. *He ～s of wine.* Sullaemsaega
k'orŭl tchirŭmnida. 술냄새가 코를 찌릅니다.

stir *vt., vi.* (*move*) umjigida 움직이다, (*churn*) hwijŏtta
휘젓다, (*excite*) pun-gishik'ida 분기시키다. *～ one's tea
with a spoon* sŭp'unŭro ch'arŭl chŏtta 스푼으로 차를
젓다.

stirrup *n.* (*for riders*) tŭngja 등자(鐙子).

stitch *n.* (*sewing*) han k'o 한 코, han panŭl 한 바늘.
—*vt., vi.*(*sew*) kkwemaeda 꿰매다.

stock *n.* (*store of goods*) chaegop'um 재고품, (*store*)
chŏjang 저장, (*share*) chushik 주식, (*stem*) chulgi 줄기,
(*lineage*) hyŏlt'ong 혈통, (*live～*) kach'uk 가축. *It's
out of ～ now, I'm sorry.* Choesonghamnidaman chae-
goga ŏpsŭmnida. 죄송합니다만 재고가 없읍니다/ *A new
～ will arrive tomorrow. Will you wait?* Sae sangp'umi
naeil toch'ak'amnida. Kidarigessŭmnikka? 새 상품이 내
일 도착합니다. 기다리겠읍니까/ *Have you any linen sheets
in ～?* Rinnerŭ shit'ŭŭi chaegop'umi issŭmnikka? 린네르
시트의 재고품이 있읍니까/ ～ *company* chushik hoesa 주식
회사/ ～ *exchange* chŭngkwŏn kŏraeso 증권 거래소.

stocking *n.* (*pl.*) yangmal 양말. *a pair of ～s* yangmal
han k'yŏlle 양말 한 켤레/ *nylon ～s* naillon yangmal

나일론 양말/ *silk* ~*s* shilk'ŭ yangmal 실크 양말.

stockroom *n.* chŏjangshil 저장실.

stomach *n.* wi 위, (*abdomen*) pae 배. ~*ache* wit'ong 위통/ ~*cramps* wigyŏngnyŏn 위경련/ *I feel a pain in my* ~. Wiga ap'ŭmnida. 위가 아픕니다/ *I kicked him in the* ~. Kŭ saramŭi araetpaerŭl ch'ajuŏssŭmnida. 그 사람의 아랫배를 차주었읍니다.

stone *n.* tol 돌. *a* ~ *bridge* toldari 돌다리/ *a grind* ~ suttol 숫돌/ *grave*~ pisŏk 비석/ *mill*~ maettol 맷돌/ *a precious* ~ posŏk 보석/ ~ *steps* tolgyedan 돌계단/ *a* ~ *pillar* tolgidung 돌기둥/ *a* ~ *wall* toldam 돌담/ *throw a* ~ torŭl tŏnjida 돌을 던지다.

stony *adj.* tori manŭn 돌이 많은. *a* ~ *road* tori manŭn kil 돌이 많은 길, tolkil 돌길.

stool *n.* (*seat*) kŏlsang 걸상, (*commode*) pyŏn-gi 변기(便器). *a piano* ~ p'iano ŭija 피아노 의자/ *a folding* ~ chŏbŭija 접의자/ *go to* ~ pyŏnso-e kada 변소에 가다.

stoop *vi.*, *vt.* (*bow*) kuburida 구부리다. *Sit up straight and don't* ~. Momŭl kuburiji malgo ttokparo anjŭshio. 몸을 구부리지 말고 똑바로 앉으시오.

stop *vt.*, *vi.* (*halt*) mŏmch'uda 멈추다, (*cease*) kŭmanduda 그만두다, (*stay*) mŏmurŭda 머무르다, (*close up*) makta 막다, (*interrupt*) panghaehada 방해하다. —*n.* (*pause*) chŏngji 정지, (*stopping place*) chŏngnyujang 정류장, (*stay*) sukpak 숙박, (*plug*) magae 마개. *How long does this train* ~ *at Taegu?* I yŏlch'anŭn Taeguesŏ ŏlmana chŏngch'ahamnikka? 이 열차는 대구에서 얼마나 정차합니까/ *We* ~*ped talking.* Urinŭn iyagirŭl mŏmch'uŏssŭmnida. 우리는 이야기를 멈추었읍니다/ *I shall* ~ *here for a few days.* Yŏgisŏ myŏch'il mŏmulgessŭmnida. 여기서 며칠 머물겠읍니다/ *I'm* ~*ping with my nephew.* Chok'ajibesŏ mukko issŭmnida. 조카집에서 묵고 있읍니다/ *I'll make an overnight* ~ *here.* Yŏgisŏ harŭtpam mukko kagessŭmnida. 여기서 하룻밤 묵고 가겠읍니다/ *Where's the nearest bus* ~*?* Kajang kakkaun pŏsŭ chŏngnyusonŭn ŏdimnikka? 가장 가까운 버스 정류소는 어딥니까?

stopover *n.* tojung hach'a 도중 하차. *one day ~ at Pusan* Pusanesŏ haru hasŏn 부산에서 하루 하선(下船).

storage *n.* chŏjang 저장. *cold ~* naengjang 냉장/ *~ battery* ch'ukchŏnji 축전지/ *~ charges* ch'anggo pogwannyo 창고 보관료.

store *n.* (*shop*) kage 가게, sangjŏm 상점. *Is this Kumgang S~?* (*in telephone*) Kŭmgang sanghoeimnikka? 금강 상회입니까/ *Do you have ~s like this in Hongkong?* Hongk'ongedo irŏn kagedŭri issŭmnikka? 홍콩에도 이런 가게들이 있읍니까/ *a grocery ~* shikp'um kage 식품 가게/ *a department ~* paek'wajŏm 백화점/ *~house* ch'anggo 창고.

stork *n.* (*bird*) hwangsae 황새.

storm *n.* p'okp'ung(u) 폭풍(우). *I was caught in a ~.* Nanŭn p'okp'ungurŭl mannassŭmnida. 나는 폭풍우를 만났읍니다/ *rain~* p'okp'ungu 폭풍우/ *snow~* nunbora 눈보라/ *wind~* p'okp'ung 폭풍.

stormy *adj.* p'okp'unguŭi 폭풍우의, (*violent*) kŏch'in 거친. *a ~ sea* p'okp'ungi inŭn pada 폭풍이 이는 바다/ *~ quarrels* maengnyŏrhan ssaum 맹렬한 싸움.

story *n.* (*tale*) iyagi 이야기, (*account*) naeryŏk 내력, (*plot*) chulgŏri 줄거리, (*short ~*) tanp'yŏn sosŏl 단편 소설, (*history*) yŏksa 역사, (*lie*) kŏjinmal 거짓말. *Please tell us a ~.* Yennal iyagi chom hae chushipshio. 옛날 이야기 좀 해 주십시오/ *a Bible ~* sŏngsŏ iyagi 성서 이야기/ *I know her ~.* Kŭ yŏjaŭi naeryŏgŭl nanŭn algo issŭmnida. 그 여자의 내력을 나는 알고 있읍니다/ *Are you reading the ~ in that newspaper?* Kŭ shinmun sosŏrŭl ikko issŭmnikka? 그 신문 소설을 읽고 있읍니까/ *Don't tell stories.* Kŏjinmal marara. 거짓말 말아라/ *I wonder how many stories it has?* Myŏt ch'ŭngina toejiyo? 몇 층이나 되지요?

stout *adj.* (*strong*) t'ŭnt'ŭnhan 튼튼한, (*durable*) chilgin 질긴, (*fat*) ttungttunghan 뚱뚱한, (*brave*) yonggamhan 용감한. *a ~ body* t'ŭnt'ŭnhan mom 튼튼한 몸/ *a~ cloth* chilgin ch'ŏn 질긴 천/ *a ~ man* kŏnjanghan sanai 건장한 사나이/ *The old lady is ~.* Kŭ nŭlgŭn puinŭn ttung-

ttunghamnida. 그 늙은 부인은 뚱뚱합니다.

stove *n.* nallo 난로, sŭt'obŭ 스토브. *an electric* ~ chŏn-gi nallo 전기 난로/ *an oil* ~ sŏgyu nallo 석유 난로.

straight *adj.* (*direct*) ttokparŭn 똑바른, (*vertical*) sujigŭi 수직의, (*upright*) chŏngjik'an 정직한, (*neat*) sunsuhan 순수한. *a* ~ *line* chiksŏn 직선/ *Is the picture* ~? Kŭrimi ttokparo kŏllyŏssŭmnikka? 그림이 똑바로 걸렸읍니까/ *Go* ~ *ahead*. Ttokparo kashipshio. 똑바로 가십시오/ *drink whisky* ~ wisŭk'irŭl murŭl t'aji ank'o mashida 위스키를 물을 타지 않고 마시다/ ~*forward* kojishik'an 고지식한/ *Most Koreans are quite* ~ *and frank.* Han-guk saramŭn taegae kojishik'ago solchik'amnida. 한국 사람은 대개 고지식하고 솔직합니다.

straighten *vt., vi.* (*make straight*) ttokparŭge hada 똑바르게 하다, (*put in order*) chŏngdonhada 정돈하다.

strain *n.* (*tension*) kinjang 긴장, (*excessive effort*) kwaro 과로, (*sprain*) ppim 삠. —*vt., vi.* (*pull hard*) chaba-danggida 잡아당기다, (*tense*) kinjangshik'ida 긴장시키다, (*overwork*) hoksahada 혹사하다, (*wrench*) ppida 삐다. ~ *every nerve* chŏllyŏgŭl ssotta 전력(全力)을 쏟다/ *We* ~*ed at the oars.* Himkkŏt norŭl chŏŏssŭmnida. 힘껏 노를 저었읍니다.

strait *n.* (*channel*) haehyŏp 해협. *a narrow* ~ chobŭn haehyŏp 좁은 해협.

strand *n.* (*beach*) padatka 바닷가. —*vi., vt.* (*on rock*) chwach'ohada 좌초하다. *Our ship has* ~*ed on the Chinese shore.* Uri paega Chungguk haeanesŏ chwach'o-hayŏssŭmnida. 우리 배가 중국 해안에서 좌초하였읍니다.

strange *adj.* (*not known*) ch'ŏŭm ponŭn 처음 보는, (*queer*) isanghan 이상한, (*unfamiliar*) sŏmŏk'an 서먹한, natsŏn 낯선. *I'm* ~ *to these parts.* I kŭnch'ŏnŭn naega morŭ-nŭn koshimnida. 이 근처는 내가 모르는 곳입니다/ *How* ~ *that you should not have heard!* Tangshini tŭtchi mo-t'aettani isanghamnida. 당신이 듣지 못했다니 이상합니다/ *I feel* ~ *here.* Yŏginŭn ŏtchŏnji sŏmŏk'amnida. 여기는 어쩐지 서먹합니다.

stranger *n.* (*unknown person*) morŭnŭn saram 모르는 사

람, (*newcomer*) natsŏn saram 낯선 사람, (*guest*) sonnim
손님, (*outsider*) munoehan 문외한. *S~!* (=*sir*) Yŏboshio.
여보시오/ *He is a ~ to me.* Nanŭn kŭ saramŭl morŭmnida. 나는 그 사람을 모릅니다/ *I'm a ~ to love.* Yŏnaee
taehaesŏnŭn munoehanimnida. 연애에 대해서는 문외한입
니다/ *You are quite a ~.* Ch'am oraeganmanimnida.
참 오래간만입니다.

strangle *vt., vi.* (*throttle*) mokcholla chugida 목졸라 죽이
다, (*stifle*) chilshikshik'ida 질식시키다, (*be choked*)
chilshik'ada 질식하다. *This stiff collar is strangling
me.* K'allaga ppŏtppŏt'aesŏ mogi choemnida. 칼라가 뻣
뻣해서 목이 죕니다.

strap *n.* (*band*) tti 띠, (*strip of leather*) hyŏktae 혁대,
kajukkŭn 가죽끈, (*razor ~*) hyŏkchi 혁지(革砥). —*vt.*
kajukkŭnŭro mukta 가죽끈으로 묶다. (*surg.*) (*plaster*)
panch'anggorŭl puch'ida 반창고를 붙이다.

strategy *n.* (*generalship*) pyŏngpŏp 병
법, (*tactics*) chŏllyak 전략.

straw *n.* chip 짚. *rice ~* pyŏtchip 볏짚/
wheat ~ milchip 밀짚/ *a ~ hat* milchip
moja 밀짚 모자/*~ rope* saekkijul 새끼줄.

strawberry *n.* ttalgi 딸기.

stray *vi.* (*lose one's way*) kirŭl ilt'a 길
을 잃다, (*wander*) hemaeda 헤매다.
—*adj.* (*lost*) kirŭl irŭn 길을 잃은. *a* ⟨saekkijul⟩
~ child mia 미아(迷兒). *a ~ sheep* kil irŭn yang 길 잃
은 양.

stream *n.* (*small river*) kaeul 개울, (*flow*) hŭrŭm 흐름.
—*vi.* hŭrŭda 흐르다. *A brook ~s by our house.* Shi-
naega uri chip yop'ŭl hŭrŭgo itta. 시내가 우리 집 옆을 흐
르고 있다.

street *n.* (*town road*) kŏri 거리, karo 가로(街路). *Which
~ should I take?* Ŏnŭ kŏrirŭl kamyŏn toejiyo? 어느
거리를 가면 되지요/ *It is the third ~ on your right.*
Orŭntchok se pŏntchae kŏriyeyo. 오른쪽 세 번째 거리예요.

streetcar *n.* chŏnch'a 전차. *a ~ stop* chŏnch'a chŏngnyujang 전차 정류장/ *a ~ ticket* chŏnch'ap'yo 전차표.

strength n. (*bodily power*) him 힘, (*power*) seryŏk 세력, (*force*) pyŏngnyŏk 병력, (*forte*) changchŏm 장점. *put forth one's ~* himŭl naeda 힘을 내다 /*one's ~ is gone* himi ppajida 힘이 빠지다/ *beyond one's ~* himi mich'iji annŭn 힘이 미치지 않는/ *with all one's ~* himkkŏt 힘껏.

strengthen vt.,vi. (*make strong*) kanghage hada 강하게 하다, (*reinforce*) kanghwahada 강화하다, (*become strong*) kanghaejida 강해지다.

strenuous adj. yŏlshimin 열심인, kyŏngnyŏrhaɳ 격렬한. *make ~ effort* punbarhada 분발하다/ *a ~ worker* ŏkch'ŏkkat'ŭn ilkkun 억척같은 일꾼.

stress n. (*pressure*) appak 압박, (*emphasis*) kangjo 강조, (*accent*) aeksŏnt'ŭ 액선트, (*~ disease*) sŭt'ŭresŭ pyŏng 스트레스 병(病). —vt. (*emphasize*) kangjohada 강조하다, (*lay ~ on*) ...e chungchŏmŭl tuda ⋯에 중점을 두다. *You must learn where to place ~es.* Ŏdie aeksŏnt'ŭrŭl tuŏya hanŭnji ik'yŏya hamnida. 어디에 액선트를 두어야 하는지 익혀야 합니다.

stretch vt., vi. (*extend*) nŭrida 늘이다, (*spread*) p'yŏda 펴다, (*reach out*) naeppŏtta 내뻗다, (*strain*) kinjangshik'ida 긴장시키다. *He ~ed out a hand for the money.* Kŭ saramŭn tonŭl padŭryŏgo sonŭl naeppŏdŏssŭmnida. 그 사람은 돈을 받으려고 손을 내뻗었읍니다/ *~ oneself* kijigaerŭl k'yŏda 기지개를 켜다.

stretcher n. (*litter*) tŭlkŏt 들것.

strew vt. (*scatter*) ppurida 뿌리다, (*overspread*) ppuryŏsŏ tŏpta 뿌려서 덮다.

stricken adj. (*hit*) majŭn 맞은, (*wounded*) tach'in 다친, (*afflicted*) pyŏnge kŏllin 병에 걸린. *~ with sickness* pyŏnge kŏllida 병에 걸리다.

strict adj. (*stern*) ŏmkyŏk'an 엄격한, (*accurate*) chŏnghwak'an 정확한. *a ~ father* ŏmkyŏk'an abŏji 엄격한 아버지/ *You seem too ~ with your young ones.* Tangshinŭn aidŭrege nŏmu ŏmkyŏk'an kŏt kassŭmnida. 당신은 아이에게 너무 엄격한 것 같습니다.

strictly adv. ŏmkyŏk'age 엄격하게. *~ speaking* ŏmkyŏk'i marhaesŏ 엄격히 말해서.

stride *n.* (*gait*) kŏrŭmgŏri 걸음걸이, (*long step*) k'ŭn kŏrŭm 큰 걸음. —*vi., vt.* (*walk*) sŏngk'ŭmsŏngk'ŭm kŏtta 성큼성큼 걷다. *He has a long* ~. Kŭ saramŭn k'omp'asŭga kimnida. 그 사람은 콤파스가 깁니다/ *make a great* ~*s* changjogŭi palchŏnŭl hada 장족의 발전을 하다.

strike *vt., vi.* (*hit*) ch'ida 치다, ttaerida 때리다, (*dash*) pudich'ida 부딪히다, (*impress*) kamdongshik'ida 감동시키다. —*n.* (*refusal to work*) p'aŏp 파업, (*baseball*) (*suitable pitch*) sŭt'ŭraik'ŭ 스트라이크. *S*~ *us if you dare!* Ttaeril t'emyŏn ttaeryŏ poshio. 때릴 테면 때려 보시오/ *The workman walked out a 24 hour* ~ *for higher wages.* Chikkongdŭrŭn noim insangŭl yoguhayŏ ishipsashigan p'aŏp'aessŭmnida. 직공들은 노임 인상을 요구하여 24시간 파업했읍니다.

striker *n.* tongmaeng p'aŏpcha 동맹 파업자.

string *n.* (*cord*) kkŭn 끈. *shoe* ~*s* kudu kkŭn 구두 끈/ *tie with a* ~ kkŭnŭro mukta 끈으로 묶다/ *undo the* ~*s* kkŭnŭl p'ulda 끈을 풀다.

strip *n.* (*narrow piece*) chogak 조각, (*of land*) chidae 지대(地帶). —*vt., vi.* (*make bare*) pŏtkida 벗기다, (*undress*) pŏtta 벗다, (*take away*) ppaeatta 빼앗다. *an air* ~ hwalchuro 활주로/ *They* ~*ped her to the skin.* Kŭdŭrŭn kŭ yŏjarŭl palgabŏtkyŏssŭmnida. 그들은 그 여자를 발가벗겼읍니다.

stripe *n.* chulmunŭi 줄무늬. *How many* ~*s are there on the sleeve of sergeant?* Chungsaŭi somaeenŭn sujangi myŏt kae issŭmnikka? 중사(中士)의 소매에는 수장이 몇 개 있읍니까/ *Stars and S*~*s* sŏngjogi 성조기.

strive *n.* (*try hard*) himssŭda 힘쓰다, noryŏk'ada 노력하다, (*contend*) tat'uda 다투다.

stroke *n.* (*of Chinese characters*) hoek 획(劃), (*of disease*) palbyŏng 발병. *This Chinese character has seven* ~*s.* I hanchanŭn ch'irhoegimnida. 이 한자(漢字)는 7획입니다/ *a paralytic* ~ cholto 졸도/ *sun*~ ilsapyŏng 일사병.

strong *adj.* (*powerful*) kanghan 강한, (*tough*) t'ŭnt'ŭn-han 튼튼한, (*influential*) yuryŏk'an 유력한, (*intense*) chinhan 진한. *a ~ wind* kanghan param 강한 바람/ *I don't feel very ~.* Tomuji kiuni naji anssŭmnida. 도무지 기운이 나지 않습니다/ *a ~ impression* kip'ŭn kammyŏng 깊은 감명/ *Make the coffee a little ~er.* K'op'irŭl chomdŏ chinhage hae chushio. 코피를 좀더 진하게 해 주시오/ *~-minded* kyŏltansŏng innŭn 결단성 있는/ *a ~ woman* kyŏltansŏng innŭn yŏin 결단성 있는 여인.

structure *n.* (*construction*) kujo 구조, (*building*) kŏnch'ungmul 건축물, (*organization*) chojik 조직. *the economic ~ of Korea* Han-gugŭi kyŏngje kujo 한국의 경제 구조/ *modern ~s* hyŏndaeshik kŏnch'ungmul 현대식 건축물/ *What's that ~ on the left?* Oentchogŭi chŏ kŏnmurŭn muŏshimnikka? 왼쪽의 저 건물은 무엇입니까?

struggle *n.* (*great effort*) punt'u 분투, (*hard work*) kot'u 고투, (*fight*) t'ujaeng 투쟁. *—vi.* (*try hard*) noryŏk'ada 노력하다, (*fight*) ssauda 싸우다. *the ~ for existence* saengjon kyŏngjaeng 생존 경쟁/ *He ~d along the crowd.* Kŭnŭn saramdŭrŭl hech'igo naagassŭmnida. 그는 사람들을 헤치고 나아갔읍니다.

stubborn *n.* (*obstinate*) kojip sen 고집 센, (*unyielding*) kup'iji annŭn 굽히지 않는. *a ~ child* kojip sen ai 고집 센 아이/ *a ~ resistance* wan-ganghan chŏhang 완강한 저항.

stud *n.* (*of shirt*) tanch'u 단추, (*nailhead*) mot 못, (*scatter over*) sanjaehada 산재하다. *a pair of ~s* changshingyong tanch'u han ssang 장식용 단추 한 쌍.

student *n.* (*Am.*) (*of high school, college*) haksaeng 학생, (*Brit.*) (*of college*) taehaksaeng 대학생. *an evening ~* yagan haksaeng 야간 학생/ *a graduate ~* taehagwŏnsaeng 대학원생/ *a junior class ~* hagŭpsaeng 하급생/ *a senior class ~* sanggŭpsaeng 상급생/ *Those ~s belong to Seoul National University.* Chŏdŭrŭn Sŏul taehakkyo haksaengdŭrimnida. 저들은 서울 대학교 학생들입니다.

studio *n.* (*for artists*) chagŏpshil 작업실, (*for painting*) hwashil 화실, (*for photographer*) sajin-gwan 사진관,

(*for broadcasting*) pangsongshil 방송실.

studious *adj.* (*fond of study*) hakkujŏgin 학구적인, (*zealous*) yŏlshimin 열심인, (*thoughtful*) shinjunghan 신중한.

study *n.* (*learning*) kongbu 공부, (*careful examination*) yŏn-gu 연구, (*room*) sŏjae 서재. —*vi., vt.* (*work*) kong-buhada 공부하다, (*examine*) yŏn-guhada 연구하다. *That boy likes sport more than* ~. Kŭ sonyŏnŭn kongbuboda sŭp'och'ŭrŭl choahamnida. 그 소년은 공부보다 스포츠를 좋아합니다/ *You will find Mr. Kim in his* ~. Kim-gunŭn chagi sŏjaee issŭl kŏshimnida. 김군은 자기 서재에 있을 것입니다.

stuff *n.* (*substance*) mulgŏn 물건, (*material*) chaeryo 재료, (*refuse*) p'yemul 폐물. —*vt., vi.* (*pack tightly*) ch'aewŏ nŏt'a 채워 넣다. *We've got some good* ~. Choŭn mulgŏni issŭmnida. 좋은 물건이 있습니다/ *I'm* ~*ed.* Manbogieyo. 만복(滿腹)이에요/ *My nose is* ~*ed up with a cold.* Kamgiro k'oga mak'yŏssŭmnida. 감기로 코가 막혔습니다/ *green* ~ ch'aeso 채소.

stuffy *adj.* (*ill ventilated*) t'ongp'ungi chal an toenŭn 통풍이 잘 안 되는, (*close*) taptap'an 답답한. *I feel* ~ *in this room.* I pangŭn sumi mak'il kŏt kassŭmnida. 이 방은 숨이 막힐 것 같습니다.

stumble *vt., vi.* (*trip*) nŏmŏjida 넘어지다, (*stagger*) pit'ŭlgŏrida 비틀거리다. *I* ~*d after him.* Nanŭn pit'ŭl-gŏrimyŏnsŏ kŭ saram twirŭl ttaragassŭmnida. 나는 비틀거리면서 그 사람 뒤를 따라갔습니다.

stump *n.* (*stub*) kŭrut'ŏgi 그루터기.

stun *vt.* (*knock unconscious*) kijŏlshik'ida 기절시키다, (*astound*) honnaeda 혼내다. *I was temporarily* ~*ned.* Nanŭn chamshi kijŏrhayŏssŭmnida. 나는 잠시 기절하였습니다.

stunt *n.* (*feat*) myogi 묘기, kogye 곡예. *an autocycle* ~ ot'obai kogye 오토바이 곡예/ ~ *flying* kogye pihaeng 곡예 비행/ *a tight rope* ~ chult'agi myogi 줄타기 묘기.

stupid *adj.* (*foolish*) ŏrisŏgŭn 어리석은, (*dull*) udunhan 우둔한. *a* ~ *person* pabo 바보/ *I was only teasing,* ~ !

Nollyŏssŭl ppuniya, i pabo ! 놀렸을 뿐이야, 이 바보 !

style *n.* (*mode*) hyŏng 형, (*fashion*) yangshik 양식, (*manner of writing*) munch'e 문체, (*vogue*) yuhaeng 유행, sŭt'ail 스타일. *What ~ of house do you want ?* Ŏttŏn moyangŭi chibŭl kuhashimnikka ? 어떤 모양의 집을 구하십니까/ *a Korean ~* Han-gukshik 한국식/ *a modern ~* hyŏndaeshik 현대식.

subdue *vt.* (*conquer*) chŏngbok'ada 정복하다, (*overcome*) igyŏnaeda 이겨내다, (*master*) nurŭda 누르다.

subject *n.* (*theme*) chuje 주제, (*thing studied*) chemok 제목, (*of study*) hakkwa 학과, (*opp. king*) paeksŏng 백성. *What ~ do you teach at school ?* Hakkyo-esŏnŭn musŭn hakkwarŭl karŭch'ishimnikka ? 학교에서는 무슨 학과를 가르치십니까/ *Let's change the ~.* Hwajerŭl pakkupshida. 화제를 바꿉시다.

sublime *adj.* (*solemn*) changŏmhan 장엄한, (*noble*) kosanghan 고상한, (*perfect*) t'ŏmuniŏmnŭn 터무니없는. *~ scenery* changŏmhan p'unggyŏng 장엄한 풍경/ *You ~ idiot !* I ch'ŏnch'i paboya ! 이 천치 바보야 !

submarine *n.* (*boat*) chamsuham 잠수함. —*adj.* haejŏŭi 해저(海底)의.

submerge *vt., vi.* (*sink*) karaanch'ida 가라앉히다, (*flood*) mure chamgŭda 물에 잠그다, mure chamgida 물에 잠기다.

submission *n.* (*subjection*) pokchong 복종, (*obedience*) sunjong 순종, (*meekness*) yuhwa 유화(柔和).

submit *vt., vi.* (*yield*) kulbokshik'ida 굴복시키다, (*brook*) kamsuhada 감수하다, (*present*) chech'urhada 제출하다. *I'll not ~ to such treatment.* Kŭrŏn taeunŭn patchi anŭl kŏshimnida. 그런 대우는 받지 않을 것입니다.

subordinate *n.* (*follower*) puha 부하(部下).

subscribe *vt., vi.* (*sign*) sŏmyŏnghada 서명하다, (*contribute*) kibuhada 기부하다, (*magazine, etc.*) yeyak kudok'ada 예약 구독하다. *Would you like to ~ to the Korea Herald ?* K'oria herŏldŭrŭl shinch'onghashiryŏmnikka ? 코리아 헤럴드를 신청하시렵니까 ?

subscriber *n.* (*contributor*) kibuja 기부자, (*for a maga-*

zine) kudokcha 구독자.
subscription *n.* (*signature*) sŏmyŏng 서명, (*contribution*) kibu 기부, (*to magazine*) kudok 구독. *Just fill out this ~ blank, please.* Shinch'ŏngyongjie kiimman hae chushipshio. 신청용지에 기입만 해 주십시오.
subside *vt.* (*become quiet*) chada 자다, (*sink*) karaanta 가라앉다. *The wind ~d to a calm.* Parami chamjamhaejyŏssŭmnida. 바람이 잠잠해졌습니다.
substantial *adj.* (*actual*) shilchaehanŭn 실재하는, (*solid*) shilsok innŭn 실속 있는, (*stout*) tandanhan 단단한. *a ~ meal* p'ujimhan shiksa 푸짐한 식사／ *a ~ business firm* chaeryŏgi tŭndŭnhan kiŏp'ch'e 재력이 든든한 기업체.
substitute *vt.,vi.* (*replace*) taeyonghada 대용하다, taeshinhada 대신하다. —*n.* (*person*) taeriin 대리인, (*thing*) taeyongp'um 대용품. *Can I ask you to ~ for me till I return?* Toraol ttaekkaji chom taeshinhae chul su issŭmnikka? 돌아올 때까지 좀 대신해 줄 수 있습니까／ *Can you secure a ~?* Taeyongp'umŭl kuhal su issŭmnikka? 대용품을 구할 수 있습니까?
subtract *vt.* (*take away*) ppaeda 빼다, (*deduct*) kamhada 감하다. *~ 6 from 9* kuesŏ yugŭl ppaeda 9에서 6을 빼다.
subtraction *n.* ppaegi 빼기.
suburb *n.* kyooe 교외. *This bus is running towards the ~s, isn't it?* I pŏsŭnŭn kyooero kanŭn-gunyo. 이 버스는 교외로 가는군요.
subway *n.* (*underground railway*) chihach'ŏl 지하철, (*underpass*) chihado 지하도. *How long does it take to go to Chongnyangni by ~?* Chihach'ŏllo Ch'ŏngnyangnikkaji ŏlmana kŏllimnikka? 지하철로 청량리까지 얼마나 걸립니까?
succeed *vt.,vi.* (*opp. fail*) sŏnggonghada 성공하다, (*follow*) ittara irŏnada 잇따라 일어나다, (*be heir to*) twirŭl itta 뒤를 잇다. *He ~ed as a doctor.* Kŭ saramŭn ŭisarosŏ sŏnggonghaessŭmnida. 그 사람은 의사로서 성공했습니다／ *I ~ed to a hard work.* Ŏryŏun irŭl in-gyebadassŭmnida. 어려운 일을 인계받았습니다.
success *n.* (*favorable result*) sŏnggong 성공, (*good for-*

tune) haengun 행운, (*lucky hit*) hit'ŭ 히트. *I don't believe his* ~. Kŭ sarami sŏnggonghariragonŭn mitchi anssŭmnida. 그 사람이 성공하리라고는 믿지 않습니다/ *I don't grudge your* ~. Taegŭi sŏnggongŭl shirŏhanŭn kŏsŭn animnida. 댁의 성공을 싫어하는 것은 아닙니다/ *make* ~ *in life* ch'ulsehada 출세하다.

successful *adj.* sŏnggonghan 성공한. *a* ~ *businessman* sŏnggonghan saŏpka 성공한 사업가/ *a* ~ *candidate* hapkyŏkcha 합격자.

succession *n.* (*sequence*) yŏnsok 연속, (*inheritance*) kyesŭng 계승, (*descent*) sangsok 상속. *a* ~ *of events* sakŏnŭi yŏnsok 사건의 연속/ *Who is next in* ~ *to the throne?* Wangwiŭi taŭm kyesŭngjanŭn nuguimnikka? 왕위의 다음 계승자는 누구입니까?

successor *n.* hugyeja 후계자, sangsogin 상속인.

such *adj.* (*of that kind*) irŏhan 이러한, kŭrŏhan 그러한. *I have never seen* ~ *a large one.* Irŏk'e k'ŭn kŏsŭn pon iri ŏpsŭmnida. 이렇게 큰 것은 본 일이 없습니다/ *Don't be in* ~ *a hurry!* Kŭrŏk'e nŏmu sŏdurŭji mashio. 그렇게 너무 서두르지 마시오/ *I have met many* ~ *people.* Kŭrŏn saramŭl mani manna poassŭmnida. 그런 사람을 많이 만나 보았습니다/ *We had* ~ *sport.* Chŏngmal chaemiissŏssŭmnida. 정말 재미있었습니다.

suck *vt.,vi.* ppalda 빨다. ~ *milk* chŏjŭl ppalda 젖을 빨다/ ~ *one's finger* sonkaragŭl ppalda 손가락을 빨다/ ~ *at one's pipe* p'aip'ŭrŭl ppŏkkŭmppŏkkŭm ppalda 파이프를 뻐끔뻐끔 빨다.

sudden *adj.* (*abrupt*) kapchaksŭrŏun 갑작스러운, (*quickly made*) chŭksŏgŭi 즉석의. *a* ~ *shower* kapchaksŭrŏun sonagi 갑작스러운 소나기/ *a* ~ *cure* ŭnggŭp ch'iryo 응급 치료.

suddenly *adv.* kapchagi 갑자기, (*unexpectedly*) pulshie 불시에. *My younger brother* ~ *disappeared.* Nae tongsaengi kapchagi shilchongtoeŏssŭmnida. 내 동생이 갑자기 실종되었습니다.

sue *vt.,vi.* (*accuse*) kosohada 고소하다, (*plead*) kanch'ŏnghada 간청하다, (*woo*) kuhonhada 구혼하다.

suffer *vi.,vt.* (*bear pain*) koerowahada 괴로와하다, (*un-*

dergo) ipta 입다, (*sustain damage*) sonhaerŭl ipta 손
해를 입다, (*permit*) hŏyonghada 허용하다, (*endure*)
ch'amta 참다. *Korea ~s from a lack of raw materials.*
Han-gugŭn wŏllyo pujogŭro kominhago issŭmnida. 한
국은 원료(原料) 부족으로 고민하고 있읍니다/ *I've ~ed
much loss through him.* Kŭ saram ttaemune k'ŭn
sonhaerŭl poassŭmnida. 그 사람 때문에 큰 손해를 보았읍니
다/ *I'll not ~ such conduct.* Kŭwa kat'ŭn haengdongŭn
yongsŏhaji anŭl kŏshimnida. 그와 같은 행동은 용서하지
않을 것입니다/ *How can you ~ his insolence.* Kŭ saramŭi muryerŭl ŏttŏk'e ch'amsŭmnikka? 그 사람의 무례를
어떻게 참습니까?

suffering *n.* (*pain*) kot'ong 고통, (*injuries*) sonhae 손해.
suffice *vt., vi.* (*satisfy*) manjokshik'ida 만족시키다, (*be
enough*) ch'ungbunhada 충분하다.
sufficient *adj.* (*enough*) ch'ungbunhan 충분한, (*adequate*)
nŏngnŏk'an 넉넉한. *Have we ~ food?* Uri shingnyang-
ŭn ch'ungbunhamnikka? 우리 식량은 충분합니까?
suffrage *n.* (*vote*) t'up'yo 투표, (*right to vote*) sŏn-gŏkwŏn 선거권. *universal ~* pot'ong sŏn-gŏkwŏn 보통 선거
권/ *Is there universal ~ in your country?* Tangshin
nara-enŭn pot'ong sŏn-gŏkwŏni issŭmnikka? 당신 나라
에는 보통 선거권이 있읍니까?
sugar *n.* sŏlt'ang 설탕. *cube ~* kaksŏlt'ang 각설탕/ *raw ~*
hŭksŏlt'ang 흑설탕/ *white ~* paeksŏlt'ang 백설탕/ *~ cane*
sat'angsusu 사탕수수/ *~ bowl* sŏlt'ang kŭrŭt 설탕 그릇/
How much ~ and cream would you like? Sŏlt'anggwa
k'ŭrimŭn ŏlmana t'alkkayo? 설탕과 크림은 얼마나 탈까요?
suggest *vt.* (*hint*) amshihada 암시하다, (*propose*) cheanhada 제안하다. *Well, what would you ~?* Kŭrŏm ŏttŏk'e
hamyŏn choch'iyo? 그럼, 어떻게 하면 좋지요?/ *I ~ you
report this to the conductor.* Ch'ajangege igŏsŭl pogo-
hanŭn ke chok'essŭmnida. 차장에게 이것을 보고하는 게
좋겠읍니다/ *I ~ed going home.* Chibe kajago cheŭihaessŭmnida. 집에 가자고 제의했읍니다/ *Here is what
I ~.* Kŭrŏm irŏk'e hashipshio. 그럼 이렇게 하십시오.
suggestion *n.* (*hint*) amshi 암시, (*proposal*) chean 제안.

I have some ~s to submit. Ch'amgoro tŭril malssŭmi issŭmnida. 참고로 드릴 말씀이 있읍니다/ *Your ~ is good.* Taegŭi cheanŭn hullyunghamnida. 댁의 제안은 훌륭합니다.

suicide *n.* (*killing oneself*) chasal 자살. *commit ~* chasarhada 자살하다/ *an attempted ~* chasal misu 자살 미수/ *A young couple committed a double ~ in a hotel room.* Chŏlmŭn han ssangi hot'el pangesŏ chŏngsarŭl haessŭmnida. 젊은 한 쌍이 호텔 방에서 정사를 했읍니다.

suit *n.* (*garments*) yangbok 양복, (*action*) sosong 소송, (*appeal*) kanch'ŏng 간청, (*wooing*) kuhon 구혼, (*a set*) han pŏl 한 벌. —*vt., vi.* (*adapt*) chŏk'ap'ada 적합하다, (*accord*) ŏullida 어울리다, (*convenient*) p'yŏllihada 편리하다. *an office ~* samubok 사무복/ *sports ~s* undongbok 운동복/ *Would you show me some men's ~s?* Namsŏngbogŭl poyŏ chushilkkayo? 남성복을 보여 주실까요/ *Does the climate ~ your health?* Kihuga taegŭi kŏn-gange chŏk'ap'amnikka? 기후가 댁의 건강에 적합합니까/ *Any time will ~ you?* Myŏt shiga p'yŏllihalkkayo? 몇 시가 편리할까요/ *Does this skirt ~ me?* I sŭk'ŏt'ŭga na-ege ŏullimnikka? 이 스커트가 나에게 어울립니까?

suitable (*fitting*) chŏktanghan 적당한, (*becoming*) ŏullinŭn 어울리는.

suitcase *n.* yŏhaeng kabang 여행 가방, syut'ŭk'eisŭ 슈트케이스. *May I take the ~ with me into the cabin?* Yŏhaeng kabangŭn kaekshillo kajigo tŭrŏgado choch'iyo? 여행 가방은 객실로 가지고 들어가도 좋지요?

suite *n.* (*train*) suhaengwŏn 수행원, (*set*) (han) pŏl (한) 벌. *the president and his ~* taet'ongnyŏnggwa kŭ irhaeng 대통령과 그 일행/ *a ~ of furniture* kagu han pŏl 가구 한 벌.

sulk *vi.* (*be sulky*) shiltchuk'ada 실쭉하다. —*n. in the ~s* shiltchuk'ayŏ 실쭉하여.

sulky *adj.* (*sullen*) shiltchuk'an 실쭉한, ttunghan 뚱한. *That girl is a little ~.* Kŭ sonyŏnŭn chigŭm shiltchuk'ae issŭmnida. 그 소녀는 지금 실쭉해 있읍니다.

sulphur *n.* yuhwang 유황.

sultry *adj.* mudŏun 무더운. ~ *weather* mudŏun nalssi 무더운 날씨.

sum *n.* (*total amount*) hapkye 합계, (*amount of money*) aeksu 액수, (*outline*) kaeyo 개요, (*calculation*) kyesan 계산. *a large*[*small*] ~ *of money* kŏaeg[soaeg]ŭi ton 거액[소액]의 돈.

summarize *vt.* (*sum up*) yoyak'ada 요약하다.

summary *n.* (*epitome*) yoyak 요약, (*brief account*) chŏgyo 적요(摘要).

summer *n.* yŏrŭm 여름. —*adj.* yŏrŭmŭi 여름의. ~ *vacation*[*holidays*] yŏrŭm hyuga 여름 휴가/ *a* ~ *resort* p'isŏji 피서지/ *Let's spend* ~ *holidays at the Haeundae beach.* Yŏrŭm hyuganŭn Haeundae haesuyokchangesŏ ponaepshida. 여름 휴가는 해운대 해수욕장에서 보냅시다.

summon *vt.* (*order to come*) sohwanhada 소환하다, (*convoke*) sojip'ada 소집하다. —*n.* (*pl.*) (*citation*) sohwanchang 소환장. ~ *a servant* hainŭl pullŏnaeda 하인을 불러내다/ *be* ~*ed* sohwandanghada 소환당하다.

sun *n.* hae 해, t'aeyang 태양, (*sunshine*) haetpit 햇빛. ~ *bath* ilgwangyok 일광욕/ ~ *flower* haebaragi 해바라기/ ~ *shade* yangsan 양산/ ~ *stroke* ilsapyŏng 일사병/ *The* ~ *comes up.* Haega ttŭmnida. 해가 뜹니다/ *The* ~ *goes down.* Haega chimnida. 해가 집니다.

sunbeam *n.* haetpit 햇빛, ilgwang 일광.

sunburned, sunburnt *adj.* haetpyŏt'e t'an 햇볕에 탄. *You've got nicely* ~. Pogichok'e haetpyŏt'e t'asyŏtkŭnyo. 보기좋게 햇볕에 타셨군요.

Sunday *n.* iryoil 일요일, kongil 공일. *Call again before* ~. Iryoil chŏne tto oshipshio. 일요일 전에 또 오십시오/ *Do you usually go to church on* ~? Taegŭn ŏnjena iryoillal kyohoee kashimnikka? 댁은 언제나 일요일날 교회에 가십니까?

sundry *adj.* katkajiŭi 갖가지의. ~ *expenses* chappi 잡비/ ~ *goods* chap'wa 잡화.

sunlight *n.* haetpit 햇빛, ilgwang 일광.

sunny *adj.* haetpyŏt tchoenŭn 햇볕 쬐는, yangjibarŭn 양지바른. *Do you think it will be* ~ *tomorrow?* Naeil nalssiga chok'essŭmnikka? 내일 날씨가 좋겠읍니까?

sunrise *n.* haedoji 해돋이, saebyŏngnyŏk 새벽녘.

sunset *n.* haegŏrŭm 해거름, ilmol 일몰.

sup *vi., vt.* (*eat supper*) chŏnyŏkpabŭl mŏkta 저녁밥을 먹다, (*sip*) holtchakholtchak mashida 홀짝홀짝 마시다. —*n.* han mogŭm 한 모금, hanip 한입.

superficial *adj.* (*external*) p'yomyŏnŭi 표면의, (*shallow*) ch'ŏnbak'an 천박한. *a ~ wound* oesang 외상(外傷)/ *a ~ knowledge* ch'ŏnbak'an chishik 천박한 지식.

superintendent *adj.* (*inspector*) kamdokcha 감독자, (*manager*) kwallija 관리자, (*director*) chihwija 지휘자. *a mine ~* kwangsan kamdokkwan 광산 감독관/ *the ~ of education* kyoyukkam 교육감.

superior *adj.* (*higher in rank*) sanggŭbŭi 상급의, (*excellent*) usuhan 우수한, (*proud*) kŏmanhan 거만한. *a ~ officer* kogŭp kwalli 고급 관리/ *~ persons* usuhan saramdŭl 우수한 사람들/ *be ~ to...* ...poda usuhada ...보다 우수하다/ *You are ~ to me in learning.* Hakshige issŏ tangshinŭn naboda usuhamnida. 학식에 있어 당신은 나보다 우수합니다.

supernatural *adj.* (*beyond nature*) ch'ojayŏnŭi 초자연의, (*abnormal*) isanghan 이상한, (*mysterious*) shinbiroun 신비로운.

supersonic *adj.* ch'oŭmsogŭi 초음속의. *~ speed* ch'oŭmsok 초음속/ *~ waves* ch'oŭmp'a 초음파.

superstition *n.* mishin 미신.

supervise *vt.* (*superintend*) kamdok'ada 감독하다, (*watch over*) kwallihada 관리하다.

supervisor *n.* kamdok(kwan) 감독(관). *a floor ~* maejang kamdok 매장(賣場) 감독/ *a mess ~* shiktang kamdok 식당 감독.

supper *n.* chŏnyŏk (shiksa) 저녁 (식사). *prepare ~* chŏnyŏgŭl chitta 저녁을 짓다/ *take ~* chŏnyŏk shiksarŭl hada 저녁 식사를 하다/ *Is ~ ready?* Chŏnyŏk chunbinŭn toeŏssŭmnikka? 저녁 준비는 되었읍니까/ *We are at ~ now.* Chigŭm chŏnyŏgŭl mŏkko issŭmnida. 지금 저녁을 먹고 있읍니다.

supplement *n.* (*appendix*) purok 부록, (*addition*) ch'uga 추가. *a ~ to the Dong-a Ilbo* tongailboŭi purok 동아일보의 부록/ *a New Year ~* saehae purok 새해 부록.

supply *vt.* (*provide*) konggŭp'ada 공급하다, (*make up for*) poch'unghada 보충하다. *—n.* (*~ing*) konggŭp 공급, (*stock*) chŏjangp'um 저장품, (*pl.*) (*provision*) yangshik 양식. *Our school supplies food for the children.* Uri hakkyo-esŏnŭn adongdŭrege kŭpshigŭl hamnida. 우리 학교에서는 아동들에게 급식(給食)을 합니다/ *We have a good ~ on hand.* Hyŏnp'umŭl ch'ungbunhi kajigo issŭmnida. 현품을 충분히 가지고 있읍니다/ *Our supplies have fallen short.* Yangshigi ttallige toeŏssŭmnida. 양식이 딸리게 되었읍니다.

support *vt.* (*hold up*) chit'aenghada 지탱하다, (*back*) chijihada 지지하다, (*maintain*) puyanghada 부양하다, (*endure*) kyŏndida 견디다. *—n.* (*help*) huwŏn 후원, (*maintenance*) puyang 부양. *I have a large family to ~.* Nanŭn taegajogŭl puyanghago issŭmnida. 나는 대가족을 부양하고 있읍니다/ *I can't ~ the fatigue no longer.* Ije tŏ p'irorŭl kyŏndiŏ nael suga ŏpsŭmnida. 이제 더 피로를 견디어 낼 수가 없읍니다/ *We need your ~.* Tangshinŭi chijiga p'iryohamnida. 당신의 지지가 필요합니다/ *I received his active personal ~.* Kŭ saramŭi chŏkkŭkchŏgin huwŏnŭl padassŭmnida. 그 사람의 적극적인 후원을 받았읍니다.

supporter *n.* (*advocate*) chijija 지지자, (*prop*) chiju 지주(支柱), (*surg.*) pungdae 붕대.

suppose *vt.* (*imagine*) sangsanghada 상상하다, (*assume*) kajŏnghada 가정하다, (*guess*) ch'uch'ŭk'ada 추측하다, (*think*) saenggak'ada 생각하다. *Let's ~ the news is true.* Kŭ nyusŭga sashirirago kajŏnghae tupshida. 그 뉴스가 사실이라고 가정해 둡시다/ *What do you ~ he wanted?* Kŭ sarami muŏsŭl wŏnhaettago ch'uch'ŭk'ashimnikka? 그 사람이 무엇을 원했다고 추측하십니까/ *Will he come? Yes, I ~ so.* Kŭ sarami olkkayo? Ne, kŭrŏl kŏmnida. 그 사람이 올까요? 네, 그럴 겁니다/ *S~ we go to bed.* Chanŭn ke ŏttŏssŭmnikka? 자는 게 어떻습니까/

Supposing it rains, what shall we do? Piga ondamyŏn ŏtchŏjiyo? 비가 온다면 어쩌지요?

suppress *vt.* (*put down*) chinap'ada 진압하다, (*stop*) kŭmjihada 금지하다, (*keep secret*) sumgida 숨기다. ~ *a revolt* p'oktongŭl chinap'ada 폭동을 진압하다/ *Meetings were ~ed by the police.* Hoehabŭn kyŏnggwane ŭihae kŭmjidoeŏssŭmnida. 회합은 경관에 의해 금지되었읍니다.

sure *adj.* (*certain*) hwakshirhan 확실한, (*reliable*) midŭl su innŭn 믿을 수 있는, (*confident*) chashini innŭn 자신이 있는. —*adv.* (*surely*) hwakshirhi 확실히, (*without fail*) kkok 꼭, pandŭshi 반드시. *I'm not ~ why he has gone.* Wae kŭga kabŏryŏnnŭnji hwakshirhi morŭgessŭmnida. 왜 그가 가버렸는지 확실히 모르겠읍니다/ *I'm not ~ if I can do it.* Hal su issŭllŭnji chashini ŏpsŭmnida. 할 수 있을는지 자신이 없읍니다/ *Be ~ to come early.* Kkok iltchik oseyo. 꼭 일찍 오세요/ *I thought he would be ~ to fail.* Kŭ saramŭn pandŭshi shilp'aehal kŏshimnida. 그 사람은 반드시 실패할 것입니다/ *Don't be too ~.* Nŏmu chashinŭl katchi mashio. 너무 자신을 갖지 마시오/ *Are you coming? S~!* Oshigetchiyo? Kagomalgoyo! 오시겠지요? 가고말고요/ *Would you be at the dance? S~ thing!* Ch'umch'urŏ kashigetchiyo? Kagomalgoyo! 춤추러 가시겠지요? 가고말고요!

surely *adv.* (*certainly*) hwakshirhi 확실히, (*without mistake*) t'ŭllimŏpshi 틀림없이, (*with negative*) sŏlma 설마. *S~ you don't mean to go.* Sŏlma kashiryŏgo hanŭn kŏsŭn anil t'ejyo. 설마 가시려고 하는 것은 아닐 테죠.

surety *n.* (*security*) tambo 담보, (*guarantor*) pojŭngin 보증인.

surf *n.* (*on the shore*) millyŏ onŭn p'ado 밀려 오는 파도.

surface *n.* (*outside*) p'yomyŏn 표면. *the ~ of earth* chiguŭi p'yomyŏn 지구의 표면/ *~mail* sŏnbak up'yŏn 선박 우편/ *Please send this parcel by ~ mail.* I sop'orŭl paep'yŏnŭro puch'yŏ chushio. 이 소포를 배편으로 부쳐 주시오.

surge *n.* (*billow*) kŏsen p'ado 거센 파도.

surgeon *n.* oekwa ŭisa 외과 의사. *a naval ~* haegun kunŭi

해군 군의(軍醫)/ *a veterinary* ~ suŭisa 수의사.

surgery *n.* oekwa 외과. *clinical* ~ imsang oekwa 임상 외과.

surgical *adj.* oekwaŭi 외과의. *a* ~ *operation* oekwa susul 외과 수술/ ~ *treatment* oekwa ch'iryo 외과 치료.

surmount *vt.* (*climb*) ollagada 올라가다, (*cross over*) nŏmŏgada 넘어가다, (*overcome*) igyŏ naeda 이겨 내다.

surname *n.* (*last name*) sŏng 성(姓), (*nickname*) pyŏlmyŏng 별명.

surpass *vt.* (*be superior to*) poda ttwiŏnada 보다 뛰어나다, (*excel*) nŭnggahada 능가하다. *He* ~*ed his father in sports.* Sŭp'och'ŭesŏ kŭnŭn abŏjirŭl nŭnggahamnida. 스포츠에서 그는 아버지를 능가합니다.

surplus *n.* (*overplus*) namŏji 나머지, (*excess*) yŏbun 여분, kwaing 과잉. —*adj.* namŏjiŭi 나머지의, yŏbunŭi 여분의. *the* ~ *food* ingyŏ shingnyang 잉여 식량/ *a* ~ *population* kwaing in-gu 과잉 인구.

surprise *n.* (*astonishment*) nollam 놀람, (*something unexpected*) ttŭtpakkŭi kŏt 뜻밖의 것. —*vt.* (*astonish*) nollage hada 놀라게 하다. *What a* ~*!* Aigu kkamtchagiya! 아이구, 깜짝이야/ *It's indeed a* ~ *to see you here.* Yŏgisŏ manage toedani ch'am nollapkunyo. 여기서 만나게 되다니 참 놀랍군요/ *You* ~ *me!* Saram nollage hashinŭngunyo! 사람 놀라게 하시는군요/ *We were* ~*d at the news.* Kŭ soshigŭl tŭtko nollassŭmnida. 그 소식을 듣고 놀랐읍니다/ *To my* ~, *I won the prize.* Nollapkedo nanŭn sangŭl t'assŭmnida. 놀랍게도 나는 상을 탔읍니다.

surrender *n.* (*yielding*) kulbok 굴복, (*transfer*) yangdo 양도. —*vt., vi.* (*yield*) hangbok'ada 항복하다, (*hand over*) nŏmgyo chuda 넘겨 주다, (*give up*) p'ogihada 포기하다. *an unconditional* ~ mujokŏn hangbok 무조건 항복/ *I shall never* ~. Nanŭn hangbok'aji anssŭmnida. 나는 항복하지 않습니다/ ~ *oneself to justice* chasuhada 자수(自首)하다/ *We shall never* ~ *our liberty.* Kyŏlk'o chayunŭn p'ogihaji anssŭmnida. 결코 자유는 포기하지 않습니다.

surround *vt.* (*encircle*) tullŏssada 둘러싸다, (*mil.*) p'owihada 포위하다. *I was* ~*ed by cameramen.* Nanŭn sajin

kijadŭrege p'owirŭl tanghaessŭmnida. 나는 사진 기자들에
게 포위를 당했읍니다.

survey n. (*general view*) kaegwan 개관, (*formal inspection*) chosa 조사, (*measurement*) ch'ŭngnyang 측량.
—vt. (*examine*) chosahada 조사하다, (*measure*) ch'ŭng-
nyanghada 측량하다. *a ~ of Business Management*
kyŏngyŏnghak kaeron 경영학 개론/ *a public opinion ~*
yŏron chosa 여론 조사/ *I ~ed him from head to feet.* Kŭ
saramŭi moriesŏ palkkŭtkkaji chasehi tŭryŏdaboassŭm-
nida. 그 사람의 머리에서 발끝까지 자세히 들여다보았읍니다.

surveyor n. ch'ŭngnyang kisa 측량 기사, (*overseer*) kam-
shija 감시자.

survival n. saengjon(ja) 생존(자). *the ~ of the fittest*
chŏkcha saengjon 적자 생존.

survive vi., vt. (*outlive*) sara namta 살아 남다. *The old
lady has ~d all her children.* Nobuinŭn modŭn cha-
shiktŭlbodado orae sarassŭmnida. 노부인은 모든 자식들
보다도 오래 살았읍니다.

suspect vt., vi. (*doubt*) susanghi yŏgida 수상히 여기다,
(*surmise*) chimjak'ada 짐작하다, (*think likely*) ...anin-ga
saenggak'ada ...아닌가 생각하다. —n. (*suspected person*)
yongŭija 용의자. *I ~ we shall have rain in the afternoon.* Ohuenŭn piga ol kŏt kassŭmnida. 오후에는 비가 올
것 같습니다/ *I ~ he is a liar.* Kŭ saramŭn kŏjinmal-
jangiin kŏt kassŭmnida. 그 사람은 거짓말장이인 것 같
습니다/ *a spy ~* sŭp'ai yongŭija 스파이 용의자/ *a ~ in
a murder* sarin yongŭija 살인 용의자.

suspend vt. (*hang up*) maedalda 매달다, (*delay*) yŏn-gihada 연기하다, (*stop*) chungjihada 중지하다. *~ payment*
chiburŭl yŏn-gihada 지불을 연기하다/ *~ a football player*
ch'ukku sŏnsuŭi ch'ulchŏnŭl chŏngjishik'ida 축구 선수의
출전을 정지시키다.

suspension n. (*suspending*) maedalgi 매달기, (*from
office*) chŏngjik 정직, (*from school*) chŏnghak 정학.
(*stoppage of payment*) chibul chŏngji 지불 정지. *~ bridge*
chŏkkyo 적교(吊橋).

suspicion n. (*doubt*) ŭishim 의심, (*distrust*) hyŏmŭi 혐의

(*inkling*) nunch'ich'aem 눈치챔.

suspicious *adj.* (*distrustful*) ŭishimhanŭn 의심하는, (*doubtful*) susanghan 수상한. *I am ～ of his promise.* Kŭ saramŭi yaksogi ŭishimsŭrŏpsŭmnida. 그 사람의 약속이 의심스럽습니다.

sustain *vt.* (*support*) puyanghada 부양하다, (*hold up*) ttŏbatch'ida 떠받치다, (*suffer*) ipta 입다, (*bear*) kyŏndida 견디다. *a large family to ～* manŭn puyang kajok 많은 부양 가족/ *Will this light shelf ～ all these books?* I yak'an sŏnbani i modŭn ch'aegŭl kyŏndiŏ naelkkayo? 이 약한 선반이 이 모든 책을 견디어 낼까요?

sustenance *n.* (*livelihood*) saenghwalbi 생활비, (*food*) ŭmshik 음식, (*nourishment*) yŏngyangmul 영양물. *How shall we get ～?* Ŏttŏk'e saenggyerŭl kkuryŏ nagajiyo? 어떻게 생계를 꾸려 나가지요?

swallow *vt.* (*gulp*) samk'ida 삼키다, (*take in*) kkŭrŏnŏt'a 끌어넣다, (*keep back*) nurŭda 누르다. —*n.* (*bird*) chebi 제비. *The waves ～ed up the swimmer.* P'adoga heŏmch'idŏn saramŭl samk'yŏ pŏryŏssŭmnida. 파도가 헤엄치던 사람을 삼켜 버렸읍니다.

swamp *n.* (*bog*) nŭp 늪, (*marsh*) sŭpchi 습지.

swan *n.* paekcho 백조.

swarm *n.* (*colony*) tte 떼. —*vi.* (*throng*) tterŭl chitta 떼를 짓다. *a ～ of mosquitoes* mogitte 모기떼/ *A crowd of people ～ed to the spot.* Saramdŭri hyŏnjange ugŭlugŭl moyŏdŭrŏssŭmnida. 사람들이 현장에 우글우글 모여 들었읍니다.

swear *vi.,vt.* (*take an oath*) maengsehada 맹세하다, (*curse*) yok'ada 욕하다, (*affirm*) changdamhada 장담하다. *I ～ to God.* Hanŭnimkke maengsehamnida. 하느님께 맹세합니다/ *S～ to speak to truth.* Sashildaero marhagettago maengsehashio. 사실대로 말하겠다고 맹세하시오/ *Stop ～ing at me!* Yogŭn kŭman hashio! 욕은 그만 하시오!

sweat *n.* ttam 땀. —*vi.,vt.* ttami nada 땀이 나다, ttamŭl hŭllida 땀을 흘리다.

sweater *n.* sŭwet'ŏ 스웨터.

sweep *vi.,vt.* (*clean*) ssŭlda 쓸다, (*drive*) ilsohada 일소하다, (*sail along*) sappunsappun kŏtta 사뿐사뿐 걷다, (*extend*) ppŏtta 뻗다. —*n.* (*clearing away*) ch'ŏngso 청소, (*stretch*) pŏmwi 범위, (*advance*) chinbo 진보. ~ *the steps* kyedanŭl ssŭlda 계단을 쓸다/ *She swept into the room.* Kŭnyŏnŭn sappunsappun panguro kŏrŏdŭrŏgassŭmnida. 그녀는 사뿐사뿐 방으로 걸어들어갔습니다/ *The coast ~s northwards.* Haeani puktchoguro ppŏdŏ issŭmnida. 해안이 북쪽으로 뻗어 있습니다.

sweet *adj.* (*taste of sugar*) tan 단, (*fragrant*) hyanggŭt'an 향긋한, (*pleasing*) kibun choŭn 기분 좋은, (*dear*) sarangsŭrŏun 사랑스러운, (*kind*) ch'injŏrhan 친절한, (*pretty*) yeppŭn 예쁜. —*n.* (*sweetmeat*) kwaja 과자, (*sweetheart*) aein 애인, yŏnin 연인. *Do you like your coffee ~?* K'op'irŭl talge halkkayo? 코피를 달게 할까요? / *I don't like ~ things.* Nanŭn tan kŏsŭl choahaji anssŭmnida. 나는 단 것을 좋아하지 않습니다/ *Don't the roses smell ~?* Changmiga hyanggŭt'aji anssŭmnikka? 장미가 향긋하지 않습니까/ *Doesn't this hat look ~?* I moja yeppŭjiyo? 이 모자 예쁘지요/ *Isn't the baby ~?* Agiga kwiyŏpchiyo? 아기가 귀엽지요/ *It is very ~ of you.* Ch'injŏrhi hae chuŏ komawayo. 친절히 해 주어 고마와요/ *I bought him ~s at the shop.* Kageesŏ kŭege kwajarŭl sajuŏssŭmnida. 가게에서 그에게 과자를 사주었습니다/ *I can't speak because I have a ~ in my mouth.* Ibe kwajarŭl mulgo issŏ marŭl hal suga ŏpsŭmnida. 입에 과자를 물고 있어 말을 할 수가 없습니다.

sweeten *vt., vi.* talge hada[toeda] 달게 하다[되다].

sweetheart *n.* aein 애인, yŏnin 연인. *See you later, ~!* Najunge manna, chagi! 나중에 만나, 자기!

swell *vi., vt.* (*grow bigger*) pup'ulda 부풀다, (*be inflated*) p'aengch'anghada 팽창하다, (*bulge out*) pulluk'aejida 불룩해지다, (*bruise*) puŏorŭda 부어오르다. —*n.* (*dandy*) mŏtchangi 멋쟁이. *My face began to ~ up.* Nae ŏlguri puŏorŭgi shijak'aessŭmnida. 내 얼굴이 부어오르기 시작했습니다/ *What a ~ you are!* Chŏngmal mŏtchangigunyo! 정말 멋쟁이군요!

swerve *vi., vt.* (*turn aside*) pinnagada 빗나가다. *Don't ~ from your purpose.* Mokchŏgŭl pakkuji mashio. 목적을 바꾸지 마시오.

swift *adj.* (*rapid*) pparŭn 빠른, (*speedy*) chŭkkakchŏgin 즉각적인. *a ~ runner* pparŭn chuja 빠른 주자(走者)/ *a ~ response* chŭktap 즉답.

swim *vi., vt.* heŏmch'ida 헤엄치다, suyŏnghada 수영하다. *Can you ~ well?* Heŏmŭl chal ch'ishimnikka? 헤엄을 잘 치십니까/ *I cannot ~ a stroke.* Chogŭmdo heŏmŭl mot ch'imnida. 조금도 헤엄을 못 칩니다.

swimmer *n.* heŏmch'inŭn saram 헤엄치는 사람.

swimming *n.* suyŏng 수영. *In summer, I like to go to sea for ~.* Yŏrŭmenŭn pada-e suyŏngharŏ kagirŭl choahamnida. 여름에는 바다에 수영하러 가기를 좋아합니다.

swindle *vt.* (*cheat*) sogida 속이다, (*fraud*) sagihada 사기하다. *Some people are easily ~d.* Ŏttŏn saramŭn chal soksŭmnida. 어떤 사람은 잘 속습니다.

swindler *n.* sagikkun 사기꾼. *a check ~* sup'yo sagikkun 수표 사기꾼.

swine *n.* (*pigs*) twaeji 돼지.

swing *vi., vt.* (*sway*) hŭndŭllida 흔들리다, (*round*) tolda 돌다, (*vibrate*) hŭndŭlda 흔들다. —*n.* (*apparatus*) kŭne 그네, (*music*) sŭwing ŭmak 스윙 음악. *She was ~ing her arms.* Kŭnyŏnŭn p'arŭl hŭndŭlgo issŏssŭmnida. 그녀는 팔을 흔들고 있었습니다/ *get on a ~* kŭnerŭl ttwida 그네를 뛰다/ *a ~ rope* kŭnechul 그네줄/ *in full ~* hanch'ang 한창/ *The work is in full ~.* Irŭn hanch'ang chinhaeng chunge issŭmnida. 일은 한창 진행 중에 있읍니다.

switch *n.* (*electr.*) sŭwich'i 스위치, (*railway*) chŏnch'ŏlgi 전철기. —*vt., vi.* (*electr.*) sŭwich'irŭl t'ulda 스위치를 틀다, (*change*) pakkuŏ nŏt'a 바꾸어 넣다, (*turn on or off*) k'yŏda 켜다, kkŭda 끄다. *We ~ed places.* Urinŭn changsorŭl sŏro pakkuŏssŭmnida. 우리는 장소를 서로 바꾸었읍니다/ *Don't ~ off yet, please.* Ajik kkŭji mashipshio. 아직 끄지 마십시오/ *S~ on the light, please.* Purŭl k'yoshipshio. 불을 켜십시오/ *~board* paejŏnban 배전반.

swoon vi. (faint) kijŏrhada 기절하다. —n. kijŏl 기절. She ~ed at the news. Kŭ soshigŭl tŭtko kŭ puinŭn kijŏrhaessŭmnida. 그 소식을 듣고 그 부인은 기절했읍니다.

sword n. k'al 칼. draw the ~ k'arŭl ppopta 칼을 뽑다/ whet a ~ k'arŭl kalda 칼을 갈다/ ~ dance k'alch'um 칼춤/ Hold! Put up your ~! Chamkkan, k'arŭl kŏdushio! 잠깐, 칼을 거두시오!

symbol n. (emblem) sangjing 상징, (mark) kiho 기호. a chemical ~ hwahak kiho 화학 기호. The Cross is the ~ of Christianity. Shipchaganŭn kidokkyoŭi sangjingimnida. 십자가는 기독교의 상징입니다.

symbolize vt. (be a symbol of) sangjinghada 상징하다, (stand for) nat'anaeda 나타내다.

sympathetic adj. (compassionate) tongjŏnghanŭn 동정하는, (congenial) maŭme tŭnŭn 마음에 드는. ~ looks tongjŏnghanŭn ŏlgul 동정하는 얼굴/ ~ strike tongjŏng p'aŏp 동정 파업.

sympathize vi. tongjŏnghada 동정하다, (agree) tongjohada 동조하다, (condole) munsanghada 문상(問喪)하다. I ~ heartily with you. Chinshimŭro tongjŏnghamnida. 진심으로 동정합니다/ I ~ with your grief. Tangshinŭi sŭlp'ŭme tongjŏnghamnida. 당신의 슬픔에 동정합니다.

sympathy n. (compassion) tongjŏng(shim) 동정(심), (favor) ch'ansŏng 찬성, (condolence) choŭi 조의(弔意). You have my sympathies=Accept my sympathies. Ch'am andwaessŭmnida. 참 안됐읍니다/ My deepest sympathies. Muŏra malssŭmdŭril suga ŏpsŭmnida. 무어라 말씀드릴 수가 없읍니다/ I have some ~ with their views. Kŭdŭrŭi kyŏnhaee ŏnŭ chŏngdo ch'ansŏnghamnida. 그들의 견해에 어느 정도 찬성합니다.

symphony n. (music) kyohyanggok 교향곡. a ~ orchestra kyohyangaktan 교향악단/ Beethoven's Fifth S~ Bet'obenŭi cheo kyohyanggok 베토벤의 제 5 교향곡.

symptom n. (sign) chingjo 징조, (med.) chŭnghu 증후. the ~s of malaria hakchirŭi chŭnghu 학질의 증후/ the ~ of peace p'yŏnghwaŭi chingjo 평화의 징조.

synagogue n. yut'ae kyohoe 유태 교회.

synchronize *vt.,vi.* (*recur together*) tongshie irŏnada 동
시에 일어나다.

synchronous recording tongshi nogŭm 동시 녹음.

synonym *n.* tongŭiŏ 동의어(同意語).

syntax *n.* (*gram.*) kumunnon 구문론.

synthesis *n.* chonghap 종합.

synthetic *adj.* (*of synthesis*) chonghap'an 종합한, (*artificial*) injoŭi 인조(人造)의. ~*fiber* hapsŏng sŏmyu 합성
섬유/ ~*resin* hapsŏng suji 합성 수지/ ~*jewel* injo posŏk
인조 보석.

syphilis *n.* maedok 매독. *contract* ~ maedoge kŏllida 매
독에 걸리다.

syringe *n.* (*injection*) chusagi 주사기, (*washer*) sech'ŏkki
세척기.

system *n.* (*arrangement*) chojik 조직, (*institution*) chedo
제도, (*method*) pangshik 방식, (*body*) shinch'e 신체. *the
social* ~ sahoe chojik 사회 조직/ *a network of* ~ cho-
jingmang 조직망/ *the easy-payment* ~ wŏlbu chedo 월부
제도/ *the inheritance* ~ sangsok chedo 상속 제도/ *the
quota* ~ haltang chedo 할당 제도/ *a new* ~ *of teaching*
saeroun kyosu pangshik 새로운 교수 방식/ *a metric* ~
mit'ŏpŏp 미터법(法)/ *What* ~ *do you go on?* Ŏttŏn
pangshigŭro hago issŭmnikka? 어떤 방식으로 하고 있읍니
까/ *a crude* ~ chojap'an pangbŏp 조잡한 방법/ *a human* ~ inch'e 인체/ *Strong drink is bad for the* ~.
Surŭn mome choch'i anssŭmnida. 술은 몸에 좋지 않습니다.

systematic *adj.* chojikchŏgin 조직적인.

systematically *adv.* chojikchŏguro 조직적으로, chŏngyŏn-
hage 정연하게.

systematize *vt.* chojik'wahada 조직화하다, (*classify*)
pullyuhada 분류하다.

◄ **T** ►

tab *n.* (*accounting*) kyesan 계산. *Keep close* ~*s on daily
sales.* Maeirŭi maesanggorŭl semirhi kyesanhashio. 매일

table 546 take

의 매상고를 세밀히 계산하시오.

table *n.* t'eibŭl 테이블, t'akcha 탁자, shikt'ak 식탁, (*food*) yori 요리, (*list*) p'yo 표. *Do you mind moving to a small ~ over there?* Chŏtchok chagŭn t'eibŭlo omgyŏ chushipshio. 저쪽 작은 테이블로 옮겨 주십시오/ *T~ for one, please.* Irinbun yorisangŭl put'ak'amnida. 1인분 요리상(料理床)을 부탁합니다/ ~ *talk* chwadam 좌담.

table d'hôte *n.* chongshik 정식.

tablespoon *n.* k'ŭn sutkarak 큰 숟가락.

tablet *n.* (*flat slab*) p'ae 패(牌), (*pill*) chŏngje 정제(錠劑). *a commemorable ~* kinyŏmp'ae 기념패/ *a sugar-coated ~* tangŭijŏng 당의정.

taboo, tabu *n.* kŭmgi 금기, t'ŏbu 터부.

tackle *n.* (*gear*) togu 도구, kigu 기구. *—vt.* (*seize*) putchapta 붙잡다, (*grapple with*) tallabutta 달라붙다. *a fishing ~* nakshi togu 낚시 도구.

tactics *n.* (*strategy*) chŏnsul 전술, (*artful devices*) sulch'aek 술책. *clever ~* kyomyohan chŏnsul 교묘한 전술/ *resort to ~* sulch'aegŭl purida 술책을 부리다/ *money ~* maesu chakchŏn 매수 작전.

tadpole *n.* olch'aengi 올챙이.

tag *n.* (*label*) kkorip'yo 꼬리표, pujŏn 부전. *a price ~* kagyŏkp'yo 가격표/ *I'll take off ten percent from the price on the ~.* Chŏngkap'yo-esŏ ship p'ŏsent'ŭrŭl kkakka tŭrigessŭmnida. 정가표에서 10 퍼센트를 깎아 드리겠읍니다.

tail *n.* kkori 꼬리.

tailor *n.* chaebongsa 재봉사, yangbokchŏm 양복점. *—vt.* match'uŏ mandŭlda 맞추어 만들다. *—vi.* (yangbogŭl) chitta (양복을) 짓다. *He is well ~ed.* Kŭŭi osŭn chal chiŏjyŏtta. 그의 옷은 잘 지어졌다.

take *vi., vt.* (*seize*) chapta 잡다, (*carry*) katko kada 갖고 가다, (*go on board*) t'ada 타다, (*eat, drink*) mŏkta 먹다, mashida 마시다, (*need*) soyodoeda 소요되다, (*consider*) ...irago saenggak'ada ···이라고 생각하다, (*accept*) patta 받다, (*catch*) kŏllida 걸리다. *Are you taking it abroad?* Oegugŭro katko kashil kŏmnikka? 외

국으로 갖고 가실 겁니까/ *You had better ~ a lunch along*.
Chŏmshimŭl katko kashinŭn ke choŭl kŏmnida. 점심을
갖고 가시는게 좋을 겁니다/ ~ *taxi* t'aekshirŭl t'ada 택시를
타다/ ~ *a plane* pihaenggirŭl t'ada 비행기를 타다/ *Will
you ~ tea or coffee*? Hongch'arŭl tŭshigessŭmnikka,
k'opi'rŭl tŭshigessŭmnikka? 홍차를 드시겠읍니까, 코피를
드시겠읍니까/ *It won't take but a few minutes*. Myŏt
pun an kollil kŏmnida. 몇 분 안 걸릴 겁니다/ *I've ~n
up too much of your time*. Nŏmu oraettongan shillyehae-
ssŭmnida. 너무 오랫동안 실례했읍니다/ *Do you ~ me for
a fool?* Narŭl paboro saenggak'ashimnikka? 나를 바보로
생각하십니까/ *May I ~ your overcoat?* Chega oet'urŭl
pada tŭrilkkayo? 제가 외투를 받아 드릴까요/ *I'll ~ five
thousand won for it*. Och'ŏnwŏn padayagessŭmnida.
5,000원 받아야겠읍니다/ ~ *it easy* (*not hurry*) sŏdurŭji
ant'a 서두르지 않다/ *You'd better ~ it easy*. Nŏmu
shin-gyŏng ssŭji mashio. 너무 신경 쓰지 마시오/ ~ *off*
(*remove*) pŏtta 벗다, (*deduct*) kkakta 깎다. *May I ~
my coat off?* Oet'urŭl pŏsŏdo chossŭmnikka? 외투를
벗어도 좋습니까/ *I'll ~ off fifty*. Oshibwŏnŭl kkakka
tŭrijiyo. 50원을 깎아 드리지요/ ~ *over* (*succeed to*) itta
잇다/ *I'm to ~ over the business*. Kŭ samurŭl naega
in-gyebatkiro toeo issŭmnida. 그 사무를 내가 인계받기로
되어 있읍니다.

take-off *n*. (*start*) ch'ulbal 출발.

tale *n*. (*story*) iyagi 이야기, (*rumor*) somun 소문. *a
fairy ~* tonghwa 동화/ *a folk ~* minhwa 민화(民話)/ *a
tall ~* hŏp'ung 허풍/ *I told them ~s of my boyhood*.
Nanŭn kŭdŭrege nae ŏril chŏk iyagirŭl haejuŏssŭm-
nida. 나는 그들에게 내 어릴 적 이야기를 해주었읍니다.

talent *n*. (*faculty*) chaenŭng 재능, (*natural ability*)
suwan 수완, (*people of ability*) injae 인재, (*performers*)
t'aellŏnt'ŭ 탤런트. *I have no ~ for music*. Nanŭn
ŭmage chaenŭngi ŏpsŭmnida. 나는 음악에 재능이 없읍니
다/ ~*ed* chaenŭngi innŭn 재능이 있는/ *a ~ed painter*
ch'ŏnjae hwaga 천재 화가/ *My, she is ~*. Ŏmŏ, chŏngmal chaenŭngi itkunyo. 어머, 정말 재능이 있군요.

talisman *n.* pujŏk 부적.

talk *n.* (*speech*) iyagi 이야기, (*conference*) sangdam 상담, (*prate*) kaeksŏl 객설, (*gossip*) somun 소문. —*vt.* (*speak*) iyagihada 이야기하다, (*consult*) sangdamhada 상담하다, (*prate*) chikkŏrida 지껄이다. *a foolish* ~ ŏrisŏgŭn iyagi 어리석은 이야기/ *an idle* ~ kaektam 객담/ *I want a little* ~ *with you.* Hago ship'ŭn iyagiga chŏm issŭmnida. 하고 싶은 이야기가 좀 있읍니다/ *No back* ~ ! Maldaekkuhaji ma ! 말대꾸하지 마/ *Don't* ~ *so fast, please.* Nŏmu ppalli iyagihaji mashio. 너무 빨리 이야기하지 마시오/ *We often* ~*ed about you.* Tangshin iyagirŭl mani haessŭmnida. 당신 이야기를 많이 했읍니다/ *I should like to* ~ *you.* Iyagi chŏm hapshida. 이야기 좀 합시다.

talkative *adj.* (*chatty*) sudasŭrŏn 수다스런. *a* ~ *girl* sudasŭrŏn kyejibai 수다스런 계집아이.

talkie *n.* palsŏng yŏnghwa 발성 영화. *A fine* ~*s was released.* Choŭn yŏnghwaga kaebongdoeŏssŭmnida. 좋은 영화가 개봉되었읍니다.

tall *adj.* (*high*) nop'ŭn 높은, (*stature*) k'i k'ŭn 키 큰, (*grand*) koengjanghan 굉장한. *a* ~ *building* nop'ŭn kŏnmul 높은 건물/ *How* ~ *are you?* K'iga ŏlmana toemnikka? 키가 얼마나 됩니까/ *How* ~ *is the tower?* Chŏ tabŭi nop'inŭn ŏlmana toemnikka? 저 탑의 높이는 얼마나 됩니까/ *a* ~ *price* pissan kap 비싼 값.

tally *vi.* (*correspond*) puhap'ada 부합하다, (*agree*) ilch'ihada 일치하다. *Does your list* ~ *with mine?* Tangshinŭi myŏngsesŏnŭn nae kŏtkwa ilch'ihamnikka? 당신의 명세서는 내 것과 일치합니까?

tame *adj.* (*domesticated*) kildŭrin 길들인, (*gentle*) sunhan 순한. —*vt.* (*break in*) kildŭrida 길들이다. *a* ~ *bear* kildŭrin kom 길들인 곰.

tan *vt.,vi.* (*hide*) mudujirhada 무두질하다, (*by the sun*) haetpyŏt'e t'ada 햇볕에 타다. ~ *skins* kajugŭl mudujirhada 가죽을 무두질하다/ *He was well* ~*ned.* Kŭ saramŭn ŏlguri pogijok'e t'a issŏssŭmnida. 그 사람은 얼굴이 보기 좋게 타 있었읍니다.

tangerine *n.* kyul 귤, orenji 오렌지.

tangle *vi.*, *vt.* (*snarl*) ŏngk'ŭrŏjida 엉클어지다, (*entangle*) ŏngk'ige hada 엉키게 하다. ~*d hair* ŏngk'in mŏrik'arak 엉킨 머리카락/ ~ *with* ...wa tat'uda …와 다투다/ *You shouldn't* ~ *with Poktong*. Poktongiwa ssawŏsŏnŭn an twae. 복동이와 싸워서는 안 돼.

tango *n.* (*dance*) t'aenggo ch'um 탱고 춤. *dance the* ~ t'aengorŭl ch'uda 탱고를 추다.

tank *n.* (*for fluids*) mult'aengk'ŭ 물탱크, sujo 수조(水槽), (*mil.*) chŏnch'a 전차. *a gasoline* ~ kasollin t'aengk'ŭ 가솔린 탱크 /~ *car* yujoch'a 유조차,/ ~ *station* kŭpsu yŏk 급수 역(驛).

tap *n.* (*cork*) magae 마개, kkokchi 꼭지, (*light blow*) t'okt'ok ch'inŭn sori 톡톡 치는 소리. —*vt.*, *vi.* (*pat*) kabyŏpke ch'ida 가볍게 치다. *turn on*[*off*] *a* ~ magaerŭl yŏlda[chamgŭda] 마개를 열다[잠그다]/ *I heard a* ~ *at the door*. Mun tudŭrinŭn sorirŭl tŭrŏssŭmnida. 문 두드리는 소리를 들었읍니다/ *Someone* ~*ped me on the shoulder*. Nugun-gaga nae ŏkkaerŭl t'uk ch'yŏssŭmnida. 누군가가 내 어깨를 툭 쳤읍니다.

tape *n.* (*band*) kkŭn 끈, t'eip'ŭ 테이프. *cut the* ~ t'eip'ŭrŭl kkŭnt'a 테이프를 끊다/ *the finish* ~ kol t'eip'ŭ 골 테이프/ *a recording* ~ nogŭm t'eip'ŭ 녹음 테이프.

tar *n.* t'arŭ 타르. —*vt.* t'arŭrŭl ch'irhada 타르를 칠하다.

target *n.* (*mark*) kwanyŏk 과녁, p'yojŏk 표적. *an export* ~ such'ul mokp'yoaek 수출 목표액/ ~ *practice* sagyŏk yŏnsŭp 사격 연습.

tariff *n.* (*tax rate*) seyul 세율, (*price list*) yogŭmp'yo 요금표. *a customs* ~ kwanseyul 관세율/ *a railway* ~ ch'ŏlto unimp'yo 철도 운임표.

tarnish *n.* (*loss of brightness*) hŭrim 흐림, (*discoloration*) pyŏnsaek 변색. —*vi.* (*discolor*) pyŏnsaek'ada 변색하다, (*dull*) hŭrige hada 흐리게 하다, (*sully*) tŏrŏp'ida 더럽히다. *His reputation is* ~*ed*. Kŭ saramŭi myŏngyega sonsangdŏeŏssŭmnida. 그 사람의 명예가 손상 되었읍니다.

tart *adj.* (*sour*) shik'ŭmhan 시큼한, shin 신. ~ *apples*

shin sagwa 신 사과.

task *n.* (*piece of work*) il 일, (*duty*) chingmu 직무, (*lesson*) kwaŏp 과업/ *My ~ is now completed.* Nae irŭn ije kkŭnnassŭmnida. 내 일은 이제 끝났읍니다/ *I have a heavy ~ before me.* Nae ap'enŭn ŏryŏun iri kidarigo issŭmnida. 내 앞에는 어려운 일이 기다리고 있읍니다/ *a home ~* (*Brit.*) sukche 숙제.

tassel *n.* (*tuft*) sul 술.

taste *n.* (*flavor*) mat 맛, (*liking*) kiho 기호. —*vt., vi.* matpoda 맛보다, ...han mashi itta ...한 맛이 있다. *Won't you have a ~ of this cake?* I kwaja chogŭm matposhiji ank'essŭmnikka? 이 과자 조금 맛보시지 않겠읍니까/ *~ burnt* t'annaega nada 탄내가 나다/ *How does it ~?* Mashi ŏttŏssŭmnikka? 맛이 어떻습니까/ *This beer ~s good.* I maekchunŭn mashi chossŭmnida. 이 맥주는 맛이 좋습니다.

tasty *adj.* (*savory*) mat choŭn 맛 좋은. *~ food* madinnŭn ŭmshik 맛있는 음식.

tattoo *n.* munshin 문신(文身). —*vt.* munshinhada 문신하다.

taunt *vt.* (*reproach*) namurada 나무라다, (*ridicule*) piutta 비웃다.

tavern *n.* (*public house*) sŏnsulchip 선술집, (*inn*) yŏinsuk 여인숙, chumak 주막. *a beer ~* maekchu hol 맥주 홀.

tax *n.* segŭm 세금. —*vt.* kwasehada 과세하다. *an additional value ~* puga kach'ise 부가 가치세/ *the business ~* yŏngŏpse 영업세/ *the corporation ~* pŏbinse 법인세/ *the income ~* suipse 수입세/ *How much income ~ did you pay?* Suipsenŭn ŏlmana murŏssŭmnikka? 수입세는 얼마나 물었읍니까/ *Does that include ~?* Segŭmi p'ohamdoeŏ issŭmnikka? 세금이 포함되어 있읍니까/ *Yes, it includes sales ~, fifteen percent.* P'anmaese shibo p'ŏsent'ŭga p'ohamdwae issŭmnida. 판매세 15퍼센트가 포함돼 있읍니다/ *~ free goods* myŏnsep'um 면세품/ *It is free of ~.* Kŭgŏsŭn myŏnseimnida. 그것은 면세입니다.

taxable *adj.* kwasehal su innŭn 과세할 수 있는. *~ articles* kwasep'um 과세품.

taxi *n.* t'aekshi 택시. *Where can I catch a ~?* T'aekshirŭl ŏdisŏ chapchiyo? 택시를 어디서 잡지요/ *Please call a ~ for me.* T'aekshirŭl pullŏ chushio. 택시를 불러 주시오/ *Can you call a ~ for me?* T'aekshirŭl pullŏ chushiji ank'essŭmnikka? 택시를 불러 주시지 않겠읍니까/ *~ driver* t'aekshi unjŏnsa 택시 운전사.

tea *n.* ch'a 차(茶). *coarse ~* yŏpch'a 엽차/ *black ~* hong-ch'a 홍차/ *cold ~* naengch'a 냉차/ *How about a cup of ~?* Ch'a han chan tŭshigessŭmnikka? 차 한 잔 드시겠 읍니까/ *I'll fix you ~.* Ch'arŭl chunbihagessŭmnida. 차를 준비하겠읍니다/ *~cup* chachong 차종/ *~pot* ch'a-chujŏnja 차주전자/ *~room* 다방/ *~ party* tagwahoe 다 과회.

teach *vt., vi. (instruct)* karŭch'ida 가르치다, *(educate)* kyoyukshik'ida 교육시키다, *(train)* hullyŏnshik'ida 훈련 시키다. *~ children* airŭl karŭch'ida 아이를 가르치다/ *~ French* Purŏrŭl karŭch'ida 불어를 가르치다/ *Who taught you Korean?* Nuga Han-gugŏrŭl karŭch'yŏ chuŏssŭmni-kka? 누가 한국어를 가르쳐 주었읍니까/ *My tutor taught me Korean.* Kajŏnggyosaga Han-gugŏrŭl karŭch'yŏ chusyŏssŭmnida. 가정교사가 한국어를 가르쳐 주셨읍니다/ *individual ~ing* kaein kyosu 개인 교수.

teacher *n.* kyosa 교사, sŏnsaengnim 선생님.

team *n. (group)* t'im 팀, p'ae 패. *a baseball ~* yagu t'im 야구 팀/ *a football ~* ch'ukku t'im 축구 팀/ *~ work* tanch'e haengdong 단체 행동/ *Is he on your ~?* Kŭinŭn tangshinne t'imimnikka? 그이는 당신네 팀입니 까?

tear *n. (pl.) (teardrop)* nunmul 눈물, *(rip)* tchaejin t'ŭm 째진 틈, *(rent)* t'ŏjin kot 터진 곳. *—vt., vi. (rip)* tchitta 찢다, *(pull violently away)* chabattŭtta 잡아뜯다, *(become torn)* tchaejida 째지다. *shed ~s* nunmurŭl hŭl-lida 눈물을 흘리다/ *wipe one's ~ away* nunmurŭl ssitta 눈물을 씻다/ *~ a letter* p'yŏnjirŭl tchitta 편지를 찢다/ *This cloth will not ~.* I ch'ŏnŭn chomch'ŏrŏm tchijŏ-jiji anssŭmnida. 이 천은 좀처럼 찢어지지 않습니다/ *~ bomb* ch'oerut'an 최루탄.

tease *vt. (annoy)* chipchŏkkŏrida 집적거리다, *(vex)* kwi-

ch'ank'e kulda 귀찮게 굴다, (*importune*) chorŭda 조르다.
~ *a dog* kaerŭl chipchŏkkŏrida 개를 집적거리다/ *Stop
your teasing.* Chom chipchŏkgŏriji mashio. 좀 집적거리
지 마시오/ ~ *mummy for money* ŏmŏnikke tonŭl chorŭda. 어머니께 돈을 조르다.

technic (*technique*) supŏp 수법, kigyo 기교, (*pl.*) chŏn-
munŏ 전문어. *advertising* ~s kwanggo kisul 광고 기술/
manufacturing ~ saengsan kisul 생산 기술.

technical *adj.* kisulchŏgin 기술적인. *a* ~ *adviser* kisul
komun 기술 고문/ ~ *development* kisul kaebal 기술 개발/
~ *aid* kisul wŏnjo 기술 원조.

tedious *adj.* (*dull*) chiruhan 지루한, (*uninteresting*)
hŭngmi ŏmnŭn 흥미 없는. *a* ~ *journey* chiruhan yŏhaeng
지루한 여행/ ~ *work* hŭngmi omnŭn il 흥미 없는 일.

telecamera *n.* mangwŏn sajinki 망원 사진기.

telecast *n.* (*television broadcast*) t'ellebijŏn pangsong
텔레비전 방송.

telegram *n.* chŏnbo 전보. *What is the rate for* ~ *for
Pusan?* Pusankkajiŭi chŏnbo yogŭmŭn ŏlmajiyo? 부산
까지의 전보 요금은 얼마지요/ *I would like to send a* ~ *to
Pusan.* Pusankkaji chŏnborŭl ch'igo shipsŭmnida. 부산
까지 전보를 치고 싶습니다.

telegraph *n.* chŏnshin 전신, (*telegram*) chŏnbo 전보. —*vi.*,
vt. (*wire*) chŏnborŭl ch'ida 전보를 치다. *a* ~ *office*
chŏnshin-guk 전신국/ *submarine* ~ haejŏ chŏnshin 해저
전신/ *Shall I* ~ *or telephone?* Chŏnborŭl ch'ilkkayo,
chŏnhwarŭl kŏlkkayo? 전보를 칠까요, 전화를 걸까요?

telephone *n.* chŏnhwa 전화. —*vi.* chŏnhwarŭl kŏlda 전화
를 걸다. *Have you got a* ~? Taege chŏnhwaga issŭmnikka? 댁에 전화가 있읍니까/ *What is your* ~ *number?*
Taegŭi chŏnhwa pŏnhonŭn myŏt pŏnimnikka? 댁의 전
화 번호는 몇 번입니까/ *May I use your* ~? Chŏnhwa
chom ssŭgessŭmnida. 전화 좀 쓰겠습니다/ *You're wanted on the phone.* Chŏnhwa wassŭmnida. 전화 왔읍니다/
Will you answer the phone, please. Chŏnhwa chom
pada chushigessŭmnikka? 전화 좀 받아 주시겠읍니까/ *a* ~
operator kyohwansu 교환수/ *a* ~ *number* chŏnhwa

pŏnho 전화 번호/ *a ~ directory* chŏnhwa pŏnhobu 전화 번
호부/ *a public ~* kongjung chŏnhwa 공중 전화/ *I will
~ you tomorrow.* Naeil chŏnhwa olligessŭmnida. 내일
전화 올리겠습니다.

telephoto *n.* chŏnsong sajin 전송(電送) 사진.

telereceiver *n.* (*T. V. set*) tellebijŏn susanggi 텔레비전
수상기.

telescope *n.* mangwŏn-gyŏng 망원경. *an astronomical ~*
ch'ŏnch'e mangwŏn-gyŏng 천체 망원경/ *a binocular ~*
ssangan-gyŏng 쌍안경.

teletype *n.* (*teletypewriter*) chŏnshin t'ajagi 전신 타자기,
t'ellet'aip'ŭ 텔레타이프.

television *n.* t'ellebijŏn 텔레비전. *~ set* t'ellebijŏn susanggi 텔레비전 수상기/ *color ~* saekch'ae tellebijŏn 색채 텔
레비전/ *Did you see the boxing match on ~?* T'el-
lebijŏnesŏ kwŏnt'u shihabŭl poassŭmnikka? 텔레비전에
서 권투 시합을 보았습니까/ *Anything good on ~?* T'el-
lebijŏne chaeminanŭn ke issŭmnikka? 텔레비전에 재미
나는 게 있습니까?

tell *vi.,vt.* (*say*) marhada 말하다, (*express*) p'yohyŏnhada
표현하다, (*announce*) allida 알리다, (*know*) alda 알다,
(*distinguish*) shikpyŏrhada 식별하다, (*count*) seda 세다,
(*order*) myŏngnyŏnghada 명령하다. *What do you want
to ~ me?* Musŭn malssŭmŭl hashiryŏmnikka? 무슨 말씀
을 하시렵니까/ *She's the British lady I told you about.*
Chŏbuni naega marhan Yŏngguk puinimnida. 저분이
내가 말한 영국 부인입니다/ *Will you ~ him to call me
later.* Najunge chŏnhwa kŏldorok illŏ chushipshio. 나중에
전화 걸도록 일러 주십시오/ *Will you ~ Mr. Lee that
Mr. Kim is here.* Kimi wattago I sŏnsaengnimkke
chŏnhae chushilkkayo? 김(金)이 왔다고 이(李) 선생님께 전
해 주실까요/ *Can you ~ who that is over there?* Chŏgi
innŭn puni nugushinji ashigessŭmnikka? 저기 있는 분이
누구신지 아시겠습니까/ *How can I ~?* Naega ŏttŏk'e
algessŭmnikka? 내가 어떻게 알겠습니까/ *Do as I ~.* Naega shik'inŭn taero hashio. 내가 시키는 대로 하시오.

teller *n.* (*of bank*) kŭmjŏn ch'ŭllapkye 금전 출납계. *a*

paying ~ chich'ulgye 지출계.

temper *n.* (*disposition*) sŏngmi 성미, (*mood*) kibun 기분, (*anger*) nogi 노기(怒氣). *She was in a good* ~. Puinŭi kibunŭn choassŭmnida. 부인(夫人)의 기분은 좋았읍니다/ *I know her* ~. Kŭ puinŭi sŏngmirŭl chal algo issŭmnida. 그 부인의 성미를 잘 알고 있읍니다/ *a cool* ~ naengjŏnghan sŏngmi 냉정한 성미/ *a calm* ~ onhwahan sŏngmi 온화한 성미/ *I have never seen him out of* ~. Kŭbuni hwa-naenŭn kŏsŭl pon chŏgi ŏpsŭmnida. 그분이 화내는 것을 본 적이 없읍니다/ *have a hot* ~ sŏngmiga kŭp'ada 성미 가 급하다/ *lose one's* ~ hwarŭl naeda 화를 내다/ *keep one's* ~ hwarŭl ch'amta 화를 참다.

temperament *n.* (*natural disposition*) kijil 기질, sŏngmi 성미. *a nervous* ~ shin-gyŏngjil 신경질/ *Korean* ~ *and Korean character* Han-guginŭi kijilgwa sŏngkyŏk 한국 인의 기질과 성격.

temperamental *adj.* (*irritable*) sŏngmi kŭp'an 성미 급한, (*sensitive*) shin-gyŏngjirin 신경질인, (*moody*) ch'imurhan 침울한.

temperance *n.* (*moderation*) chŏlche 절제, (*self-restraint*) chaje 자제. *a* ~ *hotel* surŭl naenoch'i annŭn yŏgwan 술을 내놓지 않는 여관/ *the* ~ *movement* kŭmju undong 금 주 운동/ *a* ~ *society* kŭmjuhoe 금주회.

temperate *adj.* (*moderate*) on-gŏnhan 온건한, (*mild*) onhwahan 온화한. *Be more* ~ *in your language, please.* Malssŭm chom samgashipshio. 말씀 좀 삼가십시오/ ~ *living* chŏlche saenghwal 절제 생활/ *a* ~ *climate* on-hwahan kihu 온화한 기후.

temperature *n.* (*of the air*) ondo 온도, (*of the body*) ch'eon 체온, yŏl 열(熱). *air* ~ kion 기온. *sub-zero* ~*s* yŏnghaŭi ondo 영하의 온도/ *How do you find the* ~ *of the water?* Murŭi ondonŭn ŏttŏssŭmnikka? 물의 온도는 어떻습니까/ *I'll take your* ~. Yŏrŭl chaeŏ pogessŭmnida. 열을 재어 보겠읍니다/ *You have no* ~. Yŏrŭn ŏpsŭmnida. 열은 없읍니다/ *take one's* ~ ch'eonŭl chaeda 체온을 재다.

tempest *n.* p'okp'ungu 폭풍우.

temple *n.* (*Budd.*) chŏl 절, sadang 사당, (*of head*)

kwanjanori 관자놀이. *Where is the Pulguksa ~?* Pulguksanŭn ŏdi issŭmnikka? 불국사는 어디 있읍니까/*Kyongju has many beautiful old ~s.* Kyŏngjuenŭn arŭmdaun
yet chŏri manssŭmnida. 경주에는 아름다운 옛 절이 많습
니다.

temporary *adj.* (*transient*) hanttaeŭi 한때의, ka 가(假),
(*makeshift*) imshi pyŏnt'ongŭi 임시 변통의. *a ~ employee*
imshi koyongin 임시 고용인/ *a ~ bridge* kagyo 가교(假
橋)/ *~ agreement* kagyeyak 가계약.

tempt *v.* (*lure*) yuhok'ada 유혹하다, (*induce*) ...hal saenggagŭl irŭk'ida ...할 생각을 일으키다. *He ~ed me with a
bribe.* Kŭ saramŭn noemullo narŭl yuhok'aessŭmnida.
그 사람은 뇌물로 나를 유혹했읍니다/ *I was ~ed to steal
the book.* Kŭ ch'aegŭl humch'igo ship'ŭn saenggagi
tŭrŏssŭmnida. 그 책을 훔치고 싶은 생각이 들었읍니다.

temptation *n.* (*seduction*) yuhok 유혹. *a ~ of drink*
surŭi yuhok 술의 유혹/ *overcome a ~* yuhogŭl igyŏ
naeda 유혹을 이겨 내다/ *yield to ~* yuhoge ppajida 유혹에
빠지다.

ten *n.,adj.* yŏl(ŭi) 열의, ship(ŭi) 십(10)의. *~ people* yŏl
saram 열 사람/ *~ o'clock* yŏlshi 10시/ *~ percent* ship
p'ŏsent'ŭ 10퍼센트, irhal 1할/ *~ to one* shipchung
p'algu 십중 팔구/ *~ times* ship pae 10배(倍).

tenant *n.* (*of land*) ch'ajiin 차지인(借地人), sojagin 소작
인, (*of house*) sedŭn saram 세든 사람. *~ farmer*
sojagin 소작인/ *~ right* ch'aji[ch'aga]kwŏn 차지[차가]
권.

tend *vi., vt.* (*be apt to*) hagi shwipta 하기 쉽다, (*have a
tendency*) hanŭn kyŏnghyangi itta 하는 경향이 있다,
(*look after*) tolboda 돌보다. *Fruits ~ to decay.* Kwairŭn sanghagi shwipsŭmnida. 과일은 상하기 쉽습니다/
T~ to your own affairs. Tangshin irena maŭmŭl ssŭshio. 당신 일에나 마음을 쓰시오/ *~ the sick* hwanjarŭl
tolboda 환자를 돌보다.

tendency *n.* (*inclination*) kyŏnghyang 경향, (*trend*)
p'ungjo 풍조, (*bent*) sŏngbyŏk 성벽. *a fresh ~* saeroun
kyŏnghyang 새로운 경향/ *the ~ of society* sahoe p'ungjo

사회 풍조.

tender *adj.* (*soft*) yŏnhan 연한, (*delicate*) yŏnyak'an 연약한, (*kind*) sangnyanghan 상냥한, (*sensitive*) min-gamhan 민감한. *—vi., vt.* (*present*) chech'urhada 제출하다. (*make a* ∼) ipch'arhada 입찰하다. *—n.* (*attendant*) kanhowŏn 간호원, (*money*) pŏp'wa 법화(法貨), (*bid*) ipch'al 입찰(入札). ∼ *meat* yŏnhan kogi 연한 고기/ *a* ∼ *skin* yak'an p'ibu 약한 피부/ *a* ∼ *smile* sangnyanghan miso 상냥한 미소/ *a* ∼ *spot* ap'ŭn te 아픈 데/ *I feel the wound still* ∼. Sangch'ŏga taŭmyŏn ajikto ap'ŭmnida. 상처가 닿으면 아직도 아픕니다/ *call for* ∼*s* ipch'arŭl mojip'ada 입찰을 모집하다/ *His* ∼ *was successful.* Kŭbunege nakch'aldoeŏssŭmnida. 그분에게 낙찰(落札)되었읍니다.

tenderhearted *adj.* maŭmssi koun 마음씨 고운.

tennis *n.* chŏnggu 정구, t'enisŭ 테니스. *Can you play* ∼? Chŏnggurŭl ch'il chul ashimnikka? 정구를 칠 줄 아십니까/ ∼ *ball* chŏnggu kong 정구 공/ *table* ∼ t'akku 탁구.

tenor *n.* (*singer*) t'enŏ 테너.

tent *n.* ch'ŏnmak 천막, t'ent'ŭ 텐트. *pitch a* ∼ ch'ŏnmagŭl ch'ida 천막을 치다/ *fold up a* ∼ ch'ŏnmagŭl kŏtta 천막을 걷다/ ∼ *life* t'ent'ŭ saenghwal 텐트 생활.

tenth *adj.* yŏrŭi 열의, yŏl pŏntchaeŭi 열 번째의. *—n.* yŏl pŏntchae 열 번째, (*date*) shibil 10일. *a* ∼ *part* shippunŭi il 10분의 1/ *the* ∼ *of March* samwŏl shibil 3월 10일.

tepid *adj.* (*lukewarm*) mijigŭnhan 미지근한. *a* ∼ *tea* mijigŭnhan ch'a 미지근한 차(茶).

term *n.* (*semester*) hakki 학기, (*period*) kigan 기간, (*word*) yongŏ 용어, (*pl.*) (*condition*) chokŏn 조건. *the fall* ∼ kaŭl hakki 가을 학기/ *the spring* ∼ pomhakki 봄학기/ *the end of a school* ∼ hakkimal 학기말/ *My* ∼ *of office expires in August.* Nae imginŭn p'arwŏre kkŭnnamnida. 내 임기는 8월에 끝납니다/ ∼*s of science* kwahak yongŏ 과학 용어/ *trade* ∼*s* sangŏp yongŏ 상업 용어/ *I have never heard that* ∼ *before.* Kŭ yongŏnŭn chŏne tŭrŏbon chŏgi ŏpsŭmnida. 그 용어는 전에 들어본 적이 없읍니다/ ∼*s of payment* chibul chokŏn 지불 조건/

according to ~s chokŏne ttara 조건에 따라.

terminal *n.* (*station*) chongch'angnyŏk 종착역, (*end part*) maltan 말단, kkŭt 끝. —*adj.* (*closing*) chongmarŭi 종말의, (*at the end*) kkŭt'ŭi 끝의, chongchŏmŭi 종점의. *I'd like to go to the bus* ~. Pŏsŭ chongchŏmkkaji kago shipsŭmnida. 버스 종점까지 가고 싶습니다/ *the* ~ *stage* malgi 말기(末期)/ ~ *cancer* pulch'iŭi am 불치의 암.

terrace *n.* (*balcony*) t'erasŭ 테라스.

terrible *adj.* (*awful*) mushimushihan 무시무시한, (*severe*) chidok'an 지독한, (*very bad*) hyŏngp'yŏnŏmnŭn 형편 없는. *a* ~ *war* mushimushihan chŏnjaeng 무시무시한 전 쟁/ *Wasn't that a* ~ *fire last night?* Ojetpam hwajae-nŭn mushimushihapdidagŭryŏ. 어젯밤 화재는 무시무시 합디다그려/ *What a* ~ *day!* Nalssiga chidok'agunyo! 날씨가 지독하군요/ *This hospital food is* ~. I pyŏng-wŏnŭi shiksanŭn hyŏngp'yŏnŏpsŭmnida. 이 병원의 식 사는 형편없읍니다.

terrify *vt.* (*frighten*) kŏmnage hada 겁나게 하다. *be ter-rified of* ...ŭl musŏwŏhada …을 무서워하다.

territory *n.* (*domain*) yŏngt'o 영토, (*possession*) yŏng-yŏk 영역, (*region*) chibang 지방. *within Korean* ~ Han-guk yŏngt'o ane 한국 영토 안에/ *How wide the Korean* ~ *is?* Han-gugŭi yŏngt'onŭn ŏlmana nŏlssŭmni-kka? 한국의 영토는 얼마나 넓습니까/ *a buffer* ~ wanch'ung chiyŏk 완충 지역/ *How much* ~ *does he travel over?* Kŭ-bunŭn ŏlmana manŭn chibangŭl yŏhaenghashimnikka? 그분은 얼마나 많은 지방을 여행하십니까?

terror *n.* (*fright*) kongp'o 공포, (*cause of fear*) musŏun kŏt[saram] 무서운 것[사람]. *cause* ~ kongp'oshimŭl irŭ-k'ida 공포심을 일으키다/ *a novel of* ~ kongp'o sosŏl 공 포 소설/ *left-wing* ~ chwaik t'erŏ 좌익 테러.

terrorism *n.* p'ongnyŏkchuŭi 폭력주의.

terrorize *vt.* wihyŏp'ada 위협하다.

test *n.* (*examination*) shihŏm 시험, (*trial*) kŏmsa 검사, (*touchstone*) shigŭmsŏk 시금석. —*vt.* (*try*) shihŏmhada 시험하다. *a blood* ~ hyŏraek kŏmsa 혈액 검사/*the H-bomb explosion* ~ suso p'okt'an p'okpal shihŏm 수소 폭탄 폭발

시험/ *a mental* ～ chinŭng kŏmsa 지능 검사/ *an oral* ～ kudu shihŏm 구두 시험/ *a* ～ *drive* shiunjŏn 시운전/ ～ *paper* shihŏmji 시험지/ *a* ～ *tube* shihŏmgwan 시험관/ *The doctor* ～*ed my eyesight*. Ŭisanŭn nae shiryŏgŭl kŏmsahaessŭmnida. 의사는 내 시력을 검사했읍니다.

testament *n*. (*will*) yuŏn(chang) 유언(장). *the New*[*Old*] ～ shinyak[kuyak] sŏngsŏ 신약[구약] 성서.

testify *vi*., *vt*. (*give evidence*) chŭngmyŏnghada 증명하다, (*attest*) chŭngŏnhada 증언하다, (*declare on oath*) sŏnsŏhada 선서하다. *I can* ～ *to his good behavior*. Nanŭn kŭ saramŭi hullyunghan p'umhaengŭl chŭngmyŏnghal su issŭmnida. 나는 그 사람의 훌륭한 품행을 증명할 수 있읍니다.

testimonial *n*. (*written certificate*) chŭngmyŏngsŏ 증명서, (*letter of recommendation*) ch'uch'ŏnchang 추천장, (*written tribute*) p'yoch'angchang 표창장. *a* ～ *as to character* inmul chŭngmyŏngsŏ 인물 증명서/ *Have you* ～*s from your teacher?* Sŏnsaengnimŭi ch'uch'ŏnchangŭl kajigo wassŭmnikka? 선생님의 추천장을 가지고 왔읍니까?

testimony *n*. (*proof*) chŭnggŏ 증거, (*by witness*) chŭngŏn 증언. *bear* ～ chŭngŏnhada 증언하다/ *I can bear* ～ *to his good character*. Kŭbuni hullyunghan inmuriranŭn kŏsŭl ipchŭnghal su issŭmnida. 그분이 훌륭한 인물이라는 것을 입증할 수 있읍니다.

text *n*. (*original*) wŏnmun 원문, (～*book*) kyogwasŏ 교과서, (*theme*) chuje 주제, (*main body*) ponmun 본문. *a full* ～ chŏnmun 전문(全文)/ *from the* ～ wŏnmunesŏ 원문에서.

textbook *n*. kyogwasŏ 교과서. *an algebra* ～ taesu kyogwasŏ 대수 교과서/ ～*s on grammar* munpŏp kyogwasŏ 문법 교과서.

textile *n*. (*woven fabric*) chingmul 직물, (*cloth*) ch'ŏn 천. *wool* ～*s* mojingmul 모직물/ *the* ～ *industry* pangjik kongŏp 방직 공업.

texture *n*. (*woven fabric*) chingmul 직물, (*structure*) tchaimsae 짜임새, (*constitution*) kujo 구조. *cloth with a loose*[*close*] ～ ori sŏnggin[ch'omch'omhan] ch'ŏn

올이 성진〔촘촘한〕천.

than *conj., prep.* poda(nŭn) 보다(는). *You are taller ~ I.* Tangshinŭn naboda k'iga k'ŭmnida. 당신은 나보다 키가 큽니다/ *You will get there earlier ~ he.* Kŭiboda tangshini mŏnjŏ toch'ak'al kŏshimnida. 그이보다 당신이 먼저 도착할 것입니다/*Don't talk more ~ necessary.* P'iryo isangŭro marhaji mashio. 필요 이상으로 말하지 마시오/ *I would rather stay at home ~ go for a walk.* Sanch'aekpoda chibe itko shipsŭmnida. 산책보다 집에 있고 싶습니다/ *I know you better ~ him.* Kŭibodanŭn tangshinŭl tŏ chal algo issŭmnida. 그이보다는 당신을 더 잘 알고 있읍니다/ *I have no other dictionary ~ this.* Sajŏnŭn igŏtpakke ŏpsŭmnida. 사전은 이것밖에 없읍니다/ *in less ~* inaero 이내로/ *in less ~ a month* han tal inaero 한 달 이내로/ *more ~* isang 이상/ *more ~ a week* ilchuil isang 1주일 이상.

thank *vt.* kamsahada 감사하다, komawahada 고마와하다. —*n.(pl.) (gratitude)* kamsa 감사. *T~ you very much [so much].* Ch'am komapsŭmnida. 참 고맙습니다/ *T~ you for calling.* Chŏnhwa kamsahamnida. 전화 감사합니다/ *T~ you for your kindness.* Ch'injŏrhi taehae chusyŏsŏ kamsahamnida. 친절히 대해 주셔서 감사합니다/ *T~ her for me.* Chŏ taeshin kŭbunkke kamsaŭi malssŭm chŏnhashipshio. 저 대신 그분께 감사의 말씀 전하십시오/ *Many ~s. A thousand ~s.* Chongmal kamsahamnida. 정말 감사합니다/ *No ~s.* Kwaench'anssŭmnida. 괜찮습니다/ *No more, ~s.* Animnida. Ije kŭman hagessŭmnida. 아닙니다. 이제 그만 하겠읍니다/ *~s to ŭi tŏkt'aegŭro ~의 덕택으로, (because of)* ttaemune 때문에/ *T~s to you, I had a very good time.* Tŏkpune aju chaemiitke chinaessŭmnida. 덕분에 아주 재미있게 지냈읍니다.

thankful *adj.* komapke saenggak'anŭn 고맙게 생각하는. *I'm ~ to you.* Komapke saenggak'amnida. 고맙게 생각합니다/ *a ~ heart* kamsahanŭn maŭm 감사하는 마음.

Thanksgiving *n.* kamsajŏl 감사절. *T~ day* ch'usu kamsajŏl 추수 감사절.

that *adj.* kŭ 그, chŏ 저. —*pron.* kŭgŏt 그것, chŏgŏt 저

것. *Give me* ~ *chair*. Ku ŭijarŭl chushipshio. 그 의자를
주십시오/ *What is* ~ ? Kŭgŏsŭn muŏshijiyo? 그것은 무엇
이지요/*Who is* ~ ? Kŭge nugujiyo? 그게 누구지요/*Which
will you have this or* ~ ? Igŏsŭl kajishiryŏmnikka, animyŏn chŏgŏsŭl? 이것을 가지시렵니까, 아니면 저것을/ *T*~
is the question. Kŭgŏshi munjeimnida. 그것이 문제입니다/
Is ~ *so*? Kŭraeyo? 그래요? / *T*~ *is right*. (=*Yes, just
so*.) Chossŭmnida 좋습니다, Kŭrŏssŭmnida 그렇습니다/
Get ~ ? Arassŭmnikka? 알았읍니까 ?

thatch *n*. (*for roofs*) iŏng 이엉

thaw *n*. haebing 해빙(解氷). —*vi*. (*melt*) nokta 녹다,
nogida 녹이다.

the *adj*. kŭ 그, chŏ 저. —*adv*. hamyŏn halsurok 하면 할
수록, kŭmank'ŭm 그만큼. ~ *book you mentioned* tangshini marhan kŭ ch'aek 당신이 말한 그 책/ ~ *sooner*
~ *better* pparŭmyŏn pparŭlsurok chot'a 빠르면 빠를수
록 좋다.

theater, theatre *n*. kŭkchang 극장. *go to the* ~ kŭkchange
kada 극장에 가다/ *I like* ~ *going*. Nanŭn kŭkchang
kugyŏngŭl choahamnida. 나는 극장 구경을 좋아합니다/
Would you please take me to the movie ~ ? Chebal
yŏnghwagwane teryŏda chushipshio. 제발 영화관에 데려다
주십시오.

theft *n*. (*stealing*) chŏlto 절도. *an auto* ~ chadongch'a
toduk 자동차 도둑.

their *pron*. kŭ saramdŭrŭi 그 사람들의. ~ *dogs* kŭ saramdŭrŭi kae 그 사람들의 개.

theirs *pron*. kŭ saramdŭrŭi kŏt 그 사람들의 것. *Our house
is larger than* ~*s*. Uri chibŭn kŭ saramdŭl kŏtpoda
k'ŭmnida. 우리 집은 그 사람들 것보다 큽니다.

them *pron*. (*obj. of they*) kŭdŭrŭl 그들을, kŭgŏttŭrŭl 그
것들을, (*dative*) kŭdŭrege 그들에게, kŭgŏttŭrege 그것
들에게. *The books are new; take care of* ~. Sae ch'ae-
ginikka choshimhae tarushio. 새 책이니까 조심해 다루시오.

theme *n*. (*subject*) chuje 주제, t'ema 테마, (*topic*) hwaje
화제. ~ *music* t'ema ŭmak 테마 음악/ ~ *song* chujega
주제가.

then *adv.* kŭttae 그때, *(next)* taŭmenŭn 다음에는, *(in that case)* kŭrŏmyŏn 그러면. —*adj.* *(then existing)* kŭttaeŭi 그때의. —*n.* *(that time)* kŭttae 그때. *We were living in Pusan* ~. Kŭttae Pusanesŏ salgo issŏssŭmnida. 그때 부산에서 살고 있었읍니다/ *the* ~ *president* kŭttaeŭi〔tangshiŭi〕 taet'ongnyŏng 그때의〔당시의〕 대통령/ *before* ~ kŭ ijŏne 그 이전에/ *since* ~ kŭttaebut'ŏ 그때부터/ *till* ~ kŭttaekkaji 그때까지/ *now and* ~ ttaettaero 때때로.

theologian *n.* shinhakcha 신학자.

theology *n.* shinhak 신학(神學).

theorist *n.* iron-ga 이론가. *an armchair* ~ t'aksang kongnon-ga 탁상 공론가.

theory *n.* *(opp. practice)* iron 이론, *(general principle)* haksŏl 학설, *(opinion)* kyŏnhae 견해. ~ *and practice* iron-gwa shilch'ŏn 이론과 실천/ *the* ~ *of evolution* chinhwaron 진화론.

there *adv.* *(in that place)* kŏgie(sŏ) 거기에(서), *(towards that place)* kŏgiro 거기로. *Is he still* ~? Kŭbunŭn ajik kŏgie issŭmnikka? 그분은 아직 거기에 있읍니까/ *Put the box* ~. Sangjarŭl kŏgie noŭshio. 상자를 거기에 놓으시오/ *What are you doing out* ~? Kŏgisŏ muŏsŭl hago issŭmnikka? 거기서 무엇을 하고 있읍니까/ *Don't stop* ~, *go on please.* Kŏgisŏ mŏmch'uji mashigo tŏ kyesok'ashipshio. 거기서 멈추지 마시고 더 계속하십시오/ *T*~ *you go!* Chŏ kkol chom pwayo! 저 꼴 좀 봐요/ *T*~ *goes the last bus!* Chŏbwayo, makch'aga ttŏnassŏyo. 저봐요. 막차가 떠났어요/ *Are you* ~? *(telephone)* Yŏboseyo? 여보세요/ *here and* ~ yŏgijŏgi 여기저기.

therefore *adv.* kŭrŏmŭro 그러므로.

thermometer *n.* ondogye 온도계, hallan-gye 한란계. *a Centigrade* ~ sŏpssi ondogye 섭씨 온도계/ *a Fahrenheit* ~ hwassi ondogye 화씨 온도계/ *a clinical* ~ ch'eon-gye 체온계/ *T*~*s often go below zero.* Ondogyenŭn chaju yŏngharo ttŏrŏjimnida. 온도계는 자주 영하로 떨어집니다.

thermos *n.* *(vacuum-bottle)* poonpyŏng 보온병.

these *pron.* *(pl. of this)* i(gŏt)dŭl 이(것)들. —*adj.* i(gŏt)-

dŭrŭi 이(것)들의. *What are ~?* Igŏttŭrŭn muŏshijiyo?
이것들은 무엇이지요/ *I haven't seen him ~ two weeks.* I
iju tongan kŭbunŭl pon iri ŏpsŭmnida. 이 2주 동안 그
분을 본 일이 없읍니다/ *~ days* yojŭŭm 요즈음/ *one of ~
days* mŏlji anna 멀지 않아, kot 곧.

they *pron.* (*person*) kŭdŭl(ŭn) 그들(은), (*thing*) kŭgŏttŭl
(ŭn) 그것들(은), (*people*) sesang saramdŭl 세상 사람들.
T~ were very kind. Kŭdŭrŭn ch'injŏrhaessŭmnida. 그
들은 친절했읍니다/ *That's ~.* Kŭdŭrimnida. 그들입니다.

thick *adj.* (*opp. thin*) tukkŏun 두꺼운, (*dense*) chit'ŭn
짙은, (*semisolid*) chinhan 진한, (*intimate*) ch'inhan
친한. *How ~ is it?* Tukkenŭn ŏlmana toemnikka? 두께
는 얼마나 됩니까/ *a ~ forest* ppaekppaek'an sup'ul 빽빽
한 수풀, millim 밀림/ *~ soup* chinhan kuk 진한 국/
Kapdol is very ~ with Kapsun now. Kaptorinŭn
chigŭm Kapsuniwa maeu ch'inhamnida. 갑돌이는 지금 갑
순이와 매우 친합니다.

thief *n.* toduk 도둑, chŏlto 절도.
catch a ~ todugŭl puttŭlda 도둑을
붙들다/*Stop ~!* Todugiya! 도둑이야!

thigh *n.* nŏpchŏktari 넓적다리, hŏ-
bŏktari 허벅다리.

thimble *n.* kolmu 골무.

thin *adj.* (*opp. thick*) yalbŭn 얇은,
(*slender*) kanŭdaran 가느다란,(*lean*)   ⟨kolmu⟩
yawin 야윈, marŭn 마른, (*sparse*) tŭmun 드문, sŏnggin 성긴. *a ~ voice* kanŭn moksori 가는 목소리.

hing *n.* (*material object*) mulgŏn 물건, (*articles*) sang-
p'um 상품, (*non-material*) il 일, kŏt 것, (*belongings*)
sojip'um 소지품, (*implements*) togu 도구. *What are
those ~s on the table?* T'eibŭl wie innŭn mulgŏnŭn
muŏshimnikka? 테이블 위에 있는 물건은 무엇입니까/ *I've
many ~s to do.* Hal iri manssŭmnida. 할 일이 많습니
다/ *Bring your swimming ~s.* Suyŏng togurŭl kajigo
oshio. 수영 도구를 가지고 오시오/ *Carry up my ~s.* Nae
chimŭl wich'ŭngŭro kajyŏda chushio. 내 짐을 위층으로 가
져다 주시오/ *How dare you say such a ~!* Ŏtchi kamhi

kŭrŏn sorirŭl! 어찌 감히 그런 소리를!

think vi., vt. (consider) saenggak'ada 생각하다, (regard as) yŏgida 여기다, (suppose) irago saenggak'ada 이라고 생각하다, (ponder) sukkohada 숙고하다. Give me time to ~. Saenggak'al shiganŭi yŏyurŭl chushipshio. 생각할 시간의 여유를 주십시오/ Do you ~ it will rain? Piga orirago saenggak'ashimnikka? 비가 오리라고 생각하십니까/ Yes, I ~ so. Ne, kŭrŏk'e saenggak'amnida. 네, 그렇게 생각합니다/ Please ~ over what I have said. Chega tŭrin malssŭmŭl kip'i saenggak'ae chushipshio. 제가 드린 말씀을 깊이 생각해 주십시오.

thinker n. sasangga 사상가.

third n. chesam 제3, setchae pŏn 세째 번. —adj. setchae pŏnŭi 세째 번의, chesamŭi 제3의. the ~ of April sawŏl samil 4월 3일/ Edward the T~ Edŭwŏdŭ samse 에드워드 3세/ the ~ line setchae chul 세째 줄/ the ~ floor samch'ŭng 3층(Am. sach'ŭng 4층)/ the ~ republic chesam konghwaguk 제3 공화국/ a ~ person chesamja 제3자.

thirst n. mongmarŭm 목마름, kalchŭng 갈증. slake one's ~ mogŭl ch'ugida 목을 추기다/ I have a ~. Hanjan hago shipsŭmnida. 한잔 하고 싶습니다/ a ~ for knowledge chishige taehan kalmang 지식에 대한 갈망.

thirsty adj. mongmarŭn 목마른, kalmanghanŭn 갈망하는/ a ~ food mogi marŭnŭn ŭmshingmul 목이 마르는 음식물/ a ~ season kŏnjogi 건조기/ a ~ soul sulkkun 술꾼/ He is ~ for fame. Kŭ saramŭn myŏngyerŭl kalmanghago issŭmnida. 그 사람은 명예를 갈망하고 있습니다.

this pron. igŏt 이것, (the latter) huja 후자. —adj. i 이, kŭm 금(今). What is ~? Igŏsŭn muŏshimnikka? 이것은 무엇입니까/ Is ~ the man you saw yesterday? Ibuni ŏje taegi mannan punimnikka? 이분이 어제 댁이 만난 분입니까/ T~ is Mr. Kim speaking(telephone). Chŏ Kimgunindeyo. 저 김군인데요/Come ~ way, please. Cha, iriro oshipshio. 자, 이리로 오십시오/ ~ year kŭmnyŏn 금년/ all ~ week kŭmju naenae 금주 내내/ What is all ~? Todaech'e ige ŏttŏk'e toen kŏshimnikka? 도대체 이게 어떻게 된

것입니까/*Can you spare me ~ much?* Imank'ŭm kajyŏdo chossŭmnikka? 이만큼 가져도 좋습니까/*like ~* iwagach'i 이와같이/ *with ~* irŏk'e marhamyŏnsŏ 이렇게 말하면서.

thorn *n.* (*prickle*) kashi 가시. *a ~ thicket* kashidŏmbul 가시덤불/ *Mind the ~s when you touch roses.* Changmirŭl manjil ttaenŭn kashirŭl choshimhashio. 장미를 만질 때는 가시를 조심하시오.

thorny *adj.* (*spiny*) kashiga innŭn 가시가 있는, (*painful*) ap'ŭn 아픈. *a ~ path* kashibatkil 가시밭길/ *a ~ problem* ŏryŏun munje 어려운 문제.

thorough *adj.* (*complete*) ch'ŏlchŏhan 철저한, (*out-and-out*) sunjŏnhan 순전한. *a ~ rest* chŏltae anjŏng 절대 안정/ *a ~ reform* ch'ŏlchŏhan kaehyŏk 철저한 개혁/ *a ~ fool* sun pabo 순 바보/ *Give the house a ~ cleaning.* Chibŭl ch'ŏlchŏhi ch'ŏngsohashio. 집을 철저히 청소하시오.

thoroughbred *n.* (*horse*) sunjongŭi mal 순종의 말. *—adj.* (*pured*) sunjongin 순종인.

thoroughfare *n.* (*highway*) han-gil 한길, (*main street*) taero 대로, (*passage*) t'onghaeng 통행. *a crowded ~* pumbinŭn taero 붐비는 대로/ *No ~.* T'onghaeng kŭmji 통행 금지/ *No ~ for vehicles.* Chech'a t'onghaeng kŭmji 제차 통행 금지.

thoroughly *adv.* (*completely*) wanjŏnhi 완전히, ch'ŏlchŏhi 철저히. *understand ~* ch'ŏlchŏhi ihaehada 철저히 이해하다/ *a ~ bad man* ch'ŏlchŏhan agin 철저한 악인.

though *conj.* ...ijiman ...이지만, ...hajiman ...하지만. *T~ it was pouring, they went out.* Piga ŏksugach'i watchiman kŭ saramdŭrŭn ttŏnassŭmnida. 비가 억수같이 왔지만 그 사람들은 떠났읍니다/ *T~ we fail, we shall not regret.* Shilp'aehadŏrado huhoenŭn haji anŭl kŏmnida. 실패하더라도 후회는 하지 않을 겁니다.

thought *n.* (*thinking*) saenggak 생각, (*notion*) kwannyŏm 관념, (*idea*) sasang 사상, (*regard*) paeryŏ 배려. *communist ~* kongsanjuŭi sasang 공산주의 사상/ *Korean ~* Han-guk sasang 한국 사상/ *modern ~* hyŏndae sasang 현대 사상/ *a kindly ~* hoŭi 호의/ *I have given it much ~.* Kŭ ire taehae kip'i saenggak'ae poassŭmnida. 그

일에 대해 깊이 생각해 보았읍니다/ *To my* ~, *the answer is simple.* Nae saenggagŭronŭn tabŭn kandanhamnida. 내 생각으로는 답은 간단합니다.

thoughtful *adj.* (*pensive*) saenggage chamgin 생각에 잠긴, (*full of thought*) saenggagi kip'ŭn 생각이 깊은, (*considerate*) ch'injŏrhan 친절한. *a* ~ *book* sasangi p'ungbuhan ch'aek 사상이 풍부한 책/ *a* ~ *friend* injŏng manŭn ch'in-gu 인정 많은 친구/ *You are always* ~ *of me.* Ŏnjena chŏŭi irŭl yŏmnyŏhae chusyŏsŏ komapsŭmnida. 언제나 저의 일을 염려해 주셔서 고맙습니다.

thoughtless *adj.* (*inconsiderate*) punbyŏrŏmnŭn 분별없는, (*careless*) pujuŭihan 부주의한, (*reckless*) mumohan 무모한. *Maybe it was* ~ *of me.* Ama chŏŭi pujuŭiyŏttŏn-ga pomnida. 아마 저의 부주의였던가 봅니다.

thousand *n.* ch'ŏn 천(1,000). —*adj.* ch'ŏnŭi 천의. *three* ~ samch'ŏn 3,000/ *ten* ~ man 만(萬)/ *a hundred* ~ shimman 10만/ *a* ~ *men* ch'ŏn myŏng 천 명/*A* ~ *thanks for your kindness.* Ch'injorhi hae chusyŏsŏ taedanhi kamsahamnida. 친절히 해 주셔서 대단히 감사합니다/ ~*s of* such'ŏnŭi 수천의.

thrash *vt.* (*beat*) ttaerida 때리다, (*thresh*) ttŏlda 떨다. *Stop* ~*ing that donkey.* Tangnagwirŭl ttaeriji mashio. 당나귀를 때리지 마시오/ ~ *wheat* pori t'ajak'ada 보리 타작하다.

thrasher *n.* (*thresher*) t'algokki 탈곡기.

thread *n.* shil 실. *cotton* ~ mumyŏngshil 무명실/ *silk* ~ myŏngjushil 명주실/ *coarse* ~ kulgŭn shil 굵은 실/ *fine* ~ kanŭn shil 가는 실/ *a spool of* ~ shilp'ae 실패.

threaten *vt., vi.* (*menace*) hyŏppak'ada 협박하다, (*give warning of*) chojimŭl poida 조짐을 보이다. *He* ~*ed me.* Kŭ saramŭn narŭl hyŏppak'aessŭmnida. 그 사람은 나를 협박했읍니다/ *Do you mean to* ~? Hyŏppak'al semio? 협박할 셈이오/ *It* ~*s to rain.* Piga ol kŏt kassŭmnida. 비가 올 것 같습니다.

threatening *adj.* hyŏppak'anŭn 협박하는, (*weather*) hŏmak'an 험악한. *a* ~ *weather* hŏmak'an nalssi 험악한 날씨.

three *n.* set 셋, sam 삼(3). —*adj.* sesŭi 셋의, samŭi 3의.

a child of ~ se sallan ai 세 살난 아이/ ~ *fourths* sabunŭi sam 3/4/ ~ *persons* se saram 세 사람, samin 3인/ ~ *days* sahŭl 사흘, samil 3일/ ~ *hundred won* sambaegwŏn 300원.

thresh *vi.*, *vt.* (=*thrash*) tudŭlgida 두들기다, ttaerida 때리다, (~ *wheat*) t'algok'ada 탈곡하다. *Have the farmers started* ~*ing yet?* Nongbudŭrŭn pŏlssŏ t'ajagŭl shijak'aessŭmnikka? 농부들은 벌써 타작을 시작했읍니까?

threshold *n.* (*doorsill*) munchibang 문지방, (*entrance*) ipku 입구.

thrice *adv.* se pŏn 세 번, samhoe 3회.

thrift *n.* chŏllyak 절약, (*economy*) kŏmyak 검약.

thrifty *adj.* (*frugal*) kŏmsohan 검소한, (*thriving*) musŏnghan 무성한.

thrill *n.* (*shiver*) chŏnyul 전율, tŭril 드릴, (*emotion*) kamgyŏk 감격, (*tremor*) ttŏllim 떨림, (*thriller*) tŭril innŭn sosŏl 드릴 있는 소설. *I got a big* ~ *out of it.* Kŏgie taehae mopshi kamgyŏk'aessŭmnida. 거기에 대해 몹시 감격했읍니다.

thrive *vi.* (*prosper*) pŏnyŏnghada 번영하다, (*grow vigorously*) musŏnghage charada 무성하게 자라다. ~ *on* mŏkko salda 먹고 살다/ ~ *on meat* kogirŭl mŏkko salda 고기를 먹고 살다/ *Koreans* ~ *on rice.* Han-guk saramŭn ssalbabŭl mŏkko samnida. 한국 사람은 쌀밥을 먹고 삽니다.

throat *n.* mokkumŏng 목구멍. *I have a sore* ~. Mogi ap'ŭmnida. 목이 아픕니다/ *My* ~ *pains when I swallow.* Ŭmshigŭl samk'imyŏn mokkumŏngi ap'ŭmnida. 음식을 삼키면 목구멍이 아픕니다.

throb *vi.* (*beat*) ttwida 뛰다, kodonghada 고동하다, (*pulsate*) tugŭn-gŏrida 두근거리다. *My heart* ~*bed violently.* Shimjangi mopshi tugŭn-gŏryŏssŭmnida. 심장이 몹시 두근거렸읍니다.

throne *n.* (*chair*) wangjwa 왕좌, (*power*) wangwi 왕위. *come to the* ~ chŭgwihada 즉위하다.

throng *vi.*, *vt.* (*crowd*) moyŏdŭlda 모여들다. —*n.* (*crowd*) kunjung 군중. *a* ~ *of people* saramŭi muri 사람의 무리.

through *prep.* (*by medium of*) ...ŭl t'onghayŏ …을 통하

여, (*across*) kkwetturŏ 꿰뚫어, (*during*) tongan 동안, (*on account of*) ttaemune 때문에. —*adv.* (*from end to end*) kkwettulk'o 꿰뚫고, (*to the end*) kkŭtkkaji 끝까지. —*adj.* (*finished*) kkŭnnaen 끝낸. *I knew him ~ my uncle.* Samch'onŭl t'onghae kŭirŭl arassŭmnida. 삼촌을 통해 그이를 알았읍니다/ *May I pass ~ this gate?* I munŭl t'onggwahaedo chossŭmnikka? 이 문을 통과해도 좋습니까/ *I'll stay here from Monday ~ Friday.* Nanŭn wŏryoilbut'ŏ kŭmyoilkkaji yŏgi itkessŭmnida. 나는 월요일부터 금요일까지 여기 있겠읍니다/ *a ~ ticket* chik'aeng ch'ap'yo 직행 차표/ *a ~ train* chikt'ong yŏlch'a 직통 열차/ *Are you ~ with this knife?* I k'al ta ssŭsyŏssŭmnikka? 이 칼 다 쓰셨읍니까/ *Give it back as soon as you're ~.* Kkŭnnanŭn taero tollyŏ chushipshio. 끝나는 대로 돌려 주십시오.

throughout *prep.* (*place*) toch'ŏe 도처에, (*time*) tongan 동안. —*adv.* (*everywhere*) ŏdidŭnji 어디든지, (*during whole time*) naenae 내내. *~ the country* chŏn-guk toch'ŏe 전국 도처에/ *~ one's life* ilsaeng tongan 일생 동안.

throw *vt., vi.* (*cast*) tŏnjida 던지다, (*hurl*) naedŏnjida 내던지다. *Don't ~ a stone at my dog.* Nae kaeege torŭl tŏnjiji mashio. 내 개에게 돌을 던지지 마시오/ *~ me that towel.* Kŭ sugŏnŭl tŏnjyŏ chushipshio. 그 수건을 던져 주십시오/ *T~ your chest out.* Kasŭmŭl p'yŏshio. 가슴을 펴시오/ *~ a cocktail party* k'akt'eil p'at'irŭl yŏlda 칵테일 파티를 열다/ *~ away* nangbihada 낭비하다/ *~ in* tŏmŭro chuda 덤으로 주다/ *I'll ~ in another.* Hana tŏ tŏmŭro tŭrigessŭmnida. 하나 더 덤으로 드리겠읍니다/ *~ off* pŏsŏdŏnjida 벗어던지다/ *~ up* (*vomit*) t'ohada 토(吐)하다.

thrust *vt., vi.* (*push*) milda 밀다, (*pierce*) tchirŭda 찌르다. —*n.* (*push*) milgi 밀기, (*stab*) tchirŭgi 찌르기. *~ a chair forward* ŭijarŭl ap'ŭro mirŏnaeda. 의자를 앞으로 밀어내다/ *~ a knife into an apple* k'allo sagwarŭl tchirŭda 칼로 사과를 찌르다.

thumb *n.* ŏmjisonkarak 엄지손가락. *Put your ~s up!*

Chŏngshin ch'aryŏ！정신 차려／ *T～s up！* Chalhaessŏ！잘
했어／ *T～s down！* An twae！안 돼！

thunder *n.* ch'ŏndung 천둥, uroe 우뢰. *—vi., vt.* ch'ŏn-
dungch'ida 천둥치다. *I calculate we're going to have ～.*
Ch'ŏndungi ch'il kŏt kassŭmnida. 천둥이 칠 것 같습니다／
It ～ed last night. Kanbame ch'ŏndungi ch'yŏssŭmnida. 간밤에 천둥이 쳤읍니다／ *～bolt* pyŏrak 벼락／ *～clap*
noesŏng 뇌성／ *～storm* noeu 뇌우(雷雨).

Thursday *n.* mogyoil 목요일.

thus *adv.* (*in this way*) iwagach'i 이와같이, (*accordingly*)
kŭraesŏ 그래서, (*therefore*) kŭrŏgi ttaemune 그러기 때
문에. *I studied hard ～ I passed the examination.*
Yŏlshimhi kongbuhaessŭmnida. Kŭraesŏ hapkyŏk'aessŭmnida. 열심히 공부했읍니다. 그래서 합격했읍니다.

thwart *vt.* (*baffle*) panghaehada 방해하다, (*frustrate*)
hwebangnot'a 훼방놓다.

ticket *n.* p'yo 표(票), (*in compounds*) kwčn 권(券).
admission ～s ipchangkwŏn 입장권／ *a berth ～* ch'imdaekwŏn 침대권／ *a complimentary ～* ch'odaekwŏn 초대
권／ *commutation ～s* hoesukwŏn 회수권／ *free ～s* muryo
ipchangkwŏn 무료 입장권／ *a return ～* wangbok ch'ap'yo
왕복 차표／*a ～ office* maep'yoso 매표소／ *Could I buy a ～?*
P'yorŭl sal su issŭmnikka? 표를 살 수 있읍니까／ *Where's
the ～ office〔booth〕?* Maep'yosonŭn ŏdimnikka? 매표소
는 어딥니까／ *One second-class ～ to Pusan, please.*
Pusanhaeng idŭngp'yo han chang chushio. 부산행 2등표
한 장 주시오／ *Please show me your ～.* P'yorŭl poyŏ
chushipshio. 표를 보여 주십시오.

tickle *vt.* (*titillate*) kanjirida 간질이다, (*amuse*) kippŭge
haejuda 기쁘게 해주다, (*cause laughter*) utkida 웃기다.
Don't ～ me with a feather. Kitt'ŏllo kanjiriji mashio.
깃털로 간질이지 마시오.

ticklish *adj.* kanjirŏun 간지러운.

tidal *adj.* (*of tide*) chosuŭi 조수의. *～ waves* haeil 해일.

tide *n.* chosu 조수. *high ～* milmul 밀물／ *low ～* ssŏlmul
썰물／ *a neap ～* chogŭm 조금, sojo 소조／ *The ～ is
falling.* Chosuga ppajimnida. 조수가 빠집니다／ *The ～ is*

rising. Chosuga millyŏ omnida. 조수가 밀려 옵니다.

tidings *n.* (*news*) soshik 소식. *Have you heard the glad ~?* Kŭ kippŭn soshigŭl tŭrŏssŭmnikka? 그 기쁜 소식을 들었읍니까/ *sad ~* pibo 비보(悲報).

tidy *adj.* (*neat*) tanjŏnghan 단정한, (*orderly*) chŏngdondoen 정돈된, (*trim*) malssuk'an 말쑥한. —*vt., vi.* (*put in order*) chŏngdonhada 정돈하다. *a ~ room* chal chŏngdondoen pang 잘 정돈된 방/ *a ~ boy* malssuk'an sonyŏn 말쑥한 소년.

tie *n.* (*knot*) maedŭp 매듭. —*vt., vi.* (*fasten*) puttŭrŏmaeda 붙들어매다, (*bind*) mukta 묶다, (*score*) pigida 비기다. *a bright ~* palgŭn saek nekt'ai 밝은 색 넥타이/ *a woolen ~* mojik t'ai 모직 타이/ *T~ up these parcels, please.* I kkurŏmirŭl p'ojanghae chushio. 이 꾸러미를 포장해 주시오/ *T~ your dog to the railings.* Kaerŭl nangane puttŭrŏmaeshipshio. 개를 난간에 붙들어매십시오/ *Don't ~ them so loose[tight].* Kŭrŏk'e nŭsŭnhage〔kkok〕mukchi mashio. 그렇게 느슨하게〔꼭〕묶지 마시오/ *The Korean team ~d with Hongkong in the football game.* Ch'ukku shihabesŏ Han-guk t'imŭn Hongk'onggwa pigyŏssŭmnida. 축구 시합에서 한국 팀은 홍콩과 비겼읍니다. 「shimŭl mŏkta 점심을 먹다.

tiffin *n.* (*luncheon*) chŏmshim 점심. *eat one's ~* chŏm-

tiger *n.* pŏm 범, horangi 호랑이. *~ cat* salk'waengi 삵쾡이.

tight *adj.* (*firm*) tandanhan 단단한, (*tense*) p'aengp'aenghan 팽팽한, (*close-fitting*) kkok mannŭn 꼭 맞는, (*stingy*) insaek'an 인색한, (*hard to obtain*) kuhagi himdŭnŭn 구하기 힘드는, (*drunk*) sulch'wihan 술취한. —*adv.* (*firmly*) kkok 꼭. *This drawer is too ~.* I sŏrabŭn nŏmu ppakppak'amnida. 이 서랍은 너무 빡빡합니다/ *It's too ~ in the shoulders.* Ŏkkaega chom kkinŭndeyo. 어깨가 좀 끼는데요/ *You are too ~ about money.* Taegŭn tone nŏmu insaek'ashimnida. 댁은 돈에 너무 인색하십니다/ *Shut the door ~, please.* Munŭl kkok tada chushio. 문을 꼭 닫아 주시오.

tighten *vt., vi.* kkwak choeda 꽉 죄다, t'ant'anhage hada 탄탄하게 하다.

tile *n.* (*of roof*) kiwa 기와, t'ail 타일. *a roofing* ~ kiwa 기와.

till *prep.* (*up to*) kkaji 까지. *Good-bye* ~ *tomorrow*. Naeilkkaji annyŏng! 내일까지 안녕/ *Let's wait* ~ *the rain stops*. Piga kŭch'il ttaekkaji kidaripshida. 비가 그칠 때까지 기다립시다/ *Wait for me* ~ *I come back*. Naega ol ttaekkaji kidarishio. 내가 올 때까지 기다리시오.

⟨kiwa⟩

timber *n.* (*Am. lumber*) chaemok 재목. *a* ~ *dealer* mokchaesang 목재상/ *a* ~ *yard* chaemok chŏkchaejang 재목 적재장.

time *n.* ttae 때, (*hour*) shigan 시간, (*period*) kigan 기간, (*season*) kyejŏl 계절, (*leisure*) yŏga 여가, (*age*) shidae 시대, (*frequency*) hoetsu 횟수. *another* ~ tarŭn ttae 다른 때/ *in due* ~ ttaega omyŏn 때가 오면/ *the harvest* ~ ch'usu ttae 추수 때/ *in war time* chŏnjaeng ttae 전쟁 때/ *This is no* ~ *for such idle talk*. Ssŭlteŏmnŭn marŭl hago issŭl ttaega animnida. 쓸데없는 말을 하고 있을 때가 아닙니다/ *Now's your* ~. Ttaenŭn chigŭmimnida. 때는 지금입니다/ *a closing* ~ magam shigan 마감 시간/ *What* ~ *do you have?* Myŏt shiimnikka? 몇 시입니까/ *How goes the* ~? Myŏt shiimnikka? 몇 시입니까/ *What is the exact* ~? Chŏnghwak'an shiganŭn? 정확한 시간은/ *I have occupied your* ~. P'yerŭl kkich'yŏ mianhamnida. 폐를 끼쳐 미안합니다/ *We haven't got* ~ *to do it*. Kŭgŏsŭl hal shigani ŏpsŭmnida. 그것을 할 시간이 없읍니다/ *My watch keeps* ~ *very well*. Nae shigyenŭn shigani chŏnghwak'amnida. 내 시계는 시간이 정확합니다/ *a short* ~ tchalbŭn kigan 짧은 기간/ *a long* ~ oraen kigan 오랜 기간/ oraettongan 오랫동안/ *for a* ~ tangbun-gan 당분간/ *at flowering* ~ kkot'inŭn kyejŏre 꽃피는 계절에/ *I have little* ~ *to spare*. Yŏgaga kŏŭi ŏpsŭmnida. 여가가 거의 없읍니다/ *Come and see me at any* ~ *you get*. Yŏgaga namyŏn ŏnjedŭn oshio. 여가가 나면 언제든 오시오/ *my boyhood's* ~ naŭi sonyŏn shidae 나의 소년 시대/ *in colonial*

~s shingminshidaee 식민시대에/ *ancient* ~s kodae 고대/ *modern* ~s kŭndae 근대/ *each* ~ maehoe 매회(每回)/ *I met her several* ~s. Kŭ yŏjarŭl myŏt pŏn mannassŭmnida. 그 여자를 몇 번 만났읍니다/ *Take this medicine three* ~s *a day.* I yagŭl haru se pŏnssik pogyonghashio. 이 약을 하루 세 번씩 복용하시오/ *at a* ~ tanbŏne 단번에/ *at the same* ~ tongshie 동시에/ *at* ~s (*occasionally*) ttaettaero 때때로/ *for the first* ~ ch'ŏŭmŭro 처음으로/ *for the* ~ *being* tangbun-gan 당분간/ *We had a very good* ~ *at Haeundae.* Haeundaeesŏnŭn maeu chŭlgŏwŏssŭmnida. 해운대에서는 매우 즐거웠읍니다/ *I would like to have it on* ~. Wŏlburo tŭryŏ nok'o shipsŭmnida. 월부로 들여 놓고 싶습니다/ *some* ~ ŏnjen-ga 언제가/ *You will repent it some* ~. Onjen-ga huhoehal kŏshimnida. 언제가 후회할 것입니다.

timely *adj.* chŏkshiŭi 적시의, (*seasonable*) ttaematch'un 때맞춘. *a* ~ *hit* chŏkshi ant'a 적시 안타.

timetable *n.* shiganp'yo 시간표. 「수줍어하는.

timid *adj.* (*fearful*) kŏmmanŭn 겁많은, (*shy*) sujubŏhanŭn

tin *n.* (*metal*) chusŏk 주석, (~ *plate*) yangch'ŏl 양철. *a* ~ *roof* yangch'ŏl chibung 양철 지붕/ *a* ~ *pail* yangch'ŏlt'ong 양철통.

tiny *adj.* chagŭn 작은, chogŭmahan 조그마한.

tip *n.* (*point*) kkŭt'ŭmŏri 끄트머리, (*small present of money*) t'ip 팁. —*vi., vt.* t'ibŭl chuda 팁을 주다/ *the* ~s *of fingers* sonkkŭt 손끝/ *We don't usually* ~ *in Korea.* Han-gugesŏnŭn pot'ong tibŭl chuji anssŭmnida. 한국에서는 보통 팁을 주지 않습니다.

tipsy *adj.* (*slightly intoxicated*) ŏlk'ŭnhi ch'wihan 얼큰히 취한, (*unsteady*) pit'ŭlgŏrinŭn 비틀거리는.

tiptoe *n.* palkkŭt 발끝. *walk on* ~s palkkŭt'ŭro kŏtta 발끝으로 걷다/ *dance on* ~s palkkŭt'ŭro ch'umch'uda 발끝으로 춤추다.

tire *n.* (*of wheel*) t'aiŏ 타이어. —*vt., vi.* (*fatigue*) p'irok'e hada 피로케 하다, p'igonhaejida 피곤해지다. *a spare* ~ yebi t'aiŏ 예비 타이어/ *a* ~ *punctures* t'aiŏga ppangkkunada 타이어가 빵꾸나다/ *I'm dead* ~d. Chugŭl chigyŏngŭro p'irohamnida. 죽을 지경으로 피로합니다. *I'm very ～d with teaching.* Suŏbŭro mopshi chich'yŏssŭmnida. 수업으로 몹시 지쳤읍니다/ *I'm ～d of staying home.* Chibe itkiga chigyŏpsŭmnida. 집에 있기가 지겹습 니다.

tiresome *adj.* kwich'anŭn 귀찮은, sŏnggashin 성가신. *How ～ !* Ai soksanghae. 아이 속상해/ *a ～ child* sŏnggashin ai 성가신 아이/ *a ～ speech* ttabunhan yŏnsŏl 따분한 연설.

tissue *n.* (*woven fabric*) yalbŭn chingmul 얇은 직물. *～ paper* pagyŏpchi 박엽지.

title *n.* (*heading*) p'yoje 표제, (*name*) ch'ingho 칭호, (*rank*) chiwi 지위, (*championship*) t'ait'ŭl 타이틀, (*right*) kwŏlli 권리/ *He lost the ～ to Ali.* Alliege t'ait'ŭrŭl irŏssŭmnida. 알리에게 타이틀을 잃었읍니다/ *Has he any ～ to the land?* Kŭ ttange taehae ŏttŏn kwŏlliga issŭmnikka? 그 땅에 대해 어떤 권리가 있읍니까?

to *prep.* (*direction*) …ŭro …으로, (*destination*) …e …에. …ege…에게, (*purpose*) …ŭl wihayŏ …을 위하여, (*result*) …hagedo …하게도, (*opposition*) …e taehayŏ …에 대하여, (*composition*) …wa pigyohamyŏn …와 비교하면, (*time*) kkaji 까지. *Turn ～ the right.* Orŭntchogŭro toshio. 오 른쪽으로 도시오/ *Talk ～ him.* Kŭiege ŭinonhashio. 그이에 게 의논하시오/ *I gave the book ～ my brother.* Ch'aegŭl auege chuŏssŭmnida. 책을 아우에게 주었읍니다/ *T～ my surprise he was not dead!* Nollapkedo kŭinŭn chukchi anassŭmnida. 놀랍게도 그이는 죽지 않았읍니다/ *I prefer walking to climbing.* Tŭngsanboda sanch'aegŭl choahamnida. 등산보다 산책을 좋아합니다/ *The score is 9 to 5.* Tŭkchŏmŭn kudae oimnida. 득점은 9 대 5입니다/ *a quarter ～ six* yŏsŏssi shibobun chŏn 6시 15분 전/ *I didn't stay ～ the end of the meeting.* Hoehabi kkŭnnal ttaekkaji mŏmurŭji anassŭmnida. 회합이 끝날 때까지 머 무르지 않았읍니다.

toad *n.* tukkŏbi 두꺼비.

toast *n.* (*browned bread*) t'osŭt'ŭ 토스트, (*proposing health*) ch'ukpae 축배. —*vt., vi.* (*drink to*) ch'ukpaerŭl tŭlda 축배를 들다. *I ate two slices of ～.* T'osŭt'ŭ tu chogagŭl mŏgŏssŭmnida. 토스트 두 조각을 먹었읍니다/ *I proposed a ~ for Mr. Kim.* Kim sŏnsaengŭl wihae ch'ukpaerŭl tŭljago cheŭihaessŭmnida. 김 선생을 위해 축배를 들자고 제의했읍니다.

tobacco *n.* tambae 담배. *~ ashes* tambaetchae 담뱃재/ *a ~ case* tambaetkap 담뱃갑/ *a light for one's ~* tambaetpul 담뱃불/ *a ~ shop* tambae kage 담배 가게/ *This ~ is strong.* I tambaenŭn tok'amnida. 이 담배는 독합니다.

today *n.* onŭl 오늘, (*the present time*) yojŭŭm 요즈음.

toe *n.* palkarak 발가락. *I've blisters on my ~.* Palkarak saiga purŭt'ŏssŭmnida. 발가락 사이가 부르텄읍니다.

together *adv.* (*in company*) hamkke 함께, takach'i 다같이, (*in total*) hapkye 합계, modu 모두, (*at the same time*) tongshie 동시에. *~ with* …wa hamkke …와 함께/ *Let's go ~.* Hamkke kapshida. 함께 갑시다/ *Tie the ends ~.* Kkŭt'ŭl hande mukkŏra. 끝을 한데 묶어라/ *all ~* ta kach'i 다 같이/ *We are ten all ~.* Urinŭn modu yŏl saramimnida. 우리는 모두 열 사람입니다.

toilet *n.* (*water closet*) pyŏnso 변소, (*Am. bathroom*) yokshil 욕실, (*make up*) hwajang 화장. *a flush ~* suseshik pyŏnso 수세식 변소/ *~ paper* hyuji 휴지/ *a ~ set* hwajang togu 화장 도구.

token *n.* (*sign*) p'yo 표, (*keepsake*) kinyŏmp'um 기념품, (*~ money*) t'ok'ŭn 토큰. *a ~ of respect* chon-gyŏngŭi p'yoshi 존경의 표시/ *That is a small ~ of my appreciation.* Hach'anŭn kŏshina kamsaŭi ttŭsŭro 하찮은 것이나 감사의 뜻으로/ *Give me ten ~s, please.* T'ok'ŭn yŏl kaeman chushio. 토큰 열 개만 주시오/ *birthday ~s* saengil kinyŏmp'um 생일 기념품.

tolerance *n.* (*leniency*) kwanyong 관용, (*generosity*) aryang 아량.

tolerant *adj.* (*liberal*) kwandaehan 관대한. *be ~ of* …ŭl kwanyonghada …을 관용하다.

tolerate *vt.* (*permit*) nŏgŭrŏpke poajuda 너그럽게 보아주다, (*endure*) ch'amta 참다. *How can you ~ that pompous idiot?* Chŏ kŏmanhan paekch'iwa ŏttŏk'e ŏullyŏ chinaejiyo? 저 거만한 백치와 어떻게 어울려 지내지요?

toll *n.* (*fee*) t'onghaengse 통행세, (*casualties*) sasangja su 사상자 수/ ~ *bar* ch'adanbong 차단봉/ ~*gate* t'olge-it'ŭ 톨게이트/ *a* ~ *road* yuryo toro 유료 도로/ *a death* ~ chugŭn chaŭi suhyo 죽은 자의 수효/ *the* ~ *of casualties* sasangja su 사상자(死傷者) 수.

tomb *n.* (*grave*) myo 묘. *visit a* ~ sŏngmyohada 성묘 하다.

tombstone *n.* myosŏk 묘석.

tomorrow *n., adv.* naeil 내일. ~ *morning* naeil ach'im 내 일 아침/ ~ *evening* naeil chŏnyŏk 내일 저녁/ *the day after* ~ more 모레/ *Don't wait until* ~. Naeilkkaji kidariji mashio. 내일까지 기다리지 마시오.

ton *n.* (*weight*) t'on 톤. *per* ~ t'ondang 톤당(當)/ *the* ~ shisok paek mail (100 mph) 시속 100 마일/ *Can your car do the* ~? Taegŭi ch'anŭn shisok paek mairŭl tallil su issŭmnikka? 댁의 차는 시속 100 마일을 달릴 수 있읍니까?

tone *n.* (*sound*) ŭm 음. ~ *deaf* ŭmch'i 음치/ *I'm* ~ *deaf.* Nanŭn ŭmch'iimnida. 나는 음치입니다.

tongs *n.* (*pl.*) pujŏtkarak 부젓가락. *fire* ~ hwajŏtkarak 화젓가락/ *ice* ~ ŏrŭm chipke 얼음 집게.

tongue *n.* (*organ of mouth*) hyŏ 혀, (*language*) kugŏ 국어, (*speech*) malssi 말씨. *I bit my* ~ *sorely.* Hyŏrŭl kkwak murŏssŭmnida. 혀를 꽉 물었읍니다/ *Hold your* ~! Takch'ishio. 닥치시오/ *a carping* ~ toksŏl 독설/ *one's mother* ~ mogugŏ 모국어/ *the ancient* ~ kojŏnŏ 고전어/ *a gentle* ~ pudŭrŏun malssi 부드러운 말씨.

tonic *n.* kangjangje 강장제. *hair* ~ heŏ t'onik 헤어 토닉/ *a* ~ *medicine* poyak 보약.

tonight *n., adv.* onŭl chŏnyŏk 오늘 저녁. ~'s *radio news* onŭl chŏnyŏk radio nyusŭ 오늘 저녁 라디오 뉴스.

too *adv.* (*also*) tto 또, ttohan 또한, (*over*) chinach'ige 지나치게, (*very*) maeu 매우. *I went there,* ~. Nado kassŭmnida. 나도 갔읍니다/ *I'm* ~ *glad.* Nŏmudo ki-ppŭmnida. 너무도 기쁩니다/ *I'm* ~ *happy.* Maeu haeng-bok'amnida. 매우 행복합니다/ ~ ...*to do* nŏmu ...haesŏ ...hal su ŏpta 너무 …해서 …할 수 없다/ *You are* ~ *young to work.* Nŏnŭn nŏmu ŏryŏsŏ irŭl hal su ŏpta. 너는 너

무 어려서 일을 할 수 없다/ *It is ~ early to set out.* Ch'ulbarhagienŭn nŏmu pparŭmnida. 출발하기에는 너무 빠릅니다.

tool *n.* (*instrument*) yŏnjang 연장. *a farm ~* nonggu 농구/. *a kitchen ~* puŏk yŏnjang 부엌 연장/ *a ~ box* yŏnjangham 연장함.

tooth *n.* i 이. *~brush* ch'issol 칫솔/ *~paste* ch'iyak 치약/ *~pick* issushigae 이쑤시개/ *~powder* ch'ibun 치분/ *a decayed ~* ch'ungch'i 충치/ *false ~* ŭich'i 의치(義齒)/ *the upper〔lower〕 ~* winni〔araenni〕 윗니〔아랫니〕/ *Which ~ pains you?* Ŏnŭ iga ap'ŭmnikka? 어느 이가 아픕니까/ *I must have this ~ drawn.* I irŭl ppobaya hagessŭmnida. 이 이를 뽑아야 하겠습니다.

toothache *n.* ch'it'ong 치통. *have (a) ~* iga ap'ŭda 이가 아프다.

top *n.* (*summit*) kkoktaegi 꼭대기, (*head*) susŏk 수석(首席), (*toy*) p'aengi 팽이. *the ~ of a mountain* sankkoktaegi 산꼭대기/ *My brother is at the ~ of that class.* Aunŭn kŭ hakkŭbŭi susŏgimnida. 아우는 그 학급의 수석입니다/ *spin a ~* p'aengirŭl tollida 팽이를 돌리다.

topic *n.* (*subject*) hwaje 화제. *everyday ~s* ilsang hwaje 일상화제/ *current ~s* onŭrŭi hwaje 오늘의 화제.

topknot *n.* tabal 다발, sangt'u 상투.

topsyturvy *adj.* (*upset*) kŏkkuro toen 거꾸로 된. —*adv.* (*upside down*) kŏkkuro 거꾸로, ŏngmangŭro 엉망으로. *The whole world is ~.* On sesangi ŏngmangimnida. 온 세상이 엉망입니다.

〈sangt'u〉

torch *n.* hwaetpul 횃불. *an electric ~* hoejung chŏndŭng 회중 전등.

torpedo *n.* (*pl.*) ŏroe 어뢰.

torrent *n.* (*rushing stream*) kŭmnyu 급류, (*pl.*) (*downpour*) ŏksu 억수. *a mountain ~* sankoltchagiŭi kŭmnyu 산골짜기의 급류/ *It rained in* ∼s. Pinŭn ŏksuro ssodajyŏssŭmnida. 비는 억수로 쏟아졌읍니다.

tortoise *n.* kŏbuk 거북.

torture *n.* (*agony*) kot'ong 고통, komun 고문. —*vt.* (*torment*) kot'ongŭl chuda 고통을 주다, komunhada 고문한다. *instrument of* ∼ hyŏnggu 형구/ *put to* ∼ komunhada 고문하다/ *be* ∼*d with anxiety* purane ttŏlda 불안에 떨다.

toss *vt.,vi.* (*throw*) tŏnjida 던지다, (*lift up suddenly*) ch'yŏdŭlda 쳐들다, (*sway*) twihŭndŭlda 뒤흔들다. *Let us* ∼ *up.* Tongjŏnŭl tŏnjyŏ sŭngburŭl chŏnghapshida. 동전을 던져 승부를 정합시다.

total *n.* (*aggregate*) hapkye 합계. —*adj.* (*whole*) hapkyeŭi 합계의, (*utter*) sunjŏnhan 순전한. *a grand* ∼ ch'onggye 총계/ *What is the* ∼? Hapkyenŭn ŏlmaimnikka? 합계는 얼마입니까/ *the* ∼ *amount* ch'ongaek 총액/ *the* ∼ *number* ch'ongsu 총수/ *the* ∼ *population* ch'ongin-gu 총인구/ *I'm a* ∼ *stranger here myself.* Yŏginŭn saengjŏn ch'ŏŭmimnida. 여기는 생전 처음입니다.

totally *adv.* aju 아주, modu 모두.

totter *vi.* pit'ŭlpit'ŭl kŏtta 비틀비틀 걷다.

touch *vi.,vt.* taeda 대다, (*reach*) tat'a 닿다, (*fumble*) manjida 만지다. —*n.* (*contact*) chŏpch'ok 접촉. *I haven't* ∼*ed the piano for months.* Sugaewŏl tongan p'iano-enŭn sondo taeji anassŭmnida. 수개월 동안 피아노에는 손도 대지 않았읍니다/ *Can you get in* ∼ *with him?* Kŭbun-gwa yŏllagi toemnikka? 그분과 연락이 됩니까/ *We've been out of* ∼ *lately.* Yojŭm hanch'am mot mannassŭmnida. 요즘 한참 못 만났읍니다.

touching *adj.* (*moving*) kamdongjŏgin 감동적인, (*pathetic*) aech'ŏroun 애처로운. *a* ∼ *tale* aech'ŏroun iyagi 애처로운 이야기.

tough *adj.* (*hard*) tandanhan 단단한, (*sticky*) chilgin 질긴, (*stubborn*) wan-gohan 완고한. *Leather is* ∼. Kajugŭn chilgimnida. 가죽은 질깁니다/ ∼ *meat* chilgin kogi 질긴 고기/ *a* ∼ *neighborhood* wan-gohan iut saramdŭl 완고한 이웃 사람들.

tour *n.* (*round trip*) kwan-gwang yŏhaeng 관광 여행,

yuram 유람. —*vi., vt.* yuramhada 유람하다. *When do you want to make a ~ ?* Önje kwan-gwangŭl hashiryŏmnikka ? 언제 관광을 하시렵니까/ *Can you take care of a bus ~ ?* Pŏsŭ yŏhaengŭl chusŏnhae chushigessŭmnikka ? 버스 여행을 주선해 주시겠읍니까 ?

tourist *n.* kwan-gwanggaek 관광객. *Do you have a ~ visa ?* Kwan-gwang sachŭngŭl kajigo kyeshimnikka ? 관광 사증을 가지고 계십니까/ *Where is the ~ information office ?* Kwan-gwang annaesonŭn ŏdi issŭmnikka ? 관광 안내소는 어디 있읍니까/ *a ~ party* kwan-gwangdan 관광단/ *a ~ bureau* yŏhaeng annaeso 여행 안내소.

toward(s) *prep.* (*direction*) tchoguro 쪽으로, (*as regards*) ...e taehae ...에 대해, (*of time*) muryŏbe 무렵에, kyŏng[tchŭm]e 경[쯤]에, (*about*) kŏŭi 거의, ...karyang ...가량, (*for the purpose of*) ...ŭl wihayŏ ...을 위하여. *Someone is coming ~ us.* Nugun-gaga uri tchoguro ogo issŭmnida. 누군가가 우리 쪽으로 오고 있읍니다/ *I went to bed ~ 11 o'clock.* Yŏrhanshitchŭme chassŭmnida. 11시쯤에 잤읍니다/ *Save money ~ your old age.* Nohurŭl wihae chŏch'ugŭl hashipshio. 노후를 위해 저축을 하십시오.

towel *n.* sugŏn 수건, t'awŏl 타월. *wipe with a ~* sugŏnŭro takta 수건으로 닦다/*moisten a ~* sugŏnŭl chŏkshida 수건을 적시다/ *~ hanger* sugŏn kŏri 수건 걸이/*Here's an iced ~ for you.* Yŏgi naengsugŏni issŭmnida. 여기 냉수건이 있읍니다.

tower *n.* t'ap 탑.

town *n.* ŭp 읍. *the ~ people* ŭmmin 읍민/ *a China ~* Chunggugin kŏri 중국인 거리/ *~ planning* toshi kyehoek 도시 계획.

toy *n.* changnankam 장난감. *~shop* wan-gujŏm 완구점.

trace *n.* (*track*) chaguk 자국, (*footprint*) palchaguk 발자국, (*vestige*) hŭnjŏk 흔적. —*vt.* (*track down*) ch'ujŏk'ada 추적하다, (*detect*) t'amjihada 탐지하다.

track *n.* (*rails*) sŏllo 선로, (*course*) t'ŭraek 트랙, (*footprint*) palchaguk 발자국, (*make left*) chach'wi 자취. *On which ~ does the express for Pusan leave ?* Pusanhaeng kŭp'aengŭn myŏt pŏn sŏnimnikka ? 부산행 급행은

몇 번 선입니까/ *Take the train on Track 2.* I pŏn sŏn
yŏlch'arŭl t'ashipshio. 2번 선 열차를 타십시오.

tractor *n.* kyŏninch'a 견인차, t'ŭraekt'ŏ 트랙터.

trade *n.* (*business*) changsa 장사, (*commerce*) muyŏk
무역, (*occupation*) chigŏp 직업. —*vi.* muyŏk'ada 무역
하다. *a dangerous* ~ wihŏmhan changsa 위험한 장사/
overseas ~ haeoe muyŏk 해외 무역/ ~ *fair* muyŏk pangnamhoe 무역 박람회/ *a* ~ *mission* muyŏk sajŏltan 무역
사절단/ *the* ~ *imbalance* muyŏk yŏkcho 무역 역조/ *a*
trading firm[*company*] muyŏk hoesa 무역 회사/ *a* ~
mark sangp'yo 상표/ ~ *union* nodong chohap 노동 조합/
~ *wind* muyŏkp'ung 무역풍. 「in 소매 상인.

tradesman *n.* muyŏksang 무역상, (*retailer*) somae sang-
tradition *n.* chŏnt'ong 전통, (*legend*) kujŏn 구전(口傳).
according to (*a*)~ chŏnt'onge ttarŭmyŏn 전통에 따르면/
We value our Korean ~. Uri Han-gugŭi chŏnt'ongŭl
chonjunghamnida. 우리 한국의 전통을 존중합니다.

traditional *adj.* chŏnt'ongjogin 전통적인. ~ *custom* chon-
t'ongjŏgin kwansŭp 전통적인 관습.

traffic *n.* (*commerce*) kŏrae 거래, maemae 매매, (*coming*
& going) kyot'ong 교통, wangnae 왕래. *the liquor* ~
churyu maemae 주류 매매/*the international* ~ kukchejŏk
kŏrae 국제적 거래/ *busy* ~ pumbinŭn kyot'ong 붐비는 교
통/ *Go straight until you come to the* ~ *lights.* Kyot'ong
shinhodŭngi innŭn tekkaji kotchang kŏrŏgashio. 교통 신
호등이 있는 데까지 곧장 걸어가시오/ ~ *accident* kyot'ong
sago 교통 사고/ ~ *signal* kyot'ong shinho 교통 신호.

tragedy *n.* pigŭk 비극, (*calamity*) ch'amsa 참사(慘事). *a*
domestic ~ kajŏng pigŭk 가정 비극/ *an air* ~ hanggong
ch'amsa 항공 참사/ *a love* ~ sarangŭi pigŭk 사랑의 비극.

train *n.* yŏlch'a 열차, kich'a 기차. —*vt.*, *vi.* (*drill*) hullyŏnhada 훈련하다. *Are you travelling by* ~? Kich'aro
yŏhaenghashimnikka? 기차로 여행하십니까/*Where can I*
get the ~ *for Pusan?* Pusanhaeng yŏlch'anŭn ŏdisŏ
t'amnikka? 부산행 열차는 어디서 탑니까/ *Is it faster to*
go there by ~ *than by bus?* Yŏlch'aro kanŭn kŏshi
pŏsŭboda pparŭmnikka? 열차로 가는 것이 버스보다 빠르니

까/ *an express* ~ kŭp'aeng yŏlch'a 급행 열차/ *a night* ~ pamch'a 밤차/ *the last* ~ majimak yŏlch'a 마지막 열차, makch'a 막차/ *catch*[*miss*] *the* ~ kich'arŭl t'ada[noch'ida] 기차를 타다[놓치다]/ ~ *dogs* kaerŭl hullyŏnhada 개를 훈련하다/ *highly* ~*ed officer* hullyunghi hullyŏndoen changgyo 훌륭히 훈련된 장교.

traitor *n.* (*rebel*) panyŏkcha 반역자, (*betrayer*) paebanja 배반자. *a* ~ *to the nation* maegungno 매국노.

tram *n.* (*tramcar*) shiga chŏnch'a 시가 전차.

transact *vt., vi.* (*settle*) ch'ŏrihada 처리하다, (*deal*) kŏraehada 거래하다. ~ *business with* kŏraehada 거래하다.

transaction *n.* *the* ~ *of business* ŏmmu ch'ŏri 업무 처리/ *cash* ~*s* hyŏn-gŭm kŏrae 현금 거래.

transcribe *vt.* (*copy*) poksahada 복사하다, pekkida 베끼다, (*radio, etc.*) nogŭm pangsonghada 녹음 방송하다/ ~ *it entirely* t'ongtchaero pekkida 통째로 베끼다.

transcription *n.* (*copying*) chŏnsa 전사(轉寫), (*copy*) sabon 사본, tŭngbon 등본, (*radio, etc.*) nogŭm (pangsong) 녹음 (방송). *errors in* ~ p'ilsa-esŏ saenggin oryu 필사(筆寫)에서 생긴 오류/ *the KBS* ~ *service* KBS nogŭm pangsong KBS 녹음 방송/ *a* ~ *machine* nogŭmgi 녹음기.

transfer *vt., vi.* (*convey*) omgida 옮기다, unbanhada 운반하다, (*change*) karat'ada 갈아타다, (*make over*) yangdohada 양도하다, (*change posts*) chŏn-gŭnhada 전근(轉勤)하다. —*n.* (*ticket*) karat'anŭn p'yo 갈아타는 표. *I'll* ~ *your call to extension 215.* Naesŏn ibaekshibobŏnŭro tollyŏ tŭrigessŭmnida. 내선 215번으로 돌려 드리겠습니다/ *T*~ *here for Chinhae.* Chinhaehaengŭn yŏgisŏ karat'aya hamnida. 진해행(行)은 여기서 갈아타야 합니다/ *The teacher was* ~*red to the Tong-a High School.* Kŭ sŏnsaengnimŭn tonga kodŭng hakkyoro chŏn-gŭnhasyŏssŭmnida. 그 선생님은 동아 고등 학교로 전근하셨습니다/ *a* ~ *student* chŏnhaksaeng 전학생/ *May I have a* ~ *ticket, please?* Hwanch'akwŏnŭl chuseyo. 환차권을 주세요.

transform *vt.* (*change the shape*) pyŏnhyŏngshik'ida 변형시키다, (*transmute*) pyŏnhwashik'ida 변화시키다. *He was* ~*ed into another man.* Kŭinŭn sarami pyŏnhaessŭmnida. 그이는 사람이 변했읍니다.

transformer *n.* pyŏnapki 변압기. *You have to use a ~.*
Pyŏnapkirŭl sayonghaeya hamnida. 변압기를 사용해야 합
니다.

transfusion *n.* (*blood ~*) suhyŏl 수혈. *receive a* (*blood*)
~ suhyŏrŭl patta 수혈을 받다.

transgress *vt., vi.* (*overstep*) nŏmta 넘다, (*violate*) ŏgida
어기다, wibanhada 위반하다.

transit *n.* (*passage*) t'onggwa 통과, t'onghaeng 통행,
(*conveyance*) unban 운반, (*route*) t'ongno 통로. *the ~
of goods* hwamul susong 화물 수송/ *~ duty* t'onghaengse 통행세.

translate *vt.* pŏnyŏk'ada 번역하다, (*interpret*) haesŏk'a·
da 해석하다. *T~ the following Korean into English.*
Taŭm Han-gugŏrŭl Yŏngŏro pŏnyŏk'ashio. 다음 한국어를
영어로 번역하시오/ *Can you ~ this letter into Korean?*
I p'yŏnjirŭl Han-gugŏro pŏnyŏk'al su issŭmnikka? 이 편
지를 한국어로 번역할 수 있읍니까?

translation *n.* pŏnyŏk 번역. *a close ~* chigyŏk 직역(直
譯)/ *second-hand ~* chungyŏk 중역(重譯)/ *translate a ~*
chungyŏgŭl hada 중역을 하다.

translator *n.* pŏnyŏkcha 번역자.

transmit *vt.* (*pass on*) chŏndarhada 전달하다, (*send*)
ponaeda 보내다, (*hand down*) mullida 물리다.

transparent *adj.* (*seen through*) t'umyŏnghan 투명한,
pich'inŭn 비치는.

transplant *vt.* omgyŏ shimta 옮겨 심다.

transport *vt.* (*carry*) susonghada 수송하다, unbanhada
운반하다. *—n.* (*conveyance*) unban 운반. *~ goods by
lorry* t'ŭrŏgŭro hwamurŭl unbanhada 트럭으로 화물을
운반하다/ *a ~ company* unsong hoesa 운송 회사/ *~ difficulties* susongnan 수송난/ *a ~ ship* susongsŏn 수송선/
a ~ plane susonggi 수송기.

transportation *n.* (*transport*) susong 수송, (*conveyance*)
unban 운반, (*expenses*) unim 운임. *land ~* yugun 육운/
ocean ~ haeun 해운/ *railroad ~* ch'ŏlto susong 철도 수
송/ *a ~ company* unsong hoesa 운송 회사.

trap *n.* tŏt 덫, olgami 올가미. —*vt.* tŏch'ŭro chapta 덫
으로 잡다. *I set a ~ for the rat.* Chwidŏch'ŭl noassŭmnida. 쥐덫을 놓았읍니다/ *a light ~* yuadŭng 유아등(誘蛾
燈)/ *catch a deer in a ~* sasŭmŭl olgamiro chapta 사
슴을 올가미로 잡다.

trash *n.* (*rubbish*) ssŭregi 쓰레기, (*waste*) tchikkŏgi 찌
꺼기, (*worthless stuff*) chaptongsani 잡동사니. *a ~ can*
ssŭregit'ong 쓰레기통/ *This novel is mere ~.* I sosŏrŭn
chŏngmal shishihamnida. 이 소설은 정말 시시합니다.

travel *n.* yŏhaeng 여행. —*vi.* yŏhaenghada 여행하다.
overseas ~ haeoe yŏhaeng 해외 여행/ *railway ~* kich'a
yŏhaeng 기차 여행/ *space ~* uju yŏhaeng 우주 여행/ *Let
me take you to a ~ information bureau.* Kwan-
gwang annaeso-e mosyŏda tŭrilkkayo? 관광 안내소에 모
셔다 드릴까요/ *Are you ~ling for pleasure?* Yuram
yŏhaeng chungishimnikka? 유람 여행 중이십니까/ *I'm ~-
ling on business.* Sangyongŭro yŏhaeng chungimnida.
상용으로 여행 중입니다.

traveller *n.* yŏhaengja 여행자. *a pedestrian ~* tobo yŏhaengja 도보 여행자/ *a sight-seeing ~* kwan-gwang
yŏhaengja 관광 여행자/ *Will you accept ~'s checks?*
Yŏhaenja sup'yorŭl passŭmnikka? 여행자 수표를 받습니까?

travelling *n.* yŏhaeng 여행. —*adj.* yŏhaengŭi 여행의. *a
~ bag* yŏhaeng kabang 여행 가방/ *~ expenses* yŏbi 여비/
~ salesmen sunhoe oep'anwŏn 순회 외판원.

tray *n.* chaengban 쟁반. *an ash ~* chaettŏri 재떨이/ *a tea
~* ch'atchaengban 찻쟁반.

treacherous *adj.* (*apt to betray*) paebanhanŭn 배반하는,
(*deceptive*) mitchi mot'al 믿지 못할, (*unreliable*) pulsŏngshirhan 불성실한. *a ~ action* paeshin haengwi 배신
행위/ *a ~ bridge* wit'aeroun tari 위태로운 다리/ *~ weather*
mitchi mot'al nalssi 믿지 못할 날씨.

tread *vi., vt.* (*walk*) kŏtta 걷다, (*go*) kada 가다, (*step*)
papta 밟다, (*trample*) chitpapta 짓밟다. *Don't ~ on the
flower beds.* Hwadanŭl papchi mashio. 화단을 밟지 마시오.

treason *n.* panyŏk 반역. *an act of ~* panyŏk haengwi
반역 행위.

treasure *n.* pobae 보배. *national* ~ kukpo 국보. *Our cook is a perfect* ~. Uri chip yorisanŭn chŏngmal pobaeimnida. 우리 집 요리사는 정말 보배입니다.

treat *vt., vi.* (*act toward*) taeuhada 대우하다, (*deal*) taruda 다루다, (*entertain*) taejŏp'ada 대접하다, (*cure*) ch'iryohada 치료하다. —*n.* (*entertainment*) taejŏp 대접. *Don't* ~ *me as a child.* Narŭl ŏrinae ch'wigŭp haji mashio. 나를 어린애 취급 하지 마시오/ ~ *a servant kindly* hainŭl ch'injŏrhage daruda 하인(下人)을 친절하게 다루다/ *We were* ~*ed to drinks.* Urinŭn sul taejŏbŭl padassŭmnida. 우리는 술 대접을 받았읍니다/ *I'll* ~ *you at the ice-cream house.* Aisŭk'ŭrim kageesŏ taejŏp'ae tŭrijiyo. 아이스크림 가게에서 대접해 드리지요/ *How would you* ~ *a case of cancer?* Am hwanjarŭl ŏttŏk'e ch'iryohajiyo? 암 환자를 어떻게 치료하지요/ *This is my* ~. Igŏn naega taejŏp'anŭn kŏmnida. 이건 내가 대접하는 겁니다.

treatment *n.* (*usage*) taeu 대우, ch'wigŭp 취급, (*therapy*) chiryo(pŏp) 치료(법). *discriminative* ~ ch'abyŏl taeu 차별 대우/ *fair* ~ kongjŏnghan taeu 공정한 대우/ *I cannot suffer such* ~. Kŭrŏn taeunŭn padŭl su ŏpsŭmnida. 그런 대우는 받을 수 없읍니다/ *Are you still under* ~ *in hospital?* Ajik pyŏngwŏnesŏ ch'iryorŭl patko issŭmnikka? 아직 병원에서 치료를 받고 있읍니까?

treaty *n.* choyak 조약, hyŏpchŏng 협정. *conclude a* ~ choyagŭl maetta 조약을 맺다/ *a commercial* ~ t'ongsang choyak 통상 조약. *a Non-aggression T*~ pulgach'im choyak 불가침 조약/*a T*~ *of Peace and Amity* pyŏnghwa suho choyak 평화 수호 조약.

tree *n.* namu 나무. *a dead* ~ komok 고목/ *an evergreen* ~ sangnoksu 상록수/ *a fruit* ~ kwasunamu 과수나무/ *street* ~*s* karosu 가로수/ ~*-lined street* karosu kil 가로수 길.

trellis *n.* (*lattice*) ch'angsal 창살.

tremble *vi.* (*shake*) ttŏlda 떨다, ttŏllida 떨리다. *We were trembling with cold.* Urinŭn ch'uwiro ttŏlgo issŏssŭmnida. 우리는 추위로 떨고 있었읍니다/ ~ *with anger* noyŏumŭro chŏnshinŭl ttŏlda 노여움으로 전신을 떨다.

tremor *n.* (*trill*) chŏnŭm 전음, (*shiver*) chŏnyul 전율.

trench *n.* (*ditch*) haeja 해자(垓字), (*mil.*) ch'amho 참호. *dig up a* ～ ch'amhorŭl p'ada 참호를 파다.

trend *n.* (*general direction*) panghyang 방향, (*inclination*) kyŏnghyang 경향, ch'use 추세.

trespass *vi.* (*invade*) ch'imip'ada 침입하다. *May I ～ on you for the mustard?* Kyŏjarŭl chom chibŏ chushige-ssŭmnikka? 겨자를 좀 집어 주시겠읍니까?

trial *n.* (*public ～*) kongp'an 공판, (*experiment*) shihŏm 시험, (*affliction*) shiryŏn 시련, (*annoyance*) tut'ongkŏri 두통거리. *a public ～* kongp'an 공판/ *the first ～* cheil-shim 제1심/ *I shall put it to further ～.* Tŏ shihŏmhae pogessŭmnida. 더 시험해 보겠읍니다/ *I think we'll hire you on a trial basis.* Shihŏmjŏguro ch'aeyonghae polkka hamnida. 시험적으로 채용해 볼까 합니다/ *a ～ trip* shiunjŏn 시운전/ *My young brother is a ～ to my parents.* Nae aunŭn uri pumonimŭi tut'ongkŏriimnida. 내 아우는 우리 부모님의 두통거리입니다.

triangle *n.* samgak'yŏng 3각형. *the eternal ～* (*love*) samgak kwan-gye 3각 관계.

tribe *n.* chongjok 종족. *the barbarian ～s* yamanjok 야만족.

tribunal *n.* (*court*) pŏpchŏng 법정(法廷).

trick *n.* (*artifice*) kyeryak 계략, (*illusion*) ch'akkak 착각, (*mischief*) changnan 장난, (*knack*) pigyŏl 비결. —*vt.* (*cheat*) sogida 속이다. *play a mean ～* piyŏrhan supŏbŭl ssŭda 비열한 수법을 쓰다/ *I don't know the ～ of it.* Nanŭn kŭ yoryŏngŭl morŭgessŭmnida. 나는 그 요령을 모르겠읍니다/ *You have been ～ed.* Tangshinŭn sokko issŭmnida. 당신은 속고 있읍니다.

trickle *vi.*, *vt.* ttokttok ttŏrŏjida[ttŏrŏttŭrida] 똑똑 떨어지다[떨어뜨리다]. *Blood ～d from the wound.* Sangch'ŏ-esŏ p'iga ttokttok ttŏrŏjimnida. 상처에서 피가 똑똑 떨어집니다.

trifle *n.* (*thing of little value*) shishihan kŏt 시시한 것, (*small amount*) soryang 소량, (*somewhat*) yakkan 약간. *I want you to accept this ～.* I hach'anŭn mulgŏnŭl pada chushipshio. 이 하찮은 물건을 받아 주십시오/ *Spare a ~ for the waiter*. Weit'ŏege t'ibŭl chogŭm chushio. 웨이터에게 팁을 조금 주시오.

trifling *adj.* shishihan 시시한, hach'anŭn 하찮은.

trigger *n.* pangasoe 방아쇠.

trim *adj.* (*neat*) malssuk'an 말쑥한, (*in good order*) chŏngdondoen 정돈된. —*vt.*, *vi.* (*make neat*) tadŭmta 다듬다, (*decorate*) changshik'ada 장식하다, (*cut*) charŭda 자르다/ *a ~ costume* malssuk'an otch'arim 말쑥한 옷차림/ *~ one's nail* sont'obŭl kkakta 손톱을 깎다/ *~ a Christmas tree* K'ŭrisŭmasŭ t'ŭrirŭl changshik'ada 크리스마스 트리를 장식하다/ *Shall I ~ your hair a little?* Mŏrirŭl chom challa tŭrilkkayo? 머리를 좀 잘라 드릴까요/ *T~ it up a little, please.* Yakkanman ch'yŏnae chuseyo. 약간만 처내 주세요/ *Just ~ the sides and backs.* Yŏpkwa twiman chom ch'yŏ chuseyo. 옆과 뒤만 좀 처 주세요.

trinity *n.* (*the ~*) samwi ilch'e 삼위 일체.

trip *n.* (*journey*) yŏhaeng 여행. —*vi.*, *vt.* (*stumble*) kŏllyŏ nŏmŏjida 걸려 넘어지다, (*cause to fall*) nŏmŏttŭrida 넘어뜨리다. *a weekend ~* chumal yŏhaeng 주말 여행/ *Say, how was the ~?* Kŭrŏnde, yŏhaengŭn ŏttŏhaessŭmnikka? 그런데, 여행은 어떠했읍니까/ *Have a good ~.* Chŭlgŏun yŏhaengŭl haseyo. 즐거운 여행을 하세요/ *a round-the-world ~* segye ilchu yŏhaeng 세계 일주 여행/ *I've ~ped on that sill.* Kŭ munchibange kŏllyŏ nŏmŏjyŏssŭmnida 그 문지방에 걸려 넘어졌읍니다/ *I ~ped over something hard.* Muŏn-ga tantanhan kŏse kŏllyŏ nŏmŏjyŏssŭmnida. 무언가 단단한 것에 걸려 넘어졌읍니다.

triumph *n.* (*victory*) sŭngni 승리. —*vi.* (*win*) igida 이기다. *The ~s of modern science* hyŏndae kwahagŭi sŭngni 현대 과학의 승리.

triumphal *adj.* kaesŏnŭi 개선의. *~ arch* kaesŏnmun 개선문.

troop *n.* (*pl.*) kundae 군대. *M.P. ~s* hŏnbyŏngdae 헌병대.

trophy *n.* (*of victory*) usŭnggi[p'ae] 우승기[패]. *a golf ~* kolp'ŭ usŭngp'ae 골프 우승패.

tropic *n.* yŏltae 열대. *the ~s* yŏltae chibang 열대 지방.

tropical *adj.* yŏltae (chibang)ŭi 열대 (지방)의. *a ~ plant* yŏltae shingmul 열대 식물/ *~ regions* yŏltae chibang 열대 지방/ *~ climates* yŏltaesŏng kihu 열대성 기후.

trouble *n.* (*anxiety*) kŏkchŏng 걱정, (*annoyance*) kot'ong 고통, (*disease*) pyŏng 병, (*pains*) sugo 수고, (*disorder*) pullan 분란. —*vt., vi.* (*worry*) koerop'ida 괴롭히다, (*feel anxious*) kŏkchŏnghada 걱정하다, (*take pains*) aessŭda 애쓰다. *Oh, don't ~, thanks.* A kŏkchŏng mashipshio, kwaench'anssŭmnida. 아, 걱정 마십시오, 괜찮습니다/ *What is the ~ with you?* Ottŏk'e toen kŏmnikka? 어떻게 된 겁니까/ *heart* [*mental, lung*] *~* shimjang [chŏngshin, p'ye]pyŏng 심장[정신, 폐]병/ *I'm having ~ with my eyes.* Nuni ap'ŭmnida. 눈이 아픕니다/ *What seems to be the ~?* Ŏdiga ap'ŭshijiyo? 어디가 아프시지요/ *I'm sorry to ~ you about such matter.* Kŭrŏn illo sugo kkich'yŏ mianhamnida. 그런 일로 수고 끼쳐 미안합니다/ *Don't ~ to meet me at the airport.* Ilburŏ konghangkkaji majung naoshiji mashipshio. 일부러 공항까지 마중 나오시지 마십시오/ *Did he cause any ~?* Musŭn irŭl chŏjillŏssŭmnikka? 무슨 일을 저질렀읍니까?

troublesome *adj.* kwich'anŭn 귀찮은, sŏnggashin 성가신.

trough *n.* kuyu 구유, yŏmult'ong 여물통.

trousers *n.* (*pl.*) paji 바지. *bell-bottom ~* nap'al paji 나팔 바지/ *knee ~* panbaji 반바지/ *work ~* chagŏp paji 작업 바지/ *Your ~ are unbuttoned.* Paji tanch'uga pŏtkyŏjyŏ issŭmnida. 바지 단추가 벗겨져 있읍니다.

trout *n.* songŏ 송어.

truce *n.* (*armistice*) hyujŏn 휴전. *make a ~* hyujŏnhada 휴전하다/ *a ~ line* hyujŏnsŏn 휴전선/ *~ talks* hyujŏn hoedam 휴전 회담/ *a treaty of ~* hyujŏn choyak 휴전 조약/ *~ negotiations* hyujŏn hyŏpsang 휴전 협상.

truck *n.* t'ŭrŏk 트럭, hwamulch'a 화물차.

true *adj.* (*real*) chintchaŭi 진짜의, (*correct*) chŏngmarŭi 정말의, (*exact*) chŏnghwak'an 정확한, (*faithful*) ch'amdoen 참된, (*applicable*) tŭrŏmannŭn 들어맞는. *a ~ story* shirhwa 실화/ *Is that ~?* Chŏngmarimnikka? 정말입니까/ *Be ~ to your word.* Yaksogŭl chik'ishio. 약속을 지키시오/

I'll be ～ *to you.* Sashirŭl marhae tŭrigessŭmnida. 사실을
말해 드리겠읍니다/ *Is the wheel* ～? Ch'abak'winŭn chal
kkiwŏjyŏ issŭmnikka? 차바퀴는 잘 끼워져 있읍니까?

truly *adv.* (*indeed*) ch'amŭro 참으로, chŏngmallo 정말로,
(*loyally*) ch'ungshirhage 충실하게, (*exactly*) chŏnghwak'i
정확히, (*really*) chintcharo 진짜로. *I am* ～ *grateful.*
Ch'amŭro kamsahamnida. 참으로 감사합니다/ *T*～ *I am
surprised.* Chŏngmal kkamtchak nollassŭmnida. 정말
깜짝 놀랐읍니다.

trumpet *n.* nap'al 나팔. *blow a* ～ nap'arŭl pulda 나팔을
불다/ *a* ～ *call* nap'al sori 나팔 소리.

trumpeter *n.* nap'alsu 나팔수.

trunk *n.* (*stem*) chulgi 줄기, (*body*) tongch'e 동체,
(*chest*) t'ŭrŏngk'ŭ 트렁크. *a tree* ～ namu chulgi 나무 줄
기/ *What kind of* ～ *do you want to buy?* Ottŏn t'ŭrŏng-
k'ŭrŭl sashiryŏmnikka? 어떤 트렁크를 사시렵니까?

trust *n.* (*confidence*) shinyong 신용, (*hope*) kidae 기대,
(*custody*) pogwan(mul) 보관(물), (*commerce*) t'ŭrŏ-
sŭt'ŭ 트러스트. —*vt., vi.* (*rely on*) mitta 믿다, shinyong-
hada 신용하다, (*entrust*) matkida 맡기다, (*look*) kidaehada 기대하다. *He* ～*ed me with his money.* Kŭinŭn
naege tonŭl matkyŏssŭmnida. 그이는 내게 돈을 맡겼읍니
다/ *Can I* ～ *the keys to him.* Kŭiege yŏlsoerŭl matkil
su issŭlkkayo? 그이에게 열쇠를 맡길 수 있을까요/ *I* ～ *you
can come.* Oshil su issŭrira missŭmnida. 오실 수 있으리라
믿습니다.

trustworthy *adj.* (*reliable*) midŭl su innŭn 믿을 수 있는,
tŭndŭnhan 튼튼한. *a* ～ *young man* midŭmjik'an ch'ŏngnyŏn 믿음직한 청년.

truth *n.* (*fact*) sashil 사실, (*reality*) chinshil 진실, (*honesty*) sŏngshil 성실. *talk the* ～ sashirŭl marhada 사실을
말하다. *Is there any* ～ *in the rumor?* Kŭ somuni kwayŏn sashirilkkayo? 그 소문이 과연 사실일까요/ *Tell me
the* ～. Sashirŭl marhashipshio. 사실을 말하십시오/ *to
tell the* ～ sashildaero marhamyŏn 사실대로 말하면.

truthful *adj.* (*true*) sashirŭi 사실의, (*veracious*) chŏngjik'an 정직한. *a* ～ *child* chŏngjik'an ai 정직한 아이.

try *vt.*, *vi.* (*attempt*) haeboda 해보다, (*test*) shihŏmhada 시험하다, (*use*) ssŏboda 써보다, (*in a court*) chaep'anhada 재판하다, (*taste*) masŭl poda 맛을 보다. *T~ to get here early.* Iltchik yŏgi odorok hashio. 일찍 여기 오도록 하시오/ *Please ~ me for the job.* Chŏege kŭ irŭl shik'yŏ poshipshio. 저에게 그 일을 시켜 보십시오/ *Which judge will ~ the case?* Ku sakŏnŭn ŏnŭ p'ansaga shimnihamnikka? 그 사건은 어느 판사가 심리합니까/ *Won't you ~ some cakes?* K'eik'ŭrado tŭshilkkayo? 케이크라도 드실까요/ *I have never tried real Korean dishes before.* Chintcha Han-guk yorirŭl ajik mŏkchi mot'aessŭmnida. 진짜 한국 요리를 아직 먹지 못했읍니다.

trying *adj.* (*annoying*) sŏnggashin 성가신, (*distressing*) koeroun 괴로운. *a ~ journey* kodoen yŏhaeng 고된 여행.

tub *n.* t'ong 통, mult'ong 물통, (*bath*) mogyok 목욕. *a bath ~* mogyokt'ong 목욕통/ *I never miss my morning ~.* Ach'im mogyogŭl ppattŭriji anssŭmnida. 아침 목욕을 빠뜨리지 않습니다.

tube *n.* (*pipe*) kwan 관(管), t'yubŭ 튜브. *a test ~* shihŏmgwan 시험관. *a vacuum ~* chin-gonggwan 진공관/ *a rubber ~* komu t'yubŭ 고무 튜브.

tuberculosis *n.* kyŏrhaek 결핵. *~ germs* kyŏrhaekkyun 결핵균/ *a ~ patient* kyŏrhaek hwanja 결핵 환자.

tuck *vt.* kŏdŏ ollida 걷어 올리다, (*thrust*) ssusyŏnŏt'a 쑤셔넣다. *~ up one's sleeves* somaerŭl kŏdŏ ollida 소매를 걷어 올리다/ *T~ your shirt in.* Syassŭ charagŭl chŏbŏ nŏŭshio. 샤쓰 자락을 접어 넣으시오.

Tuesday *n.* hwayoil 화요일.

tuft *n.* (*bunch*) songi 송이, (*clump*) tŏmbul 덤불.

tug *n.* (*~boat*) yeinsŏn 예인선. *—vt.* (*pull*) kkŭlda 끌다. *a ~ of war* chuldarigi 줄다리기/ *Don't ~ so hard.* Kŭrŏk'e himkkŏt tanggiji mashio. 그렇게 힘껏 당기지 마시오.

tuition *n.* (*teaching*) kyosu 교수, (*fee*) suŏmnyo 수업료. *private ~* kaein kyosu 개인 교수/ *I have private ~ in mathematics.* Nanŭn suhagŭi kaein chidorŭl patko issŭmnida. 나는 수학의 개인 지도를 받고 있읍니다.

tumble *vi., vt.* (*fall over*) nŏmŏjida 넘어지다, (*roll*) kurŭda 구르다, (*overthrow*) nŏmŏttŭrida 넘어뜨리다. *I ~d down the stairs.* Nanŭn kyedanŭl kullŏ ttŏrŏjyŏssŭmnida. 나는 계단을 굴러 떨어졌읍니다.

tumbler *n.* (*glass*) k'ŏp 컵.

tuna *n.* tarangŏ 다랑어.

tune *n.* (*melody*) kokcho 곡조, (*tone*) karak 가락. —*vi., vt.* (*adjust*) choŭmhada 조음하다, (*adapt*) chohwashik'ida 조화시키다, (*radio,etc.*) p'ajangŭl match'uda 파장을 맞추다. *What is your favorite ~?* Choahashinŭn kogŭn muŏshimnikka? 좋아하시는 곡은 무엇입니까/*I ~d the television to Channel 3.* Nanŭn t'ellebijŏnŭl ch'aenŏl same match'uŏssŭmnida. 나는 텔레비전을 채널 3에 맞추었읍니다/*I ~d in to another station.* Tarŭn pangsongguguro taiŏrŭl tollyŏssŭmnida. 다른 방송국으로 다이얼을 돌렸읍니다.

tunnel *n.* t'ŏnŏl 터널. *go through a ~* t'ŏnŏrŭl t'onggwahada 터널을 통과하다.

turf *n.* (*lawn*) chandi 잔디, chandibat 잔디밭, (*racecourse*) kyŏngmajang 경마장.

turkey *n.* (*fowl*) ch'ilmyŏnjo 칠면조.

Turkey *n.* (*country*) t'ŏk'i 터키.

turn *n.* (*rotation*) hoejŏn 회전, (*change*) pyŏnhwa 변화, (*turning*) mot'ungi 모퉁이, (*order*) ch'arye 차례. —*vi., vt.* (*go round*) tolda 돌다, (*change direction*) panghyangŭl pakkuda 방향을 바꾸다, (*reverse*) twijipta 뒤집다. *Take the first ~ to the right.* Ch'ŏt mot'ungiesŏ orŭntchoguro toshio. 첫 모퉁이에서 오른쪽으로 도시오/*Wait your ~.* Taegŭi ch'aryerŭl kidarishio. 댁의 차례를 기다리시오/*I don't know where to ~.* Ŏdisŏ toraya halchi morŭgessŭmnida. 어디서 돌아야 할지 모르겠읍니다/*T~ right into this little alley.* Orŭntchoguro tora i chagŭn kolmokkillo tŭrŏgapshida. 오른쪽으로 돌아 이 작은 골목길로 들어갑시다/*I'll have this old overcoat ~ed.* I nalgŭn oet'urŭl twijibŏ saero mandŭlgessŭmnida. 이 낡은 외투를 뒤집어 새로 만들겠읍니다/*~ away* (*face*) tollida 돌리다/*She ~ed her face from me.* Kŭ puinŭn narŭl oemyŏnhaessŭmnida. 그 부인은 나를 외면했읍니다/ *T~ off the light*. Purŭl kkŭshipshio. 불을 끄십시오/ *T~ the radio on*. Radiorŭl t'ŭshio. 라디오를 트시오/ *T~ on the light*. Purŭl k'yŏshio. 불을 켜시오/ *It ~ed out true*. Sashirimi palkyŏjyŏssŭmnida. 사실임이 밝혀졌읍니다/ *We had a swing by ~s*. Kyodaero kŭnerŭl t'assŭmnida. 교대로 그 네를 탔읍니다/ *The children got on the train in ~*. Ŏrinidŭrŭn ch'aryero yŏlch'a-e ollassŭmnida. 어린이들은 차례로 열차에 올랐읍니다.

turner *n.* sŏnban-gong 선반공.

turning *n.* (*corner*) mot'ungi 모퉁이. *Take the first ~ to the right.* Ch'ŏt mot'ungiesŏ orŭntchogŭro toshipshio. 첫 모퉁이에서 오른쪽으로 도십시오/ *~point* pun-gichŏm 분 기점.

turnip *n.* sunmu 순무.

turnover *n.* (*sales*) maesanggo 매상고, (*upset*) chŏnbok 전복. *frequent ~* pangni tamae 박리 다매.

turpentine *n.* songjin 송진.

turtle *n.* kŏbuk 거북. *~ shell* pyŏlgap 별갑.

tusk *n.* ŏmni 엄니, ppŏdŭrŏngni 뻐드렁니. *elephant ~* sang-a 상아(象牙).

tutor *n.* kajŏng kyosa 가정 교사. *look out for a ~'s position* kajŏng kyosa charirŭl ch'atta 가정 교사 자리를
tutoress *n.* yŏja kajŏng kyosa 여자 가정 교사. └찾다.

twelfth *n.* cheshibi 제12, yŏl tutchae 열 두째. *—adj.* yŏl tutchaeŭi 열 두째의, cheshibiŭi 제12의. *the ~ of September* kuwŏl shibiil 9월 12일/ *the ~ day after Christmas* sŏngt'anjŏl hu yŏltutchae nal. 성탄절 후 열 두째 날.

twelve *n.* yŏl tul 열 둘, shibi 십이(12).

twentieth *n.* sŭmu pŏntchae 스무 번째, cheiship 제20. *—adj.* sŭmu pŏntchaeŭi 스무 번째의.

twenty *n.* sŭmul 스물, iship 이십(20).

twice *adv.* tu pŏn 두 번, ihoe 2회. *I have read this book ~*. I ch'aegŭl tu pŏn ilgŏssŭmnida. 이 책을 두 번 읽었읍니다/ *You may change the water at least ~ a day.* Chŏgŏdo harue tu pŏnssik murŭl karaya hal kŏshimnida. 적어도 하루에 두 번씩 물을 갈아야 할 것입니다.

twig n. (*small shoot*) chan-gaji 잔가지.

twilight n. (*dusk*) hwanghon 황혼, ttangkŏmi 땅거미.

twin n. ssangdongi 쌍둥이. ~ *brothers* ssangdongi hyŏngje 쌍둥이 형제/ ~ *beds* t'ŭwin pedŭ 트윈 베드.

twine n. (*thread*) kkon shil 꼰 실. —vt. (*twist*) kkoda 꼬다, (*wind*) kamta 감다. *I ~d my arms round my mother's neck.* Nanŭn tu p'allo ŏmŏniŭi mogŭl kamassŭmnida. 나는 두 팔로 어머니의 목을 감았읍니다.

twinkle n. (*spark*) pantchaginŭn pit 반짝이는 빛, (*sparkle*) pulttong 불똥. —vi., vt. (*gleam*) pantchagida 반짝이다, (*wink*) kkampagida 깜박이다. *the ~ of stars* pantchaginŭn pyŏlpit 반짝이는 별빛.

twirl vt., vi. (*spin*) pingbing tollida 빙빙 돌리다, (*whirl*) pingbing tolda 빙빙 돌다. ~ *a cane* chip'angirŭl hwidurŭda 지팡이를 휘두르다.

twist n. (*thread, etc.*) kkon shil 꼰 실, (*wrench*) twit'ŭllim 뒤틀림, kkoim 꼬임. —vt., vi. (*wrap*) ŏkta 얽다, kkoda 꼬다, (*wring*) pit'ŭlda 비틀다, (*wind*) hwigamta 휘감다, *She ~ed her ring on her finger.* Kŭnyŏnŭn panjirŭl chagi sone pit'ŭro kkiwŏssŭmnida. 그녀는 반지를 자기 손에 비틀어 끼웠읍니다/ *His face was ~ed with pain.* Kŭ saramŭi ŏlgurŭn ap'ŭmŭro tchigŭrŏjyŏssŭmnida. 그 사람의 얼굴은 아픔으로 찌그러졌읍니다/ ~ *open* pit'ŭrŏ yŏlda 비틀어 열다/ ~ *wires together* ch'ŏlsarŭl pit'ŭrŏ kkoda. 철사를 비틀어 꼬다.

two n. tul 둘, i 이(2), (*pair*) ssang 쌍. —adj. turŭi 둘의. *T~, please.* Tu chang chuseyo. 두 장 주세요/ *a child of ~* tu sallan ai 두 살난 아이/ ~ *days* it'ŭl 이틀, iil 2일/ ~ *persons* tu saram 두 사람.

twofold adj. (*double*) tu paeŭi, 두 배(倍)의, ijungŭi 2중의.

type n. (*special kind*) hyŏng 형(型), t'aip'ŭ 타이프, (*model*) ponbogi 본보기, (*printing*) hwalcha 활자. —vt. t'ajahada 타자하다. *a new ~ of car* shinhyŏng ch'a 신형 차. *a woman of the Marilyn Monroe ~* Marillin Mŏnno hyŏngŭi yŏin 마릴린 먼로 형의 여인/ *a modern*

～ *of girl* shinyŏsŏng t'aip'ŭ 신여성 타이프/ *I am not the ～.* Nanŭn kŭrŏn in-gani animnida. 나는 그런 인간이 아닙니다/ *Do you want Roman or italic ～?* Romach'ero wŏnhashimnikka, it'aellikch'ero wŏnhashimnikka? 로마 체(體)로 원하십니까, 이탤릭체로 원하십니까/ *How many words can you ～ a minute?* Ilbune myŏt charŭl ch'il su issŭmnikka? 1분에 몇 자를 칠 수 있습니까?

typewrite *vt., vi.* t'ajahada 타자하다, t'aip'ŭ ch'ida 타이프 치다. *Can you ～?* T'aip'ŭ ch'il chul ashimnikka? 타이프 칠 줄 아십니까/ *She ～s for me.* Kŭnyŏga nae wŏn-gorŭl t'aip'ŭhae chumnida. 그녀가 내 원고를 타이프해 줍니다.

typewriter *n.* t'ajagi 타자기, t'aip'ŭrait'ŏ 타이프라이터. *pound the ～* t'aip'ŭrŭl ch'ida 타이프를 치다.

typhoid *n.* changt'ip'usŭ 장티푸스.

typhoon *n.* t'aep'ung 태풍. *A ～ is approaching Cheju Island of Korea.* T'aep'ungi Chejudo-e chŏpkŭnhago issŭmnida. 태풍이 제주도에 접근하고 있습니다/ *I hear we're going to have a ～ tonight.* Onŭl pam t'aep'ungi pundajiyo. 오늘 밤 태풍이 분다지요.

typhus *n.* palchint'ip'usŭ 발진티푸스.

typical *adj.* (*model*) chŏnhyŏngjŏgin 전형적인, (*representative*) taep'yojŏgin 대표적인, (*characteristic*) tokt'ŭk'an 독특한. *I'd like to see some ～ Korean dolls.* Chŏnhyŏngjŏgin Han-guk inhyŏngŭl poyŏ chushio. 전형적 인 한국 인형을 보여 주시오/ *Admiral Yi Sunshin was a ～ Korean patriot.* I Sunshin changgunŭn chŏnhyŏngjŏgin Han-guguŭi aegukchayŏssŭmnida. 이 순신 장군은 전 형적인 한국의 애국자였습니다.

typist *n.* t'ajasu 타자수, t'aip'isŭt'ŭ 타이피스트.

tyranny *n.* (*oppressive rule*) p'okchŏng 폭정.

tyrant *n.* p'okkun 폭군. *a bloody ～* chaninhan p'okkun 잔인한 폭군.

—◄ **U** ►—

ugly *adj.* ch'u(ak)han 추(악)한, pogi hyunghan 보기 흉

한. *an ~ woman* motsaenggin yŏja 못생긴 여자.

ulcer *n.* chonggi 종기, kweyang│궤양. *a stomach ~* wigweyang 위궤양.

ultimatum *n.* ch'oehu t'ongch'ŏp 최후 통첩.

ultimo *adj.* chinandarŭi 지난달의. *Thank you for your letter of the 10th ~.* Chinandal shibilcha sŏshin chal pada poassŭmnida. 지난달 10일자 서신 잘 받아 보았읍니다.

umbilical cord t'aetchul 탯줄.

umbrella *n.* (*for sunlight*) yangsan 양산, (*for rain*) usan 우산. *close one's ~* yangsanŭl chŏpta 양산을 접다/ *open an ~* usanŭl p'yŏda 우산을 펴다/ *Take an ~ with you.* Usanŭl kajigo kashio. 우산을 가지고 가시오/ *Will you let me walk under your ~?* Usan chom ssŭiwŏ chushigessŭmnikka? 우산 좀 씌워 주시겠읍니까?

umpire *n.* (*referee*) shimp'an 심판. —*vi.* shimp'anŭl poda 심판을 보다. *a ball ~* kushim 구심 (球審).

unable *adj.* hal su ŏmnŭn 할 수 없는. *I am ~ to walk.* Nanŭn kŏrŭl suga opsŭmnida. 나는 걸을 수가 없읍니다/ *I am ~ to comply with your request.* Taegŭi yogue ŭnghae tŭril suga ŏpsŭmnida. 댁의 요구에 응해 드릴 수가 없읍니다.

unanimous *adj.* (*all agreeing*) manjang ilch'iŭi 만장 일치의. *a ~ vote* chŏnwŏn ilch'iŭi p'yogyŏl 전원 일치의 표결.

unavoidable *adj.* p'ihal su ŏmnŭn 피할 수 없는, (*inevitable*) pudŭgihan 부득이한. *owing to ~ circumstances* p'ihal su ŏmnŭn sajŏngŭro 피할 수 없는 사정으로/ *in an ~ case* pudŭgihan kyŏnguenŭn 부득이한 경우에는.

unbearable *adj.* (*can't be borne*) ch'amŭl su ŏmnŭn 참을 수 없는, (*can't be endured*) kyŏndil su ŏmnŭn 견딜 수 없는. *The pain is ~.* Ap'asŏ mot kyŏndigessŭmnida. 아파서 못 견디겠읍니다.

unbutton *vt.* (*unfasten*) tanch'urŭl kkŭrŭda 단추를 끄르다.

uncanny *adj.* (*weird*) mushimushihan 무시무시한, (*mysterious*) koesanghan 괴상한.

uncertain *adj.* (*undecided*) hwakshirhaji anŭn 확실하지 않은, (*unreliable*) midŭl su ŏmnŭn 믿을 수 없는, (*doubtful*)ŭishimsŭrŏun 의심스러운. *I'm still ~ of my* *future*. Ajik nae changnaenŭn puranhamnida. 아직 내 장래는 불안합니다.

uncle *n.* ajŏssi 아저씨, (*superior*) paekpu 백부, (*inferior*) sukpu 숙부.

uncomfortable *adj.* (*unpleasant*) pulyuk'waehan 불유쾌한, (*uneasy*) pulp'yŏnhan 불편한, (*awkward*) kŏbuk'an 거북한. *I feel ~ with him.* Kŭiwa kach'i issŭmyŏn puranhamnida. 그이와 같이 있으면 불안합니다/ *This chair is very ~.* I ŭijanŭn p'ŏk pulp'yŏnhamnida. 이 의자는 퍽 불편합니다.

uncommon *adj.* (*remarkable*) pibŏmhan 비범한, (*rare*) chin-gihan 진기한, (*unfrequent*) pogi tŭmun 보기 드문. *very ~* maeu chin-gihan 매우 진기한.

unconscious *adj.* (*faint*) kijŏrhan 기절한, (*psyche*) muŭishigŭi 무의식의, (*unaware*) alji mot'anŭn 알지 못하는. *an ~ state* muŭishik sangt'ae 무의식 상태.

uncork *vt.* magaerŭl ppopta 마개를 뽑다. *~ a bottle of wine* sulpyŏng magaerŭl ppopta 술병 마개를 뽑다/ *Please ~ this bottle.* I pyŏngmagaerŭl ppoba chushio. 이 병마개를 뽑아 주시오.

uncover *vt., vi.* (*remove cover*) ttukkŏngŭl pŏtkida 뚜껑을 벗기다, (*expose*) p'ongnohada 폭로하다, (*take off*) pŏtta 벗다. *~ a box* sangja ttukkŏngŭl pŏtkida 상자 뚜껑을 벗기다.

undecided *adj.* (*not decided*) mijŏngŭi 미정의, (*unsettled*) ŏttŏk'e toelchi mŏrŭnŭn 어떻게 될지 모르는, (*irresolute*) mangsŏrinŭn 망설이는. *I'm ~ whether to go or stay.* Kalkkamalkka mangsŏrigo issŭmnida. 갈까말까 망설이고 있읍니다.

under *prep.* (*below*) araee 아래에, mit'e 밑에. *~ a bridge* tari mit'e 다리 밑에/ *Your handbag was ~ the dressing table.* Taegŭi haendŭbaegi kyŏngdae mit'e issŏssŭmnida. 댁의 핸드백이 경대 밑에 있었읍니다/ *Wear a sweater ~ the jacket.* Udot mit'e sŭwet'ŏrŭl ibŭseyo. 웃옷 밑에 스웨터를 입으세요.

underclothes *n.* (*pl.*) sogot 속옷, naeŭi 내의(內衣).

underdeveloped *adj.* chŏgaebarŭi 저개발의. *an ~ area*

chŏgaebal chiyŏk 저개발 지역/ *an ~ country* chŏgaebal-guk 저개발국, hujin-guk 후진국.

underdone *adj.* (*half boiled*) tŏl kuwŏjin 덜 구워진, (*half cooked*) sŏrigŭn 설익은. *This meat is ~.* I kogi-nŭn tŏl kuwŏjyŏssŭmnida. 이 고기는 덜 구워졌읍니다.

undergo *vt.* (*be subject to*) patta 받다, (*suffer*) tanghada 당하다. *~ an operation for stomach ulcer* wigwe-yang susurŭl patta 위궤양 수술을 받다/ *~ much suffering* manŭn konanŭl kyŏkta 많은 고난을 겪다.

underground *adj.* chihaŭi 지하의. —*n.* (*subway*) chihach'ŏl 지하철. *an ~ passage* chihado 지하도/ *an ~ shopping center* chiha sangga 지하 상가/ *~ water* chihasu 지하수/ *the ~ railway* chihach'ŏl 지하철/ *Where is the nearest ~ station?* Kajang kakkaun chihach'ŏl yŏgŭn ŏdimni-kka? 가장 가까운 지하철 역은 어딥니까?

underhand *adj.* (*secret*) pimirŭi 비밀의, (*sly*) ŭmhyung-han 음흉한. *~ dealings* amgŏrae 암거래/ *~ intrigues* ŭmmo 음모.

underline *n.* mitchul 밑줄. —*vt.* mitchurŭl ch'ida 밑줄을 치다.

underneath *adv., prep.* paro mit'e 바로 밑에, paro araee 바로 아래에. *~ the trees* namu mit'e 나무 밑에/ *the river flowing ~ the bridge* tari mit'ŭl hŭrŭnŭn kang 다리 밑을 흐르는 강.

undersell *vt.* ssage p'ara ch'iuda 싸게 팔아 치우다, t'umae-hada 투매하다. *We can ~ them in the overseas markets.* Haeoe shijangesŏ ssage p'ara ch'iul suga issŭm-nida. 해외 시장에서 싸게 팔아 치울 수가 있읍니다.

undershirt *n.* naeŭi 내의(內衣), soksyassŭ 속샤쓰.

understand *vi., vt.* (*comprehend*) alda 알다, ihaehada 이해하다, (*learn*) tŭtko alda 듣고 알다. *Can you ~ German?* Togirŏrŭl ashimnikka? 독일어를 아십니까/ *Do you ~ me?* Nae mal aradŭtkessŭmnikka? 내 말 알아듣겠읍니까/ *Do you ~ what I say?* Nae mal ashigessŭmnikka? 내 말 아시겠읍니까/ *I don't ~ why he came.* Kŭiga wae wannŭnji morŭgessŭmnida. 그이가 왜 왔는지 모르겠읍니다.

understanding *n.* (*comprehension*) ihae 이해, (*knowledge*) chishik 지식, (*intelligence*) ihaeryŏk 이해력, (*sense*) punbyŏl 분별.

undertake *vi., vt.* (*take upon oneself*) ttŏmatta 떠맡다, (*engage in*) ch'aksuhada 착수하다. *I cannot ~ what you ask.* Put'agŭl mat'ŭl suga ŏpsŭmnida. 부탁을 맡을 수가 없읍니다/ *~ responsibility* ch'aegimŭl chida 책임을 지다/ *Who ~s the patient?* Nuga hwanjaŭi kanhorŭl massŭmnikka? 누가 환자의 간호를 맡습니까?

undertaker *n.* (*mortician*) changŭisa 장의사.

undertaking *n.* (*project*) kyehoek 계획, (*enterprise*) kiŏp 기업, saŏp 사업. *charitable ~* chasŏn saŏp 자선 사업/ *a national ~* kukka saŏp 국가 사업.

undervalue *vt.* (*underestimate*) kapsŭl ssage poda 값을 싸게 보다, (*esteem lightly*) yatpoda 얕보다.

underwear *n.* (*underclothes*) sogot 속옷, naeŭi 내의.

undisclosed *adj.* (*not shown*) nat'anaeji annŭn 나타내지 않는, (*kept secret*) pimire puch'in 비밀에 붙인.

undo *vt.* (*reverse*) toedollyŏ not'a 되돌려 놓다, (*annul*) ch'wisohada 취소하다, (*open*) p'ulda 풀다, (*untie*) kkŭrŭda 끄르다. *~ a parcel* kkurŏmirŭl p'ulda 꾸러미를 풀다/ *U~ my buttons, please.* Nae tanch'urŭl chom kkŭllŏ chushio. 내 단추를 좀 끌러 주시오.

undress *vi., vt.* (*strip*) osŭl pŏtta〔pŏtkida〕 옷을 벗다〔벗기다〕. *U~ the patient, please.* Hwanjaŭi osŭl pŏtkyŏ chushio. 환자의 옷을 벗겨 주시오.

uneasy *adj.* (*restless*) puranhan 불안한, (*anxious*) kŭnshimsŭrŏn 근심스런, (*uncomfortable*) kŏbuk'an 거북한. *Don't be ~.* Kŭnshimhaji mashio. 근심하지 마시오/ *I feel ~ about my health.* Kŏn-gangi puranhamnida. 건강이 불안합니다/ *feel ~ in new suits* sae oshi kŏbuk'ada 새 옷이 거북하다.

unemployed *adj.* (*out of work*) shilchik'an 실직한, (*not used*) nolligo innŭn 놀리고 있는. *an ~ worker* shirŏp nodongja 실업 노동자/ *an ~ person* shirŏpcha 실업자/ *~ capital* yuhyu chabon 유휴 자본.

unemployment *n.* shirŏp 실업. *the problem of ~* shirŏp munje 실업 문제/ *~ insurance* shirŏp pohŏm 실업 보험.

unequal *adj.* (*irregular*) korŭji mot'an 고르지 못한, (*unfair*) pulgongp'yŏnghan 불공평한.

uneven *adj.* (*rough*) korŭji annŭn 고르지 않는, ult'ung-bult'unghan 울퉁불퉁한. ~ *ground*[*road*] ult'ungbul-t'unghan ttang[kil] 울퉁불퉁한 땅[길].

unexpected *adj.* ttŭtpakkŭi 뜻밖의, ŭioeŭi 의외의. *an* ~ *happening* ttŭtpakkŭi il 뜻밖의 일/ *an* ~ *guest* ttŭtpakkŭi sonnim 뜻밖의 손님/ *the wholly* ~ *North Korean invasion* chŏnhyŏ ttŭtpakkŭi Puk'anŭi ch'imbŏm 전혀 뜻밖의 북한의 침범.

unfair *adj.* (*partial*) pulgongp'yŏnghan 불공평한, (*unjust*) pujŏnghan 부정한. ~ *treatment* pulgongp'yŏnghan taeu 불공평한 대우/ ~ *means* pujŏng sudan 부정 수단.

unfaithful *adj.* (*disloyal*) pulsŏngshirhan 불성실한, (*unchaste*) pujŏnghan 부정한. *an* ~ *servant* pulsŏng-shirhan hain 불성실한 하인.

unfamiliar *adj.* (*strange*) nassŏn 낯선, (*not wellknown*) chal morŭnŭn 잘 모르는, (*unaccustomed*) iksukchi mot'an 익숙지 못한/ *an* ~ *face* nassŏn ŏlgul 낯선 얼굴/ *an* ~ *landscape* nassŏn p'unggyŏng 낯선 풍경/ *I am* ~ *with Spanish.* Sŭp'einŏnŭn chal morŭmnida. 스페인어는 잘 모릅니다.

unfasten *vt.* (*undo*) kkŭrŭda 끄르다, p'ulda 풀다. *You may* ~ *your seat belt now.* Ije anjŏn pelt'ŭrŭl p'urŏdo chossŭmnida. 이제 안전 벨트를 풀어도 좋습니다.

unfavo(u)rable *adj.* (*adverse*) hyŏngp'yŏni nappŭn 형편이 나쁜, pullihan 불리한. ~ *wind* pullihan nalssi 불리한 날씨/ ~ *balance of trade* muyŏk yŏkcho 무역 역조.

unfinished *adj.* (*not finished*) wansŏngdoeji anŭn 완성되지 않은, (*not polished*) tadŭmŏjiji anŭn 다듬어지지 않은. *an* ~ *house* wansŏnghaji mot'an chip 완성하지 못한 집.

unfit *adj.* (*not suitable*) pujŏktanghan 부적당한, (*unbecoming*) ŏulliji annŭn 어울리지 않는. *He is totally* ~ *to the work.* Kŭinŭn kŭ ire tomuji chŏk'ap'aji anssŭmnida. 그이는 그 일에 도무지 적합하지 않습니다.

unfold *vi., vt.* (*reveal*) tŭrŏnaeda 드러내다, (*expand*)

p'yŏda 펴다. ~ *a newspaper* shinmunjirŭl p'yŏda 신문지를 펴다. 「pakkŭi 뜻밖의.

unforeseen *adj.* yegyŏnhaji mot'an 예견하지 못한, ttŭt-

unforgettable *adj.* ijŭl su ŏmnŭn 잊을 수 없는. *a girl of* ~ *beauty* ijŭl su ŏmnŭn arŭmdaun sonyŏ 잊을 수 없는 아름다운 소녀.

unfortunate *adj.* purhaenghan 불행한, purunhan 불운한.

unfortunately *adv.* (*unluckily*) konggyoropkedo 공교롭게도, (*regrettably*) yugamsŭrŏpkedo 유감스럽게도. *You are wrong,* ~. Yugamsŭrŏpkedo tangshini t'ŭllyŏssŭmnida. 유감스럽게도 당신이 틀렸읍니다.

unfurnished *adj.* (*without furniture*) pip'umi ŏmnŭn 비품이 없는, (*not supplied*) chunbidoeŏ itchi annŭn 준비되어 있지 않는. ~ *rooms* kaguga ŏmnŭn pang 가구가 없는 방.

ungrateful *adj.* (*not thankful*) ŭnhyerŭl morŭnŭn 은혜를 모르는. *an* ~ *man* ŭnhyerŭl morŭnŭn saram 은혜를 모르는 사람/ *You* ~ *wretch!* I paeŭn mangdŏk'an nom kat'ŭni! 이 배은 망덕한 놈 같으니!

unhappy *adj.* (*wretched*) purhaenghan 불행한, (*not suitable*) pujŏktanghan 부적당한. *an* ~ *life* purhaenghan ilsaeng 불행한 일생/ *an* ~ *comment* chŏllyŏrhan nonp'yŏng 졸렬한 논평/ *And so don't be* ~ *about it.* Kŭrŏnikka, kŭ illo kkŭngkkŭnggŏriji mashio. 그러니까, 그 일로 꿍꿍거리지 마시오.

unhealthy *adj.* (*not well*) kŏn-ganghaji mot'an 건강하지 못한, (*hurtful to health*) kŏn-gange haeroun 건강에 해로운.

unheard *adj.* (*unknown*) allyŏjiji anŭn 알려지지 않은.

unheard-of *adj.* chŏllye ŏmnŭn 전례 없는/ *an* ~ *calamity* chŏllye ŏmnŭn ch'amhwa 전례 없는 참화.

uniform *n.* (*dress*) chebok 제복. —*adj.* (*all like*) ta kat'ŭn 다 같은, (*the same*) kyunirhan 균일한. *a combat* ~ chŏnt'ubok 전투복. *a waitress* ~ yŏgŭbŭi chebok 여급의 제복/ *We have a school* ~ *in our school.* Uri hakkyo-enŭn chebogi issŭmnida. 우리 학교에는 제복이 있읍니다/ ~ *in size* k'ŭgiga katta 크기가 같다.

unify *vt.* (*unite*) t'ongirhada 통일하다. ~ *North and South Korea* Nambuk'anŭl t'ongirhada 남북한을 통일하다/ *Can the world be unified?* Segyenŭn t'ongiri toegessŭmnikka? 세계는 통일이 되겠읍니까?

unimportant *adj.* chungyohaji anŭn 중요하지 않은, (*trivial*) hach'anŭn 하찮은.

union *n.* (*league*) tongmaeng 동맹, yŏnmaeng 연맹, (*marriage*) kyŏrhon 결혼. *trade* ~ nodong chohap 노동 조합/ *a labor* ~ (*Am.*) nodong chohap 노동 조합/ *the Soviet U*~ Soryŏn 소련/ *a happy* ~ haengbok'an kyŏrhon 행복한 결혼/ *live in* ~ hwahap'ada 화합하다.

unique *adj.* (*sole*) yuirhan 유일한, (*peculiar*) tokt'ŭk'an 독특한, (*rare*) chin-gihan 진기한. ~ *Korean musical instruments* Han-gugŭi tokt'ŭk'an akki 한국의 독특한 악기/ *a* ~ *experience* hŭihanhan kyŏnghŏm 회한한 경험.

unit *n.* tanwi 단위, (*mil.*) pudae 부대. *Won is the monetary* ~ *of Korea.* Wŏnŭn Han-guk tonŭi tanwiimnida. 원은 한국 돈의 단위입니다/ *a* ~ *of length* kiriŭi tanwi 길이의 단위/ *a self-governing* ~ chach'i tanch'e 자치 단체/ *combat* ~*s* chŏnt'u pudae 전투 부대/ *a police* ~ kyŏngch'al pudae 경찰 부대.

unite *vt., vi.* (*make one*) kyŏrhap'ada 결합하다, (*combine*) hapch'ida 합치다, (*by marriage*) kyŏrhonshik'ida 결혼시키다.

united *adj.* (*joined together*) hapch'in 합친, (*amalgamated*) happanghan 합방한, yŏnhap'an 연합한. *the* ~ *forces* yŏnhapkun 연합군/ *the U*~ *Nations* yŏnhapkuk 연합국/ *U*~ *Press* haptong t'ongshinsa 합동 통신사/ *U*~ *States of America* Amerik'a hapchungguk 아메리카 합중국.

universal *adj.* (*covering all the world*) chŏnsegyeŭi 전세계의, (*general*) chŏnbanjŏgin 전반적인/ ~ *agent* ch'ongdaeriin 총대리인.

universally *adv.* ilbanjŏguro 일반적으로.

universe *n.* uju 우주.

university *n.* taehakkyo 대학교. *a* ~ *hospital* taehak pyŏngwŏn 대학 병원/ *a* ~ *professor* taehak kyosu 대학

교수/ *What* ~ *are you in?* Ŏnŭ taehage tanishimnikka?
어느 대학에 다니십니까/ *I'm a graduate of S* ~. Nanŭn
S taehagŭl nawassŭmnida. 나는 S대학을 나왔읍니다/
Did you go to ~ *in Seoul?* Sŏuresŏ taehagŭl tanyŏ-
ssŭmnikka? 서울에서 대학을 다녔읍니까?

unjust *adj.* (*not just*) olch'i anŭn 옳지 않은, (*not fair*)
pulgongp'yŏnghan 불공평한.

unkind *adj.* pulch'injŏrhan 불친절한, morinjŏnghan 몰인
정한. *It's* ~ *of you to say that.* Kŭrŏn marŭl hadani
nŏmu hashimnida. 그런 말을 하다니 너무 하십니다.

unknown *adj.* (*not known*) allyŏjiji anŭn 알려지지 않은,
(*strange*) morŭnŭn 모르는.

unlawful *adj.* (*illegal*) pul〔wi〕pŏbŭi 불〔위〕법의. *an* ~
act pulpŏp haengwi 불법 행위.

unless *conj.* (*if not*) manil …i animyŏn 만일 …이 아니면,
(*except that*) ioeenŭn 이외에는. *I will not go* ~ *the
weather is fine.* Nalssiga choch'i anŭmyŏn kaji anŭl
kŏshimnida. 날씨가 좋지 않으면 가지 않을 것입니다.

unlicensed *adj.* myŏnhŏga ŏmnŭn 면허가 없는.

unlike *adj.* (*different*) tarŭn 다른. —*prep.* …wa tarŭn
…와 다른. *My brother is* ~ *me in every respect.* Nae
aunŭn modŭn chŏmesŏ nawa tarŭmnida. 내 아우는 모
든 점에서 나와 다릅니다.

unlikely *adj.* (*not probable*) issŭmjik'aji anŭn 있음직하
지 않은, (*not likely to succeed*) kamang ŏmnŭn 가망 없
는. *He is* ~ *to come.* Kŭinŭn ol kŏt katchi anssŭmnida. 그이는 올 것 같지 않습니다.

unload *vt.* chimŭl purida〔p'ulda〕 짐을 부리다〔풀다〕. ~
cargoes from ships paeesŏ chimŭl purida 배에서 짐을
부리다/ ~ *goods from a truck* t'ŭrŏgesŏ chimŭl p'ulda
트럭에서 짐을 풀다.   「열쇠로 열다.

unlock *vt.* (*open*) yŏlda 열다. ~ *with a key* yŏlsoero yŏlda

unlucky *adj.* (*unfortunate*) purhaeng〔purun〕han 불행
〔불운〕한, (*ominous*) pulgirhan 불길한. *an* ~ *woman*
purunhan yŏin 불운한 여인/ *an* ~ *day* pulgirhan nal 불
길한 날.

unmarried *adj.* mihonŭi 미혼의, (*single*) tokshinŭi 독신의.

an ～ *person* mihonja 미혼자/ *an* ～ *life* tokshin saenghwal 독신 생활/ *Are you* ～? Ajik mihonishimnikka?
아직 미혼이십니까?

unnatural *adj.* (*not natural*) pujayŏnhan 부자연한, (*not
normal*) chŏngsangi anin 정상이 아닌, (*strange*) kigoe-
han 기괴한. *an* ～ *gestures* pujayŏnhan momchit 부자연한
몸짓/ *an* ～ *death* pyŏnsa 변사/ *an* ～ *smile* okchi usŭm
억지 웃음.

unnecessary *adj.* (*not necessary*) pulp'iryohan 불필요한,
(*useless*) ssŭlteŏmnŭn 쓸데없는. ～ *expenses* pulp'i-
ryohan chich'ul 불필요한 지출/ *It is* ～. Kŭgŏsŭn p'iryoŏpsŭmnida. 그것은 필요없읍니다.

unnoticed *adj.* (*unobserved*) nune ttŭiji annŭn 눈에 띄지
않는. *pass* ～ nune ttŭiji ank'o nŏmŏgada 눈에 띄지 않
고 넘어가다.

unnourished *adj.* yŏngyangŭl patchi mot'an 영양을 받지
못한.

unobserved *adj.* chik'yŏjiji annŭn 지켜지지 않는.

unobtainable *adj.* ŏtki ŏryŏun 얻기 어려운.

unoccupied *adj.* (*vacant*) piŏ innŭn 비어 있는, (*idle*)
han-gahan 한가한. *an* ～ *room* piŏ innŭn pang 비어 있는
방/ *Is this seat* ～? I charinŭn piŏ issŭmnikka? 이 자리
는 비어 있읍니까/ *an* ～ *seat* kongsŏk 공석.

unofficial *adj.* (*not official*) pigongshigŭi 비공식의,
(*private*) kaeinjŏgin 개인적인. *an* ～ *statement* pigong-
shik sŏngmyŏng 비공식 성명.

unpack *vt.* (*undo*) p'ulda 풀다, (*take out*) kkŏnaeda 꺼내
다, (*unload*) chimŭl naerida 짐을 내리다. *I will* ～
tomorrow morning. Naeil ach'ime chimŭl p'ulgessŭm-
nida. 내일 아침에 짐을 풀겠읍니다.

unpaid *adj.* (*not paid*) chiburhaji anŭn 지불하지 않은,
(*unsalaried*) mugŭbŭi 무급의, (*honorary*) myŏngyejigin
명예직인. *an* ～ *amount* miburaek 미불액/ *This bill is
still* ～. I ch'ŏnggusŏnŭn ajik miburimnida. 이 청구서
는 아직 미불입니다.

unpaved *adj.* p'ojanghaji anŭn 포장하지 않은. *an* ～ *street*
p'ojangi an toen kŏri 포장이 안 된 거리/ *an* ～ *road*

p'ojanghaji anŭn kil 포장하지 않은 길.

unpleasant *adj.* (*displeasing*) pulk'waehan 불쾌한, (*offensive*) shirŭn 싫은. *an ~ person* kipun nappŭn saram 기분 나쁜 사람/ *an ~ smell* pulk'waehan naemsae 불쾌한 냄새.

unpolished *adj.* (*not shined*) takchi anŭn 닦지 않은, (*rude*) ttaerŭl mot pŏsŭn 때를 못 벗은. *~ rice* hyŏnmi 현미/ *~ manners* seryŏndoeji mot'an t'aedo 세련되지 못한 태도.

unpopular *adj.* inki ŏmnŭn 인기 없는. *He is ~ with his associates.* Kŭ saramŭn tongryodŭl saie inkiga ŏpsŭmnida. 그 사람은 동료들 사이에 인기가 없읍니다/ *become ~* inkiga ttŏrŏjida 인기가 떨어지다.

unprecedented *adj.* chŏllye ŏmnŭn 전례 없는. *The meeting was an ~ success.* Kŭ moimŭn chŏllye ŏmnŭn taesŏng-gongiŏssŭmnida. 그 모임은 전례 없는 대성공이었읍니다.

unprejudiced *adj.* (*impartial*) p'yŏn-gyŏn ŏmnŭn 편견 없는, (*fair*) kongp'yŏnghan 공평한.

unprepared *adj.* (*not ready*) chunbiga an toen 준비가 안 된, (*prompt*) chŭksŏgŭi 즉석의. *We are all ~ for the news.* Tadŭl ku soshigŭl yegich'ido anassŭmnida. 다들 그 소식을 예기치도 않았읍니다/ *Dinner is still ~.* Chŏnyŏk shiksanŭn ajik chunbiga an twaessŭmnida. 저녁 식사는 아직 준비가 안 됐읍니다.

unquestionably *adj.* (*certainly*) hwakshirhi 확실히.

unreasonable *adj.* (*immoderate*) kwadohan 과도한, (*excessive*) t'ŏmuniŏmnŭn 터무니없는. *~ conduct* pun-byŏrŏmnŭn haengdong 분별없는 행동/ *make ~ demands* t'ŏmuniŏmnŭn yogurŭl hada 터무니없는 요구를 하다.

unreliable *adj.* ŭijihal[midŭl] su ŏmnŭn 의지할[믿을] 수 없는. *an ~ person* midŭl su ŏmnŭn saram 믿을 수 없는 사람.

unresolved *adj.* (*undecided*) kyŏltanŭl mot naerin 결단을 못 내린, (*uncertain*) migyŏrŭi 미결의. *My doubts are still ~.* Naŭi ŭimunŭn ajik p'ulliji anassŭmnida. 나의 의문은 아직 풀리지 않았읍니다.

unripe *adj.* ikchi anŭn 익지 않은. ~ *fruit* ikchi anŭn kwail 익지 않은 과일, p'utkwail 풋과일.

unsafe *adj.* (*dangerous*) wihŏmhan 위험한.

unsanitary *adj.* (*bad for health*) piwisaengjŏgin 비위생 적인. ~ *living condition* piwisaengjŏgin saenghwal chokŏn 비위생적인 생활 조건.

unsatisfactory *adj.* (*not content*) pulmansŭrŏun 불만스 러운, (*inadequate*) pulch'ungbunhan 불충분한. *an* ~ *result* pulmansŭrŏn kyŏlgwa 불만스런 결과.

unsavo(u)ry *adj.* (*unpleasant*) pulk'waehan 불쾌한, (*nasty*) pulmisŭrŏn 불미스런. ~ *scandals* pulmisŭrŏn ch'umun 불미스런 추문.

unseasonable *adj.* (*untimely*) ttaeanin 때아닌. ~ *advice* ttaeanin ch'unggo 때아닌 충고.

unseen *adj.* (*not visible*) nune poiji annŭn 눈에 보이지 않 는, (*not seen*) ajik poji mot'an 아직 보지 못한. ~ *danger* poiji annŭn wihŏm 보이지 않는 위험/ ~ *countries* poji mot'an naradŭl 보지 못한 나라들.

unsettled *adj.* (*changeable*) pyŏnhagi shwiun 변하기 쉬운, (*unpaid*) miburŭi 미불의, (*not stable*) puranjŏnghan 불안정한, (*undetermined*) kyŏlchŏngdoeji anŭn 결정되 지 않은. ~ *weather* p'yŏnhagi shwiun nalssi 변하기 쉬운 날씨/ *The point is* ~. Kŭ chŏmi haegyŏldoeji ank'o issŭmnida. 그 점이 해결되지 않고 있읍니다.

unskil(l)ful *adj.* (*clumsy*) sŏt'urŭn 서투른.

unspeakable *adj.* marhal su ŏmnŭn 말할 수 없는. ~ *joy* marhal su ŏmnŭn kippŭm 말할 수 없는 기쁨.

unsuitable *adj.* (*not suitable*) pujŏktanghan 부적당한, (*unbecoming*) ŏulliji annŭn 어울리지 않는. *an* ~ *article* pujŏktanghan mulgŏn 부적당한 물건.

untidy *adj.* (*not neat*) tanjŏngch'i mot'an 단정치 못한, (*disarranged*) ŏsusŏnhan 어수선한.

untie *vt.* (*undo*) kkurŭda 끄르다, p'ulda 풀다. ~ *a package* kkurŏmirŭl p'ulda 꾸러미를 풀다/ ~ *a cord* kkŭnŭl kkŭrŭda 끈을 끄르다.

until *prep.*, *conj.* (*till*) ...kkaji ⋯까지. *Let's wait* ~ *the rain stops.* Piga mŏmch'ul ttaekkaji kidaripshida. 비가

멈출 때까지 기다립시다/ *Goodbye ~ tomorrow*. Naeilkkaji annyŏng！ 내일까지 안녕！

untimely *adj*. (*unseasonable*) ttaeanin 때아닌, (*too early*) nŏmu pparŭn 너무 빠른. *an ~ frost* ttaeanin sŏri 때아닌 서리/ *an ~ death* yojŏl 요절(夭折).

untrue *adj*. (*false*) kŏjishin 거짓인, hŏwiŭi 허위의, (*not faithful*) sŏngshirhaji mot'ada 성실하지 못하다. *be ~ to one's friends* ch'in-gudŭrege sŏngshirhaji mot'ada 친구들에게 성실하지 못하다.

unusual *adj*.(*uncommon*) pot'ongi anin 보통이 아닌, (*race*) chin-gihan 진기한. *~ clothes* saektarŭn ot 색다른 옷.

unusually *adv*. maeu 매우, yunanhi 유난히. *It is ~ cold this morning*. Onŭl ach'imŭn yunanhi ch'upsŭmnida. 오늘 아침은 유난히 춥습니다.

unveil *vt*. (*uncover*) peirŭl pŏtkida 베일을 벗기다, (*disclose*) tŭrŏnaeda 드러내다. *~ a statue* chemak'ada 제막하다/ *~ one's face* ŏlgurŭl tŭrŏnaeda 얼굴을 드러내다.

unveiling *n*. chemakshik 제막식.

unwelcome *adj*. (*not welcome*) hwanyŏngbatchi mot'anŭn 환영받지 못하는, (*not wanted*) talgapchi anŭn 달갑지 않은. *an ~ quest* talgapchi anŭn sonnim 달갑지 않은 손님/ *~ news* pan-gapchi anŭn soshik 반갑지 않은 소식.

unwholesome *adj*. (*unhealthy*) kŏn-gange nappŭn 건강에 나쁜. *Bad water is very ~*. Nappŭn murŭn aju kŏn-gange choch'i anssŭmnida. 나쁜 물은 아주 건강에 좋지 않습니다.

unwilling *adj*. (*not willing*) choahaji anŭn 좋아하지 않은, (*reluctant*) maŭmi naek'iji annŭn 마음이 내키지 않는. *be ~ to go* kago shipchi ant'a 가고 싶지 않다.

unwise *adj*. (*not wise*) yŏngnihaji mot'an 영리하지 못한, (*foolish*) ŏrisŏgŭn 어리석은.

unworthy *adj*. (*not deserving*) kach'iga ŏmnŭn 가치가 없는,(*unbecoming*) ...tapchi anŭn ...답지 않은. *an ~ person* shishihan in-gan 시시한 인간/ *conduct ~ of a gentleman* shinsadapchi anŭn haengdong 신사답지 않은 행동.

up *adv*. wiro 위로, wie 위에. *Look ~*. Wirŭl poshipshio. 위를 보십시오/ *Get ~*. Irŏnashio. 일어나시오 / *Stand ~*.

Irŏsŏshio. 일어서시오/ *Come ~ here.* Iriro ollaoshio. 이리 로 올라오시오/ *What's ~ ?* Musŭn irijiyo? 무슨 일이지요/ *That is ~ to you.* Kŭgŏsŭn tangshinege tallyŏssŭmnida. 그것은 당신에게 달렸읍니다/ *Time is ~.* Shigani ta doeŏssŭmnida. 시간이 다 되었읍니다/ *~ and down* wiaraero 위아래로/ *What is he doing ~ there?* Kŭinŭn kŏgisŏ muŏsŭl hago issŭmnikka? 그이는 거기서 무엇을 하고 있읍니까/ *~ to date* onŭlkkaji 오늘까지.

upon *prep.* wie 위에.

upper *adj.* (*higher*) witchogŭi 위쪽의, (*rank*) sanggŭbŭi 상급의. *the ~ stories* wich'ŭng 위층/ *the ~ lip* winnipsul 윗입술/ *an ~ class student* sanggŭpsaeng 상급생.

uppermost *adj., adv.* ch'oesangŭi[ŭro] 최상의[으로].

uppish *adj.* (*conceited*) challan ch'ehanŭn 잘난 체하는. *Don't get ~ with me!* Challan ch'ehaji marayo! 잘난 체하지 말아요!

upright *adj.* (*erect*) ttokparŭn 똑바른, sujigŭi 수직의, (*cleanhanded*) ch'ŏngnyŏmhan 청렴한. *an ~ post* sujik kidung 수직 기둥/ *an ~ judge* ch'ŏngnyŏmhan p'ansa 청렴한 판사.

uprising *n.* (*revolt*) pallan 반란, (*riot*) p'oktong 폭동.

uproar *n.* (*tumult*) k'ŭn sodong 큰 소동, (*clamor*) koham sori 고함 소리. *The meeting ended in* (*an*) ~. Moimŭn soran soge kkŭnnassŭmnida. 모임은 소란 속에 끝났읍니다.

uproot *vt.* (*root up*) ppuri ppopta 뿌리 뽑다. *We must ~ poverty.* Kananŭl ppuri ppobaya hamnida. 가난을 뿌리 뽑아야 합니다.

upset *vt., vi.* (*turn over*) twiŏpta 뒤엎다, twijip'ida 뒤집히다. —*n.* (*overturning*) chŏnbok 전복, (*disturbance*) hollan 혼란. *Don't ~ the boat.* Pot'ŭrŭl twiŏpchi mashio. 보트를 뒤엎지 마시오/ *Sit still, or the boat will ~.* Kamanhi kyeseyo. Animyŏn pot'ŭga twijip'imnida. 가만히 계세요. 아니면 보트가 뒤집힙니다/ *The news gave me quite an ~.* Kŭ soshigŭl tŭtko k'ŭge nollassŭmnida. 그 소식을 듣고 크게 놀랐읍니다.

upside down kŏkkuro 거꾸로, (*pell-mell*) twijukpakchugŭro 뒤죽박죽으로. *The boy was holding the book*

~. Sonyŏnŭn ch'aegŭl kŏkkuro tŭlgo issŏssŭmnida. 소년은 책을 거꾸로 들고 있었읍니다.

upstairs *n.* ich'ŭng 2층. —*adv.* ich'ŭnge[ŭro] 2층에〔으로〕. *Come* ~. Ich'ŭnguro oshio. 2층으로 오시오/ *Do you sleep* ~ ? Ich'ŭngesŏ chumushimnikka? 2층에서 주무십니까/ *Please carry my baggage* ~. Nae chimŭl ich'ŭnguro nallada chushio. 내 짐을 2층으로 날라다 주시오.

upstart *n.* (*parvenu*) pyŏrak puja 벼락 부자. *a postwar* ~ chŏnhuŭi pyŏrak puja 전후의 벼락 부자.

up-to-date *adj.* (*modern*) ch'oeshinŭi 최신의.

urge *vt., vi.* (*press*) chaech'ok'ada 재촉하다, (*insist upon*) yŏksŏrhada 역설하다, (*exhort*) kwŏn-gohada 권고하다. *I* ~*d him to resign.* Kŭiege saimŭl kwŏn-go-haessŭmnida. 그이에게 사임을 권고했읍니다.

urgent *adj.* (*very important*) chungdaehan 중대한, (*pressing*) kin-gŭp'an 긴급한, wigŭp'an 위급한. *an* ~ *motion* kin-gŭp tongŭi 긴급 동의/ *an* ~ *question* kin-gŭp munje 긴급 문제/*an* ~ *telegram* chigŭp chŏnbo 지급 전보.

urinate *vi.* (*piss*) ojum nuda 오줌 누다, sobyŏn boda 소변 보다.

urine *n.* sobyŏn 소변, ojum 오줌, *pass* ~ ojumŭl nuda 오줌을 누다/ *contain one's* ~ ojumŭl ch'amta 오줌을 참다.

urn *n.* hangari 항아리, tanji 단지.

〈hangari〉

us *pron.* (*dative*) uriege 우리에게, (*accusative*) urirŭl 우리를. *Give* ~ *a penny.* Hanp'un chushipshio. 한푼 주십시오/ *Tell* ~ *some more about it.* Kŏgie taehae chomdŏ malssŭmhae chushio. 거기에 대해 좀더 말씀해 주시오/ *Let* ~ *go.* Kapshida. 갑시다/ *They saw* ~. Kŭ saramdŭrŭn urirŭl poassŭmnida. 그 사람들은 우리를 보았읍니다.

usage *n.* (*use*) sayong 사용, (*treatment*) sayongpŏp 사용법, (*habit*) sŭpkwan 습관.

use *n.* (*using*) sayong 사용, (*uses*) yongdo 용도, (*utility*) soyong 소용, (*custom*) kwansŭp 관습. —*vt., vi.* (*employ*) ssŭda 쓰다, (*consume*) sobihada 소비하다, (*treat*) taruda 다루다, (*eat, drink, etc.*) mŏkta 먹다, mashida 마시다. *Is this dictionary in* ~? I sajŏnŭn ssŭshimnikka? 이 사전은 쓰십니까/ *What is the* ~ *of it?* Kŭgŏsŭl muŏse ssŭshil kŏmnikka? 그것을 무엇에 쓰실 겁니까/ *Is this of any* ~ *to you?* Igŏshi musŭn ssŭlmoga issŭmnikka? 이것 이 무슨 쓸모가 있읍니까/ *What is the* ~? Musŭn soyongi itkessŭmnikka? 무슨 소용이 있겠읍니까/ *May I* ~ *your piano?* P'iano chom ssŏdo chok'essŭmnikka? 피아노 좀 써도 좋겠읍니까/ *How much coal did we* ~ *last winter?* Chinan kyŏul sŏkt'anŭl ŏlmana ssŏtchiyo? 지난 겨울 석 탄을 얼마나 썼지요/ *Do you know how to* ~ *chopsticks.* Chŏtkarak ssŭnŭn pŏbŭl ashimnikka? 젓가락 쓰는 법을 아십니까/ ~*d to* hangsang ...haetta 항상 …했다/ *I* ~*d to drink when young.* Chŏlmŏssŭl ttaenŭn hangsang chal masyŏssŭmnida. 젊었을 때는 항상 잘 마셨읍니다/ *What* ~*d he to say?* Kŭbunŭn hangsang muŏrago hadŏn-gayo? 그분은 항상 무어라고 하던가요/ *I* ~*d often to see her.* Kŭ yŏjawanŭn hangsang mannagon haessŭmnida. 그 여자 와는 항상 만나고 했읍니다/ *be[get] used to* ...e iksuk'a-yŏ …에 익숙하여/ *You will soon get* ~*d to it.* Kŭgŏse kot iksuk'aejil kŏshimnida. 그것에 곧 익숙해질 것입니다.

useful *adj.* (*serviceable*) ssŭlmo innŭn 쓸모 있는, yuyong-han 유용한, (*helpful*) toumi toenŭn 도움이 되는, (*capable*) yunŭnghan 유능한. *Doctors are* ~. Ŭisanŭn yuyong-hamnida. 의사는 유용합니다/ *Don't throw that away, it will come in* ~ *someday.* Kŭgŏsŭl pŏriji mashio. Ŏnjen-ga ssŭlmo itke toel kŏshimnida. 그것을 버리지 마시오. 언젠가 쓸모 있게 될 것입니다.

useless *adj.* (*not useful*) ssŭlmoŏmnŭn 쓸모없는, (*futile*) hŏttoen 헛된. *a* ~ *thing* ssŭlmoŏmnŭn mulgŏn 쓸모없 는 물건/ muyongjimul 무용지물/ *a* ~ *fellow* ssŭlmoŏm-nŭn saram 쓸모없는 사람/ ~ *efforts* hŏtsugo 헛수고/ *Don't -buy* ~ *things.* Ssŭlteŏmnŭn mulgŏnŭn saji ma-shio. 쓸데없는 물건은 사지 마시오.

usher *n.* (*doorkeeper*) suwi 수위, munjigi 문지기, (*of theater*) annaein 안내인. —*vt.* (*show in*) annaehada

안내하다, (*precede*) toch'agŭl allida 도착을 알리다. ~ *in a quest* sonnimŭl majadŭrida 손님을 맞아들이다/ ~ *a person out* saramŭl chŏnsonghada 사람을 전송하다/ *The girl* ~ed *me to my seat.* Sonyŏnŭn narŭl chwasŏgŭro annaehaessŭmnida. 소녀는 나를 좌석으로 안내했습니다.

usual *adj.* (*ordinary*) pot'ongŭi 보통의, p'yŏngsoŭi 평소의. *He came earlier than* ~. Pot'ongboda iltchik wassŭmnida. 보통보다 일찍 왔습니다/ *as* ~ p'yŏngsowa kach'i 평소와 같이/ *You are late, as* ~. P'yŏngsoch'ŏrŏm nŭjŏtkunyo. 평소처럼 늦었군요.

usually *adv.* pot'ong 보통, taegae 대개. *What do you* ~ *do on Sundays?* Iryoirenŭn pot'ong muŏsŭl hashimnikka? 일요일에는 보통 무엇을 하십니까/ *Where do you* ~ *spend the summer?* Pot'ong yŏrŭmŭn ŏdisŏ ponaeshimnikka? 보통 여름은 어디서 보내십니까?

usurer *n.* (*money lender*) kori taegŭm ŏpcha 고리 대금 업자.

utensil *n.* (*tool*) kigu 기구, (*container*) kŭrŭt 그릇, *farming* ~s nonggu 농구/ *kitchen* ~s puŏk segan 부엌 세간/ *household* ~s kajŏng yongp'um 가정 용품.

utmost *adj.* (*furthest*) maen kkŭt'ŭi 맨 끝의, (*greatest, highest*) ch'oedae[ch'oego]ŭi 최대[최고]의. —*n.* ch'oedae hando 최대 한도, kŭk'an 극한. *I walked to the* ~ *edge of the cliff.* Pyŏrangŭi maen kkŭtkkaji kŏrŏgassŭmnida. 벼랑의 맨 끝까지 걸어갔습니다/ *the* ~ *limits* kŭk'an 극한/ *do one's* ~ chŏllyŏgŭl tahada 전력을 다하다/ *to the* ~ himkkŏt 힘껏/ *That is the* ~ *I can do.* Kŭgŏshi naega hal su innŭn ch'oedae handoimnida 그것이 내가 할 수 있는 최대 한도입니다.

utopia *n.* isanghyang 이상향, towŏn-gyŏng 도원경.

utter *adj.* (*complete*) wanjŏnhan 완전한. —*vt.* (*pronounce*) ippakke naeda 입밖에 내다, (*speak*) marhada 말하다. *an* ~ *fool* sunjŏnhan pabo 순전한 바보/ *an* ~ *stranger* chŏnhyŏ morŭnŭn saram 전혀 모르는 사람/ *She is an* ~ *stranger to me.* Nanŭn kŭ yŏjarŭl chŏnhyŏ morŭmnida. 나는 그 여자를 전혀 모릅니다/ ~ *a sigh* hansumŭl naeshwida 한숨을 내쉬다/ ~ *one's feelings* kamjŏngŭl nat'anaeda 감정을 나타내다.

utterly *adv.* (*completely*) chŏnhyŏ 전혀, aju 아주. *She ~ detests her husband.* Kŭ puinŭn namp'yŏnŭl aju shirŏhamnida. 그 부인은 남편을 아주 싫어합니다.

━━◄◆ V ◆►━━

vacancy *n.* (*vacant post*) kongsŏk 공석, kyŏrwŏn 결원, (*gap*) pint'ŭm 빈틈, (*unoccupied room*) pinbang 빈방. *We have no immediate ~.* Uri hoesanŭn tangjangŭn kyŏrwŏni ŏpsŭmnida. 우리 회사는 당장은 결원이 없읍니다/ *Do you have a ~?* Pinbangi issŭmnikka? 빈방이 있읍니까?

vacant *adj.* (*empty*) t'ŏng pin 텅 빈, (*unoccupied*) piŏ innŭn 비어 있는. *Have you a room ~?* Pinbangi issŭmnikka? 빈방이 있읍니까/ *a ~ house* pinjip 빈집/ *a ~ taxi* pin t'aekshi 빈 택시.

vacation *n.* (*holiday*) hyuga 휴가. *the Christmas ~* sŏngt'anjŏl hyuga 성탄절 휴가/ *the summer ~* yŏrŭm hyuga 여름 휴가/ *How long does the summer ~ last?* Yŏrŭm hyuganŭn ŏlmana kimnikka? 여름 휴가는 얼마나 깁니까/ *Where did your family decide to go on ~?* Taegŭi kajogŭn hyuga-e ŏdiro kagiro hasyŏssŭmnikka? 댁의 가족은 휴가에 어디로 가기로 하셨읍니까?

vaccinate *vt.* yebang chŏpchongŭl hada 예방 접종을 하다. *~ for smallpox* chongdurŭl not'a 종두를 놓다.

vaccination *n.* chongdu 종두. *May I see your ~ certificates?* Chongdu chŏpchong chŭngmyŏngsŏrŭl poyŏ chushio. 종두 접종 증명서를 보여 주시오.

vacuum *n.* chin-gong 진공. *~ bottle* poonpyŏng 보온병/ *~ cleaner* chin-gong ch'ŏngsogi 진공 청소기/ *~ drier* chin-gong kŏnjogi 진공 건조기.

vagabond *n.* (*wanderer*) pangnangja 방랑자.

vague *adj.* (*indistinct*) magyŏnhan 막연한, (*obscure*) ŏsŭmp'ŭrehan 어슴프레한, (*ambiguous*) aemaehan 애매한. *Your instructions are too ~.* Tangshinŭi chishinŭn nŏmu magyŏnhamnida. 당신의 지시는 너무 막연합니다/ ~

promises magyŏnhan yaksok 막연한 약속/ *a ~ explanation* aemaehan sŏlmyŏng 애매한 설명.

vain *adj.* (*useless*) muik'an 무익한, (*empty*) hŏttoen 헛된, (*hollow*) almaengi ŏmnŭn 알맹이 없는. —*n.* konghŏ 공허. *the ~ hope* hŏttoen hŭimang 헛된 희망/ *~ efforts* hŏtsugo 헛수고/ *in ~* hŏttoei 헛되이/ *My work has not been in ~.* Naŭi noryŏgŭn hŏttoeji anassŭmnida. 나의 노력은 헛되지 않았읍니다.

valiant *adj.* (*brave*) yonggamhan 용감한, (*courageous*) ssikssik'an 씩씩한.

valid *adj.* (*well-found*) kŭn-gŏga hwakshirhan 근거가 확실한, t'adanghan 타당한, (*effective*) yuhyohan 유효한. *~ argument* t'adanghan chujang 타당한 주장/ *This passport is ~ for three months.* I yŏkwŏnŭn sam kaewŏlgan yuhyohamnida. 이 여권은 3개월간 유효합니다.

valise *n.* kabang 가방. *pack a ~ and leave a hotel* kabange chimŭl ch'aenggigo hot'erŭl ttŏnada 가방에 짐을 챙기고 호텔을 떠나다.

valley *n.* koltchagi 골짜기, kyegok 계곡. *a mountain ~* sankoltchagi 산골짜기.

valuable *adj.* (*precious*) kappissan 값비싼, (*important*) kwijunghan 귀중한. *~ furniture* kappissan kagu 값비싼 가구/ *a ~ book* kwijunghan ch'aek 귀중한 책/ *~ securities* yuka chŭngkwŏn 유가(有價) 증권/ *I thank you for your ~ service.* Yuik'an pongsa-e taehayŏ kamsahamnida. 유익한 봉사에 대하여 감사합니다.

valuables *n.* kwijungp'um 귀중품.

value *n.* (*worth*) kach'i 가치, (*price*) kap 값, (*valuation*) p'yŏngka 평가. —*vt.* (*appraise*) p'yŏngkahada 평가하다, (*prize*) chonjunghada 존중하다. *the ~ of education* kyoyugŭi kach'i 교육의 가치/ *the propaganda ~* sŏnjŏn kach'i 선전 가치/ *book ~* changbu kagyŏk 장부 가격/ *put a high ~ on ...*ŭl nop'i p'yŏngkahada …을 높이 평가하다/ *I set a high ~ upon your advice.* Taegŭi ch'unggorŭl nop'i p'yŏngkahamnida. 댁의 충고를 높이 평가합니다/ *Do you ~ her as a secretary?* Kŭ yŏjarŭl pisŏrosŏ sojŭnghi yŏgishimnikka? 그 여자를 비서로서 소중히 여기십

니까/ I ~ your opinion. Taegŭi ŭigyŏnŭl chonjunghamnida. 댁의 의견을 존중합니다.

valve n. p'an 판(瓣), paelbŭ 밸브. a safety ~ anjŏnp'an
안전판.

vampire n. (vamp) yobu 요부, (bloodsucker) hŭp'yŏlgwi
흡혈귀.

van n. hwamulch'a 화물차. a goods ~ hwach'a 화차/ a
removal ~ isatchim unbanch'a 이삿짐 운반차.

vanish vi. (disappear) sarajida 사라지다, (fade away)
somyŏrhada 소멸하다, (of color) nalda 날다.

vanity n. (empty pride) hŏyŏng 허영, (worthless display)
hŏshik 허식. gratify ~ hŏyŏngshimŭl manjokshik'ida
허영심을 만족시키다/ social ~ of his wife kŭi anaeŭi
sagyojŏgin hŏyŏngshim 그의 아내의 사교적인 허영심/ from
mere ~ tansunhan hŏyŏngshimesŏ 단순한 허영심에서.

vanquish vt. (conquer) chŏngbok'ada 정복하다, (overcome)
kŭkpok'ada 극복하다.

vapo(u)r n. chŭnggi 증기, kim 김. water ~ sujŭnggi
수증기/ ~ bath hanjŭng 한증.

vaporize vi., vt. chŭngbarhada[shik'ida]증발하다[시키다].

variance n. (difference) ch'ai 차이, (change) pyŏndong
변동, (dispute) allyŏk 알력. I am at ~ with him on
that matter. Kŭ munjee taehae kŭiwa ŭigyŏni matchi
anssŭmnida. 그 문제에 대해 그이와 의견이 맞지 않습니다/
I have had a slight ~ with her. Kŭ yŏin-gwa yakkan
ch'ungdorhaessŭmnida. 그 여인과 약간 충돌했읍니다.

variation n. (alteration) pyŏndong 변동, (different
form) pyŏnhyŏngmul 변형물.

variety n. (diversity) tayangsŏng 다양성, (mixture)
honhap 혼합, (kind) chongnyu 종류, (show) pŏraiŏt'i
syo 버라이어티 쇼. We demanded more ~ in our
food. Chom tayanghan ŭmshigŭl yoguhaessŭmnida.
좀 다양한 음식을 요구했읍니다/ a ~ of toys katkaji wan-gu
갖가지 완구/ What ~ of cake do you prefer? Ŏttŏn
kwajarŭl choahashimnikka? 어떤 과자를 좋아하십니까/ Do
you keep cereals, too? Yes, many varieties. Kongmuldo
issŭmnikka? Ne, yŏrŏ kaji chongnyuga issŭmnida. 곡물

도 있읍니까? 네, 여러 가지 종류가 있읍니다/ *a ～ store* chap'wasang〔jŏm〕 잡화상〔점〕.

various *adj.* yŏrŏ kajiŭi 여러 가지의. *～ kinds* yŏrŏ chongnyu 여러 종류/ *～ opinions* yŏrŏ kaji ŭigyŏn 여러 가지 의견.

varnish *n.* nisŭ 니스. —*vt.* nisŭrŭl ch'irhada 니스를 칠하다.

vary *vt.*, *vi.* (*change*) pakkuda 바꾸다, (*alter*) sujŏnghada 수정하다, (*differ*) tarŭda 다르다. *You should ～ your diet.* Shiksarŭl yŏrŏ kajiro pakkuŏya hamnida. 식사를 여러 가지로 바꾸어야 합니다/ *Prices ～ with the weight.* Chungnyange ttara kapshi tarŭmnida. 중량에 따라 값이 다릅니다.

vase *n.* pyŏng 병, hangari 항아리. *a flower ～* kkotpyŏng 꽃병/ *fill the ～ with water* kkotpyŏnge murŭl nŏt'a 꽃 병에 물을 넣다.

vaseline *n.* wasellin 와셀린.

vast *adj.* (*very extensive*) koengjanghi nŏlbŭn 굉장히 넓은, (*huge*) koengjanghi k'ŭn 굉장히 큰. *a ～ sum of money* kŏaegŭi ton 거액의 돈/ *a ～ scheme* pangdaehan kyehoek 방대한 계획.

veal *n.* songaji kogi 송아지 고기.

vegetable *n.* ch'aeso 채소, yach'ae 야채. *green ～s* p'usŏnggwi 푸성귀/ *a ～ dish* yach'ae yori 야채 요리/ *a ～ garden* ch'aesobat 채소밭/ *a ～ salad* yach'ae saellŏdŭ 야채 샐러드.

vegetarian *n.* ch'aeshikchuŭija 채식주의자. —*adj.* ch'aeshik(chuŭi)ŭi 채식(주의)의. *～ principles* ch'aeshikchuŭi 채식주의.

vegetation *n.* (*plants*) shingmul 식물.

vehicle *n.* (*carriage*) ch'a 차, t'alkŏt 탈것. *motor ～s* chadongch'a 자동차/ *an official ～* kongyongch'a 공용차/ *army ～s* kunyongch'a 군용차/ *a passenger ～* sŭngyongch'a 승용차.

veil *n.* (*covering*) mak 막, peil 베일, (*ornament*) myŏnsap'o 면사포. *drop*〔*raise*〕 *a～* peirŭl tŭriuda〔kŏdŏ ollida〕 베일을 드리우다〔걷어 올리다〕/ *the ～ of night* 〔*darkness*〕 pamŭi changmak 밤의 장막/ *She raised her ～.* Myŏn-

sap'orŭl kŏdŏ ollyŏssŭmnida. 면사포를 걷어 올렸읍니다/
under the ~ of kushirŭl puch'yŏ 구실을 붙여, pingjaha-
yŏ 빙자하여.

vein *n.* (*blood vessel*) hyŏlgwan 혈관, chŏngmaek 정맥,
(*lode*) kwangmaek 광맥, (*mood*) kibun 기분. *I am not
in the ~ for work.* Irhal kibuni an namnida. 일할 기분
이 안 납니다.

velocity *n.* (*speed*) sokto 속도. *the ~ of sound* ŭmsok
음속/ *with a ~ of 1,000 feet a second* maech'o ch'ŏn
p'it'ŭŭi songnyŏgŭro 매초 1,000피트의 속력으로.

velvet *n.* pelbet 벨벳, udan 우단. ~ *carpet* pelbet yungdan
벨벳 융단.

vending machine (*slot machine*) chadong p'anmaegi 자
동 판매기.

vendor *n.* (*vender*) haengsangin 행상인. *a retail ~* somae
sangin 소매 상인.

venerate *vt.* (*respect*) chon-gyŏnghada 존경하다.

veneration *n.* (*reverance*) chon-gyŏng 존경, (*worship*)
sungbae 숭배.

venereal *adj.* (*of sexual intercourse*) ~ *disease* sŏngpyŏng 성병.

vengeance *n.* poksu 복수, anggap'ŭm 앙갚음. *take ~ on*
poksuhada 복수하다.

ventilate *vt.* (*change the air in*) hwan-gihada 환기(換氣)
하다. ~ *a room* shillaerŭl hwan-gihada 실내를 환기하다.

ventilation *n.* t'ongp'ung 통풍, hwan-gi 환기. ~ *arrangement* t'ongp'ung changch'i 통풍 장치/ *a window for ~*
hwan-gich'ang 환기창.

venture *n.* (*risk*) mohŏm 모험, (*daring undertaking*)
mohŏmjŏgin saŏp 모험적인 사업, (*speculation*) t'ugi 투
기(投機). —*vt., vi.* (*dare*) kamhi ...hada 감히 ...하다,
(*risk*) wihŏmŭl murŭpssŭgo ...hada 위험을 무릅쓰고 ...하
다. *a private ~* kaein saŏp 개인 사업/ *I ~ to write to
you.* Shillyerŭl murŭpssŭgo kŭrŭl ollimnida. 실례를 무릅
쓰고 글을 올립니다/ *I can't ~ a step forward.* Musŏwŏsŏ
han palchagukto naedidil suga ŏpsŭmnida. 무서워서 한
발자국도 내디딜 수가 없읍니다.

veranda(h) *n.* t'oenmaru 툇마루, peranda 베란다. *I heard some one walking in the* ~. T'oenmaruro nuga kŏrŏga-nŭn soriga tŭllyŏssŭmnida. 툇마루로 누가 걸어가는 소리가 들렸읍니다/ *an open[covered]* ~ chibung ŏmnŭn[innŭn] peranda 지붕 없는[있는] 베란다.

verb *n.* (*gram.*) tongsa 동사.

verdict *n.* (*of jury*) p'yŏnggyŏl 평결, (*judgment*) p'an-gyŏl 판결, p'andan 판단, (*opinion*) ŭigyŏn 의견. *accept a* ~ p'yŏnggyŏre pokchonghada 평결에 복종하다/ *the general* ~ ilbanŭi ŭigyŏn 일반의 의견.

verge *n.* (*edge*) kkŭt 끝, (*brink*) kajangjari 가장자리, (*borderline*) kyŏnggye 경계, (*room*) yŏji 여지. *on the* ~ *of* ① (*age*) ...i toeryŏgo hada ...이 되려고 하다. *I am on the* ~ *of 60.* Nanŭn nai yesune kakkapsŭmnida. 나는 나이 예순에 가깝습니다. ② (*ruin,etc.*) chingmyŏnhae itta 직면해 있다. *The company is on the* ~ *of bank-ruptcy.* Kŭ hoesanŭn p'asane chingmyŏnhago issŭm-nida. 그 회사는 파산에 직면하고 있읍니다.

verify *vt.* (*prove*) ipchŭnghada 입증하다, (*ascertain*) hwaginhada 확인하다, (*check*) match'uŏ poda 맞추어 보다. *The driver's report was verified by an eyewitness.* Un-jŏnsaŭi pogo naeyongŭn mokkyŏkchaga ipchŭnghae-ssŭmnida. 운전사의 보고 내용은 목격자가 입증했읍니다/ *a date* naltcharŭl match'uŏ poda 날짜를 맞추어 보다.

vermin *n.* (*harmful insects*) haech'ung 해충, (*noxious animals*) haeroun chimsŭng 해로운 짐승. *a plague of* ~ ch'unghae 충해(蟲害).

vernacular *n.* (*native language*) chagugŏ 자국어(自國語). ~ *language* t'oŏ 토어(土語)/ *the* ~ *of the lawyers* pŏm-nyulgaŭi yongŏ 법률가의 용어.

vernal *adj.* (*of spring*) pomŭi 봄의. ~ *flowers* pomkkot 봄꽃/ ~ *breeze* pomparam 봄바람.

verse *n.* (*poetry*) shi 시, (*piece of poetry*) ship'yŏn 시편(詩篇), (*metrical composition*) unmun 운문. *free* ~ chayushi 자유시. *Korean lyrical* ~ Han-guk sŏjŏngshi 한국 서정시/ *prose and* ~ sanmun-gwa unmun 산문과 운문.

version *n.* (*translation*) pŏnyŏk 번역, (*particular*

description) isŏl 이설(異說). *the French* ~ P'ŭrangsŭŏ pŏnyŏk 프랑스어 번역/ *a new* ~ *of the Bible* sŏngsŏŭi shinyŏkp'an 성서의 신역판.

vertical *adj.* (*straight up*) sujigŭi 수직의, (*upright*) kotch'u sŏn 곧추 선. *a* ~ *line* sujiksŏn 수직선.

very *adv.* (*much*) maeu 매우, taedanhi 대단히, aju 아주. —*adj.* (*identical*) paro kŭ 바로 그. ~ *good* taedanhi choŭn 대단히 좋은/ ~ *much* maeu 매우/ ~ *little* aju chŏgŭn 아주 적은/ *I am* ~ *glad.* Maeu kippŭmnida. 매우 기쁩니다/ *Give me only a* ~ *little.* Aju chogŭmman chushipshio. 아주 조금만 주십시오/ *You are the* ~ *man I want to see.* Taegi paro naega manna pogo ship'ŏhadŏn kŭ saramimnida. 댁이 바로 내가 만나 보고 싶어하던 그 사람입니다.

vessel *n.* (*container*) kŭrŭt 그릇, yonggi 용기, (*ship*) k'ŭn pae 큰 배. *a tin* ~ yangch'ŏl kŭrŭt 양철 그릇/ *a merchant* ~ sangsŏn 상선/ *a war* ~ kunham 군함/ *a wood* ~ moksŏn 목선.

vest *n.* (*waistcoat*) chokki 조끼. *a bullet-proof* ~ pangt'an chokki 방탄 조끼.

veteran *n.* (*old soldier*) nobyŏng 노병(老兵), (*expert*) noryŏn-ga 노련가. —*adj.* (*experienced*) noryŏnhan 노련한. *a disabled* ~ sangi kunin 상이 군인/ *a* ~ *politician* noryŏnhan chŏngch'iga 노련한 정치가.

veterinary *n.* suŭi 수의(獸醫). —*adj.* suŭiŭi 수의의. *a* ~ *surgeon* suŭisa 수의사/ *a* ~ *college* suŭikwa taehak 수의과 대학.

veto *n.* (~ *power*) kŏbukwŏn 거부권, (*rejection*) kŏbu 거부. —*vt.* (*reject*) kŏbuhada 거부하다. *the right of* ~ kŏbukwŏn 거부권.

vex *vt.* (*irritate*) anjŏlbujŏl mot'age hada 안절부절 못하게 하다, (*trouble*) koerop'ida 괴롭히다, (*provoke*) sŏngnage hada 성나게 하다. *I am* ~*ed to hear such bad news.* Kŭ pulgirhan soshige maŭmi ap'ŭmnida. 그 불길한 소식에 마음이 아픕니다.

via *prep.* (*by way of*) …ŭl kyŏngyuhayŏ …을 경유하여. *go to America* ~ *Hawaii* Hawairŭl kyŏngyu Miguge kada 하와이를 경유 미국에 가다/ *a bus for Sodaemun* ~ *Chongno* Chongno kyŏngyu Sŏdaemun kanŭn pŏsŭ 종로 경유 서대문 가는 버스.

vibrate *vi.* chindonghada 진동하다, ttŏllida 떨리다. —*vt.* chindongshik'ida 진동시키다.

vibration *n.* (*vibrating motion*) chindong 진동, (*of pendulum*) hŭndŭllim 흔들림, (*throbbing*) kodong 고동. *20* ~*s per second* maech'o sŭmu pŏnŭi chindong 매초 스무 번의 진동.

vice *n.* (*gross wickedness*) pudodŏk 부도덕, (*evil habit*) aksŭp 악습, (*defect*) kyŏrham 결함. *a national* ~ kungminŭi aksŭp 국민의 악습. *My horse has no* ~. Nae marŭn nappŭn pŏrŭsŭn ŏpsŭmnida. 내 말은 나쁜 버릇은 없읍니다. —*pref.* (*in place of*) pu 부(副), (*subordinate*) ch'a 차(次). ~ -*chairman* puŭijang 부의장/ ~-*chief* ch'ajang 차장(次長)/ ~-*consul* puyŏngsa 부영사/a ~-*minister* ch'agwan 차관(次官)/ ~-*president* (*of company*) pusajang 부사장/ (*of nation*) put'ongnyŏng 부통령.

vice versa *adv.* kŏkkuro 거꾸로, pandaero 반대로. *We gossip about them, and* ~. Urinŭn kŭdŭrŭl hŏmdamhago, pandaero kŭdŭrŭn urirŭl hŏmdamhamnida. 우리는 그들을 험담하고, 반대로 그들은 우리를 험담합니다.

vicinity *n.* (*neighborhood*) iut 이웃, kŭnch'ŏ 근처, (*closeness*) kŭnjŏp 근접. *Seoul and its* ~ Sŏulgwa kŭ pugŭn 서울과 그 부근/ *There isn't a good school in the* ~. Pugŭnenŭn choŭn hakkyoga ŏpsŭmnida. 부근에는 좋은 학교가 없읍니다.

vicious *adj.* (*evil*) nappŭn 나쁜, (*malignant*) shimsulgujŭn 심술궂은, (*severe*) chidok'an 지독한, (*immoral*) t'arak'an 타락한. ~ *companions* mottoen ch'in-gu 못된 친구/ *a* ~ *habit* nappŭn pŏrŭt 나쁜 버릇/ *a* ~ *headache* chidok'an tut'ong 지독한 두통.

victim *n.* (*dupe*) hŭisaengja 희생자, chemul 제물, (*sufferer*) p'ihaeja 피해자, chonanja 조난자. *a war* ~ chŏnjaeng hŭisaengja 전쟁 희생자/ ~ *of a railway accident* ch'ŏlto sagoŭi chonanja 철도 사고의 조난자/ *an* *earthquake* ~ chijin p'ihaeja 지진 피해자/ *an air-raid* ~ kongsŭp p'ihaeja 공습 피해자/ *You're the* ~ *of your own imagination.* Tangshin chashinŭi shin-gyŏng t'a-shimnida. 당신 자신의 신경 탓입니다.

victor *n.* sŭngnija 승리자.

victory *n.* (*in contest*) sŭngni 승리, (*in war*) sŭngjŏn 승전(勝戰). *a crushing* ~ aptojŏk sŭngni 압도적 승리/ *a splendid* ~ tangdanghan sŭngni 당당한 승리.

vie *vi.* (*compete*) kyŏruda 겨루다, (*contend*) uyŏrŭl tat'uda 우열을 다투다.

view *n.* (*scene*) kyŏngch'i 경치, (*sight*) chŏnmang 전망, (*opinion*) ŭigyŏn 의견, (*vision*) shiryŏk 시력, (*purpose*) mokchŏk 목적. —*vt.* (*look at*) poda 보다, (*inspect*) kŏmsahada 검사하다, (*survey*) kwanch'arhada 관찰하다. *a distant* ~ wŏn-gyŏng 원경/ *a glorious* ~ chŏlgyŏng 절경(絕景)/ *I'll tell you my* ~s *some day.* Ŏnjen-ga nae ŭigyŏnŭl malssŭmdŭrijiyo. 언젠가 내 의견을 말씀드리지요/ *my* ~ *of life* naŭi insaenggwan 나의 인생관.

viewpoint *n.* (*point of view*) kwanchŏm 관점, (*standpoint*) kyŏnji 견지, kyŏnhae 견해. *an historical* ~ yŏksajŏk kyŏnji 역사적 견지.

vigil *n.* (*watch*) pulch'imbŏn 불침번, (*keeping awake*) ch'ŏrya 철야. *keep* ~ pamsaemyŏ chik'ida 밤새며 지키다, kyŏngyarŭl hada 경야(經夜)를 하다.

vigo(u)r *n.* (*strength*) hwallyŏk 활력, (*energy*) wŏn-gi 원기, (*activity*) hwaltongnyŏk 활동력, (*force*) pangnyŏk 박력. *physical* ~ ch'eryŏk 체력(體力)/ *regain one's* ~ wŏn-girŭl hoebok'ada 원기를 회복하다.

vigorous *adj.* (*energetic*) kiuni wangsŏnghan 기운이 왕성한, (*lively*) p'alp'arhan 팔팔한, (*forceful*) pangnyŏk innŭn 박력 있는. *a* ~ *commander* pangnyŏk innŭn chi-hwigwan 박력 있는 지휘관.

vile *adj.* (*very bad*) mopshi nappŭn 몹시 나쁜, (*disgusting*) koyak'an 고약한, (*base*) piyŏrhan 비열한. ~ *weather* koyak'an nalssi 고약한 날씨/ ~ *smell* koyak'an naemsae 고약한 냄새/ *a* ~ *character* piyŏrhan in-gan 비열한 인간.

villa *n.* pyŏlchang 별장. *a seaside* ~ haebyŏnkaŭi pyŏl-

chang 해변가의 별장/ *a ~ to let* imdae pyŏlchang 임대
별장/ *a ~ keeper* pyŏlchangjigi 별장지기.

village *n.* maŭl 마을. *a neighboring ~* iut maŭl 이웃 마을/
~ people maŭl saram 마을 사람.

villager *n.* maŭl saram 마을 사람.

villain *n.* (*rascal*) ak'an 악한, aktang 악당.

vine *n.* (*grapevine*) p'odonamu 포도나무.

vinegar *n.* ch'o 초(醋), shikch'o 식초.

vineyard *n.* p'odobat 포도밭.

violate *vt.* (*break*) wibanhada 위반하다, ŏgida 어기다,
(*break in upon*) ch'imhaehada 침해하다, (*profane*)
tŏrŏp'ida 더럽히다, (*rape*) kangganhada 강간하다. *~ the*
law pŏbŭl ŏgida 법을 어기다/ *~ one's privacy* namŭi
sasaenghwarŭl ch'imhaehada 남의 사생활을 침해하다/ *It*
would be violating the Exchange Control Law. Oe-
hwan kwallipŏbŭl pŏmhanŭn ch'ŏsaga toemnida. 외환
관리법을 범하는 처사가 됩니다.

violation *n.* (*break*) wiban 위반, (*interruption*) panghae
방해, (*infringement*) ch'imhae 침해, (*desecration*) modok
모독. *a traffic ~* kyot'ong wiban 교통 위반/ *a civil*
rights ~ inkwŏn ch'imhae 인권 침해.

violence *n.* (*force*) p'ongnyŏk 폭력, (*outrage*) p'ok'aeng
폭행. *employ ~ against* p'ok'aengŭl kahada 폭행을 가
하다/ *appeal to ~* p'ongnyŏge hosohada 폭력에 호소하다.

violent *adj.* (*furious*) maengnyŏrhan 맹렬한, (*outrageous*)
nanp'ok'an 난폭한, (*severe*) chidok'an 지독한. *a ~*
attack maengnyŏrhan konggyŏk 맹렬한 공격/ *a ~ death*
pyŏnsa 변사/ *a ~ headache* chidok'an tut'ong 지독한
두통.

violet *n.* (*flower*) chebikkot 제비꽃, (*color*) portatpit 보
랏빛.

violin *n.* paiollin 바이올린, chegŭm 제금. *play the ~*
paiollinŭl k'yŏda 바이올린을 켜다.

violinist *n.* paiollin yŏnjuja 바이올린 연주자.

virgin *n.* ch'ŏnyŏ 처녀. *—adj.* (*chaste*) sun-gyŏrhan 순
결한, (*pure*) kkaekkŭt'an 깨끗한, (*untrodden*) palp'in
il ŏmnŭn 밟힌 일 없는. *a ~ voyage* ch'ŏnyŏ hanghae

처녀 항해/ *a ~ forest* ch'ŏnyŏrim 처녀림/ *~ gold* sungŭm 순금/ *~ paper* paekchi 백지/ *~ soil* ch'ŏnyŏji 처녀지.

virtue *n.* (*goodness*) tŏk 덕, midŏk 미덕, (*chastity*) chŏngjo 정조, (*merit*) michŏm 미점, (*efficacy*) hyonŭng 효능. *traditional ~s* chŏnt'ongjŏgin midŏk 전통적인 미덕/ *a woman of ~* chŏngjŏl puin 정절 부인/ *medicine of great ~* t'ŭk'yoyak 특효약.

virtuous *adj.* (*moral*) tŏk innŭn 덕 있는, (*chaste*) chŏngsuk'an 정숙한, (*upright*) kogyŏrhan 고결한. *a ~ young woman* chŏngsuk'an chŏlmŭn yŏin 정숙한 젊은 여인.

visa *n.* sachŭng 사증(査證), pija 비자. *an entry ~* ipkuk sachŭng 입국 사증/ *an exit ~* ch'ulguk sachŭng 출국 사증/ *a long-term ~* changgi sachŭng 장기 사증.

visible *adj.* nune poinŭn 눈에 보이는. *easily ~* shwii poinŭn 쉬이 보이는/ *faintly ~* hŭimihage poinŭn 희미하게 보이는.

vision *n.* (*sight*) shiryŏk 시력, (*foresight*) sŏn-gyŏn 선견 (先見), (*~ for future*) miraesang 미래상. *the field of ~* shiya 시야/ *He has normal ~.* Kŭŭi shiryŏgŭn pot'ongimnida. 그의 시력은 보통입니다/ *a test of ~* shiryŏk kŏmsa 시력 검사/ *a statesman without ~* ap'ŭl naedaboji mot'anŭn chŏngch'iga 앞을 내다보지 못하는 정치가.

visit *vt.* (*call upon*) pangmunhada 방문하다, (*inspect*) ch'amgwanhada 참관하다, (*to sick men*) munbyŏnghada 문병하다. *—n.* pangmun 방문, ch'amgwan 참관, (*short stay*) cheryu 체류. *~ a friend* ch'in-gurŭl pangmunhada 친구를 방문하다/ *This is my first ~ to Seoul.* Sŏurŭn ibŏni ch'ŏŭmimnida. 서울은 이번이 처음입니다/ *I've much enjoyed this pleasant ~.* Pangmunhae chusyŏsŏ chŏngmal chŭlgŏwŏssŭmnida. 방문해 주셔서 정말 즐거웠습니다.

visitor *n.* (*caller*) pangmun-gaek 방문객, (*guest*) sonnim 손님.

vital *adj.* (*of life*) saengmyŏngŭi 생명의, (*lively*) hwalgi innŭn 활기 있는, (*important*) chungdaehan 중대한, (*fatal*) ch'imyŏngjŏgin 치명적인. *~ energies* saengmyŏngnyŏk 생명력/*a ~ personality* chŏngnyŏkka 정력가.

vitality *n.* (*vital force*) saengmyŏngnyŏk 생명력, hwalgi

활기, (*physical strength*) ch'eryŏk 체력, (*capacity to endure*) chisongnyŏk 지속력.

vivid *adj.* (*lively*) saengsaenghan 생생한, (*bright*) sŏnmyŏnghan 선명한, (*vigorous*) hwalbarhan 활발한. *I have a ∼ memory of her face.* Kŭ yŏinŭi olgurŭl nune sŏnhage kiŏk'ago issŭmnida. 그 여인의 얼굴을 눈에 선하게 기억하고 있읍니다.

vocabulary *n.* (*stock of words*) ŏhwi 어휘, (*list of words*) tanŏjip 단어집. *a rich* [*poor*] ∼ p'ungbuhan [pinyak'an] ŏhwi 풍부한[빈약한] 어휘.

vocal *adj.* soriŭi 소리의, ŭmsŏngŭi 음성의. ∼ *cords* sŏngdae 성대/ ∼ *music* sŏngak 성악/ ∼ *solo* tokch'ang 독창.

vocalist *n.* sŏngakka 성악가.

vocation *n.* (*occupation*) chigŏp 직업, (*calling*) ch'ŏnjik 천직, (*business*) changsa 장사. *select a* ∼ chigŏbŭl sŏnt'aek'ada 직업을 선택하다/ *change one's* ∼ chŏnŏp'ada 전업하다.

vogue *n.* (*fashion*) yuhaeng 유행, (*popularity*) inki 인기(人氣). *What will be the next* ∼? Taŭmŭn muŏshi yuhaenghalkkayo? 다음은 무엇이 유행할까요/ *The song had a great* ∼ *in its day.* Kŭ noraenŭn tangshi taeyuhaengiŏssŭmnida. 그 노래는 당시 대유행이었읍니다.

voice *n.* moksori 목소리. *a loud* ∼ k'ŭn moksori 큰 목소리/ *a husky* ∼ mokshwin sori 목쉰 소리/ *a clear* ∼ malgŭn moksori 맑은 목소리/ *in a low* [*sad*] ∼ najŭn [sŭlp'ŭn] moksoriro 낮은[슬픈] 목소리로/ *Your* ∼ *is hoarse today.* Onŭl moksoriga shwiŏtkunyo. 오늘 목소리가 쉬었군요.

void *adj.* (*empty*) pin 빈, (*vacant*) t'ŏng pin 텅 빈, (*not binding*) muhyoin 무효인. —*n.* (*empty space*) konggan 공간, (*emptiness*) konghŏ 공허. *a* ∼ *space* konggan 공간/ *a* ∼ *contract* muhyoin kyeyak 무효인 계약.

volcano *n.* hwasan 화산.

volleyball *n.* paegu 배구. *a* ∼ *game* paegu kyŏnggi 배구 경기/ *play* ∼ paeguhada 배구하다.

volume *n.* (*book*) ch'aek 책, (*one of a set*) kwŏn 권(卷), (*quantity*) yang 양(量), (*bulk*) pup'i 부피. *a thick* ∼ tukk'ŏun ch'aek 두꺼운 책/ *the first* ∼ ch'ŏtchae kwŏn

첫째 권(卷)/ *a voice of great* ~ p'ungbuhan sŏngnyang 풍부한 성량/ *the* ~ *of manufacture* saengsannyang 생산량.

voluminous *adj.* (*bulky*) pup'iga k'ŭn 부피가 큰, (*copious*) taryangŭi 다량의. *a* ~ *correspondence* tut'umhan p'yŏnji 두둑한 편지.

voluntary *adj.* chabalchŏgin 자발적인. *a* ~ *helper* chabalchŏgin wŏnjoja 자발적인 원조자/ *a* ~ *army* ŭiyonggun 의용군/ ~ *service* (*mil.*) chiwŏn chedo 지원 제도.

volunteer *n.* chiwŏnja 지원자, (*charitable person*) tokchiga 독지가.

vomit *vi.*, *vt.* t'ohada 토하다, keuda 게우다. *I* ~*ed every thing I had eaten.* Mŏgŭn kŏsŭl choeda t'ohaessŭmnida. 먹은 것을 죄다 토했습니다.

vote *n.* (*suffrage*) t'up'yo(kwŏn) 투표(권). —*vi.*, *vt.* t'up'yohada 투표하다. *secret* ~ mugimyŏng t'up'yo 무기명 투표/ ~ *of confidence* shinim t'up'yo 신임 투표/ *I gave my* ~ *to Mr. Kim.* Nanŭn Kimssiege t'up'yohaessŭmnida. 나는 김씨에게 투표했습니다.

voter *n.* t'up'yoja 투표자.

vouch *vi.* (*guarantee*) pojŭnghada 보증하다, (*assert*) tanŏnhada 단언하다.

voucher *n.* (*receipt*) yŏngsujŭng 영수증. *a credit* ~ sangp'umkwŏn 상품권.

vow *n.* (*pledge*) maengse 맹세, (*oath*) sŏyak 서약. —*vt.* (*promise solemnly*) maengsehada 맹세하다, (*assert*) tanŏnhada 단언하다. *wedding* ~*s* kyŏrhon sŏyak 결혼 서약/ *make a* ~ sŏyak'ada 서약하다/ *I* ~*ed never to drink liquor again.* Tashinŭn surŭl an mashigettago maengsehaessŭmnida. 다시는 술을 안 마시겠다고 맹세했습니다.

vowel *n.* moŭm 모음.

voyage *n.* hanghae 항해. *go on a* ~ hanghaerŭl ttŏnada 항해를 떠나다/ *I wish you bon* ~. Hanghae chung musahagirŭl pimnida. 항해 중 무사하기를 빕니다.

vulgar *adj.* (*unrefined*) ch'ŏnhan 천한, (*common*) pŏmsok'an 범속한. ~ *behavior* yabihan haengdong 야비한

행동/ *a ~ fellow* sangnom 상놈/ *~ circles* sŏmin sahoe 서민 사회.

vulture *n.* (*bird*) toksuri 독수리.

---

wad *n.* (*packing*) mungch'i 뭉치, (*stuffing*) ch'aewŏ nŏnnŭn mulgŏn 채워 넣는 물건, (*of money*) chip'ye mungch'i 지폐 뭉치, (*money*) ton 돈. *a ~ of paper* chongi mungch'i 종이 뭉치/ *make ~s of money* k'ŭn tonŭl pŏlda 큰 돈을 벌다.

wade *vi.* (*cross over on foot*) kŏrŏsŏ kŏnnŏda 걸어서 건너다. *~ across a river* kangŭl kŏrŏsŏ kŏnnŏgada 강 (江)을 걸어서 건너가다.

wag *vt.* (*shake*) hŭndŭlda 흔들다, (*fingers*) kkattakkŏrida 까딱거리다. *~ a tail* kkorirŭl hŭndŭlda 꼬리를 흔들다/ *Don't ~ your finger at me.* Na-ege sonkaragŭl kkattakkŏriji[pinanhaji] mashio. 나에게 손가락을 까딱거리지 [비난하지] 마시오.

wage *n.* (*pl.*) imgŭm 임금, (*pay*) kŭmnyo 급료. *—vt.* (*war*) chŏnjaengŭl hada 전쟁을 하다. *at good[low] ~s* choŭn[ssan] imgŭmŭro 좋은[싼] 임금으로/ *Can you get along on your ~s?* Tangshinŭi kŭmnyoro saragal su issŭmnikka? 당신의 급료로 살아갈 수 있읍니까/ *a ~ increase* imgŭm insang 임금 인상/ *basic ~s* kibon imgŭm 기본 임금.

wager *n.* (*bet*) norŭm 노름, (*betting*) naegi 내기. *win a ~* naegiesŏ igida 내기에서 이기다/ *I've lost the ~.* Naegiesŏ chyŏssŭmnida. 내기에서 졌읍니다/ *Name your ~.* Ŏlma kŏlgesso? 얼마 걸겠소?

wag(g)on *n.* (*draw by horses*) chimmach'a 짐마차, (*railway truck*) mugae hwach'a 무개 화차, (*baby carriage*) yumoch'a 유모차.

waist *n.* hŏri 허리. *~ belt* hŏritti 허리띠, pelt'ŭ 벨트.

waistcoat *n.* chokki 조끼. *leave off one's ~* chokkirŭl pŏtta 조끼를 벗다.

wait *vi.* (*for*) kidarida 기다리다, (*serve*) ŭngdaehada 응대하다(*on*). *Please ~ a minute.* Chamshi kidarishipshio. 잠시 기다리십시오/ *Please ~ here.* Yŏgisŏ kidarishipshio. 여기서 기다리십시오/ *Are you ~ing for anybody?* Nugurŭl kidarishimnikka? 누구를 기다리십니까/ *How long have you been ~ing?* Ŏlmana kidaryŏssŭmnikka? 얼마나 기다렸읍니까/ *I cannot ~ any longer.* Tŏ kidaril su ŏpsŭmnida. 더 기다릴 수 없읍니다/ *Oh, I advice you not to ~ that way, boy.* Kŭrŏk'e mirul kŏt ŏpta, i sarama. 그렇게 미룰 것 없다, 이 사람아/ *~ on table* (*meal*) shijung tŭlda 시중 들다/ *Are you ~ed on?* Chumunŭn pada kassŭmnikka? 주문은 받아 갔읍니까?

waiter *n.* kŭpsa 급사, weit'ŏ 웨이터.

waiting room taehapshil 대합실.

waitress *n.* yŏgŭp 여급, weit'ŭresŭ 웨이트레스.

wake *vi., vt.* kkaeda 깨다, irŏnada 일어나다, kkaeuda 깨우다. *What time do you usually ~?* Pot'ong myŏt shie irŏnashimnikka? 보통 몇 시에 일어나십니까/ *Don't ~ the baby.* Airŭl kkaeuji mashio. 아이를 깨우지 마시오/ *W~ me up at five-thirty.* Tasŏssi pane kkaewŏ chushio. 5시 반에 깨워 주시오.

walk *n.* (*stroll*) sanch'aek 산책, sanpo 산보, (*going on foot*) tobo 도보, (*path*) podo 보도(步道). —*vi.* (*go on foot*) kŏtta 걷다, kŏrŏgada 걸어가다. *Do you often go for ~s?* Chaju sanch'aek'ashimnikka? 자주 산책하십니까/ *Let's take a ~ in the Toksu Palace.* Tŏksugungesŏ sanch'aegŭl hapshida. 덕수궁에서 산책을 합시다/ *a side ~* podo 보도/ *Shall we ride or ~?* T'ago kalkkayo, kŏrŏgalkkayo? 타고 갈까요, 걸어갈까요/ *Let's ~.* Kŏrŭpshida. 걸읍시다/ *You ~ too fast.* Nŏmu ppalli kŏrŭshimnida. 너무 빨리 걸으십니다/ *Now, I will ~ you to the station.* Yŏkkaji paraeda tŭrigessŭmnida. 역까지 바래다 드리겠읍니다/ *Please ~ in.* Ŏsŏ tŭrŏoshipshio. 어서 들어오십시오.

wall *n.* pyŏk 벽, tam 담. *a stone ~* toltam 돌담/ *a ~ clock* pyŏkshigye 벽시계/ *a ~ closet* pyŏkchang 벽장/ *~ paper* pyŏkchi 벽지.

wallet *n.* tonchumŏni 돈주머니, (*pocketbook*) chigap 지갑.

I've lost my ~ while on a train. Yŏlch'a-esŏ chigabŭl irŏssŭmnida. 열차에서 지갑을 잃었읍니다.

walnut *n.* hodu 호두. 「를 추다.

waltz *n.* walch'ŭ 왈츠. *dance a ~* walch'ŭrŭl ch'uda 왈츠

wander *vi.* (*roam*) ttŏdoradanida 떠돌아다니다, (*rove*) hemaeda 헤매다, (*stray*) kirŭl ilt'a 길을 잃다. *We ~ed miles and miles in the mist.* An-gae sogŭl myŏt mairina kirŭl ilk'o hemaeŏssŭmnida. 안개 속을 몇 마일이나 길을 잃고 헤매었읍니다.

wanderer *n.* pangnangja 방랑자.

want *n.* (*necessity*) p'iryo 필요, (*lack*) kyŏlp'ip 결핍, pujok 부족. —*vt.* (*wish*) wŏnhada 원하다, (*desire*) parada 바라다, (*need*) ...ŭl p'iryoro hada …을 필요로 하다. *daily ~s* iryongp'um 일용품/ *~ of confidence* shinyongŭi kyŏlp'ip 신용의 결핍/ *~ of nutrition* yŏngyang pujok 영양 부족/ *Do you ~ to go to America?* Miguge kagirŭl wŏnhashimnikka? 미국에 가기를 원하십니까/ *Mr. Kim, you are ~ed on the phone.* Kim sŏnsaengnim, chŏnhwa wassŭmnida. 김 선생님, 전화 왔읍니다/ *I ~ you to see what this watch ~ s.* I shigyega ŏdiga kojanginji pwajushio. 이 시계가 어디가 고장인지 봐주시오/ *What do you ~ with me?* Na-ege musŭn yongmurado issŭmnikka? 나에게 무슨 용무라도 있읍니까?

war *n.* chŏnjaeng 전쟁, (*struggle*) t'ujaeng 투쟁, (*fight*) ssaum 싸움. *guerilla ~* yugyŏkchŏn 유격전/ *the 2nd World War* cheich'a taejŏn 제2차 대전/ *an aggressive ~* ch'imnyakchŏn 침략전/ *a ~ criminal* chŏnbŏm 전범/ *a ~ orphan* chŏnjaeng koa 전쟁 고아/ *a ~ widow* chŏnjaeng mimangin 전쟁 미망인/ *lose a ~* chŏnjaenge chida 전쟁에 지다/ *win a ~* chŏnjaenge igida 전쟁에 이기다/ *after ~* chŏnhu 전후/ *before ~* chŏnjaeng chŏn 전쟁 전/ *Do you think there will be ~?* Chŏnjaengi irŏnalkkayo? 전쟁이 일어날까요?

ward *n.* (*of hospital*) pyŏngdong 병동(病棟), (*of city*) ku 구(區), (*guard*) poho 보호. *a hospital ~* pyŏngdong 병동/ *an isolating ~* kyŏngni pyŏngshil 격리 병실/ *a ~ office* kuch'ŏng 구청/ *the ~ head* kuch'ŏngjang 구청장/

a child in ～ pohorŭl patko innŭn ai 보호를 받고 있는 아
wardrobe *n.* otchang 옷장, yangbokchang 양복장. 니이.
ware *n.* (*utensil*) kimul 기물, (*goods*) sangp'um 상품.
mend broken ～ pusŏjin kimurŭl koch'ida 부서진 기물
을 고치다/ *ceramic* ～s tojagi 도자기/ *table* ～ shikki 식기
(食器)/ *The* ～s *in that store are dear*. Chŏ kageŭi
sangp'umŭn pissamnida. 저 가게의 상품은 비쌉니다.
warehouse *n.* ch'anggo 창고.
warfare *n.* (*war*) chŏnjaeng 전쟁, (*fighting*) ssaum
싸움. *aggressive* ～ ch'imnyakchŏn 침략전/ *modern* ～
kŭndaejŏn 근대전/ *total* ～ ch'ongnyŏkchŏn 총력전.
warm *adj.* ttattŭt'an 따뜻한, (*hot*) tŏun 더운. —*vt.*
ttattŭt'age hada 따뜻하게 하다, teuda 데우다. ～ *water*
tŏun mul 더운 물, onsu 온수/ ～ *milk* ttakkŭnhan uyu
따끈한 우유/ *a* ～ *sweater* ttasŭhan sŭwet'ŏ 따스한 스웨
터/ *It is* ～ *today*. Onŭrŭn ttattŭt'amnida. 오늘은 따뜻
합니다/ ～ *up soup* kugŭl teuda 국을 데우다/ *Come and
get* ～ *by the fire*. Wasŏ purŭl tchoeshio. 와서 불을 쬐시
오/ ～-*hearted* ch'injŏrhan 친절한/ ～*ing-up* chunbi
undong 준비 운동.
warn *vt.* (*caution*) kyŏnggohada 경고하다, (*admonish*)
t'airŭda 타이르다, (*inform*) allida 알리다. *I* ～*ed her
not to go*. Kŭiege kaji maldorok kyŏnggohaessŭmnida.
그이에게 가지 말도록 경고했읍니다/ *Don't say I didn't* ～
you. Miri alliji anattagonŭn haji mashio. 미리 알리지 않
았다고는 하지 마시오.
warning *n.* (*caution*) kyŏnggo 경고, (*notice*) t'onggo
통고, (*premonition*) chojim 조짐. *an air raid* ～ kongsŭp kyŏngbo 공습 경보/ *without any* ～ yego ŏpshi 예고
없이, kapchagi 갑자기/ *give* ～ kyŏnggohada 경고하다.
warrant *n.* (*licence*) myŏnhŏchang 면허장, (*certificate*)
chŭngmyŏngsŏ 증명서, (*commission*) wiimchang 위임장,
(*guarantee*) pojŭng 보증, (*law*) yŏngchang 영장(令狀),
(*ground*) kŭn-gŏ 근거. *I will be your* ～. Taegŭi
pojŭngŭl sŏdŭrijiyo. 댁의 보증을 서드리지요/ *a* ～ *of arrest*
kusok yŏngchang 구속 영장.
warrior *n.* (*soldier*) kunin 군인, (*veteran soldier*)

yongsa 용사. *a brave* ~ yonggamhan kunin 용감한 군인/ *the Unknown W*~ mumyŏng yongsa 무명 용사.

warship *n.* kunham 군함.

wartime *n.* chŏnshi 전시(戰時). *a* ~ *industry* chŏnshi sanŏp 전시 산업/ ~ *mobilization* chŏnshi tongwŏn 전시 동원.

wash *vt., vi.* (*cleanse*) ssitta 씻다, set'ak'ada 세탁하다. —*n.* set'ak 세탁, (*articles*) set'angmul 세탁물. *Go and* ~ *yourself.* Kasŏ momŭl ssisŭseyo. 가서 몸을 씻으세요/ *I must* ~ *before dinner.* Shiksa chŏnenŭn ssisŏya hamnida. 식사 전에는 씻어야 합니다/ ~*ing machine* set'akki 세탁기/ *an electric* ~*ing machine* chŏn-gi set'akki 전기 세탁기/ *Would you please teach me how to use this* ~*ing machine?* I set'akki sayongpŏbŭl karŭch'yŏ chushigessŭmnikka? 이 세탁기 사용법을 가르쳐 주시겠읍니까?

washable *adj.* ppal su innŭn 빨 수 있는. *Is this material* ~? I chaeryonŭn ppal su issŭmnikka? 이 재료는 빨 수 있읍니까?

washer *n.* set'akki 세탁기. *How thoughtful of you to give us a* ~. Set'akkirŭl chushidani chŏngmal komapsŭmnida. 세탁기를 주시다니 정말 고맙습니다.

washerman, washerwoman *n.* set'akpu 세탁부.

washroom *n.* (*restroom*) hwajangshil 화장실. *Where is the* ~? Hwajangshirŭn ŏdiimnikka? 화장실은 어디입니까?

wasp *n.* malbŏl 말벌, nanani 나나니.

waste *vt., vi.* (*squander*) nangbihada 낭비하다, (*enfeeble*) soeyakk'e hada 쇠약케 하다, (*lay waste*) hwangp'yeshik'ida 황폐시키다, (*time*) shigani hŭrŭda 시간이 흐르다. —*n.* (*wilderness*) hwangmuji 황무지, (*ruin*) hwangp'ye 황폐, (*rubbish*) p'yemul 폐물. —*adj.* (*barren*) pulmoŭi 불모의, (*desolate*) hwangp'yehan 황폐한, (*useless*) ssŭlmoŏmnŭn 쓸모없는. *Don't* ~ *food.* Ŭmshigŭl nangbihaji mashio. 음식을 낭비하지 마시오/ *Don't* ~ *any more time on it.* Kŏgie tŏnŭn shiganŭl nangbihaji mashio. 거기에 더는 시간을 낭비하지 마시오/ *Turn that tap off—the water is wasting.* Kkokchirŭl chamgŭshio, muri nangbidoenikka? 꼭지를 잠그시오, 물이 낭비되니까/ *What a* ~ *of energy!* I ŏlmana chŏngnyŏgŭi nangbiimnikka! 이

얼마나 정력의 낭비입니까/ *kitchen* ~ puŏk ssŭregi 부엌 쓰레기/ *the* ~ *from a factory* kongjang p'yemul 공장 폐물/ ~ *land* hwangmuji 황무지/ *a* ~ *basket* ssŭregi-t'ong 쓰레기통/ ~-*paper* hyuji 휴지.

watch *n.* (*timepiece*) shigye 시계, (*sentinel*) p'asu 파수, (*lookout*) kamshi 감시. —*vi., vt.* (*look on*) paraboda 바라보다, (*be cautious*) choshimhada 조심하다, (*keep guard*) kamshihada 감시하다. *a wrist* ~ p'alttuk shigye 팔뚝 시계/ *Have you a* ~ *with you?* Shigye kajigo kye-shimnikka? 시계 가지고 계십니까/ *What does your* ~ *say?* Myŏt shiimnikka? 몇 시입니까/ *a sleepless* ~ pulch'im-bŏn 불침번/ *May I* ~ *TV?* T'ellebijŏnŭl pwado chŏssŭm-nikka? 텔레비전을 봐도 좋습니까? *W*~ *your step, please.* Palpurirŭl choshimhashipshio. 발부리를 조심하십시오.

watchman *n.* kyŏngbiwŏn 경비원. *a hotel* ~ hot'el suwi 호텔 수위. *a night* ~ yagyŏngkkun 야경꾼.

water *n.* mul 물. —*vt.* (*sprinkle*) murŭl ppurida 물을 뿌리다, (*supply with*) murŭl chuda 물을 주다. *cold* ~ naengsu 냉수/ *hot* ~ tŏun mul 더운 물/ *fragrant* ~ hyangsu 향수/ *toilet* ~ hwajangsu 화장수/ *salt* ~ sogŭmmul 소금물/ *whisky and* ~ mul t'an wisŭk'i 물 탄 위스키/ *Can I have another glass of* ~? Mul han k'ŏp tŏ chushigessŭmnikka? 물 한 컵 더 주시겠읍니까/ ~ *closet* pyŏnso 변소/ ~ *color* such'aehwa 수채화/ ~ *lily* suryŏn 수련/ ~ *mill* mullebanga 물레방아.

waterfall *n.* p'okp'o 폭포.

watermelon *n.* subak 수박.

waterproof *n.* pangsu 방수. *a* ~ *coat* pangsu oet'u 방수 외투/ *a* ~ *device* pangsu changch'i 방수 장치.

watertight *adj.* muri saeji annŭn 물이 새지 않는. *a* ~ *box* muri saeji annŭn sangja 물이 새지 않는 상자.

watery *adj.* mulki manŭn 물기 많은. *a* ~ *eyes* nunmurŏrin nun 눈물어린 눈.

wave *n.* mulkyŏl 물결, p'ado 파도. —*vt., vi.* (*swing*) hŭndŭlda 흔들다, (*undulate*) kubich'ida 굽이치다, (*brandish*) hwidurŭda 휘두르다. *mountainous* ~*s* santŏ-mi kat'ŭn p'ado 산더미 같은 파도/ *a cold* ~ hanp'a 한파/

I ∼d him a farewell. Sonŭl hŭndŭrŏ kŭiege chakpyŏl insarŭl haessŭmnida. 손을 흔들어 그이에게 작별 인사를 했읍니다. 「종이.

wax *n.* milch'o 밀초. *∼ paper* p'arap'in chongi 파라핀

way *n.* (*road*) kil 길, (*path*) t'ongno 통로, (*direction*) panghyang 방향, (*means*) pangbŏp 방법. *Please show me the ∼ to Toksu Palace.* Tŏksugungŭro kanŭn kirŭl karik'yŏ chushipshio. 덕수궁으로 가는 길을 가리켜 주십시오/ *Which is the ∼ in[out]?* Ŏdiga ipku[ch'ulgu]imnikka? 어디가 입구[출구]입니까/ *Which ∼ are you going?* Ŏnŭ panghyangŭro kashil chakchŏngishimnikka? 어느 방향으로 가실 작정이십니까/ *Will you walk this ∼?* Iri oseyo. 이리 오세요/ *Come this ∼, please!* Iriro oshijiyo. 이리로 오시지요/ *Do it this ∼.* Irŏk'e hashijiyo. 이렇게 하시지요/ *Have your own ∼ then.* Kŭrŏshidamyŏn maŭmdaero hashio. 그러시다면 마음대로 하시오/ *Is this the ∼ you do it?* Ige taegi hashinŭn pangbŏbimnikka? 이게 댁이 하시는 방법입니까/ *by ∼ of* (*via*) ...ŭl kyŏngyuhayŏ …을 경유하여/ *go by ∼ of Hawaii* Hawairŭl kyŏngyuhayŏ 하와이를 경유하여/ *by the ∼* kŭrŏnde 그런데, yŏdamijiman 여담이지만/ *By the ∼, how does the matter stand?* Kŭrŏnde kŭ irŭn ŏttŏk'e toeŏssŭmnikka? 그런데 그 일은 어떻게 되었읍니까?

wayward *adj.* (*perverse*) oegojibŭi 외고집의, (*capricious*) pyŏndŏksŭrŏun 변덕스러운.

we *pron.* uri(dŭl) 우리(들).

weak *adj.* (*feeble*) yak'an 약한, (*not good at*) sŏt'urŭn 서투른, (*of liquid*) mulgŭn 묽은, sunhan 순한. *a ∼ team* yak'an t'im 약한 팀/ *a ∼ point* yakchŏm 약점/ *I feel ∼.* Nanŭn kiuni ŏpsŭmnida. 나는 기운이 없읍니다/ *I am ∼ in English.* Nanŭn Yŏngŏga sŏt'urŭmnida. 나는 영어가 서투릅니다/ *Would you like your tea strong or ∼?* Ch'anŭn chinhan kŏsŭl choahashimnikka, sunhan kŏsŭl choahashimnikka? 차(茶)는 진한 것을 좋아하십니까, 순한 것을 좋아하십니까? 「yakchŏm 약점.

weakness *n.* (*lack of power*) yakchil 약질, (*weak point*)

wealth *n.* (*riches*) pu 부(富), (*fortune*) chaesan 재산.

a man of great ～ puho 부호.

wealthy *adj.* (*rich*) puyuhan 부유한, (*ample*) p'ungbuhan 풍부한. *a ～ man* puja 부자/ ～ *in knowledge* chishigi p'ungbuhan 지식이 풍부한.

wean *vt.* chŏjŭl tteda 젖을 떼다.

weaning *n.* iyu 이유(離乳). *the ～ period* iyugi 이유기/ *a ～ diet* iyushik 이유식.

weapon *n.* mugi 무기. *a new-type ～* shinhyŏng mugi 신형무기/ *nuclear ～s* haengmugi 핵무기/ *carry ～s along* mugirŭl hyudaehada 무기를 휴대하다.

wear *vt., vi.* (*clothings*) ipta 입다, (*shoes, socks*) shinta 신다, (*hat, spectacles*) ssŭda 쓰다, (*girdle*) turŭda 두르다, (*weary*) p'irohage hada 피로하게 하다, (*be ragged*) haejida 해지다, (*last under use*) orae kada 오래 가다. *Do I need to ～ a suit?* Yangbogŭl ibŏya hamnikka? 양복을 입어야 합니까/ *I'm worn out by all this hard work.* I kodoen illo chich'yŏ pŏryŏssŭmnida. 이 고된 일로 지쳐 버렸읍니다/ *Cheap shoes soon ～ out.* Ssan kudunŭn kot haejimnida. 싼 구두는 곧 해집니다.

weary *adj.* (*tired*) chich'in 지친, (*bored*) mullin 물린, (*tedious*) chiruhan 지루한. ～ *eyes* chich'in nun 지친 눈/ *a ～ journey* chiruhan yŏhaeng 지루한 여행.

weather *n.* nalssi 날씨, ilgi 일기. *fine ～* choŭn nalssi 좋은 날씨/ *cloudy ～* hŭrin nalssi 흐린 날씨/ *How is the ～ today?* Onŭl nalssinŭn ŏttŏssŭmnikka? 오늘 날씨는 어떻습니까/ *Beautiful ～, isn't it?* Nalssiga choch'iyo? 날씨가 좋지요/ *We cannot go out in such ～.* Irŏn nalssienŭn oech'urhal suga ŏpsŭmnida. 이런 날씨에는 외출할 수가 없읍니다/ *What is the ～ forecast for tomorrow?* Naeil ilgi yebonŭn? 내일 일기 예보는/ *a ～ report*〔*forecast*〕ilgi yebo 일기 예보/ ～ *map* ch'ŏn-gido 천기도/ ～ *station* ch'ŭk'uso 측후소, kisangdae 기상대.

weave *vi.* (*threads, etc.*) tchada 짜다, (*wreath*) yŏkta 엮다. *She is weaving a rug.* Yungdanŭl tchago issŏssŭmnida. 융단을 짜고 있었읍니다/ ～ *a blind out of bamboo* taero parŭl yŏkta 대[竹]로 발을 엮다.

web *n.* (*network*) mang 망(網), (*cobweb*) kŏmijul 거미

줄. *a ~ of railways* ch'ŏltomang 철도망.

wed *vt.* (*marry*) kyŏrhonhada 결혼하다.

wedding *n.* (*marriage*) kyŏrhon 결혼. *~ anniversary* kyŏrhon kinyŏmil 결혼 기념일/ *~ day* kyŏrhonil 결혼일/ *~ feast[reception]* kyŏrhon p'iroyŏn 결혼 피로연/ *a ~ hall* kyŏrhon shikchang 결혼 식장/ *~ march* kyŏrhon haengjin-gok 결혼 행진곡/ *a ~ present* kyŏrhon sŏnmul 결혼 선물/ *a ~ ring* kyŏrhon panji 결혼 반지/ *golden ~* kŭmhonshik 금혼식/ *silver ~* ŭnhonshik 은혼식/ *When does the ~ come off?* Kyŏrhonshigŭn ŏnjejiyo? 결혼식은 언제지요/ *I was present at the ~.* Kŭ kyŏrhonshige ch'amsŏk'aessŭmnida. 그 결혼식에 참석했읍니다.

wedge *n.* sswaegi 쐐기.

Wednesday *n.* suyoil 수요일.

weed *n.* chapch'o 잡초. —*vi., vt.* (*root up*) chapch'orŭl ppopta 잡초를 뽑다. *root up ~s* chapch'orŭl ppobanaeda 잡초를 뽑아내다/ *grow like a ~* chapch'och'ŏrŏm ugŏjida 잡초처럼 우거지다.

week *n.* chu 주(週), chugan 주간(週間). *every ~* maeju 매주/ *last ~* chinanju 지난주/ *next ~* taŭmchu 다음주/ *this ~* ibŏn chu 이번 주/ *after a ~* ilchuil hu 1주일 후/ *for a ~* ilchuil tongan 1주일 동안/ *within a ~* ilchuil inaee 1주일 이내에/ *What is the day of the ~?* Onŭri musŭn yoirijiyo? 오늘이 무슨 요일이지요/ *I haven't seen you for ~s.* Myŏt chuil tongan manna poepchi mot'aessŭmnida. 몇 주일 동안 만나 뵙지 못했읍니다/ *~day* p'yŏngil 평일/ *~end* chumal 주말.

—*Days of week*—

Sunday	iryoil	일요일
Monday	wŏryoil	월요일
Tuesday	hwayoil	화요일
Wednesday	suyoil	수요일
Thursday	mogyoil	목요일
Friday	kŭmyoil	금요일
Saturday	t'oyoil	토요일

weekly *adv., adj.* (*every week*) maeju(ŭi) 매주(의). —*n.* (*periodicals*) chuganji 주간지.

weep *vi., vt.* (*cry*) ulda 울다, (*shed*) nunmurŭl hŭllida 눈물을 흘리다, (*lament*) sŭlp'ŏhada 슬퍼하다.

weigh *vi., vt.* (*determine the heaviness*) mugerŭl talda 무게를 달다. *Please ~ this letter.* I p'yonji muge chom tara chushio. 이 편지 무게 좀 달아 주시오/ *Do I ~ all my luggage?* Chimŭl choeda taraya hamnikka? 짐을 죄다 달아야 합니까/ *How much do you ~?* Ch'ejungŭn ŏlmana nagamnikka? 체중은 얼마나 나갑니까?

weight *n.* muge 무게. *total ~* chŏnjungnyang 전중량/ *net ~* chŏngmi chungnyang 정미 중량/ *What is your~?* Ch'ejungŭn ŏlmana toeshimnikka? 체중은 얼마나 되십니까?

welcome *n.* hwanyŏng 환영. *—vt.* hwanyŏnghada 환영하다. *—adj.* pan-gai majihanŭn 반가이 맞이하는. *—int.* ŏsŏ oshipshio. 어서 오십시오. *a warm and hearty ~.* ttattŭt'an hwanyŏng 따뜻한 환영/ *You are sure to find a ~.* Pandŭshi hwanyŏngŭl padŭl kŏshimnida. 반드시 환영을 받을 것입니다/ *He was enthusiastically ~d.* Kŭinŭn yŏllyŏrhi hwanyŏngŭl padassŭmnida. 그이는 열렬히 환영을 받았읍니다/ *You are ~ to come to my home.* Uri chibe oshimyŏn hwanyŏnghagessŭmnida. 우리 집에 오시면 환영하겠읍니다/ *Much obliged. You are ~.* Chŏngmal kamsahamnida. Ch'ŏnmaneyo. 정말 감사합니다. 천만에요/ *W~ to Korea!* Han-guk pangmun hwanyŏng! 한국 방문 환영!

welfare *n.* (*well-being*) pokchi 복지(福祉), husaeng 후생, (*prosperity*) pŏnyŏng 번영, (*~work*) pokchi saŏp 복지 사업. *child ~* adong pokchi 아동 복지/ *~ facilities* husaeng shisŏl 후생 시설/ *~ enterprise* husaeng saŏp 후생 사업.

well *n.* umul 우물, saem 샘. *—adj., adv.* chot'a 좋다. *Are you ~?* Ŏttŏssŭmnikka? 어떻습니까/ *I'm perfectly ~, thank you.* Aju kŏn-ganghamnida. 아주 건강합니다/ *Can you sleep ~ at night?* Pame chal chumushimnikka? 밤에 잘 주무십니까/ *I'm not very ~.* Nanŭn momi ap'ŭmnida. 나는 몸이 아픕니다/ *Shake the bottle ~.* Pyŏngŭl chal hŭndŭshipshio. 병을 잘 흔드십시오/ *Examine the account ~ before you pay it.* Ch'irŭgi chŏne kyesanŭl chal kŏmt'ohashio. 치르기 전에 계산을 잘 검토하시오/ *Can you speak English* ~. Yŏngŏrŭl chal hashimnikka? 영어를 잘 하십니까/ *W~*, *I'm through now.* Cha, ije kkŭnnassŭmnida. 자, 이제 끝났읍니다/ *Give me that as* ~. Kŭgŏtto chushio. 그것도 주시오/ *Do it as ~ as you can.* Toel su innŭn taero chal hae chushio. 될 수 있는 대로 잘 해 주시오/ *It was ~ done of you to come.* Chal osyŏssŭmnida. 잘 오셨읍니다/ *I want my steak ~ done.* Koginŭn chal igŭn kŏshi chŏssŭmnida. 고기는 잘 익은 것이 좋습니다/ *They are ~-to-do farmers.* Kŭ saramdŭrŭn yubok'an nongbudŭrimnida. 그 사람들은 유복한 농부들입니다. 「annyŏng 안녕」

well-being *n.* (*welfare*) haengbok 행복, (*good health*)

well-known *adj.* yumyŏnghan 유명한. *a ~ painter* yumyŏnghan hwaga 유명한 화가.

west *n.* sŏtchok 서쪽. *from ~ to east* sŏtchogesŏ tongtchogŭro 서쪽에서 동쪽으로.

western *adj.* sŏtchogŭi 서쪽의, (*W~*) sŏyangŭi 서양의. *the W~ style* sŏyangshik 서양식.

wet *adj.* (*soaked*) chŏjŭn 젖은, (*damp*) ch'ukch'uk'an 축축한, (*rainy*) pi naerinŭn 비 내리는. —*vt.* chŏkshida 적시다. *~ clothes* chŏjŭn ot 젖은 옷/ *a ~ floor* ch'ukch'uk'an marutpadak 축축한 마룻바닥/ *I am ~ through.* Nanŭn hŭmppŏk chŏjŏssŭmnida. 나는 흠뻑 젖었읍니다/ *Did you get ~?* Pirŭl majassŭmnikka? 비를 맞았읍니까/ *a ~ day* pi onŭn nal 비 오는 날/ *Don't ~ your feet.* Parŭl chŏkshiji mashio. 발을 적시지 마시오.

whale *n.* korae 고래. *~ boat* p'ogyŏngsŏn 포경선.

wharf *n.* (*pier*) pudu 부두, (*dock*) sŏnch'ang 선창.

what *pron.* muŏt 무엇. —*adj.* musŭn 무슨, ŏttŏn 어떤. —*int.* ch'am 참. *W~ is this?* Igŏsŭn muŏshijiyo? 이것은 무엇이지요/ *W~ is the price?* Kapshi ŏlmajiyo? 값이 얼마지요/ *W~ did you say?* Muŏrago hasyŏtchiyo? 무어라고 하셨지요/ *W~ happened?* Musŭn iri irŏnatchiyo? 무슨 일이 일어났지요/*W~ time do you get up?* Myŏt shie irŏnashimnikka? 몇 시에 일어나십니까/ *W~ size is your collar?* K'allaŭi saijŭnŭn ŏlmaimnikka? 칼라의 사이즈는

얼마입니까/ *W~ a nice car*! Ch'am choŭn ch'arŭl kajigo kyeshinŭn-gunyo. 참 좋은 차를 가지고 계시는군요/ *W~ impudence*! Ŏtchŏmyŏn kŭri ppŏnppŏnsŭrŏpchiyo! 어쩌면 그리 뻔뻔스럽지요!

whatever *pron.* muŏshidŭnji 무엇이든지. —*adj.* ŏttŏhan 어떠한. *Do ~ you like*. Muŏshidŭnji choŭl taero hashio. 무엇이든지 좋을 대로 하시오/ *W~ happens, I will go*. Ŏttŏn iri irŏnado nanŭn kal kŏshimnida. 어떤 일이 일어나도 나는 갈 것입니다/ *Take ~ measures you consider best*. Taegi kajang chot'ago saenggak'anŭn choch'ŏrŭl ch'wihashio. 댁이 가장 좋다고 생각하는 조처를 취하시오.

wheat *n.* mil 밀. *~-flour noodles* milguksu 밀국수.

wheel *n.* pak'wi 바퀴. *rubber-tired ~s* komu pak'wi 고무 바퀴/ *a toothed ~* t'omnibak'wi 톱니바퀴.

when *adv.* (*at what time*) ŏnje 언제. —*conj.* (*at the time that*) …hal ttae …할 때. *W~ did you come to Seoul?* Sŏurenŭn ŏnje wassŭmnikka? 서울에는 언제 왔읍니까/ *W~ shall we start?* Ŏnje ttŏnalkkayo? 언제 떠날까요/ *W~ do you expect him back?* Kŭiga ŏnje toraorira saenggak'ashimnikka? 그이가 언제 돌아오리라 생각하십니까/ *I don't know ~ he will come*. Kŭiga ŏnje olchi morŭgessŭmnida. 그이가 언제 올지 모르겠읍니다/ *I'll come ~ I have had lunch*. Chŏmshimŭl kkŭnnaemyŏn kagessŭmnida. 점심을 끝내면 가겠읍니다.

whenever *adv., conj.* (*at whatever time*) ŏnjena 언제나, (*interrog.*) todaech'e ŏnje 도대체 언제. *Let me know ~ you come*. Oshil ttaenŭn ŏnjena allyŏ chushipshio. 오실 때는 언제나 알려 주십시오/ *I'll discuss it with you ~ you like*. Wŏnhal ttaemyŏn ŏnjena ŭinonhagessŭmnida. 원할 때면 언제나 의논하겠읍니다/ *W~ did I say so?* Todaech'e ŏnje naega kŭrŏk'e marhaessŭmnikka? 도대체 언제 내가 그렇게 말했읍니까/ *W~ will it be over?* Todaech'e ŏnje kkŭnnajiyo? 도대체 언제 끝나지요?

where *adv.* (*at what place*) ŏdisŏ 어디서, (*in what place*) ŏdie 어디에, (*to which place*) ŏdiro 어디로. *W~ in Seoul do you live?* Sŏul ŏdisŏ salgo kyeshimnikka? 서울 어디서 살고 계십니까/ *W~ are my shoes?* Nae shini ŏdi issŭmnikka? 내 신이 어디 있읍니까/ *W~ are you going?* Ŏdiro kashimnikka? 어디로 가십니까/ *Go ~ you like.* Kago ship'ŭn tero kashio. 가고 싶은 데로 가시오.

whereabouts *n.* innŭn kot 있는 곳, haengbang 행방.
—*adv.* ŏditchŭme 어디쯤에. *I don't know the ~ of her house.* Kŭ yŏjaŭi chibi ŏdinji nanŭn morŭgessŭmnida. 그 여자의 집이 어딘지 나는 모르겠읍니다/ *W~ did you find it?* Ŏditchŭmesŏ kŭgŏsŭl ch'aja naetchiyo? 어디쯤 에서 그것을 찾아 냈지요?

wherever *conj.* (*in whatever place*) ŏdidŭnji 어디든지.
—*adv.* (*interrog.*) taech'e ŏdie 대체 어디에. *You must find him, ~ he is.* Kŭiga ŏdi itkŏna kŭirŭl ch'ajaya hamnida. 그이가 어디 있거나 그이를 찾아야 합니다/ *Sit ~ you like.* Ŏdidŭnji choahashinŭn kose anjŭseyo. 어디든지 좋아하시는 곳에 앉으세요/ *W~ did you put it?* Todaech'e ŏdida tuŏtchiyo? 도대체 어디다 두었지요?

whether *conj.* (*if*) …inji ŏttŏnji …인지 어떤지, …igŏna anigŏna …이거나 아니거나. *Ask him ~ he can come.* Kŭiga ol su issŭlchi murŏboshio. 그이가 올 수 있을지 물 어보시오/ *I don't know ~ to accept or refuse.* Pada-tŭryŏya halchi mullich'yŏya halchi morŭgessŭmnida. 받아들여야 할지 물리쳐야 할지 모르겠읍니다/ *I wonder ~ it can be true.* Chŏngmarinji morŭgessŭmnida. 정말인 지 모르겠읍니다/ *W~ you like it or not, you must do it.* Chot'ŭn shilt'ŭn kŭgŏsŭl haeya hamnida. 좋든 싫든 그 것을 해야 합니다/ *~ or no* hayŏgan 하여간, ŏtchaettŭn 어쨌든/ *Well I'll come ~ or no.* Chossŭmnida, hayŏgan kagessŭmnida. 좋습니다, 하여간 가겠읍니다/ *You must go there, ~ or no.* Hayŏgan kŏgie kaya hamnida. 하여 간 거기에 가야 합니다.

which *pron.* ŏnŭ kŏt[tchok] 어느 것[쪽]. —*adj.* ŏnŭ tcho-gŭi 어느 쪽의, ŏnŭ ŏnŭ 어느 어느. —*rel. pron.* (…hanŭn) paŭi (…하는) 바의. *W~ do you like better tea or coffee?* Ch'awa k'op'i chung ŏnŭ tchogŭl choahashimnikka? 차와 코피 중 어느 쪽을 좋아하십니까/ *W~ of them are your sons?* Ŏnŭ tchogi taegŭi adŭnimdŭrimnikka? 어느 쪽의 댁의 아드님들입니까/ *W~ of you will go with me?* Nuga nahago kach'i karyŏmnikka? 누가 나하고 같이 가렵니까/ *W~ is the oldest?* Ŏnŭ puni kajang yŏnjangishimnikka? 어느 분이 가장 연장이십니까/ *W~ one will you take?* Ŏnŭ kŏsŭl kajishiryŏmnikka? 어느 것을 가지시렵니까/ *Tell me ~ you like best.* Ŏnŭ kŏsŭl kajang choahashinŭnji malssŭmhashipshio. 어느 것을 가장 좋아하시는지 말씀하십시오/ *W~ way did they go?* Ŏnŭ kirŭl kassŭmnikka? 어느 길을 갔읍니까/ *Take the book ~ is lying on the table.* Chŏ t'eibŭl wie innŭn ch'aegŭl kajiseyo. 저 테이블 위에 있는 책을 가지세요/ *Was the book ~ you were reading a novel?* Ikko ittŏn ch'aegŭn sosŏriŏssŭmnikka? 읽고 있던 책은 소설이었읍니까?

whichever *pron.* ŏnŭ tchogidŭnji 어느 쪽이든지. *Take ~ book you please.* Ŏnŭ ch'aegidŭn choahanŭn kŏsŭl kajyŏkashio. 어느 책이든 좋아하는 것을 가져가시오/ *W~ are you going to choose?* Todaech'e ŏnŭ tchogŭl korŭl semio? 도대체 어느 쪽을 고를 셈이오?

while *n.* (*space of time*) tongan 동안, (*short time*) chamshi 잠시. —*conj.* (*during the time that*) hanŭn tongan 하는 동안. *a ~ ago* chogŭm chŏne 조금 전에/ *after a ~* chogŭm ittaga 조금 있다가/ *for a ~* chamshi 잠시/ *I haven't seen him for a long ~.* Oraettongan kŭirŭl mannaji mot'aessŭmnida. 오랫동안 그이를 만나지 못했읍니다/ *I'll be back in a little ~.* Chogŭm twie toraogessŭmnida. 조금 뒤에 돌아오겠읍니다/ *Is it worth ~ reading this novel?* I sosŏrŭn ilgŭl manhan kach'iga issŭmnikka? 이 소설은 읽을 만한 가치가 있읍니까/ *It is not worth ~ reading it.* Ilgŭl kach'iga ŏpsŭmnida. 읽을 가치가 없읍니다/ *W~ (I was) in Seoul, I met your parents several times.* Sŏul innŭn tongan taegŭi pumonimŭl myŏt pŏn manna poeŏssŭmnida. 서울 있는 동안 댁의 부모님을 몇 번 만나 뵈었읍니다/ *Don't read ~ you eat.* Shiksa chunge ch'aegŭl ikchi mashio. 식사 중에 책을 읽지 마시오.

whip *n.* mae 매. —*vt.* (*lash*) maejirhada 매질하다, (*beat*) ttaerida 때리다. *~ a horse* marŭl ch'aetchikchirhada 말을 채찍질하다/ *~ a child* airŭl maejirhada 아이

를 매질하다.

whirl *n.* hoejŏn 회전. —*vt., vi.* (*spin rapidly*) pingbing tolda[tollida] 빙빙 돌다[돌리다].

whirlpool *n.* soyongdori 소용돌이.

whisker *n.*(*pl.*) kurenarut 구레나룻. *raise* ~*s* kurenarusŭl kirŭda 구레나룻을 기르다/ *shave off* ~*s* kurenarusŭl kkakta 구레나룻을 깎다/ *chin* ~*s* t'ŏksuyŏm 턱수염.

whisk(e)y *n.* wisŭk'i 위스키. ~ *and soda* wisŭk'i soda 위스키 소다/ *drink* ~ *straight* wisŭk'irŭl sŭt'ŭreit'ŭro mashida 위스키를 스트레이트로 마시다/ *A double* ~, *please.* Wisŭk'irŭl tŏbŭllo chushio. 위스키를 더블로 주시오.

whisper *n.* soksagim 속삭임. —*vi.* soksagida 속삭이다. *exchange* ~*s* sŏro soksagida 서로 속삭이다/ ~ *in a person's ear* kwie taego soksagida 귀에 대고 속삭이다.

whistle *n.* (*sound*) hwip'aram 휘파람, (*instrument*) horurugi 호루루기, hogak 호각, (*alarm*) kyŏngjŏk 경적. —*vi., vt.* (*with mouth*) hwip'aramŭl pulda 휘파람을 불다, (*with inst.*) hogagŭl pulda 호각을 불다. *blow a* ~ kyŏngjŏgŭl ullida 경적을 울리다/ *a factory* ~ kongjang sairen 공장 사이렌/ *a steam* ~ kijŏk 기적(汽笛)/ ~ *for a taxi* hwip'aramŭro t'aekshirŭl pullŏ seuda 휘파람으로 택시를 불러 세우다.

white *adj.* hŭin 흰, (*pale*) ch'angbaek'an 창백한. ~ *clothings* hŭinot 흰옷/ ~ *hair* hŭinmŏri 흰머리/paekpal 백발/ ~ *wine* paekp'odoju 백포도주/ *Her lips were* ~ *with fear.* Kŭ yŏjaŭi ipsurŭn musŏwŏ p'arak'e chillyŏ issŏssŭmnida. 그 여자의 입술은 무서워 파랗게 질려 있었읍니다/ *W*~ *House* paegakkwan 백악관/ *a* ~ *man* paegin 백인/ ~ *race* paeginjong 백인종/ *a* ~ *paper* [*book*] paeksŏ 백서/ *a* ~-*collar worker* ponggŭp saenghwalja 봉급 생활자/ ~ *wash* paeksaek toryo 백색 도료(塗料).

who *pron.* nugu 누구, nuga 누가. —*rel. pron.* ...hanŭn saram …하는 사람. *W*~ *are you?* Taegŭn nugushimnikka? 댁은 누구십니까/ *W*~ *is that man?* Chŏbunŭn nugushimnikka? 저분은 누구십니까/ *Tell me* ~ *he is.*

Nuguinji karŭch'yŏ chushio. 누구인지 가르쳐 주시오/ *W~ shall I see?* Nugurŭl mannalkkayo? 누구를 만날까요/ *Do you know ~ broke the window?* Nuga yurich'angŭl kkaennŭnji ashimnikka? 누가 유리창을 깼는지 아십니까/ *W~ is this? (telephone)* Nugushimnikka? 누구십니까/ *W~ is calling, please? (telephone)* Nugushimnikka? 누구십니까/ *This is the man ~ wanted to see you.* l sarami sŏnsaengnimŭl poepkoja haettŏn punimnida. 이 사람이 선생님을 뵙고자 했던 분입니다.

whoever *pron.* todaech'e nuga 도대체 누가. *W~ told you?* Todaech'e nuga kŭrŏpdikka? 도대체 누가 그럽디까/ *W~ would have thought of it?* Todaech'e nuga kŭrŏn saenggagŭl haetkessŭmnikka? 도대체 누가 그런 생각을 했겠읍니까?

whole *adj.* (*complete*) on 온, chŏn 전(全), ch'ong 총(總). —*n.* (*total*) chŏnbu 전부, chŏnch'e 전체. *the ~ nation* on paeksŏng 온 백성/ *the ~ world* chŏnsegye 전세계/ *the ~ amount* ch'onggye 총계/ *the ~ sum* ch'ongsu 총수, ch'ongaek 총액/ *I didn't see him the ~ evening.* Chŏnyŏk naenae kŭ saramŭl poji mot'aessŭmnida. 저녁 내내 그 사람을 보지 못했읍니다/ *You haven't eaten the ~ lot, have you? (to inferior)* Nŏ mŏkchi anatkuna? 너 먹지 않았구나/ *as a ~* chŏnch'ejŏgŭro 전체적으로/ *on the ~* taech'ero 대체로.

wholesale *n.* tomae 도매. —*adj.* tomaeŭi 도매의. *at[by]~* tomaero 도매로/ *a ~ dealer* tomae sangin 도매 상인/ *~ prices* tomaekap 도매값/ *Our business is ~ only.* Uri kagenŭn tomaeppunimnida. 우리 가게는 도매뿐입니다.

wholesaler *n.* tomae sangin 도매 상인, tomae ŏpcha 도매 업자.

wholesome *adj.* (*healthful*) kŏn-gange choŭn 건강에 좋은, (*salutary*) kŏnjŏnhan 건전한. *~ food* kŏn-gang shikp'um 건강 식품/ *~ advice* kŏnjŏnhan ch'unggo 건전한 충고/ *a ~ girl* ch'akshirhan sonyŏ 착실한 소녀.

whom *pron.* (*objective of who*) nugu 누구. *for ~* nugurŭl wihae 누구를 위해/ *from ~* nuguegesŏ 누구에게서/ *to ~* nuguege 누구에게/ *W~ am I speaking to? (tele-*

phone) Nugushinjiyo? 누구신지요?

whooping-cough *n*. paegirhae 백일해.

whorehouse *n*. (*brothel*) maeŭmgul 매음굴, ch'angga 창가.

whose *pron*. (*poss. of who, which*) nuguŭi 누구의. *W~ house is that?* Chŏgŏsŭn nuguŭi chibimnikka? 저것은 누구의 집입니까/ *W~ book is it?* Kŭgŏsŭn nuguŭi ch'aegimnikka? 그것은 누구의 책입니까?

who's who myŏngsarok 명사록, shinsarok 신사록.

why *adv*. wae 왜, (*for what cause*) musŭn kkadalge 무슨 까닭에. *W~ do you think so?* Wae kŭrŏk'e saenggak'ashimnikka? 왜 그렇게 생각하십니까/ *Do you know ~ he was late?* Wae kŭbuni nŭjŏnnŭnji ashimnikka? 왜 그분이 늦었는지 아십니까/ *W~ don't you like him?* Wae kŭirŭl shirŏhanayo? 왜 그이를 싫어하나요/ *W~ not?* Wae an toejiyo? 왜 안 되지요/ *W~, that's Sukcha over there!* Ŏma, Sukchaga chŏgi inneyo! 어마, 숙자가 저기 있네요!

wick *n*. (*of oil lamp, etc.*) shimji 심지, tŭngshim 등심. *trim the ~* shimjirŭl charŭda 심지를 자르다/ *turn up the ~* shimjirŭl t'ŭrŏolida 심지를 틀어올리다.

wicked *adj*. (*bad*) nappŭn 나쁜, (*sinful*) saak'an 사악한, (*spiteful*) shimsulgujŭn 심술궂은. *a ~ person* agin 악인/ *a ~ smile* chitkujŭn miso 짓궂은 미소/ *She gave me a ~ look.* Kŭ yŏjaga narŭl noryoboassŭmnida. 그 여자가 나를 노려보았읍니다.

wicket *n*. (*small window*) tchongmun 쪽문, (*ticket gate*) kaech'algu 개찰구. *Where is the ~?* Kaech'algunŭn ŏdijiyo? 개찰구는 어디지요?

wide *adj*. (*broad*) p'ogi nŏlbŭn 폭이 넓은, (*extensive*) nŏlttaran 널따란. *a ~ ribbon* nŏlbŭn ribon 넓은 리본/ *a ~ river* p'ogi nŏlbŭn kang 폭이 넓은 강/ *How ~ is it?* P'ogi ŏlmana nŏlssŭmnikka? 폭이 얼마나 넓습니까/ *Open your mouth ~.* Ibŭl k'ŭge pŏllishio. 입을 크게 벌리시오/ *the ~ world* i nŏlbŭn sesang 이 넓은 세상.

widen *vt.,vi*. (*broaden*) nŏlp'ida 넓히다, nŏlbŏjida 넓어지다. *~ knowledge* kyŏnmunŭl nŏlp'ida 견문을 넓히다.

widow *n*. mimangin 미망인, kwabu 과부. *a rich ~* ton

innŭn kwabu 돈 있는 과부/ *a war* ~ chŏnjaeng mimangin 전쟁 미망인. 「홀아비 살림.

widower *n.* horabi 홀아비. *the life of a* ~ horabi sallim

wield *vt.* (*brandish*) hwidurŭda 휘두르다, (*control*) chibaehada 지배하다, (*power*) ssŭda 쓰다. ~ *an axe* tokkijirhada 도끼질하다/ ~ *a sword* k'arŭl hwidurŭda 칼을 휘두르다/ ~ *power* kwŏnserŭl purida 권세를 부리다.

wife *n.* anae 아내, ch'ŏ 처. *my* ~ anae 아내, chipsaram 집사람/ *your or his* ~ puin 부인/ *a chaste* ~ chŏngsuk'an anae 정숙한 아내/ *an immoral* ~ pullyunhan anae 불륜한 아내/ *Bring your* ~ *with you when you come next.* Taŭm oshil ttaenŭn puinŭl tongbanhashipshio. 다음 오실 때는 부인을 동반하십시오.

wig *n.* kabal 가발. *wear* [*put on*] ~ kabarŭl ssŭda 가발을 쓰다.

wild *adj.* (*feral*) yasaengŭi 야생의, (*violent*) sanaun 사나운, (*uncultivated*) migaehan 미개한, (*untamed*) kildŭlji anŭn 길들지 않은. *a* ~ *cat* yasaeng koyangi 야생 고양이, tŭlkoyangi 들고양이/ *a* ~ *flower* tŭlkkot 들꽃/ *a* ~ *boy* sanaun sonyŏn 사나운 소년/ ~ *delight* kwanghŭi 광희/ *a* ~ *talk* hoengsŏl susŏl 횡설 수설.

will *n.* (*volition*) ŭiji 의지, ŭisa 의사, (*determination*) kyŏrŭi 결의, (*testament*) yuŏn 유언. —*aux.v.* ...il kŏshida ...일 것이다, ...hal chakchŏngida ...할 작정이다. *free* ~ chayu ŭisa 자유 의사/ *the* ~ *to live* sallyŏnŭn ŭiji 살려는 의지/ *a man of strong* ~ ŭijiga kudŭn saram 의지가 굳은 사람/ *against one's* ~ pŏnŭi anina 본의 아니나/ *leave a* ~ yuŏnhada 유언하다/ *make one's* ~ yuŏnchangŭl chaksŏnghada 유언장을 작성하다/ *Look out or you* ~*be run over.* Choshimhashio, animyŏn ch'a-e ch'iil kŏshimnida. 조심하시오, 아니면 차에 치일 것입니다/ *When* ~ *he be back?* Ŏnje kŭiga toraoshimnikka? 언제 그이가 돌아오십니까?/ *I think I* ~ *see you to the station.* Yŏkkaji paeunghalkka hamnida. 역까지 배웅할까 합니다/ *W* ~ *you have another cup of tea?* Ch'a han chan tŏ hashiryŏmnikka? 차 한 잔 더 하시렵니까/ *W* ~ *you kindly tell me the way to the tourist bureau?* Yŏhaengsaro kanŭn

kirŭl karik'yŏ chushipshio. 여행사로 가는 길을 가리켜 주
십시오.

willing *adj.* (*ready*) kikkŏi …hada 기꺼이 …하다. *How
much are you ～ to pay for it?* Ŏlmamyŏn sashiryŏmnikka? 얼마면 사시렵니까/ *I'm quite ～ to do it.* Kikkŏi
kŭgŏsŭl hagessŭmnida. 기꺼이 그것을 하겠읍니다.

willingly *adv.* kikkŏi 기꺼이, chŭlgŏi 즐거이. *I shall ～
go with you.* Kikkŏi hamkke kagessŭmnida. 기꺼이 함께
가겠읍니다.

willow *n.* pŏdŭl 버들, pŏdŭnamu 버드나무. *a pussy ～*
pŏdŭlgaeji 버들개지.

win *vt., vi.* (*get victory*) igida 이기다, (*gain*) ŏtta 얻다,
(*attain*) talsŏnghada 달성하다, (*persuade*) sŏlbok'ada
설복하다. —*n.* (*victory*) sŭngni 승리, (*success*) sŏnggong
성공. *～ a war* chŏnjaenge igida 전쟁에 이기다/ *～ an
election* sŏn-gŏesŏ igida 선거에서 이기다/ *We've won!*
Uriga igyŏssŭmnida. 우리가 이겼읍니다/ *～ a prize in a
contest* k'ont'esŭt'ŭesŏ sangŭl t'ada[ŏtta] 콘테스트에서
상을 타다[얻다]/ *celebrate a ～* sŭngnirŭl ch'uk'ahada
승리를 축하하다/ *Our team has had five ～s this summer.* Uri t'imŭn kŭmnyŏn yŏrŭm tasŏt pŏn igyŏssŭmnida. 우리 팀은 금년 여름 다섯 번 이겼읍니다.

winch *n.* (*windlass*) winch'i 윈치, (*crank*) k'ŭraengk'ŭ
크랭크.

wind *n.* param 바람, (*fart*) panggwi 방귀. —*vt.* (*coil*)
kamta 감다, (*roll up*) malda 말다. *a free ～* sunp'ung
순풍/ *contrary ～s* yŏkp'ung 역풍/ *a high ～* kangp'ung
강풍/ *north ～* pukp'ung 북풍/*break ～* panggwirŭl kkwida 방귀를 뀌다/ *There isn't much ～ today.* Onŭrŭn
parami mani pulji anssŭmnida. 오늘은 바람이 많이 불
지 않습니다/ *The ～ blew my hat off.* Mojaga parame
naragassŭmnida. 모자가 바람에 날아갔읍니다/ *～ thread
on a reel* shilp'aee shirŭl kamta 실패에 실을 감다/ *～ a
clock* shigye t'aeyŏbŭl kamta 시계 태엽을 감다.

winding *adj.* kkobulkkoburhan 꼬불꼬불한. *a ～ path* kkobulkkoburhan kil 꼬불꼬불한 길/ *a ～ staircase* nasŏnhyŏng kyedan 나선형 계단.

window *n.* ch'ang 창, ch'angmun 창문, (*show* ~) chin-yŏlch'ang 진열창. *close a* ~ ch'angmunŭl tatta 창문을 닫다/ *open a* ~ ch'angmunŭl yŏlda 창문을 열다/ *Is this number a* ~ *seat?* I pŏnhonŭn ch'angtchok chwasŏgim-nikka? 이 번호는 창쪽 좌석입니까/ *How much is that brown coat in the* ~? Chinyŏlch'ange innŭn chŏ ko-dongsaek k'ot'ŭnŭn ŏlmaimnikka? 진열창에 있는 저 고동색 코트는 얼마입니까?

windy *adj.* param punŭn 바람 부는. *a* ~ *weather* param punŭn nalssi 바람 부는 날씨/ *It is* ~ *today.* Onŭrŭn parami semnida. 오늘은 바람이 셉니다.

wine *n.* (*from grapes*) p'odoju 포도주, (*from rice*) sul 술. *red* [*white*] ~ chŏk [paek] p'odoju 적 [백] 포도주/ *I'd like some red* ~, *please.* Chŏkp'odojurŭl chuseyo. 적포도주를 주세요/ *Do you prefer tea or* ~? Ch'awa surŭn ŏnŭ tchogi chossŭmnikka? 차와 술은 어느 쪽이 좋습니까?

wing *n.* (*of birds, airplane*) nalgae 날개, (*of stage*) mudae yŏp 무대 옆, (*of political party*) ik 익(翼). *the* ~*s of a bird* sae nalgae 새 날개/ *the* ~*s of an airplane* pihaenggi nalgae 비행기 날개/ *the right* ~ uik 우익/ *the left* ~ chwaik 좌익/ *the right* ~ *organization* uik tanch'e 우익 단체.

wink *n.* (*eyeing*) nunchit 눈짓, (*twinkle*) kkambakkŏrim 깜박거림, (*instant*) sunshikkan 순식간. —*vt.* (*blink*) kkambakkŏrida 깜박거리다, (*give a sign*) nunchit'ada 눈짓하다. *I have not slept one* ~. Hanjamdo chaji mo-t'aessŭmnida. 한잠도 자지 못했읍니다/ *He* ~*ed at me.* Kŭiga na-ege nunchisŭl haessŭmnida. 그이가 나에게 눈짓을 했읍니다.

winnow *vt.* (*blow off chaff*) k'ijirhada 키질하다, kka-burŭda 까부르다, (*sort out*) churyŏnaeda 추려내다. ~ *wheat* mirŭl kkaburŭda 밀을 까부르다.

winter *n.* kyŏul 겨울. *a* ~ *day* kyŏullal 겨울날/ ~ *weath-er* kyŏul nalssi 겨울 날씨/ *the* ~ *vacation* kyŏul pang-hak 겨울 방학/ *the* ~ *season* kyŏulch'ŏl 겨울철/ *We have had a mild* ~. Kŭmnyŏn kyŏurŭn chinaegiga suwŏrhaessŭmnida. 금년 겨울은 지내기가 수월했읍니다/ *last* ~ chinan kyŏul 지난 겨울.

wipe *vt., vi.* takta 닦다, humch'ida 훔치다. ~ *a dish* chŏpshirŭl takta 접시를 닦다/ ~ *up spilt milk* ŏpchillŏjin uyurŭl humch'yŏ naeda 엎질러진 우유를 훔쳐 내다/ *W*~ *your eyes.* Nunmurŭl takkŭshio. 눈물을 닦으시오/ *Take this handkerchief and* ~ *your nose.(to junior)* I sonsugŏnŭro k'orŭl takkara. 이 손수건으로 코를 닦아라.

wire *n.* (*slender rod of metal*) ch'ŏlsa 철사, (*telegram*) chŏnbo 전보. —*vt.* (*telegraph*) chŏnborŭl ch'ida 전보를 치다. *fine* ~ kanŭn ch'ŏlsa 가는 철사/ *barbed* ~ kashi ch'ŏlsa 가시 철사/ *send a* ~ chŏnborŭl ch'ida 전보를 치다/ *Let me know by* ~. Chŏnboro allyŏ chushio. 전보로 알려 주시오/ *Please* ~ *me as soon as you hear.* Tŭnnŭn taero kot chŏnboch'yŏ chushio. 듣는 대로 곧 전보쳐 주시오.

wireless *adj.* musŏnŭi 무선의, mujŏnŭi 무전(無電)의. —*n.* musŏn 무선, (*Brit.*) radio 라디오. *a* ~ *apparatus* musŏn chŏnshin-gi 무선 전신기/ *a* ~ *station* musŏn chŏnshin-guk 무선 전신국/ ~ *telephone* musŏn chŏnhwa 무선 전화.

wisdom *n.* (*sagacity*) ch'ongmyŏng 총명, (*intelligence*) chihye 지혜, (*discretion*) punbyŏl 분별, (*learning*) chishik 지식. *collective* ~ chungji 중지/ *worldly* ~ ch'ŏsesul 처세술/ *learned* ~ paeun chishik 배운 지식/ *I question the* ~ *of his methods.* Kŭiŭi supŏbi narosŏnŭn ŭishimsŭrŏpsŭmnida. 그이의 수법이 나로서는 의심스럽습니다.

wise *adj.* (*sagacious*) hyŏnmyŏnghan 현명한, (*sensible*) punbyŏl innŭn 분별 있는, (*learned*) pakshik'an 박식한, (*shrewd*) pint'ŭmŏmnŭn 빈틈없는/ *a* ~ *man* hyŏnmyŏnghan saram 현명한 사람/ *I'm* ~ *to your game.* Tangshin supŏbenŭn sokchi anssŭmnida. 당신 수법에는 속지 않습니다.

wish *n.* (*desire*) sowŏn 소원, somang 소망, (*pl.*) hoŭi 호의(好意). —*vt., vi.* (*want*) parada 바라다, (~ *to do*) ...ŭl pilda ...을 빌다, imyŏn chok'ettago saenggak'ada ...이면 좋겠다고 생각하다/ *I have no* ~ *to be loved.* Sarangŭl patko ship'ŭn saenggagŭn ŏpsŭmnida. 사랑을 받고 싶은 생각은 없읍니다/ *Give your wife my best ~es.* Puinege anbu chŏnhashipshio. 부인에게 안부 전하십시오/ *I ~ to go.* Kago shipsŭmnida 가고 싶습니다/ *Do you ~ to see me?* Narŭl mannago shipsŭmnikka? 나를 만나고 싶습니까/ *What do you ~ to eat?* Muŏsŭl mŏkko shipsŭmnikka? 무엇을 먹고 싶습니까/ *I ~ to have a cold noodle dish.* Naengmyŏnŭl mŏkko shipsŭmnida. 냉면을 먹고 싶습니다/ *What do you ~ me to do?* Muŏsŭl haedŭrilkkayo? 무엇을 해드릴까요/ *I ~ my watch to be repaired.* Nae shigyerŭl koch'yŏ chushigi paramnida. 내 시계를 고쳐 주시기 바랍니다/ *I ~ I were rich.* Naega pujaramyŏn chok'ennŭnde. 내가 부자라면 좋겠는데/ *I ~ I had met her.* Kŭ yŏjarŭl mannattŏramyŏn choassŭl t'ende. 그 여자를 만났더라면 좋았을 텐데/ *I ~ you a happy New Year.* Saehae pok mani padŭshipshio. 새해 복 많이 받으십시오.

wistaria *n.* tŭngnamu 등나무. *a ~ trellis* tŭngnamu shirŏng 등나무 시렁.

wit *n.* (*smart utterance*) kiji 기지, (*intelligence*) chihye 지혜, (*sense*) punbyŏl 분별, (*abilities*) chaenŭng 재능, (*sanity*) chejŏngshin 제정신. *a man of ~* chaech'i innŭn saram 재치 있는 사람/ *Your conversation is full of ~.* Taegŭi taehwa-enŭn kijiga kadŭk ch'a issŭmnida. 댁의 대화에는 기지가 가득 차 있읍니다.

witch *n.* (*sorceress*) mudang 무당, (*hag*) manyŏ 마녀.

with *prep.* (*together with*) ...wa[kwa] hamkke …와[과] 함께, (*by means of*) ...ŭro …으로. *I parted ~ her at the gate.* Munkanesŏ kŭ yŏjawa heŏjyŏssŭmnida. 문간에서 그 여자와 헤어졌읍니다/ *I agree ~ you.* Tangshin-gwa tonggamimnida. 당신과 동감입니다/ *Is there anyone ~ you?* Kŏgi nuga kach'i issŭmnikka? 거기 누가 같이 있읍니까/ *I have no money ~ me.* Kajin toni ŏpsŭmnida. 가진 돈이 없읍니다/ *I took my childern ~ me.* Aidŭrŭl terigo kassŭmnida. 아이들을 데리고 갔읍니다/ *I'll be ~ you in a minute.* Kot kamnida. 곧 갑니다/ *Fill the box ~ sand.* Kŭ sangja-e moraerŭl ch'aeushio. 그 상자에 모래를 채우시오/ *What did you cut it ~?* Muŏsŭro kŭgŏsŭl challassŭmnikka? 무엇으로 그것을 잘랐읍니까/ *What do you want ～ me?* Yongkŏni muŏshimnikka? 용건이 무엇입니까/ *What is the matter ～ you?* Ŏtchi toen irimnikka? 어찌 된 일입니까/ *Away ～ him!* Kŭ saramŭn tchoch'a pŏrishio. 그 사람은 쫓아 버리시오/ *Off ～ your hat!* Mojarŭl pŏsŭshio! 모자를 벗으시오!

withdraw *vi., vt.* (*draw back*) mullŏnada 물러나다, chŏlsuhada 철수하다, (*take back*) hoesuhada 회수하다. *After dinner the ladies withdrew.* Shiksa hu puindŭrŭn mullŏgassŭmnida. 식사 후 부인들은 물러갔읍니다/ *Our troops had to ～.* Agunŭn chŏlsuhaji anŭl su ŏpsŏssŭmnida. 아군은 철수하지 않을 수 없었읍니다/ *I want to ～ 50,000 won.* Omanwŏnŭl ch'atko shipsŭmnida. 5만원을 찾고 싶습니다. 「회.

withdrawal *n.* (*mil.*) ch'ŏlsu 철수, (*repeal*) ch'ŏrhoe 철

wither *vi., vt.* (*dry up*) shidŭlda 시들다, (*grow weaker*) shikta 식다, yak'aejida 약해지다. *The flowers have ～ed away.* Kkoch'i ta shidŭrŏ pŏryŏssŭmnida. 꽃이 다 시들어 버렸읍니다/ *Her affections ～ed.* Kŭ yŏjaŭi aejŏngŭn shigŏssŭmnida. 그 여자의 애정은 식었읍니다.

withhold *vt.* (*keep back*) poryuhada 보류하다, (*check*) ŏkchehada 억제하다, (*hold back*) mallida 말리다. *I shall ～ my consent.* Sŭngnagŭl poryuhal kŏshimnida. 승낙을 보류할 것입니다/ *What withheld him from making the attempt?* Wae kŭinŭn kŭ kidorŭl kŭmanduŏssŭmnikka? 왜 그이는 그 기도(企圖)를 그만두었읍니까?

within *prep.* (*inside of*) ...ŭi soge ...의 속에, (*not beyond*) inaee 이내에. —*adv.* (*inside*) soge 속에, ane 안에. —*n.* (*the inside*) an 안, naebu 내부. *～ the fence* ult'ari ane 울타리 안에/ *～ a few miles of Seoul* Sŏuresŏ su mail inaee 서울에서 수 마일 이내에/ *live ～ one's income* suibŭi t'eduri anesŏ salda 수입의 테두리 안에서 살다/ *You can reach Seoul ～ two hours.* Tu shigan inaee Sŏure taŭl su issŭmnida. 2시간 이내에 서울에 닿을 수 있읍니다/ *Is he ～?* Kŭinŭn ane kyeshimnikka? 그이는 안에 계십니까/ *～ and without* anp'akkesŏ 안팎에서/ *The door opens from ～.* Kŭ doŏnŭn anŭrobut'ŏ yŏllimnida. 그 도어는

안으로부터 열립니다.

without *prep.* (*outside of*) ...ŭi pakke(sŏ) ...의 밖에(서),
(*with no*) ...ŏpshi ...없이. —*adv.* (*to the outside*)
pakkŭro 밖으로, (*out of doors*) pakkat'e 바깥에. —*n.*
(*outside*) pak 밖, oebu 외부. ~ *the house* chip pakkesŏ
집 밖에서/ ~ *the city* shioeesŏ 시외(市外)에서/ *I can do it*
~ *your help.* Taegŭi toumi ŏpshido hal su issŭmnida.
댁의 도움이 없이도 할 수 있습니다/ *Please don't leave* ~
me. Narŭl tugo ttŏnaji mashio. 나를 두고 떠나지 마시오/
We were waiting ~. Urinŭn pakkesŏ kidarigo issŏssŭmnida. 우리는 밖에서 기다리고 있었습니다/ *The door opens
from* ~. Kŭ munŭn pakkatchogesŏ yŏllimnida. 그 문
은 바깥쪽에서 열립니다/ *Help came from* ~. Oebuesŏ
wŏnjoga tŭrŏwassŭmnida. 외부에서 원조가 들어왔습니다.

withstand *vt., vi.* (*stand against*) chŏhanghada 저항하다,
(*endure*) kyŏndida 견디다, pŏt'ida 버티다. ~ *the enemy*
chŏge chŏhanghada 적에 저항하다/ ~ *a siege* p'owi
konggyŏgŭl kyŏndiŏ naeda 포위 공격을 견디어 내다.

witness *n.* (*person*) chŭngin 증인, (*thing*) chŭnggŏmul
증거물. —*vt., vi.* (*see*) mokkyŏk'ada 목격하다, (*testify*)
ipchŭnghada 입증하다. *I have my* ~. Na-egenŭn chŭngini
issŭmnida. 나에게는 증인이 있습니다/ *Would you be my*
~ *if it becomes necessary?* P'iryohadamyŏn naŭi
chŭngini twae chushigessŭmnikka? 필요하다면 나의 증인이
돼 주시겠습니까/ *a defense* ~ p'igoŭi chŭngin 피고의 증인/
I ~*ed a horrible scene.* Kkŭmtchiksŭrŏn kwanggyŏngŭl
mokkyŏk'aessŭmnida. 끔찍스런 광경을 목격했습니다.

wizard *n.* (*conjurer*) yosuljangi 요술장이.

wolf *n.* iri 이리, nŭktae 늑대.

woman *n.* yŏja 여자, yŏin 여인, (*honorific*) puin 부인.
a ~ *doctor* yŏja ŭisa 여자 의사, yŏŭisa 여의사/ *a* ~
driver yŏja unjŏnsa 여자 운전사/ *a country* ~ shigol yŏja
시골 여자/ *a leisured* ~ yuhan yŏja 유한 여자/ *an old* ~
nop'a 노파/ *professional* [*business*] ~ chigŏp yŏsŏng
직업 여성/ *a single* ~ tokshinnyŏ 독신녀/ *an unmarried*
~ mihonnyŏ 미혼녀/ *a* ~'s *college* yŏja taehak 여자
대학/ *Let's have wine without* ~. Yŏja ŏpshi hanjan

hapshida. 여자 없이 한잔 합시다.

womb *n.* chagung 자궁.

wonder *n.* (*marvel*) nollaum 놀라움, (*strange thing*) isanghan kŏt 이상한 것. —*vi., vt.* (*feel wonder*) isanghage yŏgida 이상하게 여기다, (*feel surprise*) nollada 놀라다, (*doubt*) ŭishimhada 의심하다. *a world* ～ segyeŭi pulgasaŭi 세계의 불가사의(不可思議)/ *a college* ～ ch'ŏnjae taehaksaeng 천재 대학생/ *No* ～ *you didn't go.* Tangshini kaji anattŏn kŏtto tangyŏnhamnida. 당신이 가지 않았던 것도 당연합니다/ *I* ～ *who he is.* Kŭinŭn nuguilkkayo? 그이는 누구일까요/ *I* ～ *he will come.* Kŭbunŭn oshillŭnjiyo. 그분은 오실는지요/ *I was* ～*ing about that.* Kŏgie taehae hogishimŭl nŭkkigo watchiyo. 거기에 대해 호기심을 느끼고 왔지요/ *I* ～*ed to see you there.* Kŏgisŏ tangshinŭl mannadani nollassŭmnida. 거기서 당신을 만나다니 놀랐읍니다/ *Excuse me, but I* ～ *if Chongno is around here.* Yŏboseyo, Chongnoga i kŭnch'ŏimnikka? 여보세요, 종로가 이 근처입니까/ *I* ～ *if I could see you Thursday afternoon.* Mogyoire poel su issŭlkkayo? 목요일에 뵐 수 있을까요?

wonderful *adj.* (*amazing*) nollaun 놀라운, (*extraordinary*) isanghan 이상한, (*marvelous*) hullyunghan 훌륭한. *We had a* ～ *time today, didn't we?* Onŭrŭn ch'am chŭlgŏwŏssŭmnida. 오늘은 참 즐거웠읍니다/ *Thank you very much for the* ～ *evening.* Chŭlgŏun chŏnyŏgŭl ponaege hae chusyŏsŏ ch'am komapsŭmnida. 즐거운 저녁을 보내게 해 주셔서 참 고맙습니다/ *a* ～ *dinner* hullyunghan shiksa 훌륭한 식사/ *Wonderful!* Igŏ ch'am kŭnsahagunyo! 이거 참 근사하군요!

woo *vt.* (*court*) kuhonhada 구혼하다, (*solicit*) chorŭda 조르다.

wood *n.* (*forest*) sup 숲, (*timber*) mokchae 목재, namu 나무. *cut* ～ namurŭl peda 나무를 베다/ *fire* ～ changjak 장작/ *gather* ～ ttaellamurŭl chupta 땔나무를 줍다/ *dead* ～ komok 고목(枯木)/ *virgin* ～*s* wŏnshirim 원시림/ *The desk is made of* ～. Ch'aeksangŭn namuro mandŭmnida. 책상은 나무로 만듭니다/ *Put some more* ～ *on the* *fire*. Pure namurŭl tŏ chip'ishio. 불에 나무를 더 지피시오/ ~*cutter* namukkun 나무꾼/ ~*pecker* ttaktaguri 딱다 구리/ ~*worker* mokkong 목공.

wooden *adj.* namuro mandŭn 나무로 만든, mokchoŭi 목조 의. *a* ~ *house* mokcho kaok 목조 가옥/ ~ *walls* p'anja pyŏk 판자 벽.

wool *n.* (*of the sheep*) yangmo 양모, (*yarn*) t'ŏlshil 털 실, (*woolen cloth*) nasa 나사. *all* ~ sunmo 순모/ *synthetic* ~ hapsŏngmo 합성모/ *Is this* ~ *or cotton?* Igŏsŭn mojigimnikka, myŏnjigimnikka? 이것은 모직입니 까, 면직입니까? 「*sa* 나사/ ~ *yarn* t'ŏlshil 털실.

woolen *adj.* yangmoro mandŭn 양모로 만든. ~ *cloth* na-

word *n.* (*speech*) mal 말, (*talk*) tamhwa 담화, (*order*) myŏngnyŏng 명령, (*promise*) yaksok 약속, (*news*) soshik 소식. *borrowed* ~*s* ch'ayongŏ 차용어/ *a loan* ~ oeraeŏ 외래어/ *a slang* ~ sogŏ 속어/ *How many* ~*s can you type a minute?* Ilbune myŏt charŭl t'ajahal su issŭmnikka? 1분에 몇 자를 타자할 수 있읍니까/ *How do you say this* ~ *in Korea?* I marŭl Han-gugŏro muŏrago hamnikka? 이 말을 한국어로 무어라고 합니까/ *Translate these* ~*s into English, please.* I marŭl Yŏngŏro pŏnyŏk'ae chushipshio. 이 말을 영어로 번역해 주 십시오/ *I do not doubt your* ~. Sŏnsaengŭi malssŭmŭl ŭishimch'i anssŭmnida. 선생의 말씀을 의심치 않습니다/ *I can't find* ~*s to thank you.* Kamsadŭril mari ŏpsŭm-nida. 감사드릴 말이 없읍니다/ *I give you my* ~. Yaksok tŭrimnida. 약속드립니다/ *Drop me a* ~. Han madi soshik chŏnhashio. 한 마디 소식 전하시오/ *I received* ~ *of his coming.* Kŭiga oshindanŭn kibyŏrŭl padassŭmnida. 그이 가 오신다는 기별을 받았읍니다/ *upon my* ~ maengsek'o 맹세코.

work *n.* (*toil*) il 일, (*labor*) nodong 노동, (*occupation*) chigŏp 직업, (*employment*) ilchari 일자리, (*undertak-ing*) saŏp 사업, (*production*) chep'um 제품, (*pl.*) (*factory*) kongjang 공장, chejakso 제작소, (*literary* ~) chŏjak 저작, chakp'um 작품, (*book*) chŏsŏ 저서, (~*of art*) yesul chakp'um 예술 작품. —*vi., vt.* (*exert oneself*)

irhada 일하다, (be employed) kŭnmuhada 근무하다,
(operate) umjigida 움직이다. Are you fond of hard ∼?
Himdŭnŭn irŭl hagi choahashimnikka? 힘드는 일을 하기
좋아하십니까/ I have some ∼ for you to do. Tangshini
hal iri issŭmnida. 당신이 할 일이 있습니다/ pay ∼ sangnil
삯일/ home∼ sukche 숙제/ heavy ∼ chungnodong 중노
동/ manual ∼ kŭnyuk nodong 근육 노동/ physical ∼
yukch'e nodong 육체 노동/ What kind of ∼ were you
doing there? Kŏgisŏ musŭn irŭl hasyŏssŭmnikka? 거기
서 무슨 일을 하셨읍니까/ He is out of ∼. Kŭinŭn shilchi-
k'ago issŭmnida. 그이는 실직하고 있읍니다/ charity ∼
chasŏn saŏp 자선 사업/ educational ∼ kyoyuk saŏp 교육
사업/ an iron ∼s ch'ŏlgongso 철공소/ the glass ∼s
yuri kongjang 유리 공장/ What a beautiful piece of ∼!
Arŭmdaun chakp'umigunyo! 아름다운 작품이군요/ a
literary ∼ munye chakp'ŭm 문예 작품/ a ∼ of art yesul
chakp'um 예술 작품/ I would like to see some of your
∼s. Sŏnsaengŭi chakp'umŭl pogo shipsŭmnida. 선생의
작품을 보고 싶습니다/ You must ∼ hard. Yŏlshimhi irŭl
haeya hamnida. 열심히 일을 해야 합니다/ Don't ∼ so
hard. Kŭrŏk'e kodoege irhaji mashio. 그렇게 고되게 일하
지 마시오/ Do you ∼ here in Seoul? Sŏuresŏ kŭnmuha-
shimnikka? 서울에서 근무하십니까/ I'm ∼ing for an
automobile company. Chadongch'a hoesa-e kŭnmuham-
nida. 자동차 회사에 근무합니다/ ∼er nodongja 노동자,
chikkong 직공/ ∼ing class nodong kyegŭp 노동 계급/
∼ing hours kŭnmu shigan 근무 시간/ W∼ing hours
are from nine to five. Kŭnmu shiganŭn ahopshibut'ŏ
tasŏssikkajiimnida. 근무 시간은 9시부터 5시까지입니다.

workman n. (laborer) nodongja 노동자, (mechanic)
kongwŏn 공원(工員). a skilled ∼ kisulgong 기술공/ ∼-
ship (skill of ∼) somssi 솜씨, kiryang 기량, (work)
segong 세공(細工)/ This box is my ∼ship. I sangjanŭn
naega mandŭn kŏshimnida. 이 상자는 내가 만든 것입니다.

workshop n. kongjang 공장, chagŏpchang 작업장. a mechanical ∼ kigye kongjang 기계 공장.

world n. (earth) segye 세계, (society) sesang 세상,

(*people*) sesang saram 세상 사람, (*sphere*) ...kye ...계(界).
the New W~ shinsegye 신세계. *Are there any other
~s besides ours?* Uri oee tto tarŭn segyega issŭmnikka? 우리 외에 또 다른 세계가 있읍니까/ *We have had two
~ wars in this century.* Kŭmsegie segyedaejŏni tu
pŏn issŏssŭmnida. 금세기에 세계대전이 두 번 있었읍니다/
What will the ~ say? Sesang sarami muŏrago halkkayo? 세상 사람이 무어라고 할까요/ *the ~ of sport* ch'eyuk-
kye 체육계/ *scientific ~* kwahakkye 과학계/ *How goes
the ~ with you?* Hyŏngp'yŏnŭn ŏttŏssŭmnikka? 형편은
어떻습니까/ *Who in the ~ is that strange man?* Chŏ
nassŏn saramŭn todaech'e nugushimnikka? 저 낯선 사람
은 도대체 누구십니까/ *the other ~* chŏsŭng 저승/ *W~
War II* cheich'a segyedaejŏn 제 2 차 세계대전/ *the W~
Bank* segye ŭnhaeng 세계 은행. 「~ hoech'ung 회충.
worm *n.* pŏlle 벌레. *earthen ~* chirŏngi 지렁이/ *intestinal*
worm-eaten *adj.* pŏlle mŏgŭn 벌레 먹은.
worm-out *adj.* (*unfit for use*) tara haejin 닳아 해진,
(*exhausted*) nokch'oga toen 녹초가 된. *~ trousers* hŏn
paji 헌 바지/ *a ~ man* nŭlgŏppajin noin 늙어빠진 노인.
worry *vt., vi.* (*annoy*) koerop'ida 괴롭히다, (*vex*) aet'aeuda 애태우다, (*be anxious*) kŏkchŏnghada 걱정하다.
—*n.* (*anxiety*) kŏkchŏng 걱정, (*cares*) kŭnshim 근심.
Please don't ~ about me. Pudi nae kŏkchŏngŭn mashipshio. 부디 내 걱정은 마십시오/ *What's ~ing you?*
Musŭn kŏkchŏngishimnikka? 무슨 걱정이십니까/ *Don't ~
trying to find it.* Kŭgŏsŭl ch'ajŭryŏgo aet'aeuji mashipshio. 그것을 찾으려고 애태우지 마십시오/ *have many
worries* kŏkchŏngi mant'a 걱정이 많다/ *big worries*
k'ŭn kŏkchŏngkŏri 큰 걱정거리/ *household worries*
kajŏngŭi kŏkchŏng 가정의 걱정.
worse *adj.* tŏuk nappŭn 더욱 나쁜. *The patient gets ~
this morning.* Hwanjanŭn onŭl ach'im tŏuk nappŭmnida. 환자는 오늘 아침 더욱 나쁩니다/ *She seems to be ~.*
Puinŭn tŏuk ak'wadoen kŏt kassŭmnida. 부인은 더욱 악
화된 것 같습니다/ *Your work is bad but mine is much ~.*
Tangshini han ildo ŏngt'ŏrijiman naega han irŭn tŏ

ŏngt'ŏrimnida. 당신이 한 일도 엉터리지만 내가 한 일은 더 엉터립니다/ *That is ～ than this.* Kŭgŏsŭn igŏtpoda tŏ nappŭmnida. 그것은 이것보다 더 나쁩니다.

worsen *vi., vt.* (*become or make worse*) tŏuk ak'wahada 〔shik'ida〕 더욱 악화하다〔시키다〕.

worship *n.* (*ardent admiration*) sungbae 숭배, (*divine service*) yebae 예배. —*vt.* (*adore*) sungbaehada 숭배하다, (*attend church service*) yebaehada 예배하다. *ancestral*〔*ancestor*〕 ～ chosang sungbae 조상 숭배/ *a blind* ～ maengmokchŏk sungbae 맹목적 숭배/ *church* ～ kyohoe yebae 교회 예배/ ～ *money* tonŭl sungbaehada 돈을 숭배하다/ *Where does she* ～? Ŏnŭ kyohoee tanimnikka? 어느 교회에 다닙니까?

worth *n.* (*value*) kach'i 가치. —*adj.* (*deserving of*) …ŭi kach'iga innŭn …의 가치가 있는. *Give me a dollar's* ～ *of this tea.* I ch'arŭl il tallŏŏch'iman chushio. 이 차를 일 달러어치만 주시오/ *Please give me 1,000 won of stamps.* Up'yorŭl ch'ŏnwŏnŏch'iman chushipshio. 우표를 1,000원어치만 주십시오/ *How much is that* ～? Kagyŏgŭn ŏlmaimnikka? 가격은 얼마입니까/ *Some stamps are* ～ *thousands of dollars.* Such'ŏn tallŏssik hanŭn up'yodo issŭmnida. 수천 달러씩 하는 우표도 있읍니다/ *The book is* ～ *reading.* Kŭ ch'aegŭn ilgŭl manhamnida. 그 책은 읽을 만합니다/ *This picture is* ～ *fifty thousand won.* I kŭrimŭn oshimmanwŏnŭi kaboch'iga issŭmnida. 이 그림은 5만원의 값어치가 있읍니다/ *What's the old man* ～? Kŭ noinŭn kajin ke ŏlmana toemnikka? 그 노인은 가진 게 얼마나 됩니까/ *He is now* ～ *ten millions.* Kŭbunŭn chigŭm ch'ŏnman changjaimnida. 그분은 지금 천만 장자입니다/ *of great* ～ maeu kach'i innŭn 매우 가치 있는/ *of little*〔*no*〕 ～ kach'iga chŏgŭn〔ŏmnŭn〕 가치가 적은〔없는〕.

worthless *adj.* kach'i ŏmnŭn 가치 없는, hach'anŭn 하찮은.

worthwhile *adj.* kach'iga innŭn 가치가 있는, hal poram innŭn 할 보람 있는.

worthy *adj.* (*good enough*) kach'i innŭn 가치 있는, (*deserving*) almajŭn 알맞은, (*virtuous*) kwihashin 귀하신. —*n.* (*notable*) myŏngsa 명사(名士). *behavior* ～

of praise ch'ingch'anhal manhan haengdong. 칭찬할
만한 행동/ *a ~ gentleman* ŭijŏt'an shinsa 의젓한 신사/
The place is quite ~ of a visit. Kŭ kosŭn hanbŏn ka
bol manhan kach'iga innŭn koshimnida. 그 곳은 한번 가
볼 만한 가치가 있는 곳입니다/ *live a ~ life* hullyunghan
saenghwarŭl hada 훌륭한 생활을 하다/ *a ~ reward* almajŭn posu 알맞은 보수/ *Who is the ~ who has just
arrived?* Panggŭm toch'ak'an kŭ yangbanŭn nuguimnikka? 방금 도착한 그 양반은 누구입니까?

would *aux. v.* *(volition)* *I told you so, but you ~n't
believe it.* Kŭrŏk'e malssŭmdŭryŏtchiman mitchi anssŭmnida. 그렇게 말씀드렸지만 믿지 않았읍니다/ *The door
~ not open.* Muni tomuji yŏlliji anssŭmnida. 문이 도무
지 열리지 않습니다/ *(condition)* *If I were you, I ~ never
do it.* Naega tangshin kat'ŭmyŏn kyŏlk'o haji anŭl
kŏshimnida. 내가 당신 같으면 결코 하지 않을 것입니다/ *I
could do so, if I~.* Hal ttŭnman issŭmyŏn hal su
innŭnde. 할 뜻만 있으면 할 수 있는데/ *(wish)* *I ~ like to
go.* Kago shipsŭmnida. 가고 싶습니다/ *W~ you please
pass me the salt?* Sogŭm chom kŏnne chushilkkayo?
소금 좀 건네 주실까요/ *I wish he ~ come.* Kŭiga wa chuŏssŭmyŏn chok'ennŭnde. 그이가 와 주었으면 좋겠는데/
(habit) *We ~ sing for hours together.* Urinŭn myŏt
shiganŭl hamkke noraehagon haessŭmnida. 우리는 몇 시
간을 함께 노래하곤 했읍니다/ *I ~ sit for hours doing
nothing.* Amu hanŭn il ŏpshi myŏt shiganŭl uduk'ŏni
anja itkon haessŭmnida. 아무 하는 일 없이 몇 시간을 우두커
니 앉아 있곤 했읍니다/ *(conjecture)* *I suppose she ~ be
about 40 when she died.* Puini chugŭn kŏsŭn saship
chŏnhuyŏnnŭnga shipsŭmnida. 부인이 죽은 것은 40 전후였
는가 싶습니다/ *I don't know who it ~ be.* Todaech'e
nugunji morŭgessŭmnida. 도대체 누군지 모르겠읍니다/
(politeness) *W~ you help me, please.* Chom towa
chushigessŭmnikka? 좀 도와 주시겠읍니까?

wound *n.* *(hurt)* pusang 부상, *(cut, bruise)* sangch'ŏ
상처. —*vt., vi.* *(injure)* sangch'ŏrŭl ip'ida〔ipta〕 상처를
입히다〔입다〕. *a slight ~* kabyŏun sangch'ŏ 가벼운 상처/

a mortal ~ ch'imyŏngsang 치명상/ *a severe* ~ chung-sang 중상/ *heal a* ~ sangch'ŏrŭl koch'ida 상처를 고치다/ *I was* ~*ed in the arm.* P'arŭl tach'yŏssŭmnida. 팔을 다쳤읍니다/ *He was seriously* ~*ed in the head.* Kŭinŭn morie chungsangŭl ibŏssŭmnida. 그이는 머리에 중상을 입었읍니다.

wrap *vt., vi.* (*enfold*) ssada 싸다, turŭda 두르다, (*roll together*) kamta 감다, malda 말다, (*envelop*) tullŏssada 둘러싸다. *Shall I* ~ *it as a gift?* Sŏnmullo ssadŭrilkkayo? 선물로 싸드릴까요/ *Please* ~ *them as gift.* Sŏnmurŭl p'ojanghae chuseyo. 선물을 포장해 주세요/ *Shall I* ~ *them* (*all*) *together?* Modu hamkke p'ojanghalkkayo? 모두 함께 포장할까요/ *Please* ~ *up all my purchase together.* San mulgŏnŭl hande ssachuseyo. 산 물건을 한데 싸주세요.

wrapping *n.* (*covering*) p'ojang 포장. ~ *paper* p'ojangji 포장지.

wreath *n.* hwahwan 화환.

wreck *n.* (*ship*~) nanp'a(sŏn) 난파(선). —*vi.* (*suffer* ~) nanp'ahada 난파하다, (*suffer ruin*) manghada 망하다. *He was killed in the* ~. Kŭinŭn kŭ chonan sakŏnesŏ chugŏssŭmnida. 그이는 그 조난 사건에서 죽었읍니다.

wreckage *n.* nanp'asŏn 난파선, nanp'a hwamul 난파 화물.

wrench *n.* rench'i 렌치, nasa tolligae 나사 돌리개. —*vt.* (*wrest*) pit'ŭlda 비틀다, (*sprain*) ppida 삐다. ~ *the door open* munŭl pit'ŭrŏ yŏlda 문을 비틀어 열다/ ~ *the ankle* palmogŭl ppida 발목을 삐다.

wrest *vt.* (*twist*) pit'ŭlda 비틀다, ppaeatta 빼앗다. *I tried to* ~ *the gun from his hands.* Kŭjaŭi sonesŏ ch'ongŭl ppaesŭryŏgo haessŭmnida. 그자의 손에서 총을 뺏으려고 했읍니다.

wrestle *vi.* (*in Korean style*) ssirŭmhada 씨름하다, (*in Western style*) resŭllinghada 레슬링하다, (*grapple*) matput'ŏ ssauda 맞

⟨ssirŭm⟩

붙어 싸우다.

wrestler *n.* ssirŭmkkun 씨름꾼. *a champion* ~ changsa 장사(壯士).

wrestling *n.* ssirŭm 씨름, resŭlling 레슬링.

wring *vt.* (*twist*) pit'ŭlda 비틀다, (*squeeze*) tchada 짜다. ~ *out wet clothes* chŏjŭn osŭl tchada 젖은 옷을 짜다/ ~ *off the head of a bird* sae taegarirŭl pit'ŭrŏ tteda 새 대가리를 비틀어 떼다.

wrinkle *n.* (*crease*) churŭm 주름. —*vt., vi.* (*crease*) churŭmjige hada 주름지게 하다, (*pucker*) churŭmjida 주름지다. *Press out the* ~*s.* Churŭmŭl taryŏ chushio. 주름을 다려 주시오/ *iron out* ~*s* tarimiro churŭmŭl p'yŏda 다리미로 주름을 펴다/ *remove* ~*s* churŭmŭl ŏpsaeda 주름을 없애다.

wrist *n.* sonmok 손목. *a* ~ *watch* sonmok shigye 손목 시계/ *Which is the most popular* ~ *watches in Korea?* Han-gugesŏ kajang inki innŭn sonmok shigyenŭn ŏnŭ kŏshimnikka? 한국에서 가장 인기 있는 손목 시계는 어느 것입니까?

write *vt.* (*characters*) ssŭda 쓰다, (*letter*) p'yŏnjirŭl ssŭda 편지를 쓰다. *Please* ~ *your name and address.* Sŏnghamgwa chusorŭl ssŏ chushio. 성함과 주소를 써 주시오/ *Are we to* ~ *in ink or in pencil?* Ingk'ŭro ssŭmnikka, yŏnp'illo ssŭmnikka? 잉크로 씁니까, 연필로 씁니까/ *Please* ~ *in block capitals.* Taemuncha hwalchach'ero ssŏ chushio. 대문자 활자체로 써 주시오/ *I'll* ~ *to you soon.* Kot p'yŏnjihagessŭmnida. 곧 편지하겠읍니다/ *I'll* ~ *you when I return to Korea.* Han-guge toragasŏ p'yŏnji olligessŭmnida. 한국에 돌아가서 편지 올리겠읍니다/ *Here's my address. W*~ *to me when you have time.* Yogi chŏŭi chusoga issŭmnida. T'ŭm issŭl ttae p'yŏnji chushipshio. 여기 저의 주소가 있읍니다. 틈 있을 때 편지 주십시오.

writer *n.* (*author*) chŏja 저자, (*novelist*) chakka 작가, (*journalist*) kija 기자, (*penman*) munp'ilga 문필가, (*clerk*) sŏgi 서기. *a book* ~ chŏjakka 저작가/ *a fiction* ~ ch'angjakka 창작가/ *a woman* ~ yŏryu chakka 여류 작가.

writhe *vi., vt.* (*squirm*) momburimch'ida 몸부림치다, (*twist about*) twit'ŭlda 뒤틀다.

writing *n.* (*written matter*) ssŭn kŏt 쓴 것, (*handwriting*) p'ilchŏk 필적. *I have some ~ to do.* Nanŭn ssŏya hal kŏshi issŭmnida. 나는 써야 할 것이 있읍니다/ *political ~s* chŏngch'i nonmun 정치 논문/ *I can't make out your ~.* Taegŭi kŭlssirŭl ilgŏ nael suga ŏpsŭmnida. 댁의 글씨를 읽어 낼 수가 없읍니다/ *learn ~* sŭpcharŭl paeuda 습자 (習字)를 배우다/ *a ~ case* pyŏrutchip 벼룻집/ *a ~ book* sŭpchach'aek 습자책.

written *adj.* *a ~ application* shinch'ŏngsŏ 신청서/ *a ~ contract* kyeyaksŏ 계약서/ *a ~ guarantee* pojŭngsŏ 보증서/ *a ~ petition* chinjŏngsŏ 진정서/ *a ~ will* yuŏnchang 유언장.

wrong *adj.* (*evil*) nappŭn 나쁜, (*mistaken*) chalmottoen 잘못된, t'ŭllin 틀린. —*n.* (*injustice*) pujŏng 부정(不正), (*error*) chalmot 잘못. —*vt.* (*treat unfairly*) pudanghage taruda 부당하게 다루다, (*do wrong*) pujŏnghan chisŭl hada 부정한 짓을 하다. —*adv.* (*amiss*) chalmot'ayŏ 잘못하여, t'ŭllige 틀리게. *You are ~.* Tangshinŭn chalmot saenggak'ago kyeshimnida. 당신은 잘못 생각하고 계십니다/ *I'm afraid you've got the ~ number.* Pŏnhorŭl chalmot kŏn kŏt katkunyo. 번호를 잘못 건 것 같군요/ *You're on the ~ train.* Yŏlch'arŭl chalmot t'asyŏssŭmnida. 열차를 잘못 타셨읍니다/ *This is the ~ train.* Chalmot t'ashin kŏt kassŭmnida. 잘못 타신 것 같습니다/ *You have come at the ~ time.* Nappŭn ttaee osyŏssŭmnida. 나쁜 때에 오셨읍니다/ *do ~* nappŭn chisŭl hada 나쁜 짓을 하다/ *You are entirely in the ~.* Tangshini chŏnhyŏ chalmoshimnida. 당신이 전혀 잘못입니다/ *What's ~ with you?* Ŏttŏk'e toen kŏshimnikka? 어떻게 된 것입니까/ *guess ~* kŭrŭt ch'uch'ŭk'ada 그릇 추측하다.

wrongdoer *n.* pŏmjoeja 범죄자.

wrongdoing *n.* (*evildoing*) pihaeng 비행, (*offence*) pŏmjoe 범죄.

wry *adj.* (*distorted*) twit'ŭllin 뒤틀린, (*skew*) pitturŏjin 비뚤어진, (*ill-natured*) shimsulgujŭn 심술궂은. *make a*

~ *face* ŏlgurŭl tchip'urida 얼굴을 찌푸리다/ *a* ~ *smile* ssŭn usŭm 쓴 웃음.

━━ X ━━

Xmas *n.* K'ŭrisŭmasŭ 크리스마스, sŏngt'anjŏl 성탄절.
X-ray *adj.* eksŭsŏnŭi 엑스선(線)의. *—n.* (*pl.*) eksŭ
kwangsŏn 엑스 광선. ~ *examination* eksŭsŏn kŏmsa
엑스선 검사.
X-road *n.* shipcharo 십자로(十字路).
Xtra *n.* (*edition*) hooe 호외, (*extra*) eksŭt'ŭra 엑스트라.
xylophone *n.* shillop'on 실로폰, mokkŭm 목금(木琴). *play*
the ~ shillop'onŭl yŏnjuhada 실로폰을 연주하다.

━━ Y ━━

yacht *n.* yot'ŭ 요트, k'waesokchŏng 쾌속정. *a race of* ~
yot'ŭ kyŏngju 요트 경주/ *sail in a* ~ yot'ŭrŭl t'ago kada 요트를 타고 가다.
yard *n.* (*garden*) madang 마당, (*measure*) yadŭ 야드.
the school ~ undongjang 운동장. *five* ~*s of cloth* o ya-
dŭŭi ch'ŏn 5야드의 천/ *They are selling them by the*
~. Kŭ saramdŭrŭn yadŭ tanwiro p'algo issŭmnida.
그 사람들은 야드 단위로 팔고 있읍니다.
yardstick *n.* yadŭ cha 야드 자[尺].   「털실.
yarn *n.* (*spun thread*) pangsa 방사(紡糸). *woolen* ~ t'ŏlshil
yawn *n.* hap'um 하품. *—vi.* (*gape*) hap'umhada 하품하
다. *hide a* ~ *behind one's hand* sonŭro hap'umŭl
karida 손으로 하품을 가리다.
year *n.* hae 해, yŏn 연(年), (*pl.*)(*age*) yŏllyŏng 연령,
every ~ haemada 해마다, maenyŏn 매년/*next* ~ naenyŏn
내년/ *last* ~ chinanhae 지난해, changnyŏn 작년/ *a leap*
~ yunnyŏn 윤년/ *the new* ~ saehae 새해/ *New Y* ~'*s*
day sŏllal 설날/ *this* ~ orhae 올해, kŭmnyŏn 금년/ *the*
~ *before last* chaejangnyŏn 재작년/ *the* ~ *after next*

naehunyŏn 내후년. *the next ~ but one* hunaenyŏn 후내년/ *all the ~ round* illyŏn naenae 1년 내내/ *In what ~ were you born?* Taegŭn ŏnŭ haee nasyŏssŭmnikka? 댁은 어느 해에 나셨읍니까/ *You are older by two ~s.* Taegi tu sal tŏ wiimnida. 댁이 두 살 더 위입니다/ *I wish you a happy New Y~.* Saehae pok mani padŭshipshio. 새해 복 많이 받으십시오.

yearly *adj.* (*every year*) maenyŏnŭi 매년의. —*adv.* (*once a year*) haemada 해마다. —*n.* (*periodical*) yŏn-ganji 연간지. *a ~ income* yŏnsuip 연수입.

yeast *n.* nuruk 누룩, isŭt'ŭ 이스트.

yellow *adj.* noran 노란, hwangsaegŭi 황색의. —*n.* norāng 노랑, hwangsaek 황색. *~ race* hwangsaek injong 황색 인종/ *~ card* (*sports*) yello k'adŭ 옐로 카드/ *golden ~* hwanggŭmsaek 황금색.

yes *adv.* (*to superior*) ye 예, ne 네, (*to inferior*) kŭrae 그래. —*n.* (*answer that agrees*) yesŭranŭn mal 예스라는 말. *Waiter! Y~, sir.* Ibwa, poi! Ne. 이봐 보이! 네/ *Are you ready? Y~,* (*I am*). Chunbinŭn toeŏssŏ? Ne, (toeŏssŭmnida) 준비는 되었소. 네, (되었읍니다)/ *Isn't it raining? Y~, it is.* Piga an ojiyo? Anyo, omnida. 비가 안 오지요? 아뇨, 옵니다/ *Don't you like it? Y~,* (*I do like it*). Kŭgŏl choahaji anssŭmnikka? Anyo, choahamnida. 그걸 좋아하지 않습니까? 아뇨, 좋아합니다. (*When answering a question expressed in the negative form, the Koreans generally use* **no** *instead of* **yes**.)

yesterday *n. adv.* ŏje 어제. *~ evening* ŏjet chŏnyŏk 어젯저녁/ *~ morning* ŏje ach'im 어제 아침/ *the day before ~* kŭjŏkke 그저께/ *I have been here since ~.* Ŏjebut'ŏ yŏgie wa issŭmnida. 어제부터 여기에 와 있읍니다.

yet *adv.* (*still*) ajik 아직, (*already*) pŏlssŏ 벌써. —*conj.* (*however*) kŭrŏna 그러나. *I have received no news ~.* Ajik amu t'ongjido mot padassŭmnida. 아직 아무 통지도 못 받았읍니다/ *Has he come ~?* Kŭinŭn pŏlssŏ wassŭmnikka? 그이는 벌써 왔읍니까?

yield *vt., vi.* (*produce*) nat'a 낳다, sanch'urhada 산출하다, (*surrender*) kulbok'ada 굴복하다, (*give*) chuda 주

다. —*n.* (*output*) sanch'ul 산출, (*crop*) suhwak 수확, (*return*) posu 보수. *We will never* ~ *to force.* P'ongnyŏgenŭn kurhaji anŭl kŏshimnida. 폭력에는 굴하지 않을 것입니다/ *What is the* ~ *per acre?* Eik'ŏdang suhwangnyangŭn ŏlmajiyo? 에이커당 수확량은 얼마지요?

yoke *n.* (*wooden frame*) mŏnge 멍에, (*bond of union*) sokpak 속박.

yolk *n.* (*of egg*) norŭnjawi 노른자위. *the* ~ *of an egg* talgyarŭi norŭnjawi 달걀의 노른자위.

you *pron.* (*sing.*) tangshin 당신, taek 댁, (*pl.*) tangshindŭl 당신들, (*to inferior*) nŏ 너, chane 자네, (*pl.*) chanedŭl 자네들, nŏhŭidŭl 너희들. *Y*~ *are my friend(s).* Nŏ(hŭi)nŭn naŭi chin-guida. 너(희)는 나의 친구이다/ *Y*~ *and I* tangshin-gwa na 당신과 나/ *Y*~ *are a liar.* Nŏnŭn kŏjinmaljangida. 너는 거짓말장이다/ *Y*~ *there, what is your name?* Yŏboshio, sŏnghami muŏjiyo? 여보시오, 성함이 무어지요/ *What are* ~ *all doing?* Chanedŭrŭn muŏl hago itchi? (*to inferior*) 자네들은 무얼 하고 있지?

young *adj.* (*not old*) chŏlmŭn 젊은, (*little*) ŏrin 어린. *a* ~ *man* chŏlmŭn namja 젊은 남자/ *a* ~ *child* ŏrin ai 어린 아이/ *my* ~*er brother* tongsaeng 동생/ *your* ~*er sister* maessi 매씨/ *a* ~ *nation* shinsaeng kukka 신생 국가/ *a* ~ *lady* agassi 아가씨/ *She looks* ~ *for her age.* Kŭ yŏjanŭn naie pihae chŏmke poimnida. 그 여자는 나이에 비해 젊게 보입니다/ *I'm not as* ~ *as I was.* Ijen ch'ŏn-gwa kat'ŭn kiunŭn ŏpsŭmnida. 이젠 전과 같은 기운은 없읍니다/ *Y.M.C.A.* kidokkyo ch'ŏngnyŏnhoe 기독교 청년회/ *Y.W.C.A.* kidokkyo yŏja ch'ŏngnyŏnhoe 기독교 여자 청년회.

your *pron.* tangshinŭi 당신의, (*pl.*) tangshindŭrŭi 당신들의, (*to inferior*) nŏŭi 너의, (*pl.*) nŏhŭidŭrŭi 너희들의.

yours *pron.* (*sing.*) tangshinŭi kŏt 당신의 것, (*pl.*) tangshindŭrŭi kŏt 당신들의 것, (*to inferior*) nŏŭi kŏt 너의 것, (*pl.*) nŏhŭidŭrŭi kŏt 너희들의 것. *Is that book* ~? Kŭ ch'aegŭn tangshin kŏshimnikka? 그 책은 당신 것입니까?

yourself *pron.* tangshin chashin 당신 자신, (*to inferior*) nŏ chashin 너 자신. *Please do it* ~. Tangshin chashini hae chushio. 당신 자신이 해 주시오/ *You said so* ~. (*to inferior*) Ne ibŭro kŭrŏk'e marhaetta 네 입으로 그렇게 말했다.

youth *n.* (*young man*) ch'ŏngnyŏn 청년, (*young days*) ch'ŏngch'un·gi 청춘기, (*young people*) chŏlmŭnidŭl 젊은 이들/ *a brave* ~ yonggamhan ch'ŏngnyŏn 용감한 청년/ *promising* ~*s* chŏndo yumanghan chŏlmŭnidŭl 전도 유 망한 젊은이들/ *waste one's* ~ ch'ŏngch'unŭl hŏsonghada 청춘을 허송하다.

youthful *adj.* (*young*) chŏlmŭn 젊은. *a* ~ *bride* chŏlmŭn saesaekshi 젊은 새색시/ *a* ~ *ambition* chŏlmŭnidaun ya- mang 젊은이다운 야망.

⟫ **Z** ⟪

---

zeal *n.* (*eagerness*) yŏlshim 열심, yŏrŭi 열의. ~ *for science* kwahage taehan yŏrŭi 과학에 대한 열의/ *You lack* ~. Tangshinŭn yŏrŭiga pujok'amnida. 당신은 열의 가 부족합니다.

zealot *n.* (*enthusiast*) yŏlsŏngga 열성가, (*fanatic*) kwangshinja 광신자.

zealous *adj.* yŏlchunghanŭn 열중하는. ~ *in one's task* chagi ire yŏlchunghanŭn 자기 일에 열중하는.

zebra *n.* ŏllungmal 얼룩말.

zero *n.* yŏng 영(零), chero 제로. *The temperature is down to* ~. Ondonŭn yŏngdoro naeryŏgatta. 온도는 영 도로 내려갔다/ *below* ~ yŏngha 영하/ *above* ~ yŏngsang 영상.

zigzag *adv.* kkobulkkoburhage 꼬불꼬불하게. —*adj.* (*wind- ing*) chetchahyŏngŭi Z자형의. *a* ~ *path* kkobulkkobur- han kil 꼬불꼬불한 길.

zinc *n.* (*chem.*) ayŏn 아연, hamsŏk 함석. *a* ~ *roof* ham- sŏk chibung 함석 지붕/ *sheet* ~ hamsŏkp'an 함석판.

zionism *n.* shionjuŭi 시온주의.

zipper *n.* (*slide fastener*) chak'ŭ 자크, chip'ŏ 지퍼. *a bag with a* ~ chak'ŭ tallin paek 자크 달린 백/ *Your* ~

is open. Chak'ŭga yŏllyŏ issŭmnida. 자크가 열려 있읍
니다.

zone *n.* (*region*) chidae 지대, (*in compound words*) tae
대(帶). *the frigid* [*temperate, torrid*] ~ han [on, yŏl]
dae 한[온, 열]대/ *a buffer* ~ wanch'ung chidae 완충 지대/
a safety ~ anjŏn chidae 안전 지대/ *Do you have the* ~
system here? Yŏgisŏnŭn yogŭmŭn chiyŏkcheimnikka?
여기서는 요금은 지역제입니까?

zoo *n.* tongmurwŏn 동물원.

zoological *adj.* tongmurhagŭi 동물학의.

zoologist *n.* tongmurhakcha 동물학자.

zoology *n.* tongmurhak 동물학.

zoom *vi.* (*airplain*) ~ *up* [*down*] kŭpsangsŭng [kŭp'a-
gang]hada 급상승[급하강]하다. *Prices* ~*ed.* Mulkaga
kŭptŭnghaessŭmnida. 물가가 급등했읍니다.

HANGŬL WRITING MODELS

Perpendicular strokes are written from top to bottom; horizontals from left to right. (Read these charts left and down.)

ㄱ k(g)	ㄱ			ㅌ t'	ㅡ	ㄷ	ㅌ	아 a	ㅇ	ㅇ	아	애 yae	ㅇ	ㅇ	아					
										이	아				야	애
ㄴ n	ㄴ			ㅍ p'	ㅡ	ㅜ	ㅍ	야 ya	ㅇ	ㅇ	야	에 e	ㅇ	ㅇ	에
										이	야			에	
ㄷ t(d)	ㅡ	ㄷ		ㅎ h	ヽ	ㅡ	ㅎ	어 ŏ	ㅇ	ㅇ	어	예 ye	ㅇ	ㅇ	예
										어				여	예
ㄹ r(l)	ㄱ	ㄱ	ㄹ	ㄲ kk	ㄱ	ㄲ		여 yŏ	ㅇ	ㅇ	어	외 oe	ㅇ	ㅇ	ㅇ
										여				외	
ㅁ m	ㅣ	ㄲ	ㅁ	ㄸ tt	ㅡ	ㄷ	ㄸ	오 o	ㅇ	ㅇ	오	위 wi	ㅇ	ㅇ	ㅇ
														위	
ㅂ p(b)	ㅣ	ㅐ	ㅐ	ㅃ pp	ㅣ	ㅐ	ㅐ	요 yo	ㅇ	ㅇ	ㅇ	의 ŭi	ㅇ	ㅇ	의
	ㅂ				ㅂ	ㅐ	ㅐ				요				
					ㅐ	ㅐ									
ㅅ s	ノ	ㅅ		ㅆ ss	ノ	ㅅ	ㅆ	우 u	ㅇ	ㅇ	우	와 wa	ㅇ	ㅇ	ㅇ
														외	와
ㅇ -ng	ㅇ			ㅉ tch	ㄱ	ㅈ	ㅉ	유 yu	ㅇ	ㅇ	우	워 wŏ	ㅇ	ㅇ	ㅇ
											유			우	워
ㅈ ch(j)	ㄱ	ㅈ		ㅊ ch'	ヽ	ㅎ	ㅊ	으 ŭ	ㅇ	ㅇ		왜 wae	ㅇ	ㅇ	ㅇ
														외	와	왜
ㅊ ch'	ヽ	ㅎ	ㅊ	ㅋ k'	ㄱ	ㅋ		이 i	ㅇ	ㅇ		웨 we	ㅇ	ㅇ	ㅇ
														우	워	웨
ㅋ k'	ㄱ	ㅋ						애 ae	ㅇ	ㅇ	아				
											애				